Advances in Human Factors/Ergonomics, 19B

Human-Computer Interaction:

Software and Hardware Interfaces

Advances in Human Factors/Ergonomics

Series Editor: Gavriel Salvendy, Purdue University, West Lafayette, IN 47907, U.S.A.

Advances in Human Factors/Ergonomics, 19B

Human-Computer Interaction:

Software and Hardware Interfaces

Proceedings of the Fifth International Conference on Human-Computer Interaction, (HCI International '93), Orlando, Florida, August 8–13, 1993 Volume 2

Edited by

Gavriel Salvendy
Purdue University, West Lafayette, IN 47907, USA

and

Michael J. Smith
University of Wisconsin, Madison, WI 53706, USA

ELSEVIER

Amsterdam – London – New York – Tokyo   1993

ELSEVIER SCIENCE PUBLISHERS B.V.
Sara Burgerhartstraat 25
P.O. Box 211, 1000 AE Amsterdam, The Netherlands

ISSN 0921-2647
ISBN: 0-444-89540-X

PREFACE

A total of 1,642 individuals from industry, academia, research institutes, and governmental agencies from 41 countries submitted their work for presentation at the Fifth International Conference on Human-Computer Interaction held in Orlando, Florida, U.S.A., 8-13 August 1993. Only those submittals which were judged to be of high scientific quality were included in the program. These papers address the latest research and application in the human aspects of design and use of computing systems. The papers accepted for presentation thoroughly cover the entire field of human-computer interaction including the cognitive, social, ergonomic, and health aspects of work with computers. These papers address major advances in knowledge and effective use of computers in a variety of diversified application areas including offices, financial institutions, manufacturing, electronic publishing, construction, and health care.

We are most grateful to the following sponsors of the conference:

AT&T
Fuji Electric Company
JGC Corporation
NEC Corporation

Purdue University
University of Central Florida
University of Wisconsin-Madison

and to the cooperating organizations:

ACM SIGCAPH
Chinese Academy of Sciences
Chinese Institute of Industrial Engineers
EEC-European Strategic Programme for
    Research and Development in
    Information Technology-ESPRIT
Finnish Institute of Occupational Health
Human Factors Society
IEEE Communications Society
IEEE Systems, Man & Cybernetics
    Society
Institute of Management Services (UK)
Institute of Industrial Engineers (USA)
Intelligent Manufacturing System Center
International Ergonomics Association

International Robotics and Factory
    Automation Center
Japan Ergonomics Research Society
Japan Association for Medical Informatics
Japan Institute of Office Automation
Japan Management Association
Japan Society of Health Science
National Institute for Occupational Safety
    and Health-NIOSH (USA)
National Institute of Industrial Health
    (Japan)
Society of Instrument and Control
    Engineers (Japan)
Software Psychology Society
The Swedish Cross-disciplinary Society
    for Human-Computer Interaction

The 187 papers contributing to this book cover the following areas:

Software Interfaces
Software Tools
Media

Help and Learning
Hardware Interfaces

The select papers on a complementary part of human-computer interaction are presented in a companion volume edited by M. J. Smith and G. Salvendy titled *Human-Computer Interaction: Applications and Case Studies*.

We wish to thank the following Board members who so diligently contributed to the success of the conference and to the direction of the content of this book. The conference Board members include:

Organizational Board
Hans-Jorg Bullinger, Germany
John M. Carroll, USA
Yoshio Hayashi, Japan
Bengt Knave, Sweden
S. Joy Mountford, USA
Vladimir M. Munipov, Russia
Takao Ohkubo, Japan
Jens Rasmussen, Denmark
Ben Shneiderman, USA
Jean-Claude Sperandio, France
Hiroshi Tamura, Japan
Thomas J. Triggs, Australia
Kong-shi Xu, P.R. China

Human Interface and the Management of Information Board
Noah K. Akinmayowa, Nigeria
Yuichiro Anzai, Japan
Kazu Aoki, Japan
Salah Benabdallah, Tunisia
Tora K. Bikson, USA
Gunilla Bradley, Sweden
Fernando Camacho Acevedo, Colombia
Pascale Carayon, USA
Barbara G. F. Cohen, USA
F. Daniellou, France
Johnson A. Edosomwan, USA
Rolf Haberbeck, Germany
Hiroshi Harashima, Japan
John P. Heap, UK
Michitaka Hirose, Japan
George H. Kuper, USA
Mark R. Lehto, USA
C. Richard Liu, Taiwan
Ann Majchrzak, USA
Nobuto Nakamura, Japan
Shogo Nishida, Japan
Leszek Pacholski, Poland
Kyung S. Park, Korea
K. Venuvinod Patri, Hong Kong
Richard Rubinstein, USA
Jorma Saari, Finland
Joseph Sharit, USA
Thomas G. Sheridan, USA
Tsutomu Tabe, Japan
Menachem Terkel, Israel
Yukio Tokunaga, Japan

Eberhard Ulich, Switzerland
Andrew B. Whinston, USA
Chelsea C. White III, USA
Hidekazu Yoshikawa, Japan
Bernhard Zimolong, Germany

Human-Computer Interaction Board
Sebastiano Bagnara, Italy
Deborah A. Boehm-Davis, USA
George J. Boggs, USA
Andrew M. Cohill, USA
Ray Eberts, USA
Takao Enkawa, Japan
Klaus-Peter Faehnrich, Germany
Pierre Falzon, France
Edward Glenner, USA
Ephraim P. Glinert, USA
Sheue-Ling Hwang, Taiwan
Dylan M. Jones, UK
Richard J. Koubek, USA
Kari Lindstrom, Finland
John Long, UK
Aaron Marcus, USA
David L. Morrison, Australia
Gerald M. Murch, USA
Masaru Naniwada, Japan
Jakob Nielsen, USA
Katsuhiko Ogawa, Japan
Jose A. Pino, Chile
Fieny Reimann-Pijls
Zsofia Ruttkay, Hungary
Valery F. Venda, Canada

Work With Visual Display Terminals Board
Arne Aaras, Norway
Diane Berthelette, Canada
Ram R. Bishu, USA
Marvin J. Dainoff, USA
Biman Das, Canada
Frida Marina Fischer, Brazil
Martin Helander, USA
Kitti Intaranont, Thailand
Henry S.R. Kao, Hong Kong
Waldemar Karwowski, USA
Peter Kern, Germany
Helmut Krueger, Switzerland
Thomas Laubli, Switzerland

Holger Luczak, Germany
Choon-Nam Ong, China
Michael Patkin, Australia
Abdul Raouf, Saudi Arabia
Susumu Saito, Japan

Steven L. Sauter, USA
Louis Slesin, USA
Tjerk W. van der Schaaf, The Netherlands
Gunilla Westlander, Sweden
Lian Cang Xu, P.R. China

This conference could not have been held without the diligent work of Theresa Brown, the conference administrator, and Myrna Kasdorf, the program administrator who were both invaluable in the completion of this book. Also a special thanks goes to Dr. Richard J. Koubek, the registration chair, Dr. Chin H. Lee, the local coordinator, and Dr. Jack Posey the student liaison coordinator, for all their outstanding efforts.

Michael J. Smith
University of Wisconsin-Madison
Madison, Wisconsin 53706

Gavriel Salvendy
Purdue University
West Lafayette, Indiana 47907

May 1993

HCI International '95

The Sixth International Conference on Human-Computer Interaction will be held under the auspices of the Japan Ergonomics Research Society, the Society of Instrument and Control Engineers, and the Information Processing Society of Japan. The conference will be held July 9-14, 1995 in Tokyo, Japan. Advanced information about HCI International '95 will be available in August 1993. Further information may be obtained from:

Yoshio Hayashi
Professor, Department of Industrial Engineering
Musashi Institute of Technology
1-28-1, Tamazutsumi, Setagaya, Tokyo, 158, Japan

FAX: +81-3-3703-4887

The proceedings will be published by Elsevier Science Publishers.

Contents

Plenary Paper

Human-Robot-Computer Interaction in Multiagent Environment

Yuichiro Anzai

Department of Computer Science, Keio University, 3-14-1, Hiyoshi, Yokohama 223 Japan
(Email: anzai@aa.cs.keio.ac.jp)

Abstract

Lots of interesting problems are discovered when we extend the target of research on human-computer interaction from computers, which are essentially passive, to more active machines such as autonomous mobile robots. More appear if we further extend it to communities of robots and computers that interact with humans. This paper discusses some issues on human-robot-computer interaction in multiagent environments, and describes systems designed and implemented in our project as possible solutions to some of those issues.

1. AUTONOMOUS MOBILE ROBOTS AND HUMAN-COMPUTER INTERACTION

The field of human-computer interaction does not need to be confined to interaction with computers. It is particularly so at our age of technological development when the concept of computers itself naturally evolves. We anticipate a new area of research on human-computer interaction by extending the concept of computers to broader concepts of interactive machines.

A robot is an example. A robot, particularly a personal robot (the term appeared publicly at least by early 1980's [1]) defined as a general-purpose, compact-size, autonomous mobile robot, can be regarded as a mobile computer, more than a mere mechanical device, under the possible future status of technological development. Lots of interesting problems can be discovered if we extend the target of research from computers which are essentially passive to robots that can be active to users, and further to communities of personal robots and computers interacting with humans.

This paper discusses some issues possibly raised from the interaction among humans, personal robots and computers in distributed environments, and describes briefly some of the systems designed and implemented in our project called **PRIME** (Physically-grounded human-**R**obot-computer **I**nteraction in **M**ultiagent **E**nvironment) launched about two years ago. The goal of **PRIME** is to develop keen knowledge for understanding and designing interaction among humans, personal robots and computers, in which humans can naturally behave and cooperate each other by using multiple robots and computers [2].

2. SOME ISSUES IN HUMAN-ROBOT-COMPUTER INTERACTION

Introducing personal robots into human-computer interaction provides many fundamental issues. We present some of them below.

2.1 Interaction with Physical and Electronic Worlds

Information processed in a computer at some level is not physical, but virtual. We cannot touch it, grasp it, or throw it. Much of our modern life is associated with the integration of electronically-generated virtual information and information obtained more directly from the physical world, rather than either of these. The development of robotics is partly a history of enhancing human abilities for dealing with the physical world. By integrating personal robots into human-computer interaction, we expect integrated interaction with the physical and electronic worlds.

2.2 Active Interfaces

A computer usually waits for the input of a user from a keyboard or other devices. It generally is a machine that passively accepts input only when the user gives it. On the other hand, a personal robot is an active device since it makes an action (apparently) by itself, and accepts input implicitly from the environment as well as explicitly. These functions are relatively different from the presentday computers.

The design of an active interface needs to satisfy some conditions. Among them are (1) *sensitivity* in sensing the change of the environment, (2) *reactivity* in acting upon the change of the environment, (3) *world-modelling ability* for quickly constructing a partial model of the environment for making complex decision, (4) *expressiveness* in effectively informing humans of dynamically changing internal states of the system, (5) *resource management ability* for efficient dynamic use of physical and computational resources, and (6) *reliance* that gives humans the stable feeling of commitment to the machine. Some of these conditions are discussed in [3-4].

2.3 Robots as Agents

If we regard a personal robot as an agent, it not only accepts commands from human users, but also possibly makes requests to them. (There are a lot of different conceptual definitions for 'agent', but here we consider it as an autonomous computing system that has its own mental states. Similar concepts are seen, e.g., in [5].) For instance, suppose a person is asked by a robot for carrying a document to some place. The person may follow, refuse, or ask back something to the robot. This kind of mixed initiative interaction among humans and robots generates an interesting issue in human-computer interaction, though little work is known [6].

2.4 Acquisition of Functions

An active interface such as a personal robot can have the function of adding new functions to passive objects. For example, (usually) a cup does not move by itself. But it can move autonomously if a (very small) personal robot is placed under it. Certainly we can design a robot-cup that has sensors and actuators for appropriate movement, but such a cup would be purpose-limited and expensive. On the other hand, a personal robot can be used for adding the function of movability to an unmovable object that can be put on the robot [7].

2.5 Multiagent Framework

We are not necessarily confined to issues with a single robot. A general case is the interaction among multiple humans, robots and computers. An important issue here is how to model each agent, a community of agents, and communcation among agents.

We have employed a particular multiagent model for resolving this issue. The model is essentially the integration of a model of autonomous agents and that of agents' migration among different computing environments [8].

3. DESIGNING HUMAN-ROBOT-COMPUTER INTERACTION

Various methodologies must be integrated adequately to design human-robot-computer interaction. We consider four of them here; (1) system support, (2) interface technology, (3) intelligence, and (4) analysis of interaction, by briefly describing some of the systems designed and implemented in our project.

3.1 System Support

One of the most basic components in our human-robot-computer interactive system is the hardware architecture for personal robots. We have implemented two different types of personal robots: one is **Einstein I** with a Toshiba TMP68301 processor (16MHz) that is compatible with Motorola 68000, and the other is **Aspire** with a VME-bus shared-memory multiprocessor architecture with a AVME-130-1 compatible to Motorola 68030 processor (25MHz) on the main module, and TMP68301 and other processors on sensor, actuator and other modules [9]. The most important feature of **Aspire** is that each module has local memory, and any pair of modules has wired connections. This feature makes it possible to realize very fast reflexive reaction to changes in the environment through local channels.

Along with the development of hardware architecture, we designed and implemented a new multi-task multi-thread operating system called **PULSER** [10]. (A more recent micro-kernel version is called μ-**PULSER**.) A new interrupt mechanism called *direct-interrupt* was implemented in **PULSER**, which makes it highly reactive to changes in the environment.

Wireless communication is also a crucial component for system support. In particular, we need an efficient communication system that avoids collision of packets, a problem that often happens in broadcast communication among robots and computers. We developed such a system called **MACS** based on the slotted-ALOHA network protocol [11].

3.2 Interface Technology

As noted earlier, a robot can be an active interface system. We designed **SONIC**, an active speech dialogue system, as a working example of active interfaces, and implemented it on our robot. See [12] for the details of the system and some experiments for its evaluation.

Systems for speech dialogue with robots are not new, but most of those systems, and also most of natural language understanding systems in general, do not take into consideration information from sensors to disambiguate linguistic utterances. The meaning of an utterance generally depends upon contexts or situations [13], and it is particularly so if the situation changes dynamically. We designed and implemented on Einstein I a speech dialogue system, called **Linta**, that uses sensor information to disambiguate meanings of utterances [14].

With the development of distributed computer and communication networks, computer supported cooperative work (CSCW) has been studied much, and software tools for CSCW (groupware) are now being distributed. However, many human tasks involve not only manipulation of electronic 'virtual' information, but also handling of physical entities. We designed and implemented **RT-Michele/P** [8], a groupware that supports the transfer of both electronic and physical entities in distributed environments by using personal robots and computers. **RT-Michele/P** is based on our multiagent model, and both asynchronous and synchronous communication is supported.

Another related system called **Romeo**, an interface system for robot-supported cooperative work using teleoperation is reported in [15]. Also, we implemented **FRECS**, an interactive system that supports help of humans to save a robot from a failure using a computer network. See [16] for details.

A personal robot, when suitably designed, becomes a general-purpose function-acquisition tool. As suggested earlier, a passive object can acquire active functions by combining it with a personal robot. We designed a few types of such robots [7]. Our concept of function acquisition by personal robots is a good example of using robots as interfaces or media. A robot can be used not only for substituting human functions, but also for enhancing them as active interfaces.

3.3 Analysis of Interaction

As suggested, introducing personal robots into human-computer interaction forces us to seriously consider how physical objects should be handled. One interesting problem is what we call the *Physical Ownership Problem*, the problem of dynamically identifying the ownership of a physical object. Our temporary answer to this problem applies the concept of personal space in social psychology to define the ownership transition protocol. The protocol was implemented directly on our operating system **PULSER**. For details, see [17].

Work on human-robot communication usually focuses attention on how a human's command is communicated to a robot. But a robot, if it behaves autonomously, might ask a human for something. We conducted a psychological experiment using **HuRIS**, a human-robot interactive system developed in our project, to observe how humans deal with a robot's request [6]. The result suggests that humans follow the robot's request when they regard that the robot is a medium conveying the request of some human authority (the experimenter, for instance), but do not when the robot itself is making request. We believe that this result opened up some deep issues on human interaction with active machines.

3.4 Intelligence

Complex interaction of personal robots and computers with humans needs at least some intelligent mechanisms. Here we point to some of our work for making human-robot-computer interaction intelligent.

First, dynamic rescheduling of tasks asked to robots is important when the efficient use of robotic resources is critical. We developed an incremental constraint solver called **RACONS** and a reactive task rescheduler named **RACTAS** to solve the dynamic task rescheduling problem [18].

Another important issue related to the efficient use of robots is allocation of tasks to multiple robots. We applied the contract net protocol [19] to allocation of physical tasks to multiple robots, and developed a task allocation system using **MACS** [20].

Still another problem with the efficient use of robots is distributed planning. We take the distributed problem solving approach for this problem, and implemented a distributed planner called **Coplanner** [21]. It uses a negotiation protocol to form a group of robots that then cooperate together to generate a plan by communicating subplans possessed by themselves.

One example of using more than one robot for a complex task is generation of maps by multiple robots. We developed **Marsha**, a system developed in our project for generating maps of a terrain by cooperation of personal robots, particularly by cancelling individual differences of constituent robots [22].

An example for the advanced use of intelligence in human-robot-computer interaction is learning robots' behavior through interaction with humans. We developed, based on the algorithm presented in [23], a learning system called **Acorn-II** that makes our robots able to learn the relation between commands and behavior. We also developed an interface system for giving behavioral examples to a robot from the display.

4. SUMMARY AND CONCLUDING REMARKS

Two years have passed since we launched **PRIME**. We have described in this article some issues that emerged from our research effort, and some of the systems developed in the project. The goal of **PRIME** is still only partly achieved, but the achievement includes:

1. Formulation of a multiagent model as the computational model of human-robot-computer interaction.

2. Development of a human-robot-computer groupware in which robots can be used efficiently and intelligently.

3. Development of computational architectures for highly reactive robotic agents.

4. Establishment of the concept of active interfaces as the basic concept for human-robot-computer interface systems.

5. Exploration into active interface systems for active human-machine interaction.

The research paradigm of human-robot-computer interaction is different from human-computer interaction, telerobotics, or technology for virtual environments in many ways. Two among them are essential. One is the extension of interaction with virtual, electronic information to include more direct interaction with the physical world. Second is that an interface can be active and distributed to the user.

Discovering the coherent design principles for distributed active interfaces is not an easy task. We are presently taking the mixture of formal and empirical approaches. In the former, we have been trying to establish a multiagent model as a formal computational model of human-robot-computer interaction. In the latter, we have been trying to search for various possibilities in designing and implementing interface systems. While exhibiting some issues in human-robot-computer interaction, this paper gave a glimpse of the present status of our **PRIME** project. We expect to crop more knowledge for understanding and designing human-robot-computer interaction through our continuing research.

5. REFERENCES

1 J.Engelberger, ROBOTICS in Service, Kögan Page, pp.218, 1989.

2 Y.Anzai, Proc. of IEEE International Workshop on Robot and Human Communication (1991) 11-17.

3 T.Yakoh, N.Yamasaki and Y.Anzai, This issue.

4 C.Ono, Y.Yamamoto and Y.Anzai, This issue.

5 Y.Shoham, Artificial Intelligence, 60 (1993) 51-92.

6 Y.Yamamoto, M.Sato, K.Hiraki, N.Yamasaki and Y.Anzai, Proc. of IEEE International Workshop on Robot and Human Communication (1992) 204-209.

7 K.Kumano, Y.Yamamoto, C.Ono and Y.Anzai, SIGHI Report 93-HI-48, Information Processing Society of Japan (1993).

8 Y.Nakauchi, T.Okada, N.Yamasaki and Y.Anzai, Proc. of IEEE International Conference on Robotics and Automation (1992) 2786-2788.

9 N.Yamasaki and Y.Anzai, An architecture for personal robots, Proc. of JSME Annual Conference on Robotics and Mechatronics, (1992) 51-56.

10 T.Yakoh, T.Sugawara, T.Akiba, T.Iwasawa and Y.Anzai, Proc. of IEEE International Workshop on Robot and Human Communication (1992) 404-409.

11 T.Yakoh, T.Iwasawa and Y.Anzai, Proc. of IEEE Pacific Rim Conference on Communication, Computers and Signal Processing (1993) to appear.

12 T.Okada, Y.Yamamoto and Y.Anzai, This issue.

13 J.Barwise and J.Perry, Situations and Attitudes, MIT Press, 1983.

14 M.Sato, K.Hiraki and Y.Anzai, SIGHI Report 93-HI-47, Information Processing Society of Japan (1993).

15 K.Kawasugi, Y.Nakauchi, T.Yoshino and Y.Anzai, This issue.

16 Y.Nakauchi, M.Sato, Y.Yamamoto and Y.Anzai, This issue.

17 T.Yakoh and Y.Anzai, Proc. of the First International Conference on Intelligent and Cooperative Information Systems (1993) to appear.

18 F.Naya, K.Hiraki and Y.Anzai, Proc. of the Second International Conference on Automation, Robotics and Computer Vision (1992) RO-9-3-1/5.

19 R.Davis and R.G.Smith, Artificial Intelligence, 20 (1983) 63-109.

20 Y.Ohmori, Y.Nakauchi, Y.Itoh and Y.Anzai, Proc. of the Second International Conference on Automation, Robotics and Computer Vision (1992) RO-12-7-1/5.

21 Y.Itoh and Y.Anzai, Trans. of the Institutes of Electronics, Information and Communication Engineers, J75-D-II (1992) 2038-2048.

22 K.Ishioka, K.Hiraki and Y.Anzai, Workshop on Dynamically Interacting Robots, International Joint Conference on Artificial Intelligence (1993).

23 K.Hiraki, J.Gennari, Y.Yamamoto and Y.Anzai, Proc. of the Eighth International Machine Learning Workshop (1991) 407-411.

I. Software Interfaces

Is user interface design just common sense?

Thomas S. Tullis

Canon Information Systems, 3188 Pullman, Costa Mesa, CA, 92626, USA; email:
ttullis@canon.com

Abstract

This paper presents the results of a test to determine whether or not
experienced user interface developers could pick the best user interface for a
particular task just using "common sense." In an earlier study, seven different
user interfaces for performing a task involving reordering fields in a table were
empirically tested. The interfaces studied covered a wide spectrum of styles,
including dragging and dropping, button-pressing, and data entry. In the
present study, 28 experienced programmers were shown screen images of the
seven user interfaces and asked to rank order them from "best" to "worst" for this
particular task. Overall, there was virtually no correlation between their
rankings and the actual data from the earlier study. The developers ranked the
interfaces involving dragging and dropping consistently better than they actually
were, while they ranked one of the data entry interfaces consistently worse than
it actually was. The results indicate that, at least for this task, good user
interface design is not just common sense.

1. INTRODUCTION

One of the arguments sometimes heard about good user interface design is
that it's all just common sense, or intuition: "Why bother with all this fuss about
user-centered design, usability testing, and everything else when any good
developer can come up with the same thing just by using common sense?"
Maybe, or maybe not. This paper presents the results of a test of just that
question.

In an earlier study, Tullis and Kodimer (1992) presented the results of an
empirical comparison of seven different interfaces for allowing users to redefine
the order in which various file attributes appear in the columns of a table (e.g.,
file name, size, creation date). The seven interfaces, as illustrated in Figure 1,
were as follows:

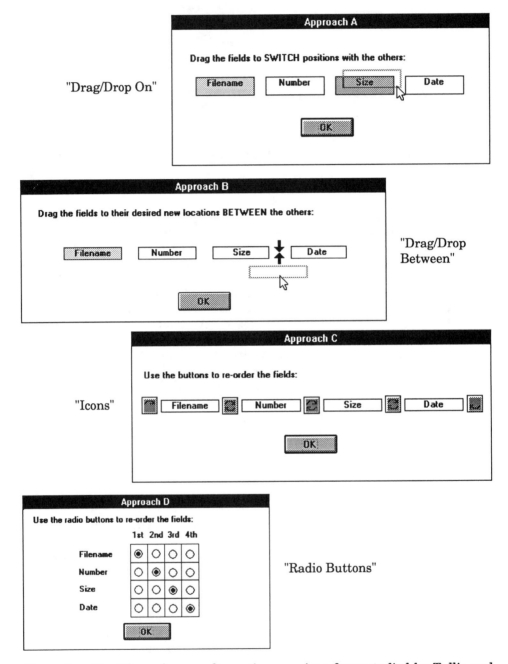

Figure 1a. First four of seven alternative user interfaces studied by Tullis and Kodimer (1992) for allowing a user to redefine the order in which four fields appear in the columns of a table.

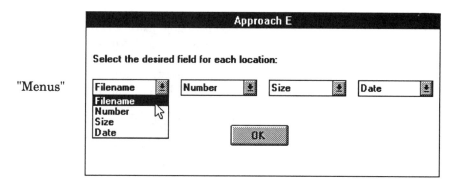

"Menus"

"One Entry Area"

"Four Entry Areas"

Figure 1b. Remaining three of seven alternative user interfaces studied by Tullis and Kodimer (1992) for allowing a user to redefine the order in which four fields appear in the columns of a table.

- *Drag/Drop On* - Dragging one of the fields, using the mouse, to the location of one of the other fields and then dropping it caused those two fields to exchange positions.
- *Drag/Drop Between* - Dragging one of the fields to its desired location between two other fields (or at the ends) and then dropping it caused the fields to reorder accordingly.
- *Icons* - Pressing an iconic button between the fields caused the two fields on either side of it to switch positions. Icons at the ends of the series caused the two end fields to switch positions.
- *Radio Buttons* - Clicking on radio buttons in a two-dimensional array allowed the user to specify the desired ordinal position for each field. Selecting a new position for one field forced another field to move to the position just vacated.
- *Menus* - Drop-down menus (also called "combo boxes") for each of the four positions in the table allowed the user to select the desired field for each position.
- *One Entry Area* - A single data entry field allowed the user to type the first letter of each field in the desired order, including spaces or commas between the letters (e.g., "N,S,F,D").
- *Four Entry Areas* - Data entry areas beside each field name allowed the user to type "1", "2", "3", or "4" to designate the desired ordinal position for each field.

Tullis and Kodimer found that users could perform reorderings significantly faster using either *Radio Buttons* or *One Entry Area*. These two approaches also were among the most preferred by the users. The other data-entry technique, *Four Entry Areas*, was consistently the worst, in terms of both user performance and preference.

The purpose of the current study was to determine whether a group of experienced programmers could choose the most effective user interfaces for this task from the seven approaches used in the earlier study.

2. METHOD

Twenty-eight experienced software developers participated in the new study, in two groups of 12 and 16. They were all employed either as programmers, engineers with some programming responsibilities, or as managers of programmers. They worked for 22 different organizations, most of which are in the engineering or technical fields. Their years of programming experience ranged from 2 to 16. All had some experience in developing graphical user interface (GUI) applications, and all considered user interface design and development a significant part of their job. The majority had experience developing Windows applications; all were Windows users. Most programmed in "C", but several other languages were represented as well.

They were shown screen dumps, on paper, of the seven actual interfaces studied by Tullis and Kodimer (exactly as shown in Figure 1) and they were given descriptions of how each worked. They were then asked to rank order the seven approaches in terms of what they thought would be the "most effective" user interface for this task to the "least effective". The terms "best" and "worst" were also used in describing the two ends of the ordering. The participants made these rankings individually. They were told of none of the results from the Tullis and Kodimer study.

3. RESULTS

The two key measures from the Tullis and Kodimer study were the users' reordering times (how long it actually took users to perform the task using each approach) and the users' subjective rankings of the seven approaches from "most preferred" to "least preferred." Overall, there was virtually no correlation between the programmers' rankings from the present study and the actual reordering time data from the earlier study, $r = -.07$. There was a somewhat better correlation between the programmers' rankings and the users' actual subjective rankings, $r = .31$, but it was still very low and not statistically significant. Scatterplots of these correlations are shown in Figures 2 and 3.

In general, the programmers ranked the two interfaces that involved dragging and dropping as being the best; those approaches actually came out in the middle in terms of both user performance and preference. Likewise, the programmers ranked the approach that used a single data-entry field as being second to the worst; in reality, this approach came out as one of the two best.

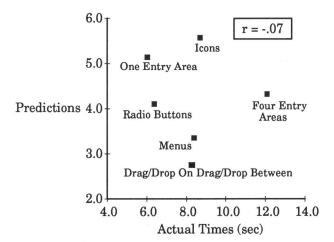

Figure 2. Scatterplot of actual reordering times for seven different user interfaces studied by Tullis and Kodimer (1992) vs. programmers' predictions (rankings from "best" to "worst", where lower numbers are better).

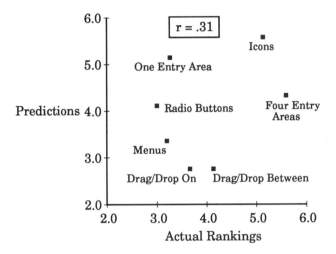

Figure 3. Scatterplot of actual user rankings for seven different user interfaces studied by Tullis and Kodimer (1992) vs. programmers' predictions (rankings from "best" to "worst", where lower numbers are better).

Analysis of the data for the individual subjects showed that no one was particularly good at selecting the best user interfaces. Individual subject correlations with the actual time data ranged from $r = -.54$ to $.46$. In fact, ten of the subjects' rankings yielded a negative correlation with the time data. The individual correlations with the actual subjective ranking data were somewhat better, but also poor, ranging from $r = -.14$ to $.54$.

Overall, the results indicate that, at least for this task and these seven alternatives, the most appropriate user interface design choices were certainly not just "common sense". Part of the problem seems to be that the programmers were biased toward design alternatives that are currently "in vogue" (i.e., those involving dragging and dropping) and biased against those that have fallen out of favor (i.e., command entry).

4. REFERENCE

Tullis, T. S. and Kodimer, M. L. (1992) A comparison of direct-manipulation, selection, and data-entry techniques for reordering fields in a table. *Proceedings of the Human Factors Society 36th Annual Meeting*, Atlanta, Georgia, pp 298-302.

The need for new application specific interface elements

J. Gulliksen[1,2] , M. Johnson[1] , M. Lind[1] , E. Nygren[1,2] and B. Sandblad[1,2]

[1] Uppsala University, Centre for Human-Computer Studies, Lägerhyddv. 18, S-752 37 Uppsala, Sweden.

[2] Uppsala University, Dept. of Systems Engineering, Uppsala, Sweden.

Abstract
The design of user interfaces for skilled workers in professional work settings should be based on style-guides that certify efficiency. Most of todays style-guides and design guidelines over-emphasise general aspects or aspects relevant to novices. To increase efficiency both of the design process and of the resulting interface, more domain specific interface elements should be used. This paper explains the basic ideas of such domain specific style-guides and gives some examples from the health care domain.

1. INTRODUCTION

Studies of different types of work situations show that properties of the work environment can hinder the persons performing the tasks to efficiently use their skills. We call these hindrances 'cognitive work environment problems' and they are often associated with the human-computer interface.

Existing guide-lines for design of the human-computer interfaces often over-emphasise what is important for non-experts and are therefore not applicable to the development of systems aimed at supporting professional workers [1]. Studies of skilled workers in a variety of contexts imply that an extremely important part of designing a system for such workers is the mapping of certain types of relevant information onto graphical properties that can be automatically perceived. When building computer systems in support of skilled workers one must allow for the user to quickly orientate and browse through large amounts of information and 'zoom in' on relevant information parts in order to rapidly be able to make decisions based on the information acquired. Reading from paper documents allows knowledge to be gained automatically by pattern recognition and by task related encoding of the information media characteristics. When reading from a screen the corresponding knowledge is often gained by effortful cognitive processes. This problem can be avoided by a careful analysis of the reading task into automatic and non-automatic components, followed by a dedicated user interface design with information presented in a perceivable rather then readable way.

The information systems we here consider can be characterised as systems aimed at supporting *administrative* work in a broad sense. In such systems we include e.g. staff and economic administration, systems for businesses, banks, logistics, health care etc. We do not consider more general purpose systems such as word-processing, spread-sheets or pure data-entry systems.

2. GENERAL ASPECTS

Most graphical user interfaces constructed today are based on the desktop metaphor, i.e. the screen is thought of as a desktop and the different graphical elements as items that are placed on the desktop. One of the main points of this metaphor is that it is up to the user to arrange the desktop in a suitable way. Thus windows can be resized, moved about, opened and closed at any time. The advantages of this are obvious. The drawbacks are the amount of time that has to be spent arranging the screen to a suitable form, the mental effort this takes and that windows must be constructed in such a way that they are independent of one another.

In some types of work situations the desktop metaphor is highly suitable since every instance of it requires a new collection of windows or a new configuration of them. In most work situations found in administrative work, however, there is a possibility to define tasks where each of these tasks share informational needs in terms of visible windows, their arrangement and their interdependence. The basis for defining such tasks is the analysis of work-related decisions and/or judgements. As a consequence of the above, inter-faces supporting administrative work built upon the desktop metaphor lead to inefficiencies since much time has to be spent handling windows and commands that is unnecessary since it is repetitive and occurs every time a certain task, defined as above, is performed by the user. Furthermore, as we have pointed out elsewhere [1,2] such handling is not only time-consuming but also interrupts the controlled mental processing needed for decision-making (i.e. the primary contents of the work).

An alternative way to design graphical user interfaces for administrative work is to employ a workspace metaphor where each defined task is matched by an especially designed workspace. The invocation of such a workspace by the user brings up an ordered set of interconnected interface elements designed to fit the requirements of the decision-making defining the task.

The idea of a workspace metaphor has been put forward earlier by for instance Card and Henderson [3] in their 'rooms' design. What is novel in our approach is that each workspace is a collection of interconnected interface elements forming what traditionally would be considered a single application, and not simply an ordering structure applied to any collection of windows. The introduction of workspaces also introduces the problem of navigating between the workspaces. In our experience, however, most users won't need more than a few workspaces and all navigational problems are overcome by having these on constant display as icons.

To enhance efficiency of the professional computer support, the interface elements should also be closely related to the concepts and the language used in the work environment. In health care, e.g., nurses and physicians do not work with 'radio-buttons' and 'scroll-bars' but with patients, lab-reports, drug prescriptions and x-ray images. If already the design of the interface could be based on more domain specific interface metaphors and interaction elements it would facilitate many things. Representatives from the work environment can more easily contribute to the design using an experimental methodology and the result will also be an interface that allows the professionals to communicate with the system in terms familiar to them. Style-guides of e.g. CUA/SAA, Motif, Windows and Presentation Manager give no or little help in the design process of an interface for a given work situation, except for the specification of basic interface elements. In the following we will present one attempt to design more domain specific interface elements.

3. RESULT

3.1 Basic interface elements
Existing style-guides have to be extended with a few new basic interface elements to support design of efficient user interfaces for administrative work domains. The following interface elements, of a more general applicability, shows to fulfil our requirements.

1. The *page,* the analogue to a single paper document, supports means for classification and efficient information retrieval. Except from the ordinary paper document properties, a page can have colour, font, size etc to form patterns that are possible to perceive automatically. Redundant presentation of familiar information facilitates automaticity in decision making.

2. The *document* consists of pages in a bundle, where knowledge used for orientation, navigation, choice of search strategy, error detection etc. is gained, not by reading but by pattern recognition and interpretation of the information media characteristics (c.f. fig. 1). Scrolling often decreases automatic perception of patterns.

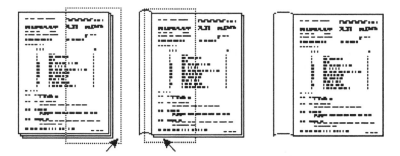

Fig 1. Turning of pages in a document is performed either by 'clicking' with a mouse pointer on the right or left part of the document or by a gesture. The edges of the bundle should show approximately the number of pages in the document and where the reader is at present.

3. An *index* lists the contents of one or many documents, and is created by a search in a database (c.f. fig. 2.). As with the document, placing the information in a bundle will reduce orientation problems.

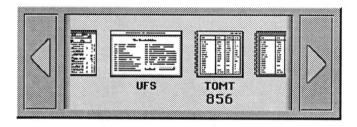

Utrustn	UHF	UHF-M(A)	UHP-F
RL-02	- 26B	- 12	-
RL-14	- 43D	- 122	-
RL-21BC	- 25C	- 130	-
RL-22	- 26C	- 130	- 81B
RL-23	- 57B	- 119B	- 7
RL-24	- 176	- 117B	- 81B
RL-42A	- 73D	- 132	- 81B
RL-43A	- 104B	- 116	- 81B
RL-43BC	- 99D	- 116	- 149B
RL-45	- 190B	- 179	-
RL-46	- 192	- 178	- 55

Fig 2. Different representations of index material in a bundle or as a scrolling index. While scrolling we have difficulties in automatically orientating and perceiving information even with small materials.

4. The *mini-icon,* an intelligent proportional diminution of an index or a document down to the size of a stamp, often provides as much information as a full-size element to a frequent user (c.f. fig. 3). The basic features, e.g. shape, size, colour, position and perhaps headline are important for classification. The icons are activated by 'clicking' and grows dynamically to full size, leaving an empty hole indicating activity. An element can be closed by 'clicking' in the empty hole or by forced closure by competition for screen space.

Fig 3. Mini-icons, here in natural size, is a diminished version of a document or an index. In routine work a lot of information can be obtained merely by pattern recognition.

5. *Micro-icons* are diminished to a point where the representation is so simplified that existing information only can be obtained by colour and position.

3.2 Design of domain specific elements

More domain specific interface elements can now be designed, based on existing style-guides and experimental elements of the type presented above. As an example of how this can be implemented we present examples from a European Community research project under the AIM-program. In this project, HELIOS-2, the objective is to develop a systems engineering environment (SEE) for ward application systems in health care units. Here both health care specific interface elements and a style-guide for such applications are being developed. The design is based on Motif and additional high level widgets.

We will give two examples. The first (c.f. fig. 4) shows a part, here two weeks, of an appointment system for outpatient clinics. The 'appointment over-view' element consists of several mini-icons showing the appointments made for one specific day. The second example (c.f. fig. 5) shows the design of the interface element 'patient'. In all applications where a 'patient' appears, this element can be used, specified to its behaviour, data-base connections and location in the work area. Current medications and important medical information are always shown, even if the information areas are empty. Several alternative 'patient' objects can be implemented.

Elements like these will be parts of the complete style-guide developed for this application domain. Applications are developed according to this.

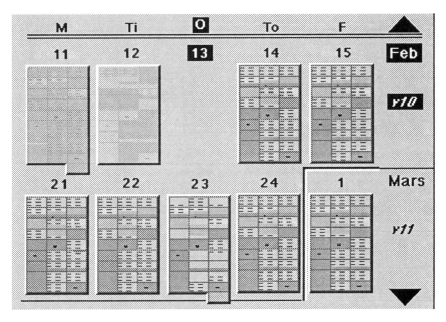

Fig 4. Domain specific mini-icons from an appointment system used in health care, where one mini-icon symbolizes one day. The experienced user can tell merely by perceiving patterns of the mini-icon whether a time is booked or not. Colour (here gray-scale) indicates the type of appointment. Different columns correspond to different physicians. Previous days can not be updated. An activated day leaves an empty hole.

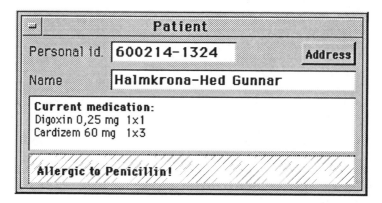

Fig 5. The 'patient' element shows important information always at hand.

4. DISCUSSION

To implement a domain specific style-guide is today an even more resource and time-consuming task than in the style of CUA or others. A feasible usage of our interface elements does however require new construction aids where the general features and functions of the elements are predefined. In the line of our research such a tool is being implemented, based on the InterViews system [4]. The basic idea is to define domain specific interface elements outgoing from an object model of the work domain.

5. ACKNOWLEDGEMENT

This work was performed with financial support from the Swedish Work Environment Fund, and from the AIM-programme, project no A1004.

6. REFERENCES

1. E. Nygren, M. Johnson, M. Lind and B. Sandblad. The art of the obvious. Proceedings of CHI'92, Monterey, California, May 1992.

2. E. Nygren and P. Henriksson. Reading the medical record 1. Analysis of physicians ways of reading the medical record. Comp. Meth. and Prog. in Biomed, 39 (1992) 1-12.

3. S.K. Card & A. Henderson. A multiple Virtual-Workspace Interface to Support User Task Switching. Proceedings of CHI+GI 1987, Toronto, Canada, April 1987.

4. M.A. Linton et.al. InterViews Reference Manual, Version 3.1. Stanford University, 1992.

Development of a Usable Graphical User Interface Design Guide

Robert M. Schumacher, Jr. and Arnold Lund

Ameritech Services, Inc., 2000 W. Ameritech Center Dr., Hoffman Estates, IL 60196 USA

Abstract
A corporate reality, that poor user interface design negatively affects employees and customers, led us to develop a graphical user interface design guide. We discovered in developing the document that current reference materials are not very helpful and are hard to use. We considered several areas for improvement, including using copious examples, providing behavioral rationale for choice of interface controls, etc. Our experiences so far have been positive and we hope will result in achieving our desired results of improving overall interface design.

1. MOTIVATION

Few milestones that we have placed on viewgraphs have generated more executive interest than "Define Ameritech Look and Feel." Ameritech is a regional telephone company serving approximately 10 million customers and providing a large array of telecommunications services. The complex network delivering these services is run by hundreds of support systems. The employees who run the network and service our customers are surrounded by dozens of different user interfaces; each with its own style and idiosyncrasies. The cost to Ameritech in lost productivity, training, and errors due to poor user interfaces is tremendous. For instance, in one recently redesigned application we calculated that if users were slowed down by only one percent it could cost the company several million dollars per year. It is relatively easy to calculate out the costs of training, lost productivity, and errors to internal users, but the potential costs of poor interface design in customer goodwill are incalculable. Customers who use our services sometimes find them difficult to learn and use, resulting in lost revenue. Customers also get annoyed when we fail to provide quality service; many times poor service can be traced to poor user interface design. Additionally, our marketing people realize that a consistent look and feel in products can result in brand equity and strengthen our corporate identity.

We felt that development of a corporate look and feel standard and design guide would increase customer satisfaction, increase the success of our products, decrease the costs of providing service through reduced training costs and increased worker productivity, and in turn, add to our corporate identity.

2. BACKGROUND

Because of the recognized need that our systems are difficult to use, Ameritech has begun to front-end many of its systems with graphical user interfaces (GUIs). Unconstrained, each developer makes his or her own design decisions, with the result that, even when developed in identical environments, parts of the same application may look very different. Ameritech also purchases many systems from the outside. Some vendors are as inconsistent in their own product lines as Ameritech has been in its development in the past; even when they are internally consistent, we are still faced with inconsistencies between vendor styles. Compounding the problem is that there is no single development environment. Systems are developed for three standard-operating environment GUI platforms (Apple® Macintosh™, Microsoft® Windows 3.1™, and OSF/Motif™) and a variety of character-based environments. Some applications are developed that will be deployed on more than one of these platforms, and developers must choose whether to be compatible with all, one, or none of the platforms.

Resolving these issues is difficult, and we do not pretend to have solved all or even many of the problems. One question that naturally comes to mind at this point is that there is plenty of guidance out there for the developer to use in design. Why clutter up the desk with one more burdensome requirement? We turn to this question next.

3. STYLE GUIDES, STANDARDS, AND USER INTERFACE DESIGN REFERENCES

3.1. Platform style guides

The use of GUI style guides (e.g., OSF/Motif™ Style Guide, 1991) to focus application development is important in promoting consistency in the user interfaces. These platform style guides describe the behavior of interface objects within a given platform. They catalog each control and indicate how it should be used. For instance, radio buttons are to be used for mutually exclusive choices. It is critical that our applications be compliant with platform style guides.

3.2. National and International Standards

We also recognized that a multitude of standards activities are reaching fruition right now, and our internal standard would need to be compatible. These standards include the work of the HFES HCI, ANSI/HFES 100, ISO/TC 150, X3V1.9 (on icons), CCITT T1M1.5, and IEEE P1201.2. For instance, the HFES HCI committee is developing design guidelines based on empirical work and best practice for design areas such as user guidance, forms, menus, windows, etc. IEEE P1201.2 is looking across the style guides to identify elements of user interface design that affect "drivability", the elements of an interface that when inconsistent across applications cause usability problems. Standards are important because they cut across platforms and vendors and help to define a minimal level of acceptability.

3.3. User interface design literature

If standards and style guides describe the syntax of controls and navigation, then much of the user interface design literature is dedicated to the semantics of design; that is, to improving the usability of applications. For advice on making an applications useful and usable there are several good human factors references available (e.g. Brown, 1989; Galitz, 1989; Shneiderman, 1986; Smith and Mosier, 1986). The information these sources contain embodies much of what is known about user interface design.

3.4. What's wrong with what's out there

As much as these sources provide necessary information for design, they are insufficient in themselves for creating usable applications. Some of their shortcomings are as follows:

• Ameritech has three standard-operating environment GUI platforms, and mainframe systems with VT100-compatible access. Style guides exist for each of these platforms, but the elements of the style guides areat times incompatible with one another.

• Most standards documents and style guides provide little more than a sort of electronic "elements of style". Style guides contain very little human performance-based rationale for choices they do recommend and how objects should work together. By necessity the more difficult problem of overall application design is ignored.

• User interface design literature contains good design heuristics, but it makes little contact with the day-to-day reality of development: the literature is too jargon ridden, information is not directly usable by developers, and design concepts are not linked to interface controls. Developers often do not have the time to investigate or they fail to see the value of this work in their day-to-day programming responsibilities. Moreover, much of the design material is based on character-based design and its extensibility is often in question.

We assert that any standard or style guide should primarily support development of *usable* applications, and secondarily or as an artifact, present the consistency and style issues. Developers need a better tool to support development of usable applications -- a design guideline that bridges the gap between the generalities of the style and design reference books, sifting out the important parts, and the realities of the computing environment of the organization. The needs of developers helped push the idea of a guidelines document from one of simply showing the elements required to achieve consistency to a document that engenders good interface design.

One last issue that we have not touched yet is the difficulty in *using* these reference materials. A number of recent studies have shown, and our interviews confirmed, that standards are quite difficult to apply (e.g., Throvtrup & Nielsen, 1991; Mosier & Smith, 1984). The source of these problems has to do with some of the things we have already discussed (e.g., perceived relevance), but also to things like indexing and examples (see Tetzlaff & Schwartz, 1990).

Our goals in developing our design guide were to (1) hold usability of the application as the key criterion, (2) ensure compatibility with standards and with the style guides of our three standard-operating environment platforms, and (3) prove useful and usable to the *development* community.

4. APPROACH

In the balance of the paper we will tie together the preceding material to our approach in developing the document.

4.1. Model

We assume that each platform provides a set of contextual conventions. These include window management tools, certain key assignments, etc. While some users may move from platform to platform, it is expected that in general users work with a single type of platform and that all applications on the platform should be compatible. Applications are accessed within the platform. We identify parameters that are platform independent, and in general use these as the raw material for standardization across platforms. Of the interface elements that are platform independent, some affect driveability and need to be optimized. Some, however, can vary (within limits) without affecting performance. A subset of these are identified and parameters are fixed to define Ameritech signature elements.

4.2. Specific recommendations

4.2.1. Provide more design support

Since our key criterion was to ensure that applications be usable, we needed to provide more support to developers on what is good design in the context of their programming environment. For example, style guides provide at least eight ways in which mutually exclusive choices can be implemented, but they provide little guidance as to which one to use in a given situation. We took these ways of implementing mutually exclusive choices and mapped them into object selection tables *based on user considerations*, for various data conditions (see Table 1). We hope that these tables help capture the kinds of questions that designers have and will guide them to the right control for that instance.

Table 1
Some of the conditions for selecting the proper interface form for mutually exclusive choices.

If Mutually Exclusive Items are...	Then Use the Following Form...
attributes or *values* that • are selected frequently • are limited in number (2-8) • are best represented verbally, and • change rarely.	Attribute menu items
attributes or *values* that • are selected infrequently • are limited in number (2-8) • change infrequently, and • require little screen space.	Pop-up menu or Drop-down list
attributes or *objects* or *values* that • are selected infrequently • are relatively few in number (8 or fewer) • have sufficient screen space available, and • do not change.	Radio buttons

In addition to having object selection tables, we have a serious and detailed treatment of usability and design in the first two chapters of our standard.

4.2.2. Leverage current practices; build molecular objects; make elements reusable

One of the main shortcomings of style guides and standards are that controls is discussed in isolation, but often the place where designs get in trouble is when controls interact or there is no clear way to perform some task with the controls provided. We looked at internal systems, both GUI and non-GUI, for *de facto* standards and "molecular interface objects", such as selecting from a menu, completing a form, etc., that could serve as a starting point for a user interface library. Standard interfaces to these functions are then defined consistent with the driveability elements, other design standards, and the Ameritech signature. The idea here is that if we take good examples of controls that combine from applications currently in use then developers could not only see the examples, but play with them, and perhaps even use the code. Our hope is that as applications are built that conform to standards, interface elements can be placed into the library. One benefit we hope to accrue is that development costs will decrease because standards serve to guide development in areas where developers might otherwise spend unnecessary time.

4.2.3. Use copious examples

Tetzlaff and Schwartz (1991), in an experiment in the usability of a standards document found, that developers code heavily from examples. This lead us to believe that figures were extremely important. Each example in the standard must conform to the standard as a whole since it may be used unwittingly as an example other than that for which it was intended. Our experience has been that if a developer has a model (i.e., a style guide) available, they will adopt that model.

4.2.4. Aid the finding of information

One of the main obstacles we found in interviews with developers was they could not find information they needed in standards documents. Thus, we improved access to the document by a variety of methods. First, since we were developing a document that would work across platforms, terminology was a problem; what one platform calls a radio button another calls an option button. We developed a "visual table of contents" (see Figure 1) that allows the reader to quickly find the object of interest visually (e.g., a command button) without having to know the technical name of the object and then find relevant sections of the document from the figure. Second, we have an extensive table of contents and index with many items cross-referenced. Third, almost unanimously the developers want the document on-line so that they can refer to it quickly. We are in the process of putting the document on-line now. We would ultimately like to provide working examples on-line and link those examples to code libraries for seamless portability. In essence, one key way to the code re-use library would be through the standards document. Last, many developers have indicated that 200+ pages is too much; they want a minimal manual. We have hopes to accommodate this request in the future by stripping out everything but requirements.

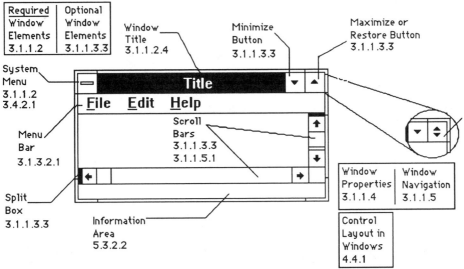

Figure 1. Example of Visual Table of Contents.

4.2.5. Obtain management support

No one is being forced to use our document. No matter the quality of the style guide *per se* we believe management support, education, and publicity are critical elements to the successful introduction and adoption of the standard. We have developed a strategy for insinuating the document into Ameritech, including: involvement in quality and product assurance processes, offering consulting services and "hot-line" support, working with purchasing to obtain their concurrence on the importance of GUI standards for requirements of custom software products to be delivered to Ameritech, and suitcasing in a course on interface design.

4.2.6. Endless reviews and empirical validation

We devoted ourselves to listening to would-be users. By the time the document was published it was reviewed by many developers, human factors experts, and management employees. We assembled a GUI steering group, made up of developers, to help refine and focus the document. These reviews are on-going; as documents are sent out follow-ups are made to understand the deficiencies of the document. Empirical validation of certain recommendations are currently underway, and usability tests of the document are planned.

5. CONCLUSIONS

By understanding the attitudes and concerns of developers toward standards, style guides, and design literature we were able to focus our efforts on what is an important corporate goal of improving the usability of our systems through development of a look and feel document. We have also written documents for development of character-based user interfaces and phone-based user interfaces. Even at this early stage the standard has been well-received, and is in part responsible for promoting the visibility of human factors work within Ameritech.

6. TRADEMARKS AND SERVICE MARKS

OSF/Motif and Motif are trademarks of the Open Software Foundation, Inc. Microsoft is a registered trademark and Windows is a trademark of Microsoft Corporation. Apple and Macintosh are registered trademarks of Apple Computer, Inc.

7. REFERENCES

Brown, C.M. (1989). Human-Computer Interface Design Guidelines. Norwood, NJ: Ablex Publishing Corporation.

Galitz, W.O. (1985). Handbook of Screen Format Design. Wellesley Hills, MA: QED Information Sciences.

Mosier, J.N., and Smith, S.L. (1986). Application of Guidelines for Designing User Interface Software. *Behavior and Information Technology*, 5(1), 39-46.

Open Software Foundation. (1991). *OSF/Motif™ Style Guide.* Prentice Hall: Englewood Cliffs, NJ.

Shneiderman, B. (1986). Designing the User Interface: Strategies for Effective Human-Computer Interaction. Reading, MA: Addison-Wesley.

Smith, S.L., and Mosier, J.N. (1986). Guidelines for designing user interface software. Technical Report ESD-TR-86-278. Springfield, VA: National Technical Information Service, U.S. Department of Commerce.

Tetzlaff, L., and Schwartz, D. (April, 1991). The use of guidelines in interface design. In *Proceedings of CHI, 1991, New Orleans, LA,*. ACM: New York.

Thovtrup, H., and Nielsen, J. (April, 1991). Assessing the Usability of a User Interface Standard. In *Proceedings of CHI 1991.* New Orleans LA: ACM: New York.

A Design Guideline Search Method That Uses a Neural Network

Kaori Ueno and Katsuhiko Ogawa

NTT Human Interface Laboratories
1-2356 Take, Yokosuka, Kanagawa, 238-03 Japan

Abstract

Human-computer interface design guidelines are useful for developing well designed interfaces. The method of effectively retrieving guidelines appropriate for the designers' problems by using neural networks was examined to improve the productivity of software designers. Two learning methods for neural networks are proposed and the performance of each are compared in this paper. First, from software designers, who had used the guidelines experimentally, we found the relations between the words and guidelines the designers associated with a sample HI designed display. Next, many networks were trained using the relations, and the trained networks were evaluated using a criterion of appropriateness which had been defined in advanced. As a result, we found Method D which trained networks using the relations between each word and several guidelines was more effective than Method C which trained networks using the relations between several words and one guideline.

1. INTRODUCTION

Human-computer interface design guidelines [1], which are compiled knowledge of cognitive psychology and ergonomics, are one tool that supports the development of good interface designs for various kinds of software. Additionally, a design guideline database of approximately 300 guidelines has been developed using the hypermedia approach [2].

Through the real use of guidelines, we found that they are useful to review interface design for software designers who did not have human factors backgrounds.

Search techniques include browsing and string searching. The latter technique can be fast but the user may not know the most appropriate words. Although the former technique is inefficient, it is used more frequently than string searching, for most designers do not know the details of the guidelines.

It is necessary for inexperienced designers to locate the appropriate guidelines effectively to produce high quality interfaces.

The most efficient search method would reproduce the experience of many users. Neural networks [3-6] are a logical method of achieving this. This paper proposes methods to search appropriate guidelines from words employed by designers using neural networks. The effectiveness of retrieval strongly depends on learning the relations between words and guidelines, therefore we developed several learning methods and tested them by computer simulations.

2. PROPOSED GUIDELINE SEARCH METHOD

We propose an appropriate guideline search method which uses guideline search words of designers and a neural net model trained with the knowledge of HI experts. Figure 1 shows the guideline search method. The left side shows a display screen when inputting words in the guideline search system. The middle shows a neural network. Three layers of processing units are used. Words which used by designers are fed to units in the input layer. Guidelines are fed to units in the output layer. Units in the hidden layer neither receive direct input nor have direct output, but are used by the network to form internal representations that are appropriate for solving the mapping problem of words to guidelines. The network was trained with these relations before the guideline search is possible. The right side shows a display screen when outputting guidelines. In detail, the guideline search procedure is as follows. When guideline user inputs words i, j and k for example, units i, j and k in the input layer are loaded with constants Wi, Wj, Wk ($0 \leq$ Wi, Wj, Wk ≤ 1). Information from these units is transformed by the hidden layer to produce patterns of activity in the output units. When the values of units m and n in the input layer are Gm and Gn (Gm, Gn $\geq$ G, $0 \leq$ G (constant) ≤ 1) for example, guidelines m and n are output on the display screen.

In this guideline search method, the performance of retrieval depends on efficiency of training the neural network. We propose two training methods. One is Method C (concentration) which trains networks using the relations between several words and one guideline, the

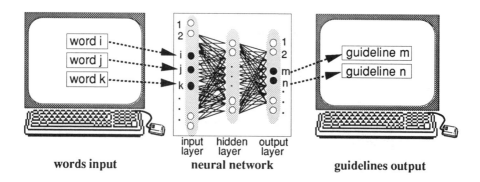

Figure 1. Proposed guideline search method

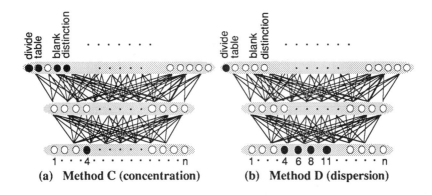

Figure 2. Comparison of Methods C (concentration) and D (dispersion)

other is Method D (dispersion) which trains networks using the relations between one word and several guidelines. An example of each is shown in Figure 2 (a) (b). For example, Method C trains the network using several words "divide", "table", "blank" and " distinction" and one guideline the 4th item as Figure 2 (a), while Method D trains the network using one word "divide" and several guidelines the 4th, 6th, 8th and 11th items.

3. SIMULATION OF GUIDELINE SEARCH USING NEURAL NETWORKS

3.1. Sampling words and guidelines

Subjects   2 HI experts and 10 software designers participated in the experiments. Experts knew the detail of the guidelines and had human factors background, while the software designers had no experience in either.

Task   An experimental software design review using guidelines was performed by the abovementioned subjects. A representation of interface design to be reviewed is shown in Figure 3. The interface was supposed to be used in an imaginary computer

```
Name Hatakeyama Koukichi      Visa Number  356478
Birthplace Toyama                    Nationality Japan
Passport M987312                     Birthdate 1966Y3M22D
Address Tokyo-to Taito-ku Asakusa 1-2-5, Japan
Other travelers on this visa
Traveler's Name                      Date of Birth - Place
   Aoki  Iku                         1965. 4.22  Yamaguchi
   Aoki  Yu                          1963. 9. 3  Beijing, China

Don't Press the RETURN KEY Before Input Complete.
```

Figure 3. A representation of a bad interface design. The original representation came from the bad sample data form in the guidelines by Smith and Mosier [1].

system dedicated to visa information input. This display screen violated several guidelines.

The subjects were provided with the interface on a piece of paper, and were instructed to improve the design through the use of the guidelines or to indicate how many guideline violations they could find. They were also instructed to complete the task in 30 minutes to an hour, and stop the task if they could not propose any more improvements. All subjects were also instructed to think aloud when performing the task.

3.2. Words and guidelines for training neural networks

Since the software designers did not necessarily select guidelines appropriate to problem of interface design, words sampled from designers were matched to appropriate guidelines selected by the HI experts. For example, one designer responded, "I think that it's possible for operators to input these '*numerals*' in the '*wrong*' way. What about *setting up lines underneath* the numerals (so that operators would know where to input), and also *putting something* (implying a hyphen or a space) between them?" These words are corresponded to guidelines which were selected by HI experts looking at the same problem, i.e. "*Marking Field Boundaries*" and "*Parting Long Data Items*". In another example, the respondent said, "There isn't any '*title*' on this '*display*'. People wouldn't know what this system is used for." These words are corresponded to the guideline "*Display Title at Top*".

74 words from software designers, 27 guidelines from HI experts and 89 sets of relations between these words and guidelines were sampled as a result of the experimental software design review.

3.3. Simulation using neural networks

Method   The networks were trained used the abovementioned sampled words and guidelines. The desired output of the network is the appropriate guidelines associated with the words input. To train or test the networks, 57 set of relations were used from among the 89 sets. The standard network had 74 input units which represented words and 27 output units which represented guidelines. The number of hidden units of the network for training was varied from 5 to 50 in units of 5.

The neural network with the abovementioned architecture was trained using 2 methods, i.e. Methods C and D.

The ten designers were equally, but randomly, divided into a training group and a test group. First, the network was trained using 28 sets of relations between words and guidelines sampled from 5 designers' data. The back-propagation learning algorithm was used to achieve convergence (R.M.S. error$\leq$0.01). Next, as a test of generalization, networks were tested without training on the 29 sets of relations from the other 5 designers' data.

3.4. Result of learning

For the purpose of evaluating the proposed search method, the performance of the trained network was rated by its appropriateness where

$$appropriateness = (N_{good} - N_{bad} \times k) / N_{total}$$

> N_{total}: the total number of guidelines selected by HI experts
>
> N_{good}: the number of guidelines that are identical with ones selected by HI experts
>
> N_{bad}: the number of bad guidelines
>
> k: weighting factor for good vs. bad guidelines

Using the weights from networks trained on the data from 5 designers with Methods C and D, the appropriateness of each network on the data from the other 5 designers is as shown in Figure 4. The appropriateness of the networks trained using Method D was significantly better than that of the networks trained using Method C (p=0.0001).

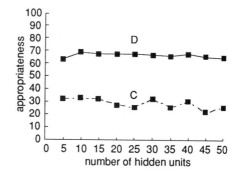

Figure 4. Performance of the neural networks trained with Method C and Method D

4. DISCUSSION

The standard networks used for analysis had 5 hidden units and had been trained using Method C and D. Each hidden unit was connected to 74 input units and to 27 output units. By studying the weight of the 5th hidden unit, the variance of the size of weights of networks trained with Method C and D were 6.12 and 20.7 respectively. It was found that networks trained with Method C did not have large weights and that specific sets of words and guidelines were not distinguished from others as a whole. There was great difference among the weights of networks trained with Method D.

Using Method D, the words which had large weights were "message", "negative" and "affirmative", and the corresponding guideline was "Affirmative Statements". Set of words and appropriate guidelines were generated when the network was trained with Method D. Considering these words and guidelines, this hidden unit encoded the expression of message.

As the number of hidden units increased, the appropriateness of the networks trained with either method did not increase as shown in Figure 4. Therefore, there may be 5 viewpoints when reviewing the interface design of this experimental display. Each hidden unit encodes "distinction and consistency", "separation", "legibleness of many data", "distinction between label and data area" and "expression of message".

We expect that analysis of the hidden units of a network which trained with data from interface design various display will be useful for classifying guideline items and improving the contents of guidelines.

5. CONCLUSION

A effective guideline search method using neural networks was proposed for software design and the appropriateness of guidelines retrieved through the method was evaluated two training method, Method C and D proposed in this paper. As a result, it was found that Method D was superior to Method C, and that weights of the networks trained with Method D were larger and the networks tended to generate sets of words and guidelines.

We need to examine these training methods and the user interface in which the input of words results in the output of guidelines further.

6. ACKNOWLEDGMENTS

The authors would like to thank Sadami Kurihara, and the members of Human Factors and Ergonomics Group at Human Interface Laboratories for providing several useful comments.

7. REFERENCES

[1]Smith, S. L. and Mosier, J. N., (1986). Guidelines for Designing User Interface Software, Technical Report ESD-TR-86-278, MITRE.

[2]Ogawa, K. and Yonemura, S. (1992). Usability Analysis of Design Guideline Database in Human-Computer Interface Design. In the Proceedings of the Human Factors Society 36th Annual Meeting, 433-437.

[3]Eberts, R., Villegas L., Phillips, C. and Eberts, C. (1992). Using Neural Net Modeling for User Assistance in HCI Tasks. International Journal of HCI, 4(1), 59-77.

[4]Mori, H. , Chung, C. L., Kinoe, Y. and Hayashi, Y. (1990). An Adaptive Document Retrieval System Using a Neural Network. International Journal of HCI, 2(3), 267-280.

[5]Mori, H. , Kinoe, Y., Seto, K. and Hayashi, Y. (1991). Cooperative Document Retrieval Making User's Ill-Defined Query Evolve. International Journal of HCI, 3(3), 253-266.

[6]Sejnowski, T. J. and Rosenberg, C. R., (1987). Parallel Networks that Learn to Pronounce English Text. Complex Systems, 1, 145-168.

Designing of Highly Effective "Human-Computer" Systems, Based on Multifunctional Elements

S.Tsiramua[a] and R.Kashmadze[b]

[a]Division of Systems of Computer-Aided Design,State Designing Institute of Land-Tenure, 15[a] Tamarashvili str., 380077 Tbilisi, Republic of Georgia

[b]Division of Medical Informatics, Ministry of Health Hospital-Polyclinic №2, 16 Kavtaradze str., 380086 Tbilisi, Republic of Georgia

Abstract

A method of the increase of efficiency of a multicomputer system "Human-Computer", functioning in the mode of simultaneous performance of functions, by means of its designing on the basis of interchangeable multifunctional elements (MFE) is presented.

Models are given of a quantitative evaluation of effectiveness indices (flexibility and structural reliability) of functioning of MFE and of the system, designed on their basis.

1. INTRODUCTION

In multicomputer systems "Human-Computer" (e.g.in local computer networks, on computer-aided working places, etc.) together with the reliability of computer techniques one is confronted with an urgent problem of human-operator's reliability, as while carrying out primary national-economic tasks high is the "price" of each operator's mistake. Operation performance of a human-operator depends on the following criteria: qualification degree, psycho-physiological condition, readiness to perform functions, sense of responsibility, etc.

As for operation performance of systems it depends on both the efficiency of a system's separate elements and its structure, flexibility and manoeuvrebility.

The system, functioning in the mode of simultaneous performance of functions, designed of one-operation elements without backup elements, is a rigid system with an inflexible structure, in which a failure of some element results in the failure of the whole system. Such systems are generally known to be less reliable.

Introduction of backup elements into the system makes it possible to construct flexible (reordering) reliable schemes (containing unreliable elements), which are nevertheless less economical [1-2].

On the other hand, a human-operator, capable of performing various functions, and a computer, having a wide range of appliction,are multifunctional elements,and their consideration in reliability model as one-functonal elements is an inadequate reflection of reality.

2. DISCUSSION

2.1. The model of reliability of a multifunctional element

In contrast to one-functional element, which may at any moment of time t be either in a workable condition or in a state of failure, MFE with the number of functional capacities $k \geq 2$ may be in one of (2^{k-1}) workable states, or in the only unworkable condition, at which MFE isn't able to perform either function, placed on it. The given situation essentially affects an approach to MFE from the point of view of its reliability. Reliability calculation element is not the MFE itself, a functional element of a system, but its functional capacity - a system's structural element [3].

The MFE reliability model, constructed with regard for partial and independent failures, involves all such functional states,in which an element occurs in the process of operation. Hence reliability of MFE a (probability of faultless work) is determined by the probability of performing at least one function f of a given set $F_a = \{f_1, f_2, ..., f_k\}$. If we take into account that the sum of probabilitites of all states of MFE equals 1,the probability that at a given moment of time t MFE is in a workable state is determined in the following way [3]:

$$P_a(t) = \prod_{l=1}^{k} p_a(f_l) + q_a(f_1) \prod_{l=2}^{k} p_a(f_l) + ... + p_a(f_1) \prod_{l=2}^{k} q_a(f_l) = 1 - \prod_{l=1}^{k} q_a(f_l), \tag{1}$$

where $p_a(f_l)$ is a probability of the performance by element a of the function f_l from the set F_a, but $q_a(f_l) = 1 - p_a(f_l)$.

2.2. The model of operation and flexibility of the system, designed on the basis of MFE

In practice it is often the case, when due to the outer or inner factors a partial failure occurs of an element, at which, starting from the moment of time t, it fails to perform the function placed on it, though it can at the same time execute another function of the given system. In such a case for the system to continue operating successfully it is necessary to redistribute functions among MFE, i.e.to execute their interchangeability without introducing additional elements.

A multifunctional element (both a human-operator and a computer) has the property to transform itself at a command into any "other" functional element. The element's operational redundancy is realized into the system's structural redundancy, which ensures its high flexibility and reliability.

Let us consider a model of operation of the system, designed on the basis of MFE, and suppose that the system $A = \{a_1, a_2, ..., a_n\}$ must fulfil in time interval T general function $F_A = \{f_1, f_2, ..., f_m\}$. Necessary condition for the fulfillment of function F_A is a simultaneous performance in a time interval T of all functions f_j , entering into set F_A , meaning that a failure to perform any function f_j will result in the failure of general function F_A. Each separate element a of system A can at any moment t of time interval T perform only one function f_l out of the set $F_a \subseteq F_A$. Hence it is evident that the necessary condition for the system A to fulful general function F_A is $n \geq m$.

Functional resources of system A are described by (0,1) matrix $B(m \times n) = \|a_i (f_j)\|$, $i=1,2,...,n$, $j=1,2,...,m$, in which $a_i (f_j)=1$, when MFE is capable of performing function f_j in time interval T, and $a_i (f_j)=0$, when vice versa. Condition of workability of system A is defined by the following function of logistics of algebra:

$$S_r = a_{i_1} (f_{j_1}) \& a_{i_2} (f_{j_2}) \& ... \& a_{i_m} (f_{j_m}) = 1, \tag{2}$$

where $i_1 \neq i_2 \neq ... \neq i_m$; $j_1 \neq j_2 \neq ... \neq j_m$; $i_1,...,i_m \in [1,n]$; $j_1,...,j_m \in [1,m]$; $r \in [1,N_S]$. N_S is a number of operation modes, representing flexibility index of the system's structure, which is determined by the following formula: $N_S = Per \|a_i (f_j)\|$; and flexibility coefficient is defined by the formula $M_S = {}^{N_S}\!/\!_{A_n^m}$.

Workability function of the system is determined by disjunction of conditions of working ability:

$$\Phi[a_1(f_1), a_1(f_2), ..., a_n(f_m-1), a_n(f_m)] = \overset{N_S}{\underset{r=1}{V}} S_r = 1. \tag{3}$$

2.3. The model of the system's structural reliability

Using probability matrixies $P(m \times n) = \|p_i (f_j)\|$, $i=1,2,...,n$, $j=1,2,...,m$ of operation capacities of the elements of system A , as well as a probability model of MFE (1), with regard for condition (3) structural reliability of system A (probability of faultless work) is determined by the sum of probabilities of the system's occurence in a workable state:

$$P\{\Phi=1\} = \overset{n}{\underset{i=1}{\prod}} p_i (f_1 ... f_{k_i}) + q_1(f_1) \, p_1(f_2 ... f_{k_1}) \overset{n}{\underset{i=2}{\prod}} p_i(f_1 ... f_{k_i}) + ...$$

$$... + p_1(f_2 ... f_{k_1}) \, p_2(f_1 \, f_3 ... f_{k_2}) ... p_n(f_1 ... f_{k_n}-1) \overset{n}{\underset{i=1}{\prod}} q_i(f_i) + ...$$

$$... + q_1(f_2 ... f_{k_1}) \, q_2(f_1 \, f_3 ... f_{k_2}) ... q_n (f_1 ... f_{k_n}-1) \overset{n}{\underset{i=1}{\prod}} p_i(f_i), \tag{4}$$

where $p_i(f_1 ... f_{k_i})$ is the probability of performance by element a_i of all or part of functions of the sets F_A .

In a particular case, when $n=m=k$ and $p_1(f_1)= \ldots =p_n(f_m)=p_a$, probability of faultless work of system A without consideration of time t is defined in the following way [4]:

$$P(F)=\sum_{g=1}^{K} N(g)p_a^g(1-p_a)^{K-g},$$ (5)

where $N(g)$ represents a number of the system's workable conditions, depending on number g of "lost" functional resources, K – a total number of functional resources of the system ($K=\sum k_i$, $K \leq mn$).

Considering that in general case at $n \geq m \geq k_i$ the number of the system's all states W_A is equal to 2^K and the number of operation modes $N_S \leq A_n^m$ (at $n=m=k$, $W_A=2^{nm}$ and $N_S=n!$), then the problem discussed is related to a great dimension class. In case of $n,m,k>3$ obtaining of the system's structural reliability polynome, designed of MFE, represents a hard task, insoluble without a computer.

In order to obtain a reliability polynome of system A methods of search and probabilistic logic, such as orthogonalization, tabular, and sectioning methods [5], have been applied.

From the viewpoint of calculation time preference is given to orthogonalization method. Nevertheless, the work in this direction is under way, as we deal with astronomical figures when $n,m,k \geq 10$, and neither of the above mentioned methods will be of use.

3. CONCLUSIONS

Investigation of the structures, designed of one- and multifunctional elements, and analysis of the results of quantitative assessment of structural reliability and flexibility have shown that efficiency of systems, designed on the basis of minimum number of multifunctional elements, considerably exceeds the efficiency of the systems, designed of one-functional elements.

Structural reliability $P(F)$ of system A, designed on the basis of MFE of a given reliability is the higher the higher its flexibility index N_S is. The latter on its part depends on the number k_i of functional capacities of MFE $a_i \in A$, $i \in [1,n]$ and a favourable arrangement of elements among functions.

Based on the given models special algorithms and programmes have been created, with which following problems are effectively solved:

1. By putting into computer memory of data on quantitative estimate of reliability (probability of performing of functions, readiness coefficient, degree of training or others) we obtain by each operation capacity of MFE a quantitative estimate of "Human-Computer" system's effectiveness indices.

2. The system's functioning is modelled.

3. Optimum systems are designed, i.e.from n $(n>m)$ elements such $m \geq 2$ MFE are selected, joint functioning of which ensures the system's maximum efficiency in performing m functions.

4. From the remaining $(n-m)$ elements the best reserve MFE are determined.

5. Optimum diagram of MFE interchangeability is modelled.

6. A scheme of training multifunctional personnel is worked out.

Besides "Human-Computer" systems it is likewise possible to use the developed application package for designing and effective control of other systems, belonging to the class of systems "Human-Technology-Environment".

4. REFERENCES

1   K.Reinishke and I.A.Ushakov, Assessment of Reliabilityof Systems with the Use of Graphs, Moscow, 1988.

2   A.I.Gubinski, Reliability and Quality of Operation of Ergotic Systems, Leningrad, 1982.

3   G.S.Tsiramua, S.G.Tsiramua and V.K.Lolua, The Model of Reliability of Multifunctional Elements, Bull.Acad.Sci. of Georgia, 132 No1 (1988).

4   G.S.Tsiramua, Discrete Systems of Variable Structure, Moscow, 1970.

5   I.A.Riabinin and G.N.Cherkesov, Logical-Probabilistic Methods of the Reliability of Structurally Complex Systems, Moscow, 1981.

Dynamic Representation of Icons in Human-Computer Interaction

Kazunari MORIMOTO, Takao KUROKAWA and Takeshi NISHIMURA

Faculty of Engineering and Design, Kyoto Institute of Technology, Matsugasaki, Sakyo-ku, Kyoto 606, Japan

Abstract

The present paper reports on two experiments that examine the psychological effects of dynamic icons and propose the desirable size and speed of icon animation representation in human-computer interaction. The first experiment compared two types of icon representation: conventional static representation and dynamic representation. Comprehensibility of icons' image and function is evaluated by a rating method. The second experiment reveals what is a desirable speed and size of dynamic representation. Results show that dynamic representation has larger effects on understanding of and feeling toward icons. The comprehensibility of dynamic icons is influenced not only by the size and speed of animated images but also by the difference between drawn objects. We propose requirements in designing dynamic icons: the size should be above 36x36 pixel area and the speed should be about 10 frames per seconds on the condition that the number of cels is under ten.

1. INTRODUCTION

Importance of graphical user interfaces (GUIs) grows rapidly, because GUIs are easier to understand and easier to use. Though some guidelines for designing GUIs have published [1], they do not describe concrete methods for designing individual elements of GUIs. For example, an icon is said to be a good interface that informs users the function performed when a mouse is clicked on it [2]. However, many users often fail to understand what icons mean and feel confused to use computers. We believe that these problems result from overestimation of users' cognitive ability and icons' capability.

In this paper, we focus our attention on designing icons to let them convey much information about their meanings to users. We propose a concept of dynamic icons that can animate images drawn on them. Several authors have proposed similar icons under the name of animated icons, but they have not described how to design, how to use, and how to evaluate them [3]-[6]. The effects of such icons have not been clarified compared with conventional ones either. Besides, some authors designed icons with animation without considering perceptual and cognitive aspects.

At first we discuss the concept of the dynamic icons and the significance of dynamic change of their images. Then we compare the comprehensibility between the dynamic icons and static ones through an experiment. Lastly, some proposals are given concerning the speed of animation and the size of dynamic icons.

2. DYNAMIC REPRESENTATION IN COMPUTER INTERFACE

Icons are classified into two categories by their appearance: static and dynamic. The appearance of static icons stays unchanged over time or changes only at the moment when some system event occurs. On the other hand, dynamic icons change their appearances independent of system events [7].

The definition of an animated icon varies with researchers. Some researchers have defined as ones indicating system function and others have defined animated icons as ones representing both system function and state. In contrast, we use the term "dynamic icons" for any icons changing their appearance to represent functions, methods, states and state transitions. As shown in Table 1, dynamic icons effectively indicate what a user can do with them, guide a user as to what to do, and inform a user where he/she is. These properties offer the potential benefit of providing the user with more information regarding semantics of icons.

Table 1 The features of dynamic icons.

Function:	What can I do with this?
Method:	How do I do this?
Function and method:	
State:	What have I done?
State transiton:	What is happening?
Occurence of events:	What happened?

3. EXPERIMENT 1: PSYCHOLOGICAL EFFECTS OF DYNAMIC ICONS

3.1 Method

Fifteen functions were selected to evaluate dynamic and static icons. Figure 1 shows these icons. The functions included text copying, file deletion, ejection and insertion of a floppy disk, file opening, printing, text mailing, and line drawing. At first, dynamic image of each icon was designed considering cognitive easiness to understand its function. Each icon had two- to five-second animation within a

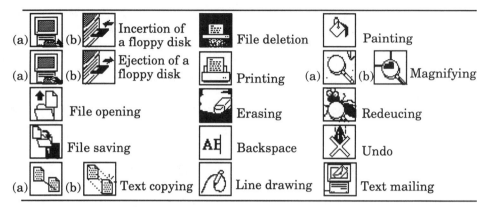

Fig. 1 Dynamic icons used in the experiment 1.

32x32 pixel area.

Forty-two subjects participated in the experiment. When subjects moved an arrow cursor, with a mouse, to the vicinity of a dynamic icon displayed on a computer screen, it started to be animated and stopped after a single cycle animation.

The subjects evaluated comprehensibility, joyfulness, familiarity and usability of each icon using a 5-point rating scale.

3.2 Results

Figure 2 shows the mean rating values of the comprehensibility of each function. The both icons showed little difference in comprehensibility of the functions in association with "magnifying text" and "opening a file". On the other hand dynamic icons were more comprehensible in case of "deleting a file"

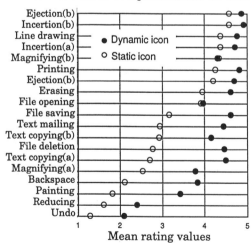

Fig. 2 Mean rating values of the comprehensibility of the functions.

and "filling a closed area" than the static icons.

A feeling of familiarity with the dynamic icons was very strong for "file saving", "magnifying text' and "file delete" compared with that toward the static ones. As a whole, familiarity largely grew by animating the images of icons.

4. EXPERIMENT 2: SIZE AND SPEED OF ANIMATED IMAGES

4.1 Method

Dynamic representation of icons was very effective for users. However, in the designing stage there is two important factors: how to decide the speed of animation and the size of icons to convey enough information.

As shown in Fig. 3, seven functions were selected to evaluate the animating speed and size of dynamic icons. The speed was varied among 2, 5, 10 and 20 frames per seconds. The size of dynamic icon was selected among 24x24, 32x32, 48x48, 64x64 and 96x96 pixel area. Figure 4 shows five examples of the pictorial image of the copy tool. Each icon was animated within one of these areas and at one of the four speeds.

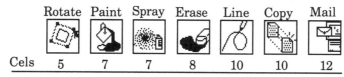

	Rotate	Paint	Spray	Erase	Line	Copy	Mail
Cels	5	7	7	8	10	10	12

Fig. 3 Icon functions and the number of cels in each icon.

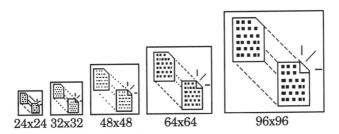

24x24 32x32   48x48   64x64   96x96

Fig.4   Five size of dynamic icons. (pixels)

Ten subjects participated in the experiment. Each icon was appeared at the center of the screen when subjects clicked the mouse button. Then the subjects evaluated the comprehensibility of meanings of the icon by the seven points' rating scale.

4.2 Results

Figure 5 shows the mean rating values of the copy tool. The size of each circle indicates the magnitude of each rating value. The rating value 2 expresses that

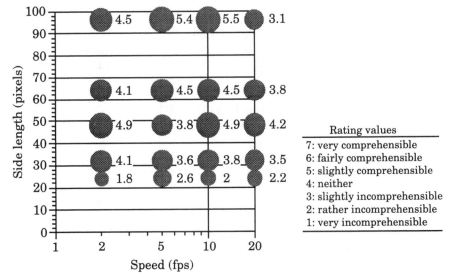

Fig. 5 Mean rating values of the copy icons.

the icon is rather incomprehensible and the rating value 5 slightly comprehensible. The copy tool icons of the size of 24x24 pixel area are less comprehensible than those of the size of 96x96 pixel area. Moreover the copy icons at the speed of 20 fps are also less comprehensible.

The spray tool icons are most comprehensible. Their rating values were 3.8 to 6.4. They are less influenced by the animation speed and the size. The eraser and pencil icons are also comprehensible as well as the spray tool icons. The size of 32x32 pixel is the lower limit in dynamic representation. As shown in Fig. 4, the size of 96x96 pixel is so large that its speed looks rather slow even if the speed is 20 frames per second.

The least comprehensible icons are the mail tool. When their speed was 20 fps, their rating values are lower than 3 points. When the size was 24x24 pixel, their rating values were lower than 4 points. On the other hand the most comprehensible condition of these icons is the 96x96 pixel size with the speed of 5 fps. In the other icons the 24 x 24 pixel icons are very incomprehensible even when the speed is 2 fps. The 96 x 96 pixel icons are very comprehensible when the speed is lower than 10 fps. The rating value is extremely low when the speed is 20 fps although the size is 96x96 pixel.

In this experiment the optimal speed of animation could not be determined. However, when the speed is 5 to 10 fps, most of icons were more comprehensible independent of size if it is above 32 x32 pixel area.

5. DISCUSSIONS

The present study has proved the evidence that dynamic icons with appearance of real world objects can play a large role in facilitating human-computer interaction. The results given above also indicate that representation of abstract functions in animation has poor effect on increasing comprehensibility of icons. These findings clearly indicate the limits of possibility of animation as a vehicle of conveying functions of the system to users. Animation is, rather, more entertaining or great fun for users and makes the system look easier to use.

In experiment 1 "text mailing" icon is constructed with 33 cels, and the duration of animation was about 5 seconds. Some subjects reported that it was hard to watch the whole sequence of the animation with concentration. This suggests that the duration of animation is critical to understand the icon meaning without cognitive efforts.

Many cels of images are necessary for representing icons without jerky effects. Large memory of the computer system is also required to design with many cels. For minimizing the image memory of dynamic icons we designed each icon with 5 to 12 cels. Therefore the speed of animation had to be rather lower. When the speed was above 25 fps, subjects could not understand what was presented on the screen. Subjects clearly sensed jerky effects in each dynamic icon which was animated with the size of 96x96 pixel area and the 2 fps speed. However, subjects felt only irritated at this slow speed rather than uncomfortable at the discontinuous changes of animated images. This suggests that the duration of a single cycle of animation, or the number of cels, is also important as well as the speed of animation. Furthermore we have to study the effects of dynamic representation the combination of the number of animation cels, the speed of animation and the memory size of images.

6. REFERENCES

1 D.J.Mayhew, Principles and Guidelines in Software User Interface Design, Printice hall, 1992

2 Y. Rogers, Icons at the Interface: their Usefulness, Interacting with Computers, 1 (1989) 105-117

3 R.Baecker and I.Small, Animation at the Interface, In The Art of Human-Computer Interface Design (1990) 251-267

4 R.Baecker, I.Small and R.Mander, Bringing Icons to Life, In Proceedings of the CHI'91,(1991) 1-6

5 S.R.Alpert, Self-Describing Animated Icons for Human-Computer Interaction: a Research Note, Behaviour & Information Technology, 10, 2 (1991) 149-152

6 T.Jones, Children and Animated Computer Icons, J. of Research on Computing in Education, 22, 3 (1990) 300-309

7 K.Morimoto, T.Uematsu and T.Nishimura, Evaluation of Dynamic Icon for Computer System, Proceedings of the 5th Annual Conference of JSAI (1991) 645-648, in Japanese

A User-Oriented Test of Icons in an Educational Software Product

S. Fullerton[1] and A. J. Happ, Human Factors Department, IBM, 1000 N.W. 51 St., MS 2212, Boca Raton, Fl, USA, 33429

Abstract

Educators evaluated two sets of icons (41 total), designed for an educational software environment, for appropriateness, discrimination, and recognition and recall. The icon sets differed in the types of objects represented. Appropriateness and discrimination indicated a clear separation of the icons, which provided direction for redesign within a product development schedule. Recognition and recall provided little distinction of the icons, probably because of the limited time available in which to run the test.

1. INTRODUCTION

Icons, as manipulated by users, represent what functions the user can perform within a graphical user interface (GUI) environment. Icons (or "objects") represent system artifacts (e.g. a folder represents storage) or devices, such as a printer. Other icons represent data and their presentation. In an educational environment, these are referred to as courseware icons. We studied a set of system icons and a set of courseware icons. This paper concentrates on the methods used to attempt to help others design appropriate, discriminable, and recognizable icons.

The most important goal of icon design in a graphical user interface is to produce icons that effectively communicate what they represent. An icon can provide the user with visual cues about the object or function it represents, and can also verify and extend a user's model of the system by helping to visualize and remember the important relationships within a product.

Reviews of icon literature and test methodology (Hakiel, 1991; Nolan, 1989) indicate that icons must be evaluated on different critical dimensions, and that such evaluation should always be done from the point-of-view of the end user. Several attributes should be evaluated in order to determine how the icons within an interface affect its usability; among them the

---

[1] Currently at the University of New Mexico, Las Cruces, NM

appropriateness of each icon with reference to its intended meaning, the discriminability of icons presented together on a display, and the icon's recognizability. Since a crucial requirement in icon evaluation, and in usability testing in general, is that the testing be performed with a representative sample of the intended end user population, all of the participants in this study were educators (elementary and secondary) and administrators.

This report describes an evaluation of two sets of icons on the dimensions mentioned above: one consisting of icons for basic system concepts, the other representing some existing applications and courseware. The goal of the study was to evaluate each icon individually, while concurrently considering the entire set in making recommendations to enhance the overall usability of the product.

2. METHOD

2.1 Participants
Fifteen teachers, two administrators, and three former teachers (currently working for IBM) participated in the study. Eight of the fifteen teachers work at elementary schools and seven teach at high schools. Fourteen of the participants had never used a computer application with a graphical interface, five had used one occasionally, and one had used one on a daily basis for 1-3 hours. Between one and three people at a time participated in the study.

2.2 Apparatus and Stimuli
Two sets of icons were evaluated; Table 1 describes the icons in each set. Educators rated 21 icons representing system objects and 20 icons representing program (courseware) objects. Since our goal was to identify the value of the methods used, the representation of each icon was given lesser importance. The icons were presented using Storyboard Live!, Version 1.0, on an IBM PS/2™ computer with a color display. Response sheets with instructions were given to each participant by the experimenter at the beginning of each task. Participants were given an eye examination as a distractor task.

2.3 Procedure
Participants performed four different tasks in order to evaluate the icons on four unique dimensions. Task 1 was intended to measure the appropriateness of each of the icons for what it is intended to represent. In Task 2, we measured the discriminability of each icon from the other icons in the same set. All twenty participants completed the first two tasks. In tasks 3 and 4, we evaluated whether people comprehended the meaning

Table 1
Description of icons used in each test set

System Icons		Courseware Icons	
Containers		**Reading**	-2 programs
	-6 unique types	**Writing**	-2 programs
	-Wastebasket	**Drawing**	-2 programs
	-School objects e.g., classes	**Class specific e.g., biology**	-8 programs
Data Objects		**Tools**	-6 programs
	-Mail		
	-Help		
	-Documents		
	-Lists		
Devices			
	-4 Drive objects		
	-Printer		
	-Network objects		

of the icon, and whether they were able to remember both the icon and what it meant. Only the first eleven participants completed Tasks 3 and 4, because examination of the data from these subjects indicated that sufficient information had been obtained on these tasks. In all tasks, participants were able to remember whether they had seen the icon and, with only a few exceptions, were able to correctly name the icon label.

Tasks 1 and 2 were administered in counterbalanced order, and were always completed before the other tasks were performed. One-fourth of the participants, therefore, performed Task 1 using the system icons first, followed by Task 2 with the courseware icons. The order in which the icon sets were presented was also counterbalanced in Task 3, . Participants were free to write or make comments, and to ask questions throughout the study.

2.4 Tasks

In Task 1, each icon was presented on-screen for twenty seconds. Participants then made ratings about the appropriateness of three different labels to each icon. The labels were on a sheet of paper that had been handed the participant at the start of the task. The ratings were made on a scale of 1= not appropriate to 7= very appropriate. Each person viewed only one of the two sets of the icons during this section of the study: either the system icons or the program icons.

Task 2 was a matching task. Participants were given a sheet of paper with a list of icon labels typed upon it. Having viewed a set of icons (different from those presented in Task 1), they tried to match an icon with a label. To reduce the probability that participants would assign icons to labels by process of elimination, there were five more icons than labels. Both the task order and the order of presentation of the icon sets were counterbalanced.

The first eleven participants then completed Tasks 3 and 4. Participants viewed a labeled icon set, then studied the icon-label pairs until they felt they could remember them all. They then viewed the same icon set in a different order, without labels, and were asked to write the name of each icon. The answers were then checked by the experimenter. If the scores reached the criterion of 95% correct, the participant continued with the study. If not, the process was repeated until they earned a 95% score. Next, participants performed one of two distracter tasks- either an eye examination or filling out paperwork- for ten minutes. They then viewed a series of individually-presented icons and indicated whether or not it was from the set just learned. If it was, they wrote its label. If not, they were asked to give it a label. The full icon set, plus an equal number of distracter icons were presented in random order. After one icon set in this section was complete, participants were presented the other.

3. RESULTS

Average appropriateness scores were computed for all three labels for each icon. The mean, standard deviation and range for the correct or intended labels for each set were also found. For the system icons, average appropriateness ratings ranged from 1.9 to 7.0 (1= not appropriate, 7= very appropriate). The mean rating was 4.63 with a standard deviation of 1.59. For the courseware icons, the range was 2.2 to 6.9 with a mean of 5.265 and standard deviation of 1.42. From the matching data in Task 2, a confusion matrix was constructed in order to determine potential confusion (range: 0 to 100%) between the different icons and their labels. If an icon was consistently assigned to one or two other labels, there could potentially be confusion between these icons and what they were intended to represent. These icons, and/or the concepts behind them, should be examined together in order to determine the consequences of confusion and whether or not changes to one or both are necessary. The test participants assigned some icons to numerous (and usually incorrect) labels. These findings indicate that these icons, and/or their correct labels, were not clearly understood, and people were probably guessing when matching icons to labels. These icons and/or labels require additional evaluation in order to ensure that they more clearly convey their intended meanings.

Based on the following criteria, the system icons were classified and grouped. Classifications were determined by data from both Task 1 and Task 2. Table 2 shows the classification scheme.

Table 2.
Rating system for classifying icons

Acceptable	Average appropriateness ratings that were above the mean with no confusion.
Severity 1	Average appropriateness ratings that were above the mean with possible confusion. These icons and their confusion need to be evaluated together in order for the necessary changes to be made.
Severity 2	Average appropriateness ratings within one standard deviation below the mean. These icons need to be reworked.
Severity 3	Average appropriateness ratings that were more than one standard deviation below the mean. These icons are in need of serious reconsideration, both conceptually and graphically.

Tasks 3 & 4 were administered with the intention of assessing how well people could recognize the icons and recall their labels. Eleven participants performed these tasks; the data were discarded for one participant who was unable to finish. Both recognition (correct indication that the icon was from the just-learned set) and recall (correct memory of the correct label) were measured. Analysis of the data from these ten subjects showed that they were able to recognize the icons 100% of the time, and gave the correct label for 96% of the icons. Half of the errors were confusion errors. Accuracy would probably decrease after a longer period of time, but time constraints did not allow for further testing.

4. CONCLUSIONS

This study evaluated two sets of icons for appropriateness, discriminability, and recognizability, in order to determine which icons effectively communicate their purpose and which icons were confusing to the intended product users.

Clearly, one would iteratively test the effect of changes to individual icons and to the interface. The desired effect of further design and testing should be to decrease the confusion among the icons, and not to decrease the appropriateness or recognizability of the icons. The task for assessing recognition and recall was not effective in identifying differences among the icons. Thus, it was not possible to tell if the icons were easy to recognize from this single test. However, the data remain valuable as baseline information for further testing.

5. REFERENCES

Hakiel, S.R. (1991). Evaluating Icons for Human-Computer Interfaces. IBM Technical Report: HF 144. IBM Hursley Laboratory.

Nolan, P.R. (1989). Designing Screen Icons: Ranking and Matching Studies. In Proceedings of the Human Factors Society 33rd Annual Meeting, (pp.380-384). Santa Monica, CA: The Human Factors Society.

6. ACKNOWLEDGMENTS

This work was supported by the IBM Boca Raton Educational Platforms department, part of EduQuest. Special thanks go to Kim Kemble, Randy Forlenza, and Pat Kelly for their continued support of the work.

Design of the User Interface of a Collaborative Text Writing System

José A. Pino and Edgardo Fabres

Departamento de Ciencias de la Computación, Universidad de Chile, Casilla 2777, Santiago, Chile. E-mail: jpino@dcc.uchile.cl

Abstract
This paper describes the design of a software system which will provide tools to produce a text document with a group of people. It will operate on a network of distributed workstations and will have some novel features in its human-computer interface.

1. INTRODUCTION

Collaborative or *groupware* systems have appeared in recent years as attempts to provide groups of people with tools to allow them to work together [8]. For instance, it has been mentioned that 30 to 70% of the time people spend in offices is used in meetings and yet comparatively few computer-based tools are designed to support these collective activities [15].

Collaborative systems can be applied to many fields, such as Computer-Aided Design, Computer-Aided Software Engineering, Computer Integrated Manufacturing and Office Information Systems. Within the latter domain, there are conferencing systems [6], group decision software [9], brainstorming [15], electronic circulation folders [7], electronic meeting scheduling systems [13], spreadsheets for group usage [4], systems for supporting large-scale negotiation [12], systems to track commitments [3], group text writing systems [2], etc.

As pointed out by Schmidt and Bannon [14], the field of Computer-Supported Cooperative Work is basically a design oriented research area. This paper concerns the user interface design of a collaborative text writing system.

Writing a piece of text with a group of people can be done with several approaches. For instance, the task of authoring it can be distinguished from that of commenting it and can be done by different people. ForComment™ [11] is software that can be used *asynchronously* to this purpose, that is, each user works on a common document at different times.

Real time systems, on the contrary, allow users to concurrently work on the same document. The complexity of these systems increases both in terms of the collaboration protocols and in the software features to allow joint work without undesirable side effects. For instance, locks, transactions or other devices have to be included to prevent users to simultaneously change a data item.

The following collaborative tools are all real-time. Cognoter and Argnoter - from the COLAB project [15] - lets users organize ideas in a document; the user workstations are in a common room and the participants can directly interact with each other. This *face-to-face* meeting simplifies group communication as compared with *distributed* cooperation (each user works with a workstation in her own office). Quilt [2], CES [5] and Shared Books [10] are examples of text writing systems with distributed collaboration. Ellis et al. made interesting experiments with GROVE - an outlining tool - having users work in face-to-face, distributed and mixed arrangements. The advantages and disadvantages of each are discussed in [1].

2. OVERVIEW OF THE USER INTERFACE

SHADOW (**SHA**red **DO**cument **W**riting) is a software system designed to provide real time tools to produce a document by a group of at most six people. It will operate on a network of distributed workstation and it will be useful to develop some novel human-computer interface features.It is being implemented on Sun Sparc workstations running Open Windows.

As other collaborative systems, the SHADOW user interface has several windows to accommodate WYSIWIS (What-You-See-Is-What-I-See) visualization [15] as well as private communications and work. A public window called *Text* allows every user to write pieces of text. No word processing is provided by the system; therefore, the text may be plain (as shown in Figure 1) or may have formatter commands such as for LaTex or troff.

A control window depicts the group members, their uniquely assigned colors and their status concerning this collaborative session. Clicking on the *Link* button to the left of one or more group members opens a private communication channel; the corresponding conversation is carried out in the *Private messages* window. The *Public messages* window is the place for discussions by the whole group.

Joint text production is done on the *Text* window, which is non-strict WYSIWIS. Each user has local scrolling control over the window. Paragraph locks are automatically set when a user tries to modify data in it.

Group members can make notes on the text placing *pins*. A pin signals the position of a *comments* window, normally invisible. A user can open a *comments* window by clicking over the pin. Appropriate buttons are provided in the lower part of the Text window to edit comments subwindows.

3. TEXT PRODUCTION

The only text structure SHADOW must be aware of is its organization into paragraphs. In order to finish a paragraph, a user simply has to click an *end paragraph* button on the lower part of the Text window. The corresponding marks are deleted whenever the file is saved for further processing by other software.

52

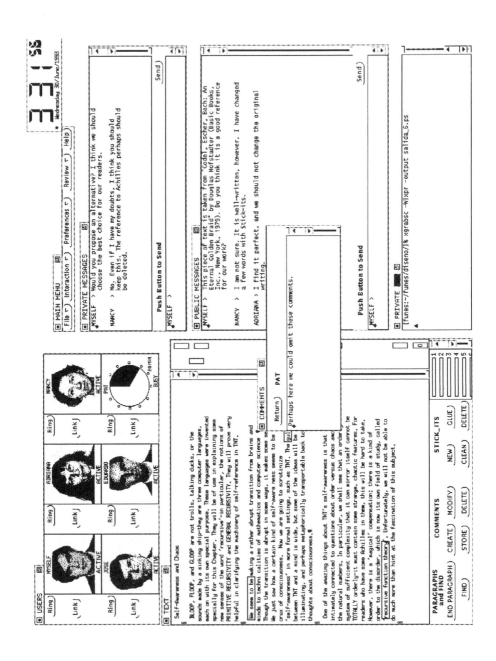

Figure 1. SHADOW User Interface

Simple editing tasks can be achieved with the Open Windows function keys. However, deletion deserves special treatment. In a collaborative environment, the deletion of a piece of text can be very disturbing: even if deletion by the author is agreed as the only acceptable way of erasing information, one user may like words, phrases or entire paragraphs other users - including perhaps the author- consider inadequate. Very cumbersome devices could be designed to force discus-sion and agreement over text to be deleted. SHADOW provides a non-destructive solution called *Stick-It*. The idea is to keep alternative scripts to allow users to review them without time pressures and present them in an intuitive fashion.

The Stick-It is a metaphor of a Post-It™ note: an image of a piece of paper which can be virtually glued over text and written over. The size of a Stick-It is completely arbitrary; in fact, the new text does not have any length relation to the overwritten text (the system scrolls the text so that the new text is seen in a nicely continuous manner). A user wishing to place a Stick-It simply selects the text to be covered and then clicks over the *new* button on the lower part of the window. The old text may be null and therefore, the Stick-It can also be used to insert tentative words or phrases in the middle of a paragraph.

Stick-Its can be placed to (partially or totally) cover other Stick-Its. The number of Stick-It layers is unlimited. To easily visualize the number of Stick-Its and which Stick-It is partially covering another one, the system automatically paints a new Stick-It with a different color within the paragraph. The Stick-It color order is shown on the lower right hand side of the Text window.

A Stick-It can be temporarily removed by selecting it and depressing the left mouse button. The uncovered area is shaded to remind the user that one or more Stick-Its have been removed. This may be considered as a metaphor of the glue debris left after removing a Post-It note from a paper page. The removed Stick-It can be placed back by selecting the location and depressing the right mouse button.

After discussing the various alternatives, perhaps the group members agree on a preferred version of one or more paragraphs and want to keep only the current view, deleting Stick-Its. SHADOW allows to do that by pressing the *Clean* button in the lower part of the window.

Stick-Its provide intuitive history management at a local level: there is no need of "undo" features. Stick-Its are also used in an object-oriented spreadsheet [4] but with different functionality.

4. OTHER FEATURES OF THE INTERFACE

Another editing facility of the SHADOW interface is the *Find* button. If one chooses it, a dialog box allows traditional string search and also search by "last glued Stick-It", "last own glued Stick-It", and "last created or edited comment". After the Text window is scrolled to display the new location, the user has the choice to continue working in the recently found paragraph or return to the previous location in the window.

An important consideration in distributed collaborative systems design is providing clues about the activities of the other users. In SHADOW, the *Users* window lets one user to inform the rest of the group members if she is to be unavailable for joint work during a period of time (Figure 1).

Two columns of indicator buttons to the right of the Text window show other users' work on that window. The first column of buttons shows the paragraph in which the users are working in the window (the button color matches the user's identifying color). More than one cursor may be over one paragraph; if one user has a lock over it, her button will partially cover the others in this case. A dark mark in the lower part of a button signals a user who has a lock over a paragraph. Placing a new Stick-It over a paragraph is considered a modification of that paragraph.

The second column of buttons on the Text window shows the relative position of the users' cursors with respect to the whole text; clicking over one of them causes a text scroll to make visible the corresponding paragraph.

At any time during a collaborative session, a user can create an annotated version of the document by choosing the *Version* option from the *File* menu. The system also stores a log with all data-related events during the session. Afterwards, group members can make *private* or *group reviews*. Private reviews are useful to track the events of a session, especially for a member who has missed it. Group reviews allow continuing work from any version onwards.

After choosing the *Review* option from the File menu, the system opens a window where the tree of versions is presented. Each version is depicted as a numbered node. Clicking on a node with the mouse buttons displays the version time and date of creation and annotation. Selecting a path on the tree delimits the initial and final version to be reviewed. Three types of reviewing are possible: all changes are shown, only changes to a selected page are shown, and only changes made by a specified user are shown. During the user-controlled display of changes, the Private messages window is normally available for communication while the Text and Public messages windows display the reviewed data. In the case of group reviews, the Private messages window works in WYSIWIS fashion and at any time the users may decide to quit the review and continue updating the current document.

5. CONCLUSIONS

Intuitive features have been included in the user interface of a collaborative text production software. Our belief is that cooperation by a group of people requires simple tools to allow alternative ways of expression to be kept and reviewed. Therefore, we have placed special emphasis in the history management devices: Stick-Its and versions.

6. ACKNOWLEDGEMENTS

This work was partially supported by *Fondo Nacional de Investigación Científica y Tecnológica* (Chile), grant No. 1162-92 and by a grant from Synapsis, S.A.

7. REFERENCES

1. Ellis, C.A., Gibbs, S.J., Rein, G.L.: "Groupware. Some issues and experiences". *Comm. of the ACM*, Vol. 34, No. 1 (1991), 38-58.

2. Fish, R., Kraut, R., Leland, M., Cohen, M.: "Quilt: A collaborative tool for cooperative writing", *Proc. of the Conf. on Office Inform. Syst.*, Palo Alto, CA, Mar. 23-25, 1988, 30-37.

3. Flores, F., Graves, M., Hartfield, D., Winograd, T.: "Computer systems and the design of organizational interaction". *ACM Trans. on Office Inform.Syst.*. Vol. 6, No. 2 (1988), 153-172.

4. Fuller, D., Mujica, S., Pino, J.A.: "The design of an object-oriented collaborative spreadsheet with version control and history management", *1993 ACM Symposium on Applied Computing (SAC 93)*, Indianapolis, IN, Feb. 1993, 416-423.

5. Greif, I., Seliger, R., Weihl, W.: "Atomic data abstractions in a distributed collaborative editing system". *Proc. of 13th Annual Symp. on Principles of Programming Languages*, St. Petersburg, FL, Jan. 1986, 160-172.

6. Johansen, R.: "Teleconferencing and Beyond". Mc Graw-Hill, New York (1984).

7. Karbe, B., Ramsperger, N., Weiss, P.: "Support of cooperative work by electronic circulation folders", *Proc. of the 3rd Conf. on Office Inf. Syst.* Cambridge, MA, Apr. 1990, 109-117.

8. Kraemer, K., King, J.: "Computer-based systems for cooperative work and group decision making", *ACM Computing Surveys*, Vol. 20, No. 2 (1988), 115-146.

9. Leal, A., Pearl, J.: "An interactive program for conversational elicitation of decision structures", *IEEE Trans. Syst., Man and Cybern. SMC-7*, (1977), 368-376.

10. Lewis, B., Hodges, J.: "Shared Books: Collaborative Publication Management for an Office Information System". *Proc. of the Conference on Office Information Systems*, Palo Alto, CA, Mar. 23-25, 1988, 197-204.

11. Opper, S.A.: "A groupware toolbox", *Byte*, Vol. 13, No. 13 (1988), 275-282.

12. Pino, J.A., Montañana, J.: "Design of a software system for negotiation", *Workshop on Next Generation Inform.Technologies and Syst. (NGITS 93)*, Haifa, Israel, June 28-30, 1993.

13. Sarin, S., Greif, I.: "Computer-based real-time conferencing systems". *IEEE Comput.*, Vol. 18, No. 10 (1985), 33-45.

14. Schmidt, K., Bannon, L.: "Taking CSCW seriously. Supporting articulation work", *Computer Supported Cooperative Work*, vol. 1, Nos. 1-2 (1992), 7-40.

15. Stefik,M., Foster, G., Bobrow, D., Kahn, K., Lanning, S., Suchman, L.: "Beyond the chalkboard: computer support for collaboration and problem solving in meetings". *Comm. of the ACM*, Vol. 30, No. 1 (1987), 32-47.

Visualizing Search Results: User Interface Development for the Project Envision Database of Computer Science Literature

Lucy Terry Nowell and Deborah Hix

Department of Computer Science, Virginia Tech, Blacksburg, VA 24061-0106 USA
Email: nowell@vtcc1.cc.vt.edu   hix@vtopus.cs.vt.edu

Abstract
    Project Envision, a large research effort at Virginia Tech, focuses on developing a user centered, multimedia database from the computer science literature, with full text searching and full content retrieval capabilities. Available bibliographic databases and on-line public access catalogs present search results as lists of text. We describe the Envision search results display, which presents search results in a Graphic View window as a scatterplot of document icons, with the semantic value of six icon attributes under user control. Bibliographic information about user-selected documents is displayed in an Item Summary window, while the document abstract and other user-selected data are available in a Preview Item window. Results of formative usability evaluation are discussed.

1. DISPLAYS OF SEARCH RESULTS IN EXISTING SYSTEMS

    Users search bibliographic databases and on-line public-access catalogs to locate documents of specific interest. The resulting collection is typically presented to the user as a text list of documents, with bibliographic information (title, author, copyright date, etc.) needed to locate the items. Systems differ in both the type(s) of searches that can be performed and the ordering principle applied to the results. The majority of systems in widespread use do boolean searches of indexed entries of titles, authors, and subject descriptors [1]. These systems present results ordered in a variety of ways: alphabetically by author, by the order in which they were located in the database, or by some other method which may or may not be identified for the user. Research systems use a variety of retrieval techniques, some of which match natural language queries against the full text of the database entries [2, 3]. Some research systems also use partial matching and statistical methods to order results by estimated relevance to the user's query.

2. OBJECTIVES AND SIGNIFICANCE OF PROJECT ENVISION

    Project Envision, a large research effort at Virginia Tech, focuses on developing a user centered, multimedia database from the computer science literature, with full text searching and full content retrieval capabilities [4]. Envision is a step toward fulfilling the dream of electronic libraries, providing remote access to research collections. An aim of the project is to develop, implement, and validate new database methods and systems that will help computer scientists and others in the computing professions more easily become aware of, locate, manipulate, and understand a variety of objects that are important to the science of computing. Data used in Envision includes publications of the ACM and other literature, such as videos, animations and so forth, that can be processed for loading and use. Envision will serve computer science researchers, teachers, and students at all levels of expertise. Envision should also provide a model for developing databases of other scientific literatures. A major portion of the resources of Project Envision has been devoted to development of the user interface.

3. DEVELOPMENT OF THE ENVISION USER INTERFACE

From the proposal stages through its current prototypes, Envision has been conceived as a user centered system. Users have been closely involved in development of Envision, through an interviewing process that guided decisions about system functionality as well as through formative usability evaluation. We will discuss some of the more interesting aspects of our task analysis based on user interviews, the Envision user interface design for search results display that evolved from this task analysis, and formative usability evaluation of the Envision search results display.

3.1 Interviews with Users

Our first step was to prepare an interview questionnaire for a sample of typical and not-so-typical users of computer science literature. In intensive structured interviews lasting from one to two hours, twelve professionals in the areas of computer science and information retrieval responded to questions about current use of information sources, their future information needs, and their wish lists for the electronic library of the future.

When seeking publications relevant to a particular topic, most of our interviewees have used electronic information systems of some kind. These include computerized library catalogs, CD-ROM systems, and on-line search services. However, our interviewees found the existing systems difficult to use for a variety of reasons. They also generally disliked any requirement or need to consult an intermediary, or search system expert, to access the literature.

Our interviewees want the ability to explore patterns in the literature. One spoke at length about the "community of discourse," of people carrying on conversations in print, all reading what the others have written. Others spoke of citation indexes, reference tools which reveal patterns of citation within the literature, so that works evolving from seminal articles may be identified. Ability to locate seminal documents, those which have been widely cited, is needed. Interconnections in the literature are of widespread interest. People want to use hypermedia linking to navigate among documents with common patterns of citation, to follow chains of reference among documents. In essence, they want to be able to follow on-going "conversations" in the literature.

Browsing was another common theme. Users want to be able to explore the literature along dimensions of their choosing, to home in on particular areas of interest and explore those in detail, then move on to broader views, or sometimes different views. For some, browsing includes the ability to examine the structure of documents, not just the citation or the abstract. Users want to identify a section of interest in a document and "zoom in on it" for closer examination. Access to tables of contents provides part of this capability, but users want to move seamlessly between the table of contents and the body of documents. They also desire the capability to search document structures, so that chapters, figures, or sections of code might be located, not just whole documents by title, subject, or author.

The feature our interviewees most want in an information retrieval system is access from their offices or workstations. Most specifically requested or implied the need for full text retrieval. Other features commonly requested include access to multiple forms of information (abstract, resume, brief description, full text, bibliographic entry) about each document retrieved, print capability, user annotation facilities, and the ability to establish and work within a personal subset of the database. A usable interface was mentioned often as a needed feature and complaints about the user interfaces of existing electronic information retrieval systems were frequently cited reasons for not using those systems.

3.2 Envision User Interface Design for Search Results Display

Interface design work to date has focused on the major tasks of targeted search and retrieval, and use of the search results. Refinement of task analyses is proceeding iteratively with user interface design, prototyping, and formative usability testing.

Responding to interviewees' concern that an information retrieval system must be accessible from their offices, our design is based on the premise that the Envision user interface will be a client running on a user's desktop computer, communicating with an Envision server via network. The user interface designs provide flexible use of varying configurations of monitors, both in size and number of displays. The lowest configuration supported uses a thirteen inch gray-scale display.

3.3 Graphic View Window

A scenario of our current search results windows, shown in Figure 1, presents the results of a targeted search, for which the query has been issued in another window. Central to the design is the concept of viewing each document as a node within the Envision database graph and representing the document graphically as an icon. Search results are presented as a scatterplot of icons in the Graphic View window, shown in the upper left quadrant of Figure 1. The design provides a graphical, direct manipulation representation of documents found by the search. By manipulating the icons, users may perform a variety of functions:

- View basic bibliographic information in the Item Summary window.
- Examine the item abstract or other short description in the Preview Item window.
- Use the document represented as the basis for a feedback search, to retrieve more documents similar to the one(s) selected.
- Print or save selected information pertaining to the item, or retrieve its full content.

Users have control over the semantics of six attributes of the Graphic View icons:
- Icon placement along the x-axis and y-axis, each of which may indicate estimated document relevance, author name, *Computing Reviews* category, publication year, number of times the document has been cited by others, number of items in the document's reference list, or document size.
- The number associated with each icon, which may be either the estimated relevance ranking of the document or a unique document identifier.
- Icon size, which may be uniform or may vary to indicate estimated relevance, document size, number of times the document has been cited by others, or the number of items in the document's reference list.
- Icon color, which may be uniform or may vary to indicate estimated relevance, document type, number of times the document has been cited by others, number of sources in the document's reference list, or document size.
- Icon shape, which may be uniformly circles or may be varied shapes representing document type (text, animation, video, hypermedia, etc.).

Assignment of document characteristics that may be represented by various icon attributes is based on research in graphical perception [5, 6]. By changing the semantics of icon attributes using pop-up menus in the Graphic View window, users may alter the configuration of the results graph. These features provide users with powerful, flexible means to explore the literature.

3.4 Item Summary Window

Bibliographic information is displayed in the Item Summary window (shown at the bottom of Figure 1) when an icon is selected. The icon/item number at the beginning of the summary line provides a mechanism for associating each line with the icon representing the document and bearing the same number.

3.5 Preview Item Window

Users may obtain additional information about selected documents in the Preview Item window by several means, including double-clicking icons or Item Summary lines. The window, shown in the upper right quadrant of Figure 1, has the relevant icon number as part of its title and typically displays full bibliographic citation data, as well as an abstract or short description, though users may opt to display other information. The full content of text items may be displayed in the Preview Item window, but other document viewers are planned for display of videos, animations, and other specialized document formats.

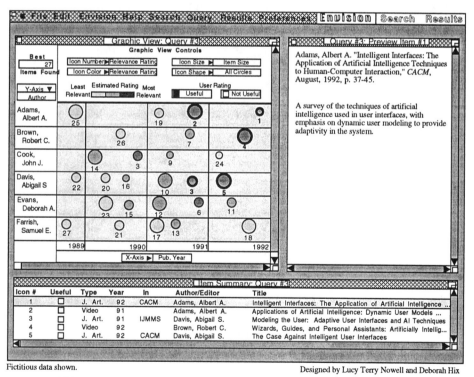

Fictitious data shown.   Designed by Lucy Terry Nowell and Deborah Hix

Figure 1.   Envision Search Results Display

4. FORMATIVE USABILITY EVALUATION

We have performed extensive usability evaluation on the user interface design for the display and use of search results. Prior to rapid prototyping and formal usability testing, prospective users, members of the Human-Computer Interaction Research Group at Virginia Tech, and the Envision project staff critiqued paper versions of the design, which was then refined and submitted for further critique. After several iterations of this process, usability testing was conducted with a rapid prototype developed on a Macintosh[1] using Aldus SuperCard[2] .

The foremost goal in the first round of usability evaluation was proof of concept: We needed to verify that users could understand relationships among the three windows and the graphic and textual objects within them. We also needed to establish user interest in this type of graphical, direct manipulation interface for viewing search results.

4.1 Participants

Since Envision is intended primarily to serve computer science researchers, usability evaluation was conducted with three computer scientists as participants. Two were graduate students, one of whom is also a programmer working in library automation. Both graduate students were primarily users of text interface systems; only one of them had any prior experience with a graphical interface. These two students had completed a graduate class in human-computer interaction. The third participant was an undergraduate who had extensive experience with both the Macintosh graphical interface and text-based systems.

4.2 Method

We formulated eight benchmark tasks, with a number of subtasks. Included were tasks such as finding three works published by a given author in a specified year and locating the title and author of the most relevant work. For these tasks we established 42 objective usability goals, based on measures of time for task completion, number of errors, and frequency of using HELP. We also had 28 subjective usability goals, measured by a questionnaire adapted from QUIS, the Questionnaire for User Interaction Satisfaction (Copyright © 1988-1991 Human-Computer Interaction Laboratory, University of Maryland at College Park).

4.3 Results

Across all participants, average times for task completion equaled or bettered our planned usability goals for 13 of the 16 measures of time. For 14 counts of errors and 12 counts of HELP usage, all measures met our usability goals. For 26 of the 28 subjective questions, the average user response was positive, on a scale of -3 to +3. Both negative responses pertained to the HELP system, which was present in only rudimentary form.

4.4 Discussion

All three participants were strongly positive in their evaluations of the design concept. They liked the variety of information presented visually in the Graphic View window and the possibilities offered for customizing the presentation. All commented positively on the power the interface provides the user. None of the participants had any difficulty in recognizing relationships among the windows and the objects in them. Minor design changes were required as a result of usability evaluation, such as changing one label from plain text to bold and revising the layout of control buttons in the Graphic View window.

---

[1] Macintosh is a registered trademark of Apple Computer, Incorporated.

[2] SuperCard is a registered trademark of Aldus Corporation.

5. FUTURE WORK ON THE ENVISION USER INTERFACE DESIGN

Participants in usability testing told us they want access to the query while they look at search results. They want to be able to revise or refine the query, in addition to examining it in relation to the results. Work is in progress to develop a smaller version of our Query window (which now occupies the full 13-inch display and provides a wide range of controls) for simultaneous display with the search results windows. Users will be able to toggle between the full-sized Query window, with the complete set of features, and the smaller window, which will provide only basic functionality. Users have told us that toggling between two versions of the Query window is preferable to either sacrificing query control features or being unable to view the query and results simultaneously.

Other features still under development include user annotation facilities, hypertextual capabilities, access to Mathematica[3], email access, and browsers for both the database as a whole and individual documents. All extensions to the design will be subjected to further rounds of formative usability evaluation.

6. ACKNOWLEDGEMENTS

This work has been funded by the National Science Foundation under Grant IRI-9116991, Dr. Maria Zemankova, Monitor. The project is also supported by the ACM and by Virginia Tech. The authors gratefully acknowledge the contributions of Dr. Edward A. Fox, Dr. Lenwood S. Heath, Dennis J. Brueni, William C. Wake, Robert K. France, Kevin A. Mayo, Eric Labow, and the Human-Computer Interaction Research Group at Virginia Tech, as well as our interviewees and usability evaluation participants.

7. REFERENCES

[1] Frakes, W. B. "Introduction to Information Storage and Retrieval Systems," *Information Retrieval: Data Structures and Algorithms*, ed. William B. Frakes and Ricardo Baeza-Yates. Englewood Cliffs, NJ: Prentice-Hall, 1992.

[2] Belkin, Nicholas and Croft, Bruce. "Retrieval Techniques," Annual Review of Information Science and Technology, ed. M. Williams. New York: Elsevier Science Publishers, pages109-145, 1987.

[3] Salton, G.; Wong,A.; and Yang, C.S. "A Vector Space Model for Automatic Indexing," *Communications of the ACM*, 18(11): 613-620, Nov. 1975.

[4] Brueni, D. ; Cross, B.; Fox, E.; Heath, L.; Hix, D.; Nowell, L.; and Wake, W. "What If There Were Desktop Access to the Computer Science Literature?" In *Proceedings of the 21st Annual Computer Science Conference, ACM CSC '93*, pages 15-22, Indianapolis, Indiana, Feb. 16-18, 1993.

[5] Cleveland, W. S. and McGill, R. "Graphical Perception and Graphical Methods for Analyzing Scientific Data," *Science*, 229(August), 828-833,1985.

[6] Mackinlay, J. "Automating the Design of Graphical Presentations of Relational Information,"*Transactions on Graphics*, 5(2), 110-141, 1986.

[3] Mathematica is a registered trademark of Wolfram Research.

Effect of Image Presentation to the Cognition of Plural Speech

Hiroshi TAMURA, Yue CHEN, Yu SHIBUYA
KYOTO INSTITUTE of TECHNOLOGY
Fax:+8175-724-7400, email:tamura@hisol.dj.kit.ac.jp
Matsugasaki, Sakyoku, KYOTO

abstract:The cognitive capability of the human to the plural speech words presented simultaneously is experimentally studied in this report. For two words presented one from right and the other from the left, higher recognition rate is confirmed for the right ear. The right/left difference in recognition rate is higher for the untrained subjects. When two speech words are mixed electronically before presentation, trained subjects responded with high recognition rate. When facial image of the talker is associated in presentation, the words associated with image showed certain increase in recognition rate.

1. Introduction

In the traditional technology of message presentation, single message was essentially chosen for the clear transmission. However in the real world event, more than one things happen at the same time. And people have the liberty of choosing one message out of others. Advanced information systems have to support such freedom of choice. Hypertext is a candidate system which have users supported by the freedom of control of selecting preferable informations at will, instead of the systems to transfer the message of the author precisely and efficiently as possible. For the effective uses of such information technology, better understanding on the human cognitive process is essential.

Although there are a large amount of studies on the speech recognitions of the man, the most of them are concerned with single speech. This paper is to report the cognitive capability of the human to the speech words presented simultaneously, and to examine the factors effecting on the capability, such as the video presentation of the talker. Some interesting studies were done in the field of physiology of human brain. They used a method called dichotic listening in which two speech words are presented at the same time, one from the right and the other from the left ear. They found a significant difference in the recognition ratio of the words presented from the right and the left. While such laterality is an essential cue to differentiate speeches presented simultaneously, we have confirmed the existence of other cues supporting speech differentiation.

Studies on the integrated use of speech and image have begun only recently. Some interactions between sight and sound were reported by MacDonald and McGurk(MMG1). Their study is concerned with the perceptions of the isolated syllable with and without image of mouth motion. The result has indicated that under noisy situations, presentation of mouth motion enhances the perception of the speech sound. Similar results were confirmed by Sekiyama et Al[SKY1] in Japanese listeners. Their recent report is suggesting that the presentation of mouth motion has different effects in different language and culture[SKY2].

Ostberg et al [OST1] has suggested that noise tolerance of the speech recognition could be enhanced by use of image of the talker, by experiments in a more realistic to daily situations.

This papers is to report how people recognize speech words presented at the same time, and whether visual facial image of speaker could enhance speech recognition.

2. Experimental System

First a talker with clear pronunciation of Japanese has read about a hundred of Japanese words, and the facial image and sound speech were recorded in the video disc. The words had a single pattern of ANBN, where A and B are various syllables with one consonant plus vowel, or single vcwel and N denotes the sound n as in an. All words have meaning, except for the few meaningless words, included intentionally for comparison. Using this image and speech samples, the video tape for presentation was edited to have the face image and the associated speech sound and an independent speech sound randomly selected from the sample set. The two speech sounds are recorded in the right and left channel of the video tape. The channel for recording the speech sound associated with video image are randomly chosen.

The video tape for presentation were reproduced and presented to the subjects by the three methods in the following:
1. from ear phones, each channel separately to right and left ear,
2. from two speakers, each channel separately to right and left speaker,
3. mixed electronically and presented from ear phones to both ears.
The subjects are students of the university. The subject wrote down the words he could recognized after each presentation.

3. Speech Recognition Cue

Some results are summarized in Table1. In the first experiments 18 novice subjects participated. The average ratio of recognition for a pair of words was for the beginners 1.3 word/pair, or 63%. The recognition ratio is 75% for the right ear and 51% for the left.. The ratio is apparently higher for the right and the difference is statistically significant in many cases. The result is consistent to the knowing that the speech are processed dominantly by the left brain.

TABLE 1 Correct ratio

Series No.	No. of sub.	novice/ trained	presentation media	correct ratio % Av.	left ch.	right ch.
1	18	novice	headphones	63	51	75
2a	38	novice	headphones	69	61	76
2b	16	novice	speakers	51	45	57
3	7	trained	headphones	81	81	82
4a	12	novice	mixed	42		
4b	4	trained	mixed	75		

The second experiment 2a was done to investigate the distribution of correct ratio among the population of 38. Fig. 1 shows distribution of the correct ratio, which is more like the normal distribution with average of 69%. When the correct ratio of the right and left ear are compared, as shown in the Fig.2, the right ear is dominating with 31 subjects, only two subjects showed left domination. The one with the left domination is left handed.

Fig.3 shows the right/left difference as the function of average correct ratio. This figure shows the right/left difference is dominant for the low correct ratio subjects. When we look into the Table1 again, in the 3rd experiment, in which experienced subjects have participated, the right/left difference is negligible. Here the trained listeners are those who have participated in the experiments more than three times. This means that the recognition capability to simultaneous speeches is enhanced quickly, and the primary enhancement is due to the improvement in the left channel. For the novice subject, hearing speaker sound (Table 1, Experiment 2b) shows lower correct ratio than to hearing headphone sound. This is due to deterioration of right/left cue by sound propagation in the free space.The left/right cue is certainly the essential cue for the novice to differentiate two speeches.

However right/left difference is not the only cue to differentiate two speech sounds presented at the same time. In order to confirm this proposition, the fourth experiment were arranged. In this experiment two speech sounds were electronically mixed and the same sound with two speech words was presented from the headphones. As shown in 4a of Table 1, the correct ratio for the novice is 43%, which means it is considerably low compared to the separate presentation. For the trained listener correct ratio is 75%.

Number of
population

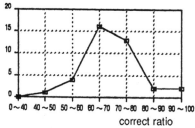

correct ratio

Fig 1. Distribution of correct ratio

Number of
population

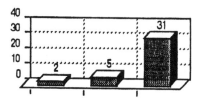

left > right   left = right   left< right

Fig.2 Number of right/left dominance

Right/Left Difference

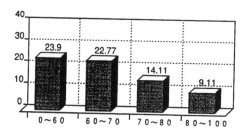

Average Correct (%)

Fig.3 Right/left dominance as the function of correct ratio

Fig 4 is the model of dual speech recognition based upon the above results. The speech sound entering from right and left ear is transmitted to left brain via cross lateral path ways. There exists the processor to differentiate speech words using right/left cue. The speech sound differentiated could be processed, searched the matching with words in speech dictionary and sent to generate the response. Beside the right/left cue, a mechanism to differentiate speeches by using time characteristics is supposed to exist in the model. The mechanism may be responsible to differentiate mixed speech sound.

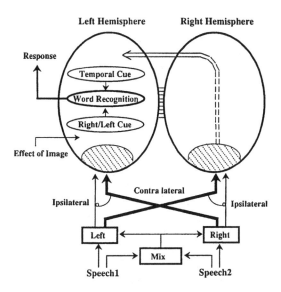

Fig.4 The Model of Plural Speech Recognition

4. Effect of Video Image

After review of the experimental data, we have noticed that the correct ratio of words shows considerable variations. Some words are consistently recognized at the high correct ratio, while some are low. So it is necessary to compensate for the effect of the word samples selected in order to evaluate the effect of presenting the image. That means if a word A is selected to be associated with the video image (VW: video word), and a word B not to be associated with image (NV: nonvideo word) in one presentation, then an other presentation should include word B as the video word and word A as the nonvideo word. Further for the purpose to evaluate the stress effect of presenting image, some speech presentations were not associated facial image at all.

Table 2 Correct Ratio of Words with and without Image (In % correct.)

	VW	NV	Diff.
group A	70	62	8
group B	64	56	8
Average	67	59	8

The results are shown in Table 2. In this presentation sample, group A and B are arbitrarily chosen words of the ANBN pattern. But the group A had higher correct responses. Taking the average of A and B, the word with image got 67% correct and the word without image got 59% correct. The difference of 8% is to be estimated as the effect of video image. The data of this experiments showed considerable differences in recognition ratio by word and by the pair. In the following an experiment was organized to investigate the effect of visual image on the recognition ratio of different consonants.

5. Difference in Effect of Visual Image

Since data from the previous experiment, as well as the reports elsewhere, are suggesting that syllables with certain consonants, like labial, are more influenced by the presentation of visual image, the next experiments was set to examine the difference in effect of the visual image on the recognition of labial and nonlabial consonants. For this purpose, an other presentation sample was edited. For the sample, 16 words of ANBN pattern each with a labial (pa, po, ba, bi, bu) , and16 words without labial were selected. A word with and without labial were paired, and each pair of words were presented four times by different presentation methods (left/right * VW/NV) in a series of 64 presentations. 34 subjects, including trained and novice, participated.

Table 3 Effect of image on recognition of labial and nonlabial consonants
Number showing % correct. VW: video word, NV: nonvideo word, diff.: difference

Laterality	Left ear			Right ear			Average		
	VW	NV	diff.	VW	NV	diff.	VW	NV	diff.
Labial	66	52	14	80	61	19	73	57	16
Nonlabial	79	70	8	88	78	10	83	74	9
Average	73	61	12	84	70	14	78	66	12

The above table shows that the recognition ratio of labial consonants are lower than that of nonlabial. Video words (VW) are recognized at higher rate than the nonvideo words (NV) in the either left or right channel and in every consonant (labial / nonlabial). But the effect of video presentation is apparently dominant for the labial. The right ear channel shows the higher recognition ratio than the left ear channel. Thus the right ear dominance sustains even under the influence of image presentation. The effect of image presentation is higher, although not so significant, to the speech words presented to the right ear channel. So supposed cooperation of the image and the left channel speech in the right hemisphere of the cerebrum were not confirmed. The effect of image presentation is relatively higher for the labial than the effect of lateral dominance of speech channel.

6. Discussions

Speech samples used in the experiments are clearly recognized when presented one by one. Simultaneous presentation makes the recognition considerably difficult. The stress to differentiate two speech words is so strong that it is felt almost impossible to do at the beginning. When the mixed sound of speeches are presented, the stress to differentiate is still stronger. If allowed to give numeric measures to the stress of the listeners to the various tasks subjectively, the stress is 1 for listening to the clear single speech, 2 for listening to a speech with some noise, 4 for the dual speech differentiation and 5 for the mixed speech differentiation. But when listeners begin the task, the correct ratio is generally 60% or more. This means the performance is not seriously damaged. And in the course of listening to the 200 or more presentations, they are trained to recognize the words at the 80% level. The subjective stress in listeners mind is assumed to enhance mental activities so as to prevent the performance to reduce. Such activities will establish some sort of processing programs in brain in the form of skill, which will further improve the performance.

One strange experience is that in spite of the same sound presented to the both ears, listeners often hear subjectively that one word come from one side and the other from the opposite.

When the presentation with and without image are compared, the video presentation in average does not have effect on the recognition ratio. The results are suggesting that the video presentation of the speech word do not enhance total recognition capability at least at the beginning, but it has the effect of concentrating attention to the video word. In the course of trials listeners acquire some skill of using visual cue to differentiate speeches when conflicting. It is opened to discussion whether the visual cue is comparable to the lip reading cue of the speech impaired peoples.

Reference

[CHN1]Y. CHEN, H. TAMURA (1992) Effects of Image Presentation to the Cognition of Plural Speech, Human Interface News & Report, 167-172

[CHN2]Y. CHEN, H. TAMURA (1992) Considerations on the mechanisms of Plural Speech cognition under effect of image Presentation, Human Interface, Vol. 8, pp677-684.

[KMR1] D. KIMURA(1961)Cerebral Dominance and the Perception of Verbal Stimuli, Canad.J. Physiology, 15,156-165

[MDN1]J. MACDONALD, H. MCGURK(1978) Visual Influence on Speech Perception Process, Perception & Psychophysics, 24,253-257

[OST1]O. OSTBERG, Y. HORIE, M. WARREN .(1992)Contribution of Visual Images to Speech Intelligibility, SPIE, Vol.1666, 526-533

[SKY1] K.SEKIYAMA, Y. TOHKURA (1991) Cultural Difference in Dependence on Visual Cues in Speech Perception,Technical Report of Acoustic Society of Japan, H91-56

[SKY2] K.SEKIYAMA , Y. TOHKURA (1991)McGurk effect in non-English Listners: Few Visual Effect in Japanese Subjects hearing Japanese Syllables of High Auditory Intelligibility, J. Acoustic Society of America, 90, pp1797-1805

[TMR1] H. TAMURA,(1982)Human Visual Scanning Program and its Modeling, in Analysis and Optimization of Systems, ed.by Bensoussan & Lions, pp917-931, Springer

A Pen-based System to Input Correct Answers to Assist in the Development of Recognition and Understanding Algorithms of Ink Data

CHO Yasuhiro, MORITA Toshihiro, HIGAKI Seiichi and MORIYA Shinji

Faculty of Engineering, Tokyo Denki University, Tokyo 101 JAPAN.

E-mail : moriya@cck.dendai.ac.jp

Abstract

This system assigns information in the form of correct answers to strokes of ink data, for simplifying the development of recognition and segmentation algorithms. When performing recognition and segmentation experiments using these algorithms, such correct answers (assigned by using our system) are utilized in speeding up these experiments and in enhancing their accuracy. In this paper, we first describe this system and its working, then we explain the correct answers actually assigned and the method of assigning them, and lastly we mention the experiments that we conducted assess this system.

1. INTRODUCTION

Two directions are emerging in the development of pen-based application programs: (i) using a pen to perform functions such as pointing, which have conventionally been achieved using a mouse, (ii) implementing pen's unique features when developing application programs. In the latter direction, especially, the tip of pen becomes a major driving force of the pen-based system. Due to this reason, a vital issue when implementing features unique to pen is to develop segmentation and recognition algorithms for handwritten ink data.

The pen-based system which we describe in this paper assigns information in the form of correct answers to strokes of ink data. Examples of such correct answers include various codes, such as, code that denotes the boundary of two consecutive English words, code denoting the English character "A", code denoting the boundary of tables of ink data, etc. We utilize these correct answers when developing segmentation and recognition algorithms. We call this pen-based system "answer assigning system".

After conducting an experiment which for example, segments English words from ink data, we need to examine the segmenting accuracy of the algorithm used in this experiment.

If the correct answers of English words had been assigned to strokes of ink data prior to the experiment, then it becomes possible to automate the process such as obtaining the exact percentage of correct segmentation, and in pinpointing which strokes of ink data had been segmented incorrectly. In the same context, it becomes meaningful to develop systems that, by making use of the already assigned correct answers, assist in analyzing ink data with the aim of developing and inventing segmentation and recognition algorithms. For instance, by making use of the already assigned code "boundary between two words", the user can extract the values of various parameters at this boundary between these two words.

The concept of assigning correct answers has been in use in developing algorithms for voice segmentation and recognition[1][2][3]. But this paper is the first such work in the field of pen–based computers.

In chapter 2 of this paper, we describe the outline of this system and the data handled by this system. In chapter 3, we explain how to use this system, and show the results of the experiment using test subjects that we performed on this system.

2. OUTLINE OF THE ANSWER ASSIGNING SYSTEM

In this chapter, we describe the role and hardware configuration of this system, and the data which this system handles.

(1) Role of the answer assigning system

Assigning correct answers to strokes of ink data is the main role of this system. This system has other roles also such as : reading/writing both ink data and assigned correct answers from/to a "stroke file"[4], (which the authors have developed,) and to assist the user in detecting, pinpointing and correcting what he/she has mistakenly assigned. To input (i.e. write) ink data from a tablet we use a separate system that is also capable of storing the input ink data to a stroke file. When conducting experiments about recognition and understanding algorithms, we use a system which reads ink data from a stroke file, conducts experiments, and also stores the experimental results to a stroke file. All of the input ink data, the assigned correct answers and experimental results can be stored in a stroke file.

(2) Hardware configuration of the answer assigning system

Figure 1 shows the hardware configuration of this system. This system uses two tablet–cum–displays, two stylus–pens, and two personal computers. Two personal computers are connected to each other with RS–232–C.

The personal computer on the left of Figure 1 is for selecting a correct answer on a menu, and the one on the right is for assigning the correct answer(s) to strokes of ink data. In this paper, the personal computer on the left is called "answer selecting terminal", and the other

Answer Assigning Terminal   Answer Selecting Terminal

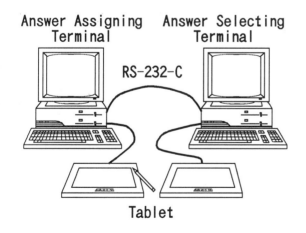

RS–232–C

Tablet

Figure 1. Hardware configuration

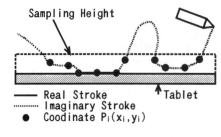

— Real Stroke
·········· Imaginary Stroke
● Coodinate $P_i(x_i,y_i)$

Figure 2. The data input from tablet

"answer assigning terminal".

(3) The data input from tablet

The data written on a tablet is sampled as a sequence of (x,y) coordinate points that correspond to the locus of movements of stylus pen over the tablet surface. When the tip of the pen is in contact with tablet surface, we call the sampled sequence of points (at this instance) as "real stroke". When the tip of the pen is moving inside the "sampling height" (in Figure 2) over the tablet surface, we call this sampled sequence of points as "imaginary stroke". In this paper, unless otherwise specified the word "stroke" implies both real stroke and imaginary stroke.

(4) What kinds of correct answers can we assign ?

The authors expect that an answer assigning system will have to accommodate a huge number of correct answers, if the system's designer desires to build the system being able to cover as wide range pen-based applications as possible. Therefore, as the first step, the authors employed only correct answers which we needed for developing our pen-based systems. The total number of the correct answers we employed reaches 8300.

Figure 3 shows some examples of the correct answers which this system accommodates. Examples of correct answers are as follows: various kinds of characters such as Japanese, English and numerals such as "A" and "2"; different kinds of gestures such as "delete" and "insert"; various kinds of boundaries such as "boundary of characters" and "boundary

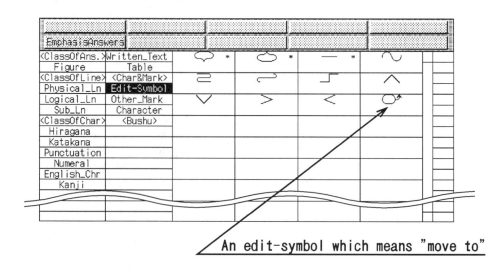

An edit-symbol which means "move to"

Figure 3. Example of screen of answer selecting terminal. The selected menu item *Edit-Symbol* is displayed in reverse, and, the different kinds of Edit-Symbols are shown on the right of this menu.

of lines", etc. The user assigns a correct answer, one at a time, to an imaginary stroke of ink data. Multiple answers can be assigned to an imaginary stroke.

(5) Reasons why this system uses two connected personal computers.

There are various reasons, such as memory insufficiency encountered when both our system and the ink data are in memory. Here, however, we focus only on the following two reasons.

First, to enable visibility of both the correct answer menu as well as the ink data (on which the correct answers are to be assigned) to the user, we decided to use two screens (which are connected to separate computers). The second is to enable the user in quickly selecting the desired correct answer out of a total of about 8300 correct answers in the displayed menu. This requires the correct answer menu to be displayed on as wide a screen as possible. In order to assign the selected correct answer to an imaginary stroke, this system should be able to display handwritten ink data as wide as possible on the answer assigning screen. It is also preferable that the user can always see ink data without concealing it by a pop-up menu of correct answers.

Another reason is to enable this system to be operated by two users in cooperation with each other, which in turn, requires two terminals. During such usage, one user selects the correct answer, and the other user assigns this answer to a stroke.

3. HOW TO USE THE ANSWER ASSIGNING SYSTEM

In this chapter, we describe how to use this system and about the results of an experiment that we performed to measure the assigning time. In this paper, we describe the usage of the following two -- Method of assigning correct answers, and, How to find mistakenly assigned correct answers.

(1) Method of assigning and deleting correct answers

User assigns correct answers as follows. As shown in the center of Figure 3, the user selects the correct answer. We call this menu as the correct answer menu. First of all, the user selects one correct answer with the pen. The item of the selected menu is displayed in reverse. Next, the user touches the imaginary stroke (on the screen where ink data is displayed) with the pen. With this, correct answers, which the user selected, are assigned to the imaginary stroke. In case it is difficult for the user to point to the desired imaginary stroke, for example due to the presence of many strokes on the answer assigning screen, then the correct answer can be assigned in the following manner. To do this, we use the "stroke cursor"[5]. (In Figure 4, the stroke cursor lies between "U" and "S" shown as straight line.) We have implemented this function of displaying only one stroke in our system. First the user touches an imaginary stroke (that lies nearer to the target imaginary stroke) with the pen. Then, by tapping the menu "←" and "→" in the lower part of Figure 4 with the pen, the user moves this stroke cursor back and forth. After moving the stroke cursor to the target imaginary stroke, the user taps "Execute" in the lower side of Figure 4 with the pen. As a result, correct answers already selected with the pen can be assigned to the imaginary stroke.

When the user assigns a correct answer to the wrong imaginary stroke by mistake, he/she can delete such mistakenly assigned correct answer using exactly the same operation as in assigning correct answers. That is, when the user points to the imaginary stroke with pen, the correct answers will be deleted in case that the correct answers already

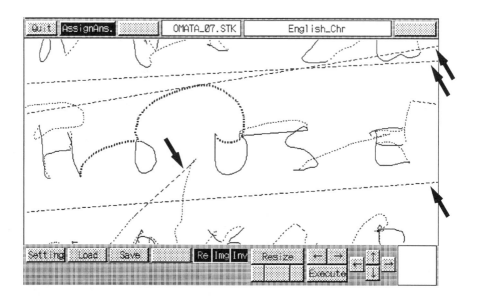

Figure 4. Example of answer assigning terminal. The lines pointed to by bold arrows denote the approximate locus of the pen tip when it is outside the sampling height.

assigned at the imaginary stroke are equal to the correct answers selected with the pen. Except for such case, selected correct answers will be added.

(2) How to find mistakenly assigned correct answers

In our system, we have implemented the function that displays in thick stroke the selected imaginary stroke. First, we describe the method by which the user can manually check with eyes the correct answer immediately after assigning these correct answer. In this method, immediately after assigning the correct answer to an imaginary stroke, this imaginary stroke is displayed in thick strokes. (In Figure 4, concentrating on the characters *HOUSE*, the real strokes are shown by solid line, and imaginary stroke by dotted lines. The imaginary strokes following "H" or "O" shown as thick strokes.) Actual operation is as follows. First, the user selects the correct answers with the pen on the answer selecting terminal. The user taps the "EmphasizeAns." menu in the top of Figure 3, and after that, he/she taps on the correct answers with the pen on the answer selecting terminal. Then, "* (asterisk)" is displayed in item(s) of menu which is displayed emphatically. The user uses exactly the same steps as mentioned above when checking the assigned correct answers. However, we omit details of the procedure here.

(3) Experiment of using test subject

Therefore, we can know the actual time that it takes for assigning correct answers. Six persons participated in this experiment. The ink data to which the test subjects assigned correct answers consists of Japanese text of about 200 characters written with non-cursive input. We show the results of this experiment. In this experiment, the six test subjects spent on an average 20.4 minutes in assigning correct answers. The six test subjects spent 6.2 seconds on average in assigning one correct answer. The above times include the time taken for correcting mistakenly assigned correct answer and for re-sizing the displayed ink data on the answer assigning screen. The average time that each subject spent in assigning one correct answer is 6.2 seconds. However, in 80% of the cases, the six subjects spent 6 seconds or less in assigning one correct answer. Therefore, we can say that users can assign correct answers sufficiently fast by using this system.

After conducting experiments, the authors found out that assigning is much faster when two users are using our system as compared to the case when only one user is selecting the correct answer as well as assigning it. However, we do not go deeply about these experiments and the results in this chapter.

4. CONCLUSIONS

In the field of pen-based computers, this system is the first that assign information in the form of correct answers to ink data. This system is equipped with about 8300 correct answers which the authors needed to conduct their experiments in developing recognition and understanding algorithms for ink data. This system is useful in developing recognition and understanding algorithms for segmenting boundaries of Japanese characters and pen-gestures in ink data. By using correct answers which have already assigned to the boundaries in the ink data, we can automatically detect and pinpoint the part of the ink data that was mistakenly segmented by the segmentation algorithm.

In the near future, we will be developing an ink data base that, in addition to other things, contains correct answers assigned to all the movements that the pen makes while the writer writes, that were assigned in the same sequence as the original order of writing. This will help in assigning and evaluating pen-based user interfaces. We hope that such an ink-database will help a lot of persons when they want to process their ink data.

REFERENCES

1 Kazuya Takeda, Yoshinori Sagisaka, Shigeru Katagiri, Hisao Kuwabara : "A Japanese speech database for various kinds of research purposes", The journal of the acoustical society of Japan Vol.44, No.10, pp.747-754, (1988)
2 Masanori Miyatake, Hidefumi Sawai, Kiyohiro Shikano : "Training Methods and Their Effects for Spotting Japanese Phonemes Using Time-Delay Neural Networks", Transactions of the institute of electronics, information and communication engineers of Japan Vol.J73-D-II, No.5, pp.699-706, (1990)
3 Chieko Furuichi, Satoshi Imai : "Speaker-Dependent Phoneme Recognition of Unspecified Vocabulary Japanese Speech", Transactions of the institute of electronics, information and communication engineers of Japan Vol.J73-D-II, No.4, pp.501-511, (1990)
4 Toshihiro Morita, Shinji Moriya : "A File Structure for Stroke Data and its File Management Program", Proceedings of joint meeting of technical committees on database systems and programming languages (Information processing society of Japan) (91-DBS-85, 91-PRG-4), 91, 84, pp.1-10, (1991)
5 Shinji Moriya, Toshihiro Morita, Kouji Inai, Satoshi Shimizu : "Stroke Editor, and Direct Pointing and Manipulation", Transactions of the information processing society of Japan, Vol.32, No.8, pp.1022-1029, (1991)

A New Approach to Visual Programming in User Interface Design

Jürgen Herczeg, Hubertus Hohl, and Matthias Ressel
Research Group DRUID

University of Stuttgart, Department of Computer Science
Breitwiesenstr. 20-22, D-70565 Stuttgart, Germany
E-Mail: druid@informatik.uni-stuttgart.de

Keywords: Graphical user interfaces, user interface development environments, interface builders, toolkits, visual programming, direct manipulation

Abstract

To face prevailing problems with existing tools for interactively building graphical user interfaces we present a new object-oriented approach to implementing visual programming tools. This approach is employed by the user interface development environment XIT. It is based on the representation of knowledge for creating and manipulating interaction objects in the underlying user interface toolkit. This knowledge forms the basis for a set of higher-level tools, including interface builders, inspectors, browsers, and tracers, which may be applied to user interfaces created by either visual or conventional programming.

1. THE ROLE OF VISUAL PROGRAMMING IN USER INTERFACE DESIGN

Employing visual programming techniques for building graphical user interfaces is not quite new [5]. Only recently, however, with the availability of so-called *interface builders* it has attracted the attention of application programmers. With these tools, a graphical user interface may be constructed by means of direct manipulation. The user selects interface elements from palettes, composes and manipulates them with the mouse, and specifies their properties by means of menus, forms, or property sheets. In contrast to more traditional approaches to visual programming, where a *visual language* is used instead of a textual, general-purpose programming language (cf. [4]), an interface builder may be rather characterized as a "visual front end" to a special-purpose language for creating and manipulating objects provided by a *user interface toolkit*. With the help of toolkits, low-level functionality is mostly hidden from the programmer; it is encapsulated in predefined, high-level building blocks. Another major difference between visual programming in general and visual programming techniques for building graphical user interfaces is that the graphical objects manipulated by the programmer are — or at least look like — the objects to be created instead of being iconic representations of abstract concepts such as operators, symbols, or data of a programming language. So for the programmer, no transformation is needed between the program to be created and the visual representation on the screen. This closely corresponds to the very idea of direct manipulation and is probably one of the most important reasons, why visual programming turns out to be more successful in the domain of user interface design than for general programming.

2. PROBLEMS WITH EXISTING TOOLS

Although visual programming techniques seem to be most natural and predestined for building graphical user interfaces, most of the existing interface builders have several shortcomings:

- They mainly address the visual aspects of a user interface, such as display attributes and layout. Describing dynamic aspects of a user interface and connecting it to the application, which is among the most difficult tasks in building highly interactive user interfaces, is not or only partly supported.

- Many interface builders are merely add-ons to certain toolkits and, even worse, only provide parts of their already restricted functionality. Therefore, incorporating application-specific interface elements or advanced interaction techniques is not possible. Whereas general-purpose visual programming tools often have been blamed for being too low-level and not scaling up for real applications, many interface building tools can be criticized for being too high-level and therefore only suitable for standard applications.

- Interface builders cannot be used for redesigning or incrementally modifying user interfaces created by conventional programming. Therefore, modifying and reusing parts of existing programs, which is one of the key principles of an object-oriented approach, is not supported. An important aspect in user interface design, however, is investigating design alternatives and extensions for existing interfaces, rather than building new ones from scratch.

- The process of constructing a user interface with an interface builder more or less still resembles conventional programming: A graphics editor (instead of a text editor) is used to specify the overall appearance. After generating and possibly editing program code, this code has to be compiled and linked with the corresponding application program. Finally, the functionality of the interface can be tested, which usually ends up in restarting the whole procedure to perform modifications. Simulation components of interface builders for testing the behavior of a user interface are mainly restricted to application-independent dynamic aspects, such as visual feedback. Modifying or customizing interfaces at application run-time is not supported.

For some of these reasons, today, most user interfaces are still implemented by means of conventional programming with the help of user interface toolkits or even no tools at all [7]. Visual programming techniques, however, can be useful for many different aspects of user interface design. Assembling user interface elements and inspecting and manipulating their (visual) properties is the basic functionality common to all interface builders. In addition, more advanced techniques have been developed for various, mostly research tools. Among them are (1) the creation of new interface elements from low-level graphical elements, as for example in Peridot [5] and Garnet [6]; (2) establishing links among user interface elements or between the user interface and the application, e.g., by direct manipulation in the NeXT Interface Builder [8]; (3) defining dependencies between them, e.g., by interactively setting up constraints in Garnet; and (4) specifying the dynamic behavior of a user interface, e.g., by demonstration in Peridot and DEMO [9].

3. A NEW APPROACH TO VISUAL PROGRAMMING

In order to face most of the problems described above we have used an approach which can basically be characterized as follows:

1. More functionality is integrated into the lower-level tools. Instead of providing a more or less complete, but rather static set of widgets, we have developed a powerful and "knowledgeable"

user interface toolkit, which provides a rich programming interface and subsumes most of the functionality needed for the higher-level tools.

2. The functionality of the interface builder is split up and distributed among a set of smaller, more universal interactive tools mutually invoking each other. They are based on the fundamental properties of the toolkit and therefore are also applicable to user interfaces created by conventional programming.

3. There is no separation between the development environment and the application environment. Therefore, each of the interactive tools may be equally used at application run-time.

In simplified terms, the key principle of this approach is: Instead of letting the interface builder know how a particular interface element may be created and manipulated, the interface element itself should know.

3.1. The User Interface Development Environment XIT

This approach has been implemented by the user interface development environment XIT, which is based on the Common Lisp Object System (CLOS) and the X Window System. XIT includes the following tools:

- *User interface toolkit* providing an object-oriented programming interface
- *User interface metasystem* for interactively inspecting and manipulating user interfaces
- *User interface construction kit* for composing interaction objects by direct manipulation
- *User interface resource editor* for adjusting resource attributes to application-specific or user-specific preferences
- *User interface browser* for inspecting the structural dependencies of a user interface and its underlying application
- *User interface tracer* for inspecting the behavioral dependencies of a user interface in a running application

Some of these tools have already been described in [2]. In the following sections, we will especially concentrate on the functionality which makes them different from related tools.

3.2. User Interface Toolkit

To provide an easy-to-use, but also general and extensible programming interface, XIT is based on two layers of user interface toolkits: (1) A *low-level toolkit*, which provides a general framework for building all kinds of interaction objects, and (2) a *high-level toolkit* providing an extensible set of common interaction objects, such as buttons, menus, property-sheets, etc., which are instantiations of the low-level toolkit.

In addition to standard and advanced features of these toolkits, which are described in [1], interaction objects in XIT have knowledge about (1) how they may be created or copied, (2) what characteristic attributes they have and how these may be visualized and manipulated, (3) what operations may be performed on them, and (4) how program code may be created for them. This knowledge is represented in the corresponding interaction objects classes, which are organized into an inheritance hierarchy. Therefore, new interaction objects generated by subclassing or aggregation automatically obtain this knowledge. Additional knowledge, e.g., for application-specific interaction objects, may be easily added if required.

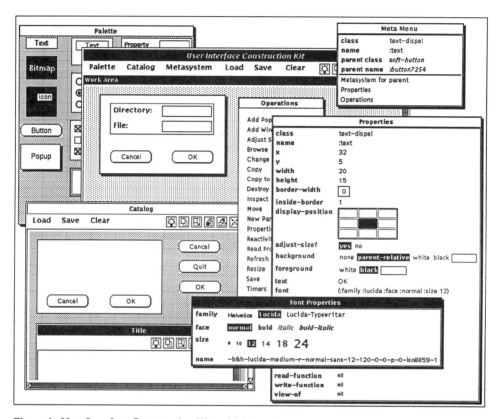

Figure 1: User Interface Construction Kit and Metasystem

3.3. User Interface Metasystem and Construction Kit

The *user interface metasystem* provides a graphical interface for inspecting and manipulating *properties* of interaction objects and performing *operations* on them. It may be invoked for any kind of interaction object, no matter whether it has been created by visual or conventional programming, and even in a running application. Properties, which may be either visual attributes, e.g., regarding the geometry of an interaction object, or behavioral attributes, e.g., describing the mapping of events onto the corresponding actions, are presented in property sheets. Attribute values are presented by editable text fields, menus, sliders, or separate property sheets, e.g., for font or color attributes. Operations, such as moving, resizing or copying an interaction object, are provided by menus. All property sheets and menus are object-specific; their contents is automatically generated from the knowledge represented for the object in the toolkit.

The *user interface construction kit* makes use of the metasystem and additionally provides common interaction objects in the form of *palettes*. Different palettes contain different kinds of objects. *Catalogs* provide user-extensible sets of (more complex) interaction objects that may be saved and reloaded. A catalog contains "real" interaction objects rather than iconic representations; selecting one of them simply creates a copy. Saving and reloading interaction objects is a basic functionality provided by the toolkits, which is used by the construction kit to store and retrieve an

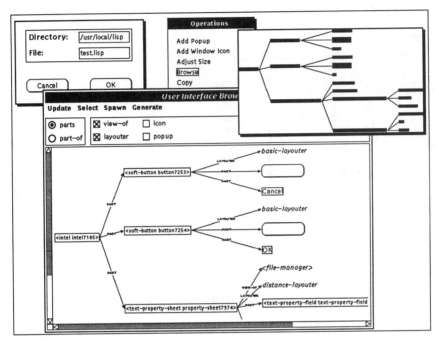

Figure 2: User Interface Browser

interface built by the user. Objects are stored in an executable, textual form, which may be edited if required and directly loaded by an application. Manipulating interfaces built by means of the construction kit and connecting them to the application is performed with the metasystem. Figure 1 shows different components of the construction kit and the metasystem building a dialog window for specifying a file.

By creating application-specific palettes, catalogs and metasystem components, the user interface construction kit may serve as an application builder.

3.4. User Interface Browser and Tracer

Interaction objects are organized into object networks. Each object is part of an interaction object hierarchy. Attribute values may be complex objects themselves, e.g., objects describing the layout or behavior. Finally, interaction objects are connected to application objects, which in turn may be viewed by an arbitrary number of interaction objects. The user interface metasystem only indirectly reflects these interdependencies by allowing the user to switch to parent or subpart objects and by providing special property sheets for complex attribute values. However, the overall functionality of an interaction objects can be made more visual and intelligible by explicitly presenting these dependencies in a graph. This is performed by the *user interface browser* which can be invoked by the "Browse" operation of the metasystem. Figure 2 shows the browser displaying the interaction object hierarchy for the dialog window created in figure 1. The dependencies to be visualized can be selected from menus. The graphical output displayed in the browser may not only be used for viewing but also for manipulating dependencies. Also for each interaction object presented in the graph, the metasystem may be invoked to inspect and modify properties.

The user interface browser as well as the metasystem basically display static aspects of a user interface. Dynamic aspects, i.e., which operations are performed in reaction to which events, are only visualized in the form of static event-action mappings in the metasystem. Understanding the internal dynamic behavior of an interface or locating errors can be very cumbersome or even impossible. For this reason, we are currently implementing a *user interface tracer* which can be used to visualize actions invoked in response to events both textually and graphically. The user may specify which actions for which events should be traced. Object-specific traces can be specified by means of the metasystem. The user interface browser and tracer are based on a general framework for building browsing and tracing tools in object-oriented programming environments [3].

4. LESSONS LEARNED

By representing knowledge about building, inspecting, and manipulating graphical user interfaces in the lower-level components, i.e. the toolkits, of the user interface development environment XIT, the implementation of visual programming tools was quite straightforward and consistent. Since these tools can be applied to any user interface built from the XIT toolkits, by either visual or conventional programming and even at application run-time, they not only qualify for user interface designers and implementors, but also for end users. Enhancing the knowledge of dealing with interaction objects by higher-level knowledge of user interface design, e.g., concerning human aspects, could substantially add to the usability of these tools.

REFERENCES

[1] J. Herczeg, H. Hohl, and M. Ressel. Progress in Building User Interface Toolkits: The World According to XIT. In *Proceedings of the ACM Symposium on User Interface Software and Technology*, November 1992.

[2] J. Herczeg, H. Hohl, and T. Schwab. XIT - A Multi-Layered Tool for User Interface Design. In *Human Aspects in Computing, Proceedings of the Fourth International Conference on Human-Computer Interaction*, volume 1, pages 678–683, Stuttgart, September 1991.

[3] H. Hohl, J. Herczeg, and M. Ressel. An Interactive Design Environment for Graphical Browsers. This volume.

[4] B. A. Myers. Visual Programming, Programming by Example and Program Visualization: A Taxonomy. In *CHI'86 Proceedings*, pages 59–66. ACM, April 1986.

[5] B. A. Myers and W. Buxton. Creating Highly-Interactive and Graphical User Interfaces by Demonstration. *Computer Graphics, Proceedings of SIGGRAPH 86*, pages 249–258, August 1986.

[6] B. A. Myers et al. Garnet – Comprehensive Support for Graphical, Highly Interactive User Interfaces. *IEEE Computer*, 23(11):71–85, November 1990.

[7] B. A. Myers and M. B. Rossen. Survey on User Interface Programming. In *CHI-92 Conference Proceedings, Human Factors in Computing Systems*, pages 195–202. ACM SIGCHI, 1992.

[8] B. F. Webster. *The NeXT Book*. Addison-Wesley Publishing Company, 1989.

[9] D. Wolber and G. Fisher. A Demonstrational Technique for Developing Interfaces with Dynamically Created Objects. In *Proceedings of the ACM Symposium on User Interface Software and Technology*, pages 221–230, November 1991.

Visual Interference with User's Tasks on Multi-Window System

Hirohiko Mori, Yoshio Hayashi

Department of Industrial Engineering,
Musashi Institute of Technology
1-28-1, Tamazutsumi, Setagaya, Tokyo, 158, JAPAN

Abstract
This paper describes the interferences of peripheral window, which are the displayed windows where users do not perform their task, with user's task performance on a window where they perform them, from the viewpoint of visual information processing, especially, of the relationship between the foveal vision and the peripheral vision. The results of our experiments indicate that the multi-window systems interfere the user's activity of his/her main task and some factors such as the number, the layout and the characteristics of each component of the windows on the display have effects on the interference. We discuss about the causes of the interference from the viewpoint of the nature of the human visual systems, especially the relationships between the foveal and peripheral vision.

1. INTRODUCTION

Multi-window system has been widely spread into many computer systems. This owes to its high usability such that the users are saved from the heavy load on their memories. However, it often occurs that various kinds of information on many windows interfere on the user's mental model [1].

This paper describes the interferences of displayed windows where users do not perform their task with user's task performance on a window where they perform them, from the viewpoint of visual information processing, especially, of the relationship between the foveal vision and the peripheral vision.

When a user works on one window, called the "foveal window," mainly using his/her foveal vision, the other windows, called the "peripheral windows," are projected on his/her peripheral vision. As the foveal vision and the peripheral vision have some cooperative or competitive relationship, windows on the peripheral vision should have influences on the activity level of the foveal vision. The aims of this paper are to examine such influences.

2. METHOD

To examine the visual interference, we had the following experiments.

Procedure

The task in these experiments is the visual search, which is similar to a counting task. In each trial, the English text scrolls automatically on the foveal window and the subjects count up how many numbers of a given word appear in the whole text (Figure 1.) The performance is evaluated by the accuracy of counting words determined by the ratio of counted number to the presented number of a given word in the whole text. Furthermore, the subjects' eye movement data are recorded by the eye-mark recorder through the experiments to examine what subjects pay attention to.

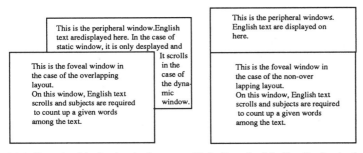

(a) An Example of the Overlapping Layout   (b) An Example of the Non-Overlapping Layout

Figure 1. Examples Screens for the Experiments

Conditions

The experiments were carried out under two conditions; (1) the text on the peripheral windows does not scroll (static windows,) (2) the text on the peripheral windows scrolls (dynamic windows). The experiments under each condition consist of random presentation of the combination of the number and layouts of the peripheral windows. Two of the variation of the layouts used are shown in Figure 1.

3 Results

The accuracy rates of the users' tasks with one or some peripheral windows are, overall, worse than without them, and its rate with the dynamic windows is worse than with the static windows. This shows that the displayed peripheral windows interfere the user's performance of the visual activity for his/her main task.

82

The number of the peripheral windows

In the case of the static windows, the results indicate that the increase of the number of peripheral windows has the significant effects on the activity in the foveal window (Figure 2(a).) The performance with one peripheral window was lower than without peripheral windows, and the performance with two peripheral windows was lower than with one window. The increase of the number of the peripheral windows, thus, involves the decline of the activity in the foveal vision.

This effect is not revealed in the case with the dynamic windows. Though the performance, indeed, is worse than without no window, there is no significant difference between one and two peripheral windows. Comparing to the static windows, though there is difference in the case with one window, the difference does not appear in the case with two windows.

The Layouts

Analysis of the layout of the peripheral windows was conducted by classifying into two types of the layout. One is "non-overlapping layout," and the other is "overlapping layout" (Figure 1.)

The results show the performance in the non-overlapping layout has higher score than in the overlapping layout in the case of the static windows. This indicates that the overlapping layout takes heavier loads on the visual activity than the non-overlapping layout.

The contrast result from this analysis for the layout is obtained in the case of dynamic windows. The performance in the case of the non-overlapping layout is worse than the case of the overlapping layout.

Each Subject's Strategy of Searching

For further analysis, the subjects were classified into three groups according to the position where they performed searching in the foveal window; (1) on the upper

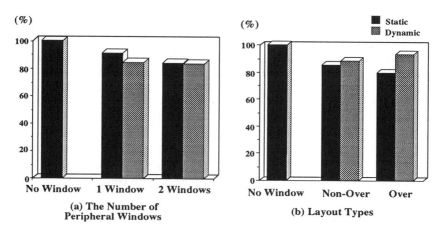

Figure 2. The Overall Results: The Accuracy of the Tasks

side, (2) on the middle position, and (3) on the lower side in the foveal window. The analyzed results indicate that there are relationships between the position where the subjects performed the searching tasks and the location where the peripheral windows are presented.

The performance on the foveal vision tends to be lower when the peripheral windows are located near the position where subjects performed their searching tasks.

3. DISCUSSION

These results may be originated from the nature of the visual information processing especially of the relationship between the foveal vision and the peripheral vision.

The Case of Static Windows

The number of the vertexes of the windows displayed on the screen becomes larger as the increase of the number of the peripheral windows. The overlapping layout also has more vertexes than the non-overlapping layout within the same account of the peripheral windows.

It has been known that when a static object is projected on the peripheral vision its vertexes rather than lines are detected [3]. The more visual resources required, when there are more vertexes of the static objects in the peripheral vision. Assuming that the total amount of visual resources is limited, the resources available for foveal vision decrease, if more vertexes of static objects have to be detected in peripheral vision.

Consequently, performance on foveal window deteriorates when there are more peripheral windows and/or these windows are overlapping.

The Case of Dynamic windows

In nature, the peripheral vision is very sensitive to moving objects. When additional unit of objects in peripheral vision is dynamic one, additional visual resources are assigned more for peripheral vision than the case of in which the additional unit of objects is static. When the peripheral windows are dynamic, performance on foveal window drops by large amount, compared to the case where these windows are static.

Then, why there is no difference in the performance between one dynamic window case and two windows case, even though we add one more dynamic window? We might be able to explain this results by following: Subjects make effort to their jobs done and there will be the minimum amount of visual resources which cannot be reduced more. This minimum amount will be a point to which the capacity of visual resources available for foveal vision in saturated. This seems to be the reason why the performance in the foveal vision has no significant difference within the condition for the number of dynamic windows.

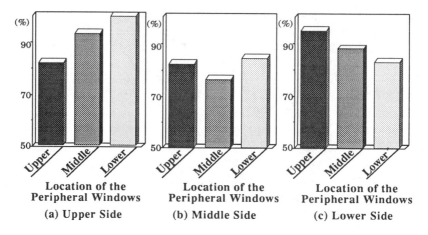

Figure 3. The Results Classified accrding to the Searching Point

According to this discussion, we can conjecture the saturation point in the case of static windows. As the equivalent performance with two windows in the static windows to each one in dynamic windows, the capacity of the visual resources will be almost saturated by the two windows even in the static windows.

Here, the another question which seems to be inconsistent with above discussion is why the layout is the significant factor to determine performance, even though one dynamic window is enough to make deterioration in performance saturated. This might be concerned with the causes from the different level of human information processing, rather than the nature of the visual functions. We could know such cause from the interview after the experiment. Most of the subjects stated that it happened, in the non-overlapping layout of the dynamic windows, they frequently failed to recognize the boundary between the foveal and peripheral window and to grasp the region to search and lost their work on. This means that their confusion of the searching region on the conscious level rather than the nature of the visual system involved the decline of their performance.

Each Subject's Attention

The eye movement data supports above discussions. The decline of the users' performance in the case of our experiments may be considered to be consequences from having their attention caught by the peripheral windows and glancing at them consciously. Eye mark, however, moved only within the foveal window without going out on the peripheral windows in the all trials. This shows that the decline of the performance is not caused by watching the peripheral windows as the results of their disturbing the subjects' concentration, but by the decline of the activity of their visual systems in spite of paying attention to the task only on the foveal vision under every condition.

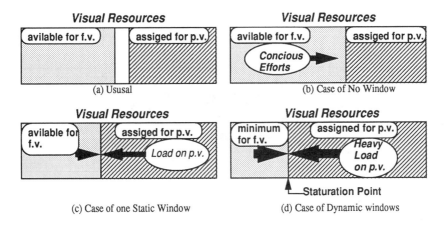

Figure 4. The Hypothesis of Visual Resources

3. CONCLUSION

This paper describes the interferences of the visual activity on the foveal window in the presence of the peripheral windows. These interferences arise from the nature of human vision, the cooperative and competitive relationship between the foveal and peripheral vision.

Though multi-window systems are, indeed, very useful, it gives some loads on the human visual system. We should pay attention in using and designing some applications with them, especially the multimedia systems with the animation because the moving objects give much heavy load on the human vision.

In this paper, we focus on the forms of the multi-window systems such as the number and layout. Now, we should examine the contextual interferences among windows that are caused by the highre levels of human information processing from the cognitive aspects.

4.REFERENCE

[1] Reichman, R., Communication Paradigms for a Window System, User Centered System Design, Norman, D. A. & Draper, S. W. (eds.), Lawrence Erlbaum Associates, 1986.
[2] Norman, K. L., Weldon, L. J., Shneiderman, B., CognitiveLayout of Windows and Multiple Screens for User Interfaces, Int. J. Man-Machine Studies, 25 1986.
[3] Fukuda, T., A Study of Pattern Recognition in Human Visual System, Dissertation, Keio University, 1979

Designing Interfaces of Autonomous Agents

Takahiro Yakoh, Nobuyuki Yamasaki and Yuichiro Anzai
Department of Computer Science, Keio University
3-14-1, Hiyoshi, Yokohama 223 Japan
Email: yakoh@aa.cs.keio.ac.jp

Abstract

This paper presents the analysis of three key factors, sensitivity, models and expressiveness, for the interface design of autonomous agents. Also the paper gives qualitative evaluation of this proposal by actually implementing the three factors in a unified way on our new operating system and autonomous mobile robots. The results are satisfactory to provide an essential step towards the design principle of autonomous agents' interfaces.

1. INTRODUCTION

Computers are evolving. We do not have to restrict our image of computers to those on our desks or in our hands. Even it seems sometimes too conservative for researchers in human-computer interaction to limit their attention to the presentday computing devices.

In particular, one possible extension of a personal computer is to extend it to a personal robot, defined here as a compact-size, general-purpose, intelligent autonomous mobile computer. This extension is by no means a dream, but is technically feasible at present in primitive forms and will be more definite in a foreseeable future. Actually, we already developed several types of personal robots with a multiprocessor architecture, and a multi-task, multi-thread operating system for robots [8], both running successfully in our laboratory. We are applying them to human cooperative work with multiple personal robots in offices and industries [4].

One very interesting and unavoidable issue there is how to design appropriate interfaces for such robots. This issue is, in more general terms, the problem of designing interfaces of autonomous agents that interact friendly with other agents, including humans.

Our paper addresses this problem, particularly by proposing and analyzing three key factors, i.e. sensitivity, models and expressiveness, for the interface design of autonomous agents. Furthermore, the paper describes how those factors can be implemented in an integrated fashion on interfaces of personal robots, based on our experience of implementation on our own robots. Note that a robot is just an example of an agent in this paper: any system that autonomously interacts with humans and other systems is an agent here.

In the next section, we describe why those factors are essential. After that, we explain the valid designs and show our implementation example. Then we evaluate our implementation, and finally describe some concluding remarks.

2. ESSENTIAL REQUIREMENTS

The three factors we propose for the interface design are sensitivity, models and expressiveness. An autonomous agent can be interactive only if (1) it is highly sensitive to input signals and symbols of various modalities, (2) it can rapidly construct, based on its goals and intentions, internal models of the relevant world for control of inferences and decision of actions, and (3) it is highly expressive in communicating its internal states to other agents. These are not sufficient conditions for the design principle that we do not have yet, but are essential requirements that we think the design of an agent necessarily satisfies.

2.1. Sensitivity

It is rather trivial that an autonomous agent be equipped with highly sensitive sensors. A presently nontrivial part of sensitivity is how a variety of sensory and linguistic data can be combined, or fused, to make the agent more reactive, and how the agent can *decide how to* combine or rank those data.

For example, the combination of a voice recognizer, natural language understander, ultrasonic sensors and vision sensors enables the agent to disambiguate the meanings of utterances, depending on situations in which the agent behaves. So how to combine and fuse many kinds of input is one of quite important technologies to realize good sensitivity.

Besides, the agent's reaction can be more flexible if it can control, depending on situations, the priority of which data are considered more important. For instance, the agent continues to move on if perceptual data are prior to linguistic input, whereas inference and planning are made when the language processing is superior. This mean that not only the priorities of input data but also those of many kinds of control process should be decided situatedly to make agent's action much flexible.

2.2. Models

There are at least two paths from input to output in an autonomous agent. One is the direct reflex from perception to action. The other is the more indirect path through inference and planning. Both are important: our robot hardware architecture supports both using a shared memory and local distributed memories.

We are particularly concerned with the latter, that is, how an internal model (or a mental model) of the relevant world can be constructed, and how the resulting model is useful in the agent's interaction with other agents. In brief, a model is built by generating a common representation shared by data with different modalities. For the representation scheme, we adopted constraint representations popular in artificial intelligence. Spatial and temporal data are transformed to constraint representations, with which inference can be made directly using constraint programming techniques.

2.3. Expressiveness

Much has been discussed in the human-computer interaction literature on how internal states of a system should be represented to human users. However, the interaction with autonomous agents needs a richer concept for the representation of internal states. It is because such an agent behaves in dynamically changing environments, and the representation of its states should be much more situation-dependent than that for relatively static machines such as the presentday computers. An agent does not just represent its internal states, but should *actively express* its states depending on what it wants to communicate to other agents and how. Thus, we propose expressiveness as the third factor for the interface design of autonomous agents.

3. DESIGN AND IMPLEMENTATION

In this section, we explain our designing policy and implementation of the three factors respectively.

3.1. Sensitive Operating System

As mentioned above, how to combine many kinds of input and how to decide process priority situatedly are the key points of sensitivity.

To make it easy to combine many inputs, we design a new asynchronized signal paradigm, called direct interrupt (**DI**). **DI** is a sort of interrupt mechanisms, but it integrate sensory inputs, states of robot, messages from computer network, linguistic inputs, and any kind of interprocess asynchronization signals. And we implemented a new operating system, called PULSER, based on this **DI** paradigm [8]. PULSER is a multi-task multi-thread [6] real-time operating system for autonomous mobile robot control. Since the context switch mechanism and the thread scheduler of PULSER is driven directly by **DI** signals, the behavior of programs is quite reactive and sensitive to **DI**. Also sensor activation mechanism and inspecting thread much increase robot's fast sensitivity.

On the other hand, situated priority decision is achieved as a dynamic process scheduler [3]. This scheduler is a kind of **DI**-driven thread scheduler, but it exchanges its scheduling policy dynamically along to the situation of robot itself. Generally speaking, two kinds of facility are required for autonomous mobile robot control. One is real-time scheduling facility which required for controlling robot hardware. And the other is quick reactivity for sporadic tasks that is invoked at changes in its relevant environment. These two requirements compose a trade-off, so it is quite difficult to decide the optimum scheduling policy as to satisfy both of two requirements. Moreover, to satisfy the requirement as to decide a robot's behavior to depend on its situation, the situated thread scheduler is a natural way to adopt.

Thus, the functions of combining input data and deciding how to combine them are now supported directly by **DI** paradigm and the dynamic process scheduler implemented in PULSER.

3.2. Hardware-Supported Software Architecture

There are many kinds of software modalities, from low-level hardware-driven modules to high level vision, inference, and planning. So it is a natural way in designing a total software system for controlling autonomous mobile robot to construct many kinds of software modules.

Though PULSER supports multi-task processing, it is impossible to process overload task set with satisfying real-time constraints. To overcome this issue, we introduce a parallel-processing hardware architecture named ASPIRE. Fig.1 shows an overview of ASPIRE architecture. ASPIRE is a kind of shared bus-connected parallel computers, but has three advantages. One is to support heterogeneity. Each board is permitted to

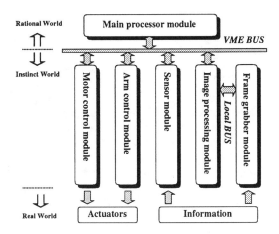

Figure 1: An overview of ASPIRE architecture.

implement its own architecture except that it must have the VME interface. The second is scalability. Each board can be attached/detached on demand. The third is transparency. Since the pure kernel of PULSER, called μ-PULSER, is running on each board, **DI** signal can reach any other tasks even on other boards.

These three advantages can solve the issue given above. For heavy tasks, which run for a long term but are not required real-time constraints, we can prepare special-purpose boards such as graphics processors or inference engines. In other cases, we can provide many real-time boards when many and many real-time tasks are required.

Furthermore, this architecture supports complex paths from input to output in a robot. In such cases, because information is communicated frequently for many tasks on many boards, slow intertask interaction makes agent's sensitivity quite inefficient.

ASPIRE architecture supports such interactions in a very fast way since it is implemented directly at the operating system level. Also ASPIRE supports wireless communication facility [7] as to interact with other agents and to communicate with computer networks. This facility is also implemented at the operating system level as to make interagent interaction fast.

3.3.   Dynamic Partial Modeling of the World

Autonomous agents (apparently) make decision dynamically by themselves. Such decision function requires the ability of modeling the world in some abstract terms. Also, the modeling must necessarily be partial, since generally an agent must respond rapidly to changes in the environment. This ability of dynamic partial modeling of the physical world is critical in designing interfaces of autonomous agents.

As an implemented example, our colleagues are working on Linta-II, a speech dialogue system for human-robot interaction. The system constructs partial world models from sensor data, and use them to disambiguate the meaning of speech utterances. Some other systems that use the ability of world-modeling have been designed and implemented in our laboratory.

3.4. Expressiveness with Colors

There are many kinds of media for expressing internal states of a machine; speech, gesture, facial expression, color, linguistic text, and so forth. We once considered facial expression as a medium for expressing a system's internal states [1], but currently we are dealing with simpler media such as color for pursuing more efficient interaction.

For example, the body of the robot is lighted in pale blue from the inside as soon as it gets in the state of embarrassment. When the agent gets embarrassed depends on how input data are combined, and how the agent decides the combination. If the sensor-actuator reflex is superior, the embarrassment is derived, for instance, from physically getting stuck. If the linguistic input is prior, the agent may be embarrassed when the inference process gets stuck. The expressions by pale blue color may be distinguished for these two cases by lighting different parts of the robot in the same color in real-time.

So we now are trying to make a robot agent able to express its internal states controlled directly by our operating system [5].

4. EVALUATION BY EXAMPLE

In this section, we evaluate the principal performance of **DI** mechanism, and our design and implementation for each of the three factors by describing an implemented example.

The **DI** response time, the time period from the occurrence of a **DI** signal to invocation of a thread relevant to the **DI**, is 119 microseconds where a Motorola MC68030 compatible with the clock speed of 25MHz is used for CPU. Note that this result is almost independent from the number of running threads.

Now we explain a typical example which is a speech dialogue interface, called Linta-II, for human-robot interaction [2]. Linta-II uses external information, such as sensory data, to reduce semantic ambiguity in human's utterance and to generate situated utterances. In this example, since verbal communication facility is given loose real-time constraints, it is necessary to combine relevant input data quickly and to reflect the result immediately to the utterance generator. The evaluation of Linta-II implementation is that the speed in speech dialogue is reasonably fast. It suggests that the sensitivity of an autonomous agent was essentially achieved.

Also, as mentioned earlier, Linta-II constructs partial world models from sensor data to disambiguate the meaning of speech utterances. The model which is adopted in Linta-II is described middle level representation, likely to a constraint representation, between low level sensory representation and high level dialogue representation. This makes it possible to share this model by both of two level directly. As described above, the performance of Linta-II is reasonably fast. It suggests that the model of Linta-II is one of good solutions for controlling autonomous agents.

5. CONCLUDING REMARKS

We have proposed three key factors, sensitivity, models and expressiveness, for designing interfaces of autonomous agents. We have explained the reasons of why all of these three factors are required and essential.

Then we described our implemented examples, and evaluated them. All of the three factors are rather difficult to implement at an application-level interface design, since rapid response is indispensable for interfaces of autonomous agents. Our approach is to integrate the three factors at the level of operating system.

Though the results are satisfactory to provide an essential step towards the design principle of autonomous agents' interfaces, much remains to be done. For example, more factors, such as reactivity and resource manageability, should be analyzed, and combined adequately to provide good design principles. Another problem is that most of those factors, including the three discussed in this article, are goal-dependent. For example, the quantitative threshold of sensitivity should be very high for autonomous agents that work for urgent or critical conditions, but can be relatively low for agents applied to amusement. We need more empirical work for knowing more about parameter settings for the design factors. Still another difficult problem is the design principle for a community of dynamically interacting agents.

Thus we have a long waiting list of problems, which seem to prove that the research will continue to be not only exciting, but also fruitful in obtaining keen knowledge for designing autonomous agents.

6. REFERENCES

1 Y. Anzai and T. Fujikawa. Nonverbal explanation of internal states in intelligent information processing and its implementation. In *Proceedings of the First Annual Conference on Japanese Artificial Intelligence Society*, pages 513–516, Tokyo, 1987.

2 K. Hiraki, M. Sato, and Y. Anzai. Speech dialogue interface for personal robot. In *Human Interface*, 47-5, pages 29–35. Information Processing Society of Japan, March 1993.

3 K. Iida, T. Yakoh, T. Sugawara, and Y. Anzai. Dynamic exchange of scheduling policies for autonomous robots. In *Proceedings of the Meeting for Real-Time Processing*, 93-ARC-99. Information Processing Society of Japan, March 1993.

4 Y. Nakauchi, T. Okada, N. Yamasaki, and Y. Anzai. Multi-agent interface architecture for human-robot cooperation. In *Proceedings of IEEE International Conference on Robotics and Automation*, pages 2786–2788, 1992.

5 C. Ono, Y. Yamamoto, and Y. Anzai. A model of expressive machines and its application to human-robot interaction. In *Proceedings of the 5th International Conference on Human-Computer Interaction*, Orlando, August 1993.

6 A. Tevanian, R. Rashid, D. Golub, D. Black, E. Cooper, and M. Young. Mach threads and the UNIX kernel: The battle for control. In *Proceedings of Summer USENIX Conference*, pages 185–197, 1987.

7 T. Yakoh, T. Iwasawa, and Y. Anzai. MACS: An efficient multicast mechanism for radiopacket communication among multiple mobile robots. In *IEEE Pacific Rim Conference on Communications, Computers and Signal Processing*, Victoria, May 1993.

8 T. Yakoh, T. Sugawara, T. Akiba, T. Iwasawa, and Y. Anzai. PULSER: A sensitive operating system for open and distributed human-robot-computer interactive systems. In *Proceedings of IEEE International Workshop on Robot and Human Communication*, pages 404–409, Tokyo, 1992.

A Knowledge Representation for Large Scale Integrated Circuit Failure Analysis

Yuko Takeguchi, Takashi Torii and Shinichi Okabe

Production Systems Development Laboratory, NEC Corporation,
Tsukagoshi, Saiwai-ku, Kawasaki, 210 JAPAN

Abstract

This paper describes how to represent knowledge for a large scale integrated circuit(LSI) failure analysis system, which supports analysts by guiding analysis procedures and inferring fault origins. There are three features of this representation method. The first is in dividing knowledge about failure analysis into blocks. The second is in describing the knowledge blocks using the most suitable form for the nature of each block. The third is in constructing a knowledge base by hierarchically combining the knowledge blocks. We are certain that our representation method facilitates the construction and maintenance of a knowledge base, because human experts have already accepted this method in developing a prototype system.

1   Introduction

LSI failure analysis is a means to identify causes and mechanisms of failure in LSIs. Analysis requires high technology and complex failure checks using various apparatuses, such as a scanning electronic microscope(SEM), therefore it sometimes takes a great deal of time to complete. In this analysis the following problems tend to arise:

- The sequence of analysis is important and complex, because LSI failure analysis includes destructive processes such as decapsulation and etching. If some analysts follow a wrong sequence, then it becomes impossible to continue analyzing the target LSIs.

- Novice analysts show a low success rate, because they can not guess the right failure causes based on the collected failure symptoms.

- Many people see a crisis because expertise in analysis is concentrated in only a few experts, and the expertise and the technology are difficult to transfer to other analysts.

It has been expected that a computer support system would be developed in order to solve these problems, which will guide procedures and inferences of failure origins based upon the knowledge of many human experts [1]. Human experts must build up a knowledge base first, and then maintain it by themselves in order for the system to be used effectually. The requirements for knowledge representation forms are described in the following:

1. Analysis procedure knowledge should be expressed explicitly, because procedures include some destructive processes.

2. Causal knowledge must be separated from analysis procedure knowledge since human experts cannot always determine the analysis sequences in reverse from the expected failure cause. Causal knowledge are simply for inferring failure causes.

3. The representation form must be understandable to human experts because they do not necessarily understand computers and AI(artificial intelligence) technology.

In this paper, LSI failure analysis is defined as a problem of collecting failure symptoms information through analysts by replying to interactive procedure guidance and inferring fault causes using the failure symptoms. First, conventional representation methods applied to the problems are described. Next, the proposed representation method is explained in detail, and a knowledge base of an LSI failure analysis support system is introduced as an implementation example using the representation method.

2 Existing knowledge representation method

Many diagnostic expert systems have been developed since 1970s for medical and industrial fields[2]. Most of these expert systems use a single representation form, such as tree structures, if-then rules, and symptom-hypothesis matrices[3, 4]. However, none of the existing single representation forms by itself is suited to the LSI failure analysis. If an expert's knowledge is represented in these forms, then the following problems may arise:

1. If-then rules: It is difficult for domain experts, as opposed to knowledge engineers, to describe expertise. In addition, it is impossible to express analysis procedures explicitly.

2. Symptom-Hypothesis matrices: It is also impossible to express analysis procedures explicitly.

3. Tree structures: If we express both procedures and failure sources in a single tree, the size of the tree would become too large to be grasped overall.

3 The proposed representation method

The proposed method is applicable to knowledge representation not only for LSI failure analysis but also for other domains in which knowledge includes complicated procedural knowledge for guiding procedures and causal knowledge for inferring causes.

This method combines conventional representation forms, depending upon each domain's nature.

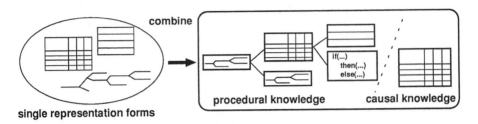

combine

procedural knowledge   causal knowledge

single representation forms

Fig. 1 Combined knowledge representation

This method has the following characteristics: (i)procedural knowledge is separated from causal knowledge, and the procedural knowledge is then divided into several procedural blocks; (ii)each and every procedural block is expressed graphically using the most suitable form determined by its nature; (iii)the whole procedural knowledge is then constructed by combining these procedural blocks hierarchically.

In this section, the proposed method is described in detail. An analysis process is defined as one process in a failure analysis, such as etching, observation using a SEM, and so forth, while an analysis procedure is defined as a sequence of analysis processes.

3.1 The expression of causal knowledge (Step 1)

In the first step, causal knowledge is expressed in a matrix form separated from procedural knowledge. All of the expected failure causes and related analysis process results are listed. Next, they are put into a symptom-hypothesis matrix, like the one shown in Fig.2. Hypotheses are defined as failure causes, and symptoms are defined as analysis results. The relationships between them are expressed in the matrix simply by the symbols, 'O' and 'X'.

		symptom							
		X-ray check			LSI tester check				
		good	*NG*	*doubt*	*open*	*short*	*leak*	....	....
hypothesis	cause 1	X	O	X	O	X	X	X	
	cause 2	O	O	X	O	X	O	O	
	cause 3	X	O	O	X	O	O	O	
	....								

Fig. 2 An example of causal knowledge (a symptom-hypothesis matrix)

The reason for adopting the matrix to describe causal knowledge is that it is most important for domain experts to easily recognize the relationships between analysis process results and failure causes.

3.2 The division of analysis procedural knowledge (Step 2)

Procedural knowledge is necessary to guide an analysis procedure in order to collect the results of analysis processes. The procedural knowledge is divided into procedural blocks. Procedural blocks are classified into two types, a fixed-sequence type and a flexible-sequence type, based upon the importance of an analysis process sequence. Procedures included in fixed-sequence type blocks must be processed in a strict order. On the other hand, procedures included in flexible-sequence type blocks can be processed in any order.

3.3 The expression of procedural blocks(Step 3)

Each procedural block is described in the most suitable form for its individual nature.

1. Fixed-sequence blocks

   Analysis processes included in fixed-sequence blocks are expressed in the form of a tree structure in accordance with the process flow(see Fig.2). A node of the tree is defined as an analysis process and the next node is chosen by the result of the previous process. This tree structure expresses only the procedures, while ordinarily diagnostic trees include failure causes on its leaves. The reason for adopting a tree structure is that procedures must represent exactly a sequence of analysis processes, and one analysis result is related to the decision of each and every subsequent analysis process.

2. Flexible-sequence blocks

   Analysis processes included in flexible-sequence blocks are enumerated and described in the form of a plain table(see Fig.3). The reason for adopting a plain table is that the table is simple and visible to express clearly what analysis processes need to be done.

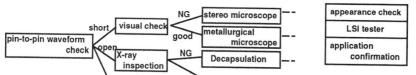

Fig. 2 The tree structure
of a fixed-sequence block

Fig. 3 The plain table
of a flexible-sequence block

3.4 The combination of procedural blocks (Step 4)

In the actual analysis domain, procedural knowledge is composed of several procedural blocks hierarchically. In this section, a combination method for procedural blocks is described using the relationships between a lower layer and an upper layer as an example.

There are two methods for combination, according to the nature of the lower layer.

1. If the execution sequence of the lower layer blocks is strict and meaningful, then the upper layer should be formed as a tree structure. Each node in the tree is defined as a

lower layer procedural block(see Fig.4). The lower layer procedural block consists of two parts, a process knowledge part and branch knowledge part. Process knowledge part determines the sequence of analysis processes and is described in the form of a tree structure or a plain table, as discussed in Step 3. A branch knowledge part determines the next procedural block and is described in the form of a symptom-hypothesis matrix, or a plain table.

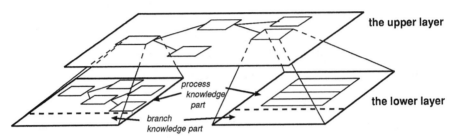

Fig. 4 A tree structure of procedural knowledge

2. If the execution sequence of the lower layer is flexible, then the upper layer should be expressed in a plain table. Each item in the table corresponds to the lower layer procedural block. (see Fig.5). In this case, the branch knowledge part is not necessary.

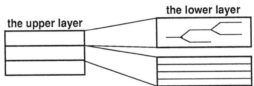

Fig. 5 A plain table of procedural knowledge

4 The developed system

We have developed an LSI failure analysis support system based on the proposed method. Analysts who have accumulated expertise through years of experience have actually built a knowledge base using the method.

Causal knowledge is described in the form of a symptom-hypothesis matrix, as mentioned before. The LSI failure analysis procedure consists of three analysis classes: the basic analysis, the electrical analysis and the physical analysis. They must be executed in that order, and the results of previous procedural blocks determine the later procedural blocks. Therefore the top layer of the procedural knowledge is expressed in a tree structure. An overview of procedural knowledge is shown in Fig.6.

There is one procedural block in the basic analysis. And there are several procedural blocks in the electrical analysis and the physical analysis, so procedural blocks, included in basic analysis and electrical analysis, have branch knowledge part in order to determine one procedural block belonging to the later level. The process knowledge part of the basic analysis is expressed in the form of a plain table, because the order of analysis processes is not strict. Each procedural block, included in the electrical and the physical analysis, is described in the form of a tree structure because they include many irreversible analysis processes.

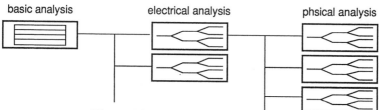

Fig. 6. The structure of the analysis procedure

The symptom-hypothesis matrix has about 60 failure causes and 200 analysis process results, and the number of all procedural blocks is nineteen.

5 Conclusion

Building a knowledge base using the proposed method has led to the following advantages: (i)the method decreases labor in constructing the knowledge base, because of understandability by domain analysts; (ii)the method decreases the size of procedural trees because of the separation from causal knowledge.

On the other hand, the method has the following problems that still need to be resolved: (i)it is necessary to extend describable knowledge, such as short cut knowledge, depended on analyst knowledge; (ii)it is necessary to describe the likelihood of each inferred cause with some quantitative indication.

Acknowledgement

The authors would like to thank Dr. M. Naniwada, Dr. M. Yamamoto and Dr. Y. Koseki of NEC Corporation for their supporting this research.

References

[1] Christopher L. Henderson and Herry M. Soden, "ICFAX, An Intergrated Circuit Failure Analysis Expert System", Proceedings of IEEE International Reliability Physics Symposium 1991, pp.142-151.

[2] W. J. Clancy, "Heuristic Classification", Artificial Intelligence 27, 1985, pp.289-350.

[3] T. Finin and G. Morris, "Abductive reasoning in multiple fault diagnosis", Artificial Intelligence Review, Vol.3.1989, pp.129-158.

[4] Y. Koseki, et al, "DT: A Classification Problem Solver with Tabular-Knowledge Acquisition", Proceedings of Third Int'l Conf. on Tools for AI, 1991, pp.156-163.

A Dialogue Manager as Interface between Aircraft Pilots and a Pilot Assistant System

M. Gerlach, R. Onken
Universität der Bundeswehr München, Institut für Systemdynamik und Flugmechanik
Werner-Heisenberg-Weg 39, D-8014 Neubiberg, Germany

Abstract

An interface for a knowledge-based support system for aircraft pilots is described which makes extensive use of speech input and speech output for communication. The system assists pilots with regard to their planning and decision tasks and provides functions for plan execution under Instrument Flight Rules.

1. Introduction

Human failure is the most important cause of aircraft accidents today. Investigations of accidents show that by far the majority of aircraft accidents can at least partly be attributed to human error [1]. Increasing automation in aircraft cockpits could not solve the problem, but changed the kind of occuring errors [2].

The causes of human failure can be correlated with findings on cognitive behaviour of human operators. The classification of human operator behaviour in skill-, rule- and knowledge-based levels show that current automatic flight guidance systems, eg. autopilot and flight management systems, support only on the skill-based and partly on the rule-based level [3]. Knowledge-based systems are one approach to support human operators on the rule- and knowledge-based level. These systems can serve as planning and decision aids and are able to recognize human errors during plan execution. This approach aims at supplementing human capabilities with functions which promise to comply with pilots' needs.

The pilot assistant system CASSY (Cockpit Assistant System), which is being developed at the University of the German Armed Forces in cooperation with Dornier company, is a knowledge-based computer system supporting aircraft pilots in situation assessment, flight planning and decision making and flight plan execution [4]. It is designed for civil regional aircrafts flying according to Instrument Flight Rules (IFR).

2. The Cockpit Assistant System CASSY

The design of the knowledge-based pilot support system CASSY is based on a hierarchical classification into several tasks (Figure 1). The Automatic Flight Planner (AFP) provides a flight plan as basic guide line for the flight. An initial flight plan may be fed into the system or is generated by the AFP by means of a problem solving algorithm as a function of destination, crew and ATC (air traffic control) constraints, weather conditions and available navigation aids. The task of the module Piloting Expert (PE) is to generate the required pilot actions based on the current flight plan. Therefore, a model of the piloting crew is realized taking into account the standard pilot behaviour. Since in IFR operation the pilot actions are highly proceduralised they are almost exclusivly rule-based. The pilot's knowledge is represented as multiple Petri-Nets which are used to model parallel pilot actions.

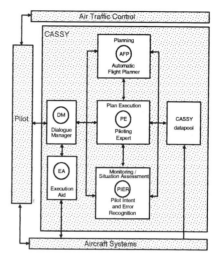

Figure 1: Structure of CASSY

The module Pilot Intent and Error Recognition (PIER) compares the expected pilot behaviour as generated by the PE with the observed behaviour of the crew. In general, deviations from the expected behaviour are due to pilot error. In this case a message is issued to make the crew aware of the situation. In some cases the crew might deviate from the flight plan intentionally (e.g. missed approach procedure). These events are recognized and serve as a new input for all CASSY modules to activate appropriate support. The Execution Aid (EA) provides additional functions to support flight plan execution having access to aircraft systems. While aircraft data (e.g. radio settings, aircraft subsystem status) are exchanged using data bus systems, the information flow to and from the crew is controlled by the module "Dialogue Manager" (DM) which is the main topic of this paper.

3. The Dialogue Manager (DM)

The interface between CASSY and the piloting crew is established by speech input, speech output and a display which is used to present alphanumeric and graphic information. The Dialogue Manager itself is structured into information input and output submodules as can be seen in Figure 2.

3.1 Output Information

The CASSY output information, repesented as 130 different messages, comprise warnings or hints to avoid or correct an observed pilot deviation from the flight plan, requested information to support flight plan execution and the actual flight plan or flight plan proposals.

Warnings and hints are transmitted verbally as speech output is percieved independently from the visual perception channel. Depending on the importance of the messages different voices are chosen to emphasize the message. Warnings can refer to the deviation from the nominal flight path (e.g. "check heading" or

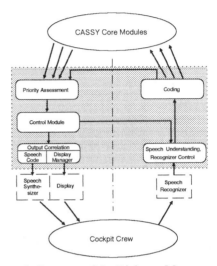

Figure 2: Structure of the Dialogue Manager

"descend to flight level 80 ") or to aircraft subsystem status (e.g. "enter 334 on ADF 1"). The perception of more complex warnings is supported by printing the message on the display while the warning is issued from the speech synthesizer at the same time. If the message refers to a geographic location the location is marked on the navigation map. Data base requests and performance calculations are presented in a similar way.

The flight plan projects the trajectory from the aircraft position to the destination. It is devided into different legs of constant values of heading, altitude or speed. Due to spatial representation, the most important information for the crew is the lateral path over ground, referenced, if possible, by radio navigation aids. Therefore, the flight plan is permanently depicted on a navigation map on the graphic display as a chain of legs. To reduce the information density on the map the representation of the map objects (i.e. their appearance, kind of additional information, colour) is a function of the importance of the object, distance and angle from the actual aircraft position. This leads to a detailed representation of the area close to the aircraft and a coarse representation of the areas far away. Similar approaches have been used for navigation maps in cars [6]. The nominal flight plan values of heading, altitude, speed and vertical velocity are printed on the respective flight guidance instrumentation. Additional information is coded by colour, if possible (e.g. leg clearances, corrrect settings of nav instruments). Numerical values are presented on an alphanumeric display page for each leg on crew request.

Flight plan proposals are graphically presented using a different colour for each proposal. Each proposal is given an evaluation score indicating its quality with respect to the problem solving algorithm of the AFP. A summary of the main differences between the proposals are available in alphanumeric mode keeping the colours of each proposal as reference. A similar approach is used for the presentation of alternate airports. The proposals can be changed according to the preferences of the crew. The crew decides which proposal becomes the new, valid flight plan.

In addition to the choice of an appropriate presentation device, a suitable order of the information flow must be achieved if several, different messages are ready to be transferred to the crew. As the CASSY core modules issue messages to the crew independently of each other, any output message is stored a certain time before it is passed to the crew to enable the priority assessment submodule to choose between the messages. Each message is evaluated mainly on the importance of the message in the actual flight phase and its thematic relationship to the last issued message.

An estimation of actual workload can be achieved using the pilot model established in the CASSY module PE. Based on this model the actual pilot actions, necessary to pursue the flight plan, are determined. The current crew workload is estimated using the classification of the Subjective Workload Assessment Technique (SWAT) for each of the actual pilot tasks [7]. A module is being developed which considers this estimation and the projection of the additional load due to the output message for the duration of pauses between the messages in order to avoid a flood of messages.

3.2 Input Information

In general, information exchange within aircraft crews as well as between pilots and air traffic controllers is mainly performed using speech as communication device. All commands, callouts, checklist procedures are coded in well defined phrases to ensure an error free information exchange. Based on this phraseology, speech input is extensively used in CASSY for discrete information e.g. to request or modify flight plan proposals or to manipulate aircraft instrumentation settings.

The input information can be broken down into flight planning commands, display configuration commands, data base requests and performance calculations, system configuration commands using CASSY's access on aircraft systems and traffic guidance commands from ATC. As long as the planned data link for communication between ATC and aircraft is not available ATC instruction must be fed into the system by the crew. This is achieved by picking up the communication between ATC and the pilot. As the pilot is obliged to give his radio call sign (i.e. usually the flight number or registration number of the aircraft) before or immediately after reading back the controller's command, the recognition of the call sign can be used to discriminate a crew command from an ATC command.

Several applications of speech recognition as input means show that the amount of possible combinations of input commands may lead to very complex language models. Often, the complexity of used language model is the reason why speech recognizers might show poor recognition rates and are therefore not considered as satisfying input devices. Even if the expected speech is reduced to command structures like "turn left to heading 1 8 0" the many different possibilities of parameters like 'heading' (i.e. 360) lead to an overall language model producing billions of possible sentences for this application (perplexity 16, vocabulary 218 words excluding names of geographic location and navigation aids). In order to reduce the complexity, the current situation of crew and aircraft must be considered. Not only the amount of parameters can be reduced but also the amount of input commands themselves as some of them only occur in certain situations. In this application the complexity of the language model is significantly reduced as the flight phase and flight plan, necessary crew actions, aircraft position and surrounding geographic area and aircraft data, actual information output to the crew and a classification into crew and ATC inputs are taken into account.

Each input command (103 for crew, 66 for ATC) is represented as a frame. Its semantic meaning is coded as a reference number plus describing parameters. The slots of the frame contain the actual possible parameters derived from several decision trees, the vocabulary and syntactical constraints as a transition network describing each way to speak the command and an evaluation of the actual probability of occurence. The reference numbers of the commands are stored in a list of currently possible commands. This list is the basis for both the complete, context depending language model and the assignment of the belonging reference number to a speech input from the crew.

The representation of expected crew actions as modelled by the PE is used to predict task relevant speech inputs of the crew using a time difference evaluation from the actual moment to the next necessary pilot actions. These inputs refer to autopilot settings, instrumentation and aircraft configuration settings or requests for support of required procedures like checklists. As aircraft systems settings can be manipulated by a speech command which is interpreted and carried out automatically by CASSY, the pilot may use commands which are closer to his mental representation (e.g. navigation beacons may be referred to by their names instead of difficult frequencies). Reactions of the crew to information output is considered estimating appropriate input commands. A warning which refers to a wrong altitude increases the probability of a respective autopilot command. This is also used to enable a DO-IT speech command as an answer to warnings like "descend to 5000 feet". Input commands which occur only in certain, time constrained situations (e.g. planning or checklists), are added to the list of probable commands when these situations apply and dropped afterwards.

An equivalent approach to predict ATC instructions would require a similar model of the controller and the actual traffic situation which is not available in CASSY. Therefore, the description of the ATC language model is based only on the current flight phase and constrained to the actual geographic area. The number of sentences for the crew language model varies between several thousands (perplexity 2 - 3, vocabulary 90 - 150 words) and for the ATC model between several ten thousands (perplexity 4 - 5, vocabulary 90 - 150 words).

The speech input is prompted on the CASSY display for verification. The recognized command is evaluated on its recognition score and on its actual relevance to find out whether it can be accepted automatically or whether it should be explicitly confirmed by the crew.

4. The Simulation Facility

The modules of CASSY are implemented as task specific processes on a Silicon Graphics UNIX workstation coded in the programming language "C". CASSY is integrated in an existing flight simulator facility.

As speech output device a DECTalk speech synthesizer is used which converts ASCII strings into speech. An SSI Phonetic Engine/Phonetic Decoder (continuous, speaker independend recognizer), implemented on a SUN-ELC 4/25 workstation, is used for speech input. Using parallel processes it is possible to update current language models, compile them as syntaxes and link them to the speech recognizer without interrupting the running system. Depending on the result of a wordspotting algorithm either the actual crew or ATC syntax is chosen against which the utterance is decoded.

5. References

1. Schänzer, G.: "Sicherheitsphilosophien im Luftverkehr", Mitteilungen der TU Braun-schweig, Jahrgang XXIV, Heft I/1989
2. Chambers, A.B.; Nagel, D.C.: "Pilots of the Future: Human or Computer?", Comm. of the ACM, Vol.28, No.11, Nov. 1985
3. Rasmussen, J.: "Skills, Rules and Knowledge; Signals, Signs and Symbols, and Other Distinctions in Human Performance Models", IEEE-SMC-13, No.3, 1983
4. Onken, R.: "New Developments in Aerospace Guidance and Control: Knowledge Based Pilot Assistance", 12th IFAC Symposium on Automatic Control in Aerospace, Ottobrunn, 1992
5. Taylor, M.M.; Waugh, D.A.: "Principles for integrating voice I/O in a complex interface", AGARD Avionics Panel Symposium, Madrid, Spain, May 16-22, 1992
6. Geiser, G.H.: "Rechnergestützte Darstellung von Straßenkarten im Kraftfahrzeug", DGLR-Bericht 92-02, Sept. 1991
7. Reid, G.B.: "Subjective Workload Assessment: A Conjoint Scaling Approach", 1982 Annual Conference of Aerospace Medical Association, Bel Harbour, 1982

A Taxonomy of Distortion-Oriented Techniques for Graphical Data Presentation

Y. K. Leung[a] and M.D. Apperley[b]

[a]Centre for Systems Methodologies, Department of Computer Science, Swinburne University of Technology, P.O. Box 218, Hawthorn, Victoria 3122, Australia

[b]Department of Computer Science, Massey University, Palmerston North, New Zealand

Abstract
In recent years, there has been a growing interest in the development of distortion-oriented presentation techniques for large scale information systems. Conflicting terminologies and principles in this area have given rise to confusion amongst interface designers. This paper presents a taxonomy of these graphical techniques. It highlights their differences and similarities, enabling sensible comparisons and selections to be made.

1. Introduction

One of the common problems associated with large scale computer-based information systems is the relatively small window through which an information space can be viewed. This is manifested in two related problem areas. The first, a spatial problem, relates to the physical size of the data space being viewed, and can be seen in the presentation of maps, charts, and complex diagrams. The second is an information density issue, and relates to the total volume and level of detail of information available. Techniques for accessing physically large graphical data sets on a limited display surface (the spatial issue) can be broadly classified as distortion- and non-distortion-oriented presentations. The main feature of distortion-oriented techniques is to allow the user to examine a portion of the space in detail on one section of the screen, and at the same time to present an overall view of the data to provide context and to facilitate effective navigation.

There has been a growing interest in the application of distortion techniques in recent years (Leung 1989, Hollands et al 1989, Mackinlay et al 1991, Sarkar & Brown 1992) which can be attributed to the availability of low cost and high performance graphics workstations. The range of distortion-oriented techniques proposed by user interface designers calls for a taxonomy to relate and delineate these techniques for two main reasons. First, there is the confusion of terminologies confronting the graphical interface designer, particularly where techniques have been applied both to the spatial problem and the information density problem. Second, a well defined classification is required to permit the comparison and generalisation of empirical results of experiments using these techniques possible.

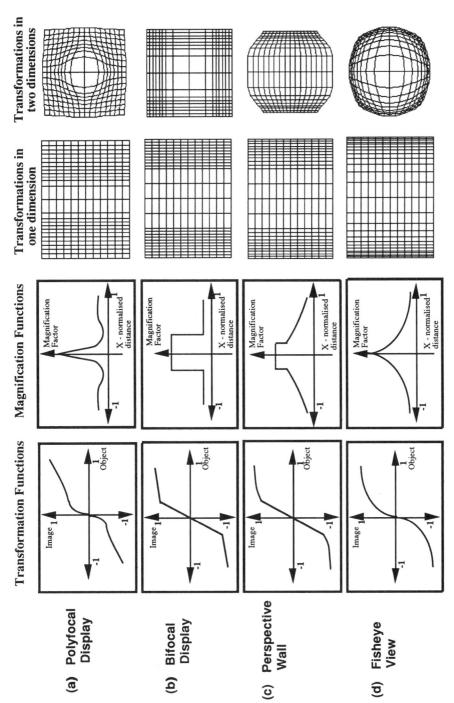

Figure 1 An overview of several distortion-oriented presentation techniques. The x and y axes of the transformation functions show the normalised distances of the undistorted and distorted images respectively

In order to obtain a better insight into the differences and similarities between available techniques, the general form of transformation and magnification functions for each technique are described and illustrated in both one and two dimensions (Leung and Apperley 1993). From these comparisons, a taxonomy is developed.

2. An Overview of Distortion-Oriented Presentation Techniques

The Polyfocal Projection (Kadmon and Shlomi 1978), which was proposed in a non-interactive presentation of cartographic maps, is the earliest of the techniques examined. Figure 1a shows the transformation and magnification functions for this technique, and the application of the technique in one and two dimensions to data spaces represented by grids of squares; areas of interest are magnified, but retain their spatial relationships with the surrounding data. Kadmon and Shlomi laid down the mathematical foundation for a variety of distortion techniques, and they also proposed the concept of a multi-focal projection. In a multi-focus view, any number of focus points, each with a different polyfocal transformation function, may be selected (Figure 2); the only practical limiting factors are the computation time involved in the generation of the view, and the ability for the user to decipher it.

The Bifocal Display (Spence and Apperley 1982), the first computer based distortion-oriented display technique, provided a similar but simpler display, comprising three fixed-focus regions for the original one-dimensional implementation (Figure 1b). Because only two fixed levels of magnification are involved, the implementation of this technique is very simple. The Bifocal Display was later extended to two dimensions for the presentation of topological networks (Leung 1989). A variant of the Bifocal Display in its one dimensional form was later proposed by Mackinlay et al (1991) as the Perspective Wall (Figure 1c) for the presentation of information with a linear structure. A very noticeable difference between these two techniques is that the Perspective Wall does not make use of the entire rectangular display surface, thus wasting valuable screen real estate.

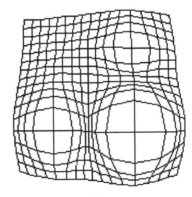

Figure 2   A multiple focus view with Polyfocal Display. Each focus point may have a different magnification function.

Furnas' original concept of a fisheye view (Furnas 1986) was based on a hierarchical information structure, and tackled the information density problem. The essence of this technique is *thresholding*. Each information element in a hierarchical structure is assigned one number based on its relevance (*a priori importance* or API), and another number based on the distance between the information element under consideration and the point of focus in the structure. A threshold value is then selected and compared with a function of these two numbers to determine what information is to be presented or suppressed.

Several variations of the Furnas' Fisheye View concept have since been described, some of which tackle the spatial problem; these differ not only in their application domains but also in their form (Hollands et al 1989, Mitta 1990, Sarkar and Brown 1992). Whilst Sarkar and Brown (1992) attempted to formalise the mathematical foundation for the graphical fisheye view, their illustration of the technique applied to topological networks was based on a variation of the ideal fisheye view (Figure 1d) which they called the Cartesian Fisheye View and the Polar Fisheye View. With the former view, the fisheye transformation is applied independently in the X and Y directions; the latter view involves the mapping of the ideal fisheye view, which has a rounded appearance, onto a rectangular surface.

3. A Taxonomy

An examination of these distortion-oriented techniques (Figure 1) shows that they can be conveniently classified into two groups in terms of their magnification functions. One class of these techniques has piece-wise magnification functions; the Bifocal Display and the Perspective Wall are in this group. The other class has continuous magnification functions; the Fisheye View and the Polyfocal Projection belong to this class. In practical terms, a distorted view generated by a discontinuous magnification function creates an abrupt visual transition at the boundary between the distorted and undistorted regions of the display, although such a technique may offer the advantage of simpler implementation. Further, it can be demonstrated (Figure 1) that the Bifocal Display is a special case of the Perspective Wall, and that Sarkar and Brown's Fisheye View may be considered a special case of the Polyfocal Projection (Leung and Apperley 1993).

It should be noted that it is the dips in the Polyfocal Projection's magnification function which make it possible for this technique to support a multiple focus presentation (Figure 2); techniques which do not have this property in their magnification function will not be able to provide a flexible multiple focus system.

4. Discussion

Whilst the fisheye view proposed by Furnas, and later extended by Mitta, should be more appropriately classified as an information suppression technique rather than a conventional distortion technique, there are some applications which call for an integrated technique to overcome the combined spatial and information density problem. Figure 3 illustrates an interface of a traveller enquiry system for train arrivals on the London Underground system. The map is presented using the Bifocal Display technique for ease of navigation, and the

108

train arrival information is embedded in the map and suppressed until the station is selected by the user. This technique is potentially powerful and greater research efforts should be focussed on exploring other application domains.

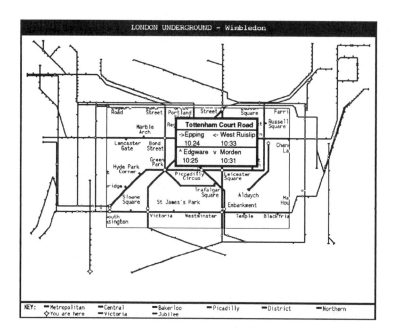

Figure 3   An application of the combined technique in presenting
information which is embedded in a spatial system

		Implementation Simplicity	Versatility	Applicability: Information Density Problems	Applicability: Spatial Problems
Techniques with Non-Continuous Magnification Functions	Bifocal Display	High	High	High	High
	Perspective Wall	Low	Medium	Medium	Medium
Techniques with Continuous Magnification Functions	Polyfocal Display	Medium	High	Medium	High
	Fisheye View	Medium	High	Medium	High

Table I   A comparison of several distortion-oriented techniques

System usability is a major factor in determining the success of a user interface, and system response time directly influences the usability of an interactive system. In a system with real time interaction, the user may initiate a shift of the focus region to view an adjacent area in detail using an interaction device. The system response time depends on three factors: the complexity of the mathematical transformations involved, the amount of information and its detail to be presented, and the computational power and suitability of computer display system. Because of the inherent complexity of its transformation functions, dedicated sophisticated hardware was used to build the Perspective Wall (Card et al 1991). In contrast, the implementation of a Bifocal Display is straightforward (Leung 89) and can be achieved using readily available hardware. It is also interesting to note that despite the complexity of the transformation functions of the Polyfocal Projection, they do not involve computation time-consuming trigonometric functions. Table 1 shows a comparison of various distortion-oriented techniques with regard to implementation issues.

5. Conclusion

This paper has reviewed several distortion-oriented display techniques and has developed a taxonomy of these techniques clearly showing their underlying relationships. A better understanding of these distortion techniques from the HCI perspective should be aimed at by gathering empirical evidence to evaluate their usability. Furthermore, with a better understanding of the usability of these techniques, appropriate application domains can then be identified.

6 References

Card, S.K., Robertson, G.G. and Mackinlay, J.D. (1991), The information visualizer, and information workspace, Proceedings CHI '91 pp.181-188.

Furnas, G.W. (1986), Generalized fisheye views, Proceedings of CHI '86, pp16-23.

Hollands, J.G., Carey, T.T., Matthews, M.L. and McCann, C.A.(1989), Presenting a graphical network: a comparison of performance using fisheye and scrolling views, in Designing and Using Human-Computer Interfaces and Knowledge Based Systems (Eds. Salvendy, G. and Smith, M.) Amsterdam, Elsevier, pp313-320.

Kadmon, N. and Shlomi, E. (1978), A polyfocal projection for statistical surfaces, The Cartographic Journal, 15, 1, pp36-41.

Leung, Y.K. (1989), Human-computer interaction techniques for map-based diagrams, in Designing and using Human-Computer Interfaces and Knowledge Based Systems, (Eds. Salvendy, G. and Smith, M.) Amsterdam, Elsevier, pp361-368.

Leung, Y.K. and Apperley, M.D. (1993), A unified theory of distortion-oriented presentation techniques, Massey University School of Mathematical and Information Sciences Report. (in print).

Mackinlay, J.D., Robertson, G.G. and Card, S.K. (1991), The Perspective Wall: detail and context smoothly integrated, Proceedings of CHI'91, pp.173-179.

Mitta D.A. (1990), A fisheye presentation strategy: aircraft maintenance data, Proceedings of Interact '90, pp875-885.

Sarkar M. and Brown M.H. (1992), Graphical fisheye view of graphs, Proceedings of CHI'92, pp83-91.

Spence, R. and Apperley, M.D. (1982), Data base navigation: an office environment for the professional, Behaviour and Information Technology, 1, 1, pp43-54.

An Information-based User Interface Architecture

H. Diel, Dr. J. Uhl, Dr. M. Welsch
IBM Entwicklung GmbH, 7030 Boeblingen, Germany

Abstract

The Information-based User Interface Architecture described in this paper is an object oriented user interface architecture with support of two aspects which are insufficiently addressed in todays existing user interface architectures, namely (1) support of object collections and composite objects, and (2) a close mapping between the applications data model and the user interface.

The Information-based User Interface Architecture implies a strong separation of application logic and user interface logic, and an abstract interface between the two.

Introduction

At the HCI'92 conference in York Prof. D. Olson requested the creation of an 'Information' based User Interface Architecture'. In [1] he requests as major characteristic of such an Information-based User Interface Architecture that (1) the user interface is derived from the information (i.e. data or objects) being processed, and (2) the user interface (and possibly further parts of the system) provides support for the handling of collections of interrelated objects.

This paper describes a proposal for such an UI architecture. By assuming a specific way in which the structure and contents of data (objects) is specified, the paper shows how this allows the association of view handlers and other user interfaces, and the provision of generic facilities (e.g. a navigation component) for the treatment of collections of objects.

In line with many other famous user interface architectures, the described Information-based User Interface Architecture implies a strong separation of application logic and user interface logic, and an abstract interface between the two.

Development-time Architecture

At development-time a large part of what is wanted to happen at run-time may already be specified. Since the described Information-based User Interface Architecture is object oriented, this means the specification of objects, their properties, methods, relations, and user interfaces. The Information-based User Interface Architecture uses for the specification of the objects (including their user interface) again objects, so-called Object Specification Objects, OSOs. However, this does not exclude the traditional approaches. An Object Specification Object can have a textual representation and various graphical views. Besides combining the advantages of textual representations and graphical representations, the Object Specification Object also provides all the advantages of object orientation such as powerful re-use and tailoring capabilities and proper definition of the functions which may be applied to the specifications.

Object Specification Object

An application will be specified by use of objects from the following four object classes:

- Abstract Specification Object
  The Abstract Specification Object describes a (possibly composite) object in a way which is independent of any specific UI technology or view type. This means that the Abstract Specification Object describes all that information which is common for all the possible UI technologies and view types.

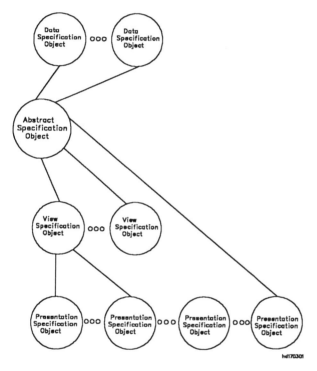

Figure 1. Objects involved in Object Specification Object

- Data Specification Object
  The Data Specification Object describes how the persistent data of an object is stored. This includes the type of data storage (e.g. SQL, flat files, repository) as well as more detailed parameters (e.g. record layout). The Data Specification Object is optional.

- View Specification Object
  The View Specification Object defines a logical view for a user interface. It may specify a subset of the items belonging to the Abstract Specification Objects to make up the logical view.

- Presentation Specification Object
  The Presentation Specification Object specifies a concrete user interface for a given user interface technology (e.g. command mode, dialog, graphic, voice) and view type (e.g. icon view, settings view, composite view).

These four object classes are interrelated as shown in Figure 1.

Association of View Specification Object and Presentation Specification Object to Abstract Specification Object

As shown in Figure 1 on page 2, are the View Specification Objects, Presentation Specification Objects, and Data Specification Objects associated to the Abstract Specification Objects. This association is a key feature of the Information-based User Interface Architecture and has to done in a specific way, namely such that for each "Element" of a view specification, user interface specification, or data specification there is a corresponding Element in the Abstract Specification Object. "Element" thereby means those elements of a specification which need to be treated as an entity with respect to addition, deletion, or movement. For a user interfaces specification these are things like the definitions for Entryfields, Radiobuttons, Pushbuttons, Checkboxes, Menuitems, Windows, etc..

It is the premise of the Information-based User Interface Architecture that in general, the Abstract Specification Object can be structured in such a way that this kind of association between the Abstract Specification Object and *all* the other specification objects is possible.

The Abstract Specification Object is made up of the following "Elements":

- Class
- Methods
- Properties
- Parts (i.e. classes contained in the present class)
- Relates_to
- Set_of
- Selection_list
- Data_item

Run-time Architecture

Separation

In order to stay extendible for future user interface technologies and view types, and to achieve consistency, and interoperability between view types, it is useful to establish a clean interface which separates user interface logic from application logic. This separation of application logic and user interface logic is a well-known concept with user interface architectures. Various "Models" have been proposed in literature and in real products. Some major examples are the the the Seeheim Model (see [2]), the Model View Controller concept (see [3]), the PAC architecture (see [4]), the Tube UIMS (see [5]), ScreenView (see [6]), MacApp (see [7]), and InterView (see [8]). As a structure which has much commonality with all these user interface architectures, we assume for our subsequent discussions the structure shown in Figure 2 on page 4.

The UI-objects shown in Figure 2 on page 4. can be mapped to various well-known concepts such as to

- A View, Controller pair of the Model View Controller concept
- A UIO of the Tube UIMS
- An Agent of FRIEND21

There are three cases of user interface communication which need to be supported by the UI-objects (not necessarily by a single specific UI-object), namely

1. Object Viewing, i.e. display of object contents and properties,
2. Object Navigation, and the treatment of object collections and composite objects,
3. Parameter retrieval and display of results for object methods.

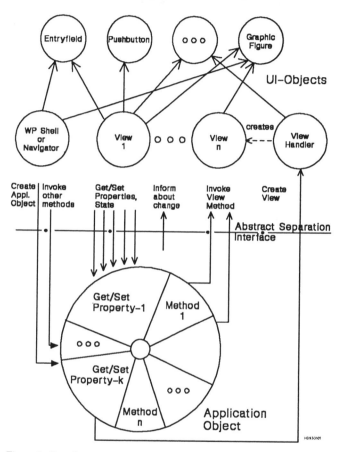

Figure 2. Run-time structure of objects involved in user interfaces

Abstraction as a necessary second concept

As described in the previous section, there exist a variety of program models and UIMS architecture which support a clean separation of application logic and user interface. In order to support the goals for extendibility to future user interface technologies, support of multiple user interface technologies, reuse, and high quality, these program models have to be supplemented by a clean architecture with respect to the information which may be communicated between the application logic and user interface logic. The goals of extendibility and support of multiple different user interface types can only be achieved, if this interface is 'abstract', which means it does not contain any UI technology dependent (or even device dependent) information. In user interface related literature this requirement is referenced as the requirement for 'Abstraction' (see [9]).

A more precise phrasing of the requirement for Abstraction in terms of the above described object oriented program model with the application objects and the UI-objects is as follows:

- The UI-object must not offer any user interface technology dependent, or device type dependent interface to the application object.
- The application object may offer an interface for retrieving and setting the application objects properties. This possibility was not foreseen with certain traditional 'Separation Architectures'. With the more modern UIMS architectures it was recognized that modern user interfaces require access to application semantic (see [10]) and that this is not in conflict with the goal of supporting Separation and Abstraction.

A Framework for Program Model supporting UI Separation and Abstraction

Based on the structure described in "Separation" on page 3 our program model consists of application objects and UI-objects. As shown in Figure 2 on page 4 there are different types of UI-objects such as Navigators and Workplace Shells, different View Handlers, and other high level UI-objects, supporting the various cases of user interfaces.

The UI-objects: The UI-objects constitute the applications user interface. As little as possible non-user-interface related logic should be contained in the UI-objects. (Notice however, that the inclusion of some function logic or checking logic may be required and would not violate the architecture.) Part of the UI-objects, at least the low level UI-objects (sometimes called Presentation Objects) may be provided by some UIMS, for example in the form of standard class libraries.

For the major UI technologies (e.g. GUI) it is also assumed that the complete set of UI-objects will be provided generically, based on the specifications given in the OSO described in "Object Specification Object" on page 2. This includes the provision of certain standard 'Views' (e.g. Settings View, Icon View) as well as the provision of a so-called Object-Navigator, which is a graphical user interface which allows to navigate among collections of interrelated objects (for example, a hardware configuration consisting of devices, processors, control units. etc.). ScreenView (see [6]) has demonstrated that such a facility driven by user interface specifications is feasible.

The application objects: The application objects provide the applications function logic. Any user interface related logic within an application object would violate the Information-based User Interface Architecture. The potential for the generic provision of application object functions is less than with the UI-objects. However, access to some standard data store facilities (for example SQL database) can be provided generically, based on the specifications given by the OSO. This may go as far as the generic provision of certain standard object methods such as Create, Delete, Copy.

The support of Generic UI-objects also requires from the application objects the support of certain standardized methods, such as Get_Property and Set_Property for all the properties specified in the Object Specification Object.

Summary

The user interface architecture described in the preceding sections is called 'Information-based' because it satisfies the following two requirements:

1. The user interface can be derived from the information (i.e. data or objects) being processed.
   It is possible to derive the Abstract Specification Object and default Presentation Specification Object from an applications data model or data base definitions.

2. The user interface (and possibly further parts of the system) provides support for the handling of collections of interrelated objects. The Object Specification Object supports the specification of object collections and it is possible to built workplace shells and navigators for object collections.

Prototypes for object navigators, a tool generating OSOs from database definitions, and further facilities have been implemented.

References

[1] Olson, D.R.
   User Interface Architectures for an Information Age.
   People and Computers VII - Proceedings of the HCI '92 Conference, 1992.

[2] Pfaff, G., editor. *User Interface Management Systems.*
   Springer-Verlag, Berlin, 1985.

[3] Krasner, G.E. and Pope, S.T.
   A cookbook for using model-view-controller user interface paradigm in SMALLTALK-80.
   Journal of Object Oriented Programming, 1988.

[4] Coutaz, J.
   Architecture Models for Interactive Software.
   Proc. ECOOP, 1989.

[5] Hill, R.D.
   The Structure of Tube - A tool for Implementing advanced User Interface.
   Proc. Eurographics, 1989.

[6] IBM Order No. SC33-6450.
   IBM SAA SystemView General Information for ScreenView.
   1991.

[7] Wilson, D.A., Rosenstein, L.S. and Shafer, D.
   C++ Programming With MacApp.
   Adison-Wesley Publishing Company, 1990.

[8] Linton, M.A., Vlissides, J.M. and Calder, P.R.
   Composing user interfaces with InterViews.
   Computer, Vol. 22, No 2, 1989.

[9] Enderle, G.
   Report on the Interface of the UIMS to the Application.
   The Separable User Interface, 1992.

[10] Edmonds, E., editor. *The Separable User Interface.*
   Academic Press, 1992.

The Impact of the Design of the Software Control Interface on User Performance.

John R. Carlson and Laura L. Hall

Department of Information and Management Sciences
The Florida State University, Tallahassee, FL 32306

1. INTRODUCTION

Modern user interfaces have made tremendous progress in improving usability. However, as the functionality provided by software systems increases in sophistication and complexity, so too do the requirements on the interface to facilitate the access of that functionality. Additionally, as the increasing scope of functionality provided by software encourages more individuals to utilize computers, so too do the requirements for the software interface to support novice users. There have been numerous factors put forward in the literature to describe the relationship between interface design and user performance. The goal of this paper is to review the relevant literature across several fields, identify the factors which contribute to the link between interface design and user performance, and integrate these factors into a conceptual model to guide further research and practice. Improving our understanding of these factors can have dramatic effects on user performance, as well as reducing the costs of the software design process.

Discussion of computer interfaces is not necessarily a straightforward matter due to the complexity of the topic and the difficulty in defining exactly what interface is under consideration. The human-machine interface is the link between the human and the machine, allowing the human to access and control the functionality of the machine. If the machine is a computer, five distinct types of computer interfaces can be discussed: the hardware-user interface, the software-user interface, the hardware-software interface, the software-software interface, and the hardware-hardware interface. This paper is concerned with the software-user interface, examples of which include: tables, graphs, menus, and icons. Within the software-user interface there are two separate interfaces: the data interface and the control interface. The software-data interface (SDI) allows the user to input and receive data from the computer through tables, charts, graphs, and so on. The software-control interface (SCI) allows the user to access the functionality of the software through menus, commands, icons, and so on. The subject of this paper, the SCI, is defined as the bi-directional transfer of control signals across the man-machine boundary via the software-user interface.

Many variables will effect user performance in addition to the design of the SCI. However, for the purposes of this paper, these other factors are held constant. The only factor which varies is the design of the SCI. As the design varies, from worse to better, it is theorized that user performance will vary, also from worse to better.

2. INTEGRATING MODEL

Based on an extensive literature review, a model which describes the factors which comprise an SCI design and their relationships to each other and to user performance has been constructed (Figure 1). Six factors in addition to user performance are shown: reliability, stability, power, speed, efficiency, and effectiveness.

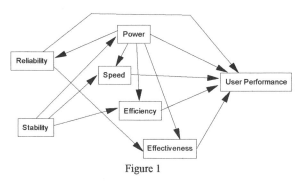

Figure 1

User Performance - User performance is a multidimensional construct. Possible definitions include the degree to which a task is successfully completed [1, 5, 17], the time necessary to complete a task [1, 5, 6, 14, 18, 19, 21], the number of mistakes committed while carrying out a task [1, 5, 14, 18], and the time spent on error recovery while carrying out a task [6].

Reliability - A reliable interface can be defined as one which is "not conductive to undetected errors in man-computer communication" (by Cheriton, quoted in [20]). To a large extent, reliable interface can be defined as one in which the commands and/or menu choices perform the function that the user intends for them to perform.

Stability - A stable interface is one which does not allow potentially damaging actions by the user, or is resilient to mistakes made by the user by allowing the user to undo any damage done. An example of an interface which has both unreliable and unstable features would be the DOS command line. The SORT command does not function as most users might expect, and there is no UNDO capability (with the exception of a limited UNDELETE).

Power - Power can be defined as the number of commands available to the user [20], and the number of ways of accessing the commands. Power can thus be seen to be comprised of two components, the *scope* of commands to which the user has access, and the *redundancy* of methods by which the user can access those commands. Additional methods of accessing identical commands can be obtained through the use of icons, shortcuts (keyboard or mouse), and redundant command-line verbs.

Speed - The speed of an SCI is a component of the total time required to enter and execute a command set. SCI speed and SCI efficiency are the two factors which determine this time. The speed is the summation of the system response times (lags) for each command in the command set, and is therefore largely a product of hardware and software constraints. SCI speed is also, obviously, controlled by the number of steps (commands, menu selections, etc.) required to implement the desired function. Higher SCI speed will be realized through a combination of fewer commands and less lag between commands.

Efficiency - The efficiency of an SCI is the time it takes to find the necessary commands/actions needed when entering a command set. This definition assumes that the user has already decided which command/action is needed. Efficiency is a measure of how quickly the identified command/action can be implemented. If the SCI is flexible and/or customizable then this time can be effected. This definition follows the general outline given in [1].

Effectiveness - The effectiveness of an SCI is the time it takes to determine the necessary commands/actions needed to accomplish a particular task. This time can be reduced if the user is able to customize the SCI. The effectiveness of an SCI is largely a factor of the screen layout and appropriateness of the interfacing system to the task. Effectiveness may be especially relevant for untrained users who may be more likely to experience performance penalties when using an SCI which is not effective.

3. THEORETICAL RELATIONSHIPS AND SUPPORT

MIS, Computer science, engineering, HCI, and human behavior literatures were surveyed to find support or lack of support for the various relationships shown in the model. This discussion follows the relationships in the model from top to bottom and from left to right.

Reliability-Effectiveness. This relationship is straightforward from a theoretical perspective: a reliable SCI will possess commands which function as the user intends them to, which will decrease the time required for a user to determine which commands are needed to accomplish a particular task (thereby increasing effectiveness). Additionally, a highly reliable SCI can actually suggest to the user what the next logical step is to accomplish the current task. This suggestion can also reduce the time required by the user to determine the next appropriate command. Empirically, a positive relationship (high reliability leading to high effectiveness) was found in [8], and reported in [10]. No negative relationships were found.

Power-Reliability. Theoretically it has been suggested that the more menu options or command-line options are available, the more reliable the SCI will be [13]. Empirically a positive relationship has been demonstrated in [8] for a command-line SCI. No empirical support has been found for other types of SCIs.

Power-Speed. Theoretically it can be seen that the more menu options available, the more icons shown, and/or the more command-line options the system must parse for, the slower the system will respond to instructions. An empirical confirmation of this negative relationship has not been found.

Power-Efficiency. This could be seen as both a positive or negative relationship. The more power, in the form of additional commands available to the user (increased scope), the more difficulty the user may have in *finding* the appropriate command (a negative relationship). Alternatively, more power, in the form of increased redundancy of commands, may assist the user in more quickly *locating* desired commands (a positive relationship). No empirical support has been found for either interpretation.

Power-Effectiveness. Likewise, this could be seen as both a positive or negative relationship. The more power, in the form of additional commands available to the user (increased scope), the more difficulty the user may have in *determining* the appropriate command (a negative relationship). Alternatively, more power, in the form of increased redundancy of commands, may assist the user in more quickly *choosing* desired commands (a positive relationship). No empirical support has been found for either interpretation.

Stability-Power. It can be argued that to have a highly stable SCI, there should be few routes to implement a particular function, while a high power SCI should have many routes. This apparent conflict could result in a theorized negative relationship either from stability to power or from power to stability. No empirical support has been found for this relationship.

Stability-Speed. Theoretically it can be seen that the use of warnings and safety procedures to protect a user from damaging mistakes will lead to an increase in the time required to implement a chosen function by requiring more command steps and more lag. This theory purports a negative relationship between stability and speed. No empirical support has been found for this relationship. A good user interface will allow the user to focus on the objects or subjects the user intends to work with [4]. This argument purports a positive relationship between the stability and speed of an SCI, that is, a highly stable SCI will decrease the time required for a user to perform a task [6].

Power-User Performance. It can be argued that the higher the power of an SCI (i.e., the more commands and options available to the user), the more confusing it will be. For a novice user this could result in decreased user performance (through more errors made while working on a task, more time required to complete a task, and a higher probability of not completing the task), but for an experienced user this could result in just the opposite: increased user performance. No empirical support has been found for either case.

Speed-User Performance. The time required to enter and execute the command set required for a particular task is a component of user performance, therefore, the less time required (i.e., the higher the speed), the higher user performance will be. Empirical support for this relationship can be found in [1, 18, and 19]. Anecdotal support can be found in [13]. It could also be argued that the more steps required to complete a particular task (hence, the more time required) the higher the probability of the user making an error. The longer the duration of the interaction the higher the probability of error. This relationship is supported by [2].

Efficiency-User Performance. The total time required for a user to locate all commands in a command set to carry out a particular task is a component of the total time required for a user to complete a task, and is therefore directly related to user performance. The less time spent trying to find desired commands, the better user performance will be. Empirical support for this relationship can be found in [1, 18, and 23]. Using the appropriate type of menu can have a positive impact on user performance [14, 21]. One study indicated differences in user performance depended on menu style, but concluded that "craftsmanship" was a more important determinant of user performance [25]. By craftsmanship the authors could have been referring to any or all of the other SCI determinants of user performance (effectiveness, power, speed, reliability, and stability). This study is therefore not necessarily contradictory to the proposed model. The use of icons has been shown to have no effect on search and selection times, but a dramatic effect on error rates (halving them) [18]. Anecdotal evidence linking SCI efficiency to user performance can be found in [5,10,11,15,17,23, 24].

Effectiveness-User Performance. The total time required for a user to determine the appropriate command at each stage in a command set is a component of the time required for a user to complete a task, and is thus a component of user performance. The less time required in the decision making process the higher will be the performance of the user. The appropriateness of the command "verb" in a menu or command-line has been shown to affect user performance [18]. A more appropriate command verb will likely lower the time required to determine the correct action to take to continue processing the task. Use of color graphics has also been shown to reduce decision making time for a user [3], however, this finding is related to the SDI, and no corresponding empirical support has been found for the SCI.

Reliability-User Performance. The relationship between reliability and user performance theorizes that an increasingly reliable SCI will lead to decreasing errors on the part of the user in determining the correct command in the command set required to complete a particular task. A more appropriate use of SCI technology should lead to less errors on the part of the user. No empirical support has been found for this relationship.

4. OVERLAPPING VARIABLES

Some variables found in the literature to be factors of SCI design which affect user performance are not included in the model because they overlap multiple constructs. Overlapping variables seen in the literature are: consistency, flexibility, ease of learning, and ease of use. What follows is an attempt to reconcile these variables with the constructs outlined in the model and is highly theoretical.

Consistency. The concept of consistency in SCI design overlaps all six determining constructs. What follows here are explanations and examples of how consistency effects each of the six constructs. Consistency in reliability requires that all command names be defined the same. Consistency in stability requires that the program provide similar UNDO and safety warnings for all conceptually similar functions. Consistency in power requires that shortcuts are available for all similar operations (e.g., should have short cut for File Save as well as File Load) and the shortcuts should be similar (e.g., ctrl-f-s and ctrl-f-l). Consistency in speed requires that system response times be similar for similar actions. Consistency in efficiency requires that menus be organized in a logical and structured manner so that users can develop an understanding of where commands will be found when they are needed. Consistency in effectiveness requires that commands be similar to problem solving techniques that the user will be familiar with.

Flexibility. The concept of flexibility overlaps the three SCI constructs of power, reliability, and effectiveness. Additional flexibility, that is the ability to access a certain command or function via multiple methods, will directly increase the power of the SCI. Flexibility can also imply that the user is able to customize the SCI with, for instance, macros. Customizability will effect reliability since macros are user-defined and should be better understood by the user. Customizability will also overlap with SCI effectiveness since the use of macros should lead to a better understanding of the available functionality of the program, and therefore a lower amount of time trying to determine the appropriate command(s).

Ease Of Learning. An easy to learn interface can be theorized to be very reliable, very stable, not very powerful, reasonably fast and efficient, very effective, and offer reasonable user performance.

Ease Of Use. An SCI which is easy to use will possess characteristics from all seven constructs, and will likely be somewhat different from an SCI which is easy to learn. An easy to use SCI can be theorized to have high reliability, reasonable stability, high power, speed, efficiency, effectiveness, and user performance. For experienced users the constructs of reliability and stability could be less important than power and speed.

5. CONCLUSION

The key findings of this paper are that SCI design effects user performance, good SCI design promotes higher performance, and that good design will involve trade-offs between the six proposed constructs. For example, the SCI designer will be faced with the trade between power and speed, and between stability and effectiveness. These tradeoffs mean that there will never be one SCI design which is optimal for all, or even most, users. However, an understanding of the six constructs, their relationships to each other, and to user performance, could lead to better, although still not optimal, SCI designs.

Five of the proposed relationships appear to have no current empirical standing. They are: power-reliability, power-speed, stability-power, power-user performance, and reliability-user performance. Future research should attempt to develop empirical standing for these relationships so that their effect on user performance can be better understood.

6. REFERENCE LIST

[1] Akin, O., and Rao, D. R., "Efficient computer-user interface in electronic mail systems," International Journal of Man-Machine Studies, 1985, Vol. 22, pp 589-611.

[2] Ambrozy, D., "On Man-Computer Dialogue," International Journal of Man-Machine Studies, 1971, Vol. 3, pp 375-383.

[3] Benbasat, I., Dexter, A., and Todd, P., "An Experimental Program Investigating Color-Enhanced and Graphical Information Presentation: An Integration of the Findings," Communications of the ACM, Vol. 29, No. 11, 1986, pp 1094- 1105.

[4] Bodker, S., Through the Interface - A Human Activity Approach to User Interface Design, Lawrence Erlbaum Ass., Inc., Pub., 1991

[5] Booth, P., An Introduction to Human-Computer Interaction, L. Erlbaum Ass., Pub., 1989

[6] Carroll, J.M., and Carrithers, C., "Training Wheels in a User Interface," Communications of the ACM, Vol. 27, No. 8, 1984, pp 800-806.

[7] Clarke, A. A., "A three-level human-computer interface model," International Journal of Man-Machine Studies, 1986, Vol. 24, pp 503-517.

[8] Good, M.D., Whiteside, J.A., Wixon, D.R., and Jones, S.J., "Building a User-Derived Interface," Communications of the ACM, Vol. 27, No. 10, 1984, pp 1032-1043.

[9] Gould, J.D., and Lewis, C., "Designing for Usability: Key Principles and What Designers Think," Communications of the ACM, Vol 28, No. 3, 1985, pp 300-311.

[10] Gould, J.D., Boies, S.J., and Lewis, C., "Making Usable, Useful, Productivity-Enhancing Computer Applications," Communications of the ACM, Vol. 34, No. 1, 1991, pp 75-85.

[11] Grudin, J., "The Case Against User Interface Consistency," Communications of the ACM, Oct 1989, Vol. 32, No. 10, pp 1164-1173.

[12] Hartson, R., "User-Interface Management Control and Communication," IEEE Software, Jan 1989, pp 62-70.

[13] Kasik, D., Lund, M., and Ramsey, H., "Reflections on Using a UIMS for Complex Applications," IEEE Software, Jan 1989, pp 54-61.

[14] Mills, Z. and Prime, M. "Are All Menus the Same? - An Empirical Study," Human-Computer Interaction - INTERACT '90, Elsevier Science Publishers, 1990, pp 423-427.

[15] Morland, D. V., "Human Factors Guidelines for Terminal Interface Design," Communications of the ACM, Vol. 26, No. 7, 1983, pp 484-494.

[16] Myers, B., "User-Interface Tools: Introduction & Survey," IEEE Software, Jan 1989, p 15-23.

[17] Ravden, S., and Johnson, G., Evaluating Usability of Human-Computer Interfaces - A Practical Method, Ellis Horwood Limited, 1989.

[18] Rubin, T., User Interface Design for Computer Systems, Ellis Horwood Limited, 1988.

[19] Schneiderman, B., Designing the User Interface - Strategies for Effective Human-Computer Interaction. Addison-Wesley, 1987.

[20] Schneiderman, B., Software Psychology - Human Factors in Computer and Information Systems. Winthrop Pub., 1980.

[21] Sisson, N., Parkinson, S., and Snowberry, K., "Considerations of menu structure and communication rate for the design of computer menu displays," International Journal of Man-Machine Studies, 1986, Vol. 25, pp 479-489.

[22] Thimbley, H., User Interface Design, ACM Press, 1990.

[23] Tyler, S., and Treu, S., "An interface architecture to provide adaptive task-specific context for the user," International Journal of Man-Machine Studies, 1989, Vol. 30, pp 303-327.

[24] Wenger, M., "On the Rhetorical Contract in Human- Computer Interaction," Computers in Human Behavior, 1991, Vol. 7, pp 245-262.

[25] Whiteside, J., Wixon, D., and Jones, S., "User Performance with Command, Menu, and Iconic Interfaces," Advances in Human-Computer Interaction, Ablex Pub. Corp., 1988, pp 287-315.

Computer-Aided Adaptation of User Interfaces with Menus and Dialog Boxes

U. Malinowski, T. Kühme, H. Dieterich, M. Schneider-Hufschmidt

Siemens Corporate Research and Development, Department of System Ergonomics and Interaction, ZFE ST SN 7, Otto-Hahn-Ring 6, 81730 München, Germany

Abstract

Contemporary interfaces include menus and dialog boxes as major interaction techniques. Particular problems with this type of interaction are involved in complex systems with a rich functionality. Inexperienced users need to learn which actions in a complex menu hierarchy relate to their tasks. For experienced users, selecting actions from menus is costly, and this effort even sums up for frequently used actions. Dialog boxes are often used to prompt for function parameters. While many functions provide a large number of adjustable parameters the majority of these are rarely changed. Even with the simplest task users have to spend a considerable amount of mental effort due to the complex structure of dialog boxes.

Adaptive prompting addresses these problems. An adaptive action prompter helps to select the needed action by presenting the most appropriate and most likely to be chosen actions in an additional dynamic menu. Adaptive dialog boxes use highlighting and colors to guide the users' focus and by this means make setting of parameters faster and easier.

The involved adaptation strategies are implemented considering the ideas of computer-aided adaptation. The main goal of this approach is that users are in full control of the adaptation. On the one hand, they decide which changes take place, on the other hand, they can inspect and change the underlying user and task models.

1. COMPUTER-AIDED ADAPTATION

Self-adaptive user interfaces which try to automatically adapt to assumed characteristics of their user community have often failed to prove that their results really match the users' needs. An analysis of current research indicates that the most promising approaches give users control over the adaptation process and extensively support them in adapting the interface on their own (Malinowski et al. 1992).

Computer-aided adaptation is meant to enable users to achieve a maximum of suitability requiring a minimum of additional effort, knowledge, and skills. First, it is important to provide transparency of the adaptation process and the underlying user modeling mechanisms. Second, the user model should provide the means for an implicit adaptation of the interface by allowing the user to change the information represented in the model. This information is used as input for automatic adaptations. Third, the adaptation process itself should be made adaptive. In order to meet the users' individual prerequisites with respect to adaptation, tools are needed to allow the user to customize the adaptation strategies (Kühme 1993). In particular, the extent of necessary or possible user involvement in adaptation should be adjustable.

2. ADAPTIVE PROMPTING

In today's user interfaces extensive prompting is provided by means of icons, menus, buttons, input fields, and other, often application-specific, controls. Some forms of a more flexible prompting have been introduced in order to reduce navigation effort (compare Kühme et al. 1993). Due to the large number of prompts, not all of them can be visible at the same time, and often a confusingly large number of them is presented in a single menu or dialog box. Thus, users have to accomplish the task of searching for the appropriate prompt in a structured environment of hierarchic lists, menus, and dialog boxes. Adaptive prompting, as proposed in this paper, aims to lead the user to those items which are the most important prompts in a given situation.

The interpretation of "most important" depends on whether the emphasis is on increasing users' performance or on providing guidance. The performance aspect might be covered by items which are most likely to be chosen, whereas in the case of guidance the items which are most appropriate with respect to the current task become the important ones. Actually, there is a strong correlation between both aspects depending on users' experience. For instance, expert users can be expected to most likely choose items which are at the same time very appropriate while this does not necessarily hold for novice users.

Once the system determines which items can be assumed to be the most important ones it presents them to the user in a way that the user's attention is drawn to these items and that the user can perceive them at a glance. At least, there are two alternatives to bring certain items to the user's attention without impairing the accessibility of all the other items. First, the system could provide the user with a complementary presented preselection of the corresponding items and, second, the system could change the appearance of these items within the regular environment. The action prompter described below is an example for the preselection method while adaptive prompting in dialog boxes is an example for the appearance changing approach.

In either case, adaptive prompting is intended to be a complementary aid, not a substitute for existing interaction techniques. Explorative working in a rich environment should always be possible if desired, but not by all means necessary in situations with a clear focus.

Adaptive prompting strategies can obviously not be expected to never fail. On the contrary, the unpredictability of users' behavior and the self-imposed restriction to the fairly small number of items perceivable at a glance will reduce the rate of successfully guessing the set of candidates for the next selection. However, this does not argue against the prompter approach as long as users do have the opportunity to select all available items as before in the non-adaptive environment. A gain in performance can already be observed if there are at least some situations in which a selection becomes considerably faster through adaptive prompting.

Beside performance aspects, adaptive prompting attempts to provide guidance by presenting and thereby suggesting items which are assumed to be appropriate in a given situation. However, the provision of guidance has to be designed very carefully since wrong assumptions about the appropriateness of items can cause severe problems. Obviously, misleading the user would be even worse than no guidance at all.

One way to deal with these limitations is to open the adaptive strategies and underlying models towards the user. Provided with an easy to understand interface to the internal mechanisms, users get a better picture of what is happening inside and are enabled to optionally modify the strategies and models in order to match their actual needs. The hope is that thereby users are empowered to take over part of the responsibility for prompting decisions.

3. THE ADAPTIVE ACTION PROMPTER

Direct manipulation interfaces provide a large number of prompts for actions, mainly through menus. For instance, a typical application would offer: a menu bar with a couple of submenus with several items each, sometimes even extended by cascaded menus and object specific pop-up menus, also often cascaded. Browsing through menu hierarchies in order to locate the desired item can be a time-consuming process, in particular, if the user does not know where exactly to find the item in question or does not even know what item may be an appropriate selection. Shortcuts address part of the problem by offering random access to menu items through pressing certain keys in combination or sequence. But shortcuts, in turn, trade faster accessibility for again more artifacts users have to remember.

The adaptive action prompter is a permanently visible, dynamic menu (or control panel) into which built-in mechanisms map the most appropriate and most likely to be chosen actions. The user can always select actions from either the prompter or the regular menus, whatever is more convenient in a given situation. The prompter contents is adjusted with every context change caused either by the user interacting with the application or by the application itself.

A sensible default value for the maximum number of items presented by the action prompter could be 4 or 5. The items can be the same as in the regular menu in which they originally appear, or they can be extended by the objects to which the actions refer, or by task-oriented explanations with respect to the purpose of an action. Figure 1 shows corresponding sample instances of the action prompter

With the adaptive action prompter, the most important actions are immediately accessible in most cases in which otherwise a search through a possibly large menu hierarchy would be necessary. Since the prompter lists the most appropriate actions one beneath the other (as opposed to being distributed over several menus) the user has a good survey of sensible alternatives.

Based on an application model and a user model, adaptive action prompting tries to automatically determine those actions that best match the actual context and evolving needs and preferences of the user (see Kühme et al. 1993 for details). Optional user involvement allows for cooperatively controlling the adaptation process. Figure 2 shows, for instance, how the user is enabled to inspect and edit prompting rules.

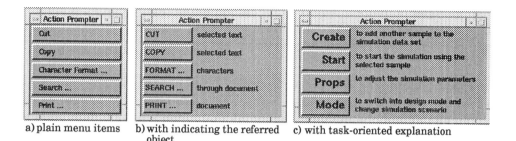

a) plain menu items   b) with indicating the referred   c) with task-oriented explanation
                          object

Figure 1. Sample instances of the Adaptive Action Prompter

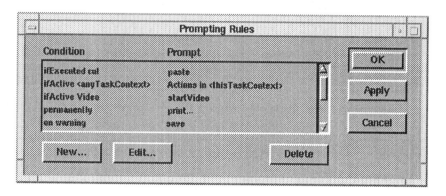

Figure 2. User Interface to Inspecting and Modifying
          Action Prompting Strategies

4. ADAPTIVE DIALOG BOXES

In direct manipulation interfaces dialog boxes are used for setting function parameters. Most functions need a large number of parameters, thus, the dialog boxes have to present many items. This results in a tangled user interface. For most tasks the majority of parameters in a specific dialog box never gets changed. Performing a simple task may take much more time and forces the user to spend more mental effort than necessary due to the complex layout of dialog boxes.

Different strategies are used to improve usability. First, items that are not applicable or not available in the current context are grey-shaded. Second, items in a dialog box are sorted according to their frequency of use. Third, rarely needed parameters are moved from their original place to an additional dialog box titled *More Parameters*. While the first approach has proven useful, the last two strategies change the layout of the dialog box, resulting in a confusion of the user.

Adaptive prompting in dialog boxes aims at presenting the information in a way that allows the user to identify the important items and their parameter setting at a glance. The structure of the dialog box is not changed in this approach. The focus of the user is directed by the use of highlighting and colors.

The parameters that are changed by the user at times are highlighted, while the items that have not been changed for some time are presented regularly (Figure 3). Additionally, for each item a *usually used value* (*uuv*) is recorded. This is the parameter setting that is usually used by the current user. If a highlighted item is set to a value different from the *uuv*, its color is set to red. Otherwise the item is marked green.

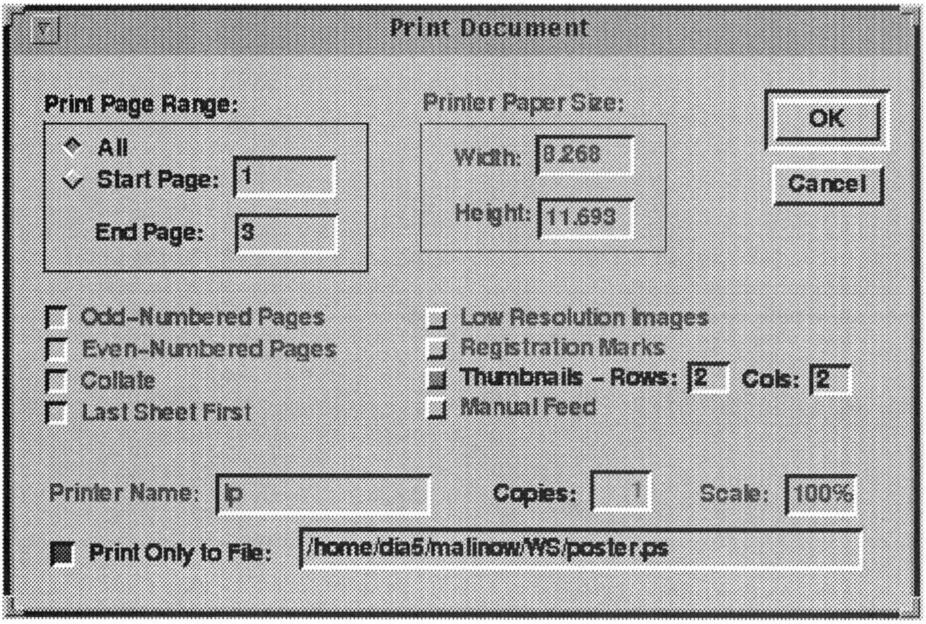

Figure 3. Adaptive Dialog Box for Print Document

The adaptation rules can easily be understood by any user. Therefore, the user can be provided with control of the adaptations to take place and decisions on the parameters determining the adaptation mechanism.

First of all, the user can decide whether the adaptation mechanisms shall be used at all. Second, the user can set and change the *highlighting parameter m* and the *uuv-change parameter n*. If the value of an item is changed within the last m usages of the dialog box, the item is highlighted. If an item is used with a specific value v different from the *uuv* n times a change of the *uuv* to v is proposed.

Third, the user can explicitly determine the presentation style of an item in a dialog box. The item can be presented normally, highlighted, or in the automatically selected style. Last, the user can decide about the system-proposed change of the *uuv*. The user can accept the change, reject the proposed change, or decide that the *uuv* for a specific item shall never be changed.

The information gained from this user involvement is represented in the user model. The data that is additionally necessary for the adaptation process, are inferred from the user's dialog with the application system and also represented in the user model. In detail, the user model contains global data: whether the user wants adaptive dialog boxes at all and the values of the adaptation parameters. Furthermore, the user model holds data about the items in the dialog boxes: the explicitly selected presentation style, the *uuv*, user's answer on a proposed change of the *uuv*, and a history of the used values. The adaptation rules described briefly earlier in this chapter are based on the information represented in the user model.

5. CURRENT STATE AND FUTURE WORK

The adaptive action prompter and the adaptive dialog boxes have been implemented in a prototype of a process control system. In this system the principle of adaptive prompting will also be applied to the visualization and control of the system. User's attention is drawn to the important parts of the visualization by the use of colors, highlighting, and shading. The tools and functions that are appropriate to deal with a given situation are presented in a tool or action prompter.

In the context of process control adaptive prompting may also be useful to support natural language input. Referring to an item by natural language can be a pain. Adaptive prompting makes the complex context of the visualization shrink to a simple, easy to survey context. If the user's focus actually is within this restricted context the remaining referencing effort in the speech input can be kept very little. For instance, the speech input "Set the flow of valve 3 in group 2 to 67!" would be reduced to "Set flow to 67!" with adaptive prompting if only one valve is highlighted. This would be even more reduced to a simple "67!" if the system additionally prompts for a change of the flow. This kind of automatic referencing by adaptive prompting can obviously go far beyond the performance of purely natural language referencing and may sometimes even surpass pointing.

6. REFERENCES

Kühme 1993
    T. Kühme. *A User-Centered Approach to Adaptive Interfaces.* In: W.D. Gray W.E. Hefley, D. Murray (eds.): *Proceedings of the International Workshop on Intelligent User Interfaces.* Orlando, FL. ACM Press, New York, pp. 243-245.

Kühme et al. 1993
    T. Kühme, U. Malinowski, J. D. Foley. *Adaptive Prompting.* Technical Report GIT-GVU-93-05, Georgia Institute of Technology, 1993.

Malinowski et al. 1992
    U. Malinowski, T. Kühme, H. Dieterich, M. Schneider-Hufschmidt. *A Taxonomy of Adaptive User Interfaces.* In: A. Monk, D. Diaper, M.D. Harrison (eds.): *People and Computers VII.* Proceedings of the HCI'92 Conference, York, September 1992. Cambridge University Press, Cambridge.

INTERACTIVE SCENARIOS FOR THE DEVELOPMENT OF A USER INTERFACE PROTOTYPE

Mona M. Kaddah

Center For Academic Computing Services, The American University in Cairo, P.O Box 2511, Cairo, Egypt

Abstract

Prototyping has become quite popular as an approach to information systems development. This may be due to the advent of fourth generation software and the increase in the number of novice users finding difficulty expressing their computer requirements. While a major and key component of a prototype, is the user interface, the specification of its structure, format and dialogue style is often difficult to determine at the outset. Tools and techniques are needed to provide novice users with an awareness of alternative design scenarios and to enable their active participation in the selection of the appropriate interface. This paper addresses this need and introduces an approach based on interactive scenarios and a development tool designed as a 'front-end builder' of the interface prototype. The main objectives of this approach are to :

□ Enhance user awareness of alternate interface designs.
□ Produce a better fit between interface structure and user needs and style.
□ Speed-up interface prototyping.
□ Enhance the elicitation of user functional requirements.
□ Provide a tool that serves in tracing interface requirements for different problem contexts.

The approach is presently being tested on two user groups in a university environment. The reaction of the users has been closely monitored illustrating todate the promising potential of this approach.

1. INTRODUCTION

Despite the fact that the user interface for an application has gained growing recognition, and constitutes a significant fraction of the code, there are no clear guidelines that insure the creation of user-acceptable, quality interfaces (Myers, 1988). Moreover, the nature of the field of user interface design, calls for understanding of human and computer capabilities. Designers with such broad insight are rare (Jones, 1989). The major concern of interface designers has been with the technology, improving type legibility, making superior scroll bars and combining color, sound and voice. This was perceived as the wrong focus, and there is a call for a more task oriented approach, whereby interfaces are designed in response to the specific tasks that people need to implement

(Rheingold, 1990). The real challenge to interface designers is how adequately an interface addresses the semantics of its task domain, and its users' capabilities (Sullivan and Tyler, 1991). Owing to environmental, cognitive, motivational and social differences between designers and users, the latter need to be interactively involved in the task analysis and design process (Thimbleby, 1990).

In response to this motivation, a reliable method for generating effective interfaces has been to test and refine prototypes with end users based on their feedback (Myers, 1988). The problem with this approach is that most end-users lack knowledge about alternate design scenarios to be able to participate in the selection of a suitable interface. The initial prototype, is developed by designers in view of their technical expertise and the mental model that they have formulated of users through imagination and experience. Users are thus limited to a narrow scope of the technology as a result of their reliance on 'professionals', and their low level of involvement. In many cases, the design outcome is either unfavorable or consumes significant resources to be refined.

Although case tools and User Interface Management Systems (UIMS) were designed to speed-up prototyping and make the creation of user interfaces easier and cheaper, reports indicate that UIMS are difficult to use, and/or limited in the kind of interfaces that they can create (Myers, 1988). The significant point is that these tools were not designed to elicit requirements from users. They can be used to represent requirements *after* they have been specified. Enabling users to select interfaces that best fit their environment and actual needs remains a challenge.

This paper addresses the above issues and proposes a new approach to the design of user interfaces that hopefully contributes towards meeting this challenge. A computer-aided mechanism called Interface Designer (ID) was developed and utilized by this approach to accomplish its goals.

2. BACKGROUND

The initial impetus that triggered the approach adopted by ID was the reaction of a user to a mail control application. Despite considerable analysis of functional requirements, the system was immediately rejected by the user due to the interface; it was menu-driven, with a form for data entry. The user realized that navigation from one menu to another, and then to the form screen when needed, was not at all the convenient environment. All the user wanted was one form screen for all data oriented operations, to be operated via hot keys, due to considerable time constraint. It is worthwhile noting that although the user agreed to a menu driven interface during analysis, did not really grasp the implications of the use of forms and menus until the application was developed and demonstrated.

3. OVERVIEW OF INTERFACE DESIGNER

ID was developed to support 'user-centered' interface prototyping focusing on:
- The elicitation of task requirements from users.
- The active participation of users in the design and selection of interface features that best fit their environment and capabilities.

130

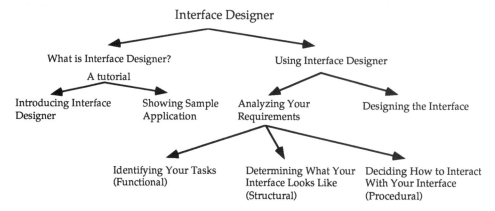

Fig. 1 - Functional Model of Interface Designer

ID provides the user with two paths along which to navigate , allowing free movement from one path to the other (see fig. 1). The goal of the first path is to provide users with a conceptual model of the mechanism, to illustrate sample applications, and in general to trigger users' interest. This is achieved through a multimedia tutorial, combining novel effects with sound, graphics and live snapshots from popular applications.

The goal of the second path is to design the user interface prototype through the provision of alternate design scenarios that the user participates in formulating. The user may express the different dimensions of the interface in terms of its target application domain, appearance and operation, guided throughout by libraries of choices. This creative process takes place in two stages:-

The purpose of the first stage is to involve users in the design by proceeding along three interdependent levels: functional, structural and procedural.

❑ Level 1 (functional) is concerned with the identification of the users' application domain and required tasks. The user may choose from data-oriented, analytic and computer-assisted learning applications.

❑ Level 2 (structural) enables users to choose from a set of alternative structures, the design that best matches the selected task. To get a flavour of the various possibilities, different environments (form-driven, menu-driven, graphical) are presented to the user to choose from.

❑ Level 3 (procedural) demonstrates how the selected interface may be activated and what procedure(s) should be followed to carry out the selected task, allowing users to visualize the functionality of the simulated interface. Throughout the first stage, users may access the first path concurrently to reinforce their knowledge about the capabilities and use of ID. This stage is moreover iterative, users may select more than one task and repeat the three levels. This sets the ground for the second stage which presents the user with an integrated scenario of the application interface.

ID is not intended to produce the actual interface with all its technical details; rather, it will produce a preliminary mock-up that reflects users' needs and, preferences. This output is to be expanded upon and enhanced subsequently.

4. BASIC CONCEPTS AND TECHNIQUES

Drawing from experience, and the two disciplines that are closely associated with interface design, Psychology and Computer Science, below are key concepts and techniques that reflect the philosophy and approach of ID:

Mutual Learning and "Alternative Rationality"
The philosophy of ID is based on the concept of a mutual learning model as developed by Boland (1978). Referred to as alternative rationality, designers and users learn about each other's capabilities and views in the course of development.

Mental Models
Successful interaction is based on models (Thimbleby, 1990). Recognizing that the influence of the interface upon the user will depend on the mental model that the user induces while interacting with it (Kaddah, 1990), simplified information about the purpose, structure, and method of use is presented at the outset to form an early mental model of the capabilities and ease-of-use of ID. Maps and tutorials are used to provide users with a model for the domain. To avoid the problem of tutorials not being context-specific, structured help has been included.

Sound, Images and Text
The combined use of sound, images and text is harnessed to create an environment that holds the users' attention and evades stress and boredom. The use of sound is especially effective, and has advantages over visual techniques in that it is 'omnidirectional' (Jones, 1989). This means that the user does not have to be looking at the screen in order to sense the output, and thus avoids undue eye strain. The use of abstraction is utilized, presenting the userwith objects that can be linked to actions, eg. an eye and ear to see and listen (see Fig. 2).

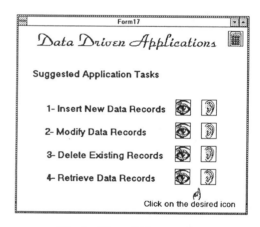

Fig.2 - Use of Abstraction

Experimenting and Adaptive Modeling
Users are encouraged to experiment by selecting interface features, evaluating the simulated interface and modifying their action as they see appropriate. To speed up the process and guide inexperienced users, a choice of either default models of screens or a capability to start from scratch is given. In case of the former, the user is allowed to modify the screen to make it more personalized. The latter option is intended for more experienced users who can visualize the interface mentally and are able to create it on their own.

Goal-Directed Interface Design
To insure that the interface will properly address the semantics of the users' domain and tasks, the top level of the analysis hierarchy is designed to assist users in this area. The subsequent levels -structural and procedural- address the lexical and syntactical aspects of the interface.

5. METHODOLOGY OVERVIEW

The activities needed to implement the ID approach may be structured in two broad stages. The first is the exploration stage, a user-driven process to draw out needs and responses according to a framework that evolved progressively, whereas the second comprised the design, development and implementation activities that ran iteratively in a prototyping environment.

5.1. Exploratory Stage
❏ A survey of the prevailing environment at the university was conducted to identify frequently requested tasks.

❏ The tasks were first structured in two domains, data oriented and analytic oriented, guided by the taxonomy proposed by Andriole (1990). The data oriented included tasks such as data storage, and retrieval, whereas the analytical domain comprised computational, decision support and design-oriented activities. A third domain was subsequently added, and that is Computer-Assisted Learning.

❏ Tests were run on users using a 'think aloud method' to obtain their feedback while running tools and applications in different environments (DOS, windows and Macintosh). Problems and needs expressed by users were recorded and evaluated. As an illustration, a common problem was related to finding the right path to the required task. A typical comment was "I don't know my way around icons and which one to use for my application". Such comments had their impact on the development of ID, which addressed the needs of non-professional users.

5.2. Design, Development and Implementation
The overall framework of ID was first developed and it was decided that Visual Basic under Windows will be the development environment because of the availability of interface building tools, which could be invoked during run time. Expertise in usage of visual Basic was also available.

The first path of ID was developed, tested on some users and the design was refined according to feedback. This process was repeated with path two until the implementation of the mechanism produced satisfactory results. The full version of ID was field tested by two groups at the university. To draw upon such experience in the future, a description of each case is provided.

6. IMPLEMENTATION: Findings to Date

Implementation of ID was first initiated by exposing users to partial prototypes of the mechanism and evaluating their feedback. The full version was then applied in real, though simple problem context as described below:

Case 1

Application context: The need of users of research networks to retrieve information about research groups according to their field of interest.

User type: Non-programmers, moderately experienced.

Sample Reaction to ID: Identified application domain (Data Driven) and tasks required; requested that error messages would appear in the group name field instead of the standard technique of having a separate error status line as the user attention would be focused on this part; requested that the audio facility be structured to specific keywords that are highlighted in red on the screen.

Case 2

Application Context: the need for a document storage and retrieval system.

User Type: A novice user and a moderately experienced non-programming user.

Sample Reaction: Novice user required coaching to identify application domain and tasks, and needed help to understand significance of a 'key' field. Both users requested pull down and pop-up menus and forms for the document; experienced user identified more elaborately interface requirements.

Presently, work is in progress to implement ID within the context of analytical oriented applications.

7. CONCLUSION

The main concern of the ID approach has been to enable users to identify their interface requirements. Through mutual learning and guided analysis that is driven by users' actual task needs, alternative design scenarios can be developed and evaluated. In the context of application prototyping, ID is intended as a preprocessor to UIMS or CASE tools. Designed as a front-end builder of the interface, it insures that captured requirements at this macro level, after subsequent processing, will generate an interface that will be fully supported by its users, because they participated in its creation. Though tentative evidence illustrates the promising potential of this approach, further experimentation, and refinements are in progress, varying problem contexts and user profiles.

8. REFERENCES

1. Thimbleby, H. *User Interface Design.* ACM, 1990.
2. Andriole, J. *The Storyboard Approach to User Requirements Analysis,* QED Technical Publishing Group, 1992.
3. Rheingold, H. 1990. An Interview with Don Norman, in the Art of Human-Computer Interface Design, (eds.), Laurel, B., Addison- Wesley Publishing Company, Inc.
4. Sullivan. J.W, Tyler, S.W. (eds.), *Intelligent User Interfaces,* ACM Press 1991
5. Jones M.K, *Human-Computer Interaction: a design guide,* Educational Technology Publications 1989
6. Myers B.A., *Creating User Interfaces by Demonstration,* Academic Press Inc.1988
7. Boland, R. J, Jr. The Process and Product of System Design, "Management Sci., 24 (1978)
8. Kaddah, M. 1990, *A mechanism for activating end-user learning and participation in office automation,* Ph.D. thesis, The University of Leeds, School of Computer Science.

Intelligent user interface for very large relational databases

Paul E. Reimers and Soon M. Chung †

Dept. of Computer Science and Engineering, Wright State University,
Dayton, Ohio 45435, U.S.A.

Abstract

Relational databases have successfully removed the need for physical navigation. However, they have failed to provide automatic logical navigation, that is, users must specify a logical access path (also known as a join path) when formulating a query. This becomes difficult and error-prone as the size and complexity of a database structure increase, especially for the casual user who may not be familiar with the structure of the database that he is attempting to query. Also, software applications, including artificial intelligence applications, involving relational databases often require some automated means of determining join paths in order to properly construct queries. In this paper, a solution based upon the concept of maximal objects is proposed to provide the automatic logical navigation. The proposed scheme is an extension of our previous approach [3], and consists of two parts: The first part is the design of database structures for storing the metadata of the database supported by this solution. The second part is the design of a join path generator which utilizes the metadata to provide a join path for an incomplete user query. The user specifies the target tables (relations) in the "FROM" clause of an SQL query, and the join path generator returns the complete "FROM" clause and the additional "WHERE" clause statements necessary in order to properly join the target tables.

1. INTRODUCTION

Formulating queries for relational database systems requires that the users understand the structure of the database, including the primary and foreign key relationships, or logical navigation. The required knowledge of the database schema and syntax of the query language can be a problem for many naive or infrequent users of database systems. In fact, experiments have shown that even after training students in relational query languages, 30 percent of the errors encountered in formulating queries involved logical navigation errors [1].

Human users are not the only relational database users. Artificial intelligence applications often need to interface with relational databases. They need to formulate queries, including proper logical navigation information, in order to effectively retrieve data from relational databases.

When a query does not contain the proper logical navigation, problems result: Cartesian products result when a query contains a disconnected join path, and wrong answers can result if a query contains a cyclic join path. Erroneous data can also result from a semantically incorrect join path. It is obvious that proper logical navigation is crucial in formulating the queries for relational database systems.

---

† This research was partially supported by National Science Foundation under grant No. IRI-9008694.

During the last decade, researchers have investigated to free the users from the need to navigate through the relational database schema when formulating a query. Three major approaches have emerged, including (1) the Universal Relation, (2) the Implicit Join, and (3) the Knowledge-Based Approach. However, many of the solutions based on these approaches turned out to be incomplete or limited.

In this paper, we propose a solution based upon the concept of maximal objects [2] to specify the scope of navigation. For a query submitted, a join-relationship graph representing a maximal object is selected and minimized, and the logical navigation information represented by the minimized graph is inserted into the query. The actual solution consists of two parts: The first part is the design of database structures for storing the metadata of the database supported by this solution. The second part is the design of a join path generator which utilizes the metadata to select a join path for an incomplete user query. The user specifies the target tables (relations) in the "FROM" clause of an SQL query, and the join path generator returns the complete "FROM" clause and the additional "WHERE" clause statements necessary in order to properly join the target tables.

The proposed scheme is an enhanced version of our previous approach [3] by adding the feature of the superset of maximal objects. For large and complex database structures, it would be advantageous to allow a maximal object to be a superset of several maximal objects. This would help minimize the size of the metadata tables and thus minimize the amount of effort required to populate and maintain the metadata tables. The proposed scheme automatically provides the join conditions, or logical navigation, for SQL queries that retrieve data from a relational database. Compared to the others schemes, it requires minimal maintenance, while providing complete join conditions as well as all the target tables required.

2. THE MAXIMAL OBJECT APPROACH

The existence of the cyclic join paths is the critical problem in most of the logical navigation solutions. To avoid this problem, the concept of maximal objects [2] was adopted in our proposed scheme. Each table (relation) in the database is referred to as an object, and a maximal objects is a set of objects in which we are willing to navigate. Each object in the database must be contained in at least one of the maximal objects defined. Moreover, no cyclic join path is allowed among the objects in any maximal object. In other word, the join-relationship graph representing a maximal object is a graph without a cycle.

Using the concept of maximal objects, the metadata concerning the logical navigation can be stored in relations, as shown in Figure 1:

MAXIMAL_OBJECT (maximal_object_id, object_id, join_id)
OBJECT (object_id, owner_name, table_name)
JOIN (join_id, object_id1, column_name1, object_id2, column_name2)

Figure 1. The database structure for storing metadata related to join paths.

In order to implement the superset feature mentioned above, the metadata tables do not need to be modified. Only the type of data stored in those tables needed to be modified. A maximal_object_id is placed in the object_id field of the MAXIMAL_OBJECT table when that maximal object is contained within another maximal object. However, one must be careful not to assign the same identifier (ID) to both a maximal object (maximal_object_id) and an object (object_id).

3. THE JOIN PATH GENERATOR

The join path generator selects a maximal object which contains all the objects which are the target tables specified in the query. The solution object list initially includes all the objects contained in the selected maximal object. The acyclic join-relationship graph corresponding to the selected maximal object is then minimized according to the target tables specified in the query. Then, the logical navigation information obtained from the minimized graph is inserted into the query.

The intermediate data obtained from the queries against the metadata tables defined in Figure 1 are stored in the intermediate data tables shown in Figure 2.

TARGET_OBJECT (object_id)
MAX_TEMP (maximal_object_id)
OBJECT_TEMP (object_id, join_id)

Figure 2. Intermediate data tables

The TARGET_OBJECT table stores the target object_ids, that is, the object_ids for the tables listed in the "FROM" clause of the query. The MAX_TEMP table stores the maximal_object_id selected by the join path generator. The OBJECT_TEMP table stores object_id and the corresponding join_id of the objects contained in the maximal object.

Steps performed by the join path generator, using the metadata and intermediate data tables based on the superset approach, are shown below:

1. Starting with empty intermediate data tables, query the OBJECT table to obtain the object_ids for all the target objects specified in the "FROM" clause of the query. Insert these object_ids into the TARGET_OBJECT table. The corresponding SQL statement for each target table is:

INSERT into target_object(object_id)
SELECT object_id
FROM object
WHERE owner_name = <owner name of target table>
    and table_name = <table name of target table>

2.a Find all the potential maximal objects that contain all the target tables, and insert them into the MAX_TEMP table. The SQL statement is shown below (with comments in brackets):

[Insert all maximal objects that contain all   ]
[the target objects (tables) into the Max_Temp]
    INSERT into max_temp(maximal_object_id)
    SELECT maximal_object_id
    FROM maximal_object a
[Return TRUE if all target tables   ]
[are contained in the maximal object]
    WHERE not exists
        (SELECT object_id
        FROM target_object
        MINUS
        SELECT object_id
        FROM maximal_object
        WHERE object_id in
            [Get all maximal objects and objects]
            [contained in that maximal object.   ]

```
                    (SELECT object_id
                     FROM maximal_object
                     CONNECT BY prior object_id =
                         maximal_object_id
                     START WITH maximal_object_id =
                         a.maximal_object_id)
              )
```

2.b Delete the potential maximal objects whose objects are also potential maximal objects.

```
        DELETE
        FROM max_temp
        WHERE maximal_object_id in
           [ Get a list of maximal objects whose objects ]
           [ are also potential maximal objects.      ]
             (SELECT maximal_object
              FROM maximal_object
              WHERE object_id in
                [ Find any objects of this maximal ]
                [ object that are also potential   ]
                [ maximal objects.               ]
                  (SELECT maximal_object_id
                   FROM max_temp)
```

3. Choose one maximal object M from those in MAX_TEMP.

4.a Obtain the object_ids of all the objects contained in the selected maximal object M, and insert these object_ids and corresponding join_ids into the intermediate data table OBJECT_TEMP.

```
        INSERT into object_temp(object_id, join_id)
        [ Get all object_ids and maximal_object_ids for ]
        [ this maximal object (stored in Max_temp)    ]
        SELECT object_id, join_id
        FROM maximal_object
        CONNECT BY prior object_id = max_object_id
        START WITH maximal_object_id in
            (SELECT maximal_object_id
             FROM max_temp)
```

4.b Get the actual objects used to join a certain maximal_object to another object or maximal_object.

```
        INSERT into object_temp(object_id, join_id)
        SELECT distinct object_id1, join_id
        FROM join
        WHERE join_id in
            (SELECT join_id
             FROM object_temp)
            and object_id1 not in
            (SELECT join_id
             FROM object_temp)
        UNION
        SELECT distinct object_id2, join_id
        FROM join
        WHERE join_id in
            (SELECT join_id
```

```
      FROM object_temp)
      and object_id2 not in
      (SELECT join_id
      FROM object_temp)
```

4.c Remove the objects from the OBJECT_TEMP table that are also maximal objects.

```
      DELETE
      FROM object_temp
      WHERE object_id in
          (SELECT maximal_object_id
          FROM maximal_object)
```

5. Delete any object from the table OBJECT_TEMP that is not a target object and only can join to one other node in the table OBJECT_TEMP. The SQL statement is shown below:

```
      DELETE
      FROM object_temp
      WHERE join_id in
          [ Obtain all the join_ids correspond to the joins ]
          [ with end nodes that are not target tables   ]
          (SELECT join_id
           FROM object_temp
           WHERE object_id in
               [ Get all the end nodes that are ]
               [ not target tables    ]
               (SELECT object_id
               FROM object_temp
               GROUP BY object_id
               HAVING count(*) = 1
               MINUS
               SELECT object_id
               FROM target_object)
      )
```

6. Repeat Step 5 until no more rows are deleted from the table OBJECT_TEMP.

7. Retrieve the names of the tables to be included in the "FROM" clause. The SQL statement is as follows:

```
      SELECT owner_name, table_name
      FROM object
      WHERE object_id in (SELECT object_id
                          FROM object_temp)
```

8. Retrieve the join path data for the "WHERE" clause. The SQL statement is as follows:

```
      SELECT d.owner_name, d.table_name, a.column_name1,
             e.owner_name, e.table_name, a.column_name2
      FROM  join a, object_temp b, object_temp c, object d, object e
      WHERE a.object_id1 = b.object_id
          and a.object_id2 = c.object_id
          and a.join_id = b.join_id
          and a.join_id = c.join_id
          and d.object_id = b.object_id
          and e.object_id = c.object_id
```

Compared to the design in [3], Steps 2 and 4 were modified in the Join Path Generator design. Step 2 gets a list of potential maximal objects. It now uses an infrequently used SQL command "Connect By" which displays data based on hierarchical relationships, and is thus able to retrieve the entire content of a maximal_object, even when it contains objects and other maximal objects.

Step 4 is concerned with retrieving the initial acyclic join-relationship graph. First, it gets all the objects and join_ids, but also includes maximal_objects joining to objects or other maximal objects. In order to handle minimizing the join-relationship graph, the query needs to contain objects only, and not maximal objects. The remaining parts of this step solve that problem. Part B gets the object_id that is involved in the join of a certain maximal object, and part C deletes the maximal objects from the table OBJECT_TEMP. As a result, at the end of Step 4, the initial graph, including object_ids (nodes) and join_ids (connectors), is stored in the table OBJECT_TEMP.

The steps involved in the join path generator have been successfully tested. The database structure and queries were designed and tested using the Oracle Relational Database Management System (version 6.0).

4. CONCLUSIONS

In this paper, an automatic logical navigation scheme based on the concept of maximal object is proposed. A maximal object is a set of relations (tables) that we are willing to navigate, and the join-relationships between relations within a maximal object can be represented in the acyclic graph corresponding to the maximal object. For an incomplete query submitted, a maximal object is selected and the corresponding graph is minimized to provide the join path and the additional target tables required.

Compared to the previous design [3], this enhanced version contains much less data in the MAXIMAL_OBJECT table. The only disadvantage of the enhanced design is that the queries are slightly more complex and may take a little more time, which is negligible.

The join path generator is designed for a single user environment. To modify the design to work in a multi-user environment, the database structure of the intermediate tables, as well as the queries referencing those tables, would need to be modified. Adding fields such as user-ID and timestamp may be sufficient.

For the case of having multiple possible maximal objects, a user can influence the selection of the maximal object by specifying more target tables that are to be included in the join path. This may result in one or more candidate maximal objects being eliminated if they do not contain those extra tables. Or all the possible results can be given to the user to be selected in interactive manner. If the maximal objects are initially defined carefully by considering the semantics of the relations, we can minimize the possibility of semantically incorrect results.

The logical navigation scheme proposed in this paper may not be perfect for every case, but compared to the other schemes, it requires minimal maintenance while providing complete join path to be specified in the user query as well as all the target tables required.

REFERENCES

[1] F. Leymann, A Survey of the Universal Relation Model, Journal of Data & Knowledge Engineering, 4 (1989) 305-320.

[2] D. Maier and J. D. Ullman, Maximal Objects and the Semantics of Universal Relation Databases, ACM Trans. on Database Systems, 8 (1983) 1-14.

[3] P. E. Reimers and S. M. Chung, Automatic Logical Navigation for Relational Databases, Proc. of ACM Symp. on Applied Computing (1993) 343-350.

SPOKEN LANGUAGE INTERACTION: EFFECTS OF VOCABULARY SIZE AND EXPERIENCE ON USER EFFICIENCY AND ACCEPTABILITY

Thomas W. Dillon[a], A.F. Norcio[b], & Michael J. DeHaemer[c]

[a]Department of Information & Decision Sciences, Franklin P. Perdue School of Business, Salisbury State University, Salisbury, Maryland 21801

[b]Department of Information Systems, University of Maryland, Baltimore, Maryland 21228

[c]Lattanze Human-Computer Interface Laboratory, Sellinger School of Business & Management, Loyola College, Baltimore, Maryland 21210

Abstract

The purpose of this study is to determine the effects of vocabulary size and interface experience on the performance and acceptance of the user. Subjects performed a hands busy and eyes busy task while interacting with a speaker-dependent connected-speech recognition system with audio output. The time required to perform the task decreased significantly when the user acquired experience with the interface. A large inclusive vocabulary decreased the number of non-recognized words spoken by the user. The results of an interface-acceptance questionnaire reveal that subjects are more accepting of the spoken language interface as they gain experience.

1. INTRODUCTION

Speech recognition systems are now being integrated into a number of applications in which the computer user is involved in a hands busy or eyes busy task. For this reason it is important to measure system performance variables such as time of task completion, number of uncorrected errors, and user satisfaction when implementing a Spoken Language Interface (SLI) [1][2][3].

One of the human factors activities identified as necessary for improved user acceptance and efficiency in speech recognition is the selection of a proper vocabulary and the design of systems feedback and dialogue [4]. In the past, studies that examined the use of vocabulary in natural language or speech recognition applications were performed by a simulation, sometimes called the "Wizard of Oz" technique [5][1]. Though limited, simulation studies assisted in providing a foundation for understanding spoken language interaction with a computer system [5]. Recent improvements in speech recognition technology now permit studies to be performed that examine vocabulary without the use of simulation techniques and permit the design of an SLI.

The skill of an SLI user varies with experience and practice [6]. For example, the inexperienced user requires a rigid interaction style [8] while the experienced user can find rigid interaction to be long, boring, poorly focused, ineffective and sometimes misleading [9].

The present study attempts to define the relationship between the independent variables of vocabulary size and experience with the interface with the dependent variables of task performance and user acceptance. The task performance measures are time on task and recognition accuracy. This study involves nursing students, or novice subjects in the domain. Future studies will include nurses that qualify for Advanced Practice Nurse, or expert nurses.

2. METHOD

2.1. Subjects

The subjects selected to participate in this study were volunteer student nurses, defined as fourth year nursing students with limited nursing experience. All subjects completed the same nursing course work requirements, which included classes in anatomy and physiology, nursing technologies, and health assessment. All subjects had approximately the same amount of actual nursing experience. Ages of the subjects ranged form 21 to 24 years of age. There were two male and eleven female subjects. Each subject was compensated for the approximate 2 hours required for the study.

2.2. Hardware and Software

A Compaq DeskPro 386s with a Verbex 6000 connected-speech recognition board with audio output acted as the spoken language interaction system. The system included a head-mounted microphone.

Five nurses performed a "Wizard Experiment" (talked through a physical assessment as if entering patient data into a natural-language voice-processing computer system)[10]. Audio tapes were made of the "Wizard Experiment." The tapes were transcribed to acquire the natural vocabulary spoken by the nurses while performing the task. These transcripts were then coded into a spoken language interface using the Verbex Voice System's development grammar. By using a "Wizard Experiment" we feel that we were able to capture the users interaction style, structure, and most of all, vocabulary [11] (See Table 1 for an example of the vocabulary and grammar). As recommended in the literature, the words which were chosen are tailored specifically for the application [12].

Two vocabulary sets were created for the SLI. The first contains all of the words spoken by the nurses. This results in a large vocabulary of 103 words that accommodates alternative word choices. The second vocabulary set contains 74 words or only those spoken by a minimum of three of the five nurses in the "Wizard Experiment," The grammar, word ordering, and feedback remained the same for both vocabulary sets.

Table 1

respirations RATE regular
respirations are RATE regular
respirations are RATE and regular
respirations are RATE per minute and regular
respirations are RATE per minute rhythm regular

Sample Vocabulary and Grammar

2.3. Experimental Design

The experimental design, a split-plot design, consisted of one between-groups factor (vocabulary) and one repeated-measures factor (experience). The vocabulary size, determined by the "Wizard Experiment," provided the available vocabulary for both levels of the study. The first vocabulary level contained 103 words or all of words spoken by the five professional nurses during the "Wizard Experiment." The second level contained 74 words, or only those words spoken by a minimum of three of the five "Wizard Experiment" participants or 60%. The two levels of the independent variable experience, were determined by each subjects first and fourth physical assessment task, each of which provide an interaction with the SLI.

Task completion time, number of non-recognitions, number of mis-recognitions, and items skipped were the performance variables collected during the study. Task completion time measured from when the subject began to assess the patient until all data was entered into the SLI. Number of non-recognitions (when the subject uttered a word not in the vocabulary or a word in the vocabulary that was not recognized by the system), number of mis-recognitions (when a subject uttered a proper word or phrase from the vocabulary and the speech recognition system recognized the utterance incorrectly), and items skipped were gathered by observation, review of the input file, and analysis of audio tapes recorded during the study.

In addition, subjective satisfaction with the SLI and attitude toward computers was assessed using two separate questionnaires.

2.4. Procedure

Subject's sessions were conducted individually. Prior to participating in the study, subjects completed a pre-experimental computer-attitude questionnaire that contained the following bipolar pairs: personal/impersonal, simple/complicated, helpful/hindering, systematic/random, easy/difficult, forgiving/unforgiving, obedient/bossy, cooperative/obstinate, unthreatening/threatening, intelligent/simple-minded, pleasing/disgusting, flexible/inflexible, satisfying/frustrating, calming/anxiety-provoking, and obliging/demanding [13].

Subjects were told that the purpose of the study was to test a newly developed computer interface that permits nurses to enter patient data into a computer system by talking. Subjects were randomly assigned to one of the two vocabularies, six to the large inclusive vocabulary and seven to the small significant vocabulary [14]. Then each subject enrolled voice models first by isolated, followed by connected speech. During enrollment, subjects were introduced to the spoken language vocabulary and grammar that would be used during the study. Each isolated word in the vocabulary was trained a minimum of two times. Then all connected-word phrases were also trained. After the training passes were completed for both isolated and connected speech, subjects performed a practice trial of the spoken language interface.

For the hands busy and eyes busy task, subjects performed a cardiovascular examination on a patient. The patient was a volunteer that laid quietly as if unable to respond to commands or requests from the nurse-subject. Twenty-one data items were gathered by the subjects including respirations and blood pressure, and various pulses, impulses, and heart sounds. For simplicity, data items were limited to cardiovascular response/results gathered by sphygmomanometer (blood pressure cuff) and stethoscope. An adaption of a standard cardiovascular examination guide sheet was provided for each subject. While performing the exam, data was entered into the spoken language interface by a head mounted microphone. Since no visual feedback was available to the subject, feedback was provided by an audio beep when data was received and recognized by the system. If the system did not recognize a spoken utterance, subjects were instructed to attempt to get recognition by repeating all items five times. Each subject performed four complete cardiovascular examinations utilizing the SLI to record response/results.

To study user acceptance, a subjective satisfaction questionnaire was completed after the first and fourth examination. The instrument used was a set of twelve bipolar adjective rating scales of seven intervals each and a concluding thirteenth seven-interval scale for overall acceptability [1]. Scale items were: fast/slow, accurate/inaccurate, consistent/inconsistent, pleasing/irritating, dependable/undependable, natural/unnatural, complete/incomplete, comfortable/uncomfortable, friendly/unfriendly, facilitating/distracting, simple/complicated, useful/useless. After subjects completed the enrollment procedure, a practice trail with the interface, and four examinations for the study, a second computer-attitude questionnaire was administered.

3. RESULTS

3.1. Task Completion Time

An analysis of variance was run on the task completion times using vocabulary size and experience with the interface as the main effects. The main effect of experience with the interface was significant, $F(1,11) = 18.78$, $p < 0.0012$. This suggested that as a subject gained experience with the interface, the time to complete the task decreased. The main effect of vocabulary size was not significant, $F(1,11) = 1.40$, $p < .2619$. The interaction of experience and vocabulary was also not significant for task completion time, $F(1,11) = 3.36$, $p < .0942$.

3.2. Non-Recognitions of the Spoken Vocabulary

The mean number of spoken language phases that were not recognized by the SLI with the large inclusive vocabulary were 5.25. This was substantially lower than the mean number of spoken language phrases not recognized by the smaller significant vocabulary, 9.642. An analysis of variance was run on the number of non-recognitions using vocabulary size and experience with the interface as the main effects. The main effect of vocabulary size was significant, $F(1,11) = 16.24$, $p < 0.002$. The performance of subjects using the vocabularies of 103 words and 74 words was significantly different. Those with the large inclusive vocabulary had far fewer non-recognized phrases. The main effect of experience ($F(1,11) = 1.07$, $p < 0.3235$) and the interaction of vocabulary and experience were not significant ($F(1,11) = 1.96$, $p < 0.1887$).

3.3. Mis-recognitions and Skips

The number of mis-recognized phrases was counted along with the number of times a subject would skip a response or result on the physical assessment. An analysis of variance displayed no significance for either mis-recognitions or skips. These two items are more an evaluation of the speech recognition system than an analysis of the effects of vocabulary size or level of experience. For this reason they will not be discussed in the conclusions of the paper.

3.4. Subjective Ratings

Two subjective ratings were used to assess user satisfaction and acceptance. The user satisfaction questionnaire consisted of an attitude scale of fifteen bipolar adjective pairs. The mean responses to each subjects pre- and post-experimental questionnaire did not differ statistically for vocabulary size ($F(1,11) = 0.02$, $p < .8974$), experience with the interface ($F(1,11) = 0.09$, $p < .7759$), or the interaction of vocabulary and experience ($F(1,11) = 0.03$, $p < .8765$). This may be seen as a positive reaction to the SLI since subjects did not react negatively to the interface. The second questionnaire was administered following the first and fourth physical assessments. The responses of the twelve bipolar rating scales were used to create an acceptability index (AI). The AI was defined as the sum of the scale responses. An analysis of variance for the AI displayed significance for the main effect of experience, $F(1,11) = 9.16$, $p < 0.0115$. No effect was found for vocabulary size ($F(1,11) = 0.40$, $p < .5396$) or the interaction of vocabulary and experience ($F(1,11) = 2.93$, $p < 0.1149$). These findings indicate that as users interact with the interface, they find the interface to be more acceptable.

4. CONCLUSIONS

The purpose of this study was to examine the effects of vocabulary size and experience on user efficiency and acceptability. The results show, that as a user gains experience with the spoken language interface task completion time decreases and user acceptance increases. In addition, a large inclusive vocabulary reduces the number of non-recognized word utterances, thus improving user efficiency.

5. ACKNOWLEDGMENTS

This research was partially funded by a grant from the David D. Lattanze Center for Executive Studies in Information Systems, Loyola College in Maryland. The speech recognition system was provided by Verbex Voice Systems, Inc. Edison, New Jersey.

6. REFERENCES

1. Casali, S.P., Williges, B.H., & Dryden, R.D. (1990). Effects of recognition accuracy and vocabulary size of a speech recognition system on task performance and user acceptance. Human Factors, 32,183-196.
2. DeHaemer, M.J. Wright, G., & Dillon, T.W. (1992). Performance effectiveness with voice input for beginning spreadsheet users. Proceedings of AVIOS '92 Voice I/O Applications Conference, 179-185.
3. Simpson, C.A., McCauley, M.E., Roland, E.F., Ruth, J.C., & Williges, B.H. (1985). Systems design for speech recognition and generation. Human Factors, 27, 115-141.
4. Frankish, C., Jones, D., & Hapeshi, K. (1992). Decline in accuracy of automatic speech recognition as a function of time on task: Fatigue or voice drift?. International Journal of Man-Machine Studies, 36, 797-816.
5. Fraser, N.M. & Gilbert, G.N. (1991). Simulating speech systems. Computer Speech and Language, 5, 81-99.
6. Leggett, J. & Williams, G. (1984). An empirical investigation of voice as an input modality for computer programming. International Journal of Man-Machine Studies, 21, 493-520.
7. Morrison, D.L., Green, T.R.G., Shaw, A.C., & Payne, S.J. (1984). Speech controlled text-editing: Effects of input modality and command structure. International Journal of Man-Machine Studies, 21, 49-64.
8. Brajnik, G., Guida, G., & Tasso, C. (1990). User modeling in expert man-machine interfaces: A case study in intelligent information retrieval. IEEE Transactions on Systems, Man, and Cybernetics, SMC-20, 166-185.
9. Rudnicky, A.I. & Sakamoto, M.H. (1989). Transcription conventions and evaluation techniques for spoken language systems research. No. CMU-CS-89-194, Carnegie Mellon University School of Computer Science.
10. Rudnicky, A.I. (1990). The design of spoken language interfaces. No. CMU-CS-90-118, Carnegie Mellon University School of Computer Science.
11. Michaelis, P.R., Chapanis, A., Weeks, G.D. & Kelly, M.J. (1977). IEEE Transactions on Professional Communication, PC-20, 214-221.
12. Zoltan-Ford, E. (1991). How to get people to say and type what computers can understand. International Journal of Man-Machine Studies, 34, 527-547.
13. Kelly, M.J. & Chapanis, A. (1977). Limited vocabulary natural language dialogue. International Journal of Man-Machine Studies, 9, 479-501.

Screen Layout and Semantic Structure in Iconic Menu Design

Ping Zhan, Ram R. Bishu and Michael W. Riley
Department of Industrial and Management Systems Engineering
175 Nebraska Hall, University of Nebraska-Lincoln
Lincoln, NE 68588, USA

Abstract
    Past research on menu interfaces has been mostly concerned with textual menus. This paper is intended to address typical issues in iconic menu design, such as screen layout and semantic structure of multiple level iconic menus. Two types of iconic menu screen layouts were studied: circular and rectangular screen layouts. The semantic structures of these menus were characterized by: 2 menu sizes x 2 directions x 2 levels of depth. The design of the menus was based on existing iconic menus. In testing, subjects studied a target icon, searched for a "matching" icon by navigating through the menu structure, and finally selected the matching icon at the lowest level of the menu. Study time, response time, and error rate were used to measure user performance.
    Results indicate that screen layout and semantic structure of iconic menus significantly affect user performance, in a way that is similar to textual menus. With the same screen space, circular screen layout was superior to rectangular screen layout.
    It is suggested that iconic menu designers should probably consider to use results obtained from textual menus as references, with care taken for the differences between textual and iconic menus. Further studies need to investigate these differences before making any sound conclusions.

INTRODUCTION

    One of the goals of menu designers is to improve user productivity through optimizing menu design. While traditional menu design is typically text-oriented, the emerging object-oriented interfaces such as iconic menus have presented a challenge for menu designers.
    A literature review indicates that it is necessary to look at this new area, especially with respect to multiple level iconic menus (Gittins, 1986). Typical issues in iconic menu design include the screen layout and semantic structure of iconic menus. Screen layout refers to the spatial organization of a menu screen such as a rectangular screen layout or a circular screen layout. Semantic structure refers to the organization of menu items within a menu system such as a tree like hierarchical structure.
    Callahan, Hopkins, Weiser, and Shneiderman (1988) investigated menu screen layout effect by comparing a circular (pie) menu system with a rectangular menu system, both of which consisted of common command names. Pie menus were found to have shorter target seek time and lower error rate, while increasing productivity by 15-20 percent, and having an equivalent subjective preference.
    It can be seen that there are several unaddressed issues in Callahan et al.'s study (1988). First, the investigators used a larger screen space for pie menus than the rectangular menus, which might have introduced biases to their conclusions. Second, as the authors indicated, only a fixed size of menu system (an 8-item size) was used to make the comparisons. Finally, the menu items were made up of textual command names only, while actual menus could be either textual, iconic, or a combination of both. Therefore, the present study was intended to

validate their conclusions and investigate the effects of screen layout and semantic structure on user performance through employing iconic menus.

METHOD

Subjects, Equipment and Menu Design

Thirty-four college students volunteered to participate in the study. An iconic menu program written in HyperCard was used to accomplish the goals of the present study. The iconic menu program represented traditional pull-down menus. Two types of menu screen layouts were tested: circular (pie) and rectangular layouts. Menu items (icons) in pie menus were evenly placed along the circumference of the pie with an equal distance to the center of the pie, where the initial mouse cursor appeared when the pie menu screen was activated. For rectangular menus, icons were placed in a rectangular format, from the up to the bottom of the menu screen with an equal distance between one and the neighboring one. The initial mouse cursor position was at the top of the rectangular menu screen when the rectangular menu screen was activated. Figure 1 shows samples of the two menu screen layouts.

Menu semantic structures were characterized by: 2 menu sizes x 2 levels of depth x 2 directions. The 2 menu sizes included a 16 and a 32 icon size. There were 16 and 32 icons in the 16-icon and the 32-icon size menu system, respectively. The 16-icon menu system consisted of four menu structures: 8x2, 4x2x2, 2x8, and 2x2x4; while the 32-icon menu system 8x4, 4x4x2, 4x8, and 2x4x4. The menu depth included 2 and 3 levels of menu depth. Menu direction could be either decreasing or increasing. For example, the 2x8 menu structure is an increasing direction menu since the number of icons is increased from 2 at the first level menu screen to 8 at the second level. Figure 1 shows samples of the 2x8 menu structure in 25% of the original area.

The icons were constructed by a unique combination of five binary attributes, which were: color (black or white), shape (circle or square), border (thick or thin), orientation (dot up or dot down), and label (numbered or lettered). For the 16-icon size menus, only four attributes were used (without the orientation attribute).

The dependent variables were response time, error rate, and study time. The independent variables were menu type, size, depth, and direction.

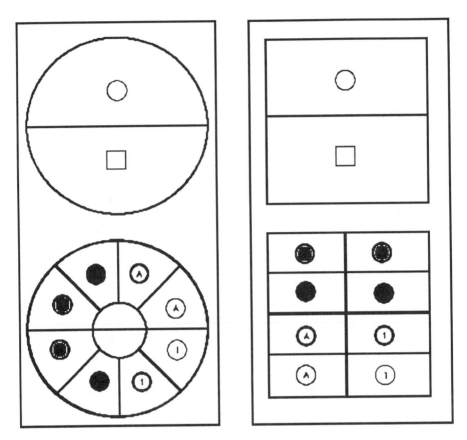

Figure 1. Samples of the 2 x 8 menu structure (left: pie screen, right: rectangular screen).

Procedure

First, each subject was given written and oral instructions for the experiment, as well as the description of the icon attributes. The subject was then informed that the experiment was self-paced and that speed and accuracy were of equal importance. This was followed by a 30-trial training session where a randomly generated "target" icon was presented on the computer screen. The subject was instructed to visually study and memorize this target icon until he or she believed that he or she had remembered it and was ready to click the mouse to start searching for a matching icon on the following menu screens. Clicking the mouse caused the target icon to be replaced with the first level of a 4x2x4 practice menu screen. Menu selections were made by moving the mouse from the initial mouse cursor position onto the matching icon and clicking the mouse. When the subject had navigated through the menu to find the matching icon for that trial, the next trial started.

Following this training session, the subjects performed a regular experiment with 75 trials in each of the 16 different menu structures. Study time, response time, and errors were automatically recorded by the iconic menu program with a Macintosh IIci computer. Study time was the time subjects spent on viewing the target icon before beginning menu navigation. Response time was the time subjects spent in navigating the menu to find the matching icon, which was adjusted to account for machine response time. Error rate was the number of errors over the total number of selections.

Each subject was asked to evaluate the menu screen layouts after the regular experiment. Subjective evaluations were compared for the pie menus with the rectangular menus.

RESULTS AND DISCUSSION

Response time, error rate, and study time were the dependent measures in the analyses. An ANOVA analysis considered menu type, size, direction, and depth as main factors. For the response time, all the main effects and all the first order interactions were significant. A similar ANOVA on the error rate showed only the menu size and the interactions of Type*Depth and Size*Direction to be significant. Menu type, size, as well as the interactions of Type*Direction, Type*Depth, and Size*Depth were significant for the study time, as shown in Table 1.

Table 1.
The ANOVA summary

Source	DF	F Value (RT)	Pr > F (RT)		F Value (ER)	Pr > F (ER)		F Value (ST)	Pr > F (ST)	
Type	1	516.79	0.0001	*	5.89	0.0152		25.72	0.0001	*
Size	1	2913.86	0.0001	*	196.16	0.0001	*	1256.72	0.0001	*
Direction	1	340.30	0.0001	*	3.51	0.0611		0.58	0.4460	
Depth	1	2394.19	0.0001	*	0.31	0.5800		0.66	0.4169	
Type x Size	1	12.52	0.0001	*	1.04	0.3069		0.64	0.4246	
Type x Direction	1	21.30	0.0001	*	0.52	0.4693		17.52	0.0001	*
Type x Depth	1	116.38	0.0001	*	14.68	0.0001	*	12.34	0.0004	*
Size x Direction	1	102.96	0.0001	*	22.33	0.0001	*	1.09	0.2968	
Size x Depth	1	33.92	0.0001	*	1.63	0.2016		42.56	0.0001	*
Direction x Depth	1	274.30	0.0001	*	1.32	0.2504		0.72	0.3962	

Menu screen layout significantly affected user performance, as shown in Figure 2. Specifically, pie menus were significantly faster and more accurate than rectangular menus by 8.9% and 8.6%, respectively. Pie menus also reduced memory load, which was reflected in the study time with a saving of 4.15% for each selection. Subjects preferred pie menus to rectangular menus, with a score of 7.16 for pie menus and 5.99 for rectangular menus on a 0 to 10 scale.

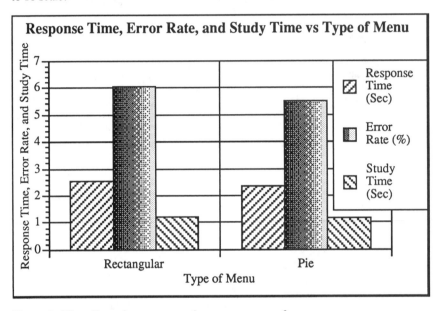

Figure 2. The effect of menu screen layout on user performance.

It is known that human eyes are sensitive within a circular area of 5 degree visual angle. The spatial layout of pie menus might match better with this sensitive circular area than rectangular menus. Thus, cognitive workload in pie menus was reduced. Therefore, subjects demonstrated a better overall user performance in pie menus than rectangular menus. The unique design of the initial mouse cursor position at the pie center could be another reason for the shorter performance time in pie menus.

Menu size significantly affected user performance. Bigger size menus mean more information to be processed. When menu size varied from 16 to 32, response time increased by 20.7% and accuracy reduced by 55.9%, with 9.7% additional study time.

Menu depth significantly affected response time, with 2 level depth being faster than 3 level depth by 4.7%.

Decreasing direction menus were significantly faster than increasing direction menus, with a difference of 1.7% in response time. This is probably due to a better transfer of learning when going from a complex situation to a simple situation than in a reverse order (Bishu and Chen, 1989). In a decreasing direction menu, the breadth reduces as one proceeds from a higher level to a lower lever of a menu. In other words, informational complexity is reduced. Therefore, the time is reduced.

Figure 3 shows a plot of the Type*Direction interaction for response time and study time. It can be seen that the difference in performance between the two directions was more prominent for rectangular menus than for pie menus. On the other hand, the interaction effect does not appear to be prominent for study time.

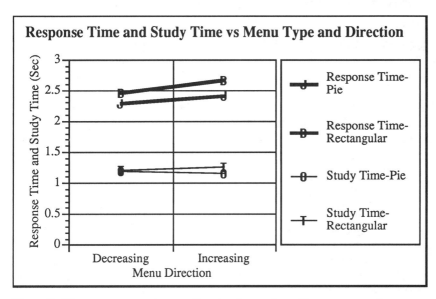

Figure 3. The menu type and menu direction interaction effect on user performance.

Results suggest that pie screen layout can be an alternative to the existing rectangular screen layout for iconic menus. It is suggested that iconic menu designers should probably consider to use results obtained from textual menus as references with care taken for the differences between textual and iconic menus as well as the overall information contents. It should also be noted that in this study the menu structures were formed by combining different attributes such as color, shape, character, border, and orientation. A generalization of the findings to a typical iconic menu system in real world may not be appropriate without a validation study.

REFERENCES

1   Gittins, D. (1986). Icon-based human-computer interaction. International Journal of Man-Machine Studies, 24, 519-543.
2   Callahan, J., Hopkins, D., Weiser, M. and Shneiderman, Ben (1988). An Empirical Comparison of Pie vs Linear Menus. CHI'88, 95-100.
3   Bishu, R. R, and Chen, Y. X. (1989). Learning and transfer effect in industry. International Journal of Industrial Ergonomics, v4, pp. 237-243.

Realtime Synthesis of a Realistic Anthropomorphous Agent toward Advanced Human–Computer Interaction

Hiroshi Dohi and Mitsuru Ishizuka

Dept. of Information and Commun. Eng., Faculty of Eng., University of Tokyo
7-3-1, Hongo, Bunkyo-ku, Tokyo 113, JAPAN
E-mail: dohi@miv.t.u-tokyo.ac.jp

ABSTRACT

An anthropomorphous agent is expected to play an important role toward advanced human–computer interaction. It permits wide communication spectrum between a human and a computer. We have proposed a concept called visual software agent (VSA). The VSA uses a realtime texture-mapping for interactive animated graphics. The anthropomorphous VSA with a realistic facial image naturally rocks his/her face all the time, winks his/her eyes, and talks to a user synchronized with a speech synthesizer. For reality and natural communication, it integrates several technologies such as a deformable three-dimensional wireframe model, texture-mapping, and parallel computing. This paper describes a realtime synthesis method of the realistic anthropomorphous agent using small-scale parallel transputers. The result of the prototype implementation shows that the speed of the realistic image synthesis is fast enough for the real usage.

1 INTRODUCTION

A human interface has become one of the most important research topics in computer science field. One of its ideal form may be the human interface which can carry out many complex tasks by a few simple operations without any exercise. An anthropomorphous agent which has a realistic moving human face as well as intelligence is expected to play an important role for this purpose because it simulates human ordinary communication style.

Toward such an advanced human interfaces between human and computer, we have been constructing a virtual agent called visual software agent(VSA)[1]. We have so far built two prototypes of the VSA. One is an anthropomorphous VSA for advanced human interfaces[2][3], and another is a goldfish VSA for making naturalistic environment artificially[4][5]. These prototypes have been installed on SUN workstations and on our original parallel computing system[6].

The anthropomorphous VSA is intended to realize an advanced human interface proto-type beyond current iconic interfaces. Salient features which the VSA should eventually have are as follows,

- a realistic human-like face which moves in realtime,

- natural communication ability, and

- intelligence.

To enable above features, we integrate the technologies of realtime image recognition, visualization (realtime image synthesis), knowledge-base, and parallel processing into the VSA system.

In the VSA system, a user communicates with a computer through a realistic three-dimensional human face image. A first step for building the VSA system is to synthesize such an image which moves in realtime on a display. For generating the realistic image of the VSA, we use texture-mapping technique[7] and a deformable three-dimensional wireframe model of a human face. Our wireframe model has about 500 vertices and about 500 surface patches.

We use only one full face photograph for texture-mapping. The face area of the photograph is decomposed into small triangle polygons, and then their texture data are mapped and transcribed onto the wireframe face model. It can re-compose any realistic facial image which can be seen from wide angles within a certain limit of direction, because it is the three-dimensional wireframe model. We can change its expression (e.g. wink his/her eyes, open his/her mouth like speaking) by making deformation of the model; i.e. controlling positions of vertices.

The face alive never freeze. Many of synthesized faces made so far can change their expression, i.e., the part of the face, but the face itself has a fixed posture. In contrast, our VSA rocks his/her face all the time. The rocking motion is orthogonal to movements caused by speech, wink, and even looking at any points. A rocking face gives a natural impression that can not be obtained from static images.

2   TEXTURE-MAPPED ANIMATED IMAGE GENERATION

2.1   Parallel Transputers

Both the texture-mapping and the deformation of a 3-D wireframe model in realtime take high computational costs. Many of latest commercial workstations have equipped a graphic accelerator for the rendering operation of polygons. Only a few high-end systems can support texture-mapping operation by hardware, but they are expensive. A compact less-expensive hardware with realtime texture-mapping is desirable for our purpose; we don't necessarily need superfluous high-quality images for our application since the VSA is always moving. In many cases it is meaningless to generate a small part in detail on moving images.

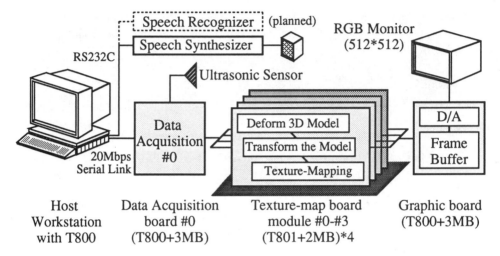

Figure 1: Hardware configuration of our prototype system.

To perform a realtime generation of texture-mapped animated images, we implemented a prototype of the VSA in a transputer network and execute necessary processes in parallel. We have selected a general-purpose parallel micro-processor, transputer[8], as the processor element of our system, because the processor is designed for parallel use.

Figure 1 shows hardware configuration of our prototype system.

The prototype system is composed of a host workstation with a transputer and three VME boards. The host workstation has a speech synthesizer via a RS-232C port. A speech recognizer is also planned. Three VME boards are a texture-map board, a data acquisition board, and a graphic board.

The texture-map board has four standard transputer modules (TRAMs) in the prototype system. Each module includes a transputer T800 and 2MB memory. The size of one module (size-2 TRAM) is 3.66 by 2.15 inches; therefore four TRAMs occupy only a half of a double-height VME board.

The graphic board includes a transputer T800, 2MB local memory, 1MB frame buffer (dual port memory), and a D/A converter. It converts image data to RGB video signal. Each module on the texture-map board has a direct point–to–point connection to transfer large amount of image data.

2.2 Control Packet

A texture-mapped animated image synthesis is basically invoked by a small control packet from the host workstation. It is an event-driven process. When some events occur (e.g., the mouse is moved, any keys or buttons are pressed, or a speech recognizer catches a certain word), the transputer on the host workstation sends the small control packet to the texture-map board. If no event occurs in some periods, the control packet is also sent in order to prevent the anthropomorphous VSA from freezing. The control packet includes the information of positions (x, y, z), rotation angles (x, y, z), mouth shape, the timing of wink, etc. The mouth shape is indicated by five patterns because Japanese has five vowels. The size of this packet is 40 bytes.

A waiting-state module on the texture-map board obtains information from a control packet received. As a result, it deforms a three-dimensional wireframe model in the model coordinate system, then transforms (transformation, rotation, and scaling) the model into the world coordinates system using an affine matrix. Then it applies texture-mapping onto the transformed model. After the completion of this process, these synthesized image data are sent to the graphic board. Because the data transfer rate of one standard serial link of the transputer is 20 Mbps and is insufficient for full-size image data, only the parts modified from its previous frame are transferred.

One transputer module is responsible for generating one frame image. Each module starts its task with at least a certain interval (about 100msec) sequentially. Consequently four transputer modules work in parallel if the events occur continuously. They have equal priority and are identical.

2.3 Intercept Packets

There is a data-acquisition board between the host workstation and the texture-map board. All control packets from the host workstation to the texture-map board pass through its data-acquisition board. In the prototype system, the board has an ultrasonic sensor and can acquire distance to a big object. The function of the data-acquisition board is very simple. That is, it reads sensor data when it receive a control packet, and then it stealthily substitutes some entries of the control packet by the data if the data is within some range. It may compare the data with one in the packet. Otherwise, the control packet is passed through without any changes. This transfer delay time is negligible because the size of the control packet is small and the number of packets per second is the same as the number of synthesized frames.

Data-acquisition boards are easily extensible and are connected serially. A successor board has a priority, therefore it subsumes or masks the entries of packets from a previous board. In some cases it may also initiate new control packet.

2.4 Software Environment

As a software development environment we have used EXPRESS ver. 3.2 (a product of PARALLELWARE Inc.). Each board has own software, and all software is written in C language. The programs are cross-compiled on the host workstation, then down-loaded to the transputers through a VME bus prior to execution. To achieve high performance we have repeatedly applied peep hole optimization to each software. Profiling tools equipped in the EXPRESS have been very useful for the software optimization on a parallel system.

3 EXPERIMENTAL RESULTS

Figure 2 shows the matching of a 3-D wireframe model with a full human-face input image. A realtime moving VSA re-composed from this full face image is shown in Figure 3. Its

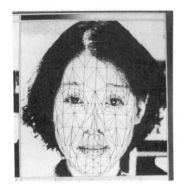

Figure 2: (left) A 3-D wireframe model with a human-face input image

Figure 3: (right) A texture-mapped animated image and our prototype system

background depicts our prototype hardware system consisting of the data acquisition board, the graphic board, and the texture-map board, from left to right, respectively.

The prototype of the VSA implemented in the above small-scale parallel transputers can turn his/her face in realtime tracking a mouse cursor position on a window, wink his/her eyes, and talk to a user (open his/her mouth) synchronizing with a speech synthesizer. Its movement is also controlled by the data of the ultrasonic sensor. The total image-synthesis speed of four transputer modules is about 12 frames/sec when the size of synthesized images is about 170 by 100 pixels which is about a bust-shot size. The time delay from getting any events to display an image is within 400msec. Therefore the prototype system can handle more than 10 events per second (<100msec interval) using four transputer modules. According to measured profiling data, each transputer module on the texture-map board spends more than 90% of the execution time for necessary computation, and the rest for data communication between processors. The data traffic from the texture-map board to the graphic board is less than 40% of the capacity of the transputer's standard serial link. Thus, if necessary, we can add more transputers easily to accelerate the processing speed.

4 CONCLUSION

This paper has described a method of the realtime image synthesis of texture-mapped animated anthropomorphous agent toward advanced human–computer interaction employing small-scale parallel transputers. The VSA with a realistic facial image can turn his/her face according to any input events (e.g., an ultrasonic sensor, tracking a mouse cursor position on a window, etc.) in realtime, wink his/her eyes, and talk to a user synchronizing with a speech synthesizer. Other input events are also possible for controlling the VSA. A rocking face gives a natural impression that can not be obtained from static images. The prototype system uses only four general-purpose micro-processors, i.e., transputers. The result of the prototype implementation shows that the speed of the realistic image synthesis is fast enough for the real usage. The synthesized image at present hardware may not be superfluous high-quality, but it is always moving and sufficient quality for human–computer interaction. The hardware is easily extensible to improve the speed or to expand the size of moving image area, if needed. We are now working to provide eyes and ears to the VSA for wide communication spectrum. They are the ability of image understanding and speech recognition. Also, we have started to implement an interactive friendly guidance system based on the VSA technology of this paper combined with a knowledge-base.

References

[1] M. Ishizuka, O. Hasegawa, W. Wongwarawipat, C-W. Lee, and H. Dohi: Visual Software Agent (VSA) built on Transputer Network with Visual Interface (TN–VIT). *Proc. Computer World '91*, Osaka (1991).

[2] O. Hasegawa, C-W. Lee, W. Wongwarawipat, and M. Ishizuka: A Real–time Visual Interactive System between Finger Signs and Synthesized Human Facial Images employing a transputer–based Parallel Computer. *Visual Computing* (Kunii T.L. ed.), 77–94. Springer–Verlag (1992).

[3] O. Hasegawa, C-W. Lee, W. Wongwarawipat, and M. Ishizuka: Realtime Synthesis of Human-like Agent in Response to User's Moving Image. *11th ICPR*, Hague (1992).

[4] H. Dohi and M. Ishizuka: Realtime Synthesis of Super–realistic Moving Goldfish using Small–scale Parallel Transputers. *CG International '93*, Lausanne, Switzerland (1993).

[5] C-W. Lee, O. Hasegawa, W. Wongwarawipat, H. Dohi, and M. Ishizuka: Realistic Image Synthesis of a Deformable Living Thing based on Motion Understanding. *Journal of Visual Communication and Image Representation*, 2(4):345–354 (1991).

[6] W. Wongwarawipat, C-W. Lee, O. Hasegawa, H. Dohi, and M. Ishizuka: Visual Software Agent built on Transputer Network with Visual Interface. *Transputing '91*, Sunnyvale CA., IOS Press (1991).

[7] P.S. Heckbert: Survey of Texture Mapping. *IEEE CG&A*, 6(11), 56–67 (1986).

[8] INMOS Limited.: *The Transputer Databook*, second edition (1989).

Iterative Prototyping of User Interfaces

D. Felix, H. Krueger

Dept. of Hygiene and Applied Physiology, Swiss Federal Institute of Technology, ETH-Zentrum, CH-8092 Zurich, Switzerland

Abstract
This paper describes an approach to design user friendly interfaces for computer based systems, especially for public use. The iterative prototyping process may not be genuinely new, however this study presents our experience with this approach. The task was to design a user-interface for a self-service terminal for train tickets, with an underlying fare system which was very complex. The system was to use a touchscreen as input media. The design process was divided into the steps *problem analysis*, *identification of archetypes* and *prototyping*. Prototyping was further divided into the three stages: Archetypes, screen layout and a functional model of the complete system. User tests in all prototyping phases showed that known ways of interaction are preferred, that a colourful screen is accepted better by users, and that a linear path through a program is initially better for untrained users, but is judged to be clumsy and slow for repetitive use or for experienced users. In general, the approach with small steps, involving users at several stages with tests has shown its advantages. The results of the tests are easier to interpret, as they are embedded in the whole process of development.

1. Introduction

Developing user interfaces is a process which has been tackled from different angles in the past (e.g. Royce, 1970; Malhotra, et al., 1980). The goal to reach is user-friendliness and general usability. This paper presents a form of interface development which uses known procedures, but extends the use of the method over the whole process of the user interface development.

Iterative proceeding has long been suggested, as well as prototyping of interfaces on different levels. The project of developing a user interface for a ticket vending system for public transportation was used to apply different depth of prototyping and user trials to develop a user friendly interface. The chosen procedure allows to check the quality of the interface at several stages, thus allowing the rating of the final results of the complete system. Normally it is very difficult to say which part of the design process has failed when problems are found in a complex system. The iterative prototyping and user testing allows control over the whole design process.

2. Method

The following procedure was chosen for the design of the system:

1. detailed problem analysis,
2. identification of archetypical situations during a task,
3. prototyping of several possible solutions for the identified archetypical tasks,
4. prototyping of different screen layout and design variants (= look),
5. prototyping of different functional procedures of the system (= feel).

In steps 3, 4 and 5 user trials were conducted to asses the best solution and to identify possible design problems, using prototypes on a Macintosh computer with a touchscreen.

2.1 Problem analysis
The problem of vending tickets for a public transport network was chosen for its complexity and its relevance for everyday life. The fare system selected is supposed to be the most complex known. Formerly only desk clerks had access to the whole of this fare system, and only tickets for travels up to 50km were sold at vending machines. The problem analysis to structure the fare system was an essential input to the next step.

2.2 Identification of archetypes
Using the structuring from the previous step, identification of archetypical steps of the task was possible. As archetypes the

- selection of the number of travellers
- selection of the travel-date
- selection of the destination/departure station
- selection of the fare reduction and
- selection of the class

were identified. The last two consist of a selection from a limited list of possibilities, and were not investigated closer.

2.3 Prototyping of archetypes
Different ways to select the number of travellers were prototyped. Three basic layouts (telephone, linear arrangement, incremental steps) of ten-key-pads with variations (with and without OK-key, with and without display for feedback of the input) were designed, resulting in eleven different layouts. The size of the keys was 16mm by 16mm, respectively 16mm by 51mm for the linear key-pad. 18 subjects (age between 20 and 25 years) performed a standard task in the laboratory, keying in one-digit numbers on a touchscreen, using all eleven layouts. They were asked to rate their preferences at the end of the test in a short questionnaire. Log files were used to assess performance.

A second experiment investigated different layouts to select the travel-date. Four layouts were tested, presenting a monthly calendar (three different layouts, presenting different ways to change the displayed month) or a four week prospective calendar. The same testing procedure was used as in the first experiment. The key size was 16mm by 16mm. 16 subjects (age between 26 and 46 years) took part in this experiment.

The third experiment investigated the preference to select a town (place of destination or departure). As the selection was to be made out of a database of 6500 places, an alpha keyboard was thought to be essential. A pre-test had eliminated several other possibilities, such as a solution using a scrolling method or an index as in a address-book. Different ways of feedback for letters entered, of presenting matching places and of scrolling in the database were tested, resulting in three different solutions. The same test-method as described above was used. 17 subjects (age between 20 and 50 years) participated in this experiment.

2.4 Prototyping of screen layouts
Four different screen designs were developed to find which "look" of the system appealed to people most. The aesthetic aspect was the centre of interest. The same elements on the screen were always present, just the design was different. 20 people (age between 24 to 63 years) were asked to rate the designs according to personal preference and ease of understanding how a task might be solved. They were further asked to state which adjectives were fitting for each design.

2.5 Prototyping of operation modes
The final prototype contained all previously found elements and allowed the selection of the complete ticket (only in a local small database, but using realistic data). Two different modes of selection were implemented: one offering a free choice of proceeding (offering all possible main function headings such as "Destination" at the same time), the other guiding the user through the selection by presenting each parameter consecutively in a linear step-by-step manner. User trials were conducted in the field, using real customers as subjects. 182 subjects (all age groups) took part in this experiment. They were asked to try and select the ticket they were about to buy at the counter, to allow realistic operations. No ticket was issued, as this function was not implemented. A questionnaire was used to asses the users impression of the system, and log-files were recorded to measure performance.

3. Results of the prototyping

For entering figures, a telephone-like layout is preferred. Additionally, users wish to have a display to check the input values and an OK-button. The key-pads using the incremental method are ranked lowest. The analysis of the number of errors shows that so few errors occur that no conclusion is possible. The performance depends clearly on the number of keys that have to be pressed: for instance, key-pads with an OK-key take more time to use than those without.

For the selection of dates, a monthly calendar using arrows to point to the following or previous month ranked best. The four-week prospective calendar clearly ranked last and was not understood by the users. Few errors were noted, however with the four-week calendar many non-selectable areas of the screen were selected.

For the selection of the place of destination or departure, feedback is best provided by highlighting the already entered letters, and by presenting the list of available places in a vertical row. However, no clear preference could be found.

The screen layout that ranked best was the most colourful prototype. Strong colour coding was used to indicate selectability and function, and at the same time attracting the users to the system. The less colourful suggestions were rated as dull, uninspiring or not easy to interpret. Although the functions were the same on all the layouts, subjects were able to discriminate the four proposed solutions. The preference for the colourful prototype was independent of the age of the subjects or of their personal background (computer experience or no computer experience).

The functional prototype showed that untrained, inexperienced users accept a step-by-step procedure better. Nevertheless, after one trial, users demanded to shortcut certain procedures and thought it would be tedious to go through the whole procedure once again. Performance was better and error rate was lower for the step-by-step solution. The solution offering free choice of the sequence of parameter selection was judged better by experienced computer users.

4. Conclusions

The results show that people prefer to work with elements they know from other machines or circumstances. Everyday utilities such as a telephone or a banking machine have accustomed people to using ten-key pads to enter numbers, and is seems obvious that this is the reason for the preference. Less common task as the selection of a date or the name of a place lead to less clear results, as there is less previous knowledge or training.

Users are further attracted by clear, function oriented colour-coding. Using clear, strong coding for functions and as a navigation aid helps people to use the system. Additionally, and not less important, users feel attracted by a colourful design of the user-interface. This may have several reasons: television, computer games and mass media are using lively, colourful presentations to attract peoples interest, and the flow of information has grown to such amount that only a limited amount is noticed. So adapting to commonly used strategies to compete with other systems enhances the attractivity of a system. It may well be that systems which are only used a short time, like the one tested in the reported research, must be treated differently to systems which are used every day, such as office or other workplace system. As research has so far concentrated on office systems, it is possible that new rules have to be defined for public, short-time used systems.

The operation mode preferred by untrained users is a step-by-step solution. However, the results indicate that a clear, easy to understand user-interface allows users to learn the procedure so quickly that they are no longer novices any more after very few manipulations. Therefor users will soon want to have a more direct, free to choose access to the information or product they want, and will be unhappy with a too rigid guidance. Further research will strive to combine a well guided path for novices with possibilities for free-choice for those with more experience.

The method of iterative prototyping of different steps in the design process of a complex system has shown its advantages. Testing of the complex functional prototype was only possible because previous tests had eliminated a number of basic questions such as "how do people expect to select a specific date". The results in each phase can therefore be interpreted more easily, as are more likely to refer to the objective of the experiment. Research will continue in this direction, formalising the approach and making use of a usability lab, where standard test can be run under controlled conditions. In every case a user testing on site where the system is to be installed is needed to check the lab findings, as only the real environment and real users will prove the usability.

Acknowledgements

Many students have participated in this project, without their help and work it would not have been possible to complete this project. Many thanks to them, especially to Werner Sturzenegger, who did most of the prototyping work, and to Sissel Guttormsen, who did the data analysis of the field tests.
The project was supported by Ascom Autelca, Switzerland, and the "Kommission zur Förderung der wissenschaftlichen Forschung (KWF)" of the Swiss Government.

References

Royce, W. W. : Managing the development of large software systems: Concepts and techniques. in Proceedings of IEEE WESTCON, 1970, pp. 1-9.
Malhotra, A.; Thomas, J. C.; Carroll, J. M. and Millner, L. A.: Cognitive processes in design. Int. J. Man-Mach. Interaction, 12, 1980, pp. 119-140.

Integrating Analytical and Creative Processes for User Interface Re-Design

Yosuke Kinoe*, Hirohiko Mori**, and Yoshio Hayashi**

* IBM Japan, Ltd.
1623-14, Shimotsuruma, Yamato-shi, Kanagawa-ken 242, Japan

** Department of Industrial Engineering, Musashi Institute of Technology
1-28, Tamazutsumi, Setagaya-ku, Tokyo 158, Japan

Abstract

This paper proposes a framework for integrating two different aspects of the redesign of artifacts, and their corresponding stages, using empirical methods: (1) the analytical process of identifying usability issues on the basis of empirical data, and (2) the creative process of formulating redesign ideas.

An analysis-supporting tool based on the framework is also introduced. By using a formalized analysis procedure, this tool helps analysts to carry out consistent data analysis of a mass of empirical data, and to classify the usability issues in stage 1. It also provides an environment that facilitates the creative process of idea formulation in stage 2, especially, by providing an intelligent support function using the "Genetic Algorithm." By using the results of the analytical process in stage 1, this function supports the creative process whereby analysts discover latent relationships among the issues that may initially be considered irrelevant, in order to facilitate ideas for global higher-level solutions.

1. INTRODUCTION

The design process can be considered as an iterative spiral [1]. Redesign is an essential element of the iterative spiral of a user-centered design cycle. Usability evaluation has been emphasized for "passive" aspects in the design process, such as how to identify specific usability problems in the user interface design. However, "creative" aspects, such as how to formulate redesign ideas for enhancing artifacts, are also important, especially in a practical product development environment. We focus not only on a process for identifying usability issues, but also on an environment that helps a design team to formulate redesign ideas.

This paper describes a methodology for integrating two different aspects of redesign: the analytical process of identifying usability issues on the basis of empirical data, and the creative process of formulating redesign ideas. An analysis-supporting tool based on the methodology is also introduced. This tool provides an intelligent support function that is implemented by the "Genetic Algorithm" to facilitate the creative process of idea formulation.

2. INTEGRATING ANALYTICAL AND CREATIVE PROCESSES

Redesign using empirical methods can be divided into two different stages: (1) identifying usability issues on the basis of empirical data, and (2) creating redesign solutions at various levels of ideas.

2.1 Analytical process for identifying usability issues

In stage 1, we need a reliable and formalized analysis procedure for identifying usability issues, in order to overcome the complexity of HCI (human-computer interaction) phenomena, which is reflected in the complicated behavior of human-computer systems in the real world. It is important to maintain the consistency of data analysis, so as to ensure the validity of the analysis results. In a practical usability study, it is also important to clarify the analysis procedure and viewpoints for assessing problematic phenomena. An analytical approach using a formalized analysis procedure can be effective in stage 1.

We adopted the basic framework of the *VPA Method* [2] as a standardized analysis procedure for stage 1. This method was developed as a formal method for verbal protocol analysis. The analysis process in stage 1 can be defined as the following three steps. (1) First of all, analysts clarify analysis viewpoints and define an *analytic model* that consists of a set of attributes for characterizing HCI phenomena, categorized according to analysis viewpoints. For example, "users' tasks," "operations," and "status of users' processes" can be used as basic analysis viewpoints for a practical usability evaluation. A set of specific attributes is defined for each viewpoint. (2) Next, analysts characterize HCI phenomena by using a standardized analysis procedure, called "segmentation & tagging," on the basis of the analytic model; empirical data on users' interaction processes are divided into "segments" and each segment is characterized with a "tag," which is a combination of the attributes selected in accordance with each analysis viewpoint. For example, a user operating a word processor tried to remember by trial and error the exact operation sequence for changing the column settings of a document, and spent many minutes completing the task. The segment that included this incident can be encoded by using a combination of attributes such as (task: to change column settings) & (status 1: trial and error, status 2: remembering operation) & (operation: menu selection) & (impact: much time spent). (3) Finally, analysts classify all the segments of HCI phenomena according to their attributes. Similar incidents can be classified into the same group. Analysts summarize each group of segments and then construct a map of usability issues.

In this method, it is essential that the data should be consistently analyzed throughout stage 1, according to consistent analysis viewpoints. An analytic model plays an essential role. A qualitative model of a user's interaction process (e.g. [3][4]) and task analysis of a target domain can be useful as a basis for constructing an analytic model.

2.2 Creative process for formulating redesign ideas

There can be various levels of ideas for redesigning artifacts; likewise, usability issues can be identified at multiple levels [5], from *local counter-solutions* for specific user-interface design flaws to *global higher-level solutions* such as design enhancements that satisfy users' potential requirements. An analytical approach helps us to analyze usability issues in detail and provides a well-structured map of the issues. This can be especially useful for building local counter-solutions. However, to support stage 2, particularly to facilitate the process of building global higher-level solutions, it is considered insufficient merely to apply an analytical approach using a formalized procedure.

The process of idea formulation itself is not considered to be well-formalized, although it is dynamic. Consistency and formality are not very important issues for the creative process in stage 2. The key to stage 2 is to provide an environment that helps a redesign team to create, accumulate, and share their findings on issues by using the analysis results of stage 1.

The redesign team members generate various types of finding as they elaborate the issues. For example, they generalize, restate, and reorganize the issues. They also try to discover latent relationships between various problematic events that seem independent. The latent relationships found are sometimes initially considered absurd, but they may later provide valuable clues for reaching global solutions. We emphasize the importance of facilitating such discoveries by analysts. In stage 2, we currently focus on the following ways of helping the redesign team to create ideas: (1) elaborating issues from various viewpoints by using *multiple representations* such as time-sequential diagrams of users' interaction processes, or maps of issues arranged according to the attributes focused on, (2) *reorganizing* the grouping of the issues, and (3) *discovering latent relationships* between the issues.

3. TOOL FOR SUPPORTING THE METHODOLOGY

We developed an analysis-supporting tool implemented in the X-window environment, which is intended to support a methodology for integrating two stages of empirical redesign, namely, the analytical and creative processes (Figure 1).

3.1 Classifying HCI phenomena by means of a standardized procedure

The tool provides analysis-supporting functions based on the three steps of the analysis process in stage 1.

First, by using the tool, analysts can define a set of attributes for characterizing users' interaction processes, and can categorize the attributes in the form of an analytic model.

Next, they can efficiently encode empirical data by using a standardized procedure of *"segmentation and tagging"*; empirical data on users' interaction processes such as thinking-aloud protocols, users' operation logs, and observers' logs are divided into *"segments"* according to the users' local tasks (*"segmentation"*), and each *"segment"* is characterized with a *"tag,"* which is a combination of attributes selected in accordance with each analysis viewpoint of the analytic model (*"tagging"*). These empirical data are synchronized with the elapsed times of testing sessions. Analysts can interactively refer to these empirical raw data linked to each segment.

Finally, they classify all the encoded segments into groups according to their attributes. They can add a summary to each group of segments and construct a map of usability issues. Figure 2 shows a sample screen of the tool.

3.2 Formulating findings and ideas

When people try to solve a complicated problem, they often use cards to formulate ideas, by gathering, grouping, and rearranging the cards on which ideas and findings are written. In stage 2, the tool provides such an environment that helps a redesign team to formulate their ideas by using the results from stage 1.

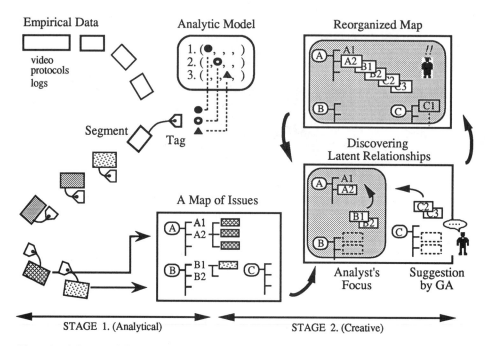

Empirical Data

video
protocols
logs

Analytic Model

1. (●, , ,)
2. (, ●, ,)
3. (, , ▲,)

Reorganized Map

Segment

Tag

A Map of Issues

Discovering
Latent Relationships

Analyst's
Focus

Suggestion
by GA

STAGE 1. (Analytical)   STAGE 2. (Creative)

Figure 1.   A framework for empirical redesign by integration of analytical and creative processes

The tool allows analysts to view the analysis results of stage 1, according to the attributes focused on, in *multiple representations* such as an "Affinity Diagram" and "Relations Diagram" of the issues, and time-sequential diagrams of the events. For example, an "Affinity Diagram" of the usability issues can be generated by arranging all the segments according to a combination of the analysis viewpoints focused on, such as "users' tasks" and "types of usability problem." This diagram can be helpful for analyzing what types of problem tend to occur in what particular tasks. Analysts can rearrange the grouping of the segments by manipulating them directly like cards, as they refer to the related empirical raw data for the issue focused on. This environment is expected to help redesign team to elaborate the issues, and to reorganize them according to various viewpoints. They can append a comment card to summarize each group of segments.

Creative ideas are often derived from intentional attempts to find relationships among the things that may initially be considered irrelevant. Trying to discover *latent relationships* between problematic HCI phenomena can be an effective way of facilitating redesign ideas, especially for global solutions. This tool provides an intelligent support function to help the redesign team to discover latent relationships. For example, when analysts use this function to try to find issues related to the ones focused on, the tool provides candidates for such related issues. This function is implemented by applying the *Genetic Algorithm* (GA) [6] (Figure 1).

The relationships among the issues in the maps, such as an affinity diagram of the usability issues, are encoded into the starting "population," that is, into a set of rules. Each rule corresponds to a particular issue in the maps and is composed of a binary sequence (e.g. "1101001...."), which is determined by an algo-

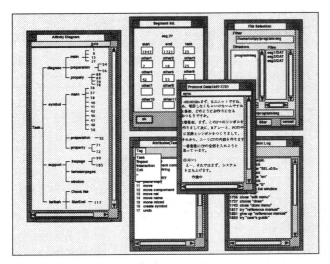

Figure 2.   Sample screen of the tool: an "Affinity Diagram" of issues (left)

rithm that can adjust the degree of matching of each rule (for an issue) with the other rules (for the other issues) in the similarity of the issues, based on the analysis results of stage 1. "Genetic operations," such as "crossover," "inversion," or "mutation," are performed to reproduce a new, revised "population" that contains new rules. The candidates for latent relationships can be formulated on the basis of the new, revised "population." The rules may be selected for the next iteration according to the analysts' estimations of how closely the candidates match their intentions. Through iteration of the above steps, the "population" can be progressively refined, so that the analysts can obtain better candidates.

3.3 An Example

We applied this framework to empirical data obtained from a practical usability testing of a CAD system for VLSI. (1) Analysts classified all the encoded segments of the empirical data according to the standard analysis procedure for stage 1, and constructed a map of 155 usability issues based on users' tasks. It was possible to generate counter-solutions for some of the issues. (2) Next, the analysts focused on three issues indicating that users of a system seemed to have some serious difficulties in performing operations for creating nets between a series of connectors, and claimed that those three issues were related. (3) On the basis of the analysts' inputs, the tool suggested candidates ·that might be related to those issues, by using the GA. The analysts evaluated the candidates, adopted some of them, and rejected the others. This step was iterated. The tool was able to provide better candidates as a result of the iterations. The analysts tried to discover the latent relationships among the related issues, including the adopted candidates. They also began to consider that in this case, rather than solving individual issue, it would be more effective to provide a global solution. (4) Finally, they were able to obtain another three issues related to the ones focused on, although they were initially classified into different groups in the map. Analysis of the latent relationships generated an idea that might solve all the related issues: redesign the task of creating nets, and provide a new overall procedure that makes it possible to create a series of nets *en bloc* and to set appropriate attributes automatically. This idea is a higher-level solution rather than a local counter-solution that solves specific problems individually. However, it did not occur to the analyst during the initial stage.

4. CONCLUDING REMARKS

In this paper, we proposed a framework for integrating two different aspects of empirical redesign, and their corresponding stages, namely, the analytical and creative processes. It is essential to emphasize both aspects of redesign in order to analyze the issues in the complicated HCI phenomena, and to create not only local counter-solutions but also global higher-level solutions on the basis of empirical data.

We also introduced an analysis-supporting tool based on the framework. This tool helps analysts to carry out consistent data analysis of a mass of empirical data by using a formalized analysis procedure in stage 1. It also provides an environment that facilitates the creative process of idea formulation in stage 2, especially, by providing an intelligent support function using the GA to help analysts discover latent relationships between problematic HCI phenomena. We are now applying this methodology to a further case study.

Obviously, various aspects of methodological enhancements are needed to make this method more effective, such as enhancement of a team work environment for accumulating and sharing not only the ideas but also the design/redesign rationale [7]. This methodology is expected to provide not only a framework for redesigning a UI, but also a generalized framework for supporting formulation of ideas by integration of analytical and creative processes. The relationship between an analytic model and intelligent support using the GA can be one of the most essential issues for this methodology.

Acknowledgements

We thank Mr. Y. Tanitsu for his continuous encouragement of our research project. We also thank Ms. K. Sakai for her contribution to the development of a prototype.

References

1 **Karat, J. and Bennett, J.L. (1991).** Working within the Design Process: Supporting Effective and Efficient Design. In J.M. Carroll (Ed.) *Designing Interaction: Psychology at the human computer interface*. Cambridge University Press.

2 **Kinoe, Y. (1989).** The VPA Method: A Method for Formal Verbal Protocol Analysis. In G. Salvendy and M.J. Smith (Eds.) *Designing and Using Human-Computer Interfaces and Knowledge Based Systems*. Elsevier, Amsterdam.

3 **Norman, D.A. (1986).** Cognitive Engineering. In D.A. Norman and S.W. Draper (Eds.) *User Centered System Design*. LEA, NJ.

4 **Kinoe, Y. and Anzai, Y. (1987).** User Interface and Cognitive Models. *J. Japanese Society for Artificial Intelligence*. Vol. 2, No. 2. In Japanese.

5 **Mack, R.L. and Nielsen, J. (1992).** Usability Inspection Methods: Summary Report of a Workshop held at CHI '92. *IBM Research Report RC-18273*, Yorktown Heights, NY.

6 **Holland, J.H. (1986).** A Mathematical Framework for Studying Learning Classifier System. *Physica*, 22D.

7 **Conklin, J. and Begeman, M. (1988).** gIBIS: A Tool for Exploratory Policy Discussion. *ACM Transactions on Office Information Systems*, 6(4).

Three Usability Enhancements to the Human Factors–Design Interface

R. G. Bias[a], D. J. Gillan[b], and T. S. Tullis[c]

[a]IBM Corporation, 11400 Burnet Road, Austin, TX, USA 78758

[b]Department of Psychology, University of Idaho, Moscow, ID, USA 83843

[c]Canon Information Systems, 3188 Pullman St., Costa Mesa, CA, USA 92626

Abstract

In a recent paper (Gillan & Bias, 1992), two of us considered the interaction between human factors (HF) professionals and other software designers. We couched our discussion in familiar human–computer interface (HCI) terms, and then addressed the design of this human–human interface. We identified the objectives of the HF–design interface, listed requirements, and evaluated early interface designs (e.g., where HF experts are involved only at the end of the development cycle). Further, we proposed three design concepts we expected to improve the HF–design interface: education, an electronic gatekeeper, and design analysis software.

1. OBJECTIVE

Aware of the value of an iterative design/test cycle in interface design, we have implemented and tested examples of three design concepts intended to improve the HF–design interface: education, an electronic gatekeeper, and design analysis software. Here we describe these implementations, summarize our evaluations of our designs, and propose improved redesigns.

2. METHODS AND RESULTS

2.1 EDUCATION

Development of an educational system involves the design of both the content of the system and the delivery method for that content. The design of both aspects of the educational system should be based on analyses of (1) the students' needs and knowledge, (2) the tasks that the students will perform using the knowledge that they gain from the educational system, and (3) the organization in which the student will perform the tasks. Thus, in designing an educational system to improve the HF–design interface, we must identify these three features of the analysis: students, task, organization. For this paper, we will focus on software developers conducting HCI design. Educating HF professionals about software development concerns and related issues in implementing interfaces is also important, but will be discussed elsewhere.

Gillan, Breedin, and Cooke (1992), in a study of the representation of software developers' knowledge about the HCI, found that developers' knowledge is organized around two major concepts, usability and the implementation of the interface. Yet, in order to have successful interfaces with HF specialists, developers need to be knowledgeable about varied HF content. Gillan and Bias (1992) identified four content areas: 1) proven approaches to HF design, including usability engineering (e.g., Whiteside, Bennett, &

Holtzblatt, 1988), 2) HF design methods and methodological tools, such as task analysis (see Diaper, 1989), 3) user modeling techniques, such as GOMS models (Card, Moran, & Newell, 1983) and semantic network models (Schvaneveldt, 1990), and 4) the scientific basis of the HF discipline, including both theories and data in sensation, perception, cognition, motor performance, as well as human interaction with computers.

We have been involved in four different methods for delivering education to software developers. These methods differ on several dimensions—the technologies involved, the duration and coverage of instruction, the spatial and temporal distances between the need for information and the instruction, control over instruction, and the convenience to the student. The dimensions on which these methods differ affect the usability of the various methods for communicating HF information to the software development community.

One method is a formal class in a university setting. This method relies primarily on an instructor, with students coming to the instructor. The major advantages are a high level of coverage and control of instruction. Software developers who participate in HF courses (such as a HF design course taught by co–author Gillan at the University of Idaho) can acquire substantial knowledge and skill. However, developers are not likely to be in close proximity to a university with a HF program. In addition, classroom students may acquire the information long before they have an opportunity to use it and, when the time comes to apply it, may lack retrieval cues to access it.

A second method, with which one of us (Gillan) has been involved, is a video–based course (Dingus, Gordon, & Gill, 1990; Dingus & Gillan, 1991). This delivery method has increased convenience and decreased spatial distance compared to the university–based course because students receive the videos at work or home. Although software developers who have taken the video courses in HF design have rated them to be valuable, the major drawback for wide coverage in the design community is the course duration of 45 hours. Developers will take such a course only if they can see a clear career benefit.

A third delivery method is an on site short course in HF, either taught by HF specialists from within the design organization or by outside consultants. One of us (Bias) has instituted a "Usability University" within his software development organization. This is an ongoing series of one– to two–hour informal "classes" on various topics related to usability. All software developers are invited to attend, and all seven sessions held at the time of this writing have had just about a roomful (about 25) of attendees. The classes are interleaved with product demonstrations, the notion being that the more the development community knows about the existing products, the better we will understand the user models held by our customers, and thus the better usability–engineered our own products will be. Key features of the Usability University offerings are informality (requiring no RSVP, fostering "drop in" participation), very close spatial and temporal distance to the user (developer), direct relevance to the software developers' daily tasks, and a responsiveness to the needs of the development community.

We believe that a fourth delivery method—computer–based minitutorials—has promise due to its convenience, close spatial and temporal distance to the user, and possibility of wide coverage through the use of different instructional modules for different topics. As part of Gillan's HF design class, graduate students have designed minitutorials on two topics—task analysis and the use of semantic network modeling procedures for menu design. The task analysis tutor, (developed by U. of Idaho graduate student, Rich Hanowski), is Hypercard[1]–based and runs on a Macintosh[1]. The content of the tutor was based, in part, on a task analysis of people doing a task analysis. The on–line tutor is modular, with modules on global information about task analysis, detailed procedural information, and an example of a task analysis. In addition, there's a Help system on interacting with the tutor. Testing of the tutor yielded high usability scores (a mean rating of 6.0 on a 7–point scale) and improved knowledge of task analysis.

In subsequent use of the task analysis tutor to help teach two graduate student researchers about HF, the students reported the most beneficial features to be its ability to permit students to follow their own path in learning, its convenience and ease of use, and the use of sound effects to maintain students' interest and motivation during learning. Due to the promising user tests with the task analysis tutor, we are currently developing a new minitutorial to teach software developers about semantic networks and the use of the Pathfinder network tool (Schvaneveldt, 1990) for the design of menu–based interfaces.

We believe that Hanowski's task analysis tutor is a prototype of the kind of educational tool that should be developed by many HF specialists to cover a variety of topics. We envision a widely–available "HCI University" consisting of tutorials from every area of HF, so that HF knowledge is available to everyone who needs it, especially software developers when and where they make design decisions.

2.2 ELECTRONIC GATEKEEPER

Allen (1977) proposes that one way in which science communicates with design is through a technological gatekeeper—a person in the design organization who reads the relevant scientific literature, interprets the results for their design implications, and communicates those results and interpretations to the design community. In the Gillan and Bias paper (1992) we proposed that the gatekeeper need not be a person, but could be an electronic entity, using current computer bulletin board technology.

At IBM–Austin we have implemented just such an electronic gatekeeper, an on-line forum designed to facilitate dialogue between the HF professionals and the other software developers. Designers were encouraged to ask usability questions on the forum, and note designs under consideration. The HF professionals were asked to monitor the forum and respond to the specific questions, announce usability tests and post results, and announce competitive product demos and other relevant events.

We have four months' data on use of forum, including such measures as numbers of entries of various types and average latency between question and answer. Thus far the usability forum has accumulated only 28 appends, averaging less than two per week. Of the 28 appends, 21 have been by HF professionals; the HF–developer give–and–take that we had hoped for did not occur.

With the forum we established a usability conference disk, to serve as a repository for documents like the usability process, UI guidelines, and icon approval forms. It has proven useful as a place where HF professionals can steer developers interested in such matters.

In discussions with the developers, we learned that more and better communication was needed among the various application development groups. Even though the usability forum was available, it was not serving this purpose. We inferred that the problem was the placement of the forum, placed, as it was, in an electronic location where developers did not already spend time. (Developers were required to take action to access this new conference disk.) Thus, in an iteration of the design, a second forum was begun, on a conference disk where the developers conduct other daily work. We are hopeful that this new usability forum, given its placement, will better serve the stated purposes.

2.3 DESIGN ASSISTANCE SOFTWARE

A third approach to enhancing the HF–design interface is for HF professionals to provide developers with tools that make it easier to apply HF principles to the systems they are building. We call this general class of tools "design assistance software." Two types of design assistance software currently exist: computerized guidelines and design critiquing software.

Several computerized guidelines have been developed (e.g., Perlman, 1989; Fox, 1992; Ogawa & Yonemura, 1992). These commonly take the form of customizable "checklists" of design guidelines that the developers can browse and/or search for guidelines addressing the issues they are facing. One shortcoming of most such tools is that they are not integrated with actual development tools. The developers still have to use something that is "outside" of what they normally use for actually building applications.

A small step toward integrating guidelines with a development tool has been taken by Bailey and Bailey (1991) in their ProtoScreens tool, which affords interactive construction of character–based screens for PC applications. For example, in the arena of color choice, in ProtoScreens the dialog box for selecting a foreground color shows the user which colors have proven to be the most effective in combination with the current background color. The user can still choose any of the other (empirically less effective) colors as well—probably a wise choice, since most developers, it is our experience, don't like having design decisions dictated to them.

Software that critiques prose has been popular as an aid to writers for several years (e.g., grammar checking programs). One of us (Tullis, 1984) applied that same basic concept to the design of alphanumeric screens. This program, called the Screen Analyzer (Tullis, 1989), is an attempt to embody guidelines and empirical usability data into a system for evaluating any alphanumeric screen. The input to the program is a literal example of the screen to be analyzed; thus, the developer must have already designed at least a first draft of a screen layout. The program then measures six different aspects of the screen: overall density of characters, local density of characters "near" other characters, number of visual groups of characters, average visual angle subtended by those groups, number of labels and data items, and layout complexity (i.e., how well aligned the various screen elements are with each other). Based on empirical data collected on over 500 alphanumeric screens, the program then makes suggestions for improving the layout of the screen being analyzed (e.g., pointing out unusually large groups of characters and suggesting that they might be broken down). Finally, the program uses regression equations to predict a subjective rating of ease of use that a user might give to the screen, and an average search time that a user would take to find a single data item on the screen.

The accuracy of the predictions from the Screen Analyzer has been demonstrated in several studies. For example, in an experiment to validate the prediction system, Tullis (1984) found that the predicted search times ($r = .80$) and subjective ratings ($r = .80$) for a new set of 150 screens were both quite accurate. But the question that remains is how useful this system actually is to developers. The main evidence that we have is anecdotal. First, it has been purchased by at least 25 different corporations or government agencies in the US and Canada for possible use in their development process. A common use seems to be in a situation where users already have an existing version of some system and are considering redesigning it. In this situation, the Screen Analyzer seems to be used as one means of pointing out some of the areas that need to be changed in the redesign. A second common use of the Screen Analyzer is as a teaching tool. In fact, two of us commonly use it in teaching screen design to graduate students and working professionals, including programmers. Other consultants who offer tutorials on UI design have also reported using it as a teaching aid. A common technique is to assign students a screen design exercise and then let them use the Screen Analyzer to improve their design iteratively. Developers seem much more responsive to the principles they learn this way than to the same principles presented in the usual lecture/examples format.

We believe that some of the concepts represented by computerized guidelines and by the Screen Analyzer could be integrated into a "User Interface Designer's Workbench" that would make this type of design assistance software more useful to, and usable by, software developers. Some features of this User Interface Designer's Workbench would be:

1. It is integrated with the actual development tools and environments that developers normally use. Obviously this implies that it must run on the platform that the developer is using. One possible approach could be a visual design tool that integrates these HF principles and generates source code (e.g., C/C++).

2. It embodies general guidelines about good UI design. To be optimally useful, the guidelines most relevant to the design task at hand need to be available immediately (e.g., having depth vs. breadth guidelines easily accessible when designing a pull–down menu system). These guidelines could be available in both "system passive" and "system active" modes. In the system passive mode, the user would have to seek the information out. In the system active mode, the system could warn the user when specific guidelines are being violated.

3. It embodies UI guidelines and standards specific to the platform for which the application is being designed (e.g., Windows, Macintosh). These guidelines tend to be quite specific (e.g., what functions go under a "File" menu) and actually much easier to embody in such a system than the more general guidelines. It should be easy for the user to request "A skeleton pull–down menu system that adheres to the platform standards," or "Dialog box buttons of conventional size."

4. It provides critiquing features that go beyond the strictly visual aspects captured by the Screen Analyzer and encompass more of the functional aspects of the UI (e.g., evaluating the complexity of the sequences of operations that the user would have to go through to accomplish various tasks).

Such a system could significantly enhance the application of HF principles to the software design and development process. An interesting question this type of tool raises is whether it enhances the effectiveness of HF professionals or whether it puts us out of a job. We think that, at least for the foreseeable future, this type of tool will be able to address only relatively "mechanical" aspects of UI design and evaluation. We hope and believe that puts the HF professional in a better position to focus on the more creative aspects.

3. SUMMARY

There has been considerable recent attention paid to the importance of the social interface in developing human–computer interfaces (e.g., Norman, 1992; Grudin, 1991). We have offered three specific, implemented features intended to improve that social interface, and have summarized empirical usability testing of those designs.

We have argued for information delivery systems that effect the knowledge transfer at times and in places convenient and useful to the user (developer). We are using and fine–tuning on–line tutors and on site short courses to supplement the more traditional university courses. We are fine–tuning also the use of an electronic gatekeeper, to facilitate the interaction between the HF practitioner and other software developers. And we are gathering data on the use of an actual design assistance software application, wherein HF principles are built into the software development tools, to bring the knowledge directly to the software development task.

Early results show that all three components of our improved HF–design interface have been valuable yet warrant redesign. The next iteration of the design was proposed in all three cases.

4. NOTE

[1]Macintosh and Hypercard are trademarks of Apple Computer, Inc.

5. REFERENCES

Allen, T. J. (1977). Managing the flow of technology: Technology transfer and dissemination of technological information with the R&D organization. Cambridge, MA: MIT Press.

Bailey and Bailey Software Corporation (1991). Protoscreens, Ogden, UT.

Card, S.K., Moran, T.P., & Newell, A. (1983). The psychology of human–computer interaction. Hillsdale, NJ: Erlbaum.

Diaper, D. (1989). Task analysis for human–computer interaction. Chichester, England: Ellis Horwood Limited.

Dingus, T.A., & Gillan, D.J. (1991). The thesis simulation: An approach for teaching research skills in a remote non–thesis program. In Proceedings of the Human Factors Society 35th Annual Meeting (pp. 505 – 507). Santa Monica, CA: Human Factors Society.

Dingus, T.A., Gordon, S.E., & Gill, R.T. (1990). A new program for the remote training of human factors professionals. In Proceedings of the Human Factors Society 34th Annual Meeting (pp. 534 – 536). Santa Monica, CA: Human Factors Society.

Fox, J. A. (1992). The effects of using a hypertext tool for selecting design guidelines. Proceedings of Human Factors Society Annual Meeting, Atlanta, GA, pp. 428–432.

Gillan, D. J., and Bias, R. G. (1992). The interface between human factors and design. Proceedings of the Human Factors Society Annual Meeting, Atlanta, GA, pp. 443–447.

Gillan, D.J., Breedin, S.D., & Cooke, N.J. (1992). Network and multidimensional representations of the declarative knowledge of human–computer interface design experts. International Journal of Man–Machine Studies, 36, 587 – 615.

Grudin, J. (1991). Systematic sources of suboptimal interface design in large product development organizations. Human–Computer Interaction, 6, pp. 147–196.

Norman, D. A. (1992). Where human factors fails: Ergonomics versus the world of design and manufacture. Human Factors Society Annual Meeting, Atlanta, GA, October.

Ogawa, K., and Yonemura, S. (1992). Usability analysis of design guideline database in human–computer interface design. Proceedings of Human Factors Society Annual Meeting, Atlanta, GA, pp. 433–437.

Perlman, G. (1989). System design and evaluation with hypertext checklists. IEEE Conference on Systems, Man, and Cybernetics, Cambridge, MA.

Schvaneveldt, R.W. (1990). Pathfinder associative networks: Studies in knowledge organization. Norwood, NJ: Ablex.

Tullis, T. S. (1984). Predicting the Usability of Alphanumeric Displays, Ph.D. dissertation, Rice University.

Tullis, T. S. (1989). The Screen Analyzer (computer program), Version 1.0. Distributed by Ergosyst Associates, Lawrence, KS.

Whiteside, J., Bennett, J., & Holtzblatt, K. (1988). Usability engineering: Our experience and evolution. In M. Helander (Ed.), Handbook of human–computer interaction (pp. 791 – 817). Amsterdam: North–Holland.

EFFECTS OF HYPERTEXT TOPOLOGY ON NAVIGATION PERFORMANCE

Sanjay Batra, R.R. Bishu, and Brian Donohue

Department of Industrial and Management Systems Engineering
University of Nebraska, Lincoln, NE

ABSTRACT

This is an empirical investigation of the effects of two hypertext topologies, a hierarchy and a hypertorus structure, on navigation performance under two different network entry conditions, enter at the top of the network and enter randomly at any node. It was hypothesized that hierarchy topology is better only if a user enters the network from the top and the hypertorus topology is better for random entry situations. Thirty two subjects were randomly assigned to one of the four conditions (hierarchy structure with top entry, hierarchy structure with random entry, hypertorus structure with top entry, or hypertorus structure with random entry). The subjects' task is to browse a hypertext network and retrieve facts about ten 1991 automobiles. Performance was determined by elapsed time, number of screens examined, and accuracy. Results showed a strong learning effect over the first ten trials but equivalent performance once subjects on either of the structures for all navigational performance measures except accuracy. The hypertorus topology fosters browsing more than the hierarchy topology. However, the more constrained hierarchy topology fosters more efficient navigation behavior.

INTRODUCTION

The popularity of hypertext systems is growing, particularly in domains that require rapid access of large amounts of loosely structured information (Nielson, 1990). On-line documentation for software applications and "courseware" that is designed to augment classroom learning are particularly well suited application domains for hypertext. The strength of hypertext systems are based on their ability to link bits of information together. Hypertext systems are thought to mimic the way the brain stores and retrieves information (Gygi, 1991).

Unfortunately, there are costs associated with systems that are extremely flexible. Users that browse complex hypertext systems tend to get disoriented and lose their current location (Nielson, 1990; Gygi, 1991; Van Dyke Parunak, 1989). Users have difficulties understanding where they are, how they got to their present location, where they want to be, and how to get there. This situation often occurs when a user activates a link accidentally and gets transported to an unfamiliar part of the network or to another network entirely. This study focuses on how the design of the hypertext system topology affects navigation performance.

BACKGROUND

Methods for improving navigation were examined by a number of investigators. Investigations suggest that hypertext navigation is aided by using overview maps (Monk, et.

176

al, 1988; Hammond, 1989; Nielson, 1990), backtracking features and interaction histories(Nielson, 1990), marking node utilities (Nielson, 1990; Gygi, 1991), and animated screen transitions (Nielson, 1990; Gygi, 1991).

Taking a different approach Van Dyke Parunak (1989) suggests that user's navigation strategies are influenced by the topology of the hypertext system they are browsing. There are several common navigational strategies: (1). Identifier, (2). Path, (3). Direction, (4). Distance, and (5). Address. The *Identifier Strategy* involves using unique descriptions to search for each entity of interest in order to find the target. This is like finding a house with the description that it has redwood siding, a large oak tree, and pink flamingos in the front lawn. The *Path Strategy* uses procedural descriptions of how to get to the target. Instructions such as "Turn right at the second light and then turn left at the next shopping center" are procedural descriptions that constitute path strategy. Note that users may need to employ some identification strategy when using path strategy. "Go due east on O Street" is an example of using *Direction Strategy*. Like path strategy, this method does not involve an exhaustive search as identifier strategy. It differs from path strategy in that it uses a different frame of reference to provide guidance. In path strategy, the frame of reference is individual nodes and is expressed in terms of links to other nodes whereas in direction strategy the frame of reference is global relating to the entire hypertext network. *Distance Strategy* limits the search area to a region around the present location of the user. This method can be expressed either spatially or in time. "Go about 1/2 mile and you will see the house" or "Go about 3 minutes and you will see the gas station" are examples of direction strategy. *Address strategy* employs orthogonal coordinates to establish location. "Go to the corner of 14th and O street" is an example of this strategy (Van Dyke Parunak, 1989).

In addition to these navigation strategies, Van Dyke Parumak (1989) suggests different network structures or topologies for hypertext. The most simple topology is a *linear* structure which each node has at the most one child and one parent. A *ring* topology is a linear one with the two end nodes connected. In a *hierarchy* topology one node has no parents and others have exactly one parent. The *Hypercube/Hypertorus* arrangement consists of nodes are arranged in a rectangular pattern. A node is connected to the nodes above, below, to the left, and to the right. The *Directed Acyclic Graph (DAG)* topology usually has one entry point and each node can have multiple parents and offspring (Van Dyke Parunak, 1989).

There is evidence in menu structure research to suggest that hierarchical structures are efficient if they are not more than a few levels deep (Mehlenbacher, et. al.,1989). In a hypertext system a hierarchy topology allows users to use identifier, unique path, directed text, and unique distance strategies (Van Dyke Parunak, 1989). The hypertorus topology is a very good hypertext systems for comparing different items. This topology enables users to use identifier, multiple path, unique distances, and address navigation strategies (Van Dyke Parunak, 1989).

A number of questions remain unsolved: (1). Does topology significantly impact hypertext navigation and usability? (2). How does topology affect learning? (3). Are certain topologies better when users find themselves accidentally deposited on a undesired part of the network? (4). What are the design implications of hypertext topology? The goal of this research is to address the issues put forth by these questions.

HYPOTHESIS

Topology affects navigational performance, specifically hierarchical structure is better when users enter the structure from the top of the network. However, when users are accidently deposited at deeper levels of the network this topology may contribute to user disorientation. Therefore, a hypertorus topology should be better for this situation because it is based on a spatial metaphor and it allows for more flexible movement. Furthermore, hypertorus topology will facilitate more exploration, especially when the system is being learned.

METHODS

Task Paradigm

The task for this study was a question and answer task where subjects were asked to answer specific questions about ten 1991 automobiles on the *AutoInformer*. The AutoInformer is the interactive hypertext system developed by the authors to give consumer information about new automobiles. It was implemented in SuperCard on a MACINTOSH IIci computer. It consists of 40 screens about 10 models of 1991 cars. Each car has 4 screens of information, one screen of general information about the automobile, a screen describing standard and optional features of each automobile, a screen with insurance data, and a consumer information screen which provides ratings of each car's quality as judged by Consumer Reports. Versions of the AutoInformer were created with a hypertorus and a modified hierarchy topology shown in figure 1. The modified hierarchy has a ring at the top level of the network. An example screen of the hypertext system is shown in figure 2.

Users were given a question on the question screen and then they were deposited at either the top of the structure or deposited anywhere in the structure. Depositing users randomly in the network was a treatment condition designed to simulate disorientation in a hypertext system. Then users were required to find the screen with the answer as quickly and efficiently as possible. After they got the screen they selected the "correct" button and then they were to go back to one of the general screens in order to exit the AutoInformer. At that point they were put back on the question screen and required to key in their response. Users were provided with a mechanism to review the question while they are in the AutoInformer to reduce the load on memory.

Experimental Design

The study compares the effects of hypertext topology and entry level on navigational performance in an information retrieval paradigm. The experiment is a 2 x 2 between subjects factorial design. The independent variables were hypertext topology either modified hierarchy or hypertorus and two treatment conditions of system entry at "random" screens or system entry at the "top" level of the network. Each subject answered 30 questions which are divided into blocks of 10 in order to have a blocking factor for learning effect.

Dependent variables used in the study were: (1). total time per trial, (2). time to find the answer, (3). time to leave the hypertext system, (4). no. of screens examined per trial, (5). no. of screens examined to the answer, (6). no. of screens examined to leave the hypertext system, (7). error rate, and (8). time spent on the answer screen.

Subjects

Thirty two subjects were recruited from the student population from the University of Nebraska. They were not considered experienced hypertext users and were familiar with driving and automobiles. Subject were motivated by the car information contained in the study which pertained to the purchase of 1991 car.

Procedure

Each subject was asked to fill out a questionnaire on their computer experience. To achieve equal levels of system interaction, each subject was asked to review a computerized tutorial. The subjects were then asked if they had any questions after they had finished. The subjects were then asked to perform one of the four treatment conditions for thirty trials. Everyone was allowed to work at their own rate to assure that they would not make forced

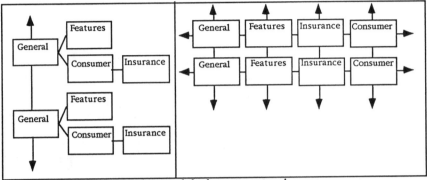

Figure 1. The hierarchy topology and the hypertorus topology.

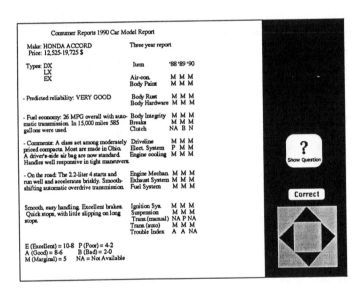

Figure 2. An example AutoInfofmer screen.

errors. An average session lasted 1.5 hours. Subjects were asked to fill out a questionnaire about their views and interpretations of the software performance at the end of the session.

RESULTS

The AutoInformer recorded all performance measures and the data was analyzed using the ANOVA procedure on SAS statistical package. Table 1 presents a summary of significant main effects for all dependent measures.

Table 1. Significant main effects

Measure	Treatment	Pr>F
Total screens browsed per trial	Entry treatment	0.0556
	Topology	0.0024
	Learning	0.0001
Screens browsed to answer per trial	Entry treatment	0.098
	Learning	0.0001
Screens browsed leaving the system per trial	Topology	0.0001
	Learning	0.0019
Total time per trial	Learning	0.0001
Time to browse for answer per trial	Learning	0.0001
Time to leave the system per trial	Topology	0.0093
	Learning	0.0001

Learning was a significant main effect for the three time measures and the three browsing frequency measures. A standardized Newman-Keuls means test indicated that performance for the 1st block of 10 trials was significantly slower and more screens were browsed. Topology conditions were a significant main effect for the total number of screens browsed and the number of screens browsed leaving the system. Figure 3 shows a histogram of the means for both these measures. A standardized Newman-Keuls means test indicated that the hypertorus topology has significantly more total screens browsed and screens browsed when leaving the system. Topology was also significant for the time it took to leave the system to answer the question with the subjects using hypertorus topology were significantly slower in leaving the system. Entry treatment was a significant main effect for total screens browsed. When randomly deposited into the system, users browsed an average of 1.251 more screens than when they enter the system from the top of the system.

DISCUSSION

Our results suggest that topology impacts navigation behavior in hypertext. Users tend to browse more screens when the structure is a hypertorus. This is due to the fact that this topology is more flexible and less structured than the hierarchy topology. However, the time it takes to get out of a hypertorus topology takes longer than the hierarchy topology. This implies that more structured topology may be more efficient when a user is done using it and wants to exit. Learning was the most consistent effect in this investigation. Users were able to adapt and learn both topologies very easily. Subjective ratings indicated that the users found all versions of the hypertext system easy to learn. Our results indicate that it did not matter whether subjects were deposited at the top of each hypertext network or deposited randomly at any screen on the network. This may be due to the fact that the networks are not large enough for the users to experience disorientation. It would be interesting to perform another study with a larger hypertext system to see if entry point is an important factor. In addition, the

180

questions given in this study required subjects to find an answer on a unique screen in the system. It would be interesting to give subjects questions that forced them to make comparisons across automobiles. This should be examined in the future.

Screens browsed by topology

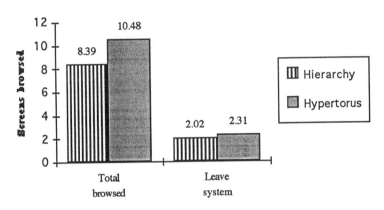

Figure 3. Screens browsed by topology

REFERENCES

Gygi, Kathleen, 1991. "Recognizing the Symptoms of Hypertext .... and What to Do About If". In *The Art of Human-Computer Interface Design*, Edt. by Brenda Laurel   Addison-Wesley Pub., Reading Ms, pp. 279-287.

Hammond, N. and Allinson, L., "Extending hypertext for learning" An investigation of access and guidance tools". Proc. BCS HCI'89 (Nottingham, UK). As reported by Nielson, Jakob, 1989. "The Matters that Really Matter for Hypertext Usability". Hypertext 89' Proceedings, November 1989, pp. 239-248.

Monk, A. F., Walsh, P., and Dix, A. J., 1988. "A comparison of hypertext, scrolling, and folding as mechanisms for program browsing". In Jones, D. M., and Winder, R. (Eds.) : People and Computers IV, Cambridge University Press, pp. 526-529. As reported by Nielson, Jakob, 1989. "The Matters that Really Matter for Hypertext Usability". Hypertext 89' Proceedings, November 1989, pp. 239-248.

Nielson, Jakob, 1989. "The Matters that Really Matter for Hypertext Usability". Hypertext 89' Proceedings, November 1989, pp. 239-248.

Nielson, Jakob, 1990. "The Art of Navigating through Hypertext. In *Communications of the ACM*, March 1990, pp. 296-310.

Mehlenbacher, B., Duffy T. M., and Palmer, J., 1990. Finding information on a menu:Linking menu organization to the user's goals. Human -Computer Interaction, 4, 231-251.

Parunak, H Van Dyke, 1989. "Hypermedia Topologies an User Navigation". Hypertext 89' Proceedings, November 1989, pp. 43-50.

The Relative Effectiveness of Hypertext And Text

Mark R. Lehto, Wenli Zhu, and Bryan Carpenter

School of Industrial Engineering
Purdue University

Abstract

User performance when using a hypertext electronic reference system was compared to that for a conventional reference book. The links in this hypertext were the same as the index entries in the corresponding book. Specific topics and particular facts were located much faster and more accurately using the hypertext system than the book, and especially so when searching for information indirectly referred to in the index. The conclusion was that hypertext appears to be superior for "reading to do" or reference type use. A second experiment compared user performance when links corresponded exactly to the original index of the book to performance when the links were generated by computer keyword searches. Strong advantages were found in speed, accuracy, and subjective ratings for links based on the author's original index.

1. INTRODUCTION

Hypertext is a potentially useful method for providing information to designers and other professionals. However, there have been few empirical comparisons of hypertext to conventional books for the types of tasks designers might perform. Previous empirical comparisons of hypertext and paper include studies on Hyperties [1,2] and SuperBook [3]. Studies of Hyperties showed that paper versions had a speed advantage for simple fact retrieval tasks which disappeared for more complex tasks. The SuperBook studies showed an overall speed and accuracy advantage over paper on structured search tasks and especially so for questions containing only text-words. For open-book essays, SuperBook users scored higher and included more facts than did users of conventional text.

The above results suggest that for information retrieval tasks where the information is organized according to a predetermined reference scheme like a table of contents or index, traditional printed text might have an advantage over hypertext system. For less structured sources of information, on the other hand, the computer-supported linking of hypertext may enable users to navigate the information space more efficiently and might even reduce the need for time consuming manual development of indexes. Although computer generated links seem to offer creators of hypertext systems a fast, easy, and thorough method for linking, little or no research compares computer generated links to author generated links from the user's standpoint.

2.THE COMPARED SYSTEMS

Two sources of information were used in this study: *Instructions & Warnings* [4] an annotated bibliography of 577 references on warning related issues, and*Work Design: Industrial Ergonomics* [5]. Both books were read into a hypertext written in Hypercard, running on the Apple Macintosh computer. The contents of the hypertext were exactly the same as those within the books. However, several features were added, including unrestricted key word searches.

Each screen in the hypertext contained four fields: topic, text, keyword, and title (each annotation has a unique serial number which is in the title field). The topic field showed the user which topic was currently being browsed. A topic corresponds to the currently active link connecting information elements. Other buttons and menus enabled users to navigate in the system and fulfill their informational needs. The hypertext system included the following major functions: *browse, index, find, map, make report*, and various *topics* manipulation functions. *Browse* allowed information within a topic to be viewed sequentially in a way analogous to reading a book page by page. *Index* enabled users to consult an index. *Find* allowed users to globally search for any words, phrases, authors or key words appearing anywhere in the text. *Map* presented a global map of the system and highlighted the currently active function of the system. *Make report* allowed users to copy pertinent information into a report. *Topics* manipulations included showing a list of previous topics in the current session so that users could easily return to any topic they had viewed before; merging two topics with specified logical connectives (AND, OR); or renaming a topic.

The first experiment discussed below compares users of the book *Instructions & Warnings* and the hypertext. Users were chosen to have a strong technical background. The second experiment compares the effectiveness of browsing links generated by exhaustive keyword searches to browsing links based on the original index of the book Work *Design: Industrial Ergonomics.*

3.EXPERIMENT 1

Subjects using a book and a hypertext were compared on two types of tasks. Reading to learn tasks required that users browse some general topics of interest and become knowledgeable on the topics. Reading to do tasks required that users try to find information on a very specific topic or a particular fact. Two levels of reading to learn tasks were considered. The topic of a *simple* learning task had a single index entry. The topic of a*complex* learning task required consulting and combining multiple index entries. Reading to learn tasks consisted of 4 questions on general topics (see table 1), evenly divided between *simple* and *complex* questions. Both required the subjects to find relevant sections of text, and then provide summary findings, conclusions, and suggestions. Asking for summary information was assumed to force the subjects to enter a learning mode.

Reading to do tasks varied in the degree of match between the indexes and the topic. An *exact match* should be easier than a *synonym match* and a *synonym match* easier than a *no match*. The size of the target information set (how many items fell within a topic), was also considered. A *small* set should be scanned faster and be more "tolerable" than a *large* set. It was expected that performance with a book might equal that for a hypertext system when searching for *exact matches* within a *small* set of items. The hypertext system, was expected to show a

Table 1. Examples of Questions

Complexity	Questions
simple	What are the *effects of case of text on legibility*?
complex	Which articles propose rules or guidelines regarding the *design of labeling and safety signage systems* that are based on *human factors*?
exact match & small	Which articles discuss the effects of visual noise on the conspicuity of names on *maps*? (1)
exact match & large	Give one study describing the percentage of subjects who would *read instructions* of electrical products. (16)
synonym & small	Which study compares the use of text, graphics, and voice in automated teller machines? (auditory vs. visual 2)
synonym & large	Which study evaluated the visibility of the road sign conveying the message "slippery when wet"? (traffic sign evaluation 14)
no match	Which study addresses the relation between the use of ear plugs and the provision of information?

Words in italic or in parentheses are index entries. The number of items in a topic are in parantheses

strong advantage both in terms of speed and accuracy over the book on tasks involving synonym *match, no match* and a *large* set of items. Each subject was asked 10 questions (see table 1 for examples). The goal was not to summarize the information, but simply to find the answer. Of the 10 questions, 4 were *exact match* questions, 4 were *synonym match* questions and the other 2 were *no match* questions. Since it was impossible to categorize *no match* questions as a small or large set size, 4 questions were *small* and the other 4 were *large*.

3.1 Method

Fifteen Purdue graduate students participated in the experiment, most majoring in Industrial Engineering, and all with experience using Macintosh computers. Four did not claim expertise in safety engineering. The others considered themselves having at least some safety engineering knowledge either from industrial experiences or safety engineering classes.

The experiment consisted of one training session and two test sessions. All subjects first completed the training session, lasting about 1 hour, in which they learned the organization, structure and functions of the hypertext system and answered three multiple-choice questions and four exercise questions similar to the test questions. They were then given the four learning task questions. Each question was randomly assigned to one of the two systems, either the book or the hypertext system and the order of the four questions was also randomized. Subjects worked on each question until they told the experimenter they finished. They were then given the 10 reading to do questions. After completing the test sessions, subjects provided subjective ratings and comments.

3.2 Results and Discussion

For the reading to learn tasks, measurements were taken of (1) the time subjects took to form a topic (when using hypertext) or a list of references (when using the book); (2) the time to complete each question; and (3) the proportion of correct references included in the answer. Table 2 summarizes the major results. The only significant result was that book users provided more correct references than hypertext users (69 vs. 54, $F(1,14)=3.46$, $p<.10$). For the reading to do task, measurements were taken of (1) the time to complete each question; and (2) the proportion of correct responses. Both dependent variables were analyzed following a two step process. The first step was to perform analysis of variance (ANOVA), means analysis and contrast analysis, using the model in which only two levels of match types (*exact match* and *synonym match*) are considered. Then multiple T-tests were made comparing average system type effects for each match type and set size combination. Numerous differences were found in performance levels between the book and the hypertext.

Analysis of the time needed to complete each question revealed that as expected, hypertext users found and retrieved specific facts considerably faster than book users (Table 3). The average search completion time using the hypertext system was only about 2 minutes while it was about 8.6 minutes for the book ($t(145)=9.97$, $p<.01$). The effects of system type ($F(1,14)=141.5$, $p<.01$), match type($F(1,14)=4.65$, $p<.05$), and set size($F(1,14)=5.97$, $p<.05$) were significant; as were the two-way interaction of system type and set size ($F(1,14)=22.27$, $p<.01$) and the three-way interaction of system type, match type, and set size ($F(1,14)=6.67$, $p<.05$). T-tests of means indicated the hypertext system's advantage in searching speed was significant for all types of tasks ($p<.01$ for each) except *exact match* & *small set*. In this latter situation, the question contained text exactly the same as an index entry. Analysis of the proportion of correct responses showed that as expected, the hypertext users answered questions more accurately than book users (95% Vs 67%, $t(146)=-4.54$, $p<.01$). Moreover hypertext users gave less erroneous answers (5% vs. 9%) and gave up without finding an answer less often (0% vs. 22%). The effects of system type ($F(1,14)=6.09$, $p<.05$) and match type ($F(1,14)=4.42$, $.05<p<.10$) were significant. T-tests of means showed that difference between system type was significant for the following match type and set size combination: *exact match* & *large* ($t(28)=-1.87$, $.05<p<.10$); *synonym* & *large* ($t(28)=-2.25$, $p<.05$); *no match* ($t(26)=-6.81$, $p<.01$).

A final result was that subjects favored the hypertext system on both the learning and reading to do tasks. Example comments include "the hypertext system was easier to use on all accounts"; "the find command on the hypertext system makes it much easier to locate specific information"; "book is limited by index"; "the hypertext system does the tedious work for you.".

Table 2.   Results For Learning Tasks

Type of System	Mean Time to Form a Topic or a List (minutes)	Mean Completion Time (minutes)			Mean Proportion of Correct References
		Simple	Complex	All	
Hypertext	4.3	12.0	14.4	13.2	**54**
Book	3.1	12.3	17.8	15.1	**69**

Boldface pairs in the same column differ significantly across system types.

Table 3.   Results For 'Reading to Do' Task

Type of System	Exact Match & Small	Exact Match & Large	Synonym & Small	Synonym & Large	No Match	Means for all
Hypertext	2.1 (.80)	**1.5 (.93)**	3.5 (1.00)	**1.4 (1.00)**	**1.4 (1.00)**	2.0 (.95)
Book	2.6 (.80)	**11.8 (.67)**	9.1 (.87)	**8.7 (.73)**	**11.2 (.23)**	8.6 (.67)

Columns contain mean search completion times and the proportion of correct Responses (within quotes.). Boldface pairs in the same column differ significantly (p<.10) across system types.

4. EXPERIMENT 2

The results of experiment 1 indicated that much of the advantage of the hypertext over the text appeared to be related to the feasibility of following more flexible search strategies, such as searching for keywords. The purpose of Experiment 2 was to further investigate the strength of keyword based search strategies. This was done by comparing performance on two hypertext stacks. The first stack provided a manually generated index (MGI) linking the authors index to relevant sections of the text. The second stack provided a computer generated index (CGI), which linked every word in the text to the paragraph in which it appeared. Each stack contained the same text, table of contents, and FIND option.

4.1 Method
A between subject experimental design was used to compare the two systems. Eighteen subjects were randomly assigned to either the manually or computer generated stack. Subjects were undergraduate students in industrial engineering, all of whom had taken a course using the text contained within the hypertext.

Each subject was instructed to read an instruction manual which described how to use the hypertext system. After reading the manual, the subject was told to use it as a guide for completing five practice questions. The subject was allowed to ask the experimenter questions on how to use the system. After completing the practice session, subjects used their respective hypertext system to answer 10 Reference Questions comparable to the simple learning questions used in Experiment 1 (see Table 1) . No time limit was placed on the search for answers, but the subject was instructed to go onto the next question if he/she did not feel that the answer could be found. The subjects were told that all answers could be found using their system. Upon completion of the reference questions, each subject was given fifteen minutes to learn as much information as they could on the topic of "Quality Circles". The system was then turned off, and the subject was given a five question quiz on the topic. Finally, the subject was asked to evaluate the hypertext system on multiple rating scales.

4.2 Results and Discussion
Both systems were easy to learn. This was evident from the fact that every subject was able to effectively use the system after approximately fifteen minutes of practice. The two hypertext systems, however, differed significantly in terms of speed, accuracy, and subjective rating. It took less time to obtain relevant information for each of the reference questions using the MGI hypertext (a mean of 849.1 s vs. 2509.5 s, $T(1,16)= -9.14$, $P<.005$). Accuracy of responses, for both the reference and the learning questions, was also greater for the MGI hypertext. On reference questions, the mean percentage of correct answers with the MGI hypertext was 96.7% versus 88.9% for the CGI hypertext ($T(1,16)=2.523$, $P< .025$). To a lesser extent, the mean percentage of correct answers for the MGI hypertext was greater for the five learning questions (3.56 vs. 2.67, $T(1,16)=1.474$, $P< .1$). A final result was that the MGI hypertext received a higher subjective rating than the computer generated index (6.11 vs. 2.33, $T(1,16)=4.255$, $P<.005$).

The advantages of the MGI, appear to be due to the more focused information provided by links based on the authors manually generated index in comparison to the large sets of potentially relevant paragraphs obtained from links based on keyword searches. Keywords, such as 'safety', presented hundreds of potentially relevant paragraphs of text. Faced with such a large set of potential sections of

186

text, subjects occasionally gave up looking. The authors' index entries, on the other hand, narrowed the set of potentially relevant paragraphs to a much more manageable size, and may well have helped to give structure to the text. This may imply that the availability of flexible keyword-based search strategies, which seemed to give hypertext an advantage over text in Experiment 1, may not make up for the focus (and/or intelligence) imbedded within manually generated links for reasonably large hypertexts.

5.FINAL COMMENTS

In Experiment 1, the hypertext system showed a statistically reliable advantage over the book on 'reading to do' tasks. Information about specific topics and particular facts was located much faster and more accurately using the hypertext system, especially when searching for information which didn't fit well into the existing organization of the book or which required significant reading and scanning through references. The 'reading to do' tasks evaluated in this experiment are clearly quite similar to tasks often performed by designers in which they are searching for reference materials. The obtained results therefore support a practical role for hypertext reference systems.

It appears that much of the advantage over the book came from the computer-supported linking and query features of the hypertext system. The hypertext allowed users to obtain access to information, including that not well identified by the index. Since good indexes are difficult and time-consuming to manually develop, and perhaps even more difficult to update or edit, the potential that hypertext offers to go beyond or around the index is very attractive. It seems safe to say that indexes, no matter how complex, will never catch up with the variety of user informational needs. On the other hand, the Experiment 2 results clearly show that these abilities to go beyond the index are limited. In comparison to a completely exhaustive keyword based index, the manually generated index was found to be a much faster and accurate tool, primarily because it weeded out irrelevant information. Experiments 1 and 2 therefore illustrate a fundamental dichotomy in hypertext applications. From a creators standpoint, a computer generated index offers a quick, simple, and thorough method for linking index entries to text in a textbook setting. These benefits, however, may be counterbalanced by improved performance due to the structure, focus, and imbedded intelligence of manually generated index.

REFERENCES

1. Shneiderman, B. "User Interface Design and Evaluation for an Electronic Encyclopedia," in Salvendy, G. (ed.) *Cognitive Engineering in the Design of Human-Computer Interaction and Expert Systems*, Elsevier, 1987, pp. 207-223.
2. Marchionini, G. and Shneiderman, B. "Finding Facts vs. Browsing Knowledge In Hypertext Systems," *IEEE Computer*, 21, Jan. 1988, pp.70-80.
3. Egan, et al "Behavioral Evaluation and Analysis of a Hypertext Browser," *Proc. ACM CHI'89 Conf. Human Factors in Computing Systems* (Austin, TX, 30 April-4 May 1989), pp. 205-210.
4. Miller, J.M., Lehto, M.R., and Frantz, J.P. *Instructions & Warnings*, Fuller Technical Publications, 1990.
5. Konz, S. *Work Design: Industrial Ergonomics*, 3rd ed. Publishing Horizons, Inc., 1990.

Implementing Adaptable Hypermedia in a Relational Database

William Leigh and James Ragusa

Department of Management, College of Business, University of Central Florida, P.O. Box 25000, Orlando, Florida 32816

Abstract
This paper reports explorations into the use of standard database technology to support applications in hypermedia and multimedia information retrieval, an application area growing in importance. Hypermedia is usually authored and browsed using proprietary software systems built for this special purpose. But there are advantages to building information retrieval systems (including hypermedia) using standardized, open database management systems technology, especially as the hypermedia base becomes large [1]. Today the "intergalactic" standard in database management is the relational model and SQL [2]. We report methods to support advanced hypermedia applications using SQL and relational database management systems.

1. INTRODUCTION

Hypermedia is characterized by the presence of several inter-related instances of different media, such as video, sound, computer graphics, and still photography [3]. Each individual instance in a hypermedia network is called a node. The user navigates these nodes through the selection of gateways to other nodes. These gateways are called links.

The links are pre-defined between the nodes by the hypermedia author. The author of the hypermedia establishes the nodes and the links so that a user may derive information through browsing. The user's browsing may be more or less purposeful depending on the task context and her mood.

2. RELATIONAL REPRESENTATION OF HYPERMEDIA

Figure 1 shows a relational schema for the particular hypermedia setup we are using as an illustrative example in this paper. In this example, a node can consist of media instances of one or more of four types: image, text, sound, or video. Each node is identified by a node number (*node#*), and there is one row for each node (including a narrative *description*) in the *node* table.

The actual node content of the image node is an image captured in an image file. In like manner the text node requires a text file, the sound node requires a sound clip, and the video node requires a stored video sequence. This subject matter is stored in _*node* tables, and there is one for each type of media to accommodate the different data types required. Additional attributes necessary for dealing with the different media types could be included in the formats of these tables.

Each node can be the origin of a number of links to other nodes. The definitions of these links in the originating node are stored in the _link_origin_ tables, with a different table for each media type of node. A particular region of each node's data is designated as the origin of the link (also known as a _hyperregion_ or _hot spot_.) The node targets of these links are identified in the _link_target_ table. In this example the targets are whole nodes (not particular regions of the nodes.) Note that in this design the link targets need not be the same media as the link origins.

---

node (<u>node#</u>, description, user_level_code)

image_node (<u>node#</u>, image_data)
text_node (<u>node#</u>, text_data)
sound_node (<u>node#</u>, sound_data)
video_node (<u>node#</u>, video_data)

image_link_origin (<u>node#</u>, <u>link#</u>, x, y)
text_link_origin (<u>node#</u>, <u>link#</u>, word_number)
sound_link_origin (<u>node#</u>, <u>link#</u>, position)
video_link_origin (<u>node#</u>, <u>link#</u>, frame_number)

link_target (<u>node#</u>, <u>link#</u>, target-node#)

Figure 1. The basic relational schema for the example hypermedia system.
Primary keys are underlined.

3. ADAPTABLE HYPERMEDIA

Once the hypermedia system is represented relationally, it becomes possible to generate specialized views of the database for different purposes [4]. In the example system an attribute called _user_level_code_ is included in the _node_ table. This code might be a number from 1 to 5, designating the sophistication of the user in the domain of the hypermedia system. Using Structured Query Language (SQL), the standardized data definition and manipulation language of relational databases, it is easy to generate the subsystem which includes only nodes with a particular value or values in this attribute. Similar attributes might be attached to the other tables and used in a similar way; for example, resolution needed for video data, dates for temporally related data, or even keywords related to the semantic content of the nodes.

One attractive alternative made possible by this approach is the creation of tailored subsets of the hypermedia database. A profile of the intended user could be prepared in a separate database and the database transferred, using the referential integrity mechanism of the relational database to filter out the links and nodes which were not consistent with the user profile or which ended up as orphans with no connections to the resulting hypermedia net. These steps to prepare the adapted database are accomplishable with a few SQL (Structured Query Language) commands, which are understood by all relational database management systems.

This reduced database might be issued on portable media or downloaded directly to a local workstation for use. A viewer-program would be needed to browse this database. This viewer would use SQL for access to the database.

More dynamic adaptation of the presented hypermedia might be required. The relational approach can allow the user profile to be changed on a realtime basis. If all access is to the complete database, not to an abstracted subset, then complete qualification can occur at the logical level of each node or link access. Selection based on matches between sets of values is supported directly in a single SQL data manipulation statement.

4. DISTRIBUTING THE DATABASE

Workstation-based computing makes possible a view of computing where the workstation looks back at and drives a host data server. In this "client/server" style of computing, which is supported by commercially available relational database management systems, application design involves partitioning the tasks between the client and the server. The previously described approach of downloading the adapted and subsetted database from the database server to the client workstation places all interactive processing on the client workstation. The alternative which allows dynamic adjustment of the user profile requires that the complete database be available, implying that all data access be performed by the database server at the behest of individual SQL requests issued by the client workstation.

Another design problem is data placement. Optimally, data should not be moved -- that is, it is always where it is needed. But this must be traded off against the needs economies of sharing. Large hypermedia databases will be made up of contributions from a large number of users in many different locations. The commercially available relational database management systems will soon support a "seamless" interface to data that is stored on multiple, connected computer systems, and which may be re-located without disturbing the users. This capability will make large hypermedia database efforts feasible. If such re-location can be performed dynamically and automatically, considerable benefits in performance can be achieved.

5. RULES AND OBJECTS

Currently available relational database management systems are extended beyond the concepts of the basic relational model to support rule processing [2]. This makes the *intensional* specification of data and relationships, in addition to the *extensional* specification manifested by the storage of actual data values. This capability increases the expressiveness of the relational user profile. Instead of a user profile which is only a list of capabilities and keywords and which requires exhaustive enumeration of all such values, the profile can consist of a set of expert system rules which allow deduction of the values. This permits (not necessarily mutually exclusive) types of users to be defined and their hypermedia needs and preferences to be deduced.

Extension of the relational database management systems to support the storage of *objects* is going on now in the industry [2]. Among other things, this allows for storing appropriate sets of viewer-programs (on a logical basis, not physically) with the hypermedia items (film clip, etc.) This simplifies the administration and use of large hypermedia databases. This extension to an object-orientation maintains backward compatibility with SQL and the basic relational model in many implementations.

1 R. Rada, Information Processing & Management, 27(6) 659-677, 1991.
2 M. Stonebraker, IEEE Transactions on Knowledge and Data Engineering, 1(1) 33-44, 1989.
3 M. O'Docherty and C Daskalakis, The Computer Journal, 34(3) 225-238, 1991.
4 J. Deogun, Information Processing & Management, 24(3) 303-313, 1988.

Interactive Haptic Interface: Two-Dimensional Form Perception for Blind Access to Computers

S. Lee, S.F. Wiker, and G.C. Vanderheiden

Department of Industrial Engineering, University of Wisconsin-Madison, 1513 University Avenue, Madison, 53706, U.S.A.

Abstract

Eight sighted college students tactually explored line drawings on a computer screen using an Optacon. Particular forms of primitive elements were shown to significantly affect the likelihood of correct identification of the shapes. Configuration of the tactile array does not appear to affect the perception of two-dimensional graphic forms. The findings of this study have implications in the design of tactile communication systems, especially graphic computer access systems for people with visual impairments.

1. INTRODUCTION

Haptic perception requires collective integration of tactile and kinesthetic information [1-3]. Gibson reported that subjects appeared to use their hands to detect and explore primitive surface features (i.e., curvature, slant, distance, edge, and corner) of solid objects [4]. These features seemed to be the main features that active touch seeks and identifies by exploratory use of fingers. If specific features must be correctly detected by haptic system for structuring a shape, then accurate transmittal of primitive geometric features is an important design consideration for tactile displays.

The objective of this study was to examine the impact of combining particular tactile primitives upon accurate recognition of non-sense two-dimensional graphical images that are of comparable complexity to those found in tangible maps [5]. With the increased efforts to use iconic symbology in graphical computer interfaces for the visually impaired [6], this study on shape identification of graphical images in a haptic environment would bear some values in practical aspect.

2. METHOD

Eight sighted college students, two males and six females with ages ranging from 21 to 25 years, participated in this experiment on an informed consent and paid basis.

As shown in Figure 1(a), four simple two-dimensional shape patterns - vertex, cross, gap, and arc - were used as hypothetical tactile primitives. These tactile primitives were chosen because they were believed to be the simplest transformation of a straight line. The angle of intersected approaching segments was fixed at 90 degrees. These primitives were then concatenated in a factorial fashion to create ten stimulus forms. A straight line was included as an additional primitive to help construct the more complex shapes (i.e., to fill the dummy part of the shape after any two tactile primitives were combined). The more complex stimulus set used is shown in Figure 1(b).

The shapes were drawn upon the CRT display of a microcomputer and subjects moved a rectangular screen cursor across the forms by manipulating a mouse lying atop a digitizing tablet. An encounter of the screen cursor with a darkened area of screen pixels of the shapes produced a corresponding vibrational pattern by a 5-column-by-20-row array of tactors in an Optacon vibrotactile display. The number of screen pixels that were mapped onto a particular tactor was fixed at 2 vertical and 4 horizontal screen pixels (i.e., 8 pixels). This asymmetry in pixel mapping was inherent given the Optacon display, computer screen, and software driver design.

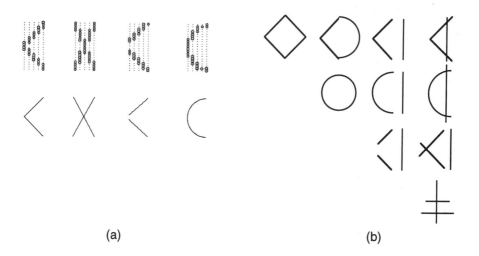

(a)   (b)

Figure 1. (a) Four hypothetical tactile primitives (from the left: vertex, cross, gap, and arc) and their mapped images on the Optacon. (b) Complex shape stimulus set. Two tactile primitives were concatenated in a factorial manner (in the stimulus matrix, columns from the left: vertex, arc, gap, and cross; rows from the top: vertex, arc, gap, and cross).

A haptic-to-visual forced-choice matching paradigm was used in the experiment. After tactually exploring the stimuli for a limited time, subjects matched the explored stimulus from a visually presented response panel. Two configurations of the Optacon display were used. For half of the trials, subjects used a standard Optacon display system configuration (i.e., subjects rested a fingertip of the non-preferred hand upon the stationary vibrotactile display to perceive stimulation and maneuvered a standard mouse upon a digitizing pad to control a screen cursor using the preferred hand). For the remainder of the trials, the subjects used a custom-built tactile-puck where the Optacon display was dismantled and integrated into the top of a puck which was then used as a mouse. This experiment was embedded in another study that had found no performance difference between the aforementioned haptic exploration methods [6].

3. RESULTS AND DISCUSSION

Result showed that the tactile primitives and more complex shapes were identified very accurately (primitives 88.8% ± 7%, and more complex shapes 91.6% ± 4.2%). *Cross* and *arc* primitives were identified more accurately than vertex and gap primitives ($F(3,21)= 3.18$, $p= 0.045$). No significant differences in correct identification rate among the ten shapes could be found ($F(9,63)= 0.99$, $p= 0.45$, power > 0.99 with fixed target rate of 10%). Examination of the confusion matrices revealed non-additive effects of the primitives upon correct identification of shapes. In the primitive set, *gap* is often confused with *vertex*, and *vertex* is often confused with *arc* primitive. The correct identification rate for the *gap* primitive was the lowest (Figure 2). For the more complex shapes, however, the *arc* primitive degraded correct identification rate (Figure 3 and 4). Complex shapes containing an *arc* primitive (shape 4,5,6, and 7 in Figure 3) were identified less accurately. Logistic analysis showed that the probability of correct identification of complex shapes decreased by 8% ($X^2= 8.99$, $p= 0.003$) with the presence of the *arc* primitive in complex forms. Interestingly, though the *gap* proved to be the most often confused among single primitives, the presence of an *arc* proved to be the most troublesome when combined with other primitives in the formation of more complex forms.

Distorted mapping of pixels on the screen to tactors and the geometric configuration of the Optacon display may have been responsible for our findings. However, the lack of agreement in perceptual performances between single primitive and more complex forms suggest that perceptual confusion is not solely display-mediated.

Tactile Primitive	Vertex	Cross	Gap	Arc	Stimuli Total
Vertex	121	2	7	14	144
Cross	4	138	.	2	144
Gap	16	5	118	5	144
Arc	6	.	3	135	144
Responses Total	147	145	128	156	576

Figure 2. Confusion matrix for the tactile primitive set. Responses are shown in columns for the stimulus presented in rows. Zero response is indicated by ".".

Shape	1	2	3	4	5	6	7	8	9	10	Stimuli Total
1	45	.	.	2	.	.	1	.	.	.	48
2	.	46	.	1	.	1	.	.	.	.	48
3	.	.	45	.	2	.	1	.	.	.	48
4	3	1	.	42	.	.	2	.	.	.	48
5	.	1	2	.	40	3	.	1	.	1	48
6	.	2	.	.	.	42	3	.	.	1	48
7	1	.	.	3	1	.	43	.	.	.	48
8	.	1	.	.	.	1	.	46	.	.	48
9	1	1	.	.	.	.	.	.	46	.	48
10	.	.	1	.	.	.	.	.	2	45	48
Response Total	50	52	48	48	43	47	50	47	48	47	480

Figure 3. Confusion matrix for more complex stimulus set. Responses are shown in columns for the stimulus presented in rows. Zero response is indicated by ".".

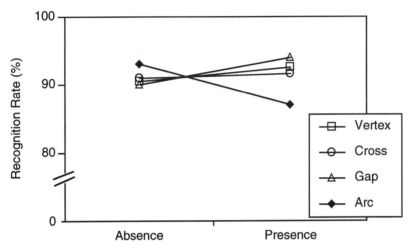

Figure 4. The effect of *arc* tactile primitive on recognition rate of the complex shape stimuli.

This result was supported by Loomis' data [7]. He used a 20-column-by-20-row vibrotactile display, which is much larger than the Optacon, for recognition of Roman letters to examine the effect of stimulus presentation mode. Though the focus of his study was on the effectiveness of stimulus presentation method, not on the shape of letters, we could find similar observations from his confusion matrix of uppercase Roman letter recognition. The full-field moving-letter mode in his study, can be considered the same as the Optacon's presentation mode, except for the size of the window through which image is scanned and presented to the finger. In the confusion matrix of 26 uppercase characters for the full-field, moving-letter mode, the mean correct recognition rate of the letters which do not have *arc* component (such as A,E,H and Z) was 49.7% ± 23%, while that of the letters which do have *arc* components (such as B,C,D and S) was 26.4% ± 12%. The correct recognition rate of the letters that have the *arc* components in them was significantly lower. The observations from the two studies supported each other.

Our findings have implications in the design of tactual communication systems, especially graphic computer access systems for the visually impaired people or for the teleoperators. Although vibrotactile arrays with the Optacon's resolution could be used to successfully distinguish between the primitives standing alone, there was difficulty in distinguishing between the same primitives when they were embedded in more complex shapes. In particular, arc versus vertex, and also gaps, were difficult to distinguish. In the case of this experiment, even when these features were fairly distinct and filled the tactile array, they posed problems for the subjects. This leaves open the question of the utility of displays of this type and resolution for doing more detailed exploration of graphic images. It appears that an even higher resolution display or greater enlargement of the features should be explored.

Two other approaches might be use of a more static rather than vibrotactile display, and the use of sound to enhance feature detection. The use of a static display may allow an individual to move finger over the pins to explore smaller features. This type of display, however, generally requires a much larger array that can hold a significant portion of the image. The second approach would be to include some dynamic image processing and feature extraction which would provide the individual with additional shape information (for example, different tones for different shapes). Some of the difficulties in distinguishing between obtuse angles and arcs encountered in this experiment may be easily resolved with such a system. This approach is not entirely dissimilar from the way visual information is pre-processed and presented to the brain (although the type of features detected in this case are different).

It is also useful to note that the Optacon's vibrotactile array was optimized for the feature extraction from text required to allow people who are blind to read printed characters. In this case, the users are able to take advantage of a number of gross and fine tactile characteristics in recognizing a word, as well as using their knowledge of the language and grammar to limit the number of candidates for the particular characters or even entire words they are trying to recognize. In trying to develop tactile arrays, it may turn out that the particular arrays as well as any feature extraction techniques, as discussed above, will need to be task-specific: that is, the design of the tactile array should take into account not only the direct tactile sensation being provided to the individual, but also their knowledge of the task, what the salient features of the target stimuli are, and alternate strategies that the user is also employing to reduce the potential candidates in the recognition set.

4. REFERENCES

1 P.W. Davidson, The role of exploratory activity in haptic perception: Some issues, data, and hypotheses. American Foundation for the Blind Research Bulletin, 24 (1972) 21.
2 J.M. Kennedy, Haptics. In E.C. Carterette and M. Friedman (eds.), Handbook of Perception (Vol. 8). Academy Press, New York, 1978.
3 J.M. Loomis and S.J. Lederman, Tactual perception. In K.R. Boff, L. Kaufman, and J.P. Thomas (eds.). Handbook of Perception and Human Performance (Vol. 2). John Wiley and Sons, New York, 1986.
4 J.J. Gibson, Observations on Active Touch. Psychological Review, 69 (1962) 477.
5 P.K. Edman, Tactile Graphics. American Foundation for the Blind, New York, 1992.
6 S.F. Wiker, G.C. Vanderheiden, S. Lee, and S. Arndt, Development of Tactile Mice for Blind Access to Computers: Importance of Stimulation Locus, Object Size, and Vibrotactile Display Resolution. Proceedings of the 35th meeting of the Human Factors Society, Human Factors Society, San Francisco, 1991.
7 J.M. Loomis, Tactile letter recognition under different modes of stimulus presentation. Perception & Psychophysics, 16 (1974) 401.

Sharing Customization in a Campus Computing Environment

Craig E. Wills
Kirstin Cadwell*
William Marrs†

Computer Science Department
Worcester Polytechnic Institute
Worcester, MA 01609

Abstract

This work studies the use and sharing of customization in a campus setting where a large computing culture exists, but one that has many diverse interests rather than focusing on a cohesive project. As part of this work we explore the development of a tool to facilitate sharing and make customization features more accessible and understandable to novice users.

1 Introduction

Customization of computing environments is increasingly available to computer users, but its use often does not match its availability. This work looks at the use and sharing of customization in a campus environment. The setting is the campus of Worcester Polytechnic Institute, which is predominately an engineering school with approximately 2500 undergraduate and 1000 graduate students. Nearly all students and faculty have computer accounts on the central computing facilities of the campus, which provides access to a UNIX[1] computing environment and many DEC workstations running the X Window System[2] [6].

Previous work on customization has observed that customization of a user's computing environment is not always a solitary task, but is also influenced by the particular computing culture [2, 3, 4]. These studies have identified small groups of users within

---

*Current address is Digital Equipment Corporation., Littleton, MA 01460.
†Current address is Atria Software Inc., Natick, MA 01760.
[1]UNIX is a trademark of USL.
[2]X Window System is a trademark of the Massachusetts Institute of Technology.

the computing environment who are responsible for translating and communicating customizations among the community as a whole. In [4], this person is termed a "handyman" referring to his or her ability to bridge the gap between workers and computer professionals. Mackay [2] concludes from her work that the design of customizable software should provide better means for sharing customizations. As part of work with the Tool Command Language (TCL), Osterhaut has developed customizer applications that can dynamically change the appearance of another application [5].

Our work explores how users customize their computing environment and how customization techniques can be made more visible to, and therefore used by, more users in a campus environment [1]. This work is motivated by two factors. First, to study the use and sharing of customization in a campus setting where a large computing culture exists, but one that has many diverse interests rather than focusing on a cohesive project. Second, to explore the development of a tool to facilitate sharing and make customization features more accessible and understandable to novice users. Not only should this tool provide for current customizations, but more importantly be extensible so new customizations can easily be added. This tool directly addresses the needs identified by Mackay; serving as a database of useful customizations that can easily be incorporated into the user's environment.

This work is important because it examines a larger and less cohesive computing environment than previous studies. On the order of 3000 users are studied in some depth concerning their use of customization features. 13% of the users had never logged in to their accounts, while 57% had logged in during the last two weeks and 72% in the past two months. Specific customization uses are collected from 224 users and 13 are interviewed in detail. One result of the project is to learn about the culture of customization in a campus environment. The other result is the development of a customization tool that is a means for users to share and learn about customization features of their computing environment.

2 Study

In our study, we examined widely used, customizable applications, such as shells, the window system, mailers and editors. Data collection programs were created to gather specific user customizations and obtain an overview of the customization level of users on the WPI system. These programs analyzed dot files (application customization files stored in a user's home directory) of applications under study with results shown in Table 1. It shows that approximately 45% of the users have not modified at least one of the default shell configuration files. For the other applications, which have no default files in a new user's account, 15-25% of the users had created customization files. However, half of all users had modified the .Xdefaults file, which controls such window aspects as the screen layout, colors, window size, and fonts. Later investigation found that the use of color, provided by the DEC session manager and stored in the .Xdefaults file, was often the first level of customization.

We also collected statistics about the use of specific shell programming constructs. For example, we found that only 11% of all users had more than one (the default) back

Table 1: Dot Files Analyzed

File (Default # of Lines)	Ave # of Lines	# Default	# not exist
.login (9)	12.4	1409 (44%)	8 (0%)
.cshrc (6)	12.6	1453 (45%)	17 (1%)
.mailrc	7.9	N/A	2489 (77%)
.emacs	20.0	N/A	2448 (76%)
.Xdefaults	35.6	N/A	1597 (50%)
.X11Startup	5.9	N/A	2668 (83%)

quoted string, used to execute a command string, in a shell dot file. Aliases were more commonly used and we found that 81% of the users had between one and six aliases. The default shell dot files contained two aliases. The maximum number of aliases was 155 with an average number of six. Common uses for aliases were for renaming UNIX commands into the equivalent DOS command name, accessing locally created programs that were not in public areas and sending messages to other users' terminal screens.

Figure 1 summarizes the customization levels of users who have logged into the system. It shows that 79% of users have modified at least one of their default files and 22% have also created one or more additional application dot files. Of the remaining 21% of users, 87% had a .Xdefaults file, indicating that users had at least customized their color setup. Thus, while users appear open to using customization there is a gap between the customization experience of core users and the dissemination of this knowledge to users on the periphery.

The two most common ways of acquiring customization, according to interviews with expert users, were to personally write their own customization and to modify customization techniques given to them. Almost all of the expert users acquired some number of customizations from other users, which compares favorably to the results obtained by Mackay [2]. However, the proportion of expert users writing their own customizations compares to Mackay's findings for system programmers in a project environment indicating that high customization users are playing a similar role in a campus environment.

3 CTool

Our findings show that users are open to customization, but we need a better means to disseminate what and how it can be done. Users are willing to share, but often the sharing is limited to a small subset of friends and in the large, unstructured computing environment the sharing often takes the same form. Sharing entire customization files provides useful customizations for the recipient, but can also leave the user bewildered with many customizations that are not understood.

In designing *ctool*, we wanted to help beginning and intermediate users become familiar and comfortable with the computer environment. Therefore, the program must be straightforward to use and should customize aspects of the system that users of the system

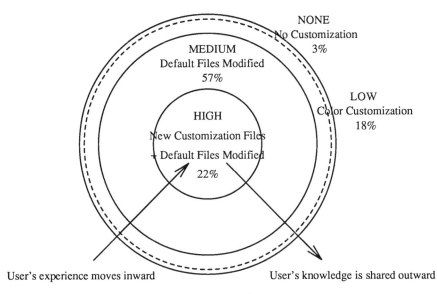

Figure 1: Level of User Sophistication

find important. A key design feature of *ctool* is extensibility so that new customization modules can easily be added by more sophisticated users to aid novice users. A tool such as the DEC session manager is useful for the features it provides, but it is limited to only those features. Because each computing environment has its own characteristics we felt that being able to adapt over time is important.

Figure 2 shows the tool organization as a tree of categories with specific customizations in each branch. The tree structure is implemented using a hierarchical file system. New categories are simply directories under the main directory, or under other category directories. Each directory contains a description file with a brief text description of the category. Other files in a directory are customization modules. The modules encompass specific customization techniques identified in our data collection programs and interviews. New customizations are added by creating a module file and placing it in the hierarchy. Modules contain descriptions and operations. Operations allow lines to be added to application dot files, possibly after gathering user input.

Based on this tool organization, we implemented a straightforward menu-driven interface for *ctool*. The interface allows the user to move up and down the hierarchy and to select a specific customization technique to incorporate. The user can inquire about a technique and optionally request that it be added to his or her computing environment. Keyword searching for techniques may be added as the tree grows in size.

We believe a tool that does not help the user to learn more about customization is not helpful in the long run. The user would become dependent on the tool, without becoming an explorer within the system. To help counter this possibility, all customization changes made to the user's environment are explained to him or her. The specific lines that are added and the name of the file they are added to are displayed to the user. When the

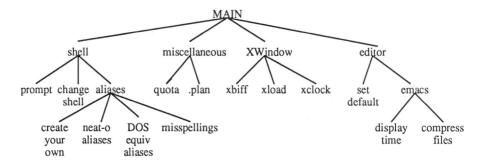

Figure 2: Hierarchical Model of *Ctool*

program adds lines to a file, it also adds comments informing the user that these lines were added by the customization tool, and what the lines do. In this way, the user can begin to understand what happens in specific customization files and begin to experiment with the command options available. At this time, the tool does not replace or delete any customizations previously added by itself or the user.

4   Evaluation

The tool was made available to the campus user community and advertised using electronic communication and word of mouth. Users were asked to provide written feedback to us about the tool. Preliminary feedback we received from thirty or so users who have used the tool included the following comments.

> "wow! neat. Now what you need to do is make a really big customization tree and submit it to stubin. I'll help writing some of the modules when...I get time."

> "I think ctool is a great idea, many of the options took me months as a UNIX user to finally implement on my own."

> "I used your ctool and I found it very easy to use and was able to create a .plan. It was so much easier than the regular UNIX way of creating one. I also used it to implement a window for mail, which I also previously could not do. It's pretty cool! You should add some more features."

The feedback has encouraged us that this tool has a role to play in the community, and should be moved in the user contributed software repository "stubin" directory, mentioned in one of the comments. Even though the customizations are not sophisticated they are useful for novice users to feel more comfortable and therefore in more control of the system. Providing users a means to select individual customization features allows them to understand how their environment is being changed. Because of its extensibility, the tool naturally allows others to add customization modules.

The purpose of this tool was to help novice users cross the threshold from confused newcomers to confident explorers. From the mail and verbal comments we have received, the tool is moving us towards this goal. The interest and enthusiasm of the user community certainly made us feel that this tool is a worthwhile contribution to the campus computing environment and would be useful in other computing environments.

5 Summary

In this work we examined the use and sharing of customization in a campus computing environment. This study provides information for customization on a large scale as compared to previous studies, which were centered around users on a specific project. As expected we found a variety of customization use in the system, but were interested to note that almost all users, who had logged in, showed evidence of customization.

On the other hand, most users still showed a relatively low level of customization, indicating a lack of time or understanding for customizing their environment. We did find the existence of a computing culture where handymen disseminate customizations to other users, but in a large environment we find many users who are not well connected. This situation leaves a gap between the core system users who have customization knowledge, but cannot connect with everyone, and the periphery users who show an interest in customization, but are unaware of how to pursue it.

To fill this gap we introduced *ctool* as a readily available customization tool, which allows novice users to tap into the customization knowledge of others. Initial reaction of users suggests this tool will help empower them to be in more control of their environment. The *ctool* does not do away with the explorer or the handyman, but gives them a vehicle to transmit their knowledge to beginning users. Future work will include studying the tool usage over an extended period and adding more customization modules.

References

[1] Kirstin Cadwell and William Marrs. User centered design: Customization of computing environments. Technical Report MQP-CEW-9102, Worcester Polytechnic Institute, December 1991.

[2] Wendy E. Mackay. Patterns of sharing customizable software. In *CSCW 90 Proceedings*, pages 209–221, October 1990.

[3] Wendy E. Mackay. Triggers and barriers to customizing software. In *ACM CHI'91 Proceedings*, pages 153–160, April 1991.

[4] Allan MacLean, Kathleen Carter, Lennart Lovstrand, and Thomas Moran. User-tailorable systems: Pressing the issues with buttons. In *ACM CHI'90 Proceedings*, pages 153–160, April 1990.

[5] John K. Ousterhout. An X11 toolkit based on the Tcl language. In *Proceedings of the Winter USENIX Conference*, pages 105–115. USENIX Association, January 1991.

[6] Robert W. Scheifler and Jim Gettys. The X Window System. *ACM Transactions on Graphics*, 5(2):79–109, April 1986.

AN INTELLIGENT USER INTERFACE FOR MULTIMEDIA MINERAL RETRIEVAL SYSTEM

Dusan Cakmakov and Danco Davcev

Faculty of Electrical Engineering & Computer Science, The "Kiril & Metodij" University, Karpos II, bb, 91000 Skopje, Macedonia

Abstract

In this paper, an intelligent user interface for mineral multimedia database retrieval is presented. The query mechanism is based on multimedia object content search using a multimedia knowledge-based structure called cognitive network. The experimental results for the system retrieval effectiveness expressed by *recall* and *precision* parameters are also discussed.

1. INTRODUCTION

The next genaration of information systems will essetially be represented by multimedia (MM) information systems.

Several MM document information systems have been proposed [13], [6], [7], [18]. Recently, a new approach to MM information management is developed in Hypertext systems [1], [14], [15], [16]. A more detailed survey of MM information systems is given in [11]. There are some critical issues which have not been satisfactory considered in the development of the MM information systems:

- Query-based access to MM information,
- Content search mechanisms,
- Integration of MM and knowledge-based systems.

The basic elements of A Multimedia Cognitive-based Information Retrieval System called AMCIRS which integrates image and text information have been described elsewhere [10], [11].

The main objective of this paper is to present AMCIRS user interface for mineral multimedia database retrieval.

In AMCIRS, the content search process is performed using vector model [19], where user query and MM information are presented by MM query and index vectors respectively. Each vector contains text and image objects. The image objects in the vectors are image object contour, represented by polygonal approximation [12]. Information selection in AMCIRS is based on similarity estimation between MM query and MM index vectors. The similarity function for image objects is deduced to polygon similarity estimation [3].

The basic contributions and innovation incorporated in AMCIRS are:

• It uses a knowledge-based structure called cognitive network (CN) which represents a multimedia construction different from other knowledge-based structures used in information retrieval systems.

  • It provides an intelligent query-based mechanism for MM information content search.

  • AMCIRS enables retrieval with different degree of importance given to the text and image parts of the MM documents.

The experimental evaluation of the AMCIRS retrieval effectiveness are given as well as the advantages of multiple media retrieval with respect to single medium retrieval.

2. THE BASIC ELEMENTS OF AMCIRS

Our global MM system model is presented on Fig. 1. The USER INTERFACE is responsible for query vector creation. The user query represents an input to the cognitive-based process conducted by the AMCIRS COGNITIVE SUBSYSTEM. This subsystem is introduced as an interface which communicates with user and MM objects using and manipulating the information from the cognitive network (CN).

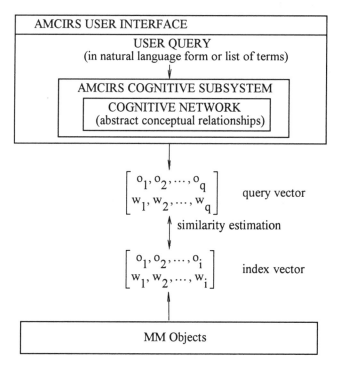

Figure 1. A global AMCIRS model

CN is an implementation of some ideas about real world objects (concepts) and connections among them.

The basic objective of CN is to simulate the end user behavior in the process of information retrieval [4], [17].

CN is MM structure which integrates the information about the given domain of MM objects. It provides information for image content search, extension of the user query with relevant information, support for our query language and user query improvement techniques. More information about CN can be found in [10], [11]. In [2], a formal CN model is given.

The content search process is activated by the user query based on the following filter specification:

$<$filter specification$>$ $\longrightarrow$
    $(<$compare operator$>_1$ "list of terms" $<$compare operator$>_2$ $<$rel$>)$

where

"list of terms"	is a list of user specified words, phrases or sentences representing the subject of the user interest.
$<$compare operator$>_1$	gives the direction of the user interest in hierarchical sense and can be one of the classical compare operators.
$<$compare operator$>_2$	is one of the classical compare operators which gives the direction of the user interest in relevance sense.
$<$rel$>$	represents the user specified relevance value.

The filter specification will activate the process of query vector creation. Some of the user specified terms in the "list of terms" will be associated to some CN nodes. These CN nodes will be the user cognition centers for spreading activity initiation [5]. The essence of this process is the identification of a set of CN nodes in or out of the sphere defined with $<$compare operator$>_2$ and radius $<$rel$>$ around the cognition centers which are below or up in the CN concept hierarchy according to $<$compare operator$>_1$. The query vector is created from the text and image representations of the identified CN concepts and the corresponding calculated weight factors. The weight factors are the closest distances in relevance sense between the identified CN concepts and the cognition centers.

On the other hand, MM objects are indexed with index vectors. Each index vector is composed of text and image objects with associated weight factors. We use single term indexing technique with inverse term frequency calculation to index text parts of MM documents. The indexing of image parts is performed by image object contour extracting. The weight factors represent a degree of importance of the index vector objects for MM object content.

In the process of retrieval, a given MM object will be selected if the level of similarity between the corresponding index and query vectors exceeds a threshold value. The similarity estimation between query and index vectors is performed according to the score:

$$a\sum_i \sum_j W_q(T_i)W_i(T_j)\text{Cort}(T_i,T_j) + b\sum_i \sum_j W_q(I_i)W_i(I_j)\text{Cori}(I_i,I_j)$$

where a and b are some suitable constants; T_i, T_j, I_i and I_j are some text and image vector objects; W_q and W_i are weight factors associated to the query and index vector objects respectively. The first summation are done over all text vector objects and the second over all image vector objects.

The correlation functions Cort( ) and Cori( ) are defined by:

$$\text{Cort}(T_i, T_j) = \begin{cases} 1 \text{ if } T_i = T_j \\ 0 \text{ otherwise} \end{cases}$$

$$\text{Cori}(I_i, I_j) = \begin{cases} 1 \text{ if the function } sim(I_i, I_k) \text{ has a} \\ \quad \text{maximum value for k = j which} \\ \quad \text{is greather then } t_r \\ 0 \text{ otherwise} \end{cases}$$

where t_r is a threshold value representing some level of similarity. For geometrical objects, $sim(\ )$ is based on polygon matching technique.

3. AN APPLICATION OF AMCIRS IN MINERALOGY

The AMCIRS application has been implemented in C using MM information from mineralogy (mineralogy domain). The choice of this domain is motivated by the following observations:
- The mineralogy domain provides a large set of MM documents with different text and image content.
- Mineralogy image information are simple, usually with geometrical forms.
- The building of mineralogy database does not require important mineralogy document modifications.

The MM mineralogy documents [8], [9] contain text and image information about particular mineral. The text information is a brief survey of the mineral description including its morphological, physical and chemical features, description of the locations where it can be found and some historical information about the mineral name. The average survey is about 150 - 200 words. The image information is represented by mineral images which correspond to the typical mineral appearances in the countries of origin.

Fig. 2 shows text and image information for given mineral in the process of mineralogy database retrieval.

Beside the text and image information for selected mineral, the estimated similarity between the text and image parts of the query and index vectors are also given.

The experimental results for the AMCIRS retrieval effectiveness are expressed by *recall* and *precision* parameters [19] and evaluated for 20 queries. A mineralogy database is consisted of 104 mineralogy documents.

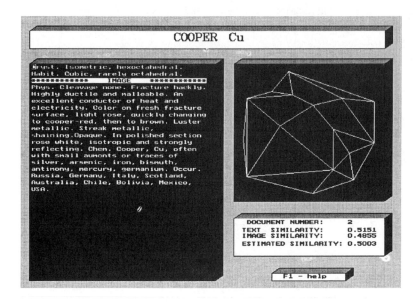

Figure 2. Screen for presentation of retrieved MM information

The experimental evaluation of the AMCIRS application on mineralogy domain shows:

• The most efficient retrieval is achieved if a slightly greater importance is assigned to the text part of the MM documents.

• Text information retrieval gives better results then image information retrieval.

• MM information retrieval gives better results then single medium information retrieval. In average, the MM information retrieval (text and image) increases the effectiveness of the system by about 7% with respect to text information retrieval and about 16% with respect to image information retrieval.

4. REFERENCES

[1] Akscyn, R.M., McCracken, D.L. and Yoder E.A., KMS: A Distributed Hypermedia System for Managing Knowledge in Organizations, *Comm. of the ACM*, Vol.31, No.7, July (1988) 820-835.

[2] Cakmakov, D. and Davcev, D., A Multimedia Cognitive-Based System Model, *Proc. of 5th Annual European Comp. Conf.*, Bologna, March (1991) 282-286.

[3] Cakmakov, D. Arnautovski V. and Davcev, D., A Model for Polygon Similarity Estimation, *Proc. of 6th IEEE CompEur92 Conf.*, Hague, (1992) 701-707.

[4] Case D.O., How do the experts do it? The use of ethnographic methods as an aid to understanding the cognitive processing and retrieval of large bodies of text, *Proc. of 11th Int. Conference ACM-SIGIR*, Grenoble (1988) 127-135.

[5] Cohen, P. R. and Kjeldsen, R. R., Information Retrieval by Constrained Spreading Activation in Semantic Networks, *Information Processing & Management* 23(4), (1987) 255-268.

[6] Cristodoulakis, S., Office Filing, in Office Automation, Edited by Tsichritzis C.D., Springer-Verlag, Berlin (1985) 67-89.

[7] Cristodoulakis, S., Theodoridou, M., Ho, M. and Papa, M., Multimedia Document Presentation, Information Extraction, and Document Formation in MINOS: A Model and a System, *ACM Trans. on Office Infor. Sys.*, Vol.4, No.4, (1986) 345-383.

[8] Dana J.D. and Dana E.S., *The System of Mineralogy*, Vol. 1, New York, (1944).

[9] Dana J.D. and Dana E.S., *The System of Mineralogy*, Vol. 2, New York, (1951).

[10] Davcev, D., Cakmakov, D. and Cabukovski, V., A Multimedia Cognitive-Based Information Retrieval System, *Proceedings of the 11th ACM Computer Science Conference*, San Antonio, March (1991) 430-439.

[11] Davcev, D., Cakmakov, D. and Cabukovski, V., Distributed Multimedia Information Retrieval System, *Computer Communication*, Vol.15, No.3, (1992) 177-184.

[12] Davcev, D., Cakmakov, D. and Arnautovski, V., A Query-Based Mechanism for Multimedia Information Retrieval, *Proc. of the 1th Inter. Workshop for MM Information Systems*, Tempe Arizona, (1992) 21-38.

[13] Forsdick, C.H., Thomas H.R., Robertson G.G. and Travers M.V., Initial Expirience with Multimedia Documents in Diamond, *Database Engineering, IEEE Computer Society Press*, Vol.3, (1984) 159-175.

[14] Garg, P.K., Abstraction Mechanism in Hypertext, *Comm. of the ACM*, Vol.31, No.7, July (1988) 862-870.

[15] Halasz, F.G., Reflections on Note Cards: Seven Issues for The Next Generation of Hypermedia Systems, *Comm. of the ACM*, Vol.31, No.7, (1988) 836-852.

[16] Nielsen, J., Through Hypertext, *Comm. of the ACM*, Vol.33, No.3, March (1990) 297-310.

[17] Norman D.A., User Centered System Design, in *Cognitive Engineering*, Ed. Norman E.S. and Draper S.W., Hillsdale, N.J.: Lawrence Erlbauru Associates, (1986) 31-36.

[18] Ozkarahan E. and Can F., Multi-Media Document Representation and Retrieval, Proc. of the 19th *ACM Anual Computer Science Conference*, San Antonio, (1991) 420-429.

[19] Salton, G., *Automatic Text Processing*, McGraw-Hill, New York, (1989).

Selecting Colors for Dialog Boxes and Buttons in a Text Interface

Stanley R. Page, Ph.D.

User Interface Group, WordPerfect Corporation, 1555 N. Technology Way, Orem, Utah 84057-2399

Abstract
The purpose of this study was to identify combinations of dialog box, button, and button highlight colors that would allow users to easily identify the highlighted button in a text interface. A combination of research analysis, performance testing, and preference testing was used to provide the design data within a short time frame. A preference test showed that users preferred black text on a gray background for dialog boxes and gray text on a blue background for document windows. Research analysis was used to reduce the potential button colors to eighteen by eliminating colors that research showed could cause problems. In the button color study, 57 participants were asked to select which of two buttons was highlighted in 306 separate pairs of buttons. Dialog boxes with gray text on blue, gray on black, or gray on dark gray as the non-highlighted button colors produced the best performance scores. Preference data indicated that white on blue, white on light blue, or white on red were good choices as highlight colors.

1. OBJECTIVE

Although graphical user interfaces are growing in popularity, text interfaces remain heavily used. Recent surveys show that text-based PC software applications continue to outsell graphical applications (ComputerWorld, 1992). As long as these text interfaces are being used we need to look for ways to make them easier to use.

A recent trend is to embellish text interfaces with as many graphical interface characteristics as possible. Such characteristics include direct manipulation, sizable windows, list boxes, dialog boxes or pop-up windows, scroll bars, and buttons. Color is used extensively in these text interfaces to compensate for the lack of graphics. Color is often used to distinguish dialog boxes from documents, to distinguish buttons from dialog boxes, and to highlight the button or other control on the dialog box that has the current focus.

Many dialog boxes have only two buttons, and one of them is highlighted to indicate the focus. When the user presses the Enter key the highlighted button is selected. Therefore, it is important for the user to recognize which button is highlighted and which is not. Otherwise, an incorrect selection could be made. The objective of the current studies was to identify combinations of dialog box, button, and button highlight colors that would allow users to easily identify the highlighted button.

2. DIALOG BOX COLOR STUDY

A study was conducted to determine user preferences for dialog box and document window colors. Twenty-six participants ranging in age from 15 to 70 were asked to rank ten potential color combinations for dialog boxes from their favorite to their least favorite. They were also asked to indicate a color preference for their document window.

Dialog boxes with black text on a gray background were the first or second choice of 15 of the 26 participants (58%). For the document window, 16 of the 26 participants (62%) preferred gray text on a blue background. Pastoor (1990) also reported a tendency for people to prefer blue background colors on their computer screens. These were the document and dialog box colors used in the button color study.

3. BUTTON COLOR STUDY

3.1 Participants

The study involved 57 participants ranging in age from 18 to 72 (mean=33). Twenty-nine of the participants were male and 28 were female.

3.2 Methods

Several recent studies have reported benefits in using combinations of methodologies to resolve user interface issues (Jeffries et al., 1990; Bailey et al., 1992). These studies point out the strengths that each method contributes to the evaluation process. Three evaluation methodologies were used in this study: research analysis, performance testing, and preference testing.

3.2.1 Research analysis

Even with its relatively limited color capabilities, a standard IBM PC compatible computer can produce 256 different color combinations. A research analysis was conducted to reduce the number of potential button colors in this study to a manageable number. The research analysis involved doing a survey of available research on the use of color in computing systems and using the data to eliminate potential color combinations that could cause performance or acceptance problems. Artistic principles were also employed to select colors that are aesthetically pleasing together. These techniques (basing user interface decisions on expert knowledge) are similar to the heuristic evaluation techniques proposed by Nielsen and Molich (1990). Eighteen button colors were selected for the study based upon the principles discovered. Some of the principles are listed below:

- Blue text on red and red text on blue cause chromostereopsis which is a false indication of depth were one color appears to be floating in front of the other causing eye strain (Helander, 1991).
- Red text on green and red text on blue cause 10% poorer performance on selection tasks (Matthews and Mertins, 1989).
- Magenta and green receive the lowest scores in preference tests of computer colors. Black, blue, and red receive the highest scores in preference tests. (Taylor and Murch, 1986.)

- Black and blue are the most readable colors on a gray background. Light cyan, green, light green, yellow, and light gray are the most readable colors on a blue background. Cyan, light cyan, green, light magenta, and white are the most readable colors on a black background. (Lalomia and Happ, 1987.)
- Almost 10% of the Caucasian male population and 4% of the non-Caucasian male population have trouble distinguishing certain colors (color deficiency or color blindness). The following color combinations should be avoided for these individuals: cyan and gray, yellow and light green, green and brown, red and black. (Travis, 1990; Thorell and Smith, 1990.)

3.2.2 Performance Test

Participants were shown randomly ordered pairs of different colored buttons on a dialog box (Figure 1) and asked to identify which button was highlighted (Button A or Button B). Each of the 153 possible button pairs was shown twice so that both colors were displayed in each button position. This resulted in each subject performing 306 comparisons of button pairs.

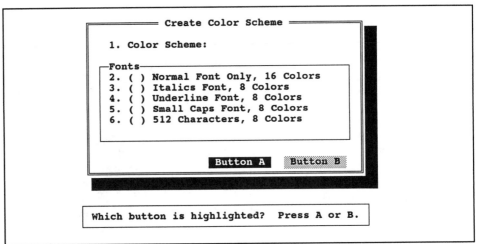

Figure 1. Screen from the button color study.

3.2.3 Preference Test

Following the button comparisons, participants were asked to rate how well they liked each of the eighteen button colors on a seven-point scale.

3.3 Results

Table 1 shows the results of the performance test. The color combinations listed across the top of the table represent the non-highlighted buttons. The combinations listed down the left side of the table represent the highlighted buttons. The number in each cell corresponds to the percentage of agreement concerning which button was highlighted in each pair. For

Table 1. Results of the performance test.

Highlighted button colors	Gray /Dk. Gray	Gray /Black	Gray /Blue	Gray /Red	White /Dk. Gray	White/ Black	White/ Blue	White/ Red	White/ Lt. Blue	Yellw /Black	Yellw /Blue	Yellw /Lt. Blue	Lt. Blue /White	Blue /Lt. Cyan	Blue /Yellw	Black /White	Black /Lt. Cyan	Black /Yellw
Gray/Dk.Gray		28%	4%	3%	2%	3%	2%	0%	1%	2%	0%	0%	0%	2%	1%	2%	1%	1%
Gray/Black	72%		16%	10%	6%	3%	3%	0%	3%	0%	2%	1%	1%	2%	4%	1%	4%	2%
Gray/Blue	96%	84%		7%	39%	27%	4%	4%	2%	2%	1%	3%	4%	4%	2%	11%	4%	4%
Gray/Red	97%	90%	83%		46%	39%	23%	3%	13%	16%	19%	14%	16%	14%	9%	25%	11%	4%
White/Dk.Gray	98%	94%	61%	54%		23%	7%	7%	6%	6%	8%	11%	11%	18%	11%	11%	12%	4%
White/Black	97%	97%	73%	61%	77%		24%	18%	16%	16%	20%	18%	23%	23%	17%	31%	18%	12%
White/Blue	98%	97%	96%	77%	93%	76%		33%	20%	30%	34%	36%	34%	32%	20%	46%	27%	26%
White/Red	100%	100%	96%	97%	93%	82%	67%		42%	48%	60%	50%	53%	40%	34%	67%	39%	32%
White/Lt.Blue	99%	97%	98%	87%	94%	84%	80%	58%		48%	52%	49%	43%	34%	25%	62%	34%	23%
Yellow/Black	98%	100%	98%	84%	94%	84%	70%	52%	52%		61%	58%	59%	43%	35%	63%	45%	32%
Yellow/Blue	100%	98%	99%	81%	92%	80%	66%	40%	48%	39%		39%	49%	43%	24%	61%	40%	23%
Yellow/Lt.Blue	100%	99%	97%	86%	89%	82%	64%	50%	51%	42%	61%		43%	40%	24%	54%	29%	25%
Lt.Blue/White	100%	99%	96%	84%	89%	77%	66%	47%	57%	41%	51%	57%		44%	28%	78%	45%	33%
Blue/Lt.Cyan	98%	98%	96%	86%	82%	77%	68%	60%	66%	57%	57%	60%	56%		39%	61%	64%	31%
Blue/Yellow	99%	96%	98%	91%	89%	83%	80%	66%	75%	65%	76%	76%	72%	61%		67%	59%	51%
Black/White	98%	99%	89%	75%	89%	69%	54%	33%	38%	37%	39%	46%	22%	39%	33%		33%	17%
Black/Lt.Cyan	99%	96%	96%	89%	88%	82%	73%	61%	66%	55%	60%	71%	55%	36%	41%	66%		36%
Black/Yellow	99%	98%	96%	96%	96%	88%	74%	68%	77%	68%	77%	75%	67%	69%	49%	83%	64%	

example, when both a gray text on black and a gray text on dark gray button were presented, 72% of the participants selected gray on black as the highlighted button.

On 43 of the 153 button pairs 95 percent or more of the participants agreed upon which button was highlighted. All of the non-highlighted buttons in this group contained gray as the foreground color. Table 1 shows that three button colors were included as the non-highlighted button in 41 of those 43 button pairs. The three button colors were gray on black, gray on blue, gray on dark gray.

Table 2 shows each button color's average preference score. The button colors with the highest preference scores contained bright colors and had a high degree of contrast between the foreground and background color. The button background colors with the highest preference scores were blue, light blue, and red. Notice that the three button colors that received the highest performance scores as non-highlighted buttons (gray on blue, gray on black, and gray on dark gray) received low preference scores.

Table 2. Average preference scores for each button color combination.

Button Colors	Ave. Score	Button Colors	Ave. Score
White on Blue	4.84	Yellow on Black	3.68
White on Light Blue	4.80	Blue on Yellow	3.64
White on Red	4.75	Black on White	3.47
Yellow on Blue	4.55	Gray on Red	3.41
Yellow on Light Blue	4.52	White on Black	3.23
Black on Light Cyan	4.38	Gray on Blue	3.23
Blue on Light Cyan	4.07	White on Dark Gray	2.61
Light Blue on White	4.00	Gray on Black	2.14
Black on Yellow	4.00	Gray on Dark Gray	1.96

4. CONCLUSIONS

It appears from this study that the best color combinations for non-highlighted buttons contain neutral foreground colors and have moderate contrast between the foreground and background colors. The highlight button colors with the highest level of acceptance appear to be those with bright colors and a high degree of contrast. If you are using gray dialog boxes, Table 1 can be used to select pairs of button colors that will allow users to easily identify the highlighted button. Using a highlight button color with a high preference score from Table 2 will increase user acceptance.

In addition to providing data concerning color selection, this study demonstrated the value of using a combination of evaluation techniques. The preference study on dialog box colors and the research analysis helped to narrow the scope of the button color study. Using both performance and preference testing provided data that will lead to improved user performance as well as a higher level of acceptance. This combination of techniques provided valuable design information within a short time frame.

5. ACKNOWLEDGEMENTS

The author wishes to thank Jim Millecam and Alan Brown for requesting the study and for their support on user interface issues. Thanks to Jack Young, Nancy Wood, and Tammy Snow for recruiting participants and administering the study. Thanks to Betty Lindsay-Carter and Gaye Lee Page for reviewing the manuscript.

6. REFERENCES

Bailey, Robert W.; Allan, Robert W.; and Raiello, P. 1992. Usability testing vs. heuristic evaluation: a head-to-head comparison. *Proceedings of the Human Factors Society---36th Annual Meeting,* 409-413.

ComputerWorld. 1992. Windows leads software sales surge. (7 Dec), 168-183.

Helander, Martin (ed.). 1989. *Handbook of Human-Computer Interaction.* Amsterdam: North Holland, p. 465.

Jeffries, Robin; Miller, James R.; Wharton, Cathleen; and Uyeda, Kathy M. 1990. User interface evaluation in the real world: a comparison of four techniques. *CHI'91 Conference Proceedings,* 119-124.

Lalomia, Mary J. and Happ, Alan J. 1987. The effective use of color for text on the IBM 5153 color display. *Proceedings of the Human Factors Society--31st Annual Meeting,* 1091-1095.

Matthews, Michael L. and Mertins, Karen. 1989. Visual performance and subjective discomfort in prolonged viewing of chromatic displays. *Human Factors,* 31(3), 259-271.

Nielsen, Jakob and Molich, Rolf. 1990. Heuristic evaluation of user interfaces. *CHI'90 Conference Proceedings,* 249-256.

Pastoor, Siegmund. 1990. Legibility and subjective preference for color combinations in text. *Human Factors,* 32(2), 157-171.

Taylor, Joann M. and Murch, Gerald M. 1986. The effective use of color in computer graphics applications. *Computer Graphics '86 Conference Proceedings,* 515-521.

Thorell, L. G. and Smith, Wanda J. 1990. *Using Computer Color Effectively: An Illustrated Reference.* Englewood Cliffs, N.J.: Hewlett-Packard Prentice Hall.

Travis, David S. 1990. Applying visual psychophysics to user interface design. *Behaviour & Information Technology,* 9(5), 425-438.

214

An interactive information filter or a trip in hyperspace

Constantin Thiopoulos

Intratech Ltd, 18 Kodringtonos str., 11257 Athens, Hellas

Abstract

The problem of "getting lost" prevents hypermedia from exploiting their full power as a flexible and user-friendly tool for the sophisticated use of large information systems. The following paper proposes a solution to this problem by presenting an interactive information filter that supports the user in tuning the granularity level of access to the stored information.

1. LOST IN HYPERSPACE

In hypermedia the information is split into fragments called nodes, which are connected via links. Information is retrieved via navigation, which corresponds to the user's exploitation of the resulting network, called the *hyperspace*. The main advantage of hypermedia is that navigation has shown to be a more natural form of search behaviour than the traditional query-based paradigm. Another advantage is that the users can choose their own path through the information and are not restricted to accessing the information sequentially.

While hypermedia offer a lot of advantages in comparison to boolean information retrieval they have a major drawback: the problem of "getting lost", i.e. the user loses orientation in hyperspace.

2. THE LOGIC OF LINKS

Hyperspace can be seen conceptually as a directed graph, whereby the nodes are the information fragments and the associative links berween them are the links of the graph. In contrast to model-theoretical logic, where the semantics are given as a denotational mapping between formal structures, the "logic" of an interlinked information structure is structural, i.e. the semantics must be defined in terms of the corresponding positional value[1]. The reason is that, from the point of view of Information Retrieval, one is interested in the interrelation of a node in hyperspace[2]. Accordingly, the meaning of a node is a subgraph containing all nodes, which are connected to this one. This corresponds to the information that is relevant to the selected node, i.e. it contains all information fragments that can be extracted starting from this node.

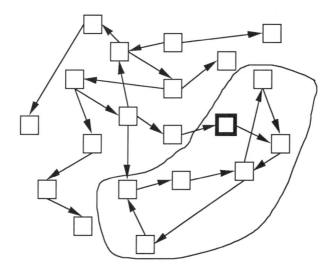

Figure 1: The meaning of a node

The meaning of two or more nodes is the subgraph containing all nodes that are connected to all of the activated ones. This is the information that is relevant to *all* of the selected nodes. Since the identified subspace contains all information fragments that can be extracted out of the hyperspace by starting from a given set of nodes, it corresponds to the *focus of interest* of a user (in respect to the considered information structure).

---

[1]This corresponds to the notion of *valeur* of a sign in a semiotic system introduced by Saussure. See [1] for the semiotic and mathematic foundation of a semantic formalism, based on category theory, suitable for capturing the structural aspect of meaning.

[2]Moreover, since circularity is possible, denotational semantics, which presuppose a hierarchic organization of the considered domain, cannot provide a frame for hypermedia semantics (see [2]).

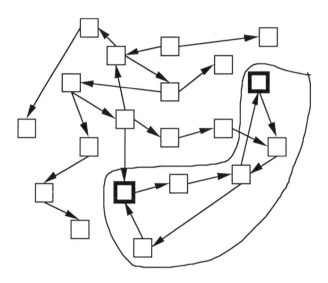

Figure 2: The meaning of two nodes

The activation of two or more nodes results, therefore, in the highlighting of a substructure of the hyperspace, constituting a horizon of relevance[3].

3. TUNING INFORMATION RETRIEVAL

By iterating this operation it is possible to model the *shift of focus of interest* of the user. Starting from a global hyperview of the hyperspace, the user can, by clicking on two or more nodes, generate a constrained hyperview containing all nodes,that are connected to all of the selected ones. These form the nodes of a new hyperview containing all links between them. Since the resulting subspace is again a directed graph it is possible to make further selections on the subspace and to specify again the resulting subsubspace etc. This trip ends when the user has identified a subspace that is sufficient for his needs, i.e. he or she will now be able to directly explore the underlying network.

In order to achieve a greater flexibility not only the global and the actual hyperview will be presented, but also the last one, i.e. after consulting the actual hyperview it will be possible for the user to correct his last choise by going to the last view and to select a new set of

---

[3]In terms of Knowledge Representation this horizon can be seen as a model of a *phenomenological situation*, in contrast to the dualistic one of situation semantics (see [3]).

nodes, which will produce in turn a new actual hyperview.

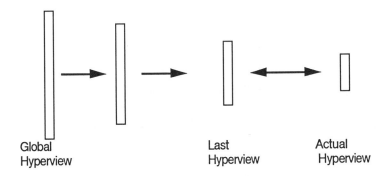

Figure 3: The sequence of hyperviews

This gradual hyperspace restriction focusses on the specific nature of hypermedia, since it requires the active participation of the user during the whole retrieval process and allows a continuous tuning of the retrieval process according to the changing interests of the user, offering a solution to the problem of "getting lost" by the user-driven inspection of the hyperspce. It can serve therefore as an information filter to large hypermedia systems, providing a frame for a software mashine, which supports the user in tunning with more exactness his access to the stored information leading not only to a solution of the problem of "getting lost" but also to a sophisticated device for handling mass information[4].

---

[4] In order to gain an overview of large information structures, the described mechanism can be combined with a stratification device in order to generate higher-level representations of the hyperspace (see [4]).

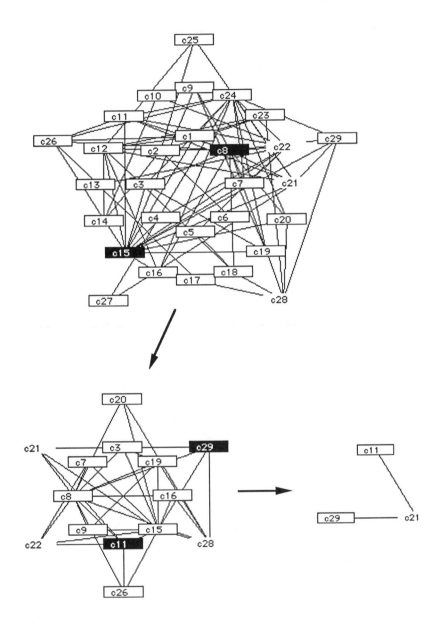

Figure 4: The tuning process

4. REFERENCES

1. Thiopoulos, C. *Semiosis und Topoi.* Pfaffenweiler: Centaurus, 1992.

2. Thiopoulos, C. Towards a logic of semiotic systems. *Mathematiques, Informatiques et Sciences Humaines,* 117, 49-60, 1992.

3. Thiopoulos, C. Meaning metamorphosis in the semiotic topos. *Theoretical Linguistics,* 16, 2/3, 255-274, 1990.

4. Thiopoulos, C. Semantic stratification of hyperbases. (To appear.)

Dialogue Design Through Modified Dataflow and Data Modelling

Søren Lauesen and Morten Borup Harning

Copenhagen Business School, Howitzvej 60, DK-2000 Frederiksberg
E-mail: sl.iio@cbs.dk   Fax: +45 38 15 24 01   Phone: +45 38 15 24 27

Abstract
Structured methods based on dataflow diagrams and data modelling are widely used for system analysis and design, but they are not suited for dialogue design. This paper shows a method for dialogue design that is based on modified data modelling and dataflow diagrams: The usual datamodel is complemented with a forms-based or picture-based model. This model is later extended with function bubbles representing dialogue actions.

The method allows a high degree of user participation, especially in the first steps, where the major design decisions seem to take place.

Keywords: Dialogue design, structured design, dataflow, data modelling, user participation, user datamodel, information demands, prototyping.

1. Introduction

The more widely used development methods are stepwise, structured methods based on dataflow diagrams and data modelling. Today they are used for business administration systems [Yourdon, 1989] as well as real-time systems [Hatley & Pirbhai, 1987]. They allow some degree of general user participation, but are not suited for dialogue design.

In contrast, the current methods for dialogue design are either very formal (mathematics based or program-like) [Harrison & Thimbleby, 1990; Kieras & Polson, 1985; Moran, 1981] or they are based on prototyping [Gould & Lewis, 1985; Bailey, 1993]. The formal methods are not well suited for user-centered development, while the prototype methods lack the necessary structure and consistency for use in larger systems.

Very little has been done to use the structured methods for dialogue design, but [Sutcliffe & McDermott, 1991] show an attempt. Their approach seems to be heavily dataflow-oriented, while the datamodels play a minor role. One observation is that the step from dataflow to dialogue is far from simple, because functions must be reorganized to match the dialogue, and because the subtasks are performed in an unpredictable sequence. Another observation is that although some data modelling was made, it was not used directly in the screen design.

In this paper we show a method that uses modified datamodels and dataflow diagrams to make a more user-centered conceptual and functional design.

We assume that the existing system has been analysed, and that we have some idea about the area to be computerized. The method will then guide us through the dialogue design in a number of steps. As with all stepwise methods, there will often be a need to go back one or more steps to revise some decision in light of knowledge gained in a later step. We will just take that for granted below.

2. Example: A Hotel Booking System

The method is suitable for design of many kinds of systems: business administration, software tools, devices with buttons, etc. Below we will illustrate the method with a simple hotel booking system. We will focus on room administration, checking in and out, etc. Thus, we will not consider accounting functions, personnel, purchase, etc.

A good starting point for the design is a traditional datamodel. It would show the basic entities (Guests, Rooms, Breakfast Selections) and the relationships between them (Bookings and Occupations of rooms, Breakfast Servings).

Such a model is rather precise. However, it is difficult to have a deeper discussion with users about it - unless they are trained well in data modelling. On the other hand, it is important to receive the users's comments on the data to be stored in the system. This is what the first step of the method accomplishes:

3. User Datamodel

A user datamodel is a way to present the system data to users. The basic idea is to show the data as "forms" or other pictures of the data. Figure 1 is a possible user data-model for the hotel booking system. The first form shows the data that the system has on a guest (name, address, passport number, payment form) and the relationships to rooms and breakfast selections. We are able to see on which dates a guest has occupied or booked which rooms, and on which dates a guest has received breakfast. We should imagine that the system stores a pile of these forms - as suggested in the figure.

The next form shows the rooms and part of their relationships to the guests. We can see the room attributes and on which days they are booked (B) or occupied (O). This form will be useful when the receptionist has to find a vacant room.

The last form shows the breakfast selections. This form will be useful, for example when we have to change prices or add new types of services.

It is essential that the forms resemble something we might later show on the screen. In fact, we can make the later, real screen pictures by "cutting" large pieces out of the user datamodel.

A user datamodel contains the same information as a traditional datamodel, but in another form. We suggest to use both models in practice, preferably with some tool to help us make sure that the models match.

User Participation

We can discuss these forms with the users. Can they see a similarity to what they use at present? Can they understand what the fields mean? Is any information lacking? Are there any difficult situations that we have not considered?

As an example, the first version of the user datamodel for hotel booking did not contain two prices for each room, nor did it include change of room. This would not have been revealed by merely discussing the technical datamodel with the users.

Naming things is another important issue that should be discussed with the users. For instance, in the hotel system the field "bath" constitutes a problem. "Bath" may be a bath, a lavatory or nothing. Is it reasonable to call it "bath"? After a discussion with the users, it became clear that the term "bath" was a reasonable choice.

Similarity to Familiar Papers/Forms

The forms resemble something the user already knows. For instance, the guest form resembles quite well the invoice received by a guest, and the room form resembles the reservation book which is normally found in small receptions.

Obviously, it makes it easier for the user to understand the system if the screen pictures resemble something he knows. However, keeping to something that the user knows also has its drawbacks. It makes it difficult to produce something that is completely different (and perhaps much better) than what the user is familiar with. For instance, we may not think of using graphics, curves, pictures, etc.

However, we can try to be creative already with the user datamodel and use graphics, curves, etc. For instance, we could show the rooms as a map of the hotel and try it out with the users.

4. Task List

In this step we first list the key user tasks for the system. In the hotel booking system, the list could start like this:

- Booking a guest per telephone, telex, or letter.
- Checking in with booking.
- Checking in without booking.
- Checking out.
- Entering the breakfast list from the kitchen.

How do we know if we have included all the tasks? Unfortunately, it is difficult to give a general answer, but we must rely on the expert users for advice. Besides, we can conduct a systematic check against the datamodel as follows:

- Do the tasks allow the user to see and change all data?
- Do the tasks allow the user to create and delete all "records"?

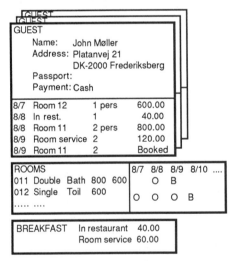

Figure 1. A user datamodel with the same information as a traditional datamodel. This example is based on a forms metaphor. Form parts are later "cut out" and combined to make screens.

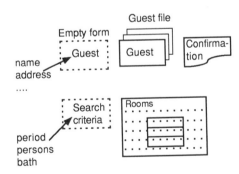

Figure 2. An information demand diagram for the booking task. Most data are parts or variants of the user datamodel. Dotted lines show temporary data, which exist only during the dialogue. The receptionist must be able to enter name, address, etc. on an empty guest form and later see the filed form. He must also be able to set up search criteria for finding suitable rooms in the proper period.

These questions will often cause further tasks to be added to the list. In our example, it is easy to see that some tasks are missing on our list. For instance, the user cannot change or delete bookings. We would have to add these tasks.

5. Information Demand Diagrams

The next step is to take the tasks one by one and identify the parts of the user datamodel that have to be visible at some point during the task. We also identify additional data needed temporarily during the task. Figure 2 shows this for the *booking* task.

We use a notation where temporary data is shown with dotted lines. The empty guest form, for instance, is temporary until the guest is registered. We show the file of registered guests as a pile of forms, and the top form is shown in heavier lines to suggest that this is the form that the user will look at. The search criteria for rooms cause the system to show a selection of rooms in the desired period. These selected rooms are marked by a frame on the room form.

It is easy to discuss the information demand diagram with the users. They usually have a good understanding of the information necessary to perform a task.

6. Function Diagram

In this step we take the information demand diagrams and add functions to them. Each function corresponds to a "button" that the user can press. On the diagram we show the "buttons" as function bubbles. At this stage we need not care whether the "button" corresponds to a function key, a menu selection, or a real button (as in computer controlled devices). In order to perform the task, the user will in general have to push several "buttons".

Figure 3 shows the function diagram for the booking task. It is a modified dataflow diagram where the arrows show data flowing into the function bubble and out of it. If an arrow goes from *inside* a form, it means that the data is copied into the function. If an arrow goes from the *border* of a form, it means that the entire form is moved.

Another notational detail is the arrows without a function bubble. They indicate that the user is changing or looking at a data field. We can place names on an arrow to specify which data fields the function is using.

According to the diagram, the *Create* button takes the temporary (dotted) guest form and places it on top of the guest file. The *Confirm* button copies the guest form to create the confirmation letter. The *Find rooms* button uses the search criteria to create a frame around the proper rooms in the proper period. Finally, the *Book* button puts booking marks on the rooms form and adds booking lines on the filed guest form.

In practice, we should add a mini-spec (pseudo-algorithm) for each "button" to specify in a bit more detail what it is supposed to do.

Note that the function diagram does not specify a sequence for pushing the "buttons", although there might be an implicit sequence because the necessary data must be available for a button to operate. Apart from such implicit sequence restrictions, the user is actually free to choose the action sequence.

As an example, the receptionist can first enter the name, address, etc. and create the guest. Next he can find rooms and book them. Or he can find rooms first and then create and book the guest. However, with this design he cannot book before he has created the guest. (It is possible to make other designs that would allow that.)

The freedom to use the buttons in any meaningful sequence is in contrast to the

224

formal dialogue specifications, where sequences and their variations are the key specification technique.

Including Other Tasks

We could handle other tasks in the same way: Make the information demand diagram and add the functions.

But in many cases it will pay to continue working on one of the previous function diagrams. In this way we can reuse many functions, and the dialogue will become more uniform from task to task. In our example, we can handle all the key tasks by means of six more buttons. The entire function diagram becomes about twice as large as Figure 3.

As an example, if a guest arrives without booking, the receptionist can check him in as follows: Find Rooms, Create (if a room is available), and Check In (a new button). The first two buttons are reused from the first task.

7. Screen Outlines and State Diagram

The next step in the dialogue design is to combine forms or form parts in such a way that they can be seen on the screen simultaneously - and divide large forms into parts, each of which can be presented on the screen. For simplicity, we have assumed in the example that we have a traditional screen without windowing and with 25 lines of 80 characters.

Figure 4 shows the three screens we could then design for the booking system. We have also shown the transitions between the screens for each of the functions, thus making the diagram a state transition diagram. In order to switch between some screens we have had to add a couple of "buttons".

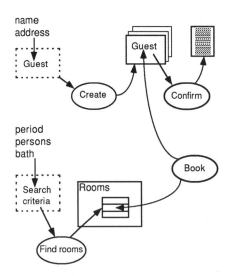

Figure 3. A function diagram showing the "buttons" to be used during the booking task. A "button" is shown as a function bubble. Arrows show the data needed and produced by the function.

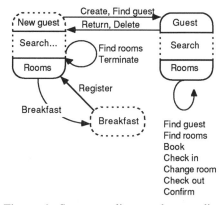

Figure 4. Screen outlines and state diagram with all functions shown. The hotel booking system needs three screens (two of them almost identical) and thus three main states. The "buttons" *Breakfast, Return,* and *Terminate* had to be added to navigate between screens. The *New Guest* screen serves as a convenient initial state.

8. Syntactical Design

The last step in the method is to make the syntactical design and test it with prospective users. The syntactical design is rather straightforward. We can "cut out" parts of the user datamodel and combine them to make the screen layouts. A lot of attention is still needed, however, to provide a good layout, phrase error messages properly, provide help screens, etc.

The function diagrams and state diagrams tell us what "buttons" to provide for each screen. At this stage we will of course have to make a choice of how to represent a "button": As a function key, a menu point, etc. However, there will usually be a standard for this, depending on the software platform used.

9. Results

At present we have only limited experience with the method. We have designed a few small systems with it, and we have given several courses where users and programmers cooperated to make a design by means of the method. Our observations on user participation in the various steps stem from that.

We have been surprised to learn that the major design decisions are embodied already in the conceptual design, i.e. the user datamodel. This step calls for a lot of imagination, and user participation is easy to achieve.

The function diagram is the most technical step, and real user participation is more difficult here. In particular, users have troubles seeing the difference between the function diagrams and the state diagrams.

Another observation is that the dialogue ends up with rather few screens compared to typical dialogues in similar applications. Finally, the usability of the dialogue is high already with the first syntactical design.

References

Bailey, G. (1993): Iterative methodology and designer training in human-computer interface design. (To appear in proceedings of Inter-CHI'93).

Gould, J.D. & Lewis, C.H. (1985): Designing for usability: Key principles and what designers think. Comm. of the ACM, 28, pp300-311.

Harrison, M. & Thimbleby, H. (eds.): Formal methods in human-computer interaction. Cambridge University Press, 1990.

Hatley, D.J. & Pirbhai, I.A. (1987): Strategies for real-time system specification. Dorset House Publishing, New York, 1987.

Kieras, D.E. & Polson, P.G. (1985): An approach to the formal analysis of user complexity. Int. J. of Man-Machine Studies, 22, 365-394.

Moran, T.P. (1981): The Command Language Grammar: A representation scheme for the user interface of interactive systems. Int. J. of Man-Machine Studies, 15, pp3-50.

Sutcliffe, A.G. and McDermott, M. (1991): Integrating methods of human-computer interface design with structured systems development. Int.J. Man-Machine Studies (1991) 34, pp631-655.

Yourdon, E. (1989): Modern structured analysis. Yourdon Press, New York, 1989.

Task analysis in the design of a human-computer interface for a ward based system

T. Frascina and R.A. Steele

Sheffield Hallam University, School of Computing and Management Sciences, 100 Napier St, Sheffield, S11 8HD, United Kingdom.

Tel 44 742 533101 / 44 742 533155
email t.frascina@uk.ac.shu / r.steele@uk.ac.shu

Abstract
This paper reports on the application of Task Analysis for Knowledge Descriptions (TAKD) to an area of ward activity, namely the requesting of pathology tests, leading to a design specification for the human-computer interface for a potential ward based computer system. It is argued that TAKD has been shown to be a powerful tool for the derivation of user interface requirements in a real world situation.

1. INTRODUCTION

A major drive in healthcare computing in recent years has been towards Hospital Information Support Systems (HISS), which often entail the integration of smaller existing information systems, with the hospital ward as the focus. The characteristics of the ward environment present particular challenges to designers [1], and the problem of how to determine the users' requirements is an acknowledged area of concern in HCI. The objective of the work reported here was to derive the requirements for the interface between the ward staff and a HISS by the application of *task analysis*. The analysis was applied to the activities of junior medical staff at the Northern General and Royal Hallamshire hospitals in Sheffield, concentrating on the completion of request forms. The aim was to produce a design specification for a human-computer interface for the ward doctors to request services from the haematology and clinical chemistry laboratories via computer systems to be based in the respective hospitals.

2. THE PROBLEM AREA

Doctors working on the wards request clinical tests from the pathology laboratories. Request forms are required to contain various demographic details about the patient, identification of the consultant, ward and requesting doctor. Test specific data is also included concerning the required investigation, specimen, and clinical details relating to the case. These data are required by the laboratories so that they can make an informed interpretation of the test results. The current problems are divided between two areas:
• For the doctor, the task is time consuming, involving the highly repetitive entry of data. There is a low skill requirement for the majority of the task, while highly specialised knowledge is needed for the selection of tests and inclusion of pertinent clinical details. Clinical details are perceived as extraneous to the request, because they are for the laboratories' use. Several forms have to be completed for many of the requests.

• For the laboratory staff, much time is spent in telephoning for missing details, while results may not go back to the correct ward or doctor because of inaccurate details on the forms. Often, tests destined for different labs are entered on the same form, so laboratory staff spend time making duplicates of request forms. Another frequent problem is that the clinical details may be absent, excessive or irrelevant.

3. THE METHODOLOGY

The analysis was performed using Task Analysis for Knowledge Descriptions (TAKD) [2], supported by the LUTAKD [3] toolkit*. Space precludes a full description of the methodology, though it may be useful to outline the main stages which were undertaken in the case study.

3.1. Data collection
• Semi structured interviews with doctors about the process of request form filling.
• Direct observation of form filling in situ. Fifty two forms were recorded in a general medical ward, and twenty seven in a specialist surgical ward.
• General observations made in a preliminary period providing essential domain knowledge.
• Extensive interviews with a range of laboratory staff concentrating on the use of the data on the request forms, essential to put the task analysis into context. These data were organised into an activity list which described the task, with each line of the list containing one specific task object.

3.2. Construction of the Task Description Hierarchy (TDH)
This is the principal analytical stage of TAKD. All available knowledge about the tasks is drawn upon to build a hierarchy of general and specific actions and objects. The nodes of the hierarchy represent actions and objects from general to specific, ending with the specific objects selected from the activity list attached to the lowest level nodes. It is the construction of the TDH that forces the analyst into thinking about the tasks in general and in detail, and into looking for underlying structure.

3.3. KRG sentence analysis
Each path from the highest level node of the TDH to the lowest, where the specific objects are attached, is described as a sentence written in a generic Knowledge Representation Grammar (KRG). Owing to the fact that each line of the activity list has a specific object, it means that the activity list is re-written in the form of KRG sentences. KRG sentences can be analysed at different levels of generality, so that different views of the task can be taken.

3.2. Outputs of the methodology
TAKD produces outputs of two distinct but equally valuable kinds. Firstly there are the 'formal' outputs, being the TDH and KRG sentences. These are tangible and measurable. They allow for descriptive reporting of the tasks analysed. Secondly, collaboration with the system users, and more particularly the construction of the TDH, produce insights into the task and task environment which contribute to the evolution of a framework both for the analysis and for the design.

---

* This has been developed as part of the TOM project. The TOM project (Task Orientated Modelling for Interactive System Design) is a collaboration between Logica, British Aerospace, University College London, Queen Mary and Westfield College, and the University of Liverpool. It is led by Logica Cambridge Ltd. and is funded under the DTI's Information Engineering Advanced Technology Program (Grant no. IED/4/1717).

4. RESULTS

This section, drawn from Frascina and Steele [4], neither makes reference to the formal TAKD terminology, nor gives the derived design specification, but rather summarises what the methodology was instrumental in revealing.

a) *The great majority of data on each form was not specific to the test, while three quarters of all data entries related to occasions when multiple forms were completed. This overhead of non test-specific data entry constituted the principal time consuming element of ordering tests.* Most of this should come from the system and should not be repeatedly entered once the doctor has identified the patient within the system.

b) *Requests for urea & electrolyte (U&E) reports and full blood counts (FBC), usually in combination, formed the great majority of the 'transactions' observed. Requesting multiple tests per patient was the norm, with up to four in a transaction.* The high frequency of occurrence of requests for FBCs and U&Es, both alone and in combination pointed to the need to have these as the principal permanent options in the interface. The selection of other tests was sufficiently infrequent to warrant their inclusion in a separate functional area. Entry of the specimen requested could be automated, because most investigations were associated with only one specimen type.

c) *The clinical details reported to the laboratories showed a degree of complexity: they comprised one or more statements about the patient's current condition, diagnosis or therapy, although queries and suggestions were made. Where there were multiple forms per transaction, there was always a degree of overlap between the details, but some types of detail remained distinct.* The analysis indicated that there was the potential to automate the entry of most of these details, which usually contained the principal diagnosis. The revelation by the analysis that multiple forms never had completely distinct clinical details was important, because it showed that where different laboratories were being given details, there was common data. The frequency with which the additional details involved the therapy that the patient was receiving suggested that there should be an option to include the current therapy on a request: this would most likely be a once only entry. Free text entry, while allowing latitude to the doctor in what is reported, is time consuming and can be minimised by incorporating the underlying task structure revealed by the analysis, although some would be necessary to permit queries and suggestions.

5. TAKD AS A MEANS OF PRODUCING A DESIGN SPECIFICATION

Task analysis does not provide the only means of producing a design specification. There is an abundance of systems analysis methodologies with this aim [5], and within the sphere of task analysis itself there are many approaches [6]. This discussion addresses two questions. Firstly, within the context of this work, how powerful is task analysis in the provision of a design specification? Secondly, is task analysis more widely applicable in the healthcare environment and beyond?

5.1. Power of task analysis

One could suggest that a design specification might easily have been derived from an informed but informal analysis of test requesting. We argue, however, that the task analysis has been crucial in coming to this point, and that the resulting design should be inherently more usable. It gives substantial justification for the inclusion of each item in the specification because of the process by which those items were selected. The data collection has necessitated a clear understanding of the place of pathology investigations in the overall job of the ward doctor.

The process of conducting the analysis has proved most revealing, in particular the construction of the TDH and its interpretation. This can be illustrated with two examples.

a) The first pass TDH took a single request form as the base unit for the task, with the completion of various data fields as sub-tasks. When the KRG sentences were being related back to the activity list, a flaw in the analysis became apparent. The frequent occurrence of clinical conditions in pairs on different forms, most usually with the combination of FBC and U&E, was not reflected in any way in the KRGs. It was thus realised that a different view should be taken, which was to take a *transaction* as the base unit, in which the requests are associated with the patient rather than the form. This refutes Benyon's assertion [7] that task analysis is device dependent, because the analysis led to a view of the task that went beyond the device used by the doctors (ie the *request form*), and had major implications for the resulting design specification.

b)   A property of the clinical details considered during TDH construction was the relationship between those spread across multiple forms. It was thought logically possible that there would be instances when the forms in a transaction would contain distinct clinical details. On completion of the TDH it was discovered that this was not the case. This could be because of an inadequate sample size, but the absence of such an occurrence over thirty two transactions indicates at the very least the rarity of such a case. Thus the process of producing the TDH was instrumental in a discovery of potential importance to the design. The analysis also revealed important information about task frequencies and was most useful in highlighting the very repetitious nature of many parts of the requesting process.

5.2. Wider applicability in the healthcare environment

TAKD has been most valuable in obtaining requirements which relate both to the general system (ie what should and should not be included in the request interface), and to interaction with the system (ie what properties the interface should have). It has underlined problems in the existing system: doctors emphasise the time consuming nature of making requests - the analysis has lead to a measurement of the extent of the unnecessary repetitions in the task. It has revealed patterns in those parts of the task that are unique but also considered non-essential by the doctors themselves. Its wider applicability was shown in that when a surgical ward was later analysed, construction of the TDH was a very straightforward matter, reflecting the similarity in task structure between the two wards, with only small adjustments needed to cope with detail. It is reasonable to suppose that such adjustments could be extended to cope with other requesting systems, such as microbiology, radiology etc, although further data collection would be needed to make the analysis appropriate. In principle, the methodology could be applied to a wide range of information based activities on the ward. Whilst there is no doubt that inexperienced people can be trained fairly quickly to perform TAKD, provided they have the assistance of the software toolkit, the acquisition of the domain knowledge essential to make the analysis effective is very time consuming. The application of TAKD requires considerable knowledge of the domain and the working environment. This is quite different from the reductionist systems analysis methodologies [5,8] which aim to describe and model data and data flows, and in doing so overlook the reasons why tasks are carried out as they are.

This work strongly supports a collaborative approach to the production of a design specification for the human-computer interface, combining the skills of the analyst with the knowledge of the clinician: the clinician brings domain expertise to the analysis, the analyst can be more detached and can provide guidance to maximise the effectiveness of the methodology. Medical informatics is necessarily a collaborative exercise. Rector *et al* [9] illustrate the need for and benefits of such collaboration with respect to the Pen and Pad [10] project, a fairly large scale enterprise seeking to apply user-centred methods in the development of a general practitioner's workstation. The research presented in this paper indicates that many of these benefits can accrue from much smaller scale projects than Pen and Pad, given the application of methodologies such as TAKD.

6. CONCLUSION

There is general acknowledgement that HCI has yet to have a significant impact in the non-academic world [11]. There is a need for the successful application of HCI techniques in real world environments. We believe that this case study makes a contribution to fulfilling such a need, whilst appreciating that the successful implementation and evaluation of the prototype interface currently being developed would make such a contribution considerably stronger.

7 . REFERENCES

[1]   Frascina T & Steele RA. The integration of hospital information systems through user centred design. In: *Medinfo 92. Proc 7th World Congress on Medical Informatics.* Lun KC, Degoulet P, Piemme TE & Rienhoff O (eds). Amsterdam: North Holland,1992:1274-1279.

[2]   Diaper D. Task Analysis for Knowledge Descriptions (TAKD): the method and an example. In:*Task Analysis for Human-Computer Interaction.* Diaper D (ed). Chichester: Ellis Horwood. 1989:108-158.

[3]   Diaper D. HCI'91 Tutorial Notes. Task Analysis for HCI. Unpublished material. 1991.

[4]   Frascina T & Steele RA. *The application of task analysis in the design of the human-computer interface for a ward-based system.* Sheffield Hallam University internal paper, 1992.

[5]   Avison DE & Fitzgerald G. *Information Systems Development: Methodologies, Techniques and Tools,* Blackwell Scientific Publications, 1988.

[6]   Wilson MD, Barnard PJ, Green TRG & Maclean A. Knowledge-based task analysis for human-computer systems. In: *Working with computers: theory versus outcome.*Van Der Veer GC, Green TRG, Hoc J & Murray DM (eds). London: Academic Press, 1988:47-87.

[7]   Benyon D. The role of task analysis in system design. *Interacting with computers* 1992,4(1):102-123.

[8]   NHS Information Management Centre. *Common Basic Specification. The generic model reference manual,* CBS001-1.0. Birmingham: NHS-IMC,1990.

[9]   Rector AL, Horan B, Nowlan WA et al. A developer's view of formative evaluation: or 'Users are always right...except when they're wrong.' In: *Current perspectives in Healthcare Computing 1992.* Richards B (ed). Weybridge: BJHC Books, 1992:99-106.

[10] Horan B, Rector AL, Sneath EL, et al. Supporting a humanly impossible task: the clinical human-computer environment. In:*Human-Computer Interaction - Proceedings of Interact '90.* Amsterdam:Elsevier Science, 1990:247-252.

[11] Earthy J. HCI, Where's the Practice ? In: *People and Computers VII*, Monk A, Diaper D & Harrison MD (eds). Cambridge University Press, 1992:477-479.

The Effect of Direction on Object-Oriented Cursor Control Actions

Joseph D. Chase[a] and Sherry Perdue Casali[b]

[a]Department of Computer Science, Virginia Polytechnic Institute and State University, Blacksburg, VA 24060

[b]Dept. of Industrial & Systems Engineering, Virginia Polytechnic Institute and State University, Blacksburg, VA 24060

Abstract

A number of past studies have compared user performance with a variety of cursor control devices. However, overall conclusions regarding the "best" cursor control device for a particular application are difficult to draw because the tasks used in previous comparisons have differed greatly from one another and have not necessarily included all of the factors affecting performance. One factor that has not received much attention is that of direction of cursor movement. The purpose of the portion of the present study reported herein was to determine if direction of cursor movement significantly effects target acquisition time with various input devices. A significant direction main effect as well as a number of interactions involving direction were found; with some conditions resulting in substantially degraded user performance. The results suggest that interface developers should consider the effects of direction of movement on user performance and design accordingly where rapid target acquisition is essential. These results also suggest that future empirical evaluations and comparisons of pointing devices should consider the inclusion of a direction component.

1. BACKGROUND

A number of past studies in the human factors literature have compared the performance of various cursor control devices, typically on some type of simple target acquisition task. Overall conclusions regarding the "best" cursor control device for a particular application are difficult to draw because the tasks used in these comparisons have differed significantly from one another and have not necessarily included all of the factors affecting performance. One factor that has been treated inconsistently in past studies is that of the direction of cursor movement. Some studies have used only a one dimensional task (e.g., MacKenzie, Sellen, and Buxton, 1991), others have randomly placed the targets in terms of direction (e.g., Card, English, and Burr, 1978; Epps, 1986; Goodwin, 1975; Sperling and Tullis, 1988), while still other studies have not explicitly reported how the direction of cursor of movement was taken into account (Albert, 1982; Mehr and Mehr, 1972). It is difficult to speculate whether the different approaches to handling movement direction might account for at least a portion of the variability in results found in these previous studies because we do not know whether/how direction of movement affects cursor control device performance. The purpose of the portion of the present study described herein was to determine if direction of cursor movement significantly effects task performance with each of a number of different input devices. The results should indicate whether direction should be included as an independent variable in future device comparisons. This is an important question to answer given the significant increase in testing time necessary to incorporate the factor of direction, and the need in most cases to maintain the most efficient data collection procedures possible. In addition, the results will indicate if particular movement directions should be avoided in software interface design when target acquisition time is critical.

2. METHOD

2.1. Subjects

Twelve subjects, six males and six females from the university community volunteered to participate in this study and were compensated for their time. Each was required to have no previous experience in operating a mouse or a trackball.

2.2. Experimental Apparatus

A Macintosh SE was used to present the computer-based tasks and to record time and error data. Specially developed programs running under HyperCard were developed and used. Three cursor control devices, the Macintosh SE expanded keyboard directional cursor keys, the standard Macintosh one button mouse, and a Kensington Turbomouse trackball, were used to perform the experimental task. For each device, the control/display ratio setting was selected according to the manufacturer's recommendations. The display consisted of a standard Macintosh SE 9 inch diagonal black and white display.

2.3. Experimental Procedures

The target acquisition task required the subject to move the cursor from a target area labeled "start" to a second target using the cursor control device, and then to confirm the selection by pressing or releasing the select key associated with the input device. Each target was square in shape. Target size (TS) had four levels: 0.27, 0.54, 1.07, and 2.14 cm side. Target distance (TD) had three levels: 2, 4, and 8 cm. These target/distances are representative of the range typically encountered in many graphics and word processing task environments within the hardware constraints of the system utilized in this study. Selection mode (M) contained two levels, 'point and click' and 'drag'. Finally, eight directions (DIR), corresponding to the four primary axial directions and the four 45 degree off-axis directions, were investigated. Each variable was treated as a within-subjects variable, hence a five-way (Device x Target Size x Target Distance x Mode x Direction) within subject factorial design was used for data collection.

Prior to actual data collection with a given device, each subject first performed 60 practice trials chosen at random from the 192 possible combinations (4 TS x 3 TD x 2 MD x 8 DIR). Ninety-six trials (4 TS x 3 TD x 8 DIR) were then performed in each of the two selection modes, with each of the three devices. Presentation order of the three devices was balanced across subjects using a Latin Square design, and presentation order of the 96 trials for each mode with each device was randomized. The dependent measure was target acquisition time, collected automatically in hundredths of a second using the timing features of HyperCard.

3. RESULTS

An ANOVA indicated all five main effects to be significant. As in previous studies, the mouse and the trackball resulted in similar performance to one another while the cursor keys resulted in significantly slower performance. Again, as in previous studies, all four levels of target size and all three levels of target distance resulted in significantly different performance from one another, with performance improving as target size increased and target distance decreased. Also as expected, the drag moves required more time to complete than the point and click moves. These results are discussed in detail in Chase and Casali (1991).

Particular to this analysis, both the Direction main effect and several interactions involving Direction were found to be significant. Table 1 shows the results of the post-hoc tests on the significant Direction main effect. The Device x Direction interaction was also shown to be significant, and surprisingly, all of that significance was found to lie with the cursor keys (see Figure 1). The cause for this effect is unclear in that the eight cursor keys corresponded directly to each of the eight required directions of movement; therefore, very similar movements on the part of the user were required to move in any of the eight directions tested. If any direction effect was to be found, it was suspected that it might occur with the mouse which, due to its nature of operation, may favor a left-to-right or eastward direction, similar to a traditional writing pattern. However, such was not the case.

The Target Size x Direction and Target Distance x Direction interactions were also found to be significant (see Figures 2 and 3). While the complexity of these graphs leave the interaction somewhat unclear, it is important to note that in both cases the combination of the more difficult target size or target distance with the most difficult direction (NW) resulted in substantially inferior performance. However, since virtually all of the variability due to direction was limited to the cursor keys, and other analyses on the data (reported elsewhere) show that the cursor keys were also much more sensitive to changes in target size and target distance than the other devices, one would suspect that these interactions would be limited to the cursor keys as well. And, in fact, the three-way interactions of Device x Target Size x Direction and Device x Target Distance x Direction were found to be significant and the majority of the interaction is limited to the cursor keys. As would be expected, the combination of the slower device (cursor keys) with the more difficult direction (NW) and the more difficult size or the more difficult distance produced measurably inferior results.

Table 1. Student-Newman-Keuls Test for the Direction Main Effect (means with the same letter are not significantly different at p<0.05).

Direction	Mean time (sec.)				
NW	1.882	A			
NE	1.764	A	B		
SW	1.718		B	C	
SE	1.699		B	C	
W	1.602			C	D
S	1.572			C	D
N	1.571			C	D
E	1.446				D

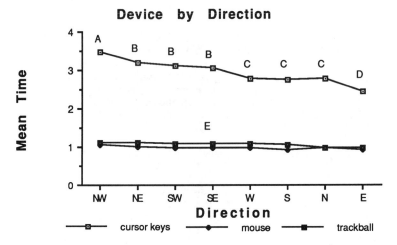

Figure 1. Device x direction interaction (means with the same letter are not significantly different at p<0.05).

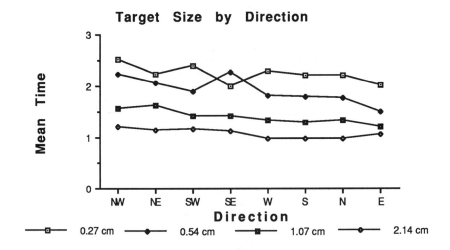

Figure 2. Target size by direction interaction.

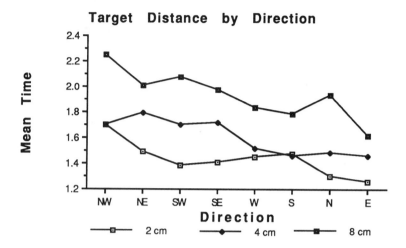

Figure 3. Target distance x direction interaction.

4. CONCLUSIONS

These results suggest that direction significantly affects performance with some cursor control devices but not with others. Because there are no strong theoretical bases for these results, it is not possible to predict how other devices may be affected by the direction of cursor movement. In addition, because some user populations such as those with physical disabilities may experience greater difficulty with particular movement patterns, direction of cursor movement may have a more significant effect for special populations of computer users than was found here. Essentially, these results raise more questions than answers, raising the issue that direction of cursor movement does impact user performance in at least some circumstances. Additional research is needed to refine our knowledge regarding the extent and magnitude of its impact. Such information should impact the design of interfaces where rapid target acquisition is essential. Even without further knowledge, the results of this particular study suggest that empirical evaluations and comparisons of pointing devices should consider the inclusion of a direction component.

5. REFERENCES

Albert, A. (1982). The effect of graphic input devices on performance in a cursor positioning task. In *Proceedings of the Human Factors Society 26th Annual Meeting*, 54-58. Human Factor Society: Santa Monica, CA.

Card, S. K., English, W.K., and Burr, B. (1978). Evaluation of mouse, rate-controlled isometric joystick, step keys, and text keys for text selection on a CRT. *Ergonomics*, 21(8), 601-613.

Chase, J.D., and Casali, S. P. (1991). A comparison of three cursor control devices on an extended target acqusition ask (Technical Report HCL-91-101). Blacksburg, Virginia: Virginia Polytechnic Institute and State University, Human Computer Laboratory.

Epps, B. (1986). Comparison of six cursor control devices based on Fitts' law models. In *Proceedings of the Human Factors Society 30th Annual Meeting*, 327-331. Human Factor Society: Santa Monica, CA.

Goodwin, N. (1975). Cursor positioning on an electronic display using lightpen, lightgun, or keyboard for three basic tasks. *Human Factors*, 17(3), 289-295.

MacKenzie, I.S., Sellen, A., and Buxton, W. (1991). A comparison of input devices in elemental pointing and dragging tasks. In *Proceedings of the CHI '91 Conference on Human Factors in Computing Systems*, 161-166. New York, ACM.

Mehr, M. H. and Mehr, E. (1972). Manual digital positioning in 2 axes; a comparison of joystick and trackball controls. In *Proceedings of the Human Factors Society 16th Annual Meeting*, 110-116. Human Factor Society: Santa Monica, CA.

Sperling, B. B., and Tullis, T.S. (1988). Are you a better "mouser" or "trackballer"? A comparison of cursor-positioning performance. *SIGCHI Bulletin*, 19(3), 77-81.

II. Software Tools

238

CoDesk - an Interface to TheKnowledgeNet

Konrad Tollmar

Computer Science Department, Interaction and Presentation Laboratory, The Royal Institute of Technology, S-100 44 Stockholm
konrad@nada.kth.se

Abstract

The Collaborative Desktop, CoDesk, consists of a set of generic tools for CSCW, Computer Supported Cooperative Work. CoDesk is an attempt to make collaboration a natural part of the daily use of a computer. Our way to achieve this is to put the user in the centre of the computing in a similar way that applications and documents are defined and visualized in the Apple Macintosh Finder metaphor of the daily-work desktop.

TheKnowledgeNet is a vision of a system for collaboration in teams where the members have access to a common base of information, including knowledge about who-knows-what. The design of CoDesk is based on its function as an interface to TheKnowledgeNet.

Basic principles in the CoDesk interface are object orientation, direct manipulation, a structured room metaphor, generic communication and co-editing tools.

Keywords: Computer Supported Cooperative Work - CSCW, User-centered design, Distributed systems, Multimedia communication

1.0 Introduction

As part of the Computer Supported Cooperative Work, CSCW, project within the Swedish research program MultiG [PGP92] a set of prototypes of environments for distributed collaborative design has been developed. They are referred to as the Collaborative Desktop, CoDesk, and TheKnowledgeNet and are developed to validate certain ideas for the design of a CSCW environment based on a broadband communication network.

This paper describes the new metaphors used for the interface. These metaphors are based on the results of the earlier prototypes and attempts to explore the usability of a generic shell for CSCW. In two reports, one video and one prototype we have analysed collaboration in design and specified some general functional requirements and interface design principles on CSCW support in a distributed design environment [MSP91] [RA92] [AEM+92]. The results are summarized in terms of a set of general requirements that a distributed environment should support: informal collaboration, sharing and record keeping of design information, sharing of background knowledge, presentations of ideas, strategies reducing the need for co-working and vice versa tool that support co-working.

Instead of design groupware based on some analysis of the design task or collaboration task to be fulfilled, we propose, like other researchers [MA90] [BR91] the design of generic collaborative tools. We use a tool-oriented approach, as, e.g., in [BEK+87] and [EK84], which aims at designing an user controlled environment that facilitates for the users to do what they want, without any limitations and assumptions imposed by the system.

TheKnowledgeNet aims at making individual mental knowledge public in the same way as libraries make documented knowledge public. The information overload in the society today is usually solved by using other people as reference rather than excessive reading of documents [CKI88]. TheKnowledgeNet aims at supporting this process and can be viewed as a distributed "library" of documents and undocumented mental individual knowledge that is made available to all group members by communication and thus supports information sharing and knowledge integration. A similar vision for large scale cooperation has been pro- posed by Engelbart [Eng90].

The Collaborative Desktop, the interface to TheKnowledgeNet, models a generic shell for CSCW by present a true directly manipulated graphical user interface. CoDesk strives to support the user with: a more seamless integration of synchronous and asynchronous modes of interaction, a social ad-hoc communication to complete more formal and planned work processes and ability to determine and control who is communicating with who at a given time

2.0 The Collaborative Desktop – CoDesk

The CoDesk, Collaborative Desktop, tries to integrate the essence in communication and collaboration via different media and tools such as text, graphics, shared windows, sound and video. The members are the prime objects in a window based direct manipulative interface, in which the members can form their collaboration environments based on a room metaphor. In this context the room metaphor is chosen to decrease the social and physical distance between the members of the cooperating groups.

2.1 User, Groups and Rooms

The most central object in CoDesk is the individual persons, members, represented both as icons and as forms (e.g. "cards") with attributes, including name, mailing per communication lists and TheKnowledgeNet who-knows-what information.

Groups are collections of persons and/or (recursively) groups, which give an hierarchical graph structure lattice. Each member is connected to a key group that can be viewed as the default group that a member is interconnected with.

We, like other researchers [BT91][Con90], have chosen a room metaphor, where rooms are used to represent the collaborating group. We are also exploring the role of rooms in supporting 'social browsing' like in Cruiser [Root88] by invitations to communicate when group members are in the same room where one can observe allowed "disturbance level" of group members. The most common way to communicate with some members will be to install a common room with some tools and working material, e.g., documents, specific for that group. To support-

temporary connections with other group members is also by getting a temporary room automatically installed by for example a direct phone call to an user.

2.2 Documents, Tools and Folders

As found by Reder and Schwab [RS90] work behaviour is characterized by multitasking, and many activities and interactions are structured into communication chains that criss-cross each other. This means that tools for collaboration should allow and support many nagging collaborative activities at the same time, an user can jump from one activity to another, "sleeping" activities that will be continued later on, etc. One an of the key issues to consider is therefore inter-transferring of data between different tools. We have divided CSCW tools into two categories, "pure" communication tools and tools which one can collaborate with, "edit", some common material.

Our basic set of communication tools that we so fare have included contains of a VideoPhone for multi-person video and speech communication, "degradable" to a telephone for sound only and a textphone for text window communication, a Mailtool for handling mail and bulletin boards and a generic tool, SharedWindow, that enable any kind of tool to be encapsulated and shared trough common views.

A common task for which collaboration through computer is very suited is writing text, designing graphics, sound or video together. Here the collaborations are mediated through the "material", documents, one works with. As stated in [BS92] to design CSCW system from the viewpoint of a common information space could be very valuable and useful. Simple, generic, tools for co-editing of these materials, one at a time as well as in combination, are needed. A couple of generic multi-user tools, drawing and text editing, have been developed within MultiG. Specific tools, facilitating administration of the collaboration process, are also interesting. The development of new and more advanced multi-user tools are one area that we will focus our attention to in the forthcoming development of CoDesk.

The ability to adopt different kinds of tools has been proven [Grun88] to be the main key in successfull CSCW system and has therefore also been one of our major goals. Because of that we would therefore like to stress that it has been a system design methodology that above mentioned and selected tools each has put various technical demands to achieve such a high flexibility as possible. We believe that our architecture [AEM+92] make it possible to integrate a large amount of ordinary single user tools into the Collaborative Desktop.

The folder object gives a simple and convenient container fo sorting and organizing documents. Folders are collections of documents and/or folders (recursively), which gives a hierarchical graph similar to groups.

3.0 The Graphical User Interface

We believe that the graphical user interface needs to be very simple due to the complex environment the users need to handle. Our idea is to rely on a couple of well known artifacts and extend them in a reasonable way. We have therefore designed CoDesk to fit in a standard Graphical User Interface, GUI, by using a normal window system, like Open Look or Motif.

3.1 Window system

The window system is the first thing an user sees when entering the most commonly used GUI systems, e.g., Mac, Windows and Open Look. Most, not all, of these systems do also define a Desktop layer, with some desktop tools. What is important to understand is that a system like CoDesk extend this with an additional layer, the network layer. That layer gives access to remote and shared data, communication and access control. This puts a cognitive load at the user that need to be reduced by a simple and easy to learn Desktop layer.

3.2 CoDesk GUI Model

As mentioned earlier our idea is to rely on a couple of well known artifacts and extend them in a reasonable way. As stated in our name - CoDesk - we have taken grants from the traditional desktop metaphor and have tried to extend it with a dual relation for members, groups and rooms.

FIGURE 1. CoDesk Iconbased User Interface

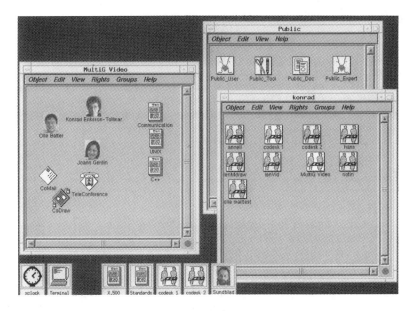

The idea is to enable sharing your local desktop meaning sharing your working material and tools. This will be possible by structure the members into groups and forming rooms in which members, groups, working materials and tools can be collected. Thus, the users can configure the "desktop" according to their needs of collaboration.

The interface to CoDesk is a directly manipulated pictorial (graphical) user interface, see figure 1, in which it is possible to organize and view structures and the basic objects: members, groups, rooms, documents, folders and tools. All objects that can be manipulated with drag-and-drop actions and by suitable tools, e.g., drop an user on the telephone to connect a phonecall to him or drop a tool into a room to install that tool to be used and shared within that room.

To simplify the use of these different kind of objects we have defined a dual relationship between CoDesk objects and the traditional [APPL87][OPEN89] desktop objects: documents, tools and folders. This means that in our CoDesk system that an user's syntax is similar to documents, rooms to tools and groups to folders. Straightforward has the graphical layout of these objects the form [Aaron82] of a rectangle, vertical square root of 2, for stability; a diamond for movement and tension; a horizontal golden rectangle for permanence.

With direct manipulation capabilities graphical user-interfaces can often be made very powerful and simple to use [Shn82]. But a necessary condition to enable direct manipulation is that you see what you get. In a distributed environment it is of outmost importance that people using the system will experience the same thing. Therefore the term related to direct manipulation WYSIWYG (What-You-See-Is-What-You-Get), has been extended in this domain to WYSIWIS (What-You-See-Is-What-I-See). As stated earlier, are two of the keys to successfully CSCW system are openness and tailarbility. In CoDesk we are trying to achieve this by strongly emphasising that the object oriented and direct manipulative approach should be supported not only in the interface to the generic collaborative tools but especially in the interface to external application.

As mentioned earlier an important part in supporting cooperative work is to handle shared working resources. Users of shared resources need to be aware of the presence of other users and their access to shared objects. This cooperative awareness and 'social browsing' [FKC90] can be provided in the graphical user interface by different forms of highlighting objects. So far we have defined 3 generic forms of awareness, active open - locked, notify and per defaults passive. An active object indicates that it is used, e.g., a that has logged in to the CoDesk, those resources has the option of being opened or locked, e.g., an active user with no disturbance level. An object can also be notified, this provides a mechanism to trigger colleague's attention to certain objects. A notified object expires after a certain time and become a normal passive object.

3.3 Screen design

One of the most spares resources on todays workstations is screen space. One of the main reasons for that is the poorly aspect's ratio found in most display systems [Aaron92], another is the almost impossible mission todo personal configuration of some window systems (e.g. Motif). A small but rather effective way to overcome to some extent the first problem is to allow the user to tailor her screen environment, the desk, by keeping track of all objects position and allocation to be able to restore them the next time the user starts the system. In CoDesk it is also possible to define in a preference file what and were to put an users default objects on screen.

4.0 Conclusion and future work

We have described The Collaborative Desktop which is an attempt to be a generic shell for CSCW application and system. We believe that the design of a desktop CoDesk, direct manipulation; consistent look-and feel; mixture of old well-known metaphors with new ones; advanced communication tools, gives a powerful environment and leads to simplification of simple operations and powerful expressions of more complex operations. In conclusion, we believe that the increasingly popular "room metaphor" is appropriate to the design of collaborative system.

Our next step in the evaluation of CoDesk is to perform real user studies. This will mainly be done at a high-tech R&D company, Ellemtel (a part of Ericsson). We have found that ordinary prototyping and system development procedures are very hard to do for CSCW system [Sørg87]. The evaluation has therefore been divided into two phases where the first one, how collaboration in a traditional and narrow banded environment takes place, is almost done, partly in [MSP91], with questionnaires and interviews. In the beginning of the summer the second phase will start with "real" use of CoDesk in this environment.

5.0 References

[Aaron82] Arron M, Corporate Identity for Iconic Interface Design: The Graphic Design Perspective, IEEE Computer Graphics and Application 4, no. 7, Dec. 1982 pp. 24ff. [Aaron92] Arron M, Graphic Design for Electronic Documents and User Interface, Tutorial Series – ACM Press 1992. [AEM+] Avatare A, Eriksson H, Marmolin H, Sundblad Y, Tollmar K, The Collaborative Desktop – Design and Implementation, Proceedings of the 4th MultiG Workshop, Electrum, Stockholm May 1992 [APPL] Apple Computer Inc., Human Interface Guidelines: The Apple Desktop Interface, Addison-Welsey, Reading, MA 1987, [BR91] Bannon L, Robinson M.: "Questioning Representation", Proceedings of ESCW´1991. [BS92] Bannon L, Schmidt K, Taking CSCW seriusly, Computer Supported Cooperative Work Journal, Vol. 1, No. 1-2, Kluwer Academic Publishers 1992. [BEK+87] Bødker S, Ehn P, Kammersgaard J, Kyng M, Sundblad Y: "A Utopian Experience", Proceedings of the Aarhus Conference on Computers and Democracy, 1987. [BT91] Borning A, Travers M: "Two Approaches to Casual Interaction over Computer and Video Networks", In Proceedings of CHI91, pp. 13-19,May 1991. [Con90] Condon C.: "Networked Cooperative Work", Proceedings Telematik Workshop, BIBA, University of Bremen, Dec. 1990. [CKI88] Curtis B, Krasner H, and Iscoe N.(1988): "A field study of the software design process for large systems". CACM, Vol. 31, no. 11, Nov. 1988. [EK84] Ehn P, Kyng M:"A tool perspective on design of interactive computer support for skilled workers", Proceedings of the 7th Scandinavia Conference on System Engineering. [Eng90] Engelbart D.: "Knowledge-domain interoperability and an open hyperdocument system", Proceedings of CSCW'90, Oct. 1990. [FKC90] Fish, R. S., Kraut, R. E., & Chalfonte, B. L. The VideoWindow system in informal communications, Proceedings of CSCW'90, (pp. 1-11), Oct. 1990. [Grud88] Grudin J., Why CSCW Application fail: Problems in the design and evaluation of Organizational Interface, Proceedings of CSCW 88. [Marm91] Marmolin et al., The Collaborative Desktop, Video 12min, IPLab, NADA, Sept. 1991. [MSP91] Marmolin H, Sundblad Y, Pehrson B: Analysis of Design and Collaboration in a Distributed Design Environment, Proceedings of EC-SCW'91, Sept. 1991. [MA90] Moran T, Andersson R: "The Workaday World as a Paradigm for CSCW Design", Proceedings of CSCW'90, Oct. 1990. [OPEN89] Open software Foundation, OSF/ MOTIF™ Style Guide, Cambridge MA 1989. [PGP92] Pehrson B., Gunningberg P., Pink S., MultiG – A research Program on Distributed MultiMedia applications and Gigabit Network, IEEE Network Magasine, Jan 1992. [RA91] Ropa A, Ahlström B: "The Video Viewer, Interface design example for video communication in a CSCW environment". Video presentation at CHI92. [Root88] Root R., Design of a Multi-Media Vehicle for social browsing, Proceedings of CSCW 88. [RS89] Reder S, Schwab K, The temporal structure of cooperative activity, Proceedings of CSCW'90, Oct. 1990. [Shn82] Shneiderman B, The future of interactive system and that emergence of direct manipulation, Behaviour and Information Technology 1, pp. 237-256, 1982.[Sørg87] Sørgard P, A Cooperative Work Perspective on Use and Development of Computer Artfacts, 10th Information System Research Seminar in Scandinavia, Finland 1987.

The Software Architecture of DIGIS

Hans de Bruin and Peter Bouwman

Computer Science Department (H4-25), Erasmus University Rotterdam,
P.O. Box 1738, 3000 DR Rotterdam, The Netherlands
e-mail: {debruin,bouwman}@cs.few.eur.nl

Abstract

The graphical UI design environment DIGIS facilitates designers to specify all aspects of UI design, including presentation and layout constraints, dynamic behavior, and coupling the UI with the (existing) application, with direct manipulation techniques. The software architecture of the interactive systems constructed with DIGIS is based on a multi-agent interaction model, and is to a large extent automatically generated from a formal domain application model which describes the application from the UI perspective.

1 Introduction

DIGIS (Direct Interactive Generation of Interactive Systems) [1] is a graphical UI design environment targeted to designers knowledgeable in cognitive ergonomics, who have an appreciation of programming but are not necessarily experts in this area. In contrast to most user interface design systems, DIGIS is a complete environment, supporting the three aspects of UI design:

- the presentation of the UI: the specification of the static graphical layout of interaction tools, including geometric constraints.

- the scenarios of the UI: the specification of the dynamic behavior (dialogue control).

- the coupling of the UI to the target application.

All these aspects are specified with *direct manipulation* techniques, without requiring any programming effort. DIGIS is aimed to be a rapid design environment with no limitations on the type of user interfaces that can be constructed, including multi-media, although the current version is restricted to $2\frac{1}{2}$D GUIs.

This paper presents the software architecture of DIGIS which is used for constructing the UI for a given domain application. The architecture is a refinement of the PAC model [2], incorporating a system task model and the domain application being modeled in an object-oriented way.

The development of an interactive system should start with a task analysis. A tasks analysis results in a thorough knowledge of the domain and the set of goals and sub-goals which can be achieved when using the interactive system [3]. A promising way to analyze the domain is by applying an object-oriented analysis methodology that identifies the objects, the relations between the objects, and the dynamic behavior of the objects. The required functionality of the domain application is derived from the set of goals and sub-goals. The way these goals are to be achieved can be reflected in a hierarchically organized system task model.

The results of a task analysis and system analysis are formalized in a Domain Application Model (DAM). A DAM captures the semantics of the domain application from the UI perspective at a high conceptual level, and provides the basis for implementing high quality user interfaces that support undo-redo, semantic feedback and context-sensitive help. The software architecture for an interactive system is to a large extent generated from a DAM. The user of DIGIS can start from this foundation and tackle the creative aspects of UI design: the specification of the presentation and the scenarios with direct manipulation techniques.

2 Domain Application Model

A DAM formally describes the goals that can be achieved in the domain application and how these goals are to be achieved from the UI point of view. It consists of two models, an Object Relationship and Access Model, describing the objects and the relationships between the objects, and a System Task Model, describing the tasks that can be performed in the domain application in order to achieve goals. A DAM for a particular domain application can be derived from the models obtained with the application of an object-oriented system analysis method (e.g., [4, 5]). These object-oriented models capture the internals of a system, that is, object properties, relationships, behavior, etc. A DAM provides an external view of the domain application, concentrating on what can be done in the domain rather than on how it is done.

2.1 Object Access and Relationship Model

An Object Access and Relationship Model (ORAM) provides the UI with an idealized object-oriented view of the domain application. It identifies the relevant objects for the UI, their attributes, the relationships with other objects, and their dynamic properties. An ORAM consists of two parts: a structure part, describing the relationships, and an object definition part. Three relationship types are used to specify the structure of the domain application:

- specialization (or generalization), the *Is-A* relation;

- aggregation, the *Is-Part-Of* relation;

- association, the *Is-Related-With* relation.

An object is defined by its attributes and its access protocol. The access protocol of an object captures the dynamics of a domain application at the object level, that is, when and how to invoke the actions of an object. A protocol is specified by means of augmented regular expressions over object actions (cf. [6]). A protocol expression is constructed with 4 operators: guard (:), repetition (∗), sequence (;), and selection (+) (in decreasing precedence). The semantics of protocol expressions are summarized in Table 1.

E + F	*selection*	E or F is selected
E ; F	*sequence*	E is followed by F
E ∗	*repetition*	Zero or more times E
φ : E	*guard*	E only if φ is true

Table 1: semantics of protocol expressions

For instance, a simplified access protocol for a *File* object can be specified as follows:

$$File\ access\ protocol = open\ ;\ (read + write)*\ ;\ close$$

This protocol states that a file must first be opened before data can be read from or written to the file. After an arbitrary number of read or write actions, the file is closed by invoking the close action.

2.2 System Task Model

The hierarchically organized System Task Model (STM) describes the tasks for achieving goals in the domain application. The achievement of a goal can be defined in this context as changing the state of the domain application. It is said that a task is executed in order to achieve a goal. Tasks may be decomposed in sub-tasks, and the execution of a sub-task results in the achievement of a sub-goal (see Figure 1).

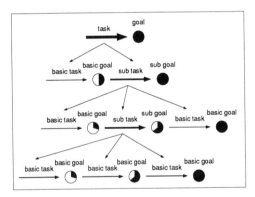

Figure 1: tasks and goals

The simplest tasks in a STM are the elementary basic tasks. They describe the most basic, indivisible yet meaningful operations on the domain application. The basic tasks are defined in terms of objects and actions defined in an ORAM, and are therefore capable of changing the state of the domain application, that is, the achievement of an elementary goal. Higher level tasks are specified with augmented regular expressions over lower level tasks, using the same regular expressions operators as used in the definition of the access protocol of an object. Tasks can take input arguments and may yield a result. A sub-task in a task definition may be protected by a guard, specifying the enabling conditions for executing the sub-task.

A task definition of an Automatic Teller Machine (ATM) is used to illustrate system task modeling. An ATM allows clients to withdraw cash from their account. Each client has a credit card, and a pin-code is associated with the card for identification purposes. A simplified transaction task (lacking the specification of the task arguments) can be defined as follows:

```
task transaction =
    enter_card_data ;
    enter_pin_code ∗ ;
    (
        cancel_transaction
        +
        ( enter_amount ∗  +  cancel_transaction )
    )
```

The transaction task is here defined in terms of basic tasks which act upon the domain application, the teller machine objects. A typical transaction with the ATM consists of entering the credit card data, followed by entering the pin-code, and finally entering the amount of cash to withdraw. The transaction can be cancelled at any time.

3 Software Architecture

The software architecture, i.e., the implementation or runtime model, of interactive systems constructed with DIGIS is based on the PAC model [2]. A PAC consists of three parts: Presentation, defining the input-output behavior, Abstraction, implementing the functional core (domain application), and Control, responsible for dialogue control and maintaining the consistency between the Presentation and the Abstraction. The PAC model is a multi-agent model. It allows PACs to be recursively decomposed in a hierarchy of PACs comprising a complete interactive system (see Figure 2).

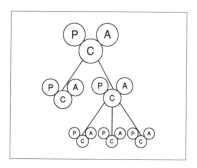

Figure 2: PAC model

Our variant of the PAC model, called the D(IGIS)-PAC model, differs in many respects. The functional core of a PAC, the domain application, is being modeled in a DAM as a set of cooperating objects. Each object in the domain application represents a single concept, and is associated with a D-PAC agent. The D-PAC agents are related with each other according to the object relationships defined in an ORAM. Due to the association relationships that can exist between the domain objects, the D-PACs form a graph. These graph structured D-PACs should not be confused with the hierarchically organized PACs in the original PAC model. If we zoom in on a PAC, a graph of D-PACs is revealed (see Figure 3).

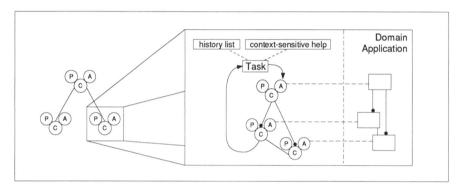

Figure 3: zooming in on a PAC reveals a D-PAC graph

The A components of a D-PAC now act as domain application object interfaces, assuring an idealized object-oriented view of the domain application, even though the domain application need not be implemented in an object-oriented way. The A components are automatically generated from the object definitions specified in an ORAM.

The C components of a D-PAC are responsible for maintaining the consistency between the domain application and the P components, and for implementing the dialogue control within the UI. The lexical tokens (events) generated by the P components are interpreted by the controllers. If an end-user interaction should result in semantical actions, the dialogue controllers execute and control the appropriate system tasks defined in a STM, either basic tasks or higher level tasks crafted on top of the basic tasks. The dialogue controller assures that all parameters required for executing the task are present. The execution of a higher level task can be regarded as a form of internal control, the dialogue controllers are temporary in charge and assure that the end-user sticks to the patterns defined in the task. A higher level task can be defined in such a way that during the execution a choice has to be made, i.e., the repetition (∗) or alternation (+) regular expression operators have been used to define the task. For instance, in the ATM example, at one point in the dialogue it possible to enter the amount of cash or to cancel the transaction. A dialogue controller controls these choices, either by interrogating other dialogue controllers or by requesting the end-user how to proceed.

The basic tasks operate on the A components and are therefore capable of changing the state of the domain application directly. A basic task is implemented as an object and supports, if possible, besides a *do* action, an *undo* action for reverting the effects of the *do* action. A global undo-redo mechanism is provided by recording the sequence of basic tasks in a history list. Undoing means stepping back in the history list and invoking the *undo* actions of the encountered basic tasks, while redoing means stepping forward in the history list.

The D-PAC model is a multi-agent model and supports multi-threaded dialogues. A thread is defined in this context as a sequence of basic tasks which match a regular expression describing a task. When the end-user, by performing some interaction with the system, implicitly executes a task, the active threads are considered. If the new task matches a thread, it is added to the thread. If no such thread can be found, a new one is started. The combination of keeping track of the active threads, and the definition of legal threads in the form of regular expressions defining the tasks, provides the basis for context-sensitive help and guidance. By looking at the steps already taken, the set of legal task continuations can be determined. This set can be used to infer the higher level goals the end-user is trying to accomplish and can be presented in some form to the end-user to provide context-sensitive help. Alternatively, the end-user can select a high level goal, and be guided step by step to achieve this goal.

The system tasks, the undo-redo mechanism, and the basic system for implementing context-sensitive help are automatically generated from a STM.

4   Conclusion

The software architecture of DIGIS has been successfully exercised in several pilot projects and is used in DIGIS, which is an interactive system itself. We feel confident that the architecture can be applied to a wide range of interactive systems. Substantial parts of an interactive system are automatically generated from a formal Domain Application Model, which models the domain application from the UI perspective, and provides a strong foundation for implementing high quality user interfaces.

References

[1] J. van den Bos and C. Laffra, "Project DIGIS, Building Interactive Applications by Direct Manipulation", *Computer Graphics Forum* (9), North-Holland, pp. 181-193, (1990).

[2] J. Coutaz, "Architecture Models for Interactive Software", *ECOOP Conference Proceedings*, pp. 383-399, (1989).

[3] P. Johnson, "Human-Computer Interaction; Psychology, Task Analysis and Software Engineering", McGraw-Hill, (1992).

[4] P. Coad and E. Yourdon, "OOA: Object-Oriented Analysis (2nd Ed.)", Prentice-Hall, (1991).

[5] James Rumbaugh, Michael Blaha, William Premerlani, Frederick Eddy and William Lorensen, "Object-Oriented Modeling and Design", Prentice-Hall, (1991).

[6] J. van den Bos and C. Laffra, "Procol; A Concurrent Object Language with Protocols, Delegation and Persistence", *Acta Informatica* (28), pp. 511-538, (1991).

Cooperative Musical Partner System: JASPER (Jam Session Partner)

Hirokazu KATO*, Sanae WAKE** and Seiji INOKUCHI*

* Dept. of Systems Engineering, Faculty of Engineering Science, Osaka University, Toyonaka, Osaka 560, Japan

**KANSAI C&C Research Laboratory, NEC Corporation, 4-24, Shiromi, 1-Chome, Chuo-ku, Osaka 540, Japan

Abstract

JASPER (Jam Session Partner) , a cooperative musical partner system is proposed in this paper. JASPER performs improvisation with a human musician and enjoys its performance. The purpose of our research is to realize communication including subjective information such as emotion between human and computer. We construct a performer model in computer which simulates a human improvising process such as [listen -> feel -> perform].

The performance style of JASPER is jam session. In jam session, it is very easy for performers to represent their emotion or intention and to communicate with each other through their performance. Performers represent uprush or depression of emotion in a performance. This system copes with such emotive variety as parameters named Tension Parameter.

In experiments, we could get impressions that users could enjoy a jam session very much. Also most of them were much interested in possibilities of this system as a new style of uses of computer. We could find out the possibilities of cooperative works and communication including subjective information such as emotion between human and computer in this system.

1. INTRODUCTION

Recently many computers have spread over our life. Applicable fields of them are also very wide. Currently, however, computers are used as 'tools' which aid human work. We are convinced that computers will be able to become human 'partner'.

In this paper we propose a cooperative musical partner system named JASPER (Jam Session Partner). This system is a kind of automatic music playing system. Most existing systems perform monotonously musical data given beforehand, but this system doesn't. JASPER performs improvisation with human musician and enjoys its performance.

There are some studies of cooperative musical system. Morita developed a computer music system that follows a human conductor by using data-gloves [1].

Vercoe developed an automatic music playing system that accompaniment follows a melody performed by human based on a real time pitch extracting process of sounds of violin or human voice [2]. These systems are cooperative systems, but two way communication between performers is not realized between human and computer. The reason is that performance of computer is influenced by human instruction but human performance is little influenced by performance of computer.

We propose a system in which human and computer perform music in interaction. That is, user presents emotion or intention through performance and computer interprets them and changes performance. In addition, the system doesn't need to be constrained performance given by a human such as automatic music playing system. In some situations, system must stimulate human emotion. Neuro Musician [3] is one of such studies. It treats an inside of the system as a blackbox by using neural networks. We adopt use of a performer model. We also introduce a new concept named Tension Parameter which represents emotional information realizing on performance. The system changes its performance in real time based on Tension Parameter.

2. OVERVIEW

The performance style of JASPER is jam session which consists of a drum, a bass and a piano. The feature of jam session is that there are few constraints in performance. Only the chord sequence is decided beforehand, and details are constructed improvisatoreally by performers. In jam session therefore it is very easy for performers to represent their emotion or intention and to communicate with each other through the sound. Blues sequence is adopted as chord sequence in this system. JASPER is assigned to a drum and a bass. A human performer takes charge of a piano. In other wards, virtual drummer and bassist in the system and a human pianist perform jam session.

JASPER has many performance patterns of one bar unit and changes performance by means of selecting and outputting the best suitable pattern of all.

2.1 Interaction between human and JASPER

Figure 1 shows an interaction between human and JASPER. The input of JASPER is a performance from MIDI keyboard and the output is a performance of a drum and a bass. User listens to the performance of a drum and a bass and performs improvisation. Its performance goes to the input of JASPER again.

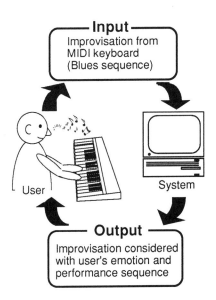

Figure 1. Interaction between human and JASPER

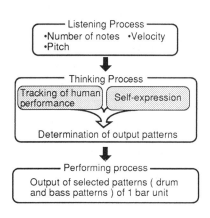

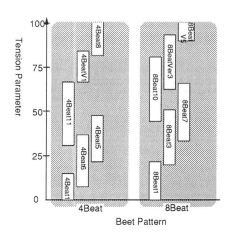

Figure 2. The structure of JASPER   Figure 3. Output Pattern Data-Map

2.2 Structure of JASPER

Fig. 2 shows the structure of JASPER. It consists of 3 parts named listening process, thinking process and performing process. The listening process corresponds to a human ear. The number, velocity and pitch of notes are extracted from performance of MIDI keyboard. The performing process corresponds to human hands and legs. The patterns determined in the thinking process are performed. The thinking process consists of tracking process and self-expression process.

2.3 Tension Parameter

In a jam session short chord sequences, ex. 8 bars or 12 bars, are repeated. Performers represent uprush or depression of emotion in this constraint. This system copes with such emotive variety as parameters. We named this parameter Tension Parameter.

2.4 Output pattern data-map

JASPER uses performance patterns of one bar unit. All patterns are classified into beat groups, ex. 4 beat group and 8 beat group. Upper limit and lower limit of Tension Parameter are attached to each patterns. Output pattern data-map is a 2-dimensional table where they are mapped. Fig. 3 shows an example of the output pattern data-map. The output pattern is determined by the correspondence of the value of Output Tension Parameter with limit values attached to each output patterns.

3. THINKING PROCESS

Fig. 4 shows the system architecture in the thinking process, that is, performer model. First of all a value of Human Tension Parameter (HTP) which represents a human emotive factor is calculated from performance data acquired by the listening process. Output Tension Parameter (OTP) which is used to select a output pattern is determined from this value and the one of System Tension Parameter (STP) which represents self-expression of the system.

3.1 Calculation of Human Tension Parameter (HTP)

To realize a cooperative performance between human and the system, it is needed to measure human emotive factor in a performance, that is, Human Tension Parameter. The Extraction Filter of HTP represents relations between human performance and human emotive factor. Since this system executes a process of one bar unit repeatedly, if the performance of next bar is determined from the present HTP, time delay of one bar is caused in tracking of emotive factor. The human emotive factor in the next bar is therefore estimated based on past performance sequence.

3.2 Determination of the output performance pattern

Output of the system is determined from HTP and STP based on the personality database. This is a set of rules and its object is to give a performance changes from a system side.

3.2.1 Judgment of leader

In ensemble, one of the performers becomes soloist and leads a performance. A soloist can decide a sequence of performance based on his intention. On the other hand, accompanists perform harmonizing with a lead of soloist. This system adopts such performance style as shown in Fig. 5. In jam session, it is not decided who becomes soloist beforehand. It must be decided who becomes soloist on a sequence

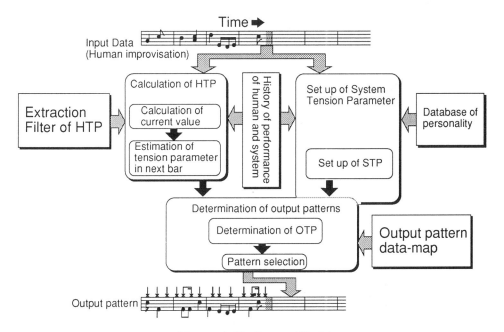

Figure 4. Performer Model

of performance through the communication of performers in real time. The judgment of leader is executed based on heuristic rules from the HTP.

3.2.2 Lead of human

If human is judged a leader of the performance, the system need to accompany a human performance. First of all, a present cooperative factor is evaluated from HTP and STP.

If the present performance is cooperative, it seems that the performance of next bar will become cooperative by the performance planed by the system. STP is therefore substituted for OTP directly.

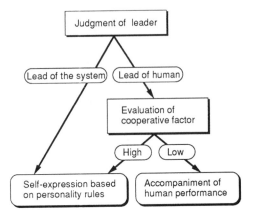

Figure 5. The sytles of Ensemble

If the present performance is not cooperative, the system modifies the performance to accompany the human performance. Thus HTP is substituted for OTP.

3.2.3 Lead of the system

If the system is judged a leader of the performance, the system will continues the performance based on self-expression. STP is therefore substituted for OTP.

3.2.4 Selection of output patterns

An output pattern is determined by the comparison of OTP to the output data-map. If several patterns are matched, only one pattern is selected by the rules to realize a natural performance.

4. EXPERIMENTS

For evaluations of the system, 5 pianist used this system in three styles of session as shown Table 1 and we interviewed them about impressions of the system and differences from a performance with a human partner. Abstracts of impressions are as follows.

Table 1. Three Sessions

	Thinking style	Turning method of extraction filter of HTP and output pattern data-map
Session 1	Only tracking	Determination by a lot of statistical data
Session 2	Only tracking	Tuning as wishes of a performer
Session 3	Tracking and self-expression	Tuning as wishes of a performer

- About quality of the performance
  There are any dissatisfaction in Session 1, but the performance of the system in Session 2 can accompany human performance well as a whole.
  The system cannot accompany quick changes of emotion somewhere.
  The performance in Session 3 is interesting because of inclusion of self-expression. The performance can be enjoyed for long time, since it is similar to the performance with a human performer.

- About the cooperative system
  This is a automatic music playing system of new style.
  We can get good excitements from a performance of the system.

As a result, we can get evaluations that this system is interesting from a view of an automatic music playing system and that its performance is inferior to the human one. All users however performed with this system for over 10 minutes in one session in spite of no instruction of time and we could get the impression of interesting. This system therefore can be evaluated very highly.

5. CONCLUSION

We proposed a cooperative musical partner system: JASPER (Jam Session Partner) which performs jam session including improvisation with human pianist. In experiments, 5 pianist used this system and we could get such impressions as they could enjoy jam session very much. Also most of them were much interested in possibilities of this system as new style of uses of computer.

It is a very effective method that we dose not simply connect output performance with input performance and that we construct a performer model which simulates human improvisation process in the system. We do not notice performance information but emotive information from a view that jam session is communication between performers and tried to extract it. In other words, we proposed Tension Parameter to realize a process to recognize partner emotion and to connect it with self emotion.

Our research is one of the trials that we let a computer recognize human emotive information. We can find out the possibilities of cooperative works and communication including subjective information such as emotion between human and computer in this system.

REFERENCES

1 H. Morita, S. Hashimoto and S. Ohteru, A Computer Music System that Follows a Human Conductor, Computer July 1991, pp.44-53 (1991)
2 B. Vercoe, The Synthetic Performer in Context of Live Performers, Proc. of Int. Computer Music Conf., pp. 199-200 (1984)
3 M.Nishijima, Teaching Musical Style to a Neural Network, proc. Intl. Symposium on Computer World '90, pp.195-201 (1990)

ESSAI - Interactive Sales System on an IBC-Network

D. Felix and H. Krueger

Dept. of Hygiene and Applied Physiology, Swiss Federal Institute of Technology, ETH-Zentrum, CH-8092 Zurich, Switzerland

Abstract
The introduction of integrated broadband communication (IBC) to sales and information terminals offers a new range of possibilities, both to the supplier of goods or information and to the customer (the end user). The project ESSAI (Experimental Service Sale Automation on an IBC network, project R2029) which forms part of the European RACE II program is currently building such a system and is investigating the technical possibilities and the usability for the customer. A consortium of partners from Italy, France, Germany, Denmark and Switzerland is working on this project. Beside the technical realisation the main goal will be to investigate how the user can cope with the sudden access to large amounts of information and the combination of different services. The project will produce two demonstrator terminals for testing which will offer different services (tickets for cultural events such as theatre, cinema, concerts; travel tickets), goods (merchandising of products related to the services offered and other products) as well as information (how to get to places, what is on, etc.). The first will be tested this autumn in Milan (Italy), the second next year in Basel (Switzerland). New forms of help for the user will be provided (animated sequences with examples how to use the terminal, on-line voice/video transmission from a control centre of a person who will help the user). Cross-links between the different application allow users to combine the different products to a package which fulfils their precise needs.

1. Introduction

ESSAI is a three-year project which forms a part of the European RACE II program (project R2029), specifically as an advance communications application experiment. Its first objectives is to provide basic concepts and the architecture of future, IBC-based (integrated broadband communication) teleshopping systems for information and goods. Beside the technical development it is a central goal to asses the end-users reaction to a new, highly powerful system which includes a multitude of services. Combining all sorts of information and goods suppliers will allow users to buy a whole package exactly fitting their needs, but will require them to master a complex and wide-expanding system. So the second point of interest is focused on how the users will cope with the complexity, and tests how the developed strategies of navigating through the system comply with the users needs and expectations. Two demonstrators (working prototypes) will be produced in the project, in order to conduct field experiments with "real customers, buying real information or goods for real money". Acceptance, performance and usability will be assessed with these experiments. Additionally, the commercial exploitation potential will be outlined to promote systems like the developed ESSAI-terminal, and a strategy for the introduction of such teleshopping systems based on the experience and a market analysis will be developed.

2. General system description

The ESSAI-terminal serves as an example how the potential offered by broadband-ISDN communication can be exploited. The central idea is to offer different information sources and goods to the users, allowing them to buy a bundle of items fitting their precise needs. In the first demonstrator, *cultural events* in the area of cinema, theatre, live music events, *goods* in the category music, books and home videos and *travel services* such as railway tickets will be available. From this range the user can, for instance, buy a ticket for a theatre play, the book to the play and the train ticket to go to the play. This puts a heavy load on the design of the user-interface, as many possibilities are offered, from which the user has to select the fitting ones. Navigation and keeping track of what has been done so far is very important, as well as a good representation of the available goods and services. As described in FELIX and KRUEGER (1993), an attractive "look" to the user interface is an important part of such a system.

Technically, the system which is developed in the ESSAI-project is divided into two main parts: the terminal, installed where the customer needs the service, and a control centre from where different information is transmitted. The terminal will only be equipped with minimal intelligence, whereas the control centre will contain the most of the database (multimedia database, availability database) and the links to the separate suppliers of information and goods, as well as the links to the credit card companies and their authorisation centres. This saves a lot of technical power at each terminal (many terminals can be connected to one control centre), cutting down the cost of terminals. The ISDN-link provides the necessary capacity to communicate large amounts of data, such as moving pictures, catalogue pages etc. Updating of locally stored information can be done by the high-capacity line as well, saving time and man-power for servicing. At the same time, a new concept of help can be implemented: a person in the control centre can act as an on-line help, and with the aid of a video connection it will be possible to see the customer who is needing help in the control centre, and the customer can see who is providing help for him. It should even be possible for the person in the control centre to remotely perform certain operations on the users screen to help solve complicated problems, thus giving optimal help to users.

Payment will be only possible by a major credit card. This is a constraint, which has been accepted as it will be quite probable that a bundle order will be in a price range which is too high to be handled in cash; the customer might not have enough money in cash, and the money collected in the terminal is soon highly desirable for thieves.

3. Procedure

The project was started in January 1992. The first year was dedicated to preparatory work. Definitions of the required functions, the necessary technical components and communication between the components were made. A clear structure of how the system was to work, what data would be flowing and what the end-user would be able to do at the terminal were described. The findings are reported in four deliverables (DELIVERABLES 2A, 2B, 5, 6, 1992). Special attention was given to definition of end-users requirements, reported in DELIVERABLE 2A (1992). The general requirements specify that the system should comply with the users expectations, the interface must be designed in a clear, easy to understand way and should be straightforward in it's logical flow. Messages should be given in a helpful, informative way to allow the users to proceed fluently, without having to call on the help-facilities too often. This requirements comply with the existing standards (e.g. DIN 66234, part 8, ISO 9241, part 10).

During the current year, the first demonstrator is being built. Following the definition of the first year, technical components as well as the terminal hardware (housing, input and output media) are being constructed or adapted to follow the specifications. And as a central point of interest, the user-interface is being programmed. The task is to provide an easy to understand interface to allow the users to access the desired information, and quickly buy the goods they wanted to buy. The first demonstrator will work with a limited technical set, using a 2MBit link for communication. Thus no on-line transmission of moving pictures will be possible. A limited set of services will be provided for the end-user. On-line help will be available by text, or voice transmission from the control centre (live). Nevertheless, it will be possible to test the developed hardware and to provide first results how the users react to a system which offers considerably more than any previous public sales system. The testing site will be in the Galleria Vittorio Emanuele II in the premises of the Italian post, and the control centre will be located in the offices of one of the project partners, both in Milan. The testing procedure will include a questionnaire to assess the acceptance and the impression of the users, a video film of the users will record the reactions in general, and log files of the transactions and manipulations will allow detailed analysis of the users actions, their mistakes and what they bought.

The second demonstrator, operable in autumn 1994 in Basel (Switzerland), will be fully equipped with all planned functions: An on-line help system which allows the user to contact a person in a control centre, including a video link from the control centre to the terminal and optionally vice-versa. Additionally, the person in the control centre will be able to remotely operate on the screen of the user needing assistance. Full video transmission will be possible, allowing the presentation of explanatory films on the goods, services and information. The experience gained from the first demonstrator will serve to iron out problems, be they technical or usability faults.

4. User interface

The user interface is the centre of our interest. How can we provide a structuring of the user-interface, to allow easy navigation through the system, helping novices to find their way around the system, and encouraging experts to browse in the system? Using a touchscreen as input media is the first solution, allowing manipulation of objects on the user-interface. Not yet a common way of communicating with a machine, it allows the users to point with their fingers to whatever they fancy, thus making manipulation intuitive. The use of animation, videos, still pictures and sound will allow realistic presentation of goods and information, creating a pleasing and entertaining system.

Guidance within the system will be provided by defining different levels in the system: a first level deals with authorisation of the users and the dialogue language. Then the users are confronted with the selection of a supplier of information or goods. Alternatively, a "what's on" function will take them to a list of currently specially promoted information or goods. Up to this point the system is under the command of the company which is running the whole system, and most likely the control centre as well. Selecting a supplier will take the users to the selection of the desired product. From this point on the supplier can determine what his catalogue looks like, and how it is accessed. Guidelines will be issued how to design this part, however freedom must be given to suppliers to incorporate their corporate identity and the philosophy they wish to use. All screens will consistently have a system area (where general, non-application dependent functions, messages or navigation aids are located), and an application area, which is defined by the supplier of the application.

5. Conclusions

The project will provide insight on how people cope with complex information structures in a situation where they are under pressure (time constraints, other people watching). It will be possible to test concepts how information is best presented to improve understanding and how information should be structured to improve usability and accessibility. Use of multimedia will be tested to assess its advantages, providing the opportunity to learn when and how it is best used.

Showing how b-ISDN can be used to create new forms of information and buying goods will promote the use of such systems, and will stress the need for research in how this is best achieved. Knowledge will be gained both in technical and in ergonomic respect, and a success of this project can augment the availability of services for people.

The goal must be to use modern technology to help solve problems and widen the palette of available services for the users, and not just to create new problems that scare people from using contemporary technical facilities.

Acknowledgements
This project is supported by the Commission of the European Communities(DGXIII, Telecommunications, Information Industries and Innovation) as part of the RACE II program. For Switzerland, the support is provided by the Bundesamt für Bildung und Wissenschaft (BBW).

6. References

DELIVERABLE 2, part A: Outline of user requirement specification. R2029/SHV/111/DS/R/002/61, 1992.

DELIVERABLE 2, part B: Outline of user requirement specification - Milan demonstrator. R2029/COS/URS/DS/R/002/b1, 1992.

DELIVERABLE 5: Architecture and scope of the 1st demonstrator. R2029/COS/As1/DR/R/005/b1, 1992.

DELIVERABLE 6: First demonstrator specification. R2029/COS/SP1/DR/R/006/b1, 1992.

DIN 66 234 (part 8): Grundsätze der Dialoggestaltung. Normenausschuss Informationsverarbeitung im DIN Deutsches Institut für Normung e.V., Draft 1984.

FELIX, D. and KRUEGER, H.: Designing the look. Shortpaper at the INTERCHI'93, Amsterdam, 1993.

ISO 9241 (part 10): Ergonomic requirements for office work with visual display terminals (VDTs): Dialogue principles. ISO/TC159/SC4.WG5 (Software ergonomics and man-machine dialogue, Draft 1991.

Involved partners

Italy:	Consorzio per l'OSI in Italia(COSI), project co-ordinator
	Servizi a valore aggiunto S.P.A.
	Centro di cultura scientifica A. Volta
Germany:	Gesellschaft für Software (STZ)
	Studiengesellschft Verkehr mbH (SNV)
France:	Thomson-CSF/LER
	Syseca S.A.
	Ouest standard telematique (OST)
Denmark:	Elektronikcentralen (EC)
Switzerland:	Ascom Autelca A.G.
	Ascom Tech A.G.
	Swiss Federal Institute of Technology (ETH)

Design-to-Cost-Support with ASCET

J. Warschat and J. Frech

Fraunhofer-Institute for Industrial Engineering, Stuttgart, Germany

Introduction

Product costs are at least to 60%-70% /1/, in some references up to 85% /2/ determined by design. In fact of this, all measures for cost reduction have to join in on the design level. Because of the designer's multiple tasks, cost efficiency can only be one aspect for the designer, who has also to consider functional, material, quality or security efficiency.
A co-ordination of these aspects on how to get low-cost, high-quality products relies on the availability of adequate information, gained from the use of one of the following categories of design analysis methods /3/:

o   Using *handbooks and checklists* provides rudimentary and relatively unstructured rules only.

o   The employment of *design teams*, which consist of representatives from each relevant area, runs all risks of time-consuming interaction problems.

o   *Automatic design systems* will only work on extremely narrow problems and are unsuitable for typical companies.

o   *Design advice approaches* provide information within the capabilities of a system, but tend to limit the designer's creativity.

o   *Design rating approaches* can combine the providing of relevant information with the full preservation of the designer's creativity.

For supporting the designer in the scope of assembly and cost efficiency, the Fraunhofer Institute for Industrial Engineering has developed the software-system ASCET (**AS**sembly **C**ost **E**stimation **T**ool), which enables the designer to estimate the assembly time and costs of a product or an assembly group already during its conceiving. This, together with the estimation of material and manufacturing costs, supports the possibilities of product modification in early design stages, allowing crucial improvements by low expenditure and the dismantling of the *"imaginary wall between the design and manufacturing functions"*. /4/

ASCET - an Application based on an Object-Oriented Data-Base

ASCET is based on the object-oriented data-base HyperWork, an innovative software technology that offers a convenient user interface in addition to its technical advantages, which are in short:

o Key points of object-oriented software /5/:

  o The encapsulation of data and program code

  o Applications are easier to extend and to maintain

  o A high flexibility allows adaptations on specific requirements

  o End-user computing allows the integration of prospective tasks

  o The providing of Rapid Prototyping

o Compatibility with forward-pointing software standards:
  o Compatible with clearly accepted graphic OS environments such as AIX
    Window or OS/2
  o Enabled for multi user systems
  o Enabled to read standard data formats (e.g. X11-images, Bitmaps, TIFF,
    Pixmaps, HPGL)
  o Mouse oriented user interface

These specific advantages of object oriented programming offers the warranty of progression according to special needs of the user. Hence, ASCET, as an application of HyperWork, can relay on the flexibility of object-oriented software and realize user defined adjustments rapidly.

On the basis of these characteristics, ASCET is a software tool for estimating manual assembly times of small-sized products. It has been developed for supporting early stages of product design by offering estimated assembly times for different versions of assemblies and products. In this manner an evaluation of assembly efficiency is possible by comparing the values of assembly times. These information is valuable for

o Development
o Design
o Work Planning and
o Calculation

to support important tasks like precalculation, product optimization or reverse engineering.

The Performance of ASCET

In order to get results, the user of ASCET initially has to set up the data base, which means the input of assembly relevant data in a master form. By setting up their configuration, products and assembly groups are defined as objects consisting of several single parts and, optionally, of other assembly groups. All these input data are stored in a growing data base, input procedures are limited to the real necessities and the reuse of known objects is facilitated.

So the principal way of working with ASCET consist of seven easy steps:
o   definition of the used single parts
o   definition of assembly groups, just by the single parts they consist of
o   definition of the assembly operations to build the assembly group
o   equivalent definitions for the whole product
o   calculation by the system for assembly, single parts and material costs
o   analysis of the results as far as costs and cost drivers are concerned
o   variation of the assembly processes or the structure of an assembly / single
     part to improve the cost situation

The internal projection of usable parts is limited on the real necessities for assembly, which means here the cubic dimensions and the weight of an object. This allows a fast definition of single parts, assembly groups and whole products, a necessary condition for encouraging the designer's creativity.

Otherwise it also can be used with virtual objects, that means not really existing parts. So, based on the existing data base, virtual objects such as single parts or assembly groups can be created, modified and, finally, also integrated in real products by substitution of real ones. In this way, the user can replace parts for receiving better solutions of assembly efficiency in early stages of product designing.

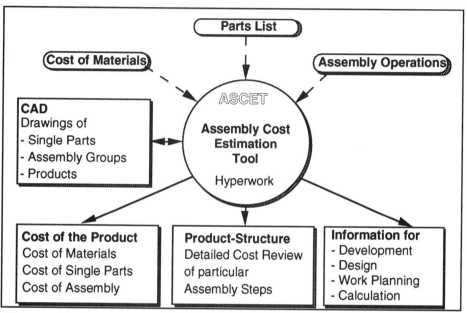

Figure 1. The performing structure of ASCET

Defined assembly objects (single parts, assembly groups and products) are now available for further analysis but can be deleted also. For a clear structure of the generated data base, single parts, assembly groups and products are allocable to suitable classes, an organisational concept which allows easy handling of a large data set.

But not only the specifications of parts can be saved, the user can also conserve their defined assembly processes in the data base. Such protocols of all assembly operations can ensure the understanding of previously evaluated products and assemblies also in later use.

For the evaluation of defined configurations of assembly groups or products under the aspect of assembly time, the user has to trace the assembly procedure of an configured object by fixing the assembly steps. This precondition for estimating assembly times can be performed in *two different ways* of assembly definition.

First, the feature-based method uses previously defined *assembly features* for the determination of assembly steps. Based on this definition, the assembly time will be calculated by evaluating the feature specific assembly linkage.

The other possibility to calculate assembly times in ASCET is using predefined *assembly operations* for the determination of the assembly linkage. Every assembly operation consists of a list of MTM-base movements. In the operation-based method those are evaluated by including the assembly object's specific data from the suitable master form.

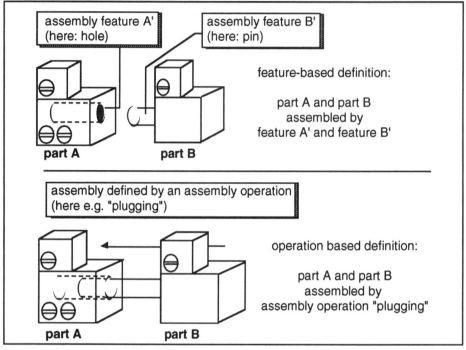

Figure 2. The two methods for the projection of assembly in ASCET

For the operation-based method the MTM analyzing system of predefined times forms the core element of assembly time evaluation. Based on this widely known and recognized scheme, every assembly can be separated in single assembly acts called basic activities, which are evaluated according to the weight, the cubic dimensions and the distance between assembly and source location of objects being used. Therefore MTM has developed a table of predefined values for these basic activities, which now can be aggregated for the projection of real assembly steps. In ASCET such a "package" of several basic activities forms an assembly operation which – once defined – can be stored for further use.

ASCET offers a set of predefined assembly operations for the most common assembly steps, so that every regular case of assembly projection can be calculated without any input effort. For specific use, new assembly operations can be added as easy as already predefined ones can be changed. This accounts for the flexibility of a user specific tool for a problem oriented assembly projection in ASCET. If certain assembly operations are known exactly, fixed values can be linked with the projection of assembly steps. Hence, in conjunction with a large data set of defined parts, all prerequisites to provide a numerous range for assembly variations are satisfied, thus pointing out capacities of reducing assembly times already in early stages of design. Therefore ASCET offers many possibilities to vary and optimize existing product data with minimal effort. For that task generated assembly protocols are kept available for further improvement, for example based on modifications of parts or assembly groups.

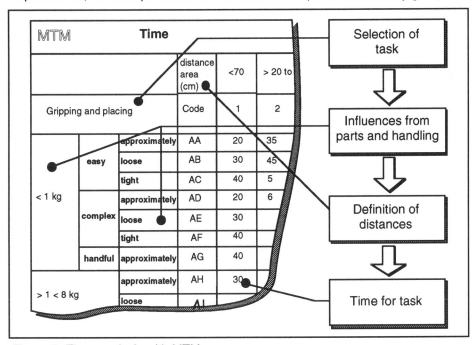

Figure 3. Time analysis with MTM

Not only the functionality of a software tool, but also its handling will be an essential condition to realize its advantages. For a convenient and easy work ASCET will provide beyond its clear structure of data organization
o a universal documentation-of-use to inform in which assemblies and products selected single parts and sub-assemblies are used,
o a comfortable tool to search for similar objects to enhance the reuse of already existing parts and to reduce the efforts of design,
o an interface using the common HPGL-format to include drawings from most CAD-systems for visualizing used parts, assembly groups and products.

The functional foundation on the recognized system of MTM enables the system to handle all aspects of manual assembly and to bring out reliable results on the estimation of expected assembly times. Its additional functions make ASCET far more capable than any other calculation tool for supporting product design. ASCET can also offer large-scale information beyond costs originated in assembly, useful also for other terms of reference such as:
o The calculation of material-costs informs about the overall cost situation

o Costs of single parts may be calculated with the statistical method of regression analysis. This is based on already existing similar parts and becomes increasingly accurate with every use of ASCET. So, with a growing set of known single part data, ASCET will be able to offer high extractive information regarding expected costs of new designed single parts with a steadily increasing reliability.

Summing up, ASCET has to be regarded as a universal tool for product development, providing information on multiple cost factors in a quick and reliable manner. Its broad functionality increases the acceptance of the user and enhances the overall benefits of the system, which will be in short
o the support for the development of cost-efficient products,
o the availability of objective calculations as a basis for discussions and decision making, and
o the reduction of product-development times and costs, since the time consuming assistance of work-planning specialists is avoided.

Significance and Discussion of Results

The scientific significance of ASCET is within the successful integration of such different extents as object-oriented programming, software-ergonomic user-interfaces and functional broadness of the system.

For referencing the calculated results with ASCET, they have been compared with conventionally calculated ones from high experienced manufacturing experts. Comparing the assembly operations of five different products, only an average drift of 0,44% for product assembly was registered.

ASCET will be able to offer valuable results for a quick and reliable estimation, facing up today's challenges of product design or optimization. Moreover, the object-oriented approach also ensures to satisfy extended demands of the future - both reagarding the implementation of new expansions and adaptations of currently available functionalities to company-specific requirement.

References

/1/ Ehrlenspiel, Klaus, Kostengünstig Konstruieren, Berlin; Heidelberg 1985, p.2

/2/ Wittenberg, Gunter, "Radical Redesign", Assembly Automation Vol. 11 No 4, 1991, p. 20 (up to 80 %)
Benson, Allan F., "Software: Programming for Profit", Assembly Nov/Dec 1991, p.15 (85 %)

/3/ Sackett, P.J., Holbrook, A.E.K., "DFA as a primary process decreases design deficiencies", Assembly Automation 8 (3) 1988, pp.137-140

/4/ Boothroyd, Geoffrey, Assembly Automation and Product Design, New York 1991, p.9

/5/ Winblad, Ann L., Edwards, Samuel D., King, David R., Object-Oriented Software, New York 1990

An algebraic system that symbolic expressions can interact with graphical representations for understanding mathematics

H. Saito and M. Nagata

Dept. of Administration Engineering, Faculty of Science and Technology, Keio University
3-14-1 Hiyoshi, Yokohama 223, Japan
Tel. +81-45-563-1141 Fax +81-45-563-5979

Abstract

This paper discusses an interaction system between symbols and images for understanding mathematics. A great deal of human understanding is facilitated through the interaction between symbols and images. The system called INGRASY (INteractive system between GRAphical representations and SYmbolic expressions), is proposed as a significant contributor to the understanding of mathematics. This system is suggested to be an effective educational tool.

1. INTRODUCTION

Recent developments in cognitive science have shown that understanding can be facilitated through the interaction between symbols and images (see Figure 1)[1][2]. Both symbols (e.g. mathematical formulas) and images (e.g. graphical representations) are important in understanding mathematics. This paper, proposes a system which focuses on the interaction between symbols and images in mathematics. This system called INGRASY (INteractive system between GRAphical representations and SYmbolic expressions) is a mathematical tool to assist understanding.

In this paper, first, an outline of the INGRASY system is presented. Second, a method for implementation is illustrated. Third, facilities of this system are explained. Finally, the system is evaluated by interviewing a system user.

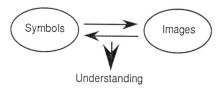

Figure 1. Understanding process

2. INGRASY SYSTEM

2.1 An outline of INGRASY

The MATHEMATICA system for doing mathematics by computer has existed for sometime[3][4]. MATHEMATICA can not only compute numerical or symbolic calculations but also graphics. If a symbolic expression is supplied, then MATHEMATICA will produce a graphical rendering. That is, mathematical formulas, or symbols are visualized as graphs, or images. These graphical representations are an effective aid in understanding mathematics. However, to date, there have been no systems converting images to symbols. If something is to be clearly understood through the interaction between symbols and images, then, it is necessary to provide a facility converting images to symbols. In this study, a system is implemented where symbolic expressions can interact with images (refer Figure 2)[5].

MATHEMATICA

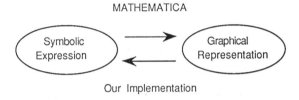

Our Implementation

Figure 2. INGRASY System Outline

Suppose that a formula is supplied to MATHEMATICA, it will then construct the corresponding graph. The MATHEMATICA system is a facility for converting symbols to images. On the other hand, it is desirable that the facility also operates in the opposite direction. That is, if an operator manipulates the graph, then the system also modifies the formula in accordance with the manipulation. Moreover, it shows modified formulas and associated graphs. This process operates in the opposite direction to MATHEMATICA and is in this respect is independent from of the MATHEMATICA system.

2.2 From graphical representations to symbolic expressions

Below the technical details of the facility converting images to symbols is described (refer Figure 3).

In this part, first an operation manipulating the graphs is selected. Then the data needed to manipulate the graph is saved. That is, points are marked by using the Mouse device to save them as data. The function related to the selected operation uses the data to show its output. This function is defined as either a function of MATHEMATICA or an external program of MATHEMATICA.

There are two problems to be solved here. One is how to gather the data from the Mouse device, and the other is how to implement the communication with the external programs. MATHEMATICA has two interfaces, a form of TEXT and a form of NOTEBOOK. The form

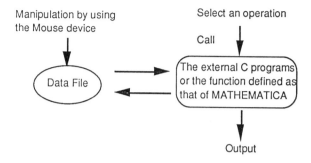

Figure 3. From graphs to formulas.

of TEXT runs on the UNIX machine and the form of NOTEBOOK runs on MACINTOSH.

The form of the NOTEBOOK interface indicates a position at any point and marks any point by the use of the Mouse device. Therefore, the NOTEBOOK interface form is used. Users of INGRASY can operate this system by simply using the Mouse device.

On the other hand, MATHEMATICA Version 2.0 has MATHLINK which provides the facility of communication between MATHEMATICA and the external programs written by the C programming language. MATHLINK enables us to call the external C programs from MATHEMATICA and vice versa. Moreover, data can be exchanged between them by employing MATHLINK.

In consideration of the above, it is decided to use MATHEMATICA Version 2.0 which has the NOTEBOOK form interface for implementing INGRASY.

3.IMPLEMENTATION

Though it has been separately confirmed that the Mouse device can be used to communicate the external C programs, they have not been combined as yet. In order to inspect the effectiveness of INGRASY in contributing to the understanding mathematics, a prototype system of INGRASY is implemented by using MATHEMATICA Version 2.0 with the form of TEXT interface. At the present, a point is substituted by the Mouse device into arguments of functions. Although MATHEMATICA can formulate four kinds of graphics - two and three-dimensional, contour and density graphics - only two-dimensional graphics have been implemented so far.

The following operations have been executed: TRANSLATION, ROTATION, SCALING, SYMMETRICAL TRANSFER FOR ANY LINE, SYMMETRICAL TRANSFER FOR ANY POINT, TANGENTIAL LINE, AREA, FIX A CURVE WITH ANY POINTS, FIX A LINE WITH A POINT AND AN INCLINATION, FIX A CURVE WITH THE MAXIMUM POINTS AND MINIMUM POINTS, VECTOR, DISTANCE BETWEEN TWO POINTS, DOMAIN.

In this paper, three operations will be illustrated; TANGENTIAL LINE, TRANSLATION, and DOMAIN, which convert graphical representations to symbolic expressions.

270

4.FACILITIES OF INGRASY

4.1 TANGENTIAL LINE

When the X coordinate of any point on the graph to TANLINE is given, a tangential line at the point is drawn. Moreover, INGRASY shows the formula of the line and the method to derive the formula - a differentiated formula, a formula of tangential line and so on .

In[1] := Plot [Sin[x], {x, -Pi, Pi}]

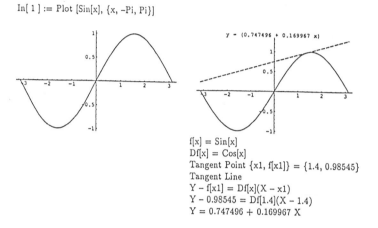

f[x] = Sin[x]
Df[x] = Cos[x]
Tangent Point {x1, f[x1]} = {1.4, 0.98545}
Tangent Line
Y - f[x1] = Df[x](X - x1)
Y - 0.98545 = Df[1.4](X - 1.4)
Y = 0.747496 + 0.169967 X

Figure 4. TANGENTIAL LINE Graph

4.2 TRANSLATION

When quantities to transfer and name of the function to PTRANS are given, the transferred graph of the function is drawn. Moreover, the formula of the graph, the way to derive the formula and a matrix of the transformation are shown, refer Figure 5.

4.3 DOMAIN

When a list of the coordinates of any points and a name of the function to DOMAIN are given, the domain of any points of the function are shown, as illustrated in Figure 6.

In[2] := Plot [x^2, {x, -10, 10}]

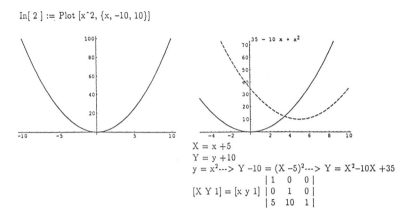

$$X = x + 5$$
$$Y = y + 10$$
$$y = x^2 \text{---> } Y - 10 = (X - 5)^2 \text{---> } Y = X^2 - 10X + 35$$

$$[X \ Y \ 1] = [x \ y \ 1] \begin{vmatrix} 1 & 0 & 0 \\ 0 & 1 & 0 \\ 5 & 10 & 1 \end{vmatrix}$$

Figure 5. TRANSLATION Graph

In[3] := Plot [{x^3-7x^2+4x+12, -x+6}, {x, -5, 10}]

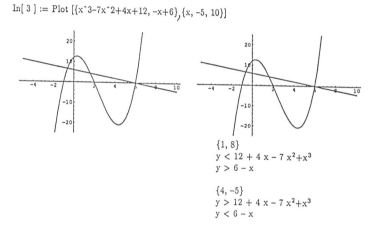

{1, 8}
$$y < 12 + 4x - 7x^2 + x^3$$
$$y > 6 - x$$

{4, -5}
$$y > 12 + 4x - 7x^2 + x^3$$
$$y < 6 - x$$

Figure 6. DOMAIN Graph

5. EVALUATION

To evaluate the system a system user survey interview was conducted. The respondent was a high school teacher. A summary of the responses follows:

Present junior high school curriculums in Japan[6], require students to mainly learn symbolic algebra as the foundation of their mathematics schooling. In high school, mathematical images are introduced[7]. The Pythagoras' theorem which students learn in the last year of junior high school makes clear the concept of distance between two points. Here images are useful in the understanding of these mathematical principles. Moreover, difficult mathematical problems can be resolved through the use of symbols. In this way, the curriculum of mathematics in Japan initially introduces symbols. Next images are taught. Finally the curriculum introduces the interaction between symbols and images. This situation further supports our approach.

The present INGRASY system discussed is found to be more or less effective. In the future the facilities to use Mouse device and to communicate the external C programs must be combined. Furthermore, a system which can do three-dimensional graphs is desirable.

According to the teacher's questionnaire replies and the high school mathematics curriculum in Japan, the system which provides the facility of the interaction between symbols and images in mathematics will be a powerful tool in assisting students' understanding of mathematics. It is planned to evaluate INGRASY further by completing more student trials of the system.

6.CONCLUSION

As a tool that helps our understanding in mathematics, the proposed system which provides the facility of interaction between symbols and images is effective. If this system is implemented successfully, it is expected that student learning will be enhanced encouraging them to use the system rather than textbooks and other study-aids. It is planned to add more operations investigating the educational point of view in detail. In addition, it is hoped that this system will become widely used in education in near future.

Acknowledgement

The project team wishes to acknowledge the kind assistance of Mr. Hisashi Kokufugata, a teacher of the Keio Girls High School, in the evaluation of the system.

References

1   Y. Saeki, Computer and Education, Iwanami Books, 1986. (in Japanese)
2   H. Azuma, T. Oyama, and Y. Saeki, Reasoning and Understanding, Cognitive Psychology Course, Vol. 3, Tokyo University Publishing Company, 1982. (in Japanese)
3   S. Koike, Mathematica An Introduction to Dealing with Numerical Formulas, Skill Criticism Company, 1990. (in Japanese)
4   S. Wolfram, Mathematica A System for Doing Mathematics by Computer (in Japanese) Second Edition, Addison-Wesley Publishing Company Japan Inc., 1992. (in Japanese)
5   H. Saito and M. Nagata, A system that formulas interact with figures, Proceedings of The 44th Information Processing Society of Japan, pp. 223-224, 1992. (in Japanese)
6   The Japanese Education Ministry, The official curriculum guidelines for junior high schools, The printing office of the Japanese Finance Ministry, 1989. (in Japanese)
7   The Japanese Education Ministry, The official curriculum guidelines for high schools, The printing office of the Japanese Finance Ministry, 1989. (in Japanese)

Preliminary experiment with a distributed and networking card-handling tool named KJ-Editor

Naohiko Takeda,* Akichika Shiomi,* Kazuhisa Kawai* and Hajime Ohiwa[†]

*Toyohashi University of Technology
Tempaku-cho, Toyohashi 441 Japan

[†]Keio University
Endo, Fujisawa 252 Japan

Abstract

An experiment that four collaborators made a specification of a middle-scale software using a distributed and networking card-handling tool named KJ-Editor was conducted. The collaborators meet at a room and are provided with separate networked computers.

According to our observation and analysis on this experiment, some features of cooperative work activity using KJ-Editor are identified; (1) a computer supported card-handling tool is a useful resource for the group in mediating their cooperative work, (2) pointing out a card or an element of the chart by a mouse has an effect for concentrating the discussion, and (3) WYSIWIS facilities sometimes become obstacles for personal viewing of the card-arrangement and cause collaborators to be uncomfortable.

1. Introduction

A distributed and networking card-handling tool named KJ-Editor that simulates arranging cards on a desk as working in collaboration is described. Card-handling is one of the most useful methods for information representeation and idea-generation.

J. Kawakita developed a card-handling method named KJ-Method[Kawakita86]. KJ-Method was originally developed for anthropological field work, but it is so useful for information-arrangement and idea-generation that it is widely used in Japanese business society. The method describes how to carry out card-handling for new idea-generation, and it is a good guide to our design and implementation of KJ-Editor.

KJ-Editor has been developed for personal use on a personal computer, and extended for cooperative-work use on an engineering work-station in network environment. Hundreds of cards can be generated on any place in a display and a sentence can be written on each of them. A generated card can be picked and moved by a mouse. Cards may be grouped by enclosing them with a curve. Relationships of cards and groups can also be marked by special lines.

In this paper, a preliminary experiment of the card-handling based cooperative work using KJ-Editor is presented. According to our observation and analysis on this experiment, some

274

features of cooperative work activity using KJ-Editor are identified.

2. KJ-Editor and its implementation

In KJ-Editor, hundreds of cards, groups, and relationship-lines can be arranged in a display. The arranged chart can be output by a printer and saved in a disk.

The most serious problem when the card-handling is simulated on a computer is how to get the panoramic view of whole cards in a chart. Our solution for this problem is providing a screen which gives a close-up view of a part of the chart and which can be panned (scrolled) very fast when a mouse is dragged out of the screen. We call the screen "Local-screen". This method is just a simulation of "real" card-arrangement on the "real" desk. The high speed panning of Local-screen was realized so that KJ-Editor is of practical use. As shown in Figure 1. an additional screen that shows the outline of arrangement is also presented in the display[Ohiwa90].

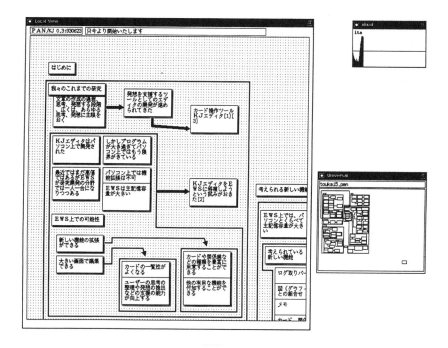

Figure 1.: Sample screen of KJ-Editor

When a collaborator makes some operations on a chart in KJ-Editor, the other collaborators can see the operations on thier own displays. That is so-called WYSIWIS (What You See Is What I See)[Stefik87a] facilities are implemented in KJ-Editor.

Some CSCW(Comuter Supported Cooperative Work) tools[Stefik87b] do not have the strict WYSIWIS facilities for the sake of the usability, whereas we implemented WYSIWIS facilities strictly by two reasons. The first reason is that Local-screen cannot display the whole of a chart. If WYSIWIS facilities are not implemented, collaborators cannot see the same part of the chart at the same time and it comes to be difficult to make a discussion on the chart. The second reason is based on Japanese way of decision making. In Japanese society, a conference is usually held for making a consensus. KJ-Method is also used for forming a consensus rather than creation. Thus, it is important for collaborators to share the same contents of the display[Ohiwa93].

In cooperative use of KJ-Editor, we restricted the the user who can arrange the chart is only one person at a time. The user who has a arranging privilege can edit the chart, and the other users can only observe his whole operations on their own displays. A pseudo mouse-cursor that is rocated at the same positon of the mouse-cursor on the display of the user who has the arranging privilege is displayed on the other user's display. The panning of Local-screen on the other user's display is also made by the pseudo mouse-cursor. Any user can get the arranging privilege, when nobody has the arranging privilege.

3. Experiment

We have made an experiment that four collaborators made a requirements specification of a middle-scale problem using KJ-Editor. The problem is "LIFT" problem that is well known as a common problem for requirements analysis[Davis87]. We have also researched the method of requirements analysis and design using KJ-Editor and its effectiveness. This experiment forms a part of this research[Takeda93].

The all four subjects are experienced programmers. They were familiar with KJ-Editor for the personal use, and used to make a requirements analysis using KJ-Editor. But, they have never used KJ-Editor for the cooperative work use. Tatar[Tatar91] has pointed out that in the experiment for evaluating a software system some experiences of the subjects for the system sometimes made bad influence on the results because they could settle some problems of the system based on their experiences. From a point of this view, we selected these subjects.

Before the experiment of the collaboration, the one of the subjects made a requirements specification for the problem as a chart using KJ-Editor for the personal use. The task of the experiment was to review this requirements specification by four subjects. The subjects met at a room and were provided with separate networked computers. They could make a face-to-face communication. Thier works were videotaped, and thier operations on KJ-Editor were recorded using logging facilities of KJ-Editor. Since the logging record includes all messages sent between the different computers, the whole of collabolative works on KJ-Editor can be reproduced.

4. Consideration

The review was worked as following order;
1. S1[1] who made a requirements specification took the arranging privilege.
2. S1 explained the chart of the requirements specification to the others.

---

[1]"S" followed by a number is used to denote subjects.

3. The other subjects put questions to S1, and discuss together.

4. Some opinions and ideas were written down the chart by any subject who took the arranging privilege.

Table 1. shows the distribution of basic operations according to the functions and operators. This statistics were collected from a experiment that lasted 97 minutes.

Table 1.: Distribution of operations

Function	S1	S2	S3	S4	Total
Get Privilege	12	12	0	4	28 (15.1%)
Give up Privilege	12	11	0	3	26 (14.0%)
Request Privilege	1	6	1	1	9 (4.8%)
Pan Local-screen	12	8	0	1	21 (11.3%)
Point out Text	0	3	0	0	3 (1.6%)
Point out Card	32	14	0	9	55 (29.6%)
Move Card	0	1	0	1	2 (1.1%)
Write down Card	0	2	0	0	2 (1.1%)
Copy Card	0	1	0	0	1 (0.5%)
Create Card	0	0	0	1	1 (0.5%)
Point out Group	3	9	0	0	12 (6.5%)
Make Group	0	1	0	0	1 (0.5%)
Delete Group	0	1	0	0	1 (0.5%)
Point out Rel-line	0	11	0	0	11 (5.9%)
Make Rel-line	0	2	0	1	3 (1.6%)
Others	1	5	0	4	10 (5.4%)
Total	73(39.2%)	87(46.8%)	1(0.5%)	25(13.4%)	186

The analysis of the logging record and videotapes led to the usefulness of a computer supported card-handling tool for the group in mediating their cooperative work. In collaboration, it was easy for the subjects to concentrate on the specific card or group in the chart. For example, the utterances that were made with pointing paticular card or group as shown in Figure 2. amount to 38 times, however it was only one time that the discussion was discontinued because of the misunderstanding of the referent.

S2: "And,... what is **this**?"
S1: "For example, what should we do in case of very high building".
S2: "And, **this** arrow, what does it mean?"
S1: "Well, there are examples of **this** card".

Figure 2.: Session including pointing out chart element

The data of Table 1. indicate that the total number of operations of pointing out cards, texts in cards, groups, or relationship-lines is considerably larger than the number of the utterances mentioned above. This also suggests that pointing out elements in a chart is useful in communicating with collaborators.

We think that this usefulness results from WYSIWIS and arranging privilege facilities of KJ-Editor. Since the other subjects could take notice of the movement of pseudo mouse-cursor which was moved by a subject who had the arranging privilege and pseudo mouse-cursor and its pointing elements were always presented on all displays because of WYSIWIS facilities, it was easy for the subjects to concentrate their focus on the pointed elements in the chart.

We also observed that new cards were always written and arranged on suitable place after getting all subjects' agreements. This cooperation is useful for preventing misunderstandings. This operation is exactly same as "storing information" which is one of the drawing space activity functions classified by Tang[Tang91]. It is thought that this effectiveness results from the arranging privilege facilities.

On the other hand, WYSIWIS facilities sometimes became obstacles for personal viewing of the card-arrangement and caused collaborators to be uncomfortable. The subject who had the arranging privilege always panned Local-screen that could present a part of the chart which was needed for his explanation. Some subjects reported that they sometimes wanted to see the surrounding area of the presented part of the chart on Local-screen, but that it was not permitted to pan Local-screen without the arranging privilege so that it caused them to be uncomfortable. For the settlement of this problem, we are implementing new panning facilities that permit a user without arranging privilege to pan his Local-screen a little.

5. Conclusion

An experiment with a card-handling CSCW tool named KJ-Editor was described. The experiment was made for only one type of card-handling uses. It is needed to make experiments for other card-handling uses, as example the brain-storming method in which many cards are created by collaborators from the beginning, and to consider the usability of KJ-Editor in the cooperative-works.

References

[Davis87] Davis,N. : Problem #4, Problen Set for the Fourth International Workshop on Software Specification and Design, IEEE–CS Press, pp.x (1987).

[Kawakita86] Kawakita,J. : KJ-Hou(KJ-Method, in Japanese), Chuo-Kohron-sha, 581pp. (1986).

[Ohiwa90] Ohiwa,H., Kawai,K. and Koyama,M.: Idea Processor and the KJ Method, J. of Information Processing, Vol.13, pp.44-48 (1990).

[Ohiwa93] Ohiwa,H., Kawai,K., Shiomi,A. and Takeda,N.: KJ-Editor: A Collaboration Environment for Brain Storming and Consensus Forming, Proc. HCI International '93, 8-13 Aug. 1993, Orlando, Florida, USA.

[Stefik87a] Stefik,M.J., Foster,G., Bobrow,D.G., Kahn,K., and Lanning,S. : Beyond the Chalkboard, Comm. of ACM, Vol.30, pp.32–47 (1987).

[Stefik87b] Stefik,M.J., Bobrow,D.G., Foster,G., Lanning,S., and Tatar,D.G. : WYSIWIS revised: early experiences with multiuser interfaces, ACM Trans. on Office Information Systems, Vol.5, pp.147–167 (1987).

[Takeda93] Takeda,N., Shiomi,A., Kawai,K. and Ohiwa,H.: Requirement Analysis by the KJ Editor, Proc. RE'93, IEEE Int. Symp. on Requirement Engineering 1993, 4-6 Jan. 1993, San Diego California, USA.

[Tang91] Tang,J.C. : Finding from observational studies of collaborative work, Int. J. Man–Machine Studies, Vol.34, No.2, pp.143–160 (1991).

[Tatar91] Tatar,D.G., Foster,G., and Bobrow,D.G. : Design for conversation: lessons from Cognoter, Intl. J. Man–Machine Studies, Vol.34, No.2, pp.185–209 (1991).

HCI Aspects of the CASSY-Environment

Erdmuthe Meyer zu Bexten[a,b] and Claudio Moraga[b]

[a]Fraunhofer Institute of Microelectronic Circuits and Systems,
Finkenstr. 61, W-4100 Duisburg 1, Germany

[b]University of Dortmund, Department of Computer Science,
Otto-Hahn-Str. 16, W-4600 Dortmund 50, Germany

1. INTRODUCTION

In the last three years a CAD-environment for a Computer Aided symbolic Simulation SYstem, called CASSY [1], has been developed at the Fraunhofer Institute of Microelectronic Circuits and Systems in cooperation with the University of Dortmund, Chair I of the Department of Computer Science. The environment is based on the X-Window system, OSF/Motif and the UIDS Motifation [2]. This tool supports the design of signal processing systems at a high level of abstraction. The main features of CASSY are a fast, symbolic simulation, which makes possible a fast design concept verification, an interactive, ergonomical user interface and an operating mode, which is adapted to the working style of design engineers (instead of forcing engineers to adapt themselves e.g., to a rigid HDL). The implementation of consecutive prototypes of CASSY has been carried out in close contact with experienced circuit designers, who contributed to the requirements definition and to the prototypes evaluation. Moreover CASSY has proven to be able to operate with additional simulators in a multilevel fashion [3].

Several reports on CASSY have been published in the past [4]. The reader not familiar with CASSY is kindly invited to read the proper references. In what follows, the newest developments within CASSY will be disclosed and discussed. These include the consistent duality in the representation of signals and systems, a tool to continuously update the methods library of the simulator and finally, a specification language to express both the functional and descriptive parts of a specification as well as a tool to display it and navigate through its information units.

2. SYSTEM DESCRIPTION

CASSY offers a special textual description method (named SIMBA) and a graphical one (named SIMGA, see Fig. 1) for the definition of architectures (signals and components). Automatic conversion between the two methods provides with a concurrently updated version in either description: For each design task there exist two descriptions, a textual and a graphical one. Any changes introduced in one of the versions will be automatically available in the other version after saving. The designer can directly enter his description in the text editor or the icon based graphic window area. For both methods the user can get proper support in form of e.g. skeletons for textual as well as graphical descriptions, hierarchical representations, automatic completion of text structures and online syntax checkers.

The above mentioned duality of representations is motivated by ergonomical principles. A textual description allows a simple compact representation of the parameters with their corresponding values and units. The structure of the system, however, is not likely to be recognized. On the other hand, the graphical method emphasizes structural features, while parameters remain hidden in the background. To access parameters, a special additional dialog window is provided. Moreover the continuous consistent availability of both methods allows the design engineers to select the alternative closest to their personal workstyle.

During all steps of a simulation it is necessary to control and verify the result signals. An interactive simulator without an appropriate tool for displaying and analyzing results is unacceptable. The CASSY system contains a tool named AUCA [5] to perform this task. AUCA supports three different display modes for presentation of input and output signals:

1. textually in form of a SIBA (Signal Description Language [1]) description,

2. as signal waveforms or

3. as lists of samples.

The CASSY system comprises a collection of sophisticated tools. Their complexity grows with the steadily increasing requirements of the users and the high efficiency of the supporting workstations. For such a complex work the user needs efficient support in form of a textual and graphical information service. Help system is the name given to a service of this kind. To perform this task CASSY uses a context sensitive help system called HICA which is based on the hypertext concept. For producing application specific help systems, a special tool named AUXA (**AUX**ili**Ar**-System [1, 6]) was created. It consists of the following three components:

- an *input language* to produce a hypertext oriented syntactical structure into the help text under development,

- a *display tool* to show the help text according to the hypertext concept,

- a *consistency checker* to guarantee that the author of a help system writes the adequate help text and the proper commands in the right way.

3. METHODS DESCRIPTION WITH MEBA

The high-level simulator HISIM constitutes the core of the CASSY-environment. HISIM is an object-oriented symbolic simulator for digital and analog circuits at the system level. The simulator supports the interactive work of engineers in the early design stages. It becomes apparent that new components may be required, for which no methods exist in the library of the simulator. The methods description tool MEBA [7] was developed to solve this problem.

The specification of a new component in MEBA (see Fig. 1) consists of a declaration part and a body. In the declaration part the engineer gives the required information for the integration of the new method into the simulator. In the body, the functionality of the component is described in a C-similar language. Moreover a special front end for MEBA will be implemented to accept thruthtables defining digital components as well as formulas defining analog components.

During the work with MEBA, an on-line syntax checker searches for errors and gives a warning at the earliest possible time. MEBA has a special icon editor to generate new icons, which will be added to the library of the corresponding editor for the graphical description of systems mentioned earlier in this paper.

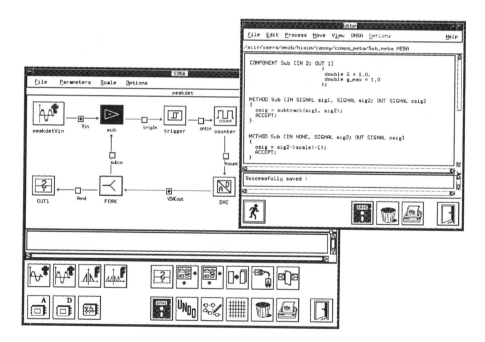

Figure 1: MEBA description for the component "Sub"

4. STRUCTURED REQUIREMENTS SPECIFICATION

The concept of system (requirements) specification in the CASSY-environment includes the following aspects:

- a formal, operational description of the system to be designed and

- a set of information blocks, which constitutes a complementary informal descriptive specification. Blocks may give details on e.g. test strategies, constraints (chip area, lowest acceptable speed, energy consumption, etc.) and reasons supporting design decisions.

This rather unusual concept of system specification has been adapted from [8]. The purpose is not that of overloading the engineer with additional paper-work. Quite on the contrary, the goal is to support his design work. This states special demands on a specification tool. The user should be given appropriate assistance to generate and edit the corresponding texts and graphics, define relationships among them and display a selection of them on an own specification window.

Under this aspect (the work with information texts) the requirements specification is similar to a special help-system and it is possible to structure it on the basis of a tree of hypertexts with special additional transversal links. The help development system of AUXA [1, 6], as well as its help-display, consistency checker and LaTeX-to-helptext converter may be adapted and properly extended to support the earlier discussed demands. Finally this will be embedded in SIMBA, which already allows the formal description of the functionality of systems, extending it to be an ergonomical specification tool.

4.1. Display Tool

The display tool uses the commands of the help development system to prepare the information text according to the hypertext concept. These texts are presented in a special window following the OSF/Motif guide lines. The window is divided in the three main areas (see Fig. 2):

- *menu bar* with the menus 'File', 'Options' and 'Help'

- *working fields* one for the formal specification, the others for the blocks of descriptive specification

Right below this field there are several buttons, one for each considered information block. By activating one of these buttons appears an pop-up menu to select in which of the following areas the informations will be presented.

- *button row* to control the navigation in the tree of hypertext documents

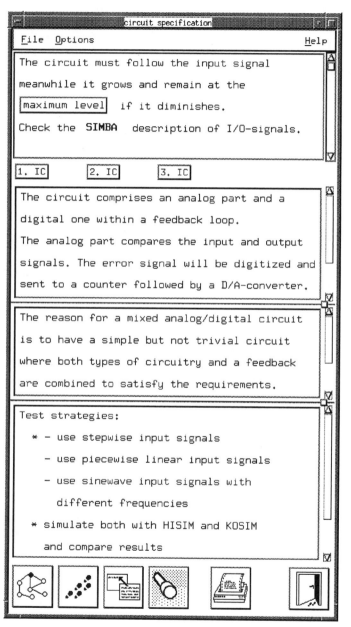

Figure 2: Window for specification information

Acknowledgments

The authors wish to thank their students of the two project groups 186 and 212 and Jürgen Rensen from the University of Dortmund, Department of Computer Science, for the prototype implementations of these concepts.

5. REFERENCES

[1] E. Meyer zu Bexten: *Eine Simulationsumgebung für signalverarbeitende Systeme*, Dissertation, Universität Dortmund, Fachbereich Informatik, Shaker Verlag, Aachen, 1992.

[2] P. Griebel, M. Pöpping, G. Szwillus: *MOTIFATION - A User Interface Development System*, in: Telekommunikation und multimediale Anwendungen der Informatik, GI - 21. Jahrestagung (Hrsg.: J. Encarnaçao), Springer-Verlag, Berlin, 1991.

[3] P. Schwarz, C. Clauß, U. Donath, J. Haufe, G. Kurth, P. Trappe: *KOSIM - ein Mixed Mode, Multilevel-Simulator*, in: B. Reusch (Ed.): Rechnergestützter Entwurf und Architektur mikroelektronischer Systeme, Informatik Fachberichte 255, S. 207-220, Springer-Verlag, 1990.

[4] E. Meyer zu Bexten, C. Moraga and J. Büddefeld: *A High Level Interactive Design Environment for Complex Systems*, Lecture Notes on Computer Science, Vol. 585, pp. 442-459, Springer-Verlag, 1992.

[5] E. Meyer zu Bexten, D. Heinen and C. Moraga: *AUCA: A Tool for Presentation and Analysis of Simualtion Results*, in this volume.

[6] E. Meyer zu Bexten, C. Moraga and M. Stark: *A Development Tool for Help Systems based on the Hypertext Concept*, Proceedings of the International Conference WWDU'92: Working with Display Units, Berlin, pp. E60-E61, 1992.

[7] J. Rensen: *Rechnergestützte Erstellung neuer Komponenten für den Simulator HISIM nach vorgegebenem Konzept*, Diplomarbeit, Fachbereich Informatik, Universität Dortmund, 1993.

[8] U. Wienkop: *Methoden und Werkzeuge für einen strukturierten Systementwurf*, Dissertation, Universität Dortmund, Fachbereich Informatik, 1992.

The TOM approach to system development: methods and tools for task oriented modelling of real-time safety critical systems

C. P. Warren

British Aerospace plc, Sowerby Research Centre, FPC 267, PO Box 5, Filton, Bristol, BS12 7QW, England.

Abstract
The Task Oriented Modelling (TOM) approach to system development is based on the production of task-related models within an overall unifying framework. The models constructed using the TOM technique represent only those aspects of the domain of application, user, and device (computer system) which are directly related to the achievement of task goals. The models are used to generate quality and cost metrics which are then used to calculate performance metrics for the task. These performance metrics direct the system developer to problem areas which can be addressed by redesign of the device, user training, or reorganisation of the domain. This performance based approach is novel in the fields of Human-Computer Interaction (HCI) and system development. As part of its support for the system development process, the TOM project has produced prototype computer-based tools which assist in the construction of the domain, user, and device models. The TOM technique was developed using the real-time safety critical domain of Air Traffic Management (ATM), the users being Air Traffic Control Officers (ATCOs). Further work is being carried out on the transfer of the TOM approach to the domain of aviation.

1. INTRODUCTION

The TOM project (IED 4/1/1717) has produced a system development technique which assists in the design and development of interactive computer systems. The project used the domain of Air Traffic Control (ATC) as an example of real-time safety-critical process control. The TOM approach provides system developers with a measure of the performance of the operator and computer system with respect to the domain of application. Support is provided in terms of computer-based tools, which aid the system developer in constructing task-based models of: the user (operator); the (computer) system; and the domain. The output from the models is used in conjunction with a system development framework to identify performance decrements during the task. The task in this case is the safe and expeditious control of air traffic.

The strength of the TOM approach is in its particular focus on tasks. When observing a task using the TOM technique, data is collected simultaneously about users, the devices they use, and the application domain within which they are working. Other task-related information concerning the working environment, and the technical and organisational infra-structure is included in the TOM analysis. At the data analysis phase, the three separate models of user, system and domain are brought together to provide a description of a single integrated system that can be evaluated in terms of its performance. Decisions about allocation of function between the user and the system can now be made more easily. Trade-offs between design options can also be evaluated in terms of the performance differences predicted by the models.

Two of the tools for producing task oriented models (the domain and the device) are in prototype form on an Apple Macintosh™ computer, whilst the third modelling tool (user, or operator) is fully implemented on a computer workstation running the UNIX™ operating system. However the TOM approach to system development can be used without the aid of computer-based tools. The tools essentially speed the process of system development.

2. INTERACTIVE WORKSYSTEMS AND DOMAINS

The TOM approach distinguishes between Interactive Work Systems (IWS) and domains of application. This distinction is based on a rationale for an engineering discipline of Human Factors developed by members of the TOM project consortium [1]. An IWS consists of a user working with a computer system to carry out a task. For example, in the domain of ATM, the user is the ATCO, and one future computer system which the TOM project has addressed is that for the production of electronic flight progress strips (EFPSs). Each aircraft under the control of the ATCO has an associated EFPS, which provides information relating to the aircraft including: route; altitude; and callsign. The domain of application is the controlled airspace through which aircraft are flying.

There are three models produced using the TOM technique: a model of the domain in which the task is being carried out (TOMDom); a model of the device used to assist in carrying out the task (TOMDev); and a model of the operator actually carrying out the task (TOMUsr). Figure 1 shows the derivation of the three model approach, and how within the TOM approach, the user and the device are viewed together as an IWS.

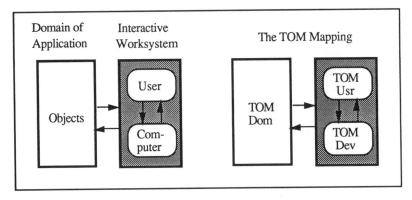

Figure 1. TOM Interactive Worksystem and Domain

3. THE TASK ORIENTED MODELS

For a given IWS and domain, the three models constructed using the TOM approach provide the system developer with the following information:

TOMDom describes the domain of a task in terms of its transformation by the task. The model expresses domain objects, their attributes, attribute relations, and the quality of transformations of those attributes.

TOMUsr describes the human behaviours exhibited by a worksystem. It expresses the physical and associated mental behaviours of the user associated with domain object transformations, and their consequent resource costs. The TOMUsr method is based on a task analysis methodology, Task Analysis for Knowledge Descriptions (TAKD) [2].

TOMDev describes the computer behaviours exhibited by the worksystem. It expresses the computer activity associated with domain object transformations, and the consequent resource costs. The TOMDev is a formal model of the computer system, modelling the user interface and the underlying application software.

4. PERFORMANCE METRICS FOR SYSTEM DEVELOPMENT

Two types of measures, Quality and Costs, are used in the TOM approach to derive a performance metric over time on task. Performance is calculated as a function of Quality/Costs. This measure of performance allows the system developer to identify any performance decrements during the course of the task. Performance of the IWS in the TOM approach is measured with respect to achievement of task goals.

TOMDom: Quality (Q), a measure of the extent to which the task goals have been met by the user.

TOMDev: Costs (K), a measure of the resource costs, in terms of both the running costs of the device in terms of processing load, and the costs of producing the software.

TOMUsr: Costs (K), a measure of the resource costs, in terms of the costs of training the operator, and those behavioural costs incurred from carrying out the task.

Figure 2 shows example cost and quality curves for a task, with the resulting performance curve for use by the system developer. The task is split into discrete task *events*. A task event is said to occur whenever the user exhibits a piece of behaviour directed towards achieving any task goal. The system developer is able to determine easily the point in the task where there is any performance decrement, and discover the cause of the problem. From the example curves in Figure 2, the task events at which the performance decrement occurs can be examined in more detail through examination of the Quality and Cost curves. It can easily be seen from this example that the major cause of the performance decrement is a marked increase in the behavioural costs for the user, probably resulting from excessive workload. The TOM tools are intended to provide graphical output of the Performance, Quality, and Cost measures for use in the system development process.

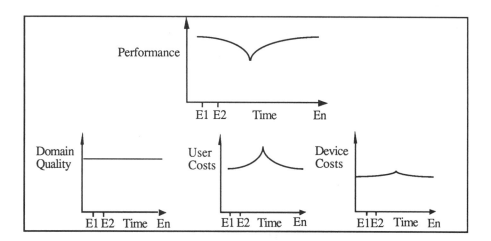

Figure 2. Example Cost, Quality, and Performance Curves

5. USING TOM IN SYSTEM DEVELOPMENT

A framework has been constructed which supports the use of the TOM technique in system development. Given that the results of a TOM analysis show a performance decrement due to excessive demands on the operator, or bottlenecks in the functionality of the device, the system developer is then able to either modify the system, or suggest revised training or selection procedures for the operators. There are five main stages in the TOM system development framework shown in Figure 3. The following subsections describe the five stages in turn.

5.1. Stage 1 of the TOM Approach: Simulation

Stage one of the TOM system development framework is optional. If there is already an existing support system used in the task, then this system can be used to carry out the observational phase of the TOM approach using a representative task. If the intention of system developer is to develop a computer system to support the task where a system does not already exist, then a simulation of the system will be necessary. A simulation of the system will also be required when the system developer does not have access to the "on-line" computer system.

Where a system simulation is necessary, aspects of the three modelling techniques are used to construct the simulation. For example, early steps of the TOMDom construction allow the system developer to scope the domain and identify a representative task. The information acquired from the partial use of the modelling techniques, and experience gained from previous system development work, assists the developer in devising an appropriate system for support of the task. If innappropriate design choices are made in the configuration and specification of the simulation, these will be identified in the performance metrics derived from output of later stages in the TOM approach.

5.2. Stage 2 of the TOM Approach: Analysis

Stage two of the TOM system development framework involves an observational study of the operator using the computer system (System A in Figure 3) to carry out the task. Having selected a representative task, the operator is observed whilst carrying out the task. The whole exercise is videotaped, including an audio recording where appropriate. The three TOM models are then constructed for the task. A full description of the use of the TOM methods used to produce the TOM models: TOMDom; TOMUsr; and TOMDev is described elsewhere [3, 4].

5.3. Stage 3 of the TOM Approach: IWS Integration

Stage three of the TOM system development framework integrates the three TOM models: TOMDom; TOMUsr; and TOMDev. The output from the three models are integrated in terms of the measures of User and Device Costs, and Domain Quality. The integrated measures provide Performance metrics for each task event over the duration of the task segment selected for full analysis.

Examination of the Performance curve (See Figure 2), allows any performance decrements to be easily seen for particular task events. The system developer is then able to cross refer to the Cost and Quality curves for those task events. In this way, the causes of the performance decrements can be identified in terms of either increased User or Device Costs, or a reduction in the Quality of Domain transformations with respect to the goals of the task. The precise behaviour of the operator, computer system activity, and domain states may be determined from examination of the User (TOMUsr) and Device (TOMDev) models for the relevant task events.

5.4. Stage 4 of the TOM Approach: Model-Based Design

Stage four of the TOM system development framework deals with the design activity suggested by the earlier analysis. The identification of the exact causes of any performance decrements now allows the system developer to generate ideas for design changes in the configuration of the computer system, the way that the user carries out the task, or indeed changes in the organisation of the domain itself. This process is represented in Figure 3 by the

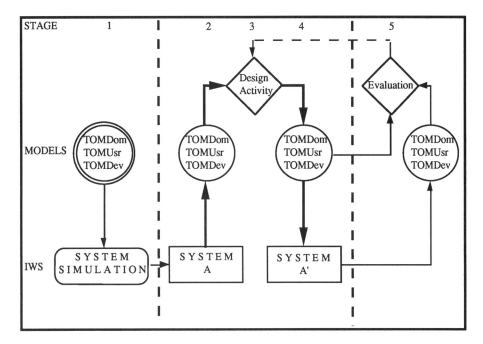

Figure 3. The TOM System Development Framework

diamond shaped box labelled "design activity" between Stages one and two of the TOM system development framework.

In contrast to many other system development approaches, the TOM approach allows the system developer to both evaluate and quantify the consequences of making changes without having to carry out further observational studies. This "model-based design" activity entails the modification of any or all of the TOM models to remove the decrement in task performance identified in Stage 3 of the TOM system development framework.

If the system developer then implements these changes, whether to the operator's task, the computer system used in the task, or the domain itself, the result should be an increase in overall task performance. This is shown in Figure 3 in terms of a re-designed computer system, System A'.

5.5. Stage 5 of the TOM Approach: Evaluation of Design Activity

Stage five of the TOM system development framework is optional. For a full application of the TOM approach, in Stage five operators should carry out a representative task on the new computer system (System A' in Figure 3). Observational data is again collected, and the three TOM models are constructed for the new computer system. Cost and Quality measures from the new models are used to calculate Performance metrics for each task event using the new system.

The Performance metrics for the new system are then compared with the predicted Performance metrics resulting from the changes made to the earlier TOM models in Stage four. This evaluation activity is represented by the diamond shaped box in Stage five shown in Figure 3. If the predicted increases in Performance suggested by the changes made in Stage four for system (System A') are not reflected by the new TOM models, then a further iteration is required (shown by the dotted line between evaluation and design activity in Figure 3).

A failure to produce the increases in task Performance suggested from the model changes made in Stage four would result in the requirement for additional design activity. Here, the original TOM models would be modified again in an attempt to maximise the overall task Performance. The number of iterations through this evaluative Stage five of the TOM system development process, would depend upon the amount of time and resources available.

6. DISCUSSION

The time taken for a complete cycle through the TOM approach to system development is appreciable in its current state as an integrated research tool, however, the approach is at an early stage of development. As has been suggested in Section 5, Stages one and five of the TOM approach are optional. This leaves Stages two, three, and four representing the essential TOM approach consisting of: Analysis; IWS Integration; and Model-Based Design.

For the TOM approach to be truly cost-effective in the process of system development, all three modelling activities require full tool support. In addition to the tool support for model construction, there is a requirement for an overall tool, integrating the three model building tools and locating them within the generic system development process. This part of the TOM tool-set is currently under-specified.

In the final stages of the TOM project, the approach was also applied to the related domain of aviation, using test pilots from British Aerospace flying an Airbus aircraft simulator. The evaluation of the TOM approach in this new domain of application are reported elsewhere [5].

Both British Aerospace and Logica are currently exploiting aspects of the output from the TOM project, and elements of the TOMUsr have been developed into a fully operational computer-based task analysis tool by Liverpool University (Liverpool University Task Analysis for Knowledge Descriptions - LUTAKD).

6. REFERENCES

1   J. Dowell, and J.B. Long, Towards a conception for an engineering discipline of human factors, Ergonomics , 32 (11), pp.1513-1535, (1989).
2   D. Diaper, and P. Johnson, Task analysis for knowledge descriptions: theory and applications in training. In J.B. Long and A. Whitefield (Eds.), Cognitive Ergonomics, Cambridge University Press, Cambridge, (1989).
3   D. Diaper, and M. Addison, User Modelling: The Task Oriented Modelling approach to the designer's model. In D. Diaper and N. Hammond (Eds.) People and Computers VI, Proceedings of the HCI'91 Conference, Cambridge University Press, Cambridge (1991).
4   M. Addison, L. Colgan, S. Gikas, and C. Warren, Methods and tools for task oriented modelling of devices - version 3, IED4/1/1717 TOM project deliverable, ref. TOM/PD15/QMW/SG030492/1, (1992).
5   C. Warren, Evaluation of the TOM technique for system development in the domain of aviation, IED4/1/1717 TOM project deliverable, ref. TOM/DEL(PD18)/SRC/CW/211092/1, (1992).

7. ACKNOWLEDGEMENTS

The TOM project (Task Oriented Modelling for Interactive System Design) was a collaboration between Logica, British Aerospace plc, University College London, Queen Mary and Westfield College, and the University of Liverpool. It was lead by Logica Cambridge Ltd., and was funded under the United Kingdom's Government's Department of Trade and Industry (DTI) and Science and Engineering Research Council (SERC) Information Engineering Advanced Technology Programme (Grant No. IED 4/1/1717). The views of the author do not necessarily reflect those of the TOM project consortium.

Thanks to C. Kelly for comments on an earlier draft of this paper.

Integrating CASE and UIMS for Automatic Software Construction

Christian Märtin and Christian Winterhalder

Fachhochschule Augsburg, Fachbereich Informatik, Baumgartnerstraße 16, DW-8900 Augsburg, Germany

Abstract
The paper presents a tool-based architecture for the design and near-automatic construction of interactive software. AME (*Application Modeling Environment*) uses an object-oriented scheme for representing applications. The system integrates CASE-tool support for object-oriented analysis and design (OOAD) and a knowledge-based UIMS for automatic user interface generation and domain code integration.

1. INTRODUCTION

Intelligent user interface design tools use graphical user interface editors, dialog specification languages or knowledge-based design approaches to facilitate user interface construction [1]. However, there is still a gap between CASE-environments for software automation and UIMSs for user interface design automation. Application domain functionality and user interface components are integrated only late in the development process. Coordination of domain and user interface design activities is often poor. Resources are sometimes duplicated and analysis and design results tend to get lost at implementation level.

AME´s objectives therefore are:
- *Full technical integration of software engineering and user interface design methodologies* starting at the early stages of system development [2].
- *Exploitation of domain models* for synthesizing the user interface objects and their behavior.
- *Reusable software components and problem solutions* for domain and user interface parts of applications using manageable repository approaches [3].
- *Adaptable design interfaces/construction tools,* which mirror the background of different developers, allow for varying abstraction levels of application represen-tations and provide missing details automatically.
- *Knowledge-based techniques* to improve the quality of the generated software.

2. ARCHITECTURE AND METHODS

AME is organized in three levels (Figure 1): *analysis and design level, construction level* and *application generation level.* Several object-oriented and knowledge-based tools are used at the different levels. An object-oriented representation scheme is used for describing interactive applications during the modeling process. It also serves as the basis for communication between the modeling tools.

2.1. Application Representation

AME uses a domain-independent, object-oriented representation, which has evolved from a frame-based approach [4]. It focuses on conciseness and flexibility for modeling interactive systems, does not restrict the developer to fixed architectures and dialog structures and ensures usability. Representation scheme and modeling tools are implemented using Intellicorp's KAPPA-PC.

To keep tool interfaces simple and to allow a uniform approach for user interface synthesis, only two generic object types are used for describing conceptual application structures: *AS_profiles* represent groups of conceptual elements. Groups can be composed of *AS_components* (content elements) and/or other AS_profiles. Whole/part relations and activation links between objects may be organized hierarchically, though cyclic structures are allowed for data recursion. Both object types may appear as classes or instances. They have standard sets of content description slots. Slot values can be manipulated and interpreted by AME tools during the construction process. Domain-dependent slots can be added. An extensible set of standard inter-object relations (e.g. whole/part structures, two types of associations, etc.) is supported.

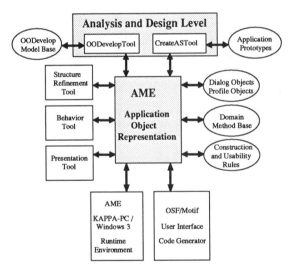

Figure 1. Application Modeling Environment

AS_profile-slots describe group-specific actions, construction/presentation services, dialog resources, or domain information for the automatic development process. AS_component-slots specify contents, functionality, dialog representations (interaction objects/media), dialog behavior, inter-object-relations, configuration services and available object prototypes.

2.2. Analysis and design level

Object-oriented techniques have been applied to user interface designs since the introduction of window systems and toolkits and have been incorporated into many user interface management systems. Object-oriented programming languages have had a major impact on the current view of the development process and the design environment for interactive applications. In the last five years several object-oriented techniques for modeling the analysis and design phases of the software development process have emerged. Some of these OOAD approaches mention the importance of the user interface for an overall application system, but only little attention is paid to the identification and modeling of user interface objects [5].

By introducing an analysis and design interface level, AME tries to integrate generic object-oriented software specification methods with user interface design techniques. In the software development process analysis concentrates on the specification and representation of the problem domain. Design, on the other hand, covers the specification and representation of the solution domain. Specifying a system's user interface is generally considered as part of the solution domain, whereas most semantic objects of an application can already be defined during analysis.

Sometimes, however, it is not possible to draw a clear line between analysis and design for an interactive application. It can be necessary to specify right at the OOA-level representation objects for some parts of a spreadsheet user interface, like dialog boxes for function selection or macro definitions, which activate low-level semantic objects.

An application developer or dialog designer, using AME, decides, at what stage in the definition process which of the domain and interface representation objects will be modeled. A dialog designer may take the results of an OOA to add the appropriate representation objects for the user interface and specify their dynamic behavior during OOD, before passing the OOD-model to the construction level. In contrast, an application developer may concentrate on specifying the high-level semantic objects of an application and only produce an OOA model. In this case the system can exploit the *OOA*-model by applying knowledge about the application domain, user interface guidelines and structural knowledge to provide the user interface representation objects in as much detail as possible. The resulting *OOD*-model is then passed to the construction level.

OODevelopTool is a CASE tool for OOAD that makes advanced software engineering methods [6] available for AME (Figure 2). It consists of a set of (graphical) editors for specifying objects, attributes, services, and the dynamic behavior of OOAD-models for complete applications or parts of applications, like the domain or user interface parts. The tool introduces a dynamic inheritance mechanism for adopting results from analysis to different design versions. This mechanism permits simultaneous modification of an OOA-model and all OOD-model versions derived from it. To extend the tool´s performance, techniques were applied, which narrow object interfaces and improve software correctness at the design level [7]. Full OOAD-models are stored in a model repository and can easily be reused and combined for building other applications. Prototypical implementations in several supported languages can be linked to each model version.

For any selected OOAD-model version an AME representation can be created automatically. OOAD-specifications are mapped to AME objects. Only information that is relevant for user interface synthesis and domain code integration is translated into an AME representation. Any combination of generalization/specialization-relations, whole/part-relations, object associations, multiplicities of inter-object-relations and message connections is translated into a structurally unique pattern of values in the slots of an AME object. The dynamic and functional behavior of an OOAD-model is specified by object services, service types, service activations, service sequencing and inter-object messages for service activation and data exchange. This information about the behavior of an object and its dynamic interaction with other objects is mapped to specific action slots of an AME object.

CreateASTool is an optional rule- and method-based design tool that can add semantic and structural design information, needed by the construction level, to AME

294

representations. It supports specific environments and domain types using an extensible set of rules and object-methods. CreateASTool offers an interactive question and answer end-user specification mode, although it is typically invoked automatically, after a pure OOA-model, without explicit user interface structures and objects, was translated into an AME representation. The rules and methods applied to a representation are both domain-independent (e.g. for detecting standard object patterns) and domain-dependent (e.g. for scanning the semantic contents of an object and for creating activation links between different objects).

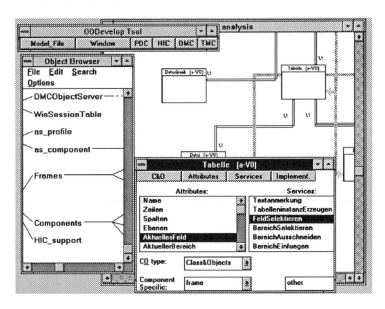

Figure 2. Using OODevelopTool for object-oriented application modeling

Object patterns [8] in AME representations are formed by inter-object-relations and message connections. They are analyzed in order to create object groups and detect semantic neighborhoods between objects. The AME representation is modified to include any detected object interdependencies and the correct object invokation hierarchies. Object patterns and semantic analysis can also provide hypothetical interaction object types for representation objects (e.g. *application main window, table, radio button group, speech command input,* etc.).

Depending on the target environment (Windows or Motif) AME representation objects for command activation like selections, menus, buttons, icons or unspecified placeholder objects are added. These representation objects may be organized hierarchically in some environments (e.g. menu bar, pulldown menus, dialog boxes, check boxes). Several of the attributes and methods of semantic representation objects, can be assigned as entries to standard menus like *File, Edit, Help,* etc. Activation links between menu representation objects and semantic objects, into which available method code will be embedded at construction level, are included. To find out, which kinds of dialog boxes can be used by an application, domain specific knowledge is required. For any interaction object type mentioned in a rule or method that is used by CreateASTool configurable object prototypes have to be provided at construction and generation level.

2.3. Construction level

Object-oriented and rule-based components at the *construction level* (Figure 3) refine the AME design representation. They automatically create a user interface prototype, add functional behavior and adapt applications to specific users. If needed, interaction objects for an AS_component or AS_profile representation object can be attached to the representation object. Their type and appearance are specified by a structure refinement tool that uses syntactical and conceptual information in AS_component- and AS_profile-slots, and, if available, any type information already provided by the design level. Pure semantic objects will have no external user interface representation.

Interaction object instances are created, configured, grouped and linked to specific slots of their representation objects by dialog behavior methods. To add a new interaction object type to AME's base of dialog resources, the interaction object type has to be implemented. A behavior method that maps the standard attribute and action slots of the representation object to the specific structure and properties of the new interaction object type has to be added to the behavior tool. Interaction objects, which activate domain services of semantic objects, are connected with them by dynamic links. Links are also used for data exchange between objects.

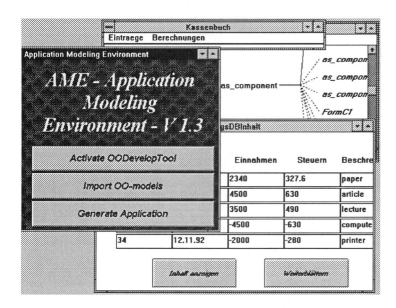

Figure 3. AME construction level interface and prototypical Windows output

Domain functionality is integrated by automatically embedding application code into method containers of representation objects. Reusable domain method code for standard services and any method implementations linked with OOAD-models are collected in a domain method base. Layout and presentation of the user interface prototype can be adapted to specific users and system configurations by rules and methods. User profile and configuration objects are provided by a presentation tool. At any stage during the construction process prototypical results may interactively be modified by the developer.

2.4. Application generation level

The *application generation level* produces runtime program code for application models. A detailed prototypical application description as produced by the construction level can directly be executed as a KAPPA-PC application under Windows. The object model of the construction level results can be compiled into independent C++-Windows applications or OSF/Motif applications under UNIX. Interaction objects are available in runtime libraries.

3. RESULTS AND CONCLUSIONS

Tests using AME for modeling interactive office applications (spreadsheets, business applications, multimedia editors) show a significant reduction of development time for user interface construction, when compared to using only graphical toolkits or user interface editors. The overall software development cycle can be standardized and further shortened. Control services and domain service activations can automatically be generated by AME and added to the source code. Combining method-based and forward-chained rule-based techniques provided good results for structure analysis, interaction object selection, dialog behavior integration and presentation. Object-orientation eases reusability of interface components and prototypical representations. The C++-library of Windows interaction objects is currently extended. A library of embeddable methods for the business and visualization domains is under development. The necessary control knowledge will be added to AME´s rule and object resource-bases.

4. ACKNOWLEDGEMENTS

The authors thank Prof. Dr. Helmut Balzert of Ruhr-University at Bochum for his perceptive comments on separating OOA from OOD. We would also like to acknowledge the contributions of Birgit Stöger and Johann S. Kempfle at FHA, who helped to acquire domain specific knowledge for spreadsheet applications and to implement the C++-interaction object library and code generator.

5. REFERENCES

1 Sullivan, J.W. and Tyler, S.W. (Eds.). Intelligent User Interfaces, ACM, 1991.
2 Hix, D. Generations of User-Interface Management Systems. IEEE Software, (Sept. 1990), 77-87.
3 McClure, C. The Three Rs of Software Automation. Prentice-Hall, 1992.
4 Märtin, C. A UIMS for Knowledge Based Interface Template Generation and Interaction, in Proc. INTERACT ´90, North-Holland, 1990, 651-657.
5 Monarchi, D.E. and Puhr, G.I. A Research Typology for Object-Oriented Analysis and Design. Comm. ACM, Vol. 35 No. 9, (Sept. 1992), 35-47.
6 Coad, P. and Yourdon, E. Object-Oriented Design. Prentice-Hall, 1991.
7 Meyer, B. Object-Oriented Software Construction. Prentice-Hall, 1988.
8 Coad, P. Object-Oriented Patterns. Comm. ACM, Vol. 35, No. 9, (Sept. 1992), 152-159.

Problem Solving Support System as Thinking Acceleration Tools

Takashi NAKAMURA

Department of Information and System Engineering, Faculty of Engineering, Osaka Sangyo University, 3-1-1, Nakagaito, Daito, Osaka, 574 Japan

Abstract

In this paper, we describe some aspects of our problem solving support system. We have developed this system as thinking acceleration tools. We have developed some thinking acceleration technique, and show how a system can offer effective support through them. Especially, we propose the idea of *Active Memo* as mechanism for thinking acceleration. We have developed this approach through experience with a prototypical support system (the task is card game calculation).

1 INTRODUCTION

What has been done so far for the information processing technology seems to increase the capabilities of a computer on a path to the ultimate machine. As a result, the computer now seems to be able to work with human beings only if humans are able to define a problem exactly. A future study theme of human interface will therefore be how to integrate the intelligence of human and computers for realizing the best results possible. Its focus should be on the technologies that allow the user to concentrate more on higher-level intelligent work for more advanced achievements. This requires the development of computer as an intelligence amplifier (IA), that is, a tool for supporting and enhancing human capabilities.

From this point of view, we study problem solving support system as intelligent thinking acceleration tools. In this paper, we describe some aspects of our problem solving support system. We have developed some thinking acceleration technique, and show how a system can offer effective support through them. Especially, we propose the idea of *Active Memo* as mechanism for thinking acceleration. We have developed this approach through experience with a prototypical support system (the task is card game calculation).

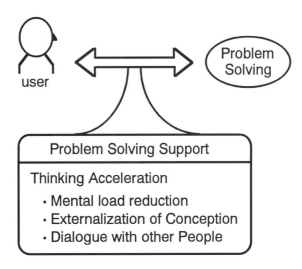

Figure 1: Problem Solving Support and Thinking Acceleration

2 PROBLEM SOLVING SUPPORT SYSTEM

We study problem solving support system as intelligent thinking acceleration tools. For problem solving support, we have found three thinking acceleration technique necessary. They are

1. Mental load reduction

2. Externalization of Conception

3. Dialogue with other people

(Figure 1).

2.1 Mental load reduction

This is the most fundamental technique. In real problem solving scenes, human user must pay attention to many aspects of the problem. If the support system reduce such user's mental load, user can concentrate more on higher-level intelligent work.

2.2 Externalization of Conception

In the information processing process of human thinking, several media play important parts. Among them are memorandum, rough sketch, model, formula expression, program. Human usually use these media for externalization of conception. Through interaction with these media, human thinking is accelerated. That is, the cycle of

1. externalization

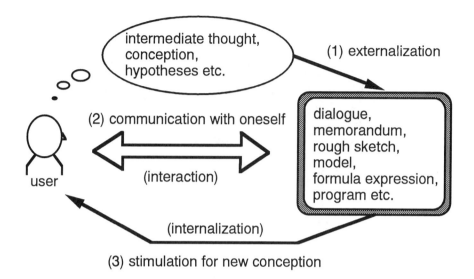

Figure 2: Externalization of Conception

2. communication with oneself (interaction)

3. stimulation for new conception (internalization)

accelerates human thinking process (Figure 2). So, the support system has to help this cycle, especially externalization.

2.3 Dialogue with other people

In real problem solving scenes, a user can solve problems easily in cooperation with other people, that is, "Two heads are better than one". So, it is necessary the support system to act a kind of "other people". In this case, it is not necessary that the "other people" have more knowledge and more ability than user. The most important role of "other people" is to suggest another path to the solution.

Sometime "Externalization of Conception" can act a kind of "other people". Through the externalized medium, the user can see past conceptions and can interact with past oneself (that is, virtual "other people") (Figure 3).

3   PROTOTYPICAL SUPPORT SYSTEM

For further study of thinking acceleration technique, we have implemented a prototypical support system. It works on UNIX workstation with X-window system. The task of the system is solving solitaire-type card game, calculation.

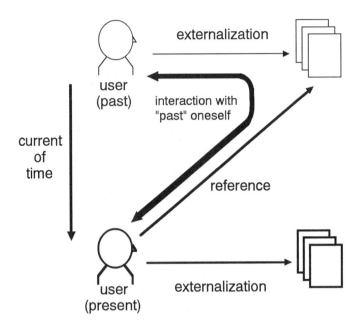

Figure 3: Externalization of Conception as Dialogue

3.1 Calculation

Calculation is solitaire-type card game. A player expose a card from shuffled 52-cards. And the player put the card into suitable position one at time, using some stacks as first-in last-out work areas.

3.2 Prototypical support system

In prototypical support system, a player play calculation on the display (Figure 4). The player expose a card, grab it and put it into suitable position or work area with mouse. The system provide "trial and error environment for problem solving" and point out some appropriate information such as the suitable position for the card that is grabbed. That is, the prototypical support system only provide some means for "Mental load reduction".

4 ACTIVE MEMO

Through experience with a prototypical support system, we suggest the idea of *Active Memo* as mechanism for thinking acceleration.

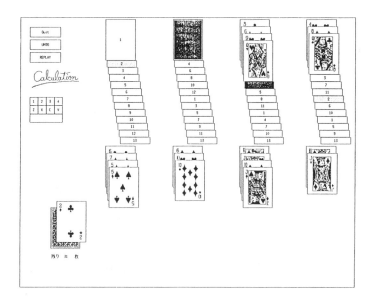

Figure 4: Example display of Prototypical support system

4.1 Active Memo

Each Active Memo is made by user. It acts according to the user's instruction. It acts as *memorandum* in one side, and acts as *program* in another side.

As memorandum, Active Memo keeps a user's concepts, hypotheses, intermediate results of problem solving and so on. It is medium for externalization of conception. It reduces the user's load for memorization.

As a program, Active Memo keeps the user's intention and acts according to it. That is, Active Memo is not only a passive memorandum but also an active agent . It reduces the user's load for attention and computation.

4.2 Monitoring Memo and Algorithm Memo

We propose two types of Active Memo, Monitoring Memo and Algorithm memo (Figure 5).

The user previously set watch conditions to Monitoring Memo. Monitoring Memo watches and monitors problem solving situation according to the user's instruction. It calls the user's attention by alarm when necessary.

Algorithm Memo executes complex computation in accordance with the user's request. Of course, the user must give computation algorithm previously.

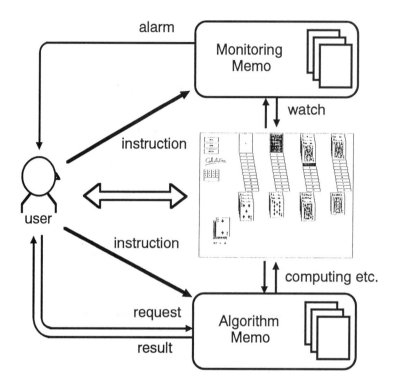

Figure 5: Monitoring Memo and Algorithm Memo

5 CONCLUSION

We have described some aspects of our problem solving support system and some thinking acceleration technique. Especially, we have proposed the idea of Active Memo as mechanism for thinking acceleration.

Now we implement Active Memo on the prototypical support system, and will be able to illustrate its effectiveness using scenarios taken from a user study.

References

[1] T.Nakamura:Problem Solving Supports by Multi-Agent Cooperative System, Proc. of 8th Symposium on Human Interface, pp.253–258 (in Japanese) (1992).

A software architecture for cooperative knowledge based systems

A. Hadj Kacem, J-L. Soubie and J. Frontin

IRIT-ARAMIIHS, Institut de Recherche en Informatique de Toulouse, 118 Route de Narbonne, 31062 Toulouse Cedex, France
e-mail : {hkacem, soubie, frontin}@irit.irit.fr

Abstract

The specificity of Knowledge Based Systems (KBS) in comparison with conventional Computing Systems (CS) lies in the fact that they integrate the feature of "intelligence". Such systems incorporate the user in the problem solving and decision process [1]. As the user guides and participates in the problem solving, it becomes essential to turn the simple communication with the system into a real *cooperation* between the two partners. Modeling this cooperation as a communication activity at the conceptual level has been proved necessary in the development of KBS. We propose a Man-System Cooperation Model (MSCM) and a new software architecture model for Cooperative KBS. Their objective is to make easier the communication between the user and the system within the context of cooperative work. Moreover, we take into account the user's objectives and his knowledge about the domain. In this paper, we firstly present the contribution of the Seeheim model to the design of Man-Machine interfaces. Secondly, we state the specificity of KBS in relation to conventional CS. We insist, thirdly, on the interest of our MSCM. Finally, we detail the software architecture we propose for the design of cooperative KBS.

1. SOFTWARE ARCHITECTURE OF CONVENTIONAL CS

Owing to the fact that software is more and more meant for non specialist final users in computing fields, designers of computing systems are concerned to a greater extent with the interface elaboration. Therefore, it becomes useful to clearly separate the abstract world of the application from the physical world of the interface while still ensuring an easy cooperation between the two universes. One of the proposed solutions to clearly organize the system is based on the notion of architectural model. Since 1985, the Seeheim model [2] has touched on the problem of organization of a CS application and its interface. This field has been the topic of several researches the principles of which focus on the Seeheim model such as PAC [3], Arche [4], etc ... This model is one of the first in the field of software architecture modeling and still remains a reference for analysis and design of interactive systems.

This kind of architecture proposes a partition of the system into three logical components. First, the Application component gathers all the functions the system performs. Second, the Presentation component is reserved for the system's external representation. It specially deals with the problems of computer readout and input device. Third, the Dialogue Controller component manages the dialogue between the user and the Application component. In the Seeheim model it represents the nerve centre of the system. The relevance of this model and this partition into three components comes from the fact that it provides an independence between the application aspects and the graphic aspects of the system allowing an easier design and evaluation.

2. KNOWLEDGE BASED SYSTEMS : THE MODELING

Cooperating, means working together in a mutual effort to achieve a common goal by sharing both the know-how and the knowledge of partners (system and user). The development of a KBS is based on the conceptual model which support the modeling of domain expertise. In our case, we think that the conceptual level reflects various levels of knowledge used by the expert when he solves problems in a particular field. This model establishes a conceptual link between the form by which knowledge is described in natural language and the form by which it is encoded in the KBS [5]. In fact, knowledge acquisition methodologies producing conceptual models such as KADS [6], MACAO [7], etc... use representations underlining, on the one hand, the purely descriptive aspect of a field and on the other hand, a formalization of the reasoning. Therefore, this model constitutes a base for development and implementation of KBS.

Since the conceptual model constitutes a good characterization of communication difficulties, it is advisable to wonder about a systematic exploitation at a formal level of information contained in conceptual models (expert and user) to further the cooperation. In order to situate our work, we will begin by emphasizing the importance of the expert conceptual model and the user's one [8].

2.1. Expert conceptual model

The Expert Conceptual Model (ECM) groups gathers the expert knowledge into "modules" associated with problem categories that refer to situations or ways close to the reasoning. To solve a problem, the expert first tries to find in the environment the characteristics (or "syndromes") of a well-known situation for which he has a solution (in a structure called "conceptual schema")" [7].

The ECM of which the expert know-how constitutes the most relevant knowledge source, contains two parts. The first, that we find in the literature under several names : static knowledge, static model or ever field model, consists in representing the whole basis knowledge of the expert's field by means of objects or concept forms that are usual for him. The second part which is also found under several names in the literature : dynamic model, dynamic knowledge or ever reasoning model, describes his reasoning strategies in the field of activities.

2.2. User conceptual model

The User Conceptual Model (UCM) has the same structure as the ECM. On the one hand, we find all concepts, objects and relations that are significant for him, and on the other hand, the problem solving knowledge [9].

Several aspects of the user are relevant to the interface technology. These aspects include : the user's expertise in common applications, the user's goals, the user's evaluation of the system, his preferences concerning communication modalities. Among these features, we find out those mentionned in [10] proving that the user's model is a knowledge source for a Man-Machine dialogue. They include hypotheses on all aspects of the user which could be relevant for the dialogue management. The user's model serves as a basis to design the interfaces and we want it to be able to evolve dynamically according to the user's characteristics and his mental state. It is the base for Adaptive Systems (AS) that need a model of system's users to make inferences not only about the domain but also about the user's knowledge of the domain [11].

The importance of user modeling is obvious for a cooperative system. The explanations that it displays must reflect the expertise of a particular user [12-13]. Consequently, the fundamental difference between ECM and UCM is not only the "behavioural" aspect of the UCM but also the empirical construction by the expert of strategical problem solving levels which justify the performance of this latter. As a consequence, we propose to take into account, among the important elements of the difficulty of communication, the resorting to this high level concepts.

2.3. Man-System cooperation model

The MSCM we propose is not considered as a cookbook to design a cooperative system but rather to dynamically exploits the two conceptual models (expert and user) and all the environmental constraints. Thus, the communication between man (user) and system (expert), within the context of cooperative work, is facilitated by taking into account the user's objectives and his abilities in the domain.

A user's cognitive or physical skill, such as his knowledge of controlled process, constitutes the third layer of MSCM. Taking them into account enables to achieve a cognitive compatibility between user and system. Yet a system cannot be independent of its exploitation environment. That's why a set of cooperation constraints stemming from the environment (physical environment, security, strategic choice, etc...) constitutes the second layer. It improves the MSCM. The conditions in which these constraints should be taken into account are related to the application spatio-temporal context. In the absence of environmental constraints and cognitive skill of the user, the analysis of inter-individual cooperation mechanisms serves as a base to the mechanisms of task's distribution. These mechanisms constitute a theoretical cooperation model which is the kernel of MSCM (first layer).

In conclusion, the originality of our approach lies in the fact that the design of cooperative KBS is based on the MSCM which contains cooperative specific knowledge, ECM and UCM. In the following section, we present a software architecture which has been chosen to suit the needs of cooperative KBS.

3. SOFTWARE ARCHITECTURE OF COOPERATIVE KBS

The needs in software architecture for making use of a cooperative KBS become more and more demanding. It leads to consider the architecture models for interactive systems of which the problem of organization of the application and its interface was boarded. It is interesting to refer to Seeheim's model [2] which always has proved its interests. It has since been considered as a reference. Like conventional CS, our architecture is composed of three logical components: the Cooperative Application, the Man-Machine interface or Presentation and the Dialogue Controller. However, it remains specific in comparison with conventional CS. This specificity comes in fact from the intelligent aspect of the system and from the cooperative aspect in resolution process. To take these specificities into account, we propose a decomposition in accordance to Figure 1.

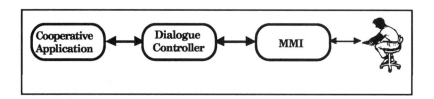

Figure 1. Model of software architecture for cooperative KBS.

In comparison with the architecture presented by Seeheim, we think that it is worthwhile, indeed even indispensable, to keep the basic idea of independence between the application and the graphic aspects. Worthwhile : because it permits an easier design and evolution of the application. Indispensable : because we manage external representation by each individual or class of system user. This last point is one of the basic elements of the third layer of MSCM. These elements take into account the user's interface preferences, namely his skills. Furthermore, the data structure which reflects the user's knowledge in the expertise domain serves as a base to estimate his intentions. In fact, this idea has been conjured up on a par with the MSCM which uses the ECM to systematically compare the user's and system's aims to drive the user during the problem solving. Such a structure must sustain some modifications since user may evolve in the resolution process. This evolution can be either at external or at internal level. Up to external level, it expresses the user's evolution in the matter of interface even though at the internal level we note an evolution in strategies and methods of resolutions. Yet the system must be able to update the UCM according to the knowledge evolution and user skills. It becomes interesting to integrate the MSCM in the Cooperative Application component level to allow a systematic evolution of the UCM and a dynamic comparison of the two conceptual models.

3.1. The Presentation or the Man-Machine interface
The entity Presentation is responsible for the application's physical presentation. This component has three distinct functions: (i) external-data translation into a computer format, (ii) processing of messages sent by the Dialogue Manager and (iii) output interpretation in external unit terms. This is the only system component which directly manipulates input/output items.

3.2. The Dialogue Manager or Controller

The Dialogue Manager (DM) behaves as a mediator between the Presentation and the Cooperative Application. In a system such as Seeheim proposes, the DM exchanges messages that the user transmits to the application and inversely. So, the Controller effects, in one way or another, some message inspection before sending them to one of the partners (Cooperative Application or Interface). In this study we use the "Dialog Manager" (DM)[†] which manages the relationships between "applicative" and graphic aspects while keeping the independence feature.

3.3. The Cooperative Application

This component includes all the functions, structures and adapted devices to a given cooperative task, taking into account the user's cognitive skills and knowledge in the field. This Cooperative Application is composed of two logic sub-entities : the Application and the Cooperation Manager (Figure 2).

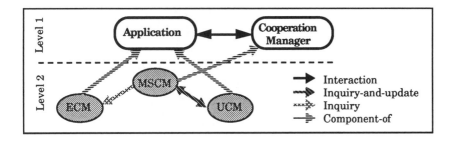

Figure 2. Architecture of the "Cooperative Application" component.

The Application component keeps the same functionalities as the ones described in the Seeheim model. It represents all the data structures and functions proposed by the system. In our case, we'll talk about ECM and UCM that are the subject of future KBS. The Cooperation Manager is based on MSCM in a computer-usable form. It constitutes the intelligent part of the system component as a whole. This component insures a cooperative communication with the user. It exploits dynamically the two conceptual models that are in the Application and the constraints coming from the application surroundings. The Cooperation Manager is the only entity which, on the one hand, is in possession of a total view on the whole system, and on the other hand, insures the coherence between the different partners.

In the systems like the cooperative KBS, we deliberately brought to the fore the entity cooperation management as an interface between the application and the Dialogue Controller. It takes charge of the cooperation and the problem of consistency of the different entities independently of the application statement. That is why it constitutes the nerve centre of the whole process. The Seeheim's model gives to the Dialogue Controller the function of system engine.

[†] diffused by ILOG society

Such an architecture meets the KBS' requirements and accurately the cooperative KBS' needs of which the communication between the user and the system is more demanding than the conventional CS to reach a real cooperation between the two partners.

4. CONCLUSION AND PERSPECTIVES

To summarize, the conceptual existence of MSCM has an influence on the knowledge phase acquisition since we talk about knowledge acquisition not only about expert but also about user. The architectural existence of MSCM has produced some modifications in the KBS architecture. So, we have proposed an architecture model taking into account the MSCM and the specificity of KBS.

Currently, our study consists of the use of operational language for the description of the MSCM, the ECM and the UCM to validate the proposed cooperation model and the model of software architecture. This language that is based on the notion of *task* and *method,* allows a formal description of strategy level, task level, inference level and knowledge level [5].

5. REFERENCES

1   M. Stelzner & M. D. Williams, The evolution of interface requirements for expert systems, Expert systems : the user interface, edited by James A. Hendler, University of Maryland, ablex pub. corp., New Jersey 07648.

2   G. E. Pfaff, User Interface Management System, Proceedings of IFIP/EG, Workshop on UIMS, 1985, Springer-Verlab, Seeheim, F. R. of Germany.

3   J. Coutaz, Interface Homme-Ordinateur conception et réalisation, Dunod Informatique, Paris 1990.

4   L. Bass , R. Little, R. Pellegrino, S. Reed, R. Seacord, S. Sheppard, M. Szezur, The Arch Model : Seeheim Revisited, User interface Developpers' Workshop, April 1991.

5   I. Delouis, Une architecture pour la représentation formelle et la simulation des modèles conceptuels : application au développement d'un système d'aide, 1ères Rencontres jeunes chercheurs en IA, 1992, France.

6   H. P. de Greef & J. A. Breuker, Analysing system-user cooperation in KADS, Knowledge Acquisition, Vol 4, n° 1, March 1992.

7   N. Aussenac, N. Matta, Making a method of problem solving explicit with MACAO, Knowledge acquisition, 1993 (to be published).

8   J. Frontin, A. Hadj Kacem, J.-L. Soubie, Acquérir des connaissances et structurer le système pour coopérer, Actes des Quatrièmes Journées d'Acquisition des Connaissances, JAC'93, 31 Mars-2 Avril 1993, France.

9   P. Booth, An introduction to humain-computer interaction, IEA 1990.

10   W. Wahlster & A. Kobsa, Dialogue-Based user models, Proceedings of the IEEE, Vol 74, n° 7, july 1986.

11   D. Benyon, D. Murray & F. Jennings, An adaptive system developper's tool-kit, Human Computer Interaction-INTERACT '90, 1990, pp 573-577.

12   D. Sleeman, UMFE : a user modelling front-end subsystem, International Journal of Man-Machine Studies (23), pp 71-88, 1985.

13   R. Kass & T. Finin, The need for user models in generating expert systems explanations, International Journal of Expert Systems, Vol 1, n° 4, 1988.

The Implementation of Knowledge Structures in Cognitive Simulation Environments

D. V. Benysh and R. J. Koubek
School of Industrial Engineering, Purdue University, West Lafayette, IN 47906

ABSTRACT

With recent trends in labor requirements moving from manual labor to cognitive oriented tasks, the need for understanding of the factors that effect skilled cognitive task performance has never been greater. A number of methods have been developed which attempt to identify, describe, or model these factors. Additionally, some of these models have been integrated and, using a multi-factor approach, have had reasonable success in explaining factors associated with human skilled cognitive task performance.

This research proposes one such model combining the outstanding features of Cognitive Modeling techniques into a Knowledge Organization framework. The resulting Procedural Knowledge Structure Model (PKSM) is then evaluated to assess likely structural dimensions which have an effect on task performance. These dimensions are then defined in terms of quantifiable measures, which are then empirically validated. Results indicate that the PKSM measures, and thus model dimensions, are highly significant indicators of aspects of task performance. Furthermore, these measures provide greater predictive power than traditional knowledge structure dimensions, and a combined model (with both sets of measures included) provides yet even stronger predictions. The demonstrated capability of the PKSM indicates that it potentially has implications for user modeling in the areas of Human-Computer Interaction, task design, personnel selection and training, and task analysis. Furthermore, the model may also be applicable as a design tool in Knowledge-Based Systems research.

OVERVIEW

In addition to Cognitive Factors, Skill Acquisition, and Cognitive Modeling, the study of the organizational structure of a person's body of knowledge has become an important area of research in the cognitive engineering fields, identifying this structure as a significant determinant of performance on cognitive tasks. With the importance of knowledge structures (KS) established, current research in the area focuses on developing quantitative tools for measuring knowledge structures and developing theoretic postulations as to the nature and effects of knowledge structures on task performance. This research provides software designers with tools and a methodology for assessing user and task requirements in the design of human-computer interaction tasks.

As an alternative to this taxonomic approach of performance determinants, others have proposed the development of simulations of cognitive processes as essential for truly understanding the inherently procedural process of cognitive performance. This Cognitive Modeling (CM) approach, drawing on a variety of techniques from computer science and artificial intelligence research, has made significant inroads in present understanding of human learning and problem solving. Being designed to yield responses identical to the group of individuals being modeled, validity of the model is a function of how well the model outputs match the human. As such, efforts continually focus on improving this degree of match.

Given the established value of knowledge structures in understanding human performance, it is intuitive that in order for a model of cognition (via cognitive simulation) to match the human output, the knowledge structure attributes between the model and human should be the same. Unfortunately, it is believed that insufficient KS information may be typically encoded into the CM as a result of the concentrated effort on developing correct procedures during model development. As such, this structural information can provide valuable input in developing and revising the cognitive simulation to better match KSs (and thus output) with the human. With this better match comes the ability to more accurately predict human output on a given cognitive performance task as may be found in the area of Human-Computer Interaction. Therefore, this research provides a model for integrating KS research findings into the cognitive simulation environment, produces a methodology, or tool, which facilitates this integration and provides evidence for the efficacy of combining KS research with cognitive simulation work.

Current Models

Current research in the area of knowledge representation is divided into three primary classifications. The first class is that of Knowledge Organization used to develop models of declarative knowledge primarily for the purpose of examining, understanding, and quantifying various aspects of human encoding, storage, and retrieval on information. These researchers are theorists, working towards an understanding of the underlying principles of human behavior through an understanding of this organization of knowledge. Typically, these models involve concepts which are interconnected by links which indicate relationships between the concepts. A number of quantitative tools have been developed for analysis of such structures such as Multidimensional Scaling [20, 9], PathFinder [21], and Hierarchical Clustering Schemes [13, 19]. These techniques provide Knowledge Structure (KS) models with a high degree of measurability, however the models themselves are not executable.

The next classification is exploratory cognitive modeling. This field is primarily concerned with modeling *how* humans organize, learn, and use knowledge (typically procedural knowledge). This leads to a concentration on extremely specific problem domains or general broad sweeping approaches intended to account for many aspects of human cognition at once. Furthermore, these models are frequently executable, or at least 'traceable' by hand. This provides the models with the ability to make direct predictions regarding performance in terms of execution time, memory load, and gains through consistency. Popular models in this category include GOMS [8], NGOMSL [14, 15], Human Associative Memory [1, 3], Adaptive Control of Thought [2, 17], Cognitive Complexity Theory [7, 12], and the General Problem Solver [4, 18].

The third class is functional cognitive modeling. In contrast to work in exploratory cognitive modeling, where the goal is to replicate cognitive processes, researchers in this area tend to work in performance frameworks. This performance approach attempts to build systems that behave intelligently with little consideration for how humans do so. These models, being computerized, are highly executable which enables them produce output similar to that of a human given the same input. However, this capability does not provide quantifiable measures which would allow predictions as to how a human would actually perform the same task with regards to execution time error rate, etc. Techniques in this area include Frames and Scripts [6, 23], Production Systems [11, 16, 22], and Logic [5, 10, 11].

Summary

Review of relevant research in the KS and CM domains resulted in a taxonomy of methodologies and a list of attributes common in many models. These attributes were identified as desirable features in a structural representation of human procedural knowledge. This list of features includes aspects such as procedural modularity, measurability, executability, class / attribute inheritance, representing general "proximity" of concepts, representing individual differences in ability or expertise, and the ability to handle different situations or initial states.

PKSM

The identification of these attributes led to the development of the Procedural Knowledge Structure Model (PKSM) which incorporated the identified attributes. The model was then evaluated with respect to the development of a catalog of quantifiable structural measures. These theoretically based measures were hypothesized as having specific affects on cognitive task performance. Finally, the model, by way of these measures, was validated in an experiment which correlated these individual measures of the human subjects' PKS with aspects of their performance on a complex pencil and paper scheduling task.

Model

The PKS model is a structural model of procedural knowledge. It is comprised of a taxonomy methods or procedures, specific to a particular task environment. However, it uses a visual representation scheme similar to that of the traditional declarative knowledge representations in order to bring out the structural and organizational aspects of procedural knowledge. This combination benefits from the advantages of each of the model aspects previously identified as being common to many approaches.

The model is best visualized as a three dimensional pyramid similar to that shown in Figure 1. The pyramid is sectioned into "floors" or levels. Each of these levels contains a flowchart representation of the task steps. The difference between the flowcharts of each level is that with each descending level, the items in the chart are broken up into smaller and smaller sub-units or sub-tasks. Each individual sub-task at one level will be broken up in to its constituent sub-tasks at the next level. This decomposition continues, level by level, until at the very bottom level, the flowchart is a very complex structure consisting basic task actions (keystrokes, hand or eye motions, and decisions) which cannot be further decomposed except at the human neurological level. Objects in the flow chart may be task goals (which will be further decomposed), basic task actions (which can be performed or executed), and decision nodes (which control the flow through the chart).

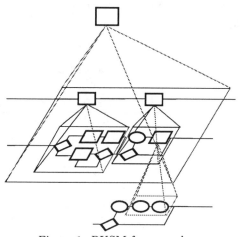

Figure 1. PKSM framework

Task goals are represented by rectangles. These goals will be subdivided into smaller goals, task elements, or decision nodes at the next lower level, much like GOMS or NGOMSL. In this same figure, basic task actions are represented by the ellipses and decision nodes by diamonds. These task actions and decision nodes, once encountered, will be perpetuated through to lower levels since they cannot be further decomposed. These individual levels have the advantage that at each level, the flow chart taken separately, can be executed from start to finish in order to perform the task. This can be accomplished by proceeding through the chart executing each basic task action and branching at decision nodes.

The procedural elements in the task are laid out in this flowchart type organization. A horizontal chart displays the actions, computations, decisions, and outputs necessary in performing the task. Unlike traditional flowcharts though, it has the capability of simultaneously representing many different ways of doing the same task, as this figure illustrates. It is not restricted to one particular strategy and does not focus on any best way of doing the work. In this manner, it is able to model the various different approaches used by different people ranging from novice to expert level performance with differing experience and ability. Furthermore, these decision nodes mimic production rule systems by defining a direction to take based on facts in the environment, or NGOMSL selection rules by selecting path to take. Also, this expands upon the usefulness of scripts by incorporating methods for each unique task situation.

Sub-task proceduralization capabilities are found by moving upwards through the pyramid structure. Working from the bottom up, groups of elemental task actions can be grouped together to form a single task item (or goal) at the next level up. The elemental items are collected or said to be proceduralized into the next higher level. Each higher structural level represents an increase in the level of task proceduralization than the one below it. The highest level will simply be the singular task statement or task goal.

Clearly, the PKS model is one of scale or scope. This is evidenced by the fact that any individual proceduralized sub-task can be separated from the structure to stand alone as a separate task. This procedure will then become the overall task with its sub-goals and sub-tasks self contained. Likewise, the original task structure can be subsumed into some larger overall task and become one of the many sub-goals within it.

RESULTS and CONCLUSIONS

The analysis of experimental results has shown that particular measures of organization and link content in the structure have significant value in determining task performance time, error rates, and expertise level. As such, the model of human procedural knowledge structures has been shown to be a useful tool in describing and evaluating how humans perform cognitive tasks. The significant contribution here is the model's focus on the structural aspects on knowledge while simultaneously incorporating important procedural aspects of cognitive psychology and knowledge-based system models.

Further, this work advances the theories of human cognitive task performance by leveraging findings in knowledge structure research to provide a foundation and a technique to model the procedural aspect human cognitive task knowledge. This may in turn, be used as a design tool to aid in cognitive simulations where improved accuracy in modeling human cognition is sought.

REFERENCES

[1] John R. Anderson. *Language, Memory, and Thought.* Lawrence Erlbaum Publishers, Hilldale, NJ, 1976.

[2] John R. Anderson. *The Architecture of Cognitition.* Harvard University Press, Hilldale, NJ, 1983.

[3] John R. Anderson and Gordon H. Bower. *Human Associative Memory*. John Wiley and Sons, New York, 1973.

[4] Avron Barr and Edward A. Feigenbaum. *The Handbook of Artificial Inteligence*. Addison-Wesley, New York, 1982, 1989. (editors).

[5] S. J. Biondo. *Fundamentals of Expert System Technology: principles and concepts*. Computer engineering and computer science. Ablex Pub. Corp., Norwood, NJ, 1990.

[6] Alain Bonnet. *Artificial Intelligence: promise and performance*. Prentice Hall, Inc., Englewood Cliffs, NJ, 1985.

[7] Susan Bovair, David E. Kieras, and Peter G. Polson. The acquisition and performance of text-editing skill: a cognitive complexity analysis. *Human Computer Interaction*, 5:1–48, 1990.

[8] Stuart K. Card, Thomas P. Moran, and Allen Newell. *The Psychology of Human–Computer Interaction*. Lawrence Erlbaum Publishers, Hilldale, NJ, 1983.

[9] Mark L. Davison. *Multidimensional Scaling*. John Wiley and Sons, New York, 1983.

[10] L. E. Frenzel. *Crash course in Artificial Intelligence and Expert Systems*. H. W. Sams, Indianapolis, IN, 1st edition, 1987.

[11] N. Goldenthal. *Expert Systems and Artificial Intelligence*. Weber Systems, Cleveland, OH, 1987.

[12] Human Factors in Computing Systems and Graphics Interface. *Transfer Between Text Editors*, april 1987.

[13] Stephen C. Johnson. Hierarchical clustering schemes. *Psychometrika*, 32(3):241–253, 1967.

[14] D. E. Kieras. *Handbook of Human–Computer Interaction*, chapter Towards a practical GOMS model methodology for user interface design, pages 135–157. Elsevier, North-Holland, 1988.

[15] D. E. Kieras and Jay Elkerton. How to do a goms analysis for interface and documentation design. Tutorial in Computer–Human Interface 1991, 1991.

[16] P. G. Kyllonen and E. A. Alluisi. *Handbook of human factors*, chapter Learning and forgetting facts and skills, pages 124–153. Wiley, New York, 1987.

[17] D. M. Neves and J. R. Anderson. *Cognitive Skills and Their Acquisition*, chapter Knowledge Compilation: Mechanisms for the Automation of Cognitive Skills, pages 57–84. Erlbaum, Hillsdale, NJ, 1981.

[18] Allen Newell and Herbert A. Simon. *Human Problem Solving*. Prentice Hall Inc, Englewood Cliffs, NJ, 1972.

[19] Judith R. Olson and Henry H. Rueter. Extracting expertise from experts: Methods for knowledge acquisition. *Expert Systems*, 4(3), 1987.

[20] Susan S. Schiffman, M. Lance Reynolds, and Forrest W. Young. *Introduction to Multidimensional Scaling*. Academic Press, New York, 1981.

[21] Roger W. Schvaneveldt, Francis T. Durso, and Timothy E. Goldsmith. Measuring the structure of expertise. *International Journal of Man-Machine Studies*, 23:699–728, 1985.

[22] R. L. Solso. *Cognitive psychology*. Allyn and Bacon, Boston, 1979.

[23] Terry Winograd. *Representation and understanding : studies in cognitive science*, chapter Frame Representations and the Declarative/Procedural Controversy, pages 185–210. Academic Press, New York, 1975.

Experimental Method for Construction of a Knowledge-based System for Shipping Berth Scheduling

Masaichiro Ogawa[a], Norio Saito[a], Tsutomu Tabe[a] and Shinji Sugimura[b]

[a]Department of Industrial and Systems Engineering, College of Science and Engineering, Aoyama Gakuin University, 1-16-6, Chitosedai, Setagaya-ku, Tokyo 157, Japan

[b]Tonen System Plaza Inc., Shuwa Iidabashi Bldg., 2-3-19, Koraku, Bunkyo-ku, Tokyo 112, Japan

Abstract

This paper gives preliminary information on the methodology needed for the construction of a knowledge-based system for shipping berth scheduling. For this purpose, a computer simulator for shipping berth scheduling was developed for eliciting knowledge from humans. The results of scheduling by humans were analyzed by the protocol analysis using a GOMS model which is a useful tool to elicit knowledge for shipping berth scheduling in a real-time interactive environment. Furthermore, the elicited knowledge was transferred into a computer as a knowledge-based system for shipping berth scheduling.

1. INTRODUCTION

Oil products are shipped out from a refinery berth which is composed of several kinds of berth (pier). The problem of shipping berth scheduling is to determine, on the gantt chart, the berths in the oil refinery and the times, where and when several ships with different times of arrival and loading different types of oil, are to be loaded. In scheduling, due consideration is given to the kind and volume of products, the characteristics of the ships and berths, and the legal regulations concerning safety, which are all effective constraints. At present, it takes several hours to manually calculate two-days' solution of this problem by hand, and it is difficult for another person to appraise and modify the solution. There is therefore a strong demand for systemization. It is difficult to use a direct mathematical solution to this problem, because of the complicated objective functions and constraints. At the same time, the necessary strategies and processing in a practical schedule are not clearly described. This study therefore attempts to clarify the knowledge of humans who have obtained better scheduling result, and the main subject is to clarify the experimental method of constructing a knowledge-based system for shipping berth scheduling with this knowledge.

2. METHOD OF APPROACH

This process is automated using the following procedures;
① Interviews with the persons involved in the scheduling problem so as to obtain an

316

understanding of the problem.

② Development of a simulator for eliciting human knowledge based on the results of ①.

③ Task experimentation with the simulator so as to obtain verbal reports.[2]

④ Analysis using the GOMS model of the verbal reports of humans who obtained better results followed by classification and systemization in accordance with the knowledge classification method of Garg. C..[3]

⑤ Construction of a prototype of knowledge-based system based on ④.

⑥ Examination of the possible applications of the shipping berth scheduling process.

The GOMS model clarifies the structure of tasks undertaken by humans, based on several individual tasks; goals, operators, methods and selection rules. According to the theory of Garg. C., "knowledge elicited from experts can be classified into Content Knowledge (CK) and Process Knowledge (PK): the former includes the facts concerned with the problems and stereotyped rules; the latter includes the strategies and procedures needed in order to solve such problems"[3]. The knowledge thus obtained is stored in the knowledge base shown in Figure 1.

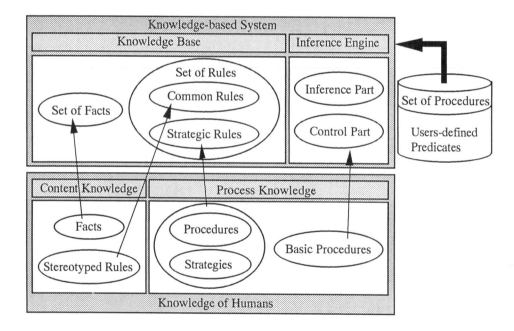

Figure 1. Connection between elicited knowledge and the knowledge base

3. SIMULATOR FOR KNOWLEDGE ELICITATION

Based on the results of the interviews with people involved in shipping berth scheduling, a simulator was developed for the purpose of eliciting the human knowledge of scheduling. This simulator is as realistic and retains as much of the full complexity of the problem as possible. The simulator screen is composed of a shipment order list as shown in Figure 2 and a gantt chart as shown in Figure 3. Humans draw up a schedule as a result of repeating the action that selects a scheduled ship from the shipment order list and by laying it out on a particular berth in the gantt chart.

Name of ship	Type of oil	Amount of shipment	Type of ship	Time	Congenial berth
1	Regular	1500 (t)	2000 (t)	6:00	1
2	Light oil	1000	1000	6:00	3
3	Lump oil	500	500	6:00	7
4	Jet oil	3000	3000	6:00	10
5	Heavy oil	5000	6000	6:00	8
⋮	⋮	⋮	⋮	⋮	⋮
18	Light oil	1500	2000	13:00	None
19	Kerosene	5000	6000	14:00	9
20	Premium	3000	3000	15:00	None

Figure 2. Example of information for humans : shipment order list

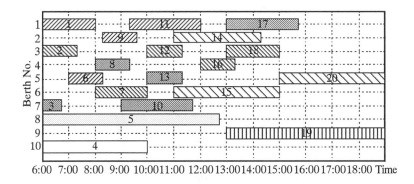

6:00 7:00 8:00 9:00 10:00 11:00 12:00 13:00 14:00 15:00 16:00 17:00 18:00 Time

Figure 3. Example of information for humans : scheduled gantt chart

4. TASK EXPERIMENTATION FOR KNOWLEDGE ELICITATION

Task experimentation was carried out in order to clarify the strategies and the procedures for shipping berth scheduling and to analyze how humans draw up a shipping schedule, while assigning the order of priority. The reasons for determining, on the gantt chart, the berths and

318

times where and when several ships with different times of arrival and loading different types of oil, were recorded as verbal reports. On the premise that the verbal reports of humans who obtained better results will provide better knowledge, the results were judged on the basis of the total waiting time of ships, the number of berths with same types of oil in the sequence, the continuity of the types of oil loaded on a particular berth, and compatibility between ships and berths. The best report was then analyzed using the GOMS model. As a result, the human who obtained the best result draws up a schedule while confirming the following four basic procedures concerning the different phases of decision making.

① Grasp the present conditions of ships and berths
② Select the selection standard for ships and berths
③ Forecast the future conditions of ships and berths
④ Determine a ship and berth

Furthermore, the characteristics of the scheduling procedures of this particular human were roughly divided into four phases as shown in Figure 4. and confirmation was made of each change in the selection standard for ships and berths in every phase.

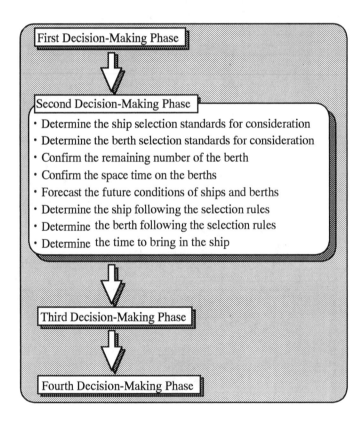

Figure 4. Outline of the different phases of decision-making

5. CONSTRUCTION OF A PROTOTYPE OF KNOWLEDGE-BASED SYSTEM

When constructing a prototype of knowledge-based system, the knowledge is classified in accordance with the method of Garg. C. described above so as to store the knowledge in the knowledge base. The set of facts use the Frame-model[6], the set of rules are expressed by the production rules in the IF-THEN format[6], and the set of procedures have coded contents so as to reach the operational conclusions of each rule by users-defined predicates.

Classification of Knowledge	Knowledge-Based System		Inference Engine
	Set of Facts	Set of Rules	

Content Knowledge	Facts on berth scheduling
	• Data on ships
	  • Number of ships
	  • Data on each ship
	   • Time
	   • Type of oil
	• Data on berths
	  • Number of berths
	  • Data on each berth
	⋮
		Common Rules
		• Rule to calculate the remaining number of ships
		• Rule to calculate the working time for loading
		• Rule to calculate the waiting time
		• Rule to prevent ships from arriving before the scheduled time
		• Rule to distinguish the next ship
		⋮	

Process Knowledge		Strategic Rules • Strategy to distinguish the conditions of the ship and berth at present • Strategy to judge the present phase of decision making ⋮ Common procedures in each decision -making phase • Procedure to select the scheduled ship • Procedure to select the scheduled berth Procedures peculiar to each decision-making phase • First Decision-Making Phase • Procedure to forecast the future conditions of ships and berths • Second Decision-Making Phase ⋮	**Control Part** Basic procedures Step 1 : ① Step 2 : ② Step 3 : ③ Step 4 : ④ **Inference Part** Operation of each basic procedure ①Judge the present condition ②Decision on selection standards for consideration ③Forecast of future conditions ④Selection of ships and berths

Figure 5. Connection between the classification of knowledge and the knowledge-based system

The facts existing in content knowledge (CK), which are stored in the set of facts, express the facts concerning the task used by the berth scheduler. The facts were stratified in a frame-model. The whole outline was represented at the upper level, the facts concerning the ships and berths were divided at the middle level, and the data on each ship and berth were stored at the lower level. There was a total of 176 frames. The stereotyped rules in CK were stored in the common rules, and the constraints on berth scheduling were included (for example : a large ship cannot be scheduled when another large ship is scheduled for next berth at the same time : legal regulations on safety). The knowledge classified as strategies in process knowledge (PK) were stored in the strategic rules. The knowledge is characteristic of the scheduling strategies of humans, corresponding to the selection rules using the GOMS model. Also included were the rules for determining the selection standards for ships and berths as well as the rules for selecting the most suitable ship and berth. The knowledge classified as procedures in PK were stored in the strategic rules. The knowledge also included the common procedures in each decision-making phase, four basic procedures, and the procedures peculiar to each decision-making phase. There was a total of about 150 rules.

6. TESTING THE PROTOTYPE

Tests using twenty kinds of shipment order lists were conducted so as to confirm the validity of the prototype of the knowledge-based system. The results calculated using the system were compared with the schedules draw up by the human who had obtained the best result, and the schedules were judged in terms of the total waiting time of ships. As a result, it was confirmed that the system was equal to the human in seventeen of the shipment order lists.

7. CONCLUSION

The following results were obtained in this study;
① A simulator was developed for the elicitation and analysis of human knowledge used in shipping berth scheduling.
② A prototype of the knowledge-based system for shipping berth scheduling was constructed.
③ The usefulness of the method of constructing a system for shipping berth scheduling was confirmed by testing the prototype.

In the future, it will be necessary for this prototype to complete the knowledge by repeating the task experimentation with the simulator for knowledge elicitation in order to obtain better scheduling results for shipment orders which are closer to reality.

8. REFERENCES

1 Card, S.K., Moran, T.P. and Newell, A., Psychology of Human-Computer Interaction, Lawrence Erlbraum Associates Inc., 1983.
2 Ericsson, K.A. and Simon, H.A., Protocol Analysis, The MIT Press, 1984.
3 Garg, C.K., Development of a Methodology for Knowledge Elicitation for Building Expert Systems, Unpublished Ph.D. Thesis, Purdue University, W. Lafayette, IN, U.S.A., 1987.
4 G. Salvendy and T. Tabe, Toward a Hybrid Intelligent System for the Scheduling and Rescheduling of FMS, International Journal of Computer Integrated Manufacturing, 1988.
5 G. Salvendy, T. Tabe and S. Yamamuro, An Approach to Knowledge Elicitation in Scheduling FMS : Toward a Hybrid Intelligent System, Ergonomics of Hybrid Automated System 1, 1988.
6 T. Tabe, A Method of Knowledge Elicitation and Knowledge Representation for Construction of a Knowledge-based System for FMS Scheduling, Journal of Japan Industrial Management Association, Vol. 40, No. 1 (in Japanese), 1989.

DEVELOPMENT OF KNOWLEDGE ELICITING TECHNIQUES FOR EXPERT SYSTEMS

Shigenobu NOMURA[a], Yoshinori HURUICHI[b], Tatsuo SUZUKI[a] and
Takashi KONDOH[a]

[a]Department of Industrial Engineering, Aichi Institute of Technology,
1247 Yachigusa-cho, Toyota City, Aichi Prefecture 470-03, Japan

[b]System Engineering Division, CKD Corporation, Ltd.
3005 Hayasaka, Kitatoyama, Komaki City, Aichi Prefecture

ABSTRACT
The major focus of this research is the acquisition of correct knowledge
about how a skilled person makes plans in the development of the expert
system. A second issue is to obtain specialized knowledge efficiently while
reducing the stress on the experts who supply this knowledge.

1. INTRODUCTION

Expert systems (ES) are being applied to an increasing number of fields.
An ES is an intelligent system for making decisions not unlike those reached
by experts in a given field by making inferences based on specialized
knowledge obtained from specialists in that field. The key features of an
expert system are: inferences based on specialized knowledge, collection of
knowledge from specialists, and a decision making capability on par a with
human experts.
Determining the specific type of knowledge to be elicited from experts in
the field is a vital operation for ES developers. Not only is this problem
basic to the structure of an expert system, but it can be influenced by the
vagaries of human nature as well. Generally, the following two problems are
encountered when knowledge is elicited from an expert: 1) the expert is
fully involved with on-going work, so there is a limit to the amount of time
available for the interview, and 2) the expert cannot clearly verbalize his
or her own method of operation.
Currently, information is acquired from experts through interviews,
apprenticeship under an expert, or by analyzing protocols. In all of these
methods the knowledge engineer concentrates on obtaining information
directly from the expert, thus subjecting the informant to considerable
psychological and physical strain. The object of the present research was
to develop methods of eliciting accurate information while reducing
the stress on the experts, using the field of freight dispatching as a
model.

2. FREIGHT DISPATCHING PROBLEM IN PHYSICAL DISTRIBUTION

These days, as shipping becomes more complex and customer service
increasingly demanding, truck dispatching can benefit greatly by effective

planning. Every day a small number of dispatchers allocate separate delivery instructions to a large number of vehicles. Vehicles have limited carrying capacity which is determined by volume, specified delivery time, and delivery address. The dispatcher must draw up an efficient delivery schedule based on these conditions. This job requires extensive experience, since factors such as the type of vehicle, condition of the drivers, type of loads, etc., must all be considered at the same time. Both efficiency and service are likely to suffer if the dispatching schedule is prepared by an inexperienced person. With such complex problems, the area of freight dispatching is an excellent model for studying of eliciting information for ES.

3. NEW KNOWLEDGE ACQUISITION METHOD

The major topic of this research was the acquisition of knowledge about how an experienced freight dispatcher makes plans. The second focus was to collect specialized knowledge efficiently while reducing the stress on the experts who supply that knowledge. This method is called expert-friendly knowledge acquisition. We structured the research by dividing the expert-friendly knowledge acquisition method (EFKAM) into two stage. In the first stage a body of knowledge concerned with the general area work was prepared along with knowledge of the subject system. The KJ method was used to systematized the collection of fundamental knowledge. The checklist method was then used to prepare interview questions which addressed unresolved areas. Generalists well-versed in the subject were interviewed in addition to specialists. Then the matrix method was used to complete the knowledge structure. In the second stage, consideration was limited to the subject of preparation of delivery truck schedules. At this stage we were able to consult experts in freight dispatching.

First, the sequence of tasks was divided into operational essentials, methods, and essential decision making rules (known through GOMS expansion). Expanding hierarchically, necessary data were extracted from previous dispatch schedules and the matrix method was used to determine and categorize the important items. More knowledge was then elicited by questioning experts about the details of these categories. The knowledge base and heuristic techniques used by the expert for making decision were successfully obtained by this method.

4. PROBLEM OF AN EXPERT-FRIENDLY KNOWLEDGE ACQUISITION METHOD

EFKAM is divided into two stage. In the first stage, the general business knowledge on a given field is acquired. In the second stage, the knowledge on expert decision making procedures is gained. In order to obtain accurate knowledge from the expert, the fundamental contents were discussed in terms of the following items.
(1) Effective application of known knowledge acquisition techniques.
(2) Development of new knowledge acquisition technique and its application.
The first stage of EFKAM consists of eleven steps. Figure 1 indicates the acquisition procedure from step 1 to step 11. The second stage is made up of eight steps. This procedure is composed of the following steps: the respective arrangement of the question items, knowledge acquisition for fundamental problems, knowledge acquisition of application problems,

arrangement of acquired knowledge, discussion of the reliability of knowledge, arrangement of question items, knowledge acquisition regarding exceptional problems and addition to knowledge.
The newly developed EFKAM offers the following advantages.
(1) It minimizes the amount of time the expert is away from the job.
(2) The expert is only queried on a small number of issues.
(3) Knowledge collection time is short.

S1 Preparation of checklist

S2 Meeting of manager concerned with the subject area

S3 The general understand of subject area

S4 Preposition Systematization

S5 Meeting of persons concerned with posision in charge

S6 Operation observation

S7 Arrangement of memo

S8 Acquisition of fundamental factors

S9 Investigation of manual and cases

S10 Comparison for acquired knowledge

S11 Systematization of acquired knowledge

Figure 1   EFKAM Procedure

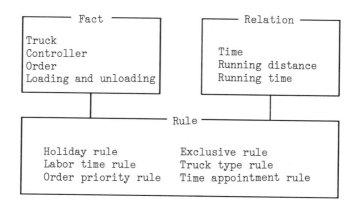

Figure 2   The structure of freight dispatching support expert system

5. APPLICATION TO FREIGHT DISPATCHING PROBLEM

We applied the EFKAM to freight dispatching problems in transport trucking in order to verify it usefulness. This is a assignment problem involving how a dispatcher, called a controller, is to assign a given load to a truck efficiently. There are numerous complex restrictions in this problem. If an unskilled person does the planning, transportation efficiency will drop immediately and transportation costs will rise.

In this study, we applied the EFKAM at the knowledge acquisition stage so as to develop a freight dispatching support expert system. Figure 2 shows the structure of this freight dispatching support expert system. We constructed an inference mechanism considering rule priority, incorporating the facts, relations and rules, then programmed using Prolog language. Rules were classified into three; truck exclusion rules, condition restriction rules, and freight dispatching rules. These items consisted of a total of sixteen rules and were expressed by predicate logic formulae. Predicate logic formulae can be expressed virtually in written form and the system can be easily changed. The freight dispatching support expert system is shown in Figure 3.

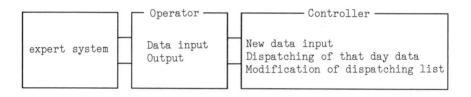

Figure 3   The freight dispatching support expert system

6. CONCLUSION

In a field test, an expert-friendly method of knowledge acquisition was used to obtain knowledge,and logical symbols were used to create rules for preparing dispatching schedules. The practicality of EFKAM was confirmed from the results of the field test when dispatch schedules were prepared by the newly developed method. Because they are effective in supporting tasks where humans are under stress, ES systems are likely to find increasing application in the future. ES should not be a part of the system; rather, a human-centered system must be developed in which there is a genuine fusion of man and machine. This research received support of THe Nitto Foundation.

REFERENCES

[1] Anna Hart: Knowledge Acquisition for Expert System, Kogan Page Ltd.(1989)
[2] H. Ueno: Introduction to Knowledge Engineering, Omu sya,(1990)
[3] Card, S.K.,Moran T.P. and Newell, A., The psychology of Human-Computer Interaction, Lawrence Erlbaum Associates Inc., (1983)

Structured Notations for Human Factors Specification of Interactive Systems

K. Y. Lim and J. B. Long

Ergonomics Unit, University College London
26 Bedford Way, London WC1H OAP, England, UK.

Abstract

The paper identifies and illustrates the use of structured notations to support a more precise human factors specification of a system design. Structured notations are considered more suitable than formal or algebraic notations, since its graphical representations facilitates communication with users. Thus, user feedback and validation of a design may be supported better throughout system development. It is expected that the structured notations illustrated in the paper, could be used more widely since they have now been incorporated into a structured human factors method [10, 11, 12]. Off-the-shelf computer support for the notation is also available, e.g. PDF™ [13].

1. REQUIREMENTS OF A NOTATION FOR HUMAN FACTORS SPECIFICATION

Generally, an appropriate notation for human factors (HF) should fulfil two pre-requisites, namely it should rectify the inadequacies of existing HF notations, and accommodate additional specification demands arising from wider HF involvement in system development. In particular, a notation should satisfy the following requirements :

(a) specificity. Current HF specifications have been criticised for being insufficiently specific. The situation is aggravated further by the demand for increasingly complex system designs. Consequently, HF methods should be enhanced with more powerful notations to support precise design specification. For instance, in safety critical system development, task specifications should be detailed enough to support design simulation, workload assessment and probabilistic human reliability assessment. In addition, Brooks [2] emphasised that HF specifications should detail the hierarchical structure and operational control of the user's task. Thus, the constructs of a notation should satisfy adequately the requirements of these design specifications;

(b) descriptive scope. Recent reports have indicated that the uptake of HF has been hindered by inadequate guidance on the process of design derivation. Specifically, criticisms have been directed at HF for focusing excessively on *what* should be done, but not on *how* requirements could be met during system design [15]. The imbalance is attributed mainly to the traditionally late recruitment of HF. In response, more explicit and complete conceptions of HF design have emerged [1, 4, 12, 14]. Accordingly, existing HF notations have also been enhanced to support the specification of a wider range of intermediate design descriptions. The notations illustrated in this paper is an exemplification of such developments;

(c) communicability. An appropriate notation should support adequately discussions between designers, and between designers and users. In particular, discussions between designers facilitate inter-disciplinary design collaboration (a result of wider HF involvement in system development); while designer-user discussions support design validation. Thus, in addition to the requirement for a more specific notation, the potential of a common notation should be exploited [3, 14];

(d) maintainability. An appropriate notation should support the documentation requirements of both design specification and maintenance (e.g. design updates and modifications). In this respect, a notation amenable to computer support would be especially desirable [13].

On the basis of these notational requirements and consistent with a wider conception of HF design [10, 11, 12], a survey of existing HF and software engineering notations was conducted. In particular, the survey focused on the notations of software engineering *structured analysis and design* methods. The focus on such methods is consistent with requirement (c) above since the graphical nature of their notations was considered more promising than algebraic notations (of formal methods) in facilitating design communication with users [5, 6]. The structured notations selected were then tested for their support of HF specification. Suitable notations were also extended as appropriate. A detailed account of notation development may be found in [8, 9].

The outcome of the research will now be reported. Section 2 summarises how structured notations have been used to support HF specification of interactive systems. The paper is then completed by a review of how structured notations may improve the uptake of HF contributions.

2. STRUCTURED NOTATIONS TO SUPPORT HUMAN FACTORS SPECIFICATION

Generally, HF design may involve specifications at the organisational level (or super-ordinate system level); task level (or sub-system level); and interaction level (or input/output level). The structured notations used to support HF specification at each of these levels, are described below.

At the organisation level, the following structured notations may be applied :

(i) *semantic nets*. This notation is used to describe the organisational structure (e.g. organisation job chart), and the relations between domain entities, concepts, events and processes of the system. Semantic nets are essentially tree diagrams comprising nodes and their relations which are numerically indexed and described in an accompanying table (Figure 1). To characterise adequately the scope of the system, a semantic net description should include taxonomic and composite relations. However, device-specific information should be excluded;

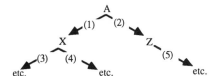

Node	Description	No.	Relation
A	Description of node A.	(1)	Description of relation (1).
		(2)	Description of relation (2).
X	etc.	etc.	etc.

Figure 1. A semantic net specification and accompanying table

(ii) *network diagrams*. This notation is used to describe the content, direction and types of information flow between system entities. Figure 2 shows two types of information flow, namely obligatory communication of information (denoted by a circle, e.g. c1 and c2), and periodic information requests (denoted by a diamond, e.g. r1 and r2). Note that system entities are denoted by rectangles and the flow of information corresponds to the direction of the linking arrow. The information exchanged is described in greater detail in an accompanying table;

(iii) *function flow diagrams*. This notation is used to describe the performance requirements of each sub-system. For instance, performance criteria such as capacity, accuracy, response time, etc., of individual function modules (performed by one or more sub-systems) may be specified, so that overall work goals of the organisation are achieved at acceptable costs. Additional information appears in an associated table (see Figure 3). Thus, function flow diagrams could support high level assessment of alternative designs of a system. For instance, alternative function

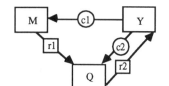

(1) Y is obliged to send reports c1 and c2 to M and Q respectively.
(2) Q may request information r1 from M, while Y may request information r2 from Q.

Info ID	Sender	Receiver	Info Status	Content
c1	Y	M	Routine	etc.
r1	etc.	etc.	etc.	etc.

Figure 2. A network diagram specification and accompanying table

flow diagrams (describing different paths or sub-system designs for particular organisational goals) may be constructed to support the computation and comparison of attainable levels of system performance.

Discussions on conceptual design alternatives are thus supported by the preceding HF design specifications. Appropriate organisational goals and performance levels may then be specified to constrain sub-system level design.

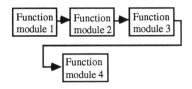

Required Performance Levels for Organisation Goal 1

Function module ID	Performed by	Capacity (units/hr)	Accuracy (% error)	Range	Response time (hr)
1	Operator 1	20	10	+10	1
2	Operator 2	etc.	etc.	etc.	etc.

Figure 3. A function flow diagram specification and accompanying table

At the sub-system or task level, the following structured notations may be applied :

(i) *structured diagrams*. This notation may be used to specify the structure and control of conceptual level tasks and low level user-computer interactions. For instance, structured diagrams may be used at the conceptual level to define the allocation of functions (see Figure 4); and at a lower level, they may be used to specify when particular computer functions should be presented to support the user's execution of the interactive task (see later).

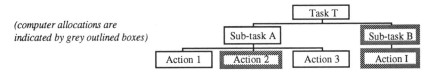

Figure 4. Structured diagram specification of function allocation between user and computer

The following constructs may be used in structured diagram descriptions (constructs are denoted by a symbol located at either the top right- or left-hand corner of its box -- Figure 5) : sequence (no symbol), selection ('o' symbol), iteration ('*' symbol), hierarchy ('↓' symbol), posit ('?' symbol) and quit ('!' symbol). Condition statements are indexed numerically at the bottom of the boxes, e.g. to specify selections and termination of iterations (Figure 5c). Generally, a structured diagram is read from top to bottom and from left to right (in that order).

In addition to constructs, structured diagrams include representation rules to support the specification of inter-leaving, concurrent and multiple tasks as follows:

(a) inter-leaved tasks are *discrete tasks* whose operations are *inter-woven*. Thus, the user is required to execute a *current* task and monitor a *background* task. At a pre-specified point of task execution, the status of the tasks is reversed. To describe such tasks, separate structured diagrams with common actions are constructed and aligned vertically (Figure 6a). Task inter-links are established by specifying common actions *across* the structured diagrams. Note that common actions are denoted by boxes assigned with the same identifier, e.g. actions {2, 4, 6} of Tasks X and Y in Figure 6a;

(b) concurrent tasks are *discrete tasks* that are performed at the *same time*, e.g. data input while monitoring displays. To describe such tasks, separate structured diagrams are constructed and aligned horizontally (Figure 6b). In addition, the root or top boxes of the diagrams are assigned a common identifier, e.g. Operator 1(data input) and Operator 2(display monitoring);

(c) multiple tasks describe *many* units of the *same task* being performed at the *same time*. To describe such tasks, the root or top box is layered and the number of units is indicated, e.g.

n=4+(action 'C')/hour indicates that more than 4 units of the same task may be performed in the specified time, and the last task unit would terminate at action 'C' (Figure 6c).

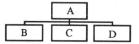

Figure 5a : Sequence construct [no symbol] -- A consists of one each of B, C and D in the given order. A is a sequence of B, C and D.

Figure 5d : Hierarchy construct [↓] -- AAAA consists of one each of B, C, and D in any order. AAAA is a hierarchy of B, C, and D.

Figure 5b : Selection construct [o] -- AA consists of either one B, or C, or D. AA is a selection of B, or C, or D.

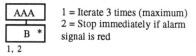

AAA   1 = Iterate 3 times (maximum)
          2 = Stop immediately if alarm
B *   signal is red
1, 2

Figure 5c : Iteration construct [*] -- AAA consists of zero or more Bs. AAA is an iteration of B.

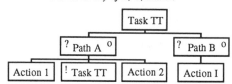

Figure 5e : Posit [?] and Quit [!] constructs -- Task TT involves either Path A or B depending on situational conditions. Path A is first 'posited'. If unacceptable conditions are detected, e.g. after Action 1, then Path A is abandoned (quit/recover to 'Task TT') and Path B is 'admitted'. If unacceptable conditions are not detected, Path A is completed.

Figure 5. Constructs of structured diagram notation (see also Jackson [7])

(ii) *semantic net and function flow diagrams.* These notations may be used for HF specifications at the sub-system level in the same manner as illustrated for organisational level specifications;
(iii) *performance tables.* These tables may be used to specify the tests and metrics to be applied on proposed design solutions [1, 16]. In particular, the tables should specify the following :

(1) *Who* should be tested, e.g. a particular user group;
(2) *What* tasks test subjects are required to perform, e.g. particular benchmark tasks;
(3) *How* tests should be conducted, e.g. laboratory simulation of the work environment;
(4) *What* test metrics should be used, e.g. objective and/or subjective assessment;
(5) *What* performance levels are expected, e.g. worst and best levels for a particular prototype;

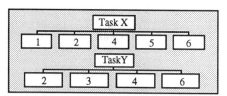

Figure 6a : Structured diagram specification of inter-leaved tasks X and Y. The common actions are {2, 4, 6}.

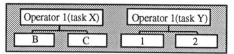

Figure 6b : Structured diagram specification of Operator 1's ability to perform task X and Y concurrently.

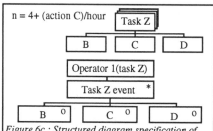

Figure 6c : Structured diagram specification of Operator 1's performance of multiple units of task Z without first completing each unit of task Z. More than 4 units may be performed per hour, terminating at action C on the fifth unit.

Figure 6. Structured diagram specification of inter-leaved, concurrent and multiple tasks

Thus, HF criteria may be specified at the task level to constrain interaction level design.

At interaction level design, the preceding structured notations may also be applied. Thus, further illustration of the notations is unnecessary. Instead, an account of how the notations have been applied in the specification of a user interface design follows.

Figures 7 to 11 show selected parts of a HF specification for a case-study concerning digital network security management. In particular, the specifications address the following HF concerns:

(a) interactive task design. Figure 7 shows part of the user's (network manager) inputs required to achieve on-line task goals for the case-study system. The structured diagram description, termed an interaction task model, specifies the relationship between particular screen displays and user inputs from a *user-centered* perspective, e.g. the selection of a 'show user list' button and Screen 4B (S4B). To this end, grey bubbles marked in Figure 7 indicate the points at which specific display screens are removed or 'consumed' (the next display screen is presented immediately);

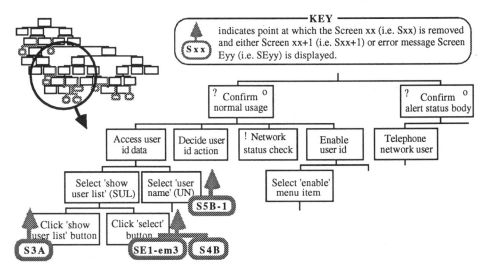

Figure 7. Part of an interaction task model for the case-study

(b) context and timing for presenting computer functions to support the user's task (including error handling). In this respect, the specifications in Figure 8 augment those in Figure 7 by defining how display screen actuations map onto user actions from a *computer-centered* perspective. In particular, the streams of user actions and screen actuations are linked as follows :

Manager Actions: 'show user list' --> select user name'
Screen Actuations 1:   Screen 4B --> Screen 5B-1
Screen Actuations 2:   Screen 4B ---> Screen E1-em3 ---> Screen 4B -----> Screen 5B-1

Figures 7 and 8, together, indicate that Screen Actuations 1 is applicable if all inputs to select 'show user list' have been made correctly, while Screen Actuations 2 is applicable if an input error has occurred (in which case an additional error screen (Screen E1-em3 or SE1-em3) is triggered).
(c) screen composition and screen object behaviours. In this respect, the pictorial specifications in Figure 9 augment those in Figures 7 and 8. These pictorial descriptions of display screens may either be drawn on paper (to-scale or dimensioned), or prototyped using a computer tool. A more detailed description of the contents of the screens is specified in accompanying tables and structured diagrams (the latter define the behaviour of individual screen objects -- see Figure 10);
(d) error, feedback and help messages. In this respect, the specifications in Figure 11 also

augment those in Figures 7 and 8 by specifying the contents of error messages. For instance, Screen E1-em3 referenced in the Figures, implies the presentation of a display screen of pictorial format E1 (not shown) and error message content ID=3 (i.e. em3) as specified in Figure 11.

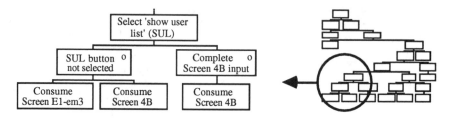

Figure 8. Part of a screen actuation specification for the case-study

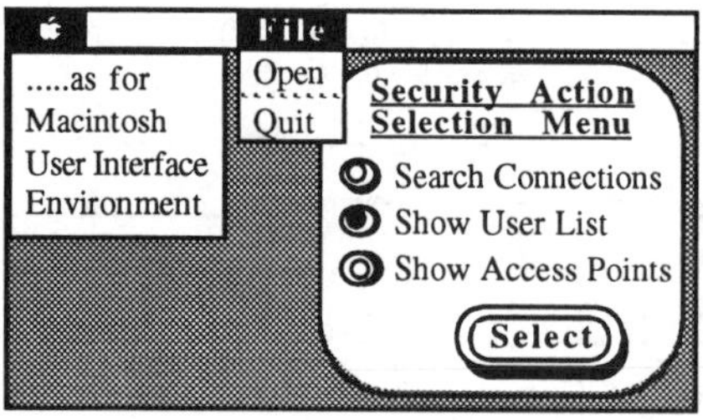

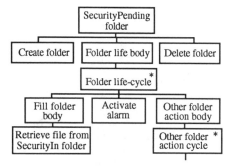

	Screen Object	Description	Design Attributes
.....as for Macintosh User Interface Environment	File (menu bar)	Offers 'Open' and 'Quit' menu items. 'Open' allows the network manager to open host and user reports. 'Quit' allows the manager to quit the security application.	Behaviour as per standard Macintosh menu items.
	etc.	etc.	etc.

Figure 9. Part of a set of pictorial screen layout specifications for the case-study

Message Number	Message Content
em1	Sorry, your log-on inputs are incorrect. Your session will be terminated.
em2	Please indicate a host and/or user report action by selecting either the 'Delete' or 'Pending' radio button.
em3	Please indicate the required security action by selecting a radio button from the "Security Action Selection Menu.' Do this action..........etc.

Figure 10. Part of an interface model for the case-study

Figure 11. Part of an error message index for the case-study

Using these notations, a comprehensive range of HF design contributions may thus be specified to support various stages of system development. In this way, HF inputs may be made more effectively.

3. CONCLUSION

This paper illustrates how structured notations have been used to support wider HF contributions to system design. In applying the notations, the effectiveness of HF input may be improved as follows :

(a) by supporting more complete and precise HF specifications at various stages of system design.

Since HF inputs may be located appropriately against the system development context, its contributions may be incorporated more efficiently;

(b) by facilitating the elicitation of user feedback. The graphical nature of structured notations together with the improvements in HF input outlined in (a) above, would support more comprehensive user feedback and design validation at each stage of system development. Thus, invalid design assumptions may be identified earlier and eliminated more effectively;

(c) by exploiting the benefits of a common notation. Since the notations were recruited from software engineering methods, the use of such notations for HF specification would reduce problems in design communication. Thus, a greater uptake of HF contributions may be expected.

Additional improvements would also accrue if an explicit HF design process were established, e.g. in the form of a structured HF method [10, 11, 12]. By integrating such a HF method with similarly structured software engineering methods, the scope, format, granularity and timing of HF contributions may be configured appropriately to support each stage of system development.

4. ACKNOWLEDGEMENTS

Part of the research was carried out for the Procurement Executive, Ministry of Defence (MoD, UK). Views expressed in the paper are the authors' and should not be attributed to the MoD.

5. REFERENCES

1. Blyth, R. C. and Hakiel, S. R. A UI design methodology and the implication for structured system design methods. In *Proc. IEE Third Int. Conf. Comd., Control, Comms. and Management Info. Syst.,* 1989.
2. Brooks, R. Comparative task analysis: an alternative direction for HCI science. In J. Carroll (ed.),*Designing Interaction : Psychology at the H-C Interface,* CUP, 1991.
3. Carver, M. K. Practical experience of specifying the H-C interface using JSD. In *Proc. Erg. Soc. Conf.,* Taylor&Francis, 1988, 177-182.
4. Damodaran, L., Ip, K. and Beck, M. Integrating HF principles into structured design methodology: a case-study in the UK civil service. In : H. J. Bullinger et al (eds.), *IT for Org. Systs.,* Elsevier Science, 1988, 235-241.
5. Finkelstein, A. and Potts, C. Evaluation of existing requirements extraction strategies. FOREST Report R1, 1985.
6. Hares, J. Methods for a longer life. *Computer News/Databases,* 1987, 18.
7. Jackson, M. A., System Development. Prentice-Hall International, 1983.
8. Lim, K. Y., Long, J. B. and Silcock, N. Requirements., research and strategy for integrating HF with structured analysis and design methods: the case of the JSD method. In *Proc. Erg. Soc. Conf.,* Taylor&Francis, 1990, 32-38.
9. Lim, K. Y., Long, J. B. and Silcock, N. Motivation, research management and a conception for structured integration of HF with system development methods: an illustration using the JSD method. In *Proc. 5th European Conf. Cog. Erg.,* Golem Press, 1990, 359-374.
10. Lim, K. Y. and Long, J. B. A method for (recruiting) methods: facilitating HF input to system design. In *Proc. ACM Conf. HF in Comp. Systs.,* ACM Press, 1992, 549-556.
11. Lim, K. Y. and Long, J. B. Rapid prototyping, structured methods and the incorporation of HF in system design. *In Proc. East-West Int. Conf. HCI,* ICSTI, Moscow, 1992, 407-417.
12. Lim, K. Y., Long, J. B. and Silcock, N. Integrating HF with the JSD method: an illustrated overview. *Ergonomics,* 35, 10(1992), 1135-1161.
13. Lim, K. Y. and Long, J. B. Computer-based tools for a structured HF method. In *Proc. Int. Conf. Computer-Aided Erg. and Safety,* Elsevier Science, 1992, 71-79.
14. Sutcliffe, A. Some experiences in integrating specification of HCI within a structured system development method. In *Proc. 4th BCS HCI Conf.,* CUP, 1988, 145-160.
15. Sutcliffe, A. Task analysis, systems analysis and design: symbiosis or synthesis? *Interacting with Computers,* 1, 1(1989), 6-12.
16. Whiteside, J., Jones, S., Levy, P. S., and Wixon, D. User performance with comd., menu and iconic interfaces. In Borman and Curtis (eds.), *HF in Comp. Systs. II,* Elsevier Science, 1985, 185-191.

The system is the expert: architecture for a model-based tutor

Michael Pearce

Galaxy Scientific Corporation, Information Division, 2310 Parklake Drive NE, Suite 325, Atlanta, GA, 30345 USA

Abstract

This paper presents a methodology for modeling the knowledge requirements for training simulations for complex systems. By explicitly modeling the function, behavior, and connectivity of the components of a systems in one common representation, two capacities are provided. The first is a quantitative simulation of the system that the user can interact with to learn how the system behaves. The second capacity is a qualitative model of the system that be used to reason about the actions and mistakes of the user. This dual-purpose view of system models allows for a decrease in the effort required to produce a simulation-based intelligent tutoring system, compared to that associated with rule-based approaches.

1. INTRODUCTION

Several types of knowledge are required to robustly and efficiently diagnose malfunctions in complex systems. The technician needs to understand the underlying principles of the target system. He also needs knowledge of the systems and subsystems of the equipment, how they are connected, and how they contribute to the performance of the equipment's purpose. Also required is knowledge of the individual components of the equipment: their functions, how their functions relate to the functions of the systems of the equipment, how they operate, and how they can fail. He requires knowledge of procedures: for example, how to determine the system status.

Designers of intelligent tutoring systems (ITS) systems have focused on the design of program modules that support the learning of troubleshooting knowledge: student, expert, instructor, and domain models are some of the modules that have been explored in recent research [1]. While this approach of designing ITSs from discrete modules is adequate for simple systems, the development of training systems for complex domains puts a heavier demand on the ITS designer. For complex systems, such as aviation equipment and power plants, the effort required to produce realistic and challenging ITS that can often exceed the costs for traditional training methods. Much of this effort results from the lack of methodology for modeling complex mechanical, electrical, and mass flow systems at an adequate (but not excessive) level of abstraction.

This paper presents a methodology for modeling the knowledge requirements for training simulations for complex systems. By explicitly modeling the function, behavior, and connectivity of the components of a systems in one common representation, two capacities are provided. The first is a quantitative simulation of the system that the user can interact with to learn how the system behaves. Such a simulation provides the fidelity of model behavior that is necessary for training transfer to on-the-job performance. The second capacity is a qualitative model of the system that be used to reason about the actions and mistakes of the user. System-independent teaching strategies can be applied to the system model to infer the incorrect knowledge of the student, and provide the appropriate information to correct the students knowledge of the system. This dual-purpose view of system models allows for a decrease the effort required to produce a simulation-based ITS compared to that associated with rule-based approaches.

2. INTELLIGENT SIMULATION-BASED TRAINING

Simulation training of troubleshooting skills can be defined as task training through the use of emulations of the equipment being training for. The goal of this training is that the student be able to apply the diagnostic reasoning skills learned from the tutor to on-the-job performance. This type of cognitive-oriented training differs from the simulator training used in pilot training, in which the tasks is primarily psychomotor. A student is allowed to interact with the simulation in the same way that he or she would interact with the actual equipment. The interface to the simulation may exist in physical mock-ups of the target equipment, or in computer programs which display graphical mock-ups of the equipment. Examples of such training systems for diagnosis training exist in power plant, aviation, and electronics technician training [2-4].

2.1. Realistic Simulation of Equipment

Training systems that provide realistic simulations of the target equipment help ensure the transfer of learning from the ITS environment to performance of the task in the workplace. Equipment simulations provide for recognition of the physical equipment, and understanding of the behavior of components and connections between them. It is best to allow for direct manipulation of the interface objects in the simulated equipment, to increase ease of use and lower user frustration. Interface objects can be presented graphicly through pictures of equipment, system schematics, or high-level animations of system processes.

Not only must a simulation trainer provide a realistic approximation of the look of the equipment being trained for, but it must also convey the time-varying behavior of the equipment. This behavior is conveyed through the simulation of the dynamics of the target system. For example, display values should change when the user changes control settings at the interface. Simulations that do not behave properly run the risk of teaching incorrect or incomplete knowledge to the student. The presentation of system behaviors require that the simulation trainer contain knowledge about the causal relationships between components of the system, and the principles that govern these relationships. This knowledge is commonly represented in the form of rules, models, or table-lookups.

2.2. Responding to User Actions

A realistic simulation of equipment without intelligent help would only be useful when an instructor is looking over the student's shoulder to give feedback. An effective training system should be able to critique the student's actions, and give useful help when an action is incorrect or could be done more efficiently [5]. This component of an ITS simulates an instructor that gives hints and advice when the user is not performing the task properly, and does it in such a way that the help increases the student's knowledge of troubleshooting strategies and of the system. Without this feedback to the student, the ITS would not be able to improve the performance of the student (in the classroom or on the job) by correcting the inaccurate knowledge of the student.

To respond to user actions, the training system must have knowledge of the subsystems and components of the equipment, and the relationships between these entities. The ITS should also contain knowledge about troubleshooting strategies, such as divide-and-conquer and island driving, and be able to use these strategies to evaluate the users actions and determine if the user may be missing some knowledge of troubleshooting or of the system that is currently being diagnosed. Based on the simulation of the currently malfunctioning component, the training system should be able to explain mistakes to the student in a form that is understandable.

3. MODEL-BASED REASONING AND SIMULATION TRAINING

A model-based reasoning system is a symbolic representation of a physical system at a qualitative level. It differs from quantitative models of physical systems in that it is meant to produce high-level predictions of system behavior, rather than exact numerical predictions. In general, model-based reasoners contain two components; the domain knowledge of the system being represented, and a domain-independent reasoning component. The domain knowledge contains information about the inputs, outputs, and behaviors of the individual components of the system, and the connections between these components. Graphically, a model-based representation of a system would look like a schematic of that system, with the internal functions of each component also included. The second component, the reasoning module, is able to use the equipment model to predict the behavior of the system in specific states (such as component malfunctions), to explain symptoms in terms of component failures, and to recommend tests to diagnose malfunctions.

The application of model-based approaches to knowledge representation for training systems differs from the traditional approach of rule-based reasoning in that a model-based representation attempts to represent the functioning of the system being simulated, rather than knowledge of how the system fails. Traditionally, training systems have represented expert knowledge in the form of rule-based systems [6]. This knowledge is collected through in-depth interviews of subject matter experts, and represents a large part of the effort in building the training systems. If a simulation component is included in the system, it is usually separate from the expert knowledge, as shown in Figure 1. The model-based approach starts from the premise that the simulation and expert knowledge are much the same, although they use different computational methods to extract the needed information. Figure 1 shows the layout of a model-based simulation trainer, in which the *system model* takes the place of the *simulation module* and the *expert model* of the rule-based system. The *help module* compares the *system model* to the *student model* to determine if help is needed and then to choose the appropriate type of help.

4. ADVANTAGES OF MODEL-BASED TRAINING

The point is not that model-based representations provide a different method for designing simulation training systems, but that they provide a better method. The model-based approach is more efficient, more robust, and easier to debug than rule-based system. While it is possible to represent the same content in rule and model-based systems, systems for which

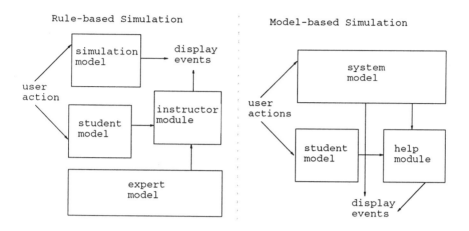

Figure 1. Rule-based and model-based simulation training system approaches.

there exists information concerning the behavior and connection of components are more easily represented with a model-based approach [7]. Because the purpose of a simulation trainer is to teach the student to diagnose malfunctions in a system (or in some cases to teach general troubleshooting skills), the model of the system and its associated troubleshooting strategies is the focus of the instructional design. This does not mean that other types of knowledge are not needed for training, but that it is supplementary to the knowledge of the system and its behaviors.

4.1. Knowledge Collection and Entry is Simplified

Because the training designer is working at the level of components of the system, and not at the level of symptoms and tests, it is much easier to enter the simulation information into the computer. The knowledge engineer can work from a schematic of the system, from documentation of component functions, and from direct measurements of physical system. Because the reasoning component is independent from domain of application, generic reasoning mechanisms can be adapted from other training systems to the needs of the current project, thus reducing the effort required to build training systems. Using a rule-based approach to system modeling, the instructional designer would work from interviews of subject-matter experts, who usually do not agree on troubleshooting strategies and methods. The designer has to go through the extra step of filtering the information gathered from interviews, and trying to integrate them into a rule base with a minimal number of internal contradictions.

4.2. Representation and Reasoning is Separate

In theory, the content and use of knowledge in rule-based systems is separate. But in practice the programmer must worry about the order of rule firing, and must usually include some type of meta-rule to ensure that the correct set of rules are applied at the right time. As the rule set grows in size, these systems quickly become unstable and difficult to debug.

A model-based system eliminates much of this difficulty, since the representation of the system is derived directly from the configuration of physical system being simulated. As long as the representation of the system and the reasoner that uses the knowledge are "correct" (they include enough information to accurately model the system), the predictions made by the model will be correct. In most cases the knowledge needed to make a decision about the behavior of a component is localized to that component and the components that provide its inputs, so debugging the system model is fairly easy.

There are several other advantages that stem from the separation of representation and reasoning. Common components, such as valves, sensors, and indicators, can be re-used from libraries of pre-defined systems, and more complex components can be built up from collections of simple components. The effects of adding knowledge of new components are localized to the connected components, which is not true in the addition of knowledge to rule-based systems. The separation also makes it much easier to use the system knowledge from a training system in a computer tool for job aiding in diagnostic reasoning. Since the two tasks of training and job aiding use much of the same knowledge, only the procedures that used this knowledge need be changed [8].

4.3. Provides Structure for Other Types of Knowledge

Although the model is central in this view of training systems design, it does not rule out the use of other types of knowledge in the system. Because troubleshooting is concerned with the search for malfunctioning components, it is natural that these other types of knowledge be structured around the model of the system. The system model provides a structure by which other types of knowledge can be included in the system. For example, heuristics for troubleshooting a particular system and procedures for testing and replacing components might be included as part of the system model. This model-centered view of knowledge engineering naturally leads to a hypermedia navigation system, in which the student can see various types of information about components, behavior, connections, procedures, and principles by selecting the appropriate topic.

4.4. Supports Flexible User Modelling

The standard form of user modeling in rule-based training systems is the overlay method, in which the student knowledge is modeled as a subset of the expert knowledge. User actions are compared to the expert knowledge, and then the student model is changed based on inferences about the user's knowledge. Thus the expert knowledge contained in the rule base is assumed to be the correct model of how troubleshooting is done, and does not allow for differences in cognitive approaches.

The user model in a model-based training system can be much more flexible, since the way that the system model is used is not as constrained as that for rule systems. Because the knowledge of the system (the model) is separated from the process that uses it, assorted types of help strategies can be plugged into the system. Several help strategies have been developed by the author, based on various biases toward different types of user help. The *decreasing abstraction* strategy presents the most abstract principles concerning the malfunctioning component first, and help becomes less abstract as more mistakes are made. The *error explanation* strategy attempts to explicitly point out to the user why his current line of reasoning is incorrect. The *statistical inferencing* strategy uses data on the types of errors the user has made in solving previous problems to select the type of help to be offered when a new mistake is made.

5. CONCLUSION

The model-based approach to simulation-based ITS design provides several advantages over rule-based expert modeling approaches. By explicitly modeling the function, behavior, and connectivity of the components of a systems in one common representation, an system designer gets both a quantitative simulation and a qualitative model of the system. This approach decreases the effort required to produce a simulation-based intelligent tutoring system by simplifying knowledge collection and entry, separating reasoning and representation, providing structure for other types of knowledge, and supporting flexible user help.

6. ACKNOWLEDGEMENTS

This work was supported by the Federal Aviation Administration Office of Aviation Medicine under contract number DTFA01-92-Y-01005. Thanks to Mr. Jefferey Norton and Mr. Brad Wiederholt of Galaxy Scientific Corporation for feedback and comments concerning simulation-based training.

7. REFERENCES

1. Foundations of Intelligent Tutoring Systems, Lawrence Erlbaum Associates, Hillsdale, New Jersey, 1988.

2. Hollan, J. D., Hutchins, E. L., and Weitzman, L., "STEAMER: An Interactive Inspectable Simulation-based Training System," AI Magazine, 1984, No. 2.

3. Pearce, M., "Results of the Environmental Control System (ECS) Tutor Experiment," Human Factors in Aviation Maintenance Phase III: Progress Report, Federal Aviation Administration Office of Aviation Medicine, in press, 1993.

4. Brown, J. S., Burton, R. R., and deKleer, J., "Pedagogical, Natural Language, and Knowledge Engineering Techniques in SOPHIE I, II, and III," in D. H. Sleeman and J. S. Brown, (eds.), Intelligent Tutoring Systems, 1982.

5. Norton, J. E., Wiederholt, B. J., and Johnson, B. J., "Microcomputer Intelligence for Technical Training (MITT): The Evolution of an Intelligent Tutoring System," in Proceedings of Conference on Intelligent Computer-Aided Training, 1991.

6. Clancey, W. J, "NEOMYCIN: Reconfiguring a Rule-Based Expert System for Application to Teaching," in Proceedings of the Seventh International Joint Conference on Artificial Intelligence, pp. 829-836, 1981.

7. Davis, R., and Hamscher, W., "Model-based Reasoning: Troubleshooting," in Exploring Artificial Intelligence, H. E. Shrobe (ed.), Morgan Kaufman, 1988, pp. 297-346.

8. Johnson, W.B. & Norton, J.E., "Integrated information for maintenance training, aiding, and on-line documentation," in Proceedings of the 36th Annual Meeting of the Human Factors Society, Atlanta, GA, The Human Factors Society, 1992.

Knowledge Acquisition for a Domain-Independent Intelligent Training System

Ronald W. Broome[a] and Marijke F. Augusteijn[b]

[a]XVT Software, Inc. PO Box 18750, Boulder, CO 80308, USA email: rbroome@xvt.com

[b]Department of Computer Science, University of Colorado at Colorado Springs,
Colorado Springs, CO 80933, USA email: mfa@antero.uccs.edu

Abstract

Recent research into Intelligent Training Systems (ITS) has emphasized instruction of specific knowledge domains. An obvious next step is the development of an ITS shell. An intelligent shell should allow the incorporation of knowledge from different instructional domains into an ITS without the need for repeatedly developing intelligent features. This would enable instructional developers, with little understanding of artificial intelligence techniques, to produce an ITS solely based on their knowledge of the domain. As might be expected, there are problems associated with the design of an ITS that is not strongly coupled to a particular domain. However, progress in the development of certain domain-independent aspects [1-4] is producing several ITS shells with limited capabilities.

ITS Challenger is a shell providing certain intelligent features for instruction in pre-dominantly declarative domains. It employs a dual knowledge representation that allows for both an instructor's anticipation of students' needs and a domain expert's point of view [4]. A set of pedagogical rules that rely upon the structure of the knowledge, but not its content, is the basis for de-coupling the system intelligence from the expert knowledge.

A primary experimental design goal of ITS Challenger is to free the instructional developer from the need to be a programmer and a knowledge engineer. However, the knowledge representation of ITS Challenger is critical to adaptation, and a strict canonical data representation is used. Authoring tools and procedures were developed to assist an instructional designer, unfamiliar with the principles of knowledge engineering, in the effective acquisition and structuring of the knowledge needed for competent instruction by ITS Challenger.

1. Introduction

Early research and design of ITS Challenger [5-7] emphasized the instruction of procedural knowledge, particularly in mathematical domains. The representation of procedural knowledge alone was insufficient for teaching and testing procedural domains [6]. This conclusion led to a new version of ITS Challenger that stresses the instruction of declarative knowledge.

To provide effective adaptation in a domain-independent shell, the knowledge structures must be sufficiently developed to allow intelligent conclusions to be drawn through structure manipulation. In ITS Challenger, the domain knowledge plays two distinct roles. It provides instructional materials that are available to the student. For this purpose, knowledge is structured in a manner that facilitates presentation to the learner by supporting a step-by-step learning experience. However, knowledge must also be used in coaching the student, diagnosing misconceptions after a student has made an error, and providing appropriate remedial materials. This requires a structure that provides dynamic access such that an embedded expert system can select and use relevant information. Therefore, knowledge also must be organized around a domain expert's conceptual understanding.

ITS Challenger requires two distinct knowledge representations to support its dual role. One structure, called the Instructional Unit Network, organizes instructional materials by pedagogical objective in anticipation of students' needs. In this network, objectives are organized in a hierarchy with the major objectives at the top and subsequently lesser supporting objectives as descendants of the major objectives. The selection of materials for each Instructional Unit is based on a specific objective and is guided by a cognitive strategy for satisfying this objective. The other structure, the Concept Network, is a relational structure of domain concepts that provides expert knowledge to embedded intelligent features. Each node in this network represents a single domain concept and incorporates knowledge about each concept's definition and relationships to other concepts.

Adaptive instruction takes place as system-guided traversal and presentation of the knowledge representation and as system-generated multiple-choice and fill-in-the-blank problems with dynamic error analysis and feedback. The level of instruction and remediation adapts to the level of the individual student's understanding of course materials.

The pedagogical principle underlying ITS Challenger is that instruction is driven by objectives. The Instructional Unit Network, accordingly, provides the instructional framework for these objectives. Figure 1 shows a small part of an Instructional Unit Network for an ITS developed for orbital dynamics.

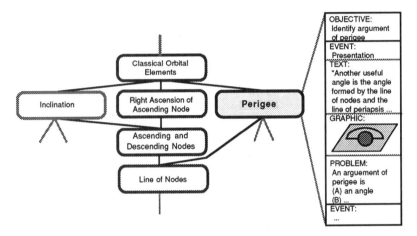

Figure 1. Portion of the Instructional Unit Network for orbital dynamics with detail of unit on *argument of perigee* shown

Each instructional objective is associated with a cognitive process taking place during learning. Students assimilate information at different levels of cognition as evidenced by different behaviors. ITS Challenger incorporates five of the learning types proposed by Gagne [8]. These are described in greater detail by Augusteijn et al [3]. It suffices to say, that, in ITS Challenger, each learning type requires a different series of events that teach to the objective. An Instructional Unit, then, consists of an instructional objective, a micro-strategy, instructional events consisting of textual and graphical presentations, a list of concepts associated with the objective, and problems that test the students' understanding of the presentation and their success in achieving the objective. Figure 1 also shows details of an instructional unit from orbital mechanics.

To accommodate the capabilities of the intelligent shell, ITS Challenger requires a relational structure for conceptual knowledge. The notion of a Concept is not easily defined, but derives from a domain expert's understanding of the instructional objectives. For example, the objective, "*identify the plane passing through earth's equator as the equatorial plane*," refers to the concepts "*equatorial plane*" and "*equator*" and identifies the relationship between them as "*the plane passing through.*" Another objective, "*discriminate between a circular orbit and an elliptical orbit*," clearly distinguishes concepts by their attributes.

The Concept Network may be described best as a hybrid of a semantic network and a frame system. Each node, a Concept, contains standard fields for supporting attributes (*has-a*) and hierarchical relationships (*is-a*). These relationships are bi-directional -- if *an orbit has a perihelion,* then perihelion is an *attribute of* orbit. Attributes may be defined as inherited or un-inherited in a conceptual hierarchy. Domain experts may also describe arbitrary relationships. For example, "*equatorial plane*" is related by "*passes through*" to "*earth's equator*" and, in the reverse direction, earth's equator *is intersected by* equatorial plane. Domain experts may also place modifiers on a relationship -- an ellipse has *two (2)* focal point(s). A Concept also has fields for alternate names and natural language definitions. An individual Concept may also contain a concept's graphical representation. Examples of the Concept Network and of internal records of Concepts are shown in Figure 2.

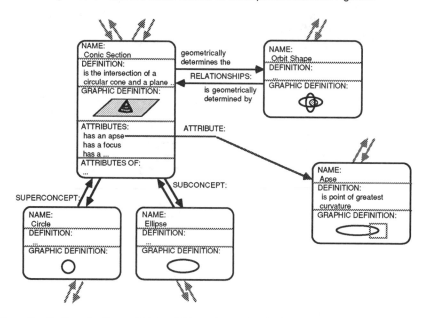

Figure 2. Portion of a Concept Network hierarchy used in the instruction of orbital dynamics

Besides supporting problem generation (multiple-choice and fill-in-the-blank), error analysis and remediation, the Concept Network provides students with the capability of hypertext. By selecting on a highlighted word in text or on a graphic, a textual and/or graphical definition of a Concept displays itself. Instructional developers associate key words in the presentation materials explicitly linking them to Concepts. This capability allows students to review previously seen or undefined Concepts. This feature may be extended eventually to allow students to submit natural language queries to obtain similar information as well as information about relationships between Concepts.

It is probably an understatement to say that the construction of the Concept Network is a difficult task. ITS Challenger operates under a closed-world assumption -- all necessary knowledge and relationships about a domain must be provided explicitly. Because the expert shell has understanding of limited relationships (*is-a, has-a* and context), the responsibility for completeness falls on the instructional developer or subject matter expert. The same can be said for the design of an Instructional Unit Network, even though, for an experienced instructional developer, the notion of objectives should transfer fairly well to designing for the ITS Challenger shell. The authoring system for ITS Challenger was designed to remove the need for explicit understanding of knowledge engineering and to stress the pedagogical organization and domain knowledge content.

2. The Authoring System and Knowledge Acquisition

ITS Challenger was developed in an object-oriented programming (OOP) environment on a Xerox 1100 series AI workstation supporting LISP and its OOPs extension LOOPS. Knowledge is encapsulated in objects that must be built by the instructional developer. The authoring system, described exhaustively by Broome [9], provides for creating, building and modifying each type of knowledge encapsulation object. These windows-based tools also give developers the "what you see is what you get" feedback of text, graphics and problems as will be presented to the students.

The *Courseware Manager* serves as the top-level entry point into the authoring system. It permits an instructional developer to manage courseware for ITS Challenger instructional domains. This includes creating new courses, making a single course "active" (when multiple domain models are loaded in the InterLisp environment), loading and saving course domains from and to storage devices, accessing Instructional Unit and Concept Network Browsers, setting author defaults, and executing courseware in "authoring" mode.

The management of an Instructional Unit Network for a single instructional domain is performed through the *Instructional Unit (Network) Browser*. The browser allows a developer to establish, modify and delete the hierarchical (learning objective) relationships between units in the Instructional Unit Network. When an Instructional Unit object is instantiated, the instructional developer selects the learning type to be employed. From this learning type an empty template of text, graphics and problems for the unit is created which supports the micro-strategy's learning events.

The *Instructional Unit Editor* allows instructional developers to manipulate the contents of Instructional Units. Features for this tool permit the definition of the instructional objective, the modification of micro-strategies and concepts associated with the unit, and the creation of data files for the unit. This editor also permits the instructional developer to modify the template of text, graphics, and problems for the micro-strategy.

The *Text* and *Graphics Editors* have features similar to many other simple commercial editors. These tools were designed and developed because tools provided by InterLisp were inadequate for the requirements of ITS Challenger. Text objects support special characters such as Greek symbols, sub- and super-scripts, underlining, and vector notation not provided by InterLisp. Graphics applications in InterLisp are of the bitmap-based type that were too memory intensive given the number of graphics in a typical courseware domain and the storage limitations of the Xerox platform. Graphics objects, in ITS Challenger, are supported by a simple graphics meta-language for describing lines and fills. Additionally, the Text and Graphics editors support the hypertext capabilities of the ITS shell by allowing the developer to highlight key words and establish links to domain Concepts.

Problem generation is an automatic process in ITS Challenger, but is not yet completely refined. The *Problem Editor* requires the developer to specify the Concepts to be tested in a problem, to select a question template (there are actually several types of multiple-choice and fill-in-the-blank problems that may be generated), and to set the search level (depth in Concept Network) from which knowledge may be extracted and from which error analysis occurs. From this information, the ITS problem generation facility may produce a series of questions, and answers and distracters, in the case of multiple-choice problems. The Problem Editor displays all possible combinations of questions and answers that can be generated (for students, the problem generator randomly selects a single question from this list). The instructional developer may eliminate answers or distracters that are inappropriate by moving them to the excluded list.

The *Concept (Network) Browser* permits a developer to manage the Concept Network for a single instructional domain. The Concept Browser allows the creation, deletion and linking of Concept objects. Objects of this class contain Concept definitions, alternate names, relationships to other Concepts and a graphical representation of the Concept. In establishing links between Concepts, a developer describes the hierarchical (*is-a*) relationships that exist in the Concept Network. Other relationships (*has-a* and author-defined) are established through the Concept Editor.

The *Concept Editor* manipulates the contents of a single Concept object. This includes the specification of alternate names for Concepts and the non-hierarchical relationships (*has-a* and author-defined). The Concept Editor automatically provides the bi-directional relationship *attribute of* for the *has-a*. For author-defined relationships, the Concept Editor prompts the developer for relationships in both directions. This editor also allows the addition, modification and deletion of textual definitions as well as provides access to the Graphics Editor for designing a graphical representation of a Concept.

In developing courseware for ITS Challenger, it was helpful to first design the course on paper before using the Authoring Tools. The courseware developer formulates the major objectives of the course and recursively refines these objectives. An objective hierarchy is created in this manner. This hierarchy has a one-to-one correspondence with the Instructional Unit Network to be created for the course. The objective helps determine the learning type for the corresponding unit. For example, an instructional objective maybe the "*understanding of Kepler's laws that govern orbital dynamics.*" The associated learning type will be *Rule/Principle* since Kepler's laws describe the physical laws of motion. The objective also provides the Concepts that the student should understand upon completion of materials in the Instructional Unit. After the learning type and Concepts have been identified, the developer designs text and graphics to support the instructional objective. A default micro-strategy associated with the learning type can now be customized to satisfy the actual instructional objective. The problems that test the student's understanding of the instructional materials do not have to be designed in detail since they are system generated. The developer selects types and templates of problems that will be allowed. It is useful, therefore, to identify a coarse list of problems that are desirable as a basis for the selection process.

It is important to design the Concept Network in parallel with the Instructional Unit Network. As Concepts are identified from instructional objectives, they should be added to the Concept Network. Some additional Concepts, not directly related to objectives, may be necessary to satisfy the closed-world condition to provide meaningful explanation to students. The design of Concept Networks was found to be considerably more difficult than the design of the Instructional Unit Network. Relationships between Concepts are often ambiguous and the decision of which Concepts to include is not straight forward. Moreover, most intelligent features of the shell depend on the Concept Network, and the ITS will only function correctly if the Concept Network is correct and reasonably complete. It is tempting to use knowledge of the problems that are generated from this structure as guidance in its design. However, this approach could hamper the construction of a valid network. It must be kept in mind that the Concept Network is a more general structure that serves several purposes: problem generation, error analysis and guidance for remediation. When knowledge of one of these areas is used to create this network, the functionality of the other areas may suffer. A general structure must be designed that is expected to support all areas equally well.

The actual insertion of materials in the ITS shell begins after a relatively complete paper design is available. It is important to create the entire Concept Network before the first directives are given to the Problem Editor. During problem generation, large localities of the network are searched for appropriate relationships. If the network is altered after problem directives are stored, the generation of the problems and remediation based on these directives may also change. However, refinements of the Concept Network may be necessary if the problem generator is given inadequate or incorrect knowledge. This process may easily lead to a recurring loop in which changes to the Concept Network cause continual alternation between the Concept Editor and the Problem Editor. Therefore, it is very important to design a correct and sufficiently complete network before entering instructional materials into the shell.

3. Conclusions and Future Work

An ITS in orbital dynamics was developed using the authoring tools. It was observed that authoring tools did indeed play an important role in the design of effective instruction by an ITS shell. However, several limitations with the developed authoring system became apparent in the "real world" application.

Browsers for both Instructional Unit and Concept Networks coerced a top-down instructional design methodology more reflective of the ITS strategy than, perhaps, of the developers' natural inclinations. It was observed that instructional designers still may perceive a linear "mental model" for the development of basic instructional materials (text and graphics), yet are able to discern and describe the potentially complex relationships between the underlying concepts. Instructional developers also had the tendency to do a first draft design of Instructional Units and their hierarchical relationships on paper. Because the Instructional Unit model was non-linear, most found this extra step necessary for pre-planning and ordering the network structure. Future research should explore the possibilities of other organizational methodologies in authoring which are not so restrictive but still yield the primary hierarchical and other secondary knowledge relationships needed by the ITS Challenger shell for adaptive instruction.

Significant insight on the authoring of the Concept Network was gained by observing the authoring or, more specifically, the selection of system-generated test problems. More often than not, instructional developers would alter the definitions of, and relationships between, Concepts when the problem generation facility would produce questions that the instructional developer found to be unacceptable. In some cases, it took the developers several passes between the Problem Editor and the Concept Editor to achieve what was considered an appropriate problem. Problem generation often drove the development of the Concept Network, even though the network is used in broader classes of adaptive system functions. It may be that the knowledge representation is not yet sufficiently designed to adequately support fully automatic problem generation. A more likely possibility is that simplifying assumptions made in the problem generation routines should be replaced by better rules for problem extraction from the Concept Network. Regardless, it has become very apparent that better feedback is needed in the authoring of Concepts.

Despite some of these limitations, the authoring tools were very important in knowledge acquisition for the orbital dynamics ITS. If for no other reason, eliminating the requirement that the instructional developer know the complicated data knowledge representation demonstrates this importance. Future research on authoring systems must emphasize not only giving instructional developers feedback on the content and context of the knowledge they input, but also on giving expert pedagogical advice on how that content will be conveyed.

5. References

1 D. Russell, IDE The interpreter, in Psotka, Massey and Mutter (eds.), Intelligent Tutoring Systems -- Lessons Learned, Hillsdale, NJ, Lawrence Erlbaum, 1988.
2 T. Murray and B.P. Woolf, A Knowledge Acquisition Tool for Intelligent Computer Tutors, SIGART Bulletin, 2 (1991) 9-21.
3 M.F. Augusteijn, R.W. Broome, R.W. Kolbe and R.N. Ewell, ITS Challenger -- A Domain-Independent Environment for the Development of Intelligent Training Systems, Journal of Artificial Intelligence in Education, 3(2) (1992) 183-205.
4 R.W. Kolbe, R.W. Broome and M.F. Augusteijn, A Dual Knowledge Representation for a Domain-Independent Intelligent Training System, Proc. of 20th Annual ACM Computer Science Conference, Kansas City, MI, (1992), 205-211.
5 M.F. Augusteijn, R.H. Gattis and R.W. Kolbe, Design for a Domain-Independent Intelligent Training System, Conf. on Technology in Training and Ed., (1987) 483-499.
6 M.F. Augusteijn and R.W. Kolbe, Domain Independent Knowledge Representation for Intelligent Training Systems, Jour. of Interactive Instruction Development, 2 (1989) 26-30.
7 M.F. Augusteijn and R.W. Kolbe, Error Analysis: Procedure Comparison Versus Bug Libraries, Proc. Fuzzy Logic OUCC, 89 (1990) 134-142.
8 R.M. Gagne, The Conditions of Learning, Englewood Cliffs, NJ, Prentice Hall, 1965.
9 R.W. Broome, A Prototype Graphical User Interface for Authoring Domain-Independent Intelligent Training Systems, (Master's Thesis) U. of Colorado at Colorado Springs, 1991.

Acknowledgments: The USAF Human Resources Laboratory, Brooks Air Force Base, Texas under contract F33615-C-003 with SASI, Inc. supported this research.

A framework for building a knowledge based system using several experts - with an application for curriculum design of engineering degree courses

M. N. Borges[1], Y. Benett[2], M. Lewis[2] and M. T. Thorn[2]

[1]Electrical Engineering Department, Funrei - Federal Institution of Higher Education, Praça Frei Orlando 170, 36300 SJDR, MG, Brazil

[2]University of Huddersfield, Queensgate, Huddersfield, HD1 - 3DH, UK

Abstract

This paper recognises and justifies the need for several experts in the process of building an expert system in the context of curriculum design. The methodology is to have a Domain Expert and Subdomain Experts working independently with the knowledge engineer. The framework proposed in this paper prevents the problem of conflict of expertise by restrictions on the subdomain boundaries and limits through the concepts of input and output variables. The paper shows that this novel approach has also addressed successfully the issues of verification and validation of knowledge based systems.

1. INTRODUCTION

It is well recognised that knowledge based systems are often built in an *ad hoc* way with a limited theoretical base (Plant, 1991) and that the knowledge elicitation is clearly identified as being the *bottleneck* of the process. Moreover, verification and validation of expert systems are currently major concerns regarding knowledge based system technology. This paper discusses a framework devised to address these issues over a particular application. In this application of expert system methodology to curriculum design it is most unlikely that a single expert is able to cover the domain; consequently the reconciliation of expertise is a problem.

In simple knowledge based system applications it is possible to find a single expert who has both the knowledge and the available time to provide all the expertise required to build an expert system. In such cases this expert usually has the competence and authority to carry out, together with the knowledge engineer, the verification and validation of the system enabling the expert to judge the system development and behaviour. On the other hand, in other more complex and extensive applications no single expert is likely to be able to cover appropriately all aspects of the area (domain) or commit enough time to the project development or both.

If the application requires several experts there is still a possibility that the knowledge engineer could work with only one expert. This expert would provide all the information to the knowledge engineer not only from the expert's own knowledge but also by obtaining the necessary expertise through discussions with other experts. Scott et al (1991) correctly point out that the knowledge acquisition is more streamlined in this approach than with multiple experts and the organisation of the project is usually facilitated for the knowledge engineer. However there are still two hurdles associated with this approach which are often difficult to overcome. Firstly, this expert has to commit a huge amount of time to work with the knowledge engineer and to acquire the complementary expertise from colleagues. Such time is hardly ever available in the case of domain experts. Secondly, the knowledge acquired from other experts may be biased or inadequate for the purposes of knowledge based systems. In other words, experts are not knowledge engineers.

The alternative strategy proposed in this paper is that a knowledge engineer would work with the several experts independently, even if the different sub-areas within the domain to be investigated are overlapping somewhat. It is postulated that there will be one expert who delineates the whole domain and is named here as the Domain Expert; those who provide expertise in each subarea of knowledge are named Subdomain Experts.

Having decided to embark on this approach it must be borne in mind that a great deal of time will have to be spent by the knowledge engineer building productive working relationships with a number of subdomain experts. Also, some constraints should be issued by the domain expert to keep the growth of the knowledge base under control. Moreover, a variety of knowledge elicitation techniques might be necessary to suit different experts making it very demanding on the knowledge engineer. In addition, conflict of expertise is likely to take place since experts seldom agree among themselves. These issues are addressed in the following section where a framework is presented which focuses on:

- the strategy adopted to delimit the domain as far as the human expertise is concerned;
- the knowledge elicitation techniques;
- the verification and validation of the subdomains implemented.

Curriculum design is seen as a poorly structured task which may not have an optimum solution and its specification is rather difficult. This application focuses on educational principles about curriculum design rather than on curriculum content. Consequently, educationists play a major role in its development. Nevertheless, the area is so vast that one particular educationist may feel more comfortable discussing say, Student Assessment than Course Structure or vice-versa. In other words, within the area of curriculum design expertise in the subareas may be better provided by specific experts who have acquired experience in one particular subarea throughout their professional practice. This is therefore, a case typically suitable for a knowledge based system application mainly because advantage can be taken of the expert system feature which allows expertise from different experts to be combined with one another in the same knowledge base.

2. METHODOLOGY

2.1. Strategy

The strategy adopted to approach these issues can be seen in figure 1. Concerning the full specification of the domain, it is proposed that the Domain Expert delineates the whole domain in a knowledge engineering exercise. The domain, represented in the diagram by the bold external line is divided into subdomains as extensively suggested in the literature (Firlej, 1991). The subdomains within the broader area (small bubbles) are decided by the Domain Expert who also defines the *boundaries* and *limits* for each subdomain. *Boundaries* means how much

346

the subdomains are allowed to expand against each other resulting in a pre-defined overlapping area and *limits* means how much the subdomains can inflate themselves within the domain. Making the point in another way, the former relate to the interfacing whereas the latter relate to the size of the subdomains and consequently the size of the eventual knowledge base. The *boundaries* previously defined act as inputs for each Subdomain Expert. On the basis of these inputs the Subdomain Experts are then able to decide how the outcomes of their particular expertise can be defined (outputs). Subdomain Experts must produce all of the outputs plus any extra ones which they consider relevant. They can also use any input from the central bubble named Common Barrel and add extra facts although they are not allowed to create other input variables. All variables inside the Common Barrel are generated as outputs from one subdomain or from the Domain Expert.

Figure 1. Strategy for domain delineation. Knowledge Base for Curriculum Design

The knowledge engineer plays a very important part in this strategy not only by acquiring knowledge from different sources but also by linking the Domain Expert to the Subdomain Experts making accessible to the latter the variables available in the Common Barrel. This is represented in figure 1 by the connections between the Common Barrel and the subdomains. The knowledge engineer also brings to the Domain Expert's arbitration the possible conflict of expertise from different Subdomain Experts. The Domain Expert decides how to settle the argument so that the knowledge engineer can implement the consensus expertise. The important aspect is that all Subdomain Experts should be warned in advance and prepared to defer to Domain Expert decisions before conflicts arise even if they disagree with a decision.

2.2 Knowledge Elicitation Techniques

In order to extract the expertise from human experts (Domain Expert and Subdomain Experts) at each stage of the process of knowledge acquisition different techniques might be applied. Particularly with several experts, it is most likely that different techniques will best suit different experts, as long as they do not overrule the major strategy.

As far as the Domain Expert is concerned, the Card-Sort technique (Gammack, 1987) has proved to be very effective in that it is both naturally easy for that expert and helpful for the knowledge engineer to become acquainted with the domain knowledge. The method also favours dividing the functionality of the expert system. Some structured or focused interviews may prove beneficial at this stage.

Regarding the knowledge elicitation from the subdomain experts, an iterative process is suggested in which the knowledge engineer begins by acquiring top level knowledge and then proceeds in a cyclic fashion to probe further and deeper into the details of the expert's skills within each subdomain. The knowledge is immediately represented and implemented in a prototype. The prototype is presented, through simulation cases, to the subdomain expert as a form of a further knowledge elicitation session and of verification. These simulation sessions for review may identify inaccuracies or omissions thus allowing for the knowledge acquisition plan to be refined in order to reflect the appropriate expertise and elicit additional knowledge, given that the expert is acting on simulated data. This cyclical procedure is shown on figure 2.

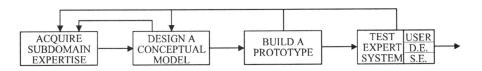

Figure 2. Iterative approach for knowledge acquisition with the subdomain experts

2.3. Verification and Validation

In this paper the concepts of verification and validation are interpreted in the manner defined by Lydiard (1992). To sum up, verification is related to the question "Are we doing the project right?" and validation concerns "Are we doing the right project?". Concerning verification, the technique suggested to elicit Subdomain Experts' knowledge is that which fosters expert-computer interaction throughout the elicitation procedure thereby making sure that the Subdomain Experts are continuously assessing the system being built (see figure 2). It also allows the Domain Expert to oversee the prototypes in order to keep the size of the whole knowledge base under control.

Validation, from the experts' point of view, enjoys a privileged position in this approach in so far that it is seen as a cross reference device between Domain Expert and Subdomain Experts which strengthens some components of the validation of the system such as competency, completeness and correctness (Lydiard, 1992). As far as end-users are concerned, the fact that prototypes for each subdomain are quickly built makes it possible to test them for acceptability and usability involving the end-user in simulation sessions. As a result, end-user requirements and impressions can be incorporated in early stages of the system development, which is highly conducive to the improvement of the user interface for the eventual expert system. In short, this framework proposes a synergy among the participants, who develop and use the expert system, that strongly contributes to its successful completion and utility.

3. RESULTS AND ANALYSIS

In applying the proposed methodology to curriculum design the Domain Expert ended up with 120 different concepts to describe the domain from 48 initially presented by the knowledge engineer. These concepts were divided into eight subdomains: "Introduction to Curriculum Development", "Methods for Curriculum Content Identification", "Learning Outcomes", "Course Structure", "Teaching and Learning Strategies", "Student Assessment", "Course Documentation" and "Course Management"; each is represented by a bubble in figure 1. Together they make up the knowledge base for this application. This first stage of the methodology required 12 hours of knowledge elicitation sessions and a variety of knowledge elicitation techniques (such as Card-Sort technique, Teaching Back technique and Focused Interviews) given that the Domain Expert did not possess the expertise in terms of rules.

Regarding the Subdomain Experts, they were happy with the strategy and mentioned that a prior definition of inputs and outputs for their subdomains had been helpful particularly because this information told them where to start and where to finish. Each of them, one at a time, was given the initial guidelines of the project in a first session and was asked to outline (as they wished) the subdomain at top level in the following session. From those sessions the knowledge engineer picked out the concepts related to the particular subdomain and checked against the Domain Expert's point of view. After that, following subsequent sessions, a conceptual model was designed for each subdomain and checked again at this stage with the Subdomain Expert. Having agreed with the conceptual model, the subdomain was then represented in a prototype and appraised by the Subdomain Expert in cyclical session until all modifications and refinements lived up to the Subdomain Expert expectations. The prototype for each subdomain must by then have included all the relevant factual and expert knowledge to the satisfaction of the Domain Expert and the user. The subdomain "Student Assessment" is taken from figure 1 as an example for a close look at the results of the applied strategy and is presented in table 1.

Table 1
Subdomain Boundaries and Limits - (an example in top level terms)

STUDENT ASSESSMENT		
INPUTS		OUTPUTS
(from) Subdomains	(from) Common Barrel	
Objectives & Outcomes	Course Rationale	Major Concepts & Facts
Educational Taxonomy	Law and Regulations	A Scheme of Assessment
Number of Units	Course Level & Focus	Conditions of Assessment
Duration of Units	Award	Means of Assessment
Number of Progress Points		Record of Assessment

3.1. Implementation and Test

Having built a prototype for a subdomain, the latter constituted a quite separate knowledge base which needed to be linked to the others in the software implementation. The methodical integration of the subdomains, which facilitates further updating and maintenance of the system, was made using the Incremental Prototype technique (Ince, 1991). The general proposed framework and the Incremental Prototype technique enabled the linking and amalgamating of these subdomains in the program to be carried out in a rigorous manner. The linked subdomains were embodied in an expert system shell which runs on a PC environment, thus making the expert system more friendly and accessible to the target customer.

The system has been tested from the end-user's viewpoint. The tests gave rise to some concerns which, once surmounted, contributed to the improvement of the user interface. These improvements were implemented and can be summarised under the following points: a)a *front page* which is intended to adequately prime the user to take full advantage of the consultation; b)a *network explanation* that is a parallel structure to the main program and allows users to get further explanation on a particular topic; c)a *two alternative paths of consultation* which allows the user, through menu options either to access individual subdomains or to go through the whole knowledge base at once.

4. CONCLUSION

The methodology of Domain Expert and Subdomain Experts has worked well in terms of being acceptable and even welcome to the Subdomain Experts and has overcome the issue of expert conflict. This method has placed a considerable burden on the knowledge engineer and this, in turn, justifies not using the Domain Expert as a knowledge engineer with the Subdomain Experts. The concept of "boundaries" and "limits" has been successful in this area of curriculum design where the knowledge was not immediately available in rule form. The knowledge engineering for the different experts has used diverse methods, but the use of a single knowledge engineer and the Incremental Prototype technique have proved successful.

5. REFERENCES

1) Firlej, M. and Hellens, D. (1991) *Knowledge Elicitation, a practical handbook*. London: Prentice Hall.
2) Gammack, J. G. (1987) Different Techniques and Different Aspects on Declarative Knowledge, *in* Kidd, A.L. ed (1987) *Knowledge Acquisition for Expert Systems - A practical handbook*. New York: Plenum Press.
3) Ince, D. (1991) *Object-oriented software engineering with C++*. London: McGraw Hill.
4) Lydiard, T. J. (1992) Overview of current practice and research initiatives for the verification and validation of KBS. *The Knowledge Engineering Review* 7(2), pp. 101-113.
5) Plant, R. T. (1991) Rigorous approach to the development of knowledge-based systems. *Knowledge-Based Systems* 4(4), pp. 186-196.
6) Scott, A. C. and Clayton, J. E. and Gibson, E. L. (1991) *A Practical Guide to Knowledge Acquisition*. New York: Addison-Wesley.

Knowledge Support Systems for Conceptual Design: the Amplication of Creativity

Ernest Edmonds and Linda Candy

LUTCHI Research Centre, Department of Computer Studies, Loughborough University of Technology, Loughborough, Leicestershire, UK.

Abstract
The paper is concerned with computer-based support for conceptual design and, in particular, with the support of creative design. The nature of conceptual design is briefly reviewed and the lack of effective computer support noted. Recent developments in computer-based Knowledge Support Systems, that offer interesting possibilities, are reviewed. The study of the early design of a clearly innovative product, the Lotus bicycle, is used to inform a discussion of the requirements for Knowledge Support Systems that can support conceptual design.

1. INTRODUCTION

As Faltings (1) puts it,

"Most research in intelligent CAD systems has focused on *detail* design, the adaptation of an initial concept to precise specifications. Little is known about the process of *conceptual* design, the transition between functional specification and concept of an artifact that achieves it.".

It is suggested that creative thought often occurs at the conceptual stage and hence any support that could enhance the designer's performance at that point could be extremely valuable. A secondary, but significant, issue is that the transition from conceptual to detail design often involves the manual entry of information into a CAD system, because the conceptual data had not been captured electronically. These are the issues that the paper will address.

2. BACKGROUND

Perhaps the most important point to note about the nature of conceptual design is that made by Visser (2), as a result of empirical studies of designers:

".. a problem solver is not 'given' problems, but 'constructs' them."

Or, as Hori et al (3) put it:

"In ... creative design, humans build new concepts out of *nebulous* mental worlds. They have some *seeds of a new concept*, incubate them and create a new concept..." (my emphasis).

Thus, the process is as much one of problem definition or selection as problem solution: it is essentially creative. The designer generates a set of scenarios or possible prototypical solutions at this stage. A potential problem, in relation to innovation, is that they tend to eliminate options early on in the process (4). One important role that computer support could play is in keeping ideas open longer by providing "external" memory and concept management facilities.

Figure 1 gives an impression of the role that computers play, at the moment, in innovation. The boundaries between these activities are of prime concern. The question is, simply, "Can the CAE support begin sooner and can it, as a consequence, amplify creative design activities.". The problem is that the earliest stages are characterised by uncertainty, tentative decisions and informal representations of design ideas.

The concept of Knowledge Support Systems, in which the end user manipulates machine representations of knowledge directly (5), has recently been developed in LUTCHI and applied to scientific exploration (6, 7, 8, 9). This work has clearly demonstrated a potential for supporting creative work (10). At the same time, other workers have began to study the approach in the specific context of design (11, 3).

Research into the design process has suggested that many of the requirements for support tools are similar to those observed in the LUTCHI study of scientific exploration above (2, 12). For example, Visser proposes that tools to assist in the management of memory load would positively support design. Her results relate closely to those of Candy et al (6) in the use of Knowledge Support Systems in the science domain.

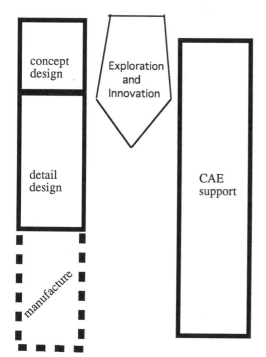

Figure 1: The design process, the designer's exploratory and innovative work and the support from computers:- an impressionistic view.

3. THE CENTRAL PROBLEM

The main concern of the paper is to consider the feasibility of applying the recent research developments in computing described above to the provision of computer support for conceptual design.

A pragmatic approach was used for the investigation in which the development of a successful innovative product was investigated. The results of the investigation are related to the practical use of advanced CAD systems in a closely related context.

In the 1992 Olympics, Chris Boardman won the first UK gold medal, in the 4000m cycling pursuit event. He was riding a revolutionary bicycle built by Lotus Engineering based upon the design concept developed by Mike Burrows (figure 2). The design of this bicycle is the subject of the study reported. Computers were not used at all in the development of the original concept whilst, in contrast, Lotus operate a sophisticated CAD infrastructure. The research reported is investigating the feasibility of bridging this gap.

4. SUPPORT FOR CREATIVITY IN PRACTICE

Lotus Engineering are firmly committed to the exploitation of knowledge-based technology to support design. They have used the ICAD system, from ICAD Engineering Automation Ltd, for several

Figure 2: Chris Boardman breaking the world 5000m record on the Lotus bicycle.

years in order to develop flexible and efficient support for the earlier design stages.

They have been able to demonstrate that a number of clear benefits accrue, including reduced timescales, the effective handling of complexity and the possibility of building generic design modules that are readily available for re-use (13). However, so far this work has not involved the creative concept designer in direct computer use. The Lotus ICAD users are specifically trained and frequently tackle particular problems that are more well defined than the ones that one finds at the very initial conception of a product. Nevertheless, that work includes investigations into support for early explorations and is at the leading edge commercially, clearly pointing towards the increased use of knowledge-based CAD in conceptual design. Our concern is, primarily, the use of systems like ICAD to act as a bridge between support for early conceptual design and the standard CAD system.

The results of the LUTCHI work have identified key design requirements for Knowledge Support Systems. The resulting underlying user interface architecture is designed to be generally applicable and easily tailored for specific domain applications. The work is extending our understanding of how knowledge-based systems can support science and the intention is to now investigate the same approach in design. The cognitive findings are concerned with the nature and accessibility of knowledge to the domain expert. The important distinguishing characteristic of this work is that it is concerned with complex domains in which the expert does not have complete knowledge but, rather, where the approach enables them to extend and refine their own understanding. This issue is central to the creative professional work that is the subject of our concern.

It is, therefore, postulated, with Fischer and Nakakoji (12), that the knowledge support systems approach could provide helpful support for conceptual design. The authors are exploring this hypothesis in order to draw out the consequential requirements for such a support system in a specific case of recent innovative design.

5. THE LOTUS BICYCLE CONCEPT

Mike Burrows is collaborating with the authors so that a cognitive history of the development of the original concept of the new bicycle can be re-constructed. It is pertinent to place this history in the context of other empirical research into early design and, in particular, Knowledge Support Systems. For example, amongst the conclusions of the LUTCHI work referenced above were that the user required:-
• to be able to take an holistic view of the data at any time
• the ability to suspend judgement on any matter at any time
• to be able to readily make unplanned deviations.

The last point was elaborated, in the context of design, by Visser. These results provide a framework for the analysis of the early design history of the bicycle. As a result, therefore, preliminary requirements for computer support are postulated. The development of the bicycle concept from Burrows' early explorations (c1979) to the time of Lotus undertaking the production of the bicycle for the Olympic Games in 1992 has formed the basis of the study.

The design process seems to have been characterized by a number of salient factors or events identified by Mike Burrows as being significant.

1. Time duration:
A lengthy gestation period existed between the formation of the initial thoughts and the final realization of the revolutionary concept. This was a normal experience for Burrows in his design work.

2. Personal and professional goals intertwined:
Burrows is a serious amateur cyclist and monocoque recumbent racer. Personal ambitions provided the stimulus to achieve advantage. Indeed, he expresses his main goal as having been "to go faster": i.e. to satisfy a personal requirements for his racing in cycling events. However, he is also a professional engineer by trade. As well as motivation, skill and knowledge, he had access to machinery for making, for example, hand made bicycle frames. Making was, most probably, an important factor in the design process.

3. Knowledge of the field:
Apart from general design and engineering knowledge, Burrows has a keen interest in the history and development of the bicycle itself. He is very aware of aspects of the process, such as the fixed ideas held about bicycles, and the required series of conceptual leaps and experiments with prototypes that can eventually lead to breakthroughs.

4. Convention and creativity:
There are, amongst cyclists, deeply held views of the bicycle concept. Very small changes in the angles used in a frame are very significant to the perception of "experts". It is not clear that this expert opinion is well founded but it is certainly strongly held. Thus, amongst experts, the search space of possible designs is thought to be well understood. Thus a critical factor in

creative bicycle design is the ability to move outside the existing search space; i.e. to break with the conventional expectations and images.

Moving outside of the search space is closely connected to the ability to respond and exploit the unexpected: for example, the combined ideas of a lady-frame shape with the BMX small size frame, triggered by hearing of a BMX used for racing. The chance availability of carbon fibre material (1982) caused the realisation that a small, but conventional, frame could be improved by filling it in. A change in the British RTC regulations, allowing the use of rear disk wheels in time-trials, generated new design possibilities.

These events led progressively, over years, to the realization that increased speed could result from the use of a small filled in frame, set back from the usual position, using a very light weight mouldable material and designed without the need to shield the rear wheel for wind resistance. The resulting bicycle concept was developed in practice to the extent that a working machine existed. The next step was to move that initial concept into the processes of the Lotus design system.

The use of CAD in the earlier stages of design within Lotus is advanced and interesting. Nevertheless, it did not influence the initial bicycle concept. Particular attention is paid to the exploitation of the ICAD software, which has successfully enabled Lotus to support design in a significantly more iterative manner. The parameters within which the postulated additional computer support might take place may be placed in that context. Outstanding questions include, what are the constraints on the form of data that could usefully be transferred into the current CAD systems? To what extent could the existing systems have offered support to the bicycle's conceptual design? What are the future requirements of CAD for early design?

6. IMPLICATIONS FOR INTELLIGENT SUPPORT TO CONCEPTUAL DESIGN

The requirements for the user to be able to take an holistic view, to be able to suspend judgement and to make unplanned deviations, that were mentioned above, have been strongly supported by the bicycle study. Additional points have also emerged, however.

The need to keep a multitude of design processes alive over long periods of time must be supported. The goals of each of these processes might be at a very high level, such as "go faster", and so may not, in themselves, define a search space. Domain specific knowledge is clearly important but the creative step may well rely upon an act that "breaks set" with conventional wisdom. In other words, creativity may be associated with a re-definition of the problem space.

It is concluded that support systems for conceptual design must allow the user:-
• to take an holistic view of the data at any time
• to suspend judgement on any matter at any time
• to be able to readily make unplanned deviations
• to return to old ideas and goals
• to formulate, as well as solve, problems
• to re-formulate the problem space.

It is the process of interaction between a Knowledge Support System and the designer that is the key element in enabling the amplification of the designer's creative achievements. This process must be allowed to occur in a way that, as a minimum, conforms to the above design ideals.

A version of this paper was presented at The AAAI Spring Symposium on AI and Creativity at Stanford University, USA in March, 1993.

7.   REFERENCES

1. Faltings, B. Qualitative Models in Conceptual Design. In: Artificial Intelligence in Design '91, Gero, G. (ed). Butterworth-Heinemann, (1991) 645-663.

2. Visser, W. Designers' Activities Examined at Three Levels: Organization, Strategies and Problem-Solving Processes. Knowledge-Based Systems 5 1 (1992) 92-104.

3. Hore, K., Sugimoto, M. & Ohsuga, S. Application of Articulation Aid to Design. In: Information Modelling and Knowledge Bases IV, Oaakkola, H. et al (eds), IOS Press, (to appear 1993).

4. Lawson, B. How Designers Think. The Architectural Press, London, (1980).

5. Shaw, M. L. J. & Gaines, B. R. KITTEN: Knowledge Initiation and Transfer Tools for Experts and Novices. In: Knowledge Acquisition Tools for Expert Systems. Boose, J. & Gaines, B. (eds). Academic Press, (1988) 309-338.

6. Candy, L., O'Brien S.M. & Edmonds, E.A. End User Manipulation of a Knowledge-Based System: A Study of an Expert's Practice. International Journal of Man-Machine Studies. 38 1 (1993) 129-145.

7. Edmonds, E.A., O'Brien, S.M., Bailey, T. & McDaid, E. Constructing End-User Knowledge Manipulation Systems. International Journal of Man-Machine Studies. 38 1 (1993) 51-70.

8. O'Brien, S.M. Candy, L., Edmonds, E.A., Foster, T.J. & McDaid, E. End User Knowledge Manipulation Systems: The Speech Knowledge Interface. In: Proc. of 20th Annual Computer Science Conference, Agrawal, J.P., Kumar V. and Wallentine, V. (eds), The ACM Press, (1992) 359-366.

9. O'Brien, S.M., Candy, L., Edmonds, E.A. & Foster, T.J. Knowledge Acquisition and Refinement Using End-User Knowledge Manipulation Systems. In: Applications of Artificial Intelligence X: Knowledge-Based Systems Conference, SPIE Proceedings Vol. 1707, Orlando, Florida. Biswas, G. (ed), (1992) 25-36.

10. Candy, L., Edmonds, E.A. & O'Brien S.M. Amplifying Creativity: The Role of End User Knowledge Manipulation Systems. In: Artificial Intelligence and Creativity. Dartnell, T (ed). Studies in Cognitive Systems, Kluwer Academic, Dordrecht, (to appear 1993).

11. Fischer, G. Communications Requirements for Cooperative Problem Solving Systems. International Journal of Information Systems. 15 1 (1990) 21-36.

12. Fischer, G. & Nakakoji, K. Beyond the Macho Approach of Artificial Intelligence: Empower Human Designers - Do Not Replace Them. Knowledge-Based Systems. 5 1 (1992) 15-30.

13. Gregory, A. Separating Fact from Fiction. Manufacturing Breakthrough. 1 6 (1992) 329-333.

A CONCEPTUAL MODEL OF HUMAN SKILL REQUIREMENTS FOR ADVANCED MANUFACTURING SETTINGS

R. J. Koubek and G. Salvendy

School of Industrial Engineering, Purdue University, West Lafayette, IN 47907, USA

Abstract
In order to achieve the economic benefits which result from immediate use of technology, personnel should be selected and trained prior to the technology implementation. This paper provides a conceptual model for determining skill requirements concurrently with the development of new technology.

1.0 OBJECTIVE AND SIGNIFICANCE

As the manufacturing environment becomes increasingly complex, the human's contribution to overall system performance continues to rise. As such, the proper selection and training of personnel capable of performing in these complex environments becomes critical. This requires a thorough understanding of the knowledge, skill and ability requirements associated with the effective operation and management of technology. Ideally, these personnel requirements should be developed concurrently with the new technology in order to reduce delays in the effective utilization of technological and human resources. Knowing skill requirements helps reduce delays in implementation because corporations can plan ahead concurrently for both the acquisition of equipment and human skills needed to operate the equipment. Economic benefits result by enabling industry to utilize high productivity systems earlier (because of the earlier and more effectively than would otherwise be possible.

These benefits to the manufacturing industry are forwarded by the development of a theoretically-driven engineering-science-based systematic model of human skills requirements associated with the operation of Advanced Manufacturing Technologies (AMT). In the following sections of this paper, first, a variety of theoretic approaches are reviewed as a basis for skill and knowledge assessment. Following this review, a hybrid model is presented which links together a number of diverse approaches in an integrated framework for concurrent prediction of skill, knowledge and ability requirements during the technology design stage.

2.0 ANALYSIS OF THEORETICAL APPROACHES TO SKILL

Numerous theoretical paradigms are available to describe the human skill characteristics which interact with technology and organizational factors. The approaches for skills-knowledge characteristics can be classified into five categories: learning theory; dual processing code theory, or automatization; cognitive abilities; knowledge structures; and cognitive resource theory. Each can be applied independently to personnel in AMT settings and hence each is discussed separately below. The integration of these five separate theories into a model for determining knowledge, skill and ability (KSA) requirements is presented in section 3.0.

2.1 Learning Theories

Learning theories primarily focus on the acquisition of domain knowledge. A well established and representative theory of learning domain knowledge is Gange's Conditions of Learning approach (1985). Here, a distinction is made between those features which are external to the learner and those which are internal. He proposes that in order to reach a specified stage of learning, certain pre-conditions must exist both externally and internally. External factors are those methods and stimuli used to instruct the person on his/her particular task. Internal factors include all knowledge acquired in learning states prior to the target state. Cognitive abilities can also be considered an internal factor.

According to this approach, eight stages of learning are possible (see Gange [1985] for details regarding these stages). Learning can be viewed as a hierarchical process where each successive stage depends on completion of the previous stages. For example, chaining, in which stimulus-response pairs are linked together, cannot be acquired without stimulus-response learning having already taken place. Gange's work places problem solving at the highest level, requiring all previous stages of learning to have been accomplished. Traditional classroom instruction of factory operation and safety procedures support learning theory assumptions about knowledge acquisition.

2.2 Dual Processing Code Theory

A second view to characterize worker KSA requirements is the dual processing code theory, more commonly known as automatization. This view has received attention among researchers attempting to train personnel to perform repetitive tasks. At its foundation is the distinction between two qualitatively different cognitive processes: controlled and automatic.

Key distinguishing features between the two processes include the use of cognitive resources and control. Automatized processes have been found to require little or no cognitive resources and are subject to lack of control over their processing. Controlled processing is resource intensive and is monitored, or controlled, by the cognitive system. Therefore, automatic processing is characterized by smooth, rapid, effortless and almost unconscious execution while controlled processing occurs in conscious tasks such as problem solving. Another distinction between the two processes lies in their development. Initially all new processes are controlled. However, automatized processes are eventually developed for consistent components of a task. If significant practice on a perceptual or rule-based stimulus and response is given, automatized processing will develop. The key to this development is consistency.

John Anderson, in his classic paper on the acquisition of cognitive skill (1982), has provided a three stage model with a series of mechanisms which act upon data during the development of automatization. In the first stage, he suggests that knowledge is represented in a declarative manner and general problem solving strategies are required to operate on this knowledge. In the second stage, this declarative knowledge is transferred into procedural knowledge and is represented as a production rule system. The process by which this knowledge transformation occurs is labeled Compilation and uses Composition and Proceduralization mechanisms. The final stage involves a tuning process. Anderson suggests learning continues after the procedural knowledge by execution of Generalization, Discrimination and Strengthening mechanisms on the production rules. In this manner, the production system representing procedural knowledge is continually honed to be more efficient. His set of mechanisms is assumed to account for each stage in the cognitive skill acquisition process.

2.3 Cognitive Abilities

A third line of work which may be applicable to determining KSA requirements is the ability requirements approach. In this view, "tasks are described, contrasted, and compared in terms of the abilities that they require of the operator". Abilities are considered stabilized operator characteristics. Here a list, or taxonomy, of abilities are provided and the analyst is required to determine the type and level of abilities required for the particular task. Probably the most significant work in this area has been done by Fleishman (1975), who has produced a validated taxonomy of 52 abilities. This taxonomy includes both physical and cognitive abilities.

Two issues important to AMT settings with this approach are evident. First, research has shown that abilities important for initial stages of learning are often different from those required for skilled task performance (although some overlap will exist). As such, there are abilities necessary to learn the task, and those required to perform the task. In a world of rapid technological and labor market changes, it is important to hire personnel who both can acquire new skills rapidly than can ultimately perform a specific task at the required skill level. The second comment regarding this approach for AMT environments is its exclusive focus on abilities, at the expense of skills. Abilities are considered stable cognitive factors which are either innate or not readily modified. Skill pertains to the capability to carry out a task sequence in an appropriate manner. Skill is task specific and must be acquired for successful operation in the production process. As such, the ability requirements approach alone is insufficient for modeling skills requirements in AMT settings.

2.4 Knowledge Structures

A fourth line of research receiving recent attention is that of knowledge structures. This view proposes that the manner in which humans structure their knowledge about the domain is a significant determinant of performance. Numerous studies have shown differences between novice and expert knowledge structures and have suggested this as a potential explanation of performance differences. In a recent set of papers, Koubek and Salvendy (1991) have proposed three levels of knowledge structures according to the level of operator skill: surface feature, task specific and abstract/hierarchical. The *surface feature* structures found in novices are composed of the explicit, physical, salient domain features. Since no abstracted concepts are used, such a structure does not provide the operator the capability to reason about their domain in anything but the most basic manner.

As humans become skilled, they develop a more conceptual, yet task-specific framework which allows for more complex cognitive activity, such as decision making, inferences and extrapolation. However, when personnel with this structure face a problem-solving task, they evoke only those parts of the structure that appear directly relevant to a narrow subset of the task at hand. Their structure, which contains conceptual information, is not yet organized in a principled manner which allows the operator to see the more broad implications and impending features from the domain for their particular problem. As such, the solution path is narrow, with a depth-first flavor to the search strategy. This knowledge structure is termed *task specific*. The majority of personnel remain at this level. Performance at a level which has been termed "super-expert" is dependent on the operator not only possessing a conceptual understanding of the domain, but that these concepts are organized in a hierarchical manner under increasingly abstracted concepts, or principles. This highest knowledge structure is termed *abstract/hierarchical*.

This theoretical approach would suggest a focus on training personnel to develop a high level conceptual understanding of the domain and coincides the Gange's learning approach. Neither of these approaches however, directly address the acquisition of high performance cognitive and physical skills as modeled by the automatization approach. Also, within the knowledge structures, domain specific knowledge which is required for the effective performance of a task needs to be acquired. This domain specific knowledge is unaccounted for in the knowledge structure approach.

2.5 Cognitive Resource Theory

Finally, a fifth view of human performance in AMT settings is that of cognitive resources. While many variants exist (see Wickens, 1992 for details), this approach basically states that a limited pool of cognitive resources are available. When task demands exceed the available cognitive resources, errors and a decline in performance is likely. Therefore, performance is a function of both task demands and operator capacity. Individual differences exist in resource capacity, suggesting the selection of personnel with high capacity. In addition, training and automatization can be used to reduce the resources required to execute the automatized or trained task, thereby freeing resources for investment in the performance of other task elements.

3.0 A MODEL FOR DETERMINING SKILL REQUIREMENTS IN AMT OPERATIONS

Each of these views by themselves is insufficient for the AMT environment. The ability requirements approach appears to transcend the other models, as its elements can be found in all the approaches. In Gange's model, moving up the hierarchy of learning requires that conditions internal to personnel be available, such as acquisition of all previous stages of learning. In addition, cognitive and physical abilities necessary to achieve the next level of learning must be present. Therefore, since attaining each learning level depends on possession of the previous level of learning, and each level may have particular abilities necessary for its acquisition, the importance of particular abilities increases as one moves up the hierarchy. The abilities necessary to attain learning at each level includes not only those specific to that level, but also includes those abilities associated with all previous learning levels. The same may be true for knowledge structures. To move from the surface feature level, to the task specific level, and ultimately, the abstract/hierarchical level, certain abilities may become increasingly important. This hypothesis is yet to be explored.

In relation to the automatization approach, Fleishman and Hempel (1954) have shown that for repetitive tasks, while abilities are important for acquiring the skill, as practice accrues, performance becomes less dependent on the initial ability set possessed by personnel. Therefore, to acquire knowledge and perform problem solving tasks, Fleishman's ability approach takes on increasing importance, while it is less important in repetitive tasks for which significant practice has accrued.

Since the ability approach does not address the process of acquiring skill and knowledge, it serves the AMT environment best when integrated in the other models. This discussion on abilities is directly paralleled by the cognitive resource theory. Problem solving tasks require greater resources, while high performance cognitive skill has lower resource requirements. Therefore, it is concluded that the combined information from the ability requirements, knowledge structures, Gange's (1985) hierarchy of learning and Anderson's (1982) automatization, together with Wickens' (1992) resource allocation provides the information needed in AMT settings.

A theoretical model for determining skills requirements in AMT operations is outlined in Figure 1. In this new theoretical paradigm, production personnel begin learning a task with a pool of cognitive resources available for skill acquisition and task execution. As these personnel acquire greater domain knowledge and move up the hierarchy of learning, consistent tasks for which practice accrues becomes automatized into high performance skills. This transfer from learning to high performance skills is represented by the horizontal lines between the columns in this figure. Since automatized tasks require minimal amounts of cognitive resources, the resources initially invested in performance of these tasks are freed for other purposes, such as learning at higher levels.

This cycle of moving up the learning hierarchy, across to skilled task performance, freeing resources, and re-investing to move further up the learning hierarchy is termed the *learning-skill* process, and is suited for both physical and cognitive task performance. It is assumed that the jobs of AMT personnel would consist of many tasks, each of which are simultaneously and independently being processed by this learning-skill cycle. Therefore, this model is applicable to individual tasks within a job, rather than to the job as a whole.

In order to move up the learning hierarchy, humans must have the physical and cognitive abilities necessary for learning at the target level. Also, in order to transfer task elements from learning to automatization, the appropriate knowledge structure must be in place. The horizontal arrows between the Level of Learning and Automatization columns can be

360

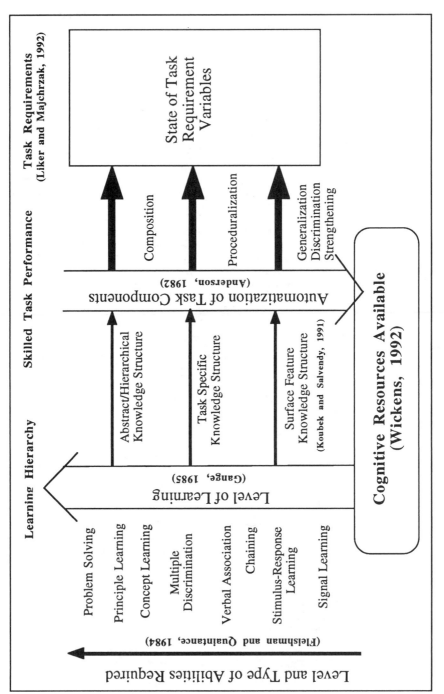

Figure 1. Learning process for AMT personnel.

considered knowledge structure "bridges" which must be crossed. At the highest levels of learning, an Abstract/Hierarchical knowledge structure "bridge" must be available to transport the learned task component to automatization. In middle levels, a task specific knowledge structure bridge is necessary, while at the lowest levels, a surface feature knowledge structure is adequate. Therefore, while knowledge may be acquired at high learning levels, in order for it to be transformed into a high performance skill, the appropriate knowledge structure must be in place.

Traditionally, shop floor workers were expected to attain only low levels of learning, and then transfer this to automatization. As such, low levels of abilities and fairly simple knowledge structures were adequate. Two outcomes result from this strategy. First, the type of tasks these personnel are capable of performing are rather simple, with minimal decision-making and problem solving demand, and second, the cognitive resources made available due to automatization are not reinvested and therefore wasted.

4.0 CONCLUSION

In the AMT work environment, technology provides the capability to integrate and present process-related information to personnel at the shop floor. Access to this information now makes it possible, and often necessary, to assign higher level decision-making, problem solving and planning tasks at the shop floor personnel level. As such, several researchers have concluded that the change of greatest significance in human resource requirements result from AMT implementation has been the increased use of cognitive skills. To perform tasks requiring these type of skills, personnel must achieve a relatively high level on Gange's learning hierarchy. Also the appropriate knowledge structure "bridges" must be in place to continually move lower level acquired tasks into automatized skills. Personnel must also possess the abilities appropriate for learning at these higher levels. Therefore, advanced manufacturing technology now supports a learning-skill process whereby cognitive resources are not wasted, but rather are continually re-invested to acquire new states of learning and make possible performance on increasingly complex cognitive tasks, thereby significantly increasing utilization of AMT system effectiveness. The model proposed here attempts to represent this process and serve as a basis for concurrent prediction of skills simultaneously with technology development.

5.0 REFERENCES

Anderson, J.R. (1982). Acquisition of cognitive skill. Psychological Review, 89(4), 369-406.

Fleishman, E.A. (1975). Toward a taxonomy of human performance. *American Psychologist*, 30, 1127-1149.

Fleishman, E.A. and Hempel, Jr., W.E. (1954). Changes in factor structure of a complex psychomotor task as a function of practice. *Psychometrika, 19*(3), 239-252.

Gange, R.M. (1985). *The Conditions of Learning and Theory of Instruction, Fourth Edition.* New York: Holt, Rinehart and Winston.

Koubek, R.J. and Salvendy, G. (1991). Cognitive performance of super-experts on computer program modification tasks. *Ergonomics, 34* (8), 1095-1112.

Wickens, C.D. (1992). *Engineering Psychology and Human Performance, Second Edition.* New York: Harper Collins.

Heuristics for generating informative responses to failing user's queries in natural language database interfaces

Z. Trabelsi, Y. Kotani and H. Nisimura

Department of Computer Science, Tokyo University of Agriculture and Technology, 2-24-16 Naka-cho, Koganei, Tokyo, 184 Japan

Abstract

In this paper we describe a natural language interface to a database, incorporating a number of heuristics and a knowledge base built on top of the database, that has been developed to respond informatively to particular failing user's queries. The interface proposes a partial solution to the complex problem of handling failing user's queries. It will be shown that the interface can be ported relatively easily from one database to another. The advantages of this work over related works are also examined.

1. INTRODUCTION

Recent works [1,2,3,4,5,6,7] have addressed the diverse and complex issues involved in developing smart natural language interfaces to databases. Such works include attempts to resolve anaphoric references in queries, to track the user's focus of attention, and to generate informative and/or summary responses.

This work describes a natural language interface to a database that uses a number of heuristics and a knowledge base to generate informative responses to particular failing user's queries. The database used to test the interface is a simple subset of the entire soccer World Cup 1990 database. For each player, coach, team and match a record was made.

In order to concentrate on the response generation issues, the internal form of a query is provided by the user when the interface requires it. An actual surface language generation capability will be incorporated in future versions of the interface.

Before activating any database access, the interface calls upon its heuristics to verify whether the user's query satisfies particular conditions. The heuristics are tried in order until one succeeds or all fail. When a heuristic succeeds the interface assumes that the user's query would fail and produces an informative response as dictated by the successful heuristic. If all heuristics fail, the interface generates the appropriate database access to respond to the query. The interface reports its inability to produce an informative response if the database access also fails.

2. THE KNOWLEDGE BASE

For each attribute of the database the knowledge base defines the set of its valid data values and the corresponding database entity. The reason why the data values of a given attribute should be within a particular set of data values is specified. In addition, the knowledge base provides the meanings of the attributes of the database as in the real world.

For some attributes the knowledge base contains the names of Boolean functions representing the condition related to the existence of their data values in the database. Each function has a number of arguments. The values of the arguments are provided either by the user's query or by the interface. The arguments are used while evaluating the above condition. If the condition is false, the function attempts to provide the skeleton of a message that indicates the reason for the non-existence of the requested data in the database. The message would be employed later to generate the appropriate response to the user's query.

3. THE HEURISTICS

The heuristics employed in the interface are procedural in nature and handle the user's queries in a domain independent way. Using the contents of the above knowledge base, the heuristics allow the interface to identify particular failing user's queries and to generate informative responses. Reasons why the user may come to type particular failing queries and strategies for responding adequately to them will be discussed.

3.1. The value heuristic

The *value heuristic* determines if in the user's query a data value X appearing for a particular attribute A is not within the set of valid data values of the attribute A. If so, the user's query would fail and an informative response is generated. The response indicates that the user's query fails since the data value X is not within the set of valid data values of the attribute A. The reason why the data values of the attribute A should be within a particular set of data values is provided in the response. Moreover, the sets of valid data values of some attributes may be listed to the user in an appropriate way. The above knowledge base contains such reasons and defines the set of valid data values for each attribute of the database.

The user comes to type such failing queries since his/her knowledge about the contents and the limits of those sets may be very limited. The *value heuristic* enables the system to produce responses such as:

Q1: Give the names of the Portugal players.

S1: I don't have any information about Portugal. Because I have information only about the 24 teams qualified for the soccer World Cup 90. Portugal did not qualify.

Do you want to see the list of the qualified teams? Yes/No: Yes.

This is the list: Brazil, Italy,...

The response S1 would be greatly welcomed by the user since it corrects his/her misconception about the database application and provides him/her with useful information.

In generating an informative response to such a failing user's query, the *value heuristic* judges whether the set of valid data values of the attribute A may be provided to the user. This depends mainly on the size of the set and the type of the user that is expected to use the interface. Such a capability aims to generate more informative responses.

3.2 The condition heuristic

The existence of the data values of some attributes of the database may be condition dependent. That is, the data values of some attributes exist in the database if particular conditions are true. Generally the user's knowledge about the existence of such conditions is very limited.

It is unnecessary to activate any database access routine when the user's query asks the interface to retrieve a data value that does not exist in the database. The interface should be able to explain the reason for the non-existence of such a data value. Otherwise the response to the query may mislead the user.

The *condition heuristic* determines if the Boolean value of the function, related to the existence of the data values for an attribute X, is false under the context of the user's query. If so, the query would fail and an informative response is generated. The response indicates that the query fails since the requested data does not exist in the database. In addition, a message indicating the reason for the non-existence of the requested data is also provided. The above function in the knowledge base defines the skeleton of such a message. An example response produced by the *condition heuristic* is:

Q2: What are the attendances of the second round.

S2: The attendances of the second round are not known yet. Because the first round has not finished yet. The second round will start in 23/06/90.

3.3. The attribute heuristic

The user may know all the entities of the database, but never all their attributes. Hence the processing of a user's query may lead the system to handle an attribute A as the attribute of a particular entity EN1. Nevertheless, in the database the entity EN1 doesn't have such an attribute. Consequently, the user's query would fail. And it is up to the interface to generate a response that corrects the user's misconception about the database entities and their corresponding attributes.

The *attribute heuristic* attempts to produce the adequate responses to such failing user's queries. Faced with the above user's query, the *attribute heuristic* reports that the user's query fails since the entity EN1 does not have such an attribute. In addition, it determines if there are other entities ENj in the knowledge base that have attributes whose meanings, in the real world, are the same as the meaning of the attribute A. If so, the *attribute heuristic* reports also that the attribute A is the attribute of the entities ENj in the database. An example is the query-response pair Q3-S3:

Q3: Give the sizes of the coaches.

S3: I cannot answer your query. Because in the database there are no sizes for the coaches. However, for the players there are sizes.

Since the user gets the response S3, we believe that he/she will not again attempt to ask about the sizes of the coaches. However, he/she may ask about the sizes of the players.

We emphasize that if the user's query contains an attribute that does not appear in the database, the *concept heuristic* in the next section may provide the appropriate response to such a failing user's query.

3.4. The concept heuristic

In accessing the contents of a database, the user's query may exceed the conceptual coverage of the database. That is, the user's query refers to concepts that are not actually represented in the database. The user may come to type such a query since his/her knowledge about the limits of the conceptual coverage of the database is usually very limited.

The *concept heuristic* determines if there is a concept, in the user's query, that exceeds the conceptual coverage of the database. If so, the *concept heuristic* reports that the query fails since it is exceeding the conceptual coverage of the database. An example is:

Q4: Display the ages of the referees.

S4: I cannot answer your query. Because the database does not know of any information about referees.

It is clear that the response S4 is more informative than the response "I cannot answer your query. Because I cannot understand the meaning of 'referees'". That is, the latter response does not mean that in the database there is no information about the referees. Hence, it does not correct the above user's misconception about the limits of the conceptual coverage of the database.

To identify a concept exceeding the conceptual coverage of a database, the *concept heuristic* determines the possible grammatical structures of the concept in the user's query. Then, it engages the user in a set of clarification dialogues based on database-domain hierarchies. From this interaction a concept that is exceeding the conceptual coverage of the database may be identified.

The database-domain hierarchies define the classes of each grammatical structure that may occur in the user's queries. Because the database domain is a limited domain, such classes may be explicitly defined. Moreover the hierarchies allow the interface to identify the contents and limits of the conceptual coverage of the database.

The clarification dialogues are sets of multiple choices. Each choice represents one class in the database-domain hierarchies. During a clarification dialogue the user is asked to select one choice in order to restrict more the nature of the class of a concept. Then, the interface generates the next clarification dialogue by going more deeper in the hierarchies.

No further clarification dialogues are generated when the user indicates that the class of the concept does not figure among the list of the classes offered. Hence the interface assumes that the concept exceeds the conceptual coverage of the database and attempts to generate the appropriate response as discussed above.

Because the user may get bored when he/she is asked many times to clarify the class of the same concept, the interface attempts to add the concept to its lexicon as a new lexical items that is exceeding the conceptual coverage of the database. So that, later if the user's query contains that concept the interface would directly identify it solely by consulting the lexicon and without resorting to any clarification dialogue.

4. DISCUSSION

In a new database the contents of the knowledge base should be recoded by the interface designer, whereas the structure of the knowledge base is independent of whatever the database is. Moreover the contents of the responses generated should be also adapted to the new type of the users that are expected to use the interface and the new database domain.

The works of Kaplan [4] and of Kao [3] are closely related to our work. Although they have shown some success, they present some limits.

Kaplan's system [4] does not employ a knowledge base. The only domain specific knowledge that Kaplan's system needs can be derived from the information in the database. However, our work shows clearly the need to encode knowledge that does not appear in the database, while dealing with failing user's queries.

Our work shows the necessity to respond appropriately to the user's queries that exceed the conceptual coverage of the database in developing a smart natural language interface. Kaplan's system is unable to deal adequately with such user's queries. Indeed, given such user's queries Kaplan's system provides completely misleading responses. For example in the query "Display the age of Takada", we assume that the term 'Takada' is a referee name in the mind of the user. If there is no information at all about the referees, Kaplan's system would interpret the term 'Takada' as the name of a player or a coach and therefore provides a completely misleading response such as "I don't know of any Takada players". It is clear that the adequate response would be "I don't know of any information about the referees".

Kao [3] proposes two algorithms to handle failing user's queries using a knowledge base model. Kao's knowledge base model neither specifies the reasons of the non-existence of some concepts in the database, nor defines the domains of the attributes of the database. The *value heuristic* introduced in our work has shown the need of such information while generating more informative responses.

In addition, Kao's work discusses solely the data values whose existences in the database are time dependent. Our work is more general since it discuss the data values whose existences are condition dependent. This includes time dependent, location dependent, and so on.

5. CONCLUSION

This work discussed mainly a number of heuristics that are intended to produce informative responses to particular failing user's queries in a natural language interface to a database. Every heuristic has demonstrated its usefulness in providing the reasons for the failures of the user's queries. The heuristics are domain-independent, and the knowledge base used by the heuristics is easily modifiable to adapt to the requirements of a new database domain.

In addition, this work illustrated clearly the need for knowledge that does not appear in the database, and database-domain hierarchies to respond informatively to the above particular failing user's queries.

6. REFERENCES

[1] Granger, R.H.: The NOMAD System: Expectation-Based Detection and Correction of Errors During Understanding of Syntactically and Semantically Illformed Text, American Journal of Computational Linguistics, Vol. 9, No. 3, pp. 188-198 (1984).

[2] Kalita, J., Jones, M.L. and McCalla, G.I.: Summarizing natural language database responses, Journal Computational Linguistics, Vol. 12, pp. 107-124 (1986).

[3] Kao, M., Nick J.Cercone and Wo-Shun Luk: Providing Quality Responses with Natural Language Interfaces: The Null Value Problem, IEEE Transactions on Software Engineering, Vol. 14, No. 7, pp. 959-984 (1988).

[4] Kaplan S.J.: Cooperative Responses from a Portable Natural Language Query System, Artificial Intelligence, Vol. 19, pp. 165-187 (1982).

[5] McCoy, K.F.: Highlighting a User Model to Respond to Misconception, in User Models in Dialog Systems edited by A. Kobsa and W. Wahlster, Springer-Verlag, pp. 233-254 (1989).

[6] Motro A.: Query generalization: A method for interpreting null answers, in IEEE Proc. Workshop Expert Database Systems, L. Kerschberg, Ed., Columbia, SC, pp. 597-616 (1986).

[7] Motro A.: FLEX: A Tolerant and Cooperative User Interface to Database, IEEE Transactions on Knowledge and Data Engineering, Vol. 2, No. 2 (1990).

Natural Language Interfaces For Integrated Network Management

Raymond Chau

Special Services Networks Group, MRP Teltech Ltd., 8999 Nelson Way, Burnaby, BC, V5A 4B5, CANADA, (604) 294-1471

Abstract

This paper describes a prototype natural language query interface (NLQI) to the AtmNet™[1] Operational Support System (OSS). The AtmNet™ OSS is an integrated network management system for MPR's cell relay multimedia networking system for MPR's cell relay multimedia networking system based on Asynchronous Transfer Mode technology. NLQI provides a more flexible and user friendly user interface to query configuration and traffic data from the system database over the existing menu based graphical user interface (GUI). Approximately one man-year was spent to produce the prototype, which is developed using an off-the-shelf natural language application development package. The background, implementation and evaluation of NLQI are presented.

1.0 Introduction

AtmNet™ is an Asynchronous Transfer Mode networking product offered by MPR Teltech Ltd.. In addition to switches, multiplexers, concentrators and service adaptors, AtmNet™ includes an Operational Support System (OSS) for network control and monitoring. The OSS stores configuration and traffic data from the network in a relational database. It currently provides a X windows based graphical user interface to support the configuration management and performance management functions.

The promise of natural language interfaces is information accessibility. Ideally in database applications, they should be able to translate an English question into a form that can be understood by a database manager and should understand the application domain enough to provide intelligent responses. A prototype natural language query interface (NLQI) was developed for the OSS to study the technology's suitability for inclusion in a future release for the product.

2.0 Implementation

2.1 Environment

NLQI was developed on a SUN SparcStation™[2] using the Natural Language product version 5.1 from Natural Language Inc.. The OSS database, in which 9 tables and 104 attributes are what NLQI uses, employs the INGRES™[3] Relational Database Management System version 6.3 from Ask Computer Inc. operating on the same hardware platform.

2.2 Methodology

We found that the traditional structured system development methodology does not fit very well when developing a natural language interface. The majority of the effort is spent in user interviewing, user testing and fine tuning. In our implementation, the process was partitioned into three main tasks:

1. Establish the interface between the application and the database. This requires teaching the application about the details of the database model. This includes the data structures and the business rules within the model.
2. Establish the interface between the application and the end user. This requires teaching the application about the range of vocabulary and concepts used by the target end users. These are specified as the applications' internal lexicon.
3. Select a group of potential users for testing and fine tuning.

---

[1] AtmNet is a trademark of MPR Teltech Ltd.
[2] SparcStation is a trademark of SUN MicroSystems Inc.
[3] INGRES is a trademark of ASK Computer Inc.

2.3   Sample Session

This section presents a transcript recorded during a user session with NLQI. User input is shown in boldface.

Transcript recorded on 8/24/92 at 13:18 by user sidl1
Connection file: atm.con
: list the nodes
Executing....

Element Name
Bashful
Doc
Sleepy
Sneezy
Grumpy
Dopey
Happy

: where are they
Executing....

Element Name	Location
Bashful	Vancouver
Doc	Burnaby
Sleepy	Victoria
Sneezy	Vancouver
Grumpy	PrinceGeorge
Dopey	Terrance
Happy	LongBeach

: which cards are mounted on bashful
Executing....

Card Name
TXICO1
TXICO4
ETACO1
ETACO4

: show the equipped cards and their adaptation layer statistics
Executing.....

Card Name	Node Name	Date	Time	PDU Rev	PDU Sent	PDU Err
ETACO1	Bashful	6/28/92	10:00	33	3	42
ETAC42	Grumpy	6/28/92	10:00	32	5	35
ETACO1	Bashful	6/28/92	10:15	30	3	45
ETAC42	Grumpy	6/28/92	10:15	49	3	55
			10:30	46	2	33
ETACO1	Bashful	6/28/92	10:30	36	4	35
			10:45	32	1	30
ETAC42	Grumpy	6/28/92	10:45	43	2	30
ETACO1	Bashful	6/28/92	11:00	38	3	44
ETAC42	Grumpy	6/28/92	11:00	46	5	44
			11:15	43	5	42
ETACO1	Bashful	6/28/92	11;15	33	3	32
ETAC42	Grumpy	6/28/92	11:30	46	3	43
ETACO1	Bashful	6/28/92	11:30	36	3	43
			11:45	38	1	33
ETAC42	Grumpy	6/28/92	11:45	46	3	43

649 more rows. Type y (continue), q (quit), s (save table), p (print table)>>
q
: total by column 1
Executing....

Card Name	PDU Rev	PDU Sent	PDU Err
ETAC01	9,325	650	9,058
ETAC42	9,903	756	9,682
TXIC04	3,780	276	3,697
ETAC42	3,852	262	3,724
TXIC01	-----	-----	-----
TXIC21	-----	-----	-----
VNAC02	-----	-----	-----

: **make a stacked bar graph**
(graph is displayed in a separate window as shown below)

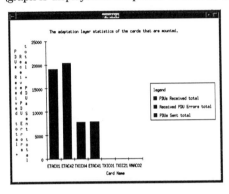

: **exit**
The transcript is in/home/larch2/ingres/nli/transcript/sisdl11265

2.4 Comments
This section presents some comments on the lessons that were learned during the implementation.

1. Thorough understanding of the database model is essential. Discover clearly how the information is conceived and clarify any ambiguities in the model with the designers.
2. Begin implementation only when a stable and correct database is available for testing.
3. Perform testing after each significant segment. The nature of language is so complex that interpretation of the same question can change throughout the development process.
4. Make use of customer support from vendor. Problems due to the internal lexicon of the product are difficult to track down. For example, a word can have a pre-programmed meaning that is different from yours.
5. It is important to provide end users with alternate methods to acquire their desired results for queries beyond the capabilities of the NLQI. Otherwise, users will lose confidence and be reluctant to accept the product.

3.0 Evaluation
3.1 Advantages
In network management applications where the technical expertise of the users can range from novice to veteran, it is important that the choice of interface not be restricted to any one level. Users should be given the flexibility to apply their knowledge of the database domain to the interface and retrieve the data in a format that most suits them. A natural language interface can do just that. A user with extensive knowledge of the network but not the database architecture can ask questions just as easily as a user knowledgeable in both areas. More importantly, this applies to those users new to both the network and the database. Essentially, the capability of a natural language interface to relate a database directly to a spoken language provides the knowledge that is required to access the database. As a result, end users do not need to understand the database structure and relationships in order to get

the information they want. Additionally, since the interface contains this knowledge, users can pose questions on the domain structure, in this case, the structure of the network.

For infrequent users of an application, it is often difficult to remember the special commands required to perform a specific task, this is particularly applicable to integrated network management applications where some users may access the information as seldom as only when a network error occurs. A natural language interface promises these users with an ad hoc interface where they can ask questions phrased in their spoken language so that there is no special syntax to remember. This flexibility also means that there is often more than one way to accomplish the same task, that is, different way to ask a question can produce the same results.

The most powerful of all the promises of a natural language interface, however, lies in its contextual ability. The use of context allows the user to logically and intuitively pose one question after another to find the answer he needs. Basically, it allows for dialogue between the user and the database so that refinement is possible to finally reach an analytical solution without going beyond using one's spoken language. When compared to a natural language interface in this capability, a GUI becomes a maze of menus and windows that requires too much work navigating for the real task at hand.

Furthermore, a natural language interface involves little learning, generally less than that of any other type of interface. The ease of use of a natural language results in higher acceptance by end users and hence appeal to a wider audience than traditional interfaces.

It is easy to see that natural language interfaces can improve communication between an integrated network management application and its users thus enhancing the utility of network information for analysis.

3.2   Disadvantages

The above advantages, however, can only be realized if the natural language interface is perfect. Unfortunately, current technology is unable to achieve perfection. As a result, most natural language interfaces do not perform to research expectations. The downfalls of natural language interfaces can be primarily attributed to three factors: the complexity of the English language, the limits of the natural language processing (NLP) technology, and the expectations of the end users.

The lexical, syntactic and semantic ambiguities of the English language serve as one of the main deterrents in the success of NLP techniques. For those interested, a detailed examination of the various types of ambiguities can be found in [3]. Although current technology is able to overcome some of the obvious ambiguities, the ability of a system is still limited. A system that is too sensitive in ambiguity detection can become slow due to the effort used in dialogue and clarification. Current applications often are capable only of rejecting ambiguous requests as opposed to presenting alternative interpretations to the user [9]. At the other extreme, a system that takes priority in semantic and pragmatic preferences can become too inflexible and picky with the vocabulary it accepts [3]. Moreover, very slight variations in the question posed to these systems, which may be insignificant to the user, will be rejected by the system [5].

In the area of natural language generation (NLG), natural language text often needs to be verbose and awkward in order to overcome the ambiguity of the language [12].

Another English language problem for the natural language interface is the broad range of grammatical mistakes that users can make. In order for the NLP technology to handle these errors gracefully its ability to make distinctions of the language that are based on subtle linguistic cues must be diminished [3].

Despite the advantage of its flexibility, this characteristic of a natural language interface unfortunately leads to difficulty in specifying the system limitations to the user, thus resulting in overestimation of the system capabilities [11]. When the user is unaware of the abilities of the system it is more than likely that questions beyond the domain of the system will be posed [2]. Moreover, the variety of words and syntactic structures available in the English language leading to the same request results in the problem of low recognition rate [7]. In order to overcome these problems users are forced to use the set of restricted vocabulary and concepts defined by the interface designer and thus require some training [11].

4.0   Conclusions

In choosing the optimal interface for an integrated network management application, the designer should consider the end user's needs, knowledge and experience. Use of a natural language interface by an infrequent or "casual" user who has limited knowledge of how the data is stored and how to access that information will obviously be much easier than using a formal query language. However, an experienced user may find that a command language interface is more powerful and efficient.

A small system with a workable restricted vocabulary and little redundancy can best benefit from a natural language interface since the difficulties of processing can be overcome [5]. In this prototype, we have shown that NLQI provides an effective interface for users to query configuration and traffic information from an integrated network management system database. Creation of a large natural language system may be beyond the current technology with its limitations since the chance of conflicting or similar relationships among different entities presented by such systems are significantly higher.

We should realize that English is complicated and that all natural language systems will have its limitations. As such, a "good" natural language system will be far from perfect but should allow the user to accomplish his task with minimal interference [3].

5.0   Acknowledgments
This project is funded by the MPR 1992 Strategic Technology Program on Intelligent Databases.

The author would like to thank Miss Teresa Fung for her effort in this project during her co-op work term with MPR. The author would also like to thank Mr. Dave Reid for reviewing the early draft of this paper.

6.0   References

[1]   A Natural language front end to relational systems based on formal semantics, A.N. DeRoech, H.E. Jowsey, B.G.T. Lowden, R. Turner and B.R. Walls, InfoJapan '90: Information Technology Harmonizing with Society, v2, p73-80, Oct 1990.

[2]   An Experimental Comparison of Natural and Structured Query Languages, Duane Small, Human Factors, v23(3), p253-263, 1983.

[3]   Designing a Practical Interface, Madeline Bates, David Meltzer and Sandra Shea, AI Expert, p60-66, 1987.

[4]   Designing the User Interface: strategies for effective human-computer interaction, Ben Shneiderman, p166-176, Addison-Wesley Publishing Co., 1992.

[6]   Experience with INTELLECT: Artificial Intelligence Technology Transfer, L.R. Harris, The AI Magazine, v5(2), p43-50, Summer 1984.

[7]   Failures in Natural Language Systems: Applications To Data Base Query Systems, Eric Mays, First Annual National Conference on AI, p327-330, 1980.

[8]   How to get people to say and type what computers can understand, Elizabeth Zoltan-Ford, Int. J. Man-Machine Studies, v34(4), p527-547, Apr 1991.

[9]   Impact of a Restricted Natural Language Interface on Ease of Learning and Productivity, H. Albert Napier, David Lane, Richard R. Batsell and Norman S. Guadango, Communications of the ACM, v32(10), Oct 1989.

[10]   Natural Language comes of age. Peter Varhol., Personal Workstation, v3(5), p22-23, May 1991.

[11]   Natural Language Generation—an Overview, Agneiszka Mykowiecka, Int. J. Man-Machine Studies, v34(4), p497-511, Apr 1991.

[12]   Natural Language Interfaces to Databases, Ann Copestake and Karen Sparck Jones, The Knowledge Engineering Review, n5(4), p225-249, 1990.

[13]   Natural Language Interfaces to Databases: State of the Art, Mohd Noor Md Sap and D.R. McGregor, University of Strathclyde, May 1992 (unpublished).

[14]   Natural Language: new release targets desktop market, EDGE: Work-Group Computing Report, v3(86), p21, Jan 13 1992.

[15]   Natural Language Processing: A Survey, Bonnie Lynn Webber, On Knowledge Base Management Systems, p353-364, 1986.

[16]   Query languages for the casual user: Exploring the middle ground between formal and natural languages, W.C. Ogden, S.R. Brooks, CHI'83 Proceedings, p161-165, Dec 1983.

Natural language as object and medium in computer-based learning

S. Leclerc and S. de Maisonneuve

Département des sciences de l'éducation, Université du Québec à Rimouski, 300 allée des Ursulines, Rimouski, Québec, G5L 3A1, Canada

Abstract

Computer-based learning recognised the importance of user models long ago. Important works has been done on dialogue based user models and advances were made on natural language as the medium of computer-based learning. On the other hand, natural language as object of computer-based learning is a growing field. This paper intend to expose problems that typically arise when natural language is both the object and the medium of computer-based learning. Writing aids available in the market are based on relatively superficial analysis of input text and extensive elaboration of descriptive material. Our system intend to analyse in depth and elaborate a complete representation of written text with a minimal explanatory material. Finally, the system is met to reduce the explanation provided to a list of examples and contra-examples

1. INTRODUCTION

In the field of education/training-oriented knowledge based systems (KBS), there has for several years existed a consensus on the need for a user model [1]. When KBSs use a natural language to interact with the user, a user model is an equally necessary element [2,3,4]. The user model generally contains information regarding the aims, plans, attitudes, knowledge and beliefs of the user. This information is used to improve the quality of interaction between the human and the KBS in the context of a problem solving-type activity.

In a KBS dedicated to a support function in language learning, the user model must contain an adequate representation of the user's verbal performance. The context of our presentation is the work1 done by our group for the development of a computer-based learning tool for written French adapted to the needs of college and university Deaf students. Typically, Deaf students production of written French is characterised with mistakes that are regular and different from hearing students of low level writing skills. Difficulties in reading French also characterise the Deaf students. In this context, the problem is to build a human-computer interaction based on the non-standard written French user's input and to offer understandable and useful instructions in written French.

This paper describes first certain representational problems that appear in the context of the development of KBS dedicated to support the learning of written French. Secondly, it presents a method for formalising the semantic and syntactic aspects of non-standard texts written in French which demonstrate particularities of conceptual graphs as the formalism of the system. Finally, the utility of the proposed representation is illustrated by an example of the processing of information that has the aim of diagnosing errors in ungrammatical sentences. This will expose the strategies used for the elaboration of diagnostics and prescriptions for remedial of the situation. We suggest that our approach of human computer interaction is particularly adapted to the needs of Deaf students interacting with a computer-based learning tool for written French.

2. REPRESENTATION OF NON-STANDARD TEXTS

Our research is based on a corpus made up of 24 texts written in French by young adults at the college level2. Half of the texts are written by Deaf individuals. The context in which the texts are produced is as follow: students are asked to write down the story presented on a single page in a wordless comic strip, made up of twelve images. It shows a man who sees flying saucers landing and discovers that aliens are ransacking his village. On finding out that the aliens are scared of mice, he frightens them off with the mice and rids the village of the invaders.

The texts produced have two important characteristics. All the texts produced by Deaf students were considered successful by the readers (evaluators) in the sense that they were able to form a representation of the event that was consistent with the description in the comic strip. Also, all the texts presented ungrammatical elements. Previous research has described problems related to the production of written French by Deaf people at the college and the university levels [5] and also by hearing students at the university level [6]. The production of texts in non-standard French is a common phenomenon not limited to the stage of acquisition of the written code (approximately within the first eleven years of schooling). In the context of a project for the development of a tutorial system aimed at the improvement of writing skills for college and university Deaf students our objective is to develop a representation of the syntactic and semantic aspects of the texts that would support diagnostic and prescriptive procedures relative to errors in written French.

The use of the reflexive form of the French verb presents a particular problem for Deaf individuals writing in French. Within the texts examined, we found 54 occurrences of a reflexive form, 22 of them being wrongly used. An example of this situation is offered in the next section.

It is necessary to describe the context in which the reflexive form is used in French. The reflexive form indicates that the person that initiates an action undergoes the action at the same time. It is marked by the insertion of a reflexive pronoun between the grammatical subject and the verb, of the same grammatical person as the subject, e.g.

Un	*homme*	*se repose*		*en fumant*	*la*	*pipe.*
aMASC.	man	REFLEXIVE3PERS.-SING.rest	smoking		theFEM.	pipe.3

'A man is resting, smoking the pipe.'

When several individuals together realise an action, the reflexive indicates that this action is undergone reciprocally, e.g.:

Les	*gens*	*du*	*village*	*se*		*consultent.*
thePLUR.	people	of-the	village	REFLEXIVE3PERS.-PLUR.	consultPLUR.	

'The people of the village discuss among themselves'

The reflexive can also be used to avoid expressing the agent role of an action: in this respect, it is equivalent to a passive e.g.:

Les	*gens*	*du*	*village*	*s'*		*apeurent*
thePLUR.	people	of-the	village	REFLEXIVE3PERS.-PLUR.	frightenPLUR.	

'The people of the village are frightened'

Finally, certain verbs are only found in the reflexive form, e.g.:

Les	*monstres*	*[s'*		*enfuient]*	*dans*	*leurs*	*soucoupes volantes*
thePLUR.	monsters	[[REFLEXIVE3PERS.-PLUR.]	fleePLUR.	]	in	their	flying saucers

'The monsters flee in their flying saucers'

An individual who reads and corrects a text diagnoses syntactic errors on the basis of his understanding of the communicative intent of the writer in relation to the linguistic means used to express the intended message. Consider sentence E111.

E111.

L'homme	*remarquait*	*dans*	*ces*	*lunettes d'approche*	*un*	*monstre*
the-man	noticedIMPERF.	in	these	spyglasses	aMASC.	monster
avoir peur	*d'une*	*petite*	*souris*	*sans*	*déffense. (sic)*	
to-be-scared	of-aFEM.	smallFEM.	mouse	without	deffence.	

A reader may notice, among other things, the inappropriateness of the preposition *dans* 'in' in this sentence. This judgement is possible because in the process of understanding the sentence, the semantic analysis made by the reader requires the presence of an instrument relation between the action *remarquer* 'notice' and the object *lunettes d'approche* 'spyglasses.' Additionally, the syntactic parse/analysis designates the preposition *dans* as the marker of the instrument relation in this sentence. The reader's representation of the sentence is procured jointly by the semantic and syntactic analyses. It is upon the reader's representation that the diagnostic procedures are applied. These procedures exploit a knowledge base in which a rule excludes the preposition *dans* as a marker of the instrument relation.

This informal description of the processes of comprehending a sentence contains within it the strategy for analysing texts and diagnosing errors. The following section describes the elements of the formalism necessary for representing the syntactic and semantic aspects of the sentences.

3. REPRESENTATION OF TEXTS USING CONCEPTUAL GRAPHS

To build the user model, we want a way to have access to the syntactic and the semantic aspects of texts written by the user. We developed a methodology to represent these aspects by using conceptual graphs formalism. This work implies the building of a parser that can accommodate ungrammatical sentences. It also has to produce a semantic representation of a sentence increased with information about the syntactic choices presiding its construction. This is a new challenge since, in the context of conceptual graphs formalism, syntactic analysis is usually a tool to provide semantic representation of sentence [7,8,9].

Essentially, conceptual graph formalism [10,11] provides two building blocks, the concept and the conceptual relation. The concept is a structure made of a type label and a referent field, the conceptual relation expresses the nature of links between concepts. By conceptual analysis, a semantic network is build which represents the meaning of a domain. Consider sentence S91:

S91.

Dans	*la*	*pleine*	*nuit,*	*un*	*homme*	*se repose*	*en berçant*
In	theFEM.	full	night,	aMASC.	man	REFLEX.rests	rocking
la	*chaise;*	*il*	*fumme*	*la*	*pipe.*		
theFEM.	chair;	he	"smokkes"	theFEM.	pipe.		

'In the middle of the night, a man rests, rocking the chair; he is smoking the pipe.'

The representation of the portion ... *un homme se repose* ... in string S91 is4:

[HOMME]←(PTNT-SELF)←[REPOSER]

The conceptual relation (PTNT-SELF) is defined as follows:

relation PTNT-SELF (x,y) **is**

[ANIMATE:*x] -

(LINK)→[AGENT:*x]→(LINK)→[RFLX-ACT:*y]→(LINK)→[PATIENT-SELF: *x]
(LINK)→[PATIENT-SELF: *x]→(GRAM)→[RFLX-PRN]

The (PTNT-SELF) relation expresses the link between an animate agent and an action of which the agent is also the patient. The action is of the type RFLX-ACT. In the conceptual hierarchy, the type RFLX-ACT is a subtype of ACT. The type RFLX-ACT has, as a defining characteristic, the ability to take as its patient a concept that is at the same time the agent of the action. Concepts such as [GIVE] or [SAY] are subtypes of RFLX-ACT whereas concepts such as [GET] or [REVERE] are not.

In the definition of the relation (PTNT-SELF), a conceptual entity of the type PATIENT-SELF is linked by the relation (GRAM) to a linguistic entity of the type RFLX-PRN. The type RFLX-PRN is a subtype of L-ENTITY which groups together reflexive personal pronouns. The concept [RFLX-PRN: se] corresponds to the reflexive pronoun *se*.

This kind of definition creates a two layers representation. The first concerns the semantic of the sentence and the second layer, the expanded form, concerns the semantic and the syntactic choices presiding its construction. The relation (GRAM) unites grammatical markers specific to the conceptual elements uncovered in the semantic analysis of the text. This approach enable the treatment of the following segment:

... un homme se repose en berçant la chaise ...

[EVENT: [HOMME]←(PTNT-SELF)←[REPOSER]]→(EQUAL) -

  [EVENT: [HOMME]←(PTNT-SELF)←[BERCER]→(LOC)→[CHAISE]]

The expanded form makes explicit the absence of the reflexive pronoun *se* before the verb *bercer* and the absence of a spatial preposition *dans* before the noun *chaise*. It is obtained by replacing the conceptual relations (EQUAL), (LOC) and (PTNT-SELF) by their expanded form provided via their definitions. Definition for conceptual relation (EQUAL) expresses the occurrence of two simultaneous events, definition for conceptual relation (LOC) expresses the localisation of an action. We therefore have:

... un homme se repose en berçant la chaise ...

[TIME-LOC: @ 0 DB 0 DE] -
 (GRAM)→[GERONDIF]
 (LINK)→[EVENT: [HOMME:*x] -
  (LINK)→[AGENT:*x]→(LINK)→[REPOSER]→(LINK)→[PATIENT-SELF: *x]
  (LINK)→[PATIENT-SELF: *x]→(GRAM)→[RFLX-PRN: se]]
 (LINK)→[EVENT: [HOMME:*x] -
  (LINK)→[PATIENT-SELF: *x]→(GRAM)→[RFLX-PRN: &]
  (LINK)→[AGENT:*x]→(LINK)→[BERCER] -
       (LINK)→[PATIENT-SELF: *x]
       (LINK)←[LOCATION] -
        (LINK)→[CHAISE]
        (GRAM)→[SPA-PREP: &]]

This approach provides us with a complete representation of both the communicative intent of the writer and his linguistic means. The next section presents the basis of the tutorial intervention.

4. DIAGNOSTIC AND PRESCRIPTION STRATEGIES

The design of the human computer interaction in our system is based on several information sources. The user model is based primarily on the analysis of his input text as described in previous section. The expert tutor is based on knowledge about typical errors and their relation with conceptualisations (or rules) that are conceived as the sources of errors. The sources of this knowledge are a descriptive analysis of the texts and a written evaluation of the ability of Deaf students to identify and correct ungrammatical sentences involving reflexive verbs. In an experimentation involving 28 subjects, twenty sentences were submitted to them for correction of errors. Ten sentences were correct, containing a reflexive form or an intransitive verb, the rest were ungrammatical. These ungrammatical sentences include verbs that should not have been in the reflexive form or omitted them when it was mandatory.

Preliminary analysis of experimental data indicates a failure rate of 25 %. These failures are of two kinds. The first category involved correct sentences that were transformed by adding or removing a reflexive form, or by adding or removing other words. The second category involved ungrammatical sentences that were not identified. Errors of the second category were four times more frequent than the first category and involved adding or removing a reflexive form. The most frequent error, within this second category, was a failure to remove an incorrect reflexive form.

As a way to choose an appropriate format for providing users explanations, we tested two kind of explanation. First one is to display a target sentence followed by four grammatical sentences labelled as such and by four ungrammatical sentences also labelled. These sentences contain a verb which is of the same kind of the target sentence. Subjects exposed to this form of explanation appear to be able to infer rules governing reflexive form use. Their error rate drops from 25% to 5%.

The second type of explanation propose an algorithm for classifying good use and bad use of reflexive form. In this algorithm, the subject must decide if the target verb can accept a direct object complement. One out of three time, the subjects made the wrong decision. It is not surprising that the algorithm is not useful for the subjects, error rate remains constant.

We pursue these experiments exploring uses of spatial prepositions and problems related to word order. This approach is aimed to provide information about conceptualisations we need to uncover in order to elaborate our tutorial intervention.

5. CONCLUSION

Our work with Deaf students learning written French involves the development of a computer-based learning tool. The human computer interaction designed has two important characteristics. First, it is based on a multidimensional analysis of Deaf students verbal behaviour. User input is a written text, it is subjected to an analysis aimed to provide the communicative intent and the linguistic means of the writer. A complete representation of the text is subjected to diagnosis procedures. These procedures reflect our knowledge of typical verbal behaviour of Deaf students. Second, it tend to reduce the load on user by procuring the minimal useful written information.

The human computer interaction designed does not reproduce the collaborative human interaction where each partner anticipates, completes and contributes to partner's utterances [12]. Instead, we hope to introduce the student in an interaction specifically adapted to his needs and oriented to the production of optimal learning conditions.

Notes

1 This project, supported in part by a grant from FODAR Université du Québec and by a grant from FCAR government of Québec, is also the work of professors C. Dubuisson and M. Nadeau, UQAM. We are grateful to our colleague Ginette Pagé for helpful comments.

2 In the Quebec educational system, college refers to a post-secondary educational institution preceding University level.

3 Orthographical errors in the French sentences are underlined, the translation provided indicates pertinent grammatical aspects.

4 The CGs presented in this text are representations of French sentences. The concept types and the content of referential fields found in French correspond to words in the text such that it would be misleading for the analysis to translate these into English. The expression of certain concepts and conceptual relations are tools of the analyst, but are translated into English to facilitate communication in the research community.

6. REFERENCES

1. S. de Maisonneuve, S. Leclerc. Quelques apports des sciences cognitives à la problématique du développpement des systèmes à base de connaissances dédiés à la formation. ICO Québec vol. 3, no. 1, p.:29-36, 1991.
2. W. Wahlster, A. Kobsa (eds.) User Models in Dialogue System. Springer Verlag, Berlin-New York. 1988.
3. K. Sparck Jones. Tailoring output to the user: What does user modelling in generation mean? In: C.L. Paris, W.R. Swartout, W.C. Mann (eds) Natural Language Generation in Artificial Intelligence and Computational Linguistics. Boston: Kluwer Academic Publishers. 1991.
4. R. Kass, T. Finin. Modeling the User in Natural Language Systems. Computational Linguistics, Volume 14, Number 3, September 1988.
5. M. Nadeau, C. Dubuisson, C. Gélinas-Chebat. Le français écrit des étudiants sourds: une analyse qualitative. Bulletin de l'ACLA, printemps 1991, vol. 13, no. 1, p.:89-103.
6. L. Pépin, M. Pagé. L'enseignement et l'évaluation de la cohérence textuelle. Yearbook de la recherche en pédagogie de la langue maternelle. Pays-Bas: Foris (sous presse).
7. A. Berard-Dugourd, J. Fargues, M.C. Landau. Natural language analysis using conceptual graphs. Artificial intelligence: theory and applications: Proceedings, International Computer Science Conference '88. p.:265-72. 1988.
8. P. Velardi, M.T. Pazienza, M. De' Giovanetti. Conceptual graphs for the analysis and generation of sentences. IBM J. RES. DEVELOP. vol.32, no. 2, March 1988.
9. J.F. Sowa, E.C. Way. Implementing a semantic interpreter for conceptual graphs. IBM J. RES. DEVELOP. 30:1, p.: 57-69, 1986.
10. J.F. Sowa. Conceptual Structures: Information Processing in Mind and Machine. Addison-Wesley. 1984.
11. J.F. Sowa. Conceptual Graphs as a Universal Knowledge Representation. Computers Math. Applic. Vol. 23, No. 2-5, pp. 75-93, 1992.
12 H. H. Clark, Schaefer, E.F. Contributing to discourse. Cognitive Science, Vol 13, no 2, pp. 259-294. 1989.

Intelligent Help Facilities: Generating Natural Language Descriptions with Examples

Vibhu O. Mittal and Cecile L. Paris

USC/Information Sciences Institute, 4676 Admiralty Way, Marina del Rey, CA 90292, U.S.A.

Department of Computer Science, University of Southern California, Los Angeles, CA 90089, U.S.A.

Abstract

On-line help facilities are essential in any complex system, especially for introductory or naive users. Previous studies have highlighted the need for appropriate examples along with the description. This paper describes a help/documentation facility built within an explanation framework that plans the presentation of text and examples using techniques in natural language generation. The paper shows how text and examples can influence each other and enumerates some of the other issues that arise in planning such presentations.

1. INTRODUCTION

Good help facilities are a crucial component of any complex system (e.g., [1,2]), and there have been many studies on generating effective online help (e.g [3--6]). Most attempts at providing intelligent help facilities have focused on either structured, hierarchical menu style help, as in the VMS online help system [7], or on hypertext style browsing capabilities (e.g [8,9]). However, static, online help, in the form of canned text is not always helpful: in one study, Houghton found that in most current systems, while online help enhanced the performance of experienced users, it was either not helpful, or sometimes even detrimental to inexperienced users [10]. It is therefore clear that online help systems that can tailor their descriptions to the user (particularly the inexperienced, introductory user), would be very helpful.

Tailoring descriptions to the user often involves more than just a change in the terminology, or the level of detail presented to the user [11]. The type of information presented is often different as well: for instance, syntactic information *vs* structural information *vs* functional information. One of the differences between introductory material and non-introductory material is the importance of examples: studies by Beard and Calamars [12], and Tuck *et. al* [13] found that the component of help most often cited as necessary, and the one most necessary for introductory users, was the presence of examples. It is thus clear that a help facility designed for introductory users must be able to include examples in its explanations.

In this paper, we shall describe a framework for an explanation/help facility that can generate natural language descriptions (of objects in the knowledge base) that incorporate examples along with descriptive text. We shall briefly describe some of the issues that arise, and using a simple example from our system on help in LISP, we shall describe how the system goes about planning its presentation.

2. ISSUES IN THE USE OF EXAMPLES

The use of examples can contribute a great deal to the effectiveness of the response. Indeed, empirical studies have found that examples can greatly increase user comprehension (e.g., [14,15]). However, studies also show that badly integrated text and examples can actually be detrimental compared to using either text or examples alone (e.g. [16]). It is thus clear that in order to provide useful documentation automatically, a system must be capable of providing well-integrated examples to illustrate its points.

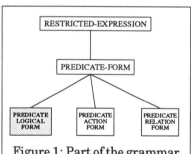

Figure 1: Part of the grammar non-terminal hierarchy.

There are many issues that arise in generating complex descriptions which include examples. Although some tutorial systems used examples in explanations, they were not considered as an integral part of the complete explanation and were inserted in the explanations without any representation of how the examples related to and complemented the accompanying explanation. Consider, for instance, a help description generated for the term 'predicate-relation-form' in our system. A predicate-relation-form is a non-terminal in our system's grammar, and its parent and child relationships are shown in Fig. 1. A part of the English description is shown in Fig. 2.

Consider the description in Fig. 2: the system first describes the predicate-relation-form by describing it as a specialization of a predicate-form (which returns a boolean value). It then describes the syntax of a predicate-relation-form. However, the description does not include the facts that:

- the syntactic detail that there is a left parenthesis before the relation-name and a right parenthesis after the last argument
- the different types of arguments that can appear after the relation

This is because these facts are communicated through the examples which follow. The parentheses are noted in the system as 'fixed features': features that are constant and will appear in the same location in every example. From this, the user can infer that those features are necessary. The different types of parameters that can appear as arguments in a predicate-relation-form are (in our system: numbers, symbols and instances) also illustrated through the use of different parameters in the examples. A natural language generator should be able to take properties of both the descriptive text and the examples into account and generate a coherent, comprehensive (yet non-redundant) explanation with examples. Such descriptions are not possible to generate if the text generator and the example generator do not interact closely in planning their presentation.

From the preceding discussion, it is clear that the inclusion of examples into explanations can cause certain portions of text to be elided. However, the incorporation of examples into descriptions can also cause additional text to be included -- information that would not originally have been communicated. This is illustrated by the last example of a function-form that is presented in the description. The system attempts to find a negative example (an example that is *not* a predicate-relation-form) that is as similar as possible to one of the positive examples that have already been presented. In this case, the system attempts to generate a negative example by changing the number of arguments from two to one. This results in the third example changing from a predicate-relation-form to a function-form. The system attempts to point this out, resulting in additional explanation.

A PREDICATE-RELATION-FORM is a predicate-form. It consists of a relation followed by some parameters, the number of which is equivalent to the arity of the relation. Examples of predicate-relation-form are:

(VERSION LOAD-SOFTWARE 5.1)
(STATUS LED-1 'ON)
(CONNECTED COMPUTER-A PRINTER-B)

However, the following is not a predicate-relation-form, because the number of arguments is not equal to the arity of the relation. It is an example of a FUNCTION-FORM:

(CONNECTED COMPUTER-A)

The difference between a FUNCTION-FORM and a predicate-relation-form is that the number of arguments in a function-form are one less than the arity of the relation, and ...

Figure 2: Part of the English description of predicate-relation-form.

Thus, as even this brief description has shown, there is strong interaction between the descriptive text and the accompanying examples. There are a number of other issues that must be addressed in a practical generation system, such as the number of examples to be presented, the order of presentation, whether the examples should be presented *before*, *after* or *within* the description, etc. Due to lack of space, we shall not discuss these issues here.[1] In the following section,

---

[1]See [17] for further details.

we shall describe the planning framework within which such descriptions are generated.

3. THE SYSTEM

Our current framework implements the generation of examples *within* a text-generation system that explicitly plans text to achieve a communicative (or discourse) goal. Given a top level communicative goal -- such as (DESCRIBE OBJECT), the system finds plans capable of achieving this goal. Plans typically post further sub-goals to be satisfied, and planning continues until primitive speech acts -- i.e., directly realizable in English -- are achieved. The result of the planning process is a discourse tree, where the nodes represent goals at various levels of abstraction, with the root being the initial goal, and the leaves representing primitive realization statements, such as (INFORM ...) statements. In the discourse tree, the discourse goals are related through coherence relations. This tree is then passed to a grammar interface which converts it into a set of inputs suitable for input to a natural language generation system called PENMAN [18]).

A fragment of the text plan generated by the system for the description in Fig. 2 is shown in Fig. 3. The skeleton shows the structure of the plan, along with the discourse goals posted by the system. The two top-level goals posted by the initial goal are (DESCRIBE (SYNTAX PRED-REL-FORM)) and (EXEMPLIFY-FEATURES (SYNTAX PRED-REL-FORM)). The first goal, to describe the features ultimately results in the first part of the description, which states that a predicate-relation-form consists of a relation-name followed by some arguments. The second goal, to

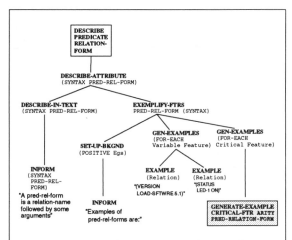

Figure 3: Plan fragment for the predicate-relation-form.

exemplify the features of a predicate-relation-form results in the generation of the actual examples, along with the associated background text ("Examples of predicate-relation-form are ... ").

Thus, examples are generated by *explicitly posting a goal within the text planning system*: i.e., some of the plan operators used in the system include the generation of examples as one of their steps, when applicable. This ensures that the examples embody specific information that either illustrates or complements the information in the accompanying textual description. Additional sources of knowledge such as the user model, text type, dialogue context, etc, can be added to the system by incorporating additional constraints in the plan operators.

Using this framework, we have generated descriptions of constructs in the programming language LISP [19] and documentation for the grammar in our own plan language [20] for the EES expert system framework [21]. The generation of these descriptions highlight some of the issues that must be addressed by *any* interface that must integrate natural language and examples together. Some of these issues are also applicable to the generation of multi-media explanations, where the constraints imposed by the non-textual component upon the text planner must be taken into account.

4. CONCLUSIONS

Examples are essential in explanations, especially for naive users. It is therefore important that on-line help systems designed for non-expert users be able to present effective and appropriate examples to the user. As systems evolve over time, it is essential that the documentation/help facility be updated to reflect the changes. A system that generates documentation from the underlying code would help alleviate the 'maintenance of documentation' problem. However, such a system would then need to be able to present examples and text in a coherent and integrated manner. In this paper, we have presented some of the issues that arise in the planning of such presentations. The issues we have described are not specific to a particular framework. Our implementation demonstrates that it is not just desirable, but also feasible to build such on-line help systems by making use of advances in natural language generation and knowledge based systems. This work is important in other related application areas such as intelligent tutoring systems, expert system explanation and user interfaces.

References

[1] G. Kearsley, *Online Help Systems: Design and Implementation.* Ablex Publishing Co., 1988.

[2] W. K. Horton, *Designing and Writing Online Documentation : Help files to hypertext.* New York: John Wiley and Sons, Inc., 1990.

[3] A. H. Duin, "Computer Documentation -- Centering on the Learner," *Journal of Computer-Based Instruction,* vol. 17, pp. 73--78, Spring 1990.

[4] E. Reiter, C. Mellish, and J. Levine, "Automatic Generation of on-line documentation in the IDAS project," in *Proceedings of the Third Conference on Applied Natural Language Processing (Trento, Italy),* pp. 64--71, April 1992.

[5] W. K. Horton, *Illustrating Computer Documentation: The Art of Presenting Information Graphically and Online.* New York: John Wiley and Sons, Inc., 1991.

[6] B. Wasson and S. Akselsen, "An overview of on-line assistance: from on-line documentation to intelligent help and training," *The Knowledge Engineering Review*, vol. 7, pp. 289--322, December 1992.

[7] DEC, *Command Language User's Guide*. Digital Equipment Corporation, 1978.

[8] G. Fischer, A. C. Lemke, and T. Mastaglio, "JANUS: Integrating hypertext with a knowledge-based design environment," in *Proceedings of Hypertext '89*, pp. 105--117, 1989.

[9] R. Rada and J. Barlow, "Expert systems and hypertext," *The Knowledge Engineering Review*, pp. 285--301, 1988.

[10] R. C. Houghton, "Online help systems: a conspectus," *Communications of the ACM*, vol. 27, pp. 126--133, 1984.

[11] C. L. Paris, *The Use of Explicit User Models in Text Generation*. London, England: Frances Pinter, 1993.

[12] R. E. Beard and P. V. Calamars, "A Method for Designing Computer Support Documentation," Master's thesis, Department of Communication, AFIT/LSH, WPAFB, Ohio 45433, September 1983.

[13] R. Tuck and D. R. Olsen, "Help by guided tasks: utilizing UIMS knowledge," in *Proceedings of the CHI'90 Conference*, pp. 71--78, ACM, 1990.

[14] J.-A. LeFevre and P. Dixon, "Do Written Instructions Need Examples?," *Cognition and Instruction*, vol. 3, no. 1, pp. 1--30, 1986.

[15] D. H. Charney, L. M. Reder, and G. W. Wells, "Studies of Elaboration in Instructional Texts," in *Effective Documentation: What we have learned from Research* (S. Doheny-Farina, ed.), ch. 3, pp. 48--72, Cambridge, MA.: The MIT Press, 1988.

[16] M. Ward and J. Sweller, "Structuring Effective Worked Examples," *Cognition and Instruction*, vol. 7, no. 1, pp. 1 -- 39, 1990.

[17] V. O. Mittal, *Generating descriptions with integrated text and examples*. PhD thesis, University of Southern California, Los Angeles, CA, 1993 (forthcoming).

[18] W. C. Mann, "An Overview of the Penman Text Generation System," in *Proceedings of the Second National Conference on Artificial Intelligence*, (Washington, D.C.), pp. 261--265, 1983.

[19] V. O. Mittal and C. L. Paris, "Generating Object Descriptions which integrate both Text and Examples," in *Proceedings of the Ninth Canadian Artificial Intelligence Conference (AI/GI/VI 92)*, pp. 1--8, Canadian Society for the Computational Studies of Intelligence (CSCSI), Morgan Kaufmann Publishers, 1992. (Vancouver, Canada).

[20] V. O. Mittal and C. L. Paris, "Automatic Documentation Generation: The Interaction between Text and Examples." To appear in the *Proceedings of the 13th International Joint Conference on Artificial Intelligence (IJCAI-93)*, 1993.

[21] W. R. Swartout, C. L. Paris, and J. D. Moore, "Design for explainable expert systems," *IEEE Expert*, vol. 6, no. 3, pp. 58--64, 1992.

Natural Language Interfaces :

Specifying and Using Conceptual Constraints

Elisabeth Godbert, Robert Pasero, Paul Sabatier

Groupe Intelligence Artificielle, CNRS URA 816, Parc Scientifique de Luminy,
163 Avenue de Luminy, Case 901, 13288 Marseille Cedex 9, France
E-mail : {godbert,bob,paul}@gia.univ-mrs.fr

Abstract

The work described in this paper takes place in the ILLICO project which aims at the development of natural language interfaces allowing a guided composition of sentences. The time necessary for the composition of sentences is all the more reduced since the selection of the expressions is accurate at different levels : lexical, syntactic, semantic, conceptual, pragmatic. We describe here how we build and use the conceptual model of the interfaced application in order to prevent the production of conceptually incorrect sentences. In this model, we define two types of conceptual constraints : a domain constraint on a relational symbol R specifies the domains the arguments of R must belong to, and a connectivity constraint on R specifies the number of individuals that can simultaneously be interrelated by R. Respecting these constraints excludes sentences such as *the dog is reading,* or expressions like *the dates of birth of Joan, the six grand-fathers of Peter* (false existential presuppositions).

1. Introduction

Our project, ILLICO, aims at developing a generator of natural language interfaces. The main purpose is to allow a rapid rate of communication, and in order to do that, we make use of techniques from computational linguistics and artificial intelligence. The system embodies the two following principles in order to assure the well-formedness of composed sentences :
   • a guided composition mode for formulating sentences ;
   • a dynamic interaction between linguistic and conceptual knowledge pertaining to the domain of the dialogue.
The time necessary for the composition of sentences is all the more reduced since the selection of the expressions is accurate at different levels : lexical, syntactic, semantic, conceptual, pragmatic ones. In this paper, we recall the main objectives of the ILLICO project. Then we describe how we build and use the conceptual model of the interfaced application in order to prevent the production of conceptually incorrect sentences.

2. Framework

The objective of the ILLICO project is the development of a generator of natural language interfaces. The main external characteristic of an ILLICO interface lies in the fact that one can compose sentences in a "free" mode or by means of various kind of linguistic and conceptual informations dynamically synthesized by the interface. This last situation, called the "guided composition" mode, occurs when the user directly asks the interface for help, or as soon as the interface has detected an unexpected expression typed by the user. Guided composition is done by partial synthesis of sentences, a principle introduced by [Colmerauer and Kittredge 83] within the multilingual interface ORBIS connected to a database on planets. The same system was used both for analyzing a given sentence and for providing partial synthesis of a sentence.

The main internal characteristic of an ILLICO interface is the modularity of knowledge specifying the different levels of well-formedness of sentences :
- A lexicon (lexical level) contains expected words and expressions.
- A grammar (syntactic level) specifies expected structures of sentences and grammatical agreement.
- A set of compositional semantic rules are expressed by lambda-expressions for producing semantic representations from the syntactic rules of the grammar.
- A conceptual model (conceptual level) specifies presuppositions associated with the expected words and expressions.

In order to take into account the consequences of these two main characteristics — guided composition and modularity of knowledge —, we have developed an approach in which all the constraints on the different levels of well-formedness (lexical, syntactic, semantic and conceptual) are coroutined when the system analyzes a given sentence or synthesizes a partial one [Milhaud *et al.* 92]. This approach has led to the development in Prolog of two systems :
- A generator of French interfaces for the consultation of different kinds of knowledges bases [Battani *et al.* 91].
- KOMBE : a communication aid system for disabled persons [Guenthner *et al.* 92].

3. Basis of the conceptual model

Conceptual well-formedness of composed (or analyzed) sentences is imposed (or verified) by consulting the conceptual model. This model describes the universe of the application as a set **E** of individuals, interrelated by elements of a set **R** of relational symbols (of any arity) defined in **E**. A set of constraints of different types specify how these individuals and relational symbols can be associated : these constraints are used to refine the description of the application, and prevent conceptually incorrect sentences in natural language.

By using singular or plural noun phrases, a natural language sentence expresses links between objects that can occur either individually or inside sets.

We assume that we can represent each sentence by one or more formulas of the type $R(x_1,...,x_n)$ such that :
- the relational symbol R is associated to a verb phrase ;
- x_1 represents the subject of this verb ;
- $x_2,..., x_n$ represent the various complements ;
- $\forall i \ x_i$ denotes a set of individuals, and its cardinality $c(x_i)$ is positive.

This representation of sentences is derived from Fillmore's theories on case structures, in which a set of cases are associated to each verb : actor, object, second object, etc. [Fillmore 68].

According to the natural language expression associated to x_i, the cardinality of x_i is more or less well known (*a child, Mary and Joan, three books, professors, some students*, etc.) ; in the case of an indefinite plural we only know that the cardinality is greater than one. Our approach for the representation of plural noun phrases is close to previous research that has been done in this area (*e.g.* [Habel 86]).

The definition of constraints in the conceptual model permits to express which associations are possible between elements of **E** and **R**, *i.e.* which formulas $R(x_1,...,x_n)$ are conceptually coherent. Respecting these constraints will prevent the processing of relational formulas which correspond to conceptually incorrect sentences in natural language. We study here two types of constraints : domain constraints and connectivity constraints.

4. Specifying and using domain constraints

A domain constraint on a n-ary relational symbol R specifies on which set, strictly included in $\mathbf{E}^n$, R is defined, *i.e.* the domains the arguments of R must belong to. Domain constraints will prevent, for example, the production of sentences as *the dog is reading* or *the cake goes to Paris*.

We first define a set of *domains* (**E** and subsets of **E**), hierarchically organized, to which the individuals belong ; the notion of domain we use here is close to the classical notion of concept defined in the knowledge representation area [Brachman 77] ; the set **D** of all the domains is partially ordered by the inclusion relation defined in the set of all the parts of **E**.

We then define decompositions of domains, which emphasize the inclusion and disjunction relations which exist between the domains, and then permit to use domain constraints :
a *decomposition* of a domain D is a set $\{D_1, D_2, ..., D_p\}$ of disjoint domains strictly included in D ; the decomposition is noted $Dec(D, D_1, D_2, ...,D_p)$.

We can define several decompositions of the same domain ; for example :
Dec(Person, Man, Woman, Child), Dec(Person, Teacher, Doctor, Farmer, Financier), etc.

Definition

A *domain constraint* on a n-ary relational symbol R is an identity $dom(R) = D_1 \times ... \times D_n$ where each D_i is a domain.

Such a constraint has the following meaning :
$$R(x_1,...,x_n) \text{ is coherent} \quad \Rightarrow \quad \forall i=1...n \quad x_i \subset D_i$$

Conceptually correct or incorrect formulas

Let R be an element of **R**, and a domain constraint on R defined by $dom(R) = D_1 \times ... \times D_n$.
We say that :
• a formula $R(x_1,...,x_n)$ is conceptually incorrect if we can prove that there exists an index i such that x_i is not included in D_i.
• otherwise, $R(x_1,...,x_n)$ is considered conceptually correct.

(in particular, when we cannot prove that a formula is incorrect, the system does not preclude its production)

<u>Example</u>

Let **E** be the set of all the objects.

Let **D** be the set of domains described by the decompositions : Dec(**E,** Animate, Inanimate), Dec(Animate, Human, Animal), Dec(Inanimate, Food, Place, Tool).

Let **R** be the set { *eat, go-to, read* }, where *eat* and *go-to* are binary relational symbols, and *read* is a unary one.

We define the following constraints :

$$eat(x,y) \quad is\ coherent \quad \Rightarrow \quad x \subset Animate \ \ and \ \ y \subset Food$$

$$go\text{-}to(x,y) \quad is\ coherent \quad \Rightarrow \quad x \subset Animate \ \ and \ \ y \subset Place$$

$$read(x) \quad is\ coherent \quad \Rightarrow \quad x \subset Human$$

Then,
- if x is an animal, the formula *read(x)* is conceptually incorrect ;
- if x is any animate object and y is any food, the formula *eat(x,y)* is conceptually correct ;
- if x is an animate object, the formula *read(x)* is considered conceptually correct if we cannot affirm that x is not a human : since x is an animate object, x may be a human.

5. Specifying and using connectivity constraints

A connectivity constraint on a relational symbol R specifies the number of individuals which can simultaneously be interrelated by R. The notion of connectivity we introduce here for natural language processing is an adaptation of the notions of cardinality and multi-valued dependency defined in the relational database area [Aho, Beeri, Ullman 79] [Delobel, Adiba 82]. In our system, connectivity constraints permit the expression, in a simple and uniform way, of the rules which can be associated to some words (verbs, nouns, or adjectives), and which impose in natural language the use of a special number (singular / plural) when these words appear in a sentence. For example, respecting connectivity constraints will prevent the production of incorrect expressions as *the dates of birth of Joan,* or *the six grand-fathers of Peter.*

Definition

Let R be a n-ary relational symbol, with n greater than 1. We note I_n the set $\{1, ..., n\}$.
A connectivity constraint on R is defined by an idendity $conn(R, s, k) = m$, where :
s is a subset of I_n, $k \in I_n$, $k \notin s$, and m is a strictly positive integer.

The constraint $conn(R, s, k) = m$ has the following meaning :

$R(x_1,...,e_k,...,x_n)$ is coherent $\Rightarrow$ if $\forall \ i \in s \ \ c(x_i) = 1$ and $c(e_k) = c$, then $c \leq m$.
So, if the constraint $conn(R, s, k) = m$ is defined, m is the degree of freedom of the k-th argument of R when the arguments corresponding to the subset s are fixed.

False existential presuppositions

A presupposition is a supposition implicitly made by the speaker. In our system, we want to prevent the generation of sentences containing some types of false existential presuppositions, *i.e.* that mention objects and assume their existences, whereas these objects certainly cannot exist. We consider that such sentences are conceptually incorrect. For example, the following expressions are incorrect in natural language : *The dates of birth of Joan are ..., Does Joan write to her six grand-fathers ?*

Cases of incorrectness

Precluding the production of relational formulas $R(x_1,..., x_n)$ that do not respect the connectivity constraints associated to R, prevents some types of false existential presuppositions. Let us consider a relational symbol R and a constraint $conn(R, s, k) = m$. From the definition of connectivity constraints, we can say that the formula $R(x_1,..., x_n)$ does not respect the constraint in the two following cases :

(1) s is any subset of I_n, and $\forall i \in s$ $c(x_i) = 1$ and $c(x_k) > m$

(2) s = {i} and $c(x_i) = p$ and $c(x_k) > p * m$

So, we say that an expression is incorrect in a natural language sentence if its representation requires the production of a formula $R(x_1,..., x_n)$ and requires us to suppose that the sets x_i satisfy one of the two cases described above.

Example:
For the relation *is-date-of-birth(x,y)* ("*x is the date of birth of y*"), we express that only one *x* corresponds to one *y* by the constraint : $conn(is\text{-}date\text{-}of\text{-}birth, \{2\}, 1) = 1$.
The noun phrase *the dates of birth of Joan* is incorrect for it contains the presupposition :
{ *is-date-of-birth(x, Joan) and c(x) > 1* }, that does not satisfy the constraint. So, our system will prevent the production of this phrase.

6. The KOMBE system

Conceptual constraints play a central role in the communication aid system for disabled persons, the KOMBE system we have developed [Guenthner *et al.* 92].
The following figure shows an example of a partial composition of a sentence by a patient communicating with a doctor. For example, the patient can compose the sentence : *J'ai beaucoup de difficultés à plier le genou gauche (It's difficult for me to bend my left knee)*.

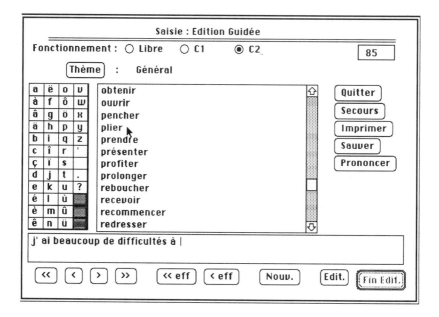

This system is devoted to Amyothrophic Lateral Sclerosis (ALS) patients. In addition to motor weaknesses, ALS patients, mainly elderly people, suffer from diseases of the central nervous system that entail increasing speech impairment and aggravate their living conditions. They have not lost their cognitive capacities but they can't speak, some of them can't write, and communicate only by eye movements. Guided composition of sentences is a convivial way for them to communicate. Step by step, they can select at a part of the screen for choosing words and expressions dymanically synthesized by the system, that always lead to the construction of a lexically, syntactically and conceptually well-formed sentence.

ALS patients can compose sentences about several conceptual situations. The introduction of a new situation only needs the definition of the associated conceptual model and lexicon. The grammar and the other components of the system are domain independent.

7. Conclusion

We have described the main characteristics of the ILLICO approach, and have shown how the specification and use of conceptual constraints prevents the production of some types of incorrect sentences. ILLICO is also a core system allowing the development of several intelligent systems for human-computer dialogue in natural language, as KOMBE, a communication aid system for disabled persons. The development of other applications is planed. Our present research aims at modeling and using other types of conceptual constraints, and adding a contextual level in the processing of texts.

8. Acknowledgements

This work is funded by the French Ministère de la Recherche et de la Technologie (ILLICO Project) and the ECC TIDE (*Technology Initiative for Disabled and Elderly people*) program (KOMBE Project).

9. References

Aho A.V., Beeri C., Ullman J.D. The Theory of Joins in Relational Databases, *ACM Transactions on Database Systems*, Vol. 4, n° 3, Sept. 1979.

Battani G., Pasero R., Sabatier P. Le Projet ILLICO : Interface en langage naturel et graphique, *Actes de la Conférence Génie Linguistique*, Versailles, France, 1991.

Brachman R.J. What's in a concept : structural foundations for semantic networks. *Int. Journal of Man-Machine Studies*, 9, 1977.

Colmerauer A., Kittredge R. *ORBIS*, 9th International Conference on Computational Linguistics, COLING, 1982.

Delobel C., Adiba M. *Bases de données et systèmes relationnels*, Dunod 1982.

Fillmore C.J. The case for case. *Universals in linguistic theory,* Bach E., Harms R.T. (ed.), Rinehart & Winston, Inc., New-York, 1968.

Guenthner F., Krüger-Thielmann K., Pasero R., Sabatier P. Communications Aids for ALS Patients, *Proceedings of the 3rd International Conference on Computers for Handicapped Persons*, Vienne, Austria, 1992.

Habel C. Plurals, Cardinalities, and Structures of Determination. *COLING Conference*, Bonn, August 1986.

Milhaud G., Pasero R., Sabatier P. Partial Synthesis of Sentences by Coroutining Constraints on Differents Levels of Well-Formedness, *Proceedings of COLING'92*, Nantes, July 1992.

Making Information Systems Fit Users Needs

A.C. Gillies, Reader in Business Information Management, Lancashire Business School, University of Central Lancashire,, Preston, PR1 2HE, UK. Tel 010-44-772-893670

ABSTRACT

In a wide range of software technologies, authors have highlighted the need for the user perspective to be considered. However, little improvement has been noted, and even where the `users' are themselves software developers, for example, in CASE tools, major problems are perceived. If the software community is serious about the adoption of quality management standards e.g. ISO9001, ISO9000/3, EN29001, then software must be fit for its intended purpose.

The hypothesis underpinning this paper is that fitness for purpose is essentially an HCI issue. This paper considers existing definitions of usability and compares them with criteria suggested by a number of Information Technology (IT) practitioners in a recent study by the author. The article then goes on to consider long term fitness for purpose of software in terms of three levels of human/computer interaction.

Finally, the article considers three different examples of information systems that have been noted for their fitness for purpose and considers the lessons that may be drawn.

1. INTRODUCTION: THE PROBLEM

Fitness for purpose has been established as a critical factor in providing a quality product or service. It is enshrined in the ISO definition of quality:

`Quality is the ability of a product or service to meet a stated or implied need [1]

In systems development, an artificial distinction has often been made between technical issues and human issues. In quality terms, the technical issues may be equated with a manufacturing view of quality, emphasising conformance to specification. The human issues may be equated with fitness for purpose.

Many authors have highlighted the low priority of human issues in software development. The problem is not restricted to one technology. Berry and Broadbent[2] highlighted the issue in the context of expert systems:

`User issues generally took a back seat in ES development'[2]

In 1991, users of CASE tools cited the following barriers to acceptance in a survey by Stobart et al:[3] poor documentation, user-analyst communication and training. There is a clear need to improve fitness for purpose.

2. WHAT IS FITNESS FOR PURPOSE OF INFORMATION SYSTEMS ?

Early attempts at defining fitness for purpose amounted to little more than a token gesture. Quality was judged in terms of the manufacturing view of conformance to specification. McCall in his GE model[4] lists eleven criteria of quality, ten of which may be regarded as being concerned with conformance to specification rather than fitness for purpose. Only usability directly relates to fitness for purpose.

This has set the tone for much of the work carried out since. A striking exception is the work of Gilb[5] who emphasises the need for fitness for purpose and proposes evolutionary delivery of software and locally defined quality templates to evaluate the effectiveness of solutions. Unfortunately, although Gilb is a well respected figure in the software world his ideas do not seem to have had a dramatic impact upon mainstream ideas.

The author has recently carried out a study of quality criteria employed in practice by the IT sections within six large companies[6]. The survey revealed that technical factors concerned with conformance still dominated. However, after discussing the issue with the users, their internal customers, more criteria were described, relating to fitness for purpose often summarised under 'business correctness':

Business correctness is the ability of the information system to meet its business objectives

At a corporate level, this represents fitness for purpose. A number of criteria were identified as contributing to business correctness [6]:

Supportiveness, User satisfaction, Ease of transition, Timeliness, User Consultation, Accuracy, Time To Use, Appeal, Flexibility, Cost/Benefit, Userfriendliness .

Almost all these criteria, although accepted by the IT personnel, were defined by the users. Having arrived at a set of criteria, the next stage is to attempt to incorporate these criteria at the design stage of systems development.

3.1 FITNESS FOR PURPOSE AT THE PHYSICAL LEVEL

The traditional scope of human-computer interaction has considered only this level, concerning itself with the actual physical interface. Much has been made of the adoption of graphical interfaces by the PC community through the proprietary Windows environment. In the UK in the second quarter of 1992, sales of Windows applications exceeded DOS applications for the first time (DOS 39% of market; Windows 51%). For the same quarter in the US, DOS applications still outsold Windows applications (46% to 32%), but a considerable share was taken by Macintosh applications (17%)[7] which when added in leads to the a greater share of the market for graphically based applications.

Some of the customers for character based applications are buying because of compatibility with existing applications or because of inadequate hardware. However, there is a significant minority of users who have consciously rejected the graphical interface as a mode of working. In order to understand this in terms other than a simple resistance to change, it is necessary to consider several features:

- It is pitched at the novice skill level
- The underlying metaphor of the desktop was intended for clerical operators.
- It is dependent upon the use of a pointing device, generally a mouse.

This use of a pointing device, e.g. a mouse, can provide a barrier to interaction in a number of ways. It is often assumed that users can use a mouse intuitively. Experience of training over 500 novice users suggests that most require up to 30 minutes practice and training before they are comfortable with different modes of operation, e.g. the difference between single and double clicking. Some people, generally the more experienced users, find the mode of interaction simply too slow or too inflexible. This may arise either because they want to interact in a more flexible way with the computer or because after many years of using a keyboard the QWERTY keyboard has become their natural mode of expression.

The final area concerns hardware and environmental problems. Much publicity has been given recently to health hazards associated with rapid and repetitive keyboard use and radiation from VDUs. This hides a multitude of problems of discomfort, eye-strain, unattractive screen design which have been creating discomfort amongst users for years.

3.2 FITNESS FOR PURPOSE AT THE TASK LEVEL

This level of interaction is concerned with the match between the way that the user works and the way that the system works. The user may well have to change their way of working in order to get the best out of the information system. This is perfectly acceptable provided that the net effect is an increase in the quality and quantity of work carried out.

Novice users often fail to appreciate how IT applications can apply to them. This may be seen in training where the author runs task-oriented training courses which take users through familiar tasks using IT applications. They are in fact courses in how to use spreadsheets, presentation graphics or databases, but the use of relevant data is sufficient to help make the required leap of understanding.

Fitness for purpose at this level affects longer term satisfaction than simple physical interaction. For example, many novice users are attracted to the Windows system because of its attractive 'look and feel'. However, they continue to use it because its ability to integrate data from one application with another fits their way of working. This level of interaction also has a critical effect upon productivity.

There are also hardware implications operating at this level. The availability of powerful portable computers and more recently, palmtops and now pen-driven computers has allowed people to work more flexibly away from their desk. In my own job, involving a degree of home working, it has removed the need for two computers. This theme is explored further at the organisational level.

3.3 FITNESS FOR PURPOSE AT THE ORGANISATIONAL LEVEL

At the organisational level, human-computer interaction is concerned with how well the information system supports the business objectives. Many of the issues raised at the task level apply equally here. For example, the issuing of portable computers to the sales forces of some pharmaceutical companies has provided much more accurate and rapid information for and about customers. The advantage to the customer is a more responsive and faster service. The advantage to the company is better information and customer service leading to competitive edge.

However, it may no longer be taken for granted that HCI at the organisational level always works in favour of the business goals. Complex technology takes time to implement and to adjust to, and this can lessen productivity and hinder the business objectives in the short term. Customers are becoming more sceptical and requiring evidence that IT can be fit for its intended purpose at the organisational level.

The field of measuring the organisational fit of IT, otherwise known as IT effectiveness, is extremely complex and problematical. IT cannot effectively be introduced into a large organisation without structural management change. It is almost impossible to separate the effects of the different factors at work. Measures of business effectiveness, such as market share, productivity, profit margins and overall profitability rarely permit a simple breakdown into the contributing factors. Some work has been done in assessing IT effectiveness in terms of internal customer satisfaction[8]. This work describes fitness for purpose in terms of how well the IT department is satisfying the needs of other departments. It provides a reasonable assessment of current performance, but less guidance on how the department is enabling or hindering the business objectives of two years' hence.

4. EXAMPLES OF SYSTEMS FIT FOR THEIR INTENDED PURPOSE

4.1. THE SEMI-AUTOMATIC REPORT GENERATOR

One of the principal advantages claimed for CASE tools is the assistance provided in documentation production. However, many users have found that although the tool produces a lot of information, it does not provide it in a suitable form. Therefore, one user, a large motor manufacturer, commissioned a group at the IT Institute to write a report generator which would digest the information from the CASE tool and assist in report production.

The client was using the IEW case tool, based upon the information engineering methodology. Four reports are required corresponding to the ISP (Information Strategy and Planning), BAA (Business Area Analysis), BSD (Business System Design) and CSD (Computer Systems Design) phases. The process is similar in each case, but the generator pulls in different data from IEW as required.

The report generator is implemented in the Word Perfect macro language, with text and diagram generation handled by compiled QuickBasic code. It consists of four phases : template generation, text processing, diagram processing, document processing.

Template generation is implemented as a WordPerfect macro called from a DOS batch file. The user first selects which type of report (ISP, BAA, BSD, CSD) is required. They are then presented with a standard template for that type of report. The template comprises chapter and section headings together with standard text where appropriate and a set of tags to indicate where diagrams will be inserted. The user has the option to de-select any part of the template. Once satisfied, the user may enter further text within the standard WordPerfect environment.

Once the user completes this task, the text processing module is run, pulling in from IEW, all the textual definitions and descriptions required within the report as specified by the user. At each tag in the document relating to textual information, the report generator places the relevant textual information. Similarly in the diagram processing module all the diagrams required by the report are generated and inserted at the points indicated within the report. Once the automated text and diagram incorporation is completed, the user is prompted by a WordPerfect macro through the final stages of document preparation, comprising:

- Report details, e.g. version number, name and type of report, used in headers later in the program.
- Incorporating text features into imported text. The macro checks for bold or underlining tags and modifies the incorporated text to ensure correct presentation

- Preview diagrams : the user previews each diagram and has the opportunity to re-size or edit the current diagram.
- Final menu : this allows the user to make any final alterations before the report is printed or stored as a WordPerfect file on disk.

The system has proved very popular with users for the following reasons:

- The system works in a manner which is sympathetic and supportive to the user. It guides them through the report generation process.
- It has improved the productivity of users dramatically, with report generation times being reduced from ca. 2 days to 2 hours.
- It has improved the quality of reports.

Although the software is a relatively small part of the implementation of CASE tools within the organisation, by designing a specific piece of software for an important task, omitted from the CASE tool, the fitness for purpose of the system as a whole has been dramatically enhanced, particularly at the task and organisational levels.

4.2 EPI INFO, VERSION 5

Epi info[9] is a tool designed by epidemiologists for epidemiologists to assist in investigations related to health care. The author has observed the enthusiastic responses of over 100 users in a training environment. The authors' observations are backed by the medical literature[10]

The factors leading to the user's enthusiasm include:

- Simplicity in use, particularly in the analysis phase
- Match to the required task
- Replacement of three separate packages with one
- Automation of several tasks through integration
- Ability to handle data from many formats, giving compatibility with existing data
- Compatibility with limited or portable hardware

The simplicity in use is in spite of the lack of a full windows-based environment. The interface is based upon text menus. The ease of use is demonstrated by the task required to produce a cross-tabulation between two variables, say `ill' , a yes/no variable and `age', a numerical variable.

The system requires either the typed command:

TABLES ILL AGE

or selection of each item from a pull down menu.

The simplicity in use is also illustrated in the construction of a data-entry check file allowing the user to improve control over data entry in a very simple fashion. The impact of this simplicity upon users cannot be over-emphasised. In training terms, it allows a trainer to take novice users far further in one day than with three packages with equivalent functionality.

The second factor is the match to a specific task, that of medical investigations, primarily for epidemiology. This allows the software to be tailored and relevant tutorials and examples to be included. Further, it enables an integrated package to be provided which replaces three separate packages. This leads to a simpler process for the implementation of investigations and a consequent improvement in user productivity.

A further factor highlighted by users is the ability to import data from existing investigations for analysis from ASCII, Lotus 1-2-3 and DBASEIII+ formats. This ability to make continued use of existing data is high on the users' list of priorities. Another factor high on the users' list, not always appreciated by suppliers, is the ability to run the software on limited, i.e. old or cheap or portable hardware.

Much of the enthusiasm for this product arises from fitness for purpose at the task level, where it neatly dovetails with the users' way of working. This more than compensates for its limitations in `look and feel'.

5. CONCLUSIONS

Fitness for purpose has historically low on the list of priorities for IT developers. They have assumed that they are the experts and that they know best. However, as users become more aware of what can be achieved and IT departments adopt the principles of `fitness for purpose' are becoming increasingly important.

This paper argues that fitness for purpose most be looked at three levels: physical, task and organisational. It suggests that the scope of human-computer interaction must be greatly expanded to include aspects not previously given priority by developers, but considered important by users. IT systems must not simply be made attractive by the provision of colourful graphical interfaces, but designed properly to meet the long term needs and aspirations of users.

References
1. ISO, *Quality vocabulary*, ISO 8042, 1986.
2. Berry, D.C. and Broadbent, D.E `Expert systems and the man-machine interface', *Expert Systems*, **3** (4) and **4** (1).
3. Stobart, S.C. Thompson, J.B. and Smith P. `Use problems benefits and future direction of computer-aided software engineering in UK', IST **33** (9) 629-636.
4. McCall , J.A. et al `Concepts and Definitions of Software Quality' *Factors in software Quality*, NTIS **1** (1977).
5. Gilb,T. *Principles of Software Engineering Management* , Addison-Wesley, (1988).
6. Gillies, A.C. `Modelling software quality in the commercial environment' , Software Quality Journal, **1** (3), 1992.
7. Brake, D. `Windows beats DOS in the UK', *Personal Computer World*, 16, 3, 170, 1993.
8. Gillies, A.C, *Software quality: theory and management*, Chapman and Hall, London, 1992.
9. Dean A.D., Dean J.A., Burton, J.H. Dicker R.C. *Epi Info, Version 5 : a word processing, database and statistics program for epidemiology on microcomputers*, Center for disease control, Atlanta, Georgia, USA, (1990).
10. Guilford, M.O. Dannenburg, A.L. `Epi Info: computer programs for epidemiology. (evaluation)', *Jou. Amer. Med. Assoc*, 262, 21, 3066-7, 1989.

Presentation and Editing of Structured 3-D Graphics

Steven P. Reiss

Department of Computer Science, Box 1910, Brown University, Providence, RI 02912, spr@cs.brown.edu, (401)-863-7641

Abstract

This paper provides an overview of our efforts at providing high-quality, 3-D visualizations of information about programs. This data is generated by querying the different information sources through a single object-oriented database schema. The result of the query is a set of abstraction objects that are then mapped, through a set of user-definable translations, into a set of abstract graphical objects that represent the display. A separate package handles layout, constraints, and presentation of these graphical objects. The resultant display is interactive at three levels. Syntactic interactions allow the user to pan, zoom and fly around in 3-D space. Semantic interactions allow user actions to affect the translations from abstraction objects into abstract graphical objects and to change the set of abstraction objects by modifying the initial query.

1.0 PROGRAM VISUALIZATION

Program visualization is an essential part of a modern programming environment. As programs become more complex, programmers must be provided with a better understanding of their static and dynamic structures. Such an understanding is much easier to convey through an appropriate picture than through reams of textual data.

The complexity of program visualizations also increases with the complexity of the underlying programs. Current program visualization techniques are already limited by the amount of screen space and the inefficient nature of a graphical presentation. To provide detailed program visualizations for today's complex programs requires a new approach to program visualization and to the display of visualization data.

We are currently involved in a project aimed at providing high-quality program visualizations for complex programs. To accomplish this task, we have broken the problem of program visualization into three parts, the generation of the appropriate visualization data, the graphical presentation of this data, and interactions with this presentation that allow the user so focus on the data of interest to the problem at hand.

2.0 ABSTRACTION DEFINITION

We feel that it is essential that the programmer be given the power and flexibility to define appropriate program visualizations dynamically. What information is relevant to the particular problem that requires visualization is not known in advance. By allowing the programmer to interactively describe the relevant information, we can both limit the amount of information to display and provide a clear focus on the most important information. Our current plan for defining program visualization is to allow the programmer to define the appropriate data as a program abstraction using a powerful query language over an object-oriented database schema. The result is a set of objects that will then be visualized.

Program information can be derived from a wide variety of sources. Syntactic information such as static calls or the class hierarchy can be derived by scanning the source and stored in a cross reference database such as xrefdb [3] or CIA [2]; semantic information can be generated by the compiler as with Sun's source browser; file and version information is gathered and reported by tools such as SCCS or RCS; configuration information is known to tools like Make; performance data is gathered and reported by the various UNIX profilers. Rather than attempting to replace or reimplement all the existing tools, we plan to use the integration framework provided by FIELD [6] to gather the information from the different tools.

To make this practical, we have developed a single, extensible object-oriented database schema that includes all the information [7]. This schema will be used in conjunction with high-level query languages, an object-oriented database algebra, and an in-core federated database system to provide the user with a powerful means for defining abstractions as queries over the complete range of program data.

3.0 ABSTRACTION PRESENTATION

Given this means for defining what information should be visualized, the task of program visualization becomes that of providing an appropriate rendering of a set of objects. We are developing the technology to provide structured (abstract) displays of objects. In order to provide the user with as much information as possible and to make that information as meaningful as possible, we are concentrating our efforts on the use of advanced graphics as a presentation medium. In particular, we are looking at 3-D presentations with smooth animation.

The system is based on the notion of abstract graphical objects. These are objects that represent a graphical entity such as a layout or a scatter plot or a simple box. Abstract graphical objects have properties, constraints, and components. The properties describe how this object is drawn locally, for example they specify the color and text contents of a box. The components are other abstract graphical objects that are drawn inside their parent. For example, a layout has both arc and node components while a scatter plot has just node components. The constraints allow the application or user to further specify how the object should be displayed. These can be simple, for example, specifying a fixed size for a box or that a box should be square or cubic, or they can be complex, for example providing a different placement or routing heuristic for a layout.

The mapping from the abstraction objects that result from a query to a 3-D display is done in two steps. The first step is to map the original objects into a hierarchy of abstract graphical objects. This is done using type-based translations. For each type (or class) of original object, there are one or more applicable translations. These translations can be specified by the application, by the user, or automatically using a built-in set of heuristics. The translations can be direct, mapping the original object into one or more abstract graphical objects, or they can involve the recursive application of the translation algorithm to the object itself or to any of its components. Different translations can be selected based on properties of the object, based on the state of the translation (i.e. is the current object being displayed inside a layout), or based on outside properties that can be set either by the user or by parent translations. While the current set of translations are hand-coded heuristics, we are in the process of implementing a translation definition language with a visual interface to allow both applications and users to define new translations.

This organization for generating displays of abstract objects was originally implemented for 2-D displays in our previous work with the GELO package in both Garden [4] and FIELD. Because most of the techniques for 2-D information graphical presentation of structured information are well understood, we were able to demonstrate here that a wide range of "standard" visual languages and presentations could be modeled through the simple combination of various shaped boxes, rectangular tilings, and layouts consisting of nodes connected with arcs. [5] Such presentations could be used as the basis both for the formal representation of graphics objects and hence graphical parsing, [1] and as the basis for defining a generic visual structured editor as seen in Garden.

The world of three dimensions is much more complex. We have developed an initial system for doing 3-D display of objects and are beginning to experiment with different display techniques that take advantage of both the third dimension and of animation over time to provide additional channels of information to the user. Using this system, we are developing a pallet of the different types of abstract graphical objects that are needed to provide effective information displays. To date, these include 2-D and 3-D boxes of various shapes; 2-D and 3-D constraint-based tilings; 2-D and 3-D layouts of graphical objects with a wide variety of layout heuristics that allow the control of placement in one or more dimensions to be based on properties of the objects; objects representing files that can reflect information and properties of the contents of those files; arcs with associated labels and properties; tagged objects where a label describes the data and the actual data is displayed in a separate plane pivoted behind the object; time sequence objects where there are base objects and then one or more instances of each in the time dimension; simple marker objects; and 2-D and 3-D scatter plots. As we experiment with different presentations, we continue to add new flavors of abstract graphical objects.

The mapping from abstract graphical objects to the display is done in three steps. The first assigns a size to each object in a bottom-up fashion, i.e. each object must compute its size given the size of each of its component objects. For complex objects such as layouts or tilings, this involves solving the corresponding placement problems. In the second phase, layout, each object is responsible for assigning a relative position and size to each of its components. The third phase consists of drawing the hierarchy of graphical objects. Drawing the display can either be done from scratch, if the display has changed substantially, or can be done via animation. Here the package automatically computes the difference between the old and the new displays and, if possible, provides a smooth animation between the two.

4.0 ABSTRACTION EDITING

The current presentation system is designed as a limited-function graphical editor. While we have defined the system so that we can eventually define a fully-functional editor for creating graphical displays on top of the display facilities, our initial concern is to allow the user to interact with the presentation to elicit as much information as possible. The simplest form of interaction is syntactic. This means providing the user with the ability to customize the display by panning, zooming, flying around, and setting appropriate cut planes and lighting.

Our current syntactic interactors are designed to use only the mouse and keyboard while at the same time allowing additional devices (i.e. a dial box or a 3-D stylus) to be used as appropriate. We have a simulated dial box that appears as a separate icon and which offers the user adjustable controls to set or adjust the position and orientation of the simulated camera and view plane. This box also allows the user to control the zoom, the focal point, and whether the projection from 3-D space to a 2-D screen is perspective or orthogonal. The right-hand mouse button is reserved for syntactic interaction. Normally it acts as a virtual sphere, grabbing and spinning the display around the current focal point. If the shift key is pressed, it allows the user to pan in either the x or y direction. When the control key is pressed, the button allows the user to pan in the z direction by moving the mouse up or down, and to control the camera's zoom factor by moving the mouse left and right. Function keys on the keyboard, such as the arrow keys, are also available to rotate, zoom, or reset the camera.

More complex interactions are semantic. These involve the user selecting one or more of the displayed objects and using these selected objects as the basis for constructing a new display. The two ways of doing this correspond to the two mappings, from program data to abstraction objects and from abstraction objects to abstract graphical objects. The translation from abstraction objects to abstract graphical objects was designed to be flexible. Translations can be conditional on properties of the object and on outside properties. Semantic interactions with the translation process are of two forms. The first is direct controls that set outside properties and hence change the whole translation process. For example, the user could indicate that the layout should be based on depth from selection as opposed to depth based on run time.

The second form of interacting for controlling the translation into abstract graphical objects uses object selection. The presentation allows for arbitrary selection sets. The user can add or remove objects from these sets using different mouse buttons or different keys. Each set is associated with a set of graphical properties and a set of traits that can be used by the translation. Graphical properties are used in the current prototype to display objects in the primary selection set with additional depth and with red (versus white) as a background color. The traits allow different translations for a given type of abstraction object to be conditioned on the object's being in appropriate selection sets.

The selection mechanism, along with additional commands, can also be used to change the set of abstraction objects that should be displayed. Selection sets can be accessed either in terms of abstract graphical objects or in terms of the underlying abstraction objects. This allows them to be used in specifying the query that generates the set of abstraction objects. This allows the user to find appropriate information through a series of queries. The sets can also be used to direct secondary queries. While the original query defines the overall set of objects, generally the user will only want to view a subset of these. A secondary query provides an easy way of specifying that subset while not discarding the original information. This is used in the current system to allow the user to only displays nodes that are connected to the current selection and to allow the display of hierarchical information where the user can compress and expand the hierarchy interactively.

5.0 CONCLUSION

The implementation of this presentation facility is being done in phases. We are working on the various aspects of the system in parallel. We have completed the development of the object schema and of an appropriate query language and query algebra and are ready to begin the implementation of the federated database system for generating abstractions. We have developed a package that supports the concept of abstract graphical objects and their mapping into a animated 3-D display. This package has been used to implement the different graphical metaphors cited in this paper. It has also been used in a prototype implementation of the higher level presentation facilities. This prototype uses program information gathered directly from FIELD to display call graphs and associated information (global variable usage, performance data, and dynamic call information). It provides hard-coded implementations of mappings from this data to a set of objects to display and from these objects to abstract graphical objects. A full range of syntactic interactors is provided. Semantic interactors are provided, but are implemented directly in the hard-coded mapping algorithms.

6.0 REFERENCES

1. Eric J. Golin and Steven P. Reiss, "Parsing in a visual language environment," *Proc. 1989 IEEE Workshop on Visual Languages*, (October, 1989).

2. Judith E. Grass and Yih-Farn Chen, "The C++ information abstractor," *Proceedings of the Second USENIX C++ Conference*, pp. 265-275 (April 1990).

3. Moises Lejter, Scott Meyers, and Steven P. Reiss, "Support for maintaining object-oriented programs," *IEEE Trans. on Software Engineering* Vol. 18(12) pp. 1045-1052 (December 1992).

4. Steven P. Reiss, "Working in the Garden environment for conceptual programming," *IEEE Software* Vol. 4(6) pp. 16-27 (November 1987).

5. Steven P. Reiss, Scott Meyers, and Carolyn Duby, "Using GELO to visualize software systems," *Proc. UIST '89*, pp. 149-157 (November 1989).

6. Steven P. Reiss, "Interacting with the FIELD environment," *Software Practice and Experience* Vol. 20(S1) pp. 89-115 (June 1990).

7. Steven P. Reiss and Manojit Sarkar, "Generating program abstractions using an object-oriented database," Brown University Department of Computer Science (1992).

RAPID 3-D EDITING THROUGH HEIRARCHICAL CONSTRAINTS

John R Rankin
Department of Computer Science and Computer Engineering, La Trobe University,
Bundoora, Victoria, Australia, 3083.

Abstract

Hierarchical 3D graphical editors allow the user to create three-dimensional designs and rapidly expand on existing designs by making use of libraries of three-dimensional objects previously constructed. When the editor has the possibility of incorporating geometrical constraints into the 3D objects, development and editing is speeded up again because invalid constructions cannot be made : fixed length edges will remain of the same length, joined edges will remain joined at the same points and so on. To handle such hierarchically nested constraint systems by the traditional method of an external constraint equation solver would be increasingly difficult due to the rapidly increasing complexity and number of constraint equations to solve at one time. Additionally, this method violates the software engineering principles of information hiding and its structure does not reflect the hierarchical structure of the three-dimensional scene. An alternative approach (the "Democracy Algorithm") using distributed constraint resolution at all levels of the scene hierarchy has been found to handle increasing complexity very effectively. This paper addresses issues concerned with certain constraint-based editing of polyhedral objects.

1. INTRODUCTION

3D graphical editors are gaining wider and wider usage in areas such as mechanical CAD, architecture and industrial design. While these programs have shown a number of different approaches to the difficult job of simulating 3D editing operations on a flat screen there is still a degree of dissatisfaction amongst users. One concern has been the degree of three-dimensional realism portayed by the program on a two-dimensional screen. For instance how do you symbolize a 3D pick operation on a 2D screen? This problem concerns both the choice of 3D graphics input device and the choice of 3D output display technology. Some researchers have experimented with new three-dimensional graphics input devices such as 'the bat' [5] to replace the traditional two-dimensional input devices of mouse, joystick and digitizer stylus, and with new 3D output devices as well [see survey in 5]. These new 3D input and output technologies show great promise for the future, however here we are concerned with new methodologies for the old two-dimensional input technologies of keyboard, mouse, joystick and stylus, and new methodologies for the traditional VDU screen output to ease the problem.

Many available editors adopt a two-and-a-half dimensions methodology to 3D graphics editing whereby the mouse or other conventional two-dimensional pick device is used for 2D screen digitization on selectable 'levels' within the 3D construct. The levels (i.e. the third dimension) is often entered by typing in a z-coordinate or by moving a slider by the mouse. Systems that require users to type in any or all of the spatial coordinates needed or require some unrelated analog input mechanism without an associated visualization of a simulated 3D geometrical action are not *fully graphically oriented* editors. One fully graphical approach is to edit the 3D data via three two-dimensional views of it an in the orthographic engineering drawings [3] with the normal two-dimensional digitizing in each two-dimensional view. The 3D editor simply puts together the input data from two orthographically digitized views to form the 3D data. The need to have two or more simultaneous views of the one object being worked on reduces the available screen space so that edited objects would have to be rather small. Additionally, many users are not used to visualizing a 3D object from its orthographic projections though many engineers become adept at the method. Another fully graphical approach is to edit facets, which are plane polygons, in two-dimensions (where detail can be added more clearly) and then place the polygon into 3D by digitizing three 3D points that define its position and orientation [3]. This final step does need a *3D digitizer* for the editor to be a fully graphically oriented editor. Such a 3D digitizer has been described in [4]. In this alternative 3D input methodology [4] 3D axes are displayed and two edges of a variable sized rectangular box are displayed. One vertex of this rectangular box remains at the origin and the diagonally opposite vertex is at the currently digitized point. The size of the box, and hence the location of the point being digitized is altered by a natural arrangement of movement commands on the numeric keypad [described in 4].

However, apart from input and output technologies and methodologies for using them, the main concern of users of 3D graphical editors is the length of time it can take to create a three-dimensional object on the screen, or to edit an existing one suitably. We will look at this carefully after detailing the standard 3D graphical editor commands in the next section. Subsequent to that we will look at extra commands for constraint-based 3D graphical editors and see how these can allow more efficient 3D editing.

2. TRADITIONAL GRAPHICAL EDITOR COMMANDS

A 3D graphical editor needs to supply a number of 3D graphics primitives in a menu. The user chooses a primitive from the menu and then digitizes points for defining it in the display area, the so-called Finite Defining Point Set [see 5]. Examples of 3D graphics primitives are 3D points, 3D line segments, 3D circles, 3D arcs, 3D polylines, 3D splines, 3D polygons, spheres, cones and cubes. This paper is only concerned with the editing of 3D objects made from vertices, edges and plane polygons. The editor needs more than just allowing one to choose a primitive from a menu and then place it onto the drawing area: it needs a number of 3D operators for editing an object. These are usually placed on the same menu as the list of available primitives. Every edit command needs to be coupled to component selection. Most editors insist that the user first select components for editing and then choose an edit command from the menu, but the reverse order is also possible. Some systems allow more than one component to be selected at the one time and therefore the edit operation applies to more than one component. Such editors are referred to here as *multiple selection* editors. The selected components are indicated by using a different display attribute such as a change of colour, and increase in intensity or flashing the component. Another indicator commonly used is to show the minmax box surrounding all the selected components in a bright colour such as red. Two obvious editor operations are delete and change. If the user chooses the delete operator then all selected components will be deleted at the same time. Many editors do not allow primitives to be redefined once created : that is the defining points cannot be individually picked and moved. In this paper, an editor that does allow this will be called *redefinable* and one that strictly doesn't will be called a *non-redefinable* editor. To change an existing component with a non-redefinable editor, a user is expected to delete the component and then create a new version of it with the desired defining points. However, some transformations are usually provided as edit operators though usually just translation and scaling are available. So when the change operator is chosen, the user must select a component or components for changing and then the user can move the minmax box of all the selected components to another position or else rescale all selected components by resizing the minmax box of all selected components using the 3D digitizer to select and move its vertices.

A recognized essential feature of 3D graphical editors is hierarchical structuring. Without this feature 3D objects are effectively just a linear list of drawing primitives without structure. Allowing a hierarchical structure means that components of an object can be worked on separately. This is equivalent to allowing multiple component selection for edit operations but it is quicker because all components in a group are automatically selected when a group is selected. In addition to this, for editors with *instancing*, editing the composition of one instance of a component in a 3D construction should also change the composition of all other instances of that component. To enable the hierarchy feature, the editor needs to provide metagraphics commands for collecting primitives into selectable groups, namely the group and ungroup commands which also only apply to selected components. To allow a hierarchy in the object construction, the groups must be allowed to contain other groups. Selecting 3D components is a straight forward generalization of the corresponding 2D process. In two-dimensional hierarchical selection, the mouse is moved over the drawing and clicked on the component desired. The hierarchy tree is then searched from the root downwards for the first group encountered whose minmax box includes the mouse position and then this minmax box and its group is highlighted. If this is not the required group the user clicks the mouse again and the hierarchy tree search continues from the place it last finished at. If this tree search comes to the end of the tree data, then it starts again back at the root of the tree. This process continues until the desired group is selected or the user exits from the select mode. This selection process is referred to as *true hierarchical selection*. It contrasts with many systems that provide grouping and ungrouping metagraphic commands but do not allow subgroup selection without having to ungroup all groups containing it from the root down and this search down the hierarchy tree is a manual selection process in these systems. This two-dimensional process carries over to three dimensions where minmax boxes are now three-dimensional minmax boxes and mouse digitization is replaced with the use of the 3D digitizer.

Other metagraphics commands needed in 3D graphical editors are transformations, copying, instancing and file input-output. The following transformations at least are required: translation, scaling and rotation. To perform a translation on a component select the translation edit operation is chosen and two points must be digitized with the 3D digitizer. Similar steps are needed for a dilatation transformation and anisotropic scaling is done by choosing the scaling operator and then moving a vertex of the minmax box of all selected components. Dilatations are isotropic rescalings relative to the centroid of the minmax box, but anisotropic rescaling is done relative to the vertex diametrically opposite the one moved. For rotations of selected components, the rotation edit operation is chosen and then three points are to be digitized. These form a plane in which the rotation takes place with the axis of rotation being the normal to the plane and through the first digitized point, and the angle of rotation is the angle subtended by the second and third digitized points at the first digitized point.

Persistence of menu choice is another way of enabling somewhat quicker 3D editing. In this method, the menu choice, whether to draw a new primitive or apply an edit command remains chosen even after one application of it is completed, until another choice is made. This saves the user from the distraction of leaving the 3D visualization to go back to the menu to choose the same option again. Editors with this feature are called *choice-persistent* in this paper.

3. CONSTRAINT SYSTEMS

Research has been growing in the area of constraints programming systems [1,2,6,7]. Early systems [8,9,10,11] used extensive equation solver code units which were cumbersome to implement. Entry of constraints to early systems was also based on typing in equations to the package. Slight errors in the entry of mathematical equations was an obvious hazard and most users didn't want to get involved with all the mathematical equations of the constraints anyway. Such systems are of great interest but were not for general use. Iterative methods have proved to be simpler to implement and they fit in neatly with object-oriented programming [6]. It is more appealing to users to be able to construct constrained systems by choosing drawing primitives that have their own built-in constraints such as fixed length line segments or line segments that remain at a fixed angle to the horizontal and then choosing constraint edit operators. An example of a constraint operator is the *join*. By asserting joins, that is, where two components share a common defining point, and a number of other constraint construction commands, new constraint objects could be built up from the available primitives.

In constructing a constrained object, all the defining points [6] digitized are saved in a global table internal to the editor. The primitives keep only pointers to the points in this points table that define them, rather than keeping the point data locally. Joined primitives share points in this table. To disturb a geometric constrained object of this kind, the user simply moves a defining point, i.e. changes its coordinates in the global points table. Whenever a primitive is activated by such a disturbance, it reads its new defining points, and works out what values they need to be to satisfy its own internal constraints, and then returns the new coordinate values to the global points pool. In the democracy algorithm [7] each component of a constrained object is implemented as an OOP object and is given an equal chance to satisfy the overall constraint requirements. Each component in turn takes the current configuration data (that is, all defining point coordinates for all components in the group) and adapts itself to the data in accordance with its own internal constraints and outputs to the group the changes that it had to make in the configuration data. The adjustment corresponds to rapid message passing between all objects in the group but without the facility of real multiprocessing an iterative round-robin implementation is adopted for the implementation. After the algorithm has cycled through every component several times, the changes in the global points table coordinates, i.e. the system configuration data has been seen to converge to a state representing a new feasible solution of the constraints. From the work done so far, convergence has seemed to be assured for small disturbances.

The hierarchical groupings of primitives in a drawing lead to a hierarchical arrangement of democracy algorithms going on at each level in the total graphics construction: each group is a constrained system with its own iterative democracy algorithm.

Redefinable constraint-based 3D graphical editors incorporate all the primitives and edit operators of the non-constraint-based editors but they add new constrained primitives to the menu and many new constraint construction operators. Examples of the latter are: join two defining points, constrain a defining point to lie on a given line and constrain a defining point to lie on a given plane.

4. ANALYSIS OF A SAMPLE CONSTRUCTION

There are many interesting examples to consider, such as the design of fold-away furniture, the design of cupboards with opening doors and pull-out drawers, and adjustable shelves placed in rooms with sliding or opening doors. In analysing the efficiency of an editor's features for a particyular problem we count the number of choices, selections and digitizations involved in the edit process. By far the most tedious and time consuming of these is the digitization where accurate positioning of the 3D digitizer is required. Selections are less arduous because the 3D digitizer cursor jumps to the nearest point (or other item for selection). Choices , being made from a finite list on the menu, can be done by left hand finger control without moving the eye from the 3D graphics visualization and so are the least time-consuming step in the editing process.

As a simple example, let us first consider the constraint-based construction of a cupboard with a single door and two shelves. The primitives provided will be horizontal and vertical panels. A panel is simply a planar rectangle and for both horizontal and vertical panels it is defined by digitizing two 3D points. The edit operation to be used is just the join. If the join operator is chosen it remains in effect until it is rechosen, and while in effect any points brought into visual coincidence will be joins. To create the cupboard the join mode is chosen, then a vertical panel chosen for which two points are digitized to give the right-hand wall. Without changing the current choice the back wall is defined as a panel with its first vertex selected from a right wall corner and the second defining vertex digitized. Next the top and bottom of the cupboard are placed as horizontal panels with points selected from existing corners rather than being digitized. Likewise two horizontal panels are used for the shelves requiring 4 selections. (A vertical edge is selected and then a point constrained to be on that edge is selected for each defining point of the shelves.) Next a vertical panel is chosen for the left-hand side wall with defining points selected from existing vertices. Finally the door is chosen as a vertical panel with one defining point selected from the lower right-hand front corner of the right wall. After that selection the join mode is switched off and the other defining point for the door is selected as the upper front corner of the left wall. The desired result is now obtained after only 5 menu choice steps, 17 point selections and only 3 point digitizations. With choice-persistence but a non-constraint-based 3D full-graphical editor this would take 1 choice, 14 selections and 18 digitizations!

Next we will consider briefly what constraint primitives are sufficient for the simple construction of a jet fighter plane. These are just the planar polygon and the prism. If the user chooses the planar polygon constrained primitive then first he must use the 3D digitizer to define the plane of the polygon. Thereafter the 3D digitizer's cursor is constrained to this plane until the ESC key is pressed to indicate the end of the polygon construction. While the 3D digitizer is constrained to the plane the vertices of the polygon are selected in order and the polygon automatically closes when the ESC key is pressed. If the prism constrained primitive is chosen then a base point must be digitized using the 3D digitizer and then n-1 vertices for the front polygon of the prism are digitized to create and display the right prism. The prism then consists of n+2 plane polygons constrained together. We will need to use the morphing edit commands: vertex merging and vertex splitting. Vertex merging reduces the number of vertices in a polygon and can convert prisms into wedges and pyramids. Polygons are used for the tail, fins and wings of the plane and the body and cockpit are shaped from sequences of edited prisms. Another useful edit command for this problem is plane polygon dilatations.

5. CONCLUSIONS

In this paper we have reviewed the general concepts for graphical editing and the usual 3D editor operators. A brief review of the constraints programming methodologies was also presented. A classification of broad editor features has been described by the new terms: fully graphical, redefining, hierarchical selection, multiple selection, instancing, choice-persistence and constraint-based. Each of these features adds to the efficiency of 3D geometric designing. This paper then indicated that the hierarchical democracy iterative constraint resolution algorithm could be incorporated into a constraint-based editor that makes certain kinds of 3D editing more efficient.

6. REFERENCES

1 M Goss, S Ervin, J Anderson and A Fleisher, "Designing with Constraints" in Priciples of Computer-Aided Design, Computability of Design, edited by Y E Kalay, pp 53-84, 1987 (Wiley).
2 Wm Leler, "Constraint Programming Languages, Their Specification and Generation", 1988 (Addison-Wesley).
3 J R Rankin, "Computer Graphics Software Construction", p 353, 1989 (Prentice Hall).
4 J R Rankin, "Computer Graphics Software Construction", pp 271-274 and 318-325, 1989 (Prentice Hall).
5 E Sachs, A Roberts and D Stoops, "3-DRAW: A Tool for Designing 3D Shapes", IEEE Computer Graphics and Applications, Nov 1991, pp 18-26.
6 J R Rankin, "A Graphics Object-Oriented Constraint Solver", Eurographics Seminar Series on Object Oriented Graphics, Springer-Verlag, (1993).
7 J R Rankin, "Generalized Dynamic Constraint Resolution Using The Democracy Algorithm", Department of Computer Science and Computer Engineering, La Trobe University, Technical Report 3/91, (1991).
8 I E Sutherland, "Sketchpad: A Man-Machine Graphical Communication System", in SJCC, Spartan Books, Baltimore, MD, (1963).
9 A H Borning, "Defining Constraints Graphically", Computer Human Interaction Conference Proceedings, Boston, Apr 13-17, 1986, ACM, New York, (1986) pp 137-143.
10 A H Borning, "Constraint-Based Tools For Building User Interfaces", ACM ToG, vol 5, Nr 4, Oct 1986, pp 345-374.
11 G Nelson, "Juno, A Constraint-Based Graphics System", ACM SIGGRAPH vol 19, Nr 3, 1985, pp 235-243.

Acknowledgements
This project was supported by an LMI Grant and Departmental Grant from La Trobe University.

Reducing Repetition in Graphical Editing

David Kurlander

Microsoft Research, One Microsoft Way, Redmond, WA 98052-6399, U. S. A.

Abstract

People producing illustrations with graphical editors often need to repeat the same steps over and over again. This paper describes five techniques that reduce the amount of repetition required to create graphical documents, by having the computer play a role in automating repetitive tasks. These techniques: *graphical search and replace, constraint-based search and replace, constraints from multiple snapshots, editable graphical histories,* and *macros by demonstration,* have all been implemented within the Chimera editor framework. Chimera, which contains an object-based editor for producing 2D illustrations, was built as a testbed for this research. All of these techniques are demonstrational or example-based. The user specifies concrete examples of tasks, and the system applies the tasks to other data. In addition to reducing repetition, these techniques allow users to customize the editor for the tasks that they frequently perform, and expert users to encapsulate their knowledge in a form that other users can exploit.

1. INTRODUCTION

People that use graphical editors often find themselves performing the same tasks repeatedly. They may need to change one set of graphical properties to another everywhere in a very large scene. Every occurrence of one shape may need to be edited into another. Often the same set of geometric relationships needs to be established repeatedly over a number of different objects. Every time an object is repositioned, there may be other objects dependent on the first that must be changed as well.

Here I discuss five different techniques that reduce repetition in graphical editing. The techniques are independently useful, but can be combined to form a more effective means of automating repetition. These five techniques have been incorporated into the Chimera editor. Chimera, an application built specifically for this research, is actually an editor framework, in which special purpose editors have been embedded. Currently Chimera includes editor components for creating and modifying 2D object-based graphics, interfaces, and text. The techniques described here work in both the graphics and interface editing components of Chimera. All five techniques are example-based. The user supplies an example of the task to be performed on a sample set of objects, and this example is generalized to work on other inputs and contexts. The user need not have special programming skills to take advantage of these techniques, and these techniques allow users to express complex scene manipulations using concrete examples that are specified using basic graphical editing skills.

Each of the next five sections describe one of these techniques for reducing repetition and promoting extensibility in graphical editors. Section 7 then explains how the techniques are interrelated, and how they can be used together to make a more powerful system for reducing repetition. Due to space limitations, this paper summarizes these five techniques only briefly. Further detail about the techniques, and many examples of their use appear elsewhere [6], and a videotape is also available that demonstrates these techniques at work in Chimera [5].

2. GRAPHICAL SEARCH AND REPLACE

One of the most common types of repetition in graphical editing involves making repetitive changes to shape or graphical properties, such as line style or fill color, many places in a scene. Two traditional graphical editing techniques, instancing and grouping, have proven useful in automating such repetition. Sutherland's Sketchpad system introduced the concept of instancing [9]. The user defines a master object and then instantiates it throughout a scene. Modifications to the master automatically propagate to all of its instances. Many commercial graphical editors, such as MacDraw [2] and Adobe Illustrator [1] allow multiple related objects to be grouped together. Entire groups of objects can be selected and modified as easily as if they were a single object. A disadvantage of both of these techniques is that they require special structuring of the scene to facilitate the process of making repetitive changes. If the user cannot predict, while creating the document, which repetitive changes will likely be required later, or if the user is just too lazy to set up the proper structuring, then these two techniques will not help. Another technique, *graphical search and replace*, can be used in these cases.

Graphical search and replace, is the analogue to textual search and replace in text editors. The user provides an example of a valid match and replacement by copying objects from the scene or drawing new objects. Chimera's graphical search and replace utility is called Match-Tool 2. It contains two editor panes: one for the sample search object and one for the sample replacement. The user further refines the search and replace specification by indicating which properties of the search and replace objects are significant. This is done by checking off the significant properties in two columns of checkboxes. A collection of parameters provide further control over the search and replace process. For example, when rotation and scale invariance are chosen, shapes in the search pattern will match similar shapes in the scene at any rotation or scale. The shape tolerance parameter adjusts how close (according to MatchTool 2's shape metric) shapes in the scene must be to those in the search pattern for a match to occur. When the polarity parameter is turned on, two shapes will only match if they were drawn in the same direction. The granularity parameter adjusts how much scene structure is ignored in finding matches, and the context sensitivity parameter allows objects matching only a specified subset of the search pattern to be replaced.

This technique can be used for commonplace editing tasks, such as finding all combinations of a particular fill color and line style, and changing the fill color, or finding all occurrences of a particular shape, and changing it. However, it can also be used for a number of other applications. Graphical search and replace can serve as a tool for generating complex shapes formed by graphical grammars. It can also add complexity to simple scenes by replacing components of graphical templates. Graphical search can find graphical scene files by content rather than by name, when serving as the basis for a graphical grep capability. Also, graphical search can be used as an iteration mechanism for graphical macros. A more detailed discussion of graphical search and replace, as well as many examples of its use, appear in [3] and [6].

3. CONSTRAINT-BASED SEARCH AND REPLACE

Though graphical search and replace facilitates making repetitive changes to shape, it operates on the complete shape of the pattern. There is no way to specify that only a particular aspect of shape (such as a certain angle or line length) is of interest. A second technique, *constraint-based search and replace*, adds greater selectivity to the search and replace specification. It allows searches and replaces on more specific geometric relationships by having constraints indicate which geometric properties are significant.

Geometric constraints can appear in both the search and replacement examples of constraint-based search and replace specifications. Constraints in the search pattern indicate which geometric relationships must be obeyed by scene objects for them to match the search pattern. For example, we can search for nearly connected lines by providing a search pattern containing two lines connected by a coincident vertex constraint. The tolerance of the search is also provided by example. For example, if the two lines in the search pattern are really a quarter inch apart (breaking the coincident vertex constraint), then all pairs of lines in the scene that are no greater than a quarter inch apart at their endpoints will match the pattern.

The replacement pattern can contain two different classes of geometric constraints. One class of constraint indicates new relationships to be established in each match when a replacement is performed. For example, if the replacement example also contains two lines connected by a coincident vertex constraint, then all nearly connected lines matching the search pattern will be connected together precisely by the replacement. A second class of constraint in the replacement pattern specifies which geometric properties of the match *should not* be changed by the replacement. For example when performing this replacement to connect nearly connected lines, it may be important that locations of the other endpoints of the lines be unchanged, or that the length of the lines not be modified. This second class of constraint specifies which geometric relationships originally in the match cannot be changed in the process of establishing the new relationships.

Constraint-based search and replace can perform very useful scene transformations, such as making all nearly horizontal lines truly horizontal, or adjusting all nearly 90 degree angles to be precisely 90 degrees. This technique can be used for illustration beautification, but whereas previous beautification systems were not extensible, or required programming to add new rules [8] [7], this technique allows the end user to extend the beautification rule set without programming, using an example-based technique. Also, using constraint-based search and replace, end users can define rules that not only beautify existing scene objects, but also add objects to the scene, constrained to existing objects in interesting ways. For example, constraint-based rules can be written to wrap rectangles around text strings, or make right angles rounded by splicing in arcs so that tangent continuity is maintained at the arcs' endpoints. Constraint-based search rules can be archived together in rule sets. Sets of rules in a ruleset can be activated and applied together to a scene. Constraint-based search and replace simplifies the process of making repetitive changes to object geometry throughout a scene.

4. CONSTRAINTS FROM MULTIPLE SNAPSHOTS

With constraint-based search and replace, a graphical editor can find intended geometric relationships in a static scene and enforce these relationships. However in graphical editing, many important object relationships govern how objects are allowed to move in relation to one another, and these often cannot be extracted from a static scene. A third technique, *constraints from multiple snapshots*, is helpful in these cases. The user provides the system with a set of valid configurations (or "snapshots") of scene objects, and the system automatically instantiates constraints that are present in each configuration. Constraints reduce the amount of repetition that users perform in graphical editing, by automatically re-establishing important geometric relationships when some scene objects move. Constraints from multiple snapshots provides a means of specifying constraints that is easier to use in some cases than traditional declarative specification.

The user need not provide, in advance, a complete set of snapshots that unambiguously determines the intended constraint set. The process of adding new snapshots, like traditional constraint specification, can be accomplished incrementally. For example, the user might initially provide two example snapshots that easily come to mind. When the user then turns on constraints and tries to manipulate the scene objects, the constraints that are present in both snapshots will be instantiated, and will restrict the objects' motion. If the user then notices that these constraints preclude another desired configuration, the user can turn off constraints, provide this configuration as an additional snapshot, and all of the constraints interfering with this configuration will be removed automatically.

Chimera has a very efficient algorithm for inferring constraints from multiple snapshots. Constraints in Chimera apply to object vertices, and as objects in Chimera are transformed, the editor monitors transformations that are applied to each vertex. Vertices that have been transformed together since the very first snapshot are placed together in a transformational group. It is very easy to determine which constraints, from our collection of generally useful geometric relationships, should be instantiated on sets of vertices in a transformational group, and which should not. For example, if a set of vertices has only been rotated together since the very first snapshot, then we know that though the slope between each pair of vertices in the group will have changed, the distance between pairs will been invariant. So there is an implied distance constraint between each pair of vertices in this group, but no slope constraints. The complete algorithm and examples of its use are described in [6].

5. EDITABLE GRAPHICAL HISTORIES

A fourth technique, *editable graphical histories*, is a means of visually representing sequences of commands in a graphical user interface. In the character-oriented world, applications typically present their histories as a textual list of commands. This technique does not extend well to the graphical domain, where screen position and other non-textual properties, such as shape, are poorly represented in textual terms. Some graphical applications animate the history directly in the application canvas, but such histories can be difficult to understand and edit, because at any single moment, no temporal context is accessible, and also because the presentation lacks structure. Editable graphical histories use a comic strip metaphor to depict the important operations in a session with a graphical application, in this case the Chimera editor. As application commands are invoked, new panels appear in the history window depicting the commands. The panels use the same visual language as the interface itself, so they are easily understood by people familiar with the interface.

To make the histories more readily understood, we employ three techniques. Related operations are coalesced into individual panels representing logical operations rather than physical operations. This also makes the history more compact. Panels show only those parts of the scene relevant to the operations they represent. Also objects in the panels are rendered according to their role in the explanation. These histories form an interface to an undo mechanism, whereby the user can select any panel and have the system restore the editor state back to that point in time. The histories also reduce repetition by allowing the user to select a series of previously executed operations and redo them. The histories can also be made editable, allowing the user to edit the scene as it existed at any time. Editable graphical histories are further described in [4] and [6].

6. GRAPHICAL MACROS BY EXAMPLE

These histories work in conjunction with a fifth technique: *graphical macros by example*. At any point in time, the user can scan through the graphical history and select a generally useful sequence of commands to be turned into a macro. A new Macro Builder window appears, containing copies of the selected panels. The user then declares each argument by making the panels editable, selecting a copy of the argument anywhere it appears in the panels, and executing the Make-Argument command. For each argument declaration, a new panel appears at the beginning of the macro showing the selected argument and its name.

Playing back the recorded commands verbatim is of limited use, since commands often work as intended only in contexts very similar to the one in which they were originally demonstrated. Chimera's macro facility provides a more powerful mechanism for reducing repetition by generalizing each of the macro's commands to work in other contexts. Chimera will choose a default generalization of each command, according to a built-in set of heuristics, but the user can view these generalizations and override them if necessary. The macro system relies on the graphical history representation to provide support for selecting commands, parameterizing the macro, editing and debugging its contents, and generalizing it to work in different contexts.

7. CONCLUSION

The five techniques described here for reducing repetition in graphical editing tasks are all implemented in Chimera, and they support one another synergistically. Graphical and constraint-based search and replace, for example, can work together, since a single replacement specification can modify geometric and graphical properties. Both kinds of search and replace can be used as an iteration mechanism for graphical macros. For example, a macro can be invoked on all text strings, or all right angles. Editable graphical histories also provide the visual representation for Chimera's macro by example facility.

If Chimera's implementation were extended, there are a number of other ways that these techniques could work together. Currently search and replace operations and snapshots do not appear in the graphical history, but they could and should. The history mechanism includes landmark objects in the panels to help communicate which region of the scene the panels represent. Currently Chimera has an *ad hoc* mechanism for choosing landmarks. Good landmarks are distinct, and graphical search could potentially be used to determine whether prospective landmarks are unique in the scene.

All of these techniques, with the exception of graphical search, trivially can be extended to graphical editing in three dimensions. The algorithms used for graphical search would need to be supplemented to allow searches on shapes formed by surfaces. It would also be interesting to explore how these techniques might be applied to domains other than graphical editing.

Acknowledgments

Steven Feiner provided helpful advice throughout this project, and supervised my research while I was a doctoral candidate at Columbia University. Eric Bier proposed that I investigate graphical search and replace while I was spending a summer at Xerox PARC, and Eric collaborated with me on that component of this research.

References

1. Adobe Systems Inc. *Adobe Illustrator User Manual.* Macintosh version 3. Part no. 0199-2045 rev. 1. 1585 Charleston Road, Mountain View, CA 94039. November 1990.

2. Claris Corporation. *MacDraw II Reference.* 440 Clyde Ave., Mountain View, CA 94043. 1988.

3. Kurlander, David, and Bier, Eric A. Graphical Search and Replace. Proceedings of SIGGRAPH '88 (Atlanta, Georgia, August 1-5, 1988). In *Computer Graphics 22*, 4 (August 1988). 113-120.

4. Kurlander, David and Feiner, Steven. A Visual Language for Browsing, Undoing, and Redoing Graphical Interface Commands. In *Visual Languages and Visual Programming*, Shi-Kuo Chang, ed. Plenum Press, New York. 1990. 257-275.

5. Kurlander, David. Graphical Editing by Example: A Demonstration. Videotape. Columbia University. March 1992. To appear in a 1993 issue of the *SIGGRAPH Video Review*. Abstracted in INTERCHI '93 Conference Proceedings.

6. Kurlander, David. Graphical Editing by Example. Ph. D. Dissertation. Department of Computer Science. Columbia University. 1993.

7. Myers, Brad A. *Creating User Interfaces by Demonstration.* Academic Press, Boston, 1988.

8. Pavlidis, Theo and Van Wyk, Christopher J. An Automatic Beautifier for Drawings and Illustrations. Proceedings of SIGGRAPH '85 (San Francisco, CA, July 22-26, 1985) In *Computer Graphics 19*, 3 (July 1985). 225-234.

9. Sutherland, Ivan E. SketchPad: A Man-Machine Graphical Communication System. AFIPS Conference Proceedings, Spring Joint Computer Conference. 1963. 329-346.

Automated Construction of Application-Specific Graph Editors in an Object-Oriented Paradigm

M. Chen, P. Townsend and C.Y. Wang

Department of Computer Science, University of Wales, Swansea, Singleton Park,
Swansea SA2 8PP, United Kingdom

Abstract

This paper describes a development environment for constructing a class of graphical user interfaces namely application-specific graph editors. It discusses the advantages of separating the process for specifying a graph notation from that for programming a graph editor, and the importance of organising software components of graph editors in an object oriented as well as modular manner. It is concluded that the use of an object-oriented approach is the key to the automation in the process of constructing this class of graphical user interfaces.

1. INTRODUCTION

Graphs† [1-2] have been used extensively in various areas of modern science, social science and engineering, and have become an indispensable means of modelling, manipulating and analysing objects of the real world and their relationships in an abstract pictorial form. In order for scientists and engineers to interactively input graphs into a computer, considerable effort has been employed over the past decade to develop various application-specific graph editors. Many other such tools are still waiting to be implemented.

This paper describes a development environment for constructing application-specific graph editors, and in particular, the use of object-oriented techniques to reduce the complexity in the realisation of the automated software construction process. It discusses the advantages of separating the process for specifying a graph notation from that for programming a graph editor, and the importance of organising software components of graph editors in an object oriented as well as modular manner.

2. USER INTERFACE DEVELOPMENT TOOLS

A number of user interface management systems [3-5] are available commercially for supporting the life-cycles of graphical user interfaces, enabling one to implement user interface facilities such as menus and forms without having to program in a traditional programming language. However, they usually do not provide support for the design and implementation of application facilities. For example, to construct a graph editor, it is still necessary for a user to design data structures for graph elements and to implement facilities such as direct manipulation of graph elements. It obviously would be of significant benefit if there was available a software

---

† In the context of this paper, by 'graphs', we mean graph-based diagrams including basic graphs, digraphs, hyper-graphs and various application-specific flow charts and networks.

development environment that would allow a user (not necessarily a programmer), with very little effort, to construct a graph editor with specific symbolic representations, semantics and constraints.

Recently, discussions on development environments for constructing application-specific graph editors started to appear in the literature, and but a handful of prototype systems have so far been developed [6-10]. With these systems, the user is either restricted to the configuration of simple editors with little alteration in basic graph notation, or is required to be involved in a substantial amount of programming in order to construct an editor suitable for a specific application. Based on an investigation of a large number of graphs used in various areas, the requirements of a development environment that enables users to construct application-specific graph editors without programming have been identified [11].

3. DECADE

DECADE — a Development Environment for Constructing Application-specific Diagram Editors — is currently being developed at Swansea. As illustrated in Figure 1, it consists of a specification tool, a construction tool, a module library manager and a high-level editor modelling language.

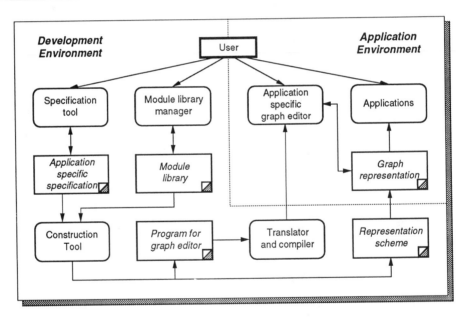

Figure 1. Principal tools of the DECADE system.

Equipped with a graphical user interface, as shown in Figure 2, the **specification tool** allows a user to define interactively a graph notation at the lexical and syntactic levels and features of the corresponding graph editor. These include

- characteristics and properties of graph components such as shapes of components and manipulation protocols defining the way in which components response to operations such as *Append, Draw, Delete, Move, Resize*, etc.,

- syntax rules governing the creation of a graph, such as constraints on connectedness and degree (number of edges incident with a vertex), and allowability of cycles, parallel edges and self loops,
- functional features of the corresponding graph editor, such as a choice between a fixed component palette and a modifiable component library.

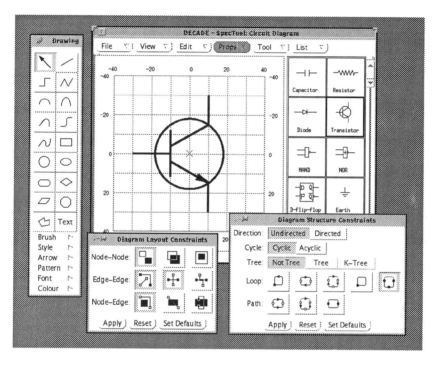

Figure 2. Specification tool of the DECADE system.

In DECADE, the **module library manager** maintains an extensible library of modules for various components of graph editors. Each module is basically a code segment that performs a specific operation on a specific type of data. As a development environment is normally expected to support a wide range of hardware platforms, it is desirable for these modules not to be tied to a specific programming language, graphics package, user interface toolkit and 'look and feel'. A **high level modelling language** for implementing modules is therefore necessary.

Based on an application-specific graph notation, the **construction tool** selects appropriate modules from the library, and generates a UNIX make file [12] for managing the configuration of a graph editor. To produce an executable graph editor, the modules are then translated into a specific programming language, compiled, and linked with a specified graphics package and a user interface toolkit. In order for the user to link an application to the constructed graph editor, an application-specific scheme for representing graphs is also determined by the construction tool according to the specification.

The principal tools of the DECADE system are being written in C++ [13]. The graphical user interface of the environment conforms to the OPEN LOOK 'look and feel' [14], and is implemented using the OPEN LOOK widget set on the top of the X Window System [15].

418

4. THE KEY TO THE AUTOMATION

In order to generate automatically a graph editor according to the specification of a graph notation, the construction tool must have the capability of assembling the graph editor with appropriate internal data structures and associated functions. In a traditional programming paradigm, the realisation of such an automated construction process is likely to encounter the following design problems:

a. It would be extremely costly, if not impossible, to implement an immense number of modules for the variations in application-specific graph notations.
b. It would be neither feasible nor desirable to design a messy data structure and a set of over-complicated functions that are generic to all graph notations.
c. It would be very difficult to maintain the interface stability of modules, as one module may have to communicate, via the same interface, with different modules for different graph notations.
d. It would not be desirable for the construction tool to maintain a huge amount of knowledge about various graph notations, which would lead to an unmanageable implementation with little extensibility.

In DECADE, the key to automation in the process of software construction is the use of an object-oriented approach [16-17]. Object-orientation is a technique for modelling software systems, which include both the graph editors to be constructed and the development environment itself in the context of this application.

In an object-oriented system, the behaviour and information of the system are **encapsulated** in its objects. A module that may define one or more objects is regarded as a 'high level object' in the DECADE environment. There are general purpose modules, such as those for defining common user interface components and their operations, and application-specific modules, such as those for defining elements and syntax of a specific graph notation. Modules are organised into a number of module trees each of which consists of ones of similar functionality, and represents an **inheritance** hierarchy of the modules. Supported by an object-oriented programming language, a module is able to inherit all the code segments defined in its ancestor modules, which facilitates code sharing between modules and reduces a large portion of the task of implementing modules for the variations in application-specific graph notations (i.e. problem (a)). Figure 3 shows a typical module tree made of modules for selecting various types of graph edges.

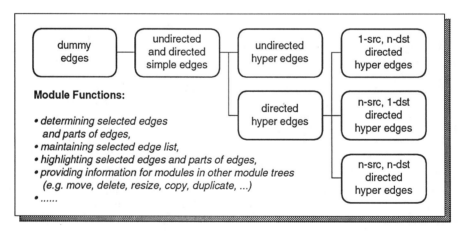

Figure 3. An example module tree.

Each module tree localises the methods with which information is represented and operations are implemented, and hides its internal structure from other module trees. This supports the concepts of **information hiding** and **abstract data types**, and therefore avoids the possibility of using a messy data structure or defining a set of over-complicated functions that are generic to all graph notations (i.e. problem (b)).

One of the characteristics of object-orientation is polymorphism, which enables an object to communicate with another object, knowing neither how the other object is defined nor how it will response. In a constructed graph editor, communications between objects are inevitable, and consistent interfaces between module trees need to be provided for all modules in the trees (i.e. problem (c)). For example, when the position of a vertex is moved, the connected edges usually have to perform certain operation accordingly. To the module which performs the vertex-moving operation, it is not necessarily clear whether connected edges are directed or undirected edges, simple or hyper edges, drawn as lines or arcs, etc. With the object-oriented approach, the moved vertex object will send a stimulus to each connected edge object which will then activate appropriate operations.

The object-oriented approach has also provided an answer to problem (d) in which the tasks of the construction tool can be defined as a set of programmable steps. Given a graph notation, the tool first searches through each module tree from which an appropriate module is identified by using a simple algorithm as shown in Figure 4. The identified modules and, in most cases, their ancestor modules are then assembled into a frame to form a graph editor, and a UNIX make file is generated for managing the configuration, translation and compilation of the editor. The knowledge about graph notations need not be hard-coded into the construction tool and is in fact represented by the semantic scheme with which the module library is organised.

```
for <each module tree> do
  the_module := <the root of the module tree>;
  found := False;
  while found = False do
    a_module := closer_to_spec(the_module, <its child modules>);
    if a_module = the_module then
      found := True;
      mark_selected(the_module)
    else
      the_module := a_module
    end if-else
  end while
end for
```

Figure 4. Algorithm for identifying modules.

In DECADE, there are a fixed number of module trees. The number of modules in each tree is generally constrained by the possible variations of graph notations which can be specified by the specification tool. The object-oriented approach provides DECADE with an architecture in which modules can be implemented efficiently, the module library can be extended easily, module interfaces can be defined consistently and modules of a graph editor can be selected algorithmically. The object-oriented paradigm provides not only an alternative programming environment, but also a solution, which could be the only solution, to the realisation of such a software development environment.

5. CONCLUSIONS

A development environment for constructing application-specific graph editors, the DECADE system, has been described. The system separates the process for specifying a graph notation from that for programming a graph editor, and provides the former with a comprehensive graphical user interface and the latter with an automated construction tool. The use of object-oriented techniques has been found to be the key to automation in the process of constructing this class of graphical user interfaces.

6. REFERENCES

1. R.J. Wilson and L.W. Beinek (eds), Applications of Graph Theory, Academic Press, London (1979).
2. C. Berge, *Graphs and Hypergraphs*, North-Holland, Amsterdam (1973).
3. B. Shneiderman, *Designing the User Interface: Strategies for Effective Human-Computer Interaction*, Addison-Wesley, Reading, Massachusetts (1992).
4. D.A. Duce, M.R. Gomes, F.R.A. Hopgood and J.R. Lee (eds), *User Interface Management and Design*, Springer-Verlag, Berlin (1990).
5. P. Gray and R. Took (eds), *Building Interactive Systems: Architectures and Tools*, Workshops in Computing, Springer-Verlag (1992).
6. J.M. Vlissides and M.A. Linton, "Unidraw: a framework for building domain-specific graphical editors", *ACM Transactions on Information Systems*, 8(3) pp.237-368 (1990).
7. F.N. Paulisch and W.F. Tichy, "EDGE: an extendible graph editor", *Software Practice and Experience*, 20(S1) pp. 63-88 (1990).
8. A. Karrer and W. Scacchi, "Requirements for an extensible object-oriented tree/graph editor", *Proc. Third ACM Symposium on User Interface Software and Technology*, Snowbird, Utah, USA, pp. 83–91 (1990).
9. S. Heknatpour, "Template-driven graphical editor", Proc. IFIP TC 2/WG 2.7 Working Conference on Engineering for Human-Computer Interaction, Napa Valley, pp.29–42 (1990).
10. J.M. Vlissides and S. Tang, A Unidraw-based user interface builder, *Proc. ACM Symposium on User Interface Software and Technology*, Hilton Head, South Carolina, USA, pp.201-210, 1991.
11. M. Chen, P. Townsend and C.Y. Wang, "A development environment for constructing graph-based editing tools", *Computer Graphics Forum*, 11(3) pp.C345-355 (1992).
12. A. Oram and S. Talbot, *Managing Projects with* `make`, Addison-Wesley, Reading, Massachusetts (1992).
13. K.E. Gorlen, *Data Abstraction and Object-Oriented Programming in C++*, Jhon Wiley & Sons (1990).
14. Sun Microsystems, Inc., *OPEN LOOK Graphical User Interface — Functional Specification*, Addison-Weslay, Reading, Massachusetts (1989).
15. J.D. Miller, An OPEN LOOK at UNIX — A Developer's Guide to X. M&T Publishing, Inc., Redwood City, California (1990).
16. I. Jacobson, M. Christerson, P. Jonsson and G. Overgaard, *Object-Oriented Software Engineering*, Addison-Wesley, Wokingham (1992).
17. W. Kim and F.H. Lochovsky (eds), *Object-Oriented Concepts, Databases and Applications*, ACM Press (1989).

Using domain knowledge to support graphical editing

Jonas Löwgren
jlo@ida.liu.se

Department of Computer and Information Science,
Linköping University, S-581 83 Linköping, Sweden.

Abstract

The purpose of this paper is to discuss *what* knowledge can be used to support graphical editing and *how* that knowledge could be used. We present examples of how presentational, syntactic and semantic knowledge is used to support graphical editing by means of support tools in the form of critiquing systems. The paper discusses results obtained from evaluations of these support tools and indicates promising directions for future work.

1. Introduction

This paper reports some aspects of our ongoing work in the area of knowledge-based support for graphical editing. We have focused on the domain of general graphical user-interfaces and, on a more specialized level, military tactical maps. It is, however, our belief that the results presented in this paper are applicable also to other graphical editing domains.

Knowledge about general user-interface design resides in the heads of design and evaluation experts. Much of it is also documented in paper-based guidelines and style guides. Several experiments in recent years have shown that these documents are hard to use, and therefore not used to the extent they deserve (see Mosier and Smith, 1986; de Souza and Bevan, 1990; Tetzlaff and Schwartz, 1991). A reasonable assumption is that the books and written instructions about tactical map editing used in military staff training suffer from similar usability problems. The approach of our work (Löwgren and Nordqvist, 1990, 1992) is to represent the available knowledge in *critiquing systems* integrated with graphical editors. A critiquing system (or a *critic*) is a knowledge-based system capable of generating comments upon a user-proposed solution to a certain problem. In this paper, we will discuss the different dimensions of knowledge we have experimented with, how we have chosen to use it and some preliminary results from evaluations of our approach.

2. Dimensions of knowledge

As one starts to analyze and work in the area of critiquing graphical user interfaces, it becomes clear that relevant knowledge can be found on a multitude of levels, including *presentation, syntax, semantics* and *user tasks*. Presentation-level knowledge is typically about layout, colors and the like. Syntactic knowledge is concerned with how the interaction is structured. Semantic knowledge has to do with the meaning of the interaction objects in terms of the application domain. Knowledge of the user tasks is central in order to determine how well the interface supports them. Presentation and syntax is more general than semantics in the sense that the same presentational and syntactic knowledge can be applied across different semantic domains.

Another dimension that we have come across repeatedly in our work is the *formative strength* of the knowledge. We distinguish between *"must"* knowledge and *"should"* knowledge. Environment-specific user-interface style guides typically include both kinds, where the "must" knowledge refers to rules that must be adhered to if the resulting design is to be compliant with the standard. "Should" knowledge refers to recommendations which could improve the design but which are not necessary from a compliance point of view. Guidelines mostly contain "should" rules. Semantic knowledge can in general be of both kinds, depending on the domain addressed by the application.

3. Illustrations

We have recently developed two different systems in order to study the feasibility of using presentational and syntactic knowledge on one hand and of semantic knowledge on the other. The first system, called KRI/AG, is presented thoroughly in (Löwgren and Nordqvist, 1992). The other system, KRI/L, has not been presented previously. In this section, the systems will be described in the context of an example, namely a tactical map editor developed for use in military staff work. The primary knowledge source for both systems is written documents. KRI/AG, which contains presentational and syntactic knowledge from user interface design guidelines and the Motif style guide, can be used to evaluate any user interface developed in Motif. KRI/L is based on semantic knowledge from books and instructions on how to draw and maintain military tactical maps; it is intended only to support applications in that area.

The current design of the map editor is illustrated in figure 1. It has a large workspace where a detailed map shows the tactical situation in a small region of the geographic area covered. The overview window (top left) indicates the position of the detailed view in the context of the whole area. There is a menubar in the top of the window, containing two standard pulldown menus. The small palette below the overview window contains six tools used to manipulate objects in the work-

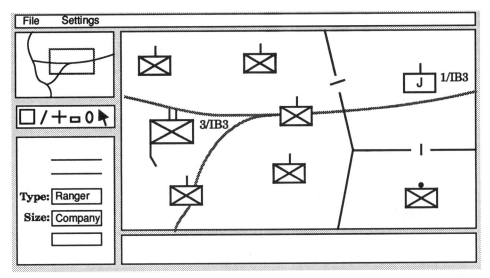

Figure 1: The tactical map editor (simplified and translated sketch).

space in various ways. The property form below the tool palette is used to display and change the attributes of the different objects. Finally, there is a message area in the bottom of the window.

Applying the critiquing systems to the map editor yields several comments. Due to space limitations, the reader is referred to (Löwgren and Nordqvist, 1992) for a discussion of the comments on presentation and syntax. Some examples of semantic-level comments are the following.

- The infantry battalion 3/IB3 should normally have four rifle companies, but there are five in the map.

- The border between [the battalion] 3/IB3 and [the company] 1/IB3 should be of battalion type. Always use the largest unit to index the border.

- It is normally not relevant to display units of group size on a map with this resolution.

The first and third of the comments above are based on "should" knowledge, whereas the second is generated by a "must" rule.

In order to illustrate possible conflicts between different knowledge levels, we will consider a hypothetical design of the popup menu used to specify the size of new units in the map. Assume that the menu contained the following items, appearing in alphabetical order in the menu: Army, Army Corps, Battalion, Brigade, Company, Defense Region, Group and Platoon. Based on general presentation and syntax knowledge, the critic would detect that the items were alphabetically ordered and generate a comment to the effect that a logical order should be sought for the menu items. It would also offer as an alternative that the items could be ordered according to frequency of use. Naturally, the comments would not contain any information on what such a logical or frequency order would be. The semantic knowledge base would comment that the items should be ordered according to ascending size: Group, Platoon, Company, Battalion, Brigade, Defense Region, Army and Army Corps. This is an extremely clear-cut example, but we expect that similar comment conflicts could arise in many situations if the two knowledge bases were integrated. Possible conflict resolution heuristics could include that "must" comments always take precedence over "should" comments, and that domain-specific comments take precedence over general.

4. Discussion

The opening of the paper formulated two issues for investigation, namely what knowledge can be used to support graphical editing and how that knowledge should be used. We have illustrated, by way of general argument and implemented systems, that we use presentational, syntactic and semantic knowledge in order to support graphical editing. We have also indicated that we believe critiquing to be a sensible way of providing the support. In this section, we discuss the approach taken and outline our future work in the area.

4.1 What knowledge ...

We have evaluated our critiquing systems in several different ways. In a study of our first system (KRI, which was similar in scope to KRI/AG but based on knowledge from human user-interface evaluation experts), the evaluators found the approach valuable, appreciated the references to guideline documents but pointed to the lack of task-related knowledge (Löwgren and Nordqvist, 1990).

KRI/AG has been evaluated in a field study (Löwgren and Laurén, 1993), where five professional user-interface designers were given a design task in the form of a written functional specification and asked to produce a user-interface prototype. The prototypes were evaluated using KRI/AG and the resulting comments formed points of departure for interviews with the designers. One purpose of the interviews was to understand the reasons behind the designers' deviations from guidelines and style guides. The results indicated that half of the deviations were due to mistakes and oversights. Comments would have been most welcome in those cases. The other half of the deviations were due to systematic misconceptions or missing knowledge, which according to Silverman and Mezher (1992) calls for debiasing strategies on behalf of the system. The designers all found the guideline and style guide documents hard to use and clearly saw benefits of a computer-based implementation of their contents.

The semantic knowledge tool KRI/L has been informally evaluated with potential users carrying out representative tasks. The interactions were videotaped and the users were interviewed after completing the tasks. The results were encouraging as far as the principles were concerned but highlighted the architectural problems with the platform we had to work with.

4.2 ... and how

In the field study mentioned above (Löwgren and Laurén, 1993), another focus of the interviews was the designers' work practice and what impact a critiquing tool such as KRI/AG would have. We found that the most important consideration for the designers was to have control over their work and over the support system. Our tentative conclusion is that a critic is to be preferred over an automatic design system. Moreover, it is essential that the critic is not perceived as intrusive.

Another, more general argument for critiquing is that user-interface design is an essentially open-ended task. Detecting deviations from design rules is not necessarily the same as constructing acceptable solutions. A poignant example is a rule in the KRI/AG knowledge base about information density, derived from a general guideline. It computes how densely filled a window is and generates a comment if the result is above a certain threshold value. There are clearly multiple ways of rectifying this potential problem; building a system that would do it automatically is a major undertaking (see, for example, Kim and Foley, 1991). The same argument holds for a large number of comments generated by design critics.

4.3 Future work

Our work so far has told us that critiquing seems like a sensible approach and that comments based on the users' tasks are important. This provides us with directions for upcoming work.

We are planning a series of experiments in order to investigate different critiquing strategies for user-interface design support. A Wizard-of-Oz environment is being developed in order to give us maximal flexibility. Among the variations we intend to study are whether the critic should be active or reactive, whether the comments should be batch-style or interactive and whether the critic should also propose improvements.

The notion of task-related comments can to some extent be captured by means of what we call *runtime evaluation* (Löwgren and Nordqvist, 1992). Briefly, this means that real or simulated users carry out relevant tasks using the design prototype under investigation. The interaction is logged, filtered and evaluated with respect to the design representation. We find the idea of working from experimentally acquired task knowledge an interesting alternative to explicitly specifying the tasks in the design representation.

In conclusion, this paper has illustrated how graphical editors can be integrated with critiquing systems containing presentational, syntactic and semantic knowledge in order to support the task of graphical editing. Our evaluations indicate that critiquing is a promising paradigm for editing support.

426

Acknowledgments

The author is indebted to Tommy Nordqvist, Peter Ericsson and Urban Persson of the National Defence Research Establishment for several years of fruitful cooperation. Thanks are also due to Ulrika Laurén for her excellent work on the field study of KRI/AG and to Torbjörn Näslund for his incisive comments on an earlier draft of this paper.

References

Kim, W. and Foley, J. (1991) DON: User interface presentation assistant. In *Proceedings of the ACM SIGGRAPH Symposium om User Interface Software and Technology (UIST'90)*, pp. 10-20. New York: ACM Press.

Löwgren, J. and Laurén, U. (1993) Validating knowledge-based evaluation as support for professional user-interface design. Submitted for publication.

Löwgren, J. and Nordqvist, T. (1990) A knowledge-based tool for user interface evaluation and its integration in a UIMS. In Diaper, D. et al. (eds) *Human-Computer Interaction — Interact'90*, pp. 395-400. Amsterdam: North-Holland.

Löwgren, J. and Nordqvist, T. (1992) Knowledge-based evaluation as design support for graphical user interfaces. In *Human Factors in Computing Systems (CHI'92 Proceedings)*, pp. 181-188. New York: ACM Press.

Mosier, J. and Smith, S. (1986) Application of guidelines for designing user interface software. *Behaviour and Information Technology*, 5(1):39-46.

Silverman, B. and Mezher, T. (1992) Expert critics in engineering design: Lessons learned and research needs. *AI Magazine*, 13(1):45-62.

de Souza, F. and Bevan, N. (1990) The use of guidelines in menu interface design: Evaluation of a draft standard. In Diaper, D. et al. (eds) *Human-Computer Interaction — Interact'90*, pp. 435-440. Amsterdam: North-Holland.

Tetzlaff, L. and Schwartz, D. (1991) The use of guidelines in interface design. In *Human Factors in Computing Systems (CHI'91 Proceedings)*, p. 329-333. New York: ACM Press.

III. Media

An Eventful Approach To Multi-Media, Multi-User Applications

Matthias Ressel, Hubertus Hohl, and Jürgen Herczeg
Research Group DRUID

University of Stuttgart, Department of Computer Science
Breitwiesenstr. 20-22, D-70565 Stuttgart, Germany
E-Mail: druid@informatik.uni-stuttgart.de

Keywords: Graphical user interfaces, event-based architecture, computer-supported cooperative work, multi-media, real-time communication.

Abstract

Existing software development tools and user interface toolkits assist application programmers in developing and implementing single-user applications with graphical user interface. However, multi-media and multi-user applications introduce new dimensions, like temporal aspects, concurrency, or sharing of objects, that are usually not supported by these tools. In this paper we describe the experience we made as we developed and implemented a distributed multi-user application in the domain of hyper-media document production. We describe the chosen event-based approach and how it makes it easier to augment existing software in order to support cooperative work as well as new kinds of temporal media.

1. INTRODUCTION

The availability of new telecommunication and network technologies makes not only possible but also creates the need for applications that make full use of the broader communication channels. These include information systems that facilitate the access to multi-media or hyper-media information as well as applications in the field of computer-supported cooperative work, that enable users to communicate and collaborate on common tasks through a local or wide-area network.

While the 80s saw the progress from computer systems with text-oriented user interfaces with just keyboard input to systems with graphical user interfaces with additional input from a pointing device (mouse, trackball, touch screens), in the next years, more and more, these graphical systems will be extended (1) to multi-media systems involving animation, video, audio, and gestures, and (2) to collaborative (or maybe competitive) multi-user systems that supply shared workspaces and allow the simultaneous, distributed work on a common task. These systems will bring new power and new qualities to the computer. For example, in tutoring systems video sequences can be part of learning units, or a learner can ask for the assistance of the tutor who, from another workstation, may "enter" the learner's workspace, solve a problem collaboratively with the learner and eventually "leave" the learner's session again.

From the point of view of application programmers, however, this implies more complexity: new user interface objects for the control and adjustment of speed, color, and volume of video or audio presentations and support for group feedback, group undo, and versioning. Other, more internal points to consider are: video and audio integration, client-to-client communication, management of shared objects and concurrency control. User interface toolkits for graphical single-user applications are available in great quantity for every platform. However, equally powerful tools for multi-user and multi-media applications are still not available.

In the course of implementing a multi-author application in the domain of hyper-media document production we have made experiences with most of the ment᾿ ned aspects of multi-user, multi-media applications. The approach that will be described uses an event-based, replicated architecture, that facilitates the extension of existing software to support new kinds of media and collaborative work.

2. A MULTI-USER, MULTI-MEDIA APPLICATION

We have developed and implemented a system that supports multiple authors in the planning and the production of hyper-media documents (*production interface*). This work has partly been carried out in the framework of the European project GUIDANCE (Race 1967). A major goal of this project was to support the development of user-friendly and usable systems for integrated broadband communication. For that purpose, a method called Enabling State Analysis [1] has been developed that, among other things, produces specifications of user interfaces for such systems.

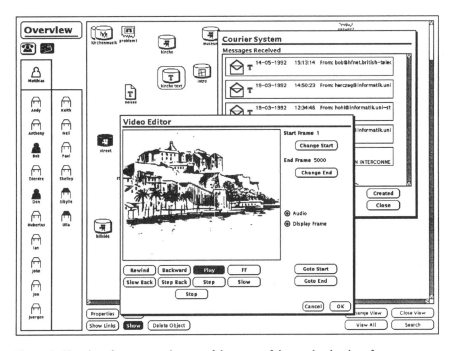

Figure 1: User interface as seen by one of the users of the production interface

Figure 1 shows a snapshot of the graphical user interface of the production interface. Several users on different sites can simultaneously create, edit and delete document nodes and links between them. For reasons of simplification of the user interface, every node contains data of exactly one kind of medium: besides text and graphics, video and audio data are supported. The sources for

430

video data are laserdisc players. For text documents a joint editor has been implemented that allows the simultaneous editing of an object by several authors whereas the editors for the other media require exclusive access. Locked document nodes, that are currently not available to other users for editing, are visually marked by a frame. In addition, the video editor provides a mode that supports "looking over the shoulder" of the workgroup member who is currently editing a video clip.

A mail system for asynchronous message exchange and a videophone for direct person-to-person communication is integrated into the user interface. The video picture is taken by a video camera at each workstation. A videophone call resembles a phone call: when the recipient of a video call is not responding, the opportunity to send a mail is offered. The presence of users in a session is represented by a set of icons showing either an empty desk (*not present*) or a silhouette of the user (*present*). These icons are also used to select recipients for video calls or mail.

3. ARCHITECTURE

Figure 2 shows the architecture of the production interface. The application processes are replicated for each user. Their shared data is managed by the central server process, that also handles video calls and the distribution of mails. Each application process is connected to a user interface.

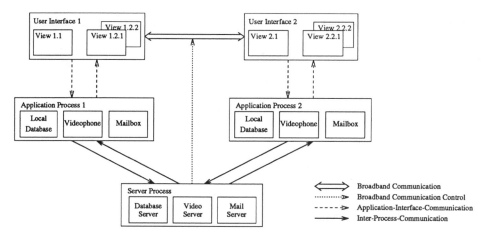

Figure 2: Architecture of the production interface

The communication between the different layers of the architecture is event-based. An event-based mechanism is a widely used approach for specifying and implementing graphical user interfaces [4]. Rules describe how an application should react on events initiated by the user, such as a key press, mouse motion or mouse button press. However, events can be generalized to any kind of asynchronous input to an application system. So we can distinguish (cf. [5] and [8]):

- user input events (e.g., key press, mouse motion)

- window system events (e.g., map notification, client events)

- timer events (e.g., periodic events)

- media events (e.g., end of tape, end of video clip, start and end of commercials)

- external events (e.g., mail arrived, mail acknowledged, incoming video call, joint editor event)

The joint text editor is different from the other editors in that it allows the simultaneous editing of one text document by several authors. This is achieved by adopting the approach to concurrency control taken by GROVE [3], namely *operation transformation*.

This event-based distributed, client-server architecture has proven to be appropriate to implement a collaborative multi-user and multi-media environment. It combines the advantages of replicated architectures and centralized architectures. The replicated architecture provides good responsiveness [8]. It also allows that the user interface can be built by available user interface development environments. On the other hand, the central server process facilitates the incremental extension and reduction of the active user group (cf. [9]) by providing simple mechanisms for connection start-up and close-down, that allow *late joining*. By using a single event queue, the server process simplifies concurrency control, especially if more than two users are involved. So it can easily manage videophone connections and guarantee permanent data storing by regularly writing its database to secondary storage.

Another important point is that the event-based mechanism can be easily extended when new media like video and audio are integrated into the user interface. Special events, for example, can be used to notify the completion of a video clip. Other events could be used to synchronize several video or audio sources (*time code*).

4. OBJECT-ORIENTED IMPLEMENTATION

The implementation is based on the Common Lisp Object System (CLOS) [10]. It has been carried out on a network of SUN workstations under Open Windows 3. Both the application system and the user interface follow an object-oriented design. Each elementary part of the application system is internally represented by an application object that in turn is associated with an interaction object on the user interface (e.g., dialogue windows for videophone, mail system, editors, document icons). Several object classes have been defined for the different document media. Common properties or functionality is inherited from common superclasses. Each class supplies a set of methods, e.g., for creating, presenting, editing or storing the members of this class. For example, presenting audio data means playing back the data through some audio device, while presenting a picture means displaying the picture in a window on the screen.

The user interfaces and the connection to the application processes has been implemented with XIT [6], an object-oriented user interface development tool for the X Window System, that is based on CLOS. Unfortunately, we had to cope with a missing integration of the video functionality and the window system, but XIT allowed the definition of new *logical events*, that provided the necessary functionality to "synchronize" the video image with the window system. For example, events that signal the end of a video clip have been used as a workaround to switch off the video board (and enhance the responsiveness of the interface), when no video was running.

The implementation of the process communication between application processes and server process is based on UNIX *sockets*. On top of the low-level socket interface a generic, protocol-based *event handler* has been implemented that establishes event-driven communication using application-specific protocols. It supports both synchronous (i.e., the sender is blocked until the receipt of a reply) and asynchronous client-server data transfer.

To support transparent sharing of object between application processes, the creation, deletion and modification of objects has been extended using the Meta Object Protocol (MOP) [7] of CLOS. When an application process invokes one of these operations, the operation is actually delegated to the server process. There, the relevant operation is performed and then all connected application processes are notified. For performance reasons, read operation on slots are performed locally on copies of the data objects. This cache is updated as a side effect of create, delete or modify operations on objects performed by the server process.

The exchange of events between processes strongly resembles the exchange of messages between the objects in these processes. For that reason, the object-oriented approach and the event-based mechanism for inter-process communication complement each other naturally. Actually, by this approach objects in one application process can send messages to one or a group of objects in other application processes. For example, this is used to distribute mail that is sent from one mailbox to others.

5. CONCLUSIONS

We have presented an event-based architecture that forms the base for a multi-media multi-author environment which supports private and cooperative work, as well as synchronous and asynchronous communication in a network of workstations. Comparing our production interface to other systems, the following observations can be made. Sharing in our system is done on application level, the underlying application data is shared without sharing the corresponding interaction objects. This distinguishes it from systems that mainly support the sharing of elements of the user interface (Colab [12] and shared window systems like Dialogo [8]) and rely on the resulting WYSIWIS functionality. Nevertheless, our system uses an architecture similar to that of Dialogo, that uses replicated applications in connection with a central conference manager. Many of the problems related to application replication could be avoided by our system by implementing it "from scratch" and making it collaboration-aware. Compared to Suite [2], the exchange of messages between objects in different applications is simplified considerably by our object-oriented implementation. There is a strong similarity between our system and SEPIA [11], surely caused by the similar area of application: cooperative hypermedia authoring. Both include video and audio both as object of cooperative work and as media for communication purposes. Both support loosely coupled modes, where the layout of objects is private and locked objects are highlighted. In addition, SEPIA also supports a tightly coupled mode for object overview windows that had not been required for our application. In both, there is integrated a joint editor for the simultaneous editing of graphical and textual information, respectively. The current design of SEPIA does not allow the dynamic expansion of tightly coupled sessions to include more authors. Both systems provide analog channels for audio/video conferencing. Yet, by also including a mail system, our system provides an integrated interface for person-to-person communication. The main goal for our production interface has been to develop an integrated system that enables the users to perform all required tasks by providing a user interface that is easy to use. For that reason, it was important to be able to use a powerful and flexible tool for implementing the user interface.

We have shown how a collaborative multi-user application could be implemented by the extension of an existing event-based user interface development tool in connection with a generic inter-process communication mechanism. We have also shown that new kinds of events play an important role especially in multi-user and multi-media applications. Especially in the emerging multi-media environments, the event-based mechanism can be extended by the definition of new media-specific events. We expect that these kinds of event-based architectures will lead to an "eventful" future for multi-user and multi-media applications.

6. ACKNOWLEDGMENTS

Part of the work described in this paper has been carried out on behalf of the European Race project R1067 Guidance. We would like to thank Paul Byerley, Sibylle Hermann, Jon May and Ulla-Britt Voigt for their cooperation. We would also like to acknowledge the support of Rul Gunzenhäuser.

REFERENCES

[1] Paul Byerley, Jon May, Andrew Whitefield, and I. Denley. The Enabling States Approach: Designing Usable Telecommunication Services. *IEEE Journal on Selected Areas in Communication*, 9(4):524–530, April 1991.

[2] Prasun Dewan and Rajiv Choudhary. Primitives for Programming Multi-User Interfaces. In *Proceedings of the ACM SIGGRAPH Symposium on User Interface Software and Technology*, CSCW, pages 69–78, 1991.

[3] C. A. Ellis and S. J. Gibbs. Concurrency control in groupware systems. In *Proceedings of the ACM SIGMOD '89 Conference on the Management of Data*, pages 399–407, Seattle, Washington, May 2–4 1989. ACM, New York.

[4] H. Rex Hartson and Deborah Hix. Human-Computer Interface Development: Concepts and Systems for Its Management. *ACM Computing Surveys*, 21(1):5–92, March 1989.

[5] Jürgen Herczeg, Hubertus Hohl, and Matthias Ressel. Progress in Building User Interface Toolkits: The World According to XIT. In *Proceedings of the ACM Symposium on User Interface Software and Technology*, November 1992.

[6] Jürgen Herczeg, Hubertus Hohl, and Matthias Ressel. A New Approach to Visual Programming in User Interface Design, 1993. This volume.

[7] G. Kiczales, J. Rivieres, and D.G. Bobrow. *The Art of the Metaobject Protocol*. MIT Press, Cambridge, Mass., 1991.

[8] J. Chris Lauwers, Thomas A. Joseph, Keith A. Lantz, and Allyn L. Romanow. Replicated Architectures for Shared Window Systems: A Critique. In *Conference on Office Information Systems*, Computer Mediated Work Environments, pages 249–260, 1990.

[9] John F. Patterson, Ralph D. Hill, Steven L. Rohall, and W. Scott Meeks. Rendezvous: An Architecture for Synchronous Multi-User Applications. In *Proceedings of the CSCW'90*, pages 317–328, N.Y., 1990. ACM.

[10] Guy L. Steele Jr. *Common LISP: The Language*. Digital Press, Digital Equipment Corporation, second edition, 1990.

[11] Norbert Streitz, Jörg Haake, Jörg Hannemann, Andreas Lemke, Wolfgang Schuler, Helge Schütt, and Manfred Thüring. SEPIA: A Cooperative Hypermedia Authoring Environment. In *European Conference on Hypertext (ECHT'92)*, 1992.

[12] Deborah G. Tatar, Gregg Foster, and Daniel G. Bobrow. Design for Conversation: Lessons from Cognoter. *International Journal of Man-Machine Studies*, 34(2):185–209, 1991.

Designing Coherent Multimedia Presentations

Thomas Rist, Elisabeth André

German Research Center for Artificial Intelligence, Saarbrücken Site, Stuhlsatzenhausweg 3, W-6600 Saarbrücken 11, Germany

Abstract

In this paper*, we describe an approach for the automatic synthesis of multimedia documents in which different media, such as text and graphics, are smoothly integrated. The approach we have taken has its roots in text generation. We start from the assumption that textlinguistic concepts such as speech acts, coherence relations, and discourse structure can be generalized in a way that they also become useful for the generation of multimedia presentations. We briefly describe a prototype of a multimedia presentation system. By means of an application example we demonstrate the system's ability to adapt its presentations to particular presentation situations.

1. MOTIVATION AND OBJECTIVE

Benefit and acceptance of numerous application systems is substantially affected by their poor ability to present information in an adequate and effective way to human users. Fortunately, rapid progress in the development of multimedia technology paves the way for new and better forms of human/machine communication. However, designing a good presentation that takes advantage of several communication media such as natural language, graphics, animation, and pointing gestures may even become a harder and a more complex task than solving the application problem. In order to optimally encode information, the system designer has to know how to coordinate different media in a coherent manner. Furthermore, particular presentations for particular purposes have to be designed, and each presentation should be tailored to the individual user and the presentation situation. As a consequence, a system designer has to anticipate the needs and requirements of each potential user in an infinite number of presentation situations - for many applications a nearly hopeless task.

This leads to the idea of factoring out presentation knowledge common to a broad range of applications and building an intelligent multimedia presentation system that automatically designs presentations on the fly in a context-sensitive way. Recently, there has been increasing interest in the design of systems generating multimedia output. Research in this area addresses the analysis and representation of presentation knowledge (e.g., see [1]) as well as computational methods for the automatic synthesis of multimedia presentations (e.g., see [2,3,4,5,6,7]). There is general agreement that a multimedia presentation system cannot simply merge the results of the medium-specific generators, but has to carefully tailor them to each other. Such tailoring requires knowledge concerning the functions of textual and pictorial document parts and the relations between them. Furthermore, a presentation system must be

* The work presented here is supported by the German Ministry for Research and Technology (BMFT) under grant ITW8901 8.

able to handle the various dependencies between content planning, medium selection and content realization.

2. APPROACH

Since a lot of progress has been made in natural language generation, we were optimistic about generalizing concepts developed for natural language generation in such a way that they become useful for the generation of multimedia presentations, too. In [8], we have shown that pictures and text picture combinations follow the same structuring principles as text. In particular, a multimedia document is characterized by its intentional structure that is reflected by the presenter's intentions and by its rhetorical structure that is characterized by various coherence relations.

Following a speech-act theoretic perspective [9], not only the generation of text, but also the generation of multimedia documents is considered as an act sequence that aims to achieve certain goals (cf. [10]). Presentation acts can be composed of other acts. While the root of the resulting hierarchical structure is a more or less complex presentation act, such as introducing an object, the leaves are formed by elementary speech acts, such as a verbal request, or elementary pictorial acts, such as depicting an object in a certain state. With each presentation act, we can associate a certain presentation goal (e.g., the user should know where a certain object is located).

A number of textlinguists have characterized coherence in terms of coherence relations that hold between the parts of the text (e.g., see [11,12]). In order to find out which relations may occur between textual and pictorial document parts, we analyzed more than 50 illustrated documents. It turned out that the relations between the parts of a picture and between picture parts and text often correspond to the relations found by textlinguists. Example are insets that *elaborate* on the main frame or text that provides an *interpretation* of a picture. On the other hand, there are relations, such as *concession* or *condition*, that are hard to express through pictorial means. Finally, we identified relations that do not appear in the textlinguistic studies mentioned above, e.g., the relation *label* between a text and its title or between picture objects and their labels.

A further extension concerns the representation of a multimedia discourse. In order to enable the generation of appropriate crossreferences from document parts in one medium to parts presented in another medium, we have to maintain an explicit representation of how information has been encoded in a single medium (e.g., graphics) or in a combination of several media (e.g., graphics and text).

3. DESIGNING A PRESENTATION SYSTEM

As pictures and text-picture combinations follow the same structuring principles as text, it has been possible to extend work on text-planning [13] to the broader context of multimedia presentation. In order to represent knowledge about how to present information, we have designed presentation strategies which relate to both text and picture production. These presentation strategies are considered operators of a planning system. The result of the presentation planning process is a hierarchically structured plan of the document to be generated. This plan reflects the propositional contents of the potential document parts, the intentional goals behind the parts and also the rhetorical relationships between them. The leaves of the plan are specifications for elementary acts of presentation that are forwarded to the medium-specific generators. The presentation planner currently orchestrates a text generator [14] and a graphics generator [15]. During the text and graphics generation processes, the individual presentation goals are further refined. A layout component formats the generated text fragments and arranges them together with the designed pictures in a document [16].

When designing an architecture for a multimedia presentation system one has to organize processes for content determination, medium selection and content realization in different media such as text and graphics. It seems inappropriate to sequentialize content determination and medium selection because on the one hand medium selection depends to a large extent on the nature of the information to be conveyed. On the other hand, content determination is strongly influenced by previously selected presentation media. Furthermore, in order to prevent disconcerting or incoherent generation results it is not enough to run the different medium-specific generators independently from each other. Natural language references to graphics, for example, can only be generated if the text generator has access to information concerning the content and the realization of the graphics.

In our approach, we interleave content determination and medium selection by using a uniform planning mechanism. In contrast to this, presentation planning and content realization are performed by separate components. On the one hand, this modularization enables parallel processing, on the other hand it makes interaction between the single components necessary. Interactions are, however, only useful if the realization components have the ability to process information in an incremental manner. As soon as the presentation planner has decided which generator should convey a certain piece of information, the information is forwarded to the respective generator. While the presentation planner selects the next pieces of information to be communicated, the generators simultaneously process previously selected parts.

The result of integrating these components is a prototype of a presentation system called WIP (Knowledge-Based Presentation of Information). The WIP system (for a detailed description, see [17]) has been implemented in Symbolics Common Lisp under Genera 8.0 running on a Symbolics XL1200 and MacIvory workstations.

4. APPLICATIONS AND EXAMPLES OF SYSTEM RUNS

There is a growing application base for intelligent multimedia presentation systems such as WIP. WIP has been designed for interfacing with various back-end systems, such as control panels, information-, tutoring-, expert-, on-line documentation and help systems, which supply the presentation system with the necessary input. In order to test the prototype system, however, we concentrated on the generation of instructions for the maintenance, service and repair of technical devices. The task of the presentation system in this application area is to transform formally represented domain plans [18] for problem solving into comprehensible instructions for human users. As WIP is designed as a presentation system, it does not generate domain plans, they are part of WIP's input and must be provided either by an help system, or manually created - as we did in the test phase. At the moment, three example domains are being tested: preparing espresso, assembling a lawn mower and installing a modem.

The design and generation of a presentation is goal-driven and controlled by a set of generation parameters such as document type, target group, resource limitations, and target language. In order to illustrate the effect of the generation parameters on the presentation let's have a look at an example taken from the modem domain. Suppose WIP is requested to instruct a user in preparing a modem for receiving data. Generation parameters are set via the pop up menu shown in Fig. 1. In the first system run, we assume that the user is an English speaker (Target Language: English) and not familiar with the modem (User Category: Novice). We indicate that we are interested in a short presentation printed in the style of an instruction manual by setting the parameters "Space restricted" to "yes", "Speech Output" to "No", and "Document Type" to "Instruction Manual". As we choose the option incremental output mode, the system begins typing out text fragments and graphical elements as soon as they are generated. Specific medium preferences are not made (Preferred Medium: None). The generated presentation is shown below the parameter menu (cf. Fig. 1). In contrast to a document retrieval system, all parts of the presentation are generated from scratch. The picture is composed of different types of images, the modem image, which results from projecting a 3D wireframe model, a 2D arrow and a formatted text label. In order to design graphics that satisfy particular presentation goals the graphics generator has to apply 3D and 2D illustration techniques. For example, in order to make the code switch visible, the top cover of the modem is shown in an exploded view style. This has been achieved by manipulating the 3D model of the modem before the projection was made. Both the label used in the annotation and the text beside the picture are generated using a lexicalized Tree Adjoining Grammar. The interplay between the presentation planner (messages beginning with "PP:") and the generators (the prefix "TD: indicates the tex generator) is reflected by the trace messages of the single components in WIP's trace window.

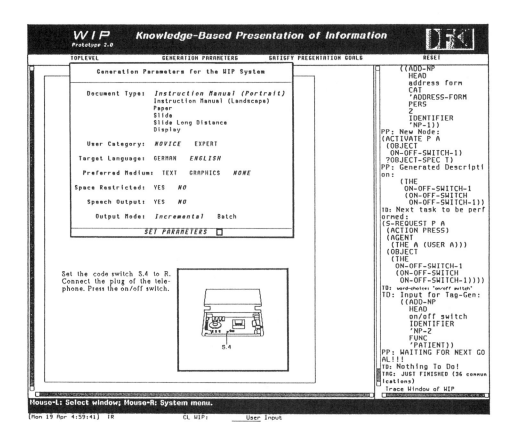

Figure 1. WIP Frame with Parameter Selection Menu and Trace Messages

The presentation planning process is illustrated in Fig. 2. Since the user is assumed not to know how to prepare the modem, the system has decided to provide the domain plan sketched in the left part of Fig. 2. This plan for preparing the modem is a sequence of three actions: setting the modem for reception of data by setting a certain code switch to a certain position, setting up a connection with the telephone line and switching on the modem by pressing the on/off switch. Starting from this domain plan the presentation planner builds up the multimedia discourse structure which is partially shown in the right half of Fig. 2. The initial presentation goal has been decomposed into a sequence of three requests. After further refinements steps, we obtain elementary speech acts and pictorial acts that are processed by the medium-specific generators. For example, the picture showing the location of the code switch relative to the modem as a whole has been generated in order to ensure that the user can localize the involved switch of the first action. Since this information serves to enable the user to carry out the first action, the generated picture is related to the first sentence via the coherence relation Enablement.

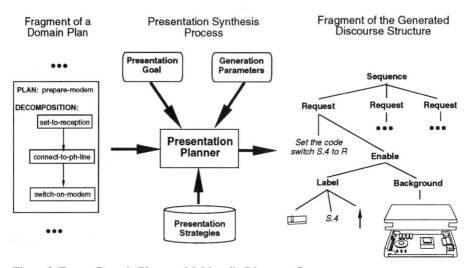

Figure 2. From a Domain Plan to a Multimedia Discourse Structure

Starting the system again with exactly the same presentation goal but different parameter settings generally leads to major changes in the presentation. For example, assuming that the user is a modem expert who knows where the parts are located, there is no need to show object locations in a picture. Fig. 3 shows the generation result after the presentation parameter "User Category" has been set to "Expert". Note that not only the picture has been omitted, but that the text produced has a higher degree of abstraction than in the first example. In a further system run, we demonstrate the influence of the generation parameter "Target Language" (see Fig. 4).

Set for reception. Connect the
plug of the telephone. Turn on
the modem.

Schalten Sie auf Empfang.
Schliessen Sie den Steckver-
binder zu dem Telefon an.
Schalten Sie das Modem ein.

Figure 3.   Generation Result
             (Language: English)

Figure 4.   Generation Result
             (Language: German)

5. CONCLUSION

In this paper, we have described our efforts aimed at the development of an intelligent multimedia presentation system. As coherent presentations cannot be generated by simply merging verbalization and visualization results into multimedia output, the processes for content determination, medium selection and content realization in different media such as text and graphics must be carefully coordinated. We have argued that techniques for planning text and discourse can be generalized to allow the structure and content of multimedia communications to be planned as well.

We have sketched the WIP system as a concrete prototype of a multimedia presentation system. WIP generates illustrated instructions on assembling, using, maintaining or repairing physical devices. The benefit of WIP lies in its ability to present the same information in a variety of ways depending on the value combination of several generation parameters. In order to adapt the system to a new application domain, one has to specify the new application knowledge, to augment the lexicon and to add wireframe models for new domain objects in order to enable the generation of 3D object illustrations. However, our experience has shown that most of the presentation knowledge can be reused when generating maintenance and repair instructions.

REFERENCES:

1 Y. Arens, E. Hovy and M. Vossers. The Knowledge Underlying Multimedia Presentations. In: M. Maybury (ed)., Intelligent Multimedia Interfaces, AAAI Press, to appear.
2 N.I. Badler, B.L. Webber, J. Kalita and J. Esakov. Animation from Instructions. In: N.I. Badler, B.A. Barsky and D. Zeltzer (eds.), Making them Move: Mechanics, Control, and Animation of Articulated Figures, Morgan Kaufmann Publishers: San Mateo, 51-93, 1991.
3 S.K. Feiner and K.R. McKeown. Generating Coordinated Multimedia Explanations. In: 6th IEEE Conference on AI Applications, Santa Barbara, CA, 290-296, 1990.
4 J. Marks and E. Reiter. Avoiding Unwanted Conversational Implicatures in Text and Graphics. In: Proc. of the 8th National Conference on AI, 450-455, 1990.
5 M. Maybury. Planning Multimedia Explanations Using Communicative Acts. In: Proc. of the 9th National Conference on AI, 61-66, 1991.
6 S.F. Roth, J. Mattis and X. Mesnard. Graphics and Natural Language as Components of Automatic Explanation. In: J. Sullivan and S. Tyler (eds.), Intelligent User Interfaces: Elements and Prototypes, Addison-Wesley, 207-239, 1991.
7 W. Wahlster, E. André, W. Graf, and T. Rist. Designing Illustrated Texts: How Language Production Is Influenced by Graphics Generation. In: Proc. of the 5th Conference of the European Chapter of the ACL, Berlin, 8-14, 1991.
8 E. André and T. Rist, The Design of Illustrated Documents as a Planning Task, in: M. Maybury (ed)., Intelligent Multimedia Interfaces, AAAI Press, to appear.
9 J.R. Searle. Speech Acts: An Essay in the Philosophy of Language. Cambridge University Press: Cambridge, MA, 1969.
10 E. André and T. Rist. Towards a Plan-Based Synthesis of Illustrated Documents, in: Proceedings ECAI-90, Stockholm, Sweden, 25-30, 1990.
11 J. Hobbs. Why is a discourse coherent? Technical Report 176, SRI, Menlo Park, CA, 1978.
12 W.C. Mann and S.A. Thompson. Rhetorical Structure Theory: A Theory of Text Organization. In: P. Polanyi (ed.), The Structure of Discourse, Ablex: Norwood, 1987.
13 J.D. Moore and C.L. Paris. Planning Text for Advisory Dialogues. In: Proc. of the 27th Annual Meeting of the ACL, 203-211, 1989.
14 K. Harbusch, W. Finkler, A. Schauder, Incremental Syntax Generation with Tree Adjoining Grammars, in: Proc. 4th International GI Congress, Munich, 363-374, 1991.
15 T. Rist and E. André. From Presentation Tasks to Pictures: Towards a Computational Approach to Graphics Design, in: Proc. of ECAI-92, Vienna, Austria, 764-768, 1992.
16 W. Graf, LAYLAB - A Constraint-Based Layout Manager for Multimedia Presentations, this volume.
17 W. Wahlster, E. André, W. Finkler, H.-J. Profitlich, and T. Rist. Plan-Based Integration of Natural Language and Graphics Generation. In: AI Journal 26(3), 1993.
18 J. Heinsohn, D. Kudenko, B. Nebel and H.-J. Profitlich. RAT - Representation of Actions using Terminological Logics. DFKI Report, Saarbrücken, Germany, 1992.

Aspects of Multimodal and Multimedia Human-Computer Interaction

K.-P. Fähnrich[1] and K.-H. Hanne[2]

[1]Fraunhofer Institut für Arbeitswirtschaft und Organisation,
Nobelstr.12, 70569 Stuttgart, Germany,
Tel.: +49 711 970 2410, Fax.: +49 711 970 2401

[2]European Community-VALUE-Relay Centre,
Willi-Bleicher-Str. 19, 70174 Stuttgart, Germany
Tel.: +49 711 123 1 321, Fax.: +49 711 123 1 322

Keywords: Multimodal human-computer interaction, gestures
recognition, combined interaction, system-architecture

1   Human Computer Interaction Styles

Human computer interaction (HCI) can be based on interaction models. The IFIP-Model is best known for a layered structure of HCI (cmp. e.g. [1]). Interaction forms are under intensive research and can be distinguished according to DIN 66234 part 8 [2] and ISO 9241 part 10 [3]. In our research-oriented model we focus on three interaction modes:

- Natural language, direct manipulation and formal interaction languages.

1.1   Is Natural-Language-Interaction "Natural" for HCI?

In NL interaction, a specific class of expressions - deictic expressions or deictics - is of major importance, and a crucial point in NL-based human-computer-interaction. Since NL in NL-Systems is always used in a certain situation, at a certain time, and at a certain place, by people (or systems) who share a great deal of both general knowledge and situational perception, the comprehension of NL depends on these factors and can be expressed by means of deictic expressions.

1.2   Direct Manipulation "Direct on the Screen?"

"Direct Manipulation" was suggested by SHNEIDERMAN [4]. The basic idea of Direct Manipulation is the visual presentation of the working environment along with objects of immediate interest in a symbolic or mnemotechnical form. The user can interact directly with the graphical objects displayed on the screen with rapid, incremental, reversible operations, whose impacts on the object of interest are immediately visible.

1.3   Formal Interaction Languages

The communication interaction style "formal interaction language" denotes essentially formal languages in the mathematical sense, especially programming and command languages, and other classical user initiated interaction styles with restricted conceptual and semantic models.

2   COMBINED (MULTIMODAL) HUMAN-COMPUTER INTERACTION

The mentioned interaction modes are usually realized separately. Combined multimodal human-computer interfaces try to share the advantages of the different generic communication modes avoiding their disadvantages. Figure 1 shows the scope of human communication and special aspects of deictic and gestural interaction possibilities as examples of multimodal interaction.

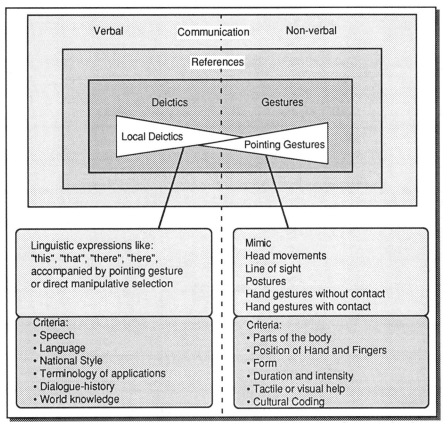

Figure 1: Gestures vs. Deictics in the Field of Human Communication

3   GESTURES: A MIX OF NL AND DM OR MORE?

In human-human communication, gestures play a crucial role (both in isolated expressions and in combination with natural language). Gestures, for example pointing actions accompanying verbal conversations, are indispensable for the creation of references to objects in our "world"[5]. In general pointing or other gestures (alone or in combination with natural language) can be ambiguous. The ambiguity can be solved by NL or by conventions. The meanings and special rules of the intended application have to be learned. The development and the implementation of gestural interaction [6], with special regards to object oriented DM-user interfaces, introduce advantages [7].

4   GESTURES IN COMBINED HCI-SYSTEMS

In many computer applications that work with graphic objects, there is the simple possibility of combining natural language and graphic objects by pointing or selecting objects and operations. In HCI the power of such combined NL/ DM interfaces lies in the possibility of allowing the above mentioned deictic interactions on screen-oriented objects. The effectiveness, the practicality of the implementation, and the advantages are described, for example, in [8]; the inclusion of restricted parts of NL in the graphical interface is implemented, for example, in an ESPRIT-project [9], while additional systems show the advantages in their technical applications in particular.

5   KNOWLEDGE REPRESENTATION IN MULTIMODAL HCI-SYSTEMS

The combination of different HCI-modes in one system requires a coordinating mechanism for the parallel access to and manipulation of the knowledge of the system (based on a suitable knowledge representation). Models for this coordinated access to the system´s knowledge are the following.
*   Knowledge Representation without Common Representation
*   Blackboard Architecture for Common Representation
*   Separaration of Domain Knowledge

In the last model, the common conceptual representation is split in two parts (views). The application system (a NL-System, an expert system, or a traditional application) represents its knowledge appropriately but independent from the other view of the interaction-module (cmp. [10] and figure 2).

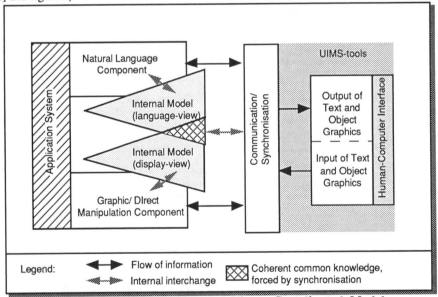

Figure 2: Model 3: Separated Views, Coordinated Models

The primary idea of this approach is the understanding that both representations are only different views of the same, basic underlaying knowledge. Besides, a third view can realise the interaction with formal interaction language (the third HCI-mode in the triad). But, because both and DM systems are based on implementations of programming languages (or formal languages), this approach can be subsumed in the other modes.

6   APPLICATIONS OF GESTURE INTERFACES

Gestures are sequences of single strokes or movements in the 2 or 3-dimensional space, performed either by humans or by any other observable object. It is possible to introduce a representation, a gesture description language ([11], [12]), in other existing knowledge representation systems or schemes.
Gesture recognition is an adequate tool for character recognition. Advantages are:

- Independence of the starting point, the size, and to a certain amount, the drawing angle.
- Independence of the drawing speed (only the sequence of strokes is important).
- Independence (in a certain environment) of the length of single strokes.
- Easy, understandable and extensible symbolic description of hand movements or other trajectories.
- All writing directions are possible.

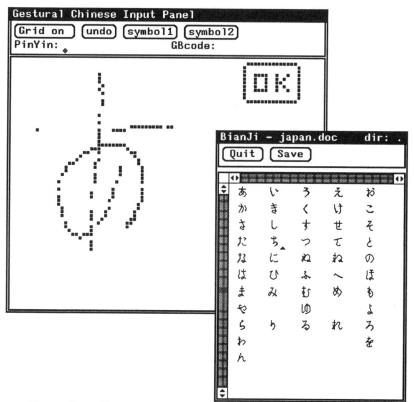

Figure 3:   **Gesture driven character recognition (Hiragana)**

Figure 3 shows an example of the developed Japanese character editor. Chinese and Japanese (Hiragana and Katakana) characters are determined by the sequence of a relatively small repertoire of single strokes. A "delete"-command can be activated by crossing out one or more characters.

444

Even the creation of handwritten letters or the application of correction signs can be seen as gesture input using a stylus or another pointing device on a suitable surface. The available gesture language, and the developed systems allow for the implementation of more characters, inclusion of handwritten capital letters and of the mentioned recognition of user dependant cursive handwriting.

If a text is already accessible in a text system allowing stylus input on a tablet or directly on the (flat) screen corrections can be done on the screen like on a sheet of paper using some private or standardized correction sign. Figure 4 shows an example of our prototype allowing this style of interaction.

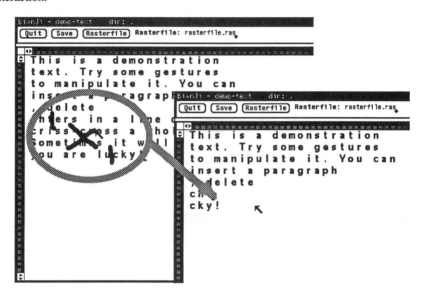

Figure 4: Correction sign with gestures (Screendump from IAO system)

7   FUTURE APPLICATIONS

Currently, approaches that incorporate gestures or combine NL and DM suffer from two weaknesses:

- Typed natural language is not sufficient for HCI. Speech is more convenient than typing and is already realized in some applications with rather restricted vocabularies.
- Pointing actions are usually restricted to single selections by means of a mouse, or a stylus on a bitmap screen. However, pointing on the screen with a mouse is not the solution we are aiming at in our research work. Instead, more advanced methods can be developed to allow input and recognition of gestures which are "painted" on the screen or on a touch-sensitive device, or are performed in a "Virtual Reality" environment ([13], 14]).

If these waknesses can be reduced by new technologies and systems possible applications of gesture interpretation and gesture description languages are, for example:

- Addition of classes of commands in graphical applications.
- Recognition of simple standard editing signs in word processing systems (with special emphasis on notebook computers without keyboards)
- Manipulation of formulae such as sketching, drafting and input in text systems

- Classification and interpretation of bio-signals (for example ECG) and technical signals
- Trajectories: Symbolic description of movements in 2- or 3-dimensional spaces
- Eye-movements which can be interpreted as gestures
- Character recognition through handwriting.

8 REFERENCES

1   Bullinger, H.-J.; Fähnrich, K.-P.: Symbiotic Man-Computer-Interfaces and the User Assistent Concept. In: Human Computer Interaction/ Edited by G. Salvendy. Amsterdam a. o.: Elsevier, 1984.

2   Standard/ Norm DIN 66234 Part 8 1988: Bildschirmarbeitsplätze, Part 8 - Grundzüge ergonomischer Dialoggestaltung. Berlin: Beuth, 1988.

3   Standard ISO 9241 (Committee Draft): Ergonomic Requirements for Office Work with Visual Display Terminals. Part 10: Dialogue Principles. Workingpaper ISO/TC 159/SC 4 /WG 5. 1991.

4   Görner, C.; Vossen, P.; Ziegler, J.: Direct Manipulation Interface. In: Methods and Tools in User-Centred Design for Information Technology/ Edited by M. Galer, S. Harker and J. Ziegler. Amsterdam a. o.: Elsevier, 1992, Chapter 8, pp 237-279.

5   Schmauks, D.: Deixis in der Mensch-Maschine-Interaktion, Multimediale Referentenidentifikation durch natürliche und simulierte Zeigegesten. Tübingen: Niemeyer,1991 and Saarbrücken, University, Ph.D. Thesis, 1990.

6   Pausch, R.; Williams, R. D.: Tailor: Creating Custom User Interfaces Based on Gesture. Univ. of Virginia, Computer Science Report TR-90-06, March, 1990.

7   Hoepelman, J.; Hanne, K.-H.: New Developments in Human-Computer Interaction, In: Handbuch des Informationsmanagements im Unternehmen/ Edited by H.-J. Bullinger. Munich: Beck, 1991, Vol 1, pp 867-893 (in German).

8   Hanne, K.-H.; Bullinger, H.-J.: Multimodal Communication: Integrating Text and Gestures. In: Multimedia and Multimodal Interface Design/ Edited by M. Blattner and R. Dannenberg. Reading: ACM Press, Addison Wesley, 1992, Chapter 8, pp 127-138.

9   Binot, J. L;. Demoen, B.; Hanne, K.-H.; Solomon, L.; Vassiliou, Y.; von Hahn, W.; Wachtel, T.: LOKI: A Logic Oriented Approach to Data and Knowledge Bases Supporting Natural Language Interaction. In: Proceedings 5th Annual ESPRIT Conference, 14.-17. Nov. 1988 in Brussels/ Edited by Commission of the European Communities. Amsterdam a. o.: Elsevier 1988, pp 562-577.

10   Hanne, K.-H.: Systems of combined multimodal Man-Computer-Interaktions, In: IPA/ IAO Forschung und Praxis, Vol. 175, Berlin, New York: Springer, 1993. (in German)

11   Wetzel, P.: Recognition of Gestures in the Dialogue of Blind User with the Computer. Stuttgart, University, Master Thesis, 1988 (in German).

12   Weber, G FINGER- A Language for Gesture Recognition. In: Proceedings INTERACT`90/ Edited by D. Diaper et al. Amsterdam a. o.: Elsevier, 1990, pp 689-694.

13   Marcus, A.; Lanier, J.: "Beyond the Desktop Metaphor". Presentation on Conference CHI 90, SIG 2, Seattle, April 3rd, 1990.

14   Lanier, J.: The Arrival of Virtual Reality in the Real World, Presentation on NATO-ASI Workshop on Multimedia Interface Design in Education, Castel Vecchio Pascoli, Italy, Sept. 1989.

LAYLAB - A Constraint-Based Layout Manager for Multimedia Presentations[1]

Winfried H. Graf

German Research Center for Artificial Intelligence (DFKI), Stuhlsatzenhausweg 3, W-6600 Saarbrücken 11, Germany, graf@dfki.uni-sb.de

Abstract

When developing advanced intelligent user interfaces composing text, graphics, animation, hypermedia etc., the question of automatically designing the graphical layout of such multimedia presentations in an appropriate format plays a crucial role. This paper introduces the task, the functionality and the architecture of the constraint-based multimedia layout manager LayLab.

1 Introduction

Due to the growing complexity of information that has to be communicated by current AI systems, there comes an increasing need for building sophisticated intelligent user interfaces that take advantage of a coordinated combination of different media and modalities, including graphics, canned and generated text, animation, hypermedia, virtual realities etc., to produce a flexible and efficient information presentation. Therefore, to communicate generated mutlimodal information to the user in an expressive and effective manner, a knowledge-based layout component should be an integral element of each intelligent multimedia presentation system. A layout manager has at its disposal a wide range of multimedia output and will seek to combine these to best effect. In order to achieve a coherent and consistent output, it must be able to reflect certain semantic and pragmatic relations specified by a presentation planner [18].

As with many other interesting AI design problems, the determination of an aesthetically pleasing layout can be viewed as a discrete combinatorial problem. In this paper, we will illustrate the exploitation of advanced constraint processing techniques such as constraint hierarchies, intelligent backtracking mechanisms and incremental compilation by the example of the *LayLab* testbed system [11], the automatic layout manager of the multimedia presentation system *WIP* (Knowledge-based Presentation of Information, cf. [20,1]). LayLab addresses a dynamic adaptation of multimedia presentations to

---

[1]The research reported in this paper has been carried out in the WIP project (Knowledge-based Presentation of Information) which is supported by the German Ministry for Research and Technology under contract ITW 8901 8.

achieve an expressive and effective output with high coherence. Here, we view layout as an important carrier of meaning.

2 Related Research

As graphics hardware becomes more and more sophisticated, computer-based multimedia communication achieves a crucial role in intelligent user interfaces (cf. [19,17,4,16]). While much work in this area has been focused on the automatic synthesis of graphics, the automatic layout design of multimedia presentations has only recently received significant attention in artificial intelligence research. Some interesting early efforts focused on rules and design grids to automating display layout (e.g., [2,7]). Recent approaches investigate more sophisticated techniques such as constraint-based and case-based reasoning methods for representing graphical design knowledge (e.g., [14,10]). The importance of a deeper treatment of multimodal constraints in information presentation in order to address the ergonomic aspects of layout has also been stressed by [5].

Further representative research related to in this paper entered the area between interactive graphics and constraint systems, e.g., the constraint-oriented simulation laboratory *ThingLab* [3,15] developed at Xerox PARC. Up to now only rudimentary work has been done in the area of layout of dynamic presentations. *Animus* [6] is one of the first systems that allows for easy construction of an animation with minimal concern for lower-level graphics programming. Here temporal constraints are used to describe the appearance and structure of a picture as well as as how those pictures evolve in time. In an application of the *Kaleidoscope* language [8], temporal constraints are used to update the display of graphical objects which are manipulated by mouse actions interactively and maintain their consistency requirements.

The importance of the text layout dimension has also been stressed by recent work at USC/ISI [13] that involves the generation of formatted text exploiting the communicative function of so–called textual devices.

3 Adaptive Multimedia Layout

A fundamental goal of our work is to construct a universal framework for automatic layout management, as an integrated component of a multimedia presentation system, that makes intelligent use of human visual abilities and design parameters whenever arranging multimedia output in any kind of presentation. Thus, from the functional viewpoint the main task of a knowledge-based layout manager is to convey certain semantic and pragmatic relations specified by a presentation planner to arrange the visual appearance of a mixture of multimedia fragments delivered by media-specific generators, i.e., to determine the precise size of the individual layout elements and the exact coordinates for positioning them in the presentation space (see Fig. 1). LayLab deals with page layout as a rhetorical force, influencing the intentional and attentional state of the reader.

One of our major design goals is the generation of highly adaptive interfaces which can be tailored to the needs and requirements of an intended target audience and situation.

448

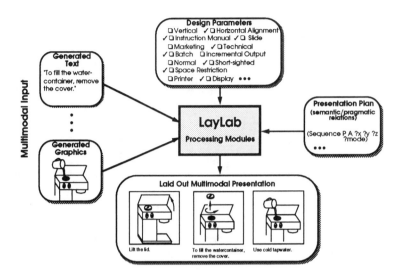

Figure 1: A Functional View on LayLab

So, the generation of a layout is controlled by a set of design parameters such as user's layout preferences, presentation type, presentation intention, output mode (incremental vs. complete only), resource limitations, output medium, and more.

4   The Architecture of the LayLab System

The design of LayLab's conceptual architecture follows a modular approach embedding a positioning component, a grid generation module, an intelligent typographer, a document beautifier and an interaction handler (see Fig. 2).

A central idea underlying automatic layout of multimedia presentations is the incorporation of application domain-specific knowledge as well as commonsense knowledge about basic design heuristics into the design process, i.e., an encoding of procedural and declarative geometric knowledge (cf. also [11]). We use automatically generated superimposed grid structures as an ordering framework for efficiently designing functional layouts. As has been proven in previous work (e.g., [10]), constraint processing techniques provide an elegant mechanism to specify layout requirements in graphical environments as well as to declaratively state design-relevant knowledge about heterogeneous geometrical relationships, characterizing properties between different kinds of multimedia items that can be maintained by the underlying system.

Therefore, Laylab exploits a sophisticated constraint solver model comprising two dedicated solvers for handling different kinds of graphical constraints defined on constraint hierarchies and finite domains. An incremental constraint hierarchy solver based on the *DeltaBlue* algorithm [9] and a domain solver that handles finite domains using forward checking (cf. [12]) are integrated in a layered model and are triggered from a common

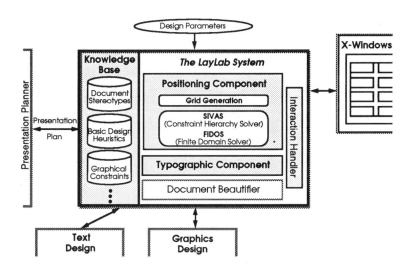

Figure 2: The Architecture of LayLab

meta level by rules and defaults. The underlying constraint language is able to encode graphical design knowledge expressed by semantic/pragmatic, geometrical/topological, and temporal relations. As in interactive graphical environments constraints frequently have only local effects and the constraint solver must be capable of finding solutions without reducing the direct manipulation responsiveness, they have to be incrementally generated by the system on the fly. The text layout problem has also been addressed by a constraint-based approach. Here, high-level specifications of relations between textual devices are expressed by constraints which can be compiled into low-level text formatting routines.

5 Integration and Implementation

Considering this architecture, a complete layout design is achieved stepwise via a refinement process. So, layout considerations can influence the early stages of the presentation planning process and constrain the media-specific generators. To handle dependencies between content generation and layout generation, WIP enables bidirectional communication to take place between the layout manager and the presentation planner. In case a revision of layout is deemed necessary layout manager and presentation planner must negotiate.

A prototype version of the LayLab system has been implemented on a Symbolics XL 1200 Lisp machine and several MacIvory workstations under Genera 8.0 using Symbolics Common Lisp/CLOS and Flavors for object-oriented interface programming and it is fully integrated in the overall WIP system.

6 Conclusions and Future Work

As a first step towards a conceptual framework for managing layout of multimedia presentations we have outlined the architecture of the multimedia layout manager LayLab. While the previous work has concentrated on constraint formalisms for supporting the layout design of static text-picture presentations, most of our current research is concerned with generalizing this constraint-based approach towards interactive layout design including further modalities like dynamic and canned presentation parts (e.g., hypermedia, animation, video). Here, the layout manager will be concerned with arranging the generated multimedia output as well as managing the interface to the user and the application. Since animated multimedia presentations can enhance the effectiveness and expressiveness of both, the visualization of the incremental layout process and dynamic application scenarios, animated layout is another area of our future research. A next version of the system will allow the user to tailor the interface to his needs by editing incrementally laid out presentations, changing default layout schemata interactively or working on virtual displays.

References

[1] E. André, W. Finkler, W. Graf, T. Rist, A. Schauder, and W. Wahlster. WIP: The automatic synthesis of multimodal presentations. In Maybury [16].

[2] R. Beach. *Setting Tables and Illustrations with Style*. PhD thesis, Dept. of Computer Science, University of Waterloo, Ontario, 1985.

[3] A. Borning. The programming language aspects of ThingLab, a constraint-oriented simulation laboratory. *ACM Transactions on Programming Languages and Systems*, 3(4):353–387, October 1981.

[4] T. Catarci, M. F. Costabile, and S. Levialdi, editors. *Advanced Visual Interfaces, Proceedings of the International Workshop AVI '92*. World Scientific Series in Computer Science - Vol. 36. World Scientific Press, Singapore, 1992.

[5] R. Dale. Visible language: Multimedia constraints in information presentation. In R. Dale, E. Hovy, D. Rösner, and O. Stock, editors, *Aspects of Automated Natural Language Generation*, pages 281–283. Springer-Verlag, Berlin, Germany, 1992.

[6] R. Duisberg. Animation Using Temporal Constraints: An Overview of the Animus System. In *Human-Computer Interaction*, pages 275–307. Lawrence Erlbaum Associates, Hillsdale, NJ, 1987.

[7] S. Feiner. A grid-based approach to automating display layout. In *Proceedings of the Graphics Interface '88*, pages 192–197. Morgan Kaufmann, Los Altos, CA, June 1988.

[8] B. Freeman-Benson. Kaleidoscope: Mixing Objects, Constraints, and Imperative Programming. In N. Meyrowitz, editor, *Proceedings of ECOOP-OOPSLA '90*, pages 77–88, Ottawa, Canada, October 1990.

[9] B. Freeman-Benson, J. Maloney, and A. Borning. An incremental constraint solver. *Communications of the ACM*, 33(1):54–63, 1990.

[10] W. Graf. Constraint-Based Processing of Design Knowledge. In *Proceedings of the AAAI-91 Workshop on 'Intelligent Multimedia Interfaces'*, Anaheim, CA, July 1991.

[11] W. Graf. Constraint-based graphical layout of multimodal presentations. In Catarci et al. [4], pages 365–385.

[12] P. V. Hentenryck. *Constraint Satisfaction in Logic Programming*. MIT Press, Cambridge, MA, 1989. Revision of Ph.D. thesis, University of Namur, 1987.

[13] E. Hovy and Y. Arens. Automatic generation of formatted text. In *Proceedings of the 9th National Conference of the American Association for Artificial Intelligence*, pages 92–97, Anaheim, CA, July 1991.

[14] R. MacNeil. Adaptive Persepectives: Case-based Reasoning with TYRO, the Graphics Designer's Apprentice. In *Proceedings of the IEEE Workshop on Visual Languages*, 1990.

[15] J. Maloney, A. Borning, and B. Freeman-Benson. Constraint technology for user-interface construction in ThingLabII. In *Proceedings of OOPSLA '89 (Object-Oriented Programming Systems, Languages, and Applications)*, pages 381–388, October 1989.

[16] M. Maybury, editor. *Intelligent Multimedia Interfaces*. AAAI Press, Menlo Park, CA, 1993. Forthcoming.

[17] A. Ortony, J. Slack, and O. Stock, editors. *Communication from an Artificial Intelligence Perspective: Theoretical and Applied Issues*. Springer-Verlag, Berlin, Germany, 1992.

[18] T. Rist and E. André. Designing coherent multi-media presentations. In present volume.

[19] J. Sullivan and S. Tyler, editors. *Intelligent User Interfaces*. Frontier Series. ACM Press, New York, NY, 1991.

[20] W. Wahlster, E. André, S. Bandyopadhyay, W. Graf, and T. Rist. WIP: The coordinated generation of multimodal presentations from a common representation. In Ortony et al. [17], pages 121–144.

Toward a Walkthrough method for Multimedia Design.

Peter Faraday and Alistair Sutcliffe,

Centre for Human Computer Interface Design,

City University, Northampton Square, London EC1 0NV, United Kingdom.

Abstract

A basic model of Multimedia comprehension is proposed. The model is used to demonstrate how a Walkthrough critiquing method may be developed for MM presentations. An expository presentation (changing a Laser Writer toner cartridge) is used to illustrate the methodology.

1 Introduction

This paper aims to show how a design walkthrough methodology can be used to evaluate comprehension problems within viewers of an expository ('how-to-do-it') MM presentation. A cognitive model is used to generate a set of evaluatory steps, which are then reviewed.

2 A Model of Multimedia Comprehension

There is no theoretical analysis of 'Multimedia cognition'. To generate such a field requires the joining of theories of verbal and visual comprehension. This work can be seen as the union of a model of text comprehension [19], object comprehension [5] and action comprehension [10]. The model generated from the cognitive psychology literature covers MM comprehension across text, still images, image sequences and animation. The following basic process steps are postulated:

(i) The presentation is scanned by visual attention and processed by low level visual recognisers to form an object model [14]. Text objects are further processed through the lexicon to form propositions [19]; other objects are bundled into object files [18]. These form the basic units drawn from the presentation (presentation units).

(ii) The model proposes that all media are subsequently processed within a common Construction - Integration mechanism [12]. The presentation is combined with existing, related knowledge schemas from Long Term Memory. The Construction phase instatiates knowledge schema's related to the presentation information. Integration then draws together the knowledge schema's and the presentation units using a set of macro-rules [19] : by either 'generalisation' (combining several presentation units with LTM schema's, eg a set of objects within the presentation generalised as a 'Laser Printer' within a Laser Printer schema), 'construction' (addition of schema information to that from the presentation unit eg the knowledge of actions that may be performed on the Laser Writer) or 'deletion' (the deletion of presentation units not related within the instantiated LTM schema's eg the deletion of the set of presentation units which formed the Laser Writer object).

(iii) The result of the Integration process are amodal 'macro-propositions' representing the 'gist' or meaning conveyed within the presentation. Empirical accounts of macro-proposition formation can be found in [1] for text comprehension; [15] for object comprehension within images; [7] for action comprehension in animation or sequences of images; [8] for the amodal nature of macro-propositions.

Most of the presentation units are now lost within the macro-proposition, although a limited set of the most relevant units are stored within media specific working memory stores - the text base [19] and visual working memory [9]. This provides the 'topic focus' for processing subsequent presentation units. The topic focus supports 'argument repetition' across presentation units : eg ellipsis within text, object coherence within and between images. If argument repetition fails (a presentation unit is re-encountered that is not in topic focus) then it must be reinstated from episodic LTM (at an expense to the speed and accuracy of comprehension).

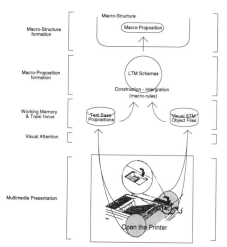

Figure 1. The basic comprehension model.

(iv) As further presentation units are processed, the macro-propositions formed are linked together within a 'macro-structure' [6] - lower level macro-propositions (representing the surface presentation content) are Integrated together to form higher level macro-propositions (increasing abstraction of semantics from the presentation). 'Structure shift' [6] or the formation of a new macro-structure, takes place at thematic boundaries within the presentation - located from signifier words in text (eg 'next', 'later'); picture sequences or animation's which do not maintain object or action invariants (no related objects between pictures, or movement of objects not related to a possible action eg 'over cutting'). Following a structure shift the working memory stores are purged and lower level macro-propositions are lost [6].

4 An initial 'walkthough' for expository multimedia presentations.

4.1 Comprehending an expository multimedia presentation

By using the theory in section (2), a 'good' expository multimedia presentation can be defined as one which (a) contains the required information for the task (4.2) and (b) is 'read' by a viewer who has sufficient 'mental skills' [17] or cognitive resources to extract and comprehend the information. The cognitive resources of the viewer refers to an ability to successfully execute processes (i) to (iv) outlined in section (2). The required mental skills can be left to chance to activate themselves within the viewer or can be assisted by providing the required result of the mental skill within the presentation itself.

 Figure 2. . The pictures show the task steps 'Open the Printer' then 'Remove the toner cartridge', but will the viewer attend to the right information, have the right knowledge schema and form the right macro-proposition?

The walkthrough is concerned with comparing the information that the model predicts will be comprehended from a designed presentation with the information requirements of the task model.

4.2 The information content of the presentation

An expository presentation can be categorised as being made up of a combination of information types [2] : Descriptive (nature of objects in a particular state - physical, spatial and temporal information), Operational (actions performed upon objects - change in spatial and temporal information) and Rhetorical or Organising information (co-variant or organising information eg cause - effect, sequence ordering of other information within the presentation).

The task is analysed using a TKS [11] style analysis, giving a set of procedures each containing actions upon objects. Information types are then attached to each (objects require descriptive information, actions require operational / rhetorical information, procedures require rhetorical information)

4.3 Evaluating what will be attended to within the presentation

The correct presentation units need to be attended to provide the information requirements for the task step. Attention is 'activated' by default to 'unusual' presentation units (those which do not fit within LTM knowledge schema expectations) or to those which the viewer is explicitly looking for due to some internal task.

Open the Printer

Figure 3.
Several presentation techniques may be combined. A zoom and a text part ('the Printer') are used to draw attention to descriptive object information; an arrow, freeze frame and text part ('Open') are used to give operational information.

Presentation techniques can be used to draw viewers attention to presentation units (figure 3). Example presentation techniques for descriptive information are : use of highlighting upon an object (physical, spatial); zooming in or out on an object (physical, spatial if background object(s) left in view); using a descriptive text part or caption to give an object identifier or descriptor (physical) or specifying relationship between objects (spatial), underlining the part to draw attention to it from other text; freeze framing an object arrangement in an animation (temporal - point in time). Example techniques for operational information are : use of learnt symbols eg blurring or speedlines (spatial); learnt signs eg arrow (spatial), using an action text part or caption, underlining the part to draw attention to it from other text; freeze framing an object away from its expected rest position (spatial); cutting or starting a new frame in a picture sequence (temporal).

These guidelines are used to assess which presentation units and associated information types will be attended to within a multimedia interface. This can then be evaluated against the information needs of the particular task step being presented.

4.4 Evaluating topic focus and argument repetition.

Argument repetition is evaluated by listing physical information within the presentation (object appearance, identifier or descriptor text part) and comparing it with that required in each task step (eg 'toner cartridge' presentation unit should be identified as the same object in all task steps that require it). The interface should insure that the physical information is given in a consistent presentation unit (use the same object appearance, identifier or descriptor) and should use several presentation units simultaneously to convey the same physical information (eg object appearance and identifier, descriptor caption or label).

Topic focus holds presentation units which are judged to be most important across the presentation - this will generally be those which have been attended to explicitly. The topic focus is maintained by the 'leading-edge rule' [19] : those units which are often repeated are held, whilst others are lost to Episodic LTM . It is thus necessary that the presentation units which are to be repeated subsequently are attended to initially (eg using techniques in 4.3). Irrelevant units will take up space within the topic focus (text proposition topic focus is limited to 4-5 presentation units [19] although the visual topic focus limit is of an unspecified size [9]). Figure 4 illustrates how an incorrect topic focus can lead to a failure in the presentation and require either an expensive search of Episodic LTM or the re-viewing of the lost presentation unit.

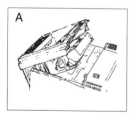 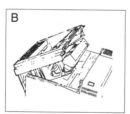

Figure 4. Picture (A) is likely to give a topic focus representing an open printer 'lid'. Picture (B) was intended to show that the 'Jam light' has changed to 'off' (right corner). An incorrect topic focus upon the 'lid' thus causes the presentation to fail - (A) should have stored the light. A highlight technique (4.3) would rectify this failure.

4.5 Acquiring the viewers available knowledge schema's

The knowledge schema's related to the task can be elicited using schema acquisition techniques such as laddering [16]. These techniques applied to each task step would give a description of information schema's the viewer should have available to process the presentation (eg typically only physical information about the exterior of the Laser Writer). It is assumed that the viewer would recognise the Laser Writer itself by its external appearance, may recognise the toner cartridge, but is unlikely to recognise any of the objects in its interior (fixing assembly cover, fixing roller etc). The viewer is also unlikely to have any knowledge schema's relating possible actions on objects required to perform the 'change toner cartridge' task.

4.6 Evaluating the macro-propositions formed

A macro-proposition will be formed by macro-rules (generalisation, construction, deletion) which combine the presentation units attended to (4.3) with any relevant knowledge schema's (4.5) the viewer may possess. The macro-propositions formed at a particular point can be elicited by the use of recall techniques, such as verbal protocols (though due to the iterative nature of macro-proposition formation, recall must be solicited before structure shift takes place).

The process of macro-proposition formation can be assisted by providing summary or 'advanced organiser' information within the presentation (eg a 'long shot' in film [13] or a summary picture [3]), which will help to activate knowledge schema's to process subsequent macro-propositions within.

Which presentation units are required to be intergrated for a particular task step macro-proposition can also be assisted by design : rhetorical information can be given to organise a set of presentation units for a particular task step (eg cause - effect : caption 'press the release latch to open the printer lid' would combine together pictures of the release latch being de-pressed together with pictures of the lid opening into a single macro-proposition).

4.7 Evaluating the macro-structure

As the presentation is comprehended and macro-propositions are formed, they are joined together and structured within LTM. The 'chucks' of presentation recalled will be probably associated with when structure shifts took place during comprehension [6]. Shifts are hypothesised as taking place following attention to certain signifiers within the presentation eg presentation units drawing attention to temporal information (either points in time eg text part "next", "then"; fades or dissolves in animation) ; or presentation units not fitting within the macro-proposition being formed (thematic shift or failure to maintain object or action continuity). Following the structure shift, the previous macro-proposition will become less available and the topic focus will be lost.

Structure shifting can be effected within presentation design by providing organising information at the start of the presentation to indicate where shifts are to take place and assist the viewer to activate them at the correct point. Techniques such as an 'advanced organiser' or summary may be used. Within a presentation shifts can be encouraged by the use of numbering, sequences or formatting (sections, titles). Drawing attention to temporal information shift signifiers will also aid their activation.

5 Conclusion

This paper has attempted to define a model of MM comprehension and show how it may be used to produce an evaluatory walkthrough technique. A great deal more work is required : both on the model itself and on fully documenting how a walkthrough might actually be done upon an expository presentation. However, it is hoped that the methodology will prove useful - especially in providing a firmer rationale behind the design of presentation planning for multimedia interfaces [4].

References

1 Anderson, R.C. (1984) Role of readers schema in comprehension, learning and memory. Psychology of Reading and Reading Instruction, pg 243 - 257.

2 Bieger, G.R. & Glock M.D. (1984) The information content of picture text instructions. Journal of Experimental Education, 53, 68-76.

3 Bransford, J.D. & Johnston , M.K. (1972) Contextual pre-requisites for understanding : some investigations of comprehension and recall. Journal of Verbal Learning and Behaviour,11, 93 - 100

4 Fiener, S. (1990) Generating co-ordinated Multimedia explanations. In 6th IEEE conference on AI applications (Santa Barbara CA) (pg 290 - 296)

5 Freidman, A. (1979) Framing Pictures : The role of knowledge in automatised encoding and memory for Gist. Journal of Experimental Psychology : General. vol 108, no 3, 316 - 355.

6 Gernsbacher, M.A. (1985) Surface Information loss in comprehension. Cognitive Psychology, 17, 324 - 363

7 Hanson, C. & Hirst, W. (1989) On the representation of events : a study of orientation, recall and recognition. Journal of Experimental Psychology : General, vol 118, no 2, 136 - 147.

8 Intraub, H. & Hoffman, J.E (1992) Reading and visual memory : Remembering scenes that were never seen. American Journal of Psychology, vol 105, no 1, 101 - 114.

9 Irwin, D. (1992) Visual memory within and across fixations. In Eye Movements and Visual Cognition (ed K. Rayner), 147 - 165. Springer - Verlag : New York.

10 Jenkins, J.J (1986) Apprehending Pictorial Events. In Event cognition (eds V. McCabe & G. Balzano), 117 - 133.

11 Johnson, P. & Johnson, H. (1988) Task-Related Knowledge structures. In People & Computer IV (eds D.M Jones & R.Winder), 35 - 63.

12 Kintsch, W. (1988) The role of knowledge in Discourse comprehension : A construction - integration model. Psychological Review, vol 95, no 2, 163 - 182.

13 Kraft, R., Cantor, P., Gottdiener, C. (1991) The Coherence of Visual Narratives. Communication Research, vol 18, no 5, 601 - 616.

14 Marr, D. (1982) Vision. San Francisco : W. H. Freeman.

15 Pezdek, K. (1989) Memory for real world scenes : the role of consistency with schema expectations. Journal of Experimental Psychology : Learning Memory & Cognition. Vol 15, no 4, 587 - 595.

16 Rugg, G. (1992) On Laddering. Technical Report LG-4-92. Department of Psychology, University of Aberdeen.

17 Salomon, G. (1981) Interaction of Media, Cognition and Learning. San Franciscio : Jossey-Bass.

18 Treismann, A. (1988) Features and Objects. The Quarterly Journal of Experimental Psychology, 40 (2) 201 - 237.

19 Van Dijk, T.A. & Kintsch, W. (1983) Strategies of Discourse Comprehension. New York: Academic Press.

MULTI-MEDIA SUPPORT FOR UP-STREAM USER INTERFACE DESIGN ACTIVITIES

K.Mouzakis and S.Howard,
Swinburne Computer Human Interaction Laboratory (SCHIL), Centre for Systems Methodologies, Department of Computer Science, Swinburne University of Technology, PO Box 218, Hawthorn, Victoria 3122, Australia.

Abstract
This paper explores how multi-media technologies may be utilised to support the early phases of user interface design. It presents a conceptual model for the support of up-stream user interface design and highlights the problems current technology has in supporting the design process.

1. Introduction

The early phases of user interface development (UID) have long been claimed to be the source of a significant proportion of the user dissatisfaction with interactive computer systems (Wasserman and Shewmake, 1985, Starts Guide, 1987).

In a recent survey (Myers, 1992), user interface software is rated as the most difficult type of software to create. Amongst the reasons given for this were:

- Iterative design is often cited as the best way to create appropriate user interfaces. The iterative design paradigm has been used to create some of the classic user interfaces, eg the Xerox Star, the Apple Lisa and Macintosh (Myers, 1992). Orthodox software design paradigms (eg Yourdon, 1989) fail to support iteration adequately.

- Multiple processing is an inherent part of user interface software. It is therefore important that the user interface software be structured so as to accept input at all times, even while executing commands. Well known problems such as consistency, synchronisation, deadlocks and concurrency will prevail during multiple processing.

- Robustness is a feature that should exist in all programs, but proves difficult to engineer for user interface software. All possible actions that the user might attempt to complete will need to have appropriate aborting and exiting procedures.

- The complexity and ease of use of the tools available for developing user interface software are becoming limiting factors.

- Language support to allow the transportation of code from one system to another is critical. Re-use is essential, but most languages that are available do not allow a smooth transition of code from one language or environment to another.

Various advanced technologies have been shown to be of benefit in domains as varied as education (eg interactive multi-media), librarianship (eg hypertext) and software design (eg groupware), for supporting people in formulating an understanding of a problem or domain. Such technologies can potentially alleviate some of the above problems. It is surprising that, to date, few have attempted to apply these technologies to UID.

This paper explores some new technologies that are available today, and the problems that are encountered when the complex interaction of user interface design is captured and represented, using the multi-media platform.

2. Up-stream User Interface Design

'Up-stream UID' refers to the activities involved in providing design with a model of target users (ie users of the intended system), their tasks and their requirements for support. Although this definition is broad enough to cover activities that would not normally be considered part of UID, we will restrict ourselves to methods generally characterised as 'task analysis' (Wilson, Barnard and MacLean, 1988) and 'user/environment profiling.'

In general , these methods involve three generic and distinct activities:
- *collecting* information on some aspect of task execution, user characteristics etc;
- *expressing* that information in a local notation; and
- *analysing* the resultant expression in order to characterise, amongst other things, the demands made of people by tasks and systems.

These three activities, whilst overlapping in practice, have particular problems, as discussed in the next section (see Mouzakis and Howard, 1992, for a detailed discussion).

3. Generic issues in up-stream UID

Up-stream UID is about understanding: the primary goal of the early phases of UID is to furnish the design process with an understanding of target users, their tasks and requirements. Sophisticated data storage and retrieval mechanisms sensitive to the semantics of the data will need to be provided.

UID is evolutionary and revolutionary: the process that delivers understanding in UID is fundamentally iterative and organic. Data collected from a large scale systems development project suggests that the process is highly context dependent (Mouzakis and Howard, 1992). Technology will need to be sufficiently flexible and accessible, so that it can support context sensitivity.

Communication and the importance of a shared model: design can be characterised as the creation of models. UID is fundamentally a communicative process, involving interaction between developers and target users, and interaction within the development team itself (Karat and Bennett, 1990). Technological support will need to be based on a clear understanding of this process.

Tool / Criterion	Declarative Languages	Automatic Generation	Interface Builders	Graphical Editors	Prototypes	Optimum System
Sophisticated Data Storage	Medium	Low	Low	Low	Nil	High
Context Sensitivity	Low	Low	Low	Nil	Low	High
Shared Information	Low	Low	Low	Low	Nil	High
Abstraction	Low	Low	Low	Low	Nil	High
Robustness	Low	Low	Low	Low	Nil	High

Table 1 A comparison of user interface tools with the optimum system
(after Myers, 1992)

Importance of structure: information collected during up-stream activities is necessarily heterogeneous and includes information on system objectives, technical and logistical constraints, requirements information and irrelevant information. Whilst it is difficult to characterise design problem solving, it is clear that reasoning about the above information is neither unitary (ie design is neither a purely analytic or holistic process) or hierarchical (ie purely top-down or bottom-up). It should be possible to create a coherent structure of the data without following a rigorous problem solving method.

Table 1 outlines the extent to which current user interface development technology satisfies the criteria discussed in this section. The scaling that is used in Table 1 is an indication of the extent to which the tool supports the criterion.

4. The Scope for Technological Support

A conceptual architecture for supporting up-stream UID is presented in Figure 1. A full discussion of its characteristics is outside the scope of this paper. We will concentrate below upon the prototyping environment.

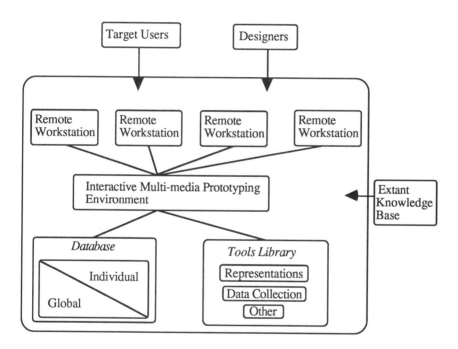

Figure 1: Conceptual Architecture

To support user interface design, the optimum system, as described in Table 1, is implemented in the conceptual architecture above.

5. Interactive multi-media prototyping environment

Through the manipulation and control of representational media, multi-media technology has the potential to support individuals, disparate in characteristics, on a common task. Users can work with animations of the final system that have a clear and explicit relationship to, say, the notations that the designer is using to support design.

By using a multi-media platform as the prototyping environment, the designer is facilitated in the use of different representational formats, formats that are necessary to support the multi-various tasks inherent in user interface design.

The current authors have been examining the use of various tools for supporting multi-media prototyping. Tools such as "Authorware Professional™" (Authorware, 1990) allow the designer to use a common notation system which could be simple and understood by the various users, and also allow the building of a system from which the users could see some immediate benefit.

Authorware Professional™ has the following attractive characteristics when viewed as a prototyping tool:

- Direct editability. Changes can be made to a design whilst it is being presented to a user.
- Response analysis. More than one type of response can be used by the user. Text entry, mouse actions, pull down menus and on-screen push buttons can be all active at once.
- Concurrency. More than one function can be performed at any one time.
- Sharing of structures. Structures can be transported to other designs and used in conjunction with a new design.
- Data collection. User data can be captured, stored and manipulated. Responses can be retrieved, extensive text analysis can be performed, and data can be plotted on the screen.

Authorware Professional™ has facilities to produce automatic documentation and automatically annotate the design by graphically printing the logic flow and describing all of the options selected by any particular user. Graphical objects can be shown in full size, by thumbnail sketches, or by an icon. All icons can be cross-referenced, facilitating consistency checking in large designs. Variables that are used by the user for interaction purposes are also cross-referenced.

6. Conclusion

As a prototyping tool which rates highly on the criteria of Shared Information, Abstraction and Robustness, Authorware Professional™ is a good current compromise. However, the fact that it is found wanting with respect to the criteria of Sophisticated Data Storage and Context Sensitivity points to areas of future research effort.

Current work is proceeding in the area of usability and functionality of authoring tools in prototyping environments. Work is also being carried out on mapping between representations and storing and retrieving multi-modal information from a database.

7. References

Authorware (1990), Reference: Authorware Professional for Macintosh. Published by Authorware Inc, Minnesota, USA.

Hartson, H.R. and Hix, D. (1989), Human Computer Interface Development: concepts and systems for its management. ACM Computing Surveys, 21(1).

Karat, J. and Bennett, J. (1990), Supporting Effective and Efficient Design Meetings, in Human Computer Interaction- Interact '90. (Eds. D.Diaper et al), Elsevier Science Publishers (North Holland).

Mouzakis, K. and Howard, S. (1992), Supporting up-stream user interface design activities, Proceedings OZCHI92, Qld, Australia.

Myers, B.A. (1992), State of the Art in User Interface Software Tools, in Advances in Human Computer Interaction, Vol 4, Norwood, NJ: Ablex Publishing Corp.

STARTS Guide. (1987), Department of Trade and Industry, UK.

Wasserman,A.I. and Shewmake,D.T. (1985), The Role of Prototypes in the User Software Engineering (USE) Methodology. Ed R.Hartson Advances in Human Computer Interaction, Vol 1, Norwood, NJ: Ablex Publishing Corp.

Wilson, M., Barnard, P. and MacLean, A. (1988), Knowledge in Task Analysis for Human Computer Systems. Eds T.Green., J.Hoc., D.Murray. and G.Van der Veer. Working with Computers: theory versus outcome. London: Academic Press.

Yourdon, E. (1989), Modern Structured Analysis, Prentice-Hall, Englewood Cliffs, N.J.

Navigational Issues in Multimedia Case Studies of Engineering Design

S. Hsi[a] and A. M. Agogino[b]

[a]Graduate Group in Science and Mathematics Education, 4533 Tolman Hall, University of California at Berkeley, Berkeley, CA 94720

[b]Department of Mechanical Engineering, 5136 Etcheverry Hall, University of California at Berkeley, Berkeley, CA 94720

Abstract

We prescribe a user interface that supports the case-base method of teaching engineering design using hypermedia enhanced with multimedia to maximize concept relationships, knowledge integration, knowledge organization, and guided-discovery learning. Hypotheses pertaining to navigational issues to support education goals are presented along with their experimental validation on two implementations that were tested on a variety of users.

Lessons learned from our experiments on the case studies are formulated as general rules for use of hypermedia for instructional software that use historical cases for teaching good design practice. Results indicate that (1) The navigational backbone should serve as a concept map to reinforce important principles to help novices to organize their own knowledge. (2) The hyper links should make important connections explicit, but not haphazard; they should be used as a pedagogical tool. (3) Navigation should accommodate the experience level of the user, both in computer use and in domain knowledge. It should be both flexible and structured. (4) Integrated use of multimedia should accommodate differences in learning styles.

1. INTRODUCTION

Hypermedia has attracted many instructional developers to create courseware for tutoring, research and instruction. The linking of multimedia elements (sound, video, animation, images) to an already complex hypermedia network of nodes adds a new dimension for researchers to explore and analyze. As more media types are added to hypermedia systems, it is critical that the user interface be designed to support the courseware designer's intentions, and support user interactions. Hypermedia has the flexibility to link information non linearly, and provide multiple representations for the user. However, this flexibility poses a challenge for the instructional designer to support user coherence of the material being presented, while allowing for different user learning styles.

Multimedia case studies are used to teach engineering design as well as excite and motivate students in engineering [2,3,4]. We prescribe a hypermedia interface that supports the case-base method of teaching engineering design. Our instructional goal is to provide students with an integrated view of engineering design and knowledge of best practices from industry. To this end, hypermedia is used to encourage guided-discovery, maximize concept relationships, and knowledge integration. Navigational links within the multimedia environment are used to reinforce and demonstrate the connections between engineering analyses and product testing, and other factors such as market, safety, environmental impact, and social-historical implications.

Our goals in the evaluation of navigation and user interface design features were to 1) test how well the case studies were able to convey the key concepts in the engineering design process and the product life cycle, 2) explore how best to use multimedia elements (audio, video, animation) to achieve our pedagogical objectives, 3) assess students' performance in navigation given concept maps and additional navigation tools, and 4) evaluate the flexibility of the interface to accommodate different levels of users, allowing for both controlled leaps to information without "getting lost" and user-directed inquiry.

In this paper, we present the evaluation results on two case studies: the Human Powered Vehicle (HPV) and the Proprinter. The HPV case, currently containing 120MB of multimedia materials, illustrates the multi-disciplinary aspects of designing and constructing an aerodynamic bicycle. The Proprinter case (80MB) focuses on concurrent engineering principles such as Design for Automated Assembly (DFAA) and use of multifunctional teams applied to product design and manufacture [2]. First, we describe navigational features of our user interface designed to support the pedagogy.

2. DESCRIPTION OF NAVIGATIONAL TOOLS

The user interface provides several features designed to aid users in their navigation and knowledge organization, as well as support teaching engineering concepts and design process.

2.1 Main Menu

The Main Menu is designed to provide an overview of the contents of the case study as well as provide a map of concepts illustrating the product life cycle from the initial market or competitive analysis to conceptual design, detailed design and redesign, simulation and analysis, testing, production and field performance. From every screen, the user can directly reach the main menu through clicking on the main menu button. In both the HPV and Proprinter cases (see Figure 1), the main

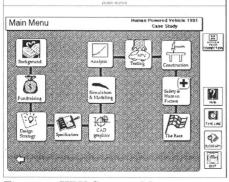

Figure 1. HPV Concept Map

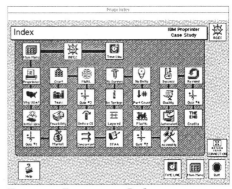

Figure 2. Proprinter Index

menu serves as the primary navigational backbone of the materials presented.

2.2 HPV Time line and Proprinter Index

In addition to the Main Menu, other navigational maps are provided to encourage multiple representations and access to knowledge. The HPV case provides a timeline to reinforce the chronology of development and project engineering view. As an alternative representation in the Proprinter case, an index provides a topic-based display to allow users to directly search and jump to sections, with a finer granularity than that provided by the Main Menu (see Figure 2). Users could use these additional features to access the material, aiding in knowledge organization.

2.3 "See Connections" Browser

The challenge in the development of the navigational structure of the multimedia case studies was to provide paths for both breadth and depth while at the same time delivering instruction to different level users with different learning styles. We found it useful to use the classifications described by Carmel et al. [1] to structure flexible paths to accommodate three general types of users: (1) the search-oriented browser, who is browsing with a goal in mind; (2) the general purpose browser, who sets a goal in the course of browsing; and (3) the casual browser, who may be unfamiliar with the domain, and browses with no particular goal in mind. On one hand, we didn't want to constrain the search-oriented user by restricting the path of navigation. Yet we also didn't want the more serendipitous user to get lost in hypermedia or see engineering as piecemeal collection of facts and figures. The See Connections Browser is designed to support those cognitive links by providing the user with suggested paths to follow. For example, in the HPV case, the team wanted to design a faster vehicle by reducing drag on an existing fairing design. This concept was demonstrated by making the links between tufts testing, wind tunnel model, and aerodynamic analyses explicit in "See Connections" (see Figure 3). A user returns to their original location after unguided independent browsing using the "Return From Connections" button. In addition to suggested connections that are an integral part of the case study, links to on-line reference materials such as pages from engineering texts are also built into the system as part of an on-going experiment with John Wiley Publishers.

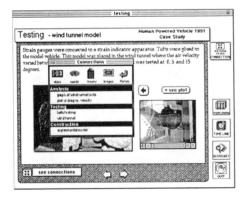 

Figure 3. Sample of See Connections from the Human Powered Vehicle Case

3. METHOD

Subjects in the evaluation studies were comprised of university faculty, high school students, college undergraduates, and graduate students. Users were allowed 30 minutes to browse the case study. Three types of data were collected: questionnaires, on-line interaction data, and interviews. Overall 80 individuals have tested the case study at this date.

On-line collected data, similar to navigation trails [5], were designed to collect the frequency, duration and location of browsing to provide insight into the navigation patterns of users. For the HPV case of which contains 228 cards (screen images), and 17 stacks (sections), the program collected stack names. For the Proprinter case which consists of one stack with over 33 cards, the navigation data consists of the card names reviewed. When the user initiates a session with the case, the name of the stack or card is recorded, and time stamped. When the user navigated to a different section, the location was again recorded. Differences between time stamps were calculated and graphed over time. Because the HPV case was organized into several stacks with large numbers of cards, only the time stamp of the stack name was recorded. This provided information about the path which students choose to follow, the time spent on each card or stack, and qualitative data about the types of browsing activities students performed. Sample processed data from the Proprinter case is provided below in Figure 4:

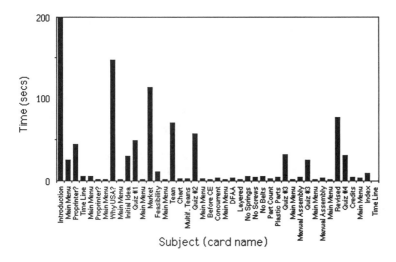

Figure 4. Sample browsing data from testing the Proprinter case.

Pre- and post-questionnaires included questions about the quality of multimedia elements, ability to navigate in the cases, and design problems which were used to measure learning from the multimedia case. (The questions relevant to hypermedia are analyzed here.) Questionnaire information about content understanding and pedagogical impact is described elsewhere [4].

468

4. RESULTS

Lessons learned from our experiments on the case studies are formulated as general rules for use of hypermedia for instructional software for teaching exemplary solutions to unstructured open-ended problem solving. Specific implementation details in the case studies are summarized and evaluated by the results of the user interface experiments.

(1) *The navigational backbone should serve as a concept map to reinforce important principles to help novices to organize their own knowledge.* In the case studies example, the navigational backbone was used to teach the life cycle design process by organizing concepts in a main menu map. The results indicate that few relied on other navigation aids to find information, and only one subject felt he was lost.

(2) *The hyperlinks should make important connections explicit. But these should not be haphazard; they should be used as a pedagogical tool.* In the design case studies hyperlinks were used to show the inter-dependencies and relationships that are difficult to convey in text books and textbook problems. User responses from the questionnaires indicated that students used the See Connections feature. Hypermedia allowed subjects to make these relationships explicit aiding in knowledge integration and coherence as validated by subjects' post responses to design questions.

(3) *Navigation should accommodate the experience level of the user, both in computer use and in domain knowledge. It should be both flexible and structured.* In the design case studies, many subjects possessed no background knowledge in engineering design nor prior experience with computers. The navigation in the cases was found to successfully scaffold novices, yet also give control to more knowledgeable users. Users who were already familiar with the content appeared to have developed a more focused and refined perception of the design process after viewing the cases.

(4) *Integrated use of multimedia should accommodate differences in learning styles.* Our data suggests users preferred different media for learning within a computerized environment. The majority relied on first learning from text, but many users report preferences for learning from alternate media (audio, video, diagrams, and images).

The on-line data indicated that all users, at some time during the session, followed the path of the main menu. In the HPV case, some users first chose to look at sections they were interested in, then came back to the main menu while others first followed the main menu to the end, then used the remaining time to review sections in more detail. The flexibility of the interface allowed for users with different browsing patterns.

Multimedia cases in engineering design have been evaluated to achieve our instructional goals and research goals. The navigational tools in the two cases have also been used successfully as models for on-going cases in mechanical dissection of physical designs, Mattel Toys, failure analysis and automotive design and manufacture.

5. REFERENCES

1   Carmel, E. , Crawford, S. & Chen, H. (1992) "Browsing in Hypertext: A Cognitive Study", IEEE Transactions on Systems, Man, and Cybernetics, Vol. 22,

No. 5, September/October.
2   Evans, J., "Multimedia Case Studies for Teaching Best Design Practices," MS Project Report, Department of Mechanical Engineering, University of California at Berkeley, 1992.
3   Hsi, S. and Agogino, A. "Creating Excitement and Motivation in Engineering Design: Developing and Evaluating Student Participatory Experience in Multimedia Case Studies" to appear in the Proceedings from the World Conference on Educational Multimedia
4   Hsi,S. and Agogino, A., "Use of Multimedia Technology in Teaching Engineering Design", to appear in HCI International '93, 5th International Conference on Human-Computer Interaction jointly with 9th Symposium on Human Interface (Japan), August 8-13,1993, Orlando, FL
5   Shapiro, A. and Spoehr, K.T. (1992) The effects of corpus organization and learning goals on learning from a hypermedia system. Presented at the Annual Meeting of the American Educational Research Association, San Francisco, CA April.

6. ACKNOWLEDGMENTS

This material is based upon research supported by the National Science Foundation Cooperative Agreement No. EEC 9053807. The multimedia case studies described in this paper were developed by faculty, graduate students, and undergraduate students at the University of California at Berkeley in collaboration with our partners in Synthesis: an NSF Engineering Education Coalition. The authors are grateful for the support of the National Science Foundation and our industrial partners: Apple Computer, Inc.; IBM Corporation; John Wiley and Sons, Inc.; Lexmark International, Inc.; and Mattel Toys, Inc. Special thanks goes to case study developers: Jay Evans, Anil Varma, Nagaraj Srinivasan, Punit Jain, Armineh Menzigian, Kirk Edwards, Bill Wood, Steve Bradley, Mitchell Suarez and Robert Stanard. We are indebted to our courseware studio specialist, Robert Lettieri.

Contingency Models for Architectural Design

Dave Bell

HCI Group, Department of Computer Science, Queen Mary and Westfield College, London University, Mile End Road, London, E1 4NS, United Kingdom

Abstract
This paper will show how modelling of the cognitive and communicative skills of individuals in the group context combined with analysis of media-usage within an architectural design group can lead to design guide-lines for a specific multimedia application and the basis for a framework to produce many such applications in the spatial planning domain.

1. Introduction

Multimedia[1] at the computer interface is widely recognised as a stimulant for the individual, adding enjoyment and motivation to work (see Peeck, 1987.) According to Marmolin (1992) the improvements to perception and learning afforded by multimedia interaction can be attributed to the increased participation of the user, such as increased control over the form in which information is presented and an increased engagement of the logical and creative capacities of the mind. The implication is that the mind is capable of manipulating sequential, symbolic information as well as parallel, associative information, and Multimedia provides a means of augmenting these abilities.

In the group context the benefits of multimedia are complemented further by the support it provides for presentation, explanation and communication between remote collaborators. The task domain of MUMS[2] is spatial planning (eg, architectural design or road planning) in which members of client and designer groups pursue the common goal of a design specification and resolve the issues which arise en route. Spatial planning was chosen as a focus for MUMS precisely because it requires exchange of information between individuals with differing background knowledge, and frequent tightly-coupled interaction.

Further design difficulties are introduced by the context of group work because the essential social elements of work and implicit mechanisms which exist must not be overlooked by the single-minded desire to maximise group productivity. Supporting a group means accommodating its day-to-day dynamics and its long-term evolution as well as enabling a number of people to exchange ideas and opinions.

Numerous attempts to design group work applications have failed precisely because the designers have neglected to recognise the covert mechanisms of group work and have attempted to extend single-user systems (Grudin, 1989,) or have ignored the dynamism which is so characteristic of groups and the amplification of that dynamism due to the technology itself (Greenberg, 1991.) Design of Multimedia applications for groups should not be left to intuition, and the risks can be reduced by use of guide-lines during design based upon theoretical and empirical evidence.

---

[1] A combination of dynamic media such as audio, video and animation; and static media such as images, graphics and text
[2] A SERC funded project "Multimedia User Modelling Systems"

The development of theoretical models of group work is encouraged by Rao and Jarvenpaa (1991) in order to underpin the development of group work applications. In the long term, such models can be used to explain and compare empirical findings, support the development of a coherent picture of the computer support of groups and ultimately to advance the field.

There are numerous arguments from the domains of Communication Theory, Social Theory and Human Cognition which have implications for the usage of Multimedia within a group-work application. The Contingency Model presented in this paper has been developed in recognition of the need to bridge the gulf that exists between theoretical evidence and implementation in the group work domain.

2. The Contingency Model

The intended use of a contingency model is to enhance the productivity of the group by directing the use of Multimedia technology in response to group needs and successive changes to those needs over time; as opposed to enforcing a static configuration of technology within which the group must work For example, providing continuous audio and video connections between members of a distributed group with the rationale that they require such communication links is absurd, because the individuals may frequently benefit from privacy or anonymity.

Contingencies can be applied to aid the initial definition of technology for a target group, and also to aid modification of the technology when needs change, due to transitions between tasks or various forms of meeting. An extensive discussion of contingencies is given in section 2.3.

2.1. The Use of Contingencies for System Design

Initial use of the contingency model involves assessment of the target user-group by an analyst using a check-list of factors. A factor is a particular characteristic of the group which justifies the use of a certain technology, the two being linked by applicable evidence. Varying degrees of a particular characteristic may have different implications for technology, the factors are therefore variations on one *dimension*. An example of such a dimension is the degree to which members are distributed: high distribution implies a need for rich communication support in order to reduce low cohesiveness and low morale, whilst low distribution will emphasise role-status differences amongst the group which can be alleviated with occasional "anonymous" working to encourage minority participation. The components of the contingency model are shown in Figure 1.

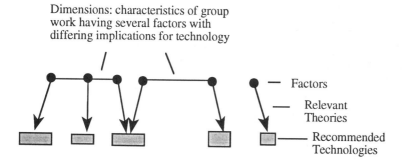

Figure 1. Components of the Contingency Model.

The assessment of the group is followed by inspection of the model in order to determine the implications for technology of the factors identified, and any emphasis for support that the analysis has exposed. It is then the designer's responsibility to integrate the resulting design guide-lines and consider additional requirements in the design process. The process is illustrated in figure 2.

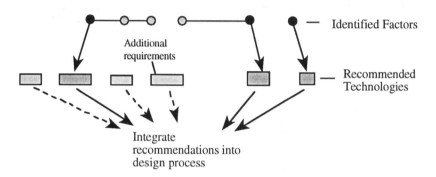

Figure 2. The use of the Contingency Model for Design

2.2. The major factors in Architectural Design

The Architects' guide-lines from RIBA (1969) present the tasks of design in a rigourously ordered and detailed framework, whilst case studies of architectural design and route planning projects indicate that in practice these tasks are loosely ordered. At a basic level these tasks are:

- clients: -gather requirements and agree a brief
- client and designer: -perform briefing, elaborate and agree upon requirements
- designers: -gather design constraints and develop design concepts
- designer and client: -present designs, elaborate them, agree upon final design

In most cases the design requirements are presented before any design concepts are expressed, but it is likely that the requirements will not be finalised until all the design queries have been answered and the design concept is agreed. The main factors in spatial planning are those having implications for system design and thus are those which the analyst must seek during group assessment. These are given in Table 1

Table 1
The Main Factors in Spatial Planning

Roles are clearly defined
Specialised knowledge/skills exists in the group
A Management Hierarchy exists
Group members are Distributed
There is a need for remote work
A high degree of cooperation is required
There is a need for focus upon a single entity
Subgroup working is required
There is a need for face to face meetings
There are specific media requirements for tasks and individuals
There is a need for Individual working
Task divisibility and subtask coordination is required
There is a need for meetings, information exchange and decision making
Interpersonal interaction is required for understanding

2.3. The Development of Contingencies

A number of the contingencies presented here were motivated by the work of Rao & Jarvenpaa (1991) who emphasised the need to increase individual productivity, to improve the mutual understanding between group members, to increase group cohesiveness, and reduce the tension due to status differences. Further contingencies have resulted from the desire to support practices particular to spatial planning.

The greatest productivity gains for a situation arising during distributed group-work are not necessarily achieved by increases in available technology, even though a majority of contingencies do promote the use of multimedia support. For example, anonymous computer-mediated communication of textual or graphical form can increase participation of reticent group-members during debate or brain-storming because an individual's fear of disapproval from superiors or anxiety regarding communication skills is alleviated (Desanctis and Gallupe, 1987.)

The impact of high spatial or temporal distribution of group members is loss of group-awareness and low cohesiveness, contributing to general dissatisfaction and conflict. It has also been found that infrequent interaction reduces the likelihood of new collaborations forming (Kraut, 1988.) Given that cohesiveness and interpersonal contact are essential to the well-being of the group, it was concluded that the productivity of remote workers will benefit from frequent access to rich communications support.

A high degree of social interaction is required in cases of misinterpretation or conflict of goals in order that participants can reach a common perspective satisfactorily (Kydd and Ferry, 1991.) Thus a high level of communicative engagement (ie, audio and video) should be available during remote presentation or explanation in order to support this interaction; textual or audio communications alone fail to provide the necessary socio-emotional support.

At the individual level, access to Multimedia representation encourages active exploration of information rather than passive acceptance, and provides a rich source for the mind that prefers dynamic rather than static stimuli (Marmolin, 1992.) The ability to manipulate the representation of information is also beneficial to the phases of problem solving: (1) concrete representations facilitate exploration; (2) visual representations support synthesis and creative thought; (3) textual forms support analysis (Marmolin, 1992.) The last points should be qualified by adding that the various Multimedia representations will have the optimal impact if they are those that the user desires (ie unrestricted by limits of the system.)

Alternative views enable non-experts to understand information which is otherwise inaccessible. Spatial Planning benefits greatly from the participation of clients at an early stage (Branki, Jones & Edmonds, 1992,) which is possible if clients have the ability to generate abstractions of technical data, such as 3D renderings of 2D plans and elevations, or graphs from tables of numbers. If clients can interpret and comment upon the evolving design at an early stage, the resultant design is more likely to be successful and satisfactory.

The need to provide contingencies for organisational factors such as roles, hierarchies, subgroups and individual working arose from the case study of Architectural Design. A client and designer group was studied which had well defined roles and hierarchy. Small groups of two or three people met for discussion of critical issues, to exchange important information and to make major decisions. Larger gatherings occurred for presentation and ratification of decisions, and for concerns to be raised. An important finding was the apparent seamlessness of the transitions that occurred between modes of work, which would clearly be technically demanding. This includes transitions between individual and collaborative working and changes to the membership of collaborative work sessions. It is clear that such ease of transition will be crucial to the acceptance of real-time group support systems.

With regard to media usage, telephone conversations form the majority of the remote communications, being used as precursors to further communications and for minor information exchanges. During presentations, the material rather than the presenter needs to be available to all, but when the mode becomes one of intense communication, as it can during explanation or debate, then greater contact is required between participants such as aural and visual channels.

2.4. The Use of Contingencies for Tailoring

To reflect the levels of dynamism in a group, the tailorability of group work system can be considered at three levels: the first is tailorability at an administrative level, the second is tailorability by a moderator and the third is by the individual. To elaborate, changes in management structure or group membership need to be performed at an administrative level; run-time reconfiguration of group-wide communications and views upon information during a work session should be allocated to a moderator (or facilitator); and individuals should have the freedom to decide what information is displayed at their computer and in what form, which windows are visible, which applications are running, and which channels (eg, aural, visual or textual) are available for communication. The issues of groupwide tailoring and individual tailoring are of most concern, for they have greatest impact on the productivity of the group, and can be driven by application of contingencies.

It is an issue whether the tailoring required by the group at run-time should be performed by software agents or by a member of the group. Software agents monitoring the group and suggesting changes to the technology configuration (possibly even making these changes) may cause users to feel detached from the system and reduce their feeling of control. Alternatively, bestowing the task of tailoring upon a group member places the onus upon one person throughout a collaborative work session (possibly all sessions) to monitor the group and modify the configuration in response to changing needs, which would prevent this member from contributing in a normal manner, and worse still make the group reliant on that one person to manage meetings. Similar issues have arisen with the facilitator described by Viller (1991.)

An agent to perform the task of run-time tailoring needs to perform a great many assessments of the group in order to make sensible changes; eg, the task divisions and subgroups that have emerged, the channels of communication that exist, the current focus of group attention. If there is no optimal media for a given task with a given information item, or for a given communication in the group, sensible defaults have to be offered which consider individual preferences and current interactions.

A problem with the contingency model in it's current form is that there is no simple algorithm that can lead to an exact solution for all situations in the group. There is no means of attaching weights to factors in order to decide between two or more technologies for a given situation, and factors which may have an influence upon the choice are difficult to assess (eg, misunderstandings or interpersonal conflict.) The principle of the contingency model is similar to techniques intended to aid design reasoning, providing a framework for bringing together design issues, potential solutions and theoretical or empirical evidence in order to assess solutions. The contingency table presents a core set of dimensions and factors (closely related to the factors in Table 1,) the implications of these factors, and contingencies which can be justified by available evidence. An entry in the contingency table is given in Table 2.

Table 2
An entry in the Table of Contingencies

Dimension	Factor	Implications	Contingency
To what degree are the group members distributed	High spatial distribution	Reduced communication implies low cohesiveness, low morale and increased chance of conflict	Make provision for frequent use of rich communications media (eg audio, video, shared graphical and textual views)

2.5. The development of MUMS' Architecture and Prototypes

An application framework has been developed upon the FOCUS[3] toolkit (Edmonds, 1992) in order to enable development of Multimedia group-work applications. Iterative development of the framework will take place, driven by the development and evaluation of prototypes. The

[3]An ESPRIT II project "Front-ends for Open and Closed User Systems"

first prototype will support several users in a road planning task, and an existing Geographic Information System, GRASS, has been integrated for this application.

Conclusions drawn from the case-studies regarding behaviour of individuals within a diverse client-designer group are informing design of the prototype. In particular, heed has been taken of the need to allow an individual to perform individual work whilst participating in the group, and to provide effortless transitions of focus (and information) between such modes of work. Group-wide tailoring of conference initialisation methods, floor control policies and access security will also be explored by the prototype.

3. Summary

Tailorability has been identified as an essential attribute of a group work system: to enable to some degree the rectification of the disparities which arise between group work needs and the technology provided; to accommodate the inherent dynamics of group work; and to accommodate the changes introduced by the technology itself. Both the run-time tailoring and initial system design can be aided by application of relevant theories and empirical evidence captured by a contingency model.

A contingency model approach can be used to integrate the design guide-lines from wide-ranging studies (eg, ethnographic studies) which are relevant to multimedia systems and present them in a form appropriate for requirements analysis and software design.

The work reported has been undertaken with support from Prof. Peter Johnson and researchers at Loughborough University, UK, namely Rachel Jones, Conn Copas and Prof. Ernest Edmonds. MUMS is funded by the Science and Engineering Research Council, U.K., under grant number GR/G35596.

References

Branki, N.E., Jones, R.M. & Edmonds, E.A. (1992) "An Analysis of Media Integration for Spatial Planning Environments". in H. Timmermans (ed). proceedings of Design & Decision Support Systems in Architecture and Urban Planning. Eindhoven, July '92

Desanctis, G. and Gallupe, B. (1987) "A Foundation for the study of GDSSs" - in Management Science Vol 33(5) pp589-609

Edmonds, E.A., Murray, B.S., Ghazikhanian, J. and Heggie, S.P. (1992) "The Re-use and Integration of Existing Software: A Central Role for the Intelligent User Interface" in proc. HCI '92 York, UK. *People and Computers VII* by the British Computer Society

Greenberg, S. (1991) "Personalizable Groupware: Accommodating individual roles and Group differences" in proceedings of ECSCW 1991, Amsterdam. Kluwer press

Grudin, J. (1989) "Why Groupware Applications Fail: problems in design and evaluation" Office Technology and People, Vol 4(3) pp245-264 Elsevier Science, UK.

Kydd, C.T. & Ferry, D.L. (1991) "Computer Supported Cooperative Work Tools and Media Richness: An integration of the Literature" in HICSS 24 Vol4 pp324-332

Kraut, R., Egido, C. & Galagher, J. (1988) "Patterns of Contact and communication in Scientific Research Collaboration" proceedings of CSCW '88 by the ACM

Marmolin, H. (1991) "Multimedia from the Perspective of Psychology" in *Multimedia: Principles, Systems and Applications* by Lars Kjelldahl (ed) Springer-Verlag

Peeck, J. (1987) "The role of Illustration in Processing and Remembering Illustrated Text" in Willows & Houghton (eds) *The Psychology of Illustration* Springer-Verlag (1987), Vol 1, Ch 4

RIBA (1969) "Architect's Appointment" published by Royal Institute of British Architects, Portland Place, London.

Rao, V.S. & Jarvenpaa, S.L. (1991) "Computer Support Of Groups - Theory-based Models For GDSS Research" Management Science,1991,V37(10) 1347-1362

Viller, S. (1991) "The Group Facilitator: A CSCW Perspective" in proceedings of ECSCW 1991, Amsterdam. Kluwer press

ON THE RELATIONSHIPS BETWEEN HYPERMEDIA AND THE PSYCHOTHERAPEUTIC PROCESS

Lic. Pablo Boczkowski[a], Fernando Das Neves[b] and Gustavo Rossi[c]

[a] Fundacion Interfas. Avda. Figueroa Alcorta 3085- 5to. B (1425) Capital Federal.

[b] LIFIA, Depto de Informatica. Facultad de Ciencias Exactas. Universidad Nacional de La Plata. Calle 50 y 115, 1er Piso. (1900) La Plata, Buenos Aires, Argentina.

[c] LIFIA and also CONICET. E-mail: grossi@unlp.edu.ar

Abstract

We present in this paper some results of a research project that explores: a) the advantages of hypertext as a metaphor by means of which psychotherapists represent and access information and knowledge acquired during the psychotherapeutic process and b) the potential of hypermedia as a tool for building learning environments for future psychotherapists.

We discuss the outstanding features of a hypermedia-based environment that provide support for learning the complex relationships presented in a psychotherapeutic process. We analyze some implementation issues and discuss some future work in this area.

1. INTRODUCTION

Hypertext and Hypermedia has been recently used to model different kind of phenomena in diverse application areas. Our work deals with studying some relationships between the hypermedia metaphor and several aspects of the psychotherapeutic process, and is strongly based on ideas of Jerome Bruner (Ref 1) on what it has been called a renewed cognitive revolution; besides it is routed on the work of lakoff & Johnson (Ref 2) on the metaphoric structure of the human conceptual system; this work provides a theoretical basis for describing the way in which human beings construct the meaning of the reality they live in.

As a natural consequence of our work, we are building hypermedia based environments for representing and accessing information gathered during the psychotherapeutic process (interviews, professional comments, etc.). Systematizing this information and packaging it with further material (theoretical comments, bibliography, etc.) will easily lead to learning environments for psychology students. However there some problems that must be solved in order to build usable learning environments in this area.

In this paper we describe the outstanding features of a hypermedia based learning environment for future psychotherapists. The structure of the paper is as follows: we first describe some theoretical basis on the relationships between hypermedia and the psychotherapeutic process; we next present the main aspects of our learning environment, stressing on human computer interface aspects and analyzing some implementation issues; some concluding remarks are presented at the end of the paper.

2. HYPERMEDIA AND THE PSICHOTHERAPEUTIC PROCESS

Our work deals with analyzing the possibilities of hypertext in the constructionist clinic as a metaphor through which the psychotherapist relates to the information generated during the psychotherapeutic process (Ref 3). Constructionist clinics apopts an analogy of text as a metaphor for analyisis; however, narrative is not really text, and this fact is not unknown to psychotherapists. The hypothesis of this work is that the hypertext as a metaphor can overcome some of the limitations of the textual metaphor, and that it will provide alternatives that are not possible in the domain of the latter. In that way, our research project becomes a valid experiment of theoretical anticipation.

We have identified four conceptual axes on which hypertext has introduced changes in the treatment of information (in particular related with the psychotherapeutic process):

a) Internal structure of the document: the hypertext favors the production of diversity, multiplicity, and in this way it challenges the authority.

b) Relationship with other documents: hypertexts imply the corporization of intertextuality.

c) Social dimension of the document: hypertext promotes collaborativity, and in this sense it proves to be an ideal tool for the social construction of information (Ref 4)

d) Amount of information in a document: Hypertexts are inclusive because they allow a collection of possible documents to be included from multiple points of views. On the other hand, hypertexts favor narrative excesses which are produced because the paratextual apparatus -footnotes, headings, etc.- that in texts is of secondary importance acquires a new dimension.

In summary regarding the limitations of text, the hypertextual metaphor will:

a) Promote the relative independence of texts.

b) Question the existence of only one and inmutable truth.

c) Challenge the presence of an established authorities and of fixed hierarchies.

Besides, it will contribute to the empowerment of the users, making more flexible the frontier between the author and the reader. It will stimulate collaborative work and the social anchorage of knowledge construction process. It will urge the therapists to generate coparticipative actions and, finally this approach will give the therapists a tool that will allow them an efficient orientation in the production of the relevant knowledge without getting lost in oceans of information and nonsense discussions.

3. LEARNING ENVIRONMENT FOR PSYCHOTHERAPISTS

A learning environment for psychotherapists must provide support for their understanding of the complex relationships involved in a psychotherapeutic process. They must understand the role of the different actors in an interview, and they must be able to build mental models about the problems of a particular patient, etc. We choose hypermedia because of its great ability for representing information, which allows to express a wide range of meanings, from a defined paragraph to a highly polysemic image. Our environment provides a virtual world where interviews between a psychotherapist and a group of people (a patient, his/her family) are presented. Interviews are enriched with comments (built upon hypermedia relationships) from the professional and different experts about the theoretical problems, including bibliography. A student is faced with prototypical situations in which he can compare his mental model of a situation with the one suggested by experts. He can switch from the "interview world" to the "theory world" and explore relationships among both worlds. Hypermedia constructs provide rich support for this kind of learning environment. However, some complex problems must be solved:

-Synchronization between worlds must be assured. A student reading an interview may like to read some theoretical ideas about a particular aspect of the interview and then return. Traditional hypermedia links are not enough for solving this problem.

-Obviously, the hypertext itself must be open. That means that a student will be able to add its own comments to the interview, or to the theoretical ideas.

-Traditionally, interviews are either written in paper or recorded in audio or video. The environment must provide a rich interface for exploring an interview. However, the original sequentially must be preserved. Actors in the interview may have virtual spaces where one can explore their role with respect with other actors.

-The target audience "loves" books; some cultural communities may not accept the transition to hypertext if they don't see great advantages. In our case, the explicit representation of mental models by means of hypermedia networks, the possibility of combining interviews with theory and bibliography provides not only a good substrate for learning but also for new research areas where psychotherapists and computer scientist (in particular hypermedia people) can interact.

A prototype of the learning environment is being developed in Multimedia Toolbook.

During the development, several issues related with the main subject of the project has risen:

-The abstract representation of an interview (and the comments on it) may help in understanding some cognitive processes involved in the psychotherapeutic process.

-The learning environment helps in showing the relevance of the hypertext metaphor for representing all aspects of the therapeutic process.

-Finally, some orientation and navigation tools that has been designed specially for this system had shown to be completely general and useful in other contexts (even in hypermedia applications not related with education).

4. IMPLEMENTATION ASPECTS

Many people related to humanities feel strong prejudices of including computers in its environment. Psychotherapists in our country are not the exception; they consider their work as a deeply human relationship between patient and doctor, and they see computers as some kind of 'cold' machine, without the attributes need to help them performing their work. Tumble this prejudices down is not easy, so we designed the environment with the same contents their natural learning environment provides. It is applicated to develop a hypermedia environment to learn about suicide, divided in four main topics: An interview of the potential suicide and his family, a theoretical background, a technical area and the bibliographic support of all of them.

Many of the issues related to computer refusing from human sciences user departs from the lack of physical appearance of information. Books, the classical method of represent information in the Printing Age, provides with a physical contact with the underlying information support: the media becomes the interface, users are accustomed to the media. A hypermedia environment takes the user apart from the media, creating an abstraction like if information really exists only when is needed.

Freedom of choosing next link in hypermedia leads them to a situation resembling a desk with paper sheets distributed all over it, where a researcher jumps from sheet to sheet gathering information. In such a situation, the reader creates his own organizational tools like stacking papers, marking sheets, etc. A computer environment does not allow that spontaneous creation of tools, so our system provides similar or (we believe) even better organizational tools.

Unlike the usual graph-based representation of hypermedia systems our work is better understood as a set-based model, where we have the information divided in domains, made by sets. An intersection among sets represents a common idea, where each set express in different way, so navigating becomes a gradual change of information point of view. We map each domain in a window, which all exists at the same time. From the user point of view each window is a world, and there is two kinds of windows: The main and the secondary windows. Also, there exists two types of navigation: inner (into the same domain or world) and extern (crossing domain boundaries).

Every window can be designated by the user as main or secondary, but only one main window may exist at a time. The main window centers the focus of user activity, and all the secondary windows sinchronize themselves with the content of an activated link in the main window; those who can not respond to the contents are shown as deactivated. The user can see the contents of all the windows, but he can not activate their links; only main window has active links. Activating an extern link or designating another window as the main one implies that the old main window loses its status, swapping its position with the incoming main window.

The purpose of this protocol is to compel the user of being aware of the actual point of view: and to enforce their cognitive monitoring (ref 5); common system does not offer an explicit representation of changing from "interview world" to "theory world"; protocol we implemented offers an explicit representation and a visual feedback of this action, dangerously related to disorientation and loss. Besides, this scheme incites the user to collate and relating information between worlds; a further development allows the 'cloning' of a world, showing more than one perspective of the same domain. To avoid a fast explosion of growing information, this cloning is live until any link is activated, where all the worlds are newly limited to a unique perspective.

Psychotherapists can be active builders of the semantic contents of the system, by adding their own media and links, which are physically represented in a different way from the standard contents; we found many psychotherapists love his discovers though the system, following their habits in a book-populated world, and they desire to be able of making a further analysis of the material.

4.1 Recovering the narrative.

A potential disadvantage of hypermedia systems is the loss of narrative power and significance (Ref 6) as links are traversed and nodes of different domains are visited. The main problem of maintaining narrative is its intrinsic linearity across the time, which do not correlate with the simultaneity of hypermedia. We fight this problem from two points: the local narrative and the global narrative.

Some researchers suggest the use of departure and arrival points to make links clear; we make this conception wider: By combining standard tours, like the widely known guided tours (Ref 7) with arrival and departures from tours we tried to emphasize main ideas, adding departures which explain the idea surrounding next steps, and arrivals which remark concepts developed through the tour, helping the user in creating levels of abstraction that gives a better idea of the narrative that is being created.

The global narrative, which implies a long discourse, is supported by an added interface element (fig. 1). The idea is identifying 'nucleus' in the worlds, that embodies very important themes. Each topic is associated to a color. As user traverse links the narrative in creation is represented as transitions or degradees from a color to another. Length of transitions and repetition of nucleus enforce the narrative helping users to recognize jumps, repetitions, local discourses, and even their loss in hyperspace. Users could even group adjacent colors, giving that group a name and realizing the meaning of that partial discourse. We found it is was easier to recognize nucleus if they are represented by pure, brilliant colors. The main disadvantages of this tool are two: repetition of colors, compelled by the lack of pure colors and the creation of this colors by transitions, which made us add a special mark over nucleus; and that some training is needed in users that have not developed their visual sense: they found difficult to think and elaborate ideas in terms of colors.

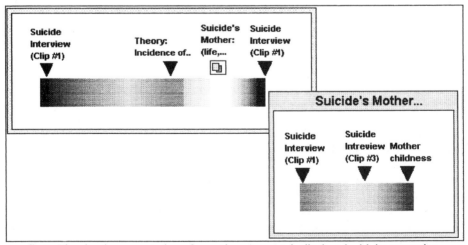

fig 1. The visual representation of narrative. A group is displayed with its expansion.

5. CONCLUDING REMARKS

We have discussed some remarkable relationships between the hypermedia metaphor and the psychotherapeutic process; in particular we have analyze some theoretical implications on the use of this metaphor to represent the information gathered during that process. Finally, we have presented the outstanding features of a learning environment for psychotherapists. The environment provides facilities for exploring large information spaces, including interviews, theoretical comments, bibliography, etc. During the development we have identified certain issues that must be further studied:

-the node and link metaphor are not enough for expressing complex synchronizations as those discussed here.

-taking into account that the environment must be open-ended, it is necessary to define a model for expressing interactions with the final user.

-it is important to find ways for reducing the gap between user expectations (related with their being accustomed to paper based material) and the learning environment.

we are now working in some of these problems and in performing serious experiences with students of psychology.

-Finally we noted that our set based modelling with domain divisions and relationships can be generalized to represent other hypermedia systems. It gives us some useful advantages over graph based modelling, that we are exploring presently.

References

1   J. Brunner: "Act of meaning" Cambirdge, Hardvard University Press (1990)

2   G. Lakoff et al: "Metaphors we live by" University of Chicago (1980)

3   P. Boczkowsky: "The hypertext as a metaphor in constructionist theory". Doctoral Thesis (in advance),(1993).

4   E. Barrett: "Textual intervention, collaboration and the Online environment", in E. Barrett (ed), The society of text: Hypertext, Hypermedia and the social construction of Information.

5   J. F. Rouet "Cognitive Processing of Hyperdocuments: When does nonlinearity help?". Proceedings of the European Conference on Hypertext, Milano, Italy (1992)

6   M. Bernstein "Excitement, Tension and Drama. Tools for hypertext writers". Tutorial given in the European Conference on Hypertext , Milano, Italy (1992).

7   C. C. Marshall "Guided Tours and on-line presentartions: How authors make existing hypertext intelligible for readers. Proceedings of the ACM Hypertext 89 Conference (1989).

An Analysis of Hypermedia Program Architecture
with Individual Differences of Learners

Susan Gautsch

Department of Communication -- University of Hawaii at Manoa
Honolulu, HI 96822

Abstract
    The purpose of this research was to investigate the effects of software architecture and individual differences of learners with respect to knowledge transfer. We conducted an experiment using hypermedia courseware based on an existing and widely used multimedia program that teaches French language and culture. Empirical data representing subjects' individual learning styles and learning performance with the courseware was collected and analyzed. In this paper, quantitative methods and results are presented, followed by a qualitative discussion. Here, three different perspectives on this experiment are applied: 1) The Message -- what is being conveyed; 2) The Medium -- how the message is being conveyed; and 3) The Mind -- how the message is accepted. Finally, conclusions and recommendations for further research are made.

1. BACKGROUND

In the infancy and rapid evolution of hypermedia technology, there has been an attempt to develop a base of research which considers educational courseware. By its very nature, this new medium is liberating to a learner -- providing an environment where not only direct questions can be answered, but new questions can be formed in the process of exploration. Some of these questions may not have absolute answers. The dynamic mixture of media, the level of user interaction, and the nonlinear structure of the software, all aid in extending the nature of digital technology beyond the discrete and absolute. Meaningful and robust communication can be achieved leading a student to global learning and understanding. As hypermedia researchers, we too are learners in a new discipline where many of our questions do not have absolute answers. For a holistic understanding of the complex nature of this new field, a synthesis of quantitative and qualitative analysis is required. Reviewing current research, we see many of the same questions are being investigated with many different and often inconclusive results. At this stage of our understanding, we cannot afford to suggest that we know the range of questions to ask. Instead, we too can be liberated in our own explorations of hypermedia courseware and the process of learning.

2. EXPERIMENTAL RESEARCH

The objective of this study was to examine the effects of software architecture and individual differences of the user on knowledge transfer. Each independent variable was analyzed with respect to the dependent variables. In addition, interactive effects between the software architecture and the individual differences were analyzed. Figure 1 illustrates this.

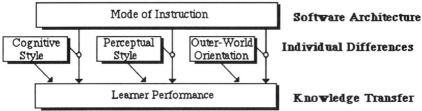

Figure 1: Research Design

2.1 Treatment and Instruments

French in Action is an existing and widely used multimedia immersion program designed by Pierre Capretz and others (1987) at Yale University. Avoiding any English translation, this program emphasizes contextual relationships in authentic settings. Following an enchanting boy-meets-girl story on video, students rely on both verbal and nonverbal communication. Lessons and exercises incorporate the material of the story with listening comprehension, vocabulary, grammar and usage, and reinvention of the story.

Representing a linear and a nonlinear Mode of Instruction, two different hypermedia versions of French in Action Leçon 2 (FA-2) were designed and implemented by the researcher using HyperCard and QuickTime video and audio segments. Differing only in their architecture, both versions were based on the existing FA-2 multimedia courseware, preserving the content and pedagogy of the original program. The linear treatment contained buttons that allow for only forward and reverse movement through a single path, whereas the nonlinear treatment contained section buttons, as well as hypertext links, a map with links, and a "go back" button based on the user's chosen path of screens visited through the nonlinear web of nodes. Formative evaluations and pilot studies were conducted to assure validity of the treatments.

The GEFT is a test based on theories of cognitive style: field independence/dependence (FI/FD). Subjects were asked to find "simple" geometric figures embedded within "complex" geometric figures. It is claimed that one's ability to break up an organized visual field in order to keep part of it separate from the whole field is a manifestation of the individual's cognitive activity. A FI individual perceives items as discrete parts of a larger structure, and is therefore able to locate the embedded figures easily. A FD individual, on the other hand, tends to leave material "as is" seeing the whole rather than the parts; and therefore has difficulty locating the embedded figures. The standardization of the GEFT shows a reliability of .82 for both male and female college students.

The MBTI is a forced-choice, self-report inventory that attempts to classify individuals along four different dimensions according to an adaptation of Jung's theory of psychological types. Of particular concern to this study are the dimensions of Perceptual Style and Outer-World Orientation. Perceptual Style is dichotomized by Sensing vs. Intuition where a sensing-type tends to focus on facts, procedures, and details. Intuition-types focus on overall patterns, relationships, and new possibilities. Outer-World Orientation is dichotomized by Judging vs. Perceiving where a Judging-type tends to plan, make decisions, and organize all in attempts to regulate and control life. Perceiving-types tend to be flexible, spontaneous, and adaptable to new experiences. Findings of reliability are largely based on post-elementary and college populations. Reliability coefficients range from .64 to .73 for the sensing/intuition dimension, with the wide range due to the variance of polar to continuous scoring (Myers, 1977).

The FA-2 Knowledge Posttest, a multiple-choice/fill-in-the-blank test of knowledge, was developed by the researcher based on the existing FA-2 multimedia course. Questions were taken from the original FA-2 exercises, the teacher's manual, and existing tests used in French in Action classes at the University of Hawaii. Both tests were in HyperCard consisting of 42 questions mixing listening comprehension, formal/informal determination, verb conjugation and usage, pronoun usage, and sentence formation. Questions were primarily text-based with sound for listening comprehension and sentence formation. Answers were in the form of true/false, multiple choice, matching, and written sentences. Performance was calculated by subtracting the Knowledge Pretest score from the Knowledge Posttest score.

2.2 Sampling, Procedures, and Data Analysis

From a population of undergraduate Communication, Education, and Computer Science college students at the University of Hawaii, a sample of 74 subjects with no previous French experience was drawn. Intervening variables such as age, gender, and other language experience were considered in the grouping the subjects and in the final analysis.

Each subject participated in two one-hour sessions. In the first session, the GEFT and the MBTI were administered. From these results, two groups for each treatment were assigned. In the second session, subjects started with the Knowledge Pretest, followed by 30 minutes with one of the two treatments, and finally ended with the Knowledge Posttest.

A two-factor analysis of variance (ANOVA) was performed. In all cases the dependent variable was Performance (continuous: Knowledge Posttest score - Knowledge Pretest score) and factor B was Mode of Instruction (discrete: linear or nonlinear). Factor A varied in three different analyses as: Cognitive Style (discrete: FD or FI), Perceptual Style (discrete: S or N), and Outer-World Orientation (discrete: J or P).

2.3 Results

For each of the three different analyses performed, with Factor A representing each of the three individual differences dimensions and Factor B consistently representing Mode of Instruction, no significance was shown with alpha levels set at 0.05. It is interesting to note, however, that in the third analysis with Factor A representing Outer-World Orientation, the main effect of the J/P scale had a p-value of .08. Though not reported as statistically significant, this is considered in the qualitative perspective to follow.

3. QUALITATIVE PERSPECTIVE

3.1 The Message

Taking a framework of communicative action, and considering the different messages of the treatment and the Knowledge Tests, we have come to question the value of quantitative evaluation of language and culture. In this study, and in education in general, multiple-choice style questions were used to produce empirical data. It is concluded that, despite numerous evaluations and pilot tests, the Knowledge Tests were valid only in the measurement of discrete facts, and not in an overall understanding of French language and culture.

Social theories of Habermas (1984) identify three worlds, or domains of communication in which we learn. 1) THE world -- where knowledge is empirical and systems operate independently of human intervention, individuals are analytical in identifying parts and subparts with the objective of finding the "absolute truth." 2) OUR world -- where knowledge is a "collective rightness" within a community of individuals interacting and sharing social norms, values, and principals. 3) MY world -- where one is involved in subjective and personal expression and knowledge is based on what is private and true to the individual.

Incongruencies can be seen in that the message of the treatments was of a holistic and conceptual nature focusing on human relationships, shared expectations, attitudes, and courtesies. Here, OUR world of social and collective rightness was clearly represented and emphasized. In the Knowledge Tests, however, THE world was emphasized, in that subjects were encouraged to be analytical and their success was based on objective, discrete, and absolute right or wrong answers. Furthermore, the administration of the pretest established this goal before the treatment was even encountered. Undoubtedly, this influenced the learning strategies adopted by the subjects. Schank and Edelson lament "Multiple choice questions are becoming a dominant method of education, not because anyone thinks they are an effective teaching tool, but because the technology made them so easy to use." (Schank, 1990b) Recommendations are made as to how these incongruencies can be avoided in further research.

3.2 The Medium

From the once fashionable wisdom of Marshall McLuhan comes the daunting phrase "The Medium is the Message" where he warns: this is a "new environmental implosion," transforming people whose senses are working overload with the modern electronic media. In this analysis, it is concluded that elements of the medium itself distracted subjects from the intended message of French language and culture.

In the treatment, subjects were introduced to many new technologies. Not only did full-color, full-motion video play on their screens, but they were able to control it with random access, easier and more powerfully than that of any VCR. This medium was truly fun and exciting (as we are endlessly told by hypermedia evangelists.) In the exercise section, subjects were highly entertained by the comical "achum" sound uttered by 'The thinker' (their coach of sorts.) Consequently, subjects were enthusiastically looking for incorrect responses.

We can view this in light of other psychological studies referenced by Heeter (1992), where "novelty-seeking" has been identified as a personality trait. Individuals have characteristically optimal levels of sensory stimulation independent of cognition, and they will seek means of increasing or decreasing stimulus to meet that level. Applying this notion to the experiment at hand, we can see how a subject's behavior and response to stimulus could have been more influenced by an attempt to increase or reduce novelty, as opposed to an attempt to understand the material.

Some subjects, however, demonstrated more frustration than novelty -- a problem not unique to this study. Stanton (1992) suggests that in the initial stages of the courseware experience, subjects focus on either the navigational system or the instructional material, but not both. These problems, however, are short-lived. Over time, they report, performance increases. Nelson (1990) reports the same difficulties in that the treatment time of their study was not long enough for learners to grasp the structural relationships in a hypermedia document. This problem leads to the notion of cognitive overhead, or the degree of complexity in a nonlinear environment such as number of choices, task scheduling, tracking, and navigating (Conklin, 1987; Doland, 1989). With the increased level of self-empowerment and control over the environment, comes an increased level of learning management.

The construct of Outer-World Orientation was closest to showing a significant difference in Performance. Significant to 92% as a main effect, this presents interesting possibilities. Judging-type subjects who like to make decisions and control their environment did not perform as well as the Perceiving-type subjects who like to be spontaneous, adaptable, and flexible. In fact, Perceiving-type subjects performed equally well regardless of their Mode of Instruction, suggesting that they were able to adapt to their environment without disorientation problems. Judging-type subjects, on the other hand, who had the linear treatment scored the lowest on Performance. This is an interesting finding in that it contradicts what would be assumed about a Judging-type's preference for a rigid structure. Instead, it possibly suggests that the restricting nature of the linear Mode of Instruction interfered with their learning by not allowing them to make decisions or control their environment.

To better understand the process of learning, it is necessary to investigate the nature of links and of user's decisions to follow them. In this treatment, there may have been some confusion introduced to the user through the hypertext links in that no value or indication of the relationship between nodes was given. For example, some of the hypertext links went to more detail about the current concept, whereas other links went to an overview or generalization. It seems, then, that false assumptions about the relationship of the material on the connecting nodes could have easily been made by subjects who followed these links. This is true for much of the existing hypermedia software used to date.

It is not surprising that each new study investigating this medium yields different and often opposing results. In its infancy intervening variables are not obvious, and in its complexity isolating these variables is not easy. An enormous responsibility is handed over to developers of such software. Each individual medium such as still image, sound, video, and animation, carries with itself its own language. Some of these languages are spatially oriented, others are time oriented. Like a mediator at an international meeting where each member carries a different language, the developer is faced with the task of integrating all these media to enhance and compliment each other in the hopes of conveying a coherent message. In addition, the element of nonlinearity and a straying from traditional notions of timing, robs the developer of conventional techniques of story-lining and transition building. In essence, there needs to be a new language developed for the production of hypermedia courseware.

3.3 The Mind

The mind is a powerful model-building device. It facilitates the act of learning by adding new information to existing models. When understandable links cannot be made, these models are restructured and new concepts are acquired. This however, is not a simple nor obvious process. Gagnè (1985), has proposed that learning is an internal event that is personal for each individual; and recent shifts in cognitive science treat a learner not as a receiver of knowledge as facts, but as one who constructs knowledge through action, communication, and reflection (Schank, 1990a).

In light of current cognitive theory and experimental results, we see how cognitive and perceptual *style* do not wholly reflect cognitive and perceptual *strategies*. Instead, we notice that the complex nature of learning does not allow such a "reductionist" approach. Furthermore, it is proposed that the continual restructuring of mental models leads to continual change of learning strategies. In a similar experiment, Stanton and Baber (1992) also found inconclusive results with field independence/dependence, yet identifiable strategy shifts occurred. Messick (1976) reports that cognitive*styles* are related to a predisposition of behavior, whereas cognitive *strategies* are a translation of that predisposition in combination with many other factors. These factors are due to external influences such as environment, timing, and social dynamics; as well as internal influences such as prior knowledge, intellectual abilities, and motivation.

Considering the results of the experiment at hand, it seems as if each individual was able to assimilate the material in a manner that supported their own learning strategies and mental models, regardless of the Mode of Instruction. Unofficial observations made by the researcher and assistants indicate that there may have been patterns established by subjects as they navigated through the treatment. Even though an ad-hoc mouse-click tracking system was embedded in the treatment, these patterns were difficult to detect quantitatively. Instead, it appeared subjects developed, over time, a strategy to follow that involved not only the nature of the links made, but the amount of time allotted to a node with respect to its content, the re-visitation of particular nodes, and the overall order and nature of material covered.

The dynamics of the apparent adaptive strategies are tremendous and impressive. To accurately understand such, it would be necessary to account for the changing nature of both the message and the medium, as well as the nature of the individual. This is an essentially difficult problem, and one that leads to many more questions. Recommendations are made as to how such an endeavor might be approached from a communicative, social, and technological perspective.

4. CONCLUSIONS AND RECOMMENDATIONS

4.1 Observational Video and User-Tracking System

Two techniques used collaboratively that undoubtedly would yield interesting results are the use of an observational video and an embedded user-tracking system. An unobtrusive video camera could be situated to record visually and audially the actions and reactions of the subjects. Here, patterns of navigation and timing could be recorded, as well as behaviors of interaction with the program. A subject's personal responses such as laughter, facial expressions, gestures, and utterances could be considered in conjunction with her use of the courseware. Perhaps it would be possible to detect such things as motivating factors, hesitancies, difficulties, and learner strengths in such a learning environment.

Embedded within the software, a user-tracking system could record such things as timing within each node, number of repeated visits, and overall material sequencing. An identification of link value or relationship between nodes would be beneficial in recognizing patterns of learning strategies. A taxonomy of buttons has been developed by (Jona, 1991) that would provide a basis for identifying types of links. For instance, links could be labeled "explanatory", "justification", "example", "overview", "elaboration", or "similarity." By capturing the sorts of paths followed as well as simple controlling functions with the video, patterns in learning strategies may begin to emerge. For example, patterns indicating a top-down or bottom-up approach could be recognized.

4.2 Longitudinal Study and Communicative Evaluation

When faced with the concerns of the medium being the message, little more than time and repeated exposure can be recommended. Any medium carries a certain amount of novelty that may never "wear-off", and therefore a longevity study would be beneficial. This would also be helpful in recognizing not only subjects' initial approaches to learning, but their adaptive strategies as well.

Much research is done in the area of evaluation of communicative language learning. Resulting pedagogical models should be used in constructing a valid measure of student performance. The foundation of such models is that of a holistic approach that measures communicative proficiency as an interdependency of listening for overall comprehension, appropriacy and accuracy, speed of language processing, range of skill, pronunciation, and vocabulary, repetition and hesitancy, and creative interaction (Porter, 1983). Naturally, these elements cannot be tested with a multiple-choice, matching, or true/false test. Instead interactions such as interviews, or role-playing, could be video taped, observed, and evaluated based on the described criteria of communicative proficiency. With this being the stated goal, subjects no doubt would respond differently to the treatments.

Capretz, P. J. (1987). French in action. New Haven and London: Yale University Press.

Conklin, J. (1987). Hypertext: An introduction and survey. Computer, 20(9), 17-41.

Doland, V. M. (1989). Hypermedia as an interpretive act. Hypermedia, 1(1), 6-19.

Gagnè, R. M. (1985). The conditions of learning (4th ed.). New York: Holt.

Habermas, J. (1984). The theory of communicative action: Reasons and the rationalization of society. Boston, Mass: Beacon Press.

Heeter, C. &. G., P. (1992). It's time for hypermedia to move to "talking pictures". Jl of educational multimedia and hypermedia, 1, 255-261.

Jona, M., Bell, B., & Birnbaum, L. (1991). Button Theory: A taxonomic framework for student-teacher interactions in computer-based learning environments No. 12). Northwestern University.

Messick, S. (1976). Individuality and learning. San Francisco: Jossey-Base.

Myers, I. B. (1977). Supplementary manual: The myers-briggs type indicator. Palo Alto, CA: Consulting Psychologists Press, Inc.

Nelson, W. A. &. J., O.J. (1990). Effects of document complexity and organization on learning from hypertext. In Eastern educational research association, Clearwater, FL

Porter, D. &. J., K. (1983). Communicative Language Teaching. London: Academic Press, Incl.

Schank, R. (1990a). Artificial intelligence: A educational perspective Northwestern University.

Schank, R. C. &. E. D. J. (1990b). Using Technology to reshape education Northwestern University.

Stanton, N. &. B., C. (1992). An investigation of styles and strategies in self-directed learning. Jl of educational multimedia and hypermedia, 1, 147-167.

488

Snapshots from the Eye:
Toward Strategies for Viewing Bibliographic Citations

D. L. Howard[a] and M. E. Crosby[b]

[a]University of Hawaii, School of Library and Information Studies,
2550 The Mall, Honolulu, Hawaii 96822

[b]University of Hawaii, Dept. of Information and Computer Sciences, 2565 The
Mall, Honolulu, Hawaii 96822

Abstract
    The objective of this project was to discover and describe how people view
computer displayed textual information. In particular, individual viewing strategies
for bibliographic citations were studied. Analysis of eye movements and fixations
illuminated actual behavior. Two conditions were studied: viewing of relevant and
not relevant material. Behavior in viewing differed between conditions. Viewing
time for the relevant condition was longer. Movement between content areas
displayed different patterns for the two conditions as did percentages of direction
of movement between individual fixations. It appeared that subjects treated
relevant material sequentially but that not relevant was treated non-linearly.

1. INTRODUCTION AND RELATED WORK

    A rich computerized information retrieval environment is created by the
abundance of commercial on-line databases, the increasingly available on-line
public access catalogs in libraries, and the plethora of CD-ROM-based indexing
and abstracting products. More and more, an information seeker searches and
retrieves references to possible information sources by searching one of these
computerized databases that most usually contain bibliographic citations.

    A common outcome of an on-line search is a set of bibliographic citations to
documents and monographs which might possibly assist the searcher with his or
her information problem. A vital function for the searcher using this product is to
predict relevant documents based on the citation, a task that is frequently
performed on-line.

    The objective of this project was to describe how people view computer
displayed bibliographic citations as they perform the task of predicting the
relevance of the cited documents to their problem. The aim was to detect and
describe individual viewing strategies as represented by eye movements and
fixations.

The study of the use of computerized text has interested a number of researchers. One area of research deals with the details of presentation, such as the size and readability of individual characters, and the ergonomics of the text as presented in computer displays. For example, Mills and Weldon (1987) reviewed empirical studies concerning the readability of computerized text, with particular attention to the features of characters, the formatting of the screen, the contrast and color of the characters and background, and dynamic aspects of the screen. These factors indirectly address the cognitive aspects of using text.

A more directly related area of study highlights efforts to identify and establish the value of strategies for a searcher. Searching is concerned with finding a target in text that is arranged in a list either sequentially or non-sequentially. For example, Crosby and Peterson (1991) found that their subjects used four systematic search strategies which varied by experience or cognitive style of the searcher and Crosby and Stelovsky (1990) found that computer science students had distinct viewing strategies for scanning algorithms. The value of strategies is seen to be related to both their efficient use and their reflection in learned behavior. Hall (1985) found significant effects on the searching and scanning performance of some disabled students when they were trained in efficient strategies, whereas Monk (1977) found an expectation of duration of search carried from one trial to the next and that a subject produced a shorter search time if an immediately previous trial had a search time of similar magnitude.

Although related, searching differs from reading text for comprehension. Reading research, focused on the process of reading and understanding words and sentences, presents data on the rate of movements and the number and positioning of fixations found while a reader processes written text. Just and Carpenter (1980) have proposed a theory of reading that posits immediate processing of words as encountered. That is, as each word is encountered in the text it will be processed without the reader waiting to see what comes next. According to this view the fixated word is available for cognitive processing within a few tens of milliseconds. Although the details of the immediacy of processing are sometimes challenged by other researchers, they all agree that there is a relation between what is being seen and what is being thought about. For our purposes, the agreement on the relation between seeing and thinking is more important than the disagreement over timing. Eye movements and fixations are tied to cognitive processing.

2. METHODOLOGY

Our study examines the viewing records of eleven volunteer graduate students from the School of Library and Information Studies at the University of Hawaii at Manoa. The eight women and three men were tasked to solve two different information problems. The two information problems were directly related to the material of the courses in which the volunteers were enrolled, thus providing them with, it was hoped, an interesting and relevant problem.

Each subject viewed seven citations which were in one of two conditions: either topically relevant or topically not relevant to the problem being solved.

Citations were presented in two formats, which differed on spacing (single vs. double) and on the problem presentation (present vs. not present on the screen). Each subject saw only one format. Citations consisted of bibliographic data arranged in separate labeled fields for author, title, publication information, indexing (descriptors about the document), and an abstract.

Data collection used an Applied Sciences Laboratory Eye Movement Monitor connected to a Macintosh II computer. By projecting an infrared beam at one of the subject's eyes, the computerized device captured and computed the location coordinates of the eye 60 times a second as a complete citation was viewed by the subject on a large video monitor. These points were converted into fixations by a program which aggregates nearby points under guidance of a set of rules.

Subjects, seated comfortably with their head supported by a chin rest, were informed of the task orally and were instructed to treat the list of citations as normally as possible, to request either the next or a previously viewed citation when ready, and to think out loud as they performed the task. Audio tapes were used to collect the verbal protocols of the subjects, including their prediction, if made. Subjects used approximately one-half hour, including time to align and calibrate the instrument, for the prediction task.

3. RESULTS

Our analysis concentrated on answering two questions. First, was there a difference in processing relevant and not relevant materials? If differences in behavior were evident for the two conditions, what patterns of processing, if any, were observed?

Question One: Was there a difference in processing relevant and not relevant materials? Although subjects were initially ignorant of the bias of the list of citations that they viewed, it seemed possible that they would react to it as they processed the list. This question addresses whether that bias was discovered (consciously or unconsciously) and resulted in reactions that were manifest in the eye movements and fixations.

First, we wanted to combine the two relevant data sets. An analysis of variances of viewing times for the two relevant lists of citations indicated that they did not differ significantly as did a comparison of variances of the average size in words of the citations. Statistical non-significance for these two features indicated that the two lists were drawn from the same population and that their processing information might be conjoined safely .

We then turned to a comparison on several measures of the conditions of relevant and not relevant. Again, to insure that the lists are from the same population, the variances for total viewing time and for average number of words per citation of the two lists, that is the relevant and not relevant lists, were compared. No difference was found, thus indicating that they were from the same population.

Based on earlier work by Howard (1991), we knew that total viewing time varied between relevant and not relevant lists. Less time was spent viewing not relevant material (F = 16.907, p ≤ .0001) and the number of fixations differed for the two conditions, again with less fixations per not relevant citation (F = 15.705, p ≤ .0002). This seems to indicate that not relevant decisions are made more quickly and require less viewing than relevant ones.

Question Two: Given that differences in behavior were evident for the two conditions, what patterns of processing, if any, were observed? Citations were partitioned into distinct content areas in order to examine processing in more detail. Author, title, publishing data, indexing, abstract and, when available, the problem were each identified spatially. For each citation, the number of fixations in each content area (box) was computed as was the direction of movement between boxes. Each move was described by a direction (up, indicated by a minus, or down, indicated by a plus) and a distance (depicted in terms of the number of intervening boxes from the starting box). This data was analyzed for each condition using seven citations for each of the eleven subjects. Average percentages were developed for the possible eleven distances.

As expected, once in a box people tended to stay there. Consistently, the largest percentage of movement for both conditions was for no movement, that is, for staying in a box. However, distance and direction of movement between boxes differed for the conditions. Figure 1 shows the percentages for movements between boxes.

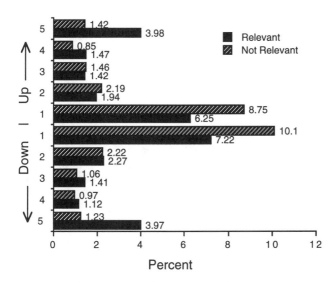

Figure 1. Distance and Direction of Content Area Movements

These percentages are computed across subjects and citations. Sustained processing of one box was truer of the not relevant group than of the relevant group. Movements for the not relevant group tended to be to an adjacent box, whereas movements for the relevant group showed more of a tendency to jump over boxes toward the periphery of the scene.

Because we found that the relevant group tended to moved toward the periphery of the citation, it seems reasonable to think they might look back at previous information more often. To examine this question, we looked at movement between fixations in the horizontal and vertical axes. That is, we described movement between each fixation pair as going left or right, up or down, and fitting one of the four combinations (left, down; right, down; left, up; and right, up). Average percentages of these movement directions were computed for all fixations within the citation. Table 1 presents the results of an analysis of variance that was done to see if the combination directions differed between conditions.

Table 1
Analysis of Variance for Directional Combinations

Anova table for a 2-factor repeated measures Anova.

Source:	df:	Sum of Squares:	Mean Square:	F-test:	P value:
Condition (A)	1	40568	40568	15.624	.0002
subjects w. groups	75	194742.13	2596.562		
Repeated Measure (B)	3	9474.114	3158.038	7.587	.0001
AB	3	4316.942	1438.981	3.457	.0172
B x subjects w. groups	225	93652.694	416.234		

There were no missing cells found.

Not only was there a significant difference between conditions (Condition (A) in Table 1) but also the four combinations (Repeated Measure (B)) as well as the interaction (AB) displayed significant variation. Using a t-test, we found significant differences of right and left movements between the conditions. Percentage of right movements were significantly higher for the relevant condition ($t = 1.9$, $p \leq .05$). Of the four combinations of vertical and horizontal movement, left and up was the only one that differed significantly for the conditions. Not relevant citations achieved a higher percentage of left and up movement ($t = -2$, $p \leq .05$).

Based on this, are they reading or searching? Reading in English is generally considered to be a series of left to right, top to bottom eye movements interspersed with data processing fixations. In our terms, movements going right and down, on the average, would be more representative of a linear processing of a text. Subjects viewing relevant citations tended to show more of this behavior. They had more right movements, and showed a tendency toward more down movements as well.

Searching, however, typically looks for a target, which would likely be manifested by more non-linear movements within the citation. In our directional terms, movements going up, on the average, would be more representative of this type of non-linear processing. This pattern was found in studies of searching, as previously noted. Subjects viewing not relevant citations displayed more of this behavior. They had more left movements, and significantly more left and up movements.

4. DISCUSSION

Viewing strategies are difficult to capture and present. To some extent, this difficulty stems from the temporal character of eye movements. Eye movements are sequenced, and the sequence is important. Direction is another feature that is relevant to describing a path for the eye. We have attempted to capture some of this by examining movements between content areas and between individual pairs of fixations. This a beginning toward describing viewing strategies for computer presented bibliographic citations. As we learn more about how an information seeker performs a task using computer text systems, the more we will be able to craft our support systems. This in turn supports a longer term goal of predicting user needs from user behavior.

5. REFERENCES

Crosby, M. E., & Peterson, W. W. (1991). Using eye movements to classify search strategies. In *Proceedings of the Human Factors Society 35th Annual Meeting, Vol. 2* (pp. 1476-1480). Santa Monica, CA: Human Factors Society.

Crosby, M. E., & Stelovsky, J. (1990). Using enhanced eye monitoring equipment to relate subject differences and presentation material. In R. Groner, G. d'Ydewalle & R. Parham (Eds.), *From eye to mind: Information acquisition in perception, search and reading* (pp. 3-22). Amsterdam: Elsevier Science.

Hall, L. C. (1985). Searching high and low: The development of efficient visual search in hearing deaf and learning disabled children. In R. Groner, G. W. McConkie & C. Menz (Eds.), *Eye movements and human information* (pp. 273-298). Amsterdam: North Holland.

Howard, D. L. (1991). What the eye sees while predicting a document's pertinence from its citation. In J. Griffiths, (Ed.), *ASIS '91: Proceedings of the 54th ASIS Annual Meeting, 28*, 87-101.

Just, M. A., & Carpenter, P. A. (1980). A theory of reading: From eye fixations to comprehension. *Psychological Review, 87*(4), 329-354.

Mills, C. B., & Weldon, L. J. (1987). Reading text from computer screens. *ACM Computing Surveys, 19*(4), 329-358.

Monk, T. H. (1977). Sequential expectancy in visual search. *Human Factors, 19*(6), 601-606.

A Model of Learning with Hypermedia Systems

G.A. Hutchings, W. Hall and C.J. Colbourn*

Department of Electronics & Computer Science, University of Southampton, Southampton SO9 5NH, United Kingdom

* Department of Psychology, University of Southampton, Southampton SO9 5NH, United Kingdom

Abstract

1.   INTRODUCTION

It is frequently suggested that hypertext and hypermedia may have a significant effect on the learning process [1–5]. However, before we can build the most effective hypermedia systems to support learning at different levels, we must first understand in detail how hypermedia systems may be used. Various studies have shown that simply letting learners wander freely within a complex, highly interwoven network of information nodes is not sufficient for quality learning to occur [6,7]. Instead, learners need to be guided, given prompts, clues and suggestions as to which parts of the information network are appropriate to their needs. At the same time however, learners must be able to branch out from these guidelines and to determine their own needs.

A variety of tools and devices have been developed which are intended to help users to accomplish this sort of discovery learning without becoming lost or disoriented in the forest of information [8–12]. It is not clear however, how these facilities will be used by learners in their quest for knowledge, or even whether they will be used at all. If they are used, do they serve the designers intended purpose of reducing the 'lost in hyperspace' effect?

We present here three studies looking in turn at the effects of task, interface design, and individual learning style on the behaviour of users interacting with an educational hypermedia application on cell biology. These findings are used to converge on a possible model of hypermedia interaction which can provide a significant analytical base for looking at other hypermedia systems.

2.   THE HYPERMEDIA APPLICATION

The hypermedia application used in the studies described below, *Cell Motility*, was developed using StackMaker, a tool kit for producing hypermedia applications within the HyperCard environment [13].   StackMaker enables the author quickly and easily to incorporate text , animations, simple graphics and video sequences into an application. Further tools are used to identify words, phrases or labels as link anchors and the information they are to be linked to as link destinations. Contents and Index Lists, together with graphical representations of either restricted parts of the application (Local Maps), or the entire application (Global Maps) are generated automatically from this information so that the computational mechanics of the authoring process, which are potentially complex and time consuming, are hidden from the author who is able to concentrate solely on the content and structure of the learning material.

The Cell Motility application consists of approximately 85 nodes comprising text, moving video, graphics and animation, with approximately 200 links. The content was designed to be complimentary to a two week section of an introductory undergraduate course in Cell Biology being taught in the Department of Biology at the University of Southampton.

3. METHODS OF STUDY

For each stage of our study, the Cell Motility application was introduced to students taking the introductory Cell Biology course initially in a traditional lecture-style presentation. The main features were demonstrated, and the purpose of the study explained, so that students were not completely ignorant of what was involved when they arrived for their 'hands-on' session, which would be during the following two weeks.

Students were required to use the system at least once as a compulsory, but non-assessed part of their course. Following the initial compulsory session a small number of students each year did spend additional unsupervised time using the system. Cell Motility was made available for use in the University Library since it was hoped to introduce the technology as an extension to the existing working and learning environment.

Exact times varied over the three years, but on average students were given a 20–25 minute introduction, including a brief guide on how to use the mouse, and the idea of buttons and icons as *hotspots* on the screen causing events to occur when they are activated by clicking on them with the mouse. Following this introduction, a period of 45–60 minutes was spent browsing through the Cell Motility application. Each student was given a subject to investigate, in order that their browsing might not be totally random (this is referred to as 'just looking'). Some students returned for a second controlled session with the system in which they were asked to perform different tasks. The first cohort was given multiple choice questions to answer, while the others were asked to make notes in preparation for an essay.

Every piece of information accessed by a student and every action performed, together with a time stamp in seconds, was recorded in a usage log. Data extracted from these logs formed the basis for the analyses described below.

4.   STUDYING INTERACTION PATTERNS

During a pilot study [14], a number of user categories became evident, based on subjective observations of the students during their use of the system:

- browsers: These students roamed freely around the system following hypertext links.
- planners: This group made extensive use of the index and contents.
- fearful: These were overawed in some way by the system, either by the hardware, or by the expansiveness of the biological content.
- fun seekers: This minority sought the quickest route to the visual material.

Since these initial categories were obtained purely from casual observations, it was necessary to determine whether they were indicative of some more fundamental underlying process. Using data from the first two cohorts therefore, a number of spectra were devised based on easily obtainable measurements which would allow the visualisation in 3 dimensions of different interactions with the hypermedia system [15]:

- *Style*:   a measure of the way in which information is accessed in terms of the number of times navigation tools were used

• *Medium*:   a measure of the type of information accessed in terms of the number of text or graphics nodes accessed

• *Spirit*:   a measure of activity in terms of the diversity of nodes accessed

These values are all objective, quantifiable measures of the manner of an individual's interaction with the system, and as such are applicable to any interactive multimedia application—not just the one described here on the subject of cell biology.

A position on each axis for each student can be calculated using data extracted from the student logs:

$$S_t = A_h/A_t$$

where S_t = style
A_h = number of hypertext actions
A_t = total number of actions

Thus, a value of S_t close to 0 indicates a user making extensive use of navigation tools, whereas S_t close to 1 indicates a user following hypertext links.

$$M = T_a/N_t$$

where   M = medium
T_a = number of text nodes accessed
N_t = total number of nodes accessed

Thus, a value of M close to 0 indicates a user accessing mainly video/graphical information, whereas M close to 1 indicates a user accessing mainly textual information.

$$S_p = N_d/N_t$$

where S_p = spirit
N_d = number of different nodes accessed
N_t = total number of nodes accessed

Thus, a value of S_p close to 0 indicates a timid user, whereas S_p close to 1 indicates a bold user.

4.1.   Effect of task on interaction patterns

A group of 45 students took part in this stage of the study, and after an initial introduction spent approximately 45 minutes browsing through the Cell Motility application. 21 of these returned for a second session, in which they were given a set of multiple choice questions to answer. A second group of 60 students were asked to browse through the Cell Motility application. During a second session, 50 returned and were asked to use the system to make preliminary notes for an essay entitled "A Comparison of the Actin/Myosin and Tubulin/Dynein Motors in Cell Motility" [15].

Multivariate analysis of variance (MANOVA) was used to test for an effect of the task on the users' interaction patterns. However, due to the fact that some participants provided data for only one of the task conditions, while others provided data for two (none actually provided data for all three conditions), the tasks were contrasted in pairs, collapsed across stages as necessary, to standardise the design for analysis. Thus, the significant MANOVA for all three interaction measures for note takers contrasted with those answering multiple choice questions (multivariate F=4.58, df=3, 60; p<0.01) showed that the note takers made considerably more use of hypertext links than those answering multiple choice questions (i.e. for *style*, 0.57 vs 0.49, univariate F=4.24, df=1, 62; p<0.05). The latter group tended to use navigation tools more extensively . However, note takers viewed a smaller number of different nodes than the multiple choice question answerers (i.e. for *spirit*, 0.45 vs 0.57, univariate F=13.38, df=1, 62; p<0.001).

The contrast between note takers and those who were 'just looking' showed a similarly reliable interaction pattern difference (multivariate F=5.30, df=3, 65; p<0.01). Those who were 'just looking' viewed more graphical/video nodes than the note takers (i.e. for *medium*, 0.57 vs 0.48, univariate F=9.16, df=1, 67; p<0.01). They also viewed a greater number of different nodes than the note takers (i.e. for *spirit*, 0.51 vs 0.45, univariate F=5.25, df=1, 67; p<0.025).

The contrast between those 'just looking' and those answering multiple choice questions didn't reveal any clear cut differences between interaction patterns. The overall MANOVA showed no effects, although 'just looking' did appear to have involved more extensive use of hypertext links than did answering multiple choice questions (i.e. for *style*, .56 vs 0.47, univariate F=4.77, df=1, 78; p<0.05).

4.2.   Effect of interface design

Two groups, each of 33 participants, were observed using the Cell Motility application on workstations with either a 13" (small screen group) or a 21" monitor (large screen group). In addition, video sequences were displayed on a separate 12" video monitor. On the 21" set-up, navigation tools were permanently displayed, and constantly updated to reflect the 'position' of the user within the information. In contrast, users of the 13" set-up had to make specific requests for navigation tools to be displayed by clicking on buttons on a floating palette, accessed via a pull-down menu. Users were given the same task in both groups—to make preliminary notes for an essay entitled "Describe the different ways in which cilia beat, and explain the underlying biomechanical mechanism" [16].

To test for a difference in the behaviour of the two groups in this study—small screen and large screen—MANOVA was again used, with *style*, *medium*, and *spirit* as the dependent variables and screen size as the between-subjects independent variable.

While the MANOVA produced a significant outcome (multivariate F=3.63, df=3, 59; p<0.02), differences between the large and small screen conditions were only evident for the *style* variable (univariate F=10.61, df=1, 61; p<0.002). This result indicated that users of the system with navigation tools constantly displayed made more extensive use of those tools (mean value of *style*=0.43), while those who had to make specific requests for navigation tools tended to make more use of hypertext links (mean value of *style*=0.58).

There were no reliable differences between the screen conditions for either *spirit* or *medium*. In the case of the former variable the means for the large and small screen conditions were 0.32 and 0.31 respectively indicating that all the users tended towards timidity. For *medium*, the means for the two screen conditions were both 0.63 indicating that the users tended to access textual rather than video/graphical information.

Despite the lack of substantial differences between the screen size conditions, a supplementary analysis of the *spirit* variable together with the 'total number of nodes accessed' revealed a noticeable within-condition consistency that suggested behaviour in the large screen group was clearly focused on the task in hand, while those in the small screen group seemed to wander aimlessly around the same small patch of hyperspace.

4.3 Effect of individual preference

The studies reported above focused on overall outcomes as described by 'group' analyses. While these gave a clear picture of the influence of the important independent variables of the task and technology environments, this was at the expense of a close look at possible idiosyncratic aspects of the behaviour of our participants. Thus the derived interaction measures—*style, medium* and *spirit*—for the two different tasks carried out by each of the participants in the previous studies were scrutinised carefully to see if there were any identifiable patterns specific to individuals rather than to the conditions under which they used the multimedia system.

Various data graphic and cluster analysis techniques were used to evaluate the intra-subject, as against the inter-subject, consistency of behaviour. One telling analysis was based on comparing each interaction index across the two tasks the participants completed. To formalise the results, the sample standard deviation for each index measure was taken as a criterion. The participants' interaction behaviour was then classified as consistent if the difference between tasks was less than this value, or inconsistent if above (this method has its foundation in the basis of most parametric two-sample tests. See e.g. [17]). Adding the more stringent requirement that this consistency criterion should be met for all three interaction indices, it was found that three (18%) of the first sample of 17 participants, and six (19%) of the second sample of 32 participants showed such consistent interaction behaviour. This clustering was similarly found using hierarchical cluster analysis (via the SPSS package) and several different agglomerative techniques [18]. Other clusters shown by these analyses were less easy to interpret.

Thus it appears that some 18% of the individuals used in our studies could be seen to approach the system in a consistent manner despite the task they were asked to carry out, while others were more task dependent.

5. A MODEL OF INTERACTIONS

The studies and data reported above suggest that the behaviour of students using a hypermedia system is subject to the influence of task, system, and idiosyncratic factors. Which, if any, of these factors predominate depends on the particular combination present at any one time. In particular, certain students appeared to show a consistency of approach irrespective of the task and system factors, and while these were only a relatively small percentage of the sample, it would be advantageous to understand further any precursors and consequences of their behaviour in using multimedia systems relative to other individuals. In order to pursue this, studies will need to be specifically designed for that purpose.

Another form of behavioural consistency was found in the investigation of 'system' factors. The 'large screen' condition would appear to offer the greatest flexibility in catering for individual preferences of multimedia use, since all methods of navigating are equally accessible in terms of the effort required to use them. There was greater within-group consistency for participants in this condition in terms of the number of nodes investigated. Of course, task influences may be modified by increasing experience of the system, allowing users to develop their own approach to learning tasks with hypermedia systems. It will be necessary to collect some longitudinal data on use of a system to investigate this more thoroughly.

It is clear that the factors we have described in this paper—task, system and individual differences—interact in ways that we have yet to fully describe, though we have demonstrated the way in which individual differences can supersede the influence of the learning environment. We believe that the approach and methods presented here can provide a basis for extending our knowledge and understanding of the use of hypermedia systems in the learning process.

REFERENCES

1. McKnight, C., Dillon, A. & Richardson, J. (1991) Hypertext in Context. Cambridge University Press
2. Nielsen, J. (1990) Hypertext and Hypermedia. Academic Press, London
3. Duncan, E.B. (1989) A Faceted Approach to Hypertext ? In Hypertext: Theory into Practice. McAleese, R. Ed. Intellect, Oxford
4. Jaffe, C.C. & Lynch, P.J. (1989) Hypermedia in the Life Sciences. Academic Computing (Sept), 10–13, 52–57
5. Stanton, N.A. & Stammers, R.B. (1990) Learning Styles in a Non-Linear Training Environment. In Hypertext: State of the Art. McAleese, R. & Green, C. Eds. Intellect, Oxford
6. Hammond, N. & Allinson, L. (1988) Travels Around a Learning Support Environment: Rambling, Orienteering or Touring? In Proceedings of CHI, 1988 (Washington, May 15–19). 269–273 ACM, New York
7. Wright, P. & Lickorish, A. (1990) An Empirical Comparison of two Navigation Systems for two Hypertexts. In Hypertext: State of the Art. McAleese, R. & Green, C. Eds. Intellect, Oxford
8. Bourne J.R., Cantwell, J., Brodersen, A.J., Antao, B. & Huang, Y.-C. (1989) Intelligent Hypertutoring in Engineering. Academic Computing (Sept), 18–20, 42–49
9. Yankelovich, N., Landow, G. & Heywood, P. Designing Hypermedia "Ideabases"— The Intermedia Experience. IRIS Technical Report 87–4, Brown University
10. Mayes, J.T., Kibby, M.R. & Watson, H. (1988) StrathTutor: The Development of a Learning By Browsing System on the Macintosh. Computers in Education 12: 221–229
11. Trigg, R.H. (1988) Guided Tours and Tabletops: Tools for Communicating in a Hypertext Environment. ACM Trans. Office Information Systems 6(4), 398–414
12. Zellweger, P.T. (1989) Scripted Documents: A Hypermedia Path Mechanism. Proceedings of Hypertext '89, Pittsburgh, Pennsylvania. 1–14
13. Hutchings G.A., Carr L.A. and Hall W. (1992) StackMaker: An Environment for Creating Hypermedia Learning Material. Hypermedia 4(3), 197–211
14. Hall W., Thorogood P., Hutchings G. and Carr L. (1989) Using Hypercard and Interactive Video in Education: An Application in Cell Biology. Educational and Training Technology International 26, 207–214
15. Hutchings, G.A., Hall, W. & Colbourn, C.J. (in press) Patterns of Students' Interactions with a Hypermedia System. Interacting with Computers 5(2)
16. Hutchings G.A., Hall W. and Colbourn C.J. (1992) The Effect of Navigation Tool Presentation on Hypermedia Navigation Strategies & User Disorientation Department of Electronics & Computer Science, University of Southampton, U.K., CSTR 92-14
17. Hays, W.L. (1973) Statistics for the Social Sciences. London: Holt Rinehart and Winston
18. Everitt, B. (1980) Cluster Analysis (Second Edition). New York: Halsted Press

Changing Persona: University Student to Museum Visitor

Trevor H. Jones and Margaret Christensen

College of Information Studies, Drexel University, Philadelphia, PA 19104

Abstract

Based on a partial model of the user, the persona construct dynamically alters the appearance of a multimedia information base. Personae were implemented in the Drexel Multimedia Demo. This project, the concept of persona, development of the specific museum persona, and discussion of the implications of using any project in multiple environments are presented.

1. Introduction

Visitors to the Franklin Institute Science Museum, freshmen, graduate students, university professors, and parents of prospective Drexel University students all use one large collection of multimedia information called the Drexel Multimedia Demo. In order to tailor user interfaces for these differing classes of users at low cost, the concept of persona was created.

This paper describes the Drexel Multimedia Demo in Section 2, describes the persona concept, implementation, and methodology in Section 3, and illustrates the process of acquisition of the "museum visitor" persona in Section 4.

1. The Drexel Multimedia Demo

Two needs initially motivated the development of the Drexel Multimedia Demo:

(i) Students requested instruction about multimedia, hypermedia, and hypertext, but the field of human-computer interaction has been under rapid development and few supporting instructional materials exist.

(ii) Secondly, admissions and public relations personnel, faculty and administrators are regularly called upon to convey a sense of Drexel University to prospective students and others outside of the university. The 1991 - 1992 school year marked Drexel University's centennial year. A hypermedia presentation has natural appeal in a University where since 1984 all freshmen have been required to have individual access to a Macintosh personal computer.

Later, the Franklin Institute Science Museum acquired it for display on the floor of its Future's Center.

The project has two major components: multimedia education and Drexel University material. Within the Drexel portion, the following hypermedia techniques are exemplified:

>hypertext with hot links
>black and white and color still images captured by a scanner or video

capture board

>colorized still images
>animations
>digitized voice
>synthesized voice
>digitized music
>music created through a MIDI interface
>analog video from a laser disk
>digital video

Students can see these individual and combined techniques in use there, and can interactively access information about them in the education section. For example, after the introductory animation and video, a student may interrupt the multimedia experience and ask "How we did it..." to find out how to create similar effects or request "About multimedia..." for general background information. Conversely, students studying the educational section can follow "Example" links to see specific techniques embedded in a complete hypermedia work about Drexel.

The theoretical foundations for the educational design (see Spiro and Jehng (1990), and Streeter (1991)) are described in Christensen et al. (1993a). Use and evaluation of the software for instruction in human-computer interaction within Association for Computing Machinery curricula is described in Christensen et al. (1993b).

3. Persona

From the beginning, it was envisioned that there would be several different kinds of users of the Drexel Multimedia Demo and that they would want to see different portions of the information space, presented somewhat differently, and with differing degrees of user control and interactivity. A "persona" offers a view of the Drexel Multimedia Media Demo to specific classes of users in an acceptable manner. Unlike "Guides", there is no artificially intelligent agent asking the user what information s/he wants from different viewpoints, but rather empirically and heuristically obtained evidence of what makes the interface acceptable.

For example, two personae are particularly important for use with our classes in human-computer interaction where hypermedia is one topic of study and where students' term projects frequently include hypermedia:

The "student of user interfaces" persona gives the computer-experienced student access to the entire complex information space but it first requires the user to pass through two screens of instructions about the availability, scope, and accessibility of the educational material. The project is available for individual student use on the multimedia workstation within Drexel's Computing Center. Here, students are in control and can browse and access material as they want. They can borrow ideas and code from the project, and try it on the same workstation, or copy it to their own computers for possible inclusion in their term projects or other uses.

The "Presentation" persona is designed for a presenter/instructor who is in control, in a lecture hall with projection and amplification facilities. The presenter has easy access to all of the information, but is not required to pass through introductory directions first. Any screens with textual directions about use of the project are omitted in this persona where the presenter is assumed to be familiar with the software already. This has been used successfully both in offering an introduction to hypermedia to a class of students and for presentations to the curious public. In this mode, the control of the software is given to the instructor while the audience sits back and sees a show. Student 'interactivity' is instructor mediated.

The scope, presentation, and control for differing personae are encoded in If-Then statements within the HyperCard scripting language. Thus the persona encoding represents a partial model of the user.

In general, data for personae were gathered during the normal process of iterative evaluation, and thus at no additional cost. That is, an initial design was iteratively evaluated and revised for each class of users until acceptable criteria were met. In this particular case, the "presenter" persona was acquired first, followed by the "student of HCI", followed by "museum visitor".

4. Acquiring the Museum Visitor Persona

4.1. Iteration One

In developing the museum visitor persona we started with the student persona since we knew that the Franklin Institute had an educational objective. Subsequent interviews with museum personnel who were experts in the design of exhibits indicated several alterations:

(i) the use of a touch screen rather than mouse both for ease of use and robustness of hardware in a public setting;

(ii) the use of a larger screen;

(iii) the use of larger buttons and typeface due to the implementation of the touch screen;

(iv) the addition of an attract loop to compete in a sensory rich environment;

(v) increased emphasis on the educational aspects of the project;

(vi) simplification of language for the general public.

It was agreed that the intended users would be English-speaking visitors with at least some high school education. Although the museum offers much for young children too, it was considered important to retain the sophistication of the project.

4.2. Iteration Two

After the museum's experts viewed and approved the alterations of the first iteration, the project was used in the museum on a rolling cart where it could be moved onto the exhibit floor for evaluation by museum visitors.

This stage of formative evaluation was designed to focus on usability, navigation and appearance of the project as well as to assess the initial changes previously specified by the experts. The sample used consisted of 22 visitors to the Institute who were chosen randomly as they entered the presentation area of the exhibit. They ranged in age from teenage to adult, and in education from junior high school to graduate school. Each subject was given an introduction to the exhibit including its purpose, its content, and where to touch the screen to navigate. Semi-structured interviews and observations were recorded while users were engaged with the system and self administered questionnaires were completed following use. Results were deemed acceptable if users responded above the middle of a 5 point Likert scale.

Table 1
First stage evaluation results summary

Evaluation Category	%age Scores Acceptable
Attractiveness of Exhibit	67
Ease of Use	57
Interest Level	67
Navigation Methodology	57
Mapping Representation of Contents	57

At this stage, observations elucidated serious navigation difficulties. The navigational map was therefore redesigned, and inconsistent buttons were brought into conformance. Because of the large size of the project, and because of the large button size required, the original navigational map of the entire project had required the use of modes which "zoomed in" on various areas. The redesign used a simpler, higher level map. In addition, numerous bugs were located and fixed. Although their experience was hampered by navigational difficulties, users reported higher scores for attractiveness and interesting content. Many saw too strong an emphasis on the Drexel material, and the introductory screen was redesigned to emphasize the equal portions of the project (educational material and example material from the Drexel content).

4.3. Iteration Three

This stage hoped to confirm the changes made during the previous stage, and to test a new automated user path data collector. However, to move a bit closer to the intended museum experience, users were not given a preliminary introduction. The first four subjects were completely unable to understand the purpose of the exhibit.or how to interact with it, having had no personal, written, or computerized instructions.

We realized that students had been introduced to the project in class, but museum visitors would not have that benefit. Further design additions included an introductory screen followed by a digital video, where a museum employee described the project's purpose. In addition, graphics were designed for the kiosk which would house the project and which would give the visitor some information about multimedia.

In this stage also, user's time constraints became obvious as potential subjects were asked to step into the office to answer questions, when they reported that they had other obligations.

4.4. Fourth Stage Summative

Following actual introduction of the exhibit into the public display area, summative evaluation was completed. This was designed to evaluate the overall effectiveness and usability of the project in its final operating environment. At this stage the full exhibit display had been completed, including identified additions from stage 2. These included an additional introductory screen ("touch screen to begin") and an introductory digital video explaining the contents of the exhibit.

Unobtrusive observation during use and user surveys following use, were used. Observation confirmed surveys. Due to the repeatable results being obtained, a relatively small sample of 10 users was recorded. These were obtained over several days and at varying times to provide an unbiased sample. Subjects ranged from teen to adult, covering educational backgrounds of high school to advanced level degrees, as well as varying computer abilities and work experiences. In all assessment areas, at least 80% of the sample gave acceptable results. Acceptable was defined as receiving scores of at least 4 on a Likert Scale of 1-6 (table 2) or by receiving above 3 on an disagree/agree scale of 1-5 (table 3). For example, the assessment of interest level was graded as 4 or higher (on a scale of 1-6) by 80% of the sample.

4.5. Other Issues

Personae addresses user interface issues. The evaluative data above indicate that the "Museum Visitor" persona is now acceptable to users. However, although the project has been used successfully educationally in a university setting, no attempt at educational evaluation has yet been made in the museum setting. In fact, during our data collection, 42 per cent of a sample of 19 reported that entertainment/diversion was equally or more important than education. In

Table 2
Summative Stage Evaluation Summary 1

Evaluation Category	%age Scores Acceptable
Attractiveness of exhibit	100
Ease of Use	90
Level of Interest	80
Entertainment Value	80

Table 3
Summative Stage Evaluation Summary 2

Evaluation Category	%age Scores Acceptable
Navigation Methodology	80
Ease of Comprehension of Content	80
Contribution to Multimedia Definition	80
Contribution to Multimedia Methodology	90

----

addition, time constraints are frequently more severe on the museum visitor since they must "watch the children", "meet my husband", "see all of the exhibits before the bus leaves", etc. It is thus not yet known whether the theoretical educational foundations for the project, especially cognitive flexibility theory [Spiro and Jehng (1990)], which were originally intended for the learning of complex, ill-structured ideas such as the design of multimedia are appropriate for a museum setting or not.

4. Conclusion

In conclusion the following is a summary of the findings derived from the development of the museum persona and installation of the project into the Franklin Institute Science Museum:

1.   The persona concept is a useful methodology for quickly and efficiently adapting large projects for use by multiple constituents. The time required to prepare a project is significantly reduced without detracting from the overall content of the project. In this instance, time spent on evaluation, development and installation (allowing for non-exhibit time, e.g. holidays, etc.) was in the order of 3-4 months. The original project took about 2 years to create. Considering the size and capability of the resultant application, this must be viewed as an acceptable process where time is a factor.

2.   When developing any project or interface, it is important to remember

that the requirements of constituents may change based on their operating environment. In our case, because of the museum's educational goals, the definition of the user as student was at least partially correct, but given the sensory rich environment together with limited time allocations and peer responsibilities, the requirements of the student in this arena may be significantly different than when in the classroom. Likewise, we might find the professionals' use of an application at work is different than when at home, based solely on the change in environment. User personae must then be developed in the context of the environment and not simply from an isolated user definition.

5. Acknowledgments

Michael Giamo of the Office of Computing Services was the artist and programmer for the Drexel Multimedia Demo. Paul Helfrich and Michael Moulton from the Franklin Institute spent many hours guiding the project's move to the museum. The original software development was made possible through a grant from Drexel University's Microcomputer Policy Committee. Drexel University provided equipment for the exhibit, and the Franklin Institute provided cabinetry, sound amplification, and much expertise in the design of the exhibit. We are very grateful to all.

6. References

1. Christensen, M., Giamo,M., Jones, T., and Simpson, L. (1993a), *Using Hypermedia to Teach About Hypermedia*, Educational Technology Review, May, to appear.
2. Christensen, M. Giamo, M., and Jones, T. (1993b), *Support for Teaching the Design and Implementation of Multimedia/Hypermedia Systems*, SIGCSE Bulletin, February.
3. Oren, T., Salomon, G., Kreitman, K. and Don, A. (1990). *Guides: Characterizing the Interface.* The Art of Human-Computer Interface Design, Brenda Laurel, ed., Addison Wesley, Reading, MA., pp. 367-382.
4. Spiro, R. J. and Jehng, H. (1990). *Cognitive Flexibility and Hypertext: Theory and Technology for the Nonlinear Traversal of Complex Subject Matter.* Cognition, Education, Multimedia, D. Nix and R. Spiro, eds., Lawrence Erlbaum Assoc., Hillsdale, NJ.
5. Streeter, Deborah (1991), *Concept Maps: A Tool for Teachers and Learners*, Proc. Conference on Teaching Economics: Instruction and Classroom-Based Research, Robert Morris College, Pittsburgh, Feb. 1991.
6.Wesley, W.G. and Wesley, B. (1990). *Concept Mapping: A Brief Introduction.* The Teaching Professor, October, 1990.

Individual differences in the use of hyper/multimedia by undergraduate students at the University of Hawaii at Manoa

T.N. Kamala, Jan Stelovsky and Martha E. Crosby

Information and Computer Science Department, University of Hawaii at Manoa, Honolulu, Hawaii 96822

Abstract

To test which individual difference characteristics influence performance in a hyper/multimedia system, we studied student performances on a specially designed multimedia system, which presented information in various interaction modes using a direct manipulation interface. While the influence of visual ability could not be tested because almost all students were high visuals, 'computer affinity' influenced performance; the 'dynamic' learning style showed significance on tasks based on the text+sound+icon mode. Sex also showed a significant effect in this mode. Personality traits, language and ethnicity did not show any effect. We suggest improvments to such empirical studies that can help determine which media and interface benefit which type of user.

1. INTRODUCTION

Since the introduction of microcomputers in the class rooms, research has been focused to a considerable extent on the effectiveness of their use for instruction by teachers. However, as students themselves started using computers for self-learning, designers of such systems, computer scientists and teachers alike realized the need to study the differences between individual students in the use of these systems. The latest such technology is the emerging hyper/multimedia on the Macintosh platform that is making great inroads into classrooms as instructional tools, revolutionizing the way instruction can be imparted and self-learning augmented. Currently, a great deal of effort and money is being spent on the development of hyper/multimedia systems for educational purposes. Therefore, it is necessary to find out whether all this expense and effort is achieving the ultimate goal of bringing the greatest good to all students who differ widely in their preferences and potential. As Marsh and Kumar (1992) observe, there are some inherent problems with hyper/multimedia that will have to be overcome before it is able to fulfill its potential. In short, it is time to find answers to two questions: (1) "Is hyper/multimedia a panacea for all ills of teaching and learning?" and (2) "Do all students benefit equally from the use of hyper/multimedia as contrasted with the pure text-based systems using command-driven interfaces?"

2. LITERATURE REVIEW

The ways in which human beings interact and absorb information delivered through technology, has rightly been both the concern and interest of researchers in many fields; because, it is the only way better systems/interfaces can be designed. It is also important for

508

another reason - to realize that what is good for one individual is not necessarily good for everyone else, nor for that matter, even for the same individual in all situations. Borgman (1989) tested undergraduate students from three major disciplines on a prototype library online catalog and found that their performance differed markedly and they were related to their technical aptitudes and personality types (as defined by the Myers-Briggs Test Instrument - MBTI) or the learning styles (Kolb's Learning Style Inventory - KLSI), or both. Sein (1988) studied the differences in performance of undergraduate students in learning an electronic mail system to test whether the learning styles (KLSI types) and visual ability were predictors of performance. Sein was the first one to look at correlation between performance of students in programming tasks and their visual ability, using the VZ-2 test instrument and, indeed, found a strong correlation. Crosby and Peterson (1989) tested students in program learning strategies and found positive correlation between their personality types, experience and performance. Kamala (1991), however, found that the visual ability of undergraduate students tested for their performance on three different CD ROM databases, were indeed stronger predictors of performance than learning styles or personality traits. She also studied "computer affinity" as a separate variable from "computer literacy" and found that the former did prove to be a better predictor of performance of students with the CD ROM databases than the latter.

Hyper/multimedia combines the traditional media (audio-video) with computers to provide a new, powerful, flexible and interrelated form of information delivery on affordable microcomputer platforms. Hyper/multimedia systems are increasingly used for classroom instruction and learning in schools and universities. Multimedia enthusiasts often regard that the advantages of multimedia as instructional tools are self-evident. Kahn (1988) reported that the experience with the numerous hyper/multimedia projects at Brown university demonstrated that the use of graphics makes it easier for users to visualize, analyze and manipulate complex information. Computer graphic displays can be used to highlight information which is needed to draw the attention of the user to the information contained within databases.

The same argument, if at all, with greater force and conviction, has been made for the efficacy of introducing audio media for class room teaching over several decades ago. In fact, audio media are used as a standard tool in schools for class room instruction all over the world. There is also no disagreement on the enhancement of the overall efficiency of a system, when audio media is combined with visual media. It is widely accepted that different media appeal to different people and the benefits accrued from the same modes of presentation vary from one individual to the other.

Despite the fact that individual differences are largely responsible for the differences in performances with computerized systems, to date, there is little empirical research pertaining to how users interact with hyper/multimedia applications (Beasely & Vila, 1992), though they have been in existence for quite a while. This study, therefore, tried to determine what factors, if any, contribute to the individual differences among undergraduate students at the University of Hawaii at Manoa in the use of a multimedia system that was developed specifically for this study. In particular, the differences in the performance of subjects in the use of a multimedia tool was tested with reference to their level of visual ability (as determined by the VZ-2 test), computer affinity and computer literacy (measured on a five-point scale using a questionnaire (Kamala, 1991). Performance was also correlated to other parameters such as personality traits, learning styles, native language, sex and ethnicity.

3. EXPERIMENTAL DESIGN

3.1 Subjects

Undergraduate students, 34 in their third semester of study, majoring in computer science and nine in their second semester from a Japanese language course, volunteered as

subjects for the study. A few of the students in the Japanese course were undecided about their major. The final sample consisted of 10 females and 33 males.

3.2 System

The experiment was conducted on a multimedia system adopted from the arcade games shell of "Kanji City", a Japanese learning courseware (Ashworth & Stelovsky, 1987). The games were filled with contents related to library information to match previous studies on searching library online catalogs and CD ROM databases. The information base on which the tasks were based, was a subset of the library classification code (LC) and call number/floor locations in the Hamilton library at the University of Hawaii at Manoa (UH). This information base was built into a special "Library Notes" program that used several presentation modes.

In order to test the effect of sound and graphics on the learning and performance of subjects, sound and icons were incorporated into the system. Sound resources were incorporated into the "Library Notes" stack and icons corresponding to the topics covered by the chosen call numbers were either copied from clipart resource or created as bitmaps. A set of three cards each of the "Library Notes" stack was presented to the subject in a different manner - i.e., the first set of three cards were presented as pure text ("t") flashing slowly in a reverse video format; the second set of three cards as text+sound ("ts"), where audio was played simultaneously as the text was shown on the screen; the third as text+sound+icons ("tsi"); and the fourth in which the subject had to click on the first visible (call number) field to see the textual description and icons pertaining to that field on the screen as well as to hear the sound ("tsii"). This last mode was labeled "interactive" because it emulated an interface where the subject has to take an active role to solicit information.

3.3 Tasks

The tasks were performed by playing them as games on another HyperCard stack, called "Library Invaders". Subjects clicked on the mouse to "shoot" the correct target-words as they descended down the screen, to complete a sentence which had blanks that were filled by the target words shot down in the right order. The blanks corresponded to the call numbers of the book/s or periodical/s in the question and the floors on which they were located. The time taken for shooting down all the missing terms and completing the sentence was recorded as "ticks" (one tick = 1/60 of a second). A built-in observer recorded every click of the mouse and provided a log of the interaction of the subject with the system for the entire session. Each game had to be played till all the blanks in the sentence were filled ("Win"). A subject could repeat a game for two reasons - either to go back and read the notes in the stack "Library Notes", or, in the event of not being able to complete the game ("Loss") before all the target words descended to the lower edge of the screen (running out of time). The time per task, however, was the cumulative time taken to complete each sentence, i.e., till the first "Win" for each task. There were two types of games: (1) with two blanks and (2) with three blanks to be filled in a sentence. The tasks within the same game type were comparable across the four modes.

The order in which the notes were presented was either as "t" as the first mode, "ts" as the second mode, "tsi" as the third mode and "tsii" as the fourth mode, or, with "tsii" as the first mode and "t" as the last in the reversed order. This took into account the 'order' effect of presentation, if any, as subjects were randomly assigned to the two orders of presentation. A set of two (total of eight) games were played based on information provided in each of the four different modes in which the notes cards were presented. Thus, the effect of the presentation media on performance could be studied. Further, the four sets of games were switched around to account for any interaction effect of presentation media being associated with certain games.

Both the stacks, "Library Notes" as well as "Library Invaders" were designed to make navigation and interaction as user-friendly as possible. All necessary instructions to proceed with the tasks were provided on the screen as buttons or pop-up fields. The subjects needed to use only the mouse and no paper and pencil, nor the keyboard.

4. METHODOLOGY

The methodology consisted of three phases. In phase I, students were administered the MBTI, KLSI and VZ-2. They also filled in a questionnaire (Kamala, 1991) designed to determine the level of their computer affinity, computer literacy and educational standing, as well as their age, sex, language, SAT scores, etc. In phase II, subjects were tested one at a time; the experimenter gave each subject a very brief introduction to the multimedia system and an explanation of the tasks to be performed. Then the subjects were asked to perform the tasks. A log of the subject's interaction with the system and the time taken to complete the tasks were recorded by the observer. Phase III was a debriefing session and the students were asked to comment on their reaction to the system. A special questionnaire was developed to gather data on which of the four modes was liked best/least by the subjects.

4.1 Variables

Personality type (MBTI types), learning style (KLSI modes), visual ability, computer affinity, computer literacy, sex, language and ethnicity were the independent variables. While personality types, learning style, sex, language and ethnicity were categorical variables, visual ability, computer affinity and computer literacy were continuous variables. They were also converted into categorical variables as "high/low" (above/below median).

Performance measure was the only dependent variable and since each task had to be completed, however many attempts a subject made, the time taken to perform each task was taken as the measure of performance in this study. [The significant outcome of the interaction log will be analyzed and reported in a later publication].

4.2 Statistical Tests

Chi-square tests were performed with all the coded individual difference variables taken as "X" variables and the performance for each task coded 'fast/slow' (above/below median) as the "Y" variable. This provided a way to study the predictive power of factors that contribute to the individual difference among subjects. Two way unbalanced ANOVA tests were also conducted on some factors such as sex and mode, to test for interaction effect, if any.

5. RESULTS AND DISCUSSION

As in any empirical research, much data has been gathered in this study. We report a few sets of data that we found important and interesting. As was mentioned in section 3.1, most of the subjects for the study were computer science majors. So, they formed a rather homogeneous group as far as one of the individual difference parameters, i.e., visual ability was concerned. They were mostly high visuals and there was no significant difference in the performance based on visual ability. However, in two of the eight tasks, there was a significant difference ($p = .044$ and $p = .026$) in the performance of subjects, based on their level of computer affinity. This is in conformity with earlier findings (Kamala, 1991). The results appear to be both interesting and important for another reason - all five subjects with low computer affinity performed fast on one of the text-only (Q1-t) task with none performing slow, while subjects with high computer affinity were rather equally distributed (19 and 17) between fast and slow. In contrast to this, in one of the tasks (Q2-tsi) based on "tsi" mode of presentation, none of the five subjects with low computer affinity performed fast, while subjects with high computer affinity showed the identical trend as in the earlier task (19 fast and 17 slow). This may mean that subjects with low computer affinity probable do not care for any media inclusion in computer systems. It may also be that any added media makes them more reticent towards computers. It is difficult to say anything conclusively based on the small sample population tested in this study and also because the trend was found only in two out of the eight tasks. But it certainly warrants further research on a larger scale.

Another interesting and significant result obtained was the effect of learning style on performance. All (100%) of 'dynamic learner' subjects performed slow on both tasks (Q1-tsi: p = .09 and Q2-tsi: p = .018) based on "tsi" mode of presentation. None of the other four learning styles seemed to affect performance. All five dynamic learners were male. Sex affected the performance of one of the tasks in this mode significantly (p = .05). In the debriefing session after the experiment, 70% ranked this mode as the best liked mode. However, many of the male subjects said that they would have preferred to hear the voice of a female instead of a male for the audio media provided in the system. This may be an explanation for the above finding.

Only two of the four bipolar MBTI scales showed any significance, that too, only for one task based on the "ts" presentation mode. In the S/N types, 66.67% of the sensing type were slow, while 69.23% of the intuitive type were fast (p = .048); however, the effect was far more pronounced in the T/F types where 68.18% of thinking type were slow and 88.89% of the feeling type were fast (p = .004). Neither J/P nor E/I contrasting pairs showed any significant difference in performance on any of the eight tasks, unlike in earlier experiments (Borgman, 1989; Crosby and Peterson, 1991). Native language and ethnicity did not affect performance on any of the eight tasks. None of the ANOVA results showed any significance.

It was found that whatever 'losses' were observed happened in the first couple of games for subjects who 'lost' games at all, barring a few who 'lost' games in the later part of the session. Perhaps, this could have been avoided by having practice sessions before performing the actual experiment.

One of the highly significant results obtained was, however, the effect of the order in which the tasks were performed. The two tasks (Q1-t and Q2-t) were performed as the first and second tasks in the "increasing" mode, while the two tasks (Q1-tsii and Q2-tsii) were performed as the first and second tasks in the "decreasing" mode. 73.91% of the subjects performed fast (Q1-t: p = .0001; Q2-t: p = .0104) in the first two tasks in the increasing mode (text-only), whereas 85% and 65% respectively were slow on the same tasks (last two tasks) in the decreasing mode. Strangely, a similar trend was witnessed for the two tasks based on the interactive mode - only 30.43% and 34.78% performed fast on the two tasks (last to be performed) in the increasing mode with 80% and 75% performing fast in the decreasing mode (Q1-tsii: p = .0012; Q2-tsii: p = .0084). This indicates that the order in which the four multimedia presentations were used did not affect the performance of subjects at all. One possible explanation for the slow performance on the last two tasks in both modes may be boredom setting in after playing six similar games.

6. IMPLICATIONS FOR FUTURE RESEARCH

The current study has yielded more data than can be analyzed and reported in one paper. More detailed analysis of the transaction log is bound to throw light on the different strategies used by the subjects to complete the tasks. Classification of strategies that were used by the sample population and discussion on which individual difference factor lead to which strategy will be the topic of the next paper. The interaction effect of a subject's familiarity with hyper/multimedia systems was also not taken into consideration in the current analysis and is acknowledged as a lacuna in this study. Future research must explicitly take this effect into account.

There were a few useful lessons learned from this research. To establish beyond doubt whether an individual difference factor can predict performance of a subject on a system, it is necessary to have a heterogeneous sample population. The current sample was too homogeneous to conclusively establish any trend. A few minor problems were noticed in the interface design. It was noticed that some subjects expected to be prompted for every action and did not grasp the meaning of the buttons provided. The design of future experimental systems could include facilities to mitigate these problems. Also, it appears that providing for some practice before the actual experiment may help subjects perform better. It would also explain the 'losses' in the first couple of games for some subjects and provide more meaningful results.

If early efforts are made to determine the differing needs and preferences of students in learning the skills to use hyper/multimedia systems, it would help in rectifying the faults that might exist in the design of these costly tools. This study was conducted in the context of library online catalogs, because library online systems are used by a wide cross-section of users, who are bound to come to the system with varying needs, preferences, skills and individual differences. Though it may not be possible to provide tailor-made systems and interfaces to suit every individual user, it should still be possible to provide at least a few alternatives that meet the needs and preferences of different groups of people. The hardware and software that make it possible are fast becoming affordable. Studies that investigate the influence of individual differences on performance with systems that use different modes of presentation can provide the much needed research findings for the development of better instructional and educational tools, by harnessing the best combination of media and technology.

7. REFERENCES

Ashworth D.; Stelovsky, J. Kanji City: An Exploration of Hypermedia Applications for CALL, CALICO Journal, (1989), 27.

Borgman, Christine L. All Users of Information Retrieval Systems are not Created Equal: An Exploration into Individual Differences. Inf. Proc. & Management, 25(3) (1989) 237.

Beasley, Robert E.; Vila, Joaquin A. The Identification of Navigation Patterns in a Multimedia Environment: A Case Study. J. Edu. Multimedia and Hypermedia, 1 (1992) 209.

Crosby, Martha, E.; Peterson, W.W. Using Eye Movements to Classify Search Strategies. Proc. Human Factors Society. 2 (1991) 1476.

Kahn, Paul. Information retrieval as Hypermedia: an outline of Interbrowse. Proc. Ninth National Online Meeting, (1988) 131.

Kamala, T.N. Individual Differences in the Use of CD ROM Databases. Dissertation. Honolulu, HI: University of Hawaii at Manoa. UMI, (1991).

Marsh, Jean E.; Kumar, David D. Hypermedia: A conceptual Framework for Science Education and Review of Recent Findings. J. Edu. Multimedia and Hypermedia, 1, (1992) 25.

Sein, Maung K. Conceptual Models in Training Novice Users of Computer Systems: Effectiveness of Abstract vs. Analogical Models and Influence of Individual Differences. Dissertation. Indiana University. UMI, (1988).

Implementation and Design Issues in Interactive Multi-Media Knowledge Based Systems for Criminal Intelligence Analysis : The Mycroft[1] Perspective.

K. Morgan*, P. Hardy**, J. Casey**, L. Holland*, T. Quinn**, R. Mead**, Memex***, R. Oldfield****

* Department of Information Science, University of Portsmouth, Hants. UK.

** Computer Services, Sussex Police, Malling House, Lewes, UK

*** Memex Computer Systems, Glasgow, UK.

**** Police National Computer Organisation, The Home Office, UK.

Abstract.

The authors describe the current status and results from a two year collaborative research project which investigated the requirements for a future generation of knowledge-based criminal intelligence analysis computer systems. Based upon an international review of current practice in criminal intelligence analysis a series of system design recommendations were produced. These recommendations have led the authors to review the design issues and requirements for such a multi-user, multi-media knowledge based criminal intelligence analysis system. The paper concentrates on the issues of matching shared multi-media knowledge representations to individual user's optimum cognitive representations; shared computer based problem solving and knowledge representation in CSCW; the suitability of object oriented design to multi-media interface design; the representations available for knowledge modeling in intelligent systems; and interface considerations when supporting multi-media data manipulations. The paper concludes by summarizing the problems and opportunities which remain for the project.

1.INTRODUCTION.

The field of computer based criminal intelligence analysis has received relatively little academic attention [19]. A review of the past 25 years of the general computing literature shows little mention of the many unique and challenging computational problems encountered in criminal intelligence analysis. Yet there can be few more deserving areas than aiding the solution of crime with its adverse impact on the standard of life and freedom enjoyed by the general population. In recent years the amount of data involved in the investigation of major crime, such as murder, has increased dramatically [7,19]. Police forces world wide are starting to find that traditional methods of criminal intelligence analysis which had served them well in the past are now struggling to cope with the increasing amounts of data involved in modern criminal investigations [27]. This project was instigated with the hope of employing 'state of the art' computing techniques to the many problems involved with criminal intelligence work.

1.1.PRESENT WORKING METHODS IN CRIMINAL INTELLIGENCE ANALYSIS.

The typical criminal investigation involves many of the problem domains currently explored by both the human-computer-interaction (HCI) and artificial intelligence (AI) communities. The nature of the work in major incident rooms involves real-time data analysis, cooperative working, and shared data-base & knowledge-base manipulation. Typically current techniques include the use of large computer based data indexing systems and single media data representations, such as wall charts and informal information exchanges [7,19]. It is important to recognize that while

---

different countries adopt variations in dealing with the problem of investigating major crime these differences are often due to variations in the legislation which constrains the methods of operation (such as civil rights) available to the criminal investigator. Whatever the legislation, or lack of it, the task of criminal intelligence shares some fundamental characteristics.

1.1.1.FUNDAMENTAL CHARACTERISTICS OF CRIMINAL INTELLIGENCE ANALYSIS.

° Data Gathering

This may be from a wide variety of sources and be of varying degrees of reliability.

° Data Accumulation

The data is centrally accumulated to ensure that all the gathered data is available to all the investigating team.

° The Transformation of Data to Information

Data of unknown reliability or relevance is transformed to useful and reliable information.

° The Transformation of Information to Knowledge

Information on all aspects of the crime is transformed to knowledge based models of the events and activities which occurred. We define useful and usable information as knowledge.

° The Transformation of Knowledge to Decisions

The knowledge based models are used to suggest possible activities or scenarios which may increase the strength (degree of certainty) within the knowledge base and reduce any gaps or weaknesses in the current state of the knowledge base.

° The Transformation from Decisions to Real-World Actions

Based on the decisions suggested by the knowledge base various real-world actions are instigated.

It is normal for an investigating team to be involved in all of these activities simultaneously.

1.1.2.CRIMINAL INTELLIGENCE INFORMATION REPRESENTATIONS.

One of the most important aspects within criminal intelligence is the maintenance of the information base. All information within a criminal investigation has some fundamental properties which are invariant. These properties can be summarized into what we will term spatial, temporal, and entity based characteristics. The combination of relationships between these characteristics theoretically enable a human or computer based system to store and manipulate any temporal/spatial event or interaction. The more accurately and efficiently these events can be stored and manipulated the more likely it is that the information base can be efficiently modeled and transformed to a knowledge base.

1.1.3.SHARED KNOWLEDGE BASES.

In the domain of criminal intelligence work a knowledge-base is only as efficient and useful as the decision making processes which it supports. Most current criminal intelligence computer systems support massive shared data bases but provide little to support the transformation of this data to useful information. Some tools are available to provide the criminal intelligence worker with graphical representations of data sets but essentially current technology only supports data bases, the further transformations we described (above) must currently be performed by human analysts. Current commercial research in the area is only just starting to address the problem of computer supported data to information transformation. Little effort has been invested in producing computer aids for the transformation of information to knowledge.

1.2.COMPUTER SUPPORTED COOPERATIVE CRIMINAL INTELLIGENCE WORK (CSCCIW)

Developments in CSCW show great promise for the efficient and rapid distribution of criminal intelligence information among a team of analysts. However, the step from sharing an information base and sharing a knowledge base may require more radical solutions.

1.2.1.INDIVIDUAL DIFFERENCES WITHIN CRIMINAL INTELLIGENCE INVESTIGATORS.

Although there are fundamental similarities in the way in which human beings process information [1,5,10,17,18,22,23] it is often found that individuals have their own unique methods for optimum working [12,14,15,16,21]. In a cooperative working environment, such as criminal investigation, utilizing this optimum from each team member is of vital importance since it can literally make the difference between the life and death of the future victims of crime [7]. The problem is how to accommodate and support the individual differences within each criminal intelligence team, and how a multi-user system can support multiple views and manipulations on a single shared knowledge set without compromising the integrity of that knowledge base. This problem is aggravated by the fact that even a single analyst will have a need to examine and manipulate the current working knowledge model in different ways at different times [7,19]. For example an analyst may wish to manipulate the teams current knowledge model to evaluate the likelihood of different scenarios and suspects. It may even be that some vital aspect of the crime under investigation only becomes apparent when the knowledge base is viewed in a particular manner. What is required then is a truly dynamic method of modeling and sharing a knowledge base in a computer supported cooperative problem solving environment. Such a system must aid a team of analysts in the stages of data transformation, while providing individually customized knowledge base manipulation tools which aid decision making. With the increasing complexity of criminal intelligence data it is important to provide tools which enhance the problem solving creativity of the human element of the criminal investigation.

2.POTENTIAL DESIGN SOLUTIONS.

There are many ways that this complex human factors requirement can be satisfied [27]. In the past teams of detectives have handled the cognitive loads and complex knowledge manipulations using techniques and principles which they had developed over long periods of time. However times change and as in other aspects of modern life an information explosion has occurred in criminal analysis [7,19]. Current criminal intelligence analysis still tends to use relatively primitive data indexing and retrieval systems in what are increasingly complex areas. Some innovative designs in data representation are starting to appear and evaluations of these methods have shown them to be significant advances [27]. However they are still only providing tools which aid humans in the transformation between data and information. The other, more complex and error prone, transformations and manipulations are still left to the human analysts. Humans vary in their ability to handle large information processing tasks [5,12,14,18] but as a species we share the characteristic of being more error prone as the size and complexity of the information increases [5,18,20,23,25]. The task of designing possible support systems for this complex and new area was and remains a great challenge. When faced with this problem we decided that a fresh review of the principal elements of criminal intelligence data might assist the process of designing appropriate computer based tools and methods.

2.1.NATURALLY OCCURRING CRIMINAL INTELLIGENCE DATA.

One can consider the natural world as a physicist might. That is as coordinates within time & space containing objects which, in turn, can be described by their behaviour within time and space. In addition there are various attributes which the object might possess, such as mass, refractive index, and chemical composition. This method of modeling appears highly successful in describing closed systems. However the data sets which are available to criminal intelligence analysts are not linear or contiguous within space/time. Criminal intelligence data has the characteristic of being a series of 'snap shots' of events with gaps, inaccuracies, ambiguities and inconsistencies. Much can be inferred by the analyst from these gaps and apparent weaknesses in the information, but only if they are presented accurately and completely. If a computer system adopted the descriptive model from physics these gaps and weaknesses in the knowledge base might not be noticed by the analyst. When one considers the basic elements which occur in any event, be it criminal or otherwise, it becomes apparent that every event has three fundamental and invariant characteristics : a time, a place, and an object or objects with characteristics or relationships. We can conceptualize these further so that we come to recognise that, for our purposes, time and space are composed of a series of discrete moments and places wherein events or objects occur. In this conceptualization gaps, errors, and inconsistencies are as important as any other item of information.

2.1.1.CONCEPTUAL MAPPINGS BETWEEN CRIME OBJECTS AND INTERFACE OBJECTS.

In order to consider implementing a multi-media representation of these knowledge bases we will need to define computer metaphors for the knowledge. In order to explain the designs we considered and the object orientated techniques we adopted it will be easier if we simplify the interface concepts to a bare minimum. If we attempt to abstract the conceptual elements of an interface we can (by some admitted simplification) reduce the numerous dialogs boxes, button types, menus, windows, colours and icons to three primary areas; the foreground, background and an axis. We have already indicated (above) that it is possible to abstract the conceptual elements of a crime into moments, places and entity/objects.

2.1.2.SIMPLIFIED MYCROFT DATA REPRESENTATION.

° Time - Moment

° Space - Place

° Entity - Object or Entity involved in the crime

If we combine these two conceptual abstractions we can consider the following conceptual mappings between interface objects and crime objects.

2.1.3.SIMPLIFIED MYCROFT INTERFACE REPRESENTATION.

° Foreground :

A representative icon which can be expanded to the full knowledge base entry for that item.

° Background :

A Tableu representation of the item. Be it a digitized map, calendar/clock, or picture.

° Axis :

A specification of the range of characteristics held by the item. In geographical terms it will be the spatial range of the place, in temporal terms it will be the range of the moment, and for other items it will be a list of the characteristics.

We can therefore easily conceive of an fundamental object-oriented software object which has data (variables) to store the details associated with that criminal intelligence item, and object methods (in-built procedures) to handle drawing and plotting itself as any of the three primary interface representations.

2.2.DOMAINS AND DIMENSIONS : DATA VIEWING.

Using this technique of object orientation the same Mycroft data sets can be viewed in six different ways, two to each of the three major modes.

° MODE 1 - TEMPORAL AXIS

Sub-view a) spatial background
Sub-view b) object background

° MODE 2 - SPATIAL AXIS

Sub-view a) temporal background
Sub-view b) object background

° MODE 3 - OBJECTIVE AXIS

Sub-view a) temporal background
Sub-view b) spatial background

Viewing data in these ways allows the analyst to see the same information from many different perspectives. It is anticipated that these facilities will enable criminal intelligence officers to literally play with possible scenarios within the data.

2.3.OBJECT ORIENTED CRIMINAL INTELLIGENCE ANALYSIS.

Initial analysis has shown that each of these major types of object can be further sub-divided :

° Time.

Time will be represented as a series of 'moments'. Where a 'moment' has a start and finish time in terms of a date and respective hours and minutes. The minimum size of a 'moment' would be 1 minute.

° Space.

Space will be represented as a series of 'places'. Where a 'place' is defined in terms of a set of x & y (latitude & longitude) coordinates. The minimum number of coordinates required to define a place is three. All locations can be specified in terms of a standard location reference system - based on HMS ordnance survey maps. When 'places' are shown as Icons they will be represented as small map icons. The location map can be shown be clicking on the Icon.

° Entities.

Within Mycroft entities are the basic objects involved within a crime. There are a series of major sub-classes of entity. The list given below corresponds to the major classes of entity which were identified as requiring a separate icon or symbol on Mycroft's graphical representations of the crime.

2.4.SOME MAJOR SUB-CLASSES OF ENTITY OBJECT HIERARCHY.

Animate Vs Inanimate
  Animate
    Human.
    Animal - Icon = Standard four legged creature icon.
  Inanimate.
    Transport.
    Building.
    Communication.

2.4.1. OBJECT INTERACTIONS & ENTITY EXISTENCE.

An entity will have a 'moment' and 'place' defined for it and will only 'exist' on the current Mycroft interface if the current global 'moment' and 'place' are the same as or 'contain' the 'moment' and 'place' which defines the entities existence.

3.DISCUSSION OF THE COLLABORATORS EXPECTANCIES.

Law Enforcement.
The successful conclusion of the project will leave the police with a tool that will have major benefit in the investigation of serious crimes. The force will also have developed considerable experience in creating multi-media IKBS systems. It is intended that this experience be used to further expand the use of these techniques in other areas of police work since the techniques it employs could equally be used in formulating organizational policy and other areas where the relationships between entities need to be simulated or modeled, and where intelligent knowledge based systems can be employed.

Academic.
The academic part of this project will make a contribution to knowledge in the following specialist areas : object oriented design & programming, knowledge elicitation in complex and vague domains, simulation of human decision making on 'complex' and 'fuzzy' data sets, design and creation of an IKBS for criminal intelligence work, HCI design & evaluation, technology attitudes, and the impact of new technology and methods.

Commercial.
Memex see the Mycroft project as having the potential to become an ongoing collaborative research programme between the existing project partners. It is hoped that this collaboration would continue to develop through subsequent generations of the Mycroft system and its IKBS rule base.

Government.
The scientists within SSG are interested in the development and enhancement of existing and new intelligence analysis methods and tools. The continued development of Mycroft beyond the stages outlined in this document would ensure that the very latest tools, methods and techniques were available to the UK's criminal intelligence taskforce.

4.CONCLUSION.

We have invested considerable effort and resources into a new and challenging areas of HCI and AI. The Mycroft project has established a unique method of intelligent multi-media information and knowledge representation and presentation. This promises to provide a truly adaptive method for knowledge representation and manipulation. We invite other parties to join us in this exciting area of enquiry.

REFERENCES.

1 - Baddeley, A.D. "The Psychology of Memory" Harper & Row. (1976)

2 - Benyon, D., Innocent, P., And Muray, D. "System Adaptivity And The Modeling Of Stereotypes." 1st Ed. 1 Vol. UK:Elsevier. Proceedings Interact'87. (1987)

3 - Egan, D "Individual differences in Human-Computer Interaction". In M. Helander (Ed) Handbook of Human-Computer Interaction. Elsevier Science Publishers B.V. (North Holland). (1988)

4 - Fowler, C. J. H., And Murray, D. M. "Gender And Cognitive Style Differences At The Human Computer Interface." NPL Report 90/87. (1987)

5 - Gibson, E.J. "Priniciples of Perceptual Learning and Development" Appleton-Century-Crofts. (1967)

6 - Goodenough, D. R. "The Role Of Individual Difference In Field Dependence As A Factor In Learning And Memory." Psychological Bulletin.(1976) 83, 675 694.

7 - Hardy, P. "Information Vs Knowledge : An Alternative View of Major Incident Rooms" (1991) Internal Paper : Sussex Police.

8 - Holland, L. "An Investigation of Knowledge Elicitation Techniques in Criminal Intelligence Settings" MSc Dissertation, University of Portsmouth. (1991)

9 - Huber, G. P. "Cognitive Style As A Basis For MIS And DIS Designs: Much Ado About Nothing." Management Sciences. (1983) 29.

10 - Johnson-Laird, D.N. "The Role of Mental Models in Everyday Thinking" 2nd Interdisciplinary workshop on Mental Models (1992) Robinson College, Cambridge.

11- Kennedy, T. C. S. "The Design Of Interactive Procedures Of Man Machine Communication." International Journal Of Man Machine Studies.(1974) 6, 309 334.

12 - Kirby, R. & Radford, J. "Individual Differences" Methuen. (1976)

13 - Lusk, E. J., And Kernick, M. "The Effect Of Cognitive Style And Report Format On Task Performance: the MIS Design Consequences." Management Sciences. (1979) 25, 787 798.

14 - Messick, S. (Ed.). "Individuality In Learning." 1st Ed. 1 Vol. Jossey Bass. (1976)

15 - Morgan, K. & Macleod, H. "Technology Attitudes Investigations"British Psychological Society London Conference. (1990)

16 - Morgan, K., Macleod, H. "Results from Exploratory Investigations into the possible role of Personality Factors in Computer Interface Preference". 2nd Interdisciplinary Workshop on Mental Models. (1992) Robinson College, Cambridge.

17 - Norman, D. A. "The Psychology Of Everyday Things." 1st Ed. 1 vol. New York: Basic Books Inc. (1988)

18 - Norman, D.A. "Memory and Attention" Wiley. (1969)

19 - Oldfield, R.W. "The Application Of Criminal Intelligence Analysis Techniques To Major Crime Investigation - An Evaluation Study". SRD Branch. Home Office Publication 30/88. (1988)

20 - Payne, J. W. "Contingent Decision Behaviour." Psychological Bulletin. (1982) 92, 382 402.

21- Rich, E. "Users Are Individuals: Individualizing User Models." International Journal Of Man Machine Studies. (1983) 18,199 215.

22 - Richardson, A. "Mental Imagery" Routledge and Kegan Paul. (1969)

23 - Stroh, C.M. "Vigilance - The problem of Sustained Attention" Oxford-Pergamon. (1971)

24 - Vernon, P.E., "Creativity" Penguin. (1970)

25 - Wason, P.C. & Johnson-Laird, D.N. "Thinking and Reasoning" Penguin. (1968)

26 - Witken, H. A. : Goodeneough, D.R. "Cognitive Styles: Essence And Origin." 1st Ed. 1 vol. International University Press. (1981)

27 - Woods, A.J., Jenkinson, R.E. "Intelligence and Operational Systems HOLMES Front End Demonstrator Evaluation Report " SSG Report, Home Office PNCO Publication 1/91.(1991)

The Development of a Plan Based Tutor to Aid in Transfer Between Programming Languages

Jean Scholtz and Adrienne Cleveland
Computer Science Department, Portland State University, P.O Box 751, CMPS, Portland, OR 97207-0751

Abstract

This paper discusses a hypertext-based system which can be used to support transfer from one procedural language to another. This tool uses plan knowledge as the transfer vehicle and is based on empirical studies of transfer between programming languages. The design and use of the system are discussed and results from empirical studies of its use are described.

1. Introduction

In developing tutors for transfer to a second language, the results of learning transfer studies are of interest. Wu and Anderson [4], Scholtz [1] and Scholtz and Wiedenbeck [2] have done extensive examination of advanced subjects transferring to a new programming language. They have examined what prior knowledge programmers use in learning a new language and where this knowledge is inadequate or perhaps, even a detriment. The results clearly show that in transferring from one procedural language to another, the planning area of program development occupies the majority of programmers' efforts. Programming plans which are templates for accomplishing specified goals play a major role in transfer, both negative and positive.

Soloway, Ehrlich, Bonar, and Greenspan [3] classified planning in program development as implementation, tactical or strategic planning. Strategic planning is language independent planning at a global level. Tactical plans are still language independent but correspond to a lower level plan, as in plans for individual modules. The process of taking tactical plans and turning them into code is implementation planning. Any given tactical plan can have many different realizations in a given language. Some of these realizations may be more appropriate and less error prone than others.

Scholtz and Wiedenbeck found several types of difficulties encountered by programmers in transfer between procedural languages. In studies of transfer to a similar procedural language, the majority of problems were concentrated in the area of implementation. The tactical plans that subjects used in their familiar language were also appropriate for use in the similar target language. Therefore, the chief problem faced by transfer subjects was locating the correct constructs in the new language in order to implement these tactical plans. One problem with locating constructs in a new language is that they often appear in a different form than in the known language.

When the target language was more distant from the subjects' known language, problems were also encountered in selecting tactical plans. Programmers often devoted much effort to implementation of ill-suited tactical plans. The problem is that programmers writing in a new language often lack the knowledge to choose the most appropriate realization. In fact, they are highly biased by their knowledge of what was appropriate in a previous language. Feedback on an incorrect decision is inadequate.

In other cases, programmers find that their implementations do not succeed. This leads to a series of searches for different constructs to use in implementation before programmers decide to implement another tactical plan. Therefore, the goal of a tutoring system in this area is to reduce the search space and to give programmers feedback about plan selection.

2. Language Transfer Tutor

Based on this transfer of learning research we designed a language transfer tutor that would aid the user in selecting the appropriate tactical plan and would suggest constructs in the language to use in implementation. The intent was to produce adequate feedback on plan selection and to direct the user to the proper section of the documentation for more detailed information. Thus the language tutor does not produce code; it merely sketches out a plan along with a list of constructs that should be considered for implementation.

We implemented this tutor in a hypertext medium for several reasons. First, we wanted to support a number of languages with the tutor. Currently we have three languages implemented: Pascal, Ada and Icon. Using a hypertext structure, we were able to design these three so that the main structure is identical. Only the end nodes differ according to the language. This will allow us to combine these knowledge bases so that a programmer could browse through and compare implementations in various languages. Secondly, this is meant to be used as a tool for programmers to use while they are developing a program in a new language. As programming is a complex problem solving activity, we wanted to present our information in a simple, straightforward manner. The hypertext structure allows the programmer to discontinue the search at any point where he feels he has the needed information.

3. An Example of Program Design Using the Language Transfer Tutor

In this section we present a simple problem and its solution in both Pascal and Icon using the plan knowledge base. Figure 1 shows a sample of selections from the tutor: the main level, the sublevel for loop plans and the sublevel for indefinite loops.

1.Contents
Boolean Expressions
Conditional Execution
Declarations
Input Plans
List Creation
Loop Plans
Output Plans
Variables
2.Loop Plans
Loop a Definite Number of times
Loop an Indefinite Number of times
3.Indefinite Loops
Test Condition Before the Loop Body
Test Condition Within the Loop Body

Figure 1: An Example of Menus in the Plan Knowledge Base

Figures 2 and 3 show how the tool would be used to devise tactical plans for a standard input plan of looping until there is no more input, with the loop body containing the input statement. Figure 2 shows the path that would be followed in the Pascal plan knowledge base in order to generate tactical plans for this *while* loop. Figure 3 shows the path that would be used in the Icon knowledge base. In the figures the items displayed in italics represent language constructs or terms. The items in regular text are items that can be selected to provide more information. The programmer is free to choose to explore the options presented at a given level in any order desired or not to explore any of them. The possibility exists that a choice of selections may eventually lead to a revision of another plan.

We have provided alphabetic labels on sections in Figures 2 and 3 to facilitate discussion. The user starts by selecting the loop plan (section A of figure 2). What he wants is an indefinite loop that continues until an end of file condition is encountered. In standard Pascal he can use a test before loop body that says "while not eof". He chooses **Exception** from the list under **Boolean expression** and finds that end of file is specified as *eof*.

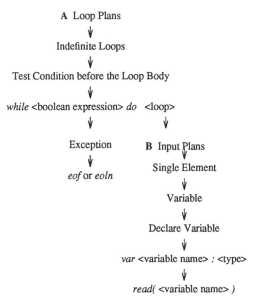

A Loop Plans
↓
Indefinite Loops
↓
Test Condition before the Loop Body
↓
while <boolean expression> *do* <loop>
↓   ↓
Exception   **B** Input Plans
↓   ↓
eof or *eoln*   Single Element
↓
Variable
↓
Declare Variable
↓
var <variable name> *:* <type>
↓
read(<variable name> *)*

Figure 2: Example from the Pascal Language Tutor

Figure 3 shows how the programmer would use that same knowledge about Pascal and get feedback on modifying the plan for the Icon programming language. Again the user looks at **Loop plans** (Section A of figure 3). The first levels of the menu are the same: **Indefinite Loops, Test Condition before Loop Body**. The next selection however differs. In Icon there are several ways to test the condition prior to execution of the loop body. One way is **Execute loop body while a boolean expression succeeds**. Assuming that the programmer selects this option, a *while* type of statement will be suggested. Selecting **Boolean expression** and continuing to **Exception** the programmer is informed that there is no end of file specification in Icon. One merely *reads* until that function fails. Therefore, a modification is needed in the user's original boolean expression. Since the user is now aware that the input statement could fail, **Input plans** is consulted. The *read* function becomes the boolean expression used in controlling the while loop and can therefore be omitted from the loop body.

4. Empirical Studies

In order to verify that our language tutor did indeed help programmers transferring to a new language, we conducted an empirical investigation. Six senior level and graduate (master's) Computer Science students participated in this study to determine the effectiveness of the tutor. Our goal in this study was twofold. First, we wanted to compare the solutions generated by these subjects with the solutions originally collected by Scholtz [1] to determine if the use of the tutor was beneficial. Secondly, we wanted to observe how subjects used the tutor and to determine what information they could find in it. We wanted to use these results to refine future versions of the language tutor.

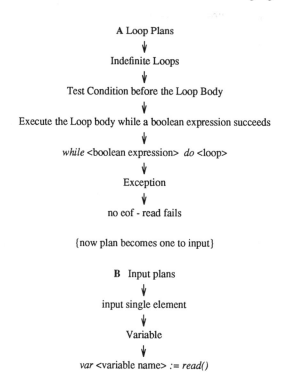

Figure 3: Example from the Icon Language Tutor

Subjects in the study were provided with a PC running the language tutor, a text of the language they were to use, and paper and pencils to use in producing the problem solution. We did not provide subjects with a compiler or an interpreter, as at this stage of implementation this would have necessitated the use of two computers.

Three of the subjects wrote the given program in Ada and three implemented it in Icon. We collected video tapes of the screen display of the language tutor. This enabled us to track the paths in the tutor that subjects explored. In addition, subjects were encouraged to think aloud and their verbalizations were captured on the video tape. We also collected the paper designs produced by the subjects. Subjects were given a demonstration of the Pascal version of the tutor before they started the experiment.

The problem given to the subjects in the study required subjects to read in lines of text from standard input, translate the characters from upper case to lower case and vice versa, and to reverse the characters in each line. Text was then to be output in fixed length blocks of 60 characters with shorter lines padded and longer lines broken up.

Subjects were told that they could stop when one of the following three conditions occurred: they had finished the problem, two hours had elapsed, or they were completely frustrated and felt that they could make no further progress. Subjects were not told that they had to use the tool; tool and book usage were left to the subjects' discretion.

5. Results

5.1 Ada

Of the three Ada subjects, two (S5 and S6) used the tool extensively while the third (S2) used the book more heavily. S2 found it difficult to accept that information in the tutor was to be used literally and felt the need to use the book to verify much of this. For example, he was puzzled by the statements *with ada_io* and *use ada_io* in the input section of the tutor and did not believe that these statements were to be incorporated as is into the program code.

In the previous experiments by Scholtz [1], subjects had difficulty mainly in three areas: finding constructs equivalent to Pascal's *char* and *ord* for use in character conversion, finding out the necessary statements and constructs for handling end of file and end of line exceptions, and dealing with input and output.

In the present experiment, subjects had somewhat better success. Both S5 and S6 found the appropriate implementation for translation of characters by using the tool. S2 also found the constructs but did not figure out how to determine if the original character was upper case or lower case.

Input and output were very confusing for subjects due to the need to reference packages in order to use the I/O routines. Subjects in the original experiment used the *get* procedure almost exclusively. This obtains one character at a time. In using the tool, all three subjects found both *get* and *getline*, which reads in an entire string of input. However, only one subject used the *getline* construct in his final code.

Handling end_of_file and end_of_line conditions still presented a problem for subjects in this experiment. These exception handlers were available in the "text_io package" and, therefore, required access by first specifying the package name. Subject S5 used the book and found that end_of_line was available but never found the necessary package references. S2 did not find the proper construct or package reference but looked only in the book. S6 used the book and found end_of_file, but again did not find the package reference needed.

One problem with the tool is ensuring that subjects take the right path in exploration or at least eventually discover it. For example, two subjects were sure they wanted to input lines as character arrays and looked under input into arrays rather than input into multiple elements. Their bias from their previous language experience was so strong that they did not even explore other options initially. One subject did eventually find the other path and decided upon string input.

A second problem was that subjects' expectations about the location of information in the tool did not match where the information was actually located. This was the case with information about end_of_file exceptions, which was located under boolean expressions in the tool. However, subjects expected to find the information under the input option.

5.2 Icon

All three Icon subjects used the tool as a first choice. They resorted to the book to get detailed syntax information, to see examples of actual usage of constructs, and to obtain more detailed semantic information.

Compared to the subjects in the original experiment, these subjects were much more successful in producing optimal solutions. Subjects in the original experiments had difficulties in three areas: finding the *map* construct used for character translation and realizing that it could be applied to strings rather than just characters, realizing that functions returned success or failure as well as a result, and finding the built-in functions that could be used for padding lines of text. S3 and S4 were able to produce optimal solutions using the tool. S7 found the necessary constructs but was struggling with the semantics of the *read* function. He did not realize that a string was an elementary data type and thought that reading in a string should be a more complex plan. S7 was also not able to produce the correct code for translating characters from upper to lower case and vice versa. He found the correct constructs in the tool but was unable to discover that he could concatenate arguments to the function in order to produce the desired results. All three subjects found the function used to pad a string of text and were able to produce the correct code for that.

6. Discussion

In general, subjects used the tool as we had envisioned it. They were able in most cases to find appropriate plans and to discover the constructs necessary to implement those plans. They used the book to find more detailed information on syntax and to investigate the semantics of constructs located in the tool. They also used the book to locate examples of complete programs and to find specific examples of constructs.

These initial results are very encouraging. Subjects did use the tool and were able to produce better solutions than subjects in a previous experiment who did not have access to the tool. The tool was easy to use and did not appear to interfere with subject's problem solving activities.

We did, however, observe several problems that subjects encountered in using the tool. First of all, subjects were sometimes unable to locate information because they expected to find it in other places in the tool. This could be solved by adding an alphabetic index which would list references to the item. Selecting a reference could take the subject directly to that card of information.

The second problem is more serious. Subjects often had a plan in mind and failed to make the correct choice at the top level because of this bias. This was especially true for input of character strings. Most subjects followed the path for input into an array rather than input of a simple variable. This specific instance might be helped by a very simple overview which lists data types available in the language.

7. Future Work

We plan to refine the tool to include an index and an overview section. We are also planning to merge the three separate versions of the tool into one unit. This would allow a developer to consider how plans would be implemented in various languages and then choose the language that simplifies implementation. We will also be reimplementing the tool in a windows environment. In this implementation, we intend to support the ability to use an editable window to collect a series of plans which could be used by the programmer as a framework for his program.

8. Acknowledgements

This work was funded by NSF grant IRI-9108294.

9. References

1. Scholtz, J. (1989). *A Study of Transfer of Skill between Programming Languages.* Unpublished doctoral dissertation. University of Nebraska, Lincoln, NE.

2. Scholtz, J. and Wiedenbeck, S. (1991). Learning a New Programming Language: A Model of the Planning Process. In B. Shriver (Ed.), *Proceedings of the Twenty-Fourth Annual Hawaii International Conference on system Sciences*, vol. II, 3-12.

3. Soloway, E., Ehrlich, K., Bonar, J. and Greenspan, J. (1984). What do Novices Know About Programming? in A. Badre and B. Shneiderman (Eds.), *Directions in Human-Computer Interaction* (pp. 27-54). Norwood, N.J.: Ablex.

4. Wu, Q. and Anderson, J. (1990). Problem-solving Transfer among Programming Languages. Submitted to *Human-Computer Interaction*.

Use of Parameters to Facilitate the Implementation of Reusable Hypermedia Modules

Jan Stelovsky

Hypermedia Lab, Department of Information and Computer Sciences, University of Hawaii, Honolulu, Hawaii 96822, USA

ABSTRACT
   This paper describes the user interface and functionality of a system that supports definition and generalization of reusable modules implemented within existing hypermedia projects. It focuses of the component that allows the module's author to parametrize the module's functionality without increasing the complexity of the resulting code. While the proposed system can find immediate practical application since it extends the functionality of a popular authoring environment, the described framework can be applied to object-oriented programming in general.

1.   THE NEED FOR PARAMETRIZED MODULES

A typical hypermedia-feasible authoring environment provides a selection of elementary object types and a rich programming language. Virtually any functionality associated with an elementary objects must be defined as program code. The most widely used authoring environment, HyperCard, for instance, provides buttons, text fields, cards, backgrounds and stacks as elementary objects and the programming language HyperTalk. This environment also encourages reusing code: to "borrow" an elementary object, the author simply cuts it and pastes it into another project.

Even a modestly complex hypermedia project contains several functional modules that could be reused elsewhere, such as choice from a set of "radio buttons", navigational palettes, maps, glossaries, and logging of user's actions. The "cut and paste" method, however, is inadequate for such modules, as they typically involve numerous objects and/or code that is part of programs on several levels of the object hierarchy. Moreover, such indispensable hypermedia facilities as integration of some media types and defining hot-spots necessitate non-trivial programming that often involves several basic objects.

When a module is installed into to another project, its components usually need to be adapted which in turn necessitates modifications of the corresponding code (e.g. references to new button names and positions). Moreover, as the requirements change during the lifetime of a hypermedia project, the modules should be modified to simplify the project's maintenance. To give an example, consider authoring facilities that are necessary only at times when new material is integrated, such as support for definition of new links, insertion of new glossary items or translation of close-captioning text into another language. These facilities can be excluded in the version of the project that is distributed on a CD-ROM.

None of the commonly used hypermedia authoring environments provides facilities that would support reusability of composite modules and simplify their adaptation to the specific requirements.

2. HYPERWAREHOUSE: A REPOSITORY OF REUSABLE MODULES

To address these problems, we have designed a "HyperWarehouse" system that supports the definition of reusable functional software modules as an extension of a popular authoring system [3]. The modules typically define objects of complex functionality classes and can contain materials of different media types (e.g. images, animation, videos) and links to related hypermedia objects.

The first version of the system forced the author to isolate all of the module's components and integrate them into the HyperWarehouse, which served as a large database of reusable modules. The current version, however, allows the module's author to refer to the elements of an existing project. We have proposed to add the support of reusable modules by extending the underlying programming language by constructs that transfer arbitrary objects and segments of code from one project to another [4].

3. THE OBSERVER: A CASE STUDY OF A PARAMETRIZED MODULE

To give a fairly complex, but at the same time typical example of a reusable module, consider the task of monitoring of user's actions during a working session. When we have implemented a "translators workbench," we needed to log the translators' interaction with the system to find out how translators are using dictionaries and knowledge databases [1]. This functionality is a generic module that can be reused to evaluate the users' interactions with any application. Another application of this "Observer" module is described in [2]. The Observer consists of numerous components: a card which contains the user identification to be inserted as a header into the log file, several routines and their calls which have to be inserted into the code of each object that handles user's interaction. In a HyperCard environment, it is a tedious and error-prone task to insert the calls manually into an existing application. This task, however, can be easily performed by an installation program that traverses the object hierarchy of the target project and inserts automatically the calls in all appropriate object scripts.

We have found a need for several parameters that modify the Observer's functionality. Within the "workbench" it was crucial that the Observer recorded the text typed in. In other projects, the typing action was irrelevant to the evaluation of the user's session. In the latter case, recording the text entry would clutter the project's code and unnecessarily increase the complexity of the resulting log files.

To give another example, there are two ways how the Observer can record the time: as total elapsed time since the beginning of the session and time since the last recorded event. While the first version produces log files that are more tailored to the analysis of user's overall performance, the latter form is better suited for the analysis of individual strategies. The choice of the recording method could be integrated in the Observer's code, which would necessitate a decision whenever an event was recorded. This solution harbors two inefficiencies: it complicates the Observer's code and slows down its real-time performance. Instead, we can parametrize the Observer's installation procedure and insert only the code that is appropriate for the selected recording method.

4. ADVANTAGES OF PARAMETRIZED MODULES

HyperWarehouse allows the module's author to offer several versions of the module according to various functionality requirements. These versions are offered as a set of parameter settings to the user of the module (i.e. to the author of a new project who wants to reuse the module). This paper focuses on the user interface that allows the module's author to define parameters and the mechanism that permits her to retrieve the parameters' values at the time when the module is being incorporated within another project.

Parameters add flexibility to the implementation of modules and efficiency of use. Without parameters, the author can either implement one generic module that contains all code (and objects) necessary to handle any possible application of the module, or provide several versions of the module. These approaches have serious drawbacks. The generic module is likely to contain code segments that will never be executed and evaluate conditions to determine the specific usage of the module. On the other hand, the task of supporting several versions of the module increases the complexity of software maintenance.

Our approach allows the author to split the module into numerous components, such as objects, routines and even code segments. She can then implement "installation scripts" that build the desired version of the module at the time when the module is installed in the target project. This approach simplifies the software maintenance as the individual components can be modified independently. Moreover, the installation script can eliminate all code that is not needed in the specific module version. As a consequence, the complexity that results from the generalization of the module's functionality is to a large extent contained in the installation scripts rather than in the module's code.

5.   PARAMETER TYPES AND DEPENDENCY

The installation scripts are written in a superset of the programming language supported by the programming environment - HyperTalk in our case - and can refer to the current parameter settings. Each parameter has a name and a value. While the name of the parameter is an arbitrary string the parameter's values are either selected from a fixed set of constant values or typed in (free input).

Currently, we support the following types of selections from a fixed set of values:
  a.i   boolean choice (either chosen or not)
  a.ii   selection of a single value
  a.iii selection of a multiple values
We also support the following free input parameters:
  b.i   single value, i.e. a string typed on one line
  b.ii   multiple values, i.e. strings typed on separate lines

If further refinements are needed (such as checking for numeric values), the module's author can append a call of an arbitrary routine. This routine will be called at the time when the user selects a parameter value and can for instance, issue a warning that the value is out of range.

The parameter types are visualized using the appropriate elements of graphical user interfaces: as a "checkbox" (boolean choice), set of "radio buttons" (selection of a single value), a "menu field" with one or more check marks (selection of a single or multiple value), and "text fields" either with corresponding number of lines or scrolling (single and multiple value free input).

To provide an additional flexibility during the parameter selection, HyperWarehouse allows the author to make the existence of a parameter dependent on the current value of another parameter. At the time when the user is selecting the parameter settings, the existence of the dependent parameters is visualized through hiding and showing the elements that are associated with the parameter. As other parameters can rely on the dependent parameter, the overall dependency graph forms a tree (Figure 1).

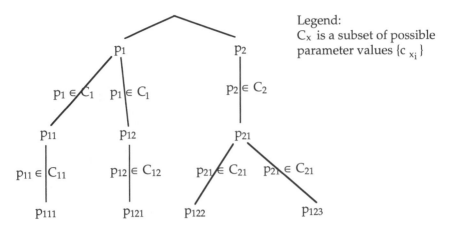

Figure 1: The parameter dependency tree

At the time when the author specifies new parameters for her module, she can select the appropriate type and appearance from a palette of available parameter types and define the dependencies based on parameter values already defined. The new parameter will then be added to a parameter settings "card" where it can be resized and moved to its final position. Figure 2 shows a sample parameter settings card for a module that implements a menu selection within a text field. The parameters indicate that the field should be inserted as a scrolling card field into the card "main" and that its script should call the routine "GoToCd."

parameters	menu in a field	⇦ 1/2 ⇨ ⏎

menu name: menu

layer: destination:

○ card   "main"

◉ bkgnd

☒ scrolling

☒ action   action line:

     ✓GoToCd Text
     FillFld "action",Text
     Action Text

Figure 1. Parameters for a "menu field" module

Notice that each time the author defines a new parameter for her module, she is performing a selection from the set of available parameter types and their representations. This task itself can be regarded as a parameter setting. Indeed, the parameter specification is a module embedded within HyperWarehouse. It has been implemented using a bootstrapping method similar to the process of how compilers are constructed. First, the parameter type "single value free input" allowed us to define the meta-parameter "parameter name". The implementation continued with the type "single value from fixed set" that was used to define the meta-parameter "parameter type" that represents the selection among the parameter types as defined in the beginning of this section. The value of the latter parameter determined the existence of further meta-parameters. The decision to use the parameter selection as a meta-module that defines its own functionality has an additional benefit: the parameter selection itself can be easily expanded. We could, for instance, accommodate additional means to display parameters, such as a pop-up menu of available parameter values, or even add new parameter types, such as a file name selection.

6. INSTALLATION SCRIPTS

After the module's parameters have been defined, the author can refer to their values within the installation script. A parameter name enclosed in curly brackets represents the parameter value. Whenever the script interpreter encounters such a parameter reference during the installation process, it substitutes it by the actual value of the corresponding parameter. The parameter values are always treated as a text string. They can be for instance used as object names, file names of media assets or names of routines to be called. Moreover, they can be compared to a string literal and the resulting boolean expression can be used as condition within a branching or loop clause.

To get the flavor of the scripting, consider the following excerpts written in our superset of HyperTalk. Note the references to the parameter "Use Dialog" of type "boolean choice" and the parameter "Choices" of type "free input with multiple values":

```
source first card of project "My Module"
target project "New Project"
if {Use Dialog} then
   replace routine "SetDefault" of this card by routine "AskFile"
end if
repeat with i = 1 to number of lines in {Choices}
   insert button "radio button" into background "main"
   set name of last background button to line i of {Choices}
end repeat
```

7. IMPLEMENTATION AND FUTURE ENHANCEMENTS

A prototype of the proposed system was implemented using HyperCard. We are currently designing the script interpreter and transporting the system to SuperCard. We plan to port it to similar authoring environments on the IBM PC platform, such as Toolbook or Windowcraft.

The current implementation allows the author to distribute the parameters of her module across a sequence of parameter definition cards. While this solution does not impose any limit on the number of parameters, we expect that complex modules will need a sizable number of cards that could complicate the user's task of selecting the parameter values. A hierarchy of parameter definition cards where a parameter templates (its name and current value) lead to cards where the parameter values can be selected might improve the convenience.

While HyperWarehouse allows the author to insert "help cards" to explain the purpose of the module, we plan to provide her with convenient access to explanations of individual parameters and their values.

The benefits of the proposed methodology are not restricted to the domain of hypermedia authoring systems. As the concept of modules as discussed in this paper include aspects of classes within object-oriented programming, similar user interfaces could be used to parametrize object classes to suit specific project needs while optimizing their efficiency.

REFERENCES

1   D. Ashworth, and J. Stelovsky, *Hypermedia Tools for T&I Training and Research*, Proceedings of the 8-th Conference of the Americal Translators' Association, (1990).
2   T.N. Kamala, J. Stelovsky, M.E. Crosby, *Individual Differences in the Use of hypermedia by Undergraduate Students at the University of Hawaii at Manoa*, Proceedings of the 5-th International Conference on Human-Computer Interaction, (1993).
3   J. Stelovsky, *HyperWarehouse: a Repository of Reusable Hypermedia Modules*, to be published, (1993).
4   J. Stelovsky, *Installation Scripts: an Extension of Programming lLnguages to Extract Generic Modules from Existing Hypermedia Applications*, to be published, (1993).

Using Multimedia to Teach Visual Literacy: A Systematic Approach

Raymond P. Kirsch[a] and Robert M. Aiken[b]

[a]Mathematical Sciences Department, LaSalle University, Philadelphia, PA 19141 USA

[b]Computer and Information Sciences Department, Temple University, Philadelphia, PA 19122 USA

Objective

The central focus of this research is the production of rudimentary multimedia tutorials that teach the fundamental skill of reading the graphical notations associated with diagrams. The target audience for these tutorials is beginning users of computer interfaces which incorporate diagrams to communicate about an advanced topic.

Significance

Diagrams add the pictorial, right-brain, dimension to the process of communicating information. When interrelated information (a diagram) is shown explicitly during the communication act, the information is more likely to be remembered and understood than if that information were conveyed without the diagram (Levin, 1987).

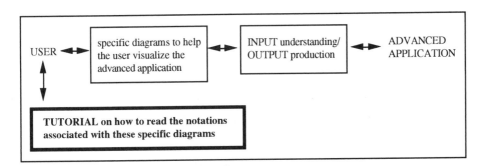

Figure 1. Typical User Interface Components with Suggested Improvement.

Many graphical user interfaces (GUIs) utilize diagrams, and have their own particular brand of the components appearing at the top of Figure 1. For instance, the picture of a database schema diagram is shown to communicate exactly how a database is structured. This frees the user from having to remember these details, and increases the likelihood of correct database queries. In some instances, diagrams are the primary language with which concepts are communicated between the user and the application (DiBattista, 1990). For example, in QBD* (Angelaccio, 1990), the schema diagram itself is used to retrieve information from a database.

Specific diagrams are aimed at helping the user to visualize advanced applications. But, are these diagrams understood by the average user? Or, is it more likely that typical GUI users may not understand, or may have forgotten a specific diagram's notations? Frequently, unsophisticated users must consult an off-line source for this information. But many users will not take the initiative to investigate fundamental diagrammatic notations and will make assumptions. This leads to potential misunderstanding and misconceptions, and certainly not to the communication and understanding, which the diagrams are expected to facilitate.

Figure 1 also shows an improvement. An on-line tutorial is available to a user working with the advanced application who finds the need for a review of its specific graphical notations can request one. A rudimentary multimedia tutorial will be presented. Afterwards, that user is more likely to understand the advanced application. There is a need for on-line presentations of the basic notations associated with domain specific diagrams. The primary goal of the research reported in this paper is to provide a tool to help produce them.

Three Presentation Levels

    Elementary -- simple composite images
    Intermediate -- composite images with groups of components
    Advanced -- whole composite images

For each level, proceed according to the following five steps

    1) Introduce the level of presentation

    2) Present prerequisite components which appear in the composite images of step 3

        For each component

        a) Indentify the component in general
          i) show a general picture
          ii) play descriptive audio(s)
        b) show example(s)

    3) Present composite images appropriate to this level

        For each composite image

        a) Indentify the composite image in general
          i) show a general picture
          ii) play descriptive audio(s)
        b) show example(s)

    4) Review the composite images in terms of the current level

        For each composite image presented in step 3, show an animated
        walk-through which highlights the concepts from the current level

    5) Review in terms of prior levels

        For each composite image presented in step 3, show an animated walk-
        through that highlights concepts on the current level and prior levels

---

Figure 2. Presentation Design Requirements.

Methodology

Two primary questions are addressed: (a) how to design computer-based presentations on reading graphical notations, and (b) how to design a system that assists in the production of these presentations. An answer to the first question is synthesized from theoretical models of graphics (Bertin, 1983), visual thinking (Levin, 1987; Paivio, 1986; Edwards, 1979; Saint-Martin, 1989) and instructional design (Reigeluth, 1980). The resulting presentation design requirements in Figure 2 were used to design the system depicted in Figure 3 which provides a tool that assists in the production of special-purposed multimedia presentations.

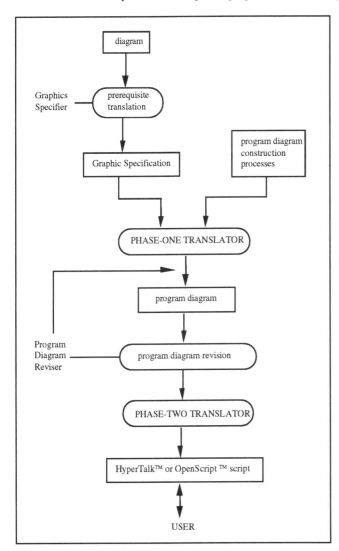

Figure 3. The Complete System.

This system translates a diagram into a rudimentary multimedia presentation based on the graphical notations associated with that diagram. Translation begins with prerequisite translation, a process which is accomplished by a person, who is referred to as the Graphics Specifier. Example diagrams are examined to determine components and composite images, and to provide descriptive annotations for them. The components, composite images, and corresponding annotations are then sequenced according to the presentation design requirements (Figure 2). The result is written in a form known as the Graphic Specification.

The Graphic Specification is input to the Phase-One Translator which automatically produces a default program diagram. Program diagram construction processes direct this translation phase. The default program diagram is an internal representation of the presentation which can either be executed as is (following Phase-Two translation), or can be revised by a person who is referred to as the Program Diagram Reviser.

Phase-Two translation converts a program diagram into an executable script in a target multimedia language, e.g., in HyperTalk™ or OpenScript™. When the target program is executed, a rudimentary multimedia tutorial is presented to the user. After witnessing this presentation, the user may select portions for review.

As a simple illustration, the translation processbegins when the Graphics Specifier examines an example diagram

to come up with the following Component and Composite Image Tables which are part of the Graphic Specification

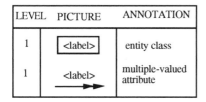

Figure 4. Component Table   Figure 5. Composite Image Table

Phase-One translation produces the corresponding portion of the default program diagram

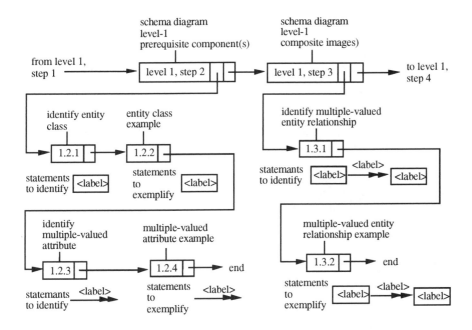

This portion of the program diagram corresponds to level one, steps two and three (Figure 2) of a presentation about database schema diagram graphical notations.

Results

An advantage of this systematic approach to the production of presentations is the resulting consistency within and across presentations. The Graphic Specification organizes a diagram's notations for presentation in a manner which facilitates their understanding, that is, in accordance with the presentation design requirements in Figure 2. This diagram specific information is input to the Phase-One translator which automatically produces a default program diagram that is guaranteed to be structurally identical to all other default program diagrams, i.e., having three levels with five steps per level. Authoring always starts as a modification of the default program diagram, and is now a process of exploring refinements, e.g., adding special effects or additional audio annotations. A structurally consistent authoring environment such as this is vital to increasing productivity, and is especially effective for inexperienced authors (Glinert, 1990). Also, since presentations all proceed in the same consistent, simple-to-complex manner, they are more likely to be assimilated by the user.

Another advantage is the reduction of cognitive overload. Since output sequencing is determined by the Graphic Specification, an author is not required to be thinking of the details of sequencing while, at the same time, exploring presentation enhancements. The process of encoding the output sequence is handled automatically by the Phase-One and Two translators, and is separated from the fine-tuning of the presentation.

Also, according to Glinert (1990), presentation development is facilitated by incorporating into the authoring environment a built-in mechanism that allows subject matter to be organized for presentation in stages that facilitate learning. A development environment with such a mechanism serves to reduce cognitive workload, eases the development of a specific presentation, and facilitates learning of how to author in that environment. The programmer is relieved of the burden of having to think about presentation sequencing and is free to explore enhancements. Glinert offers no suggestions on how to design curricular progressions, nor on how to build them into a development environment (1990, pp. 170-172), possibly because the computational realization of an instructional design methodology is a difficult problem (McCalla, 1987). Glinert speaks of the solution to this problem as future work in the area of nontextual programming. The system being reported in this paper helps to solve this problem by specifying presentation design requirements, which are a mechanism for organizing graphical notations for presentation in stages which facilitate learning (Bertin, 1983). The Graphic Specification and procedures to construct program diagrams have been designed in accordance with the presentation design requirements, and provide an example of incorporated a sequencing mechanism into an authoring tool. This particular mechanism is not ad hoc, but rather is based on theoretical, and empirically validated methods for sequencing presentations. While the complete system has not been implemented, code has been developed to translate sample Graphic Specifications for dataflow and database schema diagrams into HyperTalk™ and OpenScript™ code. Walk-throughs of all essential parts of this system indicate that its implementation is computationally feasible. This system offers an approach to solving a difficult problem. Developing a prototype is the next step in this project.

References

Angelaccio, M., Catarci, T., & Santucci, G. (1990). QBD*: a fully visual system for E-R oriented databases. Proceedings 1989 IEEE Workshop on Visual Languages.

Bertin, J. (1983). Semiology of graphics: Diagrams, networks, maps. (W. Berg, Trans.). London: University of Wisconsin Press. (Original work published 1967).

DiBattista, G., Giammarco, A., Santucci, G, & Tamassia, R. (1990). The architecture of diagram server. Proceedings 1990 IEEE Workshop on Visual Languages.

Edwards, B. (1979). Drawing on the right side of the brain. Los Angeles: J.P. Tarcher Inc.

Glinert, E. P. (1990). Nontextual programming environments. In S. Chang (Ed.), Principles of visual programming systems (pp. 144-230) Englewood Cliffs, New Jersey: Prentice Hall.

Kirsch, R. P. (1992). Computer-based teaching of visual literacy. Unpublished doctoral dissertation, Temple University, Philadelphia, PA.

Levin, J. R., Anglin, G.J. & Carney, R.N. (1987). On empirically validating functions of pictures in prose. In D. M. Willows & H. A. Houghton (Eds.), The psychology of illustration: Volume 1. New York: Springer-Verlag.

McCalla, G.I., & Greer, J.E. (1987). The practical use of AI in automated tutoring: current status and impediments to progress. (Research Rep. 87-2). Saskatoon: University of Saskatchewan, Department of Computer Science.

Piavio, A. (1986). Mental representations: A dual coding approach. New York: Oxford University Press.

Reigeluth, C.M., Merrill M.D., Wilson, B.G., & Spiller, R.T. (1980). The elaboration theory of instruction: A model for sequencing and synthesizing instruction. Instructional Science, 9(3), 195-219.

Saint-Martin, F. (1989). From visible to visual language: Artificial intelligence and visual semiology. Semiotica , 77(1-3), 303-16.

Multimedia development platforms and authoring tools: practical and theoretical frontiers

Wita Wojtkowski and W. Gregory Wojtkowski

Computer Information Systems and Production Management, Boise State University
1910 University Drive, Boise, ID 83725, USA

Abstract

This paper deals with multimedia development platforms and authoring tools. We examine available options and provide examples.

1. INTRODUCTION

Multimedia technology is forecasted to transform educational processes and business information systems applications [1-3]. Recent learning theory research asserts that individuals retain 20 percent of what they hear, 40 percent of what they see and hear, and 75 percent of what they experience [4,5]. Multimedia environment allows the learner/user to see, hear and see, and--through the simulations--experience [6]. The environment of multimedia goes beyond predetermined organization of information: what is behind the images and their linking mechanisms are equally important [7].

Although education and training tops current lists of applications for multimedia, its use is gaining ground in business presentations [8], practical utilization in workgroups, and scientific and engineering visualization [9,10]. Projected increase in spending for multimedia by the US government alone is from $900 million in 1992 to more than $2.4 billion in 1995 [11].

2. DESKTOP MULTIMEDIA DEVELOPMENT PLATFORMS

The technologies used on the multimedia development platforms are these:
high density storage; distributed computing; stereo audio capture and playback;
still image/graphics/photography capture and playback; analog full-motion video capture and playback; digital full-motion video capture and playback; desktop TV; freehand art work capture and playback; multimedia authoring software.

Multimedia authoring software, in turn, comprises tools for creating, capturing and editing all forms of graphics, animation, audio and video, as well as, clip art for graphics, animation, audio, and video.

Hardware offerings for the PC platform range from aid-in components to standard PCs bundled with multimedia upgrade kit (where integration task is really left to the buyer), to the PCs with multimedia components installed. At *minimum*, hardware components needed by the multimedia applications developer are these:

CPU:	386/33 and 8MB RAM
Storage:	hard disk: 300MB with 15 ms access time
	CD-ROM drive: 280 milliseconds (ms) access time; 150 Kbytes per second (Kbps) transfer rate
Monitor:	color monitor that supports resolutions from 640x480; noninterlaced super VGA with 1MB RAM, 14 inches screen size
Peripherals:	mouse, headphones, stereo speakers
	Video Sources: video device with serial port, laser video disk player
	Audio Sources: CD audio player, tape deck
Cards:	Audio: 16 bit stereo with 44KHz sample rate, 8 voices supported
	Video: capture and playback capability; video compression card
	CD-ROM interface card

2.1 CD-ROM Drives Standards

Most of the CD-ROM drives available today conform to the International Standards Organizations' 9660 standard (ISO 9660). Established in 1988, the standard closely approximates MS-DOS style of naming files. For most basic text search and retrieval applications and for the limited graphic use, the IS 9660 standard is adequate. Other available standards are extensions to ISO 9660. Among them are CD-ROM XA, a multimedia business standard; CD-Interactive (CD-I) aimed mostly at the consumer market; Multimedia CD (MMCD) aimed at the portable players; and multimedia CD, a standard for CD recorders (CD-R). CD-Rom XA standards can run multimedia applications more efficiently than ISO 9660 drives can [12].

2.2 PC Platform options with built-in CD-ROM and Sound

Some of the examples of the PC platform options with built-in CD-ROM and sound are shown in Table 1.

3. MULTIMEDIA AUTHORING TOOLS

Multimedia authoring tools can be divided into these groups: hard-core programmer's tools with multimedia extensions; DOS-based sequential scripting tools; Windows-based workbench systems; hypermedia tools; and Windows NT based products.

3.1 Hard core programming tools

This type of tool is exemplified by products such as Microsoft's C/C++ Version 7.0 Developer's Bench which is used with conjunction with Software Developer's Kit.

Table 1
PC platform options with built-in CD-ROM and sound

	CD-ROM drives		Sound board	Company
	Access time	Transfer rate		
	ms	Kbps		
Advantage	490	150	Sound Blaster	AST
Compaq	375	153	Media Vision	Compaq
Dell	390	150	Proprietary	Dell
Multimedia	550	171	SCSI	Micro Express
NCR	325	150	SCSI	NCR
Sensation	375	150	Proprietary	Tandy

3.2 DOS based sequential scripting tools

DOS tools take a sequential scripting approach to the authoring of the interactive applications. They are character-based and have extension that can call sound, animation and video routines. IBM's product set serves as an example. This set includes Media Script, Storyboard Live!, Linkway Live!, Audiovisual Connection (AVC).

3.3 Windows-based systems

These types of systems use drag-and drop object-oriented development techniques. IconAuthor from AimTech Corp. and Authorware Professional for Windows and the Macintosh are examples of these kind of tool.

3.4 Hypermedia tools

Hypermedia tools combine the index-based text-access technologies with multimedia capabilities to connect text with images, animations, video and sound sources. Multimedia Toolbook for Windows from Asymetrix Corp., MultiMedia Desktop for OS/2.2 from Detalus Inc. and GUIDE from Owl International Inc., serve as examples.

3.5 Windows NT based products

The expected release of Microsoft's Window's NT operating system, designed to operate equally well on high-end, single-user desktop platform; a local area network server; or a mainframe class system, has already prompted some developers of the multimedia authoring tools to announce the release of their Windows NT based products. Some examples of current releases are listed in Table 2.

Table 2
Multimedia Authoring Tools for Windows NT

	Application	Company
MediaDB	Multimedia database management system and applications development environment	Ravi Technologies
MultimediaDeveloper for NT	Applications development environment	Lenel Systems International
Spinnaker PLUS	Object oriented multimedia development tool	Spinnaker Software

4.0 NETWORKED APPLICATIONS

Vast majority of computer applications progress from stand-alone, or centralized, host-based systems, to a distributed networked environment. Examples of networked applications include electronic mail, groupware, distributed transaction processing systems, multi-tier enterprise information systems, and distributed database management systems. Because the effort to generate and implement multimedia applications can be justified only if it is shared by many users, multimedia applications also follow the route from stand-alone to networked applications [13]. Recent developments in the high speed communication technology [14] attest to that.

4.1 Promises and Problems

As all media in multimedia applications move toward the digital state, they will present new promises and new problems. New promises are in creating, for the user, the ability to access information from multiple locations and to a variety of platforms: from PCs, to television sets, to portable personal communicators that work as hand-held hybrids that support multimedia and include cellular telephone, fax machine, personal information manager, and video e-mail retrieval system. New problems emerge when video, sound, graphics, and text "became equal partners in computer transmission" [2]. This causes variety of difficulties: from the technical issues of movement and storage, to copyright problems. For example, due to the varying transmission, storage, and processing requirements of different media in multimedia applications, diverse traffic flows and performance requirements are needed. This is illustrated in Figure 1 (adapted from [14]).

Efficacy of the distributed multimedia application was currently demonstrated through a Virtual Notebook System (VNS), a multimedia group collaboration tool for users who need to communicate with others working on different networks [8].

All of the major computer manufacturers are looking to implement multimedia networking on their platforms, although no one has a cohesive vision yet. Nevertheless, recent projections from the market research firms [15,16] forecast explosive growth for worldwide multimedia on LANs and WANs. A sample of products already available for the emerging multimedia networks is shown in Table 3.

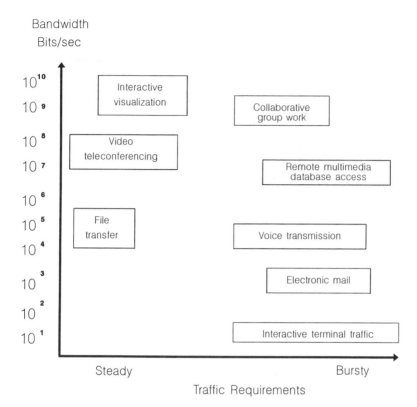

Figure 1. Traffic and bandwidth requirements for diverse multimedia applications.

Table 3
A sample of products for the multimedia networks

Application	Platform	Company
ArtiScribe New Media	DOS	Artisoft, Inc.
CD Connection and Server CD-ROM networking	all	CBIS, Inc.
DECspin multimedia networking	DEC	Digital Equipment
LINK video LAN system	all	Applied Computer Systems, Inc.
Person to Person/2 multimedia network	OS/2	IBM

5. CONCLUDING REMARKS

Multimedia technology is maturing and changing user expectations [Yankelovich et al., 1988]. In the short range, for example, CD/ROM drives as well as audio and video features may soon become expected standards for PCs. In the long range, platform-independent multimedia authoring environments will inevitably be created, so that the software becomes portable across diverse hardware architectures. The development of multimedia network services (for both the client and server) that include the manipulation of remote multimedia databases will also change expectations. It is worth noting, however, that the types of multimedia products being developed so far, are based on the traditional media or software paradigms. A new model for new media development has yet to emerge.

REFERENCES

1   J. Sculley, The Between Business and Higher Education: A Perspective on 21st Century," Communications of the ACM, September 1989.

2   B. Davis, "Looking and Learning Through Computers," EDUCOM Review, Vol. 28, No. 1, January/February 1993.

3   K. B. Sullivan, "Business Embraces Multimedia for Presentations on the Road," PC Week, March 22, 1993.

4   P. Elbow, Embracing Contraries: Explorations in Learning and Teaching, Oxford University Press, Oxford, 1986.

5   D. Perkins and G. Salomon, "Are Cognitive Skills Context-Bound?," Educational Researcher, January/February 1989.

6   D. Kirby and M. Kuykendall, Mind Matters: Teaching for Thinking, Heinemann, Portsmouth, 1991.

7   B. Davis, M. Hodges and S. Sasnett, "Advanced Multimedia at MIT," Advanced Imaging, July 1992.

8   J. Cummins, "Conference Demo Features Multimedia Application," Network World, February 8, 1993.

9   S. Polilli "Coming to Networks Near You: Multimedia Moves Toward Mainstream With Server Hosting Video, Sound," Software Magazine, September 1992

10   N. Lippis "Now Hear This (And See It Too): Multimedia Has Arrived," Data Communications, July 1992.

11   S. Zurier and J. Liebowitz "Multimedia: Government Embraces Technology Poised on Brink of Revolution," Government Computer News, August 1992.

12   B. Francis "CD-ROMs Drive Toward New Standards," Datamation, February 15, 1993.

13   S. Lerman, et al. Distributed Multimedia Computing, The AthenaMuse Software Consortium, Center for Educational Computing Initiatives, MIT, Cambridge, 1991.

14   R.J. Vetter and D. H. C. Du "Distributed Computing with High-Speed Computer Networks," Computer, February 1993.

15   Market Intelligence, World Multimedia Hardware and Software Markets, Frost and Sullivan Market Intelligence, Mountain View, CA, 1993.

16   Ovum, Ltd., Survey of European and U.S. Multimedia Markets, London, 1993.

Using animated demonstrations in multimedia applications: Some suggestions based upon experimental evidence

P.E. Waterson and C.E. O'Malley

Department of Psychology, University of Nottingham, University Park, Nottingham NG7 2RD, United Kingdom

Abstract

This paper presents results from an experiment which compared animated demonstrations with textual instructions and a combination of the two. The results show that combining spoken text with animation provides the most optimal instructional content for the tasks which were used in the experiment. In addition, the different instructions seem to lead to different processing, depending upon type of task. Preliminary suggestions are made for the use of animated demonstrations within multimedia applications.

1. INTRODUCTION

The growth of interest in multimedia applications has resulted in new instructional methods for teaching both novice and expert users how to use systems. One method which has recently attracted interest from researchers has been to use instructions in the form of animated demonstrations. Sukaviriya [4], for example, describes a system which provides context sensitive help in the form of animations. In addition, animated demonstrations are frequently available with new software in the form of "guided tours" and are beginning to be implemented as on-line animated help facilities. Evaluations of the efficacy of animation demonstrations have however, produced some mixed results. Some researchers have concluded that animations are of limited value for teaching the user long term skills that do not degrade over time, whilst others have found that animations are effective learning tools when combined with some types of interfaces and the skills that are required to learn them.

Palmiter and Elkerton [2], for example, found that animated demonstrations proved useful for immediate learning of simple HyperCard authoring skills, but that this advantage was not sustained over time as compared to users learning from textual materials. Similarly, in an extension to the study, they found that combining spoken text with animated demonstrations did not lead to a predicted advantage over animation and textual instructions alone in a delayed test session one week later. These findings lead the authors to conclude that animated demonstrations offer an advantage to those learning to use an application immediately but do not support long term learning since they are largely processed superficially, unlike textual material which appears to be remembered over longer periods.

The few other studies which exist in this area conclude that animated demonstrations do not contain the necessary learning content to support long term retention of procedures and general skill acquisition. Instead, it is argued that demonstrations tend to encourage rote learning, in contrast to materials such as written manuals. A question which surrounds this kind of research and one which researchers themselves have acknowledged ([2]) is whether or not the advantage of animated demonstrations depends upon the particular type of interface skills and tasks being taught. Some support for this view is offered by two recent studies.

Payne, Chesworth and Hill [3] carried out a study using the MacDraw drawing application. They found that when users were given an animated demonstration in the form of an off-line video tape of MacDraw in use they performed much more quickly and accurately compared with users given instructions in the form of guided exploration cards, a combination of the two media and no instructions at all. Using a similar experimental design to that of Palmiter et al. [2], Waterson and O'Malley [5] found that when subjects were taught to use the MacDraw graphics application using a series of animated demonstrations they completed tasks in a shorter time than users taught using a set of on-line textual instructions presented using HyperCard. More importantly, this advantage was sustained during a delayed test phase which took place a week after the immediate test phase of the experiment. In addition, subjects in the demonstration group seemed to have an advantage over subjects using textual materials in that they engaged in exploration of the interface, completing tasks for which they had received no previous instruction significantly faster than the latter group during both phases of the experiment. The present study was designed to further examine the effect of different types of task upon task performance using demonstration and text as instructions. In addition, a third type of instruction combining animation with spoken text (similar to the study reported in [2]) was introduced in order to more closely distinguish the processing advantages and limitations of each type of instructional media.

2. METHOD

2.1 Subjects

A total of thirty paid subjects took part in the experiment. None of the subjects had used a Macintosh computer before or the application Cricket Graph. All subjects had experience of using a mouse. Subjects were randomly allocated to one of the three experimental conditions: ten subjects received animated demonstrations during the training phase of the experiment, ten subjects were given a series of on-line textual instructions and ten were given a combination of animated demonstration with a spoken commentary.

2.2. Experimental Task

Subjects were taught six procedures for carrying out operations using the graph application Cricket Graph on the Macintosh. These procedures were taught using a series of animated demonstrations created using the MediaTracks application, a set of on-line instructions presented on individual cards running within HyperCard, or a combination of animation simultaneously presented with spoken commentary. During the test phase of the experiment subjects were then tested using forty-two tasks which were divided into three groups: (i) identical tasks — these were tasks which were identical to the ones demonstrated by animation, described in the textual instructions and presented in the combination condition (n=6); (ii) similar tasks — these were tasks which were similar to the descriptions demonstrated by animation, described in the textual instructions and presented in the combination condition (n=18); (iii) different tasks — these involved carrying out a task where no instruction had been given, and subjects were expected to generalise from what they had been taught explicitly (n=18). Table 1 below shows examples of each of the types of task used in the experiment.

2.3 Experimental Materials

A series of written instructions was created for each of the six procedures that were taught to subjects. Subjects in the textual instruction condition received a set of instructions presented on cards within a HyperCard stack. Each of the cards was presented for between 40-55 seconds. This was roughly the same amount of time which the equivalent animated demonstrations took (textual instructions lasted for 5 to 8 seconds longer). The animated demonstration and combination conditions for each of the six Cricket Graph procedures were created using the MediaTracks training tool. In the case of creating a graph, for example, the subject would see the mouse pointer move to the Graph menu at the top of the screen, select a graph option, then click on the data columns corresponding to the x and y coordinates of the graph, and finally click on the "new plot" option. In order to make sure that the instructional content for all conditions were as close to informational equivalence as possible, a group of eight non-Macintosh users, other than the experimental subjects, were asked to watch the animated demonstrations and to describe in detail the contents of each of the six demonstrations. In addition, this group was asked to describe what they has seen in such a way that someone who had not seen the animations could readily understand the content of the procedures. Written descriptions from this group were collated and common elements from the descriptions were used to form the basis of the text and combination (i.e., animation + spoken text) instructions used in the experiment.

Table 1
Examples of tasks used in the experiment

	Identical	Similar	Different
1. Changing Data	Cut/Paste	Copy/Paste	Cut/Paste/Paste
2. Transform Data	Sort Data	Count Frequency	Add Data Columns
3. Draw Graph	Line Graph	Pie Chart	Overlay Graph
4. Annotate Graph	Legend Box	Text Box	Add Text to Graph
5. Add Depth	Bar Graph	Stack Bar	Add Value Labels
6. Change Titles	Change Title	Change Label	Change Plot Symbol

2.4. Procedure

The experiment took about an hour to complete. To begin with, all subjects were shown a representation of the Cricket Graph opening screen and the various parts were explained to them. This was considered to be particularly important for subjects in the text group, as these terms were used in the written instructions. Subjects in this group would therefore be able to referentially map these terms to their corresponding positions and functions on the Cricket Graph interface. All subjects were then given a handout which gave examples of the sorts of operations which could be carried out using Cricket Graph (e.g., changing data, manipulating data, drawing graphs, etc.). This was included in the experiment as it was felt that subjects might not be familiar with various graphing/data manipulation operations, such as sorting data or adding error bars to graphs. Following this subjects were told about the type of instruction they would receive in the experiment (e.g., demonstration/text/combination). Tasks were randomised within all groups. Having received the instructions, all subjects would receive six randomised tasks followed by eighteen similar tasks and then eighteen different tasks. After the sixth instruction no further instructions were provided and each subject completed the task with no additional help from the experimenter. Subjects who failed to complete a task within five minutes were asked to move on to the next task. The time to successfully complete a task was recorded by the experimenter. Failures to complete a task were also recorded by the experimenter.

3. RESULTS

For reasons of space this section only reports time data from the experiment. An analysis of variance (ANOVA) was carried out on the log of the total performance times for each of the instructional media for each of the task groups (identical, similar and different) and revealed main effects of type of instruction ($F_{[2,27]}=12.72$, $p<0.0005$), task group ($F_{[2,27]}=77.515$, $p<0.001$) and a significant interaction between instruction and task ($F_{[4,27]}=3.65$, $p<0.05$). (The raw data were subjected to a log transform, in keeping with most reported analyses using performance times.) Figure 1 below shows a graph of the adjusted means of task performance for the three instructional conditions on each of the three task groups.

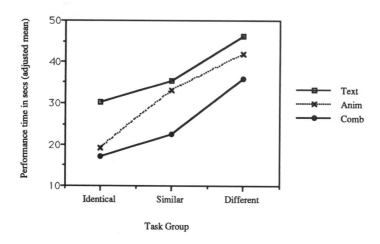

Figure 1. Graph of mean time to complete tasks by task group.

Subjects in the combination condition completed tasks in each of the task groups faster than either of the other two experimental conditions. The textual instruction group were slower in completing tasks as compared to the demonstration and combination conditions. Analysis of simple main effects revealed significant differences between the text and combination groups on the identical tasks ($F_{[2,54]}$=14.08, p<0.01) and similar tasks ($F_{[2,54]}$=9.85, p<0.01), but not on the different tasks (p=0.07).

In order to examine further the effect of task type upon performance, tasks within the similar and different groups were further broken down into the six types of task which made up the similar and different groups. These tasks were included in a three way ANOVA with type of instruction as a between subjects factor and task group (i.e., similar and different tasks) and type of task (i.e., changing data, transforming data, drawing graphs, etc.) treated as within subjects factors. The analysis revealed main effects of type of instruction ($F_{[2,27]}$=9.733, p<0.01), task group ($F_{[1,27]}$=87.485, p<0.01) and type of task ($F_{[5,27]}$=22.408, p<0.01). In addition, there were significant interactions between type of instruction and type of task ($F_{[10,27]}$=3.529, p<0.01) and task group and type of task ($F_{[5,27]}$=9.069, p<0.01). Figures 2 (a) and (b) below show graphs of the adjusted means of task performance for the three instructional conditions on each of the six task types within the similar and different task groups respectively.

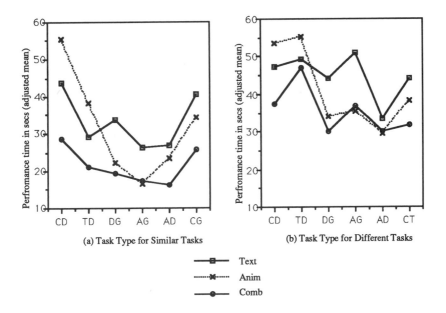

Figure 2. Graph of mean time to complete tasks by individual tasks.

As can be seen from Figure 2 (a) and (b) there was a good deal of variation in performance across the instructional groups for each of the six types of task. For both the similar and different task groups, the demonstration group were slower to complete tasks involving changing and transforming data, whilst their performance on the drawing and annotating graph tasks was very similar to that of the combination group. Likewise, the performance of the text-only group was faster relative to the demonstration group for the changing and transforming data tasks but was slower than this group for the drawing and annotating graph tasks. For the tasks involving adding depth to graphs and changing graph titles, the text group were consistently slower than the other instructional groups. Across all tasks the combination group completed tasks quicker than the either the text-only or demonstration groups.

4. DISCUSSION AND CONCLUSIONS

Perhaps the most interesting finding from the experiment is that combining spoken text with animation leads to the fastest performance times across all task groups. This result contrasts with that of Palmiter and Elkerton [2]. An explanation for this is linked to the variation in task performance which was demonstrated by all of the instructional groups. Tasks which, according to the model described by Kitajima and Polson [1], mainly involve display-based components (i.e., drawing graphs and annotating graphs) were completed in faster times by the animation and combination groups but slower by subjects in the text-only condition. In contrast, tasks which involve knowledge which needs to encoded in memory (i.e., change data and transform data tasks) were completed faster by the text-only and combination groups but slower by subjects in the animation group. Tasks in the final categories follow the general trend of the results as shown in Figure 1. These tasks were constructed so as to involve a mixture of both display-based and encoded knowledge components. The results from the different task group are not as clear cut as those from the similar tasks. This is likely to have occurred because of the difficulty of finding tasks which fit into both categories according to the model and had not already been used for the similar tasks. In many ways then, the results from the similar tasks are more indicative of the processing characteristics of the three instructional groups with respect to the model described in [1].

The superiority of the combination group can therefore be explained in terms of the need for both display-based and encoded knowledge in completing tasks in the study. Combining animation with text allows sampling and integration of both types of knowledge and therefore leads to faster performance times. The differences between the animation and text groups on some of the tasks demonstrates that different types of knowledge are sampled during the training phase of the experiment and influence subsequent performance in the testing phase. In addition, a comparison of the performance of these groups with the combination group for the first four tasks shows that, in some cases, adding text or animation to a demonstration did not improve the completion of these tasks relative to simply including either text or animation alone as instructions. One thing to bear in mind is that in this study combining text with animation may overload or confuse the user. Although no evidence for this was found in the present study it seems likely that presenting too much or superfluous information may lead to poorer performance.

The present study was designed with a specific model of display-based problem solving in mind. With regard to earlier studies it goes some way toward confirming the influence of task structure upon the effectiveness of certain types of instructions. The findings of Palmiter et al. [2] may in part be due to the tasks used in these studies (i.e., tasks where little or no display-based component was available and therefore text rather than animation was more suitable as instructional material) as well as the way in which spoken text was presented with animation in combination. With this in mind, one might conclude that, before using animations, text or combinations of these as instructions in demonstrations, it would be advisable for the designer to perform a task analysis similar to that used to generate the tasks in our study. This should proceed along the lines of deciding which tasks involve display-based knowledge and which involve sampling other sources of knowledge. At the moment there are few models of display-based problem solving and most are in the early stages of development. It seems likely, however, that when more research has been carried out in this area such models will prove useful to designers of instructional systems, particularly when animated demonstrations are to be used.

5. REFERENCES

1. Kitajima, M. & Polson, P. (1992) A computational model of skilled use of a graphical interface. In Proceedings of CHI'92, ACM: New York, pp. 241-249.
2. Palmiter, S. & Elkerton, J. (1991) An evaluation of animated demonstrations for learning computer-based tasks. In Proceedings of CHI'91, ACM: New York, pp. 257-263.
3. Payne, S.J., Chesworth, L. & Hill, E. (1992) Animated demonstrations for exploratory learners. Interacting with Computers, 4, 3-22.
4. Sukaviriya, P. (1988) Dynamic construction of animated help from application context. In Proceedings of the ACM SIGGRAPH User Interface Software Symposium, ACM: New York.
5. Waterson, P.E. & O'Malley, C.E. (1992) Using animated demonstrations to teach graphics skills. In People & Computers VII, edited by A. Monk, D. Diaper, & M.D. Harrison, Cambridge: Cambridge University Press.

A Design Model for Multimedia Computer-Based Training

Dr. Garry Patterson, Dr. Terry J Anderson, Prof. Fabian C Monds

Faculty of Informatics, University of Ulster, Jordanstown, Co. Antrim, BT37 0QB, Northern Ireland.

Keywords
Multimedia, Design Methodology, Usability, Computer-Based Training, User Interface Design, Evaluation.

Abstract
The design of a user interface for multimedia computer-based training (CBT) courseware is arguably one of the most important areas within the overall design process for todays changing learning environments. A methodology for the design, implementation and evaluation of multimedia CBT courseware, called MIDAS (Multimedia Interactive Design Aided System) is proposed. The model is centered upon the use of high quality and creative instructional design embracing the changing technologies, coupled with clear principles of learning and cognitive psychology which enables usability evaluation. A set of design usability principles, rules for the production of multimedia courseware and an evaluation document for use in individual and institutional learning environments are discussed in this paper.

1 Introduction
Current developments in interactive multimedia systems are impressive. The challenge is to use this technology effectively for CBT courseware. However the approach to the design and development of courseware for training needs reappraisal in the light of past failures. Where previously system developers and designers have been insensitive to the end user and their needs, today, the user-centered approach is moving to centre stage.

In previous papers [1, 2, 3] theoretical issues relevant to the design of a multimedia user interface for CBT courseware have been addressed. They include a user-centered approach to design, task analysis, prototyping and evaluation. UID methodologies and formal method techniques have been explored, identifying attributes and techniques which the courseware designer could usefully incorporate into a UID strategy. This paper brings all these issues together within the methodology of the **Multimedia Interactive Design Aided System** (MIDAS) model as a structure for the design, implementation and evaluation of interactive multimedia CBT courseware. Courseware abstraction will be proposed for designing cost effective CBT material. A practical method of evaluating the usability of the interface will also be presented as part of the MIDAS framework. Discussions will focus on presenting a framework for implementing multimedia CBT courseware using the methodology of MIDAS.

The challenge becomes one of knowing which tools and techniques to use and where in the system life cycle to start. Unfortunately few CBT systems have been designed with a human factors component as a high priority item [4]. An important part of developing CBT courseware involves understanding the nature of the users' tasks and the way in which users most naturally decompose them. This in turn requires understanding of the characteristics of users themselves and the influence on their behaviour of the context in which they work. In addition, designers have to take into account hardware and management policy training considerations. Since the user interface can account for approximately fifty per cent of the total life cycle costs of interactive systems, the designer has a vested interest in creating a user interface that both satisfies the customer and is constructed using the best available tools and technologies.

It is important, therefore, that a methodology of interface design be developed which integrates the development of HCI*f*'s within the overall design life cycle for the production of CBT courseware. The MIDAS model is one such methodology which centres on the stages in user interface design including ways of evaluating the usability of HCI*f*'s for courseware. *A model centred upon the use of high quality and creative instructional design embracing the changing technologies and are based upon clear principles of learning and cognitive psychology is essential.* The methodology of the MIDAS model presented here adopts such criteria. Figure 1.1 illustrates the overall structure which should help designers produce successful courseware.

2 The Methodology of MIDAS

The Multimedia Interactive Design Aided System (MIDAS), will define representations and descriptions to be used by the designer to discuss features of the system and by the implementer to produce a full and coherent implementation of a CBT system. It explores the idea that designers might, at any stage in the design process, maintain three perspectives on the design problem, each with its own form of model representation. One perspective is that of the *system,* modelled by a set of properties and principles governing the behaviour of the software interface. Another perspective is that of the *user*, with appropriate principles for modelling the mental representations and processes that govern and constrain user behaviour. The third perspective is that of the *interaction framework*, with appropriate concepts and principles for representing properties of conjoint user-system behaviour. This framework should support inter-communication between different forms of representational structures and in some sense 'integrate over' system, cognitive and other situational factors that need to be considered for the application under development. Figure 2.1 illustrates the three perspectives on the design problem.

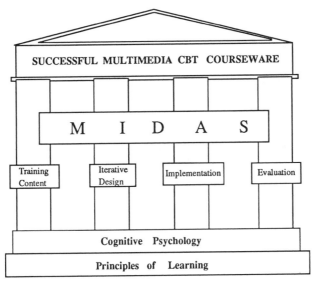

Figure 1.1   The Framework of MIDAS

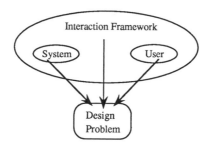

Figure 2.1   Perspectives on the Design Problem

2.1   The Courseware Designer

The changing strategies of presentation and techniques used for learning identified in [5] make it clear that most industrial and educational institutions today are employing professional graphic designers to produce high quality courseware. In the design of the user interface, the designer must therefore work in tandem with the trainer, that is the subject expert . This will be referred to as *user-centered design.* Since the design process requires many types of information from users, it requires involving users throughout the process in a variety of ways. MIDAS defines several roles users and professional designers can play in the design of the user interface and explains the impact these roles have on product and service quality. A simplified model of the design process is presented which illustrates the players in that process.

2.2   A Simplified Model of the Design Process

The design process can be viewed as several overlapping tasks as shown in Figure 2.2. By its form, the graphic suggests balance. It suggests that each design task is related to all others in a network of constraints. The tasks are (1) define the problem, (2) list the requirements any solution must satisfy, (3) select an abstract solution concept, (4) specify the general parameters of the solution, and (5) create a detailed implementation plan for the solution.

Each of these tasks can be viewed as an interactive cycle composed of four overlapping sub-activities, (1) gather background information, (2) collect and/or generate alternatives, (3) select an alternative, and (4) evaluate the validity of the decision.

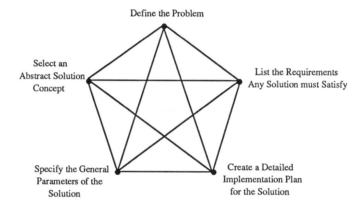

Figure 2.2   Simplified Model of the Design Process

The above simplified model provides enough common language to describe how users should be involved in the design process. The designer must be aware of the theoretical issues in each of the stages as shown in Figure 2.3. The user interface life cycle presented in [6] elaborated on these stages.

In the Midas model the *designer's* primary function is to create and implement the CBT courseware and services. In the past, designers have only been involved with a product or service until it is implemented. The designer must strive to understand why and how users interact with the design interface. They must also assume responsibilities for issues and constraints that may be in direct conflict with identified user interests, such as technical limitations, legal restrictions and corporate strategies.

The *user* will in the first instance be the trainer, or subject expert. Unlike the designer, users do not focus on software *per se* - as a tool. They are interested in what they can *achieve* with the product. Users can have three different roles in the design process: the *subject*, the *evaluator*, and the *designer*.

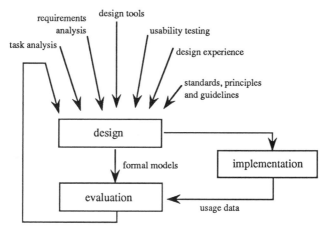

Figure 2.3   User-centered Design Cycle

3 Evaluation within the Methodology of MIDAS

The method is a practical tool, in the form of a checklist. It is based on a set of software ergonomics criteria, which a well-designed user interface should aim to meet. The checklist consists of sets of specific questions aimed at assessing usability. These provide a standardized and systematic means of enabling those evaluating a CBT system interface.

3.1 The evaluation checklist

Each of the first ten sections is based on a criterion, which a well-designed user interface should aim to meet. The criterion is described at the beginning of the section, and a number of checklist questions follow, which aim to identify whether the interface meets the criterion. The criteria are not in any order of importance within the checklist. The ten criteria are summarised in Table 3.1.

4 Conclusion

The design of effective multimedia CBT courseware depends critically on the issues raised within the MIDAS methodology. UID requires careful scrutiny of both the *human aspect* and *methods of design*. A user-centered design solution identifying the roles of designers and users has been suggested. The use of CA as a method of developing a structure for the efficient production of CBT courseware is also recommended. Guidelines for screen display and layout have been incorporated into the methodology. User participation in developing a prototype model is stressed. Evaluating the usability of the user interface is central if a prototype structure is to be fully implemented. The method adopted in this paper provides a very practical structure for assessing the effectiveness of the courseware and provides a measure that identifies problem areas, weaknesses in the UID and suggesting areas for improvement. The MIDAS model provides a methodology that designers involved in the development of multimedia CBT courseware can follow.

Table 3.1   Evaluation Criteria

Section Heading	Criteria Statement (Summary)
Visual Clarity	Information displayed on any CBT courseware screen should be clear, well-organized, unambiguous and easy to read
Auditory Presentation	The music or voice commentary for any CBT screen should be clear, structured, unambiguous and easy to follow
Consistency	The way the CBT courseware looks and works should be consistent at all times
Compatibility	The way the CBT courseware looks and works should be compatible with user conventions and expectations
Informative Feedback	Users of the CBT courseware should be given clear, informative feedback on where they are in the training course, what actions they have taken and whether they have been successful
Explicitness	The way the CBT courseware works and is structured should be clear to the user
Appropriate Functionality	The CBT courseware should meet the needs and requirements of users when carrying out tasks
Flexibility and Control	The CBT courseware interface should be flexible in structure, in the way information is presented and in terms of what the user can do, and to allow them to feel in control of the system
Error Prevention & Correction	The CBT courseware should be designed to minimize the possibility of user errors; users should be able to check their inputs and to correct errors
User Guidance & Support	Informative, easy-to-use and relevant guidance and support should be provided in the CBT courseware

These concepts are developed in subsequent research [7], both in the design of the prototype application for British aerospace and in the production of rules for designing and evaluating CBT courseware suitable to both industrial and institutional learning environments in the 1990s.

References

1 Patterson, G. (1992), A Design Model for Multimedia Computer-Based Training, *D.Phil. Thesis*, University of Ulster, Jordanstown, N. Ireland, pp. 100 -121
2. Patterson, G., Anderson, TJ., Monds, FC. (1992), A Design Methodology for CBT, *Proceedings of Interface to Real & Virtual Worlds*, EC2, Paris, pp.397 - 409
3 Patterson, G., Anderson, TJ., Monds, FC. (1991), The Production of Technology Based Courseware, *Interactive Learning International*, Vol. 7, No.4, pp. 321 - 333, Wiley, England
4 Patterson, G. (1992), *D. Phil. Thesis*, Reference 1 above, pp. 103 - 106
5 Patterson, G. (1992), *D. Phil. Thesis*, Reference 1 above, pp. 103 - 106
6 Patterson, G. (1992), *D. Phil. Thesis*, Reference 1 above, pp. 43 - 49
7 Patterson, G. (1992), *D. Phil. Thesis*, Reference 1 above, pp. 122 - 166

Visualizing Multidimensional Process Control Relationships

S.K. Habibi and D.S. Ranson

AECL Research, Chalk River Laboratories, Chalk River, Ontario, K0J 1J0, Canada

Abstract
    A case study has been performed to develop function-based displays to support power plant operators controlling component stress in a set of steam generators during heat-up and cool-down manoeuvres. Based on a function and task analysis, a set of displays has been developed to show the multidimensional relationship between the process parameters and to support the operators in detection, diagnosis, prediction, and incident recovery. Display options include 2D and 3D graphic representations. It has been concluded that 2D graphic displays are more effective than 3D displays for representing the multidimensional relationships. Further, displays have been developed to allow operators to predict the effects of changes in controllable variables on the key parameters that impact component stress.

1. INTRODUCTION

    The level of automation in power plants has risen in the past two decades to the point where operators assume the role of supervisory controllers. In this role, their responsibilities typically include the monitoring and control of process conditions and power levels, testing equipment, coordinating maintenance, and control of the plant in the event of upsets or emergencies. Plant operation is demanding due to this wide range of responsibilities and the large number of systems and functions to be managed. A well-designed human-machine interface makes an important contribution to the overall performance of the operator.
    In controlling the plant, operators must stay within predefined operating limits. Many of these limits are a function of several parameters. Consequently, the operator's goal is to keep the plant within a complex multidimensional operating envelope.
    This paper reports on a case study to develop function-based displays to support operator control of steam generators during heat-up and cool-down manoeuvres. At this plant, the steam generators consist of banks of four boilers joined at the top by a common steam drum (see Figure 1). The primary-side hot water enters the boilers from the bottom via the primary heat transport (PHT) system, while the secondary-side cool water enters mid-way up the boilers from the feedwater system.
    During heat-up and cool-down, the difference in temperature between the steam drum and PHT piping may cause stress within the individual components or the junctions between them. To avoid excessive stresses, operators must stay within an operating region that is a function of seven factors: (1) steam drum pressure, (2) overall system temperature, (3) the temperature difference between the steam drum and the PHT piping (ΔT_{DP}), (4) the temperature difference between the top and bottom of the steam drum (ΔT_{TB}), (5) PHT water pressure, (6) percent plant power, and (7) heat-up and cool-down rates.
    Staying within the stress limits requires control of the last two factors (i.e., percent plant power and heat-up and cool-down rates), as well as control of feedwater flow and cooling fan

operation. The relationships between these controlled variables and the other parameters can be difficult for operators to understand and manage. In the control room, variables are displayed as trends or as digital values. Experience has shown that using only these displays, operators have had difficulty avoiding high stress regions during heat-up and cool-down of the unit.

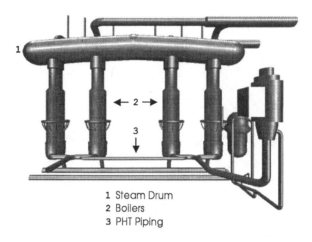

1 Steam Drum
2 Boilers
3 PHT Piping

Figure 1: 3D view of steam drum, boilers, and PHT piping.

2. ANALYSIS

To identify operator information needs, a function and task analysis has been conducted. This analysis involved a review of operating procedures and other relevant documentation, interviews with operators, and a simulator exercise. The goal of this analysis was to identify and describe precisely what would be required of the new function-based displays from an operational standpoint. Three types of information have been identified and analyzed [1]:

- functions (i.e., the purpose for which an activity or a sub-system exists),

- tasks (i.e., actions by humans or computers that achieve goals), and

- information requirements (i.e., information needed to successfully perform tasks).

Operators indicated that they monitor parameters to achieve five functions:

- avoid excessive steam drum hump and sag (ΔT_{TB}),

- avoid excessive steam drum to piping temperature difference (ΔT_{DP}),

- minimize heat-up/cool-down (H/C) rate,

- avoid excessive temperature difference between boiler headers (ΔT_{BLR}), and

- abide by special heat-up and cool-down procedures.

These functions are required to achieve the overall objective of avoiding stresses on the steam drum tee-junction and PHT piping. Operators generally deal with these functions concurrently.

However, during different phases of heat-up and cool-down, the emphasis on individual functions shifts from one to another. Each function involves maintaining a variable within safe limits. Operators understand the inter-dependence of the variables, but they concentrate on maintaining each variable within its own safe limits and only consider inter-dependencies when deciding how recovery actions will affect other variables. Operators stressed that they needed help in predicting control consequences, particularly on ΔT_{TB}, ΔT_{BLR}, and ΔT_{DP}.

3. DISPLAY PROTOTYPES

Several display options have been considered to meet the information needs identified in the analysis. Information is grouped in these displays according to functions. Within each display, picture elements have been selected according to the nature of task information needs and the characteristics of the information. The display options included three-dimensional (3D) representations, conventional parameter graphs, trends, bar charts, and schematics. Each display will be briefly described below.

3.1. 3D View of the Three Major Determinants of Stress

Displaying the relationships between all seven factors is a difficult problem. Most visualization techniques that attempt to graph data in more than four dimensions are extremely complex. A common approach to reducing the complexity is to show 3D views in which one or more variables are held constant and the entire n-dimensional space is visualized through multiple 3D views [2]. In this particular multidimensional environment, there was no operational need for multiple 3D views. Operators stated that only one 3D view of three of the seven variables defining the safe operating envelope was appropriate. ΔT_{TB}, ΔT_{DP}, and drum pressure were the main contributors to the system stress, so they were chosen to form the three axes of a 3D graph. The safe limits defined by the relationship of these three variables formed the edges of a bell-shaped object shown in Figure 2. From an operational point of view, values within the enclosed limits are acceptable, while values outside the limits represent points where excessive stresses are imposed on the boiler. Hence, the operators' goal is to avoid exceeding the high stress limits by staying within this 3D space.

Tracking and predicting changes of ΔT_{TB} and ΔT_{DP} in relation to their limits in this 3D space appeared to be very difficult. Subjective observation indicated that operators would have trouble comprehending their location within the 3D plot in relation to the limits. They would also not be able to effectively determine the direction they were heading in and how much time they had before a limit was exceeded. It appeared that the 3D representation distorted distances so that operators could potentially under- or over-estimate the distance to the limits. These observations are consistent with studies that showed that 3D displays can incur biases and ambiguity regarding the precise estimation of distance [3]. In addition, the 3D graph did not appear to provide any emergent features that enhanced the operators' ability to perform tasks. Furthermore, the work required to rotate and translate the 3D view has been deemed to be too great. For these reasons, the 3D view will not be included in the recommended set of displays.

3.2. 2D Slice Alternative

The bell-shaped 3D representation can also be represented by taking slices perpendicular to the drum pressure axis. The basic shape of each slice is an ellipse, as shown in the alternative 2D slice representation (see left side of Figure 3). To cover the range of drum pressure, 15 slice limits have been used. With this slice representation, operators have had difficulty predicting when a slice change is going to occur, and whether the new slice is going to be more restrictive.

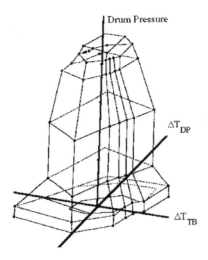

Figure 2: 3D view of steam generator operating envelope.

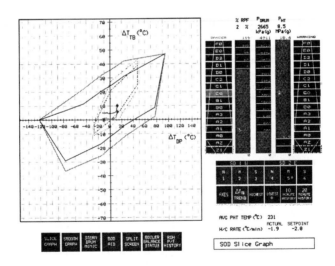

Figure 3: 2D graph of ΔT_{TB} versus ΔT_{DP}.

To aid the operators in understanding when slice changes occur, a profile view of the 3D diagram has been added to the upper right quadrant of the display. The z-axis is actually dependent on three variables over the full range of operation: percent power (% RPF), drum pressure (P_{DRUM}), and heat transport pressure (P_{HT}) (i.e., labels shown in right hand corner of Figure 3). The highlighted white areas on the scales indicate which variable leads to a slice change. Operators can also view any slice at any time to assist them in planning ahead for a slice change by selecting the appropriate profile button. These features help operators to predict when they are going to jump from one slice to another. This 2D graph, combined with the simple profile and the highlighting of variable changes, provides a more comprehensible display than the 3D representation. A smooth version has also been developed in which the limits continuously change. This display better represents the continuous nature of the process and the safe operating region, and therefore better matches the operators' mental model. However, even with this display there were some unavoidable jumps along the z-axis due to system constraints and feedback from operators, comparing the slice version to the smooth version, has been mixed. Further evaluation is needed to resolve this issue.

3.3. Additional Display Solutions

Based on the analysis, displays were also developed to support recovery and diagnosis. To help operators plan a recovery following an incident, a display has been developed, based on a model of the relationship between process constraints (see Figure 4). The sliding controllers on the right are the variables that operators can control. The effects of sliding controller changes on ΔT_{TB}, ΔT_{DP}, and ΔT_{BLR} are shown on the left side and bottom of the display. This display is intended for use in determining whether a particular control action will have a positive or negative effect on those variables. Operators indicated that this display would be very useful in recovering from incidents.

In addition, a schematic display showing the two steam drums has been developed to aid operators in diagnosis. Inside the drum, sliding indicators connected by dashed lines show the status of ΔT_{TB} (see Figure 5). The dashed lines constitute a very simple form of an object display that represents the physical humping and sagging of the drum. To further help operators detect a trouble area quickly, the ΔT_{TB} sliding indicators changed from green to yellow or red, if warning or danger limits were crossed.

A moving 3D steam drum showing hump and sag conditions has also been prototyped (see Figure 1). The humping and sagging of the drum in this display is exaggerated, but it does provide a more representative indication of the actual stress condition than a trend, bar graph, or digital value can provide. However, it has been concluded that it has a negative effect on the overall steam drum schematic format, because it contributes to misorientation of variables and clutter. Therefore, the steam drum shape has been left static and the dotted lines connecting the ΔT_{TB} sliding indicators have been used instead.

4. CONCLUSION

The configuration of steam drums at this power plant has led to a complex process control relationship that has been difficult for operators to understand and manage. Based on a systematic function and task analysis, displays have been developed to serve as real-time operator aids for monitoring related parameters, detecting failures, diagnosis, and recovery during all plant states. The displays have been well received by the operators, who have stated that these function-based displays would support them in minimizing the stress problems.

Furthermore, it has been concluded that 2D graphic displays are more effective than 3D displays for representing the multidimensional relationships. In addition, displays have been developed to allow operators to predict the effects of changes in controllable variables on the key parameters that impact component stress. Future evaluations will operationally test the displays in simulator exercises to validate that human performance is acceptable.

There is little doubt that 3D displays can provide an aesthetically pleasing view of a variety of situations. However, in this application, the disadvantages of using 3D displays outweighed the advantages of using them in place of 2D displays. More research is needed on the interaction between multiple cues and between other variables in complex environments to guide designers in deciding when to use 3D graphics in place of 2D representations.

560

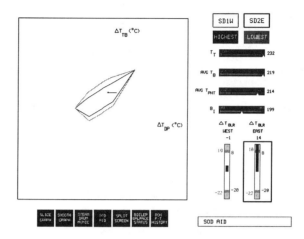

Figure 4: Predictive aid display.

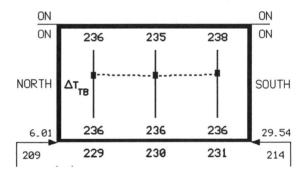

Figure 5: Portion of steam drum schematic display.

5. REFERENCES

1   D. Meister, Behavioral Analysis and Measurement Methods, John Wiley & Sons, New York, 1985.

2   P.T. Bullemer, S.V. Metz, and R.M. Richardson, A User Interface Design Concept for Visualization of Multidimensional Process Models. Proceedings of the Human Factors Society 36th Annual Meeting, (1992) 361.

3   C.D. Wickens, S. Todd, and K. Seidler, Three-Dimensional Displays: Perception, Implementation, Applications (Report No. SOAR-89-01), Crew System Ergonomics Information Analysis Center, Wright Patterson AFB, OH, 1989.

3-d diagrams for knowledge engineering: an early estimation of utility

S. Jones

Department of Computer Science, City University, Northampton Square,
London EC1V 0HB, United Kingdom

Abstract

The utility of 3-d diagrams for knowledge engineering was evaluated in six case studies. Knowledge engineers were asked to collaborate in the design of 3-d diagrammatic representations of knowledge structures. The knowledge engineers then carried out a series of simple tasks using these representations. Performance in these tasks was observed and think aloud protocols were recorded. Structured interviews were also used to elicit the opinions of the knowledge engineers regarding the utility of 3-d diagrammatic representations in their normal working practices. It was judged that 3-d diagrams are likely to be more useful than 2-d in the development of object or frame-based (rather than rule-based) systems. Engineers predicted that 3-d would be more useful than 2-d in design and debugging tasks, but that the advantage in knowledge acquisition, validation, verification and maintenance would not be as great. It was noted that the utility of 3-d diagrams need not be severely limited either by the need for specialised hardware, or by variations in user experience. It is concluded that future tools for knowledge engineering could benefit from the inclusion of a 3-d interface component. Tools supporting the development of conventional systems, in which various kinds of relationship between system objects are used in design and development, might also benefit in the same way.

1. INTRODUCTION

Two-dimensional diagrams are widely used in the human-computer interface. Three-dimensional versions are much less common, though interest has recently been growing and a number of researchers have alluded to the potential benefits of using 3 dimensions. These include: greater freedom of layout and expression [10]; greater visibility of information for a given size of screen or window [8]; and greater flexibility of spatial coding in representations of multi-dimensional information [2].

This paper describes an investigation into the use of 3-d diagrams in the domain of knowledge-based systems: specifically, in knowledge engineering. Knowledge engineering is the process of designing, developing and maintaining knowledge-based systems. Two-dimensional node and link diagrams are widely used in providing graphical representations of systems or knowledge structures for use by knowledge engineers [6]. They are, however, often inadequate for the representation of knowledge structures which are typically large, complicated and inherently multi-dimensional. The aim of the studies described in this paper was to investigate whether benefits of the kind listed above might be enjoyed by knowledge engineers: in other words, to discover whether tools for knowledge engineering using 3-d diagrams would be more useful than those relying solely on 2-d representations.

A number of projects have experimented with the use of 3-d representations of information or knowledge structures. SemNet [2] was a tool which allowed users to browse around three-dimensional arrangements of nodes and links representing various networks of knowledge. The Information Visualiser project experimented with the use of 3-d diagrammatic representations of large hierarchical structures such as Unix directories [8]. Little empirical work aimed at discovering the *utility* or usefulness of such representations has, however, so far been carried out.

The work described here investigated the use of 3-d Interactive Connection Diagrams (ICDs) supported by a prototype tool called ICDEDIT [3]. These diagrams consist of nodes representing important entities in information or knowledge structures, and links representing the 'connections' or relationships between them. Nodes are each assigned three co-ordinates denoting their position in a 3-d space. These co-ordinates are used to create a visual representation of the positions of the nodes in that space. The visual illusion of depth is created using cues such as hiding, perspective and simulated rocking motion. Diagrams created in this way are 'interactive' in the sense that direct manipulation of both individual nodes and whole diagrams is supported. Nodes can be added, deleted or moved to a different position in 3-d space and their visual characteristics (shape, size, colour, textual content etc.) can be adjusted. Whole diagrams can be rotated, translated and scaled giving zooming and panning effects.

The findings of the studies reported here were intended to contribute directly to the specification of requirements for the next version of ICDEDIT, though they are also relevant to developers of other tools incorporating 3-d diagrammatic representations. They support consideration of whether development of tools such as ICDEDIT is justified in terms of their utility or the benefits they yield, and, if so, what activities such tools might most usefully support.

2. THE CASE STUDIES

Methods for evaluating the utility of tools or interface technologies are not well-established in the HCI community, which has tended to focus on usability [5]. The method used in these studies has been described in detail elsewhere [7]. Briefly, it involved collecting information about the use of 3-d diagrams from case studies and using the notion of 'context of use' (see eg [12]) to support structured consideration of that information.

The utility of an interface technology (i.e. a technology supporting a particular form of human-computer interaction) was defined, for the purposes of these studies, as 'the ability, capacity or power of that technology to support the majority of *users* in carrying out the majority of *tasks* using the majority of underlying *software tools* in the majority of *environments* which they are likely to encounter'. (This definition is based on the definition of utility proposed by Jeremy Bentham: see, for example, [9].) The studies involved knowledge engineers developing real knowledge-based systems. Tasks of interest were knowledge engineering tasks, and the environments were those (physical, social and organisational) in which knowledge engineering typically takes place.

	Study 1	Study 2	Study 3	Study 4	Study 5	Study 6
Organisation's KBS Involvement: Nature	Academic Research	Industrial Research	Academic Research	Industrial Development	Industrial R & D	Industrial Research
Length	4 years	5-10 years	7 years	4 years	10 years	7 years
Current	6 people	30 people	10-12 people	3 people	50 people	6 people
Project: Size	1.25 person years	6 person years	20 person years	6 person months	15 person years	1 person year
User's Experience: Length	4 years	2.5 years	2.5 years	3 years	12 years	3 years
Number of Projects	0 - 5	0 - 5	3	2	5	4
Hardware and Software	Mainframes, Prolog	Mainframes, Workstations, PCs, shells, Lisp, Poplog	Macs, Suns, Prolog	PCs	Mainframes, Workstations, tools, shells, Prolog	Workstations, Prolog,
Total Time	3h 57m	5h 10m	7h 56m	2h 54m	2h 57m	2h 50m

Note 1: Total amount of time for which the subject was involved directly in the study.

Note 2: Experienced ICDEDIT user: no training required.

Table 1: Organisations, projects and users involved in the studies

2.1. Procedure

Each study was divided into three stages. In the first stage, knowledge engineers (KEs) were interviewed in their places of work to obtain information about themselves and the organisations in which they worked, to choose knowledge structures (KSs) developed in recent projects which were suitable for 3-d representation, and to discuss possible schemes for graphically representing them. Information collected at this stage is summarised in Table 1. Discussions of schemes for graphical representation of the chosen structures used examples of existing 3-d diagrams, but KEs were encouraged to make their own suggestions for visualising the KSs they had used. On the basis of these discussions, the investigator drafted graphical representations of the chosen KSs.

In the second stage, the investigator visited the KEs again to validate the draft representation. Any suggestions for modifications to the scheme proposed were incorporated into diagrams which were then developed for use in the final stages. One of the 3-d representations developed in this way is shown in Figure 1.

In stage 3, KEs visited the investigator's laboratory to carry out a series of simple tasks using the diagrams developed in stage 2. Tasks had to be simple owing to the prototypical nature of ICDEDIT and the fact that it was not connected to any real knowledge engineering tool or knowledge-based system. Those used were, however, thought to be the 'atomic tasks' [4] of which real knowledge engineering activities would be composed. The performance of the knowledge engineers was observed and think-aloud protocols [1] were recorded. After completing the tasks, semi-structured interviews [4] were used to elicit the opinions of the KEs regarding the potential utility of 3-d diagrams for knowledge engineering in various contexts of use.

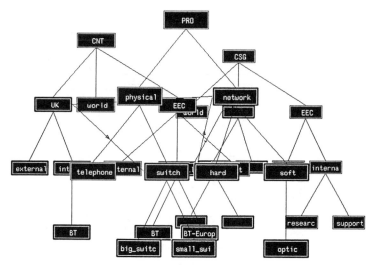

Figure 1: 3-d representation used in study 6. (Original in colour.)

2.2. Results

The information gathered in the studies was considered in categories relating to various aspects of the users, tasks, software systems and environments of interest. Aspects of the users judged to be of potential significance included: their perceptual capabilities; their experience of knowledge engineering; and their experience with other graphical representations. Components of the knowledge engineering task considered were: knowledge acquisition; knowledge validation; design; development; debugging; verification and maintenance. Important aspects of the software system were those relating to the display of the system under development and included: the size of the system; the number of different types of relationship used; and the average number of relationships per entity. Finally, features of the environment included: aspects of the organisational environment; aspects of the physical environment; and aspects of the computing environment (including need for specialised hardware and use of particular kinds of software).

All of the knowledge engineers were able to locate components of their diagrams using only information about their relative depths. This suggests that no unusual perceptual capabilities are needed to use 3-d diagrammatic representations. All of the users who took part in the studies had at least two and a half years' experience of knowledge engineering, so they provide no direct information about the utility of 3-d diagrams for novice engineers. It is, however, worth noting that the engineer with 12 years' experience (considerably more than any of the others) was the only one to have thought previously of knowledge with which he was working in terms of 3-d structures. This suggests that 3-d representations might be exploited to a greater extent by more experienced users. Finally, regarding the effect of experience with other graphical representations in tools for knowledge engineering, it should be noted that the user with the most experience of using 2-d representations initially found it difficult to adapt to 3-d, though this difficulty was all but overcome by the end of a 45 minute session with ICDEDIT.

After some experience of using 3-d ICDs in atomic tasks, knowledge engineers predicted that 3-d ICD interfaces would be more useful than 2-d in designing and debugging knowledge structures for use in knowledge-based systems, though the potential advantage in knowledge acquisition and validation, and system development, verification and maintenance was not judged to be as great. In design, it was suggested that the simultaneous display of several relationships between entities of interest (which is more feasible with 3-d representations than with 2-d) would be useful in creating models of knowledge structures. A variety of specific suggestions regarding the use of 3-d representations in debugging were also made.

Of the knowledge structures for which representations were developed in the studies, two were rule-based and four were object- or frame-based. All of the knowledge engineers who chose to develop representations of object-based structures had at some stage worked on rule-based systems, but preferred not to consider them in these studies. Two of the engineers stated specifically that they thought 3-d representations would be more suitable for use with frame-based systems than rule-based. Of the representations of rule-based structures, one was judged by the knowledge engineer to be successful and the other not. The representations of object-based systems were all judged to be successful to a certain degree, though in one case, the knowledge engineer felt that the amount of information displayed was too much, even for the three-dimensional representation. While the use of three dimensions meant that slightly more of a system could be viewed in one display than is possible with only two, the advantage was felt not to be that great. Similarly, it was judged that the number of relationships per entity which could comfortably be displayed in 3-d was not much greater than was possible with 2-d. Owing to the extra freedom of layout, it was, however, possible to display larger numbers of relationship types in 3-d representations, as at least one relationship could normally be displayed in terms of depth.

Finally, with regard to the environment, it was noted that the utility of 3-d representations would not be limited by the need for special conditions of any kind. Three-dimensional diagrams can be used successfully without special purpose hardware or software (ICDEDIT was written in the C programming language and ran on a Sun 3/60 workstation) or special equipment such as a head monitor or stereoscopic spectacles.

3. CONCLUSIONS

On the basis of the findings reported above, it is concluded that future tools for knowledge engineering are likely to benefit from the inclusion of a 3-d ICD interface component, directed specifically at design and debugging, particularly of object or frame-based systems. It should, however, be noted that the full realisation of the potential utility of 3-d diagrammatic interfaces will require the development of more advanced prototypes incorporating facilities which exploit the unique features of 3-d representations. This may, for example, mean providing not only facilities for manipulating all or part of a diagram in 3-d, but also providing support for setting up and using 3-d spatial coding schemes. Current work at City aimed at developing ICDEDIT and integrating it with prototype knowledge-based system tools will permit the need for such features to be investigated in more detail (see, for example, [11]).

Finally, it is worth noting that multi-dimensional knowledge, information or data structures are found not only in the domain of knowledge-based systems, but also in database or information systems - particularly in connection with object-oriented approaches to development and use. Tools supporting the development of systems of other kinds might therefore also benefit from the inclusion of a 3-d ICD interface component. The potential utility of 3-d ICD interfaces in domains other than that of knowledge-based systems should be in future be investigated, perhaps using further studies of the kind described above.

Acknowledgements

Part of the research described in this paper was funded by a CASE studentship sponsored by the Science and Engineering Research Council and British Telecommunications plc. The author would like to thank Uma Patel, Julie Porteous, Alistair Sutcliffe and Luke Whitaker for comments on an earlier draft of this paper.

4. REFERENCES

1   K. A. Ericsson and H. Simon, Verbal reports as data, Psychological Review, 87(3), 1980

2   K. M. Fairchild, S. E. Poltrock and G. W. Furnas, SemNet: Three-dimensional graphic representations of large knowledge bases. In R. Guindon (ed.), Cognitive Science and its Applications for Human-Computer Interaction, Lawrence Erlbaum Associates, 1988

3   M. Glykas, U. K. Patel, A. G. Sutcliffe, D. C. Dodson and T. Hackett, Towards interactive explanation by 3-d visualisation. In Proceedings of the Workshop on Task Based Explanation, Samos, July 1992

4   M. Good (ed.), Seven experiences with contextual field research, ACM SIGCHI Bulletin, 20(4), 1989

5   J. Grudin, Utility and usability: Research issues and development contexts, Interacting with Computers, 4(2), 1992

6   S. Jones, Graphical interfaces for knowledge engineering: An overview of relevant literature, Knowledge Engineering Review, 3(3), 1988

7   S. Jones, Three-Dimensional Interactive Connection Diagrams for Knowledge Engineering, PhD thesis, Department of Computer Science, City University, (To appear)

8   G. Robertson, J. Mackinlay and S. Card, Cone trees: Animated 3-d visualisations of hierarchical information. In Reaching Through Technology, Proceedings CHI91, ACM, 1991

9   A. Ryan (ed.), Utilitarianism and Other Essays: J. S. Mill and Jeremy Bentham, Penguin, 1987

10 S. Shum, Real and virtual spaces: Mapping from spatial cognition to hypertext, Hypermedia, 2(2), 1990

11 A. G. Sutcliffe and U. K. Patel, The three-dimensional graphical user interface: evaluation for design evolution. In People and Computers IX, Proceedings of the British HCI Group annual conference, Cambridge University Press, 1993 (To appear)

12 D. Wixon, K. Holzblatt and S. Knox, Contextual design: An emergent view of system design. In Proceedings CHI90, ACM, 1990

Romeo: Robot-Mediated Cooperative Work for Handling 3-Dimensinal Physical Objects

Kenji Kawasugi, Takashi Yoshino, Yasushi Nakauchi,and Yuichiro Anzai

Department of Computer Science, Keio University
3-14-1, Hiyoshi, Kohoku-ku, Yokohama 223 Japan
E-mail: {kawasugi,takashi,nakauchi,anzai}@aa.cs.keio.ac.jp

Abstract

This paper describes four important points in collaboration with 3-dimensional(3-D) objects and introduces Romeo system to handle the objects. Romeo system enables a physically dispersed worker to work with partners through a mobile robot. The robot as a medium leads to a new stage that the remote operator 1) can touch the 3-D object, 2) can see a sight from anywhere, and 3) can show the partner his behavior; a behavior of the robot shows what the operator is willing to do. We made a prototype of Romeo and made an experiment with miniature models. The end of this paper summarized to a feature of our system and the results of the experiment.

1. INTRODUCTION

It is difficult for all workers to gather in one place at the same time. Many studies have aimed to support cooperative works under the banner of CSCW.

The existing systems that utilize mutual video circuits[4] can only give us a fixed view. Computer-aided systems can treat electric data like a video signal or an audio signal. But in the case that there are objects in a shared space and objects have an important matter as much as an electric signal, computer systems cannot handle those. One phase of a video's sight may misleads workers to have inconsistencies. A movable camera would be a profitable device to get image data from any place in such environment. Then we present a mobile robot with a movable camera so that the robot can go around in shared working space more efficiently. By using the robot, we made it possible to have physical objects in shared working space.

2. REQUIREMENT FOR TELE-CONFERENCES

Systems of CSCW have been attempted to give us a shared-working environment without constraints of time and space. The problem will be what we can act in the shared working space. Media for collaboration include not only shared editors like a blackboard windows but also any 3-D objects. Groupware system should be open for any surroundings. Considering that a workspace includes 3-D objects as subjects, we classified a conference system as follows: Visibility, Manipulability, Quality, and Mutuality.

Visibility: A camera should provide the view the worker desires. There must be no limit for seeing 3-D objects. But a fixed camera of any video phone systems limits the range of a view. Though a wide-angled camera provides the widespread vision, it loses the important information such as interests of the worker. Wherever the worker is, the worker should be able to see from any viewpoint.

Manipulability: It is sure that a remote worker cannot access to 3-D physical objects directly with the video phone. The system supporting a cooperative work should provide a function for manipulating a physical object.

Quality: Any information of the shared working space should not be missed. False information lets a person to misunderstand the essence of a substance. A quality of a view provide by a system should be as real as possible. The person who is even in a distance should be able to see it clearly.

Mutuality: When two persons are discussing, each person should see the other person's facial expression or behavior, because that will also provide the non verbal or symbolic information.

A conference system is built to emulate a face-to-face environment. Above four aspects are fundamental factors to enclose a real-time tele-conferecing. Considering these requirements, we proposed a new system for collaborative work.

3. ROBOT MEDIATED COLLABORATION

At first, we define a person in remote place as workerA, in near place as workerB. There is a big obstacle for workerA to see, to hear and to touch the object in the work space. So far, apropos of seeing and hearing, many groupware systems aided by computers have been developed with sharing a workspace between each environments.

3.1. Romeo system −remote body−

Existing groupware systems still have many restrictions for seeing and hearing comparing with Face-to-Face collaboration. Video camera fixed on the terminal can only offer the one perspective of the working space.

Therefore we proposed Romeo system for workerA to work in a office. In this paper, we define the working space as the space where certain physical object resides. In Romeo, by using mobile robots, workerA enters the shared working space. Romeo system uses not a 2-dimensional working space but an objective environment through a *remote body*. Cooperation environment is depicted in fig:1.

3.2. Comparison with Previous Works

Many researchers developed groupware systems[3] [2] and another systems like Virtual Reality and Tele-existence which are related with tele-conference system. That is reason

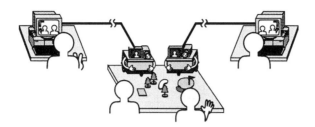

Figure 1: A structure of Romeo system.

why Virtual Reality also is able to support 3-D surrounding in computer. Some people are able to handle a subject between at the same time using a server-clients model [5] [7]. Tele-existence provides the access to objects in distance. Each system has strong points, these details are described next.

	Visibility	Manipulability	Quality	Mutuality
Tele-conference	×	×	○	○
Virtual Reality	○	△	×	○
Tele-existence	○	○	○	×
Romeo	○	○	○	○

Table 1: Classification of collaboration systems.

Tele-Conference: forces workerA to see one widespread image to grasp what happen in the working space. But workerB does not have any information such as what workerA sees or what his interests are. It is difficult for workerA to comprehend the image of 3-D objects nor touching the 3-D object. Tele-Conference only gives an electric information to users and provides neither *Visibility* nor *Manipulability*.

Virtual Reality: makes own world in computers with modeling a real world which includes human being as well as a shared space. But everything in the world cannot be introduced in a computer world as everything cannot be turn into codes. The descriptions in the Virtual Reality are abstract and already known. Though an unexpected event brings a good idea, it is hard to come out a good thought in such artificial environment. Virtual Reality systems is not suitable for a *Quality*.

Tele-Existence: is able to make the surrounding for cooperations, and it has lots of analogies of Romeo system such as workerA can handle the remote object. But it is short of *Mutuality*, that is why workerB has no method to know the action and the behavior of workerA.

Romeo: has two advantages to use a robot. One is that workerA can enter in the working space. Then workerA can see and hear from anywhere and touch objects. The other is that workerB sees the behavior of workerA's action.

Figure 2: Einstein implimented Romeo system.

4. EXPERIMENT

4.1. Realization of a remote body

Romeo provides a display to see the working space and a control panel for workerA to manage the remote body as interface, and the *remote body* is a robot equipped off-the-shelf display, microphone, speaker, and camera. The robot in use is Einstein which we developed in our laboratory last year. Einstein is 4 wheeled mobile robot. A picture of workerA was showed in the display on Einstein as if workerA sees the object taken by a video camera. Then both workerA and workerB can see and can communicate mutually. The robot interface was built up like a human being and exposes a facial expression and a behavior of workerA.

The remote body consists of a arm as a substitute for hands, a video camera for sight and audio for ears. A robot hand plays part in not only grasping the object but showing the worker's optic angle as a pointer. Because in any time people grasp something, both eyes and hands show a target object. So a robot's sight is made to synchronize the movement of robot-hands as if human's eyes follow the target to grasp. It is sure that a camera and display move simultaneously. These actions would help workerB to guess workerB's behavior. The robot is made to reflect behavior of workerA.

4.2. Experimental Setting

For the experimental task of Romeo system, we have chosen a design of golf course with a miniature set. This experiment was done with two persons. One person(workerC) was in front of miniature models, the other(workerD) sat by the display that shows aspects of models. They were visually separated, but they could talk freely over partitions. All log were recorded on video tapes. The figures in below shows the environment in use.

4.3. Observation

As the sight was to be movable, workerD could see anywhere. WorkerD moved the camera on robot as the topic was changes. The camera, however, did not always follow the subject of conversation, but it was also focussed with the feeling of workerD. A sight as well as a verbal communication were effective elements of communication.

A restricted sight

In this paper, a word *this* was frequently used by workerC in a conversation. After speaking the word, workerC checked the position of the camera and the face of workerD. By a limited sight by a camera, workerC could tell workerD's vision cover.

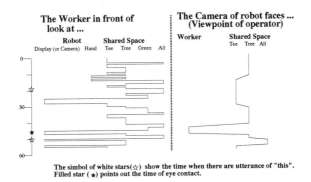

The simbol of white stars(☆) show the time when there are utterance of "this".
Filled star (★) points out the time of eye contact.

Figure 3: The change of person's eyes and camera's direction: Vertical axis means a flow of one minute in the experiment.

A camera movability

The camera could rove around the field of miniature sets by a remote control. But fig:3 shows that the camera is slow in action obviously in contradiction to human's head. The head of workerC moves over a shared workspace, moreover, the eyes move quickly and incessantly. The eyesight of workerC has no limitation except a range of naked eye. In order for workerD to see, extra camera's operation would cause a disadvantage in following the subject of conversation. A recorded dialog make it clear that workerC has an initiative and an ample store of topics about the target object. Sometime it is almost impossible for workerD to move the camera to keep up with the topic.

4.4. Discussion

In this paper, we do not mentioned about sounds. Sounds is efficient to specify who is speaking as mentioned in [6] [1], because a human can recognize more than one sound resources by listening. Romeo has a capacity to expand sound effect system. The operator can hear sounds as the robot does and then enable to tell from a speaker among the other cooperators.

The operator move the robot to any position in order to get a desired perspective, sometime try to modify the sets. Since the robot act dull, the partner may feel little weary. But the action of the robot is the same as that of human. It is a problem that the robot has poor operations. Besides, the operator talks with the partner equivalently. Romeo is the collaborative system aimed to treat 3-D objects.

5. CONCLUSION

We proposed a new robot-mediated architecture of groupware system. With 3-D objects in a working space, it is important that workerA can see anywhere workerA is interested in and can modify the subject. The robot is an efficient device as movable camera, remote hand, and facial expression.

A mixture of a movable camera and a restricted view leads to use a demonstractive pronoun *this*, and also makes workerB believe that the gaze of workerA is the same as workerB's. A mention of a demonstrative pronoun needs a feedback function so that both contexts of persons will be agreed. Romeo system has designed to have mutuality for feedback.

Romeo system has a potential to expand the number of cooperators not only two persons and also to increase the number of robots. A pair of working space and remote body can extend any cooperation, because we only propose the policy of a *remote body* and any number can always enter the working space by means of it.

6. REFERENCES

1 Marilyn M. Mantei Ronald M. Baecker Abigail J. Sellen Bill A.S. Buxton and Thomas Milligan. Experiences in the use of a media space. In *ACM Conference on Human Factors in Computing Systems*, pages 203–208, New Orleans, 1991. ACM.

2 Hiroshi Ishii Minoru Kobayashi. Clearboard: A seamless medium for shared drawing and conversation with eye contact. In *ACM Conference on Human Factors in Computing Systems*, pages 525–532, Monterey, 1992. ACM.

3 Hideaki Kuzuoka. Spatial workspace collaboration: A sharedview video support system for remote collaboration capability. In *ACM Conference on Human Factors in Computing Systems*, pages 533–540, Monterey, 1992. ACM.

4 John C. Tang Scott L. Minneman. Videodraw: A video interface for collaborative drawing. In *ACM Transactions on Information Systems*, volume 9, pages 170–184, Apr 1991.

5 Li Shu. Groupware experiences in three-dimensional computer-aided design. In *in Procedings of the Conference on CSCW*, pages 179–186, Nov 1992.

6 William W. Gaver Randall B. Smith and Tim O'Shea. Efective sounds in complex systems: The arkola simulation. In *ACM Conference on Human Factors in Computing Systems*, pages 85–90, New Orleans, 1991. ACM.

7 Haruo Takemura and Fumio Kisino. Cooperative work environment using virtual workspace. In *in Procedings of the Conference on CSCW*, pages 226–232, Nov 1992.

Eye-Gaze and Intent: Application in 3D Interface Control

J. C. Schryver[a] and J. H. Goldberg[b]

[a]Intelligent Systems Section, Oak Ridge National Laboratory, P.O. Box 2008, Oak Ridge, TN, ryv@ornl.gov

[b]Department of Industrial and Management Systems Engineering, The Pennsylvania State University, University Park, PA, jhgie@engr.psu.edu

Abstract

Computer interface control is typically accomplished with an input "device" such as keyboard, mouse, trackball, etc. An input device translates a user's input actions, such as mouse clicks and key presses, into appropriate computer commands. To control the interface, the user must first convert intent into the syntax of the input device. A more natural means of computer control is possible when the computer can directly infer user intent, without need of intervening input devices. We describe an application of eye-gaze-contingent control of an interactive three-dimensional (3D) user interface. A salient feature of the user interface is natural input, with a heightened impression of controlling the computer directly by the mind. With this interface, input of rotation and translation are intuitive, whereas other abstract features, such as zoom, are more problematic to match with user intent. This paper describes successes with implementation to date, and ongoing efforts to develop a more sophisticated intent inferencing methodology.

1. INTRODUCTION

In the few published reports of eye-gaze-contingent control of the computer interface, the combination of real-time point-of-regard and time criteria have been used to capture areas of interest within a display. Reported applications have included word processing (Frey, White, and Hutchinson, 1990), selecting items within menus (Hutchinson, White, Martin, Reichert, and Frey, 1989), controlling stories within fictional scenes (Starker and Bolt, 1990), and selection from a group of objects (Jacob, 1991; 1990). These applications have all routinely used a limited object selection algorithm based primarily on cumulated fixation time at a location on a display. Long fixation times (e.g., more than 2 seconds) are required where false object selection is to be minimized, and short required fixation times (e.g., less than 1 second) require immediate correction and recovery from false selections. Starker and Bolt (1990) introduced an exponential decay rate when generating object interest, but this was really a variant on the cumulative time criteria. The cumulated time approach to object selection is both limiting and cumbersome in real-time usage; either object selection is unnaturally slow, or a high false alarm rate produces many attempts before successful object selection.

All the applications cited above utilized two-dimensional interfaces. We have developed a prototype of an interactive three-dimensional (3D) interface that is controlled by real-time eye-gaze input. The application is an X Windows 3D object viewer (X3D) that runs on a Unix workstation. In the conventional mode, the user can rotate, translate, and zoom a three-dimensional object in continuous fashion with mouse and keyboard input. We have modified the 3D object viewer so that it accepts eye-gaze input to control translation and rotation in real time. The eye-gaze control engine is sensitive to both the spatial coordinates of eye-gaze position on the screen and to the dynamics of eye-gaze motion.

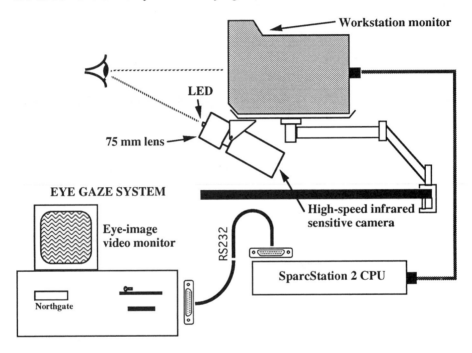

Figure 1 Eye Gaze Development System.

2. EYE-GAZE HARDWARE AND SOFTWARE

The eye-gaze system is an unobtrusive device that computes a user's spatial point-of-regard on a display. The system, shown in Figure 1, is manufactured by LC Technologies using a pupil illumination/corneal reflection method to compute point-of-regard to a calibrated display, at a rate of 30 Hz. The main components of the eye-gaze system are: (1) 80386-based microcomputer with math co-processor; (2) video frame grabber board; (3) high-speed infrared sensitive camera and 75 mm lens containing an LED infrared source; and (4) eye-image video monitor. Proprietary software performs image processing of the eye-image using pattern recognition algorithms to recognize pupil center and corneal reflection. Geometric calculations recover the eye-gaze point of regard with respect to a calibrated

UNIX Workstation

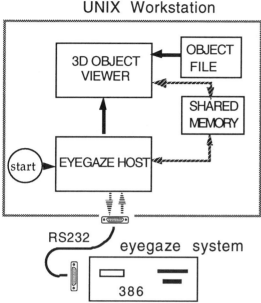

RS232

eyegaze system

386

Figure 2 Eye Gaze Host and Application.

display. The maximum average bias error over the monitor range is 0.25 inch. Tolerance to head motion is slight; therefore, a chin rest is required to eliminate significant head motion.

The graphical user-interface (GUI) application runs in an X Windows environment on a Sun workstation, and is controlled by the microcomputer-based eye-gaze system via the serial port. Eye movements are captured with the CCTV camera, which is mounted just beneath the workstation monitor. An eye-gaze data stream is delivered over the serial port to the workstation application, which uses the eye position data for interface control.

3. NATURAL ADAPTIVE CONTROL: ROTATION AND TRANSLATION

Gaze-contingent rotation and translation were obvious initial candidates for natural control, because it was possible to utilize simple control algorithms. A user inspecting a 3D object, and needing to examine a feature not currently visible in the frontal plane, would probably wish to rotate the object until the feature is in view. In this case, the natural tendency is to move the eye-gaze toward the object edge at the position where the rotated feature would appear. Eye-gaze displacement to the right is associated with the intent to rotate clockwise about the Y axis, and a shift to the left signals intent to rotate counterclockwise about the Y axis. Similar rules exist for up and down gaze shifts. These natural control rules have been implemented in the prototype gaze control system.

For the task of object inspection, screen translation may be needed to keep the object foveated. If the gaze drifts past the outer object boundary, then returns to the object, the user would not expect object rotation to accompany the shift back to the object. Translation can be used to prevent the object from shifting to the periphery of the visual field (unless the user moves the gaze off the display). Translation can also serve other purposes. If the object or scene extends beyond screen boundaries, translation can expose new regions of the object at the screen edges. In this case, the desired action is translation opposite to, as opposed to following gaze direction.

Each computer task has a unique set of performance requirements which determine optimum gain control settings for eye-gaze input. The user interface for the eye-gaze-contingent 3D object viewer contains a row of control buttons below the title bar for user-customization of gaze control. The buttons are used to adjust rotation gains (about X and Y axes), translation gains (horizontal and vertical), thresholds for small and large eye movements, and the extent of eye position averaging. Eye-gaze data is averaged to permit smooth control, at the expense of slowing the interface.

There are several human factors issues associated with this type of gaze-contingent control. For example, optimum rotation and translation gains may be task-sensitive. Second, the intent inference engine should recognize when the user wants to conduct a stable inspection of a local region of the image without rotation or translation. Jacob (1990) has called this the Midas Touch problem.

The original computer task analysis assumed that the user inspects an opaque 3D object at the frontal plane for features (both visible and hidden). Transparent object manipulation may be associated with a different set of task demands. Without hidden surface removal, the need to rotate a feature into view may not exist. Inspection of features showing through from the back face may dictate a strategy reversal where rotation pulls transparent features closer to the focus of attention, while frontal features concurrently move away from the direction of eye movements. A similar situation exists for inspection from within an object. For example, suppose the user is navigating the interior of a structure like a building. When a user looks to the right, the expectation is to see the room rotate to the left (counterclockwise) as if the head were turning right. This is the opposite of the expectation that prevails if the user is examining the building from the outside. Exterior inspection requires clockwise rotation to accompany a look to the right.

4. INFERENCE OF ZOOM INTENT

An important operation for telerobotics and other applications is zoom. Unlike rotation and translation, the mapping of intent to input syntax for gaze-contingent zoom is not intuitive. Also unlike simpler rotation and translation algorithms derived from simple analyses of the computer task, a more complex methodology is required to meditate zoom intent. This methodology presupposes that significant intent information is available within patterns of eye movements that is not present in univariate cumulative time at location selection algorithms. Eye-gaze position clusters provide a non-subjective, real-time method for defining areas of interest on a computer interface. Objects within an area of interest may be selected, and further characterization of clusters can provide additional intent information for operations such as zooming, based upon subtle changes in clusters. Selection of objects or operations can be natural and rapid, compared with the traditional minimum criterion time approach currently used.

4.1 Methodology for Detection of Gaze-Contingent Zoom

Procedures for gaze-contingent zoom detection start by collecting a sample of spatial locations while viewing a display. A minimum spanning tree [MST] is formed among the samples, using one of several efficient algorithms (e.g., Camerini, Galbiati, and Maffioli, 1988). The MST is explored for inconsistent or longer edges, followed by separation in clusters (see Zahn, 1971). The clustering procedure is locally adaptive, based upon local ratios of edges to edge length means. Boundaries of each independent cluster are defined from spatial mean, surrounded by a circle of radius equal to the mean sample distance from the spatial mean. Other cluster characteristics include mean and SD pupil diameter, mean and

SD edge lengths, and cluster sample size. Following cluster creation and characterization, each is mapped to a cluster in the previous cluster set, based upon a minimum distance algorithm. This mapping allows a characterization of changes in cluster shape and position over time. For example, clusters that decrease in size and variance, with little translation may signal desire to zoom in. Clusters that get larger and consolidate may indicate the desire to zoom out.

Multiple linear discriminant analysis currently provides an objective basis for inferring zoom-in, zoom-out, or no-zoom conditions. The discriminant functions are computed from combinations of the input variables introduced above. As this is currently an experimental, off-line procedure, the correct zoom condition is known by the system. The system provides percentage of observations correctly classified, and an associated chi-square-distributed statistic. Given convergence of the training set of experimental zoom conditions within, and possibly between, individual users, the zoom intent discrimination procedure may be implemented in the prototype interface.

4.2 Experimental Procedure

Data for the zoom intent discrimination methodology is currently collected in a controlled experiment. On each of many trials, the user determines whether a comparison stimulus is the same or different from a test stimulus. The two need only have the same elements, regardless of size, to be judged the same. An experimental trial is initiated by displaying a test stimulus, which is memorized. A comparison stimulus is next displayed, which must be compared to the memorized test stimulus. Collection of eye-gaze is also initiated at this time. If the comparison stimulus is too small, the interface is zoomed-in by pressing the left mouse button. Likewise, if portions of it are off-screen, pressing the right mouse button produces a zoom-out for a broader view. A "s" or "d" (same or different) keypress stops the trial and eye-gaze data collection. One-third of trials require zooming in, one-third require zooming-out, and one-third require neither control condition for comparison. This experimental procedure makes zooming in or out the subject's volition, and as such, it records the natural eye tendencies prior to zooming.

5. DISCUSSION

Eye-gaze camera control can be an important feature of high-workload multi-DOF teleoperation tasks performed by operators of computer interfaces. The features described here provide an early picture of how rotation, translation, and zoom control of a camera can be implemented solely from eye-gaze. Off-loading the camera functions from hand to eye provides a more natural and compatible means of viewpoint control, especially under high stress or workload conditions.

The intent discrimination methodology described here proposes a new, deeper level of computer interface control from eye-gaze, to enhance real-time control of many types of devices. Successful control applications require intent discrimination, based upon empirically-derived data. While still in an early experimental stage, the clustering and statistical methods provide a wide variety of eye-gaze-dependent data for the intent discrimination procedures.

The same technology can also have significant application in other domains, such as disability and process control applications. In the former, control of wheelchair direction and function could be inferred solely from eye-gaze. In the latter, workstation interfaces in control rooms could be rapidly zoomed-in and out to control the level of detail shown in complex displays.

ACKNOWLEDGEMENTS

We would like to thank Frank Sweeney and Reinhold Mann for their support. The research described was supported by the U. S. Department of Energy Office of Technology Programs. This manuscript has been authored by a contractor of the U. S. Government under contract DE-AC05-84OR21400. Accordingly, the U. S. Government retains a nonexclusive, royalty-free license to publish or reproduce the published form of this contribution, or allow others to do so, for U. S. Government purposes.

6. REFERENCES

Camerini, P. M. Galbiati, G., and Maffioli, F. (1988). Algorithms for finding optimum trees: Description, use and evaluation. *Annals of Operations Research* , 13, 265-397.

Frey, L. A., White, K. P., and Hutchinson, T. E. (1990). Eye-gaze word processing. *IEEE Transactions on Systems, Man, and Cybernetics* , 20(4), 944-950.

Hutchinson, T. E., White, K. P., Martin, W. N., Reichert, K. C., and Frey, L. A. (1989). Human-computer interaction using eye-gaze input, *IEEE Transactions on Systems, Man, and Cybernetics*, **19**(6), pp. 1527-1534.

Jacob, R. J. K. (1990) What you look at is what you get: Eye movement-based interaction techniques, pp. 11-18 in *CHI '90 Proceedings: Empowering People*, Seattle, WA: Association for Computing Machinery.

Jacob, R. J. K. (1991). The use of eye movements in human-computer interaction techniques: What you look at is what you get. *ACM Transactions on Information Systems* , 9(3), 152-169.

Starker, I., and Bolt, R. A. (1990). A gaze-responsive self-disclosing display, pp. 3-9 in *CHI '90 Proceedings: Empowering People* , Seattle, WA: Association for Computing Machinery.

Zahn, C. T. (1971). Graph-theoretical methods for detecting and describing gestalt clusters. *IEEE Transactions on Computers* , C-20(1), 68-86.

A USER INTERFACE TO A TRUE 3-D DISPLAY DEVICE

Bruce A. Hobbs and Martin R. Stytz
Department of Electrical and Computer Engineering
Air Force Institute of Technology
Wright Patterson AFB, OH 45433-6583
Contact: mstytz@louvre.afit.af.mil

ABSTRACT

This paper describes the development of an interactive interface to a true three dimensional, real-time dynamic graphic display, the Texas Instruments Omniview™. Our interface provides the user with a quick and flexible means of manipulating the image generated, the sub-volume displayed, and the resulting true 3-D image. It allows selection of objects and manipulation of scenes. It does not support manipulation, such as rotation or placement, of individual objects.

1. INTRODUCTION

The extension of computer graphics into three dimensions is driven by the capability of the human visual system to perceive and comprehend the world in three dimensions. Generating a two-dimensional image from a three-dimensional data set reduces the information content and produces an inherent ambiguity [1]. A three-dimensional display is needed to represent the full complexity of the 3-D world.

This paper describes the Texas Instruments Omniview true 3-D display and support system and compares it to other 3-D display techniques. The Omniview display provides a unique way of viewing the 3-D world. Several viewers are able to simultaneously see the image from their own perspective. This group viewing aids in the understanding and discussion of the image. We describe our interface concept for controlling and manipulating the 3-D image, our experience with this system and planned enhancements to the interface.

2. TEXAS INSTRUMENTS' OMNIVIEW HARDWARE

One of the newest true three-dimensional display devices is the Texas Instruments Omniview. It differs markedly from the stereo pair, holographic stereogram, and varifocal mirror 3D display techniques ([2], [3]). The Omniview design and operating characteristics are described in detail in [4]. We briefly describe the machine here. The Omniview produces a true 3-D image. The image provides depth cues by using head motion parallax, accommodation (change in focal length of the eye's lens as it focuses on a specific region of a 3-D scene), binocular disparity, and convergence (the rotation of the eyes inward to converge on objects as the objects move closer to the observer). The display principle is similar to that of the varifocal mirror, but the Omniview is viewable from all directions by a large number of observers. The display is computed in real-time and in color, unlike the holographic stereogram. No special viewing glasses are needed, unlike in the stereo pair display techniques. Points illuminate a 2-D surface in a cylindrical volume such that the viewer fuses the images into a 3-D image. However, rather than using a vibrating mirror, the Omniview is a cylindrical volumetric laser display that uses a rotating double-helix translucent disk to fill the display cylinder. The helical display disk rotates at 600rpm, thereby defining a cylindrical volume. The rapidly rotating surface (disk) within the cylindrical display volume provides the surface on which the images are drawn.

The current system provides a large view volume but is limited in the number of points that can be lit at one time. The view volume is 36 inches in diameter and 18 inches tall. A maximum of 12,000 2.5mm voxels (4,000 each for red, green, and blue) of the 67 million addressable voxels can be displayed during one rotation. Voxels to be colored are lit by lasers.

The lasers are directed to the voxels to be illuminated by acousto-optic scanners. The number of displayable voxels is limited by the response time of the acousto-optic scanners. Color images are a major benefit with the Omniview. However, attempting to combine the three colors into additional colors is not possible because of the characteristics of the display.

The current Omniview's disadvantages include flicker, limited number of concurrently displayable points, aliasing, and frame rate. Fine lines and small details are not possible to produce as each voxel is 2.5mm in diameter. Hardware limitations prevent the device from achieving the theoretical maximum of 12,000 voxels lit at a time. Another disadvantage is that the voxels are transparent. Transparency can cause confusion when viewing images with high information content ([2]). The Omniview does not provide the depth cue of interposition (or occlusion) that results when the nearer of two objects obscures the more distant object. Hidden line removal has no meaning because all images are transparent and the image can be viewed from all sides. This characteristic can make it difficult for the viewer to understand depth relationships

The graphics processing, user interface, and VME support are provided by a Sun 4/470. Because of the limited computational power available, modern UIMS techniques were not used to implement the interface. Instead, we relied upon simple method calls for message passing between input objects and rendering objects. This design choice served to save computational time at the expense of being able to easily modify the interface itself.

3. INPUT DEVICES FOR CONTROLLING 3-D IMAGES

Several devices are available for controlling an image in a 2-D or 3-D environment ([5]). The suitability of the input device is dependent on the performance required by the user and the application interface type ([6]). Input devices can be categorized by the degrees of freedom they provide the user. Discrete inputs include buttons, switches, and recognized voice commands ([7]). The range of values is yes or no, on or off. Controlling a scene through voice commands has several advantages over other input devices. Voice recognized commands do not require the use of hands, so they can be used for other manipulation tasks. Voice commands are unobtrusive in the environment and the user does not have to remember the location of the input device. Major disadvantages of voice controls are difficulty of setup and lack of reliability in recognizing the commands given.

One degree of freedom devices include sliders, dials, wheels, dial boxes and rotary pots ([5], [6], [8], [9]). Separate control can be provided for translation and rotation about each axis. The benefits of dial boxes include precise and direct control for movement in each direction separately. The disadvantages include unnatural interaction and in many cases the need to use two hands to perform the desired tasks.

Two degrees of freedom devices allow positioning or moving in two dimensions while moving one device or input mechanism. Two degrees of freedom can be provided with a mouse, trackball, or joystick input device ([5], [6], [8], [9]). These 2-D devices often require elaborate software solutions to make them perform in 3-D worlds. The main advantages of the mouse are user familiarity with its operation and ease of 2-D translations. Disadvantages include unnatural interaction. For example, complex tasks must be broken down into simpler operations, for example rotation about an arbitrary axis. Trackball operation is similar to a mouse and can be thought of as an upside down mouse. One benefit over the mouse is that the trackball does not require an area to move the device over. A disadvantage over the mouse is the difficulty some users find in precisely controlling positioning. The joystick is commonly used to change position based on the stick position. Stick offset from vertical indicates both the velocity and direction of movement. Releasing the joystick to the center position stops the movement at its current position.

Three degrees of freedom can be provided by a 3-D joystick ([5]). The 3-D joystick functions the same as a 2-D joystick with the addition of a third degree of movement. This movement is provided by moving the joystick about the z-axis, by either pushing or pulling the stick. Positioning movement about the x-, y-, and z-axes is then provided.

Six degrees of freedom can be provided with a Spaceball, DataGlove and poolball. Six degrees of freedom devices are multidimensional and provide users with intuitive three-dimensional interaction capabilities. The spaceball provides six degrees of freedom using a force/torque controller. It provides three force components and three torque components ([6], [7]). Mapping force and torque to velocity is an intuitive and precise operation for many users. This mapping allows for simultaneous translation and rotation of objects. A button on the spaceball can be used to select and deselect an object [6].

Six degrees of freedom are provided with the DataGlove by using an electromagnetic tracking device such as the 3Space Isotrack from Polhemus ([6], [7]). The DataGlove tracking is then used with gesture recognition software to manipulate the synthetic environment. The glove gives information about the angle of all of the joints in the user's hand. The gesture recognition software then maps this information into a gesture vocabulary. This input device offers the potential for intuitive interaction by tracking the glove to extract rotation and translation commands for the synthetic environment ([6]). The main disadvantage of the glove is difficulty in gesture recognition and the limited gesture vocabulary.

The poolball is a hollowed-out billiard ball with a Polhemus sensor on the inside and two buttons on the outside. The poolball was found to be easier to use and more precise than the DataGlove. Advantages of the poolball include that it does not require calibration for each user, its position can be accurately specified at all times, and actions initiated with the buttons are easy to control precisely.

4. INTERFACE CONCEPT

Our goal for this interface was to provide the ability to interactively control and manipulate the true 3-D image in the Omniview. The observed environment is dynamic with a large number of objects that can enter or leave the world at any time. Multiple simultaneous events can take place at any time. One example of this type of complex, rapidly changing environment is an airport where aircraft are taking off and landing. Other aircraft traverse the area at higher altitudes and ground vehicles move to support aircraft and transport cargo and people. The user of this system needs to have control of the content of the image without requiring an understanding of the underlying computer data structures and algorithms. We assume the user is knowledgeable in the field of the image being depicted, such as airport traffic.

Previous interfaces to true 3D devices, such as the varifocal mirror and holographic display, can be characterized as being command line driven. We developed an interactive interface to a true 3-D device that provides the user with the flexibility and convenience that a window, icon, mouse, and pointer (WIMP) GUI interface provides to users of 2-D displays. As a step toward attaining this goal, we developed an interface to the device that permits direct user interaction with the display. To accommodate the display limitations of the device we use

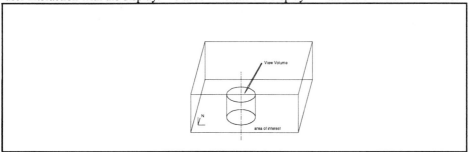

Figure 1: Omniview View Volume Inset Within the Volume of Interest.

a combination of voice commands, joystick, and a 2-D menu system running on a host computer to provide the interface.

The Omniview display can be thought of as a cylindrical portion of the entire 3-D world of interest (see Figure 1). In the airport example, the display can be as large as the town theairport is located in or as small as a single runway. The area covered can range from one kilometer square to an area 300 kilometers on a side. Our interface allows the user to alter the amount of information presented and the portion of the volume displayed. Too much information in the display can hide important information. Therefore, the user must be allowed to select which information is important and should be displayed. The image is then generated with consideration paid to the resolution available and the limited voxel budget.

We required several types of controls over the image and its contents. These controls provide the user with the maximum control over the location of the displayed volume and the items displayed in the volume. These controls include:

1.   Selecting specific objects to view. The objects are organized in the database according to the operating environment. The user can request a listing of all vehicles or only vehicles from one environment (i.e., air) and select a specific object from the list. The object can be removed from the image or added back into the image.

2.   Selecting classes of objects to view. The user can select a class of objects (e.g., air vehicles or commercial aircraft). The selected class of objects can be removed from the view, added to the view, or isolated in the Omniview.

3.   Selecting a specific object to track. A single object selected to be tracked results in the object remaining at a fixed location in the display volume with all other objects and the area displayed moving relative to the fixed, tracked object.

4.   Setting the image update rate. The user can specify the length of time each image is displayed on the Omniview. This control is used to force the system to provide sufficient time for the user to manipulate the interface.

5.   Altering the resolution/complexity of icons used. The image is drawn with objects depicted with variable icon complexity, more complex icons are automatically used as the displayed volume shrinks. The user can optionally override the automatic resolution settings for the icons.

To provide the desired capabilities, we implemented two different classes of interfaces to the Omniview. The paradigm for the interface is a dual-display work station. The direct manipulation interface allows the user to be in front of the Omniview display and control the display. The direct interface does not provide as rich an interface as the indirect interface. The indirect interface is implemented using the Sun. This interface provides a finer degree of control of the display than the direct interface but the user is placed at a distance (3-4 ft) from the display.

By using the Sun's monitor, keyboard, and mouse; a GUI was constructed to indirectly manipulate the scene. Pull-down menus and point and click dialogues allowed selection of classes of objects or individual objects. The ability to position the view volume in the area of interest was provided as a basic user control. A tracking window allowed rapid large scale movements to the desired display area. The tracking window enables the user to control the space depicted in the view volume and to enlarge or reduce the space shown.

The movement of the view volume was provided using a mouse tracking window (Figure 2). This window provides the user an input area and feedback map of the area being viewed. The map is a 2-D representation of the area of interest, similar to a topographic map. A circle on the map depicts the location of the center of the Omniview display and the area being viewed. Dragging the circle in the window changes the area being displayed on the Omniview.

The indirect manipulation capabilities provide the algorithms and data structures to allow direct input devices to control the image. The user can vary the size and location of the display cylinder to change the portion of the world being viewed. A pointing device can be used to select individual items of interest in the display. One limitation to the interface is that textual information can not be usefully displayed in the volume. This is due to two factors. First, since the display is viewable from 360 degrees, a single location for the text is not appropriate for all viewers, only some viewers would see the text correctly. The other difficulty with text is the limited Omniview resolution and small voxel budget. A simple alpha-numeric character set can easily require 30 voxels per character. With only a best case of 4,000 voxels of any one color, 100 characters is close to the voxel budget. We therefore chose to eliminate text from the Omniview portion of the interface. Instead, the Omniview supports direct manipulation of the volume and individually displayed items.

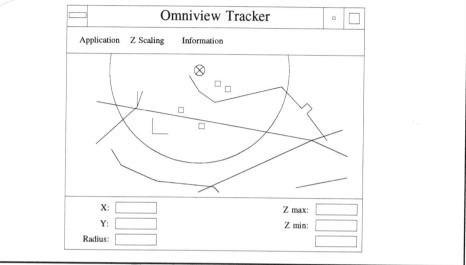

Figure 2: Omniview Tracker Window.

A joystick provides control over the location and size of the viewing cylinder. The location of the view volume is changed by moving the stick. The size of the display volume is changed by using one button on the joystick base for enlarging the area being viewed and the other button for reducing the size of the area. The joystick input is acknowledged with an arrow in the volume indicating the direction of movement or the direction of scaling the display volume. The change in location and size of the volume being displayed is also shown on the Sun's tracking map. While the joystick is capable of providing several control capabilities, other controls were still needed.

Voice control provides an additional means for direct control of the Omniview. Voice control allows the user to walk around the display, viewing it from all sides while maintaining control over the image. Voice commands are used to provide the same basic inputs as are available with the menu system. However, the selection of individual items or object classes is not provided using voice control.

5. EXPERIENCE AND FUTURE WORK.

The voxel size, budget, and scheduler caused problems. As the number of voxels to be illuminated grew, the scheduler had difficulty generating the desired image. For example, flat grids started having peaks, valleys, ridges, and dropouts. A line of voxels that should have been in a straight line could look very ragged and disjointed, depending on the number of voxels requested. This problem will be addressed in future versions of the Omniview.

The Sun 4/470 lacks the CPU power to perform the desired functions and compute displays at an interactive rate. Even trying to generate images of only 7,000 voxels, at 10 frames/sec and support a responsive user interface proved difficult. Slowing the display to 1-2 frames/sec allowed satisfactory response to user input, but update lag was very disconcerting. However, as the size of the area being viewed increased the slower frame rate is less noticeable because the amount of object movement per frame is small.

The Sun's GUI for indirect manipulation worked well. It provided complete control of the generated image. Individual objects and classes of objects could be easily removed from the scene. The selection of objects and classes of objects was provided by pull-down menus and point and click item selection boxes. This greatly aided the viewers in identifying and locating specific items of interest. Rapid, large scale movement across the environment could also be made. The window interface was also invaluable in testing and supporting development of the direct manipulation interface.

The direct manipulation methods provided a useful alternative to the indirect manipulation interface. The joystick proved useful in controlling the location and size of the area being displayed. Positioning with the stick was intuitive with sufficient precision for the resolution of the display. Voice control was useful for providing untethered, limited control of the items in the display from any location. Viewing the image as it changed aided in quickly identifying differences in the images. A drawback to voice control is the training required by the system for each user. However, some users were able to achieve acceptable command acceptance without training the voice recognition system.

Users of this system ranged from one time users to long-term repeat users. Most users found the indirect interface easy to use and understand. It did not suffer from the limited resolution of the Omniview. Selecting an object was most easily performed with the joystick. The user needed to know nothing about the object being selected with the joystick, but given the low resolution of the Omniview, distinguishing between two similar objects was difficult. In this situation the information on the objects available on the Sun monitor was invaluable.

Several extensions to the direct image manipulation methods can be made. The joystick control should be expanded to include position and orientation tracking of the joystick. This would enable the user to walk around the display and not be concerned with the orientation of the stick. A 3-D joystick or spaceball could easily be added. The 3-D joystick would allow the user to change the location of the viewing cylinder in all three directions and change the size of the volume separately in radius and in height. The spaceball would give similar capabilities.

The addition of a pointing and selecting device for the direct interface is needed. This would allow the user to point at an object to have a specific action take place, such as removing an object from the view, identifying the object, or changing the object's attributes. Object selection could be provided with a selection volume directed by the joystick or spaceball. This capability requires a faster image update rate because lag time would make it difficult for the viewer to successfully select the item of interest.

6. REFERENCES

[1] Wickens, Christopher D. "Three-Dimensional Stereoscopic Display Implementation: Guidelines Derived from Human Visual Capabilities," *SPIE Stereoscopic Displays and Applications*, 1256: 2-11 (1990).

[2] Hodges, Larry F. and David F. McAllister. "Three-Dimensional Display for Quality Control of Digital Cartographic Data," *SPIE True 3-D Imaging Techniques and Display Technologies,* 761: 146-152 (1987).

[3] Stytz, M.R. *et al.* "Three-Dimensional Medical Imaging: Algorithms and Computer Systems," *ACM Computing Surveys*, 23: 421-499 (1991).

[4] Williams, R. Don *et al.* "Direct Volumetric Visualization," *Proceedings of Volume Visualization '92.* 99-106. Los Alamitos CA: IEEE Computer Society Press (1992).

[5] Buxton, William. "Lexical and Pragmatic Considerations of Input Structures," *ACM Computer Graphics* , 17(1): 31-37 (January 1983).

[6] Felger, Wolfgang. "How Interactive Visualization can Benefit from Multidimensional Input Devices," *SPIE Visual Data Interpretation,* 1668: 15-24 (1992).

[7] Bryson, Steve. "Survey of Virtual Environment Technologies and Techniques," *Implementation of Immersive Virtual Environments.*, ACM (July 1992).

[8] Chen, Michael *et al.* "A Study in Interactive 3-D Rotation Using 2-D Control Devices," *ACM Computer Graphics* , 22(4): 121-129 (August 1988).

[9] Beaton, Robert J. et al. "An Evaluation of Input Devices for 3-D Computer Display Workstations," *SPIE True 3-D Imaging Techniques and Display Technologies*, 761: 94-191 (1987).

An Interactive Design Environment for Graphical Browsers

Hubertus Hohl, Jürgen Herczeg, and Matthias Ressel
Research Group DRUID

University of Stuttgart, Department of Computer Science
Breitwiesenstr. 20-22, D-70565 Stuttgart, Germany
E-Mail: druid@informatik.uni-stuttgart.de

Keywords: Domain-specific design, construction kits, end-user programming, browsing, information exploration and visualization, graphic presentation techniques, direct manipulation

Abstract

Browsing, viewed as an integral approach to exploring and directly manipulating large and complex information spaces, crucially depends on adequate graphical presentation and interaction techniques to support navigation. Going beyond available user interface development environments, which are poor in representing and graphically presenting application-specific information structures, we describe an integrated approach to developing domain-specific browsing tools. A set of extensible and reusable construction kits for browsing form an application-independent framework that provides powerful mechanisms for representing, presenting, and accessing complex information structures. This framework is integrated within a browser design environment which offers higher-level tools for building or modifying domain-specific browsers interactively. These tools are designed to be used by both application developers and end users, i.e. domain experts, to adapt and tailor browsers according to a particular application domain or to specific user needs.

1. EXPLORING INFORMATION SPACES BY GRAPHICAL BROWSERS

Browsing is a commonly used navigation strategy for exploring large and complex information spaces. No matter what the application domain is — whether the information spaces represent social, physical or biological information processing systems such as corporate management structures, communication networks or the human visual system, or whether they represent software artifacts such as hypertexts, object-oriented program structures or knowledge bases — the inherent information is often structured as a network of information nodes representing entities and connections between nodes representing relations.

Usually, computer applications provide browsing environments as an adequate means to explore and directly manipulate these structures. However, browsing through large or complex information spaces involves two common problems of usability: (1) cognitive overload, caused by being flooded by too much or badly structured information possibly distracting from interesting details, and (2) disorientation, caused by having lost context. Browsing environments usually face these problems by making use of special guiding, filtering and information reducing techniques which are based on appropriate user interface metaphors providing an intuitive understanding of visual and behavioral aspects of the task domain.

Navigational and spatial metaphors in particular have proven to be an efficient solution to the disorientation problem [1]. Hypertext systems, for example, complement link-based browsing by various real-world metaphors to support navigation such as overview maps, footprints, interaction histories, and guided tours [12]. Another approach to supporting information exploration and understanding is to add depth and motion to the flat world of conventional computer screens through the use of 3D visualizations, interactive animation techniques, and virtual reality [14, 4].

In any case, information exploration by browsing crucially depends on appropriate visualization techniques to realize spatial and navigational metaphors. Taking advantage of the principle that it is easier to recognize what is interesting or useful than to recall or specify it in advance, graphical presentations are especially useful and often superior to textual descriptions (cf. [3]).

Graph visualizations are one important means to make complex information networks conceivable and accessible. For example, numerous domains of software systems are based on graphs to model the underlying information structures such as hierarchical file systems, semantic nets, entity-relationship diagrams, rule dependencies, hypertexts, data flow diagrams, function call sequences, and inheritance hierarchies, to name but a few. By making structural relationships visible and presenting information in its context, human perception can easily recognize patterns in a graph drawing, such as symmetries, hierarchical dependencies, and other spatial relationships, revealing the underlying structure. In a "well-drawn" graph, contextual information can be used to reduce ambiguity, find particular information nodes, identify characteristic groups of nodes, or follow paths.

2. AN INTEGRATED APPROACH TO BUILDING GRAPHICAL BROWSERS

Building browsers for particular application domains is a major undertaking. The application representation framework covering semantics and functionality has to be designed along with the presentational framework covering visualization, navigation and manipulation. However, current application development technology does not adequately facilitate the development of information-intensive applications embodying complex graphical visualization and interaction techniques (cf. [10]). User interface development environments that are available today focus on the application-independent, visual domain of interface elements such as windows, menus, icons, buttons, etc., rather than integrating the application representation framework. Especially, toolkits and interactive user interface builders do not provide appropriate means to reflect semantic aspects of a browser's dynamic application logic on the user interface.

Furthermore, developers are left to themselves implementing graphical presentations and interaction mechanisms which are essential ingredients of browsing systems. For example, graph visualization heavily relies on appropriate automatic layout algorithms and graph editing support. Although in recent years, graph widgets and libraries have emerged which try to capture common characteristics of graph drawings, like shape, connectivity, and layout [2], we believe that most of these systems are not flexible and extensible enough to be generally useful (cf. [11]). Besides, these systems are intended to be used by programmers and require both detailed knowledge about the functionality and semantics of the graph library and the underlying programming language.

Going beyond these systems, we suggest to provide a browser design environment that serves as an *application builder* for developing domain-specific browsing tools. Whereas a user interface builder provides an interactive, visual front-end to a user interface toolkit, an application builder in the domain of browsing provides an interactive, visual front-end to a design framework based on a set of application-independent, reusable *construction kits* for representing, visualizing, accessing, and manipulating complex information structures. By integrating interactive development tools within the browser design framework, application developers can easily build or extend browsers not only by programming but also interactively. Moreover, end users, which are usually domain experts, can exploit the interactive design tools to combine, adapt, and tailor browsers according to their specific needs or preferences.

2.1. The Browser Design Framework

A layered architecture of extensible, object-oriented construction kits forms the basis for building graphical browsers by means of programming. The construction kits have been implemented in the Common Lisp Object System (CLOS); their user interface is based on XIT [9], a user interface development environment for the X Window System.

Textual visualizations of object structures are provided by XTEXT, a toolkit that presents objects in the form of textual descriptions, e.g. in the form of attribute-value pairs, and links by means of sensitive items that let the user browse through information nets according to the ideas of hypertext systems.

Graphical visualizations of information networks are provided by XGRAPH, a construction kit for visualizing and editing structures that can be represented as directed graphs. It provides an application-independent framework for generating, laying out, displaying, and manipulating directed graphs from semantic relations of arbitrary application domains.

Representing Graphs: Three levels of representation are distinguished: The *application level* represents the objects and relations of the work domain. On the *structural level*, this application structure is mapped onto a directed graph. On the *presentation level*, nodes and edges of the graph are represented by interface elements such as icons and arrows, mapping application attributes onto visual attributes such as color, text, and shape. By distinguishing application-specific, structural, and presentational knowledge on different levels, which are interlinked with each other to maintain consistency, the user interface can be changed easily without affecting semantics defined on the structural level, e.g. automatic graph layout algorithms.

Generating Graphs: Different types of *graph generators* are available, which map application structures onto graphs by generating node and edge objects from application-specific representations, such as explicit descriptions of nodes and edges, or implicit descriptions based on the specification of a set of *source objects* and a set of *inferior producers* each of which corresponds to a particular semantic relation between application objects.

Laying out Graphs: An extensible library of *graph layout engines* is provided to produce characteristic drawings for specific graph topologies, as for example hierarchical or netlike structures. Each layout engine is controlled by a set of characteristic parameters which may be adjusted to incorporate domain- or user-specific layout constraints.

Presenting Graphs: On the user interface, graph editing operations are provided which let the user modify the application through direct manipulation of user interface elements. Several presentation techniques for filtering or reducing the visible information of a graph are employed: scrolling, panning, zooming, and fisheye viewing. The motivation for incorporating fisheye presentations for graphs is to provide users with a balance of local detail and global context (cf. [6]). Fisheye views are distorted views which present information related to a point of interest (focus node) in great detail while less relevant information is abstracted. We have implemented an algorithm for fisheye views extending Furnas' original idea to graph presentations with multiple foci.

Building domain-specific browsers by programming is within the province of the XBROWSE construction kit. XBROWSE offers a set of prebuilt higher-level components (based on XTEXT

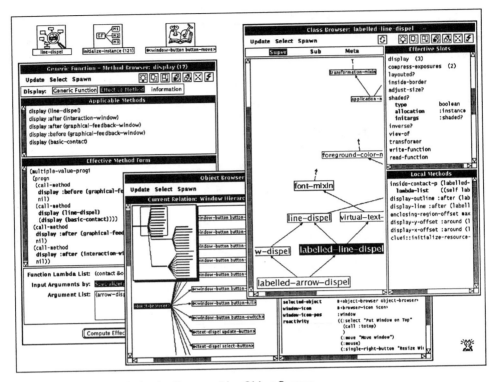

Figure 1: Browsing tools for the Common Lisp Object System

and XGRAPH) that can be used and specialized by programmers, through subclassing, to develop domain-specific browsers integrating appropriate visual and navigational aids. To specify starting points for browsing, a *selection component* offers different mechanisms to bring specific objects of the underlying application domain into the focus of a browser. New browsers can be invoked from a browser so that the user may explore an information structure following different kinds of links simultaneously. XBROWSE controls the communication between these browsers. Update methods are performed for all browsers affected by an internal change. Multiple browsers providing different views may be invoked from each other and used simultaneously.

By exploiting the XBROWSE construction kit, we have implemented browsers for different application domains. The most elaborate example is a set of graphical browsers for CLOS [7], which serve as programming tools for inspecting and modifying class, instance, generic function, and method objects and their relations (cf. figure 1).

2.2. Developing Browsers Interactively

We have complemented the browser design framework by interactive development tools that support design activities of developers and end users above the code level:

Interactive Presentation: Various visual aspects of browsing components can be customized to meet users' current interests by means of a *browser metasystem.* Users can directly manipulate characteristic parameters to customize the look and feel of graph presentations (by selecting and

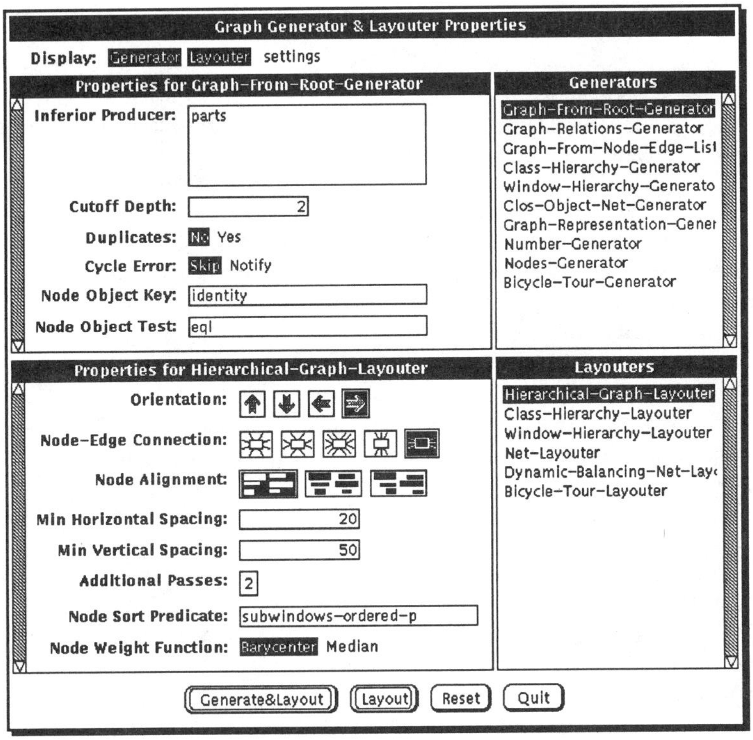

Figure 2: Metasystem for generating and laying out a window hierarchy

adjusting properties of graph generators and layout engines), to define and manipulate fisheye views, etc. Since the metasystem is just another tool provided by the browser design framework, an application programmer can incorporate it easily into any application browser, possibly restricting or extending its functionality to make application-specific information available to its users.

Interactive Design: Application programmers can specialize a prebuilt *browser prototype* for a specific application domain. Via the metasystem, which is part of the prototype, the developer can select appropriate graph generators and layout engines and adjust their parameters.

As an example, figure 1, among other things, shows an *object browser* for exploring window hierarchies. This browser has been built interactively by instantiating the predefined browser prototype, selecting an appropriate graph generator and a layout engine via the metasystem (cf. figure 2), specifying the `parts` inferior producer function for the generator, and optionally adjusting various other parameter defaults. The window hierarchy of a particular window of a running application will be displayed by invoking the selection component of the browser and simply clicking on the window in question. The properties of windows will be displayed as textual descriptions with sensitive items being subjected to editing or browsing by following links. A more elaborate example of a *user interface browser* featuring graphical display of interaction objects and their interdependencies is described in [8].

3. TOWARDS KNOWLEDGE-BASED BROWSER DESIGN ENVIRONMENTS

We have presented an application framework for constructing graphical browsers which derives its essential value from the integration of powerful construction kits for browsing with interactive design tools. Currently, building a specialized application browser *from scratch* is either a matter of programming or of interactively specializing a predefined prototype.

We want to augment these techniques by providing *domain-specific* design environments that support interactive design activities for particular classes of application browsers (e.g. computer network management systems), based on direct manipulation techniques to graphically select, compose, and instantiate predefined building blocks. Moreover, such a browser development environment could be enhanced by knowledge-based components that act as design experts providing help in guiding the designer and criticizing specific designs (cf. [5, 13]).

ACKNOWLEDGEMENTS

The authors would like to thank Christian Rathke for interesting discussions about the idea of knowledge-based design environments applied to the domain of browsing tools. Special thanks go to Rul Gunzenhäuser for making this work possible.

REFERENCES

[1] L. J. Allinson. Designing and Evaluating the Navigational Toolkit. In *Proceedings of the NATO Advanced Workshop "Cognitive Modelling and Interactive Environments"*, 1990.

[2] G. D. Battista, P. Eades, and R. Tamassia. Algorithms for Drawing Graphs: An Annotated Bibliography. Available via anonymous ftp from wilma.cs.brown.edu, file /pub/gdbiblio.tex.Z, Mar. 1993.

[3] H.-D. Böcker, G. Fischer, and H. Nieper. The Enhancement of Understanding Through Visual Representations. In *CHI-85 Conference Proceedings, Human Factors in Computing Systems*, 1986.

[4] S. Feiner and C. Beshers. Worlds within Worlds: Metaphors for Exploring n-dimensional Virtual Worlds. In *UIST'90: Proc. of the ACM Symposium on User Interface Software and Technology*, 1990.

[5] G. Fischer and A. Lemke. Construction Kits and Design Environments: Steps Towards Human Problem-Domain Communication. *Human-Computer Interaction*, 3(3), 1988.

[6] G. Furnas. Generalized Fisheye Views. In *CHI-85 Conference Proceedings, Human Factors in Computing Systems*, 1986.

[7] J. Herczeg and H. Hohl. Building Browsers for the Common Lisp Object System. In *Proceedings of EastEurOOPe'91, Conference, Tutorials and Exhibition on Object-Oriented Programming*, 1991.

[8] J. Herczeg, H. Hohl, and M. Ressel. A New Approach to Visual Programming in User Interface Design. This volume.

[9] J. Herczeg, H. Hohl, and M. Ressel. Progress in Building User Interface Toolkits: The World According to XIT. In *UIST'92: Proc. of the ACM Symposium on User Interface Software and Technology*, 1992.

[10] J. A. Johnson et al. ACE: Building Interactive Graphical Applications. *CACM*, 36(4), 1993.

[11] A. Karrer and W. Scacchi. Requirements for an Extensible Object-Oriented Tree/Graph Editor. In *UIST'90: Proc. of the ACM Symposium on User Interface Software and Technology*, 1990.

[12] J. Nielsen. The Art of Navigation through Hypertext. *CACM*, 33(3), 1990.

[13] C. Rathke. A Knowledge-based Design Environment for Graphical Network Editors. In *Proceedings of the twenty-second annual Hawaii International Conference on Systems Sciences*, 1989.

[14] G. G. Robertson, S. K. Card, and J. D. Mackinlay. Information Visualization Using 3D Interactive Animation. *CACM*, 36(4), 1993.

HelpDraw graphical environment: A step beyond data parallel programming languages [*]

Akram-Djellal Benalia, Jean-Luc Dekeyser and Philippe Marquet[a]

[a]Laboratoire d'Informatique Fondamentale de Lille 1,
Bâtiment M3, Cité Scientifique, 59655 Villeneuve d'Ascq cedex, France.
e-mail: `benalia@lifl.fr`

Abstract

In this paper we describe the data parallel programming environment "HelpDraw" which, through some interactive and graphical manipulations, allows to express (or translate) the user data parallel thought in a data parallel code without compelling him to learn a particular language. HelpDraw also provides the dual part of the code generation: the code visualization, by visualizing the graphical effect of each action of a given data parallel code.

1. Introduction

Several interactive and graphical environments have been carried out these last years. They are devoted to user assistance in several phases of the parallel application development cycle; for example: (a) [1, 2] task flow graph editors that allow, at the design level, task partitionning and mapping tasks; (b) [3, 4] code visualizations to analyze and debug programs, this allows users to better understand the program, to detect deadlocks, bottlenecks, etc; (c) [5] visualization during code transformation phase (parallelization and optimization): graph of dependences and codes transformations. This allows users to interact with the system and to better understand the transformations; (d) [6] visualization (graph, bargraph, etc) of simulation and performance analysis results such as rooting load, communication load, etc.

The work facility provided by these development environments to assist the user is not minor. Almost none of there allow the user to develop his code without being compelled to learn a particular language (without syntax constraint).

This lack justifies the interest of the graphical environment **"HelpDraw"**. Through some interactive and graphical manipulations, HelpDraw allows to express (or translate) the user data parallel thought in a data parallel code.

HelpDraw also provides the dual part of the code generation: the code visualization. This part allows the user to analyze step by step his data parallel program, since it visualizes the graphical effect of each action in the code.

The HelpDraw environment is based on the data parallel programming model

---

[*]This project is supported by Digital Equipment Corporation in the frame of a Data-Parallel Research Initiative.

"HELP" [7]. The HELP model is characterized by the hyper-space notion. A HELP program defines one or several hyper-spaces. The programmer-handled data parallel objects (DPO) are positionned in these hyper-spaces. In the HELP model, applications of operators are clearly distinguished from data transfers because of the two levels of programming: computational operations on objects are executed along a subset of hyper-space points, while communications are realized in the form of intra hyper-space DPO migration.

An hyper-space is defined as a cartesian reference of positive coordinate points. The DPO are multi-dimensional arrays allocated on compact sets of hyper-space points. Two DPOs allocated on the same hyper-space point set are said to be conform. The HELP microscopic level reflects the data parallel model through the parallel execution of a same arithmetic or logical expressions on conform DPO elements. In order to execute microscopic processings on non-conform DPO, programmer has to ensure their conformity by the application of previous macroscopic primitives: DPO transformation or migration inside the hyper-space. At this macroscopic level, the programmer globally handles objects, without accessing their element values.

Different macroscopic operation classes coexist: (1) copy primitives (e.g.: Extract): produce a full or partial copy of the source DPO; (2) shake primitives (e.g.: Shift_wrap): produce a result DPO that contains the interchanged source DPO elements; (3) migration and reshape primitives (e.g.: Move, Rotate, Expand, Replicate): produce a result DPO which is the reshaped or moved DPO source.

The HELP model provides a geometrical support for the data parallel programming, and thereby allows to graphically visualize the hyper-spaces (1D, 2D, and 3D), the data parallel objects (DPOs) which are a geometrical shapes, and also the macroscopic operations defined in HELP (ie, DPO migration and reshape).

HelpDraw is a data parallel instruction generator. The generated instructions are either a composition of macro and microscopic functions (e.g: Vect=Vect1.macro1 opμ Vect2.macro2.macro3) or a control structures which may include instruction block (eg: *Loop* or *Where-Else_Where*).

2. Instruction Generation

The user might be able to develop his data parallel code without having to know the language, but only through an interactive manipulation of HelpDraw. The HelpDraw environment consists in two editors: textual and graphical. The first is a standard text editor. In the graphical editor (fig. 1), the user defines an hyper-space in which he allocates and manipulates DPOs. It is difficult to distinguish these DPOs when they are numerous or allocated on the same area. So, HelpDraw provides the possibility to associate a color to each DPO. To find or select a DPO, HelpDraw provides a list (DPO_List) in which is visualized the DPO name and the associated color. In the aim of an improved visibility, the user is allowed to hide temporarily some DPO reperesentations.

In order to build an instruction, the user applies on the DPOs the micro and macroscopic functions defined in HELP. These functions are activated either through the pull-down menus or, especially for the macroscopic ones, by direct manipulation. HelpDraw is a direct manipulation interface [8, 9] in which the user points to DPOs and executes

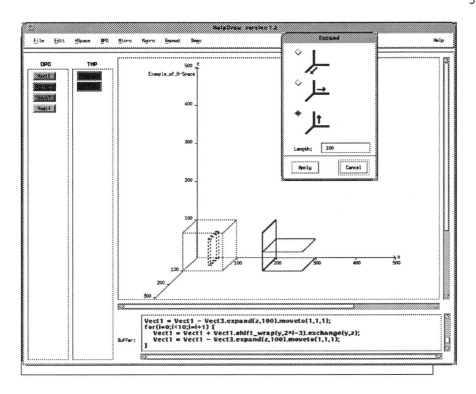

Figure 1. HelpDraw Interface

macroscopic functions. Some concrete examples are the "Move" and the "Extract" functions: to apply the "Move", the user moves using the mouse the pointed DPO where he wants to, even in 3D hyper-space; and to extract a sub-DPO, the user points to the sub-DPO origin then by moving the mouse he traces out and visualizes the part to be extracted. Although the hyper-space is graduated in data (not in pixels), the interface allows the user to move the mouse in the (3D) hyper-space with the necessary accuracy (even by a step of one data).

In the aim to generate an instruction that corresponds to the user executed operations, HelpDraw has to memorize all the operations trace, and also to visualize the graphical effect of each operation (e.g: in the Move operation, show the DPO movement in the hyper-space). Indeed, when the user applies a function on DPOs, HelpDraw automatically generates a temporary DPO (TMP) which represents the intermediary result. This TMP is a data parallel object represented with its own color. But since it has no name (as the user DPOs) and in order to distinguish it, HelpDraw inserts it in a list (TMP_List) different from the first one (DPO_List). Moreover, this TMP has as feature an historic which indicates the chronological actions that have led to its creation. For instance, if the user applies the macroscopic operation "macro1" on a DPO "Vect1", the generated TMP will have the historic: "Vect1.macro1". If, after that, the user applies another operation "macro2" on the same TMP, this will be consumed and HelpDraw generates a new TMP that will have as historic: "Vect1.macro1.macro2".

The whole instruction is generated from the creation historic of eaach TMP involved in this instruction. These instructions are generated in a Buffer (or instructions window); and it is up to the user to decide to copy them to the text editor in order to build functions or a complete program.

The microscopic operations (arithmetic, logic) are not executed only if there is DPOs conformity (same shape and same origin); and unlike the geometrical operations, they are not executed by direct manipulation but through pulldown menus. This prevents the user from producing directly an expression (e.g.: dpo1+dpo2*dpo3-dpo4) and forces him to use temporaries which have not an important visual significance at this level. To palliate this, the user has to introduce textually an expression, for example: "A+B*C-D", the arguments are formal parameters. HelpDraw translates the expression in a diagram [10], thus the user may associate (directly by the mouse) each DPO to the correspondent argument. These diagrams may be reused, modified, and also built by assembling the necessary components.

Concerning the hyper-spaces, it is important to notice that the user may define as many hyper-spaces as he wants, and may easily navigate from one to another. However, in the HelpDraw environment, only three dimensions hyper-spaces are visualized. Nevertheless, the user may choice to represent the dimensions he wants (e.g.: for the 4 dimentions hyper-space x,y,z,t , the user may choice to represent x,y,z or x,z,t or another combination).

3. HelpDraw: Demonstrational Interface

The previous section has shown how HelpDraw succeeds in keeping the user operations trace until the instruction generation. Now, we face other problems, especially the repetitive task (operations) execution. For example, the user wants to reexecute the same operations sequence on other DPOs without being obliged to perform it step by step once more; or to generate the Loop code (i.e.: FOR). This would be possible by using "demonstrational interfaces" or "programming by example" principle [11].

We remind the Brad Myers definition [12]: "*Demonstartional* interfaces let the user perform actions on concrete example objects (often by direct manipulation), while constructiong an abstract program. The term *demonstrational* is used because the user demonstrates the desired result using example values".

As a matter of fact, to reexecute the same user operation sequence ("Again") on other DPOs, HelpDraw, while the user is performing the operations on the first DPO, records the trace of each action with the necessary parameters; thus the user has only to replay the recording (e.g.: to perform Expand(z,100), the interface records the operation type as well as the parameters: dimension=z and length=100).

Concerning the Loop development, ex:

```
for (i=0; i<100; i++) {
  MAT=VCET1.macro1(2i+1).macro2 opmicro VECT2.macro3(3i-5);
  MAT2=MAT opmicro VECT.macro4(3i);
}
```

the user performs the first Loop iteration to constitute, thereby, the example or the template that will be used by HelpDraw. At the end of this iteration and knowing the Loop step and bounds, the interface executes the Loop, visualizes its graphical effect, and generates the corresponding code.

In addition, the fact to record each operation will allow the user to go back and cancel an already performed action ("Undo"). And it is up to the interface to recover the exact state that was before the canceled operation.

4. Conclusion and Related work

We have tried to show that from a data parallel thought (here according to the HELP model), the user is able to develop its code independently of languages, i.e. without syntax constraints. In addition, HelpDraw allows better understanding of the data parallel paradigm, since while manipulating the interface, the user has a feedback and he can see the graphical effect of his actions as well as the generated code.

However several perspectives appear and have to be realized in order to improve the HelpDraw environment:

- To generate the code, HelpDraw is actually placed at the instruction or the instruction block level. One among the finalities to reach is to generate functions and then a complete programs. This lead us to direct more the HelpDraw graphical editor by the function and program context (or syntax).

- In spite of the direct manipulation tools provided by HelpDraw (to ensure the conviviality) and its demonstrational aspect (to avoid repetitive tasks), we are obliged to notice the limitations of this kind of interfaces especially to anticipate the user actions (e.g.: suggest an operation parameter value) or to realize directly a known goal (e.g.: to ensure the conformity) without compelling the user to execute all the operations himself.

  Only the intelligent interfaces may realize that, such as Peridot [12] or Eager [11]. They have to use inferencing in order to realize a goal or to anticipate the user action. In our case, based on the HELP model rules, the concerned DPO knowledges (shape and position), and the other user action knowledges (actions already done), having also the goal (e.g.: conformity) or the action to anticipate, HelpDraw uses inferencing and provides the user with the necessary suggestions.

- Another aspect, as important as the code generation, is the data parallel code analyze and debugging. So in the aim to complete the HelpDraw environment, it is necessary to develop the dual part of the code generation: *the program visualization* [13, 14] in which from an existing code, the interface graphically and step by step visualizes (animates) the operations especially the macroscopic ones (DPO migration and reshape). This will allow the user to find the data parallel thought and also to analyze, debug, and better understand his program behavior.

REFERENCES

1. A.Beguelin, J.S. Dongarra, G.A.Geist, R. Manchek, and V.S. Sunderam. Graphical development tool for network-based concurrent supercomputing. In *ACM Supercomputing'91 Proc.*, pages 435–444, November 1991.
2. D. Bruschi, P.Lenzi, E. Pozzetti, S. Gobbo, and G. Serazzi. A user-friendly environment for parallel programming. In *Proc. Euromicro Workshop on Parallel and Distributed Processing*, pages 451–456, Gran Canaria, January 27-29 1993.
3. Hermann IImberger and Claus-Peter Wiedemann. A visualization and control environment for parallel program debugging. In *Proc. of the Twenty-sixth Hawaii International Conference on System Sciences*, pages 387–396, Los Alamitos, California, 1992. IEEE Computer Society Press.
4. M. Friedoll, M. Lapolla, S.Kochhar, S.Sistare, and J. Juda. Visualizing the behavior of massively parallel programs. In *ACM Supercomputing'91 Proc.*, pages 472–480, November 1991.
5. Chyi-Ren Dow, Shi-Kuo Chang, and Mary Lou Soffa. A visualization system for parallelizing programs. In *IEEE Supercomputing'91 Proceedings*, pages 194–203, Mineapolis, November 1992.
6. C.D. Norton and E.P. Glinert. A visual environment for designing and simulating execution of processor arrays. In *Proc. 1990 IEEE Workshop on Visual Languages (VL'90)*, pages 227–232, Sokie, October 1990.
7. J.-L. Dekeyser, D. Lazure, and Ph. Marquet. Help for data parallel scientific programming. In *Euromicro Workshop on Parallel and Distributed Computing*, pages 22–29, Gran Canaria, January 1992.
8. J.E. Ziegler and K.-P. Fahnrich. Direct manipulation. In M. Helander, editor, *Handbook of Human-Computer Interaction*, pages 123–132. Elsevier Science Publisher B.V., 1988. revised 1992.
9. B. Shneiderman. Direct manipulation: A step beyond programming languages. *IEEE Computer*, 16(8):57–69, August 1983.
10. G.Viehstaedt and A.L. Ambler. Visual representation and manipulation of matrices. *Journal of Visual Languages and Computing*, 3(3):273–298, 1992.
11. Allen Cypher. EAGER: Programming repetitive tasks by example. In *proc. SIGCHI, Human Factors in Computing Systems*, pages 33–39, New York, 1991.
12. Brad A. Myers. Demonstrational interfaces: A s tep beyond direct manipulation. *IEEE Computer*, pages 61–73, August 1992.
13. Brad A. Myers. Taxonomies of visual programming and program visualization. *Journal of Visual Languges and Computing*, (1):97–123, 1990.
14. S. El-Kassas. Visual languages: their definition and applications in system development. In A. Nuñez, editor, *EUROMICRO'91 – Hardware and Software Design Automation, 17th Symposium on Microprogramming, Vienna, Austria*, Vienna, Austria, September 1991.

Improving the Quality of Computer-Generated Charts

Ralph Marshall

Brown University
(Current address: The MacGregor Group, 10 Post Office Square, Boston, MA)

Abstract

Properly designed data graphics can be a valuable aid to understanding quantitative information and as a consequence are used by people in a wide range of work. However, designing these graphics requires time and expertise which is often not available to the people most familiar with the underlying data. While automated graphic design has been an area of research for some time, most of this work has focused on expanding the range of data sets which can be handled, while neglecting the need for esthetically pleasing results and user control. This paper describes a library-based approach to generating business graphics which addresses these open areas.

1.   Statement of the Problem

Producing charts and graphs which show data sets is a difficult task, and it is one which most people have not studied in any depth. However, these same people are often called upon to make presentations and write reports which can make good use of visual displays. While a host of computer systems such as spreadsheet packages and dedicated presentation tools have been developed to assist in this task, virtually none of them offers any assistance in selecting an appropriate design. This paper describes a research prototype named Playfair which begins to provide such guidance to non-expert users.

While creating data graphics is far from a science, we do have a sizable body of knowledge on the subject which has been amassed over time. Different individuals and organizations will probably always disagree about what they consider to be a good graph, but most accomplished practitioners work from a set of rules and basic designs which they apply to specific problems. Playfair attempts to work along the same lines by having a library of graph templates with rules which describe when they can be used and how well they work for a given data set.

2.   Solution: Library of Graph Templates

In order to exchange information through some medium, the parties involved in the communication must agree on a fixed set of rules for interpreting the signals which they are exchanging. It is these conventions which allow us to look at a bar chart and know how to read it without detailed instructions. So, while innovations in graphical form are necessary when existing approaches lack sufficient expressiveness, in most cases people prefer to work with a small collection of general styles.

This same idea can be extended to computerized presentation. By working from a library of design templates the system can take advantage of the accumulated knowledge and conventions which inform the work of human graphic designers.

The template describes a family of related graphics, such as scatter plots and bar charts. The templates consist of three components:

- Layout and drafting information such as font choice and line styles.

- A list of variations in the family and rules for mapping data into them.

- A set of effectiveness guidelines known as a *critic*.

Storing expert opinions on decisions such as layout, line styles, and font choices, relieves the software of the need to make these decisions anew for each data set. Since the number of templates is relatively small, it is practical to devote significant effort to getting these details right for each one. These carefully crafted templates also function as an important body of design expertise, allowing for organization-wide consistency and a source of knowledge for casual users.

Candidate presentations are produced by generated only those style variations which make sense given the particular data set. The associated critic uses a set of template-specific rules developed by humans to produce a numeric rating for each chart. The charts can then be presented to the user in a sorted order for his or her final selection. The ordering serves as an aid to users who do not have the graphic design training and/or time to set all of the parameters necessary for a finished image.

In order to make this a practical graphing system we must provide as much flexibility to the user as possible. However, most existing automated design systems require complete control over the design rather than providing the option of working in a cooperative fashion with a user. Since Playfair's generation system consists of making decisions about the alternatives possible for a given template, it is straightforward to allow the user to make some of these decisions and let the computer make any remaining ones.

Another important feature of the library-based approach is that it simplifies the task of customizing the system to produce results which meet the user's specification. Without having to tinker with the underlying reasoning system, you can add a new template to the system which will allow it to create the required images. This modular approach means that none of the existing designs will be affected by the addition, and that the new style does not have to have anything in common with existing templates.

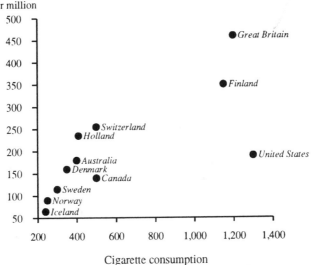

1950 Lung Cancer Death Rate and 1930 per capita Cigarette Consumption

Figure 1: An Example Scatter Plot Created by Playfair

3. The Theory of Data Graphics

Data graphs, work by encoding the different components of the data set using various visual techniques such as position, color, text labels, etc. Different classes of graphs allow different forms of variation. For example, in simple bar charts the color and length of individual bars can vary but the width of each bar is fixed. Additionally, each form of visual encoding is only suitable for certain types of data values. For example, shapes are inherently unordered and thus are inappropriate for numeric values. The space limitations of this paper preclude a complete discussion of this important subject, but [5] provides an excellent summary.

Playfair makes use of an important idea taken from [1], namely that the data presented by a graphic can be broken down into *components*, each of which represents a single field in a relation. By describing the mandatory and optional components which can be presented by a given design, the library supports a mechanism for matching data to be displayed with templates which can handle it.

The scatter plot template used to generate Figure 1 includes the following components:

Marks	Non-numeric field shown as distinct dots.	
X, Y position	Two fields encoded as position along the axes.	
Size	Numeric field associated with each mark.	(*Optional*)
Value	Non-numeric field for each mark.	(*Optional*)
Label	Mark identity as a text label.	(*Optional*)

Given such a definition of the scatter-plot family we can generate instances of it which match a given data set. This example shows a three-field relation using positioned marks and optional labels to allow identification of individual dots (which can be omitted if only the distribution of the marks is considered interesting).

4.   The Role of the Critics

The previous section describes how to generate a set of designs which are potentially appropriate for a data set. However, we must provide more guidance to the user than simply eliminating completely invalid styles; we must also attempt to help the user pick the most effective alternative. It is impossible to capture many of the factors which cause somebody to prefer one design over another in a given situation, so the goal of ranking is for the computer to provide a small set of good alternatives from which the user can make the final selection. This task is performed by the critics, which assess the graph designs based on both the data types and individual values. This section provides a detailed example of how this analysis is applied to a set of designs.

Figure 2 shows another display generated by Playfair, in this case the best available design for this data set.

Operating Revenues of the Norfolk & Western Railway

Category	1938	1937
Freight	72,898,946.38	89,835,838.44
Passengers	1,942,334.20	2,274,594.70
Mail	1,245,285.43	1,306,575.04
Express Delivery	303,758.38	429,632.40
Other Transport	324,564.03	352,719.83
Facility Rentals	448,053.25	662,142.58

Figure 2: Highest Rated Display

The current implementation of Playfair generates charts based on 4 templates: bar charts, scatter plots, line charts, and tables. The following subsections describe the steps followed to design displays for this data set and subsequently rate them.

Bar charts

Generation. The basic design uses bar lengths to represent revenue for one year and shading of the bars to depict the second year. Related designs are produced by varying elements such as orientation of the bars and the choice of which year to show using length.

Criticism. All of the designs score poorly on two counts:

- The ratio between the longest bar (Freight) and the shortest (Express Delivery or Other Transport) is about 250:1, resulting in a graph displaying one long bar and a set of blips for the remaining categories.

- Representing the second numeric field through variation in gray value makes it difficult to judge ratios between values. (Playfair does not currently generate multi-bar charts, which would be a better design in this regard.)

Scatter plots

Generation. Marks represent various categories with the two years along the axes, with either labels or visual coding of the categories.

Criticism. This is a fairly decent design given the data types alone, but fails in this particular case. Due to the extreme value of one category most of the marks will be crowded together near the origin with a lone mark at the far opposite corner. This design is therefore ranked above bar charts but below tables in effectiveness.

Line charts

Generation. There is only one type of design possible, namely showing the categories along one axis and displaying the revenue for the two years by two lines distinguished by color, pattern, or label.

Criticism. This is a poor design both because it suffers from the same extreme ratio problem as a bar chart and because the categories do not represent any sort of continuous field. This design is rated below bar charts for this reason as it is wholly inappropriate.

Note: all of the foregoing graphic designs will also be penalized due to the small size of the data set, since there is little likelihood of depicting a useful trend. This penalty is intended to favor tables over graphics for small data sets.

Tables

Generation. Columns can be displayed in any of six sequences and the rows can be sorted by any of the three columns or left unsorted, producing a total of 24 possible tables.

Criticism. As a class tables are a good match for this data set. The extreme range of values poses no problems and the small number of data points makes the table easy to read.

This process of generation and criticism leads Playfair to suggest the table shown as one of the most appropriate choices for this data set.

5. Related Work

My work on graphic design has of course been influenced by that of others, both in traditional graphic design and in the emerging area of computer-generated presentations. Starting with the seminal research of Jock Mackinlay (see [3]), a number of groups have explored the problem of automating the production of business graphics based on a first principles method. In general their systems work by starting with low-level encodings of the data values based on their types and aggregating the mappings into a finished image. This approach permits a wide range of data sets to be visualized but does so at the cost of having no high-level categories of presentations.

One of the drawbacks with such systems is that the esthetic quality of the resulting graphics tends to compare poorly with professionally generated ones. While this may in part be due to the fact that the systems are research prototypes, the ability to work from templates that have been refined by humans makes it much easier to achieve visually effective displays. I feel that the graphics included in this paper demonstrate that a template-based system can in fact produce first rate graphics without extensive user intervention. Edward Tufte's widely read book on data presentation [6] is an excellent starting point for this area of research.

The notion of using templates for choosing the most appropriate form of display was first advanced in [2], but that work was limited to matching a given data set to a general presentation style (e.g. "The data set should be shown as a bar chart."). My notion of templates introduces the use of detailed designs that have been crafted by a human and that can be evaluated by the system based on rules tailored to that design. This combination allows the system to produce high-quality finished images within an expandable range of styles. A more complex description of the ideas and methods developed for Playfair is given in [4].

6.   References

[1]   Jacques Bertin. *Semiology of Graphics*. The University of Wisconsin Press, Madison, Wisconsin, 1983. Translated by William J. Berg.

[2]   Sakunthala Gnanamgari. *Information Presentation Through Default Displays*. PhD Thesis, University of Pennsylvania, 1981.

[3]   Jock D. Mackinlay. Automating the design of graphical presentations of relational information. *ACM Transactions on Graphics*, 5(2):110-141, April 1986.

[4]   Ralph J. Marshall. Bringing graphic design expertise to computer generated presentations. Master's Thesis, Brown University, Mary 1993.

[5]   Steven F. Roth and Joe Mattis. Data characterization for intelligent graphics presentation. In *SIGCHI Bulletin (CHI '90 Conference Proceedings)*, pages 193-200. Addison-Wesley Publishing Company, 1990.

[6]   Edward R. Tufte. *The Visual Display of Quantitative Information*. Graphics Press, Box 430, Cheshire, CN 06410, 1983.

OOQBE*: An intuitive graphical query language with recursion.

F. Staes[a] and L.Tarantino[b]

[a]Department of Mathematics and Computer Science, University of Antwerp (U.I.A.), Universiteitsplein 1, B - 2610 Wilrijk, Belgium

[b]University of L'Aquila, Dipartimento di Ingegneria Elettrica, Poggio di Roio, I - 67040 L-Aquila, Italy

Abstract: In this paper we present OOQBE*, a graphical query language for object oriented databases, that allows users to formulate queries by providing examples of the desired answer. The language is designed so that it regains in an object oriented environment the advantages of relational query languages: declarativeness, associative access and closure under query. Furthermore, a new operator is introduced (filter), which significate extends the query language. OOQBE* also provides for a transitive closure operator, giving the language an expressive power equivalent to the power of Linear Datalog.

1. Introduction.

In this paper we present OOQBE* (Object-Oriented **Q**uery **B**y **E**xample), a graphical query language that allows users to formulate queries by providing examples of the desired answer. A preliminary design of a subset of OOQBE*, has been discussed in [6], together with its implementation environment, namely the KIWIS system. Basically, in the data model underlying OOQBE*, a Data Base (DB) is viewed as a hierarchy of objects, each identified by an object identifier and described by properties representing its relation with other objects in the DB. The target of a property is not restricted to be a primitive object but can be any user-defined object; properties are allowed to be set-valued.

Object Oriented Data Base Management Systems (OODBMS's) usually offer only limited ad hoc query capabilities, aimed at extracting objects existing in the database and based upon a navigational process (thus including the formulation of "implicit joins", i.e., queries based on the traversal of inter-object references). OOQBE*, instead, is designed so that to regain the advantages of relational Query Languages (QL), among which: *declarativeness, associative access* (for arbitrarily comparing properties of an object, as well as of different objects), *closure under queries*. Furthermore, OOQBE* is conceived to be fully integrated in a browsing environment and browsing primitives can be used during the formulation of the query and while analyzing the answers.

The effectiveness of a graphical QL depends on the Display Model, i.e., on the rules defining the mapping from DB objects onto their visual representations. The object visualization must: 1) help the user to perceive the nature of the data, 2) support a direct manipulation based interaction. In OOQBE*, an object visualization composes the representations of its properties in such a way that both the structure and the semantics of the object can be intuitively perceived. There is a precise correspondence between the object structure and the nature of the graphical elements used within its representation. A friendly *formulation environment* is provided for building examples and rehandling previously generated queries under the system assistance. Queries are formulated either by filling in *object templates* visualized according to the display model, or, starting from objects retrieved while browsing, asking the system to generalize the retrieved example by substituting some constants with variables. The answers are presented to the user according to the display model, ready for further exploration through customary browsing primitives.

The OOQBE* querying primitives can be classified into four groups, depending on the effects of the resulting queries. The first three kinds of queries are typical of most (relational) QL's:

1. queries aimed at extracting objects existing in the database,

2. queries aimed at combining objects in the database,

3. queries aimed at extracting portions of objects based on intensional characteristics (i.e., by projections).

Queries of types 1) (that include selections and implicit joins) and 3) are usually offered by the existing OODBMS's, while queries of type 2) cannot be formulated by navigational OO QL's. They correspond to the formulation of "explicit joins", necessary for guaranteeing ad-hoc queries, since existing objects in the DB may not reflect all relationships requested by a query. Furthermore, In OOQBE* we introduced a fourth type of extraction, applicable in OODB's, though a new operator (*filter*), for permitting a direct formulation of queries aimed at the extraction of portions of objects based on extensional characteristics.Finally, OOQBE* provides a transitive closure operator, extending the expressive power to the equivalent of Linear Datalog.

Section 2 of this paper introduces the global aspects of the interaction environment. Section 3 describes the graphical query language in more details. Finally, section 4 presents some future research and a comparison with a number of similar systems.

2. The Interaction Environment.

The effectiveness of a user interface to a DB system heavily depends on the visualization techniques adopted for presenting information to the end-user. Such techniques should help the user to perceive the nature of the data model and the DB contents; furthermore the representation techniques must allow an intuitive interaction.Thus, in an OODBMS, an object's visualization should compose the representation of its properties in such a way that both the structure and the semantics of the object can be perceived by the user.

Most of the examples presented in the following sections use a common example database describing flights between airports. Essentially, the database stores information on flights (number, departure airport and time and arrival airport and time) and airports (name and list of other airports connected to it by some flight). Of course, not all of this information is extensionally defined (stored in the database), but some of it (e.g. the connectedTo properties of an airport) is intensionally defined (computed). However, to OOQBE* users there is no difference between the two kinds of information. The schema of this database is depicted in figure 1. According to a Display Model that satisfies the above mentioned requirements, figure 2 shows a representation of a flight object. Notice that there is a precise correspondence between the structure of an object and the nature of the graphical elements used within an object's representation. The interested reader is referred to [6] for more information on the concept of Display Models and on how they are used within OOQBE*.

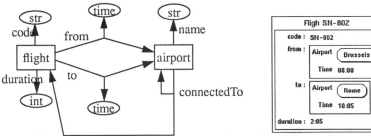

Figure 1: Example database schema.   Figure 2:   Flight representation

3. The Query Language.

In the design of a query language some guideline principles are to be taken into account which derive from their main purposes. Generally, end users require a means to easily extract information and are not interested in, nor expert enough to, fully exploit all the features of the database programming language, e.g. for performing computations. Thus, most of the time they just need ad hoc query facilities (that may be a subset of the database programming language) from which they expect ease of expression and efficiency.

3.1 Basic features of the OOQBE* query language.

The main concept needed in a by-example query language is that of an object template, i.e. a pattern identifying a set of objects exhibiting a common set of characteristics. The formulation of a query coincides with the specification of such a template and the evaluation of the query is accomplished by retrieving the data base objects matching the pattern.

The specification of an object template is done by interacting with a *selection form* associated with an object. Figure3 depicts the selection form associated with the *airport* class. Selection forms allow to specify conditions on all the object's property values. Not only can the end-user impose conditions on the properties of the target class (the *airport* class in this case), s/he also can expand links to other objects in order to impose conditions on properties of these objects, In the above figure, the arguments of the *connectedTo* property are expanded once. (The property arguments of the nested airport object and of the flight object are not expanded, and still represented by a button). End users can expand links by clicking on the buttons representing them.

Conditions on property values are specified by typing condition expressions at the text fields. These expressions can consist of constants, arithmetic operators and logical operators. For example, to select all airports connected to the Brussels airport by flights having a duration between 1 and 2 hours, the user can specify the condition as '> 60 AND < 120' (supposing that the duration is specified in minutes) at the duration field of the nested flight representation and '*Brussels*' at the airport's name field. Furthermore, links between property values (possibly in different query forms) can be specified. This can be used to construct so-called explicit joins. See [4] and [7] for a discussion on the difference between implicit and explicit joins.

3.2 Projections and filters.

The facilities introduced above allow for the selection of instances of a class that satisfy a given condition. However, OOQBE* also allows to include or exclude properties (or property values) from the resulting answer. To this end, the system provides *projection/filter forms* as

606

depicted in figure 4. As one can see from this figure, projection forms are based on the object representations provided by the Display Model, just as selection forms are based on these representations. The checkboxes in front of the property names can be used to include or exclude properties from the resulting answers of the query.

While the checkboxes in front of the property names can be used to include or exclude properties based on their names, the text fields are used to include or exclude specific property values from the resulting answers. Please note that the filtering conditions do not influence what objects are selected, but only what properties of these objects will be visible. By default, constraints specified at the projection form's text fields are automatically copied to the corresponding text fields of the selection form.

As an example use of this feature, consider again the query formulated in the previous section. If the selection condition equals the filtering conditions, the resulting object will only have as *connectedTo* values those connections that satisfy the selection condition. All other connections will be hidden. However, if no filtering condition is specified, all *connectedTo* values of the original object will be visible in the answer.

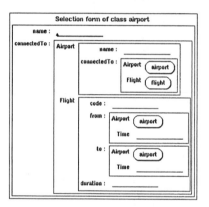 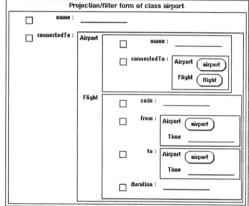

Figure 3: Example selection form.   Figure 4:   Example projection form.

Also, it is possible to specify a filtering condition without specifying a selection condition. Using the same example, this results in all airport objects, but in each airport object only those *connectedTo* properties that satisfy the condition will be visible.

3.3 Recursive Queries.

While the facilities introduced until now allow for the formulation of a large number of queries, there still are a number of queries that can't be formulated. For example, it is not possible to formulate queries like *'Give me all connections (made up of possibly multiple flights) between Brussels and Rome'*. The specification of this kind of queries requires the use of a so-called *transitive closure* operator.

OOQBE* provides for a transitive closure operator that can be applied to both implicit and explicit joins. Using this operator, OOQBE* allows to specify the above query in two ways. On the one hand, the user can start from the *airport* selection form (as shown in figure 3), open the representation of the nested airport object using the transitive closure option, and specify the two airport names in the appropriate text fields (shown in figure 5). Note that when expanding an implicit link using the transitive closure operator a number of extra boxes are drawn round the nested representation.

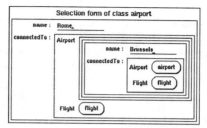

Figure 5: Using the transitive closure operator on implicit joins.

An alternative way to specify this query starts from two query forms on the *flight* class, and applies the transitive closure operator to the explicit link between the *to* property of the first form and the *from* property of the second (depicted in figure 6). Note that explicit joins are represented by the *LINK-* tokens, indicating that all appearances of these tokens have to have the same value. Hence, the meaning of the explicit join in figure 6 is: find all combinations of flight objects where the *to* value of the one flight equals the *from* value of the other flight. Applying the transitive closure operator to this construction yields the query as described above.

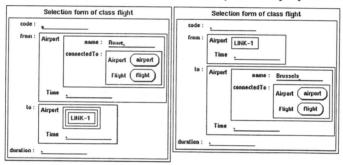

Figure 6: Using the transitive closure operator on explicit joins.

3.4 Advanced features.

As discussed extensively in[2], introducing a transitive closure operator results in an expressive power equivalent to the power of Linear Datalog. However, when formulating a linear query, the user has to make himself the translation to the equivalent query using the transitive closure operator. While OOQBE* neither allows for the definition of linear recursive queries, it allows for a more natural and intuitive formulation of a large number of queries by providing the user with a possibility of defining a number of extra conditions.

One of these new facilities allows the user to impose conditions on the length of a **transitive closure**. Obviously this can be used very effectively in the formulation of queries like *'find me all flights between Rome and Brussels with a maximum of 2 stops'*. However, it can be used also in the formulation of less trivial queries. For example, one of the queries that cannot be formulated intuitively using a transitive closure operator is the well-known *same-generation* query (given a detectable storing information on persons where each person as a parent, find the persons of the same generation as a given person). However, using this new facility the query can be formulated in an intuitive way as shown in figure 7: starting from three selection forms on the *person* class, one indicates that the transitive closures applied to the parent

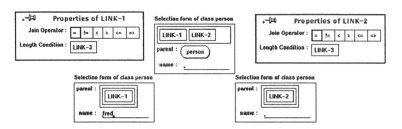

Figure 7:Querying for the persons of the same generation as *fred*.

properties of the two selection forms have to point to the upper selection form. Afterwards, it is indicated that the length of both transitive closures has to be equal using a third link. Note that the upper selection form is only needed to be able to express that the ancestor of both persons have to be the same.

4. Conclusions and related work.

Throughout this paper we gave a short introduction to the graphical query language OOQBE*. OOQBE* offers an intuitive and user friendly alternative for querying object oriented databases. While there exist a number of other graphical query languages (for example, [2], [3], [5] and [1], OOQBE* has a number of important advantages:

- In contrast to the other systems, OOQBE* allows to define custom-made representations for classes, and have these representations used not only by OOQBE* but also in the querying and update paradigms.
- Although theoretically the expressive power of OOQBE* is not higher than the power of e.g. GraphLog, it allows to define a number of queries in a more intuitive way.

5. References.

[1] M. Angelaccio, T. Catarci, and G. Santucci. Qbd*: A graphical query language with recursion. *IEEE Transactions on Software Engineering*, 16(10):1150–1163, 1990.

[2] M. Consens and A. Mendelzon. Graphlog: a visual formalism for real life recursion. In *Proceedings of the Ninth ACM Symposium on Principles of Database Systems*, pages 404–416, 1990.

[3] I. Cruz. G+: Recursive queries without recursion. In *Proc. 2nd Int. Conf. Expert Database Systems*, pages 355–368, 1988.

[4] W. Kim. A model for queries for object-oriented databases. In *Proc. of VLDB*, pages 423–432, 1989.

[5] M. Kuntz and R. Melchert. Pasta-3's graphical query language: Direct manipulation, cooperative queries, full expressive power. In *Proc. of the 1989 VLDB*, pages 97–105. 1989.

[6] F. Staes, L. Tarantino, and A. Tiems. A graphical query language for object-oriented databases. In *Proceedings of the 1991 IEEE Workshop on Visual Languages and Computing*, Kobe, Japan, October 1991.

[7] F. Staes, L. Tarantino, and B. Verdonk. A logic based approach for supporting queries in object oriented databases. In *Object Oriented Approach in Information Systems*, pages 193–208. North Holland, Quebec City, 1991.

[8] F. Staes, L. Tarantino, B. Verdonk, and D. Vermeir. Supporting user interaction with oodb's: a declarative approach. In *Proceedings of the International Conference on Database and Expert System Applications*, pages 210–215, Berlin, 1991. Springer Verlag.

Sketching Editor for Engineering Design

M. Stolpmann, D. Roller

University of Stuttgart, Institute of Computer Science, Breitwiesenstraße 20-22, W7000
Stuttgart 80, Germany

Abstract

In this paper an editor for engineering sketches is presented that includes an innovative, easy-
to-use user interface which is capable of automatic online beautification of hand drawn sketches.
This editor is part of GRIPSS (GRaphical Idea-Processing & Sketching System), a research
project at the University of Stuttgart, Germany. Primary application areas for this novel
approach to computer assistance are the early design stages in engineering. The user interface is
based on a LCD tablet, representing an integrated input/output device. In combination with a
software system the problems with menu hierarchies and a lot of different operating states have
been overcome. An extremely natural handling of the editor and immediate optical feedback
directly on the input device has been achieved.

Keywords:

Graphical user interface, sketching editor, conceptional design, idea documentation, CAD, CIM
chain, computer-aided creativity

1. ROLE OF SKETCHES IN ENGINEERING

A significant part in engineering deals with highly creative work. There, it is essential to
document new ideas. Typically sketches are the medium to capture the results and preserve
them for later use. Computer support of highly creative activities like the conceptional design
phase in engineering has not been investigated much by now. Thus, almost all contemporary
CAD implementations are not really appropriate for the important task of translating an idea
into a sketch, just at the moment the idea is born.

In this paper an editor for engineering sketches is presented. Today, sketches normally are
drawn by hand using pencil & paper. Still there is very little computer support for this task.
However, sometimes CAD-systems or drawing programs are misused for this application! On
the one hand, sketches on paper often lack clarity. Besides their frequently untidy look they are
only accessible and interpretable by the developer him/herself. Efficient search for information in
such documents is impossible. Nevertheless, sketches represent an important part of the know-

610

how - and thereby capital - of a company. On the other hand, misused standard software is not able to satisfy the users needs. Frequently, the reason lies in their powerful but complex user interface. Often command structures are hierarchically organized and therefore typically several keystrokes and/or selection picks are needed even to draw a simple line. This work presents some actual results of the development of a CA-tool dedicated to the task of drawing sketches directly into a computer.

Engineering sketches typically are created in a state of highly mental concentration - therefore a system which allows the user to draw them directly into the computer has to be very natural and easy to use. Particularly, it is untolerable for the user to work through menu hierarchies and different operating states [1]. So, we have chosen the user interface to mimic and extend the conventional paper & pencil environment as far as possible. The developed editor provides a lot of innovative features:

- automatic on-line beautification: graphics input is beautified so that sketches become more accurate and tidy (Fig. 1); this includes the recognition of geometric primitives (like lines, circles, ...) based on the strokes drawn as well as the consideration of geometric constraints (such as horizontal lines and concentric circles)
- LCD-tablet with direct optical feedback; text is entered via the normal keyboard, not drawn character by character with the stylus (as in some pen-computer applications)
- gestures instead of hierarchical menus: where necessary, the system is controlled by gestures rather than menus (example: gesture to delete an object)
- enterprise-wide database: all sketches are stored in a central database; retrieval software supports search in the complete archive, so sketches become available for all developers of a company [1]
- CAD data interface: the data structures of GRIPSS have been designed for transfer to CAD-systems; so sketches or parts of it can be converted into a specific CAD data format.

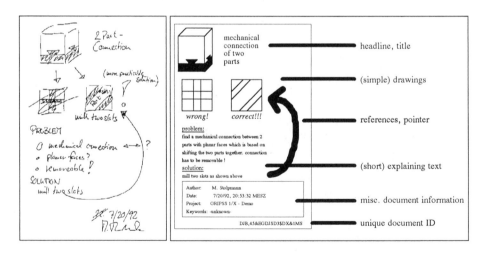

Figure 1: Original sketch (left) and preprocessed result (right)

Results of a study which compared the effectiveness of the used LCD-digitizer among common input devices like mouse, trackball and normal digitizers without direct optical feedback have shown that the I/O-device chosen is most appropriate for sketch input. In fact, the concept of this sketching editor does not only try to change the medium for sketches: it has far-reaching implications on the communication flow within a company. One goal in the GRIPSS project is to develop a powerful and flexible groupware-tool based on this sketching editor.

2. SYSTEM ARCHITECTURE

The software architecture of the sketching system consists of the following main modules (cf. Figure 2):

- the actual interactive sketching editor with the capability of on-line beautification of strokes;
- an I/O-module for the communication between LCD-tablet and the editor kernel;
- some application specific modules which allow the definition and handling of special gestures (like dimension arrows or other particular symbols);
- the document database and the corresponding database interface;
- the (selective) output modules;
- and an option to use scanned data, which is targeted to convert (old) paper-drawn sketches into the electronic system.

By now, the module for scanner input is rather limited in respect to the complexity of graphics compared to the interactive input (due for instance to the missing temporal sequence of the elements and drawing speed).

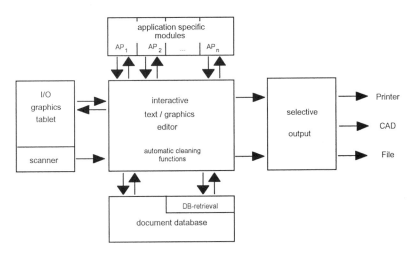

Figure 2: GRIPSS software architecture

Currently, the GRIPSS prototype environment consists of an personal computer using the DX 486/50 processor and a Wacom LCD-digitizer. The software is developed in C++ under DOS. A port to a pen-based operating system is planned.

3. SKETCH INTERPRETATION

Sketches are combined of single strokes; each stroke is a representation of the curve the user has drawn with the stylus without lifting it from the tablet. The internal representation of a stroke consists of a set of digitized points on an integer lattice as well as sequence information for these points. Because of the fixed digitizing rate, the sequential points may not represent continuous lines. Rather, holes that just stem from the digitizing process may occur. Therefore a recognition method is needed that is robust against this kind of distortion. Figure 3 shows two examples for the interpretation of simple strokes. The problems to be solved for the sketch interpretation can be divided into three parts:

- geometry recognition: the sketching system has to classify strokes into a set of geometric primitives or recognize them as a gesture; additional problems arise in the case that the stroke does not represent a single primitive but a higher geometric object (like a square)
- constraints recognition: the beautification module has to recognize constraints like horizontal and vertical lines or concentric circles
- data structures for reuse in CAD: it should be possible to (selectively) transfer the sketching information into CAD-systems for further use. So the internal data structures of the sketching system must be prepared for this task. Essentially, this requires a clean distinction between different types of information, like texts, geometry and annotation.

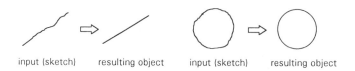

input (sketch)   resulting object   input (sketch)   resulting object

Figure 3: Cleaning functions for simple sketches

The method in the current implementation of the sketching system to perform the above mentioned problems is an extended version of the Hough transform [2,3]. This approach supports the recognition of lines and circles in the following manner: Every pixel of the digitized stroke is converted from object space to parameter space. There, a maximum search leads to the parameter values of the represented object (see Fig. 4 and 5). The implemented form of the Hough transform is specially adopted to the needs of the sketching editor. This includes the use of a recursive refinement of the parameter space (sometimes called adaptive Hough transform [4]) which resulted in a significant efficiency increase of the recognition process. Experiments have shown a very robust and stable nature of the extended Hough transform.

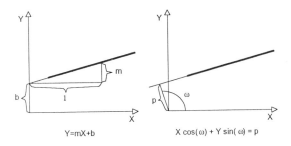

Figure 4: Transformation to parameter space for lines

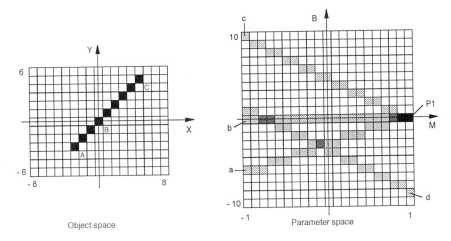

Object space

Parameter space

Figure 5: Discrete Hough transform (example)

Constraint recognition is embedded within local and global context, so constraints between several objects (for example concentric circles) as well as ´one-element-contraints´ (like horizontal lines) are handled [5]. Some typical constraints are shown in figure 6. A particular difficulty lies in the definition of efficient search strategies for possible constraints between a new object and the remaining objects in the GRIPSS data structure. Currently, heuristic rules which take sequence as well as placement information of the objects into account are used.

parallel   tangential   co-linear   orthogonal   vertical   horizontal   concentric

Figure 6: some examples for constraint recognition

A post processor enables the conversion of the internal data structures of the sketching editor to external CAD data formats. The key lies in the definition of the internal data structures for the editor: They need to be powerful and flexible enough to represent syntactical as well as semantical information about the sketches. Only if this additional information is archived during the sketching process, the interpretation of the sketching data into a CAD format is less crucial compared to scanned raster images [6].

User control of the editor is provided by gestures, which are recognized by the same techniques that are described for geometric elements. A syntactical analysis of recognized strokes distinguishes between gestures and geometry. Afterwards, the semantic information of the filtered gestures is parsed and executed.

4. CONCLUSION

In this paper the concept for a sketching editor with the capability of online beautification of hand drawn sketches has been presented. This editor provides an innovative user interface by utilizing a special I/O device that enables direct optical feedback. The sketching editor is part of a more comprehensive research project named GRIPSS (GRaphical Idea-Processing & Sketching System) at the University of Stuttgart, Germany.

First experiments have shown rather promising results. However, for industrial use, a lot more functionality is needed. As an example, more gestures and application specific modules have to be developed. Currently, other techniques for the sketching interpretation are examined. Some of these methods are based on spline approximation [7] and fuzzy logic [8].

5. REFERENCES

1 D. Roller and M. Stolpmann, GRIPSS: A Graphical Idea-Processing & Sketching System, in: "Interfaces in Industrial Systems for Production and Engineering", Elsevier, 1993

2 P. V. C. Hough, Method and means for recognizing complex patterns, US Patent No. 3.069.654 (1962)

3 R. O. Duda and P. E. Hart, Use of the Hough Transformation to Detect Lines and Curves in Pictures, CACM, Vol. 15, No. 1 (1972)

4 J. Illingworth and J. Kittler, The Adaptive Hough Transform, IEEE Transactions on Pattern Analysis and Machine Intelligence, Vol. 9, No. 5 (1987)

5 D. Roller, Advanced Methods for Parametric Design, in: H. Hagen and D. Roller (eds.), "Geometric Modeling", Springer, 1991

6 G. Spur, F.-L. Krause and H. Jansen, Verfahren zur automatischen Zeichnungsinterpretation für CAD-Prozesse, ZwF 82, No. 5 (1987)

7 M. J. Banks and E. Cohen, Realtime Spline Curves from Interactively Sketched Data, Computer Graphics, Vol. 24, No. 2 (1990)

8 R. Zhao, Incremental Recognition of Hand-Sketched Diagram Graphics in Gestural Interfaces, in: R. Beale and J. Finlay, "Neural Networks and Pattern Recognition in Human Computer Interaction", Ellis Horwood, 1992

Contextual help for free with formal dialogue design

Ph. A. Palanque[a], R. Bastide[a] and L. Dourte[b]

[a] L.I.S., Université Toulouse I, Place Anatole France, 31042 Toulouse Cedex, France. Email: palanque@cix.cict.fr, bastide@cix.cict.fr

[b] D.I.R.O., Université de Montréal, C.P. 6128 succursale A, Montréal (Québec), H3C 3J7, Canada. Email: dourte@iro.umontreal.ca

Abstract

This paper presents how the contextual help system for a user-driven application may be generated automatically from the formal specifications of the application. In our case the formal specifications are based on Petri nets and the help system is built by transforming the Petri nets in an augmented transition network. This network is then used by the contextual help system in order to answer users' questions.

1. INTRODUCTION

The use of formal methods in the design process of user interfaces has been advocated by numerous research works [1, 2]. They allow for the making of concise, unambiguous and complete specifications of the dialogue part of human-computer interaction.

One formalism, Petri nets, have been used for a long time in the design of human-computer interfaces [3, 4].

In previous papers we have presented such a formal method based on Petri nets and integrated in an object-oriented framework [5, 6, 7]. Building on the huge amount of research work done in Petri net theory, this method allows to analyse and validate the dialogue specification in order to statically verify properties of the behaviour of the interface [8, 9].

This paper's aim is to demonstrate another benefit of this method, the ability to automatically generate an important part of the contextual help system in a way which is not usually achieved.

Contextual help is specifically concerned with the current state of human-computer interaction and should ideally answer three basic questions that the user may be interested in: *"what?"*, *"why not?"* and *"how?"*.

The question "what?" corresponds to the interrogation "What can I do from now on?". In user-driven interfaces, the screen presented to the user must reflect the internal state of the application. It is therefore possible to determine visually which actions are currently enabled. This feature is commonly achieved in most present software by greying out or otherwise inactivating the widgets which allow to trigger the actions that are not available.

The question "why not?" naturally comes to the user's mind as soon as he wishes to trigger an action whose triggering widget is currently greyed out. In current software, usually not only is the question unanswered but it cannot even be asked. Actually a user's action on a greyed out widget is simply ignored.

The question "How?" stands for "How can I make that action available again?". The answer to this question should naturally complement that of the question "why not?" by providing the sequence of commands to trigger in order to enable the desired command.

2. USER ACCESS TO CONTEXTUAL HELP

We model in this paper the Select-Cut-Copy-Paste functions of a word processing application to demonstrate how users may access the contextual help.

Novice users may be puzzled if they find several inactivated menu items when they open the Edit menu. For example, when there is no selection on the screen, the Cut and Copy functions are not available.

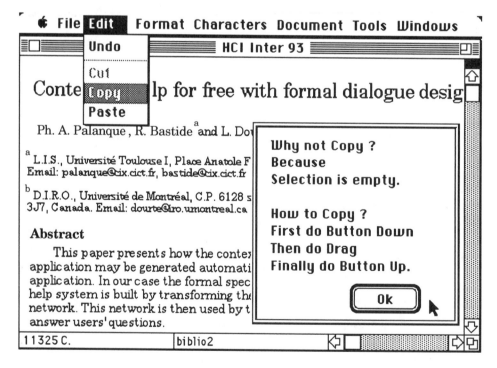

Figure 1. An example of a contextual help window within a word processing application.

In our proposed help system, the tentative triggering of an inactivated widget is interpreted as a request for contextual help on that item. This request results in the opening of a help window, presenting the answers to the questions "Why?" and "How?". An example of such an help window is shown in Figure 1: in the situation depicted, the user wished to copy while there was no selection. Figure 1 shows the open Edit menu of a word processing application from which the help has been triggered, as well as the help window with the answers generated automatically.

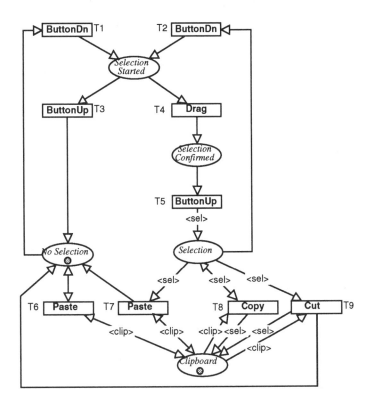

Figure 2. A high-level Petri net modelling the Select-Cut-Copy-Paste functions.

3. FORMAL DESCRIPTION OF THE DIALOGUE

The formal description of the Select-Cut-Copy-Paste functions is modelled by the high-level Petri net (HLPN) depicted in Figure 2. In the framework of our method we use a dialect of HLPNs, called Petri Nets with Objects (PNOs) [5], which is particularly well suited for the design of user-driven interfaces because of its ability to handle objects (in the object-oriented sense) instead of simple tokens (as in regular Petri nets) in the reachability of places. Such a simple example does not require the most advanced features PNOs, so the net modelling it can therefore be read and interpreted as a conventional predicate/transition net [10].

A net models the potential evolution of the dialogue in the following way: any user action is associated with one or several transitions in the net (the name of the action is inscribed inside each transition). An action may be triggered if at least one of its associated transitions is enabled in the net (i.e. each of the transition's input places holds at least one token). If the action may not be triggered (none of its associated transitions is enabled), the widget or menu item triggering this action must be greyed out. With this semantics, the question "What?" is automatically answered by the set of all enabled transitions in the net.

A marking m is an assignment of tokens to the places of a Petri net. The number and position of tokens may change during the execution of the Petri net [11]. The initial marking (i.e. before the start of the execution) shown on Figure 2 models the state of the interaction when the application is launched. In that state, only places *Clipboard* and *No Selection* hold a token: the clipboard is supposed to contain the results of previous interactions, and the selection is initially empty. From that state, the user may (for instance) try to select something by pushing the mouse button (transition ButtonDn), then dragging the mouse (transition Drag) and finally releasing the button (transition ButtonUp).

When a selection is done (i.e. there is a token in place *Selection*, and no token in place *No Selection*), the functions Copy and Cut are activated.

4. AUTOMATIC HELP GENERATION

The question "Why not?" may be answered by examining the net's marking (as may be done for the question "What?"): an action is unavailable only if none of its associated transitions is enabled by the current net marking. The question may be answered by listing all the places that lack a token in order for one of its associated transition to be enabled. For example, from the initial marking stated on Figure 2, the function Copy is not available because the place *Selection* holds no token. The answer to the question "Why not Copy?" is therefore "Because Selection is empty".

The answer to the question "How?" requires the use of formal techniques from Petri net theory, namely the construction of the net's **reachability graph** [11], which may be done automatically. In a reachability graph, each node represents a reachable marking of the net, and an arc flowing from node n1 to node n2 corresponds to the transition whose occurrence transforms marking n1 into marking n2. A reachability graph is, in finite cases, a finite state automaton, or an augmented transition network [12] if there is an infinite set of nodes [6].

The reachability graph corresponding to the net in Figure 2 is depicted in Figure 3. The markings must be read in the order (*Selection Started, Selection Confirmed, No Selection, Selection, Clipboard*). This graph is a finite state automaton whose initial state is the marking (0,0,1,0,1). From this initial state, for example, there is no arc labelled with Copy, which means that the action Copy is not available.

To answer the question "How?", the reachability graph must be used in the following way: starting from the current state, we must proceed in a breadth first search in the graph, looking for a state featuring an output arc labelled with the desired action. When the path is found, the answer consists in listing the sequence of commands labelling the arcs on the path. The breadth first search ensures that this sequence is the shortest one.

For example, starting from the initial state outlined, the Copy command is not available. The search on the reachability graph provides the following path to activate it: ButtonDn, Drag, ButtonUp; the answer to question "How to Copy?" would therefore be:
First do Button Down
Then do Drag
Finally do Button Up.

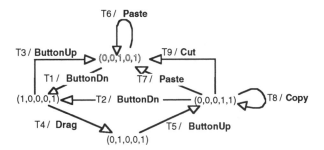

Figure 3. Reachability graph of the Petri net modelling the Select-Cut-Copy-Paste functions.

The answers to both questions "Why not?" and "How?" are shown in Figure 1, as computed by the help system. Obviously, a little more work would be necessary to generate more correct English output. This could be achieved by associating a natural language help message with each transition of the Petri net.

5. CONCLUSION

This paper only presents the automatic generation of contextual help which is part of a more general interface design method integrating Petri net modelling into the object-oriented approach. The method, called Petri Nets with Objects, addresses the well-known drawbacks of classical Petri nets by allowing the structuring of models in an object-oriented way (encapsulation, inheritance, client-server relationship, etc.). A design process for building user-driven interfaces is supported by the method by providing a set of methodological rules helping the designer to build his models [13].

Actually our efforts are on the building of a development environment supporting this method. This environment will integrate a graphical presentation editor, a syntactic editor allowing the edition of PNOs, several analysis modules allowing to prove design properties of the models and a PNO interpreter acting as a run-time kernel.

6. REFERENCES

1   U.H. Chi, Formal specification of user interfaces: a comparison and evaluation of four axiomatic approaches. *IEEE Transactions on Software Engineering 11*, 8 (August 1985), 671-685.

2   W.R. Van Biljon, Extending Petri nets for specifying man-machine dialogues. *International Journal of Man-Machine Studies 28*, (1988), 437-455.

3   M. Zizman, *A System for Computerisation of Office Procedures*, Ph.D. thesis, Warton School of Management, 1977.

4   H. Oberquelle, Human-machine interaction and role/function/action-nets. In W. Brauer, W. Reisig and G. Rosenberg, eds., *Petri nets: applications and relationships to other models of concurrency*, Lecture Notes in Computer Science 254 & 255, Springer-Verlag, Berlin, 171-190.

5   C. Sibertin-Blanc, High level Petri nets with data structure. In *6th European Workshop on Petri Nets and Applications* (June 1985, Espoo, Finland).

6   R. Bastide and P. Palanque, Petri nets with objects for the design, validation and prototyping of user-driven interfaces. In D. Diaper et al., eds., *Human-Computer Interaction - INTERACT'90*, North-Holland, 1990, pp. 625-631.

7   R. Bastide and C. Sibertin-Blanc, Modelling a flexible manufacturing system by means of Cooperative Objects. In *Computer Applications in Production and Engineering: Integration Aspects (CAPE'91)*, North-Holland.

8   P. Palanque, *Modélisation par Objets Coopératifs Interactifs d'interfaces homme-machine dirigées par l'utilisateur*. Thèse de doctorat de l'Université Toulouse I (France), 1992.

9   P. Palanque, C. Sibertin-Blanc and R. Bastide, Validation du dialogue par analyse d'une spécification fondée sur les réseaux de Petri. In *Actes IHM'92 Quatrièmes journées sur l'ingénierie des interfaces homme-machine* (30 nov., 1 et 2 déc. 1992, Paris), Telecom Paris, 1992, pp. 121-127.

10 H.J. Genrich, Predicate/transition nets, in W. Brauer, W. Reisig and G. Rosenberg, eds., *Petri nets: applications and relationships to other models of concurrency*, Lecture Notes in Computer Science 254 & 255, Springer-Verlag, Berlin, 207-247.

11 J.L. Peterson, *Petri Net Theory and the Modeling of Systems*. Prentice-Hall, Englewood Cliffs, N.J., 1981.

12 W.A. Wood, Transition network grammars for natural language analysis. *Communications of the ACM 13*, 10 (October 1970), 591-606.

13 P. Palanque, R. Bastide, L. Dourte and C. Sibertin-Blanc, Design of user-driven interfaces using Petri nets and objects. In *Fifth Conference on Advanced Information Systems Engineering (CAISE'93)* (8-11 June 1993, Paris).

A Method for Generating Messages on the On-line Help System Based on a User Model and a Situational Model

Y. Kobayashi and M. Nagata

Dept. of Administration Engineering, Faculty of Science and Technology, KEIO University
3-14-1 Hiyoshi, Yokohama 223, JAPAN
Tel. +81-45-563-1141 Fax +81-45-563-5979 Email yuyu@ae.keio.ac.jp

Abstract

Messages sent from the existing on-line help systems are either extremely simple or too difficult for the novice user to comprehend. On the other hand, these messages are often too narrow in context for the expert user. One of the reasons for this is that the messages are designed on the assumption that only one "typical" human model represents all users. In this paper a method is proposed for generating suitable on-line help system messages for each user level. In order to implement this a user model is introduced reflecting the skills of each user and a situational model for each type of usage. The idea being to create a user model and situational model where suitable messages are generated. In this paper these models and our prototype on-line help system for the Emacs editor are discussed. Results of experimental use are also presented.

1. INTRODUCTION

Interactive computer systems providing on-line help facilities have been widely used for some considerable time. Existing on-line help systems (for example, the Emacs editor system) provide various facilities. However, if the messages sent from the on-line help system are unsuitable for the user, they are of little worth or assistance. Most of messages from such systems are too simplistic for a novice user to understand. Moreover, they often include difficult technical terms. On the other hand, these messages are commonly too short for an expert user. Such messages do not supply suitable information for the user. One of the reasons for this situation is that the messages are designed on the assumption that only one "typical" person represents the user in general [1]. It is believed that the on-line help system should send messages which are adaptable to the individual user. To generate suitable messages to each user, a user model reflecting the skill of the user has been created incorporating a situational model for each type of use.

According to the user's ability to employ each command the model is divided between three classes. In the situational model there are seven situational patterns for usage. The system then generates suitable messages by the employment of these models.

A prototype on-line help system of the Emacs editor was implemented. This is an on-line help system where each command is assigned to a key. In addition, experimental results using the system are reported in this paper.

2. SCREEN MESSAGE PROBLEMS

Information on a screen is generally used less effectively [2]. Generally, it is impossible to produce a lot of detailed information on a screen, like that contained in a manual. Messages must be short and as direct as possible. However, suitable messages depend upon the intention of the user. If the intention changes, of course, ideal messages for the user also change.

For example, a message concerning the next-line command of the Emacs editor is shown in Figure 1. This message is not adequate for all users. For beginners, this message should be written more concretely without difficult technical terms, such as "ARG line", "buffer" and "newline". On the other hand, for experts, it should be a short comment rather than the long message of Figure 1. Different messages are needed for different users. As a first step it is necessary to identify the main factors on understanding messages to enable the generation of suitable messages.

next-line
Move cursor vertically down ARG line.
If there is no character in the target line exactly under the current column, the cursor is positioned after the character in that line which spans this column, or at the end of the line if it is not long enough.
If there is no line in the buffer after this one, a newline character is inserted to create a line and the cursor moves to that line.

Figure 1. Next-line command example message

3. USER AND SITUATIONAL MODELS

As mentioned above, the operator's ability to employ each command is closely related to understandability[3]. Moreover, the situation is also related to comprehension. For example, where an expert operator has not used a particular command for long period, it may be inferred that the operator needs a reminding as to the command assigned to the key. On the other hand, where the command has been recently referred to it could be expected that the user has greater interest in more detailed information concerning the command and its convenient use. Here a method is proposed to reflect the various skills of the operator and the surrounding situation. This method is implemented by the use of two models, a user model and a situational model.

The user model consists of a command skills index assigned for each user. Three skill levels:- novice, amateur and an expert levels are assigned. All operators would belong to one of these three levels. For example, if an editor application operator is a beginner then they would be classified as being at the novice level for all commands. The situational model consists of usage patterns. The following seven patterns were created for the editor experiment.

1. Frequent use of the on-line help
2. Using the on-line help reference on an command sequence error
3. Using the on-line help reference for a command not used for a considerable period
4. Using the on-line help reference for a command used frequently
5. Using the on-line help reference for a command whose relational command has not been used to date
6. Using the on-line help reference a command used immediately before
7. Others

A operator can only belong to one pattern at a time. Where a operator can belong to two or more patterns, they are classified to one of the patterns in order of precedence. The precedence is as listed in the above pattern order. For example, if an operator can plausibly belong to both pattern 2 and/or 3, then they are classified as pattern 2.

4. METHOD FOR GENERATING MESSAGES

A method for generating messages is proposed as follow: When a operator selects the on-line help system, the situational model judges the situation and the user model indicates the skill level for each command. According to this, the system interprets the intention of the user and shows the corresponding message adapted to the operators needs. This process is summarized in Figure 2.

The principle is to identify the operator's needs according to the following guidelines: The situation is selected by reviewing the prevailing conditions. A level of skill is then determined according to the number of times and the ratio of errors for the command selected. For example, if a operator uses of a command 30 or more times and the ratio of errors is less than or equal to twenty percent, then that person is classified as an expert concerning that command.

We use the following parameters by this method.

- A name of the operator
- Recent history of using each command
- Recent history of using all commands
- Times of using each command
- Error rate for each command
- Interval between use of each command

These parameters are updated according to the individual operator [4].

624

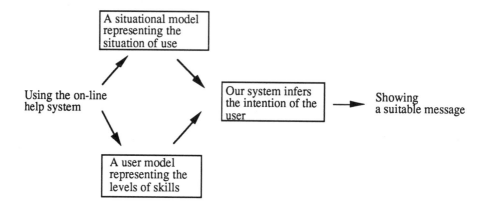

Figure 2. System outline

5. EXPERIMENTAL IMPLEMENTATION

This model has been used on an limited version of the Emacs editor [5] on-line help system according to the above-mentioned parameters. This was written in the Lisp language on the Sun workstation. This editor has ten commands for moving cursors: Four commands (forward-char, backward-char, next-line, previous-line) are specified as basic commands and six other commands (forward-word, backward-word, beginning-of-line, end-of-line, beginning-of-buffer, end-of-buffer) are nominated as advanced commands. The system provides only one function, which is to search through keys assigned to commands.

To evaluate the effectiveness of the method, two types of experiments were carried out using the prototype system; one is to compare our system with the traditional on-line help system (Experiment 1). The other is to test the suitability of the messages (Experiment 2). In the experiment six beginners are asked to use the editor to solve programming exercises of the Lisp language employing the on-line help system. The following two directions were given to the six students.

1. "Write a program transforming mathematical expressions into fully parenthesized expressions."
2. "Write a program transforming fully parenthesized expressions into expressions in the Polish notation."

The following outlines the procedures and results of the experiment.

Experiment 1

Four students were divided into two groups, A and B. They resolved the set exercises through the application of the following procedures.

A group
Questions 1 (using trial system) → Questions 2 (using the traditional system)
B group
Questions 1 (using the traditional system) → Questions 2 (using trial system)

Numerical times of command usage were made for A group and compared with that of the B group (Table 1).

Experiment 2

During the exercise, two students were asked to reply to a questionnaire concerning the suitability of the message. The questionnaire was provided by the system. The results are shown in Figure 3.

In Experiment 1, for Group A (operators who used the trial system first) the total number of times commands are used is fewer than that for the Group B group (operators who use the traditional system first). Moreover, the number of times advanced commands are used by Group A is greater than that for Group B. This clearly shows how the Group A operators operated more efficiently than Group B operators. In Experiment 2, it is found that the correct ratio is 68.4 percent, confirming that most of messages given by the trial system are suitable.

Table 1.
Comparring the number of times of using commands

	A group		B group	
	A1	A2	B1	B2
basic commands	301	429	572	668
forward-char	83	199	196	432
backward-char	184	180	359	209
next-line	10	14	4	6
previous-line	24	36	13	21
advanced commands	45	24	5	14
sum	346	453	579	682

626

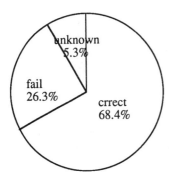

Figure 3. Evaluation of message suitability

6. CONCLUSION

The effectiveness of on-line help facilities primarily depends on the messages sent from the system. Here a prototype on-line help system has been proposed for generating suitable messages reflecting the skills of the operator and the operator situation. Even though the experiments are of limited nature and scale, the results attained have confirmed the effectiveness of the system. Many interactive software systems are able to gather data to create user and situational models during their execution. However, the method introduced here is unique in that it employs both a user and situational model which is found to be useful in integrating the on-line help system of many interactive systems.

7. REFERENCES

1   E. Rich, Users are individuals: individualizing user models, Int. J. Man-Machine Studies, 18, pp. 199-214 (1983)
2   B. Shneiderman, Designing the User Interface, Nikkei McGraw-Hill Inc. (1987)
3   M. Nagata and S. Nakajima, A Method for Generating Messages of the Interactive Software Based on the Individual User Model, J. of Institute of Electronics, Information, and Communication Engineers, Vol. J70-D, 11, pp. 2077-2082 (1987) (in Japanese)
4   R.B. Allen, User models: theory, method, and practice, Int. J. Man-Machine Studies, 32, pp. 511-543 (1990)
5   T. Yuasa and M. Hagiya, A Primer of Common Lisp, Iwanami Inc. (1986) (in Japanese)

User responses to an editor supporting a syntactic selection method

Alice Dijkstra@, Carla Huls#, Han Damen#

@ Unit of Experimental and Theoretical Psychology, Leiden University, P.O. Box 9555, 2300 RB Leiden, The Netherlands
# Nijmegen Institute for Cognition and Information (NICI), Nijmegen University, P.O. Box 9104, 6500 HE Nijmegen, The Netherlands

Abstract
Present-day text editors only allow users to apply delete, copy, move, etc., operations to arbitrary text fragments, and to typographically defined text fragments such as characters, word-like fragments, lines, and paragraphs. This paper investigates the usefulness of a text editor equipped with a facility that enables users to select and manipulate linguistically defined text fragments, e.g. sentences, constituents (containing one or more words) and words, by simple key-strokes. We present the results of an empirical evaluation study where users are offered this facility in addition to traditional methods of operating on text fragments. We tested whether or not users would actually decide to apply the functions to linguistic arguments and how we could positively influence that decision by means of our user interface design.

1. INTRODUCTION

Van Waes (1991) observed that writers when using a computer instead of pen and paper do not revise more often but rather more locally. Almost 45% of the revisions involved sentence or word-sized text fragments. Another 30% of the revisions involved parts of sentences. Dijkstra and Huls (1992) observed that this percentage included a specific set of sentence positions and sentence fragments: BEGIN-SENTENCE, END-SENTENCE, NOUN PHRASE and PREPOSITIONAL PHRASE. All these revision arguments share the characteristic that they are linguistically defined (positions in) constituents in a linguistic representation. Furthermore, they observed that a large number of errors were made with respect to capitalization, punctuation and spacing which were the result of the user being unable to precisely select the appropriate piece of text to be moved, deleted, or copied. Present-day word processors do allow users to apply functions to the argument word. Unfortunately however, their definition of a word is not a linguistic one but a typographic one, which is often not correct if the word is followed or preceded by a punctuation mark. If the typographic definition and the linguistic definition do not coincide, or the user wants to manipulate a larger linguistic text fragment, then especially spacing errors are likely to occur.

These errors might have been prevented if the text editor had access to a (partial) linguistic representation (cf. Terhorst 1992), and moreover, the user had applied the desired operations to the linguistic arguments in this representation. A linguistic editor would, for example, support a function MOVE CONSTITUENT to BEGIN-SENTENCE, and be able to evaluate the linguistic consequences of the move-operation, thereby maintaining proper capitalization and spacing. Huls and Dijkstra (1992) conclude that such functionality would minimize the distance between user goals and device operations (cf. Hutchins et al. 1986; Norman 1986; Moran 1983; Payne et al. 1990). If a writer's goal is to move the prepositional phrase [*with your word processor*] in the sentence: [*It is not easy to delete certain parts of the sentence with your word processor.*] from the end to the beginning of that sentence, then he needs to execute a number of device operations.

Even if the phrase is precisely selected, spacing and capitalization have to be changed by hand. If on the other hand the user was working with a linguistic editor which can determine and manipulate the linguistic representation of that sentence, then he could attain his goal by means of one device operation, i.e. directly applying the move-action to the prepositional phrase as a unit. As a result, the user would not need to check the selection boundaries when selecting such a fragment, and the editor itself would maintain proper spacing and could even maintain proper punctuation.

Obviously, such linguistic functionality requires an adjustment of the user interface such that it is possible to select linguistically defined fragments easily. We may not expect users to consciously know what the proper linguistic representation of a sentence is. Therefore, we think we should devise an interface that guides the users in their conception of this representation.

An important recommendation resulting from our research is that linguistically based revision strategies deserve linguistically based support. The notion of a linguistic editor is not completely new. Several types of structure-recognizing editors that facilitate writing and editing source code are already being used by programmers to their satisfaction. Word processing systems, however, do not support such a facility for natural language. The question still is whether or not users will actually use the support that is offered by such a linguistic editor. More specifically, we have investigated which interface characteristics will encourage people to use it. In this paper we present the results of an experiment in which we tested whether — given two different types of interfaces — users would use a selection method that allows them to directly select linguistically defined constituents, noun phrases and prepositional phrases in this experiment, as arguments by means of one keystroke.

2. METHOD

We implemented a simple editor that imitated the behaviour of a linguistic editor. Subsequently, we asked seventy-two psychology students who only had minimal experience with word processing systems and could be expected to have a basic knowledge of grammar to participate in the experiment. They were asked to select and delete sentence fragments (six noun phrases, six prepositional phrases and four arbitrary strings) from sixteen sentences. A text fragment could be selected by positioning the cursor in it and then pushing one of three predefined selection keys that were labelled SELECT CHARACTER, SELECT WORD or SELECT CONSTITUENT. A selected range could repeatedly be expanded by pushing the EXPAND key. The selected range was highlighted in reverse video. After that, it could be deleted by pushing a key labelled REMOVE.

Nineteen grammatically correct sentences were shown on the screen. Their syntactic structure had been analysed in advance and was coded in a background version of the sentence file. On the desk there was a printed piece of paper that also showed nineteen sentences. Each sentence on the screen could be changed into the one on paper by deleting a specific part of the sentence. The first three sentences were used by the instructor to demonstrate each of the system's three selection methods. The order in which the methods were shown was counter-balanced between subjects.

There were two different user interface versions for this editor. In one version the smallest syntactically coherent phrase (noun phrase or prepositional phrase) in which the cursor was positioned was underlined (cf. Figure 1). When each test sentence was presented to the subject, the cursor was positioned at the beginning of the sentence, and the first constituent was underlined. If the subject moved the cursor into another constituent, then that constituent was underlined. In the other version no phrases were underlined.

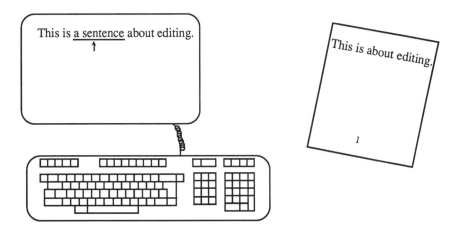

Figure 1. A snapshot at the moment that the cursor has been positioned in the phrase to be deleted of the version of the experimental editor with the interface that underlined syntactic constituents.

There were two experimental conditions in the design: *marked constituent* and *unmarked constituent*. Marking the constituent implied that the interface underlined the constituent, i.e. noun phrase or prepositional phrase, that, given a cursor position, would be selected if the SELECT CONSTITUENT key was pressed. In the other condition, the constituent in which the cursor was positioned by the subject was also deleted as a whole whenever the SELECT CONSTITUENT key was pressed, but it was not underlined. The subjects were randomly assigned to either experimental condition.

There were three possible types of phrases that had to be removed in order to change the sentence on screen into the sentence on paper. These phrases were either a noun phrase (in six sentences), a prepositional phrase (in six sentences) or an arbitrary control phrase (in four sentences). The experimenters scored the first selection method chosen for each sentence, either the character, the word or the constituent method. The number of times the select constituent method was chosen is the dependent variable, and it was measured for three types of phrases, i.e. noun phrase (NP), prepositional phrase (PP) and control phrase (CP).

At the end of each session the subjects were asked for their subjective impression of the use of the text editor and the selection methods: why did they use a particular function, did they like the new constituent method?

3. QUALITATIVE AND QUANTITATIVE RESULTS

Of the seventy-two intended subjects only sixty-four actually participated in the experiment. They generally appreciated the extra selection method supported by the experimental editor. They commented that selecting a constituent by means of one keystroke was very useful and easy. Those subjects that had been assigned to the marked-constituent condition, i.e. the user interface that underlined linguistic constituents, said that underlining made it easy for them to choose the constituent selection method. As the user was shown what would be selected, he was prevented from making unnecessary selection mistakes.

There were also some negative comments, most of which were concerned with technical shortcomings of the experimental editor. The most important one was that the editor was too slow. Another comment from those subjects assigned to the marked constituent condition was that they thought the underlining was not always correct. In fact, the underlining sometimes did not coincide with what they incorrectly assumed to be a constituent. This was an effect of our experimental design combined with the subject's imperfect conception on what a syntactic constituent is. In the control sentences the subjects had to select an arbitrary string of characters, i.e. a non-syntactic fragment. At the same time the syntactic constituent in which the cursor was positioned was underlined, as in all other sentences. This had some subjects think that the wrong part of the sentence was underlined. Apparently, the instructions nor the interface itself offered the user enough information in that respect.

We performed a number of statistic analyses on our data. The means and standard deviations of the number of times the constituent selection method was chosen per phrase type and per condition is shown in Table 1. In both conditions the constituent selection method was chosen far more often than chance would predict, whenever a NP or PP constituent had to be selected (prediction = 2). Whenever CPs, i.e. non-constituents, had to be selected the constituent selection method was less often chosen than would be predicted by chance alone (prediction = 1.333). This indicates that, whichever condition the subjects were assigned to, they preferred the constituent selection method when the task was to select and delete a NP or PP, while this method was not preferred whenever a CP had to be selected and deleted.

Table 1. Means and standard deviations of the number of times the constituent selection method was chosen for the three types of phrases in the two conditions.

| | | Condition | |
		marked constituent	*unmarked constituent*
Noun Phrase:	Means	3.656	4.938
(NP)	Standard Deviation	1.638	1.645
Prep. Phrase:	Means	4.500	5.312
(PP)	Standard Deviation	1.646	1.306
Control Phrase:	Means	0.688	0.250
(CP)	Standard Deviation	0.998	0.672

A multivariate analysis on the dependent variable for the three phrase types shows that underlining has a significant (with $\alpha = 0.05$) effect on the choice of the selection method (MANOVA: $p = 0.003$). A univariate analysis shows that this effect originates in significant positive effects for NP and PP selection and a significant negative effect for CP selection (ANOVA: NP: $p = 0.003$; PP: $p = 0.032$); CP: $p = 0.044$). So, in the marked constituent condition, the constituent selection method was more frequently used whenever a constituent had to be selected, and less frequently whenever a non-constituent had to be selected. These effects were significant. We also found a strong correlation between NP and PP, concerning the selection method chosen ($r = 0.7568$, $p < 0.001$).

4. DISCUSSION

We summarized the results from previous investigations which show the theoretical usefulness of editors supporting linguistic functionality. The remaining question we tested in the present experiment was whether or not users would actually decide to use such linguistic functionality and how we could positively influence that decision by means of our user interface design.

The experiment confirmed our hypothesis that subjects would actually use the constituent selection method if appropriate and not use it if inappropriate. The use of the constituent selection method was stimulated even more if the user interface — by means of underlining — guided the subjects in their understanding of the linguistic concept constituent. Following the experiment, the subjects commented positively on the availability of this linguistic selection method. On the basis of these results we conclude that more usability studies are justified.

Acknowledgements
We were very fortunate to have a number of first year psychology students who enthusiastically helped us conduct the experiment. We also thank Guus Peeters for the implementation of the imitation linguistic editor, Nick Terhorst for his work on the NP/PP grammar, and Gerard Kempen, Jan Peter de Ruiter, Fenna Poletiek and Edwin Bos for commenting on earlier versions of this paper.

This research was carried out within the framework of the research programme *Human-Computer Communication Using Natural Language (MMC)*, subproject *Description of the Functionality of an Editorial Support Environment*. The MMC-programme is sponsored by SENTER, AND Software, Digital Equipment B.V. and SUN Microsystems Nederland b.v.

5. REFERENCES

Dijkstra, A. and Huls, C. (1992). Searching for Linguistic Arguments: a preliminary assessment of the usefulness of linguistic representations in an Editorial Support Environment. In G.C. van der Veer, M.J. Tauber, S. Bagnara and M. Antalovits (eds.) Proceedings of the Sixth European Conference on Cognitive Ergonomics (ECCE 6). European Association of Cognitive Ergonomics, CUD, Roma, Italy.

Huls, C. and Dijkstra, A. (1992). A Structured Design of Word Processing Functionality. In A. Monk, D. Diaper and D. Harrison, (eds.) People and Computers VII: Proceedings of the HCI '92 Conference. Cambridge University Press, USA.

Hutchins, E., Hollan, J. and Norman, D. (1986). Direct Manipulation Interfaces. In: D. Norman and S. Draper, (eds.) User Centered System Design: New Perspectives on Human-Computer Interaction. Lawrence Erlbaum Associates, Hillsdale, New Jersey.

Moran, T. (1983). Getting into a system: External-internal task mapping analysis. Proceedings of the CHI '83 conference on human factors in computing systems, 45-49. ACM, New York.

Norman, D. (1986). Cognitive Engineering. In: D. Norman and S. Draper, (eds.) User Centered System Design: New Perspectives on Human-Computer Interaction. Lawrence Erlbaum Associates, Hillsdale, New Jersey.

Payne, S., Squibb, H. and Howes, A. (1990). The nature of device models: the yoked state space hypothesis and some experiments with text editors. Human-computer interaction, 5, 415-444.

Terhorst, N. (1992). A linguistic editor, SPIN-MMC Research Report no. 26. NICI, Nijmegen, The Netherlands.

Waes, L. van (1991). De computer en het schrijfproces: De invloed van de tekstverwerker op het pauze- en revisiegedrag van schrijvers. [The computer and the writing process: The influence of the word processor on the pausing and revision behaviour of writers.] (PhD-thesis) Universiteit Twente, Wijsbegeerte en Maatschappijwetenschappen, Enschede, The Netherlands. (in Dutch, with an English summary).

Cognitive processing and hypermedia comprehension: A preliminary synthesis

David G. Payne[a], Michael J. Wenger[a], and Maxine S. Cohen[b]

[a]Department of Psychology and Center for Cognitive and Psycholinguistic Sciences, [b]Department of Computer Science, State University of New York at Binghamton, Binghamton, NY, USA

Abstract

Three experiments investigating the nature of the psychological processes that may be critical to successful comprehension and retention of hypertext are described. Together, these experiments illustrate the utility of theoretical tools and empirical preparations borrowed from studies of reading linear text. In addition, the results call into question previous claims about the processing demands imposed by hypertext and other forms of nonlinear text.

1. EXPERIMENTS 1 AND 2: AMOUNT AND TYPE OF PROCESSING DEMANDS

Experiments 1 and 2 explored the applicability of theoretical constructs that have been useful in understanding the psychological processes involved in reading linear text and directly tested some of the claims that have been made about the cognitive demands imposed by hypertext. These two experiments differed only in the familiarity of the stimulus texts; therefore, we report them together, noting differences as appropriate. In both experiments, we used a dual-task approach, pairing reading with other types of processing and retention requirements. In addition, we manipulated the type of cognitive processes induced by the text by manipulating text form. These manipulations allowed us to test the usefulness of two theoretical constructs employed in studies of the reading of linear text: the notions of (a) a limited capacity working memory (Baddeley, 1986) and (b) material-appropriate processing (Einstein, McDaniel, Owen, & Cote, 1990).

1.1. Subjects and Design

Experiment 1 employed 40 and Experiment 2 employed 50 Introductory Psychology students at SUNY-Binghamton. The experiment was conducted as a 2 (Form: Causation, Description) x 2 (Type: Hypertext, Linear Text) x 3 (Concurrent Load: Digit, Spatial, Control) mixed-factorial. Form was manipulated between subjects while Type and Concurrent Load were manipulated within subjects.

1.2. Materials

Twenty-four texts (12 in each experiment) drawn from scientific and technical publications were used as stimulus materials. Six of the texts in each experiment were structured according to antecedent/consequent relationships, a text form referred to as Causation (Meyer, Brandt, & Bluth, 1980; Meyer & Freedle, 1984). The remaining six texts in each experiment were structured according to associations among subtopics of a single major topic, a text form referred to as Description (Meyer et al., 1980; Meyer & Freedle, 1984). Each text contained 700-900 words and was converted into both linear and hypertext online documents. The twelve texts used in Experiment 2 were selected to be more familiar than those used in Experiment 1 using a method described in Spyridakis and Wenger (1991).

The concurrent memory load tasks required subjects to maintain either a series of random digits or an abstract figure (a 4 x 4 matrix) composed of 10 periods and six pound signs while reading, with a test for retention given at the end of the node read while the load was maintained. The control task involved presentation of a memory load at node boundaries without the requirement to maintain the load while reading (the test for retention of the load immediately followed the load).

All experimental texts were presented and subject responses were recorded using HyperWIN, an IBM hypertext product. All materials were presented on a 33 cm VGA color monitor controlled by a PC-compatible microcomputer. The concurrent load tasks were presented using a second PC-compatible microcomputer equipped with a 33 cm monochrome monitor.

1.3. Procedure

Each subject read a total of either six Causation or six Description texts, with three texts presented as Linear text and three presented as Hypertext. Subjects were tested individually in experimental sessions lasting approximately 100 min. The presentation of each of the six experimental texts followed the same basic pattern. Before the first node of every text a brief set of instructions was presented. In the hypertext versions, it was emphasized that if subjects should come across a node that they believed they had previously read then they should search for a node they had not read. The instructions for the hypertexts also emphasized that it was the subjects' responsibility to indicate when they felt that they had read all available nodes.

Following these instructions, the first concurrent memory load was presented (all load presentations were 8 sec in duration). In the digit and spatial load conditions, subjects then began reading; in the control condition, the probe item was presented immediately after the load was cleared from the screen. At the end of the node, subjects in the digit and spatial load conditions were presented with the probe item for the previous load. Immediately after responding subjects were presented with the next load after which they selected the next topic (a single choice in the linear texts) and continued reading. In the control condition, subjects received the next load and its probe.

At the end of each text subjects were given two min to write down as many node titles as they could remember. Subjects were then asked to rate their familiarity with the material discussed in the text. Following this, they responded to 10 multiple choice questions probing their comprehension of the text. Finally, they were presented with 15 pairs of node titles and were asked to indicate whether these nodes were linked in the text they had just read; this test was designed to probe subjects' recall of text structure.

1.4. Results

Unless otherwise noted, all results discussed here were significant at $p < 0.05$. Due to space limitations, we have omitted reporting values for inferential statistics and instead discuss results only in terms of statistical reliability. In addition we use the data from Experiment 1 to illustrate the results from both experiments, noting that the primary difference between the results for the two experiments was the level of overall performance.

With respect to performance on the concurrent load task, subjects produced a higher percentage of correct responses to probes in the control condition (89%) than they did while reading with a digit load (68%) or a spatial load (67%). Reaction times to correct responses to probes revealed a pattern consistent with the accuracy data, with responses being fastest for probes in the control condition (1363 msec), followed by responses to digit probes (1889 msec) then responses to spatial probes (2440 msec).

The important point to be made by the results so far is that there were no interactions of any of the experimental manipulations with text type (linear versus hypertext), indicating that the type of memory load did not affect subjects' behavior while reading hypertext any differently than it did when they were reading linear text.

Recall (proportion recalled), comprehension, and recall of structure were dependent on the number of nodes actually read. Thus, these three measures were conditionalized, i.e., they were calculated based on the nodes actually read by the subject. For recall of node titles, there were three effects of interest. First, recall was highest in the control condition (41%), followed by the spatial (38%) and digit (31%) conditions. When reading hypertexts, subjects recalled a higher percentage of node titles (41%) than they did when reading linear texts (33%). Finally, the type of load appeared to have different effects on the hypertexts and linear texts, depending on whether the text was Causation or Description (see Figure 1).

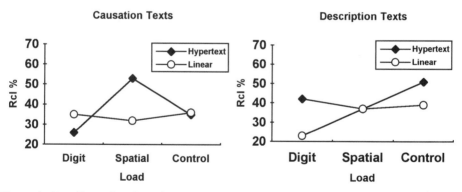

Figure 1: Recall as a function of text type and concurrent load, Experiment 1. The left panel shows recall for Causation texts while the right panel shows recall for Description texts.

For comprehension, subjects performed better when reading hypertexts (49%) than when reading linear texts (41%) and comprehension for subjects reading hypertext was best when reading was paired with a spatial concurrent load (see Figure 2). For recall of structure, performance was best when subjects read hypertext (68%) rather than linear text (52%).

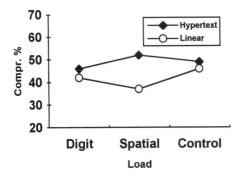

Figure 2: Comprehension as a function of text type and concurrent load, Experiment 1.

In summary, the results from the measures taken *while reading* suggest that reading hypertext does not induce any additional working memory load than does reading linear text, in contrast to claims that have been made about the possible additional cognitive overhead required by hypertext (e.g., Conklin, 1987). However, the measures taken *after reading* suggest that reading hypertext may impose a different type of processing than does linear text, with outcomes dependent both of the form of the text presented and the type of concurrent load, with results suggesting that hypertext may proportionally more processing of information about relations among subtopics when compared to linear text.

Two results from Experiment 1 suggested that these results should be accepted only tentatively. First, general levels of performance were relatively low, and second, subjects reported that their familiarity with the material in the texts was low. However, the results of Experiment 2, which employed materials of higher rated familiarity producing higher levels of overall performance, parallel those of Experiment 1 and directly support the conclusions drawn from Experiment 1.

2. EXPERIMENT 3: DIFFERENCES IN INFORMATION PROCESSING

The intent of this experiment was to collect performance data using measures that have been demonstrated to reliably predict comprehension and retention performance using linear text and determine if there were any systematic relationships between these measures and comprehension and retention of hypertext. Subjects read hypertext passages as in Experiments 1 and 2 and in addition performed several information processing tasks designed to identify possible important individual differences variables.

2.1. Subjects, Design, Materials, and Procedure

A total of 26 subjects, drawn from the same subject population as that used for Experiments 1 and 2, participated in the current experiment. The performance of each subject was assessed using four common measures of information processing, and correlations between these measures and the hypertext performance measures were calculated. The four information processing tasks were the following: (a) a test of working memory span (a measure commonly associated with performance in reading linear text), (b) a spatial processing task, measuring ability to remember and transform spatial information, (c) a letter matching task, measuring ability to match alphabetic stimuli along either physical or name dimensions, and (d) a choice reaction time task, a basic measure of processing speed. Four of the texts used in Experiment 2 were used as stimulus texts.

2.2. Results

Mean performance on the hypertext measures was calculated for each subject as an average for all texts read. These means were then subjected to a correlation analysis with the information processing measures. Table 1 presents the critical results of this analysis, showing those correlations that were significant at $p \leq 0.10$. The central point to note in this analysis is the degree to which measures of spatial/relational processing ability relate to the hypertext performance measures, providing support for the general conclusions drawn from Experiments 1 and 2, namely that relational processing is an important component of comprehension and retention of hypertext.

Table 1:
Significant task correlations, Experiment 3.

	Information Processing Measures					
	RCL	*SPA*	*SPR*	*PRT*	*NRT*	*CRT*
WPM		0.50		-0.34	-0.35	-0.72
REP						
COV	0.65					
RCL					-0.33	
COM	0.43		-0.36	-0.43		-0.45
STR						
WMS			0.38	0.50		

WPM = words/min (within-node reading rate), REP = number of repeated nodes, COV = proportion of text covered, RCL = recall, COM = comprehension, STR = structure recall, WMS = working memory span, SPA = spatial processing accuracy, SPR = spatial processing reaction time, PRT = physical match RT (letter matching), NRT = name match RT (letter matching), CRT = choice RT.

3. CONCLUSIONS

First, contrary to claims (e.g., Conklin, 1987), reading material presented within a hypertext format appears to place no more demands on the human information processor than does the act of reading linear text. Second, while reading hypertext may not impose more processing requirements than does reading linear text, it does appear to require a different balance of processing resources than does linear text, with hypertext requiring a higher proportion of relational processing than does linear text. Third, and perhaps most important for future research, the tools and the explanatory constructs used to gain an understanding of the cognitive processes at work in reading linear text can be applied usefully to the challenge of gaining an understanding of the cognitive processes at work in reading linear text.

4. REFERENCES

Baddeley, A. D. (1986). *Working memory.* Oxford: Clarendon Press.

Conklin, J. (1987). Hypertext: An introduction and survey. *IEEE Computer*, September, 1987, 17-41.

Einstein, G. O., McDaniel, M. A., Owen, P. D., & Cote, N. C. (1990). Encoding and recall of texts: The importance of material-appropriate processing. *Journal of Memory and Language, 29*, 566-581.

Meyer, B. J. F., & Freedle, R. O. (1984). Effects of discourse type on recall. *American Educational Research Journal, 21* (1), 121-143.

Meyer, B. J. F., Brandt, D. M., & Bluth, G. J. (1980). Use of top-level structure in text: Key for reading comprehension of ninth-grade students. *Reading Research Quarterly, 16*, 72-101.

Spyridakis, J. H., & Wenger, M. J. (1991). An empirical method of assessing topic familiarity in reading comprehension research. *British Educational Research Journal, 17* (4), 353-360.

Using argumentation to overcome hypertext's HCI failings

J.A.A.Sillince* and R.H.Minors[+]

*Sheffield University Management School, Crookesmoor Building, Conduit Road, Sheffield S10 1FL UK j.sillince@uk.ac.shef.pa

[+]Department of Computer Science, Regent Court, University of Sheffield, 211 Portobello Street, Sheffield S1 4DP UK. r.minors@uk.ac.shef.dcs

1. Hypertext's HCI problems.

Hypertext enables the user to move between distant pages according to her choice of an indexed item. Each page contains a set of keywords which lead to other pages. Thus each page contains information about the next layer of pages. This is very different from a book, which contains parts, and within them chapters, and within them pages, all in page number order. A book has a structure, which may be restrictive, whereas hypertext has little structure, which creates its own problems of high cognitive overhead (the user must memorise her own specially created structure for the document) and getting lost (caused by the lack of an ordering mechanism analogous to page numbering in a book).

2. What is special about argumentation.

Static features of argumentation (see Figures 1 and 2) comprise:

(1) **Toulmin structures**, of datum, warrant, and claim. For example, in the argument *'The sky is red and so it will be fine'*, the **datum** is *'The sky is red'*, the **warrant** is *'If the sky is red, it will be fine'*, and the **claim** is *'It will be fine'*.

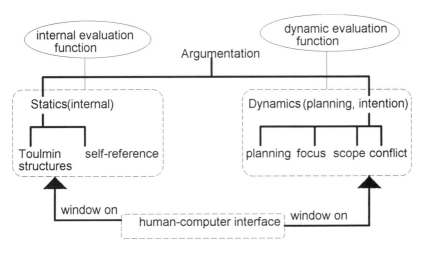

Figure 1.

defining feature	Toulmin structures	self-reference	focus	scope	conflict
tolerant of self-inconsistency	Possible to say 'A attacks A'	e.g. 'this argument is circular'	arguer avoids criticism if source of self-inconsistency kept out of focus	arguer avoids criticism if source of self-inconsistency made to seem irrelevant	Two opposed viewpoints inconsistent
not deductive	datum-to-claim warrants (or mappings) can be imperfect	first order logic does not include self-reference	focus defined inductively	No concept of relevance in first order logic	First order logic does not allow negotiation and compromise
emotional	emotions expressed as attainment of goals	emotion defined as 'awareness of imminent change in my belief X'	Belief X is defined by the semantic net in the focus of X.	Imminent change occurs not only in belief X but in relevant other beliefs	The goal is changing the beliefs of the opponent
value transfer	'good' transfered by proximity within text e.g. 'The shady crook Mr. X did Y'	Value transfer can itself be argued about	Focus influences the effect of value transfer	Scope influences the effect of value transfer	Two opponents means contrast between values of 'bad' and 'good'
about beliefs rather than knowledge	beliefs are datums which are warranted	argument nodes can contain argument nodes within themselves	There is no objective focus: it must be dynamically made	There is no objective scope: it must be dynamically made	Knowledge is not subject to conflict as is belief
strength-based	evaluation function	strength values propagate from one argument node to another	focus is where dynamic updating of strength values occurs	claims outside scope of argument have no strength	Strengths rather than true-false means that a continuum exists over which compromise is possible

Figure 2.

(2) **Self-reference**. For example, '*Argument X is good because Y said so*' is itself an argument.

Dynamic features of argumentation (see Figures 1 and 2) entail the areas of planning and intention. and comprise:

(1) **Focus**, or the agreed **current claim**.
(2) **Scope**, or the agreed set of **relevant** claims.
(3) **Conflict**, between opposed **goals** (**support** or **attack** of **main claim**).
(4) **Plans** (datum-claim chains supporting or attacking the main claim).

These features require their own evaluation function: there is a **static evaluation function** which evaluates **how good is an argument**, and a **dynamic evaluation function** which says **how good is a plan**. An account of our own approach to argumentation and a comprehensive bibliography is contained in Sillince and Minors (1991; 1992; 1993).

3. The distinction between focus and scope.

Past work attempting to apply discourse analysis to computer dialogue has had only a one-dimensional approach to dialogue focus: it is defined as the part of the mutual knowledge available to participants relevant at a particular point in the dialogue (Grosz and Sidner, 1986; Belkin *et.al.*, 1987). We shall suggest that an important distinction exists between **debate scope** and **argument focus.** In the middle of a debate, a participant changes track, and starts on a new line of argument. We understand its relevance, but we may complain that he has '*shifted his ground*' or that he '*hasn't answered the question*' but we continue to argue with him. This shift takes place within the scope of the debate. Say the current argument is that '*Because the sky is red the weather will be fine tomorrow*'. Let us suggest three distinct cases for a response to this argument:

- Case 1: Within focus and within scope: '*But the sky is not red*'.
- Case 2: Out of focus but within scope: '*But our climate is not dry*'.
- Case 3: Out of focus and out of scope: '*But London is in England*'.

It is clear that getting the opponent to agree a reclassification from Case 2 to Case 1 will be relatively easy ('*I believe that red sky meaning good weather originated in dusty climates*').

The reason why we need both concepts (focus and scope) is because in a long debate, the set of related claims (claims in the scope of the main claim that the debate is trying to establish) will grow very large, and yet we know from practical experience of such debates that it is not legitimate to keep switching between the different claims in this set. What this means is that even Case 2 type claims are not legitimate. Also we need to separate Cases 2 and 3 because the rules for dynamically legitimating Case 2 type claims will be different from those dynamically legitimating Case 3 type claims.

4. What kind of interface does it need?

An argumentation system needs a window onto both the static and the dynamic aspects. People get lost in hypertext because they cannot rephrase or recapitulate text. Hypertext offers a book, but the user wants to rewrite the book her own way: we shall call this dynamic user reclassification. The static and dynamic elements of argumentation enable us to specify the kind of system we are proposing. Focus and scope are things which people do to cope with the complexity of argumentation. They are means of linearising something which is not linear.

Focus shift is accepted gracefully by opponents as a concession of a point and in order to 'oil the wheels' of the argument, allowing it to progress. Politeness rules and conventions about withdrawal, attachment, commitment, deference and appeasement are all involved.

Scope, on the other hand, is to do with the inability to hold too many ideas in one's head at the same time. Some boundary must be drawn around what it is and is not permissible to argue about.

Conflict means there is not just one acceptable viewpoint. This immediately puts the user in centre stage and interests him.

Planning means that there is a clear intentional picture in which the current page and its predecessors fit. The user can look forwards (via perhaps several paths) to a goal (expressed as a claim). He can also look backward to evidence for the current page, or at pages which support or attack the current page.

Toulmin structures enable users to categorise text as datum, warrant, or claim. Users can say what implies or supports what, and in doing this, they are dynamically creating their own links between pages.

Self-reference enables users to treat these Toulmin structures as arguments themselves.

5. Does hypertext have this kind of interface?

HCI is mainly about making people feel comfortable. Argumentation is what people feel comfortable with. Hence they must be allowed to argue. Unfortunately hypertext is **monological:** it is a single viewpoint system which fails to compromise with the user's view. In contrast with hypertext, argumentation is **dialogical**. This requires some method of saying how strong an argument is (an evaluation function).

Also, hypertext does not have any intentional thread running through it which allows one to make judgements about goals or plans, in the way it is possible to do with argumentation.

Because the use of hypertext is not a real dialogue between the user and the system, in which both participants have some real discretion, the concepts of focus and scope have no meaning.

Hypertext is hierarchical and does not allow recursive graph structures required by self-reference. It does not enable users to encapsulate existing text. It does not automatically and dynamically generate new nodes. And it does not allow users to create their own inter-text links.

6. A proposed argumentation-based hypertext system.

The design starts with Marshall's idea that hypertext links can be created by datum-to-claim steps, thus allowing chaining of links and planning (Marshall, 1989). At each node there is a contextual menu which looks forwards or backwards. A **forwards** menu would contain the first few words of any claim C which lies on the path between the current claim and the main claim. These claims have been processed by using the current claim as a datum. A **backwards** menu contains the first few words of any claim which lies between the current claim and the initial information. These claims have been processed by using the initial information as a datum and the current claim as the resultant of this processing. Because argumentation requires dynamic node generation, **node granularity** is optimised dynamically too. There are different presentation modes such as **context mode, detailed mode,** and **explanation mode.** Context mode contains the last two user-system exchanges. The system uses several criteria for inclusion of nodes in the set of nodes presented in the web: user or system statements which are logically related, and nodes with similar types of user error. Several nodes or links can be chosen for inclusion (**encapsulation**) in a new node represented by a collective icon. Several types of encapsulation are available: e.g argumentation fallacies (e.g. over-generalisation), and debate strategies (e.g. thin end of the wedge). **Browsing** has several support tools: e.g. **reference points** (current focus of argument, claims noted as out of scope, common ground, initial problem, etc.), **given known find unknown** (given datum and claim find warrant, given datum and warrant find claim, given warrant and claim find datum), **given system choices find system preferences** (which claim the system most likely to agree with), and **given main claim find user's plans** (system generates alternative datum/claim chains or plans between current claim and main claim). **Finding a datum** comprises scanning existing text for evidence to instantiate in a warrant. **Evaluation** enables user and system to exchange viewpoints and be given persuasiveness scores: an inter-node link is an argumentation move which carries a (static) persuasiveness strength; a series of them either forwards (a plan to a main claim) or backwards (arguing why something is as it is) carry (dynamic) plan evaluation strengths.

7. Argumentation reduces hypertext's HCI problems.

The HCI problems of hypertext (cognitive overload, getting lost) arise from the user's inability to argue back. These problems would be reduced by a hypertext system with argumentation abilities. We justify this statement by appeal to three claims:

(1)   High user control of task simplifies the cognitive task.

Because high control means that the user does not need to attend to the intentions of someone or something else (the controller), her cognitive task will be simpler. Because the task is simpler it will be more easilly integrated into her model of the task, and hence it will be more easily remembered. One aspect of this is that the navigational logic will be clearer to the user, because she will understand why she undertook each action.

(2)   Dynamic text reclassification simplifies the cognitive task.

The user simplifies her task and also more easily remembers if she can dynamically reclassify text or 'chunk' in her own way. She wants to be able to encapsulate a chunk of supplied text descriptively as 'The argument about X' or as 'A way of doing Y', or personally as 'What I call Z', or evaluatively as 'A circular argument about X' or 'A fallacy involving Y'. This chunking is a user-controlled action, and hence, by (1), simplifies and eases memorisation.

(3)   Evaluation of her actions helps the user to learn.

There are two extreme states: either the user is forced to do what the system tells her, or she is free to do whatever she thinks. Neither of these is conducive to maintaining the user's interest, so the user is not likely to learn in such circumstances. The best state is one where the dialogue dynamics is essentially distributed between the user(s) and the system, and where each participant evaluates what the other(s) say or do. This type of dialogue is essentially what would result from basing the dialogue on the dynamics present in argumentation. The user's chunking must be evaluated in a negotiated (not a dictatorial) process. The user must expect that at the end of the process the author of the hyperbook agrees that her way is the right way to chunk.

8. References.

Belkin N.J., Brooks H.M., and Daniels P.J., 'Knowledge elicitation using discourse analysis', *International Journal of Man-Machine Studies*, 27, 1987, 127-144.

Grosz B.J. and Sidner C.L. 'Attention, intentions and the structure of the discourse', *Computational Linguistics*, 12, 1986, 175-204.

Marshall, C.C., 'Representing the structure of a legal argument', *2nd International Conference on AI and the Law, Proceedings of the Conference*, New York, 1989, 121-127.

Sillince J.A.A. and Minors R.H., 'What makes a strong argument? Emotions, highly-placed values and role-playing', *Communication and Cognition*, 24, 3/4, 1991, 281-299.

Sillince J.A.A. and Minors R.H., 'Argumentation, self-inconsistency and multi-dimensional argument strength', *Communication and Cognition*, 25, 4, 1992, (in press).

Sillince J.A.A. and Minors R.H., *An extended-hypertext approach to CAI using recursive data structures derived from an argumentation model*, Sheffield University Management School Discussion Paper No. 93.3, 1993..

Surface Display and Synthetic Force Sensation

Michitaka Hirose and Koichi Hirota

Faculty of Engineering, University of Tokyo
7-3-1 Hongo, Bunkyo-ku, Tokyo 113, Japan

Abstract

In the real world, the sensation of force is felt when a real object comes into contact with a part of our body. This fact motivated us to the idea of creating artificial touch sensation by using some type of force feedback device. A prototype display device for simulating force sensation based on this idea was developed and called Surface Display.

In previous research, the touch sensation was often discussed and many prototypes for force feedback were developed. However, most of these devices were designed from a conventional force feedback perspective, which has been developed mainly in the robotics field. In this paper, another approach for designing a force feedback device, a "mock-surface" method, is presented. Several prototype devices were implemented based on the approach and assessments were made from various point of view.

This paper describes the conceptual design and implementation process as well as some experimental results.

1 Introduction and Background

Many devices which provide touch sensation have been developed. Richard J. Feldman of the American National Institute of Health designed a unique device named Joy String.[1] The GROPE Project at the University of North Carolina built one of the most successful applications of force feedback in virtual environments.[2] Hiroo Iwata of Tsukuba University developed a force feedback manipulator, which provided gripping force feedback for three fingers, and absolute translational force and rotational moment to the user's hand.[3] A similar type force display was developed at Utah University, which generated only the gripping force. [4] Margaret Minsky of MIT developed a force display which presented tactile sensations by simulating frictional force.[5] A pen type force display developed by Hiroo Iwata of Tsukuba University simulated force that was fed back to a pen or pen-type tool.[6]

Most of the devices developed in these research projects are designed from a perspective of conventional force feedback. Namely, the attention is focused on the magnitude of the reaction force affected from the virtual object. In the real world, the sensation of force is obtained when a body part makes contact with a real object. This fact suggests the existence of another perspective for creating artificial touch sensation.

2   Conceptual Design of Surface Display

In this perspective, the device is designed to presents the "existence" of the local surface of an object, and the force is determined according to the degree of interaction with the object. This concept can be called the idea of surface display in contrast with the idea of force display (see Fig.-1) . The sensation associated with contact is generated when the surface of a part of our body comes into contact with a real object. Therefore, artificial surface display must present sensations which are similar to the surfaces of real objects.

In the case when a virtual object makes contact with many different parts of our body, it becomes difficult to simulate the existence of the object by a simple mechanism. Accordingly, a simplification was made so that the virtual object could be felt only by a finger tip with the shape of the finger tip represented as a sphere in the virtual environment. It was also assumed that the displayed surface is continuous. These assumptions made the design and control of the mechanism quite simple (see Fig.-2(a)) . In addition, it was still possible to display a vertex or edge of an object by re-calculating and presenting numerous tangent surfaces according to the motion of the user's finger (see Fig.-2(b)). This was called the "mock surface" method.

3   Implementation

3.1   Prototype I

As it was very difficult to accurately measure the position of the user's finger tip by

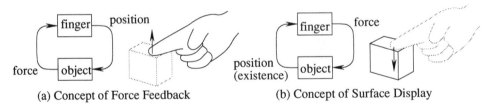

(a) Concept of Force Feedback   (b) Concept of Surface Display

Fig.-1 Concepts of Force Display

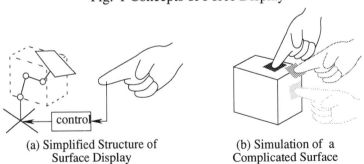

(a) Simplified Structure of
Surface Display

(b) Simulation of a
Complicated Surface

Fig.-2 Ideas in Surface Display

using a conventional space sensor, a special sensor, which detected the displacement in translation and rotation in a small range, was used coupled with a tracking mechanism.

The mechanism of the prototype I contained three degrees of freedom for translational tracking (see Fig.-3(a)(b)) . The contact surface was a cylindrical tube. Control of the mechanism had two modes: tracking mode and display mode (see Fig.-3(c)). In tracking mode, the mechanism was built to track the user's finger and the finger is kept free from touching the sides of the tube. Display mode was used after the finger made contact with a virtual object. In this mode, the mechanism would stop, because it would not be allowed to go inside of the surface of the virtual object. Due to this sudden stop, the user's finger would go off from the center of the force feedback head and make contact with the surrounding tube; thus performing the simulation of a solid surface.

3.2   Prototype II

Prototype II was a more direct implementation of the idea of surface display.[7] The mechanism was divided into two parts: a tracking mechanism and a display mechanism. The tracking mechanism contained five degrees of freedom for translational and rotational motion (see Fig.-4(a)) . Similar sensors like the type used in prototype I was used for tracking the movement of the user's finger. The display mechanism had three degrees of freedom for azimuth, elevation, and distance relative to the user's finger (see Fig.-4(b)).

Prototype II contained a force sensor which measured the force applied by the user's finger. This sensor enabled more realistic interaction between the user and the virtual object by means of allowing different types of physical reactions which were dependent upon various levels of force (ie. a small force caused a small displacement and a large force caused a large displacement). One of the most simple examples of such interaction is the interaction with an elastic object such as a spring.

A one dimensional spring with a mass and damper was built, and its behavior was observed. Normally, the relation between force and displacement is defined as an equation of motion. In Surface Display, the displacement was calculated under a given force condition (see Fig.-5) .

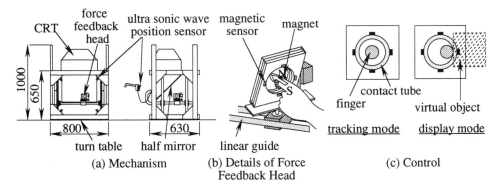

Fig.-3 Mechanism and Control of Prototype I

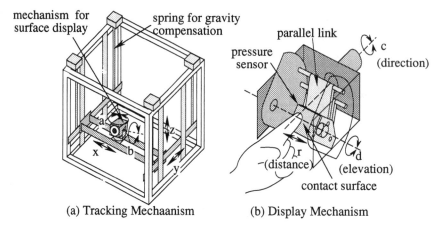

(a) Tracking Mechaanism   (b) Display Mechanism

Fig.-4 Mechanism of Prototype II

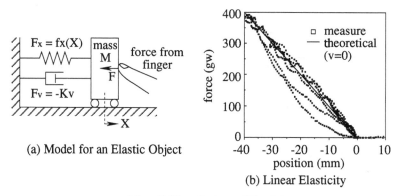

(a) Model for an Elastic Object   (b) Linear Elasticity

Fig.-5 Simulation of Spring

4 Experiments and Application

To clarify the application of Surface Display, the simulation of several kinds of tasks were performed.[8][9] Two of them are discussed below.

4.1 Writing in a Virtual Environment

The sensation of contact and constraint in motion is essential in writing tasks. A virtual blackboard was created in the Surface Display environment and observations concerning the effect of virtual surface were conducted. Subjects were asked to write Japanese characters under several visual and force related conditions. The clarity of written characters was estimated subjectively by a third person (see Fig.-6) . According to the average

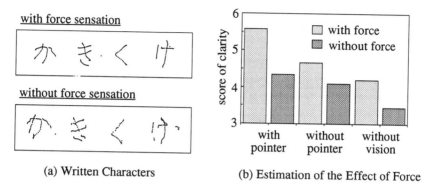

(a) Written Characters

(b) Estimation of the Effect of Force

Fig.-6 Writing in Virtual Environment

scores of clarity under each condition, it was shown that the sensation of force was very important for the writing tasks.

4.2 Modeling of 3D Shapes

As a more complex application, a virtual plastic surface was created in a Surface Display environment. The surface was partitioned into 64×32 pieces and each piece was a polygon with dimensions of 4mm in the x and y direction. When the surface was pressed, transformations were calculated from the amount of force between the user's finger and the surface. By using this surface, the shape of a 3D object could be formed in the same manner as the shaping and forming of metal plates (see Fig.-7).

In the case of a metal plate, the relation between force and displacement is non-linear. When the force is small, the plate behaves as an elastic object. When the force is large, plastic deformation occurs. Such non-linear behavior was implemented in our application.

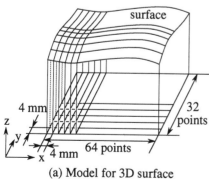

(a) Model for 3D surface

(b) An Example of a Created Shape

Fig.-7 Editor for 3D Shapes

5 Conclusion

The conceptual design and implementation of a force feedback device with a perspective differing from conventional force feedback systems was conducted. The feasibility and practicality of the idea was tested by the development of prototype devices and by experimentation with several types of tasks.

Acknowledgments

We are very grateful to Toshiba Corporation and the Tokyo Electric Power Company for their support of our research in creating Surface Display and Synthetic Force Sensation.

References

[1] J.D. Foley, "Interfaces for Advanced Computing", Scientific American, Vol. 257, No. 4, pp.83 - 90 (1987)

[2] F.P. Brooks, M. Ouh-yong, J.J. Batter, P. Jerome, "Project GROPE - Haptic Displays for Scientific Visualization", Computer Graphics, Vol. 24, No. 4, pp. 177 - 185, ACM SIGGRAPH '90 (1990).

[3] H.Iwata, "Artificial Reality with Force Feedback : Development of Desktop Virtual Space with Compact Master Manipulator", Computer Graphics, Vol. 24, No. 4, pp. 165 - 170, ACM SIGGRAPH '90 (1990).

[4] G.Burdea, J.Zhuang, E.Roskos, D.Silver, N.Langrana, "A Portable Dexterous Master with Force Feedback", Presence, Vol. 1, No. 1, pp. 18 - 28, MIT Press (1992).

[5] M.Minsky, M.Ouh-yong, O.Steel, F.P.Brooks, M.Behensky, "Feeling and Seeing: Issues in Force Display", Computer Graphics, Vol. 24, No. 2, pp. 235 - 243, Proceedings 1990 Symposium on Interactive 3D Graphics, Snowbird, UT (1990).

[6] H.Iwata, "Non-restricted Haptic Environment", Proceedings of the 8th Symp. on Human Interface, pp.23 - 26, SICE (1992) (Japanese).

[7] K.Hirota, M.Hirose, "Development of Force Feedback Environment", Proceedings of the 8th Symp. on Human Interface, pp.19 - 22, SICE (1992) (Japanese).

[8] K.Hirota, M.Hirose, T.Ishii, and T.Yuh, "A Study on the Force Feedback for Virtual Space Manipulation", Proceedings of the 68th Annual Meeting, No. 910 - 17, Vol. C, pp. 404 - 406, JSME (1991) (Japanese).

[9] M.Hirose, K.Hirota, R.Kijima, "Human Behavior in Virtual Environment", Human Vision, Visual Processing and Digital Display III, Vol. 1666, pp. 548 - 559, SPIE (1992)

A Six Degree-of-freedom Pen-based Force Display

Hiroo IWATA

Instibaute of Engineering Mechanics, University of Tsukuba
Tsukuba, 305 JAPAN

Abstract: This paper describes about design of a pen-based force display and its application to direct manipulation of 3D shapes. We have developed a 6 degree-of-freedom force reflective master manipulator which has pen-shaped grip. The system employs two 3 degree-of-freedom manipulators. Both end of the pen are connected to these manipulators. By this mechanism, the hardware of the force display is small and light weighted. The performance of the force display is exemplified in interactive deformation of free-form surface.

1. Introduction

Virtual world technology usually employs glove-like tactile input devices. Users feel troublesome when they put or off these devices. If the glove is equipped with force feedback device, the problem is much severe. This disadvantage obstructs practical use of force displays. This paper describes method of implementation of force display without glove-like device. A pen-based force display is proposed as an alternative device. We have developed a 6 degree-of-freedom force reflective master manipulator which has pen-shaped grip. Users are familiar to a pen in their everyday life. Most of the human intellectual works are done with a pen. We use spatulas or rakes for modeling solid objects. These devices have stick-shaped grips similar to a pen. In this aspect, the pen-based force display is easily applied to design of 3D shapes. This paper proposes a method of deformation of free-form surface by the pen-based force display.

2. A Pen-based Force Display

Human hand has an ability of 6 degree-of-freedom motion in 3D space. If we build a 6 degree-of-freedom master manipulator which has serial joints, each joint must support the weight of upper joints. This characteristics leads large hardware of the manipulator. We use parallel mechanism in order to reduce size and weight of the manipulator. The pen-based force display employs two 3 degree-of-freedom manipulators. Both end of the pen are connected to these manipulators. Total degree-of-freedom of the force display is 6. Three degree-of-freedom force and 3 degree-of-freedom torque are applied at the pen. Overall view of the force display is shown in Figure 1. Each 3 degree-of-freedom manipulator is

Figure 1. Overall view of the force display

composed of pantograph link. By this mechanism, the pen is free from the weight of the actuators.

Figure 2 shows a diagram of mechanical configuration of the force display. Joints MA1, MA2, MA3, MB1, MB2, and MB3 are equipped with DC motors and potentiometers. Other joints move passively. The position of joint A and B are measured by potentiometers. Three dimensional force vector is applied at the joint A and B. The joint A determines the position of the pen point, and the joint B determines the orientation of the pen. Working space of the pen point is a part of a spherical volume whose diameter is 44 cm(Figure 3). The rotational angle around the axis of the pen is determined by the distance between the joint A and B. A screw motion mechanism converts rotational motion of the pen into transition of the distance between the joint A and B.

Applied force and torque at the pen are illustrated in Figure 4. F_A indicates a force vector applied at the joint A. F_B indicates a force vector applied at the joint B. If F_A and F_B are the same vectors, translational force is generated(See Figure 4(a)). If direction of F_A and F_B are reverse, torque around the yaw axis or the pitch axis is generated(See Figure 4(b),(c)). If F_A and F_B are opposite, torque around the roll axis is generated by the screw motion mechanism(See Figure 4(d)).

The pen is equipped with a push button. Function of the pen in virtual environment is activated by pushing the button.

3.System Configuration of Pen-based Virtual Environment

The hardware configuration of the overall system is indicated in Figure 5. The host computer is SGI IRIS Indigo (R3000, Entry). The host computer generates real-time image

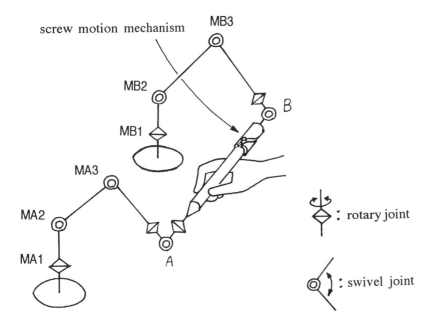

Figure 2. Mechanical configuration of the force display

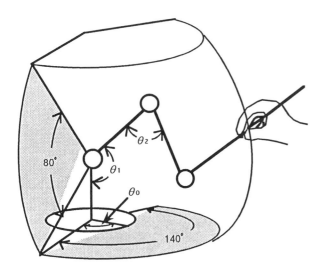

Figure 3. Working space of the pen point

654

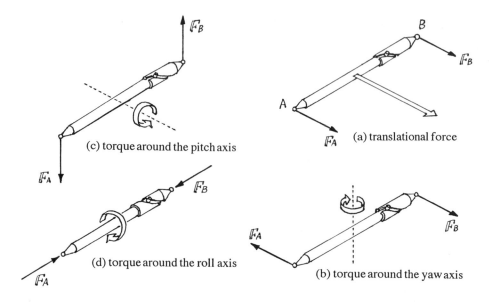

(c) torque around the pitch axis

(a) translational force

(d) torque around the roll axis

(b) torque around the yaw axis

Figure 4. Applied force

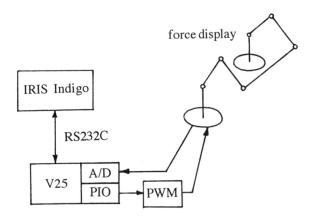

force display

IRIS Indigo

RS232C

V25 | A/D
PIO

PWM

Figure 5. Hardware configuration of the system

of virtual space. A V25 board computer has A/D (analog to digital) convertors and PIO (parallel input/output unit). V25 is an intel 8086 compatible micro processor. Joint angles of the force display are acquired by A/D convertors. Accuracy of position sensing of the pen point is 2 mm. Motor torque is generated by PWM (Pulse Width Modulation) amplifier. The maximum generated force at the pen is 500gf. The weight of the pen (220gf) is compensated. The V25 board computer is connected to the host computer by RS232C.

The host computer executes following processes:
1) Calculation of the position and orientation of the pen
2) Handling of the geometric model of virtual objects
3) Collision detection and calculation of reaction force
4)Graphics drawing
Sampling rate of the force display and update rate of graphics is 10Hz.

4. Design of a 3D Shape

Design of 3D shapes is difficult if we use conventional input devices such as keyboards or mice. Spatial input device is inevitable for direct manipulation of geometric models[1][2]. In the real world, we feel reaction force from materials in modeling solid objects. Force feedback plays important roles in manipulation of virtual objects[3]. Takahashi, Kanai, and Morisawa developed a glove-like force feedback device for deformation of free-form surface[4].

As an example of application of the force display to design of 3D shapes, we implemented a deformation algorithm of free-form surface. The deformation is caused by direct motion of the pen. If the user pushes or pulls the surface while pushing the button on the pen , it deforms. The user feels reaction force while the surface is deforming. This action is similar to embossing a metal plate.

The method of deformation is illustrated in Figure 6. Figure 6 shows a 3D shape of the deformation caused by a single user action. Deformed shape is generated by sine curves. When the user releases the button, the deformation stops. If the user pushes or pulls the surface again, deformation pattern shown in Figure 6 is overlapped. Reaction force is applied to the pen while the surface is deforming. The force vector is vertical to the original surface. If the user moves the pen against the reaction force, the surface is deformed. Applied reaction force increases proportional to the displacement of the pen point.

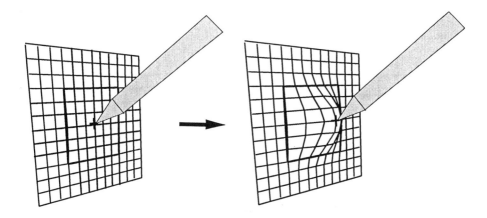

Figure 6. Deformation of free-form surface

5. Conclusions

The 6 degree-of-freedom pen-based force display is developed and performance of the device is exemplified in interactive deformation of free-form surface. Unlike glove-like tactile input devices, the pen-based force display does not require users to fit the device to their hand. It neither require calibrations. For this advantage, the pen-based force display is easily combined to everyday work space.

Pen-based operation is currently a major issue in the field of user-interface. Some pen-based OS are proposed and actually used. Our device can easily combine those environments. Future work of our research will be development of pen-based haptic user environment such as 3D widgets or new design methods for 3D shapes.

5. Acknowledgments

This work is greatly assisted by a graduate school student Takahiro Nakashima. This paper would not be possible without his efforts.

References

[1]Clark,J.H. Design Surface in 3-D. Commn.of ACM. Vol.19, No.8, 1976
[2]Sachs,E et al. 3-Draw:A Tool for Designing 3D Shapes. IEEE CG&A. Vol.11, No.6, 1991
[3]Iwata,H. Artificial Reality with Force-feedback:Development of Desktop Virtual Space with Compact Master Manipulator. Computer Graphics. Vol.24, No.4, 1990
[4]Takahashi,H.,Kanai,S., and Morisawa,T. A Development of Geometric Modeling System with Artificial Reality - Generation of Free-Form Surface -. Proc. of 7th Symposium on Human Interface. 1991

Virtual Kitchen System using Kansei Engineering

N.Enomoto*, M.Nagamachi**, J.Nomura*, K.Sawada*

*Virtual Reality R&D Group, Matsushita Electric Works Ltd.
**Faculty of Engineering , Hiroshima University

Abstract
A new paradigm for relationship between human and computer has been called artificial reality, virtual reality or cyberspace. Using three-dimensional computer graphics, interactive devices, and high-resolution display, a virtual world can be realized in which one can pick up imaginary objects as if they were physical world. Using this technology and Kansei Engineering, Virtual Kitchen System has been developed in Matsushita Electric Works. Kansei Engineering is defined as a "translation system of a customer's favorite or image into real design components" (Nagamachi,1986). Virtual Kitchen System can be used for the customers to design virtual kitchens which just they image and experience them in virtual space. And in future, it will be able to deal with whole of house, then customers can design their house and check the housing performances such a light, sound, vibration, temperature, air and living-space amenity.
This paper details Kansei Engineering and the Virtual Kitchen System.

1.INTRODUCTION

When planner plans living space, it is important to get customer's need or lifestyle. But because of diversified lifestyle and flooded products, it is being difficult to grasp customer's lifestyle and needs. Then it has become important for manufacturer to change the process of how to design products and how to sales to deal with this problem. Product designer is required to implement customer's need and feeling, and interior planner must grasp customer's lifestyle and what he images through their conversation and embody his willing. But customer's needs are diversified and their expression of kitchen images are vague. Kansei Engineering is valid such a problem. Using this technology, Virtual Kitchen System can translates the customer's image of kitchen what he desires into the virtual kitchen, and after that, he can step in into his virtual kitchen space to check it. As a Kansei information, this prototype system is using lifestyle and kitchen image in adjective word.

2.KANSEI ENGINEERING

Kansei Engineering is defined as "a translation system of a consumer's image or feeling into real design components"(Nagamachi,1986). Namely, when a customer expresses their image toward a object in adjective, detail design items (for instance,object style, color, material, size and so on) are selected through the Kansei Engineering procedure, and using this outputs, designer or planner can design the object.

The Kansei Engineering Procedure is;

Step1. Collect the adjective words
Collect many adjective words which have relation to the object domain.

Step2. Assess slides or pictures on SD scales
Make pair these adjectives in a good-bad fashion for the SD (Osgood's Semantic Differentials) scales. Then assess many slides or pictures related to the object domain on these SD scales.

Step3. Elicit effective adjectives from collected adjectives
Calculate the assessed data at Step2 by factor analysis or principal component analysis, and obtain the semantic factorial structure of adjectives on the related design domain. And elicit adjectives which have a close relation to the object domain from the collected adjectives.

Step4. Subdivide the object design into the design components
Subdivide the object design on the slides or pictures into the detail design components, then classify each component into category according to it's quality. For example, L-style (category) layout (component), mahogany (category) cabinet (component).

Step5. Get the relevancy between a adjective and design components
Using the assessed data at Step2 and qualitative data at Step4, analyze by Hayashi's Quantification Theory Type 1, which is a kind of multivariate regression analysis dealing with qualitative data (Hayashi,1976). The results of this analysis means relevancy between a adjective and each design component.

3.VIRTUAL KITCHEN SYSTEM

3-1 MATIS/ViVA Overview

ViVA (Virtual Reality for Vivid A&i space) system is developed which allows our customers to pseudo-experience their custom kitchens before purchasing them. The kitchen planning process is detailed in Fig.1. When a interested customer comes to the showroom, the kitchen planner first explains the kitchen products' descriptions using catalogues and exhibits.

The kitchen planner next draws a rough layout according to the desires of the customer. Then a floor plan, an elevation view, a perspective drawing, and a written estimate are created on a CAD system based on the rough sketch. This CAD system called MATIS (Matsushita Amenity Total Interior System) includes approximately 30,000 of Matsushita's kitchen products as well as data on previous and current customers in its database. This customer data includes fields for room dimensions, cabinet placement, standardized parts information, special order information, etc.

After drawing the plan on the MATIS system, the two-dimensional picture is first translated to a three-dimensional layout to be experienced in the ViVA system. The customer's own kitchen plan can be translated into a ViVA database within a day. The next time the customer comes to the showroom, he can now experience many aspects of his own kitchen. The customer can check his kitchen with the ViVA system and decides if it matches his own idea of how the kitchen should be. And using the Texture Mapping technology, ViVA system allows the customer to coordinates colors of the kitchen cabinets, the wall, the floor and the ceiling.

Once the customer is satisfied with the virtual kitchen and approves his kitchen design, final approval and appliance drawings are made and the order is sent to the CIM line. The CIM line starts its operation according to the specifications decided by the customer. Tolerances of 1mm can be kept using this CIM system In only one week from placing the order, the completed kitchen is delivered to owner's home ready for installation.

Usual kitchen planning system without the ViVA pseudo-experience system, the customer often cannot image his own kitchen vividly. Sometimes there are many discrepancies between the customer and the kitchen planner. In such a case, the consultation is started afresh. The ViVA system helps eliminate these mistakes that are often made. Fig.2 shows the impressions of customers experienced the ViVA system.

With ViVA, the following items can be experienced in the virtual kitchen:

1. The arrangement of cabinets and appliances.
2. The general feeling of available space.
3. Overall ergonomic design: The user can open and close cabinet doors, turn on faucets, move goods on the counter etc.
4. The color-coordination of the room components (kitchen cabinets, the floor, the ceiling)

The ViVA kitchen planning system, located in Matsushita Electric Works' Shinjuku Showroom near Tokyo, has been available to customers since October 1991. Since then many people have experienced the system.

3-2 Virtual Kitchen System using KANSEI Engineering Overview

As the next version of ViVA system, Kansei ViVA system is being developed (stage1-type system on Fig.1). This system is valid to the following customers' types:

1. The customers who have no idea of the kitchen
2. The customers who are in confusion because they saw many catalogues and exhibits
3. The customers who cannot image what the size of their kitchen space   (usually, kitchen looks smaller than actual size in showroom because the height of the room in showroom is higher than housing one).

Using this system, vagueness and confusion of customer's image are cleared. So we expect that this system can decrease the number of the consultation between planner and customer (usually it repeat 4 or 6 times, sometimes over 10 times), and decrease the time of the consultation (usually it takes 2 hours, sometimes over 4 hours). The ViVA system using Kansei Engineering is detailed in Fig.3. First, customer inputs the field for room dimension and height of customer who use kitchen as restriction conditions. Next, he inputs lifestyle of his family and his image toward the kitchen in adjective words as Kansei conditions. Then the Kansei ViVA system identifies the kitchen plan in detail (for instance, kitchen layout, cabinet color, floor color, counter height and so on) using Kansei Engineering, and selects the kitchen plan used before similar to his kitchen plan from the ViVA database. We gathered over 200 of adjectives and 18 items featured lifestyle. After experience, customer can change the wall size, cabinet arrangement, cabinet color and so on of the similar kitchen plan into his own kitchen plan.

3-3 Living Amenity Simulation System Overview

Current ViVA system and Kansei ViVA system are dealing with kitchen space. In the future, we wish to develop to model an entire house. Fig.4 shows such a system.This development is joined with the project which is a 7-year plan since 1989 called "Technology Development Project for New Industrialized Houses" under the Ministry of International Trade and Industry. The aim of this project is to develop a system which achieves new housing production for the coming 21st century. For the implementation of the project, research and development is being proceeded by "The New Industrialized House Production Technology and System Development Technology Research Association(WISH21)". MEW takes charge of development of "resident participation" amenity simulation system in this project. Using this system, resident can experience and evaluate housing performance such as light, sound, vibration, temperature, air and so on.

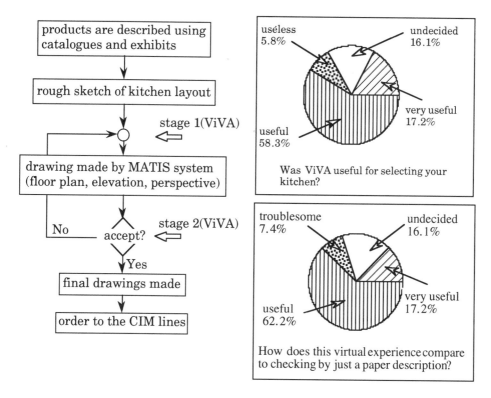

Figure 1. Kitchen Planning Process

Figure 2. ViVA User Survey Results

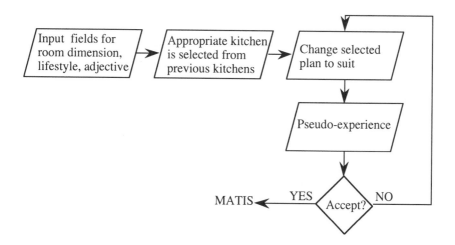

Figure 3. Kansei ViVA System

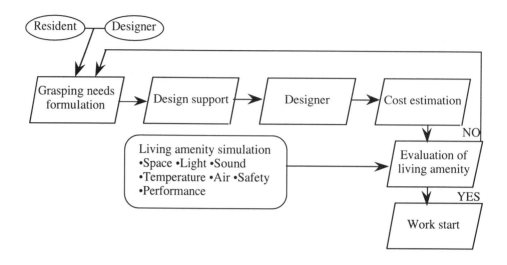

Figure 4. Living Amenity Simulation System

4.CONCLUSION

This paper described about Kansei Engineering and the Virtual Kitchen System. As indicated in this paper, current system kitchen simulation system is valid. And Kansei ViVA system could cover gap which arose between customer and kitchen planner in their consultation, and decreased consultation-time to a certain extent. In future, Kansei ViVA system will be developed which can deal with the Kansei information in a broad sense. Namely, advanced Kansei ViVA system will be able to deal with customer's "amenity" such as favorite lighting effect, comfortable temperature and so on.

REFERENCES
1 Nagamachi M., A Study of Custom Consultation System in Terms of Knowledge Engineering, Human Interface, Vol.3 (1989)
2 Nagamachi M., An Image Technology Expert System and Its Application to Design Consultation, International Journal of Human-Computer Interactions (1991)
3 Nomura J., Ohata H., Imamura K. and Schultz J. R., Virtual Space Decision Support System and Its Application to Consumer Showrooms, Visual Computing, Spring-Verlag Tokyo (1992)
4 A Pamphlet of Housing Development Project for the 21st Century
5 Enomto N., Nagamachi M., Sekine T., Kitchen Planning Expert System using Kansei

Simulated World of Hypothetical Life Forms
— Virtual Creatures —

Takushi Fujita, Hayuru Itoh, Hitomi Taguchi, Toshiyuki Fukuoka,
Soichi Nishiyama, and Kazuyuki Watanabe

Fujitsu Laboratories Ltd.
1015 Kamikodanaka, Nakahara-ku, Kawasaki 211, Japan

Abstract
We developed a system with which we can interact with autonomous
creatures in a virtual world. The creatures, generated in real-time by
computer simulation, respond to our hand gestures and voices. They also sing
a song under the baton of a man. We will apply outcomes of this experiment to
general purpose human interfaces.

1. INTRODUCTION

How to bring a computer into home is a major concern for computer
industries. However, much efforts to breakthrough "human interface barrier"
are needed to change a computer to a commodity or a consumer electronics
like a TV set.

Windows and icons are examples of human interface tools designed to
make computers easier to use. If computer tools are made less abstract, then
users can relate to them as real tools, not just as concepts and functions.

Agents are a human interface tool. An agent, created by artificial
intelligence, is a presentation of something we are familiar with, for example
a person or an animal [1]. People feel more comfortable communicating with
a living thing than with a computer. We created such agents in the form of
virtual creatures.

2. VIRTUAL CREATURES

Our goal was to create agents that people would feel comfortable
interacting with. We created virtual creatures that would act and respond like
domesticated pets. Several such creatures inhabit the virtual world we
created. The creatures interact, in real time, with each other and with the
user (Fig. 1).

We constructed an experimental theater (Fig. 2). Images of the virtual
world are displayed on a wide screen in front of the user. Sounds of the virtual
world such as voices of the creatures are heard from surrounding speakers.

Fig. 1 Environment to interact with virtual creatures.

Fig. 2 Experimental theater.

3. ARCHITECTURE

We proposed a unified model to describe a virtual world containing a variety of objects. Based on this model, we developed an interface for communicating with objects in the virtual world.

3.1 Virtual world model

A unified model is needed for the computer simulation of a virtual world. The model must be flexible enough to represent all of the objects in a hypothetical virtual world.

Everything that appears in the virtual world is defined as an object (Fig. 3). Each object has attributes such as position, orientation, appearance, name, and each attribute is defined by its name, type, and value. An attribute's name indicates its meaning. In our model, all objects in the virtual world are autonomous. That is, an object changes its own attributes' values.

A person interacting with the virtual world is also treated as an object. The person's actions and voice are detected with sensors and microphones, and converted to object attributes. However, a person cannot interact the virtual world model. An environment in which a person can interact with the virtual world can be created by converting object attributes to images and sounds.

3.2 Communication server

An object in the virtual world exists as a process on a computer. These processes are called clients. Clients communicate asynchronously with a server, which is connected to a communication network (Fig. 4). Servers on different computers can communicate via this network. We implemented a communication server on a UNIX system. Clients communicate with the server using interface functions, such as:

Registration of new objects and attributes.
Update of attributes.
Reference to attributes of other objects.

Every server on the system stores attribute data for all objects in the virtual world. Whenever a server updates data for a client, the server sends the updated information to other servers on the network.

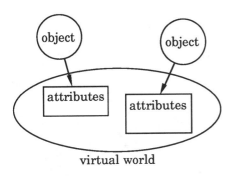

Fig. 3 Conceptual model.

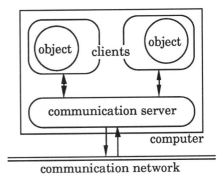

Fig. 4 Implementation.

4. SIMULATION

A virtual creature is represented as an object with attributes. The simulation task of each individual creature is to calculate its attributes and send their updated values to the communication server in real-time. We proposed the following model to simulate individual creatures.

4.1 Simulation of individual creatures

A virtual creature is considered to be a blackbox with attributes whose values vary dynamically. A creature's motions are represented as variations of its attributes, which are obtained by mechanisms inside the blackbox.

Inside the blackbox, the creature's states such as physical condition, memories, and emotions are represented with state variables. Mechanisms to generate attribute variations are defined by a group of functions. The functions are executed frequently enough to generate smooth motion of the creature.

4.2 Motion

Realistic motion is generated based on physical models, which have to be simple enough to generate motions of the objects in real-time.

A creature's motion influenced by such forces as gravity, buoyancy, damping, and repulsion can be simulated by combining translation and rotation, which are computed assuming a rigid body. For example, rigid body translation is calculated with the following equation.

$$dP/dt = F \qquad (1)$$

where $\mathbf{P}$ and $\mathbf{F}$ represent momentum and force. Equation (1) is approximated with the following equations.

$$\Delta \mathbf{v} = (\mathbf{F}/M) \, \Delta t$$
$$\Delta \mathbf{x} = \mathbf{v} \, \Delta t \qquad (2)$$

where $\Delta \mathbf{x}$ and $\Delta \mathbf{v}$ are variations of the position and velocity, Δt is the time interval, and M is the total mass of the object. These equations are calculated each cycle and the state variables are updated.

Similar rules are applied to other variables which are used to simulate deformations of the creature's body and changes in emotions.

4.3 Behavioral planning

Generating a variety of actions of an intelligent creature is not easy only with simple equations as described above. We implemented a behavioral planning function which determines the creature's behavior according to its emotions and circumstances.

The function is executed in two steps. First, the most unpleasant thing for the creature is chosen from the creature's circumstances. That is the thing which should be removed first from the circumstances [2]. Secondly, a plan to cope with the situation is selected by a hierarchical architectural planner [3].

5. USER ENVIRONMENT

Objects in a virtual world are represented by models that are quite different from the real world. The virtual world environment should be as familiar as possible to the users, who live in the real world.

5.1 User in the virtual world

In the virtual world, a user is regarded as an object with attributes similar to virtual creatures. Where as virtual creature attributes are calculated by the simulation program, the user's attributes are based on the user's states and actions in the real world. We used a microphone and a 3D sensor attached to a baton to convert the user's actions to object attributes.

5.2 Visual environment

The virtual world environment viewed by the user is generated by computer graphics machines and projected onto a screen (Fig. 1). The images of objects in the virtual world are generated based on the object's attributes, which include position, orientation, color, and deformation. Texture patterns and polygonal shape data for the object images are loaded to each graphics machine in advance.

We used texture-mapped polygons to generate the images of the deformable creatures' soft bodies. The coordinate values of the vertices of the polygons are regarded as elements of a vector $\mathbf{P}$, and the shape is defined by a function $\mathbf{P}(d_1,\ldots,d_n)$, where $d_1,\ldots,d_n$ are the deformation parameters included in the attributes of the object and $\mathbf{P}(d_1,\ldots,d_n)$ is defined as in the following example.

$$\mathbf{P}(d_1,\ldots,d_n) = \mathbf{P}_0 + d_1\mathbf{D}_1 + \ldots + d_n\mathbf{D}_n \qquad (\mathbf{D}_i = \mathbf{P}_i - \mathbf{P}_0) \qquad (3)$$

where $\mathbf{P}_0$ defines a neutral shape, and $\mathbf{P}_1,\ldots,\mathbf{P}_n$ each define a deformed pattern. $\mathbf{P}_0$ and $\mathbf{D}_1,\ldots,\mathbf{D}_n$ are loaded on each graphics machine in advance, and $d_1,\ldots,d_n$ are obtained from the network in real-time as object attributes.

5.3 Sounds

Multi-channel speakers, arranged in the theater, output the sounds of the virtual creatures. A digital sound generator creates the creature's voices. The generator is triggered by changes in some specific attributes of the creatures, and the sounds are distributed to each speaker channel by a digital sound mixer so that the voices are heard in the right place at the right volume.

The sound system can create a chorus of singing creatures. The tempo and timing are controlled based on the creatures' attributes.

6. EXPERIMENT

We constructed an experimental theater in which a person can interact with virtual creatures in a simulated virtual world (Fig. 2). We used three engineering workstations (Fujitsu S-4/630, 670), three graphics workstations (IRIS 340VGX, Skywriter), three personal computers (Fujitsu FM-R70, 80), and some equipments for the theater system. A typical scenario is as follows:

Two families, with parents and three children inhabit the virtual world (Fig. 5-a). The virtual creature's village also has plants, columns, blocks, and mountains around. A sun cycles around the world every 20 minutes, creating days and nights.

At daybreak, the creatures wake up. When the user calls a creature, the creature turns and approaches the speaker. If he says "hello", the creature responds by answering, smiling, and swinging its head (Fig. 5-b). In contrast, if the user yells, the creatures act frightened, protruding their eyes, and some of the creatures get angry and harden their faces (Fig. 5-c).

If the user starts beating the baton, some of the creatures will start singing. Upon hearing the song, the other creatures will join the chorus.

As nightfall approaches, the creatures return home and go to sleep.

(a) A mother smiling at her daughter (left),
and fathers glaring at each other (right).

(b) The creatures greeting us.   (c) The creatures frightened at yell.

Fig. 5 Behavior of virtual creatures.

7. CONCLUSION

For the purpose of studying autonomous agents as human interface tools, we developed a system with which we can interact with virtual creatures.

We proposed a virtual world model for computer simulation. Everything in the virtual world are represented as an object with attributes. All objects are autonomous, each of which changes their attributes by themselves. That makes simulation programs quite simple. Communications between objects based on the model are served by communication servers on a computer network.

Based on the model, we created autonomous virtual creatures. The creatures interact with each other and with a human. An environment to interact with them is generated in real-time based on object attributes. And the user can feel as if he were in the virtual world.

We are planning to apply the technics we studied from this experiment to general purpose human interfaces.

Acknowledgements
We would like to thank Prof. Koichi Ohmura for his helpful suggestions. We would also like to thank following people for their contributions to the construction of this system: Suma Noji, Yoshiro Watanuki and Masaki Sakai of Nippon Electronics College, Minoru Kubota of M-cape composition workshop, Takeshi Kawamura of Apricot Wild Child, Shigeo Sato, Masayuki Kobayashi, and Masayuki Yada of Bigtowns Ltd., and Jonathan Swartz of Carnegie Mellon University. Thanks to Shuzo Morita, Nobuyuki Makimura, and Motomitsu Adachi of Fujitsu Laboratories Ltd. for supporting our work.

References
[1] B.Laurel: Computers as Theatre, Menlo Park, CA: Addison-Wesley, 1991.
[2] L.Festinger: A theory of cognitive dissonance, Evanston: Row, Peterson, 1957.
[3] A.B.Loyall and J.Bates: A reactive, adaptive architecture for agents, Technical Report CMU-CS-91-147, CMU, Pittsburgh, 1991.

Virtual Space Teleconferencing System
- Real Time Detection and Reproduction of 3-D Human images

Fumio Kishino, Jun Ohya, Haruo Takemura and Nobuyoshi Terashima

ATR Communication Systems Research Laboratories,
2-2 Hikaridai, Seika-cho, Soraku-gun, Kyoto 619-02, Japan

Abstract

Real-time reproduction of a 3D human image is realized by the experimental system the authors recently built for the realization of a virtual space teleconferencing, in which participants at different sites can feel as if they are at one site and can cooperatively work. In the teleconferencing system, the 3D model of a participant is constructed by a wire frame model mapped by color texture and is displayed on the 3D screen at the receiving site. Using the experimental system, the optimum number of nodes for real-time reproduction is obtained. Promising results for real-time cooperative work using the experimental system are demonstrated.

1. INTRODUCTION

The coming visual communications is expected to provide real-world sensations. To achieve a real-world sensations, it is essential to reproduce three-dimensional surroundings of remote site around a receiver. Recently, virtual reality (VR) or artificial reality (AR) has been progressing worldwide. This technology presents a human being the sensation of being involved in a virtual environment. There are two types of realistic virtual worlds: the real world itself and an imaginary world generated by computer.

Tachi et al. proposed to use remotely controlled sensors which works as a receivers eyes, ears and so on. They proposed design strategies for a stereoscopic TV system for teleoperation and evaluated their system[1]. This method is rather one way communication from remote sensor to a receiver. With tele-manipulator, this method can be extended for two way communication between human and tele-operated robot. However, extending this two way communication for human and human communication or for multi-point communication is difficult because of physical constraints. For natural human-human communication, it is essential not only to acquire the situation at remote site but also to transmit receivers status to remote site.

If it is possible to create truly realistic virtual world which is preciselly modeled on a real world by using computer vision (CV) and computer graphics (CG) technologies and also is possible to create virtual human being who is reproduction of receivers, such virtual world can be shared and used for two-way or multi-point communication and can make users feel as if they are really coexisting with their communication partners. This paper describes a virtual space teleconferencing which realizes the communication with realistic sensations.

2. VIRTUAL SPACE TELECONFERENCING

In order to achieve "Teleconferencing with realistic sensations"[2], the concept of virtual space teleconferencing is examined. As shown in Fig.1, a "virtual space teleconferencing" system creates an image of a conference room (virtual conference room) using computer graphics in real time. It also constructs images of the remotely located conference participants. Users of the system can talk to each other or proceed with a conference with the sensation of "sharing the same space". Characteristics of virtual space teleconferencing are shown in Table 1 in comparison with conventional video teleconferencing characteristics.

Fig .1 Virtual space teleconferencing concept

There are many problems to be solved, however, before this system can be realized. This paper focuses on real-time reproduction of 3D human images and a cooperative work environment which are key technologies for achieving this system.

Table 1 Characteristic of virtual space teleconferencing

Items	Virtual space teleconferencing	Conventional video teleconferencing
Motion parallax	Participants can observe a stereoscopic CG image according to the eye-position allowing the viewer to get a motion parallax effect.	Impossible
Eye contact	It can be easily realized.	Difficult
A sense of immersion	Participants feel as if they are actually in the conference room.	Impossible
Cooperative work in a common space	Participants can cooperatively manipulate virtual objects in the conference room.	Impossible

3. REAL-TIME REPRODUCTION OF 3D HUMAN IMAGES

A method for human image recognition and reproduction is one of the most important research problems to be solved. In this system, perspectives of human images from the viewpoints of participants must be synthesized, and should include correct shade and shadow to suit the lighting conditions of the virtual room. To solve these problems we applied a model-based coding approach using image recognition and image reproduction of a three-dimensional human body model.

An experimental system enabling real-time reproduction of 3D human images was developed to evaluate the effectiveness of virtual space teleconferencing[3]. This system consists of three modules: 3D modeling of the human body, real-time detection of body motions and real-time synthesis of human images.

3D modeling of the human body is done using a Cyberware color 3D digitizer, which rotates around an object, projects laser stripes, and acquires color information and 3D coordinates of each point on the surfaces of parts. The acquired 3D coordinate data is transformed into a 3D wire frame model consisting of triangular patches. More specifically, if the difference in the directions of surface normals to neighboring points is smaller than the threshold, the points are merged to form an area with a uniform direction. After this process is applied to all points, each area is divided into triangular patches. Then, the color information of each point is mapped to its corresponding triangular patch. 3D information is acquired by dividing the head, body and arms as shown Fig.2. The 3D model of each part is articulated with another.

It is very difficult to achieve real-time detection of body motion with most image processing technologies. Therefore, to detect the positions of the head, hands and body in real-time, magnetic sensors[4], which can detect the three translation and rotation parameters, are used. Finger movements are detected by using a data glove[5]. For real-time detection of facial expressions, nine blue tape marks are attached to the facial muscles that can strongly affect changes in facial expressions. The 3D coordinates of the nodes in the parts for the head, hands, fingers and body are obtained from the information detected by the magnetic sensors and data glove. The results from tracking the marks on the face are used to move the nodes of the wire frame model for the face.

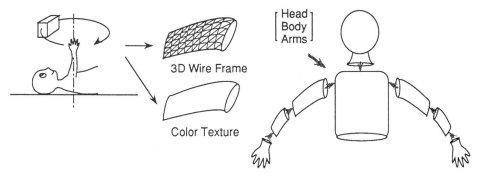

Fig. 2 3D Modeling of human body

Fig. 3 Scene of virtual space teleconferencing

Fig. 3 shows a human image synthesized in a virtual conference room. Most of participants agreed that the 3D human image reproduction is quite natural and smooth, but further study is necessary for a more accurate image quality evaluation.

In this experimental system, to achieve real-time reproduction, tape marks, a data glove and magnetic sensors are used. However, these tools are not appropriate for natural human communications. It is a final goal to develope a system that does not require such tools.

4. COOPERATIVE WORK THROUGH VIRTUAL SPACE

A virtual workspace for virtual space teleconferencing is to be generated by computer graphics. "Virtual manipulation" is a facility enabling users to interact with a virtual environment. Users can cooperatively work on tasks such as city planning or modeling a new car. In such a case, it is desirable for the users to be able to handle objects in the virtual environment just as they would be in a real environment. If this can be achieved, users can collaborate in various ways without any prior training of teleconferencing operations.

Fig.4 shows an overview of "Virtual Manipulation." First, the user's viewing position, hand position and hand shape are measured. The user's intentions are then analyzed to allow grasping, translating or releasing of an object in the virtual environment. The system will be able to select the object of the user's interest with higher order analysis of the user's intention.

"Virtual manipulation" has many applications such as teleoperation, city planning, product design and man-machine interface where a small number of operators must

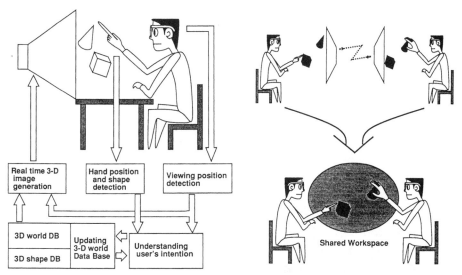

Fig. 4 Virtual manipuration concept   Fig. 5 Shared workspace configuration

monitor huge amounts of information, e.g., monitoring and operating electric power plants. By providing a "virtual manipulation" environment for collaboration, the system can be used more effectively. The concept of a cooperative work environment in computer networks is known as "computer-supported cooperative work" (CSCW) or groupware. Groupware is also intended to create a shared workspace that supports dynamic collaboration in a work group over space and time constraints[6]. A cooperative work environment using a virtual workspace is more flexible than the traditional CSCW environment based on conventional user interface devices, such as mice, keyboards or CRT displays.

Two of the systems in Fig.4 were used to implement a cooperative work environment[7]. Object layout tasks, e.g. toy block layout, office furniture layout and city building layout tasks, were chosen as model tasks to be performed in this environment. It is known that understanding the final image of a layout from a 2-D plan requires plan reading skills. From this point of view, such tasks are better suited for a 3-D virtual workspace. Fig.5 shows the system configuration. Fig.6 shows two users facing each other and manipulating the CG image of office furnitures, located between the two users. Two users can also look in the same direction and share the same view.

When the opposite view configuration is used, a workspace that can be shared is limited. This configuration is useful, provided that the task performed requires observation of objects from different points of view. For example, an office furniture layout requires an evaluation from various points of view and is therefore very suitable for this configuration. On the other hand, when two users are facing the same direction, the background is shared by the two users. This configuration enables them to share the same view and is useful for explaining, training or teaching an operation on objects.

674

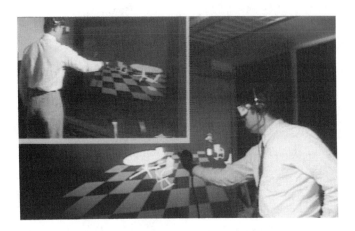

Fig. 6 Cooperative work through virtual space

5. CONCLUSION

This paper describes the key technologies for achieving virtual space teleconferencing. Other technologies, for future purposes include, stereoscopic displays, 3D image databases, and so on. This new communication medium is expected to be applied to a lot of fields.

REFERENCES
[1]Tachi S. et al:"Tele-existence(1): Design and Evaluation of a Visual Display with Sensation of Presence",Proceeding of the 5th Int. Symposium on Theory and Practice of Robot and Manipulators(1984)

[2]Harashima H. and Kishino F.:"Intelligent Image Coding and Communications with Realistic Sensations-Recent Trends-", Trans. IEICE, E74,6(1991)

[3]Ohya J. et al:"Real-time reconstruction of 3D face images in Tereconference with realistic sensations",Technical Report of IEICE, HC92-61(1993)

[4]Raab F.H. et al:"Magnetic position and orientation tracking system",IEEE Tr. on AES-15(1979)

[5]Zimmerman et al:"Hand gesture interface device",CHI+GI'87(1987)

[6]Ishii H. and Miyake N.:"Toward an Open Shared Workspace",Communications of the ACM,34,12(1991)

[7]Takemura H. and Kishino F.:"Cooperative Work Environment Using Virtual Workspace",CSCW 92 Proceedings(1992)

A Virtual Reality system using physiological data
– Application to Virtual Sports CAI –

Ken'ichi KAMIJO and Akihisa KENMOCHI

C&C Information Technology Research Laboratories, NEC Corporation,
1-1, Miyazaki 4-Chome, Miyamae-ku, Kawasaki, Kanagawa, 216 Japan

Abstract

The authors propose a new Virtual Reality (VR) system which uses physiological data indicating user tension and weight balance. The system consists of a physiological data measurement system, a model for processing that data into an estimated "user condition," and a feedback system for adjusting the virtual environment to suit that condition, so as to provide users with a more comfortable environment in virtual space.

The system has been applied to a Virtual Sports CAI system. The resulting prototype provides a simulated skiing environment through the use of a head-mounted display, a slope simulator, and sound effects. It uses physiological data (finger plethysmogram and weight balance measurements) to model a trainee's tension level and skiing ability.

The system has been tested in two experiments. The first experiment showed that feeding back tension level data is effective in helping adjust the environment so as to maintain trainee motivation. The second experiment confirmed that somatosensory information given to the trainee was effective in evoking the sensation of acceleration.

1 Introduction

Virtual Reality (VR) technology has received much recent attention in a number of fields for its potential use as a next generation human interface (HI) [1]. With VR technology, a user can enter a computer-generated environment and directly manipulate objects within it. The HI schema for a typical VR system is shown in Fig.1a. VR systems are different from conventional HIs in that they have feedback processing to reflect such information as a user's motion, position in space, and posture, both in the real and in the virtual environment. While VR technology is currently used primarily in video games and amusement parks, it has recently shown additional enormous potential in the field of computer-aided design – by allowing designers to modify their creations far more easily and effectively than before[2].

VR systems, however, the user model has been represented in a simple physical model based only on posture and position in space. Such systems might be significantly enhanced, particularly with regard to user comfort, if data regarding the user's psychological conditions were also incorporated into the model.

The authors propose here a new Virtual Reality (VR) system which does employ physiological data. The system is applied to a prototype simulated skiing environment, and

676

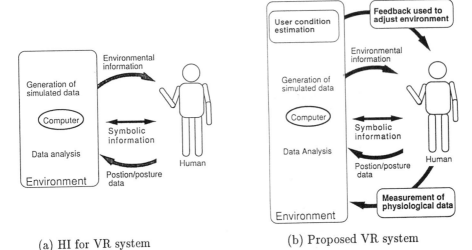

(a) HI for VR system   (b) Proposed VR system

Figure 1: Data flow schemata on Human Interface (HI).

the physiological data used are tension and weight balance. The system consists of a physiological data measurement system, a model for processing that data into an estimated "user condition," and a feedback system for adjusting the virtual environment to suit that condition so as to provide users with a more comfortable environment in virtual space. The schema for the VR system is shown in Fig.1b.

The system has been applied to a Virtual Sports CAI system. The resulting prototype provides a simulated skiing environment through the use of a head-mounted display, a slope simulator, and sound effects. It uses physiological data (finger plethysmogram and weight balance measurement) to model a trainee's tension level and skiing ability.

2   Virtual Sports CAI for skiing

In sports training, it is often difficult to express advice to a trainee effectively in verbal form, just as it is difficult for the trainee to express his physical sensations verbally, and this is particularly true in the beginning and early-intermediate stages of training. The authors' "Virtual Sports CAI" system measures information which cannot easily be expressed verbally, and gives advice non-verbally through a variety of VR techniques. Specifically, the authors have developed an experimental prototype system for a image training system for skiing. A feedback system helps maintain trainee motivation by changing ski slope difficulty according to the skier's tension level.

2.1   System Structure

The prototype system consists of the following: a head-mounted display (Eyephone, VPL Research) with position and direction sensor, two steel plates, on which a trainee stands, a slope simulator to move the plates, eight weight balance sensors (load transducers, NEC San-ei Instruments) in the plates, a finger plethysmogram sensor (NEC San-ei Instruments), and computer systems consisting of a graphical workstation (Iris/Elan, Silicon Graphics), a workstation (SPARC Station 2, SUN) and three personal computers

(a) System apparatus (b) Scene example

Figure 2: Virtual Sports CAI system appearance and scene example during training. The scene indicates weight balance bar-graphs in front of virtual ski plates.

(PC-H98, NEC Corp.) for data measurement, data analysis and control devices. Individual computers communicate through an Ethernet cable with TCP/IP protocols. The system apparatus is shown in Fig.2a.

The system estimates the trainee's skiing ability on the basis of how well his/her weight is balanced on the plates, produces appropriate CG images for skiing, and displays them in the head-mounted display.

The slope simulator presents slope shapes and evokes a sense of acceleration by moving the plates with five AC motors located below each plate and used for roll, yaw, pitch, up-down and left-right movements.

The system also presents trainees with such helpful graphically depicted information as the present status of his/her weight balance (see Fig.2b), which can aid in developing a sense of the relation between balance and making turns, etc.

2.2 Tension estimation and feedback to virtual environment

To estimate the trainee's tension, the system measures the finger plethysmogram data which reflects the amount of blood flow in the finger. The amount change is the response of an autonomic nervous system: a person under high tension experiences low volume of blood-flow through the veins and vice versa. The sensor, attached to the fingertip, consists of a small light bulb and a light detector.

The trainee's tension level is estimated from the finger plethysmogram in ten degree units from 1(low) to 10 (high). Let M_t be a finger plethysmogram data at time t through a band-pass filter for noise reduction. Then, to obtain the amplitude of the data, maximum value M_t^{max} and minimum value M_t^{min} in the period from $(t - \Delta t)$ to t are calculated. The general minimum value S^{min} is also calculated from the beginning point. To normalize individual factors, the ratio R_t is given by $(M_t^{max} - M_t^{min})/S^{min}$. Therefore, estimated tension level L_t is given by $L_t = i$, if $C_i < R_t \leq C_{i-1}(i = 1, \cdots, 10)$, where $C_0, \cdots, C_{10}$ are constants and $C_0 > \cdots > C_{10}$. In this system, constants $C_0, \cdots, C_{10}$ are set to $\infty, 5.5, 5.0, 4.5, 4.0, 3.5, 3.0, 2.5, 2.0, 1.5$, and 0, respectively.

In order to avoid trainees' over-stress and boredom, the system has feedback rules for maintaining motivation during the training. For the purpose, the undulation size in a virtual slope is changed immediately according to the current tension level. For example,

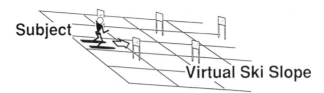

Figure 3: Skiing condition for experiments.

if the system estimates the trainee at a high tension, then the system presents a gentler slope, and vice versa.

3 Experiment 1: Evaluation of the feedback based on tension level

In general, although it is important to maintain the trainee's motivation during training, accomplishing this goal is difficult for ordinary CAI systems. Experiment 1 was conducted to evaluate the effectiveness of the feedback system, based on the tension level estimation, using a subjective evaluation task.

Method.

Five subjects, who have experience on skis, participated in this experiment. Each subject skied on a virtual slope using the VR system for 120 seconds under the following conditions ; *C*: Control (the virtual slope constantly had small undulation), *R*: Random change (the slope changed to small, middle and big undulations randomly) and *FB*: Feedback (the slope changed small, middle and big undulations, according to tension level, to maintain the motivation).

In each condition, system let subjects ski straight, as shown in Fig.3. The undulation size was changed smoothly by using B-spline interpolation function. Each subject participated skiing twice under each condition in a random order.

During skiing, the subjects were asked to evaluate the degree of enjoyableness every 15 seconds. The following seven categories were used: +3 denoted " very enjoyable," 0 "ordinary," −3 "very boring."

Results and Discussion

The subjective evaluation scores were obtained under each condition. An example result of the scores, tension level change and feedback values under condition *FB* is shown in Fig.4. For each subject, the average scores during skiing were calculated. The average for five individuals under conditions *C, R* and *FB* were -0.78, 0.99 and 1.31, respectively. According to *t*-test (one-sided test), the score under condition *FB* is significantly higher than under condition $R(t(4) = 2.29, p < .05)$.

Under condition *R*, some sequences of random feedback values to virtual environment were similar to the values according to the tension level. As the case resulted in a high score, the score under condition *R* should be underestimated. Therefore, it was found that the feedback based on tension level to virtual environment was effective in maintaining the motivation.

4 Experiment 2: Evaluation of somatosensory information for skiing

Somatosensory information is important to simulate the reality in a virtual world, as well as visual and auditory information. In practice, expert skiers tilt forward by their skiing speed-up. Therefore, it seems reasonable to assume that the plates tilt backward

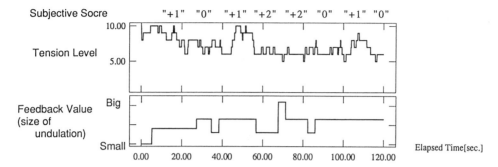

Figure 4: Example result showing subjective evaluation scores, tension levels and feedback values under condition *FB* in Experiment 1 (Subject Y.T.).

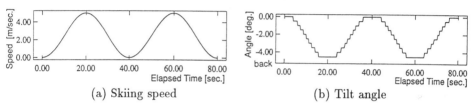

(a) Skiing speed   (b) Tilt angle

Figure 5: Change in skiing speed and tilt angle in Experiment 2.

according to the speed involved, in order to present the acceleration feeling by changing the trainee's subjective gravity. Experiment 2 was conducted to confirm the effectiveness of somatosensory information, especially for evoking the acceleration feeling.

Method

Three subjects, who have experience on skis, participated in this experiment. Each subject skied on a flat slope using the VR system for 80 seconds under the following conditions; *C*: Control (subjects gazed at the fixation point, while the simulator stayed flat), *V*: Visual (subjects watched the CG image slope at speeds which change, like a sine curve shown in Fig.5a, without plate movement), *S*: Somatosensory (subjects gazed at the fixation point with back-tilting plates according to a sine curve shown in Fig.5) and *VS*: Combination of Visual and Somatosensory information. In conditions *V* and *C*, the system let subjects ski straight as shown in Fig.3.

The weight balance locations were measured.

Results and Discussion

Figure 6 shows the average balance points at each time for three individuals under conditions *C*, *V*, *S* and *VS*. As a result, it was found that there was no swing under conditions *C* and *V*. Under condition *S*, the subjects swung backward, according to the plate movement. It was found that the subjects swung forward according to speed change under condition *VS*. The results indicate that the combination of visual and somatosensory information changed the subject's gravity feeling. Therefore, in order to simulate the virtual skiing environment, both slope image and slope simulator are required.

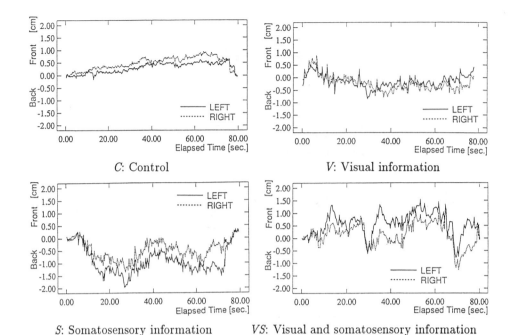

C: Control V: Visual information

S: Somatosensory information VS: Visual and somatosensory information

Figure 6: Average balance points in Experiment 2.

5 Conclusion

The authors have proposed a new Virtual Reality system using physiological data. The system has been applied to a Virtual Sports CAI system. The resulting prototype provides a simulated skiing environment through the use of a head-mounted display, a slope simulator, and sound effects. It uses physiological data (finger plethysmogram and weight balance measurement) to model a trainee's tension level and skiing ability.

The system was tested in two experiments. The results of Experiment 1, subjective evaluation, indicate that the feedback of tension level data is effective in helping to adjust the environment, so as to maintain trainee motivation. In Experiment 2, it was determined that the combination of visual and somatosensory information given to the trainee is effective in evoking the sensation on acceleration.

Acknowledgment
The authors would like to thank Dr. S. Fukuzumi, NEC San-ei Instruments Ltd., Dr. K. Iida and Dr. T. Yamazaki, NEC Corp., for meaningful discussions about applicability of physiological measurements to the VR system.

References
[1] Myron Wrueger: *Artificial Reality II*, Addison-Wesley(1991).

[2] K. Shinohara et al.: *A Virtual Reality System for Network Communications - Multi Party Co-operative Work in Real-time-*, Proc. the second International Conference on Artificial Reality and Tele-existence(ICAT'92), pp.129-132(1992).

The Basic Study of Natural Operation in Virtual Space

Nobuko KATO , Miwako DOI and Akio OKAZAKI

Research & Development Center, Toshiba Corporation
1, Komukai Toshiba-cho, Saiwai-ku, Kawasaki 210, Japan

Abstract

New input devices such as the $DataGlove^{TM}$ have recently been developed for application in virtual reality field, but the naturalness of their operation has yet to be perfected. This paper proposes a new method for obtaining naturalness in operation of objects in a virtual world. The method adopts a non-linear correspondence of hand position from a real world to a virtual world. In addition it also adopts sound feedback. Experimental results show that operation based on this method is more effective than operation employing linear correspondence.

1 Introduction

Recently, Virtual Reality(VR) has become familiar and applied to many fields on a trial basis. VR technology depends on the human sensual mechanism. People can recognize the outer world by not only eye sensation and acoustic sensation, but also cutaneous sensation and deep sensation (i.e. weight, resistance). Especially, information based on the reaction of active behavior is important for recognition. In the case of motion control in virtual space, it is important that system gives sensations to operators correctly.

There are two ways for realizing motion control in virtual space : the method using a haptics device [1] and that with a sensor of 3D position and gesture [2][3].

A haptics device makes a stress in real space. It calculates using the position of operator's hand and object to make cutaneous sensation and deep sensation as feedback given into the human body, so that human motions in real space can be controlled. However, many haptics devices are impractical, since they impose limitations on the operator's movements and the space where the operator works.

On the other hand, motion control by a 3D position sensor and gesture uses no tactical feedback. Therefore, it tends to make operations lack of naturalness. Generally, physical constraints in the virtual space are calculated to reduce this unnaturality. The heavy calculation of the physical constraints are required for it and it make the system response slow and a discrepancy between a real world and a virtual world becomes larger.

The method we propose for controlling motions interactively in virtual space is designed to accomplish the following objectives.

- Independence of haptics device
- Reduction of calculation

A linear function which maps a real world to a virtual world cannot absorb the play in an operation and sometimes makes mismatches. In addition, sound is the only method available for feedback if tactile feedback is not used.

We have adopted the following approaches to realize the proposed system.

- Non-linear function for mapping the real world to the virtual world
- Sounds which correspond to motions

The next section describes the non-linear function and sound system. Experimental results and discussion are presented later.

2 Realization of Natural Operation

2.1 Non-linear correspondence from real space to virtual space

Usually, operation in virtual space is used with linear correspondence from real space to virtual space. However, weight or resistance in virtual space cannot be represented when a haptics device is not used. Furthermore, sometimes correspondence from virtual space to real space is lost when physical constraints apply to only virtual space, because there are no constraints for the hand in real space.

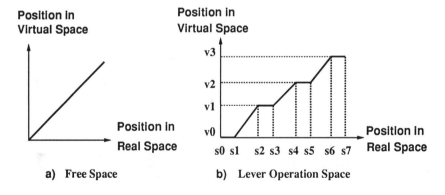

Figure 1: Projection function

In the following, the idea of the non-linear correspondence is explained by an example task:operation of shifting lever. In the action of lever shifting in a real space, a certain amount of force is needed to shift the lever from one shifting position to another, in other words, the lever will not move until a certain amount of force is exerted by the hand. If the lever in the virtual space linearly moves according to the hand movement in real space as shown in Figure 1-a , the operation may become unnatural. In contrast, the non-linear function shown in Figure 1-b can imitate the real lever action better than the linear function. The reason is as follows.

According to the function expressed in Figure 1-b, the lever will not move and remains at a position v0 the first shifting position, when the hand in the real space moves within an interval [s0, s1]. When the hand in the real space moves within an interval [s1, s2], the lever moves within an interval [v0,v1] in linear correspondence with the hand in real space, until the lever shifts to the second shifting position v1. As a result, operator can clearly distinguish shifting position in a virtual space if a hand moves straight forward in a real space.

In this case, gradient and step width are able to represent a lever weight and a power of resistance. Thus a non-linear function enables an operator to easily control his hand in a real space correctly.

2.2   Emphasis feeling of operation by sound

We have also used a sound instead of the cutaneous and deep sensation for the purposes of achieving feedback sensation from the outer world. In the following , three cases of sound use are explained.

The first one is to realize a touch sensation. The system make a sound instead of actual touch sensation when an operator touchs or releases an object.

The second one is for resistance. For example, when a operator opens or closes a door, the system makes a sound at the moment instead of representing their actual resistance.

The last one is for weight. The system generates different sounds to distinguish each heavy or light object when it moves.

3   Experimental Result

3.1   Virtual control console

We have made a control console in a virtual space to confirm the effects of non-linear functions and sounds. The virtual control console has three levers on it and an operator can shift them at three levels . The goal of this development are:

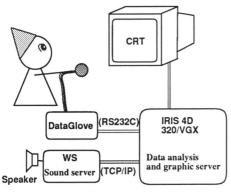

Figure 2:
System construction of a Virtual
control console

Figure 3:
Three levers of a virtual
control console

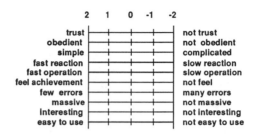

Figure 4: Questionnaire

- these levers can be easily shifted,

- with few errors,

- with achievement of feeling during operation,

- with different feeling for each lever.

A configuration of a virtual control console is shown in Figure 2. Data analysis and graphic server are on an IRIS4D/320VGX. A sound server is on the other workstation. The IRIS 4D/320VGX and the workstation for sound effect are connected via an Ethernet. An operator uses a DataGlove manufactured by VPL Co Ltd. to input hand position and gesture in real space. The virtual control console is displayed as actual size.

3.2 Parameter feature

Three types of levers(LL:large size lever, ML: middle size lever, SL:small size lever) are set on the console as shown in Figure 3. The LL and ML are levers to be shifted forward or backward by the hand, while SL is a lever whose rear end is pivotally fixed and whose front end is to be shifted from right to left or from left to right. Each of these levers has three shifting positions and a step function which has different step width and gradient for each.

Also each of these levers has its own sounds as follows.

- A sound at grasping a lever

- A sound at releasing a lever

- A sound at shifting a lever

A heavy sound is assigned to LL while a light sound is assigned to ML to clearly distinguish the lever type.

Indicator lamps aligned beside each shifting position turn on if the lever moves to that position.

3.3 Measurement of required time and its errors

The following four groups are prepared for comparison.

[**A**] With a linear function

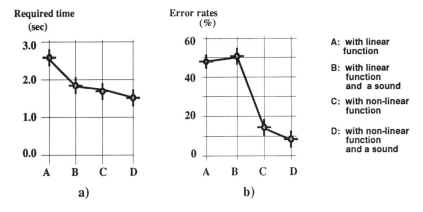

Figure 5: Operation Time & Error

[B] With a linear function and a sound

[C] With a non-linear function

[D] With a non-linear function and a sound

The task which subjects perform is as follows.

1. The position to which a lever is shifted is indicated at random.

2. Subjects grasp a lever and shift it until it moves to the correct position.

3. A green indicator lamp turns on if a lever shifts to a correct position.

4. Subjects release the lever.

Before the experiment session, subjects exercise with the lever operation using DataGlove for 30 minutes. One session has 15 tasks for each compared group, that is 60 tasks totally. Subjects try four sessions that were assigned on a random basis. The following items are measured from subjects trials.

Time: The interval from when the lever position is shown to the time subjects release the lever.

Error: Rate of error tasks to all tasks. An error task is a task whose shift time exceeds the minimum shift time.

Subjects completed the questionnaire shown in Figure 4 for each session . The results are shown in Figures 5 and 6.

4 Discussion

Figure 5-a indicates that subjets who operate with a non-linear function(C,D) or with a sound(B) operate faster than subjects who operate with a linear function only(A). But differences are small in B,C,D.

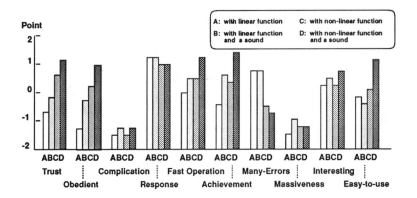

Figure 6: Results of questionnaire

Figure 5-b shows that error rate with a non-linear function(C,D) is better than with a linear function(A,B). This is also confirmed by the responses to the questionnaire as shown in Figure 6.

According to the responses to the questionnaire shown in Figure 6, trust and the feeling of achievement with a non-linear function or a sound are higher than with a linear function only. But subjects cannot identify the differences in the levers' weights. One reason for this problem is that loudness and clarity are insufficient to distinguish the lever sounds.

5   Conclusion

This paper has presented a method of natural operation in virtual space. Operators can easily control the virtual levers with a non-linear function and a sound. This method does not require a large amount of calculation for solving physical constraints. The following conclusion is obtained from the experiments.

- The operation with a non-linear function or sound is faster than that with a linear function only.

- The incidence of errors in operation is reduced by the system with a non-linear function.

References

[1] Hiroo IWATA and Keigo MATSUDA, "Artificial Reality with Force-feedback: Development of Desktop Virtual Space with Compact Master Manipulator" ,
Computer Graphics , Volume 24, Number 4, August 1990

[2] Junji NOMURA, "Virtual Space Decision Support System and Its Application to Consumer Showrooms" ,Virtual Computing ,pp109-196(1992)

[3] Noriko ENOMOTO, Junji NOMURA and Kazuya SAWADA, "Investigation of Proper Operating Environment and Calibration Techniques for 3-D Magnetic Sensor ",
The Seventh Symposium on Human Interface , October 1991

New Techniques for Interaction in Virtual Worlds - Contents of Development and Examples

Wilhelm Bauer and Oliver Riedel

Fraunhofer Institute for Industrial Engineering
Nobelstrasse 12, 70569 Stuttgart 80, Germany,
Tel: +49-711-970-2090, Fax: +49-711-970-2299

Abstract
A number of industrial applications of Virtual Reality have recently appeared on the market which are no longer toys but real tools. Multidimensional input devices like the Spaceball, the Spacemouse, ot the DataGlove are available and provide the users with intuitive three-dimensional interaction capabilities. But what about the ergonomic software interface for the user of VR? The most common interface to virtual worlds - a glove - is not sufficiently accurate to ensure that all gestures necessary for the handling of a complex program can be measured. As a result, the user must spend a great deal of time becoming familiar with the complex worlds and learning to use the interface effectively and efficiently. This paper will discuss a 3-D user interface to virtual worlds which is similar to the well-known 2-D GUI's, but which is driven not only by gestures, but by a combination of gestures and icons.

1   Introduction

There appear no limits to the possibilities of using Virtual Reality but the acceptance of the application by a large majority of the users will depend for the most part on the user-friendliness of the application.

Because three-dimensional worlds can only be controlled by a corresponding three-dimensional interface, the only realistic input media on the market are as follows:

- Spaceball: Spaceballs (also called force balls) look like someone stuck a baseball on a joytick, but force balls differ from joysticks in one major aspect - they don`t move. Instead, they measure the amount of force applied to them. To move upwards with a force ball, you simply pick up the ball as if you were picking it off a table. Several small strain gauges located inside the ball measure six different values (three rotations and three translations) and the hardware-interface translates these values in the six degrees of freedom (DOF). In addition to this feature most of the spaceballs have up to nine software-programmable buttons for the use of additional options. Force balls work for navigating or moving objects around. Just as the ball can control your viewpoint, it can also be attached to virtual objects so that moving the ball moves the virtual object in a similar way.

- SpaceMouse: Several companies have taken a basic mouse design and modified it by adding some form of 6 DOF or 3 DOF tracking sensors: either ultrasonic, electromagnetic or gyroscopic tracking are used. You do the same thing when you pick up your mouse, it reaches the edge of your mouse pad, and you set it back down in the center. The effective use of these devices is primarily dependent on the qualities of their 6 DOF tracking system.

- DataGlove: The basic premise of wired-clothing devices is to wear some external form of tracking device to monitor the position and orientation of key hand or body parts. Users could communicate with the computer through simple gestures made with their hands while wearing the wired glove. Wired clothing works by measuring bend angles of fingers using either mechanical, fiber-optic or resistive sensors. Fiber-optic sensors are used in the two most popular versions of the wired glove and wired suit. These work by looping a single strand of fiber-optic cable across a joint, like a knuckle. As the knuckle moves, the cable bends, which causes a reduction in the amount of light passing through it. This effect is enhanced even more if minute scratches are placed where the cable passes over the knuckle. The varying light output is measured by a photodetector and then communicated to a controller, which summarizes the current state of all the sensors and sends it on to the computer. The computer recognizes the gesture, and the graphic image of the object is attached to the graphic image of the user's hand. This is a simple and natural method for interacting with objects.

Most of the hitherto constructed applications employ a language of gestures to provide the user with control. The complexity of the amount of functions available determines the cost of this „language" of gestures. Because Virtual Reality refers not only to visualizing three-dimensional data-material but is also a media of interaction between this data the development of the interface must be done with special care. This level of care must be implemented in the choice of almost intuitive gestures for actions which approach reality, as well as in the presentation of appropriate Feedback to the user as confirmation of his actions. Some programs recognize differing conditions during use, which in time control different functions. At this time the measurement and storage of a gesture language can only be accomplished with the DataGlove. These input devices, however, are not get sufficiently developed to overcome the following weaknesses:

- low resolution of joint angles,
- low levels of accuracy in repetition,
- user-depedent calibration is required,
- the maximum number of gestures is limited,
- a high degree of training is required.

As a result is was necessary to develop a new interface device for complex programs, which despite the use of DataGloves, is able to place the entire functionality of the program at the user's disposal.

2. Solutions

To overcome the above mentioned shortcomings inherent in existing hardware, particularly the DataGlove, a new solution had to be found which differed from the pure gesture control techniques of the existing interface media. A complete abandonment of this media was, however, not an option, as existing gestures such as driving or flight gestures are already so closely associated with virtual worlds, that the introduction of completely new techniques would more likely have been a hindernis to the usage of Virtual Reality. The starting point was found in a joint medium which used both icons and gestures. Icons have the great advantage of already being well-know through the use of two-dimensional „Windows" technology such as X or MS-Windows. During the creation and presentation of the icons however, it was not possible to draw upon existing implementations, since icons had never before introduced into a three-dimensional environment. Two primary organisational possibilities were available:

- grouping the icons in floating space and
- grouping the icons around the Cybermant in the form of a virtual „toolbelt".

The first option was eliminated since users would have differing distances to cover to reach the icons depending upon their location in the virtual space. Even the gesture-controlled „calling" of icons to the user was seen to be impractical. As a result the icons were located at a fixed point („toolbelt") in relation to the user. The number of available icons is depedent upon the system status and can be changed by the user through the use of gestures or icons. During the development of the icons, logos and 3-D objects were used which could easily be associated with the related actions and/or functionality.

The following describes the evaluation of the new interaction technique at the institute and the result of the tests are discussed.

3 Description of the Test Environment

To establish a test environment, an industrial softeware package was selected, which was developed for companies in the future business. This ensured that the experiments could be applied to a number of different people, including those without VR experience. The application VILAGE was developed with and for the following hardware and software:

• VPL DataGlove and EyePhone.
• VPL Body Electric with proprietary expansion of the operating system software. This expansion was made through the help of patches which are possible from the version 3.5 on of the VPL program 'Body-Electric'. The patches themselves are programmed in C++ and integrated through the socalled 'Resource-Editor' of Macintosh.
• Isaac renderingsoftware with special modifications to accomodate the SiliconGraphics Skywriter to improve the frame rate.

4 Experiments and their Results

4.1 Procedures

The experiments were made by using 50 people per software version. All of the people had some experience in the field of interior planning. To some extent this experience was based on the classic planning media such as paper floorplans and furniture or using CAD-based media such as the widely-used AutoCAD system. Non of the people had experience with the use of VR-Systems. Experiments were carried out in the VR-Laboratory at the institute as well as at various trade shows and other public events. The experiment was split up into 4 sections:

1. Introduction of the VILAGE program and a short summary of the goals of the experiment.

2. Questioning the test persons regarding the meaning and clarity of the various gestures and icons used in the program. The leader of the test project then evaluated the effectiveness and the clarity of the gestures and icons based on the answers received from the test participants.

3. A more indepth look at the two system versions with help provided by the test project leader. At this time, the time frame (learning curve) was measured to determine how much time was required before the test participants felt comfortable with the system(s).

4. Three repetitions of a standard exercise: a desk was to be transported out of a warehouse into the room and subsequently placed very precisely in the right-hand corner of the wall containing a window.

The criteria which were evaluated are as follows:
- time required complete the exercise,
- accuracy of placing the furniture,
- number of individual actions required to complete the exercise.

4.2 Results

4.2.1 Clarity and Effectiveness of the Gestures and Icons

A major criterion governing the potential use of icons in user interfaces is the clarity of the pictures used. „ A picture is better than a thousand words" is particularly important in this case, since a complex series of procedures are represented in a single pictorial symbol. To establish the clarity/effectiveness of an icon, the test participants were first given the summary of the program attributes of VILAGE and the major functional points, after which they were shown 12 icons and 9 gestures which had to be interpreted by the test person. The statements of the experimentees were categorized by the test-supervisor as follows:

- Correspondence of the real icon-meaning and the user's evidence (Mf = 100 %)
- Partly correspondence ((Mf = 50%)
- No corredspondence (Mf = 0%)

The histogram of this experiment can be seen in figure 1. There will be abstained from a detailed explanation of the examined icons respectively gestures. As it can be seen in the histogram the meaningfulness of the icons is much higher as the meaningfulness of the gestures. It can be also seen much clearer if the average of the meaningfulness of the icons Mf(i)=64,6% and the gestures Mf(g)=1,4% are put into relation to eachother: there is an increase of the meaningfulness between icons and gestures of about 40 times.

One reason for the relatively low correlation of the icon-meaning and the user's statement are lacking precise tests for the project which could be a main connecting theme for the creation of three-dimensional icons. Through the experiments is has been found out that the icons have been recognised much more often than gestures. This is an advantage if the program is used very often. It is possible that then more functions of the program are used than with the gesture-version of the same application.

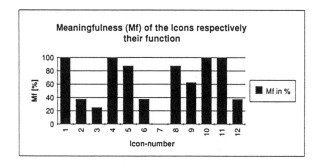

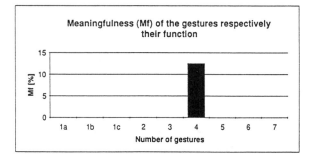

Figure 1: Meaningfulness (Mf) of the icons respectively their function

4.2.2 Training Time

The following part of the test records the training-time of the experimentees. The training-time was over as the experimentee has gained a certain security in using the program. The test supervisor helped the experimentees during the test, the activities during training-time referred not only to the following type of problem but also to the other functions of the programs.

4.2.3 Processing Time

The measuring of the training-time of a defined problem was a central part of the survey and the advantages and disadvantages of both version soon turned out. The results shows an identical working time for each run of the superimposed histograms of both program version. This makes clear that there is no appreciable difference in learning time required for the two systems. A more detailed investigation of the time required to work with the icon-loaded system indicated strong volatility in time required based on the application. This turned out to be due to the incorrect construction of one of the icons, which compared to the other icons had geometrically oversized attributes. As a result, there were repeated instances where this icon was activated by accident. When this icon was corrected, the problem disappeared. A new series of measurement was not, however, carried out as the problem affected only the one icon.

Another reason for the initially faster execution time of the gesture-based software version is also the number of actions to complete the test.

5 Summary

This paper describes the comparison of two different versions of a user interface for a VR-program. Experiments in a defined test environment were carried out to determine the clarity and effectiveness of icons, learning time associated with their use, and other criteria. It became apparent there are advandtages incorporating both gestures and icons when compared to one incorporating only gesture-based action. Particular advantages are:

- the high recognition value,
- a significantly shorter learning time is required for first-time users of the program,
- accidential use of two functions at once is not possible,
- a hierarchical organisation of the user interface is possible without redundancy of various action elements.

6 References

1 Bauer, W.; Riedel, O.: Virtual Reality Design of Office Workplaces, Proc. of ICPR 93, Lappeenranta, 1993.
2 Herrmann, G.; Riedel, O.: VIRUSI: Virtual User Interface - Iconorientierte Benutzerschnittstelle für VR-Applikationen, Forschung und Praxis, Band T 35. Hrsg.: Warnecke, H.J.; Bullinger, H.-J., Springer-Verlag, 1993, page 227-243.
3 Bauer, W.; Bullinger, H.-J.; Riedel, O.: Virtual Reality as a Tool for Office Design Applications - Visions and Realities, Proc. of HCI International 93, Orlando, 1993.
4 Böhm, K.; Hübner, W.; Väänänen, K.: „GIVEN: Gesture Driven Interactions in Virtual Environments - A Toolkit Approach to 3D Interactions", Proc. of Interface to Real & Virtual Worlds, Montpellier, 1992.
5 Bryson, S. et al.: Implementation of Immersive Virtual Environments, Course Notes SIGGRAPH 92, Chicago, 1992.
6 Furness, G.A.; Bricken, M; Bricken, W.: „Virtual Interface Technology", Course Notes SIGGRAPH 91, Las Vegas, 1991.

modelling techniques by adopting a "spatial" approach where people employ the affordances of virtual computer space as a means of control. In so doing, our underlying philosophy has been to encourage individual autonomy of action, symmetry of power, freedom to communicate and minimal hard-wired computer constraints. Where the interacting objects are artifacts, the model provides mechanisms for constructing highly reactive environments where objects dynamically react to the presence of others (e.g. you may activate a tool simply by approaching or looking at it).

2. ROOMS AND VIRTUAL SPACES

We have chosen to base our work around the metaphor of interaction within virtual worlds. Under this metaphor, a computer system can be viewed as a set of spaces through which people move, interacting with each other and with objects which they encounter. The use of spatial metaphors to structure work environments is not new, having previously been explored in areas such as user interface design, virtual meeting rooms, media spaces, CSCW environments and virtual reality. A number of collaborative virtual environments have been constructed and demonstrated including Rubberrocks [Codella 92], the Virtual Art Museum [Loeffler 92] and Reality Built for Two [Blanchard] and the work of [Takemura 92]. Other related work includes office environments based on virtual world metaphors [Root 88], [Benford 93a], [Benford 93b] and the use of rooms based metaphors to structure user interfaces [Henderson 85]. An alternative approach is the "media-spaces" of [Gaver 92].

One reason for this popularity of spatial approaches to collaborative systems is their strong relation to physical reality and therefore their highly intuitive nature. From a more abstract standpoint, space affords a number of important facilities for collaboration including awareness at a glance; support for ad-hoc as well as planned interaction; use of body language and other social conventions in conversation management; flexible negotiation of access to resources, and structuring, navigation, exploration and mapping of large-scale work environments.

We believe that current spatially-oriented systems will not effectively scale to heavily populated spaces, especially because of the problem of computational and cognitive overload. More specifically, as the number of occupants in a virtual space increases beyond a few people, the need to effectively manage interactions will become critical. Also, new techniques are needed which support non rigid and natural social conventions for the handling of, for example, conversation management.

3. KEY CONCEPTS OF THE SPATIAL MODEL

Central to the model is the concept of *awareness*, a measure of how much one object in a virtual world is aware of another. An object inhabiting virtual space might represent people and also other artifacts (e.g. tools and documents).

Let us then establish that any interaction between objects occurs through some *medium*. A medium might represent a communication medium (e.g. audio, visual or text) or some other kind of object specific interface. Each object might be capable of interacting through a combination of media/interfaces and objects may negotiate compatible media whenever they

Awareness, Focus and Aura
A Spatial Model of Interaction in Virtual Worlds

Steve Benford [a] and Lennart E. Fahlén [b]

[a] Dept. of Computer Science, University of Nottingham, Nottingham, NG7 2RD, UK
email sdb@cs.nott.ac.uk, phone +44-602-514203, fax +44-602-514254

[b] Swedish Institute of Computer Science (SICS), Box 1263, S-16428 Kista, SWEDEN
email lef@sics.se, phone +46-8-7521539, fax +46-8-7517230

Abstract
    We present a spatial model of group interaction in virtual environments. The model aims to provide flexible and natural support for managing conversations among large groups of people in virtual space. It can also be used to control more general interactions among other kinds of objects inhabiting such spaces. The model defines the key abstractions of aura, focus, nimbus and adapters to control levels of awareness between objects. These key concepts are defined in a sufficiently general way so as to apply to any CSCW system where a spatial metric can be identified - i.e. a way of measuring position and direction. Also, some possible domains of usage are discussed, such as virtual reality, database and text conferencing applications. The model described in this paper is being developed as part of the COMIC project, a European ESPRIT Basic Research Action on computer-based mechanisms of interaction in cooperative work.

1. INTRODUCTION

    The emerging generation of interface and multi-media technologies require new models of interaction, both human to human and human to computer.
    Our paper presents a model for supporting group interaction in large-scale virtual worlds. The model provides generic techniques for managing interactions between various objects in such environments, including humans and computer artifacts. Furthermore, the model is intended to be sufficiently flexible to apply to any system where a spatial metric can be identified (i.e., a way of measuring distance and orientation). Such applications might range from multi-user virtual reality through conferencing systems, collaborative hypermedia, document editors, databases and information spaces.
    Where the interacting objects are humans, the model provides mechanisms for conversation management. These contrast with existing floor control and workflow

meet or become aware of each other in some other way.

Next we need a mechanism for determining which objects are capable of interacting with which others at a given time (simultaneous interaction between all objects is not computationally scaleable). *Aura* is defined to be a sub-space which effectively bounds the presence of an object within a given medium and which acts as an enabler of potential interaction [Fahlén 92], [Fahlén 93]. Objects carry their auras with them when they move through space and when two auras collide, interaction between the objects in the medium becomes a possibility. Note that an object typically has different auras (e.g. size and shape) for different media.

Once aura has been used to determine the potential for object interactions, the objects themselves are subsequently responsible for controlling these interactions. This is achieved on the basis of quantifiable *levels* of awareness between them [Benford 93a], [Benford 93b]. The measure of awareness between two objects need not be mutually symmetrical. As with aura, awareness levels are medium specific. Awareness between objects in a given medium is manipulated via *focus* and *nimbus*. Focus is another space, within which the object directs its attention. Nimbus is still another space where the object projects some aspect of its presence to be perceived by other objects. Or, expressed in another way:

> *The more an object is within your focus, the more aware you are of it.*
> *The more an object is within your nimbus, the more aware it is of you.*

Objects negotiate levels of awareness by using their nimbus and focus in order to try to make others more aware of them or to make themselves more aware of others. We use the word negotiate to convey an image of objects positioning themselves in space in much the same way as people move around in a room to get access to some physical resource. As the simplest case, the awareness level between two objects is computed by taking the "product" of one object's "focus value" and the other object's "nimbus value", or put in other words:

> *The level of awareness that object A has of object B in medium M is*
> *some function of A's focus on B in M and B's nimbus on A in M.*

The resulting quantified awareness levels between two objects can then used as the basis for managing their interaction on an application specific basis. An example would be to use awareness levels to directly control the the volume level of an audio channel between two objects. Note that the use of nimbus and focus allows objects in an interaction to influence their awareness of each other in an independent fashion. That is, they support our goals of autonomy, power balance and symmetry.

A further addition to the model is the introduction of various objects that can alter the aura, nimbus and focus "fields". We call such objects *adapters* and examples include using a "virtual microphone" or sitting down at a "virtual conference table", both of which can increase the awareness level between objects.

Adapters support interaction styles beyond basic mingling. In essence, an adapter is an object which, when picked up, moved close to or approached in some other way, amplifies or attenuates the aura, nimbus and focus.

It is important to note that aura, focus, nimbus, adapters and the resulting awareness can all be asymmetrical, multidimensional, multi layered, different for each media and interaction mode, as well as dynamic in space and time and dependent on other conditions.

The model allows persons in the environment to govern their interaction and collaboration with other persons as well as tools and services provided in the environment, through awareness. An object, for example a person, can change its aura, focus and nimbus "fields" implicitly by moving and changing orientation in the environment, and explicitly by choosing to be attentive to a certain object.

For example, by moving close to another person, you become more aware of that person, which might allow you to talk to each other through a speech connection. The same technique is used to get access to tools and services in the CSCW environment. It is important to note that, although persons control their interaction through aura, focus and nimbus, they need not be explicitly aware that they are doing so. Aura, nimbus and focus may often be invisible or may be implied through "natural" mechanisms such as body direction or the use of eyes to provide gaze awareness. Also, aura, focus and nimbus are manipulated in "natural" ways that are associated with basic human actions in space, for instance movement and change of orientation.

To summarise, our spatial model defines key concepts for allowing objects to establish and subsequently control interactions. Aura is used to establish the potential for interaction across a given medium. Nimbus and focus are then used to negotiate the mutual and possibly non-symmetrical levels of awareness between objects which in turn drives the behaviour of the interactions. Finally, adapter objects can be used to further influence aura, nimbus and focus and so add a degree of extendibility to the model.

4. APPLYING THE SPATIAL MODEL

4.1. Multi-user virtual reality - the DIVE system

One application of the spatial model is to virtual reality systems. A prototype multi-user virtual reality system, DIVE (Distributed Interactive Virtual Environment) [Fahlén 91] [Carlsson 92] has been developed as part of the MultiG program (a Swedish national research effort on high speed networks and distributed applications [Pehrson 92]).

DIVE is a UNIX-based, multi-platform software framework for creating multi-user, multi-application, three-dimensional distributed user environments. There is support for multiple co-existing "worlds" with gateways between them to enable inter-world movement.

Users or participants are represented by unique graphical 3D-bodies or icons (i.e. a self representation) whose position, orientation, movements and identity are easily visible to other participants. In our current implementation, auras are represented as invisible objects that can be part of a user's or tool's representation in the virtual environment, i.e as a sphere around each user's icon. Aura handling is achieved through a special collision manager process. When a collision between auras occurs, this manager sends a message containing information such as the ids of the objects involved, positions, angles and so on, to other processes within the DIVE environment. These processes (e.g. the owners of the objects involved) then carry out appropriate nimbus, focus and awareness computations. It is possible to have support for a multiple of users, objects, media and service specific aura types with associated collision managers. These managers can be mapped onto separate processing nodes in a network, something that is important from a computational load balancing viewpoint. The handling of focus and nimbus can be mapped in a similar way.

A toolkit has been developed as a first step to construct a distributed collaborative environment and to allow experimentation with the concepts of aura, focus, nimbus and awareness. Presently it consists of a whiteboard tool [Ståhl 92a], a conference table tool, the handling and distribution of documents and basic support for aura functionality. Further details on the aura implementation in the DIVE system can be found in [Ståhl 92b].

4.2. Other applications

We can envisage the application of the spatial model to a wide range of other CSCW systems. One interesting example might be that of collaborative hypermedia. A hypermedia document can be considered as a one dimensional space where the spatial metric is the number of links between two nodes. Simple aura, nimbi and foci might then convey a sense of awareness between people browsing through such a space. Hypermedia browsers could use measures of awareness to take actions such as notifying people of the presence of others or automatically opening up communication channels.

It may also be possible to spatially organise more general information domains, classification schemes and taxonomies. One approach to the spatial visualisation of large databases is given in [Mariani 92]. As a second example, work has been carried out into the spatial mapping and classification of scientific disciplines based on a statistical analysis of the co-occurrence of keywords in academic papers [Callon] and also in the cloud space approach of [Chalmers 92]. The spatial model could be applied to manage interactions across such a space and similar techniques might have applications in areas such as news systems, bulletin boards and shared databases. An application of the spatial model to a text conferencing system is being realised in the *CyCo (Cyberspace for Cooperation)* system at Nottingham University [Benford 93a], [Benford 93b].

5. SUMMARY

Our paper has described a spatial model of group interaction in large-scale virtual environments. The model provides mechanisms for managing conversations between people, as well as interactions with other kinds of objects, in spatial settings. The notion of awareness is used as the basis for controlling interaction and the model provides mechanisms for calculating awareness levels from the spatial properties of objects (e.g. position and orientation). This allows objects to manage interactions through natural mechanisms such as movement and orientation in space. The model defines the key concepts of aura, nimbus, focus and adapter objects all of which contribute to awareness. These concepts are defined in a sufficiently general way so as to apply to any system where a spatial metric can be identified. The paper also considers some potential applications.

We anticipate that aura, focus and nimbus are appropriate mechanisms to support and encourage the normal social conventions that govern interaction.

As a final comment, we need not only use awareness to control conversation across communication media; it can also be used to govern any kind of interaction between objects in distributed systems. Thus, the spatial model might eventually provide a generic platform for building a variety of virtual environments. We are optimistic that spatial models of interaction will form an important aspect of support for CSCW, particularly as new technologies such as virtual reality become more widespread in the next few years.

6. REFERENCES

[Benford 93a] S. Benford, A. Bullock, N. Cook, P. Harvey, R. Ingram and O.-K. Lee, *From Rooms to Cyberspace: Models of Interaction in Large Virtual Computer Spaces*, The

University of Nottingham, Nottingham, UK, to appear in Interacting With Computers, Butterworth-Heinmann 1993.

[Benford 93b] S. Benford, A. Bullock, N. Cook, P. Harvey, R. Ingram and O.-K. Lee, *A Spatial Model of Cooperation for Virtual Worlds*, Proc. of Informatique '93, Interface to Real & Virtual Worlds, Montpellier, France, March 22-26, 1993.

[Blanchard] C. Blanchard, S. Burgess, Y. Harville, J. Lanier, A. Lasko, M. Oberman and M. Teitel, *Reality Built for Two: A Virtual Reality Tool*, ACM SIGGRAPH Computer Graphics 24:2, pp. 35-36.

[Callon] Michel Callon, John Law and Arie Rip (eds), *Mapping the Dynamics of Science and Technology*, Macmillan press, ISBN 0-333-37223-9.

[Carlsson 92] Christer Carlsson and Olof Hagsand, *The MultiG Distributed Interactive Virtual Environment*, In Proc. 5th MultiG Workshop, Stockholm, December 18, 1992.

[Chalmers 92] M. Chalmers and P. Chitson, *Bead: Explorations in Information Visualization,* Proc. SIGIR'92, SIGIR Forum, ACM Press, June 1992, pp. 330-337.

[Codella 92] Christopher Codella, Reza Jalili, Lawrence Koved, J. Bryan Lewis, Daniel T. Ling, James S. Lipscomb, Favid A. Rabenhorst, Chu P. Wang, Alan Norton, Paula Sweeney and Greg Turk, *Interactive Simulation in a Multi-Person Virtual World*, Proceedings of CHI'92, Monterey, May 3-7, 1992, pp. 329-334.

[Cook 91] S. Cook, G. Birch, A. Murphy and J. Woolsey, *Modelling Groupware in the Electronic Office*, in Computer-supported Cooperative Work and Groupware, Saul Greenberg (ed), Harcourt Brace Jovanovich, 1991, ISBN 0-12-299220-2.

[Fahlén 91] Lennart E. Fahlén, *The MultiG TelePresence System*, Proc. 3rd MultiG Workshop, Stockholm, December 1991, pp. 33-57.

[Fahlén 92] Lennart E. Fahlén and Charles Grant Brown, *The Use of a 3D Aura Metaphor for Computer Based Conferencing and Teleworking*, Proc. 4th Multi-G Workshop, Stockholm-Kista, May 1992, pp 69-74.

[Fahlén 93] Lennart E. Fahlén, Charles Grant Brown, Olov Ståhl and Christer Carlsson, *A Space Based Model for User Interaction in Shared Synthetic Environments*, Proc. of INTERCHI '93, Amsterdam, April 27 - May 2, 1993.

[Gaver 92] William Gaver, *The Affordances of Media Spaces for Collaboration*, Proc. CSCW'92, Toronto, November 1992, ACM Press.

[Henderson 85] Henderson and Card, *Rooms: The Use of Multiple Virtual Workspaces to Reduce Space Contention*, ACM Transactions on Graphics, Vol. 5, No. 3, July 1985.

[Loeffler 92] Carl Eugene Loeffler, "Networked Virtual Reality", Proc. of the 5th MultiG Workshop, Stockholm, December 18, 1992.

[Mariani 92] John A. Mariani and Robert Lougher, *TripleSpace: an Experiment in a 3D Graphical Interface to a Binary Relational Database*, Interacting with Computers, Vol 4, No. 2, 1992, pp147-162.

[Pehrson 92] Björn Pehrson, Per Gunningberg and Stephen Pink, *MultiG-A research Programme on Distributed MultiMedia Applications and Gigabit Networks*, IEEE Network Magazine vol 6, 1 (January 1992), pp. 26-35.

[Root 88] R.W. Root, *Design of a Multi-Media Vehicle for Social Browsing*, Proc. of CSCW'88, Portland, Oregon, September 26-28 1988, pp25-38.

[Ståhl 92a] Olov Ståhl, *Mdraw - A Tool for Cooperative Work in the MultiG TelePresence Environment*, Technical Report T92:05, SICS, 1992.

[Ståhl 92b] Olov Ståhl, *Implementation Issues of Aura Based Tools*, Proc. 5th MultiG Workshop, Stockholm, December 18, 1992.

[Takemura 92] Haruo Takemure and Fumio Kishino, *Cooperative Work Environment Using Virtual Workspace*, Proc. CSCW'92, Toronto, Nov 1992, ACM Press.

The Sense of Presence Within Virtual Environments: A Conceptual Framework

Woodrow Barfield[1] and Suzanne Weghorst[2]

[1]Laboratory for Interactive Computer Graphics and Human Factors
[2]Human Interface Technology Laboratory
Department of Industrial Engineering, FU-20
University of Washington
barfield@u.washington.edu
weghorst@u.washington.edu

1. Introduction

Recent developments in display technology, e.g., the use of a head-mounted display slaved to the user's head position, techniques to spatialize sound, and computer-generated tactile and kinesthetic interfaces allow humans to experience impressive visual, auditory, and tactile simulations of virtual worlds. However, while the technological developments in virtual environments have been quite impressive, what is currently lacking is a conceptual and analytical framework in which to guide research in this developing area. What is also lacking is a set of metrics which can be used to measure performance within virtual environments and to quantify the level of presence experienced by participants of virtual worlds. The purpose of this paper is to discuss the concept of presence in the context of virtual environments focusing on conditions which may produce a sense of presence within virtual worlds and to suggest techniques to measure presence. In addition, we present the results of two exploratory studies which investigated several important factors related to the sense presence within virtual environments.

A typical virtual environment system consists of three components: 1) one or more input devices, e.g., a space ball or a power glove, 2) several forms of output such as stereoscopic images, spatialized sound, or tactile feedback, and 3) a computer to model and render images (Furness et al., 1992). Instead of viewing directly an image presented on a CRT, the virtual display creates only a small physical image (e.g., nominally one square inch) and projects this image into the eyes by optical lenses and mirrors so that the original image appears to be a large picture suspended in the world. A personal virtual display system, termed a head-mounted display, usually consists of a small image source, e.g., a miniature cathode-array tube or liquid crystal display, which is mounted on some headgear, and small optical elements which magnify, collimate and project this image via a mirror combiner into the eyes such that the original image appears at optical infinity. With two image sources and projection optics, one for each eye, a binocular virtual display is achieved, providing a stereoscopic scene. With a partially reflective combiner, i.e., a mirror that reflects light from the image source into the eyes, the display scene can be superimposed onto the normal physical world. The user can also position the image anywhere, i.e., it moves with the head. When combined with a head position sensing system, the information on the display can be stabilized as a function of head movement, thereby creating the effect of viewing a circumambience or "virtual world" which surrounds the user. This circumambience creates the feeling that you are immersed in a computer simulated environment, that is, the feeling that you are experiencing the computer simulation from the inside, not merely passively observing it from the outside.

An acoustic virtual display can also be created by processing a sound image, in the same way that the pinnae of the ear manipulates a sound wavefront. A sound object is first digitized and then convolved with head related transfer function (HRTF) coefficients which describe the finite impulse response of the ears of a generic head to sounds at particular angles and distances from the head. Monaural digitized sound can thus be transformed to spatially localized binaural sound presented through stereo headphones to the subject. By using the instantaneously measured head position to select a library of HRTF coefficients, a localized sound which is stable in space can be generated. These sound objects can be used either separately or as an overlay of 3D visual objects. Similarly a tactile image can be displayed by providing a two-dimensional array of vibration or pressure transducers in contact with the skin of the hand or body. Tactors may be actuated as a function of the shape and surface features of a virtual object and the instantaneous position of the head and fingers.

2. A Conceptual Framework For Presence

Figure 1 provides an organizational framework for empirically exploring the concept of presence in virtual environments. This model is derived from extensive informal observations of virtual environment participants, along with some preliminary formal investigations (Weghorst and Billinghurst, 1993; Weghorst et al., 1993). It is meant merely to serve as a starting point for a program of human factors research, and is by no means definitive. It should also be noted that our notions about virtual presence are derived primarily from inclusive interactive environments, and as such may prove to have some inherent biases.

On the left-hand side of Figure 1 is a list of some of the factors which we suspect may influence the degree of presence within a virtual environment.

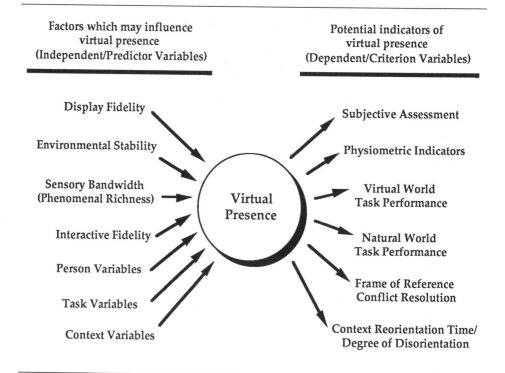

Figure 1. A framework for exploring virtual presence.

Among the variables shown in Figure 1 included in the "display fidelity" factor would be such things as spatial and contrast resolution, field of view, optical distortion, stereopsis and other distance cues, lighting and shading models, pinnae model accuracy (for spatial sound displays), and other modality-specific parameters. "Environmental stability" might encompass object attribute constancy and consistency, as well as intermodality consistency. "Sensory bandwidth" refers to the variety and dynamic range of the output displays, and the kinesthetic and proprioceptive correlates of the participant's interaction behaviors. "Interactive fidelity" reflects the intuitiveness and ease of interaction within the virtual environment, and includes such things as the range and naturalness of control behaviors, display update rate, lag, and temporal and spatial predictability of the system response. Virtual environments pose a particularly interesting set of questions with regard to the credibility of entities that behave in unnatural but internally consistent ways. Comparisons of general virtual interface approaches, such as immersive versus desktop displays, can be framed within this set of factors. Immersive interaction, for example, typically affords the participant greater sensory bandwidth and interactive fidelity, but often at the expense of display fidelity and environmental stability.

Figure 2 shows the importance of attentional resources for virtual presence. Incoming sensory information is processed at several levels within the human's information processing system. When attentional resources are allocated to computer-generated sensory information, such as visual information provided by a head-mounted display, tactile information provided by tactors, or auditory information provided by HRTFs, presence for that stimulus event(s) occurs.

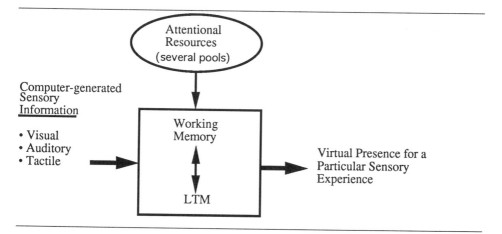

Figure 2. Virtual presence occurs when attentional resources are allocated to stimulus events which are generated by a computer.

Both models (Figures 1 and 2) predict that numerous person, task and context variables will influence the sense of virtual presence within a virtual environment. These effects will most likely be mediated by intervening variables such as comfort, engagement, and cognitive and physical load. We should, of course, also expect to find numerous interaction effects among all of these factors. Factors which reduce the need for participant adaptation may, for instance, be more important to older, rather than younger, participants.

2.2 Techniques To Measure Presence

Virtual presence is generally conceived of as a hypothetical subjective state of awareness and involvement in a non-present environment. Subjective assessment, while typically problematic, can be useful for initial exploration and hypothesis generation. We suspect that it will eventually be supplanted by more robust metrics. These might include physiometric indicators, such as posture, muscle tension, and cardiovascular and ocular responses to virtual events. Heart rate and evoked cortical responses to optical looming of virtual objects, for instance, might indicate their salience, and the degree of presence within their environment. The basic idea behind these measures is as follows: Just as humans experience changes in physiological parameters in response to novel or unusual stimuli, as the sense of presence increases within a virtual environment, the participant should experience similar physiological changes. For example, one measure may be a blink response to an object on a collision course to your virtual eye. Furthermore, it has been shown that the diameter of the pupil correlates with performance on a number of cognitive tasks, will pupil diameter also vary with the sense of virtual presence? Heart rate variability is generally found to decrease as the mental workload increases, will this also vary as the sense of virtual presence in a virtual environment increases or decreases?

Performance appropriateness, speed and accuracy on tasks defined solely within the virtual environment might also be influenced by the sense of virtual presence. Likewise we might expect a performance decrement on concurrent tasks defined solely in the natural environment. And when the natural and virtual frames of reference call for conflicting responses, the direction of resolution of the conflict may also serve as an indicator of the degree of presence within each. Furthermore, as the sense of presence increases, the attentional resources allocated to the objects or tasks performed in the virtual environment should increase. Therefore, we postulate that as the sense of presence within the virtual environment increases, the virtual environment participant will pay less attention to sensory input external to the virtual environment. Thus, one may measure the sense of presence by using the secondary task technique proposed by psychologists in the study of mental workload (Wickens, 1992). Imposing a secondary task as a measure of residual resources or capacity not utilized in the primary task is a technique that has a long history in the field of mental workload. Furthermore, a series of studies using psychophysical techniques to evaluate the subjective level of presence reported by the virtual environment participant as a function of the issues referred to in Figure 1 needs to be performed. For example, one study may involve a subjective rating of presence as a function of frame update rate, given some representative task.

In addition to these "real-time" measures of presence, we might also be able to infer degree of presence from certain post-interaction effects, such as the degree of disorientation and time to reorient when re-emerging into the natural context. As with physiological reactions, behavioral responses to exclusively virtual events may provide a measure of the degree of presence experienced within an environment. Our notion here is that presence in a virtual environment necessitates a belief that the participant no longer inhabits the physical space but now occupies the computer generated virtual environment as "place". Of particular interest are responses to virtual events that directly contradict the appropriate response to a concurrent natural world event. An example scenario suitable to this approach would be "mixed" natural and virtual environments in which "perceptual capture" across environments affects performance on simple tasks. Degree of presence should be predictive of the predominant direction of capture. Other measures not mentioned in Figure 1 which may be useful, albeit somewhat more remote, include memory for virtual events and post-interaction reconstruction of the virtual environment.

3. Some Preliminary Empirical Findings

Two exploratory studies conducted by Suzanne Weghorst and colleagues offer some initial findings relevant to the first model of virtual presence. Neither study was designed primarily to study virtual presence, and both rely upon subject self-report for assessing presence. Their value is thus in providing some directions for future research, rather than firm conclusions.

3.1 Study 1: Navigation In A Virtual Environment

Study 1 was designed to investigate the effects of certain virtual world features on navigability and the participant's construction of a cognitive spatial map. Eighty-six subjects ranging in age from 14 to 59 were given immersive interactive flythroughs of two different virtual worlds. Standard VPL Eyephones and a VPL DataGlove with attached Polhemus 6D tracker served as the participant interface.

The first world provided an opportunity to accommodate to the interface, and was the same for all subjects (Virtual Seattle). The second world was one of three similarly complex worlds which differed in their use of a ground plane and other spatial landmarks, and in the visibility and degree of abstractness of the objects in the world. Only a portion of the data collected during these sessions is relevant here. Following each "flythrough" participants completed a 24-item automated (HyperCard) survey. Survey questions used a 10-point scale anchored on each end. Wording of the questions and item anchors was adjusted during pilot sessions to assure a reasonable sample distribution across the scale. Pearson correlation coefficients were computed among all variables for the 70 cases for which we had complete data (two-tailed $p < .05$, df 68, $r = .24$).

Several of the items were germane to the proposed model. An embedded sub-scale consisting of three items was designed to assess virtual presence: "Sense of being there", "Sense of inclusion in the virtual world", and "Sense of presence in the virtual world". These three items were highly intercorrelated, particularly after the second immersive experience, and were also significantly correlated with many of the other scale items.

Responses to the item assessing the sense of "Being there" were most highly correlated with "display comfort" ($r = .38$), "comfort with computers" ($r = .36$), "ease of navigation" ($r = .27$), "being lost" ($r = -.26$), "overall enjoyment" ($r = .26$), "display color quality" ($r = .25$), and "ability to get around" ($r = .24$). "Inclusion" was most correlated with "overall enjoyment" ($r = .47$), "overall comfort" ($r = .40$), "introspection" ($r = .40$), "ease of interaction" ($r = .36$), "ease of navigation" ($r = .35$), and "movement ease" ($r = .31$), and "display comfort" ($r = .31$). The item assessing the sense of "Presence" was most highly correlated with "orientation within the virtual world" ($r = .47$), "being lost" ($r = -.45$), "engaging" ($r = .42$), "color quality" ($r = .40$), "image clarity" ($r = -.40$), "overall enjoyment" ($r = .40$), and "ability to get around" ($r = .38$).

These findings suggest that ease of interaction may be slightly more predictive of the sense of virtual presence than the other factors studied. Almost equally predictive were the indicators of display comfort and quality. The results also suggest that the term "Inclusion" may have some additional semantic load, perhaps related to feelings of comfort and safety. The finding that all three measures were significantly predictive of overall enjoyment may indicate the importance of the sense of virtual presence in the immersive experience. It should also be noted that subject age was negatively correlated with all three measures of virtual presence, although significantly so only with "Inclusion" ($r = -.30$).

3.2 Study 2: Subject And Social Factors

Study 2, which focused more on subject variables and social factors, was conducted in conjunction with a project designed to expose junior high aged children to virtual world design during a science summer camp. In the second year of the project, 69 children (age 8-16, with a mean of 11.8 years) spent a week working in small groups on the design of a three-dimensional model and the specification of object dynamics within that model. Porting of the model into an immersive system, and implementation of the dynamics, was done by laboratory staff and graduate students. Each work group then spent a session immersed in their virtual world, during which they were free to navigate, explore, and interact with the model. Standard VPL Eyephones and a joystick handle with embedded Polhemus 6D tracker served as the participant interface.

Following their "flythrough" participants completed a 27-item automated (HyperCard) survey and a free response questionnaire. Survey questions again used a 10-point scale anchored on each end. Wording of the questions and item anchors was adjusted during pilot sessions to assure a reasonable sample distribution across the scale. Pearson correlation coefficients were computed among all variables for the 36 cases for which we had complete data (two-tailed $p < .05$, df 34, $r = .33$). Only a few of the items were relevant to the model. Responses to the item "Did you feel you were a part of the virtual world?" were significantly positively correlated with "How much did you enjoy designing and building a virtual world?" ($r = .50$) and "How much did you enjoy the PSC Technology Camp?" ($r = .36$). Both of these latter items were highly predictive of each other ($r = .67$) and of the item "Were your ideas for the world the same or different from others in your group?" ($r = .59$ and $.63$, respectively). These findings suggest that the social dynamics of the virtual environment experience may influence presence.

Although not significantly predictive of "feeling a part of the virtual world", "knowing where you were in the virtual world" was significantly positively correlated with "ease of movement" ($r = .33$), "getting where you wanted to go" ($r = .52$), and "wanting to be in VR again" ($r = .40$), and significantly negatively correlated with "dizziness while in the virtual world" ($r = -.50$). Self-reports of "dizziness" and "disorientation" after the immersive experience were significantly correlated ($r = .58$), and post-immersion dizziness was significantly predictive of "wanting to be in VR again" ($r = -.36$). While self-reports of feeling dizzy while immersed were highly predictive of reported dizziness afterwards ($r = .55$), only "immersive" dizziness was significantly correlated with gender ($r = .35$), with girls being more likely than boys to report feeling dizzy. In order to sample a broader community approximately one-third of the camp participants were sponsored by scholarships for underrepresented groups (girls and non-white ethnic groups). "Immersive dizziness" was also higher for these students ($r = .38$), but this effect appears to be due to the preponderance of girls in the "scholarship" group. Ethnicity *per se* was predictive only of "wanting to build another world" ($.43$) and "wanting to do VR again" ($r = .34$), with white participants generally more positive about the experience than children of color.

4. Conclusions

These findings point toward some of the complexities in teasing apart the effects of subject variables on our proposed measures of virtual presence. Additional studies designed specifically around these questions are in order. In summary, based on the results of the two studies, the following was found: 1) ease of interaction and indicators of display comfort and quality were shown to be slightly more predictive of the sense of virtual presence than the other factors studied given a navigation task, and 2) the social dynamics of the virtual environment experience was shown to influence virtual presence. Finally, a conceptual model of virtual presence was presented primarily to suggest areas for future research on this important topic.

5. References

Furness, T., Weghorst, S., Bricken, W., and Barfield, W., Communicating Situational Awareness in Virtual Environments, *Working Paper, HIT Lab*, University of Washington, 1993.

Weghorst, S. and Billinghurst, M, Spatial Perception of Immersive Virtual Environments. *HIT Lab Technical Report*, University of Washington, 1993.

Weghorst, S., Byrne, C., Osberg, K., and King, W., Construction and Exploration of Virtual Worlds by School-age Children. *HIT Lab Technical Report*, University of Washington, 1993.

Wickens, C., *Engineering Psychology and Human Performance*, 2nd edition, Harper Collins Publisher, 1992.

The Art of the Belly

Wolfgang Slany and Christian Stary

CD-Lab for Expert Systems, Vienna University of Technology, Paniglgasse 16, 1040 Vienna, Austria

ABSTRACT

If we want to link brains and computers as closely as possible, we have to search for new styles of interaction. In particular, novel interaction concepts have to be based on the integrated management of sensorial inputs, and the direct manipulation and distribution of information among several agents. These requirements have lead to the definition of a complex interface between innovative input/output devices, computers and human agents. The integration of previously separated technologies as well as the development of complex control knowledge for direct human–to–human interfaces using information processing technology are discussed in this paper.

1. INTRODUCTION

Since prehistoric times humans are dreaming of the capability to allow them to transmit their knowledge, thoughts, etc. over large distances and spaces [17]. Scientific proof that such capabilities may naturally exist is however lacking [1]. On the other hand, recent technological advancements give birth to completely new tools and systems for communication. Computers as information processing devices can already be interconnected worldwide. Information technology is becoming a major economic factor in our information society.

According to [15] information will continue to play a crucial role in future scenarios of the information society. All activities of rational agents will be centered around information [6]. As a consequence, we need a direct interface to all facilities that handle information. Information is exchanged smoothly among agents, taking into account cognitive and virtual realities ($\Rightarrow$ adaptivity). Its persistence increases accurate maintainability as well as continuous availability for several purposes. As such, the hardware and software facilities become "an extension of the human nervous system" (McLuhan in [19]).

But before a globally interconnected humanity will access all information sources without any restrictions on a planet of unlimited communication capabilities, the interaction between communication systems and humans must be dramatically simplified. We thus propose a model for networking brains and machines. Directly. By assembling existing technologies, improving them, and developing them to practical use, we will briefly outline how to design and implement The Art of the Belly[1].

---

[1]The Art of the Belly: orig. Japanese (pronounced *haragei*; written 腹芸). The art or technique of silent communication; communication by understanding what is in the mind—or inside the belly (*hara*)—by intuition without relying on verbal expressions [10].

2. HARDWARE

Hardware is the faintest point in our discussion, but much more has been done than is commonly assumed. The actual design work needed for this part of our model is heavily oriented toward the realization of a smooth communication system. Humans generally dislike highly visible artificial adjuncts like hearing aids. The main design aspect for the hardware besides purely technical and obvious ergonomic considerations should therefore be its complete invisibility.

If we had a way to allow the more or less direct exchange of data between the neural tissue of the brain and some electronic sending and receiving unit, we could ultimately reduce the size of this unit sufficiently to integrate it into the body, much like a pacemaker correcting irregular heart beats is surgically inserted into patients with cardio rhythmical problems. Actually, all major telephone companies are working already unintentionally on the size reduction of the proposed sending and receiving unit, in form of the portable telephone. Already as soon as in 1994, some companies like Motorola plan to finish setting up a worldwide satellite net directly accessible from portable phones small enough to carry in a coat pocket and powerful enough to allow the user to make and receive calls from anywhere in the world [14].

Moreover, the worldwide ISDN[2] network should be completed according to plans of the telephone companies by the year 2004, and it will provide exactly the *bandwidth* and basic *information exchange capability* that is necessary to carry the data from individual interface to individual interface [9]. Considering the above, establishing the communication network and sufficiently reducing the size of the interface unit seem both very feasible.

However, the question how to connect locally organic tissues and man–made systems remains. Neural tissues are extremely well suited for pattern recognition and for learning new tasks, whereas computers perform better in retaining large amounts of data and in brute number or symbol crunching. Our interface respects those different faculties and is built around them in order to maximize the overall performance. But have neural tissues and electronic devices been directly connected in the past? Yes, they have. The actual information exchange between these two is a large and very active research area in the field of biomedical engineering, see e.g. [20] for some advanced examples relevant to our investigation. It is further possible to supply artificial limbs with sensorimotor functions to those who lost some part of their body by accident or were handicapped since birth, e.g. [4].

In particular, we found the example of persons trained to gain sight without ever having seen before in their life most intriguing. A blind man is provided with low resolution graytone pictures by a small camera mounted on his glasses so that the scene taken by the camera changes naturally with the movements of his head. The image is projected continuously as sensorial information on the skin of his abdomen. After only one week of training, the blind's brain interprets this sensorial tickling as a picture. In the first stage, he has to learn to recognize already known objects such as coffee cups. Even persons born blind could learn after some time to interpret correctly perspective, parallax, shadows, rotation, looming, zooming and subjective localization in three-dimensional space. One very rewarding experience for the blind test persons is their first "sight" of flickering flames in a fire, or their own image in a mirror, something they could not understand through touching alone [3], [4].

Similarly, for those having lost a hand by accident, experimental artificial hands have been constructed which can be controlled by interpreting the signals from sensors on motoric nerves in the remaining part of their arm [2]. Of course the rewiring of the excitatory nerves to the robot arm is not the same as it was to one's own before, and the robot arm itself has not the same flexibility as a biological one, but with some training, the person can even learn to

---

[2]ISDN: Integrated Services Digital Network.

write again. This result is important, since it shows one possible way for human agents to output easily interpretable symbolic information to an artificial system. The movements of the hand have been shown to be symbolically interpretable by a computer system, e.g., by the talking-glove [11].

There is a lot of neurological data proving the plasticity of the brain, especially clinical data about patients recovering from brain damage like after a stroke, a surgical operation or an accidental wounding, where other brain regions take over the function of the lost neural tissue [18]. The examples for sensorial input (blind man) and motoric output (artificial limb) work best when the information flows bidirectionally, id est the same brain controls input and output and thus, a closed control loop exists. This is the case when the blind can direct himself the camera by moving his head, or when the fingertips of the artificial hand have sensors attached to them, the information being passed back to the brain by excitation of sensorial nerves in the remaining arm.

When users of the system want to send messages among themselves, the interpretation of the neural signals by the hardware causes no problems, since the correct format is provided by the user's brain after it learned to communicate with the machine, and another brain will interpret the sent message the same way, in form of pictures, speech or other sensual impressions. But in order to communicate with machines, the neural signal stemming from a human must be interpretable by the computer system. This can be done in two ways. Either the human learns a symbolic way to communicate its thoughts to the machine. Or the machine must be able to interpret the original neural signal. Both ways have been shown feasible in scientific experiments, and both have their merits, e.g. [5]. Human test persons can learn to control the signal caught via EEG[3] by electrodes on their head if they get an immediate feedback through changing colors on a screen in front of them, or a changing sound, corresponding in a certain way to the recorded brain activity [7]. We believe that this mechanism could probably be extended to allow the correct classification of a fixed set of basic symbols sent from the neural system to the computer system, and is therefore ideally suited for symbolic communication, for example characters forming a written text, see also [11].

The second way asks for an understanding of how the brain stores or transmits information. While most of this understanding is still lacking, there are experimental results from [5] showing how to interpret two–dimensional receptive field profiles of mammalian cortical simple cells as members of the family of two–dimensional Gabor[4] elementary functions. This can be used to retransform the neural signal from a brain into the actual picture seen by its owner, or to transform a picture taken by a camera into a correctly interpretable neural signal. While this approach has to be developed thoroughly, it will prove most valuable to communicate with machines in non–symbolic ways, like by pictures or through speech.

3. SOFTWARE

The usability of the system as a whole is largely dependent on the number of services and connected users. With a view to the future, the Art of the Belly is conceived to be a development of nowadays direct communication systems, such as the telephone. Thus the number of connected users will be high, which is important for the realization of universal human–to–human, human–to–machine, and machine–to–machine communication. On the other hand, a very broad variety of services will eventually be offered by some private or official sources, as has been shown by the much simpler "minitel" system introduced in France several years ago.

---

[3] EEG: electro encephalo gram.
[4] D. Gabor: pioneer of information theory, Nobel Price winner and inventor of the hologram.

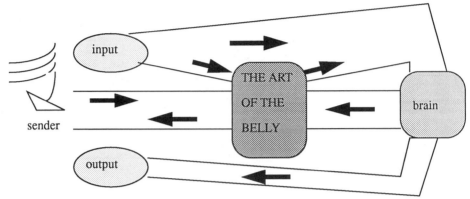

Figure 1: *The context of the Art of the Belly*

The "minitel" network allows more than six million persons to gain access via a special terminal to over 15,000 services like news, weather by region, electronic mail or automatic written translation between the languages of the European Community. The Art of the Belly will provide its users with these services and much more. Every possible application of a computer system will be evocable through it, see e.g. [6]. At any time, and independent of place.

Users of the Art of the Belly will be able to remember as much as they can afford by buying memory space. But memory will be cheap, because it will be normally possible to compress most of the information, or to store only access pointers to data already available in some database, which itself is another service in the network.

In order to handle large information spaces, the spatial dimension of user interfaces have been investigated thoroughly. Since the capabilities of information storage and retrieval systems are more complex than in nowadays applications, the input and output has to be handled by more complex interaction features. As a consequence, concepts such as focus of work and compression of information have become crucial features of interfaces. In combination with real–time interactive 3D animation systems, these concepts can be mapped into user interfaces. In particular, virtual 3D workspaces correspond closely to human experiences and skills of working in the real world [12]. Another improvement is the implementation of real "Look and Feel" interfaces which are still under investigation [13]. This type of interaction combines seeing with gestures, which leads to direct information acquisition and processing.

The most promising approaches stem from projects which are focused on integrated access and distribution facilities for information processing. For instance, FRIEND21 [15] has been concentrated on the agent of the 21st century who is directly engaged in the information environment of a certain society. All hardware parts have to be portable. Equipment such as VLSI, memory, and input devices have undergone already great advances. For instance, lipreading using vector quantization has turned out to be more effective than automatic acoustic letter and number recognition [16]. In FRIEND21, the control knowledge to handle artificial stimuli acquisition and their reaction will be embedded in "metaware", id est complex software managing agency models. The latter provides the fundamentals for handling distributed agents and their associated "worlds".

4. FUTURE WORK

Based on the architectural framework shown in figure 1, we develop a scenario for further investigations, in order to prove the feasibility of the Art of the Belly. The individual's brain is related to the Art of the Belly via a permanent input and output channel (indicated in figure 1 by directed arcs). The output of the brain can also be directed towards the neuronal output of the human individual directly. The input for the brain can either stem from the individual's inherent (natural) input or the artificial output from the Art of the Belly.

The Art of the Belly is connected with a sender handling the sensorial input and motoric output. It also receives input from the individually acquired information. If we would have provided additional output of the Art of the Belly to the individual's output, control knowledge, e.g. for playing tennis like a professional, would have been applicable directly after receiving the appropriate information.

One of the first activities will be the empirical proof for the extensive use of sophisticated devices, as proposed by [20], and concepts, such as Gabor transformations [5]. Once we have a reliable basis for the investigation of the illustrated communication channels, we can start to elaborate the particular connections of the Art of the Belly. For instance, in order to cover the most complex communication part (id est the correlation of individual input, brain, and Art of the Belly), the visual perception of cats can be used to test the accuracy of artificially acquired information by replaying the input to the cat.

The user of The Art of the Belly should be free to choose whatever interface he or she likes best, much as nowadays workstation users are not bound to a specific windowing system or shell. But of course the basic kernel system should always be the same in order to allow the industry to produce software in form of services available to everyone on the net, whatever his or her favorite obscure interface looks like. The specification of this kernel is a wide research field in its own, since many features of today's operating systems, network management systems and database systems comprise major aspects of this kernel system, for example authentication, data compression or accounting methods. But the problems are more numerous than it looks like.

Empirical findings will be the catalyst or bottleneck for future developments of integrated direct interaction facilities, as proposed in this paper. However, the design of laboratory studies to gain empirical results valid over a wide application area has still to be discussed, since the usability of such results is a controversial issue [8].

References

[1] Alcock, J. E. *Parapsychology: Science of the Anomalous or Search for the Soul?* In: Behavioral and Brain Sciences, Vol. 10, Nr. 4, December 1987. A negative critique of the article [17].

[2] Ärzte Woche. *A myoelectrically controlled hand prothesis (in German).* In: Österreichische Zeitschrift für Medizin (Fax: +43–1–513 47 83–31), Vol. 2, Nr. 23, June 15, 1988.. p. 1.

[3] Bach–y–Rita, P. *The plasticity of the brain and sensomotoric substitution (in German).* In: Mannheimer Forum 76/77. Bœringer Mannheim GmbH, Mannheim, 1976. pp. 88–144.

[4] Bach–y–Rita, P. et al. *Tactile and Acoustic Presentations of Computer Images for the Blind.* In: Access to Visual Computer Information by Blind Persons, K. Fellbaum (ed.), Technical University of Berlin, Institute of Telecommunications, 1990. pp. 81–84, pp. 137–142.

[5] Daugman, J. G. *Complete Discrete 2–D Gabor Transforms by Neural Networks for Image Analysis and Compression.* In: IEEE Transactions on Acoustics, Speech, and Signal Processing, Vol. 36, No. 7, July 1988. pp. 1169–1179.

[6] Dertouzos, M. L. *Building the Information Marketplace.* In: Technology Review, January 1991. Edited at the Massachusetts Institute of Technology. pp. 30–40.

[7] Gevins, A. S. and Morgan, N. H. *Applications of Neural–Network (NN) Processing in Brain Research.* In: IEEE Transactions on Acoustics, Speech, and Signal Processing, Vol. 36, No. 7, July 1988. pp. 1152–1161.

[8] Wolf, C. (Organizer), Carroll, J. M. (Mod.), Landauer, T. K., John, B. E., Whiteside, J. and Wolf, C. *The Role of Laboratory Experiments in HCI: Help, Hindrance, or Ho–Hum? (Panel description).* In: CHI'89 Proceedings, April 30–May 4, 1989. pp. 265–268.

[9] Kamae, T. *Multimedia Telecommunications toward the 21st Century* In: Proceedings of the GI'91, Telekommunikation und Multimediale Anwendungen der Informatik (Reihe Informatik Fachberichte, Springer Verlag, Heidelberg), October 14–18, 1991. In press.

[10] Kojima, S. and Crane, G. A. *A Dictionary of Japanese Culture.* The Japan Times, 1987.

[11] Kramer, J. *Lending a Helping Glove . . .* In: Communications of the ACM, Vol. 32, Nr. 3, March 1989. p. 286, see also CACM, Vol. 32, Nr. 4, April 1989, p. 515.

[12] Mackinlay, J. D., Robertson, G. G. and Card, S. K. *Rapid Controlled Movement through Virtual 3D Workspaces (Videotape description).* In: CHI'91 Proceedings, April 27–May 2, 1991. pp. 455–456.

[13] Minsky, M. (Mod.), Brooks, F., Behensky, M., Milliken, D., Russo, M. and Druin, A. *Recent Progress Creating Environments with the Sense of Feel: Giving "Look and Feel" its missing meaning (Panel description).* In: CHI'89 Proceedings, April 30–May 4, 1989. pp. 189–190.

[14] Newstrack. *Small Talk.* In: Communications of the ACM, Vol. 33, Nr. 8, August 1990. p. 10.

[15] Nonogaki, H. and Ueda, H. *FRIEND21 Project: A Construction of a 21st Century Human Interface.* In: CHI'91 Proceedings, April 27–May 2, 1991. pp. 407–414.

[16] Petajan, E., Bischoff, B. and Bodoff, D. *An Improved Automatic Lipreading System to Enhance Speech Recognition.* In: CHI'88 Proceedings, May 15–19, 1988. pp. 19–25.

[17] Rao, K. R. and Palmer, J. *The Anomaly called Psi: Recent Research and Criticism.* In: Behavioral and Brain Sciences, Vol. 10, Nr. 4, December 1987. See [1] for a negative critique of this article.

[18] Taine, H. *De l'Intelligence.* Presses Universitaires de France, 1950.

[19] Tello, E. R. *Between Man and Machine.* In: Byte, September 1988. pp. 288–293.

[20] Urban, G. A., Ganglberger, J. A., Olcaytug, F., Kohl, F., Schallauer, R., Trimmel, M., Schmid, H. and Prohaska, O. *Development of a Multiple Thin–Film Semimicro DC–Probe for Intracerebral Recordings* In: IEEE Transactions on Biomedical Engineering, Vol. 37, Nr. 10, October 1990. pp. 913–918.

IV. Help and Learning

Animated Help as a Sensible Extension of a Plan-Based Help System

Markus A. Thies

DFKI, Stuhlsatzenhausweg 3, W-6600 Saarbrücken 11, Germany
thies@dfki.uni-sb.de

Abstract

Object-oriented graphical interfaces entail new demands for providing the user with adequate help. Static and knowledge-based help systems with a pure textual help reach their limits as soon as the user needs assistance in performing interactions within a graphical interface.

In this paper the animated help system AniS$^+$ is presented that dynamically generates sequences of animated interaction steps by considering not only the current interface and application context but also the task currently being pursued by the user.

1 Motivation

Object-oriented graphical interfaces entail new demands for providing the user with adequate help. Static and knowledge-based help systems with a pure textual help (cf. [1, 3, 5, 10, 11]) reach their limits as soon as the user needs assistance in performing interactions. For example, if the user asks questions of the form: *"How do I include object A into container-object B ?"* or *"Please show me, how I get objects X, Y, and Z visualized."* A generated textual help could possibly look like the following: *"Move the mouse to the position of object A and press the left mouse button. Now move the mouse with the left mouse button still pressed to the position of the container object B. Then release the mouse button."* We argue that an animated presentation of these interaction steps would be more helpful than a pure textual description.

When the user needs assistance in performing interactions within the graphical interface, an animated sequence demonstrating the necessary interaction steps on top of the current interface seems to provide the best solution to the user's needs.

To establish a closer relationship with the current problem of the user, the animation must be dynamically generated and must consider, the task currently being pursued by the user, as well as the current interface or application context.

2 Animated Help

In this paper we describe the system AniS⁺ (**Ani**mated **H**elp **S**ystem). In contrast to earlier approaches to animated help (cf. [6, 7, 8]), AniS⁺ generates animated presentations of interaction steps in the context of the task currently being performed.

The animation presentation comprises the movement of the mouse on the display and the manipulation of objects (e.g, menus, scrollbars, windows, application objects) with the mouse. The shape of the mouse is varied to reflect mouse actions like single-click or double-click with the left or right mouse button.

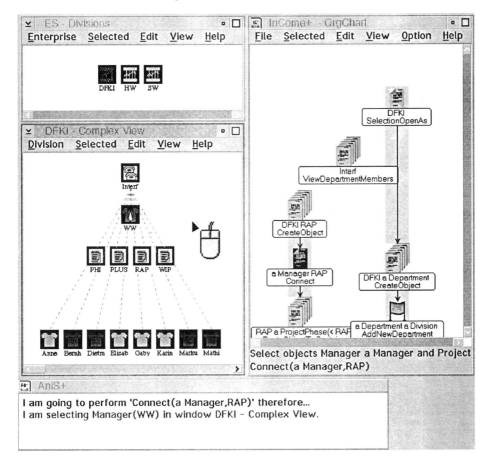

Figure 1: AniS⁺ generates navigational actions (selecting an object)...

To consider the task a user is currently pursuing, AniS⁺ is integrated within the plan-based help system PLUS (cf. [2, 4, 9]) and it communicates with the plan processing component of PLUS. Within the plan processing component of PLUS, a plan recognition component is responsible for the determination of plausible hypotheses about the goals currently being pursued by a user.

Figures 1 and 2 show two stills of the animation of a sequence of interaction steps. Both top left windows represent an application that models the organizational structure of enterprises, including departements, projects, managers and professionals. The lower left window is part of AniS+. It narrates the ongoing animation. The window on the right side belongs to the PLUS System and it graphically visualizes the current interaction context. Within that window the user requested animated help in order to connect a manager with the project RAP. Therefore, both objects must be selected before the action **connect** can be performed.

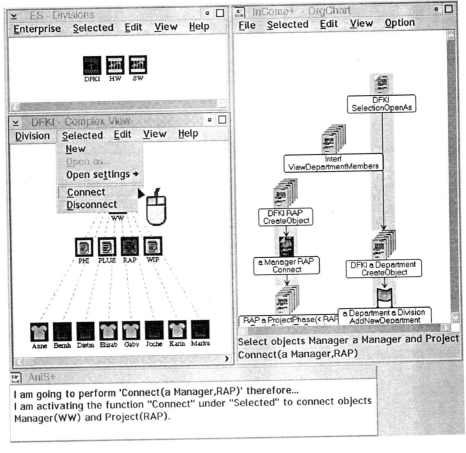

Figure 2: ...and varies the mouse shape.

The mouse movements and clicks are simulated by sending corresponding mouse events to the interface in such a way that the interface and also the application are acting on these events as if they were performed by the user. Thus, the actions are really executed within the application.

A text describing the goal of the animation and the current mouse action is displayed in order to provide the user with a better understanding of why AniS$^+$ performs the current mouse action. By variable substitutions, the prestored text fragments are adapted to the current application context (cf. lower left window in figures 1 and 2).

3 Realization of AniS$^+$

AniS$^+$ is part of the plan-based help system PLUS which is integrated into a user interface management system (UIMS). Figure 3 shows the architecture of AniS$^+$ but it omits other components of the PLUS System that are of no interest in this paper.

AniS$^+$ works with a two phase planning loop to incrementally generate the interaction steps (e.g., mouse movements and clicks) necessary for the execution of the generated action sequence (cf. figure 3). An action sequence generated by the plan completion component serves as an input to AniS$^+$.

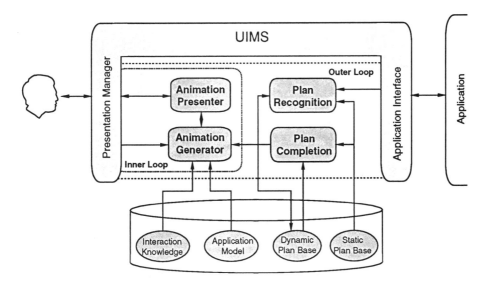

Figure 3: Architecture of AniS$^+$

The inner loop consists of an animation generator and an animation presenter. It considers the changes within the interface context (e.g., selecting an object, scrolling the window). The animation generator uses a backward-chaining algorithm to generate a sequence of interaction steps that will be presented on the current display by the animation presenter. During this backward-chaining process, the animation presenter accesses a knowledge base that defines specific pre- and postconditions for each action. Informal examples of such preconditions are "to apply an action to an object, it must be selected" and "an object can only be selected if it is visible". The representation of generic interface concepts allows us to generate navigational interaction steps (e.g., steps to scroll the visible area of a window). The interaction knowledge part of the knowledge base models the interface syntax (e.g., clicking on an object changes its state to be selected). The application semantics (e.g., which objects can be visualized in which types of windows and which actions are applicable to which objects) is formalized within the application model part of the knowledge base. There is an interface to the presentation manager of the UIMS for accessing information on, e.g., selected objects, visibility of objects, and window states (overlapped or iconified).

The animation presenter transforms the generated interaction steps into appropriate events for mouse movements and mouse clicks. Therefore it accesses the interaction style guide that is stored within the interaction knowledge. It is also responsible for reflecting interactions on the screen by changing the mouse shape and for narrating the animation.

In addition, the outer loop contains the plan processing component (plan recognition and plan completion) of the PLUS System. It considers the changes in the application context that take effect after the execution of an action and involves both the plan recognition process by reacting to the performed action, and the plan completion component by reflecting new parameter values provided by the user.

The plan recognizer works upon a hierarchical static plan base. It maps performed user actions to predefined plans using a spreading activation algorithm. Thereby, a dynamic plan base is built up holding hypotheses about plans (tasks) the user may be currently working on. By satisfying temporal constraints and by propagating already known parameter values along the defined parameter constraints, the plan completion component generates, on demand, a valid sequence of actions that must be performed in order to finish the plan hypothesis. Although selected objects are considered to be replacements for missing parameters during the execution of the animation, not every parameter can be anticipated from the result of the plan completion process. For that reason, the user is prompted to provide missing parameters.

4 Conclusion

Animation as a part of a plan-based help system is a sensible extension for supporting the user in performing interaction steps in a graphical environment. It fills the gap between the concepts of an interactive graphical interface and a textual representation of help. Although animation can be valuable, merely using animation in help does not deliver a perfect help system. Minimal textual explanations are presented with the animation to help the user to generalize concepts. AniS$^+$ demonstrates the feasibility of our approach.

5 Acknowledgement

This paper is based on work that has been done within the project PLUS which is conducted cooperatively by the IBM Laboratory Böblingen, the IBM Germany GmbH, and the DFKI. Special thanks to Wolfgang Wahlster, Thomas Fehrle, and Frank Berger for their valuable remarks and discussions on this paper.

Bibliography

[1] M. Bauer, S. Biundo, D. Dengler, J. Koehler, and G. Paul. PHI – A Logic-Based Tool for Intelligent Help Systems. In *Proceedings of the 13th International Joint Conference on Artificial Intelligence*, Chambery, France, 1993.

[2] F. Berger, T. Fehrle, K. Klöckner, V. Schölles, M. A. Thies, and W. Wahlster. PLUS – Plan-based User Support. Research Report RR-93-15, DFKI, 1993.

[3] J. Breuker, editor. *EUROHELP, Developing Intelligent Help Systems*. EC, Kopenhagen, Amsterdam, 1990.

[4] T. Fehrle and M. A. Thies. InCome: A system to navigate through interactions and plans. In H.-J. Bullinger, editor, *Human Aspects in Computing: Design and Use of Interactive Systems and Information Management*, Amsterdam, London, New York, Tokyo, 1991. Elsevier Science Publishers B.V.

[5] G. Fischer, A. Lemke, and T. Schwab. Knowledge-based help systems. In *Proceedings of the CHI'85 Conference on Human Factors in Computing Systems*. acm Press, 1985.

[6] D. Neiman. Graphical Animation from Knowledge. In *Proceedings of the 2nd National Conference of the American Association for Artificial Intelligence*, Pittsburgh, PA, 1982. AAAI Press.

[7] P. Sukaviriya. Dynamic Construction of Animated Help from Application Context. In *Proceedings of the ACM SIGGRAPH Symposium on User Interface Software (UIST'88)*, New York, 1988. ACM SIGGRAPH, acm Press.

[8] P. Sukaviriya and J. D. Foley. Coupling a UI Framework with Automatic Generation of Context-Sensitive Animated Help. In *Proceedings of the ACM SIGGRAPH Symposium on User Interface Software (UIST'90)*, New York, 1990. ACM SIGGRAPH, acm Press.

[9] M. A. Thies and F. Berger. Plan-based graphical help in object-oriented user interfaces. In T. Catarci, M. F. Costabile, and S. Levialdi, editors, *Proceedings of the International Workshop AVI'92, Advanced Visual Interfaces*, volume 36 of *World Scientific Series in Computer Science*, Rome, Italy, May 1992. World Scientific.

[10] W. Wahlster, D. Dengler, M. Hecking, and C. Kemke. SC: The SINIX consultant. In P. Norvig, W. Wahlster, and R. Wilensky, editors, *Intelligent Help Systems for Unix - Case Studies in Artificial Intelligence*. Springer, Heidelberg, 1993. forthcoming.

[11] R. Wilensky, Y. Arens, and D. Chin. Talking to UNIX in english: An overview of UC. *Communications of the ACM*, 27(6), June 1984.

An Adaptive Intelligent Help System

Chi-Tien Chiu, Chaochang Chiu, and A. F. Norcio

Department of Information Systems, University of Maryland Baltimore County, Baltimore, MD 21228-5398

Abstract

This paper introduces the architecture of an adaptive intelligent help system. The paper also discusses how this system can operate with different users and applications adaptively and intelligently. Novice users certainly need help to learn and to use the target application. Even experienced users need help to make the most effective use of the application. This system also emphasizes the motivation of learnability through help strategies.

1. INTRODUCTION

A help system should assist the user in specific situations. There are two aspects on which an intelligent help system should focus in order to provide effective support to the user. These two aspects are *who the user is* and *when the help should be activated.* The first requirement for the system which is its ability to adapt and give advice intelligently, is that the system must know the expertise level of the user. The system adopts the methodology directly from the model which infers an individual user's task-specific expertise dynamically[1]. The second requirement is that the system should be able to monitor a user's activity in order to detect any error or inefficiency. To meet these two criteria, our system includes a Help Strategy Map (HSM) and a Task-domain Knowledge Checker (TKC). Both are discussed below.

An adaptive human-computer interface can potentially fulfill three key roles in support of the user: (1) it helps users accomplish intended goals on the target application; (2) it enables users to understand how the application operates; and (3) it can increase the abilities of the user [2]. In this paper, we suggest that an intelligent help system should dynamically trigger an adequate help strategy for each individual user as the situation requires. By doing so, our system aims to achieve the following goals: 1) problem solving -- helping user out of the current interaction mistake or dilemma; and 2) task learning -- helping the user to gain familiarity with the task. By monitoring the previous five commands, this system generates a help message if the user commits an error or has obvious difficulties. Figure 1 illustrates the architecture and the components of the system.

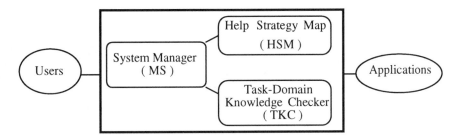

Figure 1. System Architecture

2. THE HELP SYSTEM

There are three basic concepts underlying this help system:

1. Task-orientation: The system emphasizes the representation of more specific, domain-oriented knowledge [3]. The purpose is to acquire sufficient knowledge about a particular problem area. The system is task-dependent so that its knowledge base is a state transition diagram.

2. Explicit user's goals: In order to address the system's generic functionality, the goal of each task is pre-determined for the user. The object is to modify the behavior of the interface to meet the inferred goals of the user. It appears that the mechanism of our system could have the ability to detect not only the error, but also the user's intentions. However, this is not in the scope of our focus.

3. Problem-solving and learnability: This is the main task which our help system is designed to accomplish. Our design focuses on the specific context of help message. This help system does not act like a tutor that provides the so-called best learning strategy. The user has to solve the specific problem by using the target application (in our example, a word processor). The system tries to help the user achieve the appropriate goals as well as gain familiarity with the task.

3. SYSTEM MANAGER (SM):

The System Manager handles the dialogue between the user and the system. It issues an appropriate help message to the user according to the help strategy from the Help Strategy Map (HSM) and the type of help content from the Task-Domain Knowledge Checker (TKC).

4. HELP STRATEGY MAP (HSM):

The HSM is a table as shown in Table 1. It is important that the comprehensibility of the help information match the expertise of the user [4]. The system has to determine the expertise of the user and monitor the user's performance. Two parameters are directly derived from the previous information using a fuzzy inference engine and neural network processes, namely the User Knowledge Level (UKL) and the Observer Performance Pattern (OPP) [1].

The fuzzy inference engine identifies user's level of expertise for a specific task domain dynamically, and the neural network determines the user's continuous performance pattern. The HSM is a two dimensional table with five help strategies. The strategy in each cell is determined by the user knowledge level (UKL) and observed performance pattern (OPP).

OPP UKL	VS	LS	US	LU	VM
1	A	A	B	B	C
2	A	B	B	C	D
3	B	B	C	D	D
4	B	C	D	D	E
5	C	D	D	E	E

TABLE 1. Help Strategy Map

where:

OPP: **VS**: Very-likely stable   **LS**: Likely stable   **US**: Unstable
    LU: Likely misunderstood   **VM**: Very-likely misunderstood

UKL: **1**: Expert   **2**: Near expert
    3: Experienced   **4**: Near experienced   **5**: Novice

According to Fisher, Lemke and Schwab, a good help system must have a passive and an active component [5]. Most on-line help systems are passive. A user must activate the help system by either typing an help command or clicking the help icon. Some help systems track the user's navigation and the possible error the user committed. But those error messages focus only on general types of errors. This means that the user frequently does not know the system tried to help. The five help strategies in Table 1 provide a user with the adequate help messages (passive or active). They include:

Strategy A: Message only. This category occupies the leftmost and highest three positions in HSM. These positions stand for the user's high expertise and stable performance of the task. Hence, the system should let this level of user be active and give the error message only. The system does not provide any help or hint. The user must either activate the on-line help or issue another command. By doing so, the system not only can obtain feedback, but also achieve its goals. This feedback assists the system in deciding whether this user should be reclassified. In another case, if this user was misclassified, we can assume that this user is likely to commit another error and the system must reevaluate the current classification. Thus, the system can offer an alternative help strategy based on the classification.

Strategy B: Message and ask if need help. This category occupies those upper and left positions in HSM. We can see that users in this category might need some assistance. The system provides an error message and optional help. The latter is to ask whether the user needs the system to be active; that is, provides the right step. The user can bypass the help.

This explains how the system can stimulate the user's learnability to enhance understanding of the task.

Strategy C: Message and suggestion for the next right step. This category fills up the diagonal positions in HSM. These users definitely need help in order to maintain their current classification. If a user takes the suggestion, the user remains in the current category. Otherwise, most likely the user is downgraded. At this point, the system acts semi-actively, that is the user still can ignore the suggestion. Therefore, the system helps the user to comprehend the task.

Strategy D: Mandatory next step. This category occupies the lower and right positions in HSM table. A user in this category should do the next step in order to continue the task. From this point on, a user is passive until the system reclassifies the user to a higher classification.

Strategy E: Give information about the task and tell next step. This category consists of the lowest and rightmost three positions in HSM. A user who is classified in this category is unaware of the task. The system provides more information about the task until the user has learned enough to move to another category.

5. TASK-DOMAIN KNOWLEDGE CHECKER (TKC)

The TKC is used to track the user's actions during the task-performing process and to evaluate its correctness and efficiency. This procedure not only can detect if any error occurred and but also can determine proper help messages. Based upon the state transition diagram of the specific task (for example, the text editor in Figure 2), a rule-based system is constructed to store the necessary navigation to accomplish the task. By monitoring every step the user attempts, the TKC is able to determine if the user is correct, wrong, or lost.

5.1 Technique of TKC

As we mentioned before, our example in Figure 2 is only one small portion of a text editor. Even in a complex system, text editing consists of a number of tasks based on their functionality. As long as a task state transition diagram can be formed for each one, there is a way to monitor how the user navigates.

It is generally agreed that an intelligent interface should be able to infer and evaluate a user's plans and intentions. It should also adapt its behavior to the individual user and to the user's current task [6]. Our methodology can also be used in a task-independent environment. By monitoring the user, the system should be able to detect the user's goals. In our system, we assume that user's goals are already known. The system monitors the user's movements and makes comparison to the state transition diagram. Therefore, the system knows where the user is and whether any error has occurred.

5.2 Example

For instance, there is a file called EXAMPLE, the task is to delete the whole second paragraph and then save it. This example is trivial. The TKC forms the most optimal route for navigation based upon the state transition diagram. That is:

OPEN -> BLOCK -> CUT -> SAVE -> EXIT

If the user didn't type or select "OPEN", the TKC constructs the different message for him according to the user's category in HSM.

Strategy A: On the screen, maybe it says "ERROR! Press RETURN to continue.". After the user enters RETURN, the system returns the user to the previous state.

Strategy B: On the screen, it says "ERROR! "XXXXX" is not correct here. Press RETURN to continue or "ESC" for help.".

Strategy C: On the screen, it says "ERROR! "XXXXX" is not correct at this point. "OPEN" is the right command. Press RETURN to continue.".

Strategy D: On the screen, it says "ERROR! "OPEN is the right command. Please Enter "OPEN" to continue.".

Strategy E: On the screen, it says " To delete one paragraph in a file, you have to "OPEN" the file first, and "BLOCK" the paragraph, "CUT" it, and "SAVE" the file.

The above error message for each strategy is only a possible suggestion.

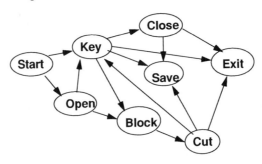

Figure 2. State Transition Diagram Example

6. DISCUSSION

Since the novice-expert continuum exists, an intelligent help system should provide the adaptive mechanism for the individual user. Novice users certainly need help both in learning and use of the system. Even users proficient in specific tasks may have more to learn [7]. That is why our proposed help system issues a help strategy based on not only the classification, but the current performance of the users. The only way to use a computer is by issuing a command. This can be achieved either by typing a command, clicking an icon, selecting from a menu, or even talking to the computer system. According to Norman [8], the interface should be designed to allow the individual user to: (1) execute an action by more directly expressing high-level intentions; and (2) receive direct help in planning how to carry out the task. The help messages in our system are designed either to recommend a correct command or to assist using a correct command.

7. CONCLUSION and REMARKS

This proposed help system is designed to provide help to different classes of users. One strength of the system is the generic task-specific knowledge checker which can detect errors and inefficiencies. Another strength is the HSM table which generates different help strategies determined not only by the level of a user's knowledge, but also by the user's observed performance. Regardless of the multimode which an intelligent interface is supposed to have, we believe our help system can function adaptively and intelligently. Also, there are several challenging directions for future research:

1. How to integrate the help system to an intelligent user-computer interface. A help system is only one of the functions of the entire interface. The multimode of interaction for individual group of users is necessary for an intelligent interface. By the same token, a help system should be able to determine what type of interaction mode is more suitable for the individual user.

2. How to implement this mechanism in a task-independent environment. There are additional concerns, such as detecting the user's goal, necessary before the TKC can work on error-checking.

REFERENCES

1. C. Chiu, and A. F. Norcio (1992), "A Fuzzy Neural Network Architecture for Modeling Users in Adaptive Human-Computer Interfaces.", Submitted to the IEEE Transactions on Systems, Man, and Cybernetics.
2. Jeffery G. Bonar, "Interface Architectures for Intelligent Tutoring Systems", In Intelligent Tutoring Systems, Ed. Hugh Burns, James W. Parlett, and Carol L. Redfield, Lawrence Erlbaum Associates, Publishers (1991), Hillsdale, NJ
3. Shortliffe, E. H. (1976). Computer-based medical consultations: MYGIN. New York: Elsevier.
4. Fowler,C., Macaulay, L., & Siripoksup, S. (1987). An evaluation of the effectiveness of the adaptive interface module (AIM) in matching dialogues to users. In D. Diaper & R. Winder (Eds.), People and computers III (pp.345-359). New York:Cambridge University Press.
5. G. Fisher, A. Lemke, and T. Schwab, "Active help Systems", In Readings on Cognitive Ergonomics - Mind and Computers, Ed. G. C. van Veer, M. J. Tauber, T.R.G. Green and P. Gorny, Proceedings of the 2nd European Conference Gmunden, Austria, Sep. 1984
6. Greenberg, S., and Witten, I. (1983). "Adaptive personalized interfaces - A question of viability.", Behavior and Information Technology, vol. 4, pp. 31-35.
7. Tyler, S. W. and S. Treu, "An interface architecture to provide adaptive task-specific context for the user", International Journal of Man-Machines Studies, vol.30, pp.303-327, 1989
8. Noman, D. (1983). Some observations on Mental Models. In D. Gentner & A. Stevens, Eds. Mental Models. Hillside, NJ:Lawrence Erlbaum Associates.

A usability evaluation of text and speech redundant help messages on a reader interface

E. M.-Y. Wang[a], H. Shahnavaz[b], L. Hedman[c], K. Papadopoulos[c], and N. Watkinson[d]

[a]Department of Industrial Engineering, National Tsing Hua University, Taiwan, R.O.C.

[b]Department of Human Work Sciences, Luleå University, Luleå, Sweden

[c]Telia Research, Haninge, Sweden

[d]British Telecom Research Labs, Ipswich, England

Abstract
The purpose of this study is to investigate whether text and speech redundant help messages are more usable than non-redundant messages on a reader interface. This paper looks at the principles underlying multi-media. The hypothesis is that if a speech and text redundant message is presented on a reader interface, then the users should have less difficulties or errors and shorter performance time in such tasks, by using such a (redundant) interface than using the text interface or speech interface. Four evaluation tools, i.e., observations, subjective ratings, interviews, and objective performance measures, were used to evaluate the effects of the messages. Twenty subjects (9 males and 11 females) from the general public participated in the study. The results partly support our hypothesis by showing that the redundant interface is the easiest and quickest among the three in terms of learning and using. Appropriate use of text and speech redundant help messages does contribute to the usability of the reader interface for the tested condition. However, the adverse effects of the speech, e.g., repeat messages are annoying, must be dealt with care.

1. INTRODUCTION

Usability has been studied intensively in the field of Human-Computer Interaction (HCI) in recent years as more complex computer systems, which are uneasy to use, have been developed. Many researchers are trying very hard to understand the usability characteristics generally required in an HCI system. These results have been formulated into several usability principles that are considered very important and have been used for usability design and evaluation in the field [1-4].

With the growth of advanced information technologies, e.g., speech technology, multi-media, hypermedia, etc., the systems will be more complex, yet they must be very usable to the end-users. Though people expect the new media, e.g., audio, speech, video, etc., will have high potential on HCI applications, their effects on human performance are largely unknown.

Most online help systems are often nothing more than electronic versions of hard-copy manuals with keyboard or menu-based mechanisms for accessing the help information [5]. It is probably for the reasons that speech output is inferior to text in transmission and storage size and speed, comprehension, possibility of review and preview, and annoying [6], most help messages are presented in text. However, there are advantages of using speech in interfaces: almost everyone understands spoken language, speech can be heard over distances, and the user is free to use other modalities when listening to speech messages [6]. To take the advantages of both media by applying the redundancy principle to the help messages, the reader interface may be more usable.

2. REDUNDANCY PRINCIPLE AND THE READER INTERFACES

In this study, the redundancy principle was selected for evaluation. Redundancy principle in HCI refers to a feature that conveys the identical information as another feature, but in different forms, in order to make the user performance more effective.

Three versions of a holiday information reader interface, i.e., the text (Figure 1), speech, and text-and-speech redundant, were developed on SuperCard for studying the effects of message redundancy on user performance with the two media. The effects could be compared to determine which version of the three could provide better usability.

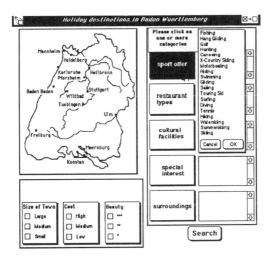

Figure 1. The text reader interface shows a sport list and a text message "Please click on one or more categories" after the category "Sport Offer" was selected.

The text interface displays only the textual messages. The messages were displayed automatically if the mouse cursor stayed over a "button" on the screen for more than two seconds without been clicked. This was made to provide help to the user who might be unsure what next action should be performed and was making a decision. The messages disappeared after a few seconds which was long enough to read. The speech and the redundant interfaces were the same as the text interface except the media of messages. In speech interface, messages were conveyed with built-in recorded spoken language instead of text while in the redundant interface both text and speech messages were provided.

3. METHODS

3.1. The hypothesis

The following was formulated for this evaluation: "*If* a speech message, along with a text message, is presented on a reader interface and they convey the same information, *then* the users should have *less difficulties or errors and shorter performance time* in using such (text-and-speech redundant) interface than using the text interface or speech interface."

It was considered that the users from the public may be mostly novices. They may need various types of help information to ease the operation or the reader interface must be usable. Speech messages are more "natural" than text messages. However, a speech message ends when the last phoneme is silent and its intelligibility reduces in a noisy environment. On the other hand, a text message may be less "natural" but it displays regardless the noise level. To take advantages of both speech and text, a redundant message may be most effective.

3.2. Evaluation tools

Four evaluation tools, i.e., observations, subjective ratings, interviews, and objective performance measures, refined from an earlier study[7] were used.

Observations. On-site observation was employed to get a quick impression of the most obvious problems on the interfaces. The time stamped videotape observation was used to keep detail behavioural information as well as for further objective data analysis.

Subjective ratings and interviews. Having done the tasks, subjects rated the interfaces that had been used in two aspects, i.e., general and specific. General questions deal with the systems as a whole and focused on the subject's feelings about the preferences, satisfactions, learning/using the systems, and the usefulness of the messages. Specific questions deal with the specific interface and focused on whether the messages were clear, helpful, and necessary to the performance. The rating scales are 11-point bi-polar scales on which the mid-point indicates neutral, i.e., no special feeling, no opinion, or no effect. Semi-structured interviews were done to obtain subjects' opinions about the interfaces and the reasons behind the scores and their unique behaviours.

Objective performance measures. Along with videotape observation, some measures were taken for detail analysis. The data that have been collected from the videotapes were: (1) Numbers/time of each type of performed actions, (2) Numbers/types of "errors" (i.e., operations that violate the instructions intentionally or "consciously"), (3) Numbers/types of "wrong-doings" (i.e., messages were misunderstood or misleading the operations), and (4) Numbers of click before a message was presented (within 2 seconds after the cursor was stopped over a button).

3.3. Subject backgrounds, equipment, experimental design, and tasks

Subject. Twenty subjects (9 males and 11 females) were recruited from the public and were paid for participation. Their ages were between 24 and 59 with an average of 40 and a standard deviation of 9.7. A half of them had no experience with computers at all. The majority (9 of 10) of the others had used IBM-PC/Compatible and terminal type machines. One subject had 4 years Apple/Macintosh experience. Another two subjects among the inexperienced group had played some video games. However, because computer-linked machines can be found in many public places, most of them (18 subjects) have used such facilities occasionally (mostly banking, ticket selling, and library book searching systems). There were only two subjects didn't have any kind of computer related experience.

Equipment. The three versions of reader interface were installed on a Macintosh IIfx with colour monitor and mouse. Two video cameras and a mixer were used to record the subjects' actions and the screen. For recording the interviews, a cassette audio recorder was used.

Experimental design. The subjects were randomly divided into two groups. One was tested on the text and the redundant interfaces the other on the speech and the redundant interfaces. To avoid any effect that might cause by a specific interface or the positions of the items to be selected on the screen, the sequences of interfaces used and the items to be selected were also randomised.

Task. The holiday criteria that subjects may select on the reader interfaces contains size of town, cost, beauty, sport facilities, types of restaurant, cultural facilities, special interest, and surroundings. Having set the criteria, the system will search from its database the towns that meet the criteria and indicate the locations of the towns on the inlet map. Two holiday information tasks were used. They differed in the items to be selected and the sequence of the selections to eliminate the learning effect of doing the same task twice (with a single medium interface and the redundant interface). The subjects were asked to follow the task instructions, select the items which describe a holiday, then find out the cities that fit those selected items. Each task consisted of 4 parts of operations: initiate search, select/add items, de-select items, and reset the screen.

Procedure. The subjects were asked to fill out the personal information form at the reception. The experiment started by showing a briefing information to the subject. It informed the subject what would be seen, the experimental procedure, and his/her legal rights. Mouse operation was then explained and practice was provided. While performing the tasks, subjects were allowed to ask for help. It finished with a semi-structured rating and interview.

4. RESULTS AND DISCUSSION

4.1. From observations

Subjects' actions and behaviours were observed on the experiment site as well as on the laboratory from videotapes. Most subjects used trial and error strategy for learning, which took rather long time if they could not breakthrough the bottle necks. The problems reflected some design deficiencies on the reader interfaces, which also provided valuable experience on HCI usability design and revealed certain usability issues. Some, but not all, of the observed problems of this kind are mentioned below:

(1) They had difficult to recognise the "category buttons", which was perhaps due to the shape of these buttons looked more close to square tags. (2) Many subjects tended to click directly on the map, on scroll bars, scroll arrows, or text field of the category windows while trying to find the category buttons at the beginning of the experiment. (3) Many subjects were confused by the "Cancel" (i.e., cancel the selections and close the list) and the "OK" (i.e., confirm and save the selections then close the list) buttons on the category lists. Having selected the items on a category list, they didn't click "OK" button, thus the list was left on the screen, blocked other lists, and made confusion. They had to try many times to know what had went wrong. (4) On text interface, text messages popped up, stayed, and disappeared quietly. Some subjects were reading the instruction sheet while the test messages presented and disappeared so they had never noticed the existence of such messages nor gotten the helps. (5) If a speech message was presented at the time when mouse cursor had been moved to a next location other than that message linked button, the subject might think that the cursor position is where he/she should click on. (6) Some subjects might be curious or used the speech messages for operation confirmation purpose. They left the mouse cursor on a button intentionally and waited for the message before clicking. (7) Some subjects were so concentrated on the task they didn't even notice or follow the messages. (8) The repeat speech messages bothered many subjects.

4.2. From subjective ratings

General ratings. Ten subjects preferred the redundant interface while 7 and 3 preferred the text and the speech ones, respectively. The satisfactory scores indicated that the text interface was most satisfied while the speech interface was most unsatisfied. In general, learning to use the system was neither difficult nor easy. Once learned, it was very easy to use. This was further supported by the fact that they considered the messages were only slightly useful for performing the tasks, i.e., they didn't get much help from the messages.

Specific ratings. The subjects gave the highest ratings to the redundant interface for the specific questions asked while those to the text interface were the lowest. Though it shows that the redundant messages were clearer than text-only messages (p=0.0288), speech-only messages were not different from the redundant ones in terms of clearness. It also shows that the redundant messages were a little more helpful for performing the tasks than either one of the others, but statistically there were no differences. However, the subjects who had used both speech and redundant interfaces suggested that the redundant messages were more necessary to their performance than speech-only messages (p =0.0075). When asked to compare the helpfulness of the redundant messages with the others, the speech/redundant group considered redundant messages were more helpful than speech-only messages while the text/redundant group considered redundant messages were a little less helpful than text-only messages (p =0.0225). This might be caused by their different experiences with different interfaces but may also indicate that if speech has to be used to help users, a text-and-speech redundancy may help a lot.

4.3. From objective performance measures

Before recording the objective measures, the activities were defined, the begin/end points and action cues were identified to facilitate the work. These activities were: RT (*R*ead *T*ask sheet), LS (*L*ook at *S*creen, or think), CN (*C*lick but *N*o system response, or move mouse), CS (*C*lick and *S*ystem responded, or effective click), and H (*H*elp). While observing the videotapes, the observer took notes on errors, special behaviours, and relevant information about the performance for further analysis and reference. After the subject clicked on the "Search" button, the objective measure was terminated.

The analysis concentrates on the task performance times. Having recorded various performance times and relevant information, necessary adjustments were done before analysis. Data sets that contained irrelevant time elements, such as system crashing, incomplete task operation, etc., were eliminated. Outliers ($\bar{x}\pm SD$) were excluded due to the large variations of performance times. The proportions of performance times for various activities show similar patterns for all interfaces. The extremely little time spent on requesting or accepting help and communication might reveal the ease of learning and use, but one should also be aware of that the strategy used by almost all the subjects was trial and error. Moreover, this overall data include the time spent on trials, making errors, correcting errors, figuring next actions, etc., which actually took much of the performance time. As shown in Table 1, the improvement of the average performance time is remarkable from the first task to the second. Most obviously, the thinking time decreased quite much, which is indicated by the reduction of "Look screen" and "Move mouse". This may suggest that the system has a very high learnability. If they had further opportunities to use either of the interfaces again, many subjects expressed that they had the highest confidence in being able to perform much faster and accurate.

Table 1
Improvement of average performance time in sec (Task2 vs. Task1).

	Read Task	Look Screen	Move Mouse	Effective Click	Help & Comm.	Total Time
Avg. time in Task1	109.58	137.25	130.92	192.42	43.92	614.08
Avg. time in Task2	67.39	31.00	18.94	128.22	4.17	249.72
Time improved	42.19	106.25	111.97	64.19	39.75	364.36
% of improvement	38.50%	77.41%	85.53%	33.36%	90.51%	59.33%

Some other objective measures are also useful. For example, the exact clicking time readings were observed and timed, it was found that many effective clicks were made before the help messages presented, especially for the second task. This indicates that the messages are probably unnecessary if the system is easy to learn, or the speech messages can be turned off while the silent text messages are left on as the user is getting familiar with the system. The experiments can be extended to break down the time elements to separate the error time, correction time, etc., to examine whether errors are of a specific type, or if the correction can be made easily and quickly, etc. Furthermore, it can be possible to identify the most serious problems in a specific interface within the system, e.g., the ineffective activities and time. It is also possible to extract the real "effective" operation time to set as usability design target.

4.4. From interviews

Some specific comments are useful for usability design, for examples:
(1) "It is difficult to start." This information gives some ideas about why much of the operation time was dedicated to thinking, trial and error, and move mouse. Perhaps the first

important thing to consider for a usable system is to provide an easy initiation for the users, otherwise, the users will loose their interests in learning it, not to mention using the system.

(2) "Once learned, it's easy." "I don't need the message once learned." "The second task was easy, I didn't realise there was no speech." These comments supplement the previous point. The messages are most helpful for novice users, once they learned they may never need the help again.

(3) "Speech is slightly annoying." "Voice would be bothering if learned." Though the rating scores showed the speech and the redundant messages were helpful, many subjects mentioned that they dislike speech which bothered them. The authors believes that the repeat speech messages had given the subjects a stressful feeling of being supervised and pushed.

(4) "I could use it without speech." These comments may indicate the unnecessary of the speech. Together with the previous comments, an alternative modification would be to present these help messages passively by adding a user controlled Help button on the interface. The help messages (text or speech) will not present unless the user wants to.

5. CONCLUSION

From the information and data collected, it shows that the redundant interface is the easiest among the three in terms of learning and using. But the hypothesis was only partially verified. Appropriate use of text and speech redundancy does contribute to the usability of reader interface. The adverse effects of the speech must be dealt with care, for example, function allocation of various media has to be studied as a new medium is introduced into a system.

In a multimedia system, the redundancy principle may be applied in various combinations of two or more media. The more complex a system is with more media, the more difficult to deal with newly emerged usability issues. The experience of this study has showed that the implementation and effects of usability principles can be evaluated with simple tools. It should be emphasised that early and rigourous planning and preparation of the usability evaluation can be paid off with saving in analysis time and with more significant and valid results. It is expected that the evaluation tools can be further improved, extended, and used to evaluate other usability principles.

6. ACKNOWLEDGMENTS

This study was done within RACE/GUIDANCE project (R-1067) and by financial support from Swedish Telecom. Thanks are extended to them and the subjects for their contributions.

7. REFERENCES

1 Molich, R., and Nielsen, J. (1990). Improving a human-computer dialogue. Communications of the ACM, 33 (3), 338-348.
2 Swain, R.E. (1990). The user-system interface for computerized products -- Part I: Design principles. Human factors in practice (A joint publication of the Computer Systems and Consumer Products Technical Groups of Human Factors Society), (Dec., 1990), 16-22.
3 Apple Computer. (1989). HyperCard stack design guidelines. Reading, Massachusetts: Addison-Wesley.
4 Holcomb, R., and Tharp, A.L. (1989). An amalgamated model of software usability. In Proceedings of the 13th Annual International Computer Software and Applications Conference (pp. 559-566). Washington, DC: IEEE Computer Society Press.
5 Elkerton, J. (1988). Online aiding for human-computer interfaces. In M. Helander (Ed.), Handbook of human-computer interaction (pp. 345-364). Amsterdam: Elsevier.
6 Streeter, L.A. (1988). Applying speech synthesis to user interfaces. In M. Helander (Ed.), Handbook of human-computer interaction (pp. 321-343). Amsterdam: Elsevier.
7 Wang, E.M.-Y., Boucherat, P., Shahnavaz, H., Hedman, L., and Sahlin, C. (1990) A verification of the evaluation tools for evaluating multimedia co-operative authoring emulation. In Proceedings of the International Conference on Integrated Broadband Services and Networks (pp. 335-340). London: The Institution of Electrical Engineers.

Development of a processflow manager for an IC-Diagnosis System

Holger Retz and Axel Hunger

University of Duisburg, Department of Data Processing, Bismarckstraße 81, 4100 Duisburg 1, Germany

Abstract

The analysis of faulty digital circuits is a very complex task which can only be performed in a semi-automatic system environment. This paper presents a processflow management system which provides the operator with a high process transparency. The system mainly consists of a graphical representation of the data flow and a graphical course of the process, which is supported by predefined rules. Herewith the operator is prevented from making any wrong decisions. A further component is a communication manager which allows the information exchange among specific tools.

The implementation of a dedicated process description language allows the easy and consistent modification of existing processes as well as the definition of new processes. This language has been integrated in an existing framework.

1. INTRODUCTION

The diagnosis of failed ICs can not be fully automatically executed yet. Normally a lot of different tools and data sets from the CAD- and test world are used to efficiently prepare the investigations in a circuit. This procedure requires a tight coupling between the two different areas of CAD design and physical analysis. A typical debug session of a mid-size IC takes one complete working week and can only be performed by an experienced and specialized physical engineer.

The fastest solutions can be found when all tools are used in the right course and any mis-operation is avoided as far as possible. As the optimal flow of data is not constant but varies depending on the current failure problem (loops, backtracks), a corresponding help & support system would result in drastic savings of time.

Such a help system is presented in the following which enhances a conventional diagnosis system.

The new system integrates the design, test and diagnosis tools and takes considerations of software ergonomics and inter process communication into account. A graphical interface leads the operator through a session, checks the required input- and output-datasets of each tool in the process and proposes the optimal session flow. Nevertheless the possibility of an interactive user operation is given at any time during the session.

The use of a standard dataformat and a structured access to the data via a procedural interface optimizes the integration of tools.

2. BACKGROUND

Ergonomics
The useability of the software and a suitable user interface are among the most important points for the success of interactive software products. Specially a complex process like an IC diagnosis system, which can only be executed semi-automatically, needs an appropriate man-machine interface.

Three different points were considered before starting the software integration and the processflow modelling [2]:
- The knowledge and the capabilities of the potential operators were analysed. With help of this analysis a division of labour among operator and computer was performed and complex tasks were divided into procedural subtasks.
- The kind of interaction was fixed. Depending on the process status and the process flow, kinds of input/output (text, graphic) and information representation (window technique, scrollbars) were choosen.
- The most important question was the suitable dialogform between operator and computer. Both the computer-driven dialog (menues, dialog-boxes, decision help) and the operator-driven dialog (manual access to the process, command line features) were combined to a hybrid form of dialog.

Process communication
During the analysis process, information like the actual process status and, in particular, part results of the fault diagnosis have to be present immediatly [3].

A conventional approach is the data exchange through files. A process control supervises the different tools and guarantees a controlled data exchange. This method needs a structured serial process flow and needs all tools to have access to a fixed area. Both, the parallel activity of different tools and the use of a transparent network are not possible.

Therefore it was decided to use the X-Window System, where the socalled X-Protocol is provided for the communication (and the data exchange) among socalled X-Clients. The details on the implementation of the communication management are described in chapter 3.3.

Access to standard data via a procedural interface
As well known from the practical experiences, a widely spread problem is the high number of different, incompatible data formats. Normally, each commercial product uses a special data format and in order to interface to a new tool, a corresponding data converter is necessary. This problem is not only limited to the CAD world but also exists in the test world, because the different hardware testers have their own data input which has to be interfaced. From that background a standard format called 'EDIF Test' was developed which provides a standard description of a device in a toolindependant way [4,5]. This stategy frees the operator from performing confusing and time-consuming data conversions.

The use of 'EDIF Test' provides a clearly structured data and any application does not have access to an 'EDIF Test' file but reads and writes the data via an internal data structure by calling a corresponding function of a procedural interface, PI, (figure 2).

732

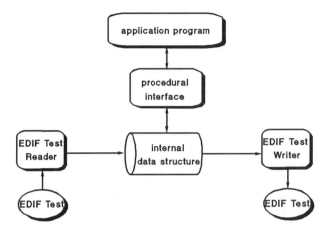

Figure 1: Use of the procedural interface

During the modelling phase of the standard data format, the access via a PI was advantegous as for any change in the format only the corresponding PI-functions had to be modified instead of each tool interface.

3. THE PROCESSFLOW MANAGEMENT SYSTEM

The whole CAD, test and diagnosis process is supported by a processflow-manager which supports the operator in terms of decision making (and avoides herewith wrong decisions) and makes the correspondence between the tools and data sets more transparent.

The complete system has been modelled, provided with a set of underlying rules, described by a dedicated language and realized in a graphical flow graph representation. These features are described in the following sections.

3.1. A general process description language

A process description language has been developed (figure 2), which allows the definition of tools and datasets as well as underlying rules within a process in a general way.

```
( defaults
          ( processname
            version_number
              ⋮
          )
( definition_part
          ( tools ...   )
          ( datasets ...)
          ( events ...  )
          ( start )
          ( end )
)
( implementation
          ( symbols ... )
          ( events ...  )
          ( graphical_information ... )
)
( rules ... )
```

Figure 2: Top most level of the description language

With help of this language already described processes can be modified. Based on that language an interpreter has been developed, which automatically generates a processflow visualization as it is described in 3.2.

In the particular case of the "IC diagnosis" process a corresponding model has been defined. Furthermore a set of rules has been defined which basically checks the following questions:
- does it make sense to execute a tool at the current process status?
- is the required input data available?
- has the input data been generated by the right tool?
- is the point of time of data generation plausible?

3.2. Graphical process representation

As described above, the processflow can be automatically visualized (figure 3).

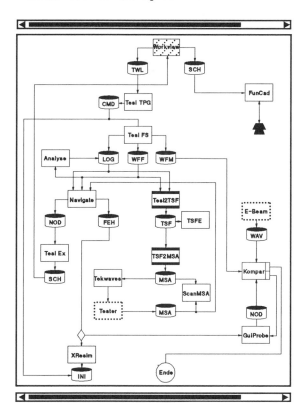

Figure 3: The visualization of the processflow

The discussed interpreter provides different graphical symbols for application programs, converters and data sets. The distinction between available and active programs and between generated and not yet generated data sets is realized with a color system. The graphical representation can be scrolled through and zoomed in and each tool can be activated by clicking the symbol with the mouse.

3.3. Communication management

A communication manager has been developed in order to realize an inter client communication (ICC) (figure 4).

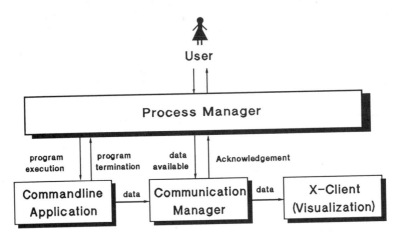

Figure 4: A communication manager for inter client communication

The communication is controlled by 'events (i.e. data available', 'data received', 'incorrect data format'). With help of an event-handler the specific tools can receive and interpret the events (and herewith the information).

In the presented system the ICC-based communication manager is used to realize the communication between several diagnosis tools and a dedicated editor. Herewith partial results of the diagnosis tools can be visualized during a session.

4. CONCLUSIONS

A processflow management system for an IC-diagnosis system was realized to support operators of this semi-automatic process.

The different kinds of operator-computer interfaces have been analysed as well as different data exchange methods. From this background a hybrid dialogform was choosen which includes both menues, dialog boxes, decision help *and* command line features and manual operator access.

The definition of a general process description language has been the basis for automatic generation of a graphical process representation. As part of the system a communication manager has been defined and implemented which realizes the intertool communication and allows the online visualization of partial results during a process session. A graphical interface supports the operator in terms of observation of process status, guidance through the system and decision help via predefined rules.

An output of this well-defined operator-computer interface is a faster 'time to market' as the time required to locate a fault in a device can be reduced.

REFERENCES

1   Hunger, A.; Retz, H.; Ritschel, O., Fault dictionary navigation as an efficient preparation for E-beam testing, ESREF '92, Schwäbisch-Gmünd, Germany

2   Fähnrich, K.P. (eds.), Software-Ergonomie, State of the art, Oldenburg Verlag, München, 1987

3   Scharf, R.; Kunztsch, C.; Helmreich, K., A Distributed Environment for Automated CAD Data based Fault Localization, Proc. 5th International Conference on Quality in Electronic Components: Failure Prevention, Detection and Analysis / 2nd European Symposium on Reliability of Electron Devices, ESREF '91, Bordeaux, France

4   Retz, H., An 'EDIF Test' viewer, 5th European EDIF Forum 1991, Montpellier, France

5   EDIF, Electronic Design Interchange Format, Version 2.0.0, Electronic Industries Association, EDIF Steering Committee, Washington, USA, 1990

Intelligent Task Based Model for the Design of Screen Review Systems for People with Blindness

J. Gunderson

Division of Rehabilitation Education, University of Illinois, 1207 South Oak Street, Champaign, Illinois 61820, phone: (207) 244-5870, email: jongund@ux1.cso.uiuc.edu

ABSTRACT

This paper describes an intelligent task based approach to designing user interfaces for people with blindness to access computer systems. The intelligent task approach uses information on the tasks associate with a particular application program (or operating system) to create a optimized non-visual user interface. A task model, rather than the current direct screen model, provides more support to the blind computer user to independently learn functions within application programs, and independently discover and recover from command errors.

1. INTRODUCTION

People with severe visual impairments and blindness have not directly benefitted from the human factors research which has increased the usability of computer application software over the past 10 years. Current systems to access computers for people with blindness place significantly more memory and cognitive demands upon the user than sighted users using the same computer[1]. Most people with blindness use MS-DOS based computer systems with synthetic speech output to read information from the computer screen. Products for accessing Graphical User Interfaces (GUIs) like the Apple Macintosh, Microsoft Windows and IBM OS/2 are becoming available. Programs which translate computer display information into speech are called screen review programs (SRP). SRPs designed for access to character based MS-DOS application programs read information directly from the computer screen, typically an 80 column line at a time. The direct screen approach places the burden on the blind user to know where information is located on the computer screen, and the meaning of the symbols and abbreviations which often appear on the screen. For example, line 25 in WordPerfect for MS-DOS contains status information for editing a document. The status line includes information on the file name, document number, page number and the location of the cursor on the corresponding printed page.

```
c:\wpdata\sample.doc                    Doc 1 Pg 1 ln 2.1" Pos 1.35"
```

Figure 1. Status/Prompt line of WordPerfect 5.1

When a SRP reads the following WordPerfect status line shown in Figure 1, the user typically hears something like this: "c colon backslash whoop data backslash sample period doc doc one p g one l n one point one quote pas two point three five quote". Based on the previous spoken information the user needs to sort out and translate the information into what it actually represents. Many users with blindness never get to the point of being able to understand what is being spoken and how it relates to the tasks associated with wordprocessing. The reading of the status line is just one example in the extensive list of human factors problems in the usability design of screen review systems. Screen review technology has tried to become more user friendly, but the movement is still based on the direct translation model which requires the user to understand the visual layout of the application program.

An alternative to the direct translation model is an intelligent task based model. The intelligent task based model is designed around the task to be accomplished. The visual display is only one place to gather information about the task for presentation to the user through speech, braille or vibrotactile image, rather than the focus of what is to be translated. The intelligent task model is designed to support the underlying task the user is trying to accomplish and not necessarily the visual representation of the task seen on the computer screen.

2. DIRECT TRANSLATION PROBLEMS

The current model for SRP technology is the direct translation of the information on the computer screen to a speech synthesizer. The main problem with the direct approach is that novice users have very little knowledge of either the task, or the types and location of screen information they need to complete the task. In the direct translation model most novice users with blindness develop a rote memory behavior of using the computer (I type this and this should happen). The rote behavior is due to the blind user's limited knowledge on the location and format of screen information. Rasmussen[2] describes this behavior as skill level behavior. Current SRPs though are limited in their ability to move people up to the more general rule and knowledge levels of operation. The limiting of users to the skill level is due to the lack of automatic presentation of information for orienting the user to the task and options available to them. In the rote behavior approach users either complete the task successfully or need to start all over again when the completion of the task fails (if the user even detects the failure). A simple mistake in toggling the insert key will allow the blind user to start typing over text with no discernible change in speech feedback while using most SRPs.

The rote behavior doesn't provide a mechanism for error discovery or recovery when the user accidently types a wrong key. Error information (if any) is typically not presented to the user or in a form the blind user can understand. The rote behavior leads to a error recovery technique of completely resetting the computer when the error does become evident. The resetting of the computer often results in many hours of lost work and user frustration. Resetting the computer is typically entirely unnecessary if the blind users would have information available to them to understand the task the computer is performing. An example of the lack of task/command information in WordPerfect is when the user accidently hits the Help Key (F3). The only way to exit the help screens is by hitting the ENTER key. When the user accidently presses the help key the user will hear the unexpected message: "selection colon zero left parenthesis hit enter to exit right parenthesis". The user is not expecting the message and therefore probably will not understand the message. The message that the user hears provides no direct information that the user is now in the help screen. As the user presses more keys they do not hear anything automatically spoken, even though the top 24 lines of the screen are changing with each key press. The Cancel key (F1) key and Exit key (F7) which normally exits the user from other functions and menus do not work in the help screen, instead hitting the Cancel and Exit keys present information on their function in the rest of the program. If the user does use the read line function to read the bottom line on the screen they will only hear the previous message. The problem with reading the prompt line is that even though the information on how to exit the help function is in the message, it is masked by the extraneous information before and after the message. The masking makes it difficult for the user to extract the helpful information.

3. OTHER APPROACHES

Current work in the area human computer interaction for people with blindness is focusing on graphical user interfaces [3,4,5,6]. The primary focus of research on the human interface is how to present graphical images/objects in either tactile[7,8] or auditory form [9,10,11]. Edwards[12] though tries to look at translation of the task associated with visual WIMP (Window, Icon, Menu, Pointer) user interfaces to a non-visual user interface. He uses the functional objects associated with WIMP based computer systems and created an auditory user interface for a wordprocessor called SoundTrack. The SoundTrack approach is interesting since it is trying to translate the basic concepts of the visual WIMP user interface to a user interface similar in function but optimized for auditory presentation. The approach of SoundTrack is fundamentally different than current screen review systems that base what they display on what is on the character or graphical screen[14]. SoundTrack is based on the translation of the concepts of a WIMP interface, not the visual representations of a particular WIMP interface. The intelligent task based access system comes from the concept translation, rather then screen image translation approach.

4. INTELLIGENT TASK BASED MODEL

The intelligent task based model for the design of SRPs is based on the translation of the task from the visual domain to an optimized non-visual domain. The task approach is in contrast with the "tool" approach of standard screen review programs[15], which is based on providing information on what is on a computer display without any information on task. A task based SRP model presents information in a form compatible with how the information is spoken, similar in concept to creating visual displays which are compatible with task[16]. For example in describing the location of a file someone would not say "it's in the c colon backslash whoop data", but would be more likely to say "it's on drive c in the w p data sub directory". The task approach reduces the cognitive demands on the blind user by translating the screen information to its conventional speech pronunciation. Norman[17] describes the increase in compatibility as reducing the cognitive gulf between the user and the access system. In addition to the translation of screen information, the task is also identified. In WordPerfect when someone presses the F7 key to access the Print Menu the typical SRP only says "Selection colon zero". A task based SRP would say "Print Menu" to orient the blind user to the fact that they are in the print menu. The task based SRP allows the user to use the arrow keys to investigate and select print menu options, even though the use of the arrow keys is not a selection technique associated with WordPerfect menus. The task based SRP can add the additional search functions with the use of knowledge about the menu task, where menu information is located, and how to speak menu information as the user presses the arrow keys. The fundamental principle behind the design of task based SRPs is the use of knowledge about the application program to orient and direct the blind computer user to the current task and options available to them.

By using intelligence the task based SRP can help the user by controlling and transforming the presentation of information to the blind user. The benefit to the user is less time needed to orient themselves to the functions of an application program, easier error identification and correction, and ability to identify options in a standard way.

4.1 Orientation

Intelligent task based SRPs use information about the application program to orient the user to the task they are trying to perform and the command options available to them. Orientation to the task provides the user with a context for understanding the information presented to them. So when the user is in a menu, set up screen, or edit screen the information presented to the user reflects the context of the task the computer is performing. The other half of the orientation problem is the type of commands available to the user in a particular dialog with the computer. The availability of command orientation information to the user assists them in understanding the commands needed to manipulate information, select/change options or exit from a particular part of an application program.

4.1.1 Task Orientation

One of the problems with current SRPs is the lack of a means to orient the user to the task the computer is performing. The errors for most people with blindness are due to the user thinking the computer is performing one task and the computer actually performing another. For example in WordPerfect for MS-DOS most screen review programs are designed to read the bottom line of the screen when information in the status line changes (i.e. when a menu or prompt appears after pressing a function key). From the earlier example the user hears something like "c colon backslash whoop data backslash ....". From the message the user is suppose to understand that they are in the edit screen of WordPerfect. With a task based SRP the information could be translated to "Editing file sample period d o c". The user is directly presented with the information that they are editing a document and given only the additional information of the file name. The machine intelligence needed for the translation is knowledge about the current task the application program is performing and what information is needed to orient the user to the task. The additional information on the WordPerfect status line about position, document number and etc.. can be accessed with special screen review commands that present these functional units of information independently.

4.1.2 Command Orientation

The other half of the orientation problem is providing information to the blind user about the keyboard commands available to them. There are two types of commands the user needs information on: application commands and review/help commands. Information on the application keyboard commands are important for the user to make selections and change items in dialog boxes and selection screens. Review commands are not the simple read line or read window commands associated with current SRPs, but commands that relate to functional information on the screen. For example a task based review command could read the current cell number or range of selected cell numbers when using the spreadsheet application Lotus 123. Access to command information needs to be standardized, so that across applications and even within applications users know how to get command information. One solution would be to use the ALT-SPACE BAR function on IBM compatibles or the COMMAND-SPACE BAR on the Macintosh to provide serial access to command information. Every time the space bar is activated a new command would be presented. When the command list is finished the presentation would start again from the beginning.

4.2 Symbol Translation

Symbol translation is important to make spoken messages easier to understand. The example provided at the beginning of this paper on the WordPerfect status line demonstrates the use of quotes to represent inches and abbreviations to represent "document", "page", "line" and "Position". An intelligent access system can recognize the symbols or abbreviations and translate them to their appropriate prose pronunciation. Therefore the status line fragment /Pos 1.35"/ will be spoken as "position one inch and 35 hundredths" rather that the current "pos one point three five quote". The user directly receives the information that the symbols represent in the status line context.

4.3 Intelligent Presentation

One of the important aspects of an intelligent access system is the ability to control the presentation of information. Control of information presentation is important so the user has time to process the information, before hearing the next item. The most important information related to the task should be presented first in a salient way to the user. The user does need to have access to all the information available. The user also needs to have control over the presentation of the information to allow the user to interpret the information at their own rate. The default presentation needs to present the most important information. For example, Figure 2 shows the WordPerfect list files screen. The list files screen has 3 different areas: Directory/Disk info on the top 3 lines, file information on the next 20 lines, and menu options on the bottom two lines. The cursor tracks the current file selected. The current file selected is also highlighted for sighted user to identify it. Most SRPs have a feature to read highlight bars. The highlight feature though is often difficult to use since the user must manually turn it on and off. The use of the highlight feature requires the user to have the knowledge that; one, they need to use the feature for the list files function; two, that their screen review program has the feature; and three, the knowledge of key command to turn the highlight feature on and off. Even if the user successfully turns the feature on and off the system reads all the information highlighted. In this case "abstract period doc one comma zero two four eleven dash one one dash nine two three colon four zero p".

The intelligent system would automatically announce only the file name "abstract dot d o c" as the user moved through the file list with out the user needing to turn any features on or off. The user can access additional information on a file by repeatedly pressing the space bar to read the file size, date created, and time created. The first press the user would hear "file size equals one thousand twenty four bytes". The second key press the user would hear "File created on November eleventh nineteen ninety two. The third press the user would hear "time created three forty p m". The next press would start with the file name again. The intelligent presentation approach provides the user with control over the presentation of the information and have file information translated to a pronunciation compatible with speech communication.

```
04-14-93  11:19p                    Directory C:\USERS\JON\PROCEED\HCI93\*.*
Document size:      0   Free: 33,116,352 Used:     80,265   Files:      16


  .    Current   <Dir>               | ..    Parent   <Dir>
_ABSTRACT.BAK    1,024  11-11-92 03:40p | ABSTRACT.DOC   7,168  03-24-93 08:45p
 PAPER   .BAK  15,872  04-13-93 11:03p | PAPER   .DOC  16,384  04-14-93 09:35p
  .                                  | .
  .                                  | .


1 Retrieving; 2 Delete; 3 Move/Rename; 4 Print; 5 Short/Long Display;
6 Look; 7 Other; 8 Copy; 9 Find; N Name Search: 6
```

Figure 2. List files screen for WordPerfect 5.1

4.4 Task Translation

Task translation is an important, but potentially controversial capability of task based screen review systems. Task translation can be used to increases user interface consistency within and between application programs. The concept of task translation is to change both the commands and/or the presentation of information from the information available from the visual display. The potential advantage of the task translation approach is to decrease learning time and the potential for errors. The reduction in errors and learning time is accomplished by changing the commands and information presented to the user to be more consistent with the task the user is trying to accomplish. The commands for selecting an item from a menu would be the same whether you are in WordPerfect, Lotus 1-2-3 or DBase. The controversial aspect of task translation technique is that the preference by many blind computer users to use exactly the same commands as their sighted counter parts to perform the same functions. There is good reason for their concern. The unilateral substitution of the commands means that it will probably be more difficult to receive help from sighted computer users, since the blind users will be using different commands. Peer support is a common means for people to learn new functions and problem solving skills in the workplace. The concern can be minimized by making the new commands associated with task translation an addition, rather than a substitution. The standard application commands would be active, but a new set of commands would be available that are consistent through out and between application programs.

4.5 Error Detection and Recovery

The detection of errors and recovery is not a direct function of an intelligent task based access system, but the result of improved presentation of information and providing standardized ways to receive command information. The use of intelligent presentation by providing orientation information and command options provides a means for independent error detection and recovery. For example in WordPerfect accidently hitting the Help key (F3) puts the user in help mode where the standard cancel key (F1) doesn't exit. The user in this case hears the announcement that they are in Help mode, giving them information that they are in a mode they do not want to be in. When the user discovers that the standard cancel command only brings up information about the cancel key, the user can use the standard command help feature to determine the key they need to press to exit. In the case of WordPerfect's help screen the key is the ENTER key.

5. GUI AND INTELLIGENT ACCESS SYSTEMS

This paper primarily discusses the application of the intelligent task based approach with MS-DOS based computer application software. The concepts behind the intelligent access approach need to be a part of access systems for graphical user interfaces (GUIs) with WIMP type organization. Current GUI screen review programs use "off screen models" based on intercepting draw commands to the screen, and gaining access to control and draw lists from the operating system. The off screen models need to take into account more than just the physical location of objects drawn on the screen or the position of an object in a control list. The access system needs to take into account orientation, symbol translation, format translation and task translation; or again as in MS-DOS SRPs the blind computer user will be required to understand the screen format and layouts. Just because some of the GUI environments have been shown to be easier for sighted users to learn and use, does not necessarily mean that blind users will automatically enjoy those benefits.

6. CONCLUSIONS

The Intelligent Task Based (ITB) user interface goes beyond trying to create a set of general tools for users to ask to "read" text or graphics from a computer display. The ITB model focuses on the task by using information about the application program to identify and translate the task to a non-visual user interface. Direct screen model SRP systems start their design at the point of "what is on the screen" and then determine how to display "what is on the screen" in a non-visual form for the blind. The ITB system starts with the task and uses the screen or operating system as a place to gather information about the task. The ITB access system has the capability to provide additional information to the user even when the information is not available from the visual display. This paper tries to describe a different way of thinking about user interfaces for people with blindness. The techniques described in the paper are not intended to be thought of as the optimal solution, but to demonstrate how a different way of thinking can increase the usability of computer systems by people with blindness.

7. REFERENCES

1. D. Griffith J. Human Factors, 32 (1990) 467.
2. J. Rasmussen Information Processing and Human-Machine Interaction, Horth-Holland 1986.
3. J. Lazzaro Byte, June (1991) 416.
4. L. Boyd, W. Boyd, and G. Vanderheiden, J of Visual Impairment and Blindness, 84 (1990) 496.
5. E. Mynatt and K. Edwards Fifth Annual Sym. on User Interface Software and Technology, November (1992) 61.
6. A. Edwards, 3rd Inter. Conf. on Computers for Handicapped Persons, July (1992) disk.
7. G. Vanderheiden and D. Kunz Proc. of the 13th Annul. Conf. of RESNA, June (1990).
8. J. Fricke 3rd Inter. Confer. on Computers for the Handicapped Persons, July (1992) disk.
9. A. Karshmer, R. Hartley, et. al. Confer. on Computers for the Handicapped Persons, July (1992) disk.
10. M. Blattner, D. Sumikawa and R. Greenberg J. Human-Computer Interaction, 4 (1989) 11.
11. M. Cohen and L. Ludwig Int. J. Man-Machine Studies, 34 (1991) 319.
12. A. Edwards J. Human-Computer Interaction, 4 (1989) 45.
13. A. Edwards Int. J. Man-Machine Studies, 30 (1989) 575.
14. G. Vanderheiden J Visual Impairment and Blindness, 83 (1989) 383.
15. D. Crow and B. Smith Int. Workshop Intelligent User Interfaces, January (1993) 97.
16. C. Wikens Engineering Psychology and Human Performance, Merrill, Columbus, 1984.
17. D. Norman and S. Draper (eds) User Centered System Design, Lawrence Erlbaum, Hillsdale, NJ, 1986.

THE USE OF COMPUTER SIMULATED CASES TO STUDY FACTORS THAT INFLUENCE CLINICAL PRACTICE STYLES

James G. Anderson, Ph.D.[a,b], Stephen J. Jay, M.D.[b,c], Christine Beville, B.S.[c], Marilyn M. Anderson, B.A.[b]

a Purdue University, West Lafayette, IN 47907
bDivision of Academic Affairs, Methodist Hospital of Indiana, Indianapolis, IN 46202
cIndiana University School of Medicine, Indianapolis, IN

ABSTRACT

This study was undertaken to determine if computer simulated cases could be used to determine factors that influence clinical practice patterns. Three computer simulated cases were presented to 46 residents in emergency medicine, internal medicine, family practice, and transitional medicine at Methodist Hospital of Indiana, a 1120 bed, private, teaching hospital. A questionnaire was used to collect additional data on how physicians deal with clinical uncertainty. There was no significant difference by year of residency in physicians' reactions to uncertainty in patient care. The results indicate that physicians in internal medicine were the most reluctant to disclose the uncertainty that they experienced in diagnosing and treating patients. Also, reluctance to disclose uncertainty significantly affected physician performance on the three test cases. The study provided evidence that computer simulated cases can be used to evaluate physicians' clinical performance and to identify factors that cause practice variation.

1. INTRODUCTION AND PROBLEM STATEMENT

Recent concern over the dramatic increase in health care costs has prompted efforts to curb spending. Some of these efforts have attempted to change the diagnostic strategies of physicians; however, it has been well-documented that physicians vary greatly in their approach to clinical problem solving [1]. Although it is generally accepted that physician's practice styles can be changed, there is little agreement on which approach is ideal in bringing about long-term changes. Tierney and others [2] were successful in using computerized reminders to reduce test-ordering, but effects were short-lived once the reminders were no longer implemented. Traditional CME programs have also been shown to be ineffective in bringing about long-term changes in practice behavior [3]. Furthermore, simple dissemination of practice recommendations has not changed physician behavior [4].

Factors known to affect clinicians' practice styles include gender, age, training, and specialty, as well as personal attitudes about certain clinical decisions [5]. These personal attributes give rise to a physician's "clinical personality". Salem-Schatz and colleagues [6] used surveys to evaluate physician attitudes about treatment risks and willingness to conform to peer pressure. Both were found to be consistent predictors of transfusion rates. Other studies suggest that experience is a good predictor of test-ordering behavior. Staff physicians order fewer and more relevant tests than do residents [2].

Results of preliminary research performed at Methodist Hospital of Indiana indicated that physicians can be classified into "clinical personality" groups [7]. The study also suggested that clinical personality factors may be important determinants of physicians' practice patterns.

The purpose of this study was (1) to determine if computer simulated cases could be used to determine factors that influence clinical practice patterns; and (2) to determine the effect of clinical personality factors on clinical practice patterns. First, it was hypothesized that stress from uncertainty and reluctance to disclose uncertainty would vary by year of residency and by specialty. Second, it was hypothesized that stress from uncertainty and reluctance to disclose uncertainty would affect physicians' performance in diagnosing the simulated cases.

2. METHODS

2.1. Subjects

The study was performed at Methodist Hospital of Indiana, a 1120 bed, private teaching hospital. The subjects were first, second, and third year residents in the following programs: emergency medicine, internal medicine, family practice, and transitional medicine. Complete data were obtained from 46 out of 85 residents over a 12 week period during the summer of 1992 (see Table 1).

Table 1
Subjects by Year of Residency and Specialty

	Emergency Medicine	Internal Medicine	Family Practice	Transitional Medicine	Total
G-1	2	4	3	8	17
G-2	5	4	4	--	13
G-3	5	7	4	--	16
Total	12	15	11	8	46

2.2. Questionnaire

A Questionnaire was developed to measure clinical personality factors. This questionnaire incorporated the

Physicians' Reaction to Uncertainty Scale [8] which measures how physicians respond to uncertainty in diagnosing and treating patients. Thirteen items measure stress from uncertainty; the other nine items measure the physician's reluctance to disclose uncertainty. The responses range from 1 = strongly agree to 6 = strongly disagree. Other sections of the questionnaire measure (1) risk taking behavior, (2) patient relations, and (3) relations with other physicians. Only the findings related to uncertainty in clinical decision making are reported here. Both Stress from Uncertainty and Reluctance to Disclose Uncertainty were dichotomized at the median score into low and high groups.

2.3. Simulated Cases
Three case studies were presented in random order for evaluation to every resident taking part in the study. These cases were pericarditis, aseptic meningitis, and pulmonary embolus. To standardize the presentation and scoring of the cases, a computer program entitled Iliad was used. Iliad is a "diagnostic expert system" that can simultaneously present case studies and evaluate performance [9]. Iliad presents a chief complaint representative of the history findings for a simulated case. The subject must enter a diagnostic hypothesis and request specific additional historical, physical examination, and laboratory findings. The computer responds to each query.

All subjects were asked to complete the three cases in a random order in a period of an hour or less. In an attempt to prevent bias due to specialty, common clinical cases were presented. The cases were completed without assistance except for technical assistance in using the computer. Subjects were not told the correct diagnosis or informed of their actual performance on the test cases.

2.4. Dependent Variables
Iliad scores the work-up at each step by comparing the subject's choice with an internal standard. It scores final performance on four separate criteria: (1) Final Diagnostic Errors (accuracy of the final diagnosis), (2) Posterior Probability (completeness of the work-up), (3) Cost, and (4) Average Hypothesis Score (average of the scores at each step). It also counts the total number of findings and breaks them down by history, physical exam and laboratory findings. Each of these findings are also given a score from 1 to 100 based on their appropriateness given the subject's diagnostic hypothesis. For this analysis, the subjects' scores on the three cases were averaged.

3. RESULTS

First, second, and third year residents' scores on the reaction to uncertainty scales were compared. An analysis of variance indicated that there was no significant difference among the groups on the Stress from Uncertainty Scale (F =

0.06, p < 0.95) or on the Reluctance to Disclose Uncertainty Scale (F = 1.12, p < 0.33).

Analysis of variance was used to compare the mean scores of the specialty groups on the two uncertainty variables. As can be seen from Figure 1, there were no significant differences among the four groups of residents on the Stress from Uncertainty subscale (F = 0.90, p < 0.45). However, the groups did differ significantly on the second measure, Reluctance to Disclose Uncertainty (F = 1.71, p < 0.05). Figure 2 indicates that internal medicine residents were the most reluctant to disclose the uncertainty that they experienced in diagnosing and treating patients.

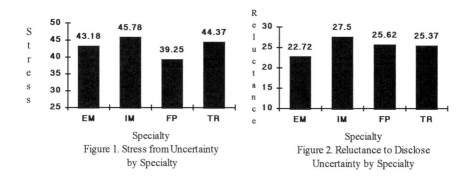

Figure 1. Stress from Uncertainty by Specialty

Figure 2. Reluctance to Disclose Uncertainty by Specialty

The performance of residents with high and low Stress from Uncertainty scores and Reluctance to Disclose Uncertainty was compared in Figure 3. The mean Average Hypothesis Score for the three cases was used as the dependent variable. This is an overall measure of the subject's sequential step-wise reasoning about the cases and ranges from 0 to 100. Residents who reported low levels of stress scored higher (F = 2.15, p < 0.15) as did those who were less reluctant to disclose their uncertainty to other physicians and patients (F = 1.98, p < 0.16).

In order to compare the performance of the subjects with high and low Reluctance to Disclose Uncertainty scores, we examined the physicians' diagnostic reasoning. The results are shown in Figure 4. Physicians who were more willing to disclose the uncertainty that they experience in diagnosing and treating patients collected more patient information in order to be more certain about their diagnosis (F = 3.62, p < 0.06). In general, they asked more history questions (F = 2.62, p < 0.11) and ordered more laboratory tests (F = 5.35, p < 0.02) than physicians who were more reluctant to disclose the uncertainty that they experienced. There was no significant difference between the two groups in the number of physical examination findings requested (F = 0.91, p < 0.34)

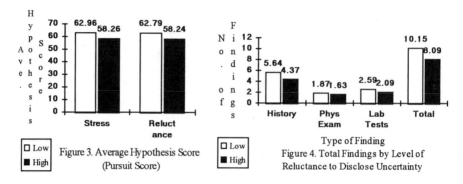

Figure 3. Average Hypothesis Score (Pursuit Score)

Figure 4. Total Findings by Level of Reluctance to Disclose Uncertainty

4. DISCUSSION

This study found that physicians' reactions to clinical uncertainty were not significantly different for levels of medical training. Our findings differ from those of Gerrity and others [8] who found that physicians who had been in practice longer felt less stress from uncertainty than those who had practiced for a shorter time. There were no significant differences among these same physicians on the Reluctance to Disclose Uncertainty subscale. The difference in findings may reflect the populations studied. Our population consisted of first, second and third year residents. Gerrity's population consisted of physicians who had been in practice form 2 to over 31 years.

The findings of our study regarding differences among specialty groups in their reaction to uncertainty also differs from those of Gerrity [8]. The earlier study found that general practitioners, family practitioners, and general internists reported significantly more stress from uncertainty than internal medicine subspecialists and surgeons. Our study found no significant difference in stress from uncertainty among specialty groups.

In constrast, our study found that internists were significantly more reluctant to disclose their uncertainty in diagnosis in comparison to the other specialty groups. Gerrity and others found no significant differences among specialties on this subscale. Again, the difference in findings may reflect the different physician populations studied. These findings need to be clarified by future research. Some of the factors that may account for physicians' different responses to clinical uncertainty may be differences in experience, training, and physicians' beliefs about their professional role.

The results of this study indicate that computer simulated cases can be used to determine factors that influence clinical practice patterns. Clinical personality factors were found to have important influences on physician performance on three simulated cases. In particular, the way that physicians deal with the uncertainty that is inherent in clinical practice appears to affect their diagnostic reasoning. Physicians who were reluctant to disclose their uncertainty to other physicians and patients did not perform as well on the simulated cases as those physicians who acknowledged the uncertainty that they experienced. The former group asked fewer history questions and ordered fewer tests in reaching their final diagnosis.

This study suggests a new strategy for exploring factors that may account for variation in physicians practice patterns. This strategy involves assessing performance with simulated cases and relating performance measures to physician characteristics, clinical personality factors, educational and organizational factors that shape or modify physicians' practice patterns. A clearer understanding of specific influences on medical decision making is needed in order to develop effective strategies to change practice patterns.

5. ACKNOWLEDGMENT

We wish to acknowledge the assistance of Richard Campbell, M.D., Carey Chisholm, M.D., and Alvin Haley, M.D.

6. REFERENCES

1. Wennberg, J.R. Dealing with Medical Practice Variations: A Proposal for Action. Health Affairs 1984, 3:6-32.
2. Tierney, W.T., M.E. Miller, and C.J. McDonald. The Effect on Test Ordering of Informing Physicians of the Charges for Outpatient Diagnostic Tests. NEJM 1990, 322:1499-1504.
3. Haynes, R.B., D.A. Davis, A. McKibbon, and P. Tugwell. Critical Appraisal of the Efficacy of Continuing Medical Education. JAMA 1984, 251:61-64.
4. Lomas, J. and R.B. Haynes. A Taxonomy and Critical Review of Tested Strategies for the Application of Clinical Practice Recommendations: From "Official" to "Individual" Clinical Policy. American Journal of Preventive Medicine 1988, 4 (Suppl.):77-94.
5. Eisenberg, J.M. Doctors' Decisions on the Cost of Medical Care: The Reasons for Doctors' Practice Patterns and Ways to Change Them. Ann Arbor, MI: Health Administration, 1986.
6. Salem-Schatz, S.R., J. Avorn, and S.B. Soumerai. Influence of Clinical Knowledge, Organizational Context, and Practice Style on Transfusion Decision Making. JAMA 1990 264:476-483.
7. Anderson, J.G., S.J. Jay, S. Trajkovski, R. Campbell, A. Haley, and M.M. Anderson. Determining Clinical Practice Styles from Computer-Based Data. Proceedings MedInfo, Amsterdam: Elsevier, 1992, 1173-1179.
8. Gerritty, M.S., R.F. DeVellis, and J.A. Earp. Physicians' Reaction to Uncertainty in Patient Care: A New Measure and New Insights. Medical Care 1990, 28:724-736.
9. Bergeron, B. Iliad: A Diagnostic Consultant and Patient Simulator. M.D. Computing 1991, 8:46-53.

A COMPUTER-BASED INTEGRATED INSTRUCTION AND DESIGN FOR TEACHING AESTHETIC DESIGN

Rungtai Lin

Department of Industrial Design, Mingchi Institute of Technology,
84 Gungjuan Rd., Taishan, Taipei 24306, Taiwan, ROC

Abstract

As a professional engineering designer, one must know not only the state-of-the-art technology, but also the product aesthetics to enhance their appeal and desire in the eyes of the purchaser. Despite its importance, the aesthetic training has not been taken as a part of engineering design education because of its time-consuming, and art-based rather than science-based. However, availability of relatively low cost personal computer (PC) and PC-based CAD systems has offered the feasibility of integrating aesthetic instruction into engineering graphics and design courses. This paper is intended to develop an integrated CAI/CAD system for teaching aesthetic principles to engineering students. The knowledge associated with aesthetic design has been organized in a hierarchic structure for easy learning. A knowledge base containing 153 slides and 90 text pages has been developed as course materials for teaching the aesthetic principles to the students. Ten exercises have been selected properly for practicing aesthetic design. The system was implemented by using AutoLISP programming language operating in AutoCAD environment on the personal computer.

1. INTRODUCTION

In today's highly competitive market, the aesthetic quality of a product may determine whether a product will be successfully marketed or not. It has been said that between two products equal in price, function, and quality, the better looking will outsell the other. Therefore, the aesthetics enhancement of products is being used as a marketing tool in many industrial firms [1]. As a professional engineering designer, one must know not only the state-of-the-art technology, but also the product aesthetics to enhance their appeal and desire in the eyes of the purchaser. Despite its importance, the aesthetic training has not been taken as a part of engineering design education. The major reason for this lag is not the less important of aesthetic design, but rather the relative long training process a student has to take. In the design college it may take a student several semesters for learning and practicing aesthetics before he can apply these techniques to practical design problems.

The availability of relatively low cost personal computer and PC-based CAD systems began to revolutionize the fields of design, engineering, and drafting [2]. Instead of using paper, pencil, and drafting board, the designer can execute design on computer by using interactive graphical input / output devices [3]. Many commercially available CAD systems such as AutoCAD from Autodesk, Inc., Personal Designer from Computervision, Inc., CADKEY from Micro Control System, Inc. etc. have been widely employed both by academic institutions and industrial companies as tools for design [4,5,6]. While CAD systems have been applied to a wide variety of applications such as mechanical drafting, architecture, industrial design, art, etc., no attempts have been made to extend its capability from design-aid phase into instruction-aid phase. Many design related courses (e.g., graphic design, engineering drawing) are tedious, time-consuming, and labor-intensive for instruction even though they are fundamental to engineering disciplines [7,8]. Most of the instructors still convey their knowledge to the students based on conventional instruction techniques which is not only inefficient but also obsolete.

In this paper, we propose a computer-based instruction and design system for teaching aesthetics in design to engineering students. Although the implementation of the current system is specific to aesthetic design domain, it can be easily adopted to any other disciplines.

2. CONVENTIONAL INSTRUCTION ENVIRONMENT

Aesthetic design deals with the application of aesthetic principles to the product design. The major concerns of aesthetic design are the product appearance such as form, color, style and the compatibility with its visual environment. Many principles for aesthetic design have been accumulated by aesthetician and psychologist of art during the past few centuries [9-13]. These principles are generally accepted by professional designers and artists. A typical introductory curriculum in the aesthetic design may include the study of design elements, basic variables, design principles, and visual perception as shown in Figure 1.

AESTHETIC DESIGN			
1. DESIGN ELEMENTS	2. BASIC VARIABLES	3. DESIGN PRINCIPLES	4. VISUAL PERCEPTION
1-1: POINT	2-1: SIZE	3-1: BALANCE	4-1: ILLUSION
1-2: LINE	2-2: SHAPE	3-2: SYMMETRY	4-2: FIGURE AND GROUND
1-3: PLANE	2-3: MOVEMENT	3-3: PROPORTION	4-3: GROUPING
1-4: VOLUME	2-4: NUMBER	3-4: REPETITION	
1-5: COLOR	2-5: DENSITY	3-5: RHYTHM	
1-6: TEXTURE	2-6: INTERVAL	3-6: CONTRAST	
		3-7: UNITY	

Figure 1 Course contents of aesthetic design

Traditionally, the students in design college may take several semesters to learn how to select proper design elements, determine suitable values for design parameters, and apply design principles of aesthetics to a given design problem. A typical process for teaching aesthetic design may include three major stages: 1) Instruction (knowledge communication), 2) Paper work (design skill practice), and 3) Consultation (evaluation and discussion). The instructor usually will select a topic, explain terminologies, introduce principles related to the given topic, illustrate several examples, arrange laboratory sessions for practice, and evaluate students' works (Figure 2).

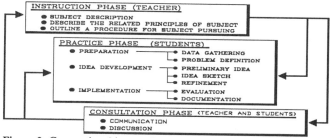

Figure 2 Conventional instruction procedure of aesthetic design

In conventional instruction environment, the instructor usually spends many hours in the preparation of visual aids such as slides, drawings, good examples for illustrations of design elements, variables, and principles involving in a given design problem. Afterward, the student may have to spend a lot of time in practicing the skills that involve in tedious refining and redrawing process. Most of the instructors are unable to provide enough visualization aids for illustrations because of the time limit. The majority of the students are unwilling to improve any part of their design once the preliminary drawings have been finished. Although aesthetic training is a critical part of any engineering discipline, we can't expect engineering students to earn the aesthetics in this way.

3. THE COMPUTER-BASED INSTRUCTION AND DESIGN ENVIRONMENT

Even though CAD systems are being used as the design tool in many areas and CAI systems have been successful in many educational environments, no attempts have been made so far to integrate the instruction of aesthetic design into CAD systems. The CAI/CAD approach seem to be a better way for using the computer in aesthetic design. Figure 3 shows a comparison on procedure between conventional and integrated CAI/CAD approach to aesthetic design [14].

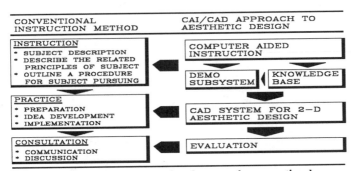

Figure 3   A comparison on procedure between the conventional
method and CAI/CAD approach in aesthetic design

To improve the conventional instruction environment, we propose a computer-based integrated instruction and design environment CAIDAD (CAI/caD in Aesthetic Design) which will benefit both instructors and students. As shown in Figure 4, the CAIDAD environment consists of three major subsystems: CAI for instruction, CAD for design practicing, and knowledge base for storing instruction materials associated with the aesthetic design.

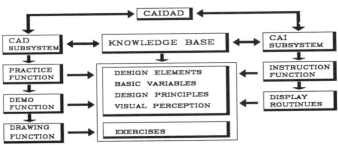

Figure 4 System structure of CAIDAD

The CAD subsystem provides facilities for the users to create, edit, and manipulate graphic entities (e.g., points, lines, planes, volume). As an instructor, he can use CAD subsystem as graphic editor to prepare instruction material and store them into knowledge base. As a student or user, he can use CAD subsystem to develop his skills, and perform the design task. The CAI subsystem controls and manages the instruction and learning process of course material through menu-driven mechanism and hierarchic index structure. As a student, he may select any subject available in knowledge base, study them page by page from the screen, and sharpen his skills by doing exercises. As an instructor, he may use the subsystem to review the course content and update the knowledge base. The knowledge base contains course contents, good examples of aesthetic design, practicing exercises, help text of the system, and rules for evaluating students' works. The knowledge base can be accessed by the instructor to renew the teaching materials and used by the student as a learning tool while CAIDAD is running on the personal computer.

4. SYSTEM IMPLEMENTATION

The CAIDAD system has been developed and implemented on the personal computer. AutoCAD has been selected as a base system for supporting the implementation because of its popularity, flexibility, and programmability. AutoLISP has been used as the programming language to develop many utility functions and subroutines for managing the knowledge base. The system is organized into five submenus that connected to a main menu. This menu-driven structure makes it possible to switch at will in learning units of CAI domain and between the CAI subsystem and the CAD subsystem.

4.1 Knowledge Base

To implement the knowledge base, we break the course material into two main portions: texts and graphics. Texts are used to present the details of knowledge associated with aesthetics in design. Graphics are used for illustration of applying aesthetic principles to practical design problems. More than 153 slides and 90 text pages have been implemented and stored on diskette as the knowledge base. Table 1 shows the distributions of slides and text pages among different chapters in the course material.

Table 1. Contents of slides and text pages in knowledge base

	SLIDES	TEXTS
INTRODUCTION	9	4
DESIGN ELEMENTS	48	26
BASIC VARIABLES	23	15
DESIGN PRINCIPLES	27	25
VISUAL PERCEPTION	14	9
EXERCISES	30	11
TOTAL	153	90

Graphics are implemented as slide files and constructed by using drawing editor of AutoCAD and organized in the same format. A typical sample slide from the knowledge base is shown in Figure 5. These slides are managed and displayed on the graphic mode by CAI and CAD subsystem. Texts are implemented as the text file which is composed of pages and edited by word processor such as Word Perfect. The text file is used to explain detailed description of concepts of the aesthetic design and to get help text of CAIDAD. These text files are controlled and displayed on the text mode by CAI and CAD subsystem. By using the HELP command, the help text of a specific command of CAIDAD is provided to remind users.

752

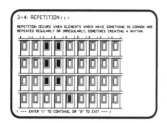 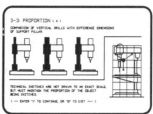 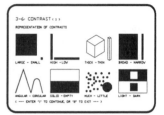

Figure 5 Three sample slides from knowledge base

4.2 CAD SUBSYSTEM

AutoCAD offers a wide range of features such as the hierarchic menu structure, on-line help, 2-d drafting, 3-d modeling, customized menu, slide-making facility and AutoLISP. These capabilities make AutoCAD a suitable package for supporting the CAD activities in CAIDAD environment. In addition, AutoCAD's drawing functions have been enhanced in CAIDAD system. There are some routines which provide examples in aesthetic design for demonstration, and also serve as a tool for exploration of the visual composition. For example, the tessellation function can generate repeating patterns by using a given unit. Figure 6 shows an example generated by tessellation function.

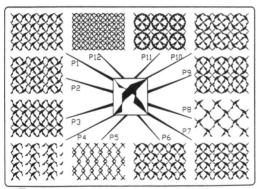

Figure 6 An example of repeating patterns generated by tessellation function

4.3 CAI SUBSYSTEM

The CAI subsystem was implemented by using AutoLISP programming language. The subsystem consists of about 40 modules that are organized in a hierarchic structure as shown on Figure 7. Each module will perform tasks such as load texts or slide files from the knowledge base, prompt users for menu selection, and the switch control over the next level of modules. Upon startup, the module MAINMENU controls and manages with modules such as INTRO, DEMENU, BVMENU, DPMENU, VPMENU, and EXMENU that correspond to the six chapters of the textbook respectively. After selecting a topic, a second menu appears offering choices for topics associated with the given selected topic. At this point, the student can sequentially learn concepts of the aesthetic design by following the program, and by his own pace. After learning concepts of the aesthetic design, students can switch to the CAD domain to practice and check how well he/she did learn. This module consists of 10 creative design problems related to the aesthetic design. Students are encouraged to create their own designs based on the concepts presented in the previous sections.

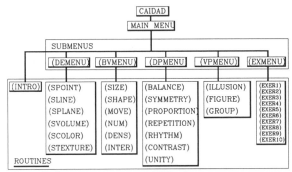

Figure 7 System structure of CAI subsystem

5. CONCLUSION

A computer-based integrated instruction design system CAIDAD has been developed and implemented successfully. The system extended AutoCAD's functionality from traditional design-aids into instruction-aids. The system is not intended to replace instructor, but rather to assist the instructor in many ways such as the course preparation, instruction in a high visualization quality, and more dynamic teaching / learning environment.

The system can be used in the classroom by the instructor as an instruction-aid or in the laboratory by the students as a learning-aid. In the classroom, a projection system which can transform the computer screen image into large projection screen is highly recommended. In the laboratory, its primary purpose is to provide a powerful tool for students to learn concepts of the aesthetic design on their own more effectively and enjoyably than if they would have to practice conventional exercises with the paper and pencil.

At Industrial Design Department of Mingchi Institute of Technology, Taiwan, we offer a core course for engineering freshmen "Introduction to Engineering Design" which features both lectures and laboratories. The CAIDAD system is being planned for usage in this course. Future improvement and modification of the system rely on the response and feedback from the students.

6. REFERENCES

1. H. Read, Art and Industry, Faber and Faber Limited, London, 1944.
2. D. L. Goetsch, MicroCADD Computer-Aided Design and Drafting on Microcomputers, Prentice Hall, NJ, 1988.
3. J. D. Foley and A. Van Dam, Fundamentals of Interactive Computer Graphics, Addison-Wesley, MA, 1982
4. D. L. Ryan, Computer-Aided Design for AutoCAD Users, Prentice Hall, Nl, 1989.
5. J. V. Valentino, CAD with ComputerVision, Holt, Rinehart and Winston, NY, 1987.
6. H. F. Keedy, An Introduction to CAD Using CADkey, PWS-KENT, Boston, 1988.
7. J. H. Earle, Engineering Design Graphics, Fifth Edition, Addison-Wesley, MA, 1987.
8. W. J. Luzadder and J. M. Duff, Fundamentals of Engineering Drawing, Prentive Hall, NJ, 1989.
9. O. Hiroshi, Basic of Design, Art Publishing Company, Tokyo, Japan, 1979.
10. G. H. Lee and I. H. Lai, Principles of Form, Ta-Sen Book Company, Taipei, Taiwan, 1973.
11. B. Munari, Design as Art, Penguin Publishing Co., NY, 1963.
12. D. C. Malcolm, Design: Elements and Principles, Davis Publication Inc., Worchester, 1972.
13. M. Maier, Basic Principles of Design, Van Nostrand Reinhold Company, NY, 1977.
14. R. Lin and S. S. Chern, A Prospect of The Application of CAI/CAD in Teaching Aesthetic Design", Industrial Design Magazine, Vol.16, No.3, (1987), 143-145.

Student Modelling in Hybrid Training Systems

D. Milech, B. Waters, S. Noel, G. Roy & K. Kirsner
Centre for Computer Managed Training and Decision Support Systems
University of Western Australia

Abstract

We are constructing a student model for a hybrid training system, a mixture of formal instruction and simulation-based training. This model measures a student's fluency; knowledge; the robustness and articulability of the knowledge; and the flexibility and generalisability of the knowledge.

This approach to student modelling is more complex than that found in the typical ITS system, in which student models only measure the mastery of knowledge. In a hybrid system such as ours the student model must do more than determine whether or not each item of knowledge is known, because: (i) the knowledge to be imparted is procedural (eg, industrial process control) and in such domains competency includes more than knowing facts and (ii) the interaction between student and training system is quite complex, and so more information is needed in order to guide training properly.

Our approach to modelling allows us to estimate each student's knowledge, how the knowledge can be used, and whether knowledge is at an operational or abstract level. In addition, our approach yields comparable measures of competency for both formal instructional methods and simulation-based methods, and allows us to design more complex interactions between student and training system which are necessary in a hybrid training system.

Introduction

In constructing an ITS system in an industrial process control domain, we have been forced to develop a new approach to modelling student knowledge. One reason for this development is the domain of application of the training system. The usual ITS systems are used in relatively rigid instructional domains such as arithmetic, programming languages and diagnosis, and in such domains skill acquisition can be modelled with a set of simple probabilities identifying the likelihood that the student has learnt the instructional material (Villano, 1992). This simple approach to modelling is usually satisfactory because ITS systems do not need much information about the student in order to direct training. However, in teaching procedures such as process control in an industrial domain, distinctions need to be made between the possession of knowledge, the ability to apply it thoughtfully and deliberately, and the ability to apply it habitually and automatically. In such domains, skill acquisition is complex and the student model must incorporate a vector of parameters that will be capable of diagnosing not only the mastery of knowledge but also the mental representation of that knowledge and how well that knowledge generalises.

In addition, the instructional methodology embedded in our training system has forced us to develop a new approach to modelling student knowledge. Our instructional methodology is reasonably complex because we aim to teach students operational procedures as well as declarative knowledge. Therefore we have found it necessary to adopt a hybrid approach to training, one which uses simulation based training for some skills and formal instruction for others (Milech, Kirsner, Roy and Waters, 1993). The development of a hybrid system has forced us to reshape ideas about student modelling, in particular, to develop a generalised student model which can be used to assess skill acquisition regardless of the method of training. In addition, we have found it necessary to give students help while they learn operational procedures, but this means that it is difficult to interpret simple performance parameters (like those in the usual student model) since a student's performance is conditional not only on the state of the student's knowledge but also on the level of help being given.

The Student Model Vector

To meet the needs of a more complex student modelling requirement we have replaced the usual probability node in the student model with a vector of student parameters outlined in figure 1. This vector is capable, for a given node, of diagnosing the mastery of knowledge, the representation of that knowledge and how well the student can generalise that knowledge.

Type of Representation	Mastery of Knowledge	Knowledge Generalisation

Figure 1 The student model vector showing the three groups of parameters.

For each of the three groups shown in figure 1 there exists a set of diagnostic parameters.

Type of Representation

Initial research involving an ITS system under development for training Power System Controllers to operate a complex electrical grid has shown that students can be trained to perform complex tasks (involving 30 or more discrete steps) without any detailed knowledge of the system. Their performance is smooth and automatic and can be performed concurrently with other attention consuming tasks. On the other hand if the task is changed the students are no longer able to perform the task as they have no understanding of how to compensate for the change in the task. They tend to be rigid and inflexible.

Using other training techniques students can be taught to perform these same tasks thoughtfully and deliberatively. Their task performance is not necessarily as smooth and their performance can be easily degraded by introducing a concurrent task. If the task is changed, however, this group of students is more flexible, being able to compensate for changes in the task by reasoning about the new task.

While on the surface it appears that both groups of students are being taught the same thing, in reality the state of the student's knowledge is vastly different. Past studies in human learning and in expertise (eg. Hasher and Zacks, 1979; Hayes and Broadbent, 1988; Reber, Kassin, Lewis and Canto, 1980; Schneider, Dumais, and Shiffrin, 1984; Schneider and Shiffrin, 1977; Shiffrin and Schneider, 1977) have shown that there are two basic types of information processing. In 'automatic' information processing, operations seem to require no conscious intervention. Subjects are fast and accurate and their performance does not degrade under stress. However, subjects are incapable of introspection and cannot report how they perform the task. In contrast, with 'controlled' information processing subjects are thoughtful and deliberative. They think through the task and can explain what they are doing. Their performance has been shown to be slower and less accurate, and stress degrades their performance considerably. Researchers have called the knowledge associated with automatic information processing "implicit" and the knowledge associated with controlled information processing "explicit". In industrial process control this distinction is an important one and for this reason it is essential for the student model to capture more than a probabilistic measure of the mastery of domain knowledge. We also need to know what sort of knowledge representation a student has.

The distinction between implicit and explicit knowledge representations is important when attempting to make training effective and our student model attempts to distinguish between implicit and explicit knowledge representations. The characteristics described above to define implicit and explicit representations can be used to diagnose the student's knowledge representation.

One of the previously mentioned distinctions between students with an implicit knowledge representation and students with an explicit knowledge representation is how well they perform a task under conditions of stress. Because the application of implicit knowledge requires little conscious intervention, it should be less affected by stress. However, explicit processes show a marked deterioration under stressful conditions (Mandler 1982). This can be measured by having the student perform the operation that they are learning while attempting to perform another attention consuming task concurrently. When a student has an implicit knowledge representation this measure should be high. Alternately when a student has an explicit knowledge representation this measure should be low.

A second distinction between implicit and explicit knowledge representations involves how well a student can articulate his/her understanding of the task being taught (Berry 1987). Articulability requires conscious deliberation about the task and therefore should be low when a student has an implicit representation and high when a student has an explicit representation.

A third distinction between the knowledge representations is demonstrated by how well students can perform a task that they have been trained to perform when procedure or rules are changed. Implicit representations are developed through training with consistent exposure to the same stimulus configurations (Hascher and Zacks 1979; Schneider, Dumais, and Shiffrin, 1984; Schneider and Shiffrin, 1977; Shiffrin and Schneider, 1977) and are relatively rigid. Therefore, students with an implicit representation would not be expected to adapt to such changes easily. However, explicit knowledge representations can be changed more easily, and so students with an explicit representation would be expected to adapt to task changes relatively easily.

Mastery of Knowledge

The student model we are building estimates the mastery of knowledge with several indices. However the interpretation of these indices is complex for several reasons. First our estimate of a student's knowledge must depend not only on the standard of the student's performance but also on the level of help given to the student. For example, in our training system students receive various forms of help in learning complex procedures, but the amount of help they receive decreases as learning progresses. When help decreases, performance will suffer a short-lived deterioration, and the student model must take this into account, otherwise estimates of the mastery of knowledge will be subject to continuous oscillation. Our current, ad hoc solution to this problem is to dampen the adjustment of indices immediately following an adjustment in the level of help.

The second problem in interpreting indices is that the interpretation may depend upon the type of lesson being conducted. The main indices for estimating the mastery of knowledge are the accuracy and speed with which tasks or procedures are performed and the accuracy and speed with which questions are answered. As an index, accuracy is simple to interpret whether training is implicit or explicit: the greater the accuracy, the greater the knowledge. That is, accuracy is an important and easily interpreted diagnostic parameter for both implicit and explicit training. However, the interpretation of speed may depend on whether implicit or explicit training is being conducted. As knowledge increases during implicit training, so does speed; however, the relationship between speed and knowledge is complex for explicit training; therefore, speed is not necessarily diagnostic of mastery in explicit training.

Knowledge Generalisation

Our student model will also assess a student's competence at generalising knowledge. In particular, it will assess a student's competence (i) at applying more abstract knowledge in concrete situations (eg, applying theory to a practical problem) and (ii) in transferring knowledge to new but similar situations (eg, applying a specific procedure to the same task in a new setting). Procedures for estimating knowledge generalisation are still under development.

Currently, our approach to this estimation problem is to develop a framework for representing the curriculum which permits us to define knowledge generalisation in operational terms. For example, in the domain of power system control, Controllers must learn to understand load flow at a highly abstract level involving various electrical and load equations relating to the behaviour of power systems and must also learn specific procedures for diagnosis and monitoring of the power grid. Our framework for representing the curriculum in the domain of power system control describes knowledge in terms of two dimensions. The first dimension is 'Abstraction' in which knowledge is ranked along a continuum from theoretical to procedural. The second dimension is 'Specificity' in which knowledge is ranked on a continuum from generic procedures to implementation specific procedures.

We are currently developing tasks (with associated indices) to estimate a student's competence to generalise along each of these dimensions as well as their competence in generalising knowledge to very similar situations which involve changes in some surface features.

Using the Model in Training

It is the practical utility of our approach to student modelling which will determine its worth: useful if it can be used to improve the quality of training and useless otherwise. There are several ways in which we are currently using the information in our student model to improve training, but there are several problems in the implementation of our approach which must be resolved before its true utility can be assessed.

Implementation Problems

There are a number of problems which have yet to be solved in developing our model and integrating it with our training system, in particular, the problems of (i) determining what the grain of resolution should be for the model and (ii) determining how to link the model to the curriculum.

Grain of resolution : How precise must we be in the measures for the student model vector? Should the student model keep information for each step involved in a task, or for chunks of the task, or for all of the task? Creating vectors for each step is memory intensive and analysing the model is slow. However, if the student model keeps information only at the level of the procedure, interesting performance details (eg temporal grouping of steps) are lost.

Linking the model to a curriculum : The training goals in our system are more complex than simply imparting knowledge. The training goals also specify what sort of knowledge representation (Implicit or Explicit) the student should acquire. Therefore the training goals are no longer implicit in the knowledge base of the training system but must be represented separately. For each vector in the student model the training system requires a training goal stated as a target performance vector.

Practical Use of the Parameters in Training

Even though there are problems which have yet to be resolved in determining how to implement our student modelling procedure, the model itself is being used to manage training in several ways.

First, our model presently allows us to estimate whether a student is acquiring an appropriate knowledge representation, that is, whether it is implicit or explicit. If the student's representation is inappropriate, the training system introduces corrective or remedial lessons which are specifically aimed at changing the type of knowledge representation. These corrective or remedial lessons are currently being developed.

Second, our model allows us to continuously assess the mastery of the knowledge, and estimates are used for two distinct purposes:

- they are used to determine when a lesson has been successfully learnt; and
- they are used to determine what sort of help a student needs.

The underlying reason for measuring mastery is to maximise the efficiency of training. First, there is no point in continuing a lesson once a student has attained an appropriate level of mastery and second, there is no point in continuing to provide extensive help to a student whose mastery has improved beyond the level of rank novice.

And finally, our model will allow us to measure generalisation, that is, how successfully relatively abstract knowledge can be applied to more specific problems and how successfully knowledge can be transferred to similar situations which involve changes in surface features only. There are two reasons why it is important to measure generalisation. The first is to ensure that once students have knowledge that they can apply it; that is, rather than assuming that mastery of knowledge ensures that it will be applied appropriately, we measure students' competence at generalisation and will introduce corrective or remedial lessons which are specifically aimed at improving their ability to generalise if their competence is low.

The second reason why it is important to measure competence at generalisation is to maximise the efficiency of training. Efficiency is achieved by ensuring that instructional material is generalised, and this should have the effect of creating instructional savings, both in the number of lesson required and in the number of presentations of lesson needed for a student to master the material.

Berry, D. (1987). The problem of implicit knowledge. *Expert Systems, 4*, 144-150.

Hayes, N.A., Broadbent, D.E. (1988). Two modes of learning for interactive tasks. *Cognition. 28* 249-276

Hasher, L. Zacks, R.T. (1979). Automatic and effortful processes in memory. *Journal of Experimental Psychology: General, 108*, 356-388.

Mandler, G. (1982). Stress and thought processes. In L. Goldberg and S. Breznitz (Eds.), *Handbook of stress: Theoretical and clinical aspects*, New York: Free Press.

Milech, D., Kirsner, K., Roy, G., Waters, B. (1993). Applications of psychology to computer-based tutoring systems. *International Journal of Human-Computer Interaction, 5*, 23-40.

Reber, A.S., Kassin, S.M., Lewis, S., Canto, G. (1980). On the relationship between implicit and explicit modes in the learning of complex rule structure. *Journal of Experimental Psychology: Human Learning and Memory, 6*, 492-502.

Shneider, W., Dumais, S.T., Shiffrin, R.M. (1984). Automatic and controlled processes in attention. In R. Parasuraman and D.R. Davies (Eds.), *Varieties of attention*, Orlando, Fl: Academic.

Schneider, W., Shiffrin, R.M. (1977). Controlled and automatic human-information processing: 1. Detection, search, and attention. *Psychological Review, 84*, 1-66.

Role of Analogical Reasoning as a Tool for Training

D.M. Boase-Jelinek and D. Milech

Centre for Computer Managed Training and Decision Support Systems, University of Western Australia, Nedlands, 6009, Australia.

Abstract
Computer managed training systems may use analogies to build on a student's existing knowledge and experience. Careful design of such training systems involves consideration of how much a student must know about a referent before it can be used as an analogy. Our research shows that two thirds of subjects solved a novel problem when trained with familiar analogies whereas one quarter solved the problem when trained with an unfamiliar analogy. Furthermore, training systems should present feedback to students regarding the adequacy of their use of an analogy. Our research suggests that feedback encouraged one quarter of subjects to use the analogy correctly.

1. INTRODUCTION

The role of analogies is to link a person's past experiences to new information being learnt. Analogies act like a bridge linking a familiar world to the new domain. For example, a person learning to be an electrical power system controller will have trouble if he or she knows nothing about electricity. However, if he or she is given an analogy which links knowledge about familiar objects to an understanding of electricity the learning process will be easier.

The challenge facing designers of computer based training packages is to answer questions such as : How is an appropriate analogy selected? and, What is the most effective use of an analogy? The answers to these questions involve research into the nature of analogies and the way people use them.

There are two contrasting accounts of how people make analogies. Gentner (1983) suggests that a person will make an analogy between an analogue (which we will refer to as system X) and new knowledge (which we will refer to as system Y) by recognizing equivalent relations in each system. This is a top-down approach to making an analogy because it requires an understanding of the theory and relations for a system X. For example the flow of water through a pipe may be used as an analogue to describe the behaviour of electricity in a wire. Gentner suggests that this analogy will be fruitful <u>only</u> if the theoretical relations in system **X** (Pressure = Flow * Resistance) is thoroughly understood an can be mapped to the theoretical relations in system **Y** (Volts = Current * Resistance).

A contrasting account, proposed by Holyoak & Thagard (1989), is that people build analogies on the basis of surface features. This is a bottom-up approach because it is based on concrete exemplars. For example, in making an analogy based on flow of water through a pipe (system **X**) to describe the behaviour of electricity (system **Y**) people might have noticed that if the pressure is increased, the flow will increase through the hose. This experience can be used to predict what might happen to current flow in a wire: if the voltage is increased, the current will also increase.

The differences between the top-down and bottom-up accounts of analogical reasoning lie in the knowledge about the analogue which people apply when making an analogy. Gentner assumes that people have abstract knowledge of relations and formulae. Holyoak and Thagard assume that people have concrete knowledge of surface features of the analogy.

To test these accounts we devised an experiment which addresses two questions: When do people go top-down or bottom-up in using an analogy?, and How much must people know about system **X** before attempting to make an analogy? The answers to these questions go some way to answering the challenges faced by designers of computer based training systems regarding optimal use of analogies.

2. METHOD

In this experiment, subjects were taught about the behaviour of a fictional system called a "Pectronizer" based on the operation of an electrical transformer (see Figure 1). In this system, fictional objects called "Pectrons" flow through the "Pectronizer" device. The Pectrons have attributes Imps and Vrooms. As the Pectrons flow through the Pectronizer they are transformed. Imps decrease by a fixed ratio, and Vrooms increase by the same ratio. An important relation in the "Pectronizer" system which was pointed out to subjects during this training phase, is that energy is the same on either side, and is calculated by multiplying Imps times Vrooms.

There were four groups of subjects in this experiment, each with differing levels of knowledge about an analogy. The method used for teaching one group of subjects was to present only the Pectronizer system, and no analogue. This group were called the NO KNOWLEDGE group because no links were made to their existing knowledge.

A second group of subjects were called LOW KNOWLEDGE because they were presented with an unfamiliar analogue to train them about the Pectronizer system. This analogue (see Figure 2) looks similar to the Pectronizer system except that

Pectrons are replaced by water flow. It was presented by saying that Pectrons are **like** water, imps are **like** pressure, and vrooms are **like** flow.

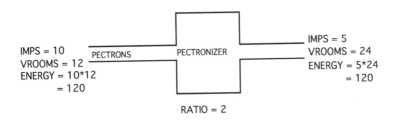

Figure 1. System X - the Pectronizer

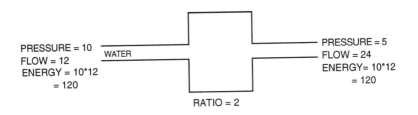

Figure 2. System Y - an analogy presented during training

A third group (called the HIGH KNOWLEDGE group) was given a more familiar analogue involving temperature of water. The fourth group (called the TRAINED ANALOGY group) was trained about the analogue by being given a visual demonstration of the analogy in action. One important feature pointed out for each analogue was the energy balance on each side of the system.

Following training, subjects were presented with a problem solving test (see Figure 3). The problem solving test was slightly different from system **Y** about which subjects were trained. The key feature of this system is the junction. The junction behaves differently to a "Pectronizer" because it halves the "Vrooms" without changing the "Imps". The total energy flowing down both arms adds up to the energy flowing in, so energy is balanced on either side of the system.

The differences between system **Y** and the problem solving test mean that bottom-up solution schema approaches to analogical reasoning will not work. Subjects who try to apply a solution based on the operation of a "Pectronizer" will not get an energy balance across the system. However, the similarities between system **Y** and the problem solving test mean that top-down approaches to analogical reasoning may work. The high order relation of energy balance across the system holds for all the systems, and can lead to a correct solution.

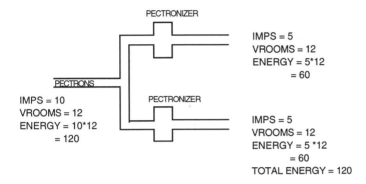

Figure 3. The problem solving test

Subjects were given the problem solving test and asked to indicate the Imps and Vroom values on each arm on the right hand side of the system. If they were unable to find a correct solution, subjects were given feedback in the form of questions asking them to describe the energy going in to the system, and energy going out of the system, and to describe what is happening to the energy flows in the system. These questions are based on the observations by Mayer (1989) that people do not test the adequacy of their solutions. Novick & Holyoak (1991) suggested giving these kinds of questions to motivate subjects to think more carefully about the problem.

In observing performance of this task, we were interested to see whether subjects achieved an energy balance in their solution, and whether they used an analogy in thinking about the problem. We were also interested in the effect of the feedback on performance, and the effect of the subject's level of knowledge about the analogy on performance.

3. RESULTS

The results shown in Table 1. reveal the differences between the number of subjects who achieved an energy balance compared to the number expected to achieve an energy balance. The expectations of energy balance were based on whether subjects used an analogy to reason about the problem. According to Gentner (1983), analogy use involves recognition of high order relations. In this case the high order relation was an energy balance across the system. The Low Knowledge group are particularly interesting here because only 4 out of the 11 subjects who used an analogy to reason about the problem achieved an energy balance. This suggests that where people do not understand an analogy they do not use a top-down approach to making the analogy.

Table 1
Number of subjects who achieved or were expected to achieve an energy balance

	Achieved an energy balance	Expected to achieve a balance
No Knowledge	4	1
Low Knowledge	4	11
Trained Knowledge	8	8
High Knowledge	10	8

To check whether an analogy was useful for solving the problem, a comparison was made between subjects who did or did not use an analogy (see Table 2.) These results show that analogies with which subjects were familiar or given training did help in solving the problem. One subject in the NO KNOWLEDGE group specifically mentioned an analogy which he made up to help solve the problem. Few subjects in the LOW KNOWLEDGE group solved the problem. So, an analogy only appears to be useful if it is familiar, or if people are trained to understand it.

Table 2
Number of Correct Solutions for Subjects who Used or Did Not Use and Analogy

	Solved problem using Analogy	Solved problem without using Analogy	Did not solve Problem
No Knowledge	1	3	12
Low Knowledge	3	1	13
Trained Knowledge	7	1	4
High Knowledge	10	0	7

Finally, we were interested in the effect of feedback on finding solutions. The results in table 3. reveal that feedback assisted all subjects uniformly. The results suggest that the feedback increased motivation to try to solve the problem and provided a hint to focus on the high order relation and use a top-down approach to solving the problem.

Table 3
Number of Correct Solutions for Subjects Before and After Feedback

	Solved problem before Feedback	Extra Solutions after Feedback	Did not solve Problem
No Knowledge	1	3	12
Low Knowledge	2	2	13
Trained Knowledge	4	4	4
High Knowledge	6	4	7

4. CONCLUSIONS

These results suggest that familiar analogies are more likely to be used than unfamiliar ones. The use of familiar analogies is more likely to be top-down, and more successful than unfamiliar analogies. Feedback questions can increase the likelihood of using an analogy, and by increasing motivation and providing a hint, and can increase the likelihood of finding a correct solution.

The application of these findings to computer based training systems is that analogies are useful providing they are familiar. One issue that has been demonstrated in this experiment is that analogies can be made useful and familiar by providing training about them. Finally, it has been shown that asking subjects questions about the high order relations in the task is a useful and motivating form of feedback which increases the likelihood of finding a correct solution.

5. REFERENCES

Gentner, D., (1983)., Structure Mapping: A Theoretical Framework for Analogy. In A. Collins & E. Smith (eds.). Readings in Cognitive Science: A Perspective from Psychology and Artificial Intelligence (pp. 176-225). San Mateo: Morgan Kaufmann Publishers. (Reprinted from Cognitive Science, 7, 155-170, 1983)

Holyoak, K. J. & Thagard, P., (1989). A computational model of analogical problem solving. In S. Vosniadou & A. Ortony (Eds). Similarity and analogical reasoning (pp. 242-266). Cambridge: Cambridge University Press.

Mayer, R.E., (1989). Models for understanding. Review of Educational Research, 59(1), 43-64.

Novick, L. R. & Holyoak, K. J., (1991). Mathematical Problem Solving by Analogy. Journal of Experimental Psychology: Learning, Memory and Cognition, 17(3), 398-415

COMPUTER TECHNOLOGY IN THE EDUCATIONAL CURRICULUM DEVELOPMENT OF NIGERIA IN THE 21ST CENTURY

Dr. Noah K. Akinmayowa,
Department of Psychology, University of Lagos, Nigeria.

Abstract

Computer technology is a problem-solving methodology which allows the best utilization of resources. This is achieved by the establishment of effective decision-making, communications processes which enhances full creativity, efficiency, goal setting, accelerated learning, reduction of errors from personnel assigned.

The acceleration of decision-making process in the provision of technical information as an input which aid high-level implementation of decision in the management of systems is enhanced. The tools of computer technology assist the user interface (HCI) in the proper initiation and evaluation of action process that will ensure that all necessary factors in system development are considered in a logical and methodical manner prior to the estbalishment of a firm approach.

The utilization of computer technology enhances an engineering analysis approach for the definition of problems, identification of feasible alternatives, selection of Evaluation criteria, application of Analytical techniques, Sensitivity Analysis and the assessment of risk and uncertainty in the evaluation process.
These objectives can be achieved within an educational
.curriculum where computer hardware is in place coupled with the application of the systems approach in the educational environment.

This paper subscribed to the need for computer design to aid the objectives above and the adoption of the technology approach to curriculum development and implementation strategies.

EDUCATIONAL OBJECTIVES/PHILOSOPHY

The application of systematic instruction/approach in order to develop the technical, theoretical, and attitudinal skills of the individual should be the philosophy of any educational curriculum[1].

In this venture, the instructions/curriculum projects must be tailored to train technical expertise which would enable the individual assess his/her impact, enable the individual identify in a problem-solving tasks technological considerations, economic, political,

ecological and social factors and environmental impact assessment strategy.[2]

The educational curriculum should enhance within the individual skills for the development of creativity, sensitivity to needs, use of analytical tools through modelling using analytical tools and information technology. The curriculum must enhance ability for experimentation capability, measurement and observation, capacity for data analysis presentation, utilization and the development of ability to work with others and be able to make effective communication.[3]

The development of attitudinal characteristics of objectivity and open-mindedness, curiosity and persistence, professional attitude, initiative and interest will to create, develop and support system success are essential to an effective educational system.

This strategy will be required in any major educational programme at both the lower and higher levels . The emphasy of this strategy at the lower level (primary education) in Nigeria or any other developing country is very essential since the first twelve years of a child is the period necessary for developing attitude, apptitude and the necessary reinforcement needed for the intelligent care of his physical needs and trained guidance for enhancing his mental, emotional and social potentials.

The experience of the child at the stage of development has long-term implication for influencing the aspiration and achievement in later life.

SYSTEMS INTEGRATION

Many behavioural scientists[4,5,6,7], counsellors, teachers, educational psychologists emphasized that the factors which influence learning must be integrated through the learner-teacher-

768

aid-environment systems. This integration must see
the learner at the centre of the integration [8,9] Revolving
around the learner are relevant variables:

(a) educational aims and objectives
(b) selected learning and experiences
(c) selected content
(d) integration of learning experience and content
(e) evaluation strategy

In 1969, the Nigerian Curriculum conference identified
new national goals for education in Nigeria. Achieving
these goals has been fraustrated by failure of

(a) Educational Planning
(b) Financial/Human Resources Allocation
(c) Educational Routine Administration
(d) Emphasy on Entry Requirement
(e) Examination/Assessment System
(f) Management Training
(g) Parental and Community Expectations
(h) International Influence
(i) Lack of information technology

The above   social factor also affect planning strategies and inequality in Nigeria.[10] It is a matter for
concern that the Nigerian child is forced to take educational
instructions in English and Mother-tongue languages.
At the end of it all, he is neither proficient in any
of the languages leading to emotional and intellectual
problems B. Fafunwa submitted the use of mother tongue
language as a medium of instruction in primary school
since it is the most natural way of learning. The
natural method proposed would allow learning to be
based on the innate, inherent moral sense, instinctive,
using normal, not miraculous, logical, using deductible
methods.

The reappraisal of the curriculum strategies which
would change the foreign method of teaching that is
in practice in Nigeria and a change to the educational
technology approach will enable educational objectives
to the achieved.

Chadwick[11] gave 33 major differences between the traditional
and systems approach in educational methods.   Experts
agreed that in the utilization of the systems approach, [12,13]
research must be done to ascertain the role of teachers
The effect of the socio-cultural milieu must also be
studied in order to help in the preparation of effective
curriculum and the study of appropriate and effective
audio-visual aids,[14] which will enhance education.

The child must be able to suggest his own pace, his
interest and can work with less anxiety. The adoption
of a system view will enable the child to learn at
the onset of educational training, work organisation
before being overpowerd by learning materials. In
this model, the teacher is seeing as the learning resources co-ordinator, where the pupil is provided with
resources to achieve objectives in a relaxed atmosphere
and educational culture which emphasise consultation.
Assessment of performance is the entire business of
the teacher. The system approach model is flexible
and must be weighed harmoniously within the dynamic
socio-cultural-political environment conditions to
achieve its objectives.

IMPLICATIONS

The implication of these demand.is that in the application
of computer technology design at the software and hardware
levels for educational development,the impact of Socio-
cultural factors must be considered.

Time is here for the use of African languages and those
of other non-western countires in the design of computer
technology know-how in order to ease the teaching tecniques
and application.

It is also necessary to show here that through the
application of computer technology Knowhow in terms
of methodology and challenges which it poses to the
user, the assigned educational objectives are achievable.
Computer technology that will teach problem-solving as a
procedural-knowledge-knowledge how to do something rather
than declarative knowledge- that is, knowledge of facts and
principles. Emphasy should be placed on the development of
general skills such as mnemonic techniques, decision making,
representation and search and creativity.

The student must learn how problems are represented and
analysed, the ability to categorize a problem correctly and
planning as well as the improvement of problem-solving capacity through appropriate instruction. The search for problem-solving methods has become important to effectively
harness the importance of Computer technology in educational
curriculum. The computer would serve as tutor using (AI)
Artificial Intelligence. The development of educational
Curriculum which utilize computer technology in stimulating
the human mind and trascending it.

Since computers can use facts to make inferences and draw on
experience to reach unprogrammed conclusions, it should
support the problem-solving effort.

Finally, educational curriculum must be able to use intelligent Computer Tutors (AI) and the application of Cognitive Psychology Principles in Learning Strategies. Diagnosis of misconceptions of problems must be taught and computers which diagnose errors and teach teachers to diagnose
errors and enhance the teaching of principles, the use of
conceptual ideas to improve the diagnostic quality of tests
are essential for design and application.

REFERENCES

1. Fafunwa, B.A. (1971) The need for Systematic Curricu-
    lum development process in Nigeria. NERC
    Publication on Guidelines on Primary School
    Curriculum. National Workshop on Primary
    Education, April 26 to May 8, 1971. pp
    XVIII - XXVII.

2. Blanchard, S.B. (1976) Engineering Organization and
    Management, Prentice-Hall Inc. Englewood
    Cliffs, New Jersey. pp. 4-9, pp. 448-491.

3. Akintola, J.M. (1981) Educational Change in Africa:
    A Decade of Action Journal of The Nigeria
    Educational Research Council Vol.1 No.2
    pp. 169-181.

4. Awokoya, S.O. (1981), Futuristic Prospects of Quantity
    and Quality of Nigerian Education. Journal of
    the Nigerian Educational Research Council
    Vol. 1 No. 2 pp. 169-181.

5. Obaya, P. (1980), Towards a National Education Policy
    for the Year 2000. NERA Conference Report
    May 7-8 ISBN 978 - 2360 - 02 - 2. Univer-
    sity of Benin. pp. 1- 23.

6. Akintola, J.M. (1971), NERC Publication on Guidelines
    for Curriculum Development in Primary School,
    University of Ibadan, pp. IX - XIV.

7. Lambo, T. A. (1971) NERC Publication on Guidelines
    for Curriculum Development in Primary School.
    University of Ibadan. pp. XIII - XIV.

8. Cookey, NERC Publication on Guidelines for Primary
    School Curriculum Development Workshop,
    University of Ibadan. pp. XV - XVII.

9. Fafunwa, B.A. (1981) New Perspectives in African Edu-
    cation, Macmillan and Co. Limited, Lagos and
    London. pp. 35 - 45.

10. Dalta Ansu, (1984), Education and Society: A Sociology of African Education. Macmillan Publishers Ghana. pp. 54 - 61.

11. Chadwick, C. Educational Technology, Progress, Prospects and Comparison British Journal of Educational Technology. No.2, Vol.4, May 1973.

12. Holmes Brian, Problems in Education Pub. Routledge and Kegan Paul Limited. Broadway House, London. pp. 68-74.

13. Akrofi, K. Asiedu, Organisation of Examinations for Teacher Curriculum Development in Ghananian Teacher Training Colleges. West African Journal of Education. Vol. 4, Vo.2, May 1971. pp. 25-30.

14. Wiman R. V. and Meherhenry XVC (1969) Educational Media: Theory into Practice Charles E. Merril Publ. Co. Columbus, Ohio. pp. 30-48.

CONTROL OF COSMONAUTS TRAINING TO OVERCOME OPERATIONAL COMPLEXITY

Yuri Glazkov, Alex Rudchenko, Alex Vislotsky, Alex Vankov

Gagarin Cosmonaut Training Center, 141160, Star City, Moscow Region, Russia

Controlling the process of preparation of the crew of manned spacecraft (MSC) for flight is at the present time one of the most timely problems in respect of both the contents and complexity thereof. The introduction of a large number of contingent modes of MSC functioning into the preparation program substantially increases its complexity, makes it difficult to evaluate the degree of preparation of the crew, increases the time necessary for the training process. The large number of parameters for controlling the process of crew training in mission simulators (MS) makes it necessary to develop mathematical models of training (MMT), on the basis of which both the planning of the preparation and the evaluation of the results are accomplished.

The main requirements which such a MMT should satisfy are:
(i) the MMT should comprise as few parameters as possible;
(ii) the MMT should be complex, i.e. take account simultaneously of the process of acquisition and the process of losing skills.

It is shown in [1] that one of the most suitable ways to describe the process of crew training in the MS is to use the information approach and corresponding thereto MMTs describing the training process in relation to the complexity of the trainings and the intervals therebetween:

$$\mu_{i+1}^{j} = \mu_{\infty} + (\mu_0 - \mu_{\infty}) \times \left[b \exp\left(-aZ_i^{j}\right) + \exp\left(-aZ_i\right) \right], \tag{1}$$

$$Z_i = \sum_{k=1}^{i} \left\{ X_k \left[1 - \exp\left(-\frac{\gamma}{K_k} \sum_{l=k}^{i} \tau_l \right) \right] \times \exp\left(-\alpha \sum_{l=k}^{i} \tau_l \right) \right\} \tag{2}$$

$$Z_i^{j} = \sum_{k=1}^{i} \left\{ X_k^{j} \left[1 - \exp\left(-\frac{\gamma}{K_k^{j}} \sum_{l=k}^{i} \tau_l \right) \right] \times \exp\left(-\alpha \sum_{l=k}^{i} \tau_l \right) \right\}, \tag{3}$$

where μ_0, μ_{∞} are the initial and maximum levels of crew training preparation; a is the speed at which the skill is obtained; Z_i, Z_i^{j} are the amounts of information accumulated by the crew during i trainings in respect of the general and specific portions of the level of crew training, respectively; b is a coefficient determining the ratio between the general and specific portions of the level of crew training; K_i, K_i^j are the indices of the quality of activity of the crew during the ith training and jth mode (the coefficient of erroneous activity in the course of fulfilling the training task is used as the criterion); X_i, X_i^j are the informational saturations of the training and of each of its modes, and are proportional to their complexity — Si,Sij , respectively; γ, α are coefficients characterizing the speed of acquisition and destruction of skills, respectively; τ_1 is the interval between the $(l-1)$th and the lth trainings.

In the mathematical model $(1)-(3)$, the complexity of each of trainings is considered as a weighed sum of the complexity of performing elementary actions, which compose the training, taking into account the intensity of the activity and its significance in respect of the realization of the training program. The structural model of the conversion of information, realized by the presented MMT, is shown in Figure 1.

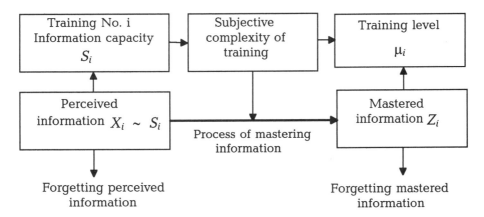

Figure 1. Model of conversion of information in the training process

The presented MMT is based on the experimentally established facts as follows:
— skills acquisition rate depends on the mean complexity of a training task;
— the maximum value of the rate of skills acquisition is achieved at the specific mean value of the interval between trainings;
— the level of training for a well—trained crew remains almost stable during a certain period of time and only then drastically decreases (see figure 2);
—there exists an optimal value of interval between trainings that ensures the maximum increment of the crew training level. This optimal value is variable itself as the training process goes on (see figure 3).

If the possible conditions for conduction of each of the modes in the planned flight are known, then it is possible to predict the level of their complexity. Let's assume that an $(i-1)$th training has been conducted.

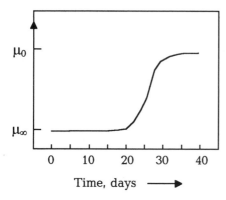

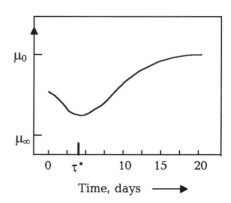

Figure 2. Level of training vs time
after the last training in the schedule

Figure 3. Level of training vs time
after the previous training

If the requirements for the probability Pr of performing each of the modes are prescribed and the law for distribution of the coefficient of erroneous actions [1] is used, then:

$$P\left(K_i^j > K_{max}, \mu_i^j S_r^j\right) < P_r \tag{4}$$

wherefrom it is found that:

$$\mu_i^j\left(Z_i, Z_i^j\right) < \mu_r^j \tag{5}$$

where K_{max} is the level of erroneous activity of the crew corresponding to the error aborting the jth flight mode. The condition (4) is the criterion of the preparedness of the crew for the coming flight after the $(i-1)$th training has been conducted. Since the problem being solved during the crew training process in the MS is to provide the crew with general skills for the control of an MSC, then it is necessary to require that the crew be given the maximum amount of general information during the preparation:

$$Z_i\left(\vec{S}, \vec{\tau}\right) \Rightarrow max \tag{6}$$

where $\vec{S}$ is a vector of training complexity; $\vec{\tau}$ is a vector of intervals between trainings under the following limitation on the duration of the training process:

$$\sum_{l=1}^{i-1} \tau_l \le T.$$

If the value of $\vec{\tau}$ is fixed it is not difficult to solve the optimization problem (6) since it has an analytical solution. Therefore, it is easier to solve the problem (6) as follows:

$$\max_{\vec{\tau}} \left[\max_{\vec{S}} (Z_i) \right]. \tag{7}$$

The task of determining the optimum planning of the complexity of trainings and the corresponding intervals is simplified if instead of a limitation on the general duration of the training process, a system of limitations on the length of the intervals between each of the trainings is set:

$$T_l^+ \le \tau_l \le T_l^-, \quad l = \overline{1, i-1},$$

where $T_l^+ (T_l^-)$ is the maximum (minimum) possible interval between trainings. In that case the optimum plan $\left(\vec{S^*}, \vec{\tau^*} \right)$ for the whole training process will consist of a combination of the optimum plans for each of the trainings and will be obtained by the step−by−step solution of the following problems:

$$Z_l(S_l, \tau_l) \Rightarrow \max, \quad l = \overline{1, i-1}.$$

After the optimum general plan has been compiled, the next problem which can be solved during the planning of the training process will be the task of distributing the modes through the training and selection of their complexity in order to obtain such Z_i^j which would ensure the fulfillment of the system of conditions (5). Here, the most substantial restrictions will be those related to the logic of introducing the modes into the training. All in all, only a small number (as compared with the possible number) of standard trainings can be determined. The following conditions should be satisfied for each standard training when it is included in the lth position in the training process

$$S_l^j \ge S_{min}^j, \quad \sum_j S_l^j = S_l^*, \tag{8}$$

determining the possible number of standard trainings for each lth training. It is proposed that an attempt be made to find a permissible solution of the system

(6) by successively including standard trainings in the training plan in accordance with the strictest limits of the system (5), which are determined by:

$$\mu_i^j\left(Z_i^j\right) \le \mu_r^j \quad .$$
(9)

In order to ensure the necessary scopes of Z_i^j a nonlinear programming problem that is discrete in respect of τ and continuous in respect of S, has to be solved. The minimum necessary scope of information which would be mastered by the crew being prepared to a specific flight mode, is obtained from equation (1) describing the change in the training level of the crew and from the condition (9):

$$Z_i^j = -\tfrac{1}{a} \times \ln\left[\tfrac{1}{b}\left(\tfrac{\mu_r^j - \mu_\infty}{\mu_0 - \mu_\infty} - \exp\left(-aZ_i^*\right)\right)\right] \quad ,$$
(10)

where the last term is the component of the general part of the training level at the moment flight or the ith training is conducted. Equation (3) that describes the change in the specific part of the information, can be approximately presented as follows:

$$Z_{l-1}^j = Z_l^j \times \exp\left(\alpha\tau_l^j\right) - S_l^j \times f\left(Z_{l-1}^j, S_l^j\right)$$
(11)

where τ_l^j is the interval between trainings $l+1$ and l, in both of which the mode j is included; $f\left(Z_{l-1}^j, S_l^j\right)$ is the function describing the process of mastering the information. It is possible to achieve the required scope of information in respect of the jth mode after conducting an lth standard training TRl with different distributions of the scope of that information in the preceding training. The training process will be planned in a maximum balanced way if the following condition is satisfied:

$$\max Z_{l-1}^j \underset{TR_l}{\Rightarrow} \min$$
(12)

If several equivalent solutions are found for the problem (12), the selection of the best one is made on the basis of criterion minimizing the sum scope of the information accumulated up to the lth training:

$$\sum_j Z_{l-1}^j \underset{TR_l}{\Rightarrow} \min$$

As a result, the minimum number of trainings necessary for the guaranteed preparation of the crew for the forthcoming flight, is attained. Wherein, the

As a result, the minimum number of trainings necessary for the guaranteed preparation of the crew for the forthcoming flight, is attained. Wherein, the boundary condition $Z_0^j = 0$ should be fulfilled during the final step of planning the training process in respect of modes for all the modes. If this is not possible, the number of trainings should be increased and a return made to the solution of the general problem of planning the complexity of the trainings and the intervals (6). Thus, planning of the training process in a mission simulator is an iterative process, during which the following two problems are successfully solved: (i) the general problem of planning (6), as a result of the solution of which the general portion of the training level of the crew is maximized, and the conditions and requirements for the specific portion of the training level are formed; (ii) the problem of the distribution of the standard trainings and selection of the complexity of the modes in order to ensure the minimum amount of trainings necessary to satisfy the requirements formed during the solution of the preceding problem.

The practice has shown that the utilization of this approach significantly reduces the required amount of the trainings (reduction of 50% and more). As an example, a typical training schedule is shown in Figure 4.

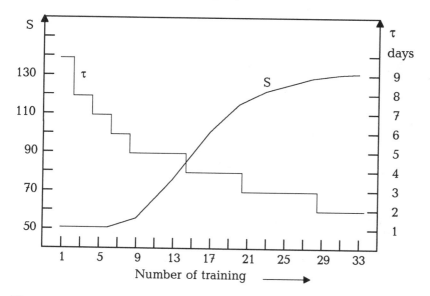

Figure 4. Example of training schedule

REFERENCES

1 A.I. Vislotsky, Planning of the Training Process for the Crews of Manned Spacecraft in the Mission Simulators, Collect. Techn. Pap., NPO "Molniya", Vol.7 − "Ergonomics", Russia, Moscow, 1991.

Use of Multimedia Technology in Teaching Engineering Design

S. Hsi[a] and A. M. Agogino[b]

[a]Graduate Group in Science and Mathematics Education, 4533 Tolman Hall, University of California at Berkeley, Berkeley, CA 94720

[b]Department of Mechanical Engineering, 5136 Etcheverry Hall, University of California at Berkeley, Berkeley, CA 94720

Abstract
   Computer-based case studies are being developed to enhance the current case study method of teaching engineering design by using multimedia technology to illustrate concepts, and hypermedia to support cognitive flexibility. An architecture for the life cycle design concept is presented. As components of the Kolb experiential learning cycle, these case studies are designed to provide experiences in active experimentation and reflective observation, as well as complement hands-on activities. The results from evaluation of several cases used to support instruction are included. The research from this study suggests several improvements necessary in the interactive case studies presented, but overall the cases were found to be successful in delivering key concepts of best practices in engineering design and in accommodating different learning styles.

1. PROBLEM DESCRIPTION

   The practice of engineering design requires integrating multiple disciplines multidimensional thinking, analysis skills, and hardware proficiency. Exercises and curricular material used in teaching engineering design must involve open-ended tasks that require combining creative, spatial, conceptual and analytical abilities to synthesize solutions. Students learning engineering design are rarely presented with the whole life cycle of a design, but instead are taught knowledge in pieces. The case study method of instruction offers one solution towards integrating knowledge, by providing knowledge representations that are highly interconnected to permit greater flexibility in the way that knowledge can be synthesized and assembled for use in learning [5,7,8].
   We are developing computer-based multimedia case studies to enhance the current case study method of teach engineering design by using multimedia technology to illustrate concepts, and hypermedia to support cognitive flexibility [8,9]. In this context, cognitive flexibility refers to the ability to spontaneously restructure and apply one's knowledge to changing situations and problems as the knowledge in hypermedia is organized, interconnected, and presented in multiple ways. Cases focus on multidisciplinary problem-solving and current "best practices" [6] in engineering, specifically issues in life cycle design, collaborative work and concurrent design, or the simultaneous engineering where groups contribute to

all stages of product design. These case studies cover important aspects of the design of selected engineering products in which exemplary design practices have been followed. Cases provide positive examples of market driven design, design for assembly, design for manufacturability, serviceability, recyclability and disposability; and normative (or prescriptive design practices) like quality circles and multifunctional teams. The cases studies are also selected to capture student interest by showing the inter-dependencies between technical and societal factors, and relevance of economic considerations and global impact of design decisions. Towards these instructional goals, we provide a user interface architecture that supports the life cycle design concept with case studies.

2. INSTRUCTIONAL APPROACH WITH MULTIMEDIA

Similar to the modified Kolb model for experiential learning [2,4,10], case studies serve as part of the learning cycle to stimulate reflective observation and support active experimentation by guided non-linear, multi-dimensional exploration in hypermedia that engages the student (see Figure 1). In this model, instruction should support different learning styles through activities addressing the four processes cyclically because students learn by different ways of perceiving information ranging from the sensory (e.g. seeing, hearing, touching) to the more abstract, conceptual and symbolic. Multimedia technology (digitized audio, video, images, text) is used to appeal to the more sensory learners to illustrate concepts and enhance text explanations with graphical, audio, and visual information. Equations of engineering analyses, and links to textbook explanations are also provided. Interactive questions in the on-line cases are design to promote reflection and self testing of knowledge. Hands-on activities in combination with multimedia case studies provide concrete experiences for students. For instance, students can perform mechanical dissections of the products explained in the cases such as toys, a printer, or bicycle parts to reinforce experiential learning.

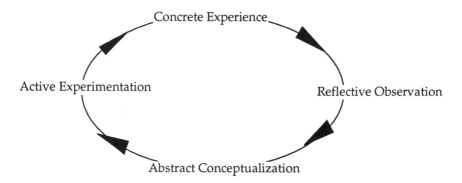

Figure 1. Experiential learning cycle

Multimedia cases are being used in various ways for classroom instruction. Using an overhead projection system and storage on hard disk or CD-ROM, instructors use cases as examples to support standard lecture formats. The digitized clips of robotics assembly, animated mechanisms, and interviews with engineering designers serve as a basis for stimulating group discussion, and Socratic teacher-student dialogues. Multimedia cases are also installed in the computer laboratory for individuals to explore in more depth on their own to support the reflective observation part of the learning cycle. Before approaching hands-on laboratory activities such as mechanical dissection or design projects, students use cases as computer-based activities to provide the historical background, design principles, and rationale behind the product. Multimedia cases are also used as expert models to fuel and motivate students to construct their own understanding through the creation of their own multimedia case.

Several case studies are currently under development on the Macintosh and IBM platforms using HyperCard™ and Toolbook™ authoring tools. These include cases of consumer products and a team design project: Mattel Toys, the IBM Proprinter, and the Human Powered Vehicle (HPV). Cases from Mattel Toys present design for assembly, safety issues, and market-driven design concepts. The Proprinter teaches students about industrial practices of automated assembly, multifunctional teams, design trade-offs, and concepts in engineering design such as concurrent engineering and design for manufacturability. The HPV case is designed to excite lower division students about engineering design, making connections to math, physics and engineering science. The HPV case uses multimedia to communicate these concepts in a stimulating environment that contains video clips of wind tunnel testing, road testing, vehicle construction, and clips of the actual race.

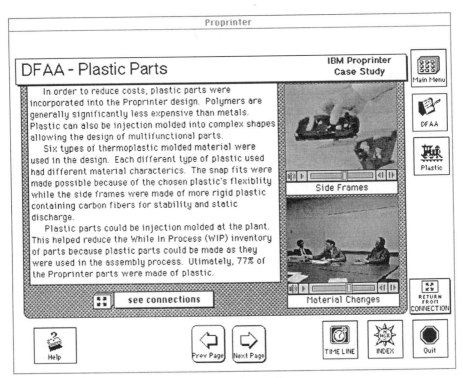

Figure 2. Sample screen from the Proprinter Case

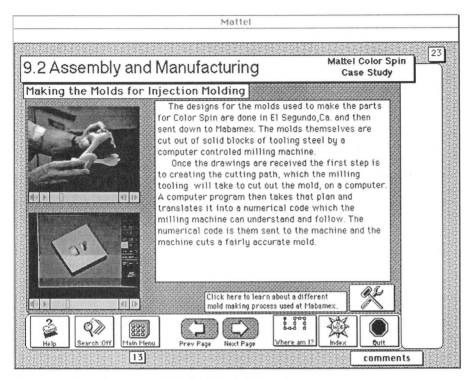

Figure 3. Sample screen from the Mattel Toys Case

3. METHOD OF EVALUATION

Multimedia cases have been tested and evaluated by over 80 students and faculty. Evaluation feedback and data include 1) pre- and post-test questionnaires to monitor learning where answers to questions were explained in the multimedia case, and to provide feedback on multimedia features and 2) on-line interaction data, which collected information on navigation patterns, sections of interest and other computer interactions. Questionnaire information about content understanding and pedagogical impact are included here. More results pertaining to user interface design and navigational issues are found elsewhere [3].

4. RESULTS

Results from students' responses to design questions in the questionnaire indicated that they learned several key concepts related to life cycle design. Although students had various levels of prior knowledge before seeing the case studies, all students' post-questionnaire responses indicated their approach to a given engineering design problem was more "correct", integrated, and consistent with concurrent engineering principles.

Analyses of the on-line data indicate students chose to follow the life cycle path provided. However, students varied in their preference for different features of the multimedia cases, and varied in the time they spent on each section. The pattern for navigating in the HPV revealed two groups of users: (1) students who consistently followed the main life cycle path through the case, and (2) those more independent users who first chose to look at sections they were interested in, and then later returning to the order provided along the main path.

In several of the cases, there are text explanations that summarize the main concepts and contents of the digitized video clips. Through our surveys and on-line collection method, we found that some students preferred reading the text first before watching video clips, while others preferred to learn from the visual images, audio, and digitized movies. Exemplary of sensory learners, surveyed students wrote they liked " pictures and sounds because they help me to learn more in depth". Other surveyed students wrote "drawings and sounds because they explain", "(I liked) sounds because it sounds real", and "(I liked) sounds and movies because they show how it is" indicating the multimedia aspect accommodated their preferred learning style. Also, foreign students relied more on the text for better comprehension over the video and audio. Pre-college students tended to preferred the video and audio components of the multimedia cases over text.

5. FUTURE WORK

User interface studies are being planned to test improvements in random text-based search features to assist users in quickly finding sections associated with specific topics not apparent in the index or concept map. Evaluation methods of educational multimedia are also being investigated for improvement.

As we plan to distribute multimedia cases to other instructors and university campuses, multimedia case study materials are being indexed for future dissemination initially on a CD-ROM format, and later on a networked courseware database. Multimedia case studies on automotive design and manufacture and on mechatronics products are also currently under development.

6. CONCLUSIONS

In summary, we present a new multimedia delivery system for using the case study method in the classroom that strengthens and enhances the existing case study method by providing participatory interactive and experiential learning. We do not claim that these cases will replace actual design experience, but serve as one aspect of a curriculum to prepare the engineering designer for more realistic thinking, decision-making and problem-solving. Learning as knowledge reproduction will hopefully be replaced with knowledge use , transfer, and application.

7. ACKNOWLEDGMENTS

This material is based upon research supported by the National Science Foundation Cooperative Agreement No. EEC 9053807. The multimedia case studies described in this paper were developed by faculty, graduate students, and undergraduate students at the University of California at Berkeley in collaboration with our partners in Synthesis: an NSF Engineering Education Coalition. The authors are grateful for the support of the National Science Foundation and our industrial partners: Apple Computer, Inc.; IBM Corporation; John Wiley and Sons, Inc.; Lexmark International, Inc.; and Mattel Toys, Inc. Special thanks goes to case study developers: Jay Evans, Anil Varma, Nagaraj Srinivasan, Punit Jain, Armineh Menzigian, Kirk Edwards, Bill Wood, Steve Bradley, Mitchell Suarez and Robert Stanard. We are indebted to our courseware studio specialist, Robert Lettieri.

8. REFERENCES

1 Evans, J., "Multimedia Case Studies for Teaching Best Design Practices," MS Project Report, Department of Mechanical Engineering, University of California at Berkeley, 1992.
2 Harb, J. N., Durrnat, S. O., and Terry, R.E.(1992)"Use of the Kolb Learning Cycle and the 4MAT System in Engineering Education", Journal of Engineering Education, pp. 70-77, April.
3 Hsi, S. and Agogino, A., "Navigational Issues in Multimedia Case Studies of Engineering Design", to appear in HCI International '93, 5th International Conference on Human-Computer Interaction jointly with 9th Symposium on Human Interface (Japan), August 8-13,1993, Orlando, FL
4 Kolb, D.A. (1984) Experiential Learning: Experience as the source of learning and development, Englewood Cliffs, New Jersey: Prentice-Hall
5 Linn, M.C. and Clancy, M., (1992) "The Case for Case Studies in Programming Instruction (in press), *Communications of the ACM*, Vol. 33:3, March, pp. 121-132.
6 *National Research Council, Improving Engineering Design: Designing for Competitive Advantage,* National Academy Press, Washington, D.C. 1991
7 Sansalone, M., (1990) "Teaching Structural Concepts Through Case Studies and Competitions", *Engineering Education*, May/June, pp.472-475.
8 Spiro, R. and Jehng, J. (1991) "Cognitive Flexibility and hypertext: Theory and Technology for the nonlinear and multidimensional traversal of complex subject matter." In Nix and Spiro (Eds) *Cognition, Education, and Multimedia* Lawrence Erlbaum.
9 Steidel, Jr. R.F. "The Role of the Case Study in a Graduate Curriculum in Mechanical Engineering Design", Technical Report, University of California: Berkeley.
10 Svinicki, M. D. & Dixon, N. (1990) "The Kolb Model Modified for Classroom Activities" in *College Teaching,* pp. 69-74.

AN ADAPTIVE USER-ORIENTED MESSAGE PRIORITIZATION SCHEME*

Wei-Ping Wang

Department of Electrical and Systems Engineering, The University of Connecticut
Storrs, CT 06269-3157, USA

Abstract
Message prioritization and filtration is important to reduce the detrimental effects of information overload in human-computer interactions. This paper develops an adaptive computer support scheme which learns about the end-user's message accessing patterns, and adaptively arranges messages in a priority set. The scheme is based on learning automaton, and requires little a priori knowledge about the end-user. This scheme can be integrated with existing information systems to develop "smart" user interface, which is adaptive to end-user's information needs. A simulation example is provided to show the effectiveness of the scheme.

1. INTRODUCTION

Information overload is an increasingly salient problem encountered in management, man-machine interaction, command and control systems, etc. [1-3]. With the help of computer systems, organizations are transforming towards flatter structures. People are exposed to an increasing amount of information, or more precisely an increasing number of messages with different importance. The term "message" generally refers to any form of media carrying information, such as a report, a signal, and a graph. So far, computer systems has greatly helped humans in the storage and distribution of data. They do not, however, provide much support to the higher level functions of human information processing: determining what to communicate and present, and in what priority. Computers with their large capacity tend to flood some end-users, e.g., senior managers [2, 4].

At the issue is then how to support the end-users' information acquisition in the face of overload. Recently the problem has attracted much research attention, and different prototypes of support systems have been proposed and empirically studied [1, 2, 5].

This paper develops an adaptive message prioritization scheme based on learning automaton. The focal issue is how to arrange or prioritize the messages to facilitate the end-users' information acquisition without intruding their operations. The following section briefly discusses different views to characterize messages. Section 3 presents a generic message prioritization problem where an end-user is provided with messages about a number of activities, but he can only process a portion of them due to his limited capability. The problem is analyzed in the context of learning automaton, and an adaptive prioritization scheme is developed in Section 4. A simulation example is given in Section 5, followed by concluding remarks in Section 6.

---

* This work was supported in part by the National Science Foundation under grant IRI-8902755, and by the Office of Naval Research under contract N00014-90-J-1753.

2. MESSAGE EVALUATION PERSPECTIVES

A human user is commonly characterized as having limited information processing capability and bounded rationality [6]. When confronted with an excessive number of messages, A human has to select a subset to process since he/she cannot receive, process and digest a large number of messages in a short period. Even when there is enough time, it is psychologically detrimental to let a user navigate through a flood of messages in search of needed information. It is thus desirable to have a system filter or prioritize messages for the end-user. The difficulty, however, lies in the analysis and evaluation of different messages: what are important. A message can be examined from different perspectives, such as what kind of statistical event the message covers, what the message means, and what consequences it may cause. These three perspectives correspond to three different views of information: syntactic, semantic, and economical.

Shannon's information theory deals exclusively with the syntactic aspect of information in a statistical sense [7]. It uses entropy to examine the informativeness of messages (symbols), but does not consider the semantic information that comes from those messages, except indirectly or by implication. The "exception-reporting" strategy used in information systems shares the same rationale of Shannon's information theory, that is, messages about abnormal situations are more informative and more important for the end-users.

Any useful message has its meaning. This semantic aspect has recently been studied by some researchers [8]. The existing theory provides profound insights into this challenging problem, but does not offer a solution yet. Methods to evaluate the semantic information of messages are not available. Instead, there exist different empirical techniques, such as using key words, subjects or templates to index or classify messages, which help end-user to access information more effectively. These methods are commonly used in applications where conventions (of indexing, e.g.) can be easily setup and used [4].

Messages can also be examined by the consequences they may cause, such as the value or cost of information in economical sense [9]. Although desirable, it is hard to evaluate a message, and thus intractable in practice to have a system organizing messages by value.

In general, human's concern about information can not be characterized by any single aspect, rather it is a mixture of them. Human information processing is also affected by a number of other unquantifiable factors (e.g., social or cognitive ones). What determines the importance of a message is often fuzzy and even subconscious, and it is of high uncertainty and complexity to existing understanding. Therefore, it is difficult to devise message prioritization methods based on theories of human information processing. Instead, we can develop computer support schemes which learn from the end-users, and prioritize messages according to their information acquisition features. This motivates the development of the adaptive support scheme in this paper.

3. A GENERIC MESSAGE PRIORITIZATION PROBLEM

A message in any format can be viewed as a representation of the state of an activity, such as the progress of a project, the working condition of a machine, or the geographical location of a battle unit. The end-user's information acquisition is based on his concerns about the activities. Intuitively he would be most interested in messages about the most concerned activity. Therefore it is helpful to arrange messages of the most concerned activities in an easily accessible set so as to prevent redundant (unlikely to be read) messages from blurring needed information, and also ensure that the most wanted information is acquired when the user does not have time or patience to search through the messages.

The end-user's concern (information need or preference) about different activities is, however, unknown and stochastic. The user may neither always access messages about the most concerned activity, nor always ignore messages about the least concerned activity. The saving feature is that the end-user is more likely to access messages of a concerned activity than

reflects what he is concerned about, and to what degree. The following gives a simple formulation of the problem.

Consider a set of N independent activities $\{A_1, A_2, ..., A_N\}$. Each time, the system presents a particular message to the user about each activity. There are N messages in total to cover the whole situation. The number of messages the end-user may access each time is affected by many unknown factors, and can be at best treated as a random variable. Assume the average is M, reflecting that the end-user may access M messages on the average at each information acquisition epoch.

The user's concern about the N activities can be described by an unknown vector $C = \{c_1, c_2, ..., c_N\}$, where the element c_i represents the probability that the user reads messages about activity A_i. The sum of $\{c_i\}$ represents the average number of accessed messages, which is bounded by the end-user's limited capability M, i.e.,

$$\sum_{i=1}^{N} c_i \leq M. \tag{1}$$

To facilitate the end-user's information acquisition, consider that the system may have a limited priority message set, which is attention-catching and easily accessible. The priority set is sized according to the user's capability. Without loss of generality, assume that the priority set has an average size equal to the user's information acquisition capacity, i.e., M messages. For a particular time, the set may contain more or less priority messages around the average number. This is consistent with the fact that the number of high priority reports is not fixed but generally confined to accommodate the user's capacity in information processing. Now the challenge is to devise a message prioritization scheme which can distinguish and rank-order the end-user's concerns about the activities and to report the most concerned in the priority set.

4. AN ADAPTIVE MESSAGE PRIORITIZATION SCHEME

The focal issue to realize the aforementioned scheme is to learn what activities should be covered in the priority set from the user's feedback information. Such a problem falls nicely into the domain of learning automaton. The following first introduces the concepts of learning automaton without getting into mathematical details.

4.1 Learning Automaton

A learning automaton consists of two components: a stochastic automaton which makes decisions, and a random environment which responds to the decisions [10]. Given a set of alternative actions, the automaton decides which action to take. The chosen action is the input to the environment which usually responds in a binary manner, indicating whether the action is right or wrong. The environment is, however, probabilistic. It may not judge any action as definitely right or wrong. The important feature is that the environment's negative responses have the least probability for the correct actions. The automaton is expected to learn the most correct action -- action with the highest probability to be right.

The stochastic automaton attempts a solution of this problem adaptively. To start with, no information on the actions is assumed, and equal probabilities are attached to all the alternatives. One action is selected at random, and the response of the environment to this action is observed. Based on this response the action probabilities are updated according to certain reinforcement scheme. For example, the probability for choosing the action is increased if the response is positive, otherwise, the probability is decreased. Then a new action is selected according to the updated action probabilities, and the procedure is repeated. In the past decade, different schemes have been developed and applied to solve various problems, such as telephone traffic routing [10]. Here the principle is applied to develop a message prioritizing scheme to support human computer interaction.

4.2 End-User as the "Random Environment"

In our problem, the end-user is provided with N messages about the N activities each time. With limited capability, he may choose a portion of the messages to read. As discussed above, the user's information acquisition is probabilistic, that is, there is a non-zero probability for any message to be read or ignored. For more concerned activities, the user would regard the messages to be more important, and need to access them more frequently. On the other hand, the frequency the end-user accesses messages about an activity reflects his concern to it.

By treating the messages as inputs and the processing status (read or not) of the messages as output, the user's information acquisition can be described as the "random environment". Let S = {s_1, s_2, ..., s_N} denote the message presentation pattern, where $s_i = 1$ if activity A_i is reported in a priority set, otherwise $s_i = 0$. Let X = {x_1, x_2, ..., x_N} denote the vector of user's response to the messages. The variable $x_i = 1$ if the message about A_i is read by the user, otherwise $x_i = 0$. Note that the user may read messages both in and out of the priority message set. This is equivalent to that the environment may give hints on unselected actions. The probability that the end-user may read messages about A_i is c_i, and the interest vector C = {c_1, c_2, ..., c_N} denotes the user's responding probability vector toward the messages. The vector is subject to the capacity constraint (1).

The computer support scheme is to report the most concerned activities in the limited priority set. The user's responding probability C={c_i} is not known, and it is incumbent on the system to learn and improve message presentation according to the user's message accessing pattern.

4.3 Message Prioritization as the "Stochastic Automaton"

Given N activities to be reported, the system needs to determine the presentation pattern S from the feedback information X. The support scheme is to improve its message prioritizing strategy by changing the probabilities for different activities to be reported in the priority set. Let v_i be the probability for A_i being reported in the priority set, i.e., $v_i = prob\{s_i = 1\}$. Vector V = {v_1, v_2, ..., v_N} denote the prioritizing probability vector.

The support system can be modeled as a stochastic automaton with input vector X and output vector S. Both inputs and outputs are binary variables. To maintain the size of the priority set, the prioritizing probability vector V is subject to the following constraint,

$$\sum_{i=1}^{N} v_i \leq M. \tag{2}$$

Of interest is to find the reinforcement scheme by which the computer system improves its message prioritizing vector V in the process of making choices S and receiving responses X.

4.4 Reinforcement Scheme

First note the following two distinct points: 1. the conventional learning automaton deals with a single input-output pair [10], while our problem has multiple inputs and multiple outputs (vectors), and 2. the action probabilities in conventional learning automaton is from one probability space, and sum up to one, while the prioritizing probability vector V is about different probability events and subject to the constraint (2). These two features need to be incorporated in the reinforcement scheme to maintain a balanced increase and decrease of the prioritizing probabilities.

Studies in learning automaton have yielded various updating schemes with expediency or convergence (ε-optimal) properties [10]. Adopting linear reward penalty method, here we consider a simple reinforcement scheme,

$$v_i(k+1) = v_i(k) + a(k)[v_i(k)+e], \text{ if } x_i = 1, \tag{3}$$
$$v_i(k+1) = v_i(k) - b(k)[1-v_i(k)+e], \text{ if } x_i = 0, \tag{4}$$

where $a(k)$ and $b(k)$ are updating parameters, and e is a small constant. The updating parameters are not independent because of the constraint (2). Assume that the value of $a(k)$ is pre-determined as a constant a_c. Let $R(k) = \{i, \text{ for } x_i=1\}$ denote the message set read by the user at the time k Then to maintain the priority set size the value of $b(k)$ can be determined

$$b(k) = a_c \sum_{i \in R(k)} v_i(k) \Big/ \sum_{i \notin R(k)} v_i(k) \qquad \qquad (5)$$

The updating is also subject to the natural probability constraint: $0 < v_i < 1$, for $i = 1, 2, ..., N$. The small constant e in (3-4) is used to prevent the updating from being stuck before it reaches the desired solution, and to keep the updating alert to possible changes in the user's interest C. With $e=0$, a v_i will remain unchanged once it becomes 1 or 0, and the scheme may be trapped.

4.5 Implementation Issues

Given the resulting probability vector V, there may be different ways to decide what to report in the priority set. Naturally, we can choose priority messages probabilistically based on the vector V. We can also combine with some practical features. For example, managers of N projects need to send messages (reports) to a senior manager through a computer system. The messages may be rated in different importance levels by the project managers. The project manager's rating only reflects their local views on messages about particular projects, which may be different from the senior manager's global concerns across projects. The senior manager's concerns are learned and reflected in the prioritizing vector V. Combining the global and local aspects, the probability v_i the chance for the senior manager to access project i, can be secured for messages of the highest importance. This method shares the rationale of exception-reporting. Another way is to choose a threshold, and to report an activity in the priority set if its prioritizing probability is greater than the threshold. This will stablize the message presentation (not frequently change priority set).

5. A NUMERICAL EXAMPLE

Consider a simple information acquisition example with twelve activities. The end-user is able to receive three out of the twelve messages on the average. So the average size of the priority set is three. The end-user's interest (vector C) to the activities is assumed in the table,

Table 1. End-user's interest (vector C) on the twelve activities

A	A_1	A_2	A_3	A_4	A_5	A_6	A_7	A_8	A_9	A_{10}	A_{11}	A_{12}
C: $1<k<200$	0.38	0.11	0.66	0.44	0.15	0.09	0.27	0.20	0.18	0.11	0.29	0.13
C: $200<k<400$	0.38	0.11	0.66	0.11	0.15	0.09	0.27	0.20	0.18	0.44	0.29	0.13

The user's interest to different activities spread quite evenly. For the most concerned activity A_3, the user may access its messages with probability 0.66. The lowest probability is near 0.1. For the three most interested activities, the user allocates less than half of his attention. This arrangement aims to test the scheme's ability in soliciting the most concerned activities in an unclear circumstance. The simulation runs 400 steps. Within the interval $1<k<200$, activities A_1, A_3, and A_4 are the most interested. At the time 200, the user's concern to activity A_4 and A_{10} is swapped. This arrangement intends to test the scheme's adaptivity.

To start with, the system assumes equal probabilities to report the activities in the priority set. The user would read the messages according to his interest probability vector (unknown to the updating scheme). From such information, the system updates the prioritizing probability vector by the above reinforcement scheme (3-5). In the simulation, $a_c = 0.5$, and $e = 0.2$. Figure 1 shows the major prioritizing probabilities v_1, v_3, v_4, and v_{10}.

The results show that the reinforcement scheme can improve the message presentation effectively. It is also able to track the change of the end-user's information need on different activities. The scheme takes less than 50 steps to single out the three most concerned activities. Moreover, the value of parameter a_c can be increased to speed up the adaptation. The tradeoff is larger ripples in the prioritizing probabilities. If the user's interest is more concentrated (more focused), the adaptive scheme will yield better performance.

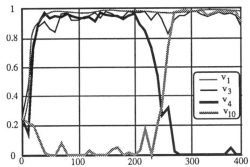

Figure 1. Prioritizing probabilities -- v_1, v_3, v_4, and v_{10}

6. CONCLUDING REMARKS

Information overload is an increasingly concerned issue. In a broad perspective, it is not only a problem for senior managers or high rank officers, but also a problem to ordinary computer end-users. People are experiencing an increasing number of electronic messages, and electronic information services. The information filtration and prioritization work, which used to be carried out by experienced humans including end-users themselves, has to be supported by computer systems.

This paper presents a simple approach to formulate human information acquisition problems, and develops an adaptive message prioritization scheme. The scheme learns about the user's information needs, and report the most concerned activities in a priority message set. The salient feature of the scheme is its simplicity. It requires little a priori knowledge of the human users, and does not intrude their operations. This work is applicable, with possible modifications, to a variety of prioritization problems where messages can be categorized into different classes. It may also be combined with other methods, such as using key words, to develop effective computer support systems which can perform message filtration and prioritization functions more effectively.

7. REFERENCES

1. J.F. George, J.F. Nunamaker, and J.S. Valacich, *Decision Support Systems*, 8, (1992) 307.
2. J. Martin, *Information Systems Manifesto*, Prentice-Hall, Inc., New Jersey, 1984.
3. J.P. Kahan, D.R. Worley, and C. Stasz, *Understanding Commanders' Information Needs*, RAND/R-3761-A, Santa Monica, CA: RAND, Arroyo Center, 1989.
4. T.W. Malone, K.R. Grant, F.A. Turbak, S.A. Brost, and M.D. Cohen, *Communications of the ACM*, 30 (1987) 390.
5. J.A. Ricketts and R.R. Nelson, *Information Management*, 12 (1987) 235.
6. H.A. Simon, *Models of Bounded Rationality: Behavioral Economics and Business Organization*, The MIT Press, Cambridge, MA, 1982
7. R.J. Mceliece, *The Theory of Information and Coding*, Addison-Wesley Publishing Company, London, 1977
8. G. Jumarie, *Relative Information: Theories and Applications*, Springer-Verlag, New York, 1990.
9. J. Marschak, *Economic Information, Decision, and Prediction, Volume II: Economics of Information and Organization*, D. Reidel Publishing Company, Dordrecht-Holland, 1974.
10. K. Narendra and M. Thathachar, *Learning Automata: An Introduction*, Prentice-Hall, Inc., New Jersey, 1989

Medical diagnostic expert system

Renu Vig, Deepak Bagai and Y.C. Chopra

Electronics and Electrical Communication Department, Punjab Engineering College, Chandigarh, India

Abstract

The expert system presented in this paper consists of a fuzzy rule base. Assuming a matrix representation of rules, a rule based system has been developed in Turbo-Prolog for finding anemia in a person. The final diagnosis is given by the rule with highest confidence factor. Since most cases are not classic ones and exceptions, seem to recur in medicine, a system that can make use of previous experience is suggested. Such a system can cut down on its work by using previous cases to suggest a solution to a new but similar case, rather than starting from scratch each time.

1. FUZZY SETS

In expert systems, facts and rules are concepts and relations between concepts, respectively. Concepts play an important role in knowledge representation. How to select concepts is very important for a successful representation. Another problem is how to represent new concepts based on old concepts. Fuzzy sets can be used to capture the vagueness and imprecision of natural concepts [4]. Furthermore, fuzzy sets and natural concepts have a similar group of operations. Mathematically speaking, the category of concepts is equivalent to the category of fuzzy set (V) and concepts can be represented by fuzzy sets.

After giving the truth value set (V), typically $V = [0, 1]$, the most important and interesting problem is to select the universe for representation. There is a similar problem in the representation of rules. A rule, if $p(u)$ then $q(u)$, is valid if and only if the following inclusion holds :

$$P = \{ u \,|\, p(u) \text{ true } \} \subseteq$$
$$Q = \{ u \,|\, q(u) \text{ true } \}$$

For example, the rule "if a tomato is red then it is ripe" can be represented by $P \subseteq Q$, where P = red tomatoes and Q = ripe tomatoes as well as by the two factors "colour" and "ripeness". So, knowledge can be represented based on factor space. Every factor corresponds to a universe X_α in which α takes possible values depending on various objects. For example if α = "haemoglobin" then X may be a set of linguistic labels { high, normal, low, very high, very low}. X_α is called the state space of α. The collection of all state spaces indexed by all related factors is called a factor space.

Sr No	HGLN	HMCT	MCV	MCHC	RCC	WBC	PLT	NRC	SEI	TIBC	HSWC	RCBM	DIAGNOSIS
1.	v.low	v.low	normal	normal	low	v.low	v.low	n.prsnt	normal	normal	n.prsnt	n-prsnt	APLASTIC_ANEMIA
2.	low	low	normal	normal	low	normal	normal	prsnt	normal	normal	n-prsnt	n-prsnt	MYLOPHTHISIC-ANEMIA
3	v.low	v.low	low	normal	low	normal	normal	n-prsnt	low	low	n-prsnt	n-prsnt	ANEMIA_CHRONIC_DISEASE
4	v.low	v.low	high	normal	low	normal	normal	n-prsnt	normal	normal	prsnt	n-prsnt	MEGALOBLESTIC_ANEMIA
5	v.low	v.low	low	low	low	normal	normal	n-prsnt	low	high	n-prsnt	n-prsnt	IRON_DEFICIENCY_ANEMIA
6	low	low	normal	low	normal	normal	normal	n-prsnt	high	high	prsnt	prsnt	SIDEROBLASTIC_ANEMIA
7	low	low	normal	normal	low	v.low	normal	n-prsnt	normal	normal	n-prsnt	n-prsnt	APLASTIC_ANEMIA
8	low	low	normal	normal	low	low	low	prsnt	normal	normal	prsnt	n-prsnt	MYLOPHTHISIC_ANEMIA
9	low	low	normal	normal	normal	normal	normal	n-prsnt	normal	low	n-prsnt	n-prsnt	ANEMIA_CHRONIC_DISEASE
10	low	low	high	normal	low	low	low	n-prsnt	normal	normal	prsnt	prsnt	MEGALOBLESTIC_ANEMIA
11	low	low	low	low	low	normal	normal	n-prsnt	low	high	n-prsnt	n-prsnt	IRON_DEFICIENCY_ANEMIA
12	low	low	high	low	high	normal	normal	n-prsnt	high	high	n-prsnt	prsnt	SIDEROBLASTIC_ANEMIA

Figure 1. Rule matrix.

Facts are propositions that express existing relationships between concepts and objects in a universe. A fact may be a combination of several simple facts. A simple fact is a proposition of the form :

$$A \text{ is } B \, (A \subseteq B)$$

where A and B are fuzzy subsets of the universe U and A_α and B_α are subsets of the state space X_α of the factor α. For example for α = "haemoglobin", A may be the range [4,20] and B may be a set of linguistics [high, normal, low, very high, very low].

2. ANEMIA DIAGNOSIS

The fuzzy knowledge base comprises of fuzzy subsets of all factors of anemia. A matrix representation of rules has been assumed as shown in Fig.1. Regarding the uncertainty of the rules there are three cases :
a)   rules are certain and the antecedent and consequent are precisely defined;
b)   rules are uncertain but the antecedent and consequent are precisely defined;
c)   the antecedent or the consequent is imprecise.

Calculation of CF for Anemia Diagnosis

S.No.	TRUTH VALUES Factors												Diagnosis
1	1.0	1.0	0.3	0.3	1.0	0.7	0.4	1.0	0.2	0.3	1	1	0.2
2	1.0	1.0	0.3	0.3	1.0	1.0	1.0	0	0.2	0.3	1	1	0
3	1.0	1.0	0.9	0.3	1.0	1.0	1.0	1.0	1.0	0	1	1	0
4	1.0	1.0	0	0.3	1.0	1.0	1.0	1.0	0.2	0.3	0	1	0
5	1.0	1.0	0.9	0.9	1.0	1.0	1.0	1.0	1.0	1.0	1	1	0.9
6	1.0	1.0	0.3	0.9	0	1.0	1.0	1.0	0	1.0	1	0	0
7	1.0	1.0	0.3	0.3	1.0	0.7	0.4	1.0	0.2	0.3	1	1	0.2
8	1.0	1.0	0.3	0.3	1.0	0.6	0.4	0	0.2	0.3	1	1	0
9	1.0	1.0	0.3	0.3	0	1.0	1.0	1.8	0.2	0	1	1	0
10	1.0	1.0	0	0.3	1.0	0.6	0.9	1.0	0.2	0.3	0	1	0
11	1.0	1.0	0.9	0.9	1.0	1.0	1.0	1.0	1.0	1.0	1	1	0.9
12	1.0	1.0	0	0.9	0	1.0	1.0	1.0	0	1.0	1	0	0

Aplastic Anemia   CF   0.2
Mylophthisic Anemia   CF   0.0
Anemia-Chronic-Disease   CF   0.0
Megaloblestic Anemia   CF   0.0
Iron-Deficiency Anemia   CF   0.9
Sideroblastic Anemia   CF   0.0
Final Diagnosis = Anemia due to Iron Deficiency (0.9)

Figure 2. Anemia diagnosis.

Case (a) may be treated using classical logic methods. Case (b) may be treated using statistical approach. The treatment of case (c) is the main task of fuzzy reasoning methods. In fuzzy reasoning, there are two steps:

1.   First to obtain the truth value of the rule from the truth values of the antecedent and consequence.

2.   From the truth values of the rule and the fact to get the truth value of the result.

The general form of a fuzzy production rule is :

$$\text{If } F \ (CF = X) \text{ then } C \ (CF = Y)$$

where F represents the antecedent portion of the rule containing fuzzy quantifiers and C represents the consequent. From the matrix representation of rules, CF of each diagnosis can be found from CF values of various factors. For example, Aplastic Anemia (CF) is found as follows using fuzzy logic:

$$\text{Aplastic - Anemia (CF)} = \min \{ \text{HGLN (CF), HMCT (CF),}$$
$$\text{MCV (CF), MCHC (CF), RCC (CF), ..., } \}$$

Then, CF of final diagnosis is maximum of CF of various rules.

As an example, say the following measurement is noted for various factors:

HGLN - Very Low; HMCT - Very Low; MCV - Low, MCHC - Low, RCC - Very Low, WBC - Normal, PLT - Normal, NRC - Not present, SEI - Very low, TIBC - High, HSWC - Not present, RSBM - Not present.

The matrix giving the CF values of various factors and rules is shown in Fig.2.

3. ROLE OF EXPERIENCE

When a doctor observes a patient and takes a preliminary history, he builds up an impression of the primary considerations in diagnosis. Based on similarities between a new patient and other patients the doctor has seen, an impression is formed. With the help of fuzzy knowledge base for various symptoms and a rule base matrix based on past experience a diagnosis can be reached at. Different symptoms represent factors such as fever, running nose, cough, etc. Fever in the range [$95^{\circ}F$ to $105^{\circ}F$] will take up the linguistic set [high, normal, low, very high, very low]. Similarity between the current and past case can be computed as follows :

$$S \ (F, M) = \frac{F.M}{\max \ (F.F, M.M)}$$

where F gives the values of membership of the fuzzy set contained in a rule and M represent those of the observed fact. In this case, rule will be obtained from previous experience.

For experience to improve problem solving skills, the problem solving system must provide for acquisition and evaluation of feedback. Experience includes both making a decision and evaluating its outcome. A reasoner that suggests solutions to problems but never knows the outcome of its suggestions has no basis for evaluating its decisions. It cannot, therefore, be counted on to correct past errors or dependably suggest new solutions based on old ones. As new features of a case are learnt during the course of a problem solving episode, the case is better integrated into memory, resulting in additional, more similar, and more applicable cases being made available for reasoning. In general, particular past experiences called to mind by a current problem can be useful in the following manner:

1. They can aid in problem understanding by suggesting additional features to be investigated or by pointing out alternative classifications.

2. They can help in planning by suggesting solutions or courses of action to be followed or avoided.

3. They can suggest an explanation for and a means of recovery from failure.

4. UNCERTAIN EVIDENCE

Practically when faced with a patient, a doctor cannot usually give a definite and unique identification of the illness. This does not indicate a lack of ability or intelligence on the doctor's part. It is more because the only evidence which a doctor has to follow is the symptoms observed, and this often is insufficient to identify the illness uniquely. Several illnesses may produce similar symptoms, in the early stages at least, and some diseases do not produce all the symptoms in the early stages. So when working backwards from the symptoms, a doctor must consider several possibilities. It may be, of course, that some of these possibilities are more likely than others. So the result of a diagnosis could well be a list of possible diseases, with some indication of how likely each is. The information can therefore be extended for each illness by including a measure of how common or likely it is. The most convenient way to do this is to specify its probability.

Even if the probability likelihood is included in the description, the information is not enough to arrive at a reliable conclusion. There are two main reasons for this. If we are considering the likelihood of the patient having a particular illness, then:

1. A patient can have a disease without necessarily showing all the symptoms of that disease, perhaps because the symptoms have not all been developed yet.

2. A patient can have some of the symptoms of an illness, but not acutally have that disease. This could be because the symptoms result from a different disease, which has some symptoms in common.

When someone is ill, all the expected symptoms may not be displayed necessarily. Some symptoms are more likely to appear than others. Some may be definitely expected. So, it is very significant, if they are not observed. Each symptom needs to be weighed in proportion to how likely it is to be observed. The weight factor should be included for every symptom in the list. To accomodate this information, the description of the symptom needs to be extended as follows:

symptom (name, weight factor)

A symptom is rarely unique for a single disease. One which is common to several diseases may not be as helpful as one which is unique to a particular disease. So, some symptoms of a disease will be more informative than others. Each symptom will now have to be weighed to give an indication of its uniqueness. A symptom which is relatively common will tell us less than one which is comparatively rare. The weight factor is the probability that the symptom results from some other illness and not the one under consideration. Symptom is now described as follows :

symptom (name, weight factor 1, weight factor 2)

Weight factor 1 is the probability that the symptom will be observed in someone who has this disease. Weight factor 2 is the probability that the symptom will be observed in someone who does not have this disease. Consider the rule hypothesis (influenza) :-

symptom (runny-nose, 90, 40).

The above rule indicates that 90% of people who have influenza have a runny nose. Also, 40% of patients who have runny nose have it for some reason other than influenza. So, the knowledge base will be complete if both the weight factors are available for each symptom from a medical expert.

The process of estimating how likely a patient will have a disease is a repetitive one, beginning with an initial estimate and gradually working towards a more accurate answer. More systematically the diagnostic process is as follows :

* Start with the initial probability
* Consider the symptoms one at a time
* For each symptom, update the current probability, taking into account :
  - Whether or not the patient has the symptom
  - The weight factors 1 and 2.

The awkward stage of this process is clearly updating the probability in the light of each piece of new evidence. This is the heart of the inference engine. In particular, what should be the adjustment numerically? How is the sequence of revised estimates arrived at? Is it a guess work? Fortunately this problem can be solved by using Bayes theorem. If weight factor 1 is denoted by Py and weight factor 2 by Pn and P is the current probability of hypothesis then :

* If the patient has the symptom

$$\text{new probability} = \frac{100 * Py * P}{Py * P + Pn(100-P)} \qquad 3.1$$

* If the patient does not have the symptom,

$$\text{new probability} = \frac{100 * (100-Py) * P}{(100-Py) * P + (100-Pn)(100-P)} \qquad 3.2$$

To acquire knowledge in this form is going to be tedious.

5. REFERENCES

1. Janet L. Kolodner and Robert M. Kolodner, "Using Experience in Clinical Problem Solving", IEEE Transactions on Systems, Man and Cybernetics, Vol. SMC- 17, No.3, May/June 1987.

2. Peter N. Marino, "Fuzzy Logic and its Application to Switching Systems", IEEE Transactions on Computers, Vol.C-18, No.4, April, 1979.

3. William F. Funch III, "Large Interactions of Compiled and Causal Reasoning in Diagnosis", IEEE Expert, 1992.

4. Xiantu T. Peng. Abraham Kandel and Peizhuang Wang, "Concepts, Rules and Fuzzy Reasoning: A Factor Space Approach", IEEE. Transactions on systems, Man and Cybernetics, Vol.21, No.1, January/February, 1991.

Supporting Instead of Replacing the Planner - An Intelligent Assistant System for Factory Layout Planning

Jürgen Herrmann[a] and Matthias Kloth[b]

a   Universität Dortmund, Informatik I, 44221 Dortmund, Germany

b   Fraunhofer-Institute for Materialflow and Logistics,
    Joseph-von-Fraunhofer-Str. 2-4, 44227 Dortmund, Germany

ABSTRACT
A new, interactive approach for software tools supporting real-world design tasks is presented. The intelligent design assistant provides analysis information about the current and previous design states and can perform single design steps automatically. Explanations about design decisions make these steps transparent to the user. An adaptable user interface supports the planner's design style. The system has been applied successfully to factory layout planning.

1. INTRODUCTION

Increasing requirements in the working process with growing complexity require for more and more support by computers. Nowadays, even for complex design tasks like factory layout planning software tools are available. However, current software tools for complex real world problems are often organized in the wrong way: They automate the considered task (or parts of it) instead of supporting the problem solving process performed by the expert. In this way a tool provides a more or less sufficient replacement for the user's work, often with limited usefulness. These systems decrease the acceptance and conceal the hazard of long-term dequalification of the users [1]. Intelligent assistant systems [2-5] are organized in an alternative way and can be integrated into the daily work of the planner without effort.

2. CURRENT TOOLS FOR LAYOUT PLANNING

Facilities planning or, in a narrower sense, layout planning is a task planners have to deal with during the design or redesign of factories [6]. As the requirements of working processes grow, the planning and design of factory layouts become more complex. Different sub tasks of the facilities planning or layout design processes are, e.g., the selection of conveyer and storage technologies, the determination of the production type and structure, and the positioning of components on the basic floorspace. The result of the design process is a detailed facilities' layout that represents the assembly and the production process organization. Multiple objectives that can only partly be formalized have to be considered. Planners need much intuition and creativity besides their domain-specific qualification to be able to integrate the requirements and restrictions that cannot be determined in advance into the solution.

Current tools try to automate layout planning in a very restricted way. One of the main disadvantages of existing facilities planning systems is the reduction of the whole problem to mathematical, formal aspects - in this case the allocation problem (see Fig. 1). This problem takes into consideration an optimized allocation of objects (e.g., production areas or machines) to each other or onto a basic floorspace [7]. The quality of the solution is described by a quantitative function that represents the dependencies between these objects. Additionaly, because of the complexity, existing layout planning systems are only able to handle a restricted, one-dimensional optimizing function. This insufficient combination of methods (algorithms) with the abilities and requirements of the planners questions the quality of support provided by such layout planning systems [8]. If the planners wants to use the calculated results, they must modify them according to the other objectives and their preferences.

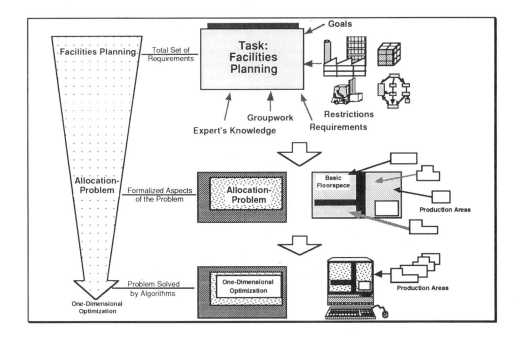

Figure 1: Software development as problem-reduction

Although new software-technologies as expert systems provide the technical potentials to design user-oriented, one can establish that such systems are built as complete problem-solving systems [9,10]. This mode of use stands for the attempt to generate a complete solution with the consequence that the users often are degraded to data typists. Afterwards, these users have to mend the systems solution because even knowledge-based methods are not able to take into account all requirements of a complex planning task (e.g., group work, lean production or aesthetical aspects). Together with an insufficient transparency, such "complete" problem solving systems have a low acceptance and can lead finally to the long-term dequalification of the users [1].

As a result of the deficient consideration of the requirements for planning tasks neither the methods and strategies of a planner are regarded nor is such a system able to reflect the models and images of the planner. Accordingly, the planners are not able to integrate the system into their daily work flow. To reach an adequate integration, the working methods and the models of the planners must be represented and supported. The users must be able to understand the system and to get a fitting mental image of it. A way to reach a corresponding transparency and usability are alternative guiding models for software development and software engineering.

3. CONCEPTION OF AN INTELLIGENT ASSISTANT SYSTEM

To overcome the limitations of current layout planning tools in this paper a new, interactive approach is presented that is based on the principles listed below. The goal of the layout planning system's organization is to support the planner's strength and provide an adequate and flexible distribution of tasks and functions between user and system, leaving the control of the problem solving process in the hands of the user. He or she can select how much support is needed for each sub task and can use the system as an intelligent assistant [2-5] integrated into the daily work of the planner. It provides different functions and modes of use that enhance and ease the user's work.

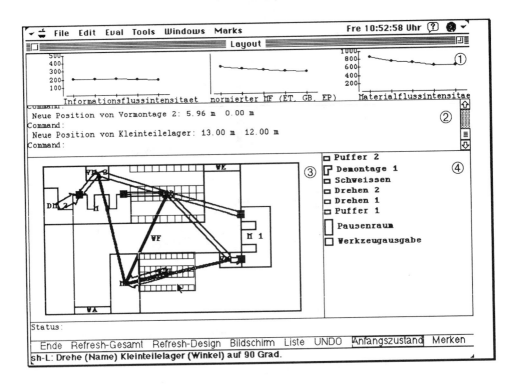

Figure 2: Graphical User Interface of the Assistant for Logistic-Oriented Layout Planning

- Representation of the current design state and the design history
  The graphical representation of the current state (see Figure 2) is oriented towards the methods and metaphors the user is acquainted with, e.g., the "Draw-And-Rub-Out-Method". In this way the assistant is embedded into the user's every-day problem solving

procedure. In Window ③ the current state of the layout planning process is displayed graphically and the different material flow activities are visualized by means of distinct line widths. The ordered list of means of operations to be arranged is shown in Window ④. In Window ② messages about the status of the planning process are printed out.

Selected previous design states are represented that enable a comfortable backtracking and a comparison of different states. Analysis information about different aspects of the most recent design states is visualized graphically in Window ①.

- Analysis of design states

To evaluate a design state the consistency (according to several kinds of constraints) is checked. Evaluation functions deliver information about the quantitative objectives (e.g., used area, material flow). Using the analysis functions the planner can compare the quality of different design states. This makes it easy for him or her to concentrate on the informal, qualitative objectives that depend on his/her design experience and cannot be handled by the system. There are two different ways the user can backtrack to another design state:

a) *Chronological backtracking:* With this function the user can undo one or several of the most recent design steps and reach a previous design state in that way.

b) *Backtracking to a previously selected design state:* During the work with the system the designer can select important intermediate design states that form reset-points for a non-chronological backtracking and are stored by the system. These design states need not be predecessors of the current design state. Alternatively they can belong to a different design path that has been postponed by the user. In this way the reset-points form the nodes of a tree-like structure with edges representing the is-successor-of relation (see Figure 3). The user can *backtrack* to a reset point or inspect it using the stored evaluation information. Besides that the system can generate an explanation of the design decisions that led to the stored design state (see below). Comparing and evaluating alternative reset points the user can reason about design variants and select the most appropriate one.

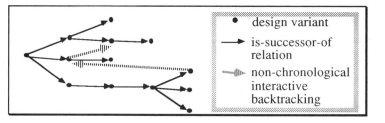

Figure 3: Tree of different design variants (reset points for backtracking).

- Automation of selected sub tasks

The system has problem solving knowledge to perform some sub tasks of layout planning (e.g. placement of a single functional unit). If ordered by the user a single design step or a sequence of steps can be executed by the system that leads to a (possible) new design step. Using this knowledge the planner can evaluate several design alternatives quickly. Currently the system can perform the following sub tasks:

i) *Clustering of the means of operations to be arranged:* The automatic clustering process is guided by background knowledge about the production plans of the factory to be designed. Each production plan describes groups of objects cooperating strongly during a production process. According to this information, clusters of objects are formed that must be placed close to each other during factory layout planning. The use of clusters decreases the complexity of the whole planning process significantly.

ii) *Sorting of the list of means of operation to be arranged:* There are several criteria that influence the priority of the objects to be placed, e.g., the material flow intensity, the sympathy of two areas and the different area sizes. According to a system or user generated priority list for these criteria, the assistant sorts the list of unplaced objects. After each placement of an object, a new design state is reached that differs from the previous one according to these criteria. As a consequence, the order of the unplaced objects is recalculated for each new design state.

iii) *Placement of the next unplaced object:* This operation is performed in two steps: (a) Calculation of an *ideal* position for the object and (b) calculation of a *realizable* position close to the ideal one. The first step is performed by means of a numerical procedure using the intensity of the relations between the new object and already arranged means of operation. A realizable position must satisfy all applicable constraints, e.g., the prevention of overlapping areas. For the second step an approved algorithm is used that searches for the optimal field in the matrix of possible positions. To keep the complexity of this calculation tractable heuristics are applied that determine a set of favorable candidate positions used as an input for the algorithm. In this way knowledge-based and conventional procedures supplement each other.

- Explanation of design decisions

As the users are controlling the whole design process they must comprehend the analysis and design steps performed by the assistant. Furthermore the *explanation* of the planning process that led the final factory layout belongs to the deliverables of a commercial planning project. For that reasons, explanations form an integral part of the planning process that must be supported by an intelligent assistant system.

Existing explanation methods suffer from different problems making them unusable for our purpose [12]:

- Many explanation components in use are restricted to the presentation of the trace of rules that led to the current design state in a reasonably readable form. They cannot provide a deeper explanation of the reasons for the decisions made.
- More sophisticated explanation methods can provide deeper explanations and base on a natural language interface that analyses and answers various questions about the problem solving process, e.g., clarifying the reasons for a decision and the alternatives that were discarded. On the other hand the enormous effort for the implementation of these methods can exceed the development costs for the problem solver to be explained. This prevents their practical application.
- Most explanation methods are restricted to knowledge-based problem solvers. The explanation of algorithmic procedures that are used in our system, e.g., for the positioning of objects, is not possible.

For the layout planning assistant a new explanation component has been developed that avoids the problems listed above.

The explanation component provides *different* kinds of information about the system. It increases the transparency of the domain and the system's structure and clarifies the dynamic problem solving process based on a new four-staged representation:

1) A help-module that delivers introductory information about all parts of the system.
2) Dynamically generated explanations about the current knowledge-based *or* algorithmic design steps based on a list of different kinds of questions supported by the explanation component
3) Background knowledge about the system (e.g. underlying design school).
4) Information about the principal entities of the domain.

- Adaptation and extension of the system

To support the planner's design style, a system must be adaptable to his or her needs. The system supports the reconfiguration of the graphical user interface. Currently there are 15 evaluation functions that analyze the design states. The user can select the three or four ones that are displayed in the graphical user interface (see Window ① in Figure 2). The integration of new evaluation functions into the assistant is supported, too. A special editor features the construction of new evaluation functions from basic evaluation aspects.

A knowledge acquisition component (not yet integrated into the system) features the flexible extension of design state representations and problem solving knowledge. Using machine learning methods the system will acquire general design rules from example design steps performed by the user [5].

4. CONCLUSION

A prototype of the layout planning assistant has been implemented [13] and is currently extended. The system demonstrates that an intelligent design aid can support the users' problem solving performance according to their personal wishes instead of degrading them to data typists and debuggers of an automatic problem solver. The intelligent design assistant provides an open work environment available to planners in which they are able to select various modes of support depending on their different requirements and tasks. Moreover, they have the possibility to involve their qualifications and creativity in the problem solving process. In this way planners can make their job with the computer concentrating on their *work* and not on hampering characteristics of the system.

Future enhancements of the assistant will support group decisions and the coordination and management of collaborative design processes.

5. REFERENCES

1   M. Kloth, F. Feldkamp: Zur Aufgaben- und Kompetenzverteilung in der Interaktion zwischen Expertensystemen und ihren Benutzern; in: Publishing Series of the Technical Assessment Project „Changes of Knowledge Production and Knowledge Distribution Of Expert Systems" of the AI-Association NRW, Bonn, März 1991

2   P. Hoschka, P. Wißkirchen: Assistenzcomputer; in: GMD-Spiegel 1/90, pp. 20-25

3   G. A. Boy: Intelligent Assistant Systems; Academic Press; London, San Diego, New York, 1991

4   J. Herrmann, B. Reusch: Combining Expert Systems and Machine Learning in CAD Systems for Micro Electronics; Proc. of the Int. Workshop on AI Applications to CAD Systems for Electronics, Okt. 1987

5   J. Herrmann, R. Beckmann: LEFT - A Learning Tool for Early Floorplanning; Proceedings of the 18th Euromicro Conference (Special Issue of Microprocessing and Microprogramming), Paris 1992

6   J. A. Tompkins, J. A. White: Facilities Planning. John Wiley & Sons, New York 1984

7   R. Burkard: The asymptotic probabilistic behavior of quadratic sum assignment problems; in: Zeitschrift für Operation Research 23, 1979, pp. 73 - 81

8   W. Dangelmeier: Interaktive Anordnungsplanung; in: Fördertechnik 5/1990

9   E. L. Fisher: An AI-Based Methodology for Factory Design. In: AI Magazine, Fall 1986, pp. 72 - 85

10 O. Akin, B. Dave, S. Pithavadian: Heuristic Generation of Layouts. In: J. S. Gero (ed.): Artificial Intelligence in Engineering. Elsevier, Amsterdam, Oxford, New York, Tokio, 1988, pp. 413 - 444

11 W. Dangelmeier: Algorithmen und Verfahren zur Erstellung innerbetrieblicher Anordnungspläne; Springer Verlag, Berlin, Heidelberg, New York, Tokio, 1986

12 W. Coy, L. Bonsiepen: Erfahrung und Berechnung - Kritik der Expertensystemtechnik; Springer Verlag (Informatik Fachberichte 229), Berlin, Heidelberg, 1989

13 M. Kloth, I. Land, J. Herrmann: Ein wissensbasiertes Assistenzsystem für die Fabriklayoutplanung, 22. GI Jahrestagung "Information als Produktionsfaktor", 1992

PREVENTING HUMAN ERRORS IN SKILLED ACTIVITIES THROUGH A COMPUTERIZED SUPPORT SYSTEM

M. Masson and V. De Keyser

Université de Liège, FAPSE, 5 Bld du Rectorat, B 32, Sart-Tilman, Liège, Belgium

Abstract

For a human operator, gaining expertise not only involves the acquisition of knowledge regarding his technical and social environments, but also the progressive development of large repertoires of process experiences acquired through practice.

Expertise increases operator overall efficiency by providing highly adapted behaviour *schemata* issued from past experiences. But expertise is unfortunately not free from negative effects, as it introduces a risk of *capture error* or capture by routine (Norman, 1981), even in presence of contradictory evidence in the environment (De Keyser & Woods, 1989 ; Masson & De Keyser, 1992).

Supporting human operators - and particularly expert operators - should not only consider problem solving activities but should thus also include the prevention of *routine errors*, which go along with skill acquisition.

This is precisely the function of CESS (Cognitive Execution Support System), the error prevention prototype presented in this paper.

1. INTRODUCTION

The behaviour of control room operators remains a central component of the safety and reliability of any complex socio-technical system, such as systems for electrical energy production and process industries.

In those large energosystems, where latent risks are very high and the effects of human decisions are often transmitted and amplified by chains of automated control and supervision systems, *human errors* may have dramatic consequences (Masson and De Keyser, 1992).

The technical, economic and social impacts of human errors and system breakdowns are now well known. They have been revealed to a large public in the most spectacular and tragic manner by catastrophes like Tchernobyl, Three Mile Island, Bhopal, Zeebrugge, Teneriffe, Challenger, etc.

Thus there is a need both for understanding the nature of human error and for developing new generations of *Intelligent Decision Support Systems* aimed at detecting, preventing or recovering human failures in a more flexible and comprehensive way.

2. SUPPORT SYSTEMS AND SKILLED ACTIVITIES

Most of the support systems developed today in the domain of man-machine interactions are dedicated to supporting human activities such as diagnosing, planning, situation assessment, estimation and regulation, that mainly resort to *problem solving*.

Problem solving can briefly be defined as any kind of activity requiring a deviation from customary behaviour and involving the mobilization of attentional resources.

As pointed out by Reason (1987, 1990), problem solving activities that are needed to deal with unusual, novel or changed situations for which no compiled knowledge structure is available, are slow, tedious, demanding and error prone. Thus it is *fully* justified, from both an engineering and ergonomical point of view, to try to support those activities in operators or teams of operators.

But as pointed out by several authors in the fields of human factors engineering and applied cognitive psychology like Rasmussen (1987) and Reason (1987), *a substantial part of human activity does not resort to problem solving.*

In fact, we know for example since W. James (1890) that the successful practice of any type of activity results in the gradual devolution or delegation of control from a "high level", closed loop and attention-driven control mode typical of problem solving, to a "low level", open loop and schema-driven processing style characterising *routinized or proceduralized activities*. Devolution of control results in the setting up of what have been called "action demons" or semi-autonomous cognitive processors that progressively acquire a substantial amount of autonomy in the release and control of activity (Reason & Embrey, video tape on Human Error). The more an operator is skilled, the more his activity relies on those ready-to-access and ready-to-use low level knowledge and control structures.

Assistance systems supporting problem solving activities are both needed and justified in circumstances where problem solving activities have to be carried out, which is particularly the case for operators facing unusual and rare situations for which realistic mental models are lacking. However, they lose most of their helping power and utility once activity gets routinized, which is more likely to be the case for skilled operators operating in strongly proceduralized tasks, like process control operations in nuclear power plants and maintenance tasks in process industries.

But because routine activity sometimes fails to match the requirements of the encountered situation, there is *also* a need for developing assistance and error prevention systems aimed at supporting routinised behaviour carried out in familiar environments by skilled operators (Masson & De Keyser, 1992).

3. ROUTINE OR ROUTING ERRORS

Routinization has the double advantage of increasing efficiency and autonomy, by reducing mental workload (Bainbridge, 1989) and of freeing attentional resources from the situation at hand (Reason, 1987, 1990), both in its spatial and temporal components.

With the acquisition of skill, a substantial amount of cognitive activity gets governed by low level control structures, variously called schemata (Bartlett, 1932), scripts (Shank § Abelson, 1977) or frames (Minsky, 1975), which allow to avoid resource consuming problem solving by providing solution frameworks or action sketches experienced in past circumstances. They operate mostly locally in environments corresponding to or *matching* their descriptive elements. Their control action is *situational* and requires the involvement of the attentional control mode through *attentional checkings*, carried out on the running of the activity. In Reason's terms : "In its simplest form, routine action (i.e., well practised tasks carried out in familiar surroundings by skilled operators) can be regarded as comprising segments of preprogrammed behavioural sequences interspersed with attentional checks upon progress, carried out either consciously or preconsciously." (Reason, 1987, p 66). "The control of routine action is thus like a rather curious railway system where all the points are set by default to follow the most popular routes. To change these settings requires a positive attentional act on the part of the driver." (ibid., p 72).

But this attentional system sometimes fails and when it does, the unmonitored skilled behaviour is likely to fall back on a particular - or a mixing of - well established routines. *Those routines can unfortunately be unsuitable for the situation at hand and lead the operator to erroneous perceptions, actions and strategies.*

Erroneous activation of normally highly adapted and efficient activity segments (Norman, 1981) results in what are traditionally called *routine errors*, errors due to habit or inattention errors.

There is thus a kind of "price to pay" for becoming skilled (Reason & Embrey, video tape on Human Error), as those low level cognitive structures controlling activity can be automatically activated in an unsuitable context or in an inappropriate way simply because they were successfully, frequently or recently used in past circumstances, or because they are released by the environment through local calling conditions.

4.   CESS : COGNITIVE EXECUTION SUPPORT SYSTEM
A ROUTINE ERROR PREVENTION PROTOTYPE

4.1.   Role and functions

Introducing an original support system aimed at preventing and/or correcting routine errors in skilled activities is the objective of a research currently carried by M. Masson in the University of Liège.

A software prototype called *Cognitive Execution Support System* [1] has recently been implemented in lisp on a SUN Workstation, on the basis of insights gained in the study of human errors commited in familiar surroundings by skilled people (Masson & De Keyser, 1992 ; Masson, Malaise, Housiaux and De Keyser, 1993).

CESS best applies in circumstances where a familiar and apparently nominal task environment features one or more *changes* that tend to pass unnoticed due to the effects of habit, which generate usually useful but *locally* unsuited expectations in the subjects' mind.

CESS has three generic functions :

1. CESS sketches out anticipatively the way the user perceives and acts or reacts to his task environment by simulating in real time the basics of human routinised behaviour.

CESS thus belongs to the class of *anticipatory systems* (Rosen, 1985).

2. By comparing this expected answer produced by simulation to the requested answer accessed in a data base or computed in real time, CESS warns the user when perceptual or action errors are suspected.

3. In the cases where this preventive warning would fail to avoid slipping, CESS gives the user the opportunity to rectify an erroneous answer before actuating it in the task environment.

According to the version in use, the system thus provides either a *preventive* and/or a *corrective* aid module, both aimed at counteracting *capture errors* (Norman , 1981) as explained in the preceding section.

4.2.   Functioning

CESS works by *sketching out* anticipatively the way the user will perceive and act or react to his task environment, by simulating in real time the basics of human routinized behaviour. The user is then warned when error risks are suspected.

The current prototype works by anticipating its user's behaviour on the basis of a combination of *similarity* and *frequency* criteria (Reason, 1987, 1990), in the way COSIMO simulates knowledge base extraction in an operator confronted with accident conditions (Cacciabue, Decortis, Drozdowicz, Masson, Nordvik, 1992).

In case of routinized activity, the action a subject is the most likely to select is determined both by the resemblance between the local situation and situations framed in memory (the similarity criteria), and by the frequency distribution of those situations in past circumstances (the frequency criteria).

The system accounts for the first resemblance factor by computing and updating, in the course of the task, a *similarity score* between the situation faced by the user and similar exemplars hold in memory. This similarity score is then combined to a *frequency score*, which indicates the number of times those exemplars were experienced in past occasions.

The combination of the similarity and frequency scores gives each candidate situation its final *activation level* (Norman, 1981). When activation reaches a given threshold, the candidate

---

[1] The idea of designing such a system originated when the author was employed by *Aérospatiale Protection Systèmes*, a Subsidiary of the French Aérospatiale Group (Rouhet & Masson, 1991). However, CESS benefits from earlier discussions and theoretical reflections developed in the *Ispra JRC* Group on COSIMO, see particularly (Cacciabue, Decortis, Masson, Nordvik, 1990).

obtaining the highest activation score is selected, according to the *"winner takes all"* principle, as the best candidate for estimating the subject's current perception and action.

This candidate is then evaluated against the current situation. If it appears to be inappropriate or *faulty*, personalized warnings are sent by the *preventive aid module, before* the user has carried out any action on the system.

Errors that would still occur in spite of those preventive warnings are processed by the *corrective aid module* . This module gives the user the possibility to rectify his action before it would be released in the task environment. The corrective aid module thus operates like a *filter* blocking selectively any unsuited action before it can bring about consequences.

4.3. Experimentation and salient results

The CESS concept and its current software architecture were tried out on a population of 130 students aged between 18 and 30, using a very simple and repetitive computerized task favouring routinization : the transcoding of 240 series of 9 letters into corresponding series of digits, using an increasing alphanumerical code.

The series of letters (the stimuli) were of two types : normal and modified series. Modified series featured either one or two letter modifications, the first modification remaining the same in the two changed series.

The number and position of the modified series in the whole set of stimuli were controlled by the experimenter.

The task comprised 228 normal series, 10 series with one letter modification and 2 series featuring two modifications. Modified series appeared on average every 20 series.

10 versions of CESS, including one control version, were tested over 10 subjects each.

Objective and subjective performance scores were used in order to assess the efficiency of the various types of preventive and corrective aids constituting those 10 versions.

Salient results are summarized in the following ten points.

1. Routinization effects can easily be reproduced in laboratory by using a simple and repetitive task, as the one selected in this experiment.

2. Changes (simple modifications) and "changes in changes" (modifications in already modified situations (Masson, 1991)) brought about a significant increase in the overall error rate.

3. The first appearances of the one modification series led to a large increase in the error rate. After some repetitions however, errors turned back to their basic rate, indicating that the modified stimuli were correctly identified and processed. The apparition of the second modification brought about a new sudden increase in the error rate.

4. Errors did not appear at random : the most common erroneous answer given to the one modification series did correspond to the *correct* answer to *normal* series, while the most frequent erroneous answer obtained with the two modification series did correspond to the answer suitable for the one modification series.

Such a result tends to indicate that both the normal and the one change configurations succeeded in getting *routinized* and served in turn as a basis for *coping with a (new) stimulus or situation change.*

5. With a task of that type, CESS has proved to be efficient both at *anticipating the subjects' responses and errors* and consequently at *lowering the error rate.*

6. With the given configuration of task simplicity and regularity, *preventive aids* alone lowered the overall error rate by a factor 10.

7. *Corrective aids* had a still greater impact, with an error reduction factor comprised between 50 and 100, according to the kind of message sent and to the number of correction trials allowed. But corrective aids could also virtually suppress any risk of routine errors, by forcing automatic correction in case of error persistence.

8. *Sound* preventive aids increased the confidence the users had in the capacities and "intelligence" of the error reduction system and, as a corollary, induced in them a collaborative attitude.

9. Preventive aids also decreased the use and need for corrective aids in the course of activity, but were *not sufficient* to achieve a zero error risk level when used alone.

10. In its current version, the system suffers from several ergonomical limitations regarding the user interface. Those limitations are likely to have reduced its efficiency during the experiment.

4.3. Current limitations

In conclusion, this first set of experiments has indicated that CESS was efficient at reducing human errors in a very simple task favouring routinizaion, in spite of its current ergonomical limitations. One can however question the validity and generalization power of the results obtained up till now with the CESS experiments.

Two main restrictions are identified.

1. The first one concerns the population of subjects who participated in those experiments : these were students from the University of Liège, mostly from the Faculty of Psychology. One can effectively wonder if university students do not differ too much and in too many aspects from operators. However, as the kind of task used in those experiments did not require any sort of specific technical ability or expertise, it seems reasonable to guess that no significant difference would have been found between those two categories of subjects.

2. The second restriction concerns the nature of the task itself, and particularly its complexity level. This very simple task was selected in order to easily and quickly allow a switching in cognitive control mode, from full attentional to automated or semi-automated activity. The "price to pay" for enabling such delegation of control was a drastic reduction of complexity, by comparison to realistic operator tasks.

5. CONCLUSION AND NEED FOR FURTHER RESEARCH

Due to its specificity, CESS would be best applicable in two types of tasks :

- *procedural* tasks : tasks for which procedures exist and actually rule out the behaviour of human practitioners. Main application domains are safety monitoring and fault management in nuclear power plants, maintenance operations in process industry and flight management in civil or military aeronautics (Amalberti, 1992).

- *"proceduralized"* tasks : tasks involving large segments of routinised or skilled activity, such as discrete operations in manufacturing industry and decision making tasks in process industry (Cacciabue et al., 1992) or medicine (Boreham et al., 1992).

As human tasks never entirely belong to those two categories, to become applicable in real work environments, CESS would thus need to be *associated*, in a larger architecture, to support systems having other purposes and application domains. Such an association would allow to account for operator activities that do not resort to skill and routine and that are tackled by problem solving oriented support systems.

In a next development step, which is planned to be carried out inside a European Network on Human Error (CEC, Human Capital and Mobility Programme), it is hoped that the system will be robust enough to be applied - with necessary modifications - to more complex applications.

6. ACKNOWLEDGEMENTS

This research was carried out under a grant from the Service de Programmation de la Politique Scientifique Belge and took place within the Belgian Programme of Impetus to Research in Artificial Intelligence. This support is greatly acknowledged.

7. REFERENCES

1   R. Amalberti. Safety in Process Control : an Operator-centred Point of View In *Reliability Engineering and System Safety*, Vol. 38 (1992) 99-108.
2   F.J. Bartlett. *Remembering*. Cambridge : Cambridge University Press, 1932.
3   N.C. Boreham, R.W. Foster and G.E. Mawer. Strategies and Knowledge in the Control of the Symptoms of a Chronic Illness. *Le Travail Humain*, PUF, Paris, 55 (1992) 15-34.
4   L. Bainbridge, L. Development of Skill, Reduction of Workload. In *Developing Skills with Information Technology*, L. Bainbridge and S. A. R. Quintanilla (eds.), John Wiley and Sons Ltd, 1989.
5   P.C. Cacciabue, F. Decortis, M. Masson, J.-P. Nordvik. Cognitive Modelling as Simulation Technique for the Development of Intelligent User Interfaces. In *Simulation and the User Interface*. A. Life, C. Narborough-Hall, L. Hamilton (eds.). Taylor & Francis, London, 1990.
6   P.C. Cacciabue, F. Decortis, B. Drozdowicz, M. Masson & J.-P. Nordvik. COSIMO : a Cognitive Simulation Model of Human Decision Making and Behaviour in Accident Management of Complex Plants. Institute of Electrical and Electronic Engineers Transactions on Systems, Man and Cybernetics, IEEE-SMC, 22 5 (1992) 1058-1074.
7   V. De Keyser V. & D.D. Woods. Fixation Errors in Dynamic and Complex Systems. In A.G. Colombo and R. Micenta (eds.) *Advanced Systems Reliability Modelling*, Kluwer Academic Publishers, Dordrecht, 1989.
8   W. James. *The Principles of Psychology*. Henry Hott, New-York, 1890.
9   M. Masson. Understanding, Reporting and Preventing Human Fixation Errors. In D.A. Lucas, T. van der Schaaf and A. Hale (eds.) *Near Miss Reporting as a Safety Tool*. Oxford : Butterworth-Heinemann, 1991.
10 M. Masson & V. De Keyser. Human Error : Lesson Learned from a Field Study for the Specification of an Intelligent Error Prevention System. *Advances in Industrial Ergonomics and Safety IV. Proceedings of the Annual International Ergonomics and Safety Conference*, Denver, CO, 10-14 June, 1085-1092, 1992.
11 M. Masson, N. Malaise, A. Housiaux and V. De Keyser. Organisational Change and Human Expertise in Nuclear Power Plants : Some Implications for Training and Error Prevention. Nuclear Engineering and Design, Special issue on ANP '92, (1993) : in press.
12 M. Minsky. A Framework for Representing Knowledge. In P.H. Winston (Ed), *The Psychology of Computer Vision*. New-York : McGraw-Hill, 1975.
13 D.A. Norman. Categorization of Action Slips. *Psychological Review*, 88 (1981) 1-15.
14 J. Rasmussen. Cognitive Control and Human Error Mechanisms. In J. Rasmussen, K. Duncan and J. Leplat (eds.) *New Technology and Human Error*. John Wiley and Sons Ltd, 1987.
15 J.T. Reason. Generic Error Modelling System (GEMS) : A Cognitive Framework for Locating Common Human Error Forms. In J. Rasmussen, K. Duncan and J. Leplat (eds.) *New Technology and Human Error*. John Wiley and Sons Ltd, 1987.
16 J.T. Reason. *Human Error*. Cambridge : Cambridge University Press, 1990.
17 J.T. Reason and D. Embrey. *Human Error - A Fall from Grace*. A Reliability Associates Video Tape, narrated by QED. Signal Vision, Knutsford, Cheshire, UK.
18 J.-C. Rouhet & M. Masson . Erreur Humaine. Les erreurs que commettent les pilotes sont-elles différentes des nôtres ? Le Programme ARCHIMEDE. *Revue Générale de Sécurité*, Société Alpine de Publication, Grenoble, Nov. (1991) 55-61.
19 R. Rosen. *Anticipatory Systems*. Pergamon Press, New York, 1985.
20 R.C. Shank & R.P. Abelson. *Scripts, Plans, Goals, and Understanding*. Hillsdale, NJ : Lawrence Erlbaum Associates, 1977.

Audicon: Easy Access to Graphical User Interfaces for Blind Persons - Designing for and with People

O. Martial and A. Dufresne

Université de Montréal, Département de Communication, C.P. 6128, Succursale A, H3C 3J7 Montréal (Québec), Canada

Audicon is a project conducted by Visuaide 2000 and the Canadian Workplace Automation Research Centre with the collaboration of the Université de Montréal and the Université de Sherbrooke.

Abstract

There is a real need to render Graphical User Interfaces (GUI) accessible to blind people and the aim of the Audicon project is to develop hardware and software to adapt a graphical user interface to their specific needs. In order to define the main design principles and to choose the inptut/output device of the interface we used a three-step methodology: analysing offices of visually impaired persons, creating a prototype, evaluating the prototype. The results of the tests prove that an interface which allows direct manipulation of objects on an electronic desktop, using "earcons" (1) instead of graphical icons and allowing multimodal access to both audio and tactile information, is a good one for blind users. This test also gives us many pratical ideas to improve the device and shows the importance of the participation of users in the design process.

1. BACKGROUND

For a long time, blind people have been left on the fringes of our communication-oriented society. Some tools (particularly those with braille versions of data on diskettes, voice synthesizers and more recently scanners) have made more information accessible to them (2). But with the development and rapid spread of Graphical user interfaces, people with impaired vision are once again shut out. GUIs, or direct-manipulation interfaces, are the outcome of research on human-computer interaction (3). This type of interface has become widely used for a variety of professional applications (office automation, desktop publishing, cartography, CAD, etc.), and has been adopted by all major manufacturers (4; 5). In just a short time, this type of interface became the basis for the tools of tomorrow. It can be described as a way of making computers user-friendly: familiar concepts of folders, documents, filing and so on are illustrated on the screen by icons. Users can manipulate "objects" directly using a mouse. Three of the main basic principles of GUIs are: Metaphors from the real world, Direct manipulation and See-and-Point. But as it demands visual activity ("What You See is What You Get") and eye-hand coordination, GUIs can not be used by visually impaired people. Opinion is unanimous about the urgent need to study the question and to find solutions for the blind persons (6; 7).

2. OBJECTIVES

Some products and projects already exist : OutSpoken, Soundtrack, InTouch, (7; 8; 9; 10) and more recently Window Bridge (11). We however believe that they don't respect basic principles of human interface design (4). In this context, we are trying to develop a computer interface truly adapted to blind users by studying their needs and blending new technologies to meet them. As a first step, the Audicon interface will be designed for people with no residual functional vision to use Windows on IBM PC.

3. METHODOLOGY

In order to guide the creation of the Audicon interface, we have analyzed the offices of visually impaired persons, created and evaluated a prototype of the device.

3.1. Analysing Offices of Visually Impaired Persons

To understand the nature of the communication between a person and a machine when a task is being carried out, we began by analysing the specific needs of a sample of visually impaired people in their offices. As a first step, this problem is approached by means of a two-level analysis of mental representation that people have of their own office (12):
- The level of conceptual mapping : What kind of mental "picture" of his office does the blind person have? (workspace, objects, tasks as goals and subgoals, actions linked to tasks);
- The level of perceptual mapping : What kind of perceptual conditions allow him to build a mental model and operate on it?

We filmed ten blind persons and five seeing persons (witness group) in individual interviews in the process of carrying out everyday tasks in their office. Our analysis showed patterns in the mental representation of space and in activity organization, allowing us to deduce general design principles and pratical implications for the design of the prototype.

Analysing offices of visually impaired persons showed us (13) that blind people :
- construct their spatial mental representation with many cognitive resources (memory and integration of partial data)
- do a tactile exploration of the space and define physical marks in their environment
- use together auditive and tactile informations
- accord importance to the place and the order of objects
- are very dependent of technical aids (such as computers and recorders) to accomplish their daily tasks.

These results lead us to define six design principles for Audicon Interface: an adapted metaphor of the desktop, direct manipulation, sound iconography, multimodal access to information, flexibility of the interface and tools for self-organization.

3.2. Creating a Prototype

To allow direct manipulation of objects on the screen by blind users, we have selected a touch tablet with a mouse as the main input/output device for the Audicon interface (Figure 1). It provides data in digital voice and sound, voice synthesis and/or braille according to the technical configuration and depending on the user's choice. The contents of the screen are projected onto the horizontal plan of a tablet, respecting the layout of the data.

The tablet has grooved grid marks which can be felt with the fingers. In order to explore the screen contents, the user moves the mouse on the tablet and a feedback is provided to him in the form of digital voice and sounds, which are "earcons" evoking the objects or events on the screen (for example, the sound of a scrolling menu or the sound of dragging an object).

The front of the mouse has a circular sensor corresponding exatly to the position of the pointer on the screen in absolute coordinates. In its prototype format, the mouse has four buttons in a diamond-shaped layout :
- the top one has the same function as a mouse button for sighted users. It is used in two ways: by pressing it once (known as clicking), or by pressing it twice (known as double-clicking)
- the left one is used to activate the voice synthesis to have the name of an object read;
- the right one is for the braille (not implemented in the prototype);
- the low one is for special functions (not implemented in the prototype).

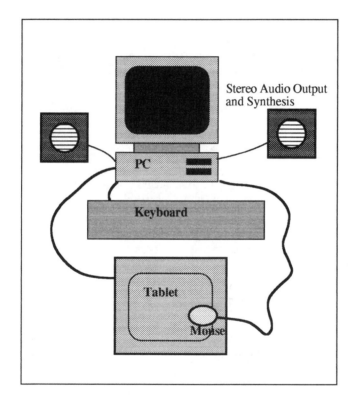

Figure 1. Schema of the prototype.

3.3. Evaluating the Prototype

The prototype has been evaluated with seventeen blind persons in a simulated use situation. Each person was met individually in a filmed interview. After an explanation of the device, several exercises were successively proposed to each user. A logfile containing every action of the user is saved on the computer and a questionnaire is filled at the end of the test. The results generally show very few errors and fast performances in recognizing and manipulating objects with the device (Table 1).

Table 1
Mean time and percentages of errors.

	Mean time	Errors
Exploration		
Tablet	53 sec.	
Mouse	1 min. 59 sec.	
Objects	4 min. 14 sec.	
Spatial exploration of the "screen"	2 min. 33 sec.	1,66 %
Finding objects (sound + synthesis)		
Exploration	5 min. 21 sec.	
Identification	1 min. 14 sec.	0 %
Finding objects (sound alone)		
Exploration	5 min. 51 sec.	
Identification	2 min. 18 sec.	0 %
Identification of objects	3 min. 29 sec.	2.08 %
Identification of position	4 min. 28 sec.	3.13 %
Selecting, moving and deselecting an object		
Exploration	3 min. 46 sec.	
Execution	1 min. 2 sec.	0 %
Selecting, opening and closing a folder, choosing an item		
Exploration	6 min.45 sec.	
Execution	1 min. 31 sec.	3.13 %

4. DISCUSSION OF THE RESULTS

Although the simulated situation tested was far less complex that the real use of a GUI, the results are very signifiant. The results of the questionnaire and the good performances (very few errors in short time) obtained by every visually impaired user of the prototype confirm the success of the general design principles.

4.1. The design principles
The first four principles appear to be confirmed with the testing of the prototype.

An adapted metaphor of the desktop
The prototype used the office metaphor with objects as desk, chair, telephone, books and filing cabinets. This metaphor was very well accepted by the blind users who understood through it the advantages of the graphical interface, particularly during the exercises of manipulating objects (open, select, deselect, move, close, choose in a list of items). They mentally did an immediate link between these objects and their daily world of files and directories. Our test showed that, as for seing persons, the classical desktop may bring help and attractiveness to a user interface for blind persons.

Direct manipulation

Exploring the tablet by moving the mouse, the blind users found very easily the objects on the tablet. But, as they usually do in their own offices, they also rapidly developed strategies positionning objects on the tablet, placing their own marks and moving the mouse. The results of this test prove that direct manipulation is an essential design principle of Audicon Interface because it can help blind users interact naturally with the computer, even more than seeing persons do.

Sound iconography

The GUIs use only a few sounds. Some researches (1; 14; 15) however prove that "earcons" or "auditory icons" can bring useful and attractive informations to computers' users. For blind users, sounds are essential in order to know their environment and during the test they rapidly identified the objects with their sounds alone, almost without any errors. Sounds also helped these users in performing the tasks requested with the interface. These results prove that for visually impaired users, an audio iconography can replace the visual iconography of GUIs.

Multimodal access to information

Braille was not available in the tested prototype but the results prove that blind persons spontaneously and conjointly used tactile informations to identify and manipulate the objects of the interface. It appears that multimodality is also an essential design principle, especially because blind people have various needs (only some persons know braille and every user become tired working in one modality).

4.2. The device improvements

The test also gives us many pratical ideas to improve the device and shows a great variety of interesting strategies in exploring and operating the electronic desktop.

The tablet

In the results of the test it appears that the tablet is too large for some users and that the boundaries of the "screen" must be better pointed out. It suggests that we can add a specific sound when the cursor is out of the "screen" and modify the texture of the tablet inside and outside the boundaries of the "screen".

The mouse

Some users have suggested to add a little point in the centre of the circular sensor of the mouse in order to know the exact position of the pointer on the screen. A mouse without cable would also be appreciated. The questionnaires suggested ways to improve the form and size of the mouse as well the place and form of the buttons.

The sounds

Though the users have very good results in identifying objects and actions with the proposed sounds of the prototype, their appreciation of the quality of these sounds varied. In the GUIs, defining visual icons is not an easy task (16) but as auditive information is sequential and inherently transient (14), defining a good sound iconography is even more difficult. The results of the tests showed the importance to use the competences of music specialists to elaborate the principles of the sound iconography in order to maximize the perception and discrimination of the various earcons.

5. CONCLUSION

Our methodology and the first results make us confident that Audicon will be an interface really adapted to the needs of blind people. These results show the importance of the participation of the users during all the design process, from the first steps of the project to final evaluation of the interface in a real use situation. Evaluating prototypes also helps us to validate some hypothesis and to make decisions on design.

6. REFERENCES

1   M. M. Blattner, D. A. Sumikawa & R.M. Greenberg, Earcons and Icons: Their Structure and Common Design Principles, Human-Computer Interaction, volume 4, Hillsdale, New Jersey, USA, Lawrence Erlbaum Associates, 1989, p. 11-44.
2   J. Lazzaro, Opening the Doors for the Disabled, Byte, August 1990, p. 258-268.
3   B. Shneiderman, Designing the User Interface: Strategies for Effective Human-Computer Interaction, Reading, MA, Addison-Wesley Publishing Co, 1987.
4   Apple, Human Interface Guidelines: The Apple Desktop Interface, Reading, MA, Addison-Wesley Publishing Co, 1987.
5   IBM, Systems Application Architecture, Common User Access: Advanced Interface Design Guide, 1989.
6   L.H. Boyd, W.L. Boyd & G.C. Vanderheiden, The Graphical User interface, Crisis, Danger and Opportunity, Journal of Visual Impairment & Blindness, december 1990, p. 496-502.
7   J. Lazzaro, Windows of Vulnerability, Byte, June 1991, p. 416.
8   A. D. N. Edwards , Adapting the Macintosh and Other Graphical User Interfaces for Blind Users, 6th International Workshop on Computer Applications for the Visually Handicapped, Leuven, Belgium, 1990, p. 1-9.
9   L.H. Boyd, W.L. Boyd, J. Berliss, M. Sutton & Vanderheiden, The Paradox of the Graphical User Interface: Unprecedented Computer Power for Blind People, CTG'91, October 1991.
10   G.C. Vanderheiden, Graphic User Interfaces: A Tough Problem with a Net Gain for Users who are Blind, Technology and Disability, 1 (1), Summer 1991, p. 93-99.
11   J. Lazzaro, Window Bridge: The First Speech Program for MS Windows, SAF Technology Update, October 1992, p. 3-7.
12   D.A. Norman, Cognitive Engineering, in D.A. Norman and S. Draper, User Centered System design: New Perspectives on Human-Computer Interactions, Hillsdale, NJ, Lawrence Erlbaum Associates, 1986, p. 31-61.
13   O. Martial & A. Dufresne, Pour l'accès aux interfaces graphiques par les non-voyants: analyse des représentations mentales du bureau, ERGO-IA'92, Biarritz, France, Octobre 1992.
14   W. W. Gaver, The SonicFinder: An Interface That Uses Auditory Icons, Human-Computer Interaction, volume 4, Hillsdale, New Jersey, USA, Lawrence Erlbaum Associates, 1989, p. 67-93.
15   W. Buxton, Introduction to this Special Issue on Nonspeech Audio, Human-Computer Interaction, volume 4, Hillsdale, New Jersey, USA, Lawrence Erlbaum Associates, 1989, p. 1-10.
16   A. Marcus, Sign Language: graphics designers try to break the language barrier with icons, Unixworld magazine, Special report: International Unix, 1991, p. 63-67.

Development of a Simulation-Based Intelligent Tutoring System for Assisting PID Control Learning

Takeki Nogami[*] , Yoshihide Yokoi[**] , Ichiro Yanagisawa[***] and Shizuka Mitui[***]

[*] Shikoku Research Institute Incorporated, 2109-8, Yashimanishi-machi, Takamatsu-shi, JAPAN

[**] The University of Tokushima, 2-1, Minamijyosanjima-cho, Tokushima-shi, JAPAN

[***] Mitsubishi Atomic Power Industries, Inc., 4-1, Shibakouen 2-Chome Minato-ku, Tokyo, JAPAN

Abstract
A simulation-based ITS (Intelligent tutoring system), SRIM, has been developed in order to realize an individualized learning environment for PID control. For mitigating the burden of students in learning with a simulator, SRIM navigates the learning by providing local goals for PID controller tuning and advisory messages. The architecture of ITS is employed to perform the local goal selection and the tutoring strategy switching, naturally and timely.

1. INTRODUCTION

In the education of automatic control theory, simulators have been used as effective tools, so far. However, for a novice student, it is not always easy to decide his operation on the simulator, and to interpret simulation result properly and, as a result, to acquire new knowledge by himself. Therefore, the use of simulators has been usually limited to the use guided by human instructors. Under these backgrounds, we have been developing a simulation-based ITS for assisting PID control learning (SRIM) in order to realize an individualized learning environment that is suitable for personal use.

The teaching objective of SRIM is to assist the student in understanding effect of control actions (proportional, integral and derivative actions) and in acquiring procedural knowledge for optimal tuning of PID controller.

Generally, the difficulty of the personal use of simulators lies in the following steps:

1)Operational goal selection step where students select operational goal by themselves.
2)Interpretation step where students observe the simulation and interpret the relation between his operation and the simulator response.

Although the difficulty depends on the complexity of domain problems, It is not so easy to select a good operational goal and to make a proper interpretation without having a deep understanding of the problem.

SRIM assists learners in these steps, by providing local goals for simulator operation and advisory messages about the simulation results. In order to give natural and proper local goals, the architecture of Intelligent Tutoring Systems [1] is employed.

2. SYSTEM CONFIGURATION

The system configuration is shown in Fig. 1. SRIM is implemented on UNIX workstation by using OpenWindows and G2 real-time expert systems shell [2]. The system is composed of the following modules:

--Simulator module
--Tutoring module
--Knowledge base
--User interface

The simulator module has a simulation model composed of a PID controller and a process represented by first order time lags. The simulator module itself evaluates the characteristics of the feedback loop behavior such as the overshoot, off-set and stability.

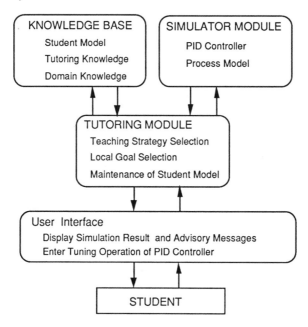

FIG. 1 SRIM System Configuration

816

The tutoring module determines the local goal and the teaching strategy suitable for the knowledge state of the student. The module maintains the student model from the history of the PID controller tuning operation.

The knowledge base contains the following kind of knowledge that is represented by rules, procedures and other G2 objects.

--Tutoring Knowledge for local goal and teaching strategy selection,
--Domain Knowledge for the evaluation of the simulation result, and
--Student Model to represent the knowledge state of the student.

3. TEACHING STRATEGY AND STUDENT MODEL

Fig. 2 shows the flow chart of SRIM.

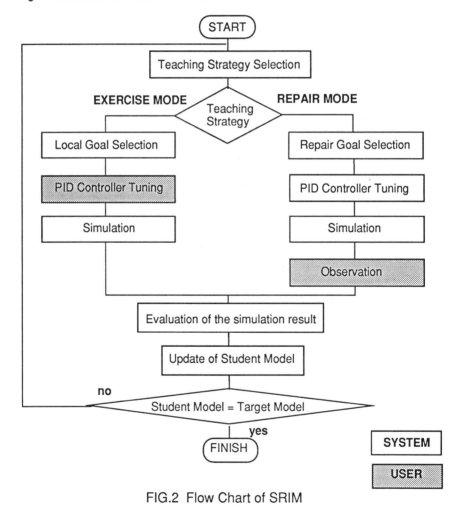

FIG.2 Flow Chart of SRIM

The following two tutoring strategies are employed in SRIM:
--Exercise mode
--Repair mode

In the exercise mode, a local goal for tuning operation of PID controller is presented to the student, at first. "Decrease the off-set " is an example of the local goal and which is defined as an operational goal satisfied by one step operation. The next, the student selects his operation and executes the simulation. By observing the simulation, the student understands that his operation was success or failure.

The repair mode is invoked when a contradiction is detected in the student model or wrong operation is selected repeatedly. In order to repair the student's erroneous knowledge, SRIM executes a teaching simulation and presents advisory messages. After the simulation was finished, the student reports what he learned from the simulation to the system.

The selection of local goals and the switching of tutoring strategy is performed based upon the knowledge state of the student. For that purpose, SRIM maintains the student model by the following information sources:

1)Selected tuning operation for given local goals in the exercise mode
2)Report from the student in the repair mode.

The student model is represented by causal links between tuning operation of PID controller (a pair of a control action and its direction of change) and its effect on the characteristics of feedback loop behavior (such as overshoot, off-set and stability). Fig. 3 shows an example of the representation of the student model.

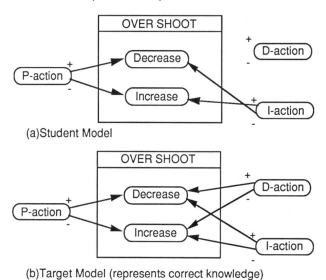

FIG.3 Representation of Student Model

818

In Fig. 3-(a), no link from D-action is established yet. This means that SRIM does not know the student's knowledge about the effect of D-action on overshoot. SRIM also have a target model as shown in Fig. 3-(b) which represents a correct knowledge. By comparing the student model and the target model, SRIM can know where is erroneous knowledge. Fig. 3 shows that the student has a erroneous knowledge on the effect of I-action.

The local goal is represented by a target characteristics of feedback loop behavior, its direction of change (increase or decrease, stabilize or instabilize) and changeable control actions as follows:

--Improve the stability by P-action
--Decrease the over shoot by P-action
--Decrease the offset

In the local goal selection, we take account of the followings:

--the goal must be reachable
--the goal should be related to the unevaluated part of the student model
--the goal should be related to the erroneous part of the model

4.CONCLUSIONS

We have developed a simulation-based Intelligent Tutoring System, SRIM. SRIM assists a student in understanding the effect of control actions in PID control and in acquiring procedural knowledge for optimal tuning of PID controller through the tuning operation of PID controller which is navigated by SRIM. For that purpose, we proposed a teaching strategy based on local goals for simulator operations. For mitigating the burden of students in learning with a simulator, SRIM navigates the learning by providing local goals for PID controller tuning and advisory messages.

The evaluation of SRIM is to be performed. In the evaluation, the teaching effect of SRIM is to be evaluated by comparing with other learning methods such as pure use of simulators or textbook. The preliminary result shows the effectiveness of the tutoring strategy of SRIM.

5.REFERENCES

[1]E. Wenger, Artificial Intelligence and Tutoring Systems, Morgen Kaufmann, Los Altos, California (1987)
[2]G2 Reference Manual Version 3.0, Gensym Corporation (1992)

THE USE OF EXPERT SYSTEMS FOR TRAINING HUMANS IN RULE-BASED REASONING

J. Sharit[a] and S. Chen[b]

[a]Department of Industrial Engineering, State University of New York at Buffalo, Amherst, NY USA

[b]Department of Civil Engineering, State University of New York at Buffalo, Amherst, NY USA

Abstract

This paper summarizes a study concerning the prospect of employing expert systems (ESs) for training individuals in the emergency management of risk. This idea is based on the assumption that for many emergency situations it would be unrealistic for humans to access or otherwise engage in a dialogue with an ES. At the same time, in the process of reasoning with rules, ESs possess certain qualities that could prove worthwhile for humans to adopt. Accompanying this overview is a somewhat circuitous discussion of various perspectives to rule-based performance that are believed capable of benefitting from this paradigm as well as from each other's views.

1. SOME PERSPECTIVES ON RULE-BASED REASONING

The notion that people reason, or are guided in their behavior, by rules has managed to greatly influence our thinking about human task performance. In Rasmussens's [1] "SRK" framework, rule-based performance occupies a position somewhere between the knowledge-based level of performance, which typically deals with unfamiliar situations and involves the explicit formulation of plans directed toward a goal and the manipulation of meaningful symbols within a problem space, and the skill-based level of performance, that represents highly integrated patterns of behavior that usually occur without conscious control. This framework is intuitively easy to apply to a wide variety of tasks, and can guide the selection of appropriate methods for more detailed analysis [2].

The rules that underlie the rule-based level of performance are assumed to be stored in long-term memory, and are triggered by external and internal *signs*; therefore, a critical characteristic of most rule-based tasks is the recognition of internal or external *states* and the association of rules with those states. Rules can derive from various sources such as instruction manuals or conscious planning, and tend to evolve based on previous experiences one has had with them. Many industrial tasks are governed largely by rule-based behavior (especially industries whose operations are heavily proceduralized) which, in part, explains the general interest in this level of performance.

The distinction between these three levels of performance in terms of the particular forms in which information is likely to be used also provides a logical framework for describing human error tendencies [3]. This framework was more formalized by Reason [4] who noted a number of failure modes of errors that occur at the rule-based level of performance (or "rule-based mistakes"). Within his modeling framework, the potential for all errors, including skill-based "slips" and "lapses", and knowledge-based "mistakes", begins with cognitive underspecification—somewhere in the human's cognitive processing system the specification of information is incomplete. How a particular error at the rule-based level of performance occurs (i.e., the failure mode) would then depend upon the context of this underspecification, including the relative influences of two biases considered primarily accountable for shaping the forms of the errors, namely *frequency* (how frequently a rule being considered has been successfully activated in the past) and *similarity* (how well the information under consideration matches an existing rule), as well as other factors such as recency and emotional value. Although the potential for instantiation of a rule exists in spite of inconsistencies between informational cues and the antecedent of the rule, the more successful the rule has proved in the past the less important is the requirement for contextual appropriateness. This failure mode is referred to by Reason as "rule strength", and is an example of a misapplication of a good rule.

Assuming the human seeks to minimize cognitive effort, the human is expected to resort to less effortful rule-based processing when confronting difficult problem-solving situations, potentially employing a variety of pattern-matching activities prior to shifting to more laborious cognitive control modes in order to make available processing resources for the more analytic and conceptual analyses demanded of the problem. The tradeoffs between bias-driven low energy rule instantiation and the potential for error associated with these processes is consistent with a connectionist (neural network) perspective on how information is organized [5,6]. When knowledge-based performance is required, processing mechanisms superimposed or otherwise aligned with these networks can, at high energy costs, more selectively access and manipulate this information, and generate the potential for new pattern-matching activities. At the other extreme, maintaining highly automatized patterns that can ultimately qualify as *signals* affords the lowest degree of energy expenditure, but at the expense of increased vulnerability to various slips and lapses.

In adopting a connectionist perspective, an important but somewhat subtle distinction must be made between the rules that are being inferred based on descriptions of human behavior and the issue of how those rules are actually implemented. To the extent that the mechanisms underlying neural networks operate in accordance with these descriptions, even if rules are not being explicitly manipulated many of the inferences, such as those concerning failure modes at the rule-based level of performance, are likely to remain valid. However, there may be important insights into rule-based performance that will depend on a closer examination of the underlying architecture responsible for its implementation.

2. PRODUCTION SYSTEMS AND EXPERT SYSTEMS

The production system (PS) framework represents another perspective to rule-based performance. Although many PSs have been proposed [7], the fundamental component of all PSs is a set of condition-action pairs (called productions). If working memory contains elements that match the pattern associated with the condition, the production is activated according to the action specified which, in turn, augments working memory with new elements that enables still other productions to apply. A number of embellishments serve to distinguish between the various PSs, providing each with the opportunity to test the general claim that PSs are capable of modeling all cognitive activity [7].

The PS framework formed the basis for computer programs called expert systems (ESs) that are essentially rule-based reasoning systems [8]. Although it is tempting to attribute the relative success of a given ES to the fact that it represents a realistic simulation of human behavior, this explanation is too convenient—ESs are generally designed with the principal objective of building a program that displays competence in a particular task or domain [9], irrespective of the mechanisms of human reasoning that might underlie that competence.

Many human tasks are procedural, relying on the abilities to detect the need for invoking particular rules and to reason with those rules. For many such tasks, ESs can be relied on either to perform these tasks or to serve as decision aids for humans. However, for a number of scenarios, especially those involving the real-time emergency management of risk, many workers will not likely have rapid access to such decision aids [10]. In these situations, the prospect of engaging in a dialogue with an ES would not be realistic. One approach to this problem is to "reverse the paradigm"—since ESs are excellent rule-based processors, the possibility exists that human rule-based reasoning can benefit from ES training. This approach assumes that much of the knowledge on which humans are expected to act in emergency management of risk is likely to be rule-based.

The details of an exploratory study intended for testing the potential usefulness of this approach are given in [11]. Prior to summarizing this study, a number of issues related to this idea are worth noting. First, although we know (because we specify) how ESs process rules—for example, we could program them to process rules through forward or backward chaining or through a combination of these strategies—we do not know what strategy any given person might use, and whether ES training could alter the strategy that person would normally use. A second and related issue concerns the number of levels required in rule processing, or what may be referred to as "rule-processing complexity". With increased complexity, a strategy that is primarily forward-driven could lead to a combinatorial explosion of potential solution paths that, in crisis management situations, could result in excessive workload and increased likelihood of error. In this case, the capability for ES-based training to *bias* the human towards a more efficient strategy for processing rules would be advantageous. Finally, for situations where the human's knowledge is incomplete, implying that the problem cannot be resolved through knowledge of the rules available to the human, it would prove interesting to determine whether ES-based training would make the human when operating alone less likely to force a solution through the existent rule set under such "deadened" conditions.

3. A STUDY ON EXPERT SYTEM BASED TRAINING

The application area selected for investigating the potential effectiveness of employing ESs for training humans at rule-based reasoning was management of a hazardous chemical spill. An ES in the chemical spill domain was developed, written in PROLOG, and was comprised essentially of two modules: a knowledge base and an ES shell. The knowledge base consisted of 34 rules that dealt with various aspects of chemical spill emergency management, such as identification/classification of chemicals, selection of appropriate rescue apparatus, and assignment of victims to appropriate areas. The ES's shell included an inference engine, a user interface, and an explanation facility, and incorporated a backward-chaining and combined depth-first breadth-first search strategy.

In response to a chemical spill incident the decision maker is usually confronted with a number of facts concerning information on spill states, and must make decisions concerning various aspects of safety management. The query system represented a set of scenarios that included a variety of queries (e.g., should victims be assigned to the yellow first aid zone?) and associated facts that simulated such chemical spill incidents. Based on this information the subject had to reason with the rules to find solutions to the query. Queries were classified in terms of the level of complexity in rule chaining required by the ES and whether deadend conditions were present. Low complexity queries required two or three levels of chaining, medium complexity queries required four levels of chaining, and high complexity queries required five or six levels of chaining for solution. A deadend query represented a situation whereby a conclusion to the query could not be arrived at through the processing of the rules in the rule set.

The training conditions consisted of a backward chaining ES and a control condition. ES training incorporated an interface consisting of four windows. The *scenario window* presented the facts describing a spill scenario and the associated query. Through the *expert system window* the subject received prompting instructions for interacting with the ES (such as the need for feeding in the facts associated with a particular spill scenario) and obtained the ES's yes/no answers to queries. The *explanation window* displayed the ES's explanation facility, allowing subjects to observe how the ES processed rules in a backward-driven manner in order to derive yes/no answers to the queries. The *tree window* displayed AND/OR tree graphics that was created for the purpose of providing a visual compliment to the verbal explanation facility.

Subjects in the control condition were not exposed to any mechanisms suggestive of a particular problem-solving strategy. Their interface consisted of two windows: a *scenario window*, which presented the query system as well as answers to queries, and a *rule window*, which displayed, in a random sequence, the 34 rules comprising the rule set. Twelve undergraduate and graduate students served as subjects and were paid $5.00 per hour of participation, including training; half the subjects were assigned to the ES training condition and the other half were assigned to the control condition.

To qualify for the training session, subjects had to demonstrate adequate knowledge of the 34 domain rules. This was accomplished through a test that required the subject to (verbally) provide the appropriate "if" (i.e., condition) component given the "then" (i.e., action) component of a rule, or provide the "then" component when presented with the "if" component. Memorization of the rules was performed as a take-home assignment.

In the ES training session, the subject was first instructed to retrieve a scenario and have it displayed in the scenario window. As prompted by the ES, the subject then input the facts concerning the spill scenario into the scenario window, and obtained the response to the query from the ES. Next, the subject activated the explanation facility and the corresponding tree graphic, and navigated through the solution path displayed in the explation window. Training in this session was completed when the subject was exposed to nine such scenarios. Essentially the same procedure was followed in training subjects assigned to the control condition except that instead of having access to the ES and its associated facilities, the subjects were instructed to search among the 34 rules displayed in the rule window to verify the answers provided in the scenario window to the queries.

In the experimental session subjects again interacted with the computer, but this time they were required to solve, on their own, a total of six queries. Two queries were of low complexity, two were of medium complexity, and two were of high complexity, and within each level of complexity one of the two queries represented a deadend condition (subjects had been exposed to each of these possibilities during training). Subjects were instructed to respond rapidly and to verbalize their thoughts or strategies associated with attempting to answer the query; this information was tape-recorded and subsequently analyzed. Warm-up exercises were provided to allow the subjects to become familiarized with this verbalization process.

The primary data consisted of the various decision strategies employed by the subjects and the degree of correctness of their yes/no answers (queries representing deadend conditions also required "no" responses). Although a high percentage of correct responses was expected for all subjects in view of the degree of familiarity with the rules that subjects had to demonstrate in order to qualify for training, all six subjects in the ES training group responded to all queries correctly, while two of the subjects in the control condition failed to solve the high complexity deadend query correctly.

Based on the analysis of the verbal protocols, the strategies subjects used in attempting to solve each of the queries were grouped into four categories: forward reasoning, backward reasoning, combined forward-backward reasoning, and automatic (implying that there was no evidence for the use of any strategy—only 3 of the 72 individual analyses fell into this category). The average forward/backward (F/B) ratio for the control group was 4.0; in contrast, the average F/B ratio for the ES training group was 0.6. These results indicate that forward reasoning may be the more natural manner in which humans reason with rules, and that ES training tends to *bias* their rule-based reasoning strategy.

More detailed analysis of the verbal protocols provided further insight into the potential effects of ES training on rule-based problem solving. First, a closer examination of the incorrect response to the high-complexity query made by one of the two subjects in the control condition confirmed the danger of the forward-driven reasoning strategy leading to an increased number of solution paths. Although the other subject employed a backward reasoning strategy, the solution path was pruned too early to reach a correct answer. Assuming that humans tend to be more comfortable processing rules in a forward-driven manner, this latter result could imply that without formal intervention (such as ES training), humans may be at a disadvantage in attempting to (correctly) employ backward-driven reasoning strategies to problems characterized by greater complexity in rule processing.

4. RULE-BASED PERFORMANCE REVISITED

The interest in emergency management of risk notwithstanding, the study described above has potential utility as a paradigm for elaborating on a number of seemingly competing approaches for explaining rule-based performance. To capitalize on this paradigm, it is necessary to: (1) incorporate more explicit time constraints on human problem solving; (2) introduce varying degrees of cognitive underspecification; and (3) and assess the degree of *confidence* with which subjects provide answers to queries. Additional training strategies

824

can also be explored, including various *hybrid* strategies that incorporate both forward-driven and backward-driven processing of rules. While these experimental interventions are manageable, simulating the *experience* of crisis decision making is a formidable problem that is not easily resolvable.

The application of Reason's modeling framework to this general paradigm could potentially clarify a number of issues related to the PS formalism. For example, in reference to Anderson's [7] ACT model, a better understanding of the processes associated with partial matching could be derived from an examination of the distinctions discussed by Reason that underlie the mechanisms of human error. Use of the ES training paradigm could (e.g., by virtue of its capability for *biasing* the human towards a backward-driven strategy for processing rules) also help clarify differences that might exist in activation levels and accompanying pattern-matching processes associated with goal-directed processing, that could lead to challenging the assertion of "condition-action asymmetry" in PSs. Perhaps most importantly, Reason's modeling framework, especially as it concerns failure modes associated with errors at the knowledge-based level of performance, could help identify mechanisms for carrying out goal-directed processing within PSs such as ATP, and more generally, reconcile the PS and schema system frameworks by shifting the emphasis away from architectural distinctions and more towards control mode, even to the point of abandoning the need for maintaining a clear distinction between declarative and production memories.

5. REFERENCES

1 J. Rasmussen, *Information Processing and Human-Machine Interaction: An Approach to Cognitive Engineering*, North-Holland, New York, 1986.
2 M.R. Lehto, J. Sharit, and G. Salvendy, The application of cognitive simulation techniques to work measurement and methods analysis of production control tasks, *International Journal of Production Research, 29*, 1565-1586, 1991.
3 J. Rasmussen, Human errors: a taxonomy for describing human malfunction in industrial installations. *Journal of Occupational Accidents, 4*, 311-333, 1982.
4 J. Reason, *Human Error*, Cambridge University Press, Cambridge, 1990.
5 J.A. Feldman and D.H. Ballard, Connectionist models and their properties, *Cognitive Science, 6*, 205-254, 1982.
6 J.A. Anderson, Cognitive and psychological computation with neural models, *IEEE Transactions on Systems, Man and Cybernetics, 17*, 799-814, 1983.
7 J.R. Anderson, *The Architecture of Cognition*, Harvard University Press, Cambridge, 1983.
8 N.J. Nilsson, *Principles of Artificial Intelligence*, Tioga, Palo Alto, CA, 1980.
9 R. Davis and J. King, An overview of production systems, *Machine Intelligence 8*, 300-332, 1977.
10 N. Moray, Can decision aids help to reduce risk and human error? A program for research on the management of risk. Department of Mechanical and Industrial Engineering, University of Illinois at Urbana-Champaign, *EPRL-88-20*, 1988.
11 J. Sharit, S. Chen, and D.-Y.M. Lin, Expert system based training for emergency management, *Journal of Computing in Civil Engineering, 7*, 6-22, 1993.

A Situated Cognition Approach to Problem Solving with Implications for Computer-based Learning and Assessment

Michael F. Young[a] and Michael McNeese[b]

[a]Educational Psychology Department, University of Connecticut, U-4, 249 Glenbrook Rd., Storrs, CT 06269-2004 (e-mail myoung@uconnvm.uconn.edu)

[b]Armstrong Laboratory/ Human Engineering Division ,AL/CFHI, BLDG 248, Wright Patterson AFB, OH 45433-6573

Abstract
In this paper we discuss the nature of an ecological approach to problem solving and describe some new alternatives to assessing problem solving as a perception-action process. We suggest that a situated cognitive view of problem solving requires new assessment techniques that are non-invasive and allow expert problem solvers to externalize more of the perceptual processes they use.

1. THE NATURE OF REAL WORLD PROBLEM SOLVING

Real-world complex problem solving requires coordination of multiple cognitive processes, applied through multiple paths (Siegler & Jenkins, 1989), and it occurs within contexts that provide critical perceptual cues for potential solutions. Real world problem solving is often interpersonal, ill-structured, and involves interwoven problems, extended time frames, and several possible competing solutions (Meacham & Emont, 1989). Real-world problem solving also involves discovering problems/ subproblems, detecting key attributes of the problem (Bransford, Sherwood, Vye, & Rieser, 1988), and the 'generation' of relevant subproblems (Cognition and Technology Group at Vanderbilt, in preparation). Successful problem solving in groups requires the social construction of knowledge to facilitate transfer from the context in which learning occurred to the many varied real world contexts in which knowledge is applied.

In reviewing instances of real-world problem solving such as surgery, combat piloting and team engineering design, we have identified 10 characteristics of "situated" problem solving:
1. Coordination of multiple cognitive processes, applied through multiple paths (Siegler & Jenkins, 1989), dynamically and continuously unfolding. Examples include analysis, planning, problem identification, metacognitive monitoring, and problem solving while comparing multiple solutions to multiple subproblems.
2. Complex contexts that provide critical perceptual cues and rich situational affordances (Rogoff & Lave, 1984).

3. Interpersonal interaction. Greeno, Smith, & Moore (in press) write, "... the issue of [problem solving] is social in a fundamental way. Learning occurs as people engage in activities, and the meanings and significance of objects and information in the situation derive from their roles in the activities that people are engaged in. (p.2)"

4. Being interpersonal, real world group problem solving requires the social construction of knowledge (see Bereiter and Scardamalia, 1989; Edwards & Middleton, 1986). More than simply communicating or coordinating within a group, problem solving requires that group members construct a shared perception of the problem and the solution, often mediated by technology.

5. Ill-structured content requiring generation of relevant subproblems (CTGV, 1992). Despite careful and extended planning, real situations vary widely from case to case, and require continuous identification of problems, sub-problems to these problems, and solutions. When complex problem solving is done on the fly, problems that are detected must be conceptualized into manageable subproblems that afford specific actions: planning is integrated throughout the problem solving process.

6. Integration of distributed information, typically from various specialties and domains.

7. Real world problem solving takes place across extended time frames. Such problems cannot be solved in a few minutes or even in a few hours, and are often completely beyond the time and space constraints of a single individual. They have a developmental history and future all contextualized in the ongoing situation.

8. Competing solutions (Meacham & Emont, 1989). Rather than a single correct solution, most real world problems have multiple correct solutions as well as "almost workable" solutions.

9. Real world problem solving involves discovering problems and noticing perceptual attributes of the problem, such as detecting relevant from irrelevant information (Bransford, Sherwood, Vye, & Rieser, 1986).

10. Finally, real world problem solving involves inherent values, intentions and goals that often have personal and social significance (Johnson, Moen, & Thompson, 1988).

We believe that to assess problem solving as it occurs in the real world, the assessment must begin by presenting an environment with these characteristics. Then, with aid of technology as we describe, the assessment must focus on the process as well as the products of problem solving. In this paper we present several approaches to assessing problem solving as a perceptual process. We describe concept mapping the knowledge of experts (AKADAM), a computer partner for problem solving capable of creating a "dribble" file of the process (JPA), and several measures designed to assess perceptual components of problems solving using videodisc-based vignettes. We convlude with a description of problem solving as a perception-action cycle.

2. CONCEPT MAPPING WITH AKADAM

The Advanced Knowledge and Design Acquisition Methodology (AKADAM) represents a prototypic method for mapping the conceptual understanding of an expert using an ecologically valid method. The AKADAM process initially asks the expert (or more broadly, person to be assessed) to spontaneously define the domain or problem space through a conceptual map, highlighting the conceptual relationships they consider meaningful. The method results in a socially constructed externalization of the expert's knowledge that overcomes the restricted linear presentations of spoken or written language. In the collaborative and generative AKADAM process, expert and assessor can repeatedly refer to the developing concept map which itself can afford new exploration of concepts, understanding, linking, and new interpretations, all constructed "on the fly." The concept map and an accompanying design storyboard component serve to anchor attention to a common environmental object that represents the deepening structure of the conceptual knowledge.

The transfer of knowledge from expert to assessor is incomplete unless it also includes the perceptual cues used to make important discriminations within the problem domain (Zaff & McNeese, 1991). Once the concepts are mapped in a visuo-conceptual form, the expert is brought back to lead a second collaborative effort to transform the information into a picto-literal representation using a storyboarding technique. Design storyboarding uses a graphic medium to create a sequence of display frames showing a defined time sequence. In this context, the expert is actually placed in the role of designer. Tunnicliffe and Scrivener (1991) suggested that designers are most comfortable when they express ideas as sketches and diagrams while also being given the flexibility to engage in verbal explanations. This has also held true for experts serving in the role of designers elaborating their conceptual and perceptual knowledge through design sketches in the AKADAM process. Our experience indicates that in many cases experts switch between the concept maps and storyboard designs to progressively elaborate the conceptual representation of their knowledge. This process captures more knowledge that was previously believed to be accessible only to the expert implicitly.

3. ANCHORED ASSESSMENT WITH JPA

The Jasper Planning Assistant (JPA) is a HyperCard®-based automated data retrieval system for the Jasper problem solving series. The Jasper Series is a videodisc-based mathematical problem solving context available from Optical Data, Inc. Fall of 1992, the first author implemented Jasper in a 5th grade classroom in rural New England, with a same-school control class. In three months, students "immersed" themselves in three problem, working in dyads, and completing numerous extension activities. The JPA was used to assess their achievement on one of these problems.

A typical session for solving the Jasper problem would begin with a student viewing the 15-minute story, beginning to end. Near the end of the story a problem arises and all the information needed to make a quantitative decision about that problem has been embedded in the story. As the story ends, the problem is posed to the students for them to adopt and solve. JPA provides "scaffolding" (Bruner, 1986; Vygotsky, 1978) for solving the problem by prompting students to generate planning questions, and make calculations. It also provide control of the videodisc to retrieve information and a facts sheets for storing found and computed data.

The JPA in helping students to solve the problem, creates a "dribble" file of information about where students re-visited the videodisc, what calculations they made, and time the spent planning, retrieving information, calculating and reviewing facts. This externalizes more of the problem solving process than judging answers, and is less invasive than think-aloud verbal protocols (Young & Kulikowich, in preparation).

4. ALTERNATIVE METHODS FOR ASSESSING PERCEPTION

We have found the perceptually-rich stimuli provided by video (specifically videodiscs) useful for acquiring evidence about student perceptions. Two applications of video include the experimental task, "Whata-ya-see?" and a multi-phase task to assess the perception-based skill of information finding. "Whata-ya-see?" involves providing each student a blank sheet of paper, then replaying a short scene from the Jasper story. When the scene ends, students are asked to list all the things they saw or heard during the segment. We have noted that experimental students increased the number and diversity of items listed during the course of our intervention. Students who initially only focused on the overt story-relevant information, began to list feelings produced by the musical score, background items (e.g., book titles from the book shelf), and descriptive adjectives for listed items, toward the end of the intervention. This we have taken as evidence of changing perceptions.

Information Finding is a task we have administered to both experimental and control students. The procedure involves repeated showings of the same information-rich video with the same questions asked after each viewing. In one recent study we used only two repetitions. Phase 1: Students were given a blank sheet of paper, told to "watch carefully for they would be asked questions later," then shown a 12-minute video vignette on Admiral's Byrd's flight across the Antarctica to the south pole (NG Explorers videodisc). The students were then asked 12 fact questions about information contained in the video. Phase 2: Papers were collected, and a second blank sheet distributed. Students were then shown the same video vignette a second time, and again asked the 12 questions, plus a 13th "bonus" that all students were expected to get correct. Our results indicated that seven students in the Experimental group spontaneously took notes on the first phase while none of the Control students took notes. During Phase 2, 12 Experimental students spontaneously took notes, while 3 Control students took notes. The Experimental class scored consistently and significantly more information found on both phases. This we suggest provides evidence for perceptual learning taking place in the experimental classroom.

5. DISCUSSION

Real world problems have many attributes that make them different in many important ways from problems used traditionally to teach and assess problem solving. We have identified 10 characteristics we believe are essential for "realistic" problem solving to occur. We view complex situated problem solving from the perspective of ecological psychology (Gibson, 1979/1986). From this perspective we acknowledge the primacy of the interaction between the skills and abilities brought to the situation by each problem solver (effectivities) and the affordances for action provided by the problem environment or problem space -- a symmetry of acausal interactions (Shaw, Turvey & Mace, 1982). This relationship is captured in the perceiving-acting cycle that temporally unfolds through the problem-solving process. When perception is emphasized over memory, it is the information picked up from the environment that is perceived and acted upon, plus an agent's goals and intentions that must become the subject of assessment, not simply the actions or results of problem solving. From this perspective, we characterize meaningfulness of a problem as an overlap of an individual's goals and intentions with the activities afforded by a problem space or problem-solving environment. We posit that meaningful problem solving results in transfer of learning, perhaps the *sine qua non* of education, and we characterize this transfer from the ecological perspective as changing the nature of the attractors in the external and internal fields (see Kugler, Shaw, Vicente, & Kinsella-Shaw, 1991, for description of changing attractor fields and Greeno, Smith, & Moore, in press, for a discussion of transfer of situated learning).

From our perspective, knowledge and intelligent behavior are best characterized as a **relationship** between the abilities of an individual (effectivities) and the nature of situations (affordance of the environment). All learning and problem solving are situated. And as in most real-world activities, a prominent feature of the situation is often other people (co-workers, team members, and cooperative group partners). Knowledge is often socially constructed-- based on the shared affordances provided by multiple agents in a situation. To understand situated learning and cognition, we must construct realistic problem solving contexts that are well-define, more constrained, and replicable in contrast to the real world. The Jasper videodisc problem solving context represents an example of such a problem solving environment. The AKADAM approach to assessment relies on the social construction of knowledge to produce concept maps and storyboards that capture the perceptual cues and conceptual knowledge of experts as well as novices. Research on Jasper suggests that situated learning can occur in such environments providing a mechanism to study real-world problem solving in an ecologically valid way. Such research also raises the important issue of assessment of real-world situated knowledge. The JPA provides a technology-based tool that supports problem solving while seamlessly collecting assessment data. Additional assessments using video to focus on perception rather than memory are also a key component of an assessment of situated problem solving.

Our data present a complex multivariate array of indicators, that challenge existing psychometric models. However, the concept maps and solution paths provided by these situated assessment techniques have potential to significantly enhance knowledge-based expert systems, intelligent tutors, and school-based assessment in mathematics, science, and related fields. In short, a theory of situated learning applied to well-define realistic problems can provide the mechanism for enhancing problem solving for novices, experts, teachers, students, and professionals in many fields.

6. REFERENCES

Bereiter, C., & Scardamalia, M. (1989). Intentional learning as a goal of instruction. In L. B. Resnick (Ed.), Knowing, Learning, and Instruction: Essays in Honor of Robert Glaser (pp. 361-392). Hillsdale, NJ: Erlbaum.

Bransford, J. D., Sherwood, R. D., Vye, N. J., & Rieser, J. (1986). Teaching thinking and problem solving. American Psychologist, 41, (10), 1078-1089.

830

Bruner, J. S. (1986). Actual Minds, Possible Worlds. Cambridge, MA: Harvard U. Press.

Cognition and Technology Group at Vanderbilt. (1992). The Jasper experiment: An exploration of issues in learning and instructional design. Education Technology, Research and Development, 40 (1), 65-80.

Edwards, D. & Middleton, D. (1986). Joint remembering: Constructing an account of shared experience through conversational discourse. Discourse Processes, 9, 423-459.

Gibson, J. J. (1979/1986). The ecological approach to visual perception, Hillsdale, NJ: Erlbaum.

Greeno, J. G., Smith, D. R., & Moore, J. L. (in press) Transfer of situated learning. To appear in D. Detterman & R. Sternberg (Eds.), Transfer on Trial.

Johnson, P. E., Moen, J. B., & Thompson, W. B. (1988). Garden path errors in diagnostic reasoning. In L. Bolc & M. J. Coombs (Eds.), Expert Systems Applications, Berlin, Germany: Springer-Verlag.

Kugler, P. N., Shaw, R. E., Vicente, K. J. & Kinsella-Shaw, J. (1991). The role of attractors in the self-organization of intentional systems. In R. R. Hoffman & D. S. Palermo (Eds.) Cognition and the symbolic processes. Hillsdale, NJ: Erlbaum.

Meacham, J. A. & Emont N. C. (1989). Interpersonal bias in everyday problem solving. In J. D. Sinnott (Ed.), Everyday problem solving, New York: Praeger.

Rogoff, B., & Lave, J. (1984). Everyday cognition: Its development in social context, Cambridge, MA: Harvard University Press.

Sigler, R. S., & Jenkins, E. (1989) How children discover new strategies, Hillsdale, NJ: LEA.

Vygotsky, L. S. (1978). Internationalization of higher psychological functions. In M. Cole, V. John-Steiner, S. Scribner, & E. Souberman (Eds.), Mind in Society: The development of higher psychological processes. Cambridge, MA: Harvard University Press.

Young, M. F., & Kulikowich, J. M. (in preparation). Improving reading comprehension through real world situated problem solving. Paper to be presented to AERA annual meeting, San Francisco, May 1992.

Zaff, B. S., & McNeese, M. D. (1991). Design acquisition: Translating user knowledge into design solutions. Proceedings of the Interface 91' Conference, 1 (pp. 42-49), Dayton, OH.

A COMPUTER-ASSISTED INSTRUCTION SYSTEM
FOR BEGINNER'S CRUDE CHARGE SCHEDULERS

Kotaro Saito [a], Tsutomu Tabe [a] and Katsuo Furihata [b]

[a] Graduate school of Industrial and Systems Engineering, Aoyama Gakuin University, 1-16-6, Chitosedai, Setagaya-ku, Tokyo 157, Japan

[b] Tonen System Plaza Inc., Shuwa Iidabashi Bldg., 2-3-19, Koraku, Bunkyo-ku, Tokyo 112, Japan

ABSTRACT : This paper offers preliminary information on the methodology needed for the development of computer-assisted instruction (CAI) system for the purpose of training beginner crude charge schedulers. It is assumed that a skilled scheduler makes schedules using elementary knowledge of such schedule coupled with his or her scheduling abilities. In order to train beginners, as opposed to skilled schedulers, it is necessary to develop a system consisting of two subsystems; one is to impart elementary knowledge; the other is to improve the scheduler's abilities. In this connection, prototype based on this method was constructed and the validity of the method was confirmed through experimentation this prototype.

1. INTRODUCTION

Crude charge scheduling involves the making of a daily schedule in a petroleum refinery. This includes three operations: (1) the crude unloading operation, (2) the crude charging operation, (3) the crude shifting operation. The schedules are evaluated based on (a) the total waiting time of tankers, (b) the volume of crude charging, (c) the amounts of crude oil to be mixed with different types. Although crude charge schedules are usually made by skilled schedulers, expert systems (ES) for the task concerned have been developed and will replace schedulers in the future. However, if the conditions governing the ES such as the facilities, policy and related circumstances change, skilled schedulers will be needed to revise the ES. Furthermore, it will be necessary to train apprentice schedulers.

At the same time, most scheduler training programs consist of two steps: (1) acquiring knowledge, such as petroleum refining and facility operation by operating facilities in a petroleum refinery over a period of two to three years; (2) developing scheduling abilities by making schedules based on real data as an exercise and receiving advice from skilled schedulers over a period of one year. Since beginners need to spend three to four years in order to become professional schedulers, there is the problem of how to train beginners quickly.

This paper therefore presents preliminary information on the methodology required for the development of a computer-assisted instruction (CAI) system for the purpose of training beginner crude charge schedulers, by taking the following steps: (1) clarifying the means by which the problem can be solved, (2) constructing a prototype system, and (3) confirming the validity of the method through experimentation with the prototype.

The target of the system is those persons who have no knowledge of crude charge scheduling,

832

and its goal is to make schedules while giving due consideration to the basic point, such as the facilities, the type of crude oil and so on, based on a simplified model.

2. HOW TO APPROACH THE PROBLEM

The relationship between the knowledge and the scheduling abilities of the skilled scheduler can be divided into knowledge of crude charge scheduling itself, such as the number of tanks, the method of using the simulator and so on, and scheduling abilities, which include recognition of the various conditions and so on. When a scheduler makes crude charge schedules, he or she uses both of the above aspects knowledge and scheduling abilities. To give an example, if a scheduler is aware of the fact that a tanker will be arriving soon and that the tanks are almost full, he will take the following actions: acquiring the necessary knowledge, such as "when the crude oil is unloaded from the tanker, the tanks must be spaced," and "if crude oil is charged, the tank should be spaced"; deciding to charge crude oil using his or her scheduling abilities, acquiring the necessary knowledge, such as "the crude charging operation inputs mean charging the tanks, the charging volume and the start time"; and determining such inputs using his or her scheduling abilities.

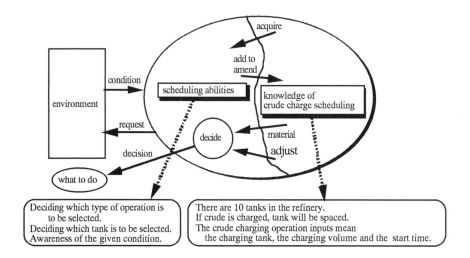

Figure 1. Relationship between the knowledge and the scheduling abilities of the scheduler

Training therefore includes: imparting knowledge through the presentation of teaching materials; then, improving one's abilities by making imaginary schedules with a simulator. This is followed system training based on this idea and consisting of the following four steps: (1) strengthening the basis of crude charge scheduling; (2) learning the method of using the simulator; (3) making schedules using a simplified model aimed of beginners; (4) giving advice. The first two steps impart the knowledge required for crude charge scheduling. The last two steps help improve one's abilities.

3. HOW TO SOLVE THE PROBLEM

Figure 2 shows the basic architecture of the system. It consists of two subsystems: (1) a subsystem for imparting knowledge (upper part of the figure), consisting of an explanatory function and student model, and (2) a subsystem for improving one's abilities (lower part of the figure), with a simulator that includes warning and diagnostic functions. If beginners use this system, they will quickly become professional schedulers.

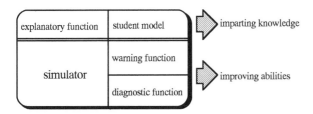

Figure 2. Basic architecture of the system

3.1 EXPLANATORY FUNCTION

The explanatory function presents teaching materials for the purpose of imparting knowledge to students. There are 25 teaching materials (the scheduling basics numbering 20, and the simulator manuals totaling 5.) The teaching materials consist of both text and graphics. Figure 3 shows a sample of these teaching materials. It represent the sphere of crude charge scheduling in a petroleum refinery. Almost all of student spend about 60 minutes learning from these teaching materials.

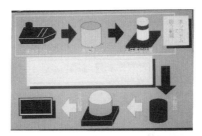

Figure 3. Sample of the teaching material

3.2 STUDENT MODEL

With the student model, a selection is made of the teaching material most appropriate for the progress made by the student. The student model adopts the idea of an overlay model. The student's progress is expressed by the model as follows: (1) Since a student in the earlier stage of study has not yet learned anything from the teaching materials, all teaching materials are considered as "unknown material", as shown in figure 4(a), (2) If he or she understands the material explained, this changes to "known material", as shown in figure 4(b). In this way, the overlay model expresses the progress made by dividing the materials into "unknown" and "known". In this research, once the explanatory function has explained "unknown material", the student model makes sure that the student has fully comprehended by asking the question, "Do you understand?" If the student's answer is, "Yes", this material changes to "known material". The system can therefore select the teaching material most appropriate for the progress made by the student.

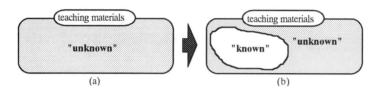

Figure 4. Concept of the student model

3.3 SIMULATOR

By using the simulator, it is easy for the student to calculate the charging volume, as well as the charging time. The simulator uses a Gannt chart with tables on the display. Even if the student is unfamiliar with computers, he can still use the simulator easily by means of a mouse. Figure 5 shows the actual display of the simulator. The X-axis of the Gannt chart shows the time; one measure represents one day. The Y-axis shows the number of tanks. If the student selects "menu" using the mouse, the menu will appear, enabling the student to select the type of operation required. If the student makes a schedule using a pencil and a ruler, he will spend half a day to complete it. However, by using the simulator, it can be completed it in only 30 - 60 minutes.

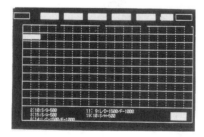

Figure 5. Actual display of the simulator

3.4 WARNING FUNCTION

The warning function warns the student if he or she attempts to perform an invalid operation. There are 34 basic warning statements. For example, if the student attempts to load crude oil which is over the limit of the tank, the following warning will be given, "Tank will overflow." Since this warning function works each time the student attempts to perform invalid operation, it is not possible for the student to make an infeasible schedule.

3.5 DIAGNOSTIC FUNCTION

The diagnostic function diagnoses the schedule made by the student and offers advice. This function is coded by means of knowledge-based programming; it is easy to add to and amend advice given. There are about 150 rules. The process of diagnosis is as follows: (1) Expressing each valuation index of the schedule by means of rules using natural language, such as, "too much", "too little" and so on, so that the student will be able to understand the valuation easily; (2) Advice is given in natural language, such as, "You must pay a penalty to the shipping company if you keep the tanker waiting." The student is therefore made aware of the bad points of his or her schedule as soon as it has been completed.

4. CONFIRMING THE VALIDITY

4.1 STEPS OF THE EXPERIMENT

The prototype has been tested as follows: (1) The testers acquire knowledge of scheduling by using the system; (2) The testers make a schedule, and then the researchers obtain the values of the valuation index; (3) The testers are divided into two groups, one is given advice by means of the diagnostic function, and the other is not given any advice; (4) The testers then make another schedule, and the researchers obtain the values yet again.

4.2 METHOD OF ANALYSIS

The valuation indexes are: (a) the total waiting time of five tankers under given condition; (b) the total difference between the charged volume and the target volume of each of the eight types of crude oil under given condition; (c) the amounts of crude oil mixed with different types. As for each valuation index, the smaller the value, the better.

For the purpose of analysis the researchers use the study growth rate for each valuation index. The study growth rate is expressed as follows:

$$\text{Study growth rate} = \frac{(\text{value of the first schedule}) - (\text{value of the second})}{(\text{value of the first})} \times 100 \tag{1}$$

The bigger the rate, the better. The averages and variances of these rates in each tester group are calculated. The averages are examined by using the following equation:

$$t_0 = \frac{\overline{x_1} - \overline{x_2}}{\sqrt{\dfrac{(n_1 - 1)\widehat{\sigma_1}^2 + (n_2 - 1)\widehat{\sigma_2}^2}{n_1 + n_2 - 2}} \sqrt{\dfrac{1}{n_1} + \dfrac{1}{n_2}}} \tag{2}$$

If $-t_{n_1+n_2-2} < t_0 < t_{n_1+n_2-2}$, then there are differences between the groups.

where n_1, n_2 = number of testers

$$\overline{x_1}, \overline{x_2} = \text{average of the study growth rate}$$
$$\widehat{\sigma_1}^2, \widehat{\sigma_2}^2 = \text{variance in the study growth rate}$$

4.3 RESULTS OF THE EXPERIMENT

The experiment was carried out using 15 undergraduate students (ten testers were given advice, five were given no advice). Table 1 shows the averages and variances of the study growth rate in each tester group. It also shows the values of t_0 and whether there are any differences between the groups. As a result of examination, differences between the groups are found in (a) and (b). In a comparison with the averages of the groups, the average of the group that was given advice is better than that of the grope that was not. Differences between the groups are not found in (c), since the values of the first and second schedules are good. Since it was confirmed that a beginner who uses the method proposed by this study can make better schedules than those who use only the simulator, it was also confirmed that the method is valid.

Table 1
Average and variance of the study growth rate

		Advice given	Not given	t_0	Difference
(a)	Average	85.59	11.34	15.33	Yes
	Variance	435.71	219.46		
(b)	Average	79.14	36.2	31.19	Yes
	Variance	73.36	101.936		
(c)	Average	60.84	48.34	2.07	No
	Variance	1750.77	1178.02		

$t_{13}(\alpha = 0.05) = 2.16$

5. CONCLUSION

In this study, (1) a method of developing a CAI system for beginners of crude charge scheduling has been proposed; (2) a prototype based on this method has been constructed; and (3) the validity of the method has been confirmed through experimentation with this prototype.

6. REFERENCES

1 G. Salvendy (ed.), Handbook of Industrial Engineering, pp.109-138, Institute of Industrial Engineers, 1991
2 Artificial Intelligence Society of Japan (ed.), Handbook of Artificial Intelligence (in Japanese), pp.841-869, Ohm-Sya, 1990
3 K. Miyakawa, Statistics (in Japanese), Yuhikaku-Sya, 1988

HUMAN-COMPUTER INTERACTION AND THE AUTOMATION OF WORK

Karl U. Smith[a] and Thomas J. Smith[b]

[a]Professor Emeritus, Behavioral Cybernetics Laboratory, University of Wisconsin - Madison, 1001 Tower Blvd., Lake Wales, FL 33853

[b]U.S. Bureau of Mines, 5629 Minnehaha Ave. South, Minneapolis, MN 55417. This is not an official Bureau publication. The views expressed are not necessarily those of the U.S. Bureau of Mines.

Abstract
Computers have greatly expanded the scope and complexity of work automation. This report presents a behavioral cybernetic analysis of human-computer interaction (HCI) and work automation, dealing with how the computer serves to augment human self-control of work behavior. Major conclusions are that computer automation of work: (1) feedback influences human behavior and performance; (2) is key to human efforts to effectively manage high population density and worldwide socioeconomic integration; and (3) from a human factors perspective represents one of the most significant scientific and socioeconomic issues confronting humankind.

1. INTRODUCTION

Work is the engine of the human condition. Through organized work, species *Homo* has defined its civilizations, cultures, ethnic and national identities, commerce, socioeconomic status, organizations, institutions, and communities, and in so doing has self-guided its own emergence in evolution.

We work to control our environment. Throughout evolution humans have invented technologies to facilitate performance of work and to thereby enhance their control of environmental conditions. Mechanization of work through technology may have flowered in the industrial revolution, but key antecedents are found in timekeeping technology (dating back to ancient megaliths), engineering feats of early civilizations, early mechanical inventions of Leonardo (termed by some the father of automation) and others, and the pervasive impetus of trade and warfare.

Computer-based automation represents the latest stage in mechanization of work, denoted as the information or post-industrial age. The basic purpose of computer-based technology remains the same---expanded control of environmental conditions---but the terms of reference are vastly altered because of new and diverse modes and patterns of HCI for managing and integrating work made possible by this technology. Consequently, the human aspects of computerized automation have received both a scientific and commercial emphasis far surpassing that accorded earlier technologies [1].

Human factors principles of automation, including an historical and scientific analysis of manufacturing automation, are detailed by Smith and Smith [2] and generally discussed in Blache [3]. These reviews point out that manufacturing science---the integrated application of engineering and human factors principles to achieve manufacturing efficiency and quality---has emerged at the forefront of efforts by the U.S. and other industrialized

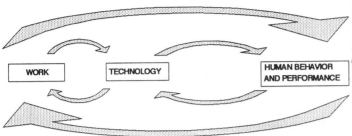

Figure 1. Behavioral cybernetics of human interaction with work and technological design factors.

countries to compete and survive economically in the global marketplace. The present report extends this analysis by addressing the role of HCI in work automation from a behavioral cybernetic perspective, that is in terms of how the computer serves to augment human self-control of work behavior.

Figure 1 defines our behavioral cybernetic interpretation of HCI and work automation. Arrows in the diagram symbolize mutual feedback relationships linking human behavior and performance, the design of technology, and work design. There are three major implications of this feedback model of HCI and work automation: (1) there are not strict cause and effect relationships among the three attributes shown in the figure, in that each serves simultaneously as both cause and effect of the others; (2) consequently, design factors both originate from; and (3) in turn feedback influence human behavioral expression. Some key implications of computer automation for each of the attributes shown in Figure 1 are considered in the following sections.

2. TECHNOLOGICAL DESIGN AND HCI

The model depicted in Figure 1 assumes that technological design factors feed back to influence behavioral specialization in use of the technology, which in turn positively influences subsequent technological development. Figure 2 depicts 15 distinct stages of technological innovation created in human evolution through this feedback process. The illustration suggests that human development of technology has been cumulative and integrative, leading to successively more complex machines and technological systems. As new tools, machines, and systems are produced, older technology is not discarded but continues to be refined and redesigned (dotted lines in the figure). Consequently, all of the technological creations of the past remain in use as essential components in machines and machine systems of today. The computer epitomizes this process as the most technically advanced end product of a million or more years of human evolution in creating technology for controlling environmental conditions through work.

From this perspective some future trends in computer-based technological design, under the combined feedback influences of human creativity and the imperatives of work organization, may be predicted with reasonable accuracy. For example, Nickerson [4] cites ethereality, connectivity, and versatility as prominent themes in the progress of computer automation. The first refers to incorporation of micro-computing power into everyday devices, so that we increasingly interact with computers without realizing it. The second refers to mushrooming use of computer networks to mediate communication at regional, national, and global levels. The third refers to growing power of computers in diverse applications, such as automated manufacturing or virtual reality.

Less obvious is the projected course of software design to make all of this technology work. Software traditionally has lagged hardware, and a reversal of priorities (as shown by the rise of Microsoft and the decline of

LEVEL OF
TECHNOLOGY

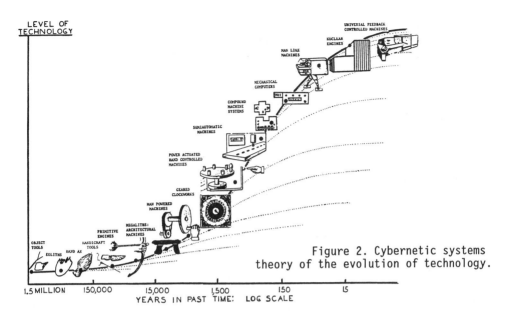

Figure 2. Cybernetic systems
theory of the evolution of technology.

| 1.5 MILLION | 150,000 | 15,000 | 1,500 | 150 | 15 |
YEARS IN PAST TIME: LOG SCALE

IBM) already is underway. Two outcomes are likely. The first is that software technology will represent the next distinct stage in Figure 2. The second is that participation of human factors in the software design process will intensify (i.e., this conference has a secure future).

With regard to the second point, one important implication of Figure 1 is that good design cannot necessarily be predicted a priori. Instead, as Gould [5] has emphasized, user-compatible systems must be designed iteratively, such that the feedback effects on performance of a new system are recurrently tested at successive design stages, until an acceptable design is achieved.

3. WORK DESIGN AND HCI

Our focus in this section is on manufacturing operations, where effects of computer automation on work design have been dramatic. Computer automation of office work has been relatively less successful.

Prior to the advent of computing, manufacturing mechanization--the first phase of automation--expanded greatly during the industrial revolution. A milestone in the transition from mechanized to computerized automation was introduction of analog computers to automate gun sighting and aircraft tracking mechanisms during WWII.

Ford Motor Company was the first to use the term automation in the early fifties, to describe operations of a computerized engine-drilling transfer line. Two subsequent phases in computer automation of manufacturing followed [2]. The second involved creation of diverse types of computerized, specialized, automatic manufacturing production lines. The third phase, still ongoing, involves computer-integrated manufacturing, based on computer-robot production systems and integration of these systems with computer-based business control of manufacturing.

In the course of these phases of computer-based work automation, the following specific advances in work design and the control of work have occurred: (1) expansion of types of work subject to automation; (2) greater complexity of control of work operations; (3) more direct involvement of management in work automation; (4) better integration and control of production; (5) facilitated changeover of jobs and production sequences; and (6) better integration of machine and non-machine production roles.

Some emerging trends in work design linked to computer automation also may be discerned. These include: (1) globalization of production; (2) decline in the manufacturing workforce; (3) rise of software-intensive business; (4) flexible work schedules and sites (i.e., telecommuting); and (5) uncoupling of economic recovery and employment.

The record suggests that attention to the human factors of HCI has figured prominently in the scope and success of these changes [2,3]. This may seem contradictory, in that elimination of human control is the putative goal of computer automation. The fact is, however, that increasing computerization of work, exemplified in manufacturing, has made human factors more, not less, critical to effective work operations. This has promoted emergence of a new, multi-disciplinary branch of human-computer science dealing with the human factors of HCI generally [6] and manufacturing in particular [7].

The disappointing record of office automation may be understood in terms of human factors issues [8]. Office computer systems are deficient in providing effective social communication in the office environment. To benefit both office and manufacturing automation, several corrective steps are essential: (1) design systems to ensure human, not computer, control over the pace and conditions of work; (2) employ computers for their most efficient function---i.e., processing and monitoring information, not controlling it, which is what workers do best; and (3) strictly delimit the role of computers as mediators of social communication, since their abilities to serve as surrogates in social interactions among workers, supervisors, engineers, and managers remains primitive.

We believe that critical human factors issues define in large part the overriding scientific significance of HCI and work automation. That is to say, as suggested in Figure 2, computerized automation of work represents the forefront of a revolutionary revision of the marketplace and human society generally, encompassing the formation of global corporations, feedback restructuring of government by such entities, computerized control of financial exchange and communication, and revamping of educational systems required to produce new managerial and technical skills for organization and operation of automated corporate enterprises.

These changes may be viewed technically as representing the latest revolutionary adjustment of the course of human biosocial evolution in response to the tremendous increase in the world's population. In other words, we are entering an era in which computerization of work is accompanied (in a feedback manner) by computer-mediated reorganization of society itself, as a primary strategy of social and technological adaptation for meeting the daily needs of billions of people.

4. HUMAN CONSEQUENCES OF COMPUTER AUTOMATION OF WORK

The premise of the feedback model in Figure 1 is that as new designs of technology and work are created, specialized changes in human behavior and performance emerge customized for their use. There is extensive empirical support for the thesis implied by the figure that design factors critically influence variability in interactive behavior and performance [9].

What are the likely human consequences of computer automation of work? Findings from both early and recent studies of this question offer some answers. For example, Buckingham [10] identified a broad range of both positive and negative human-related effects of automation of work: (1)

degraded worker skills; (2) decreased interaction among workers; (3) marked increase in level of worker boredom; (4) lowering of requirements for workers to perform at capacity levels; (5) unequal lowering of worker skills for different jobs; (6) increase in the demands for supervision; (7) lower set-up rate for particular jobs; (8) improved quality and quantity of output; (9) easier equipment maintenance and storage; (10) marked increase in indirect labor costs; (11) greater need for preventive maintenance; (12) improvement in housekeeping; (13) no appreciable effects on wage structure; (14) possible upgrading of labor in the future; (15) improvement of working conditions in certain areas; (16) increase in job safety in some operations; (17) increase in job-related stress, especially in automated offices; (18) higher demands for mental alertness and resistance to strain; (19) increased mobility, flexibility, and education of workers; and (20) reduced ability of workers to achieve work satisfaction and to identify with the objects of production.

The record of work automation in the past three decades provides support for many of these predictions [2,3,6,7]. They fall into three general categories, namely psychosocial, safety and health, and management effects.

Psychosocial Effects. Taylor's model of management from early in the century featured strict control of worker activity by management, with little or no opportunity for self-control by workers over their jobs. In some industries automation has changed this trend and has promoted participation by workers in decisions affecting work organization and conditions [7]. In other industries automation has been used to refine and entrench Taylorism. The epitome of the latter development is use of computers to monitor the performance of workers, especially in clerical tasks. It is estimated that 4-6 million clerical workers, or 20-35 percent of the total clerical labor force in the U.S., is subjected to such computer monitoring and control [11].

Safety and Health Effects. The negative human factors of computer automation of work also extend to adverse safety and health effects. Health consequences of video display terminal (VDT) use are pervasive and constitute the most prevalent health problem associated with computer technology. Less frequent but far more dramatic are major industrial accidents (Three-Mile Island, Chernobyl, Challenger, KAL-007) traceable, at least in part, to automation failures [12].

Management Effects. Effects of computerization of work on management started to emerge by 1960 and have been as distinct as those on workers. Bright [13] explored this subject. His findings are that automation required new patterns of management planning, and that special problems arose where such planning was inadequate. Also, the roles of marketing and advertising were enhanced because the viability of high volume production through automated manufacturing relies heavily upon high customer acceptance.

Buckingham [10] viewed automation as a vehicle often used by management as a base for empire building, sometimes resulting in wasteful capital expansion. Specifically, automation should not be rationalized by confusing its engineering with its social, economic, and managerial aspects, because not infrequently the engineering changes are impractical and lack a sound economic and management basis. The multibillion-dollar loss of General Motors in creating new automated auto plants illustrates the point [3].

Mann and Hoffmann [14] concluded that industrial automation increased management planning problems related to: (1) failure to recognize key human factors issues, such as social integration factors; and (2) meeting new training and educational needs. Although this analysis generally drew positive conclusions about human aspects of automation, it also uncovered the human basis of future disasters of automated industrial systems.

5. CONCLUSIONS

Mushrooming scientific and technical interest in HCI and work automation has occurred because of problems encountered in utilization of computers in manufacturing and other industrial sectors, and because of the profound individual, institutional, and societal effects. We conclude that computer-mediated automation of work is vital to human efforts to: (1) control environmental conditions on a global scale in order to effectively manage increased population density and socioeconomic integration worldwide; and (2) achieve all major socioeconomic objectives for the next century, including building a global economy, socioeconomic improvement in the third world, and meeting employment and production needs of a growing population while reducing environmental damage.

We conclude also that success of this effort rests upon appropriate application of human factors principles in the design, organization, operation, and management of automation. We believe therefore that the human factors of work automation and HCI represent one of the most critical scientific and socioeconomic issues confronting humankind today.

6. REFERENCES

1   Salvendy, G. (1987). What we know and what we should know about human-computer interaction: strategies for research and development. In G. Salvendy (Ed.), *Cognitive Engineering in the Design of Human-Computer Interaction and Expert Systems* (pp. 13-19). Amsterdam: Elsevier.
2   Smith, K.U., and Smith, T.J. (1988). Analysis of the human factors in automation. In K.M. Blache, (Ed.), *Success Factors For Implementing Change: A Manufacturing Viewpoint* (pp. 259-338). Dearborn, MI: Society of Manufacturing Engineers.
3   Blache, K.M. (Ed.) (1988). *Success Factors for Implementing Change: A Manufacturing Viewpoint.* Dearborn, MI: Society of Manufacturing Engineers.
4   Nickerson, R.S. (1993). Human interaction with computers and robots. *International Journal of Human Factors in Manufacturing, 3.* In press.
5   Gould, J.D. (1990). How to design usable systems. In M. Helander (Ed.), *Handbook of Human-Computer Interaction* (pp. 757-789). Amsterdam: North-Holland.
6   Helander, M. (Ed.) (1990). *Handbook of Human-Computer Interaction.* Amsterdam: North-Holland.
7   Karwowski, W. and Salvendy, G. (Eds.) (1993). *Human Factors in Advanced Manufacturing.* New York: Wiley. In press.
8   Hoos, J.E. (1960). When the computer takes over the office. *Harvard Business Review, 38,* 102-112.
9   Smith, T.J., Henning, R.A., and Smith, K.U. (1993). Sources of performance variability. In W. Karwowski and G. Salvendy (Eds.), *Human Factors in Advanced Manufacturing* (pp. 336-425). New York: Wiley. In press.
10 Buckingham, W. (1961). *Automation: It's Impact On Business and Industry.* New York: Harper.
11 Booth, W. (1987). Big brother is counting your keystrokes. *Science, 238,* 17.
12 Hornick, R.J. (1987). Dreams--design and destiny. *Human Factors, 29,* 111-121.
13 Bright, J.R. (1958). *Automation and Management.* Boston, MA: Graduate School of Business Administration, Harvard University.
14 Mann, F.C., and Hoffman, L.R. (1960). *Automation and the Worker: A Study of Social Change in Power Plants.* New York: Holt.

Social Implications of Feedback and Delay Characteristics in Electronic Communications Usage

Barrett S. Caldwell

Department of Industrial Engineering, University of Wisconsin-Madison, 1513 University Ave, Room 393, Madison, WI 53706-1572 USA

Abstract
This paper discusses and presents research concerning issues of communication feedback and transmission delay affecting use and acceptability of communications media. Previous research in organizations has indicated significant stress effects from electronic communications and office automation computer systems due to system delays and lack of information or social feedback. The current paper discusses the impact of feedback and time delay in electronic communications, and the development of a mathematical model of medium acceptability under conditions of transmission delay. This paper also presents research indicating situational differences in medium acceptability based on information and feedback demands of the situation and the user. The findings presented in this paper elaborate aspects of use and acceptability of communications media. These findings emphasize integration of social and organizational demands in information technology design and implementation.

1. INTRODUCTION

Tremendous improvements in computer portability, processing speed, and cost have led to new generations of electronic communications and information technology devices. These new communications capabilities greatly expand the range of media available to provide exchanges of information and social contact between persons. As the variety of communications media increases, these technological advances permit more opportunities for persons to communicate across barriers of time and space. The changing capabilities of communication media force us to re-examine the nature of communication and contact, particularly in situations where the factors of communications feedback and delay are more variable than in more traditional media such as face-to-face communication, written messages, or telephone conversations.

2. INTERPERSONAL COMMUNICATION AND CONTACT REGULATION

Interpersonal communications, by definition, serve an essential and central role in groups and organizations: the sharing of ideas and information, and the maintenance of social relationships and meanings. This role is critical to effective task coordination and performance in the complex organization, and the lack of effective communication leads to work stress and decreased performance [1-3].
Communication has been effectively described as a feedback systems process, where previous information exchange can be used to improve understanding of future information

844

exchange and enhance task performance in human-human or human-machine processes [4-6]. From this systems perspective, the communication act has both costs and benefits to the individual. Costs include information (both task and social) overload; effort to extract important information from potentially ambiguous or misunderstood inputs; and noise and delay associated with poor communications channels that degrade the quality or utility of the information received. Benefits of communications include the increased availability of information from sources beyond the individual's experience; task-related information exchange interactions that lead to improved performance and learning for future tasks; and social support which reduces stress and uncertainty about the individual's task performance, personal interactions, or understanding of organizational culture variables [7-11].

A single ideal balance between costs and benefits of interpersonal communication does not exist. Individual, situational, and task demand differences over time necessitate a dynamic view of contact regulation [12-14]. Nonetheless, ideal performance and minimal overall (human) system degradation will occur when communication acts are maintained within a range around optimum contact levels defined by individual, task, and situation characteristics which exist at a particular time. Increasing performance decrements will occur as achieved contact or communication deviates farther from this optimum. Optimal contact, considered as a normalized (but not static) quantity, can be presented in a fashion similar to that used in statistical process control. An ideal process output may exist, but is economically or practically infeasible to produce exactly ideal outputs each cycle. The process engineer uses the control chart to determine when outputs are within optimal, acceptable, or unacceptable tolerances around the ideal [15]. The ranges of optimal, acceptable, and unacceptable system performance indicated in the process control chart are presented in Figure 1.

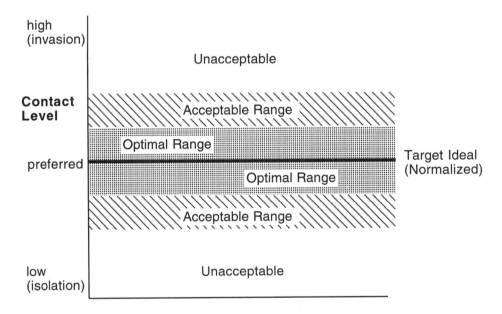

TIME

Figure 1 . Graphical presentation of control chart (contact level) variance ranges and resulting performance.

3. FEEDBACK, DELAY, AND COMMUNICATION ACCEPTABILITY

A cost-benefit model of interpersonal communication extends the feedback systems paradigm developed by other human-machine systems researchers [5,6,16,17]. Delays in information transmission can lead to performance decrements and increased workload required to plan actions in advance to offset the delay period. Especially in cases of unpredictable or uncontrollable delays with task deadlines, delay acts as a system cost with significant stress and health outcomes [18-21]. However, insufficient delay can lead to perceived loss of control and machine pacing, and erodes the contact regulation buffers that exist because of "inertia" or natural delays in human communication exchange. The author has developed a mathematical model of communications media acceptability under conditions of message transmission delay. This model highlights the cost and benefit issues of information feedback and delay, and identifies differences in medium acceptability based on expectations of synchronous versus asynchronous medium design implementations. Discussion of these findings is found elsewhere [13, 22, 23].

4. SITUATION APPROPRIATENESS AND MEDIUM ACCEPTABILITY

Recent research conducted by the author's research team has identified situational constraints significantly affecting the perceived acceptability of communications media [24]. Survey respondents rated the acceptability of either a specific medium currently in use, or a variety of media which could be used in organizations, for eight hypothetical situations. These situations varied in message urgency and content, and distance between sender and receiver; these variables have been identified as important mediators of electronic communications medium acceptability and appropriateness [25-27]. In each of five groups studied, using three different sets of situations, significant differences in medium appropriateness (not attributable to order or specific media) were observed between situations. One example of situational differences in medium acceptability is presented in Figure 2. This figure illustrates the perceived acceptability across eight situations for approximately 1000 state office workers evaluating a pilot test of electronic voice mail systems. The situations were:

1. Nearby co-worker needs large amount of data to study for long term project
2. Need to contact co-workers about cancellation of today's meeting
3. Urgent, complex, subtle message to nearby co-worker
4. Establish rapport with new office worker
5. Give co-worker positive feedback from meeting; you're away on business trip
6. Routine message to distant colleague
7. Need large amount of numeric data immediately from distant colleague
8. Build trust and goodwill with distant colleague for long term, detailed project

These overall situation rating differences are supplemented by results showing that the specific technology used by the workers significantly influenced the resulting acceptability ratings. Significant effects of gender were also discovered. Gender effects can be attributed to differences in task and social maintenance communications frequencies often seen between males and females [28-30].

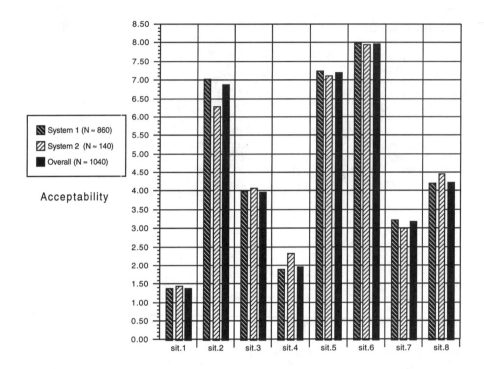

Figure 2 . Ratings of acceptability for voice mail use by situation, 1040 State office workers.

5.   CONCLUSIONS

These results disconfirm hypotheses that medium acceptability is primarily determined by medium characteristics such as information richness, rather than the match between medium capabilities and situational demands. Instead, these data emphasize integrating organizational demands, situation constraints, and users' social as well as task requirements into the design and implementation of advanced electronic information technologies [8, 31]. No single medium, regardless of technological advancement, will adequately meet the demands of a range of communications requirements in complex organizations. Recognition of the criteria to match technology implementation with social, organizational, and societal demands will help to reverse the trend cited by Eason [8], that the majority of information technology implementation efforts fail to achieve desired results. The information presented in this paper should help to provide effective translations between technology developers and organizational design and management professionals to help improve the configurations and use of advanced information technologies to improve workplace productivity and well-being.

6. REFERENCES

1. Bradley, G., *Computers and the Psychological Work Environment*. 1989, London: Taylor & Francis.
2. Sauter, S.L., L.R. Murphy, and J.J. Hurrell, *Prevention of Work-Related Psychological Disorders: A National Strategy Proposed by the National Institute for Occupational Safety and Health (NIOSH)*. American Psychologist, 1990. **45**(10): 1146-1158.
3. Sundstrom, E., K.P. DeMeuse, and D. Futrell, *Work Teams: Applications and Effectiveness*. American Psychologist, 1990. **45**(2): 120-133.
4. Shannon, C.E. and W. Weaver, *The Mathematical Theory of Communication*. 1949, Urbana, IL: The University of Illinois Press.
5. Sheridan, T.B. and W.R. Ferrell, *Man-Machine Systems: Information, Control, and Decision Models of Human Performance*. 1974, Cambridge, MA: MIT Press.
6. Rouse, W.B., *Systems Engineering Models of Human-Machine Interaction*. North Holland Series in System Science and Engineering, ed. A.P. Sage. Vol. 6. 1980, New York: North Holland.
7. Bradley, G. and M.M. Robertson. *Computers, Psychosocial Work Environment, and Stress: A Comparative Theoretical Analysis of Organizations and Action Strategies*. in *11th Congress of the International Ergonomics Association*. 1991. Paris: Taylor & Francis.
8. Eason, K., *Information Technology and Organizational Change*. 1988, London: Taylor & Francis.
9. Kiesler, S., J. Siegel, and T.W. McGuire, *Social Psychological Aspects of Computer-Mediated Communication*. American Psychologist, 1984. **39**(10): 1123-1134.
10. Ouellette Kobasa, S.C. and M.C. Puccetti, *Personality and Social Resources in Stress Resistance*. Journal of Personality and Social Psychology, 1983. **45**(4): 839-850.
11. Schein, E.H., *Organizational Culture*. American Psychologist, 1990. **45**(2): 109-119.
12. Altman, I., A. Vinsel, and B.B. Brown, *Dialectic Conceptions in Social Psychology: An Application to Social Penetration and Privacy Regulation,* in *Advances in Experimental Social Psychology,* L. Berkowitz, Editor. 1981, Academic Press: New York.
13. Caldwell, B.S., *Group Isolation and Performance Factors in Human-Environment Systems*. 1992, Washington, DC: AIAA Report 92-1530.
14. Harrison, A.A., *et al.*, *Implications of Privacy Needs and Interpersonal Distancing Mechanisms for Space Station Design*. 1988, Moffett Field, CA: NASA Ames Research Center.
15. Box, G.E.P. and N.R. Draper, *Empirical Model-Building and Response Surfaces*. 1987, New York: John Wiley & Sons.
16. Hubka, V. and W.E. Eder, *Theory of Technical Systems*. 1988, Berlin: Springer-Verlag.
17. Moray, N., W.R. Ferrell, and W.B. Rouse, ed. *Robotics, Control and Society: Essays in honor of Thomas B. Sheridan*. 1990, Taylor & Francis: London.
18. Emurian, H.H., *Physiological Responses During Data Retrieval: Comparison of Constant and Variable System Response Times*. Computers in Human Behavior, 1991. **7**: 291-310.
19. Grandjean, E., *Ergonomics in Computerized Offices*. 1987, London: Taylor & Francis.

848

20. Sauter, S.L., J.J. Hurrell Jr., and C.L. Cooper, *Job Control and Worker Health.* Wiley Series on Studies in Occupational Stress, ed. C.L. Cooper and S.V. Kasl. Vol. 14. 1989, Chichester, UK: John Wiley & Sons.
21. Smith, M.J., P. Carayon, and K. Miezio, *VDT Technology: Psychosocial and Stress Concerns,* in *Work With Display Units 86,* B. Knave and P.-G. Wideback, Editor. 1987, Elsevier Science: New York. p. 695-712.
22. Caldwell, B.S. *The Role of Socio-Technical Systems Engineering in Implementing Office Automation and Information Technologies.* in *IFAC Symposium on Automated Systems Based on Human Skill.* 1992. Madison, WI: International Federation of Automatic Control.
23. Taha, L.H. and B.S. Caldwell, *Social Isolation and Integration in Electronic Environments.* Behaviour and Information Technology, 1993. In Press.
24. Caldwell, B.S., J.A. Maryniak, and L.H. Taha. *Organizational Acceptance of Communications Media: Situational and Technological Constraints in Stress Mediation Through Electronic Social Interaction.* in *Stress in the 90's: A Changing Workforce in a Changing Workplace.* 1992. Washington, DC: American Psychological Association.
25. Daft, R.L. and R.H. Lengel, *Organizational Information Requirements, Media Richness and Structural Design.* Management Science, 1986. **32**(5): 554-571.
26. Lea, M., *Rationalist Assumptions in Cross-Media Comparisons of Computer-Mediated Communication.* Behaviour and Information Technology, 1991. **10**(2): 153-172.
27. Trevino, L.K., R.H. Lengel, and R.L. Daft, *Media Symbolism, Media Richness, and Media Choice in Organizations: A Symbolic Interactionist Perspective.* Communication Research, 1987. **14**(5): 553-574.
28. Bales, R.F. and P.E. Slater, *Role Differentiation in Small Decision-Making Groups,* in *Family, Socialization, and Interaction Process,* T. Parsons, Editor. 1955, Glencoe, IL: The Free Press: 259-306.
29. McGrath, J.E., *Groups: Interaction and Performance.* 1984, Englewood Cliffs, NJ: Prentice-Hall.
30. Spence, J.T. and R.L. Helmreich, *Masculinity and Femininity: Their psychological dimensions, correlates, and antecedents.* 1978, Austin, TX: University of Texas Press. 26-28, 30-38, 57-60, 109-129.
31. Rouse, W.B., *Human Resource Issues in System Design,* in *Robotics, Control and Society: Essays in honor of Thomas B. Sheridan,* N. Moray, W.R. Ferrell, and W.B. Rouse, Editor. 1990, Taylor & Francis: London. p. 177-186.

A human memory model based on search patterns

Tomoko Saka, Hideaki Ozawa and Naoki Kobayashi

NTT Human Interface Laboratories, 1 - 2356, Take, Yokosuka, Kanagawa, 238-03, Japan

Abstract

We investigated subjects' behavior when they searched for articles that they had previously read in a newspaper. We found that they used memories about target articles. The memories involved semantic information, pattern information, and spatial information. Traditional memory models, however, have examined the roles of only semantic information and pattern information. An experimental method is created to find the relationships and the characteristics of these three types of information and their role in memory.

The experiment investigates the changes in subjects' behavior that accompany changes in the structure and content of an article.

The result is that semantic memory is always necessary to recall the appearance, contents, and location of an article. If there is no semantic memory, the pattern memory and spatial memory fail to hold any useful information. Furthermore, we propose a human memory model based on these results.

1   Introduction

Humans use memories when searching for previously seen information[1]. One memory involves content. This memory is often used to access an information system or database, using keywords. Most computer systems are used to handle only text information. Retrieval using keywords can deal effectively with such information. The recent trend, however, is to store multimedia information instead of just text. Multimedia information consists of various representations, such as, text, pictures, video, and so on. When we retrieve multimedia information, we can use keywords for the text portion, but we do not have appropriate methods for the other media.

One solution to this problem may be developed from the way multimedia information is handled daily in the real world. We felt that the methods we use in real life to retrieve multimedia information could be helpful in developing retrieval methods for computer systems. Therefore, we decided to examine the function of memory in multimedia information retrieval.

We investigated the behavior of subjects when they searched for previously seen information. We found that they used memories about semantic information, pattern information, and spatial information. Traditional memory models have examined the dependency of memory on semantic information and pattern information[2,3].

Based on a series of experiments, a new memory model is proposed which consists of memories about semantic information, pattern information, and spatial information.

2 Background

We looked for an example of multimedia information in the world outside computers, and chose newspapers. The reason why we chose newspapers is that newspapers represent information with text and pictures. Moreover, newspapers are one information source that may be accessed repeatedly.

A preliminary experiment investigated subjects' behavior when they searched for articles that they had previously read in an actual newspaper. We found that the subjects used non-semantic as well as semantic search keys. They used memories of text, titles, pictures, and article position, as search keys for retrieval.

Text is basically semantic information, and contains very little pattern information or spatial information. Titles and pictures contain both semantic information and pattern information. Position information is created by the article itself and its components.

To determine the characteristics and the relationships of the memories created for semantic information, pattern information, and spatial information, we decided to investigate the search keys and actions commonly performed in retrieving articles.

3 Experiment

3.1 Materials

We performed an experiment to investigate the changes in the subject's response that accompanied changes in the article. The changes involved the article's structure and similarity. The following situations were considered.

[**Changes in structure**]
    (A)No title and no picture.
    (B)A title and picture in each article (picture size was different for each article).
    (C)One picture in each article.
    (D)One title in each article (title size was different for each article).

We made four types of special newspapers, representative pages of which are shown in Fig.1. Many editions of each type were developed containing different material.

[**Changes in similarity**]
    (A)The target articles were about the same theme.
    (B)The target articles were about different topics.

Each newspaper consisted of 12 pages, one of which was selected as the target page containing the target article. For each type of newspaper, we collated the target pages for the memorization phase of the experiment.

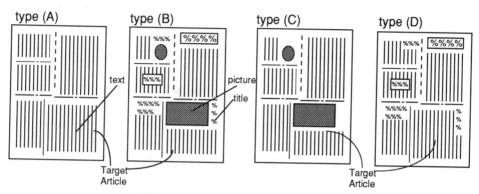

Fig.1 : Examples of test materials

3.2 Method

In the memorization phase about twenty subjects were assigned to each collated set of target pages (about seven pages per set). They were asked to read one article (the target article) on each page with the intention of retrieving the target articles at a later date from their respective newspapers. After two days, the subjects were asked to find the target articles in newspapers. Before searching for the article, they were shown a card that contained only the text of the first paragraph of the article. The subjects were interviewed about their search keys before and after undertaking the search. Their impressions about the target article were also collected. The search time was measured and the per page rate was calculated.

3.3 Result

The following results were recorded. From these results, we came to four conclusions. Each conclusion is given at the end of each paragraph.

[**Effect of contents**]

Result

When a subject could not comprehend the content of an article because of the difficulty of the article, similarity with other articles, and so on, the subject could not memorize the article (Fig.2).

Conclusion

There is a process by which the content of an article is comprehended and memorized.

852

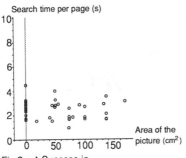

Fig.2-a : Success in
comprehending the content

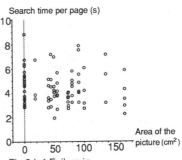

Fig.2-b : Failure in
comprehending the content

Fig.2 : The changes in search time

[**Processes of memorization**]
Result

(1)The search time per page depends on
the search key used(Fig.3). The memories
about the text, title, picture, and position
of an article were used as search keys.
The memory about position was used in
conjunction with other search keys.
The position memory yielded the shortest
search times per page.
(2)Subjects who remembered the title
or/and the picture of an article, also remembered the content of the article.
(3)The position of an article is memorized
unconsciously.

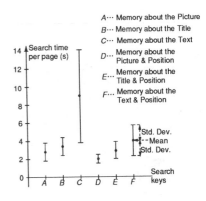

Fig.3 : Search time for each search key

Conclusion

The memory of article position is attendant on the memories about text, title, and
picture. There are three stages in the memorization of an article. In the first stage,
the article's content is memorized. In the second stage, the title and/or picture are
memorized. In the third stage, the article's position is memorized.

[**Memories from picture and title**]
Result

(1)Some subjects thought that the pictures influenced the memorization of an article.
(2)Distinctive titles, such as a title containing numbers, are easier to memorize.

Conclusion

There are two kinds of memories about a title/picture. One is the memory of its content (semantic memory), and the other is the memory of its appearance or image (pattern memory).

[**Effects of picture**]
Result
(1)Some subjects thought that the pictures influenced the memorization of an article.
(2)The more the title /picture suits the content of an article, the easier it is to memorize the article.

Conclusion

The content of a picture sometimes supplemented the content of an article.

These four conclusions were used to develop a model of memories about newspaper articles (Fig.4).

4 The memory model

Outline: Traditional human memory models treat the memorization of only the semantic information and pattern information. We created a human memory model consisting of three kinds of memories (Fig.5). They are semantic memory, pattern memory, and spatial memory.

When we started this research, we supposed that pattern memory and spatial memory were more impressive than semantic memory. It seemed that pattern memory and spatial memory were more useful as search keys. However, we found that semantic memory is essential to memorize an article and that pattern memory and spatial memory are subsidiary to semantic memory. This is because, if semantic memory cannot be formed, neither pattern memory nor spatial memory can be retained.

Semantic memory: Semantic memory is the memory about the article's content. It is only retained when the content of the article is comprehended.

Pattern memory: Pattern memory is formed and retained if the reader has an interest in the article or he is impressed by the article. The image of a picture is an example of what constitutes pattern memory. That is, it is the memory of images, appearances and/or composition.

Spatial memory: Spatial memory is formed and retained when the reader's interest in the article or impression of the article's composition is especially strong. It is the memory about relative position on the page in the case of a newspaper. Spatial memory must be attached to either semantic memory or pattern memory or both. This is because memory about position can be used only in conjunction with the other forms of memory.

5 Conclusion

Against the traditional models of memory, we have proposed a model of human memory based on the keys used for relocating information.

Traditional memory models deal only with information containing semantic and pattern attributes. However, information has other attributes. The proposed memory model

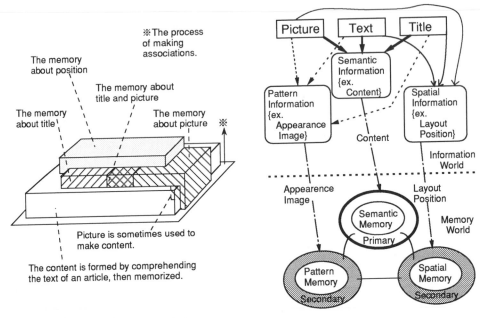

Fig.4 : Constructing memories
about an article

Fig.5: Proposed Model

adds spatial memory and the relationships and the characteristics of the three kinds of memories have been clarified.

Furthermore, the following knowledge was gained.

- The content of an article is more important for efficient information processing activities than its representation.

- When we add a picture to an article, we should consider the relationship between the picture and the content of the article.

Reference

1 M. W. Lansdale, Remembering about documents : memory about appearance, format and location, Ergonomics, Vol.34, No.8, pp.1161-1178 (1991)

2 D. E. Rumelhart, Introduction to human information processing, John Wiley and Sons (1977)

3 K. T. Spoehr and S. W. Lehmkuhle, Visual information processing, W. H. Freeman and Company (1982)

Control of complex system by situated knowledge: The role of Implicit learning

A. Rizzo[a], O. Parlangeli[b], C. Cambiganu[a], S. Bagnara[a]

[a]Universita' di Siena & Istituto di Psicologia CNR,
via Roma 47, 53100 Siena, Italy

[b]Universita' di Padova
P.za Capitaniato 3, 35100 Padova, Italy

Abstract
An experiment is reported which tests the hypothesis that content and context play a crucial role in learning to control a complex system. The same formal rule, originally devised by Berry and Broadbent [1], has been used to govern the behavior of four different scenarios. A pre-test analysis showed different degrees of cognitive match between each scenario and the rule used. Four different groups of subjects were respectively requested to interact with the four scenarios. Subjects were subsequently tested for their verbalized knowledge. Results show that subjects' performance and verbalized knowledge are unequally affected by the different scenarios. Subjects' verbalization seems related to situated principles of the system behavior but not to the underlying rule.

1. INTRODUCTION

In recent years consensus is growing about the existence of multiple learning processes related to different memory systems (see e.g., [2, 3]). Despite this, our understanding of the underlying processes is quite shallow, particularly in relation to the claim that cognitive skills can be learned both explicitly and implicitly [4]. An important research domain where this claim has been supported by experimental results is decision making in controlling complex systems. Here subjects, with practice, can improve their ability to make the correct decision even though they are not able to show a coresponding improvement in verbal knowledge and to develop an adequate, explicit, model of the system under control (cf. [1, 5, 6]). The dissociation between implicit and explicit knowledge is manifest with a defined pattern of relationships; e.g. subjects commonly show changes in performance without changes in verbal knowledge, but rarely show changes in verbal knowledge without changes in performance. These results suggested the existence of alternative modes of processing in human decision making [6, 7].

This dissociation does not concern all the situations in which subjects engage in the control of a dynamic system, but is manifest under particular conditions (e.g. Berry and Broadbent 's task). Yet, we still need to identify the key factors that give rise to the different types of learning and the different types of knowledge [8].

There are two fundamental aspects of human knowledge which have not received the attention they deserve in this field of study. The first concerns the situated property of knowledge - that is, knowledge transformations are constrained by knowledge content. According to this view (see e.g., [9, 10, 11]) we can better understand human knowledge and its transformations not by imputing to them any formal logical calculus but by taking into account two main factors. First, content: the greater the familiarity and the richer the relevant schemata available, the more readily can one solve a problem; Second, form: one succeeds in solving problems to the extent that one can construct mental models that represent the relevant information in an appropriate fashion and use his/her mental model flexibly [12].

The second aspect concerns the proposal for a dual system of knowledge control [13; 14]. This approach maintains that the high level conscious system "has access to a representation of the environment and of the organism's intentions and cognitive capacities. It is held to operate not by directly controlling behavior, but by modulating the lower level contention-scheduling system by activating or inhibiting particular schemata. It would be involved in the genesis of willed actions and required in situations where the routine selection of actions was unsatisfactory - for instance, in coping with novelty, in decision making, in overcoming temptations, or in dealing with danger." ([15] p. 335).

Taking into account these proposed characteristics of human knowledge and applying them to the issue of controlling complex systems, at least two predictions can be made. First, the difficulty of a control task is not directly related to the underlying formal structure of the system under control but to the recruitment of schemata that can be properly adopted and if necessary modified. Second, a dissociation between verbalized knowledge and performance is likely to occur only when the mental model by which the performance is controlled is at a higher abstract level of description than the level at which the performance is actually executed. For example when the intentions are stated at an abstract level and the performance is mainly driven by environmental activation of the proper schemata.

The reported experiment aims to test the first prediction and produce preliminary evidence on the second one.

2. EXPERIMENT

As we have already pointed out, research on human implicit learning has up to now neglected the role of context in acquiring the necessary skills to control a complex system. In order to explore such relationships an experiment was set up to compare the effects of different scenarios on learning to control a complex system. The two tasks devised by Berry and Broadbent [1], usually named Sugar Production and Person Interaction, were used. Sugar production is a task where subjects are instructed to imagine that they are the manager of a small sugar production factory and that they can control the level of production simply by determining the number of workers employed at the sugar factory. The level of production is affected by the number of workers according to the following equation: $P = [(2 \times W) - P_1] + R$; where P is the current sugar production output (ranging between 1,000 and 12,000 tons); P_1 the previous sugar output; W the number of workers employed by the subjects (ranging between 100 and 1200); and R a random +1, 0 or -1. Note that before introducing the P_1 and W values they are scaled so as to range between 1 and 12. The lower and the upper bounds are fixed for both production and work force, and subjects are aware of these bounds. The starting levels are 6,000 tons and 600 workers. The goal of the subjects is to achieve and maintain the production level at 9,000 tons. While Interacting, subjects type a number of between 1 and 12 to represent the number of workers in hundreds. The numbers denoting the production reached and the work-force on the previous trial are always in view. To allow for the random element in the task, the scoring criterion is set so that a sugar output of 8,000, 9,000, or 10,000 tons counts as being on target. Subjects are not aware of this criterion.

In the Person Interaction task subjects are told that they will interact with a computer "person" named Clegg, who exhibits any of 12 styles of behavior. In this task the 12 styles of behavior have numerical equivalents, which correspond to the 12 levels of work-force and sugar-production output.

Two new scenarios have been devised named Slope and Tank. One of these, Slope, was designed with the aim of maximizing the match between presumed available schemata of knowledge related to the scenario and the underlying formal rule governing the system behavior. The other one, Tank, has been elaborated with the opposite purpose.

In the Slope scenario, subjects are instructed to imagine they are at the top of a slope on which is laid a trolley tied with a rope and that they can control the position of the trolley on the slope simply by pulling the rope. The surface of the slope is slightly uneven, and becomes steeper nearer the top. The position of the trolley on the slope may vary from position 1 to position 12 and the force with which the trolley can be pulled varies from 100 to 1,200 Newtons. Subjects are also told that the trolley movement on the slope is limited by two walls across the bottom and the top of the slope.

In theTank scenario subjects are told that they will control the level reached by the water contained in a cubic tank varying the quantity of water introduced in it. The number of levels reached by the water may vary from 1 to 12 and the quantity of water that the subject can introduce varies in 12 discrete steps from 100 to 1,200 liters.

The rule governing the functioning of these four scenarios is the same, namely that one described for the Sugar Production task. A pre-test using a questionnaire has been conducted to evaluate the cognitive match between each scenario and the underlying rule. Nine questions investigated each scenario, some referring to the relationship to the rule and some to its behavioral characteristics. This analysis has been conducted on all four scenarios. Each scenario was evaluated individually by fourteen subjects. No subject evaluated more than one scenario. On a seven point scale the two scenarios proposed by Berry and Broadbent [1] obtained an average evaluation of 3,72 (Sugar) and 4.89 (Clegg), the two new ones obtained 4.51 (Slope) and 3.68 (Tank).

According to the situated view of human knowledge we maintain that scenarios with a higher match between available schemata and the underlying formal rule governing the system behavior should produce a better performance. The level of performance should be a consequence of situated explanations, made available by the current schemata, about the system behavior. Moreover, congruent schemata should allow richer verbal reports and such a verbalized knowledge should be related more to situated principles accounting for the system behavior than to the underlying rule.

2.1 Method

Subjects. The 48 volunteer subjects were undergraduate students or employees at Siena University or at Padua University. For each experimental condition half of the subjects were Siena University students or employees and half were Padua University students.

Design. The subjects were randomly allocated to one of four experimental groups - Factor Scenario at four levels: sugar task (n=12), person interaction task (n=12), slope task (n=12) and tank task (n=12). All groups of subjects were tested in two sessions of 20 trials - Factor Practice at two levels. Following the performance, subjects were tested for their verbal knowledge with a post-task questionnaire.

Thus, we had a mixed Factorial design: Scenario (4 levels, between) x Practice (2 levels, within) plus a Factorial design: Verbal Knowledge (4 levels, between).

Procedure. All subjects were given written descriptions of one particular scenario and of the modalities of interaction. They were told the target level they must achieve and maintain, the starting levels and the fixed bounds of the output response. Taking into consideration the differences due to the peculiarities of these scenarios (i.e., liters *vs.* Newton *vs.* styles of behavior *vs.* work-force) the modalities of interaction and the information displayed remained the same. Each subject received a post-task verbal questionnaire at the end of the experimental session. The structure of the questionnaire was the same for all scenarios. Each questionnaire consisted of four questions: subjects were given a sequence of one input and one output and were asked to state what input value would be required next in order to bring the output variable to target. Subjects' answers were scored as being correct if the chosen value determined an "on target" output. For each question subjects were requested to explain the reason for their response. Verbalizations were tape recorded and transcribed.

2.2 Results

In table 1 are shown the subjects' mean performance scores for each condition. An ANOVA showed that both the main effects and their interaction were significant: Scenario, $F(3, 44)= 5.571$; $p< .0025$; Practice, $F(1, 44) = 18.76$; $p<.001$; interaction Scenario x Practice, $F(3, 44) = 2.953$; $p<.05$. showed that Tank was significantly different from the other three scenarios. The post-hoc analysis for the Factor Scenario relating to the single sessions revealed that Clegg and Slope where different from Tank in both sessions while Sugar was different from Tank only in the second session.

Table 1
Scenario x Practice mean scores

	Clegg	Slope	Sugar	Tank	Mean
Session I	5.00	5.25	3.75	3.08	4.27
Session II	8.08	7.08	6.67	3.00	6.21
Mean	6.54	6.16	5.21	3.04	

Mean questionnaire scores were: Clegg, 1.42; Slope, 1.50; Sugar, 1.00; Tank, 0.33. The ANOVA for verbalized knowledge data showed a significant main effect

F(3, 44)=6.103; p<.0015. The post-hoc analysis revealed a significant difference between "Tank" and the other three scenarios

The correlation between cognitive match and performance, and between cognitive match and verbalization score was in both cases R = 0.83, while the correlation between performance and verbalization score was R = 0.99.

3. CONCLUSION

Results reveal that, as previous research has indicated, practice increases control of the system. For three of the four scenarios considered, performance improved from the first session to the second one. This obviously means that subjects learnt something about the system useful in performing the task. However, as predicted, the content and form of knowledge influences the learning processes.

Such a claim is supported by our data in two ways. First, the factor "Scenario" was significant, with the scenarios manifesting a higher cognitive match with the rule allowing better control. Second, the learning trend for the four scenarios was different. The Tank scenario, for which the pre-test analysis had shown the most evident mismatch, did not allow any learning at all. The Sugar scenario induced a low performance in the first session but recorded an increase in the second. The Clegg and Slope scenarios, which rated higher in the cognitive pre-test match, induced a high performaces in the first session and a further increase in the second one. It is worth noting, that it is not the the availability of specific knowledge on the underlying formal rule governing the different systems that plays the crucial role. But, as Johnson-Laird [9] has argued, in coping with novel situations and transforming knowledge already possessed, it is the richness and the familiarity of such knowledge which is crucial. In fact, This knowledge does not allow the derivation of the underlying rule but provides situated reasons for explaining the occurrence of events in the system behavior. This brings us to the second aspect of the present study: the dissociation between implicit and explicit learning - namely the improvement in the ability to control a system in association with poor verbalization about the modalities in which such an ability is reached or controlled. Poor verbalisable knowledge about the rule does not imply an implicit knowledge of such a rule: as stated above, other knowledge could be used or acquired explicitly, thus allowing the improvement shown in the system control. Indeed, our results indicate that verbalizations are related to performance. This is evident in two senses. From a quantitative point of view there is a clear relationship between levels of performance and scores at the post-task questionnaire. Moreover, from a qualitative point a view, the explanations advanced by the subjects were in keeping with the behavior of the scenarios, even if not with the underlying rule. They could provide explanations such as: "Since the trolley was very high and in a steep position I had to apply a higher force", in the Slope scenario; or "Clegg is spoiled and touchy so to keep him friendly I have to follow his states" in the Clegg scenario; had some difficulties with the Sugar scenario "I had to employ 500 workers when the production crashes to 1000 tons", and found themselves in trouble with the Tank scenario. Thus, situated knowledge provides the reasons for explaining the otherwise bizarre behavior of the system under control. The subjects' behavior seems to vary according to the suggested mental model and the intentions pursued by subjects are stated at a level of description closely related to level of performance so there is not much room for dissociation between performance and verbalized knowledge. Situated knowledge can account for both.

Finally, the pre-test analysis provided only rough information about the match between each scenario and the rule used. Investigation concerned the global index of match between each scenario and the underlying rule, without assessing either the familiarity of the relevant schemata or their richness. Nevertheless this index proved to be of practical use in discriminating between different scenarios and predicting their influence on learning processes. Further study should be aimed at exploring the role of different aspects of situated knowledge in relation to its use in governing "complex" systems.

4. ACKNOWLEDGMENTS

This research was supported by grants from CNR target Project 'Prevention and Control Disease Factor'; subproject 'Stress'; grant N° 9103615.

5. REFERENCES

1   D.C. Berry and D.E.Broadbent.. On the relationship between task performance and verbalisable knowledge. Quart. Jour. of Exper. Psy., 36 (1984) 209.
2   L. Nadel. Multiple memory systems: What and Why. 92 Jour. of Cog. Neurosci., 4 (1992) 2.
3   L.R. Squire. Declarative and Nondeclarative Memory: Multiple Brain Systems Supporting Learning and Memory. Jour. of Cog. Neurosci., 4 (1992) 232.
4   A.S. Reber. Implicit Learning and Tacit Knowledge. Jour. of Exper. Psy.: General, 118 (1989) 219.
5   D.C. Berry and D.E. Broadbent. Interactive Tasks and the Implicit-Explicit distinction. Brit. Jour. of Psy., 79 (1988) 251.
6   D.E. Broadbent, P. FitzGerald and M.H.P.Broadbent. Implicit and explicit knowledge in the control of complex systems. Brit. Jour. of Psy., 77 (1986) 33.
7   D.C. Berry. The role of action in implicit learning. Quart. Jour. of Exper. Psy., 43 (1991) 881.
8   D.C. Berry. Implicit Learning: Twenty five years on. Conference on Attention and Performance, Erice, Italy, July, (1993).
9   P. N. Johnson-Laird. Mental Models. Cambridge, MA: Harvard University Press. 1983
10 R.G. D'Andrade. The cultural part of cognition. Cog. Sci., 5 (1981) 179.
11 V. Girotto and P. Light . The pragmatic bases of children's reasoning. In P. Light and G. Butterworth (Eds.) Context and Cognition. London: Harvester,1992.
12 H. Gardner. The Mind's New Science. New York: Basic Book, 1987.
13 D.A. Norman and T. Shallice. In R.J. Davidson, G.E. Schwartz and D. Shapiro (Eds.) Consciousness and Self-Regulation IV. New York: Plenum Press. (1980/86)
14 P.N. Johnson-Laird. In A. J. Marcel & E. Bisiach (Eds.) Consciousness in Contemporary Science. Oxford: Oxford University Press, 1988
15 Shallice 88 Shallice, T. In A. J. Marcel & E. Bisiach (Eds.) Consciousness in Contemporary Science. Oxford: Oxford University Press, 1988.

A Model of Behavioral Techniques for Representing User Interface Designs

J.D. Chase[a], H. Rex Hartson[a], Deborah Hix[a], Robert S. Schulman[b], and Jeffrey L. Brandenburg[a]

[a]Department of Computer Science, Virginia Polytechnic Institute and State University, Blacksburg VA 24061 USA

[b]Department of Statistics, Virginia Polytechnic Institute and State University, Blacksburg VA 24061 USA

Abstract

A user-centered approach to interactive system development requires a way to represent the behavior of a user interacting with an interface. While a number of behavioral representation techniques exist, not all provide the capabilities necessary to support the development process. Based on observations of existing representations and comments from users of the User Action Notation (UAN), a user- and task-centered behavioral representation, we have developed a model that classifies behavioral representations according to *scope*, in terms of activities they support within the development process; *content*, in terms of components of interaction designs they can represent; and *requirements* for documentation and communication within and among various development activities. We present results demonstrating the model's reliability in the context of two problems, critical incident classification and evaluation of existing techniques.

1. Motivation

In recent years a number of researchers in human-computer interaction have found that the process of user interface development should be *user-centered*, rather than simply following standard software engineering practices [5, 6, 11]. A user-centered focus requires a method for describing the behavior of a user interacting with an interface. Some techniques for behaviorally representing the user's view of a design include:

- GOMS [1]
- Command Language Grammar (CLG) [9]
- keystroke-level model [2]
- Task Action Grammar (TAG) [10]
- scenarios or story-boarding

These techniques generally were created as analysis tools and therefore do not directly support the design process. They also typically model error-free user performance and are limited to user actions without addressing feedback or other interface components. These omissions are addressed by the User Action Notation (UAN) [7,8], a user- and task-oriented notation that describes the behavior of both the user and the system in their cooperative performance of a task.

Through empirical work with UAN users and other interface developers, we have found a general lack of formal understanding of behavioral representation techniques. We can classify some of the issues involved along the following dimensions:

- *scope* within the interface development process, in terms of activities the representation techniques should support

- *content*, in terms of components of user interaction designs that need to be represented

- *requirements* for documentation and communication within and among the various activities of the interface development process

This paper focuses on the empirical derivation and evaluation of a model of behavioral representation techniques based on their *scope, content,* and *requirements*. The purpose of this model is to aid in analyzing and comparing existing behavioral representation techniques, organizing data collection and extension of existing behavioral representation techniques, and guiding development of new behavioral representation techniques.

2. Model Development

We developed the model of behavioral representation techniques in two ways. First, we asked UAN users to contribute lists of their needs for a behavioral representation technique, including supported activities, interface components, and representation requirements. Second, we examined existing behavioral representation techniques by reviewing appropriate literature to determine the requirements for which they were designed. For example, since user task performance prediction is a component of several existing techniques, it is included as a characteristic within *content*..

Requirements

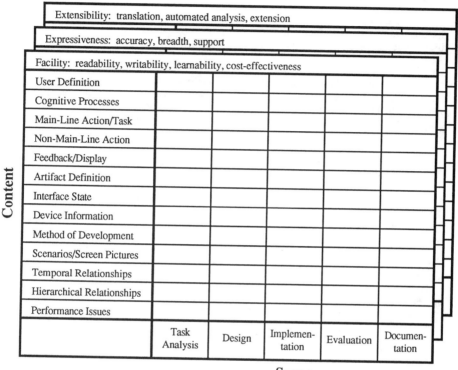

Content		Task Analysis	Design	Implementation	Evaluation	Documentation

Extensibility: translation, automated analysis, extension

Expressiveness: accuracy, breadth, support

Facility: readability, writability, learnability, cost-effectiveness

	Task Analysis	Design	Implementation	Evaluation	Documentation
User Definition					
Cognitive Processes					
Main-Line Action/Task					
Non-Main-Line Action					
Feedback/Display					
Artifact Definition					
Interface State					
Device Information					
Method of Development					
Scenarios/Screen Pictures					
Temporal Relationships					
Hierarchical Relationships					
Performance Issues					

Scope

Figure 1. Model of Behavioral Representation Techniques

Figure 1 illustrates our model of behavioral representation techniques. The dimensions of the model do not represent continuous variables; rather, they demark a three-dimensional box with discrete points on each edge. The model provides the ability to characterize the capabilities, scope, coverage, and appropriate applicability of an existing behavioral representation technique. Further, the model provides the ability to anticipate problems or missing elements within a behavioral representation technique by examining the technique and assigning a value to each intersection of the various components of each axis. For example, if a *requirement* is automated translation of the design representation into a prototype and a *content* item is interface feedback, then the model suggests examining the technique's capabilities with respect to automated translation of feedback notation. In this way, the model ensures that all intersections are examined for the behavioral representation technique under investigation. The model suggests areas of improvement for behavioral representation techniques; it also suggests areas of extension. For example, the UAN currently provides no method for recording user task performance prediction information, a characteristic that has already been established as an important *content* item in other techniques. This points to performance prediction as a possible area of future extension for the UAN.

3. Model Evaluation and Results

To demonstrate the model's reliability, we tested whether different individuals obtained statistically similar results using the model to perform a variety of tasks. We discuss two of these tasks: critical incident mapping and analysis of existing techniques.

3.1 Reliablity of Incident Mapping

In the first of these tests, involving incident mapping, we selected a representative subset of 40 critical incidents reported by UAN users and then had each of several subjects map these incidents into the model. Critical incidents were defined to be:

- an encounter with an interface component that the UAN does not represent;
- a difficulty using the existing UAN notation;
- a variation in notation or method from the current UAN standard; or
- an incident in which the UAN provides a notation or a view of the interface that would not have occurred otherwise.

Five subjects were selected on the basis of their varying levels of experience with the UAN. We intentionally chose a mix of subjects from UAN novices to experts in order to demonstrate that the model would be reliable across experience levels. These subjects then mapped each of the 40 incidents to the cell or intersection in the model in which it best fit. The results of this mapping were then compared using an extension of Cohen's Kappa [3,4], a coefficient of agreement of nominal scales. Kappa measures the proportion of agreement among multiple raters. Essentially, kappa is normally distributed between zero and one with with zero representing only chance agreement and one representing perfect agreement. Since kappa is approximately normally distributed, it provides for a significance test against the normal distribution in order to determine the significance of the given results. We separately analyzed each of the three dimensions of the model, yielding three sets of results. Table 1 shows the proportion of agreement, the adjusted kappa (agreement beyond chance), the z value (standard normal representation of kappa), and the p value for each of the three dimensions.

Table 1. Results of analysis of incident mapping

Dimension	Proportion of Agreement	Kappa	z value	p value
Scope	0.8725	0.8362	28.56	<0.00001
Content	0.6575	0.6224	36.04	<0.00001
Requirements	0.8925	0.8327	20.10	<0.00001

The probability of obtaining the kappa values listed in the table without reliable agreement among subjects is less than one in one hundred thousand. While these results show highly significant levels of agreement (i.e. well beyond chance) among the five subjects, the level of agreement on the *Content* axis appears lower, since the proportion of agreement and kappa values are well below that of the other two axes. However, since there are 13 levels on the *Content* axis and only 3 and 5 levels respectively on the *Scope* and *Requirements* axes, it is less likely that all subjects would agree on the best fit of an incident along this axis. Therefore, the numbers on the *Content* axis actually show a more significant level of agreement among subjects than the other two axes, as demonstrated by the z-values or normally distributed values. From these results, we can conclude that the model is reliable across subjects for the task of mapping critical incidents.

3.2 Reliablity of Technique Analysis

In the second test, we had five subjects use the model for analysis of an existing technique. This process involved going through each intersection in the model and rating the UAN on a scale of 1-3 with respect to that intersection, based on existing descriptions of the UAN. Again, as in the first experiment, five subjects were selected for their varying levels of familiarity with the UAN. For this test, agreement was defined by two different methods. For the first method, which we will refer to as *3 or more agreement*, three of the subjects had to agree and the other two could be off by at most one, e.g. three subjects select three and the other two select two. For the second method, which we will refer to as *4 or more agreement*, four of the subjects had to agree and the other could be off by at most one, e.g. four subjects select one and the other subject selects two. In both cases we compared the resulting proportion of agreement to the probability of agreement by chance using a z-test. Table 2 lists the method, the probability of agreement by chance, the proportion of agreement (as defined by the two methods listed above), the z value and the p value.

Table 2. Results of analysis of ratings comparisons

Method	Probability of Agreement by Chance	Proportion of Agreement	z value	p value
3 or more	0.3416	0.7795	12.89	< 0.00001
4 or more	0.0947	0.5641	22.39	< 0.00001

The probability of obtaining the tabled proportions of agreement without reliable agreement among subjects is less than one in one hundred thousand. Again, as with the previous test, the results here indicate a highly significant level of agreement among the five subjects. While the proportion of agreement is somewhat lower for the *4 or more agreement* method of evaluation, the resulting z-value and therefore the resulting significance is actually higher than that of the *3 or more agreement* method. Again, as with the previous test, we can conclude from these results that the model is reliable for the analysis of an existing behavioral representation technique.

4. Conclusions

We have shown that this model of behavioral representation techniques is reliable for incident mapping and technique analysis. The model should serve as a useful tool for analyzing and comparing existing techniques, organizing data collection and extension of existing techniques, and guiding development of new techniques. It also should be particularly useful for interface developers who have specific needs for a behavioral representation technique, since it provides a method for comparing and selecting among such techniques.

5. Acknowledgment

We would like to thank the National Science Foundation for its continuing support of Human-Computer Interaction research at Virginia Tech, as well as the subjects who participated in this research.

6. References

1. Card, S. K., Moran, T. P., and Newell, A., (1983). *The Psychology of Human-Computer Interaction.* Lawrence Erlbaum Associates, Hillsdale, N.J., 1983.

2. Card, S. K., and Moran, T. P., (1980). The Keystroke-Level Model for User Performance Time with Interactive Systems. *Communications of the ACM,* 23, 396-410.

3. Cohen, J. (1960). A Coefficient of Agreement for Nominal Scales. *Educational and Psychological Measurement,* 20, 37-46.

4. Fleiss, Joseph L., (1971). Measuring Nominal Scale Agreement Among Many Raters. *Psychological Bulletin,* 76, 378-382.

5. Gould, J.D., and Lewis, C. (1985). Designing for Usability: Key Principles and What Designers Think. *Communications of the ACM,* 28(3), 300-311.

6. Hartson, H. R., and Hix, D. (1989). Toward Empirically Derived Methodologies and Tools for Human-Computer Interface Development. *International Journal of Man-Machine Studies,* 31, 477-494.

7. Hartson, H.R., Siochi, A.C., and Hix, D. (1990). The UAN: A User-Oriented Representation for Direct Manipulation Interface Designs. *ACM Transactions on Information Systems,* Vol 8, No 3, July 1990, 181-203.

8. Hix, D., and Hartson, H.R., (1993). *Developing User Interfaces: Ensuring Usability Through Product & Process.* New York, NY, John Wiley & Sons Inc..

9. Moran, T.P., (1980). The Command Language Grammar: A Representation for the User Interface of Interactive Computer Systems. *International Journal of Man-Machine Studies.* 15, 3-51.

10. Payne, S.J., and Green, T.R.G. (1986). Task-Action Grammars: A Model of the Mental Representation of Task Languages. *Human-Computer Interaction.* Hillsdale, NJ: Lawrence Erlbaum Associates, Inc.

11. Rosson, M.B., Maass, S., and Kellogg, W.A. (1987). Designing for Designers: An Analysis of Design Practice in the Real World. In *CHI+GI Conference on Human Factors in Computing Systems,* Toronto, 137-142.

A New Paradigm for Diagnostic Expert System Based on Designer's Knowledge

Yasufumi Kume

(Kinki University,Higashiosaka,Osaka,Japan)

Hyun Seok Jung

(University of DongSeo,Pusan,Korea)

Gavriel Salvendy

(Purdue University,West Lafayette, Indiana,U.S.A.)

ABSTRACT

Conventionally, the diagnostic expert system have been developed using maintenance engineers' knowledge. But these expert systems have many problems. First,these systems need failure data, but there is no data for advanced production equipment. Second, the generic system is needed for the advanced production equipment.

This paper reveals the necessity of the diagnostic system built by the designer of production equipment. In order to justify the necessity of this system, the problems of conventional diagnostic expert system based on trouble-shooters' diagnostic knowledge and the use of causality,especially the necessity relation between the elements of machine parts, which belongs to designers' knowledge is emphasized. As a knowledge representation, it is proposed that a diagnostic matrix with dual relation includes the knowledge of designer and that of maintenance engineers.

Finally, the extension of the constructed diagnostic system to another version can be easily performed by the concept of standardization which has been successfully applied to the design stage.

1. INTRODUCTION

As the requirement of consumers have been diversified, the competition of products development continued to intensify and we are confronted with the lack of the labor force,the automation of production system in which FMS, FA, CIM and SIS etc. are included make rapid progress and information is handled in the production system such as a fault diagnosis system for computer hardware DOC(Needalman and Peak,1987), BRAKE(Tuchinsky et al.,1987) for control mechanism, the diagnostic system for chip mounter made by NEC(Naruo,Lehto and Salvendy,1990), the diagnosis of automobile, the fault diagnosis of learning board using micro-computer, the diagnosis of abnormal vibration in steam turbine generator. The development of this expert system justified by the need to reduce the significant production delays and expense associated with trouble shooting malfunctions. The first step toward the development of the expert system is to elicit and organize the designer's knowledge. In the conventional expert systems, a diagnostic matrix is representing only the knowledge of troubleshooters(Reggia et al.,1983;1985;Wang and Yong,1989). However, the designer who understand the structure of a production equipment makes CAD data. At this time, it is possible to make the diagnostic matrix. From such a view point, in this paper,the expert system for diagnosing a production equipment is modeled. In particular, a method of reasoning is considered. At first, the definition of expert system is described. By the taxonomy,the expert system for diagnosing a production equipment is discussed. Next, a model of an expert system for diagnosing a production equipment is proposed. The relation from cause to symptom as well as the relation from symptom to cause is considered. In addition, the concept of possibility and necessity are introduced (Kume,Jung,Inuiguchi and Savendy,1991). It is proposed that the relation from cause to symptoms can be modeled in the sense of necessity and possibility. These concepts are incorporated into reasoning(Jung,Kume,Inuiguchi and Savendy,1992).

2. CLASSIFICATION OF DIAGNOSTIC OBJECT

In this diagnosis, the method is depending on the object. Namely, by means of the object of a human being or a production equipment, they are divided as medical diagnosis or the diagnosis of production equipment shown in Figure 1. Considering the basic difference of

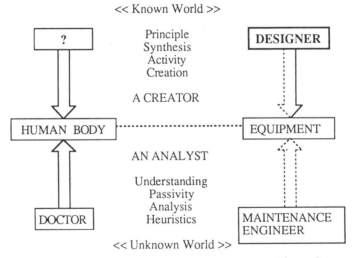

Figure 1 The comparison of the creator with analyst

both of diagnosis, in the case of a medical diagnosis, the feature of a living body, that is , reinforced performance, healing and the difficulty in organ transplantation etc., should be considered. On the other hand, in the case of the diagnosis of production equipment, these are not problems. When the system becomes a fault condition, the part in fault can soon be replaced. Also, considering the growth of a structure, the evolution of a human being does not change comparatively. Therefore, a medical technique is advanced by the accumulation of knowledge. As the change of structure for production equipment is remarkable, a maintenance technique can not catch up with the development of a production equipment structure. Therefore, maintenance technique must use more vague and rough knowledge. Namely, from the change of an objective structure, it is difficult to be put to practical use for the diagnostic technique of a production equipment, but in the case of a medical diagnostic system, it difficult to use for practical purpose. As shown in Figure 1, for practical use of such a system, the existence of a creator for an object and the extent of understanding each system should be considered. In the case of production equipment, the designer of it is a human being.

3. PROBLEM OF CONVENTIONAL METHOD

The object of development of a conventional diagnostic expert system is to automize and diagnose by a non-expert in order to understand the structure of equipment and its function, to control a production equipment advanced abruptly in manufacturing plant sufficiently and to complement the lack of skillful maintenance engineer. In the conventional system, the diagnostic system based on the knowledge of a maintenance engineer may not be able to cope with the failure that we do not experience. In the case of the constitution of an expert system, the staff and allotment of duties are shown in Figure 2. On the other hand, the relationship between the life cycle of an equipment and failure rate is represented by a bath-tub curve shown in Figure 3. In this figure, as the experience for the maintenance of a specific equipment and the knowledge about a structure are poor until A point on the bath-tub curve, the condition of development for diagnostic system does not get ready. In short, in the strict sense of the word, a maintenance engineer is absent. With lapse of time C point at which the experience with a certain degree is healed and it is possible to constitute a diagnostic system.

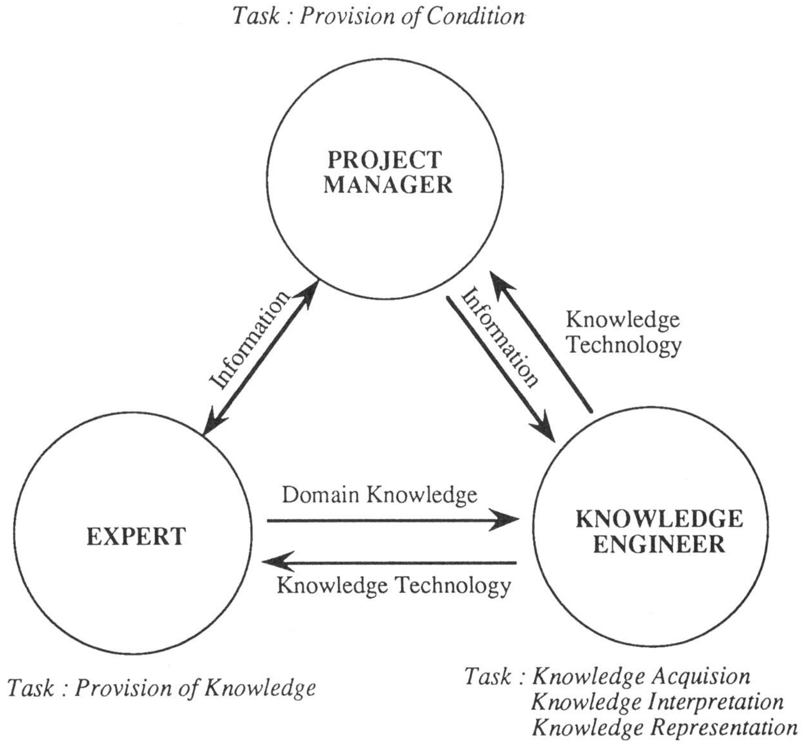

Task : Provision of Condition

Task : Provision of Knowledge

Task : Knowledge Acquision
Knowledge Interpretation
Knowledge Representation

Figure 2   Task and information exchange in the development team

for an expert system

Consequently, after lapse of C point, it is possible to develop a diagnostic system with considerable cost and labor, but after B point, as the equipment gets older, the concept of time must be introduced in order to assure correct diagnosis. Especially, in order to express the close relationship between failure and symptom, probability or membership degree is introduced in the diagnostic system. As the intensity of relation changes with the lapse of time, the degree of the relation must be determined considering the lapse of time. As another one is the system based on elicited knowledge by the present time, the failure of first experience

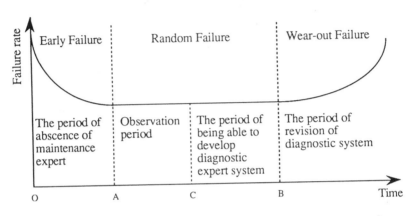

Figure 3   The relationship between the bath tub curve and
possibility of constructing a diagnostic system

generated after that time can not be diagnosed. Learning function for system must be introduced in order to cover it. However, if it will not be the same failure, it is difficult to diagnose it. Namely, the effect of learning is very low. In order to resolve it, the certain knowledge concerning the properties of structure and parts in equipment must be held.

4. HIERARCHY OF EQUIPMENT STRUCTURE AND DIAGNOSTIC MODULE

A diagnostic matrix is used as the method for systematization of diagnostic knowledge. In another work, if a used matrix is not hierarchical, it needs to call for all diagnostic matrices. Indeed, if even the part which is not broken down is not inspected, the diagnosis is not sure. Also, the efficiency of calculation is not good. In addition, when large scale system is treated,the method which approaches hierarchically is more excellent in the aspect of efficiency. The inference from diagnostic module to failure unit is performed. System diagnosis and the failure in unit are separated in inferred unit diagnosis. In the system diagnosis, as only simple set of the part which constitutes system can not constitute the total system, the diagnosis is performed based on the relationship between the whole and unit. Thus, at present, the system is constructed on the basis of consultation of a number of designers and maintenance engineers. In the result of discussion, a matrix is constituted by the content and symptom of each failure of unit and reasoning is performed in terms of the relationship between symptom and the failure of unit. In the diagnosis of unit, the inference to make sure the point and content of failure is performed by means of the failure of each component of in unit, its symptom and the relation matrix.

5. CONCEPTUAL SYNTHESIS FOR DIAGNOSTIC EXPERT SYSTEM BY MEANS OF MAKER OF EQUIPMENT

Summarizing the result mentioned above, it is shown in Figure 4. Namely, when a designer of equipment designs, he refers to standard structure data. Matching its data base with standard diagnostic module, the diagnostic system for specific equipment is built by optimal revising, connecting and assembling in the diagnostic system. Also, considering the result of middle and final inspection under making equipment, the diagnostic system becomes more actual. In addition, repairing new type equipment, it needs to visualize a sequence of repair to remove the anxiety which worker feels and to make sure work. For example, in the assembling process, a sequence of work is simplified and filed. It is possible to make good use of it at repair. On the other hand, the visualization by means of computer graphics may come out. Considering the diagnosis of failure, the process of feedback for the result of repair and operation becomes as follows. At first, the routine of system diagnosis operates and decides the unit regarded as a candidate. Next, the diagnostic module of an objective unit is recalled, and the part of failure is inferred. After the result of repair is confirmed, the process from the occurrence of failure to the finished repair is reported to the data base of failure history, the diagnostic module and the designer. The redesign of the structure of equipment can refer to it. If the failure is not in the standard diagnostic module, its failure is added to the diagnostic module newly. Repeating the supplement and alternation in the diagnostic module, the perfect diagnostic knowledge is kept in the standard diagnostic module gradually. As a production form is automized, the effect of the failure of equipment on production has been augmenting. The diagnostic expert system is developing by means of the knowledge of a maintenance engineer in response to the necessity of maintenance which

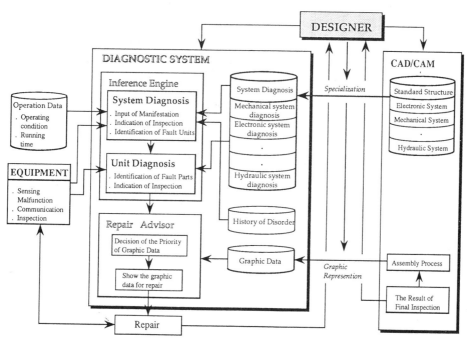

Figure 4   The structure of a diagnostic expert system based on designer's knowledge

is enlarging. However, as there are the fundamental problems of the system itself, it is difficult to evaluate obtaining good results. Also, as the reliance of the maintenance of advanced production equipment on the after-sale service becomes high, the separation between production and maintenance is expected. In addition, as internationalization of products proceeds, the maintenance becomes the most important task.

6. CONCLUSION

In this paper, three problems of diagnostic expert system by maintenance engineer are pointed out, and its critical points are clarified. And the concept of diagnostic expert system by the designer that can respond to the division of production and maintenance and the internationalization of products and the effective method building it is proposed. By means of this concept, it is expected to perform the detail failure diagnosis exactly and speedy. Still more, as the change of contact of operator with equipment decreases, it is difficult to understand the equipment sufficiently. In consideration of this, it reveals that the sequence of repair must be visualized, for the work of maintenance engineer is carried out efficiently on the aspect of time, economics and psychology.

REFERENCES

Jung,H.S., Kume,Y.,Inuiguchi,M. and Salvendy,G.,1992,A Diagnosing the Malfunctions of Equipment with Failure Data. In Proceedings of 1992 Japan-U.S.A. Symposium on Flexible Automation.
Kume,Y., Jung,H.S.,Inuiguchi,M. and Salvendy,G.,1991,DEVELOPMENT OF GENERAL PURPOSE EXERT SYSTEM FOR DIAGNOSING MALFUNCTIONS OF PRODUCTION EQUIPMENT.In PROCEEDINGS OF THE FIRST CHINA-JAPAN INTERNATIONAL SYMPOSIUM ON INDUSTRIAL MANAGEMENT" INDUSTRIAL MANAGEMENT,International Academic Publisher 314-319.
Naruo,N., Lehto,M. and Salvendy,G., 1990, Development of a Knowledge-Based Decision Support System for Diagnosing Malfunctions of Advanced Production Equipment, Int.J.Prod.Res.,**28** 2259-2276.
Needalman,B.I. and Peak,G., 1987, DOC, A Computer Hardware Diagnostic.In Proceedings of ESD/SMI Dearborn, Michigan, 295-300.
Reggia,J.A.,Nau,D.S.and Wang,P.Y.,1983, Diagnostic expert systems based on a set covering model, Int.J. Man-Machine Studies, **19** 437-460.
Reggia,J.A, Nau,D.S.and Wang,P.Y.,1985, A Formal Model of Diagnostic Inference, Information Science, **37** 227-285.
Tuchinsky,P.M., Vora,L.E., Anderson,A.E., Hatfield,S., Cunther,C and McWhorter,R.A.,1987, BREAKS: A Diagnostic Expert System for Engineering, In Proceedings of ESD/SMI, Dear born, Michigan, 271-280.
Wang,H. and Yong,C.,1989, AN EXPERT DIAGNOSTIC SYSTEM OF MECHANICAL EQUIPMENT, In DIAGNOSTIC AND PREVENTIVE MAINTENANCE STRATEGIES IN MANUFACTURING SYSTEMS, by MILAC,V.R.and McWATERS (eds.)(NORTH-HOLLAND, AMSTERDAM) PP.239-245.

Introducing Problem Solving Strategies of Users into the Interface Design

Nong Ye[a] and Gavriel Salvendy[b]

[a]Department of Biomedical and Human Factors Engineering, Wright State University, Dayton, Ohio 45435, U.S.A.

[b]School of Industrial Engineering, Purdue University, West Lafayette, Indiana 47907, U.S.A.

Abstract

Human problem solving strategies must be taken into consideration of human-computer interface design to avoid unnecessary training time, job disorientation, and job dissatisfaction of users in computerized job environments. An experiment was conducted to investigate differences of expert and novice computer programmers in program comprehension strategies. Both expert and novice programmers used a knowledge retrieval strategy first to recognize familiar program segments and a problem reasoning strategy then to comprehend unfamiliar program segments. Experts controlled their program comprehension process in a more systematic manner than novices. Human-computer interface designs for compatibility with user problem solving strategies, such as a hierarchical grouping of familiar interaction elements and a non-hierarchical grouping of unfamiliar interaction elements, are discussed.

1. INTRODUCTION

Current theories and guidelines of human-computer interface design [1, 2, 3] give little attention to users' dynamic problem solving process and strategy. This may not present a big problem for users in small tasks because required information and functions can be arranged within one screen space and made directly accessible to users. When a task is sophisticated and requires the support of massive, various information and system functions at different stages of problem solving, the compatibility between the interface design and users' problem solving strategy becomes crucial to shorten user knowledge transfer from an original task environment to a computerized task environment and to increase user expectation of system behavior. Decision making with decision support systems (DSS), product design with computer-aided design (CAD) tools, and software development with computer-aided software engineering (CASE) tools are some examples of such sophisticated tasks.

Without proper arrangement of system information and functions in correspondence with the problem solving process and strategy of users, several problems may arise. First, users are easily distracted from their regular problem solving process because of their confusion with unpredictable system behaviors. Second, required system supports (information or functions) are not directly accessible to user when needed. Third, users can hardly transfer task knowledge to a new computerized task environment. As a result, the full functionality of computer systems can hardly be explored or utilized by users. Without clues of how systems fit into a problem solving process, users usually limit themselves only to a small portion of system functionality [4] such as report generation of DSS and drawing of CAD, ignoring main system functions such as decision making and engineering analysis.

Computer programmers are a large population of computer users. Most programming tasks, such as program design, program comprehension, and program modification, require

874

information and knowledge from a variety of sources, and require sophisticated information processing and knowledge processing. This paper presents an experiment on differences of expert and novice programmers in program comprehension strategies. Implications of experiment results in human-computer interface design are also discussed.

2. METHOD

2.1. Subjects

Subjects participated the experiment on paid voluntary basis. Expert and novice computer programmers were selected according to Shneiderman's classification of programming expertise levels [5]. Ten expert programmers were graduate students in the Department of Computer Science at Purdue University who had several years of C programming experience while ten novice programmers were sophomores in the School of Industrial Engineering at Purdue University who were on the half way of an introductory course in C and learned the C concepts which were required by experiment tasks.

2.2. Tasks

The subjects were asked to comprehend three C programs with different degrees of difficulty. The program difficulty is determined by the program length and the complexity of program structure. Program one has 12 lines of C code to convert a string into an integer. Program two has 34 lines of C code to evaluate a reverse-Polish arithmetic expression. Program three has 92 lines of C code to report student course grades. Considering the program length, the program difficulty increases in order of programs one, two, and three.

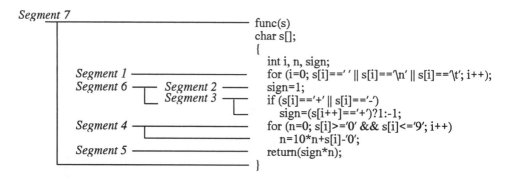

Figure 1. Program plans of program one.

The complexity of program structure is determined by how many levels of program plans are involved in a program. Figure 1 presents the structure of program one. An open-end box for multiple lines of code or a line for a single line of code are used to indicate a program plan. Program plans at different levels of details form a hierarchy. For example, the hierarchy of program one includes segment 7 as the whole program at the highest level, segments 1, 6, 4, and 5 at the next level, and segments 2 and 3 at the lowest level. Program plans of a program are provided to the subjects along with program code. Program one has 7 program plans in 3 levels. program two has 17 program plans in 4 levels. Program three has 35 program plans in 5 levels. A group of program code, which corresponds to a program plan, is called a program segment. Considering the levels of program plans involved in a program, the program difficulty increases in the same order as indicated by the program length, from program one, to program two, then to program three.

A randomized list of program plan descriptions, which were prepared by the experimenter, were also provided to the subjects along with the code and structure of programs. The subjects were asked to show their program comprehension process by continuously matching a program segment of interest to its narrative description from the randomized list. If the subjects comprehend a program segment correctly, they should be able to identify the narrative description of that program segment from the randomized list. The action sequence of program segment identification reveals subjects' process or strategy of program comprehension.

2.3. Procedure

The same set of experiment materials regarding three C programs were given to each subject. Each subject was asked to comprehend three programs by entering every matching pair of program segments and their narrative descriptions for each program. The experiment was monitored by a software system on a Sun workstation. The computer asked the subject to enter the number of a segment and the number of a segment description. The computer verified the correctness of the entered pair, displayed a verification result, and prompted the subject to enter the next pair of segment and its description. If a subject makes a wrong match, he/she can correct it at any time, not necessarily right after the wrong match. The subject had to find out all the correct matches of segments and their descriptions for a program before proceeding to the next program. Subject actions were recorded and timed by the software system.

2.4. Experiment Design

The experiment examines the effect of programming expertise and program difficulty on program comprehension performance and strategy. The independent variables are a between-subject factor of expertise (expert v.s. novice) and a within-subject factor of program difficulty. The dependent variables include performance measures of completion time and error rate. Other dependent variables are measures of problem solving strategies and problem solving processes, which are generated from subjects' action sequence.

Problem solving strategies can be generally classified into two categories: knowledge retrieval and problem reasoning. Knowledge retrieval in program comprehension is a process of retrieving stereotyped knowledge schemas to recognize familiar program segments. The direct fit between a knowledge schema of subjects and a program segment is likely to produce high performance accuracy. Problem reasoning in program comprehension, however, has to integrate incomplete knowledge and create new knowledge for constructing a conceptual model of program functioning so as to clarify the role of unfamiliar program segments in a program context. At the beginning, model testing (identifying the description of program segments in this experiment) is likely to incur low performance accuracy since an initial conceptual model is likely to be incomplete and inaccurate. As the conceptual model becomes more complete and accurate with the process of knowledge integration, knowledge creation, and model testing, performance accuracy will increase.

To examine problem solving strategies, the frequency of program comprehension errors (segment-description mismatches) across trials is calculated. The error frequency on a trial of a program is the total number of persons in an expertise group (experts or novices) who made an error on that trial. If only knowledge retrieval is used by a subject, performance accuracy should be kept low constantly throughout the course of problem solving, and the error frequency distribution should look like a horizontal line with a constantly low level of error frequencies. If only problem reasoning is used, more performance errors should be made during the early stage of problem solving and fewer performance errors during later stages, and the error frequency distribution should look like a learning curve.

Methods of controlling problem solving process can be classified into two categories:

systematic and opportunistic. To examine process control methods, the mean jump between program plans of adjacent segments in subject action sequence is calculated. A jump is considered as how many levels the program plans of adjacent segments are away from each other. A subject's mean jump per pair of adjacent segments is calculated by dividing the number of adjacent pairs involved in the process into the sum of jumps made by those pairs. For example, if a subject comprehends and identifies all the segments of program one in the sequence of segments 2, 1, 3, 6, 4, 5, and 7, the mean jump will be $(1+1+1+0+1+1)/6=0.833$.

A subject who employs a pure systematic strategy like top-down or bottom-up should complete the comprehension of all the program segments at one level before moving to the next level. If a pure top-down or bottom-up process is conducted, a subject's maximum mean jump should be (level jumps)/(total number of adjacent pairs)=$(1+1)/(7-1)=0.333$ for program one because the subject needs to jump only twice from one level to another, $(1+1+1)/(17-1)=0.19$ for program two, and $(1+1+1)/(35-1)=0.12$ for program three. A subject using an opportunistic method is likely to have a larger mean jump than a subject using a systematic method.

3. RESULTS AND DISCUSSION

Subject performance time on a program is calculated by subtracting the time when the subject is given experiment materials from the time when the subject enters the last segment-description pair. The main effect of expertise on performance time is not significant ($F_{1, 18} = 0.95$, $p > 0.30$). The performance time increases significantly with problem difficulty ($F_{2, 36} = 256.17$, $p < 0.0001$) from program one, to program two, then to program three. No significant interaction is present between expertise and problem difficulty ($F_{2, 36} = 1.32$, $p > 0.25$).

Subject performance error on a program is calculated by dividing the total number of segments in a program (7 in program one, 17 in program two, and 35 in program three) into the frequency of errors (mismatches). The main effect of expertise on performance error is significant ($F_{1, 18} = 14.76$, $p < 0.005$). Experts produce fewer errors than novices. The main effect of problem difficulty on performance error is also significant ($F_{2, 36} = 18.68$, $p < 0.0001$). The performance error on program three is higher than on program one and program two while no significant difference exists between program one and program two. There is a significant interaction between expertise and problem difficulty on performance error ($F_{2, 36} = 5.54$, $p < 0.01$). A Student Newman-Keuls test on this significant interaction reveals that the problem difficulty sharpens the difference between experts and novices.

Figure 2 shows the distribution of error frequency across trials. Error frequencies of experts on each of the three programs are kept at a constantly low level before the first trial with the highest error frequency (trial 3 of program one, trial 5 of program two, trial 24 of program three) than after. After this trial, error frequencies of experts approximately decrease with trials, appearing like a learning curve. For each program, most experts first identified familiar program segments of variable initialization, screen setting, and information input/output, leaving unfamiliar segments of complex information transformation and control logic for later stages of program comprehension. Novices' error frequency distributions on the three programs show similar patterns to experts'. Thus, it appears that both experts and novices employ a knowledge retrieval strategy at the early stage of problem solving and a problem reasoning strategy afterwards.

Experts had better performance accuracy than novices before and after the first trial of highest error frequency. It is likely that experts' possession of more complete and accurate knowledge than novices' strengthens experts' ability in both knowledge retrieval and problem reasoning, resulting in experts' better overall problem solving performance than novices'.

The mean jump of each subject is submitted to ANOVA with expertise as a between-subject factor and problem difficulty as a within-subject factor. The main effect of expertise is significant ($F_{1, 18} = 10.53$, $p < 0.005$). Novices produce larger jumps than experts (the mean jump of experts is 0.595 and the mean jump of novices is 0.776). The main effect of problem

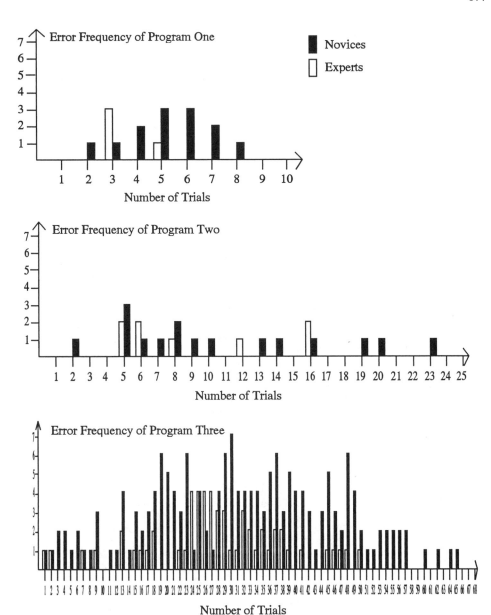

Figure 2. Error Frequencies of Experts and Novices on Three Programs.

difficulty is significant ($F_{2, 36}$ = 6.68, p < 0.005). The jump on program three (with the mean of 0.781) is larger than on program one (with the mean of 0.650) and program two (with the mean of 0.625), but no significant difference exists between program one and program two.

The interaction between expertise and problem difficulty is not significant ($F_{2, 36} = 0.46$, p > 0.60).

The significant main effect of expertise shows that the experts control problem solving process in a more systematic manner than novices. However, even experts did not strictly follow the pure top-down or bottom-up process because their mean jump (0.595) is greater than the maximum jump (less than 0.333) allowed by the pure top-down or bottom-up process. In addition, the significant effect of problem difficulty shows that subject problem solving process becomes less systematic with increasing problem difficulty.

4.   IMPLICATIONS IN HUMAN-COMPUTER INTERFACE DESIGN

Since the problem difficulty affects the problem solving performance and process of users, task analysis is the first step towards user-compatible interface design of computer systems especially for sophisticated tasks. From task analysis, user expertise in each interaction element (piece of information or item of functions maintained by computer systems) can be determined. A hierarchical grouping of user familiar interaction elements is advocated to allow the stereotyped retrieval of these elements in a systematic manner like top-down. Since users are familiar with these interaction elements, a phrase is sufficient for users to identify the function of such an interaction element. Hence, a hierarchical menu structure would be a good choice for organizing user familiar interaction elements. A non-hierarchical grouping of user unfamiliar interaction elements is advocated to facilitate imaginative thinking for knowledge integration and creation in a problem reasoning strategy. An associative network as the basic memory structure of humans is a good choice for organizing user unfamiliar interaction elements because it allows the flexible access to its elements in a casual manner. Since users are not familiar with these interaction elements, graphic information such as an icon together with a phrase is a great help for users to identify the function of such an interaction element and to associate it with other interaction elements. Icon shape and color can be used as a means to categorize these unfamiliar interaction elements if required. To further support associative thinking in problem reasoning strategy, concurrent views on different parts of a task can be provided to users through multiple windows.

5.   REFERENCES

1.   D. J. Mayhew, Principles and Guidelines in Software User Interface Design, Prentice Hall, Englewood Cliffs, NJ, 1992.
2.   B. Shneiderman, Designing the User Interface: Strategies for Effective Human-Computer Interaction, Addison-Wesley, Reading, Massachusetts, 1992.
3.   N. Ye and G. Salvendy, An adaptive interface design using neural networks. In H.-J. Bullinger, Ed. Human Aspects of Computing: Design and Use of Interactive Systems and Work with Terminals, Proceedings of IV International Conference on Human-Computer Interaction, Elsevier, Amsterdam, (1991) 435-439.
4.   R. H. Sprague, Jr. and E. D. Carlson, Building Effective Decision Support Systems, Prentice-Hall, Englewood Cliffs, NJ, 1982.
5.   B. Shneiderman, Exploratory experiments in programmer behavior. International Journal of Computer and Information Sciences No. 5 (1976) 123-143.

6.   ACKNOWLEDGMENT

This work was supported by the NEC Research Fellowship and Professorship.

Development of a methodology for optimizing the elicited knowledge

C.-J. Chao[a] and G. Salvendy[b]

[a]
Chung Shan Institute of Science and Technology, P.O. Box 90008-9-6, Lung-Tan, Taiwan, R.O.C.

[b]
School of Industrial Engineering, Purdue University, West Lafayette, Indiana 47907

Abstract

Knowledge elicitation is the first step in building expert systems, and it is a major bottleneck in the construction of expert systems. In this research, a conceptual framework and methodology is presented for selecting knowledge elicitation methods. A statistical nested factorial design is utilized with three tasks, four knowledge elicitation methods and ten cognitive factors. Twenty-four subjects were used in the experiment, and five hypotheses were tested.

Based on these findings in the experiment, a matching index for combining tasks, knowledge elicitation methods and cognitive abilities is derived. This matching index maximizes the elicited knowledge by selecting the most appropriate method of knowledge elicitation for specific tasks and also selecting the best individuals for this knowledge elicitation.

1. OBJECTIVES AND SIGNIFICANCE

Although many different methods of knowledge elicitation exist, the following issues are not known about these methods: (1) different knowledge elicitation methods may be suitable for different tasks (2) different knowledge elicitation methods may extract different kinds of knowledge and (3) the expert's cognitive abilities may be an important factor in the knowledge elicitation procedure. The primary objective of this research is to combine the above three concepts into a new conceptual model which will provide a framework and a methodology for selecting the most appropriate knowledge elicitation method for each task.

This derived conceptual model has an important impact on human computer interaction and training of knowledge engineers.

2. BACKGROUND LITERATURE AND DERIVATION OF HYPOTHESES

An expert system is a computer program that contains both declarative knowledge and procedural knowledge. It has often been stated that knowledge elicitation is the critical bottleneck in establishing expert systems (Hoffman, 1987). Little research exists about the comparative effectiveness of different knowledge elicitation methods. Thus there are few guidelines to aid the knowledge engineer in the selection of knowledge elicitation techniques (Fox et al., 1987). The conceptual

framework presented here consists of the following four dimensions:
1. knowledge elicitation methods
2. cognitive factors of human ability
3. task types
4. knowledge structures
A description of each of the dimensions is presented in the following sections.

2.1 Knowledge elicitation methods

Knowledge elicitation is the process which extracts problem solving expertise from some knowledge sources. The most commonly used knowledge elicitation methods include interview, protocol analysis, induction and repertory grid analysis. During the interview, the knowledge engineer proposes some hypothetical problems pertaining to the tasks in question and asks the expert to solve them. Protocol analysis asks the experts to " think aloud " while performing a task (Tuthill, 1990). Induction is the process of discovering knowledge from examples. A repertory grid uses identified elements and constructs to describe objects. Each knowledge elicitation method has its advantages and disadvantages. Hence in order to obtain more effective knowledge elicitation results, a match needs to be made between task type and the method of knowledge elicitation.

2.2 Cognitive factors of human ability

Lehner and Kralj (1988) demonstrated that the "cognitive model" is a dominant factor in the quality of user/expert system interaction. Ekstrom et al. (1976) identified twenty-three cognitive factors of human abilities, but their impact on the effective utilization of different knowledge elicitation methods is unknown.

2.3 Task types

Bylander and Chandrasekaran (1987) suggested that different knowledge elicitation methods should be required for different kinds of tasks. One of the application tasks in building an expert system is analysis task which is composed of diagnosis, debugging, and interpretation. Analysis tasks involve the explanation of information through components. Hence, all the possible solutions in certain problems can be identified reliably, validly, and objectively.

2.4 Knowledge structures

The expert's knowledge consists of two types of knowledge, procedural knowledge and declarative knowledge. Procedural knowledge is defined as the strategies and sequences of operations used in problem-solving (knowing how). Declarative knowledge includes facts and meanings stored in memory (knowing what).

2.5 Development and statement of hypotheses

A major problem in knowledge elicitation is not only which knowledge elicitation method is best for which task, but also whether there is a model which can account for their relationship. A knowledge elicitation method which is most appropriate for one expert for a specific task may not be effective for the same expert on a different task or by another expert on the same class of tasks. Therefore, The purpose of this research is to develop a model for matching the attributes of tasks, the cognitive characteristics of individuals and the knowledge elicitation methods.

Five hypotheses are proposed to test the validation of the model.

1. The quality of acquired knowledge is closely related to the expert's cognitive abilities.
2. Different knowledge elicitation methods extract different amounts or types of procedural and declarative knowledge from the domain experts.
3. In order to obtain the maximum efficiency in extracting knowledge from experts, different cognitive abilities require different knowledge elicitation methods.
4. Each knowledge elicitation method is best suited for a specific task or class of task.
5. If the above four hypotheses are supported, then the following function is hypothesized:
   Matching Index = f (knowledge elicitation method, cognitive ability, task attributes)

3. METHOD

Based on the hypotheses proposed above, a statistical experiment is used to test whether one knowledge elicitation is superior to other methods for various task types. The detailed description of this experiment is presented below.

3.1 Task description

The tasks selected are two computer programs written in the FORTRAN language (Lin, 1985). One represents diagnosis task and the other represents a debugging task. In the interpretation task, subjects have to explain the possible reasons of the observed error message in the FORTRAN program

3.2 Subjects

Twenty-four subjects were randomly selected from the top nine percent of a group of 800 students .These students are expert computer programmers and have especially good skills and knowledge in debugging, diagnosis and interpretation tasks utilized in the FORTRAN language.

3.3 Dependent variable and independent variables

The dependent variables are used to assess the model's usefulness and are outlined below:

1. Completeness -- percentage of total knowledge captured
2. Total Time -- The elapsed time from the start of the knowledge elicitation session to the finish of the rule reviewing by the experts.
3. Inconsistency
4. Efficiency -- number of rules/ time
5. Importance of data

The independent variables include three tasks and four knowledge elicitation methods.

3.4 Experimental design and procedure

A nested factorial design (Hicks, 1973) is utilized in the experiment. Each treatment combination includes the same number of subjects to obtain a balanced design. Six subjects are randomly assigned to each knowledge elicitation method. Since the same subjects can not appear in different groups, these subjects are nested within groups. Each subject is randomly assigned one of the four knowledge elicitation methods. All experts performed the same tasks under the same experimental conditions. All subjects completed the same cognitive tests which were randomly ordered. For the interview and the protocol methods, video and audio recorders were used to record all of the experimental procedure for subsequent review and analysis. After the analysis, rules were derived by the knowledge engineer or the computer, and the experts were asked to update all of the rules without missing any useful information in solving each task.

4. RESULTS

4.1 Data analysis

A statistical software SAS was used to analyze the results of the nested factorial design, correlation coefficient and multiple regression analysis. In case where there is an overall significant effects due to method or method X task, a Student-Newman-Keuls test is performed to investigate all possible pairs of means in a sequential manner. Table 1 shows the descriptive statistics and practical differences for each dependent variable .

4.2 Match index among task, cognitive ability and method of knowledge elicitation

The experimental results indicate that task type, cognitive ability and method of knowledge elicitation have effects on the acquired knowledge. Therefore, a multiple regression equation including these three variables is used to predict their matching index. A three stage process is utilized to determine which knowledge elicitation method is the most effective for which task and individual. Stage one provides the regression equations for the following five dependent variables. When the regression equations are obtained, the match index can be estimated. At stage two, an intercorrelation matrix is developed by using Saaty's analytical hierarchy process (AHP, Saaty, 1980), and this method is used to calculate a weight for each of the five dependent variables. In stage three, the weights derived from the intercorrelation matrix are used to derive an overall effective measure for the four different knowledge elicitation methods and the three different tasks. This is done by multiplying the relative index Yi derived from stage one with the weights obtained in the intercorrelation matrix. The index for the and inconsistency are negative due to their opposite effects in knowledge elicitation.

4.3 Testing of hypotheses

The five hypotheses have been tested by using a statistical experiment and the results are illustrated below.

Hypothesis one is supported, since significant correlations are present between cognitive abilities and the dependent variables associated with the quality of acquired knowledge.

Hypothesis two is supported for the debugging task only. The Interview and induction methods are better than the protocol and repertory grid analysis methods.

Table 1   The descriptive statistics and practical differences in the use of different knowledge elicitation methods for three tasks

Tasks	Knowledge elicitation method / Dependent variable	Protocol		Interview		Induction		Repertory grid		% change
		X	S.D.	X	S.D.	X	S.D.	X	S.D.	
Diagnosis	total knowledge acquired (%)	40.3	4.6	39.3	9.4	41.5	10.3	40.5	15.5	------
	Total time (min.)	265.5	140.2	258.8	77.7	118.3	22.3	120.8	34.6	124
	Inconsistency	8.3	2.5	9.8	3.1	6.0	1.8	2.3	2.4	322
	Rule/time(#/hr.)	4.9	1.9	4.1	3.4	9.4	2.3	9.0	2.1	128
	Importance of data	55.8	5.6	53.6	14.0	56.0	14.7	55.5	22.6	------
Debugging	total knowledge acquired (%)	37.2	12.8	52.7	6.3	50.0	8.7	37.7	12.9	41
	Total time (min.)	266.8	97.6	309.7	52.4	136.7	25.7	128.2	42.1	141
	Inconsistency	9.8	4.0	5.3	2.7	6.2	2.6	4.5	2.6	118
	Rule/time(#/hr.)	4.1	1.3	5.0	0.6	10.8	2.8	8.4	1.3	162
	Importance of data	60.0	22.2	85.6	7.9	80.7	13.2	63.2	10.9	44
Interpretation	total knowledge acquired (%)	25.3	6.1	27.8	4.4	21.2	6.2	21.2	6.2	------
	Total time (min.)	77.8	48.3	125.3	32.0	48.2	18.4	67.8	31.8	------
	Inconsistency	2.2	1.6	2.5	1.8	0.7	0.8	1.0	1.3	------
	Rule/time(#/hr.)	15.8	5.3	9.2	1.7	18.3	4.8	14.1	3.4	99
	Importance of data	57.3	12.1	61.7	9.0	44.5	8.4	49.2	11.0	------

⌊____⌋ significant difference at α = 0.05 level

Hypothesis three is confirmed, and it indicates that the efficiency of each method is associated with certain cognitive abilities.

Hypothesis four is supported, and it indicates that each knowledge elicitation method is suitable for a different task under the requirements of different dependent variables.

Hypothesis five has index of been demonstrated successfully to form a total match index which combines the importance of data, completeness, time, inconsistency and efficiency.

5. CONCLUSION

From the study presented here, the following conclusions may be drawn:

1. The repertory grid and induction methods of knowledge elicitation require significantly less time (by one to six fold) to elicit knowledge than the interview and protocol methods in diagnosis or debugging tasks.

2. For eliciting knowledge in the debugging tasks, the induction or interview method elicits an average of 40 percent more knowledge than using either the protocol or the repertory grid method.

3. The induction method of knowledge elicitation acquires about 100 percent more procedural knowledge/per hour than the protocol method in the interpretation task.

4. For the interview and protocol methods, the percent of procedural knowledge acquired in diagnosis task increased from around 40 percent for one expert to about 70 percent when the knowledge was acquired from six experts. Percent of procedural knowledge increased to 90 percent for the repertory grid and induction methods.

6. REFERENCE

1 Bylander, T., and Chandrasekaran, B. (1987). Generic tasks for knowledge based reasoning: the 'right' level of abstraction for knowledge acquisition. *International Journal of Man-Machine Studies.* vol. 26, pp. 231-244.

2 Ekstrom, R.B., French, J.W., Harman, H.H., and Dermen, D. (1976). *Manual for Kit of Factor-Referenced Cognitive Tests.* Princeton: Educational Testing Services.

3 Fox, J., Myers, C.D., Greaves, M.F., and Pegram, S. (1987). A systematic study of knowledge base refinement in the diagnosis of leukemia. In A. Kidd (Ed.). *Knowledge Acquisition for Expert Systems: A Practical Handbook.* New York, N.Y., Plenum Press.

4 Hicks, C.R. (1973). *Fundamental Concepts of Design of Experiment,* 2nd ed., Holt, rinehart and Winston, New York.

5 Hoffman, R.R. (1987). The problem of extracting the knowledge of experts from the perspective of experimental psychology. *AI Magazine.* vol. 8, no. 2, pp. 53-67.

6 Lehner, P.E. and Kralj, M.M. (1988). Expert systems: The user interface. In J.A. Hendler (Ed.), *Human/Computer Interaction,* pp. 307-318.

7 Lin, W.P. (1985). *ANSI FORTRAN structure program design.* sixth edition. Song-Kang Co.

8 Saaty, T.L. (1980). *The analytic process.* New York: McGraw-Hill.

9 Tuthill, G.S. (1990). Knowledge engineering: concepts and practice for knowledge-based systems. Blue Ridge Summit, PA: Tab Books. pp. 193-224.

A Taxonomy for Human Behaviour and Human-Computer Interaction

William H. Edmondson*

Cognitive Science Research Centre, School of Computer Science,
The University of Birmingham, Birmingham B15 2TT, U.K.

Abstract

Conventional theoretical and taxonomical approaches to HCI are contrasted with a taxonomy based on underlying interaction behaviour. It is shown that clarifying insights can be obtained by consideration of underlying interaction behaviour and that these can be formalized for use in interface design.

1. MODELS IN HCI

Human-Computer Interaction is typically modelled by theorists on the basis of other sorts of human behaviour. The models chosen are for the most part unsurprising, but they may afford fresh insight, as when assessing the degree of autonomy appropriate for agents in an agent-based interface (cf. Edmondson & Meech 1993). This model building approach is, however, problematic, and this is for two reasons.

The first problem concerns the original basis for the models. Typically these include human communication, tool usage, and agents. The issue here is that the behaviour in the original domain is only imperfectly understood, so attempts to derive models will inevitably be flawed and/or incomplete, (cf. Good 1989, where this point is made in connection with models based on communication behaviour). Attempts to study the use of artefacts (generalization of the tool metaphor) make the point clearly (Caroll 1991).

The second difficulty with the modelling approach is the assumption that HCI is a *unitary* and *coherent* phenomenon. The first issue to note is the corollary that a *single* model - e.g. human communication - is required. However, the practical consequence is that any discussion of design details is replaced by concern for the 'best' or most appropriate model (also forgetting that these models are not themselves worked out). The second issue is the presumption that HCI is a *coherent* behavioural phenomenon (or perhaps a coherent collection of phenomena), a behaviour which is distinctly HCI and nothing else; in short - a discipline. This is the 'space-science' error: in the early 1960s it was considered sensible to establish departments of 'space science' in universities, etc., (especially in the USA) but eventually common sense prevailed and 'space' was recognized as a new place where all the old disciplines applied. HCI has no inherent coherence - it is a domain, not a discipline. Clearly the unwarranted views are not widely held, but it is probable that in one form or another they underpin many theoretical stances (cf. some of the papers in Carroll 1991).

2. CATEGORIZATION AT THE INTERFACE

Some researchers have apparently elected to do without a theory - a plausible move - and have instead offered only a simplistic view of HCI, based on categorization of HCI in superficial terms - windows, icons, menus, direct manipulation, etc. (e.g. Shneiderman 1987, 1992, Sutcliffe 1988). Whilst this strand in the HCI literature may reflect acknowledgment of the aforementioned difficulties associated with establishing HCI as a science with a theory or a model, this is by no means clear, nor, ultimately, helpful because nothing theoretically significant is offered instead. The ultimate vacuousness of this entirely descriptive approach is readily found in the sense of fashion which accompanies this or that account of windows or icons or whatever. Within just one such domain, e.g. icons, it is possible to find only a little analytical insight (cf. Edmondson 1992); most of the work is descriptive or shallow.

3. CATEGORIZATION OF INTERACTION

An alternative perspective is that human behaviour through the computer *interface* is based on a few behavioural primitives which, in isolation or in combination, are to be found in the *interaction*. This taxonomical approach offers three mutually exclusive or 'orthogonal' *underlying* categories of interaction. These are *manipulation, selection, communication.*

Manipulation is direct interaction with the environment (real or virtual); it is 'physical' manipulation in the conventional sense and relies upon 'physical' actions and appropriate sensors coupled in real time.

Selection behaviour is the making of selections from a set of selectable items - generally, a selection space of selectable option, values, or items. The selection space and the items in it must be known or recognizable for any selection to be made, as opposed to guessed at.

Communication, in the general sense, involves the use of some sort of linguistic behaviour, with recognizable intent, usually associated with particular sub-classes of the category:
- specification - command languages are an example of this sub-class; the user is intent on specifying the resultant state of the system;
- information - form filling behaviour exemplifies this sub-class;
- instruction - as would be given to an agent;
- question - from the user to a system or agent, as in help systems.

The three basic or underlying styles of interaction can surface in many different interfaces, and it is important to recognize that the *interaction* style is primarily governed by the user's view of the task, and not by the *interface* style (see also Edmondson 1991). With different emphasis the same point can be made as follows - superficial characteristics of the *interface* are not a reliable guide to the nature of the *interaction*. Examples make this clear.

A menu-based interface is well suited to a selection based interaction, but this does not mean that interfaces incorporating menus always imply selection as the underlying form of the interaction - consider the following:

Dialogue boxes (often invoked from a menu) are in many respects equivalent to menus and they often offer selection spaces without sequential constraints - an important property of such interfaces. However, they sometimes permit values to be entered, e.g. margin width (in values specified to 3 decimal places!). The uniform appearance of the interaction as selection, suggested by the interface, is misleading - the interaction *at this point* is communication (specification). It might be argued that in fact dialogue boxes are actually to be read as interfaces indicating communication (specification) - but then the observation remains valid because there will be instances when the user is clearly making selections.

The user's perception of a task may be such as to change the natural interaction style from, say, selection to specification. This would be the case when a user requires 12pt Palatino italic and simply wants to specify that (knowing about, but being currently uninterested in, the alternatives available in selection space).

Implementational difficulties may force the user to modify the underlying interaction style (that is, to change their behaviour). This can come about, for example, when the user's natural choice of style would be communication (question), but the system obliges the user to work in selection style by offering a menu-based interface - 'city guides' are a good example.

A passenger in a crowded lift can call out "17 please" and know that someone near the buttons will ensure that floor 17 is selected. The appearance - communication (instruction) - is misleading; the interaction with the lift is one of selection. The human intermediary, apparently an agent, is not really free to do anything else; the instruction is unambiguous; the *interaction* does not *require* an agent - the particular circumstances do (someone unable to verbalise the request would wait until the lift emptied sufficiently for the buttons to be within reach).

The Mac interface is usually described as direct manipulation - the use of mouse, icons, windows, menus, and etc. This description is doubly misleading: (a) the *interface* is stylistically mixed and not homogeneous; (b) the *interaction* is taxonomically mixed and not homogeneous. The use of the mouse to navigate around a menu system *making selections* is not direct manipulation of anything except the mouse (just as the passenger in the lift will directly manipulate a finger to the button, but does not directly manipulate the lift to floor 17). Moving the file/folder icons from one location to another - perhaps the waste bin - does not constitute manipulation; the *interaction* here is communication (specification) - as it is when ejecting a floppy disc via the waste bin (!). Dragging a window corner to change its shape does indeed manipulate the window, and this may indeed be the point of the interaction (to ensure tessellation rather than overlap, say). But the purpose might also be something else entirely - selection of a different portion of selection space, perhaps, by enlarging the section of a menu which is in view (cf. full and short menus).

4. TASK FOCUS

It is not difficult to extend the list of examples which illustrate the three points made so far (points made in the context of considering HCI to be a domain, not a discipline) - *interface* style and *interaction* style are not inevitably linked, in practice; *interface* style and *interaction* style are heterogeneous; the user's conception of the task determines the preferred *interaction* style, although the *interface* implementation may force the user to use a different style.

An obvious observation at this juncture might be that task analysis with users should lead via elicitation of the interaction style to the interface required to support that style. This discussion is taken up again below, but first an intermediate step in the argument must be made.

The theme here is the user's answer to the question "What are you doing?". When carrying out a task the user will have a *task focus*, and this can change from moment to moment. For example, a person using a word processor is seen to go through a sequence of actions with keyboard and mouse which result in a paragraph of text being repositioned in a document. The question is posed and the user replies "editing my paper on X". For the user that is the *task focus*. Although perhaps more specifically the user has obviously been writing as well as editing (and indeed might have said so) it would clearly have been odd to have replied "I'm moving a paragraph to a different location" (odd because this states the obvious), and odder still to have said something like "I'm moving the mouse 2" vertically". Equally odd would have been an answer of the form "I'm trying to beat Dr Jones in the published-paper league, to ensure my promotion". All these answers could be *true* but they are somehow not relevant.

One important feature of the task focus is that it is changeable - under the control of the user (from editing, to saving,...), or under control of a system (alarm status indicators), or unintentionally as a by-product of an aspect of interface design. Thus, if the HCI designer is attempting to support a user in, say, a word processing application, the designer must be aware not only of the differences between underlying interaction styles, in the general sense, but also that the user may switch style whenever the task focus changes. The designer's problem is to support such changes but in such a way as to avoid prompting them unbidden.

Consider a WYSIWYG interface for a word processor. This typically will provide a visual representation of a document as it will appear on the printed page. If an unfortunate line-break or page-break is indicated then the user may thoughtlessly shift task focus to deal with that. The interface is slippery with regard to task focus because two very different tasks are readily reflected in a uniform interface, and with uniform interaction style - the user *specifies* the order of words and paragraphs..., and also *specifies* the page layout parameters..., perhaps without ever lifting fingers from the keyboard, although the style of the interface may be such as to encourage mousing through menus (note that in a different package, e.g. Word Perfect, the specificational nature of the interaction is brought to the surface of the interface).

5. TASK ANALYSIS FOR TASK FOCUS

The task focus is the *contextualized local goal* in the accomplishment of some general goal(s), but, and this is the other major feature of the task focus, it serves as the basis for contextualization of action at any moment. In other words, the task focus is the operative element of overall context *and* the internal determiner of the appropriateness and legitimacy of any any action; the task focus is itself given context by the overall goal(s) and simultaneously serves as context for action. The goal of "writing the paper on X" thus contextualizes, sanctions, creates... a set of local goals (sometimes thought of as sub-goals - but the hierarchical relationship is not necessary or significant). These local goals serve as the contexts for actions to be taken which in conjunction accomplish the goal (e.g. getting the right words, in the right font, with the right heading layout style, within the right margins, within the page limitation...); they are task foci.

Task analysis for interface design is typically thought of as the means whereby a task can be 'broken down' into several different 'smaller' tasks, etc., in such a way that (a) provision for the components will ensure provision for the whole; and (b) support for interaction at the componential level will support the task in the unitary sense. Thus, according to received wisdom, "writing the paper on X" must be supported at the componential level - the whole will necessarily be possible if the various parts are possible. In addition, the interface style should be made consistent across the components to ensure that the overall goal is supported by the interface (see, however, Reisner 1990).

A contrasting claim is made in this paper. The insight afforded by the taxonomical approach to interaction behaviour is that task analysis must relate *task foci* (not actions) to styles of *interaction* (not to interface styles), and furthermore that provision for task foci means provision for change of focus.

Task analysis for selection behaviour is possible, using Decision Track (Edmondson 1990, Edmondson & Spence 1992, Edmondson & Billups 1992), in a way which exactly captures the points made above. The user's identification of a task focus - say adjustment to the characteristics of the font being used - is identified in the formalism as embarking on the making of a decision. The decision is complete when the appropriate or desired characteristics of the font have been *selected*, and the task focus can then change. The formalism provides for documentation of the user's conception of selection space in sufficient detail for the necessary properties of the *interface* to be specified so that the underlying style of *interaction* - selection - is fully supported.

A useful complication can arise in the formalism if the range of available task foci is small enough to be offered as a set of selections, as is found, for example, in the menu-bar for the Mac operating system. In fact the Multifinder operating system permits several applications to be open at once (the task focus equivalent to "using the Mac" involves *selecting* an application); within any one application several local goals are offered for *selection*; within a specific task focus (e.g. editing) a *selection* has to be made. This richness of structure can indeed be captured using Decision Track - the formalism explicitly relates a set of selectable items to a task focus. There is no formal constraint which prevents a selectable item being a task focus.

The value of Decision Track, in relation to task analysis and task foci, is that with it an HCI practitioner can document the functionality of a system as a set of selection spaces, even where the 'final' or 'significant' interaction is not itself selection-based (an example would be the use of a control panel to set up parameter values - the (sub)set to be adjusted is *selected*, the values are not). However, where the local goals are not constrained, in relation to some general goal(s), it is not possible to identify them in advance and establish their selection space. In these circumstances it may only be feasible to sample the range of task foci, paying special attention to the interaction styles required to support any of the local goals *and* the transitions from one task focus to another.

6. CONCLUSIONS

Successful HCI designers may well have developed particular skills in recognizing and providing for task foci and transitions between them. It could indeed be argued that natural talent in this area is a valid basis for HCI design. However, such a design approach depends heavily on designers being able to function as different sorts of users, and this is not always possible. Furthermore, if designers function as very experienced users they may miss opportunities for uncovering task perceptions (chains of task foci) which novices or other users might utilize. The claim made in this paper is that insights into the behavioural basis of HCI, and in particular the value of formal capture of user's underlying interaction behaviour, will go some way to make possible the successful implementation of interfaces which support the interactions which users want to perform.

Acknowledgement
* William H. Edmondson is supported by a grant from Apricot Computers Ltd., a subsidiary of Mitsubishi Electric U.K. Ltd.

References

Carroll J. M., 1991, ed. *Designing Interaction: Psychology at the Human-Computer Interface.* Cambridge: Cambridge University Press.

Good, D. A., 1989. The Viability of Conversational Grammars. In *Structure of Multimodal Dialogue*, eds. D. G. Bouwhuis, M. M. Taylor, & F. Néel. Amsterdam: North-Holland.

Edmondson W. H., 1990. Decision Track: A formalism for Menu Structure and User's Selection Behaviour. In *Human-Computer Interaction - INTERACT '90*, eds. D. Diaper et al. Amsterdam: Elsevier Science Publishers.

Edmondson W. H., 1991. Interaction Taxonomy. A working paper for the Second Venaco Workshop on the Structure of Multimodal Dialogue. Acquafredda di Maratea, September 1991.

Edmondson W. H., 1992. Abstraction and Organization in Signs and Sign Systems. Paper for the First Workshop on Iconic Communication, University of Brighton, December 1992.

Edmondson W. H. & Billups I.R., 1992. The Decision Track Formalism. University of Birmingham, School of Computer Science, CSR-92-4.

Edmondson W. H. & Spence R., 1992. Systematic Menu Design. In *People and Computers VII*, Proceedings of HCI'92, York, September 1992, eds. A. Monk et al. Cambridge: Cambridge University Press.

Edmondson W. H. & Meech J. F., 1993. A Model of Context for Human-Computer Interaction. Workshop 2, IJCAI '93, Chambéry, August 1993.

Reisner, P., 1990. What is Consistency? Research Report RJ 7326 (68807) 5/31/90. IBM Research Division, Almaden Research Center, San Jose, CA 95120, USA.

Shneiderman B., 1987 & 1992 (1st & 2nd editions). *Designing the User Interface.* Addison-Wesley Publishing Co.

Sutcliffe A., 1988. *Human-Computer Interface Design.* Macmillan Education Ltd.

Task Analysis Method using the GOMS Model with Grouping

Kanji Kato and Katsuhiko Ogawa
NTT Human Interface Laboratories, 1-2356 Take, Yokosuka, Kanagawa 238, Japan

Abstract

This paper proposes a task analysis method that extends the GOMS model through the grouping of repetitive sub-procedures. Its aim is to increase the ability to discriminate among differently sequenced procedures performing the same task. The task analysis method consists of three steps: procedure decomposition in a single task, grouping of sub-procedures into multi-tasks, and constructing a GOMS model. The application of this method to an actual multi-request registration task indicates the validity of the method.

1. Introduction

In actual working places, tasks are often carried out using procedures that were never anticipated by system designers and/or site foremen. Such unexpected procedures may cause human errors or inefficiency. Any procedure other than the predetermined procedures may be categorized as errors in a certain context (Leplat, 1989). The method to predict the likely procedures or to estimate procedure selection tendencies would be extremely useful for the design of more reliable, more efficient computer systems, work, or training.

In relation to procedure selection, procedure selectivity has been discussed from the view point of the strategy selection in the search process for locating faults (Rasmussen, 1986), or from the sphere of acceptable work activities (Rasmussen, 1989). However, procedure prediction or procedure selectivity estimation has not been developed sufficiently. This situation may be caused by the existence of too many factors influencing procedure selection, the factors' variable impact on procedure selectivity, or work context. The complexity of cognitive processing, "Cognitive complexity" for short, is an important factor because many other factors such as total execution time and learnability, are strongly related to this factor. The estimation of cognitive complexity require some model of the human cognitive process.

Cognitive complexity has been estimated by the number of steps, that is, the number of primitive procedures as derived by the Natural GOMS Language (Kieras, 1988) based on the GOMS model (Card, Moran, & Newell, 1983), a kind of human cognitive process model. It is expected that fewer steps indicate lower cognitive complexity and more steps indicate higher cognitive complexity. However, among procedures with the same task attainment criterion, the differences in the number of the steps are usually not large enough to estimate or to predict procedure selection. To increase the power of procedure discrimination, we propose a modified GOMS task analysis method, that is, the GOMS task analysis is modified to take account of the grouping of successively repeated sub-procedures.

2. Proposed method

GOMS task analysis is one application of the GOMS model. The GOMS model decomposes human cognitive processes into four cognitive components; Goal, Operator, Method, and the Selection rule. It was originally developed to construct an explicit model of the user's procedural knowledge for a particular system design (Card, Moran, & Newell, 1983). The Natural GOMS Language (NGOMSL) was developed to yield a convenient procedural method to analyze tasks based on the GOMS model (Kieras, 1988). Using NGOMSL, tasks are decomposed hierarchically as shown in Figure 1. The leftmost

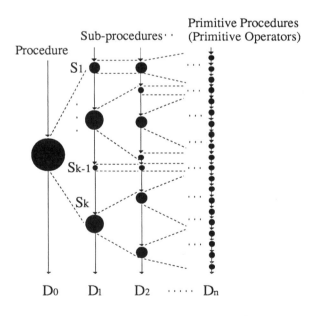

Figure 1. Procedure decomposition process (single task)
(●: procedure / sub-procedure)

undifferentiated procedure (D$_0$) is gradually decomposed (D$_1$, D$_2$, ...) until sub-procedures are reached that can not be decomposed any further. We call them the "primitive procedures." Each procedure can be decomposed into five or so components at large, therefore, deeper hierarchies are produced for more complex tasks. The number of the primitive procedures ("primitive operators" in Kieras's paper), "the number of steps" in other words, is thought to be an indication of cognitive complexity (Smith, Carayon, Eberts, & Salvendy, 1992). However, the difference in step numbers will not be sufficiently large if the procedures are the same except for the sequencing of several sub-procedures. This indicates that step number may not be so adequate to discriminate between alternative procedures.

Is there any possibility of utilizing step numbers, the number of sub-procedures, as the indication of cognitive complexity? There is still the possibility that the step number of the roughly decomposed sub-procedures may reflect the cognitive complexity, especially for the macro level task structure. As one of the possible macro level task structures, the existence of sub-procedure repetition can be thought of as decreasing the cognitive complexity. The step numbers derived from this idea may enhance procedure discrimination, especially for multi-tasks. Multi-tasks are those where several instances of the same goal must be accomplished at the same time (as shown in the left-side of Figure 2). The proposed method can be described as follows.

(a) <u>Procedure decomposition in a single task</u>

A single task in multi-tasks (e.g., Task 1, Task 2, or Task 3 in Figure 2) are decomposed into several sub-procedures. Since this is the first decomposition, equivalent to D$_1$ shown in Figure 1, we call the sub-procedures "the primary subprocedures." The clues for procedure decomposition are large discontinuities in interface usage, or changes in the combination of senses used and devices accessed.

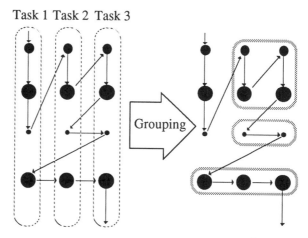

Task 1 Task 2 Task 3

Grouping

3 tasks proceed in the sequence indicated by the small arrows

Successively repeated sub-procedures are grouped into a new single sub-procedures

Figure 2. Examples of grouping
(● : group ⬭ : sub-procedure)

(b) Grouping of sub-procedures in a multi-task

Successively repeated sub-procedures are grouped into a new single sub-procedures (Figure 2). To find groups, the figure such as Figure 2 or the table type figure equivalent to Figure 2 is useful.

(c) Constructing a GOMS model

A GOMS model is constructed using the ordinary procedures but regarding each set of the grouped sub-procedures as the NGOMSL "unit task."

3. An application

3.1 Actual task

We applied the proposed method to an actual task. The simple procedure of the task is as follows; acceptance of customer's request via phone call and recording his/her requests on paper (this is one of the peculiar features of the Japanese HCI task due to the difficulty of rapid Japanese character input especially under time pressure), data input to computer with reference to the record, self-confirming the system's response to the data input, confirmation of the system's response with the customer using display terminal/using print-out, and registering the request with the system.

The working site was video taped for a certain time period. 31 dual request registration tasks were recorded and analyzed.

3.2 Application of the method

• Procedure decomposition

Five primary sub-procedures were derived from the first step of the method as shown in Figure 3. The duplication between S3 and S5 comes from two alternative sub-procedures in confirming information with the customer: confirming using display terminal or using print-out.

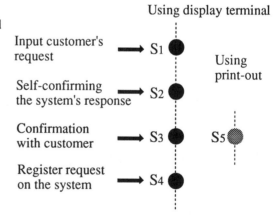

Figure 3. Sub-procedures in the actual task

• Grouping of sub-procedures in a multi-task

Due to several constraints on the sub-procedure sequences, 315 differently sequenced procedures were logically possible. Nineteen procedures remained after removing those considered unlikely for human operators. For example, the procedures that keep the customers waiting too long are avoided by the operators, and were removed from the analysis. All 19 feasible procedures were examined and grouped as shown in Figure 4.

Condition Sub-procedure	Using display terminal		Using print-out	
	1st	2nd	1st	2nd
Input customer's request				
Self-confirming the system's response				
Confirmation with customer				
Register request on the system				

Figure 4. Examples of sub-procedure grouping
(Successively repeated sub-procedures are grouped)

• Constructing a GOMS model

For each of the 19 feasible procedures, a GOMS model was constructed in NGOMSL. For this, primary sub-procedures were decomposed only once (one level), and the number of steps was acquired. For all 19 procedures, the actual selection frequencies are shown in Figure 5(b).

The distribution of the steps of GOMS model with grouping (shown in Figure 5(b)) is broader than the one without grouping (as shown in Figure 5 (a)). This result indicates

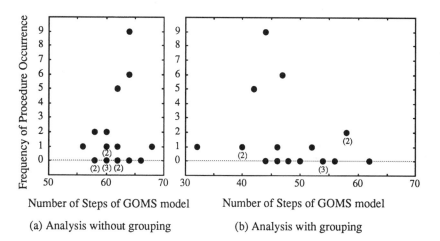

(a) Analysis without grouping   (b) Analysis with grouping

Figure 5. Effects of grouping on task analysis
(parenthesized numbers indicate multiple procedures)

that GOMS task analysis with grouping enhances procedure discrimination.

The three most frequent procedures are among the most simple procedures. This may reflect the logical tendency for the operators to prefer the procedures with few steps, that is, those with less cognitive complexity.

4. Conclusion

With the aim of realizing procedure prediction or procedure selectivity estimation among procedures performing the same task, the number of steps in the GOMS model was treated as an indication of "Cognitive complexity" which is expected to affect workers' procedure selection. To enhancing the discrimination of procedures, a new method was proposed by modifying the GOMS task analysis. The proposed method includes grouping of successively repeated sub-procedures before constructing a GOMS model. The application of the proposed method to an actual multi-request registration task indicates the validity of the method to enhance the discrimination of procedures. Furthermore, the result of the application indicates the possibility of procedure selectivity estimation by showing that the most frequent procedures are among those with the fewest steps.

Acknowledgments

The authors gratefully acknowledge Sadami Kurihara for his encouragement and support in this work. We thank Tohru Komine for his helpful work especially for data collection.

References

Card, S. K., Moran, T. P., & Newell, A. (1983). The psychology of human-computer interaction. Hillsdale, NJ: Lawrence Erlbaum Associates, Inc.

Kieras, D. E. (1988). Towards a practical GOMS model methodology for user interface design. In M. Helander (Ed.), The handbook of human-computer interaction. 135-158. Amsterdam: North-Holland.

Leplat, J. (1989). Error analysis, instrument and object of task analysis. Ergonomics, 32, 813-822.

Rasmussen, J. (1986). Information processing and human-machine interaction. Amsterdam: North-Holland.

Rasmussen, J. (1989). The role of error in organizing behaviour. Roskilde, Denmark: Risø National Laboratory, Report No. M-2799.

Smith, M. J., Carayon, P., Eberts, R., & Salvendy, G. (1992). Human-computer interaction. In G. Salvendy (Ed.), Handbook of industrial engineering. 1107-1144. New York: John Wiley & Sons.

Task-dependant descriptions: A preliminary study

Laurent Karsenty
CNAM - LENET, 41 rue Gay-Lussac, 75 005 Paris (France)

1. Introduction

Although the designers of aiding systems are able today to store many kinds of knowledge required for explanation purposes (e.g. [Scott & al., 1984], [Swartout & al., 1992]), a problem remains as one looks for an intelligent dialogue : how to select the "good" explanation, i.e., the one that satisfies the user's needs and makes human-computer interaction more efficient.

The work presented here is especially concerned with explanations needed to describe a complex device in the domain of space industry. In cooperative design activities, descriptions of devices, which convey both structural and functionnal information, allow one participant to communicate knowledge on a state of solution. Our project is aimed at specifying an aiding system which will store information on previous "cases" (i.e. the problem and its solution(s)). This goal raises two issues : what is the information necessary to produce adequate descriptions of a device ? how must the system use this information when interacting with an end-user ?

In order to answer these questions, an analysis of cooperative human-human dialogues was conducted. These naturally occurring dialogues gathered two participants designing a complex physical device. Both participants were expert designers, but their competence was unequal : one was an engineer, and the other was a draughtsman.

2. Generating descriptions: the schema-based approach

One of the most elaborated work concerned by generating descriptions is McKeown's one [McKeown, 1985] who has developed an approach called the *schema-based approach*. This work is based on text analysis, and has led to identify four Rhetorical Schemas (RS), allowing types of information to be organized according to dialogue goals. The "Constituency schema" was proposed for describing an entity or event in terms of its sub-parts or sub-types (Fig. 1), the "Identification schema" for defining a concept, the "Attributive schema" for illustrating a concept on a particular point and the "Compare/Contrast schema" for comparing two entities.

McKeown' s study was intended to help an information system in answering questions such as "What is a x ?", "What do you know about x ?" and "What is the difference between x1 and x2 ?". The basic process in answering such questions consists in (i) selecting a set of relevant information from a knowledge base, (ii) selecting an appropriate RS and instanciating it, (iii) using focus constraints which help maintain text coherency. Thus, the main advantages of RSs are (i) guiding the selection of information, and (ii) allowing to organize it in a coherent way. Numerous researchers have adapted this model to make it suitable for other applications (e.g., Sarantinos & Johnson, unpublished) or to tailor descriptions according to the user' s level of expertise (e.g., [Paris, 1988)

However, it is important to note that RSs provide the generator with several optionalities, alternatives and possibilities of recursion under-constrained. This can be explained by the fact that text analysis does not account for the writer's intentions, and consequently, is unable to understand why such type of information appears in a given description. One consequence of this feature of RSs is that a system may easily produce unrelevant descriptions.

FIGURE 1 :The Constituency Schema[1] (from [McKeown, 1985])

Identification/Attributive
Constituency
Cause-effect*/Attributive/
  {Depth-identification/Depth-attributive
      {Particular-Illustration/Evidence}
      {Comparison; Analogy/Renaming}}+
  {Amplification/Explanation/Attributive/Analogy}

Example:
  "Steam and electric torpedoes. Modern torpedoes are of 2 general types [Constituency]. Steam-propelled models have speeds of 27 to 45 knots and ranges of 4000 to 25000 yds. (4,367-27,350 meters) [Depth-identification; Depth-attributive]. The electric powered models are similar [Comparison], but do not leave the telltale wake created by the exhaust of a steam torpedo [Depth-identification; Depth-attributive]."

The purpose of our study was to test the validity of this approach when one tries to apply it for generating descriptions in task-oriented dialogues. In this type of dialogue, participants may not only have communicative goals, but also and above all task goals. Furthermore, unlike textual descriptions, the hearer in task-oriented dialogues is clearly identified and he cooperates with the speaker in order to solve a problem. These differences rose the following issues: first of all, are rhetorical schemas found in task-oriented dialogues ? Next, how could descriptions be affected by task goals ? And how could descriptions be affected by the presence of an hearer engaged in a cooperative problem solving ?

3. Methodology of the study

3.1 Collecting descriptions
Interactions between designers were videotaped during a whole project. Two projects have been followed. Each one lasted for 10 days and resulted in about two hours of dialogues. Every hand-made draft and printed drawing was also collected.
In addition, the observer collected information about specific aspects of a description which, at first glance, did not seem relevant to him. For instance, if a speaker said "here, you have a surface made of steel" and nothing more which explains why he gave this information, the observer asked "why it is important to know that this surface is made of steel ?". These questions were asked during the course of the dialogue or after (one or two weeks after).

3.2 Identifying a description
In McKeown' s study, a description is an anwer to some specific types of question (e.g., "what is a X ?"). In our dialogues, such questions never appeared (except once); descriptions were always given spontaneously. So, a description was identified each time that the speaker's utterances were intended to define an object, illustrate a particular point about an object (e.g. a specific attribute) or show the difference between two objects.

---

[1] The "{}" indicate optionality, "/" indicates alternatives, "+" indicates that the item may appear 1 or more times, and "*" indicates that the item is optional and may appear 0 or more times.

3.3 Rhetorical predicates in verbal descriptions

In order to code the information included in verbal descriptions, two kinds of change were brought to the initial list of Rhetorical Predicates (RP) found in [McKeown, 1985].

One of the issue of this study was to determine why such descriptive information was given at such moment. So, a first change consisted in replacing the general predicate "attributive" by some more specific attributes, such as "Location", "Size", "Function", etc. The following list represents the RPs found in the descriptions collected :

- Identification
- Constituency
- Attributive :
    Location ; Link mode ; Size ;
    Relation ; Function ; Process ;
    Flexibility ; Picture
- Depth-identification
- Depth-Attributive

- Historical background
- Inference
- Contrast
- Comparison
- Evidence
- Explanation
- Analogy

Note the presence of an attribute "Picture" which denotes an important feature of our description, multimodality. Indeed, very often, in addition to a verbal description, a drawing was made. Another significant difference with the previous list of RPs is the "Historical background" predicate (see also [Sarner & Carberry, 1992]), which conveys information on (i) the previous state of the device and (ii) the reasons which explain the need of some changes.

This list of RPs is a first result of our study. It shows (i) the main predicates which are involved in design descriptions and (ii) that some RPs observed in textual description do not seem necessary in task-oriented descriptions (e.g. amplification).

5. Results

5.1 Rhetorical schemas in dialogues

Taking into account the changes brought to the initial list of RPs (see 3.3), we observed that the four rhetorical schemas (RS) defined by McKeown fit the descriptions recorded in task-oriented dialogues. But it is important to stress three facts :

1. concerning the order of RPs : some descriptions begin with an "Explanation" predicate, or in other words, with information which explains (or justifies) some features of the description which is going to be produced. Example (this is a simplified version of a real dialogue):

A1   what is required, it is to reduce the number of physical links (**Explanation**)
A2   so, there are only two external half-dishes (**Depth-identification**)
A3   directly linked by the shock absorber to this disk [...] (**Relation + Link mode**)

This specific order is not allowed by McKeown's RSs. Yet, this kind of spontaneous explanation, very common in task-oriented dialogues (cf [Karsenty & Falzon, 1992]), not only makes the descriptions more understandable and more relevant, but also allows to avoid some hearer's questions.

2. this result should not lead to conclude that describers construct or recall schemas similar to RSs. [Gilbert, 1987] has already shown that, from a psychological point of view, this way of planning discourse is unbearable (limitations of human working memory which preclude the construction of extensive detailed plans, descriptions as answers given a few milliseconds after a question, etc.). Actually, this apparent adequation between RSs and task-oriented descriptions could be due to the numerous alternatives and optionalities allowed by the RSs.

This feature hides the fact that any attribute or any part of an object is not described at anytime (see 5.3).

3. finally, in dialogue, a description is the result of a *collaborative process*, where both participants take an active part in order to establish a description which satisfies both of them.

5.2 Describing : A collaborative process

A description in McKeown's approach is a one-shot answer. In dialogues, it is the result of an interactive process. To capture this feature, we needed to code the *speech acts* involved in task-oriented descriptions. Hereafter, the list of speech acts found, and an extract of a collaborative description (notation : [Speech act: RPs]) :

- Inform/Ask for Information
- Agree/Ask for agreement
- Confirm or Critic/Ask for confirmation
- Justify/Ask for justification
- Correct

A1	Are you agreed with this design ? (**Request for assessing**)
A2	here, you have an axle ... slightly bigger (**Inform: Location + Depth-identification + Comparison**)
A3	you have a kneecap, as previously (**Inform: Depth-identification + Comparison**)
A4	and here you have a ring (**Inform: Depth-identification**) which serves to stop the rotation (**Function**)
B1	... (*shows a sign of misunderstanding*)
A5	Actually, it doesn't really stop the rotation, it minimizes it (**Correct: Function**)
B2	It is elastic ? (**Ask for confirmation: Depth-attributive**)
A6	No (**Negative answer**), it is not necessary because we should have some acceptable plays here. (**Justify: Depth-attributive**)
B3	Ok, so it's minimized by the plays ? (**Ask for confirmation: Process**)
A7	Exactly (**Confirmation**)

This example illustrates two main points :
- the hearer (B), by asking some additional information (B2), helps the speaker in producing a relevant description.
- in design dialogues, a description refers not only to an object, but also to a *solution*, which is the result of a reasoning. A cooperative activity is characterized by the search for a mutually agreed solution. This emphasizes the need for *justifications* when describing a designed device to another designer.

The interactive nature of task-oriented descriptions addresses the issue of the user's intervention during the description process. The schema-based approach, as proposed by McKeown, does not make this functionality possible. Another approach to the discourse planning called the *plan-based approach* has been developped especially to deal with it (e.g. [Moore & Paris, 1990]). However, although this first attempt enhances the possibilities of dialogue between the user and the system, it does not solve the problem of relevance addressed in this paper.

5.3 Operative descriptions

When comparing a description given with the information on a device that the describer possesses[2], we note that *descriptions are always incomplete*. For instance, he never describes all the parts composing a device, or all the attributes of a part of a device.

---

[2] This has been infered by identifying (i) the amount of information contained in a drawing that the describer had achieved before presenting a verbal description to another designer, (ii) other descriptive information given during the rest of a dialogue.

Another point is that descriptions of the parts of a device differ according to the level of detail. One part may just be identified, whereas another one will be described with details on its material and size for instance.

Actually, given the goal of the participants (e.g. assess a design ; determine a functional play), we noted that there is always a specific relevance of the information conveyed with one of the subgoals that the describer assigned to the hearer. To determine this, an analysis of the tasks having been performed during the recorded dialogues was achieved. This analysis was conducted by interviewing the describers on these tasks, and led to identify task models (see Fig. 2) :

FIGURE 2 : Task Model and Description: an example

Task Model :	A description given :

1. Determine the functional play between O and O'
   1.1 Locate O
   1.2 Locate O'
   1.3 Identify the move between O and O'
   1.4 Search for the allowance value
     associated with this move
	A1 To determine this play,
	 A2 you have the axle (*draws at the same time*)
	 A3 here, the ring ...
	 A4 It is the ring that makes the position ...
	 A5 So, this is our value, here.

The *operativeness* of the information included in descriptions is also apprehended when asking a describer/hearer why he gave/asked for a given detail. Let us see the following example :

A1   Are you agreed with this design ? (**Request for assessing**)
A2   here, you have an axle ... slightly bigger (**Inform: Location + Depth-identification + Comparison**)

The observer asked why it was important to know that the axle is bigger. A answered that this corresponded to a change which was motivated by a wrong behavior of the previous axle. The fault had been identified by saying that the previous axle was too small (we simplify).

The entire description (see example of 5.2) is aimed at showing that a desired function (to stop the rotation) is ensured. This needs to identify each part playing an important role in this function and their relationships. But this function bears also on *prerequisites*. A good behavior of the axle is one of this prerequisites.

Because this prerequisite was known to be not ensured, it was necessary to add an information to the description which would indicate that the new design had resolved the previous problem. Therefore, this information is necessary just because it helps the hearer in achieving its assessing task. Task-oriented descriptions are *operative* in the sense given to this term by [Ochanine, 1966] : an "operative picture" contains the information about the state of an object which is needed by the human agent *in order to perform his task as well as possible* .

5.4 Descriptions based on a shared context
Two last points are noticeable :
• Descriptions are often made with the "Comparison" predicate ; Example : "here you have an axle ... slightly bigger.". Very often, the object compared with the one introduced in the description is not made explicit. The speaker, when uttering such a sentence, must think that the hearer (i) will think about the object being compared, and (ii) will think that the speaker thank that s/he would be able to think about this object. Thus, we concluded that descriptions are often based on a shared context of knowledge.

• All the information necessary to achieve the interaction goal is not given in a description. The most significant example concerns the "Function" predicate : it is quite rare in the descriptions collected, even if most of the time a description is produced when the describer expects the hearer to assess the device described ; yet this task requires a full understanding of the way the structure performs one or several function(s) desired. Actually, when talking to an expert, the only structural information is normally sufficient to infer the functions performed (see also [Paris, 1988] for a similar observation).

But we will not conclude that an hearer's model is sufficient to decide the type of information to be included in a description. Instead, we believe that it is necessary to model a shared context, because an hearer, when infering a specific fact, must at the same time have some reasons to think that the speaker intended him/her to produce this inference.

6. Conclusion

In conclusion, it seems that the "picture" of the device that conveys a description in cooperative dialogues may be qualified as (i)*operative*, i.e., just enough informative to reach a given goal, and (ii) *contextualized* i.e., based on previous knowledge mutually established.

Textual analysis has led to define some rhetorical schemas which exhibit a richness of optionality, alternatives and possibilities of recursion for which very few criteria of choice have been proposed. Actually, this approach is unable to predict how relevant a description will be in task-oriented dialogues, because the only goals considered in describing are dialogue goals. Conversely, we believe that because a description in task-oriented dialogues is needed *just to help achieving a task* , its content must be determined according to task goals. Therefore, the basic process which conducts to produce a description is not, given a dialogue goal, to select and instanciate an associated rhetorical schema, but given a task model, to retrieve information which satisfies its informational requirements not yet fulfilled. A similar approach has been developped by [Sarner & Carberry, 1992] concerning the generation of definitions, and has led to an implementation.

7. References

Gilbert G.N. (1987). Advice, discourse and explanations. *Proceedings of the Third Alvey Explanation Workshop*, University of Edinburgh.

Karsenty L. & Falzon P. (1992). Spontaneous explanations in cooperative validation dialogues. *Proceedings of the ECAI-92 Workshop on Improving the use of knowledge-based systems with explanations*. Vienna: Austria, August 4 1992.

McKeown K.R. (1985). Discourse Strategies for Generating Natural-Language Text. *Artificial Intelligence*, 27, 1-41.

Moore J.D. & Paris C.L. (1990). Planning Text for Advisory Dialogues. In *Proceedings of the 27th Annual Meeting of the Association for Computational Linguistics*, Vancouver, Canada. 203-211.

Ochanine D. (1966). The operative image of controlled object in Man-Automatic systems. In *Proceedings of the 18th International Congress of Psychology*, Moscow. 48-56

Paris C.L. (1988). Tailoring object descriptions to a user's level of expertise. *Computational Linguistics*, 14(3), 64-78

Sarantinos E. & Johnson P. (unpublished). *Explanation Dialogues: A theory of how experts provide explanations to novice and partial experts.*

Sarner M.H. & Carberry S. (1992). Generating Tailored Definitions Using a Multifaceted User Model. *User Modeling and User-Adapted Interaction*, 2, 181-210.

Scott A.C., Clancey W.J., Davis R. & Shortliffe E.H. (1984). Methods for Generating Explanations. In: Buchanan B.G. & Shortliffe E.H. *Rule-Based Expert Systems: The MYCIN Experiments of the Stanford Heuristic Programming Project*. Reading, Mass: Addison-Wesley.

Swartout W.R, Paris C. & Moore J.D. (1992). Design for explainable expert systems. *IEEE Expert*, 6(3), 58-64.

DEALING WITH THE DILEMMA OF DISPARATE MENTAL MODELS

WM. J. GARLAND

Department of Engineering Physics, McMaster Univ.
Hamilton, Ontario, CANADA L8S 4M1

Abstract

The integration of diverse and disparate operational support agents for real-time complex plant process management is investigated. This is motivated by the increased sensor density and complexity inherent in today's nuclear and chemical plants which lead to operator information overload. Such plants are best understood by a functional decomposition into sub-systems and components, typical of the engineering approach. Thus, computer-based aids must be based on such a functional decomposition. This, however, is not the mental model employed by the operator and leads to a dilemma: the system needs to be functionally decomposed along the lines of the physical or engineer's mental model, whereas, this is an inappropriate model for the operator. Some mechanism is needed to bridge the gap. Herein, a solution to this dilemma is proposed: concurrent scorecarding based on the blackboard paradigm.

1. INTRODUCTION: The Problem Domain

The proper design of real-time process plant user interface tools for nuclear and chemical process plants naturally requires the incorporation of the relevant characteristics of the physical plant. One of the most obvious features is its distributed architecture. Plant operations are diverse and multifaceted. Events can happen anywhere in the system. The breadth and depth of plant operations required that the plant be ENGINEERED by decomposition into layered sub-systems (functional abstraction, otherwise known as piece-wise refinement).

In operations, operator overload, response time, etc., necessitate procedural responses. The operator is never left with an open ended question. For instance, if the plant state is unknown, there is a definite procedure to follow. At any given moment, there are a limited number of alternatives to choose from. Successful plant operations are, by definition, procedural and pre-enumerated.

The overall control strategy used at the plant is of central importance. For the most part, regulations require that the human remain 'in the loop', ie, in control. The operator has at his or her disposal many tools to enhance performance but the operator is very much in the driver's seat. This is so not just because regulations require it. It is so also because operators, like engineers do not wish to divest their authority to a machine. Machines are tools, no matter how intelligent they appear to be. This issue has been referred to as the machine-centred approach vs. the human-centred approach [1].

Process plants operate, of course, in real time and require real time control. To respond to real events in a complex plant, analysis is required. Much of the control is automatic but a significant role is played by the operators who must reason about the situation at hand. The right side of Figure 1 illustrates the roles played the human operator with respect to the plant and plant control. It is not just a question of being fast. Rather, bounding the solution time is the issue. Can a sufficiently good solution be found within the time required? The heuristics, however, are not well delineated and human operators will remain for the foreseeable future.

2. COGNITIVE ISSUES: Problem Solving Strategies

The mental model of the designer or engineer as developed in Rasmussen's book [2] is one that is based on functional decomposition. Problem solving strategies here relies on a deeper than average understanding and use of specific knowledge. The user, however, is the operator, not the design engineer. The operator's mental model of the plant is closer to that of a technician - the plant is a collection of many systems, most of which are treated with generic algorithms for fault diagnosis and treatment of event symptoms, irrespective of the system in question. Rasmussen's figure (reproduced in part on the left side of Figure 1) illustrates this generic algorithm. The generic algorithm for problem solving is to observe and identify the state of the situation, interpret, evaluate, plan actions and execute the actions. Rasmussen notes that shortcuts can be taken at any stage. In fact, most of what we do involves shortcuts to some degree. ALL problem solving is covered by this figure but the technician often employs strategies and tactics that do not rely heavily on a detailed knowledge of system and component behaviour. That is, short cuts to Rasmussen's full solution path are taken.

Expertise is composed of both knowledge and the ability to manipulate that knowledge. It has been observed and is widely recognized in the literature that it is the vast knowledge-base that exemplifies the expert rather than raw inferencing capability. The nuclear reactor environment is a case in point; operator actions require mostly procedural knowledge and moderate inferencing capability. The knowledge-base (composed of facts and heuristics) is then very important. The knowledge-base is necessarily system or component specific. This leads to the paradigm of message passing as a means of allowing disparate agents (models or codes or humans, etc.) to interact. It is at this level that one is concerned about how the operator or engineer interacts with the system being controlled. The result of this is that the objects being manipulated (the

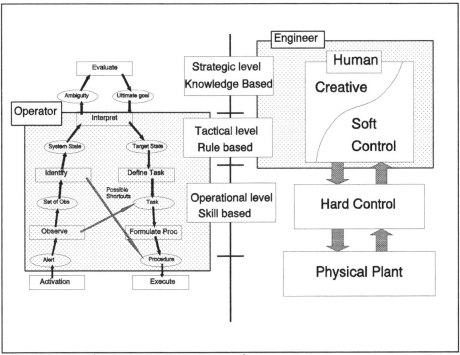

Figure 1 Various Mental and Physical Models.

knowledge base) need to be defined before they can be manipulated (by the inferencing or procedural engine). But how we define these objects will depend on the mental model chosen. <u>This leads to a dilemma: the system needs to be functionally decomposed along the lines of the physical or engineer's mental model, whereas, this is an inappropriate model for the operator.</u> The plant is organized along the same hierarchial lines as the design engineer's mental model. That organization expects the human to provide the top level knowledge based control. The operator, however, spends much of the time at the rule based and skill based levels. Figure 1 illustrates this point. The issue is not a trivial one and, as such, deserves careful consideration in the design of operational support systems. No-one to date has demonstrated a schema to solve this dilemma. This mental model mismatch plus a machine-centred bias are arguably the leading causes of the failure of artificial intelligence based support systems.

3. THE SCORE CARD

We need to decouple the decision making process from the details of the solution. Thus, we pose the user interface in the users' terms: "What decision must I make and what factors influence that decision?" 'What decision' implies that the user must pick an option (ie., an object) from a pre-enumerated set. The 'factors that influence' are the attributes of the objects and if an appropriate decision is to be made, the attributes must be common amongst the objects (i.e., in the same class). Such clustering has been found to be a central feature for neural nets to be successful [3]. If a common set of attributes do not exist in the domain of an engineered system, then the set is ill-posed and

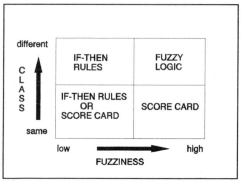

Figure 2 Scorecard Domain

the user cannot choose because there is no declared valid basis for reaching a decision in this case. The problem domain, then, is one involving clustered objects which are to be evaluated by weighing the pros and cons of each object. As illustrated in Figure 2, simple IF-THEN rules are appropriate if there is no fuzziness to the problem domain and can be applied whether clustering exists or not. To handle fuzziness, confidence factors would have to be added and this is deemed inappropriate if a more appropriate technique is available. One such technique that has proved successful is scorecarding. Our problem is clustered and fuzzy, exactly the domain for which scorecarding is the most useful.

Scorecarding (the tallying of how well alternatives measure up for a number of attributes) is useful for reconciling judgements with facts, symbolic with numerics. As discussed in [4], the solution strategy centres around the elimination of alternatives that cannot be used for one reason or another, and the ranking of those that are left by the use of score cards. The specification of the scoring details is a knowledge engineering exercise that is not trivial but it is one that must be done in some form at some point in the design of any operator aid. Scorecards merely give form to the substance; but most importantly, the form is an appropriate one for decision making for all types of users, including operational support staff. User supplied attribute weights are used to generate the weighted sum to give the total scores used to rank the alternatives in the decision to be made. The score card approach provides a good way to perform the ranking since it emulates the expert methodology of weighing the pros and cons of the alternatives.

To illustrate the use of the score card, let us suppose that the operator must monitor the secondary side of a power plant, looking for signs of bad chemistry or condenser leaks. An array of alarms and measured data are available. The operator must choose from a finite number of possible states (no problem, bad chemistry exists, a leak exists, etc.). Now, of course, there is much more to a monitoring situation than this but the plant procedures are built around first determining which of the above states the plant is in. The presence of an alarm does not guarantee the existence of a plant state. Indeed, alarms can give conflicting indications. The detailed procedures determine how these data should be interpreted as attribute scores. Arbitrarily, a 0-1 scale is chosen. Weights can be assigned to each attribute to indicate its relative importance. For instance, a conductivity measurement might be less useful or reliable than a chlorine concentration measurement.

While the details of the scoring algorithms are of fundamental importance to the success of the scoring procedures, herein we are concerned with the use of the scores in reaching a decision. That is, we wish to delineate an appropriate score <u>evaluation</u> procedure, given a set of n attribute scores for each of m objects. We define the 'degree of closeness to the ideal' for the ith attribute of the kth object as d_i^k, where $k = 0, 1, 2 ... m$ objects, and $i = 0, 1, 2 ... n$ attributes.

The 'membership' function is defined [5] to be a measure of the closeness to the ideal as

$$L_p(\lambda, k) = \left[\sum_{i=1}^{n} (\lambda_i)^p (1 - d_i^k)^p \right]^{1/p} . \tag{1}$$

where λ_i is the derived weight for attribute i, and p is a parameter, typically between 1 and ∞.

We note that smaller is better in the membership function. When $p = 1$, equal weight is given to each attribute deviation from the ideal for each object regardless of the deviation size. When $p = 2$, increasing weight is given to larger deviations (a root mean square measure). When $p = \infty$, only the largest deviation is important since, in this case:

$$L_\infty(\lambda, k) = \max_i [\lambda_i (1 - d_i^k)] . \tag{2}$$

It remains to define the algorithm for weight adjustment. We set the context

$$\tilde{\lambda}_i = \sigma_i = \sqrt{\frac{1}{m} \sum_{k=1}^{m} (d_i^k - \bar{d}_i)^2} , \tag{3}$$

dependent weight to the standard deviation of the scores, that is,
Finally, since the user may have supplied a priori attribute importance in the form of weights, say w_i, the final weights need to be calculated as the product of the context dependent and context independent weights (normalized),

$$\lambda_i = \frac{w_i \tilde{\lambda}_i}{\sum_{i=1}^{n} \tilde{\lambda}_i w_i}, \quad where \sum_{i=1}^{n} \lambda_i = 1. \tag{4}$$

The procedure is straightforward. Applying the above equations, $L_p(\lambda,k)$ is calculated for all objects and the best choice is that object with the lowest L_p using the p that the user deems appropriate. This has been implemented for heat exchanger selection and the prototype performed very well, meeting or exceeding all expectations in ease of construction, ease of use, speed, and accuracy in emulating the human expert. It is currently being considered for a nuclear power plant application.

4. CONCLUSIONS

This implementation of scorecarding provides a means of dealing with disparate agents but it does not address the issues of real-time, asynchronous events or concurrency (ie multiple agents acting in parallel and sharing information during the solution). However, they are not precluded either. Such a technique clearly allows the user to remain in control since the aid simply presents the relevant information in a manner conducive to decision making, providing an automatic focus on the important issues and letting the user decide which path to actually follow.

5. ACKNOWLEDGEMENTS

This work has been made possible through funding from the Atomic Energy Control Board, HTFS (Heat Transfer and Fluid Flow Service) and the Natural Sciences and Engineering Research Council of Canada, Grant STR0118177.

6. REFERENCES

1 John A. Bernard, "Issues Regarding The Design and Acceptance of Intelligent Support Systems for Reactor Operators", ICHMT 2nd International Forum on Expert Systems and Computer Simulation in Energy, University of Erlangen, 17-20 March 1992.

2 Jens Rasmussen, "Information Processing and Human-Machine Interaction: An Approach to Cognitive Engineering", North-Holland Series in System Science and Engineering, 1986, ISBN: 0-444-00987-6.

3 R. E. Urig, "Analysis of Complex Systems Using Neural Networks", ICHMT 2nd International Forum on Expert Systems and Computer Simulation in Energy, University of Erlangen, 17-20 March 1992.

4 Wm. J. Garland, "Knowledge Base Design for Heat Exchanger Selection", Engineering Applications of Artificial Intelligence, Vol. 3, # 3, September, 1990.

5 M. Zeleny, "Multiple Criteria Decision Making", McGraw Hill, Inc., New York, New York, 1982.

An Associative Approach in Dynamic User Modeling

Qiyang Chen and A. F. Norcio

Department of Information Systems, University of Maryland Baltimore, MD 21228-5398

Abstract

A research framework for building a user model by utilizing artificial neural networks (ANN) is presented. The limitations of stereotype-based user modeling are discussed which underlie the motivations of introducing ANN approaches. An associative user modeling approach is proposed which is incorporated in a blackboard processing environment.

1. Introduction

In order to capture a user's individual characteristics in task performance, a user modeling mechanism has been recognized as an important component in adaptive interface systems [7]. An interface equipped with a user model helps the system tailor its response to individual users. It not only exhibits a wide range of cooperative functionality, but also improve system efficiency and effectiveness [4].

In order to make a large number of inferences based on a small number of evidence or observations, it has been common practice in user modeling to have a set of pre-defined stereotypes associated with a particular user. The assumed information about users and the tasks they perform are represented in a generalization hierarchy. Along with certain types of confidence measurements, this information can be further classified in terms of its persistency or temporal extent and its sources, and the degree of specification [9]. In next section we will highlight some of the issues that motivates our approach.

2. Limitations of Stereotyping Approaches

Stereotyping provides a simple way for obtaining initial information about a user. The modeling process proceeds with a stereotype assignment in terms of default or evidential reasoning. Default reasoning allows the modeling process to maintain stereotypical information about a user in the absence of evidence to the contrary, whereas evidential reasoning assigns and revises the belief values to the facts held by the model [1].

2.1 Default modeling process

In the stereotyping approach, rule-based reasoning is conducted with extensive default assumptions that may conflict with the new evidence during the interaction. Therefore, techniques such as truth maintenance and ad hoc approaches are necessary for handling inconsistencies in a non-monotonic process. However, since these approaches examine one piece of evidence at a time, they may fail to detect inconsistent inputs that should be ignored. For example, a database query from a user may imply a conflict with system's original belief about this user's understanding of the contents of the database; this may be due to misusing the grammar of query language. This conflict may have nothing to do with user's belief about database contents; therefore it should be ignored in the modeling process. Thus, without examining the continuity and *overall behavior pattern* in task performance, the modeling process may not reflect the real situation and the current effort of maintaining consistency may bring some new conflicts in the subsequent interaction. Meanwhile, model construction may frequently fall into a non-monotonic process of conflicts-resolution [3].

2.2. Evidential Modeling Process

If the model construction is driven by evidential reasoning, specifying the belief values for both evidence and rules become very difficult. Even if one can identify the correlation between observed user's behavior data and its implications, it is still difficult to assign probabilistic values. In addition, even with a well understood situation, it is still likely to fail maintaining probabilistic formalisms (e. g. independence of probabilities) over the whole production system.

Some user modeling systems utilize techniques for handling uncertainties as a learning mechanism in which the model is refined by modifying the belief values until adequate modeling performance is obtained. It is obvious that off-line tuning is both time consuming and inexact. It is often based on inadequate tests and a subjective judgment of how the interaction is pursuing, and local improvement obtained by tuning one capability of the modeling process might be detrimental to other capabilities. Moreover, if such a revision is not based on a view of the behavior pattern, the modeling process may face the dilemma of frequent conflict-resolution.

2.3. Representation Power of Generalization Hierarchy

It is efficient to build an initial user model through stereotype hierarchy. However, its inherent structure limits the degree of individualizing a user. Since the pre-defined properties are framed within each stereotype and can be only inherited through the hierarchy, there is no effective way to update those properties that are no longer significant in the context of task performance. It is not an extreme situation that a user may fail to fit any set of stereotypes, so that the modeling process fails to associate any system beliefs to that user. However it would be better to extract some of the properties or assumptions distributed among the stereotypes to characterizing a particular user.

A hierarchical stereotyping approach also provides a natural way for classifying a user's long-term characteristics [9]. However, in a real time interaction, a user's performance primarily reveals short-term characteristics which change over time and exhibit many varieties regarding the current task. It is difficult to classify short-term characteristics through a pre-defined hierarchy. For example, a user may exhibit both expert and novice traits in a task performance. Therefore the classification of long-term characteristics via few dimensions might not help system's adaptation to the current context [7]. Besides modeling long-term characteristics of user provides no direct insight with respect to the context of task and underlying goals [4]. We suggest that modeling process should emphasize short-term characteristics of the user because it results in more efficient system adaptation to the current task than modeling long-term characteristics. In addition, the short-term model is temporal to the context of interaction so that it is less risky than a long-term model [5].

3. Modeling Users with Associative Approach

3.1. Viewing User-Task Information through User's Behavior Patterns

It seems more appropriate to represent knowledge about a user and the task in a form of patterns as well as their associations. Since a user's behavior data in an interaction is highly related in a context of task and mixed with noise, all the aspects of the pattern have to be examined before any decision can be made. However, the conventional stereotype, in which the inference proceeds a step at a time through sequential logic, may become seriously inadequate for describing such pattern-formatted knowledge and the workload of recovering from inconsistency might be very heavy [8].

In our approach, the user's information is viewed and organized as a set of patterns. Various ANN techniques can be used to analyze the patterns, which requires the ability of fault tolerance, graceful degradation and signal enhancement. Some ANN operation primitives have been suggested for user modeling process [2,3]. In this paper, we are more concerned about modeling user with associative memories.

3.2. Auto-associator

This ANN primitive can be implemented by various paradigms of associative memory. It captures the associations between input and output patterns despite incomplete or inconsistent inputs. The associative memory that has only a single set of interconnected units can be one of the implementations. Each unit serves as both an input unit and an output unit. Its feature of self-organizing is especially useful in recognizing user-task context.

Suppose a state transition diagram is used to define the user's task performance. It can be transformed into a stored pattern in associate memory in which each state is represented by a unit and the transitions are mapped to weighted connections. During an interaction, a user's operations involving several units can be organized as an stimulus vector. The associative memory can produce a relatively complete path of state transitions as a prediction for navigating the user toward task accomplishment. This provides a basis for comparing the user's real action with the predicated one and then modifying corresponding user models. This property can also be used in plan recognition while some relevant traits are observed.

Associative memory also provides a way to model what the user knows. Considering a user's problem solving as a procedure of associative thinking, the representation power of a user model could be enhanced by adjusting the pattern of weights or propagating activation levels through interconnected concepts to reflect the real time change of the user's mental model or the beliefs. Thus a user model can be updated dynamically and consistently. In the modeling process, the stimulus from a user can trigger some assumptions about what a user already knows and then the corresponding units are fired. The spreading activation rule can eventually create two network states: the network reaches a single, stable state, or it reaches a mode in which it cycles through a constant series of states. The set of those units reaching the highest activation level specifies a possible range of concepts known to a user. If the network cycles through a series of states, it may imply alternative ranges of concepts. In the other words, it can be expected that a series of concepts is the likely result of a particular stimulus. Usually the activation and propagation rules are ad hoc and the activated nodes compete with each other in a multiple-winners-take-all fashion.

3.3. Associative User Modeling

In our approach, the associations are established among the system's beliefs about the task-related characteristics of all possible users. Unlike the stereotype approach, these beliefs are not framed within any structure. All elementary properties and underlying assumptions about users and their tasks are viewed to be associative to each other in a spectrum which is valued from negative to positive (i. e. contrary to consistent). Stereotype hierarchy limits the representation of the associations so that it is impossible to extract properties from different stereotypes to form a new profile (i.e. a set of new stereotypes) about the current user or task.

Associative user modeling reduces the workload of knowledge acquisition, because it is much easier to identify the casual relationship between two system beliefs than to define complete stereotypes with respect to a user's task. Learning processes can be conducted in term of automatically revising weights, adding or deleting a unit representing an assumption. It proceeds locally so that the change to the network can be limited to the minimum.

In associative user modeling, there is no explicitly pre-defined stereotype involved. All assumptions are organized into associative memories in which the relationship among the assumptions are weighted under certain conditions. The activity level of network units at each propagation phase is considered to be a prediction of the possibility of relevance to the user's current task. After filtered by a threshold function at the end of iteration, the fired units that represent assumptions reach the value of 1. The weights can be initially set by the following equation [6]

$$w_{ij} = -\ln \frac{p(x_i = 0 \cap x_j = 1)p(x_i = 1 \cap x_j = 0)}{p(x_i = 1 \cap x_j = 1)p(x_i = 0 \cap x_j = 0)}$$

In the original version of this equation, p is derived from a Bayesian analysis of the probability that unit x_i is fired given unit x_j is fired and vise versa. However, in our approach, we loosely define value of p as the value of plausibility which may not satisfy the probability formalism, because it is often difficult to assign precise probabilistic values and maintain the formalism for the casual relationships among assumptions used in user modeling.

The pattern of weights reveals three aspects of the relationships: if the two assumptions tend to be on and off together, then the weight will be a large positive value; if the two assumptions come on and off independently, then the weight of their connection is almost zero; if the two assumptions are somehow contrary which is implied by a larger value difference of corresponding units, then the weight takes on a negative value. In addition, a constant bias is given by

$$bias_i = -\ln \frac{p(x_i = 0)}{p(x_i = 1)}$$

Using a bias can help detect the significance of an assumption within the context of task.

If an assumption is usually fired, it has a positive bias; and if it equally often on and off, it has zero bias. If it is usually off then it has negative bias.

In associative memory, the pattern of fired assumptions underlies a user's profile. If network contains n units then there are 2^n possible binary states (i.e. stored patterns) in which system could potentially settle. Thus the capacity of representation in associative user modeling is much greater than stereotyping approach that has same number of initial assumptions.

4. A Blackboard Structure of User Modeling System

As a component of an adaptive interface, our associative user modeling framework is shown in Figure 1. In order to tailor system response to an individual user, the characteristics about the tasks must be also captured. Therefore, two knowledge sources are necessary in an interaction: user profiles and the task profiles. Accordingly two networks are utilized: one that incorporates the user's task-related characteristics and one that stores the assumptions underlying system actions or responses. From the view point of system adaptation, one network addresses *when to adapt*, while another addresses *how and what to adapt*. The generated responses vary based upon the types of application systems (e.g. database retrieval, tutorial system, etc.).

A blackboard structure is appropriate for knowledge representation and reasoning. The objects in blackboard can be manipulated cooperatively in terms of sending or receiving stimulus vectors, or utilized independently depending on the control information appearing in the blackboard. The dynamics of networks are interpreted and stored in the knowledge bases of the user profile and the task profile. This blackboard system supports a multilevel user modeling process in the sense that it incorporates procedures of preprocessing, updating and post-processing a user model in an interaction [3].

It is acknowledged that associative memories cannot accomplish all procedures of user modeling. Production systems processing both user and task profiles are necessary to coordinate the multilevel process, which are implemented in the control module. Its major functions are forming task-related user images delivered to the networks, analyzing and interpreting network outputs, and supporting response generation. However, there is no non-monotonic reasoning involved in symbolic reasoning. Meanwhile the declarative information about both user and task profiles are manipulated and stored in knowledge bases.

The patterns stored in networks are viewed as blackboard objects, while the user and task profiles as well as related production systems are underlying knowledge sources. User modeling proceeds with dynamics of networks, making changes to both blackboard objects and knowledge sources. As data appears on the blackboard, the network modules produce increasingly accurate information. The system dynamically chooses a focus of attention in current modeling process. If the focus of attention is a knowledge source, a blackboard object is activated as the context of its invocation. If the focus of attention is a blackboard object, a knowledge source that can process that object is chosen. If the focus of attention is both a source and an object, a complete modeling process is executed within the current context. The stored patterns in networks are continuously invoked as interaction progresses. Once the networks reach a stable status, some contents of the model are established with respect to the current context. This fulfills the dynamic process of user modeling.

914

5. Conclusions

The inherent features of conventional stereotype approaches limit user modeling in the aspects of reasoning mechanisms, capabilities of individualization, and learning, It is suggested that the concepts and the techniques of pattern recognition be utilized to capture task-related characteristics of a user. Some ANN primitives, especially associative memories have shown the promise of enhancement in modeling process. The proposed framework not only possesses all advantages of stereotyping approach but also provides a flexible platform for overcoming the limitations of the conventional approach. A prototype system and related experiment is under implementation. Further research is aimed at verifying that this framework can scale to large, complex applications in which various associative paradigms are investigated in terms of their efficacy in user modeling.

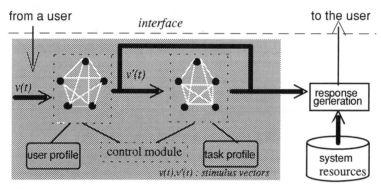

Figure 1. *Blackboard structure for user modeling*

References

1. Bonissone, P. and Tong , R. M., " Editorial : Reasoning with Uncertainty in Expert Systems," *International Journal of Man-Machine Studies*, Vol. 30, 69-111 (1985)
2. Chen, Q. and Norcio, A. F., "A Neural Network Approach to User Modeling," *Proceedings of 1991 IEEE International Conference on Systems, Man, and Cybernetics*, pp.1429-1434 (1991).
3. Chen, Q. and Norcio, A. F. "Modeling Users with Neural Architectures ," *Proceedings of 1992 International Joint Conference on Neural Networks*, pp. I-547 - I-552 (1992).
4. Clowes,I., Cole, I., Arshad, F., Hopkins, C.,and Hockley, A., "User Modeling Techniques for Interactive Systems," *People and Computers: Designing the Interface*, Ed. by Johnson P. and Cook, S., Cambridge University Press. pp. 35-45 (1985)
5. Kobsa, A., "User Modeling in Dialog Systems: Potentials and Hazards," *AI and Society*, Vol. 4, pp.214-240 (1990)
6. McClelland, J. L. and Rumelhart, D. E. *Parallel Distributed Processing* Vol. 2, Cambridge, MA: MIT Press (1986)
7. Norcio, A. F. and Stanley, J., "Adaptive human-computer interfaces, A literature survey and perspective," *IEEE Transactions on System, Man and Cybernetics*, Vol. 19, No. 2, pp. 399-408 (1989)
8. Pao, Y., *Adaptive Pattern Recognition and Neural Networks*, Addision-Wesley Publishing Co., (1989).
9. Rich, E. "Users are individuals: Individualizing user models," *International Journal of Man-Machine Studies* Vol. 18, No. 3 (1983)

Information tools: A new approach to interface design and development

Andrew Michael Cohill

Computing Center, Virginia Polytechnic Institute and State University, 1700 Pratt Drive, Blacksburg, VA 24060-6361

Abstract

This paper presents a model for the design of information tools and describes a case study in which this model was used to develop an campus–wide information system intended for use by the 30,000 member user community of Virginia Tech. A set of design and development principles (an information architecture) provide a framework for understanding why the project has been successful in spite of some difficult organizational and sociological barriers to acceptance.

1. Introduction

The design of software is still being driven largely by technology and the needs of highly skilled users, rather than by basic design principles like simplicity, elegance, and aesthetics. Most software designed for use on personal computers is marketed toward niche groups; some of the most popular personal software categories like databases, spreadsheets, drawing programs, desktop publishing, and communications appeal primarily to business people with specific tasks to perform or technocrats who will attempt to find ways to use these sophisticated programs even if cheaper, more convenient alternatives exist.

For those of us involved in the research and development of computers, software, and interfaces, we often speak of what we do as "systems development." This has been appropriate as long as computers were large, expensive, bulky machines requiring the ministrations of a whole host of high priests and acolytes to keep them running (often by muttering incantations over them). But as what we think of as computers continues to evolve, I wonder if we need to change our thinking.

Throughout most of human history, what we as a race have been concerned with is the development of tools. On an individual level, what most of us still use for most of our daily activities are things we think of as tools, not systems. While it may be amusing (and true) to call a spatula a *Hot Food Flipping System* and a toothbrush a *Dental Crevice Food Extraction and Cleaning System*, labeling them as such would probably only discourage sales.

In my office, where computers have theoretically created a revolution, most of the things on my desk are tools: pens, pencils, paper, stapler, tape, scissors. And my desk is a tool, although it could be called a *Personal Work Organizing, Storage, and Display System* (PWOSDS).

We use the things we work with because the mean something to us. Every item in our work environment is part of a network of associations that enables us to work. This network of associations composes a structure, an intellectual collection of information nodes and connections that represents our view of the work world. We use tools to manipulate this network.

With respect to software and the interfaces that accompany them, most products that are sold today are typically empty of information content (nodes and relationships between nodes). It becomes the job of the user to create the information to be manipulated by the software; it usually goes further than that, though–the user also may be required to determine how the information is manipulated. In other words, the user has to assume some of the responsibility for the design of the tool. Examples of this abound: spreadsheets are not only empty of information but must also be programmed to behave in certain ways to be of use; the same is true for database products, even for so–called easy–to–use products like HyperCard, which runs on the Macintosh.

I believe what people want are tools complete with information. One of the most apocryphal uses for a home computer is as a place to store recipes. But who ever really does this? We need only look to the print/book medium to understand why: what are most popular are cookbooks, complete with recipes, not empty books where you can write your recipes. If one really wanted to market recipe software the recipes should be provided with it, and in addition to the usual index and browsing capabilities of paper cookbooks, you ought to be able to tell your automated cookbook that all you have in the house are potatoes, eggs, an onion, and some Italian sausage. And it would tell you that what you can make with those ingredients is a fritata. If you are designing a computer for the kitchen, it had better do more than existing tools, and do things that I cannot do (easily) with existing tools. In a recent paper I described this as the *Fritata Principle* (Cohill, 1993a).

In a more complex example in the same task domain (the kitchen), Kellogg, Carroll, and Richards describe what they call an "augmented kitchen", which incorporates not only a "smart" cookbook but kitchen aids that manage tasks like the design of a dinner menu for a set of guests with special dietary requirements and food pantry inventory management. They elaborate on three information objects called the Dinner Party Planner, the Shopper, and the Chef. In describing the information space in which such tools work, they require these information objects to have four attributes: richness, connectivity, persistence, and direct interaction.

Marcos Novak, when speaking of the potential of cyberspace, notes the potential of separating data, information, and form (Novak, 1992). Too often, the data and information have been bound too tightly to the form (the interface). By separating data and information from the form, it becomes possible to imagine a variety of small, elegant tools that are used in different circumstances to manipulate the same information.

In a recent study of architects at work, computers were used mainly to support word processing The architects had little interest in the new 3D, solid modeling, multi–media virtual reality systems that are commonly displayed at popular HCI conferences. They viewed them as an impediment to getting their work done (Cohill, 1993b). What they wanted was tools to help them with the more mundane but critical tasks of managing a business. Catalano (1990) claims that architects must learn to act more like computer programmers to maximize the use of technology but also insists they must continue to function with the high levels of intuitiveness, cognitive flexibility, and aesthetic sensitivity that characterizes architects (Burnette, 1979). This strikes me as horrifying—why do we continually try to change the way people think and work?

Robertson, Card, and Mackinlay (1993) have been considering the workspace problem for several years, and among other ideas have proposed a three dimensional, rotating, cone tree for visualizing directory and document hierarchies. While I am sympathetic to the idea, as I look around my office, I do not see anything that resembles a three–dimensional, rotating, cone tree. Frequently, what I see is a mess. Many of us work quite effectively in very messy information workspaces, including the architects mentioned previously (Cohill, 1993b). I am nervous when I see these new interfaces; what troubles me is not the prospect of adjusting to this new tool, but that all that it does is make it easier to use an already artificial storage model: hierarchical directories. I think we can do better.

I would argue that software designed as an information tool must meet four conditions:

❑ It must be functionally 'pure'; that is, I should be able to grasp the tool's purpose and use immediately.

❑ It must contain or provide easy access to information that is of use to me.

❑ It must not require programming to use or access the information.

❑ It must be a natural extension of the way I currently work.

Heidegger's (1927) now classic example of the man using a hammer still bears examination: the goal is to produce a tool so perfectly suited to the task and so perfectly designed for the user that there exists an unconscious connection between the user and the tool. That is, good tools are unobtrusive in use; we are unaware of the tool as we use, and can focus on the task.

2. A case study of the design of information tools

Eris is the campus–wide information system of Virginia Tech. The Eris system, developed as a set of information tools conforming to the definition described above, had to appeal to all members of a 30,000 user campus community, not just technocrats or users with specialized needs. To do this, the development team had to consider a wide variety of issues not always associated with software development.

❏ Ease of use was vital to success. With potentially 30,000 users, many of them new each year (students), the software had to be so easy to use that no training or paper documentation would ever be required.

❏ Design of the tools was extremely important. Because the software was free, if people did not like it, they had no financial investment in continuing to use it. The tools had to be functionally complete and visually compelling.

❏ Sociological problems usually overshadowed technical problems. The system was so radically different that from the existing formal and informal information delivery systems that it began to affect and change organizational responsibilities and boundaries.

❏ Information content was critical; while the designers would not be responsible for providing information, compelling tools for creating and posting information had to be delivered along with the tools to access that information.

Cohill's information architecture model (1991) was used as a framework for development. This model requires a design–based approach with attention in four areas: software engineering, ergonomics, and the typically neglected areas of environmental design and organizational behavior.

After two years of use and development, the Eris project has become a key strategy to expand access to information on campus. It currently provides a variety of information tools that give users access to a campus-wide calendar; a news reader; an electronic catalogue and timetable; access to electronic books, documents, and software; and electronic mail. New tools are delivered to users electronically over the university network.

In the coming years, additional tools creating electronic classrooms, electronic help desks, and more sophisticated versions of existing tools will become available. The success of the project can be attributed to four design principles:

1) *Let information drive the design, not the technology.* Every Eris information tool is purposefully designed around the information it must deliver to users. In addition, the tool guides the user to the information, rather than forcing the user to shape the tool to obtain information. Users are not expected to have to add value to the tool in order to use it.

2) *Design small, elegant tools that deliver a single kind of information well.* The Eris development group has studiously avoided big, ugly, "do everything" interfaces and system designs. Each Eris information tool delivers a single kind of information, and the interface of each tool is uncompromised by the complexity incurred when trying to develop a Swiss army knife application.

Elegance is achieved on many levels. As networked information tools, none of the Eris products require the user to know anything about how the software accesses or obtains the information from central servers. No userids, passwords, access codes, handshakes, or other technical jargon is required to receive information. Users only have to point to the information they want to receive it.

3) *Get smart fast by doing small things over and over.* Because the effort has been centered around the design of small tools, mistakes are smaller and easier to correct. Development time for tools is measured in weeks and months, rather than years. As experience is gained with the design and development process, it becomes easier and easier to enhance products as users ask for additional features. This design principle is applied not only to the interface, but to every component of the system. The software is highly modular, resulting in a set of small code chunks designed to do just one thing well. New tools are assembled in a building block fashion from these components, achieving the efficiency and reusability promised by true object–oriented design.

4) *Integrate individual tools with a seamless interface.* All Eris tools share similar characteristics that make learning to use new tools quick and easy. Visual appearance is consistent from tool to tool, menus are organized in the same way, and similar commands appear in the same place and use the same words. The modularity of code at both the system and interface level ensures that similar actions in different tools look and feel the same to users.

Following these design rules, the Eris team has met it goal of creating information tools: compelling, easy-to-use software that requires no training, that deliver usable information quickly, and appeal to a broad range of users with varying amounts of computer experience.

3. Summary

In this decade the focus must turn away from the interface and towards the information, towards delivery of a *product*, not a piece of software. If all interfaces have a similar set of widgets, what distinguishes systems is not the inclusion of those things but how they are put to use, and this means understanding much more thoroughly the information to be manipulated and the associated tasks. In the future, information architects and designers will provide a holistic vision of the proper uses of information tools as well as coordinating the integration of form and function.

We must begin to understand better what design really means, in contrast to the engineering focus currently used on most software development projects. We should strive for smaller, neater, more elegant tools that do just one thing very well, rather than strive for systems that do everything (poorly). There is a reason why most of the non–cybernetic tools that we own and use have a single purpose. The challenge is to design cybernetic tools that are smaller, neater, and more elegant than anything we have now, and to make those tools work together seamlessly and invisibly. Until we stop believing that users can adapt to our designs and instead adapt our designs to the users, we will not reach our goals

5. References

Burnette, Charles H. (1979) *The Architect's Access to Information*. Washington, D. C.: NIST

Catalano, F. (1980) The Computerized Design Firm. In: *The Electronic Design Studio: Architectural Knowledge and Media in the Computer Era*; editors, M. McCullough, W. Mitchell, and P. Purcell. Cambridge, MA: MIT Press, pp. 316–332

Cohill, A. M. (1991) Information architecture and the software design process. In: *Taking Design Seriously*, J. Karat, editor. Boston: Academic Press

Cohill, A. M. (1993a) Software as a consumer product: A case study of design for a mass market. In: Proceedings of the 8th Symposium on Human Factors and Industrial Design in Consumer Products. Santa Monica, CA: Human Factors and Ergonomics Society (May 5–8, 1993)

Cohill, A. M. (1993b) *Patternmakers and Toolbuilders: The design of information structures in the professional practice of architecture*. Ann Arbor, MI: University Microfilms

Heidegger, Martin (1927) *Being and Time*. Translated by John Macquarrie and Edward Robinson. (1962) New York: Harper and Row

Kellogg, W. A., J. M. Carroll, and J. T. Richards (1992) Making Reality a Cyberspace. In: *Cyberspace: The First Steps*. Editor, Michael Benedikt, pp.411–431. Boston: MIT Press

Novak, M. (1992) Liquid Architectures in Cyberspace. In: *Cyberspace: The First Steps*. Editor, Michael Benedikt, pp. 225–254. Boston: MIT Press

Robertson, G. G., Card, S. K., and Mackinlay, J. D. (1993) Information visualization using 3D interactive animation. *Communications of the ACM*, Vol. 36, No. 4, pp. 57–71

Design Issues of Bilingual Editor

Miwako DOI

Research and Development Center, Toshiba Corporation
1, Komukai Toshiba-cho, Saiwai-ku, Kawasaki, 210, JAPAN

Abstract

User friendly machine translation systems are obtained by two approaches: improving translation quality and providing more interactions. Regarding the second approach, to date little research has been carried on. This paper describes the design process of a suitable bilingual editor by evaluation of specific errors produced in the translation process, display of prototype operation sequences, function selections in accordance with the design concept and reviews based on specified user profiles. The developed bilingual editor is implemented on the SUN workstation with a practical Japanese-English bi-directional machine translation system called ASTRANSAC.

1. INTRODUCTION

In the international sphere there is growing demand for large and rapid information exchange. Machine translation can facilitate assimilation of large volumes of information. In Europe, batch machine translation systems and postediting are used[1][2]. On the other hand, interactive machine translation systems and bilingual editors have been developed and used in Japan[1][2]. Bilingual editors for interactive machine translation are a bridge between two languages, between a machine translation parser and a machine translation generator, and between translators and system developers.

Recently, researchers in the machine translation field have been focusing on user friendliness of machine translation systems[3][4]. User friendliness of machine translation systems can be obtained by two approaches. The first approach is improvement of the translation quality with better grammars, better lexica, more sophisticated disambiguation strategies, etc. The second way is introduction of the more interactions by employing better editing tools. Many researchers have adopted the first approach in their efforts to improve translation quality[1][2], but few researchers have considered the second approach.

Thurmair[3] identified three key factors for the success of interactive machine translation. Firstly, fast translation process because response time is critical for interaction. Secondly, an intelligent method of dictionary updating. Thirdly, a suitable bilingual editor. Thurmair identified which factors are essential for interactive machine translation, but did not clarify how they were to be achieved. Thurmair has developed a batch translation system called METAL.

In 1985, prior to Thurmair's presentation of the above-mentioned factors, Toshiba's first prototype translation system was demonstrated and provided confirmation of the factors identified by Thurmair.. First, high-speed parsing is achieved as a result of strict separation of syntactic and semantic analysis. Secondly, intelligent dictionary updating is realized by employing three independent kinds of dictionaries : a general dictionary, a dictionary of technical terms, and a user-defined dictionary. The user-defined dictionary is updated during translation and editing. Thirdly, a suitable bilingual editor is designed by evaluation of specific errors produced in the translation process, display of prototype operation sequences and reviews based on specified user profiles. The system configuration of ASTRANSAC is shown in Figure 1.

This paper describes the design process of this bilingual editor. The design concept of a bilingual editor is

922

described in section two. The third section explains how functions of a bilingual editor are defined. The fourth section presents the experimental results and the implementation of the proposed bilingual editor in a commercial Japanese-English bi-directional machine translation system called ASTRANSAC. Finally, conclusions are given.

2. DESIGN CONCEPT

A bilingual editor has to perform several tasks: obtaining data related to translation tasks, correcting misplaced constituents, selecting translation alternatives, updating and

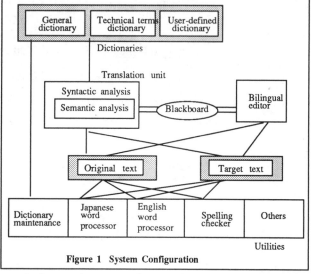

Figure 1 System Configuration

referring to dictionary data, kana-to-kanji conversion, etc.   Increase of these functions slows user's response[5].   The problem is how to reduce the number of functions in the editor without reducing specifications.   In order to solve this problem, the following design concepts are defined.

1) <u>Sentence-based translation.</u> Sentence-based translation is a good choice till anaphoras are resolved.

2) <u>Efficient use of data related to translation tasks (translation-related data).</u>   The functions of a bilingual editor are limited to translation tasks.   Any other functions (formatting, spelling checks, and so on) are with in the scope of utilities.   The purpose of a bilingual editor is to improve the translation quality and ease of translation.

3) <u>Word-level editing.</u>   The minimum unit of syntactic and semantic analysis is a word, so that the editing unit is a word.   By word-level editing, translators can quickly execute tasks such as displaying a target word or registering a new target word.

4) <u>The bilingual editor independent of the translation unit.</u>   By the parallel processes of translation and editor, translators can obtain translation-related data and update dictionary at any time.   This independence realizes quick editing.

5) <u>Computer novices.</u>   Translators have expertise concerning language grammars, etc., but are likely to lack expertise concerning computers and UNIX.   Therefore, minimization of user input burden is critical for realizing a usable interface.

The next section explains how editing functions are designed.   Design alternatives are evaluated based on the above-mentioned design concepts, and any function violating a design concept is rejected.   Thus, employment of these design concepts prevents increase of editing functions.

3. FUNCTIONS OF BILINGUAL EDITOR

At the start of the bilingual editor design, the core of the translation unit worked and produced specific errors and translation alternatives.   The design of a bilingual editor starts from analysis of these translation errors, translation alternatives, and specified functions.   Then the operation sequences were reviewed with the display prototypes and comparisons of the operation alternatives.

3.1 Evaluation of translation errors and alternatives

Typical translation errors and alternatives are as follows.

1) <u>Misplacing and ambiguous placing of constituents.</u> In the case of adverbs, for example, word order is not unique.

Example 1

　I just arrived in Boston yesterday.

　私はBostonにきのう<u>ちょうど</u>着いた。

　私はBostonに<u>ちょうど</u>きのう着いた。

2) <u>Word-level translation alternatives.</u> A polysemous word produces ambiguity.

3) <u>Translation alternatives derived from modification ambiguity.</u> There are several interpretations of a modification.

Example 2

　Through the window,　I　saw the campus of Harvard University on the right bank of the river.

4) <u>Translation alternatives derived from sentence-structure ambiguity.</u> The combinations of multiple parts of speech produce several interpretations at the sentence-level.

Example 3

　Time flies like an arrow. -NP (Time flies) + V (like) + NP (an arrow).

　　　　　　　　N (Time) + VP (flies like an arrow).

By examining these errors and alternatives, the following six principle functions are deduced.

a. Exchanging words

b. Referring and using the dictionary

c. Highlighting the correspondent words in original text and target text

d. Presenting and selecting the translation alternatives derived from modification ambiguities

e. Presenting and selecting the translation alternatives derived from sentence-structure ambiguity

f. Definition of a new target word in a dictionary.

3.2 Display prototype

The importance of screen design has been demonstrated in a variety of studies. Keister and Gallaway[6] found that redesigning a series of screens resulted in a 25% reduction in total processing time over 500 displays. Screen design defines both the display layout and the interactive method. After the above-mentioned functions are defined, the operations and the display layout are designed by the display prototype. The display prototype comprises three steps: defining the funda..ental screen design by comparisons of screen design alternatives, defining the screen design in detail, and the check by the design concepts. As a result of the display prototype, the fundamental screen design does not change in spite of the display hardware alteration from a line-mode display to a bit-map display.

The fundamental screen design is based on the above-mentioned six functions. Plural design alternatives for each functions are proposed and evaluated for legibility, symmetry and consistency with other operations. Consistency is especially important, because differences in the editing operations of bilingual editor, Japanese word processors, and English word processors confuse users. For example, the representation methods of original text and target text are shown in Figure 2. Hardware constraints (e.g. a line-mode display) are neglected at this step and feasibly covered by software at the next step in accordance with the state charts.

Details of screen design are reviewed by the sketches of the display layout and the operational sequences. Operational sequences are doubly checked by the state charts. This design process is iterative. If the problems of state charts or the display layout are found at the design review, the whole design is re-examined.

Lastly the functions are checked by the design concepts mentioned in Section 2. The check result is shown in Table 1. The functions, which do not correspond to any design concept are not adopted. Fortunately, all functions are adopted as a result of the check shown in Table 1. At the version-up, new functions are checked and selected, as shown in Table 1.

4. EXPERIMENTAL RESULTS

Experiments were performed to evaluate the operations on a practical field data set including English technical papers. The first experiment was performed in 1985. In the first experiment, operation sequences were counted manually, so that cursor movement operations (ex. arrow keys) were neglected. The second experiment was performed in 1993, and operation sequences were automatically measured. Cursor movement operations and mouse-button clicks can be counted. The quality of translation in 1993 is

Alternative 1   Left-right layout

| Another problem of these systems is that users have to employ these operations whenever they edit the contents of the documents. / これらのシステムの問題は彼等が文書の内容を編集するときはいつでもユーザがこれらのオペレーションを用いなければならないということである。 | Legibility good | Symmetry good | Consistency good |

Thus, they have to spend lots of time to completely finish / このように、彼等は完全に文書を配置することを終えることに

Alternative 2   Up-down layout by sentence

Another problem of these systems is that users have to employ these operations whenever they edit the contents of the documents.

これらのシステムの問題は彼等が文書の内容を編集するときはいつでもユーザがこれらのオペレーションを用いなければならないということである。

| Legibility bad | Symmetry bad | Consistency good |

Alternative 3   Up-down layout by paragraph

Another problem of these systems is that users have to employ these operations whenever they edit the contents of the documents.Thus, they have to spend lots of time to completely finish laying out the documents.

これらのシステムの問題は彼等が文書の内容を編集するときはいつでもユーザがこれらのオペレーションを用いなければならないということである。このように、彼等は完全に文書を配置することを終えることにたくさんの時間を費やさねばならない

| Legibility bad | Symmetry bad | Consistency bad |

Figure 2 Example of design layout comparison

Talbe 1 Function checklist by design concepts

Functions	Related design concepts				
	Sentence-based translation	Use of translation -related data	Word-level editing	Independence	Novice users
Cursor movement	X		X		
Cursor enlargement			X		X
Cursor unit switch			X		X
Cursor jump	X	X			X
Target word display		X	X		X
Dictionary reference		X			X
New word into a dictionary	X	X	X		X
Word deletion from a dictionary		X	X		X
Insertion		X	X	X	X
Deletion		X	X	X	X
Moving	X	X	X	X	X
Copying	X	X	X	X	X
Execution		X			X
Undoing		X			X
Modification alternatives		X	X		X
Sentence-structure alternatives		X			X
Translation start	X				X
Translation of sentence parts		X			X

much better than in 1985, but the screen layout and fundamental operations are unchanged.

Figure 3 shows operation percentages of two experiments. In order to compare two experiments, cursor movement operations are neglected. In the second experiment, there are twice as many cursor operations as insert operations, and four times as many mouse-button clicks..

The first experiment was executed on the prototype translation system in 1985. The prototype translation system ran on a minicomputer, the monitor of which was a line-mode display. The bilingual editor displayed original text and target text in two pseudo-windows. The average operations were 18 times per sentence. The content of the dictionary was not rich, so that dictionary reference operations were little used and new words were registered. The target sentences generated by the system were too bookish and delete operations were frequently used.

The second experiment was executed on the commercial system ASTRANSAC in 1993. ASTRANSAC runs on a Sun workstation. Operations average one third the number executed by the prototype system. Because the content of the dictionary is rich, dictionary reference operations were frequent and no new words were registered during the second experiment. In the first experiment, unknown words were words unregistered in th dictionary. In the second experiment, unknown words were unknown, being spelling errors. After the user corrects a misspelled word, the user translates the correct sentence again.

The experimental results show that operations of the bilingual editor are useful in spite of the machine change and the translation quality change.

5. CONCLUSION

This paper shows the design process of a suitable bilingual editor. The design methods are evaluation of specific errors produced in the translation process, display of prototype operation sequences, function selections in accordance with the design concepts and reviews based on specified user profiles. As a result, the bilingual editor realizes a suitable interactive environment. The screen layout and the operations are not

926

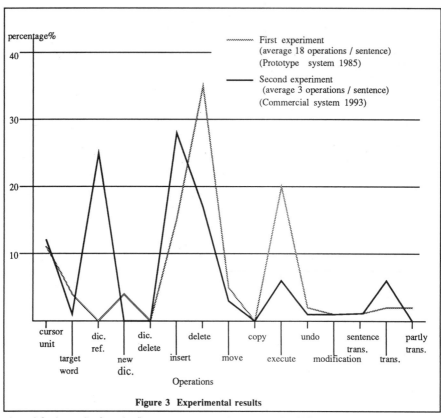

Figure 3 Experimental results

changed fundamentally from the first prototype system demonstrated in 1985.

Acknowledgement

The author thanks Mr. S. Amano, Mr. K.Takeda, and the machine translation group for helpful suggestion and assistance with experiments.

REFERENCES

[1] Machine Translation Summit III Proceedings, Center of Machine Translation, Carnegie Mellon University, 1991.

[2] Machine Translation Summit Proceedings, Japan Electronic Industry Development Association, 1987.

[3] Thurmair, G., "Recent Developments in Machine Translation", Computers and the Humanities, Vol.25, pp. 115-128 (1991).

[4] Amano, S., Hirakawa, H., Nogami, H., and Kumano, A., "The Toshiba Machine Translation System", Future Computing Systems, Vol.2, No.3, pp.227-246(1989).

[5] Perlman, G., "Making the right choices with menus", Proceedings of INTERACT'84, pp.291-295 (1984).

[6] Keister, R.S., and Gallaway, G.R., "Making software user friendly: An assessment of data entry performance", Proc. of the Human Factors Society 27th annual Meeting, pp.1031-1034 (1983).

Coordinating an interface agent with direct manipulation environments

Takashi Sonoda, Fumitaka Matsumoto, Kengo Omura and Mitsuhisa Kamei

Foundation Research Laboratory, Fuji Xerox Co., Ltd.
2274 Hongo, Ebina, Kanagawa, 243-04 Japan

Abstract

In this paper, we propose a collaborative manipulation interface which includes an interface agent as the "dialogue partner" and a direct manipulation interface as the "tools". These tools are shared and collaboratively manipulated by the user and the agent. It is thought that this interface system simulates human cooperative works. This interface has the same properties as the cooperative works. We describe the benefits of the collaborative manipulation interface. A prototype system for the group schedule management is also developed.

1. THE COMPUTER: TOOL OR DIALOGUE PARTNER

Various models of interface have been proposed by many interface designers. These interfaces are classified into two major groups. In the first group the computer is regarded as a "tool". A good tool lets a craftsman fully exhibit his skill. Similarly, in the interface design, the "tool" type interface allows the user to easily exhibit his skill. The direct manipulation interface is a representative of this type of interface. Task domain is represented by the model world based on the metaphor of the well known real world, and the user manipulates objects in the model world by using the "tools". Then the user can feel that he is manipulating the real world. While in the second group the computer is treated as a "dialogue partner". The user has a goal that he wants achieved with the computer. The "dialogue partner" computer understands the user's goals and translates them into the series of operations of the computer. The aim of the "dialogue partner" type interface is for the computer to intelligently converse with users and accomplish tasks as a human secretary would [1-5].

What differences are there between the "tool" type interface and the "dialogue partner" type interface? One difference is the position of task knowledge in the human-machine communication. In the "tool" type interface the

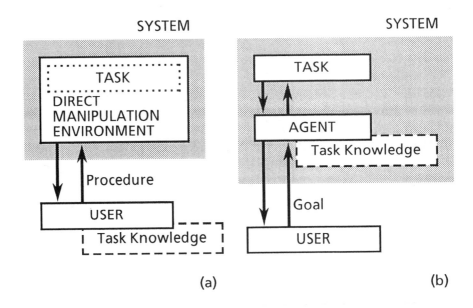

Figure 1. (a) "Tool" type interface. (b) "Dialogue partner" type interface.

user translates his goal to procedures and manipulates the computer by himself. The user must have the procedural knowledge to achieve a task. While in the "dialogue partner" type interface the procedural knowledge to achieve the task is kept by the dialogue partner, namely the computer. Figure 1 shows the position of knowledge of the task in two types of interface. These two interfaces have, therefore, complementary properties, the "tool" type is a procedure oriented interface and the "dialogue partner" type is a goal oriented interface.

2. COORDINATING AN INTERFACE AGENT WITH DIRECT MANIPULATION ENVIRONMENTS

As is discussed in Section 1, in the "tool" type interface, knowledge of procedures is given to the computer from the user, while in the "dialogue partner" type interface a goal is given to the computer from the user. Some tasks are suitable for the "dialogue partner" type interface and others are suitable for the "tool" type interface. These two interfaces are used accordingly to suit the task. If a computer includes two types of interfaces, it can deal with various tasks.

In this section, we propose a collaborative manipulation interface, in which the tools are shared and collaboratively manipulated by the user and the agent.

2.1. Collaborative Manipulation Interface

In the direct manipulation interface, the user carries out a task with tools in the model world by himself. The user must have the skill and knowledge to carry out a task. There are some tasks that the user must only do by himself. But in many other cases, there are tasks which can be done by other users as well. Additionally, it is not always possible for the users to have all the knowledge, the skills or the proper system required for the task. In these cases, if there is an intelligent agent in the computer, the user can order the agent to do the work that the user does not want to do by himself and/or is not able to do. And, the user and the agent continue the work collaboratively, giving knowledge to each other in some situations. For this reason, we propose an interface which has a combined agent with multi-modal dialogue and a direct manipulation environment.

Figure 2 shows the outline of this interface named the collaborative

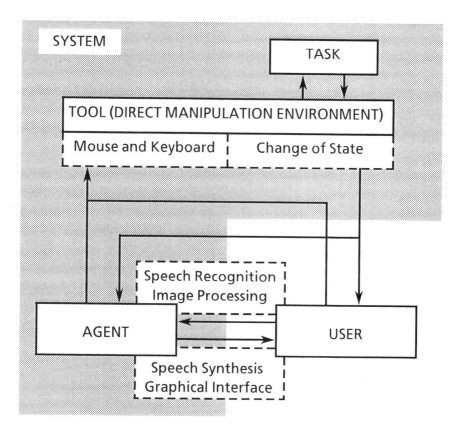

Figure 2. Collaborative manipulation interface.

manipulation interface. In the collaborative manipulation interface, the user and the agent are able to use the same tools in real-time, to watch interaction between the other and tools at any time, and to interrupt the interaction of each other. So this interface would have the following effects.

(a) By observing the manipulation by the agent, the user can know how to manipulate the tool and the various restrictions of the tool. Moreover the user learns how to achieve the task using the tool.

(b) The user can interrupt the agent's manipulation at any time and cooperatively carry out the task with the agent. Also the user can communicate with the agent using a multi-modal dialogue, such as ordering work by speaking command and/or pointing tool. The agent is able to learn the user's skills by observing the manipulations.

2.2. Brief Description of our Prototype System

An initial experimental system for supporting the group schedule planning and the schedule management has been developed on a collaborative manipulation metaphor [6, 7]. An animated agent and several graphical tools on the display are provided in Figure 3. Here when a user wants to decide the date of a meeting, he can either request the agent to find the appropriate candidates or do it himself using graphical tools. In the case of the former, the agent performs the required task by manipulating tools on behalf of the user. The user can monitor the sequence of actions of the agent and he can break into agent's manipulation whenever he wants to to manipulate by himself.

The multi-modal dialogue between the user and the agent is modeled after face to face human communication situations. The prominent features in this dialogue are given as follows. First, the user can regulate the verbal communication with the system by observing postures, gestures and facial actions of the agent which indicate states of the conversation and the system. Secondly, the animation of the facial expressions of the agent that changes on the basis of the emotional model is used to make the communication warmer and more enjoyable. Finally, the object the user is looking at on the display is recognized by utilizing eyetracking technology, and under some prescribed conditions the agent can begin to talk about the looked-at objects.

3. DISCUSSION

In this paper, we propose a collaborative manipulation interface. Our model is a simulation of the cooperative works which should be done by two men and a computer. One man is a human worker (user) and the another is an electronic co-worker (agent).

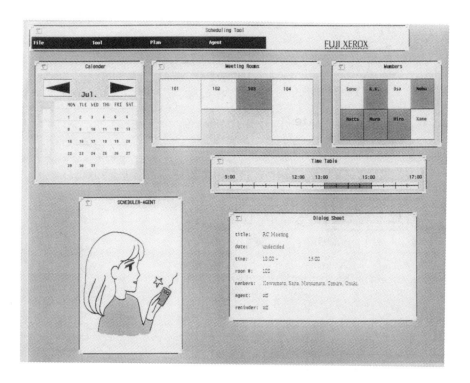

Figure 3. Display image of the prototype system.

Figure 4 shows an aspect of the cooperative work. The co-worker who is advanced in task knowledge translates the worker's goals to the series of procedures of the shared computer which would then realize the goals. From the worker's point of view, the co-worker can spontaneously be identified with a human teacher or friend even though it is an electronic existence. The worker understands the role of the co-worker and that of the computer distinctively. The worker can use these two modes without confusion.

It is also possible that the places of two men are reversed if the worker is advanced in task knowledge. In this opposite case the worker translates the co-worker's goals to the operations of the computer.

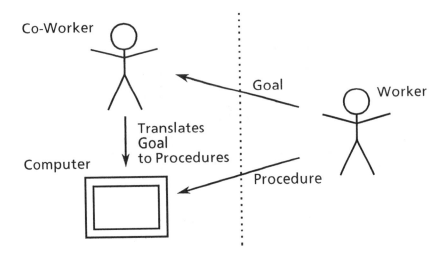

Figure 4. An aspect of the cooperative work.

4. REFERENCES

1   B.Shneiderman, Direct Manipulation: A Step Beyond Programming Languages, IEEE Computer, Vol.16 August, p.57 (1983)

2   E. L. Hutchins, J. D. Hollan, and D. A. Norman, Direct Manipulation Interfaces, in D. A. Norman and S. W. Draper (eds): User Centered System Design, (Lawrence Erlbaum, Hillside, New Jersey 1986) p.87

3   E. Hutchins, Metaphors for Interface Design, in M.M.Taylor, F.Néel, and D.G.Bouwhuis(eds) The Structure of Multimodal Dialogue, (Elsevier Science Publishers, Amsterdam 1989) p.11

4   B. Laurel, Interface Agent: metaphors with character, in B. Laurel (ed.), The Art of Human-Computer Interface Design, (Addison-Wesley, Reading, Massachusetts 1990) p.355

5   A. Kay, Computer Software, Scientific American, Vol.251, no.3, p.52 (1984)

6   K. Omura et al., A Collaborative Manipulation Interface: Coordinating an Interface Agent with Direct Manipulation Environment, Proceedings of the 8th Symposium on Human Interface, Kawasaki, Japan (1992) p.105 [In Japanese]

7   T. Sonoda, F. Matsumoto, K. Omura, and M. Kamei, Coordinating an Interface Agent with Direct Manipulation Environment, Proceedings of the Annual Meeting of the Information Processing Society of Japan, No.5, Tokushima, Japan (1992) p.223 [In Japanese]

The Fifth Generation Fallacy: Looking Back from 1993

J. Marshall Unger

Department of Hebrew & East Asian Languages and Literatures, 2106 Juan Ramón Jiménez Hall, University of Maryland, College Park, MD 20742-4831, USA

Abstract

Now that Japan's Fifth Generation project has ended, there is general agreement that it failed to produce applications that revolutionize the way Japanese work. I predicted this outcome in 1987 after analyzing the problems of handling Japanese script on computers, particularly those associated with input. Did the project fail for the reasons I described or for different ones? A survey of empirical research published between 1987 and 1992 supports the original hypothesis that poor Japanese white-collar productivity and inefficient use of computer power are due to the use of Chinese characters in Japanese script, and that there are fairly severe limits on what any computer program, of whatever type, can do to remedy the situation.

1.   BACKGROUND

The Fifth Generation computer project (5G) ran from 1981 to 1991. It was heralded by such authorities as Edward Feigenbaum and Pamela McCorduck, who in 1983 praised Japan's decision to invest heavily in logic-based or "strong" AI and berated private industry and government agencies in the United States and Europe for failing to rise to "Japan's computer challenge" [1]. In 1987, I published a rebuttal [2] of this thesis, arguing as follows:

(1) Feigenbaum and McCorduck grossly overstated the accomplishments and promise of strong-AI research. Not only were their hypotheses about the nature of intelligence (which were shared by other AI proponents) excessively strong, but even as early as the mid-1980s, results from so-called neural-net or connectionist models, based on much weaker hypotheses and therefore long neglected in AI circles, were clearly superior to what was being achieved with logic-based systems.

(2) Furthermore, documentary evidence showed that the Japanese government launched 5G mostly for domestic political reasons, not because those responsible accepted the theories of American scientists like Feigenbaum or believed that AI would guarantee them global economic hegemony in the 21st century. Planning documents repeatedly mention the need to improve Japan's poor performance in white-collar productivity and software; many other project goals indirectly addressed these same chronic problems of the Japanese domestic economy.

(3) The root cause of these problems was that Japanese script could not be handled elegantly on computers. This difficulty could be avoided if Japanese were willing to learn to read their language in romanized form in certain computer applications, but for various cultural and political reasons, they generally did not want to do so. Ironically, increasing numbers of Japanese were learning to TYPE romanized

Japanese on computers as transcriptive (*kanji henkan*) word processing systems flooded the market; it had been proven, however, that transcriptive systems were intrinsically inefficient and could not support the speed, ease, and quality attainable with touch typing in an alphabetic script because of structural properties of the Japanese writing system itself.

(4) Indeed, a fully automatic system for writing Japanese would require a computer that could literally read the user's mind. The odds that 5G or any other strong-AI effort would produce a breakthrough in input technology were therefore virtually nil. It followed that 5G would not lead to major improvements in Japanese productivity or software as had been claimed.

In the process of advancing this argument, I also examined the reasons for Japanese resistance to the idea of reading Japanese-language data in romanized form in computer applications. I showed that the chief causes of this resistance were historically recent and political in character; there was nothing about the script itself that made it indispensable for effective written communication in Japanese, nor was there any merit in predictions that Japan would suffer an irreparable break with its past if alphabetic script were allowed a larger niche in daily Japanese life.

Although my book was well received in many quarters [3-8], favorably cited by other scholars [9-10], and issued in Japanese in 1992 [11], it was also attacked by two kinds of reviewers [12-15]. One group saw any criticism of the strong-AI research agenda as a Luddite assault upon science itself; the other saw any challenge to the historical and theoretical account of the Japanese writing system currently taught in Japanese schools as anti-Japanese prejudice.

Now that 5G has come to an end, a definitive response to critics in the first group is possible. The consensus of published opinion to date is that 5G failed to produce most of the applications described in its planning documents; that enthusiasm for logic-based systems has been replaced, in Japan and elsewhere, by interest in neural net models, which make weaker and fewer assumptions about the nature of intelligence; and that the only true achievement of 5G has been to set a precedent in Japan for government-financed basic research in computer technology [16-19]. Furthermore, it is now widely acknowledged in hindsight that before and during the lifetime of 5G, while proponents of strong-AI were insisting that intelligence is NOTHING BUT formalized rule schemata, the most innovative research going on was the interdisciplinary work of the Santa Fe Institute and scientists working on the periphery of the emerging field of Chaos [20]—work based on the same concept of "mind" as an emergent property of "brain" that Hubert Dreyfus and John Searle (as I noted in 1987) had invoked in their criticisms of strong-AI dogma. In sum, my analysis of and predictions about AI research and 5G have turned out to be more accurate than those offered by Feigenbaum, McCorduck, and other AI advocates.

Critics of the second kind believe that the way in which the Chinese characters (Japanese *kanji*) are processed in the brain is essentially different from the way in which other kinds of characters are processed. They think *kanji* stand for thoughts, or at least for whole words that express thoughts, whereas all other kinds of characters merely represent sounds; therefore, the presence of *kanji* in a Japanese text adds essential information that cannot be conveyed by any other means and without which the text is incomplete. It follows that *kanji* are indispensable for proper written communication in Japanese and that giving them up, even on a limited scale, would undermine Japanese culture. On this view, writing systems that make use of Chinese characters are fundamentally different from writing systems that do not; we may therefore call those who subscribe to this view BIMODALISTS. Is there empirical support for their position?

2. NEGLECTED RESULTS

First, let us recall two important lines of research I cited in 1987 but the Bimodalists have persistently ignored.

One is the work of Yamada Hisao, then at the University of Tōkyō. More than a decade ago, Yamada and his colleagues showed how to design a Japanese input system with which a trained typist could copy-type at a speed and level of accuracy comparable to English touch typing under similar conditions; training on this system for an educated native speaker of Japanese required roughly the same amount of time as needed to train an educated native English speaker to touch type [21]. Furthermore, Yamada explained why his kind of descriptive input system had these characteristics and why transcriptive or inscriptive systems could not. Yamada's work thus indirectly showed that the psycholinguistic processes involved in reading and writing Japanese script are basically no different from the processes involved in the case of other languages and other writing systems.

This conclusion was supported in two ways by the work of Michel Paradis and his colleagues at McGill University [22]. The first half of their study surveyed the psycholinguistic literature down to 1984 and showed that there was no experimental evidence supporting the hypothesis that *kanji* are processed in a different hemisphere of the brain from other kinds of characters used in Japanese writing. A similar survey of the clinical literature going back to 1901 in the second half of the book revealed that loss of reading or writing ability due to brain injuries in Japanese patients followed no discernible pattern with respect to the distinction between *kanji* and other kinds of characters.

3. RESEARCH SINCE 1987

Empirical evidence that I did not cite in *The Fifth Generation Fallacy* or was published after it appeared casts further doubt on the Bimodalist position.

3.1 Psycholinguistic Findings

A major long-term research project by Harold Stevenson and his colleagues at the University of Michigan, which began well before 1987, showed that the acquisition of literacy among elementary school children in Minneapolis, Sendai, and Taipei was not significantly affected by national differences. "These results are in marked contrast to prevailing but previously untested belief that children who must learn to read an alphabetic form of writing are disadvantaged, in comparison to children who are learning to read a script based on distinctive whole units, such as Chinese characters, or symbols with high grapheme-phoneme correspondence, such as Japanese *hiragana*" [23].

These conclusions are corroborated by experimental results of a different kind reported by Richard Alan Horodeck [24], who studied the handwriting mistakes involving *kanji* made by educated Japanese. He found that errors in which the only link between the false and target (intended) *kanji* was that they each could be read (i.e.

pronounced) the same way in some context (not necessarily that of the stimulus) outnumbered all other kinds of errors 10 to 1. Horodeck thus took a large step beyond Paradis by providing strong affirmative evidence of a similarity between *kanji* and other types of characters, viz. the major role played by subvocalization in recall during writing. Furthermore, Horodeck devised a reading test to determine whether, during ordinary reading, certain types of *kanji* errors were harder to detect than others. The results of this experiment showed that Japanese subjects were far more likely to accept a false *kanji* if they knew a reading for it that made linguistic sense in the context of the stimulus; false *kanji* that are not pronounced, in any context, like the target were significantly easier to detect even though they were visually and in all other respects just as prone to being confused with the target. This result strongly suggests that fluent readers of Japanese associate phonological information with *kanji* at a very early stage in the reading process. Similar results for Chinese have since been reported in a study comparing the reading abilities of native and non-native readers of Mandarin [25]. Manufacturers of transcriptive Chinese and Japanese word processing systems ought to pay careful attention to these results because they imply that the kind of false characters that these now widely used systems generate are precisely the kind most difficult for skilled native readers to detect when proofreading.

3.2 Historical Research

In the literature on the origins and history of writing, the Bimodalist position gets support from certain examples of so-called picture-writing that allegedly convey precise messages without any reference to spoken language. Perhaps the most widely cited example of such writing is a "love letter" of the Siberian Yukaghir, most recently cited in a treatise on writing systems by the British linguist Geoffrey Sampson [26]. In 1989, John DeFrancis of the University of Hawaii, traced Sampson's illustrations back to their original 1895 Russian source and demonstrated conclusively that there were not specimens of writing at all but simply the remnants of games played by Yukaghir women, who challenged each other with birch-bark picture riddles about their personal lives [27].

DeFrancis had earlier called into question the claim that Japan and Taiwan enjoy nearly total literacy because of the use of Chinese characters in the writing of Japanese and Mandarin [28]. Richard Rubinger of Indiana University has now called attention to historical data from 19th-century Japan that strengthens DeFrancis's case [29]. Rubinger cites, among other things, data from a little-known 1881 literacy test given to all 882 males in the small village of Tokiwa in what is now Nagano Prefecture. The Tokiwa survey ranked examinees according to six levels of skill. It also recorded ages; thus, assuming that examinees achieved their lifetime level of literacy during school-going age (i.e. from 6 to 13), the Tokiwa survey allows one to chart changes in levels of literacy attained from the 1810s to the 1870s—almost the entire span of the nineteenth century.

The survey found a very broad range of skills—everything from total illiteracy to fluency with government documents. Most test-takers were at the bottom of the scale, and the numbers in the higher categories dropped off precipitously. Even more interesting, Rubinger found little correlation between schooling and literacy. On the one hand, there was a steady decline in the percentage of those totally illiterate and a steady rise in the percentages of those minimally literate from the 1810s onward, but concluded that increasing attendance at traditional *terakoya* ("temple schools") was enough to account for this change; Rubinger found no sudden jump that could be correlated with the initiation of compulsory schooling. On the other hand, the Tokiwa data suggest that a small but highly trained elite who performed the reading and writing tasks of the village maintained a tight monopoly on high-level literacy skills through hereditary positions, apprenticeships, or special tutoring, rather through schooling.

All this casts doubt on the Bimodalist contention that there is something special about the Japanese writing system conducive to widespread literacy. My own most recent research suggests further that this Bimodalist belief is of Western origin and was absent from Chinese and Japanese works on writing and language until the 19th century [30]. The idea that Chinese characters are ideograms that convey thoughts or meanings directly to the mind without reference to any particular language can be traced back to the Neo-Platonists and early Church fathers at a loss to explain Egyptian hieroglyphs. During the Enlightenment, reports from China were seized upon by Europeans such as Leibniz, who saw the Chinese writing system as a precedent for an algebra of ideas by means of which all disputes could be settled through deductive calculation. It is easy to understand why Europeans, who had endured the horrors of religious warfare during the 17th century, should yearn for such a calculus of thought; what is remarkable is that, having picked up this notion from the West in the 19th century, many Chinese and Japanese today believe it originated in East Asia.

4.   CONCLUSIONS AND IMPLICATIONS

The Bimodalist view of Chinese characters is thus untenable in the face of both directly observable and historical evidence. Perhaps the supreme irony is that it was a product of the very Western tradition, dating back to Plato, from which logic-based AI research drew its inspiration. Acceptance of the separability of mind and body and of the Platonic worldview, in which ideas exist independently of human thought, is a necessary condition for belief in the possibility of a computer program that not only SIMULATES intelligent behavior but, in its very structure, actually EMBODIES intelligence. In this sense, the fallacy of equating *kanji* with ideograms and the fallacy of the Physical Symbol System Hypothesis underlying strong-AI research [31] are the same, as I argued in 1987.

5.   REFERENCES

1   E.A. Feigenbaum and P. McCorduck, *The Fifth Generation*, Addison-Wesley, Reading, Mass., 1983.

2   J.M. Unger, *The Fifth Generation Fallacy*, Oxford, New York, 1987.

3   M. Kesteron, "Is Japan Just Chasing Moonbeams with Its AI Research?" *Toronto Globe & Mail*, 24 October 1987.

4   B. Johnstone, "The Robot Generation," *Far Eastern Economic Review*, 19 November 1987.

5   E.J. Brebner, "Exposing an AI Illusion," *Mainichi Daily News*, 28 February 1988.

6   J. Edwards, "Treatise Touts New Theory of Japanese AI Quest," *PC Week*, 1 March 1988.

7   M. Cross, "Japan—Handicapped by Its Language," *New Scientist*, 14 April 1988.

8   N. Iizuka, *Nikkei Konpyūta*, 16 November 1992.

9   S. Kumon, "Wāpuro jidai no Nihongo no kakikata," *Shūkan Tōyō Keizai* 24 September 1988.

10   A. Penzias, *Ideas and Information*, W.W. Norton, New York, 1989, p. 44.

11   J.M. Unger, *Konpyūta shakai to kanji*, SIMUL, Tōkyō, 1992.

12   D.E. Williams, *Asian Wall Street Journal*, 10 May 1988.

13   E.H. Kinmonth, *Pacific Affairs* 61:3, 1988.

14   M.M. Strauss and M. Tomita, *Journal of Asian Studies* 47:4, 1988.

15   H. Somers, *Computational Linguistics* 14:4, 1988.

16   D.E. Sanger, "Japan Sets Sights on Winning Lead in New Computers," *New York Times*, 30 April 1990.

17   T.R. Reid, "Japan Ends Computer Project," *Washington Post*, 2 June 1992.

18   A. Pollack, "'Fifth Generation' Became Japan's Lost Generation," *New York Times*, 4 June 1992.

19   D. McNeil and P. Freiberger, *Fuzzy Logic*, Simon & Schuster, New York, 1993, p. 244.

20   M.M. Waldrop, *Complexity*, Simon & Schuster, New York, 1992.

21   H. Yamada, "Certain Problems Associated with the Design of Input Keyboards for Japanese Writing," *Cognitive Aspects of Skilled Typing*, ed. W.E. Cooper, pp. 305-407, Springer, New York, 1983.

22   M. Paradis, H. Hagiwara, and N. Hildebrandt, *Neurolinguistic Aspects of the Japanese Writing System*, Academic Press, Orlando, Fla., 1985.

23   H.W. Stevenson, G.W. Lucker, S. Lee, J. Stigler, "Poor Readers in Three Cultures," *The Role of Culture in Developmental Disorder*, v. 1, ed. C. Super and S. Harkness, pp. 153-177, Academic Press, New York, 1987.

24   R.A. Horodeck, "The Role of Sound in Reading and Writing *Kanji*," Ph.D. diss., Cornell, 1987.

25   E.B. Hayes, "Encoding Strategies Used by Native and Non-Native Readers of Chinese Mandarin," *Modern Language Journal* 72:2, 1988.

26   G. Sampson, *Writing Systems*, Hutchinson, London, 1985.

27   J. DeFrancis, *Visible Speech*, U. Hawaii Press, Honolulu, 1989.

28   J. DeFrancis, *The Chinese Language*, U. Hawaii Press, Honolulu, 1984.

29   R. Rubinger, "Literacy West and East: Europe and Japan in the Nineteenth Century," *Senri Ethnological Studies* 34, 1992.

30   J.M. Unger, "The Very Idea: The Notion of Ideogram in China and Japan," *Monumenta Nipponica* 45:4, 1990.

31   A. Newell and H.A. Simon, "Computer Science as Empirical Inquiry," *CACM* 19:3, 1976.

KJ-Editor: A Collaboration Environment for Brain Storming and Consensus Forming

H.Ohiwa[*], K.Kawai[†], A.Shiomi[†] and N.Takeda[†]

[*]Department of Environmental Information, Keio University
Endo, Fujisawa 252 Japan

[†]Toyohashi University of Technology
Tempaku-cho, Toyohashi 441 Japan

Abstract

KJ method, which is very popular in Japan for group work, and the editor for supporting the method in network environment is presented. Relationship of the method to software requirement engineering and decision making process is also discussed.

1. INTRODUCTION

Collaboration is an essential activity for human society and computer support for it has recently attracted many researchers' attention. Mutual understanding must be established for getting the meaningful results from the collaboration.

For such problem, KJ method is very effective. This method was formalized by J. Kawakita for generating new ideas in his ethnogeographical works[2]. However, it has been widely accepted by Japanese business community for usefulness of consensus forming among the participants of idea generation.

We have developed an editor for supporting the KJ method on a personal computer[3] and extended it so as to use it in network environment[5]. The editor has been used for requirement analysis of the software system[4].

In the next section, requirement engineering for software systems is described, and the difference of decision making process between Japanese and western society is shown. Then, the KJ method itself and the KJ editor are briefly described. Some comments are made on the difference between the KJ method and hypercard system.

2. REQUIREMENT ENGINEERING

Recently, one of the key issues in software engineering is how to make a perfect specification by analyzing, understanding, and recording the problem that a sponsor is trying to solve. The functions, goals, and constraints on the proposed system must be precisely specified and both the sponsor and the developers must agree on the specification, as they form a basis for the subsequent construction of the system. Such field is called "requirement engineering".

This requirement analysis is very difficult especially for large scale computer systems. Completed specifications are often incomplete and even if they are complete, it may be misinterpreted by the designers or the implementers.

One of the approaches for this problem is writing a specification in mathematical terms in order to avoid misinterpretation. However, it is not easy to write it in this way if it is done by average engineers whose mathematical background is not enough for the job. Furthermore, even if it is completely written in mathematical terms, it may not be understood by the average engineers.

One of the approach for this problem is to clarify the process of making the specification. In order to understand the specification, it is necessary to know how it comes out. Then, the problem becomes how to record requirement analysis process. There are several approaches for this problem: introspection, interview, protocol analysis, and discourse analysis[1], but they are all at the very early stage of research.

3. WESTERN VS JAPANESE WAY OF DECISION MAKING

The ways of making specification in Japan is different from those in western world. In the western society, some analyst is responsible for the specification. Although he may investigate various aspects of the system by holding conferences with the clients, users, designers , and implementors, he himself decides what the final specification is.

In Japanese society, no single person is responsible for the specification. Conferences are held and relevant persons meet and discuss the matter, but even the chairperson has no responsibility for the resolved specification. He is responsible for coordination and not responsible for the resolution.

In western society, a conference is held for making a resolution which is made by voting. Therefore, some participants may not agree to the resolution and an accommodation may not be formed.

In Japan, a conference is held for forming a consensus or an accommodation. All the participants must approve the resolution although some may not agree to it. Therefore, Japanese conference takes many hours and often makes no resolution. Decision making process is very slow.

The aim of the conference for specification in Japan is for understanding the matter by all the participants. Such conference may start with brain storming. In the west, brain storming is done for creating new ideas. However in Japan, it is not necessarily carried out for this purpose; rather, it is done for forming a consensus among the participants.

KJ method is a very popular method in Japan for forming an accommodation from brain storming. It was developed for creating new concepts from brain storming, but it is used not for creating but for forming a consensus or an accommodation. This comes from the fact that consensus or accommodation is much more important in Japanese business community than creation.

4. KJ METHOD

KJ method was developed for new idea generation and claims to establish an orderly system from chaos. The method consists of four steps.

The first step of the method is to write down on a card what has come to mind on the subject to be discussed. Only one thing must be written down on a card. At this step, no judgment should be made on the importance of what is to be written, because what is important can only be established at the completion of the method. All the facts and information relevant to the problem should be written down.

The second step is to associate several cards into one group. All the cards must first be shuffled and spread on the desk. This grouping should be done subjectively rather than objectively or rationally by examining the content of cards, because this subjectiveness may reveal real desire hidden by the rationality. Grouped cards may be labeled by a new card which represents the essence of the group. Then the groups may further be grouped in a hierarchical manner.

The third step is to arrange the card groups on a large piece of paper, and to enclose each group by an outline. Spatial relationships of arranged cards and groups must reflect semantic relationship and extreme prudence is required for this step. It is also necessary to make clear the mutual relationships between the cards and groups by drawing special lines. The relationships include opposition, causality, and equality. At this stage, the internal structure of the matters written on the cards which is invisible in the first step, becomes visible. The result is called the A-type chart.

The fourth step is to write down an essay on the subject according to the A-type chart. This step is called B-type writing. It should be noted that the A-type chart represents the subject spatially, and that the B-type writing represents the same information in a sequential order. Because of the difference in representation, while doing B-type writing, oversight in the A-type chart may be found and some revision must then be made.

The method can be done personally, but often done in group. Then, competent persons must be in the group to obtain a good results. This does not mean that the rest of the group is not needed. They are very good audience for stimulating the competent and sometimes may find their oversights. Furthermore, they can fully understand how the results are obtained. This fact is very important in requirement engineering.

5. KJ EDITOR

The KJ method can be carried out on an KJ editor[3] we have developed. On using it, a display becomes a desk-top on which cards are arranged. The following editing capability is provided for arranging cards on the display.

Hundreds of cards may be generated on any place on the display and a sentence may be written on each of them using a keyboard. The size of the card may be changed using a mouse. A generated card may be pick and moved by the mouse. A sentence on a card may be edited using a keyboard. A card judged as useless may be discarded.

Cards may be grouped by enclosing them with a curve. The curve can be drawn by pointing out some points on the curve by the mouse. Groups may be grouped hierarchically in the same way. A group may be moved by the mouse like a card, thereby relative position of the grouped cards is preserved.

Relationship of cards and groups can be marked by special lines. The editor has seven different types of lines for relationships. When a card or a group that has been marked with relationship lines is moved, the lines are automatically redrawn so as to keep track of the relationship.

6. COMPARISON WITH HYPERCARD SYSTEMS

Making an A-type chart may look constructing a hypercard system, because the process of grouping cards and defining relationships between cards and groups are the same as that of constructing hypercard system. However, there is an essential difference between hypercard and the A-type chart.

In a hypercard system construction, any relationship between cards can be established. Because of this easiness of establishing relationship, resultant system becomes very complex, and it often becomes extremely difficult to understand the whole system structure.

The most important part of the A-type chart forming is to arrange card groups on a desk. Spatial nearness must represent nearness of the meaning of cards. However, because of the spatial restriction, the number of the nearest cards is limited. If a card has so many relations with other cards, most of them must be ignored, because of this spatial restriction.

Which relation should be picked and which be discarded is not an easy decision. It requires deep understanding of the whole problem, because such restriction holds for every arranged cards. When the number of the cards are increased, the difficulties increase exponentially. The designer must then think what is essential to the problem.

Although arranging cards is not an easy task, the resultant chart is easy to understand, because human eye and brain can understand a structure of two-dimensional image instantly.

Although the A-type chart may be represented by a hypercard, the KJ method forces the designer to take off less important relations from the whole structure.

7. CONCLUSION

KJ method was originally developed for a new idea generation, but it is widely used in the Japanese business community for reaching a consensus or forming an accommodation. The method is very effective when used in group for mutual understanding of the problem .

In requirement engineering, the specification must be understood by all the relevant persons for the subsequent system development. KJ method is a very good paradigm for this problem and we have developed an editor for the KJ method in network environment[5].

References

[1] J. A. Goguen, C. Linde "Techniques for Requirements Elicitation" Proc. RE'93, IEEE Int. Symp. on Requirement Engineering 1993 4-6 Jan. 1993, San Diego CA

[2] J. Kawakita, *The KJ Method: Let Chaos Tell* (in Japanese), Chuokoron-sha,Inc, 581pp., 1986; *The Original KJ Method* (in English), Kawakita Research Institute, Tokyo, 44pp. 1982.

[3] H. Ohiwa, K. Kawai, M. Koyama, "Idea Processor and the KJ Method" J. Information Processing Vol. 13, pp.44-48, 1990

[4] N. Takeda, A. Shiomi, K. Kawai, H. Ohiwa "Requirement Analysis by the KJ Editor" Proc. RE'93, IEEE Int. Symp. on Requirement Engineering 1993 4-6 Jan. 1993, San Diego California, USA

[5] N. Takeda, A. Shiomi, K. Kawai, H. Ohiwa "Preliminary Experiment with a Distributed and Networking Card-Handling Tool Named KJ-Editor" "Proc. HCI International '93" 8-13 Aug. 1993, Orlando, Florida, USA

Use of Bi-directional Image Exchange in Facilitating Precontact Communication

Yu SHIBUYA and Hiroshi TAMURA

Faculty of Engineering and Design, Kyoto Institute of Technology
Matsugasaki, Sakyo-ku, Kyoto, 606 JAPAN
Tel.: +81-75-724-7498. Fax.: +81-75-724-7400. E-mail: shibuya@hisol.dj.kit.ac.jp

Abstract

A bi-directional image communication network of a small size was introduced experimentally in a laboratory environment. In studies of bi-directional image exchanges, the major concerns were to enhance communication by use of facial expressions or body gestures during the conversation. What we propose in this paper is the use of bi-directional image exchange to facilitate contacts among parties such as finding the person and catching the chance to communicate. This paper is to report the use of bi-directional image exchanges in a laboratory environment in the past 3 years.

1. INTRODUCTION

Studies on the use of images in communication so far were concerned mostly with the use of facial and gesture expression to enhance communication among parties which are already in contact. CAVECAT[1] aimed to enable a small number of individuals or group located in separate offices to engage in collaborative work without leaving their offices. Media Spaces[2] provided a continuous video and audio connection between two of its research facilities located hundreds of miles apart. Cruiser system[3], a desktop video telephony system, was provided to parties who were in a single building, and, from a functional point of view, it was compared with the other media such as face-to-face, phone, and handwritten document.

Our basic idea is that it is not the feasible use of images to help people already in contact and to substitute media contact for the face-to-face meeting. The media might help the people to make a contact effectively and to maintain the link between the parties after contact. In this paper, our focus of study is to examine the use of images to enhance communication by providing support to establish the contact. To make a contact with a person, we must override the barrier such as not knowing situations around him, not having proper topics to begin with, or not having appropriate expressions for the topics. To override such barriers of communication, some sort of communication is necessary before making a contact with a person. We call it *precontact communication*.

Precontact communication is a general process before making a contact in our daily face-to-face communication. That is knowing the presence of a person, knowing the availability for contact, and catching the chance to make a contact. But knowing such things by face-to-face contact may be intrusion into a person's place or waste of time. An image exchange system is available to reduce such ineffectual or unnecessary contact. So a bi-directional image exchange is appropriate method to make a precontact communication.

2. SYSTEM CONFIGURATION OF THE BICS

System configuration of our bi-directional image communication system, called BICS (Bi-directional Image Communication System), is shown in Figure 1. Members of our research group are distributed in separated three rooms, but the distance between the rooms are so near that we can go back and forth very easily.

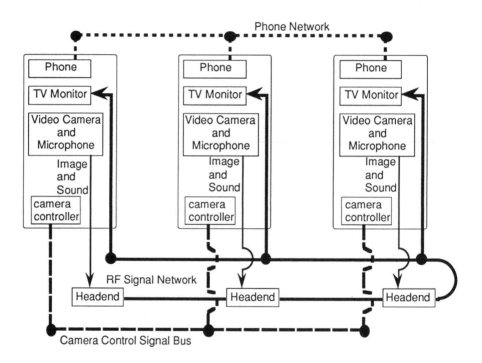

Figure 1. System configuration of the BICS.

A terminal of the BICS introduced in each rooms consists of a phone, a camera, two TV monitors, a microphone, a TV transmitter, and a camera controller. Because we regard our laboratory environment as the public spaces, so any people visiting the rooms can access the BICS.

One important feature of the BICS is that all camera's angle can be controlled by anyone in the every site. With this camera control system, the users are free to find the people in another site and know what they are doing. But the images other people want to see are not always those they want to show, so sometimes they are intentionally out of the sight of the camera. To avoid such undesirable action, some sort of implicit social rule of accessing the live video image networks must be introduced.

3. EXPERIMENTAL EVALUATION

3.1. Beginning of use

Three years ago, in 1990, the BICS was first introduced in our laboratory environment[4]. At that time, some people were hesitating to use the system because they were seen by somebody from another site. So the use of the BICS was observed less frequently than it was expected. But two or three months later, the people were used to the BICS, and they accustomed to use the BICS to communicate each other.

3.2. Classification of actions

Before describing the current daily usage of the BICS in the laboratory environment, the access methods to the BICS is classified as follows.

Glance : A quick short look at the monitor. Most people takes a glance at the monitor, when go across the front of the monitor. But the duration of looking in is very short, and they don't have explicit purpose.

Watch : Look monitor carefully, and the duration is usually longer than that of the glance. In this case, most user have the some purpose such as to search people, to catch chance to talk to, and to know what happen in remote site. And after watching the monitor, they begin to make some actions such as to call up somebody or to walk to the remote room.

Camera control : Controlling the remote site camera angle. Camera control is always carried out with watch, and is used to search people and to know who is there in remote sites.

Call up : Talk to the specific people with whom want to make conversation or to ask something to do. In some cases, if there is no response from the remote site, the conversation does not begin.

Broadcast : Different from the call up, distribute the message to all people accessible to the BICS. This is used to search people and to know who there is. And in some cases of broadcasting, the conversation through the BICS will begin.

Conversation : Through the BICS, talking with the remote site people each other. When somebody want to make conversation with a people in another room, usually first he watch the monitor to find the people, call up the people, and then begin conversation. So at the beginning of the conversation, there must be a call up or broadcast action.

3.3. Daily use of the BICS

From above categorizations, the daily use the BICS in our laboratory environment is shown in Table 1.

Table 1. Frequency of use of the BICS
(Record of 5 days observation.)

Action	# of action	# / (Total # of people = 50)
glance	64	1.28
watch	47	0.94
control camera	21	0.42
call up	40	0.80
conversation	23	0.46
broadcast	2	0.04
Total	197	3.94

The duration of this observation is 5 days, about 40 hours. All camera's images transmitted through the BICS are picture-in-pictured, and recorded by VCR with mixed sound. In Figure 2, we show a shot of a picture-in-pictured images used for evaluation. Counting the number of actions was done by reviewing the recorded VCR tape. Among the actions the glance is very difficult to detect, so the number of the glance in Table 1 is underestimated.

Table 1 shows that the most frequent use of the BICS is the glance and watch. These actions often lead the people to make a conversation.

Figure 2. A shot of picture-in-pictured images.

3.4. Purpose of using the BICS

From the functional point of view, the actual usage of the BICS is categorized as follows.

Knowing the remote site status : The BICS is used to know the status of the remote site, the presence of the people or the availability of the copy machine in the remote site.

Find People : We find the man whom we talk to through the BICS. Before talk to him, we know his status from the video image. If we recognize he is busy, we give up to talk to him. This is general awareness, we usually do in our face-to-face communication.

Ask a person to do something : We can ask to people easy task through the BICS. For example, we often people in the remote site to look for something in the site, we ask our simple problem in studying, and so on.

Monitoring the remote room : If there is no people in remote site room, we can keep watch of remote room with the BICS.

Substitute for phone : For the public message exchanges, the user likely to use the BICS rather than the phone. But for the private message exchange, the phone is often used because they want to make a pier-to-pier or person-to-person link between them.

3.5. Process of communication

The real efficiency of the BICS is not estimated with the frequency of the use. The process of the communication is more significant factor to study. Here we show a role of the images in facilitating the communication. The general process of communication may be grouped into three stages as in Figure 3.

Precontact Communication
    Finding the people ("Is he/she there?")
    Getting the status information ("Is he/she busy?")
    Catching the chance to contact ("May I talk to him/her?")
Incontact Communication
    Call up
    Conversation
      Public conversation
      Private conversation (often use a phone)
Postcontact Communication
    Maintaining the link
      ("Is it go well?" or "Is there no more problem?")

Figure 3. Three stages in communication

In our face-to-face communication, we follow these stages. Among these stages, pre and postcontact communication play an important roles in making a good communication. If the precontact communication is properly arranged, incontact communication might follow smoothly. And if postcontact follow-ups are credible, good relationships among the colleagues might be maintained . The image exchanges are useful to make such good precontact and postcontact communication. By using the BICS, we can get the information without disturbing the other people and maintain our good links between parties without making a face-to-face contact. People might think it efficient to substitute incontact communication by the media contact, but such trial often end in unexpected result, to be described in the next section.

3.6. Making electronic circuits

We have tried to examine whether the media communication can be applied for various purpose and whether it can substitute for the incontact communication properly. For example, trials were made to give instructions to students to build electronic circuits. In many cases, instructors were frustrated because the instructions were often too early or too late, and because they were not able to grasp the trouble remotely. The instructor often went to the working site of the students and gave direct advice.

These experiences suggest that it is not feasible to think total communication process can be covered by the media contact. Instead, media contact is useful and powerful to establish direct contact efficiently and timely, and further to follow up the result of the contact.

4. CONCLUSION

In this paper, the general process of communication is grouped into three stages, they are precontact communication, incontact communication, and postcontact communication. The proper precontact communication leads an incontact communication smoothly, and the credible postcontact communication maintain the good relationships among the parties. From the experimental evaluation of the BICS, that the image exchanges of the BICS are useful to facilitate the pre and postcontact communication.

5. REFERENCES

1   M. M. Mantei, R. M. Baecker, A. J. Sellen, W. A. S. Buxton, and T. Milligan, Experiences in the Use of a Media Space, Proceedings of the CHI '91, pp.203-208, 1991.
2   S. A. Bly, S. R. Harrison, and S. Irwin, Media Spaces: Bringing People Together in a Video, Audio, and Computing Environment, Communication of the ACM, Vol. 36, No. 1, pp.28-47, 1993.
3. R. S. Fish, R. E. Kraut, R. W. Root, and R. E. Rice, Video as a Technology for Informal Communication, Communication of the ACM, Vol. 36, No. 1, pp.48-61, 1993.
4. Y. Shibuya and H. Tamura, An Experimental Evaluation on the Roles of Bi-directional Image Communication in the Laboratory Environment, Human Interface, Vol. 6, pp. 251-256, 1990.
5. H. Tamura and Y. Shibuya, Tacit Communication with Bi-directional Image Exchange, Proceeding of the SICE '91 in Yonezawa, pp.787-788, 1991.

Human Centred Collaborative Design in System Development
- Intelligent back scratcher to be attentive to user's needs -

Yoshihiro Sato

Research Institute of System Science
NTT DATA COMMUNICATIONS SYSTEMS CORPORATION
Dai-Tokyo Kasai Shinjuku Bldg., 13th Floor
25-3 Yoyogi 3-Chome, Shibuya ku, Tokyo 151 Japan
TEL: + 81-3-5371-5611 FAX: +81-3-5371-7591

Abstract

The transfer of user's needs to the system designer is essential design system well suited for users. Unfortunately the requirement transfer is not easy. Users , who demand system, are not the expert in the area of system design. On the other hand, system designers, who are demanded system, are not the expert in the area of user's business. The gap of the domain knowledge exists between them. Communication is the crucial key factor for reducing this gap.

This paper describes the Collaborative Design Method (CDM) that supports the knowledge transfer and the knowledge share with effective communication, and the expression of the structured group knowledge.

1. Introduction

The system development process can be divided into the upper process and the lower process. The upper process completes at the point when the system specification is described by the designers. After that, the concrete system is built up on the specification. Software productivity has improved remarkably in the lower process supported by programming languages, debugging tools, testing tools, etc. The upper CASE (Computer Aided Software Engineering) tools support the analysis of requirements in the upper process. However, this assumes that user's needs are clarified; therefore, CASE tools do not support the appearance of needs themselves. In the upper process, the clarification of what users truly want is important in addition to clarification of how they actually operate. Nowadays, the method which appropriately arranges the subjective and vague information such as user's needs has not been established.

The author of this paper has been developing the Collaborative Design Method (CDM) that expresses the structure of group knowledge and shapes common understanding. The effective communication during CDM processes can share the demanded part of domain knowledge with participants. This method adopts the concepts of the KJ method[1], which is a well-known Japanese problem-solving method. The measure function to arrange and structure a large amount of qualitative information that has been put into words is the same of KJ method. The difference from the KJ method is that the CDM is charactered by the analogy of the knowledge jigsaw puzzle . The development of the CDM has assumed that it would be applicable to system design, but it is highly compatible with a wide range of other applications as well. In addition to system design, the CDM can be used to arrange large amounts of verbal information.

2. Processing subjective information

The work in system development begins by understanding user's needs. Presently, designers collect information about user operations through field investigation, questionnaires, interviews, document investigation, and try to understand user's needs. The upper CASE tools support the processing of objective information, such as the operate flow, the relation among the tasks, etc. Some tools are used for analyzing the needs described on the requirement form in the upper process. The useful method that supports the processing of "subjective information" for the appearance of needs themselves has not been established. The understanding about user's needs is rely on the range of domain knowledge that the designer has in the user's area.

On the other hand, users do not always express their needs concerning the resulted system clearly because they are not the expert of system design. This situation is similar that they can't tell precisely where is itchy on their back. Certainly, only the users that have information related to the true request should be targeted as the source of information. That is participatory design is essential for designers to understand their request. "This involvement of users in design is seen, not only as a means of promoting democratization in the organization's change process, but also as a key step to ensure that the resulting computer system adequately meets the needs of the user."[2]

User's requests are subjective information. In many cases, this vague information is not clearly expressed. To conceptualize needs for a group, knowledge (needs) must be collected from the members and then integrated; however, very few methods have supported this integration process. "Conventional knowledge acquisition support tools basically assume that knowledge is acquired from an expert, and very few tools have been applicable to the acquisition of knowledge from more than one participant."[3]

3. The Collaborative Design Method (CDM)

3.1. Scratching back in Collaboration

The author is developing a method to establish a structured language expression through the integration of images that a group has conceptualized. This method supports the processing of subjective information during the upper process of system development by structuring and expressing the group knowledge. The CDM can play the role of a back scratcher that points out the itchy part on the back.

The purpose of the CDM is to acquire knowledge from a group of people, and to form an image of a vague idea. Because the CDM supplements the knowledge of these people, it is, in principle, applicable to collaborative operations requiring input from a number of experts (users). At first, this method cuts knowledge about objects in the system into many pieces and extracts them from the brain. These pieces of knowledge are then assembled like a jigsaw puzzle to form an image.

The CDM is charactered by following features;

(1) All participants are considered to be subjects of the process.

The Collaborative Design Method puts "participation by all members, understanding of all members, and satisfaction of all members" into practice. "All members" means concerned persons who participate in the collaborative design. Persons who speak louder, who are good at theorizing, or whose title is higher, frequently take the initiative in group operations where the emphasis is on discussion. Results drawn out from these kinds of group operations are largely affected by the insistence of these leaders. Even if a result is not based on the opinions of other participants, consent given to the result assumes that their opinions have been reflected. The CDM adopts democratic consideration to prevent the situation where a certain discussion technique or a relationship between high rank and low rank determines the results of discussion.

(2) Results that are decided by the sum of knowledge

Because it is a result of collaboration, the result must not be reduced so that it only reflects an average of members' capabilities. The capabilities of all members should be combined to form a better final result--the final result obtained is based on the knowledge and viewpoints of many people.

Persons who participate in the CDM must be experts on objects in the system. Mr. Onoue and others point out that, when a group conducts creation-oriented work, members must have "information over a certain level about the working subject," and together they must individually maintain information as well as their special capabilities [4].

(3) The opinion of the minority is respected

The opinion of the majority must not override the opinion of the minority. Giving precedence to the majority opinion is a defect that easily occurs when conventional group work is done. The CDM does not only adopt the opinions of the majority. Rather, it places stronger importance on the opinions of the minority.

(4) The process is maintained

The process for gathering information in a particular order is clearly visible. When a specific person pushes his/her own concept forward, omissions, discontinuity of procedure steps, or jumping to a conclusion can prevent other persons from understanding the process through which the results are drawn out. Including a sudden idea or a personal theory in the gathered information has no background to explain how the conclusion was reached.

(5) Information,process and results are shared

The following things are shared.
- Input: Design information
- Process: Procedure up to product completion
- Output: Understanding of the results

(6) Group organization using the KJ method is adopted

Mr. Takahashi reported that he had collected 200 different methods for solving problems. Although there are many display-type methods that illustrate ideas, the number of convergent-type methods, which are necessary for integrating the knowledge of a group, is quite limited. According to the method investigation that Mr. Takahashi conducted at 70 companies, the method used most frequently was brainstorming, invented by A.F. Osborn (57.1%); the second most frequent method was the KJ method (48.6%); the third most frequent was the check-list method[5]. In Japan, the KJ method is the most acknowledged convergent method. It was estimated that people would easily receive the KJ method, because of its style of group organization that is very close to the thinking processes of humans.

Proper execution of the KJ method requires skills that are characteristic to the KJ style. "Most people are required to take part in a training course before they can properly employ the KJ method."[6] The CDM adopts the concept of group organization, an important part of the KJ method, and improves it for easier operation.

The CDM is different from the KJ method with respect to the following points:

a. It includes a phase in which all members must understand the information presented.

b. It includes a phase in which the coverage of information presented is checked.

c. It visually selects information that is to be used for grouping.

d. It includes a process in which an investigation is made to consider the removal of useless information.

e. It forms groups from information about lower-level concepts.

f. It may adopt submitted information to create a representative label or title for a group of information.

g. Finally, it represents images in structured layers.

3.2. The Analogy of an Intelligent Jigsaw Puzzle

The CDM calls a card that extracts knowledge about an object in the system a knowledge piece (KP). The participants deal operate knowledge pieces by association of a jigsaw puzzle(see Figure.1).

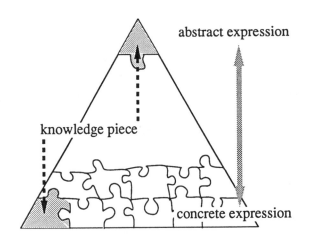

Figure 1. The analogy of a jigsaw puzzle

Considering the analogy of a jigsaw puzzle, the CDM works with knowledge pieces in the following phases.

- 1st phase (making)   : Creation of knowledge pieces
- 2nd phase (refining) : Sharing of knowledge pieces
- 3rd phase (mapping)   : Outlining of knowledge pieces
- 4th phase (selecting) : Selection of knowledge pieces
- 5th phase (grouping) : Assembly of knowledge pieces

Collected knowledge pieces are a part of the image that each expert has about an object. All participants check the information on these knowledge pieces. If some knowledge piece is not understandable, it is rewritten so that it can be easily understood. Because knowledge pieces include duplicate pieces or defective pieces, only the necessary knowledge pieces are selected and used during the grouping phase.

During the grouping phase, the shapes of pieces are matched and are then gradually accumulated. Pieces to be placed adjacent to each other are searched for, based only on their shape. The shape represents the meaning of a knowledge piece. When the difference in meaning between the pieces is small (compared to others) those pieces are fitted together. The difference in meaning between pieces can only be measured by a person having expert knowledge in the applicable domain. A piece is supplied whenever it is needed. Individual pieces are parts of the group knowledge, and those parts are collected to form the group knowledge as a whole. Individual pieces in a chaotic state are integrated to create an entire image as if they are self-organized. Finally, the knowledge pieces are structured, pyramid-style, and the language expression (see Figure.2).

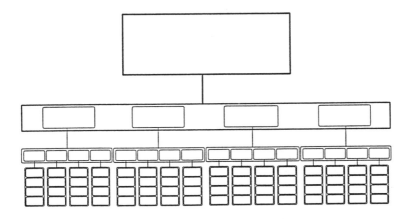

Figure 2. The CDM chart : Each square is a knowledge piece.

This process is visually executed by replacing the creative work that is performed within the human brain with manual work. Thereby, all members can take part in the thinking and can share the process work until the result is achieved.

4. Conclusion

The designer should have a proper comprehension of user's needs in system design. In order to do so, it is necessary to process not only objective information but also subjective information. However, the proper method which can arrange and structure subjective information in words such as user's needs has not been established. This paper has introduced the Collaborative Design Method(CDM) that can process subjective information to shape user's vague needs in the system development .

Reference

1 Kawakita, J., The Original KJ Method, Kawakita Research Institute, Tokyo, Japan, 1982

2 Gill, K. S., Summary of Human-Centred Systems Research in Europe, NTT Data , 1990

3 Kunifuji, S., Knowledge Acquisition Support Groupware GRAPE, pp. 374-389,1991

4 Onoue, Y., Kuwana, E., Communication Analysis of Argument Structure-Based Collaborative Design, 1992

5 Takahashi, M., Creation Method and Support System, Building a Idea Support System Symposium Report, International Institute for Advanced Study of Social Information Science, pp.75-87, 1991

6 Kawakita, J., Idea Support System That Enhances People's Creativity, Building a Idea Support System Symposium Report, International Institute for Advanced Study of Social Information Science, pp.13-18, 1991

Cooperative Work Analysis of Plant Operator Crew

Hiroshi UJITA[a], Ryuji KUBOTA[b], Kouji IKEDA[b], and Ryutaro KAWANO[c]

[a]Energy Research Laboratory, Hitachi, Ltd., 7-2-1 Omika-cho, Hitachi-shi, Ibaraki-ken, 319-12 JAPAN

[b]Hitachi Works, Hitachi, Ltd., 3-1-1 Saiwai-cho, Hitachi-shi, Ibaraki-ken, 317 JAPAN

[c]Nuclear Power Research and Development Center, Tokyo Electric Power Company. 1-1-3 Uchisaiwai-cho, Chiyoda-ku, Tokyo, 100 JAPAN

Abstract
Elucidation of crew communication and collaboration aspects is required to improve the man-man interface which supports plant operators' diagnoses and decisions. Experiments to clarify operator performance under emergency situations were performed using a training simulator. The operator performance was evaluated from the viewpoint of crew communications. Six approaches have been tried to evaluate operator performance: cognition-communication flow, movement flow, position covered, task gain evaluation, information effectively exchanged, and communication correlation aspect. Crew communications and collaborations in emergency situations were categorized into four types: Top Down, Bottom Up, Tight Coupling, and Loose Coupling.

1. INTRODUCTION

Elucidation of plant operators' cognitive processes and communications is required to improve the man-machine and man-man interfaces which support operators' diagnoses and decisions. Experiments to clarify operators' cognitive processes have been performed [1], in which operator performance under abnormal conditions was evaluated by protocol analyses, interviews, etc. using a plant dynamics simulator of a nuclear power plant. The cognitive processes had been previously analyzed [1], by using the information processing model developed on the basis of Rasmussen's idea [2]. We have had working hypotheses, based on experimental observations, that crew communications can be divided into various types and the communications can be used to evaluate crew collaboration types. Differences in operator crew performance were evaluated in the present study.

2. CLASSIFICATION OF CREW COLLABORATION TYPE

Experiment observations and data analyses showed that the operator crew collaboration can be broadly divided into 4 types, regarding a crew of 4 members set up for a certain problem. The types, compiled in terms of the flow of the information and instruction, are shown in Fig.1.

Top Down: The operators engage themselves in gathering data and carrying out operations as instructed by the supervisor, while keeping the supervisor informed of the data. This weakens the solidarity among the crew members, leaving only the supervisor in a position to grasp the whole situation.

Bottom Up: The collection and exchange of data as well as the decision making are carried out by the crew members, with the supervisor only informed for approval. The supervisor in this type is engaged in making general judgments and giving approvals.

Tight Coupling: There is a close exchange of communications among the crew members including the supervisor, with the decision making conducted in a natural way on the basis of mutual exchange of data and ideas. This results in summarized data being brought forward to the supervisor, enabling him to make general judgements easily.

Loose Coupling: There is little communication between the supervisor and the other crew members, contrary to the Tight Coupling type, the circulation of data is not effectively carried out.

Good performance was observed in the crew with the Tight Coupling communication type because a large amount of information and common-objective tasks were shared among operators. This conclusion was supported by training instructors who attended the experiments.

According to observations of simulator experiments, the influence of the leadership formation in a usual situation is considered to appear as the collaboration type among the crew members in an emergency situation. Hence, the correlation between the leadership type of the PM theory, suggested by Misumi [3], and the crew collaboration formation was taken as a reference to conduct analysis and evaluation, supposing the Top Down type as Pm, Bottom Up type as pM, Tight Coupling type as PM, and Loose Coupling type as pm (with the capital letter P indicating that the importance is placed on Performance, M, Maintenance of crew harmony, while the small letters respectively indicating the opposite).

3. CREW COLLABORATION ANALYSES

The analysis method of crew behavior is based on Yukimachi's method [4].

3.1 Qualitative Analysis
(1) Cognition-Communication Flow

The communication type as well as the progressive trail of the cognitive process and the defined task were subjected to analysis on the basis of conversations among the crew members. The group thinking process was clarified by using the flow, which connects the cognitive process for each operator and communications among operators. The differences in communication amounts for a task were indicated.

Compared with the Loose Coupling type, the Tight Coupling type is found to have a higher level of interpretation and definition of the task through conversation, which is then effectively linked with the operations.

(2) Movement Flow

The solidarity of the crew members was analysed by indicating for positions at each control panel the conduct of each crew member there and then comparing the movement flow. Three types of movement flow analysis examples are shown in Fig. 2. The group response process to the task was clarified using the flow, which relates the operator positions to the panels and indicates discussions among operators. The differences in discussion form for a task were indicated.

The analysis shows that the crew members in Loose Coupling type hardly gather together, and behave separately whereas the members in the Tight Coupling type often gather and talk about solving the problem, allotting 20-40 seconds for conversation.

(3) Position Covered

The numbers of stays longer than ten seconds at each position for each operator were counted. In order to help each other in the crew, the number of stays for each operator should be spread over all control panels.

(a) The simple failure case shows that only the operator positioned to be directly aware of it responded to the abnormality.

(b) The multiple failure case shows that operators support each other and the action area is broad.

3.2 Quantitative Analysis

(1) Task Gain Evaluation

Response time varies one order due to operator crew differences. However, which response is better, quick or slow, is not decided, because response is considered to be correct if the time is in an allowable range.

Basically, tasks which should be done in the situation must be done. Therefore the numbers of tasks executed are a good performance measure. However, if the plant reaches a good condition safely, which satisfies the plant goal, tasks not executed must not be so important.

Here, correlation of two measures is considered; many tasks should be done quickly, therefore the upper left curve means good performance in Fig. 3. This index is considered to be a good performance measure, though it has no relationship with crew collablation type. Crew 1 responded quickly and Crew 2 performed many tasks, while Crews 3 and 4 performed less tasks within a longer time.

(2) Information Effectively Exchanged

Quantitative indexes for evaluating crew performance were identified, which were considered to be represented by the amount of information effectively exchanged among operators as shown in Table 1. The first two are quantitative indexes of the communication amount and the differences in information amount are indicated in the third one. The fourth one is for clarifying leadership type.

(3) Correlation Analysis

The transition of crew communication due to differences in the contents of the three types of tasks in multiple failure case is shown in Fig. 4 as a communication aspect graph. Distributed according to the average value of each axis, the Tight Coupling type is allotted at the top right, the Bottom Up type at the top left, the Top Down type at the bottom right and the Loose Coupling type at the bottom left. Although the allotment of the axis and the division method can be further improved, the method was found to enable comparison of the differences in communications according to the crew and task contents.

Table 1
Comparison of information effectively exchanged in multiple failure case.

Index for information		Top Down	Loose Coupling	Tight Coupling
Speech rate (min^{-1})		21	21	50
Portion of discussion in speech (%)		53	55	74
Speech amount for each cognitive element		2.2	2.0	3.1
Speech ratio for each operator (%)	Supervisor	43	47	33
	Auxiliary operator	19	10	24
	Reactor operator	18	22	14
	Turbine operator	20	21	29

4. CONCLUSIONS

In order to evaluate collaboration among the plant operator crew members, several methods were developed and experiment results were analysed to get the following conclusions.
(1) Six approaches were tried to evaluate operator performance from the viewpoint of clarifying crew communication or collaboration aspect.
(a) The group thinking process was clarified by cognition-communication flow.
(b) The group response process was clarified by movement flow.
(c) The group coordination was clarified by position covered.
(d) Correlation of number of tasks and response time was clarified by a task gain evaluation chart.
(e) Quantitative indexes for evaluating crew performance are considered to be represented by the amount of information effectively exchanged among operators.
(f) Collaboration type was clarified by a communication aspect graph.
(2) The collaboration aspect can be broadly divided into 4 types: Top Down, Bottom Up, Tight Coupling, and Loose Coupling.

REFERENCES

1 H. Ujita, et al. : Plant Operator Performance Evaluation Using Cognitive Process Model, 3rd International Conference on Human-Computer Interaction, Boston, U.S.A. (1989).
2 J. Rasmussen: Skills, Rules, Knowledge; Signals, Signs, Symbols and Other Distinctions in Human Performance Models, IEEE Trans. on SMC., SMC-13(3) (1983).
3 J. Misumi: The Behavioral Science of Leadership, Blue Backs (in Japanese) (1986).
4 T. Yukimachi: A Study on Analytical Method for Team Activities During Plant Disturbance, Ningen-Kougaku Vol.25, No.6 (in Japanese) (1989).

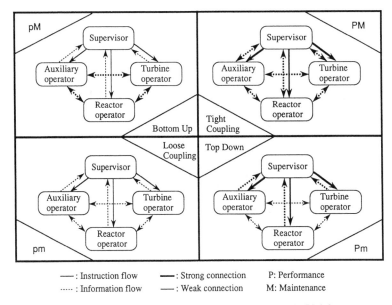

—— : Instruction flow   ▬▬ : Strong connection   P: Performance
‥‥‥ : Information flow   —— : Weak connection   M: Maintenance

Fig.1   Crew communication type and leadership type in PM theory.

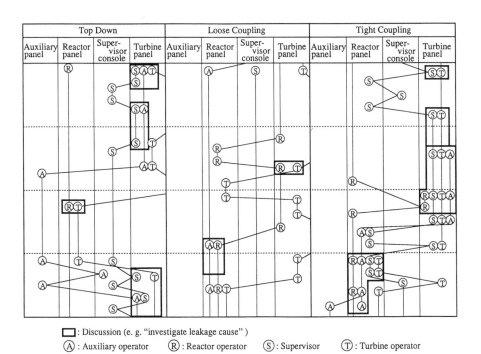

▢ : Discussion (e. g. "investigate leakage cause")

Ⓐ : Auxiliary operator   Ⓡ : Reactor operator   Ⓢ : Supervisor   Ⓣ : Turbine operator

Fig.2   Movement flow analysis in multiple failure case.

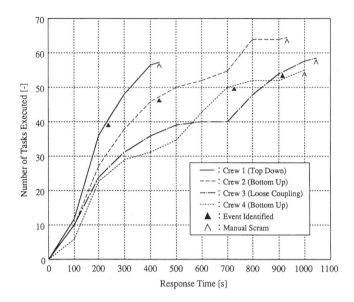

Fig.3   Comparison of crew performance
using task gain evaluation chart in single failure case.

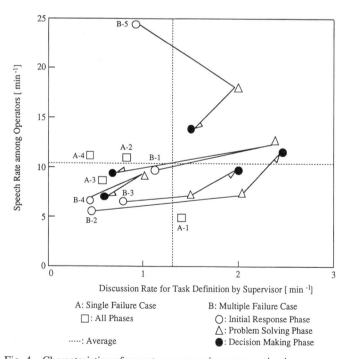

Fig. 4   Characteristics of operator crews using communication aspect graph.

Group Communication Support System for Software Development Project Based on Trouble Communication Model

Shoichi Takeda   Mie Nakatani   Shogo Nishida

Central Research Laboratory, Mitsubishi Electric Corporation
Amagasaki, Hyogo 665 JAPAN

Abstract
   This paper deals with a group communication support system in a software development project when there happens some trouble on it. First, we analyze a communication process in the real projects, and then we propose a communication model based on the analysis. We focus on the communication in case of troubles, and the process is modeled using "charge", "competence" and "knowledge" of each member in the project. A group communication support system named CACTUS (Computer Assisted Communication Tool for Urgent Support) is developed based on the model, and also the use of the system is discussed.

1. INTRODUCTION

   The problem with developing a large scale software system is becoming more and more difficult with increasing complexity. The problem is traditionally dealt with from software engineering point of view. Many researchers study programming languages[1], reusability of software modules[2], specification techniques[3], and so on.
   Here the problem of developing a large scale system is dealt with from the CSCW (Computer-Supported Cooperative Work) viewpoint[4]-[6]. We think that communication is an important factor in collaboration. Especially in software development, communication plays some important roles; transfer of specification from system engineers to programmers, monitoring the development process by a project manager, and so on. Our final goal is to improve productivity by supporting communication in a software development project.
   In this paper, we focus on supporting communication in the software development team. As the first step, we analyze the communication process in the real project, and investigate which type of communication is most important for the software development project. Then we propose a communication model based on the analysis. The feature of the model lies in the ability to predict communication route dynamically. A group communication support system named CACTUS is developed based on the simulation model , and also the possibility of the use of the system is discussed .

2. OBSERVATION OF COMMUNICATION IN A REAL PROJECT

   The most popular model for software development process is a water-fall model(7). The model expresses the software development process by dividing into six phases, that is, requirement analysis, functional design, system design, coding, test and maintenance as shown in Fig.1. We observed a real software development project, and noticed there exist two types of communications, that is, "standard communication" and " non-standard communication". Fig.1 shows an image of both types of communication. Standard communication usually has rigid standard forms, and a project is going on only with standard communication when there is no trouble during software development. But we have many unexpected troubles in a real project. In some cases, the problem is settled just by sending some messages by a facsimile. In other cases, people have to have long meeting to settle the problem. In case of such non-standard communication, people are apt to be confused, but it is very important to collect related informations and give good solution to the problem as soon as possible.

3. ANALYSIS OF TROUBLE COMMUNICATION

3.1. Definition of Trouble Communication

There are many aspects on non-standard communication, and it is not so easy to define non-standard communication in general. But here we propose one type of definition of non-standard communication. The idea is as follows.

(a) At the first step, we define " trouble communication" as in Fig.2. In this model, communication is triggered by some trouble in the process of the software development, and is finished by finding solution for the trouble. The state before occurrence of trouble is called "consensus state". This state is one where the project is proceeding successfully and phases are moving one by one in the water-fall model. If this consensus state is broken by some trouble, then people need communication to solve it. This communication is defined as "trouble communication" in the model, and it finishes when the state reaches "new consensus state".

(b) Non-standard communication is composed of a sequence of the above trouble communications. Even if people think they reach new consensus state by finding some solution to the problem, there may happen new problem or they may notice inadequate points on the next day. Then new trouble communication starts until they have new consensus state.

(c) Trouble communication, as defined in Fig.2, occurs in parallel with standard communication which is provided formally according to the software development process based on the water-fall model.

3.2. Features of Trouble Communication

The features of trouble communication are extracted from real examples. We summarize them as follows.

(a) Many members of the team are related to one trouble communication. Key persons in trouble communication are:

    trouble finder   : a person who finds the trouble
    decision maker : a person who gives final decision
    worker   : a person who works to remove the problem concretely according to the
                    decision

(b) The first important process is to report the trouble to appropriate decision maker. This is basically in the hand of trouble finder at first step. Even if he finds an important trouble, he may not notice it as important one and he does not report it to anyone. The important thing in this stage is that the trouble is reported up to the person who recognizes the importance of it and has an "competence" to make decision on it. " Competence" is the right to make decision by himself. Competence is usually limited to some area depending on his position in the team. Competence plays an important role in looking for appreciate decision maker for the trouble.

(c) Once trouble is reported to decision maker, then the most important thing for him is to collect informations for search of solution. Decision maker usually contacts people related to the trouble, gathers informations and look for good solution. In this process, communications arise in the project.

(d) After decision maker gives final solution, it has to be informed to the workers. In this phase, it is important that the decision is reported exactly to all the related workers.

If the trouble is small enough, then trouble finder, decision maker and worker may be the same person. But in this case, communication problem does not occur, because all the role in trouble communication is closed into one person. The problem of trouble communication arises when three types of people, that is, trouble finder, decision maker and worker, are different persons.

Another important factor for trouble communication is what is the main components for determining communication process in case of trouble. This means that by which component communication process between trouble finder and decision maker is determined or by which component communication process is decided for decision maker to gather related informations. According to our analysis for the real projects, the main components which affects communication process in trouble are:

Competence   : each member's right to make decision
Knowledge   : each member's knowledge on the system
Types of trouble : type of trouble which happens

"Competence" is used when trouble finder looks for appropriate decision maker. On the other hand, "Knowledge" is what each member knows on the system. "Knowledge" of each member is used when decision maker collects various informations to give precise decision. Also "Types of trouble" affects communication process because the area of related members are basically determined by the "type of trouble".

4. TROUBLE COMMUNICATION MODEL

We propose a model of trouble communication based on the above-mentioned analysis. Trouble communication is the communication from some "consensus state" to "new consensus state" when a trouble occurs. In the model of trouble communication, the following four types of communications are considered as shown in Fig.3.

(i)   communication from trouble finder to decision maker
(ii) communication for collecting informations by decision maker
(iii) communication from decision maker to worker(s)
(iv) communication from decision maker to members to be reported

These four types of communications are assumed to happen sequentially in our trouble communication model, and their process is expressed as follows.

(1) A trouble finder finds or recognizes a trouble in a software project. He decides a decision maker who has competence for the trouble. He notifies the trouble to the decision maker.

(2) The decision maker decides members who have informations related to the trouble. The decision maker gets informations from them and give solution for the trouble.

(3) The decision maker decides a worker who works to repair or get rid of the trouble. The decision maker sends the solution to the worker.

(4) The decision maker decides the members to be reported. The report is send to them from the decision maker.

In this process, there are four types of decisions. Here we propose the decision mechanism for each process ((1) to (4)) in our trouble communication model. We use the following data in the model.

(a) project organization

(b) system structure(software structure)

(c) "charge" map of each member

(d) "competence" map of each member

(e) "knowledge" map of each member

(f) "type of trouble" with parameters

The words "competence", "knowledge", and "type of trouble" have already defined in the previous section. " charge" means the part of the system which each member is in charge of. The image of each data will be easily understood by the schematic diagram of Fig.4 (a)-(e), which shows concrete data used for simulation.

Here a simple example of simulation result of the trouble communication model is shown. Fig.4 shows the data used for the simulation. Fig.5 is the simulation result when person "Pro 1" finds a trouble in the "Package 1". In this case, "decision maker" becomes "SE 1". Then "SE 1" collects informations from "Pro 2" and himself, workers become "SE 1", "Pro 1" and "Pro 2". The solution is also reported to the three persons. Based on the simulation results, communication route is estimated as shown in Fig.5.

5. A GROUP COMMUNICATION SUPPORT SYSTEM CACTUS

A group communication support system named CACTUS is developed based-on the trouble communication model. CACTUS simulates a trouble communication process and gives advice to the team members. The simulation is based on the above mentioned data ((a) to (f)). These data need to be prepared in advance.

CACTUS is implemented on a UNIX workstation. Fig.6 shows an example display of CACTUS. The system is used on-line in a software project. The system gives us an advice for each decision step. The followings are the supporting functions for each step of trouble communication.

(1) When a trouble finder inputs a trouble (name of troubled module) and a specific type of trouble, the system gives suggestions on who is the "decision maker".

(2) When a decision maker has to collect related informations to make an appropriate solution, the system suggests him a list of members who have related information about the trouble.

(3) When a decision maker has to give some orders to workers, the system suggests who are the workers on the trouble.

(4) The system also suggests to whom final decision should be sent .

6. CONCLUSIONS

This paper proposes a group communication support system named CACTUS based on the trouble communication model. The feature of the system is that "charge" "competence" and " knowledge" of the project members are included in the communication model, and that concrete communication route is estimated from the data. We think the simulation mechanism is based on organizational structure, and our approach may be called " organizational" one.

7. REFERENCES

[1] B. Meyer, " On Formalism in Specifications,"IEEE software, Vol.2, No.1, pp.6-26, 1985.
[2] M. Shaw,"Abstraction Techniques in Modern Programming Languages," IEEE software, Vol.1, No.4, pp.10-26, 1984.
[3] R. Pietro-Diez and P. Freeman, "Classifying Software for Reusability," IEEE software, Vol.4, No.1, pp.6-16, 1987.
[4] Proceedings of CSCW'86, ACM SIGCHI, 1986.
[5] Proceedings of CSCW'88, ACM SIGCHI, 1988.
[6] Proceedings of CSCW'90, ACM SIGCHI, 1990.
[7] Fujino and Hanada,"Technology for Software Production," Institute of Electronics, Information and Communication, 1986(in Japanese).
[8] M.Nakatani and S.Nishida," Trouble Communication Model in a Software Development Project," IEICE Trans. Fundamentals, Vol.E-75A, No.2, pp196-206, 1992.

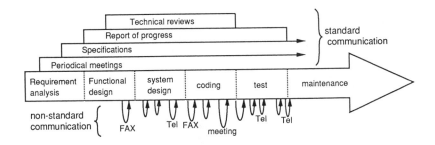

Fig. 1 Standard communication and non-standard communication

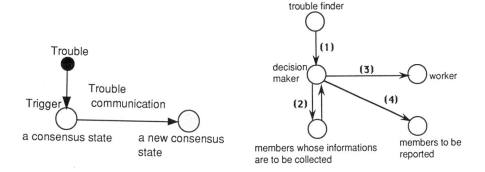

Fig. 2 Definition of trouble communication

Fig. 3 Four basic communications in the process of trouble communication

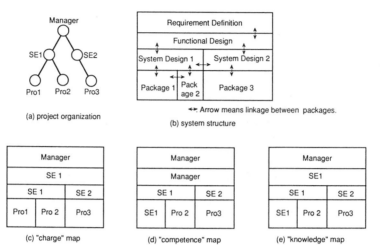

(a) project organization

(b) system structure

⟷: Arrow means linkage between packages.

(c) "charge" map

(d) "competence" map

(e) "knowledge" map

Fig. 4   An example data for trouble communication model

Fig. 5   The result of simulation for the example data

Fig. 6   An example display of CACTUS

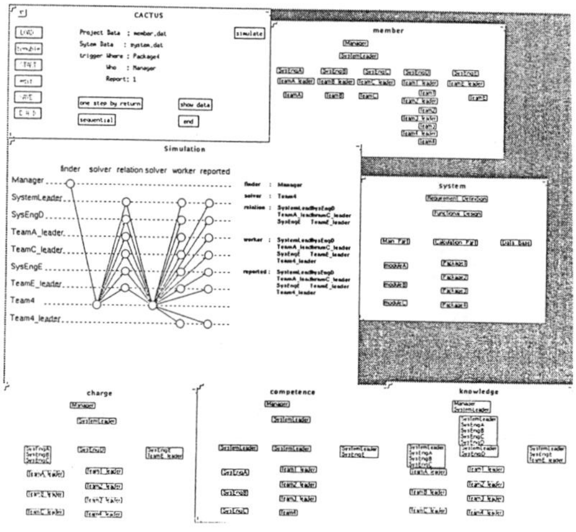

A meeting support system based on analyses of human-communication
- Using the context and contents of meetings -

T. Uetake[a]; M. Nagata[a]; K. Takeuchi[a] and H. Takagi[b]

[a]Dept. of Administration Engineering, Faculty of Science and Technology, Keio University
3-14-1 Hiyoshi, Yokohama 223, JAPAN
Tel. +81-45-563-1141 Fax +81-45-563-5979 E-mail : tomo@ae.keio.ac.jp

[b]Graduate School of Business Administration, Keio University
2-1-1 Hiyoshi, Yokohama 223, JAPAN
Tel. +81-45-562-1185 Fax +81-45-562-3502

Abstract

All activities of humans are based on inter-personal communication. This paper presents a new support tool in human-communication. Most of the research completed in this area to date has been grouped into basically two varieties. First, the hardware viewpoint, the other from the social psychological perspective. This paper presents a new third perspective which is termed the software approach. The system illustrated provides useful information concerning participants in discussion meetings by the discrete analysis of verbal dialogue statements made in these meetings.

The central idea of this research is to classify verbal statements between two levels; (1) statements on the "progress" of the meeting, and (2) verbal statements on the "objects" of the meeting. In this paper these are referred to as meta-*utterances* and *ontent-level utterances* respectively. It is shown that the context of a meeting can be traced by analyzing verbal statements by their context-level. Moreover, if the theme of the meeting is fixed, useful information can be determined by analyzing context-level verbal statements.

1.INTRODUCTION

The increasing development of information technologies has enabled the development of communication systems with which people can communicate each other without time and space constraints.[1] In this situation cooperation amongst people becomes a significant and important activity.

Human activities are all naturally based on inter-personal communications. This paper presents a new support tool in analyzing verbal communication. Discussion meeting support systems have been previously researched under the headings of Computer Supported Cooperative Work (CSCW) or Groupware. Most of the research completed is divided between two areas. The first being the hardware viewpoints. For example, Watabe et al. (1990) implemented a distributed desktop conferencing system - MERMAID - by taking advantage of multimedia technologies. Another is from social psychological perspective. For example, Lee and Sara (1991) reported in their field study how computer networks changed work and organizations. The research presented in this paper takes another perspective that being the software viewpoint which is based on the inter-personal communications and formation and context. Based upon this, it is proposed to illustrate a support system model for monitoring the progress of discussion meetings.[4][5]

2.EXPERIMENTAL MEETING

The study examined data collected from an experimental discussion meeting. Participants in the experiment were shown one-third of the movie entitled, "Twelve Angry Men". This movie begins by introducing the deliberations of a jury from a trial of a man accused of murder. At the beginning there is only one jury person who insists that the suspect is not guilty, and the rest state he is guilty of the crime. As the movie progresses, one jury person changes his mind, followed by one after another. In the experiment, the movie is stopped just before a second jury person changes their mind and insists that the accused is innocent. The participants are asked to identify who will be the second jury person to change his mind and then who will be the third and so on. Their goal being to identify the order in which the twelve jury persons change their minds. Initially, each participant is asked to produce their own forecast. Then, through the group discussion they are asked to create a mutually agreed to forecast within a two hour time-frame.

This type of discussion is widely used as a managerial exercise for business executives in Japan (Yanagihara 1982). Its aim is to have them go through a process of developing consensus by sharing and analyzing information amongst the group.

The experimental meeting was carried out at the Keio Business School in June, 1990. The participants were seven MBA candidates. The process of the discussion was video-taped and later analyzed. All verbal statements of the discussion were entered into the system in character code form. It is suggested that this manual process could be replaced by the voice-recognition device.

3. CONTEXT EXAMINATION

3.1 Extracting meta-utterances

The group discussion agenda is determined during the meeting. Verbal statements made are classified into two levels, either; (1) verbal statements about the "progress" of the meeting (*meta-utterances*)[7] or, (2) verbal statements about "objects" (*content-level utterances*).

A meta-utterance indicates how matters are being discussed or in a what manner discussions are occurring. Content-level utterances provides information about a certain discussion subject or context.[8][9]

The key to tracing the context of a meeting is to focus upon meta-utterances. In the experiment a system was constructed to distinguish *meta-utterances* from *content-level utterances* by the use of keywords in verbal statements. The system can be figuratively represented by a tree. In this model, the roots of the tree represent the subject of the discussion and the nodes represent *meta-utterances*. This model is called a "*context-tree*" (See below of further explanation). This kind of tree corresponds to a goal-subgoal tree. It is found that in most cases when the final goal of the discussion is precisely determined the context of discussion can be adequately explained using the tree model.

3.2 Framework

The method framework is as follows;

Step 1. The context-tree and candidates' stack is set to zero.
(candidate's stack is where last five meta-utterances are stacked)
Step 2. When a verbal statement by a speaker is made, then proceed to the next step.
If there are no more verbal statements, output the context-tree.
Step 3. The addressee(s) of the verbal statements is (are) inferred.
Step 4. If the verbal statement is classified as a meta-utterance, add it to an appropriate place in the context-tree (find appropriate parent from candidates' stack) and insert it in the candidates' stack, then go to Step 2.

3.3 Rules

The addressee of each verbal statement must be determined before distinguishing meta-utterances from object-level-utterances. Next, meta-utterances from object-level-utterances must be distinguished. Further, it must be determined where to add a new meta-utterance to the context-tree.

An outline of the rules is as follows;

Address-rules : To infer the addressee(s) of the verbal statement
Class-rules : To classify verbal statements
Add-rules : To determine where to add a new meta-utterance to the context-tree

3.4 An example

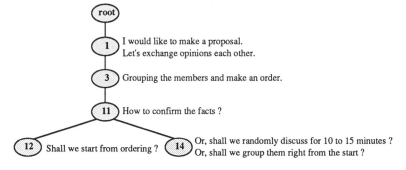

Figure 1. Context-tree model

To verbal statements the system employs *address-rules, class-rules, add-rules* to construct a context tree. The input (verbal statements) versus output (*context tree*) relationship is shown above in Figure 1.

4. CONTENT EXAMINATION

4.1 Extracting contents

At meetings people typically collect information about the subjects (objects) of discussion. Thus, a systematic method for accumulating this information as a knowledge base can assist participants.[10] The system introduced in this paper classifies verbal statements by the objects and the respective participants.

In the examination of *content-level utterances*, two rules are utilized to determine agenda changes from one issue to another during discussions. One rule is the appearance of keywords which change the subject. The other rule refers to verbal statements about the next discussion object. Such verbal statements are referred to as the *"key utterances"*. It is possible to classify verbal statements by objects through the verbal statements made. To do so, the system employs three databases; "Objects database", "Key utterances database" and "verbal statements database".

According to the key utterances, the system allocates content-level utterances to the appropriate databases. If the participants request the system to show verbal statements on a particular object, then it shows them by using the objects database. For example, consider the next situation: At some point at the meeting, one participant forgets or does not understand a particular object which is already been discussed. That person subsequently, interrupts the meeting to discuss the object again. In such a situation, the system would prove effective in providing information.

4.2 Outline

The method is outlined below;

(1) Input Process

Step 1. System receives a new verbal statement.

Step 2. Next, system assesses whether the verbal statement is a *key utterance*.

Step 3. If assessed as a *key utterance* then the system allocates the statement to the key utterances database. Return to Step 1.

(2) Output Process

Step 1. User inputs an object about which information is desired.

Step 2. System searches all *key utterance* concerning the object.

Step 3. System then outputs all related verbal statements.

4.3 Rules and Databases

An outline of the rules and databases is listed below;

Rules

Rule 1: Search for the appearance of keywords which change the object.

Rule 2: Search for a verbal statement about the next object.

Databases
Object database   : Information on the objects
Key utterance database : Information on key-utterances
Utterances database   : Verbal statements list

4.4 An example

Suppose, there is a verbal statement as follows;

'Next, shall we change the subject to number two?'
(In Japanese, (次は２番いきましょうか (tsugi wa ni bann ikima shouka ?)))

First, the system takes the verbal statement and classifies it.

In this case, the verbal statement is determined to be a *key utterance* by Rule 1 because it contains a keyword ('Next'). This verbal statement also has a keyword which suggests the next object ('number two'). Subsequently, this verbal statement is determined to be change agent by the application of Rule 2.

In the next step, the system writes this statement to the *key utterances* database.

5. METHOD EVALUATION

Twenty-one business executives were asked to evaluate the the performance of this system by replying to a questionnaire,. In the questionnaire, the executives scored each verbal statements by five grades. Grade 1 indicates a verbal statement on the progress of the meeting, conversely, Grade 5 indicates objects.

Comparing the verbal statements which were recognized as meta-utterances by the system with the grades of respondents (shown in Table 1) the meta-utterances indicated by the executives concurred with those judged by the system. In addition, most of the verbal statements which were regarded as meta-utterances were also picked up by the system (Table 2).

Table 1
Comparison between System and executives(1)

System	Executives<avg.(std.)>
Meta	1.10(0.36)
Quasi-meta	1.90(1.90)

Table 2
Comparison between System and executives(2)

criteria	exectives	System
1.5	11	8
1.3	9	7

To further evaluate the content database of this system, eight students of Keio University viewed the video of the meeting and listed the key utterances. This list was compared with the results of the system key utterances database (results shown in Table 3).

In this experiment, the system has successfully listed information about the objects of the meeting which provides a valuable knowledge base. The result have also shown that the system is effective in determining points of change from one issue to another as the meeting has progressed.

Table 3
Comparison between System and students

	Success rate
Success	83.3 %
Failure	16.7 %

6.CONCLUSION

This paper has established that it is possible to trace the context of communication in meetings by the application of a simplified method. Moreover, it is confirmed that a communication support system can be constructed which improves interpersonal communications without complex methods.

7.REFERENCES

1. Y. Kanda, Trends of Collaboration Technology,. Journal of Electronics, Information, and Communication. Vol.73, No. 9 , pp. 968-970 (1990). (in Japanese).
2. K. Watabe, et al., Distributed multiparty desktop conferencing system: MERMAID, Proc. of 3rd Conf. on CSCW. ACM, pp. 27-38 (1990).
3. S. Lee and K. Sara, Computers, Networks and Work, Scientific American, September (1991).
4. H. Takagi, Information system as social system, Proc. of 1st Conf of Japan Association for Management Informatics, pp. 45-46 (1990). (in Japanese)
5. H. Takagi and J. Ogawa, Double-bind situation in business organization, Journal of Keio Management Association, Vol.9, No.1, pp. 45-56 (1991). (in Japanese)
6. H. Yanagihara, Creative OD: Vol.1. Behavioral Science Application Group (1982). (in Japanese)
7. M. Nagata, H. Takagi and K. Takeuchi, A system to trace communication context, Journal of Japan Association for Management Informatics, Vol.1, No.1, pp. 39-44 (1991). (in Japanese)
8. K. Takeuchi H. Takagi and M. Nagata, Computer Supported Meta-Communication Analyses of Meeting, The Research Paper Series, No.12, Keio Management Society (1992).
9. K. Takeuchi, H. Takagi, M. Nagata and T. Uetake, A meeting support system based on analyses of human-communication (1). Proceedings of The 45th Information Processing Society of Japan, Vol.6, pp. 251-252 (1992). (in Japanese)
10. T. Uetake, M. Nagata, K. Takeuchi and H. Takagi, A meeting support system based on analyses of human-communication (2), Proceedings of The 45th Information Processing Society of Japan, Vol.6, pp. 253-254 (1992). (in Japanese)

Doing by understanding: embedded systems for understanding coordinated work

Timo Käkölä

Department of Computer Science and Information Systems, University of Turku, FIN-20520 Turku, Finland

Abstract

Organizations are adopting new structural forms and ways of working to cope with rapid changes in their environment. This creates increasing pressures on actors' competence. On the basis of a theoretical framework called Humanistic Perspective, we argue that the actors must understand work as a whole, including computerized tasks, if they are to manage complex work situations. Based on our experiences with a prototype system we claim that this is not possible until radical changes are made in the structure as well as the components of software systems. Specifically, we claim that applications should be embedded in extended support systems making organization of work, task coordination and the coordinating role of information systems explicit. As a step towards this goal we propose Role Interaction Nets as (1) the structural basis of embedded systems and (2) the new metaphor for human-computer interface design.

1. INTRODUCTION

Organizations are gradually adopting structural innovations such as autonomous teams and networks to cope with external and internal pressures such as changing market requirements and rising overhead costs. As a result, work is becoming increasingly dependent on complex social interactions among multiple actors within and between organizations. These interactions must be coordinated to facilitate smooth activity of interdependent actors. Computer-based information systems (CBIS) are crucial as means of managing these coordination processes.

However, many issues must be resolved before CBIS can be fully utilized. According to Humanistic Perspective [1] the most important one is how to ensure that the actors are able to be in control of and responsible for their work as a whole. This requires that the actors must understand (a) their work as a part of a larger context as well as (b) the computer-supported parts of work. We argue that without this knowledge managing complex work situations is practically impossible.

For instance, Orlikowski [13] states that one reason for the usability problems of Notes is that the actors see Notes as a tool supporting only individual work. But why do they regard a tool specifically designed for coordinating work as a tool for individual use? According to our interpretation there are two underlying reasons for this misconception: the tool does not make explicit (1) the work context and (2) its coordinating role in this context. These reasons are even more obvious in traditional integrated systems making the computer-mediated communication and coordination invisible [2].

Some systems do provide a work context. For instance, group editors use various techniques to show each actor what the other actors are doing when editing synchronously a shared document [11]. However, these techniques are too application specific to be able to account for work as a whole. Therefore, generalizing them to be used in other types of information systems is difficult.

Support systems have been proposed as means of improving actors' understanding of the function of the CBIS [9]. However, they treat computerized tasks separately from other organizational activities, and therefore do not support the actors in learning how these tasks affect and are connected to the work as a whole [3]. Therefore these systems are necessary but far from adequate from our point of view.

Based on a theoretical framework and experiences with a prototype system, we claim in this paper that being a responsible actor is not possible until radical changes are made in the structure as well as the components of software systems. Specifically, we argue that applications should be embedded in extended support systems making organization of work, task coordination and the coordinating role of information systems explicit. As a step towards this goal we propose Role Interaction Nets [5] as (1) the structural basis of embedded systems and (2) the new metaphor for human-computer interface design.

2. ACT ORIENTATION AND EMBEDDED SYSTEMS

2.1. Act orientation: computerized tasks as human acts

Implementation of structural and process innovations required by the new organizational forms poses new requirements on actors' competence. The actors have to understand all aspects of their work. Especially important is that they gain a holistic view of the organization and their role in it. However, the actors rarely understand the functions and transactions performed by means of CBIS and the role of a CBIS as a mediator of communication and collaboration [2]. They perceive a CBIS as a black box. As a result, gaining deep understanding of the content and coordination of work is jeopardized.

Nurminen [1] presents a theoretical frame of reference called Humanistic Perspective to help to resolve these problems. He states that information cannot be separated from its use in a work situation. Rather, the actors must be made visible by interpreting all computerized tasks as human acts. As a result, there are one or more actors responsible for every computerized task and piece of information. We call this interpretation *act orientation*.

However, it is impractical for actors to be responsible for computerized tasks, which they don't understand and cannot control. Furthermore, managing exceptional, erroneous and new situations is difficult in this situation. Finally, user driven application development is practically impossible without actors' deep understanding of the content and organization of work [12].

2.2. Implications of act orientation on software systems

Based on both act orientation and our experiences in developing a prototype support system called XTEND [4] we argue that significant changes need to be done in the components of software systems and their relations. The components are (1) applications performing the production function; (2) support systems assisting actors in understanding the function of applications; and (3) human-computer interfaces [6]. These components and their underlying structure must be in line with those of the work system, if information systems are to be useful. Therefore, our approach extends the content and meaning of support systems by focusing not only on applications but on information and work systems as a united whole. It also redefines the relationship between applications and support systems by embedding applications in the support systems. Finally our approach calls for a new metaphor for guiding human-computer interface design.

2.2.1. The XTENDed support system

Actors need an overview of the organization and its task coordination. Coordination is often handled by documents, e.g. Order-Invoice. Information for these documents is at least partly fetched from databases. For these reasons, the support system should present the departments and units of the organization, different roles of actors, tasks and sub-tasks belonging to these roles, documents, and databases. Availability of such knowledge is the basis for reconstructing the missing link between CBIS and work systems.

The XTEND system partly provides this knowledge. To support task coordination it describes jobs and tasks on different levels of detail. A kind of task lattice [7] is established. This description provides the main control structure of the support system. Connections are made visible by zooming-in and zooming-out for vertical connections and by a network structure for horizontal connections. The connections and transaction flows between different departments are described on the overview level. The actors may look at the detailed task performance on the department level and carry out transactions which don't belong to their own responsibility areas to understand their fellow workers' jobs. The control structure is implemented as a hypermedia system.

To support work performance XTEND offers the actors opportunities to experiment by navigating forward in the task lattice, using a database identical to the one in use but not live and searching the database in an ad-hoc fashion. Starting from a problem situation the actors may take one step at a time, look at the database to see what happens, and go further if the response is what they wanted. If the action proves incorrect the actor can try another move and no errors are caused in the database of the application system. Experimentation is a way of learning new and calling to mind forgotten sub-tasks.

2.2.2. Embedded systems

Typically support and application systems are separate from each other: an actor invokes the support system from the application, finds out for example how to perform a certain function and then returns to execute it. This applies to XTEND as well. However, our experiences prove that this approach is inadequate. For instance, the XTEND support system has all the functionality of the application but it also has additional functions described in the previous section. Having two parallel systems is not feasible in practise, since every change to one system must be propagated to the other. Moreover, the parallel systems increase the complexity of the software and the actors can even get lost while navigating between them.

The logical solution is to integrate these systems. The first step toward this goal is to replace the subsystem of the support system corresponding to the application with the application itself. This implies a radical shift in the relationship between applications and support systems: the application is embedded into the support system. We call these integrated systems *embedded systems*.

2.2.3. The new metaphor for human-computer interface design

Embedded systems bring about a dilemma: how can all the knowledge about work and information systems be represented without making the embedded systems so complex that they become completely unusable. One solution is to apply hypermedia, since it provides a powerful knowledge representation structure for constructing human-computer interfaces [8]. However, it is too generic alone to guide interface design. We also need a new metaphor with much wider level of description than, for instance, the desktop metaphor has. Folders or waste baskets on the screen are not enough anymore. Yet, the metaphor must be based on intuitive concepts to make the interfaces mutually understandable to the actors.

Organizational role theory provides such a metaphor. The theory states that actors occupy roles in organizations. Each role is associated with a set of tasks that define the role player's expected behaviour. Roles interact when task coordination between them is required to perform tasks (e.g., a role transfers responsibility for materials or documents to another role). Organizational structure simultaneously defines and is created by roles and their interactions.

In the next Section we present the Role Interaction Net Language that uses roles and interactions as the primitives for visualizing both structural and process aspects of organizations. These visualizations can serve as the new metaphor as well as the structural basis of embedded systems.

3. THE ROLE INTERACTION NETS AS THE BASIS OF EMBEDDED SYSTEMS

Our framework poses several requirements on embedded systems. In this Section we present the Role Interaction Net (RIN) Language [5] as a way of meeting these requirements. First we explain what the RIN Language is and then we illustrate its use with the help of an example.

3.1. The RIN Language

The language is based on organizational role theory and Petri nets. In accordance with the theory, the language provides two primitives: *roles* and *interactions*. A RIN is composed of a set of concurrent roles. The behaviour of a role is described by its interactions with itself (i.e., solitary actions) and with other roles. Techniques from Petri nets are utilized to give the language the process description capability.

The language has several properties that make it highly amenable to embedded systems. (1) It can be used to describe any kind of work and information system. (2) Consistent with act orientation, it can be used to associate both human and computerized tasks with a role. As a result, it is able to describe *consistently* coordination between organizations, teams, and individual actors in different roles even when coordination is mediated by computerized tasks (i.e., software modules) and shared databases. Consistency helps in making the description mutually understandable. (3) With the help of a macro construct it allows formal and detailed as well as informal and abstract descriptions for computerized tasks and manual tasks respectively. Therefore the language in no way forces the actors to behave in a rigid and bureaucratic manner.

3.2. Using the RIN Language as a basis of embedded systems: an example

The RIN description of an organization should be developed during an organization design process jointly by OD experts and actors [5]. In addition, systems analysts would describe computerized tasks and ensure that the applications performing these tasks can be enacted from the RIN. Various views of this RIN would then be used in organizational domains to construct the human-computer interfaces. In the example we use a view defined as the set of roles and interactions that all actors in an organizational domain share and the set of roles in other domains that interact with the roles in this domain directly. We call this view a domain RIN. Each actor in the domain can use this RIN to enact the needed applications.

Figure 1 shows the domain RIN that creates the human-computer interface for the part of the inventory application that workers in a bulk inventory would use. The RIN shows that each worker can take two roles. In the first one she receives material pallets and information on each pallet from a packer in a packing unit. Then she uses the inventory application to determine shelf positions for the pallets. Finally she stores the pallets to the positions. In the second role a bulk worker receives a delivery order from a worker in the buffer unit. Then she uses the application to find out which pallets are needed for the delivery and where they are located. Finally she fetches the pallets and delivers them to the buffer.

The domain RIN visualizes direct material or document related coordination in concurrent interactions between the roles. Information is always connected to the organizational tasks where it is used to show the indirect coordination mediated by shared databases. For this reason the Bulk_Database role is introduced to illustrate the coordination aspect of the shelf position information between the roles of bulk workers. The role is a logical view of the database and only concerned with this domain. Different views of the same database can be used in different domains.

Each bulk worker would use this RIN to perform the proper application function depending on her role by double clicking one of the macro squares labelled "Determine..." with a mouse. She could also enter into the support mode and experiment with the application. For instance, by double clicking a macro square a more detailed RIN would appear showing both the dialogue and computerized tasks implementing the application interface and function respectively. She could execute these tasks one by one and check the results by looking at the database as discussed in Sub-section 2.2.1. If everything was all right, she would commit the changes to the database. As a result, the actors would have the opportunity to take responsibility of their work.

The domain RIN would also facilitate learning and preventing coordination breakdown situations within and between domains. For example, in the support mode a bulk worker could take the buffer workers' role simply by double-clicking the 'Buffer_man' role description. A domain RIN of the buffer unit would appear. Now she could see what happens in this domain if she makes an error in using the information system in her own role and a buffer man receives wrong pallets or information. Understanding the coordinated nature of work helps actors redesign their work and eliminate many breakdown situations.

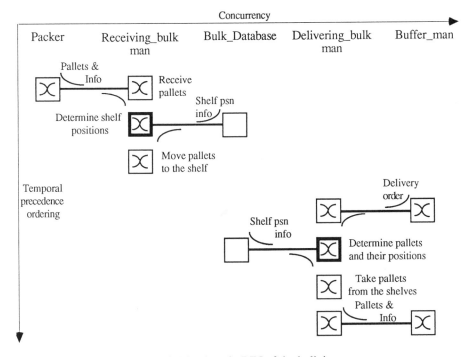

Figure 1. The domain RIN of the bulk inventory

4. DISCUSSION AND CONCLUSIONS

In this paper we have claimed that the actors must understand all aspects of their work and that embedded systems provide this understanding. Still, many issues of both technical and organizational natures emerge and need to be resolved when these systems are implemented.

Embedded systems call for explicit integration of organization and information systems design: computer applications are seen in the human-computer interfaces as means of performing computerized tasks belonging to human actors in the roles determined by the organization structure. This means that changes in the work and information systems must immediately be reflected in the interfaces. Therefore implementing and maintaining embedded systems may seem a laborious and expensive effort.

Yet, there are many factors that help make our approach feasible. (1) Organizations have to be able and willing to continuously redesign their businesses if they are to excel in the competition. Redesigning is practically impossible if they don't maintain precise knowledge of their structures, processes and systems. The RIN Language facilitates creating and maintaining this knowledge [5]. (2) When the actors understand work and information systems as a whole they are able to redesign their work and the corresponding RIN descriptions. Moreover, they can also actively participate in the systems development process [12]. Consequently the pressures on organization designers and systems analysts are reduced. (3) Technical developments in such areas as hypermedia, group editors and CASE tools support the participative development of embedded systems.

Another important but often neglected issue of organizational nature arises. When workers understand and are competent in their jobs they are likely to say: "What's next? We master our jobs and now we could take more responsibilities". Management may consider this situation threatening and take defensive actions. On the other hand, the workers may see embedded systems as new management control and rationalization tools, because these systems visualize what everyone is expected to do. The point is that embedded systems are likely to be unsuccessful if they are perceived as threatening by some influential groups. However, this doesn't imply that we should stop developing these systems. Argyris [10] shows that organizations can and have to overcome their defensive routines by changing their norms and rules, if they want to do better than the mediocrities. Once this behavioural change is taking place embedded systems can be beneficial in supporting this process.

We are currently redesigning the XTEND prototype to validate our ideas and inspire commercial implementations. It is too early yet to say whether embedded systems are adequate alone to provide such a level of understanding that the actors can take responsibility of their work. Nevertheless, we are confident that well-coordinated work combined with improved use of CBIS can bring about substantial benefits to those organizations that adopt these systems.

5. REFERENCES

1. Nurminen M. I., 1988, People or Computers: three ways of looking at information systems, Studentlitteratur & Chartwell-Blatt, Lund, Sweden.
2. Eriksson I., Hellman R., Nurminen M. I., 1988, A Method for Supporting Users' Comprehensive Learning, EDUCATION & COMPUTING, Vol. 4, No. 4, pp. 251-264.
3. Eriksson I., Nurminen M. I., 1991, Doing by Learning: Embedded Application Systems, Journal of Organizational Computing, Vol. 1, No. 4, pp. 323-339.
4. Eriksson I., Käkölä T., 1992, A Support System for Systems Use, a manuscript submitted to Interacting with Computers.
5. Rein G., 1992, Organization Design Viewed as a Group Process Using Coordination Technology, Unpublished PhD dissertation, MCC Technical Report, Austin, Texas.
6. Lutze R., 1987, Customizing help systems to task structures and user needs. Human-Computer Interaction - INTERACT ´87, pp. 871-878, Amsterdam: Elsevier Science.
7. Gasser L., 1986, The integration of computing and routine work, ACM Transactions of Office Information Systems, Vol. 4, No. 3, pp. 205-225.
8. Conklin J., 1987, Hypertext: An Introduction and Survey, IEEE Computer, Vol. 20, No. 9, pp. 17-41.
9. Canter D., Rivers R., Storrs G., 1985, Characterizing User Navigation Through Complex Data Structures, Behaviour and Information Technology, 4, pp. 93-102.
10. Argyris C., 1990, Overcoming Organizational Defenses: Facilitating Organizational Learning, Allyn and Bacon, Boston.
11. Ellis C.A., Gibbs S.J., Rein G.L., 1991, Groupware: Some Issues and Experiences, Communications of the ACM, Vol. 34, No. 1, pp. 39-58.
12. Hellman R., 1989, User Support: Revealing Structure Instead of Surface, Behaviour & Information Technology, Vol. 8, No. 6, pp. 417-435.
13. Orlikowski W., 1992, Learning from Notes: Organizational Issues in Groupware Implementation, CSCW '92 Proceedings, pp. 362-369, ACM.

Computer simulation model of cognitive process in group works

K. Furuta and S. Kondo

Department of Quantum Engineering and Systems Science,
The University of Tokyo, Hongo, Bunkyo-ku, Tokyo 113, Japan

Abstract
In this paper, a computer simulation model of cognitive process in group works is proposed, and the simulation system based on the model is presented. In order to simulate parallel and cooperative activities by many agents, the system has separate sets of knowledge base and blackboard for individual agents, and they can exchange messages through the communication channel. This system was tested using the result of communication network experiment by Leavitt, and then applied to operation of a nuclear power plant.

1. INTRODUCTION

Since modern technological systems are usually operated and maintained by groups of humans, group as well as individual factors should be considered in discussing the reliability and safety of such systems. The methodology, however, to analyze and assess human behavior as a group has not yet been established enough.

We have developed a method to assess group reliability by numerical simulation using an information processing network representing a human group [1]. In this method, information and human decision are respectively represented as information worth and binary correct or wrong decision, and the approach was useful to reveal general characteristics of group performance. It is, however, difficult to apply this method to specific cases, because the meaning of each information and knowledge is not considered, and because the model parameters can hardly be evaluated from empirical studies.

On the other hand, we have tried modeling cognitive behavior of a process plant operator using AI (Artificial Intelligence) technologies to assess man–machine systems by computer simulation. This study showed that deterministic simulation of human information processing with considering the specific meaning of information and knowledge is useful for the analysis of human error mechanism and workload assessment [2], but group performance was not considered before.

This paper presents an AI-based simulation model of human behavior including group process. The model will be useful not only for analyzing specific cases of group works in mission–oriented situations but also for evaluating model parameters from empirical data for group reliability analysis.

2. COGNITIVE MODEL

In this study, a human group is modeled as a network of multiple agents who are deciding and behaving based on the information obtained from the environment and other agents as well as their own knowledge. Each agent is represented as an information processor, which consists of sensory subsystem, working memory, long term memory, motor subsystem and attention mechanism. The Rasmussen's decision ladder is adopted as the basis of cognitive process model, but the knowledge–based analysis and the knowledge–based planning processes are not included in the present model.

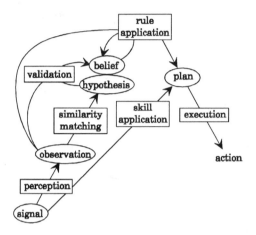

Figure 1. Cognitive model of an agent.

The cognitive process model used is illustrated in Figure 1, where information is classified into five types: signal, observation, hypothesis, belief and plan. Visual and auditory signals are separately processed, but those from the environment and other agents are not distinguished. The human information processor is assumed to process these kinds of information by the cognitive tasks as follows:

Perception: It is the process to generate observations in the working memory from the signals appeared in the sensory subsystem by giving them qualitative or conceptual meaning. Fuzzy sets are used to interpret the signals representing quantitative information.

Similarity matching: Hypotheses on the current state of the world are proposed by similarity matching, where observations are matched with the symptomatic patterns stored in the long term memory, and the cases similar enough to the present observations are retrieved as hypotheses.

Validation: If the similarity exceeds the critical value, hypothesis is changed into belief. Otherwise, hypotheses are to be validated by checking unobserved symptoms.

Rule application: Rules stored in the long term memory are applied to the current observations and beliefs. As a result of rule application, new beliefs or action plans are generated in the working memory. An action plan, here, is a sequence of procedures to be executed by the agent.

Skill application: Skill means direct association from some sensory signal to the related action plan in this model. If any skill is applied to input signals, the action plan is generated.

Execution: The action plans present in the working memory are executed.

Confirmation: It will be tried to confirm beliefs which are observable but not yet confirmed by invoking sensory action.

The agents can exchange messages with each other, and messages are sent either to specified or unspecified listeners. The communication is used for information transfer, query and answer, or instruction. It is possible to ask others to carry out planned actions. In the present model, whether one executes the action by oneself or asks others its execution is determined by the predefined role system, which is given as knowledge in the long term memory.

3. SIMULATION SYSTEM

A computer simulation system has been developed based on the cognitive model explained in the previous section. It is a knowledge–based system based on the blackboard model as shown in Figure 2. The system has multiple sets of blackboard and knowledge base, each set of which corresponds to an individual agent, while the inference engines are shared by every agent. The control system executes the blackboard control cycle of every blackboard one by one. Task execution for different blackboards, however, does not always synchronized, because the number of cycles required for task execution depends on task type. This architecture enables to simulate parallel but cooperative behavior by multiple agents.

The attention mechanism in the human information processor is modeled by the blackboard controller, which makes the list of executable cognitive tasks and allocates computation time to the task of the highest priority. This process is repeated over the agents.

The simulation system has been built on a UNIX workstation in Prolog, and it can be coupled with other simulation programs such as plant simulator. The result of simulation can be shown in a graphical form similar to the communication flow and action flow diagrams in TADEM (Team Activity Description Method), which has been proposed by Sasou, et al. [3] as a method to describe and evaluate team activities in experiments.

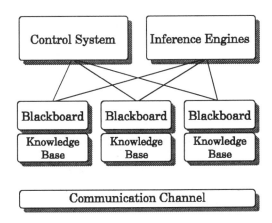

Figure 2. Architecture of the simulation system.

3. CASE STUDY

3.1. Communication network experiment

For the purpose of model validation, the classical experiment of communication network by Leavitt [4] was analyzed with the simulation system. In this experiment, subject groups of five members were requested to find out the information commonly possessed by the all members, which is one out of five symbols marked on a sheet of paper. The subjects were allowed to exchange messages by passing memos, but the communication pattern was restricted by the experimenter. The four communication patters shown in Figure 3 were used: circle, chain, Y and wheel. The group performance was compared between these patterns.

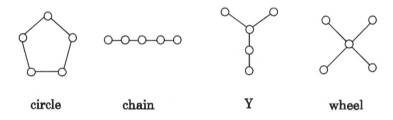

circle   chain   Y   wheel

Figure 3. Communication patterns used in the experiment by Leavitt.

In this experiment, the problem is well defined and the knowledge necessary to solve it is relatively clear. The subjects are thought to have used the common sense knowledge as below to solve the problem:

(1) The information given by the experimenter should be transferred to every accessible member.
(2) The information given by another member should be transferred to the other accessible members.
(3) If the common symbol is known, it should be answered immediately and informed to every accessible member.
(4) New information other than the answer can be used to narrow the candidates of common symbol.

The above knowledge was written in rules and given to the simulation system. If one has many neighbors to communicate, the order of communication was decided at random. The numerical results shown below, therefore, were obtained by averaging 20 trials for the same communication pattern.

In Figure 4 the numbers of sent messages are compared between the experiment and the simulation. The result is shown for each position in the communication patterns as well as for the total of each pattern. The result of simulation well agrees with the experiment (r=0.97 for totals, and r=0.95 for positions). The number of blackboard cycles and the time required to solve the problem are well correlated; it is also the case with the number of cognitive tasks executed and the number of errors observed.

The wheel and the Y apparently showed the communication pattern that information was collected toward the central position and the solution was distributed in the opposite direction. The circle showed varieties of communication patterns, none of which were dominant, and the chain was between the both extreme cases. Such characteristics of communication patterns were common to the experiment and the simulation. These results show that the simulation model described in this paper is appropriate to predict the group performance in Leavitt's experiment.

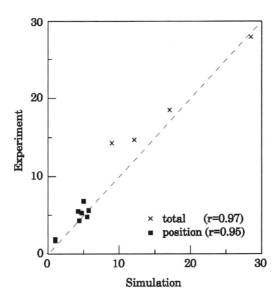

Figure 4. Number of messages sent in the experiment by Leavitt and its simulation.

3.2. Operation of nuclear power plant

The second case is more complex and realistic than the previous one: operation of a nuclear power plant under abnormal plant condition. In this case, the simulation system was coupled with a BWR type nuclear power plant simulator, and comprehensive simulation of both man and machine systems was carried out. It was assumed four operators make an operator crew: chief operator, reactor operator, auxiliary system operator, and turbine operator. The abnormal event used was the multiple losses of feedwater to the reactor vessel and initiation signal of the HPCS (High Pressure Core Spray), which is expected to start automatically in emergency to maintain the water inventory.

In the simulation, three crews were assumed which differ in the distribution of knowledge necessary to deal with the abnormal event. The chief operator of crew 1 has almost all of the relevant knowledge exclusively, while that of crew 2 has just the knowledge for critical judgements. Every member of crew 3 has the knowledge necessary to monitor and operate the equipments in his/her own charge.

While all of the three crews could properly deal with the anomaly, the difference of knowledge distribution resulted in that of group behavior. Figure 5-(a) and (b) compare the number of judgmental tasks and the number of messages exchanged between the crew members. The chief of crew 1 showed strong leadership and the other operators just followed

984

the instruction of the chief. On contrary, the operators in crew 3 behaved autonomously and the chief just diagnosed the event and overlooked the work of his/her crew. Such difference in group behavior has been reported also in simulator experiments with subjects. Though the difference is not necessarily attributed to the difference in knowledge distribution, the simulation model will be able to take other causes also into account by changing knowledge utilization strategy.

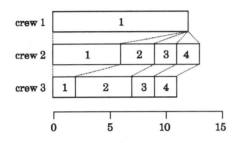
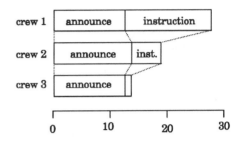

(a) Number of judgmental tasks.　　　　(b) Number of messages exchanged.

Figure 5. Comparison of group behavior between the three operator crews.

4. CONCLUSION

A simulation model of cognitive process in group works has been proposed based on the well-known concept of human as an information processor, and a simulation system has been developed on the model. The system is a knowledge-based system with multiple sets of blackboard and knowledge base, and this architecture was effective to model parallel and cooperative activities by many agents.

The system was first tested using the communication network experiment by Leavitt, and the result of simulation agreed well with the experimental result. It was hence shown that the simulation model was appropriate for well defined problems such as the case used. Test simulation was also performed for operation of a nuclear power plant, and it was able to analyze the influence of knowledge distribution on group behavior.

Validation of the model under complex and realistic situations is still to be continued, and the model does not consider social factors such as social cognition and normative influence. The prospects, however, have been obtained that group works can be analyzed based on cognitive models by computer simulation.

REFERENCES

1. K. Furuta and S. Kondo, Reliability Engineering and System Safety, 35 (1992) 159.
2. K. Furuta and S. Kondo, Int. J. Man-Machine Studies (to appear).
3. K. Sasou, et al., Ningen-kogaku, 26 (1990) 251 (Japanese).
4. H.J. Leavitt, J. Abnormal and Social Psychology, 46 (1951) 38.

Negotiability: A Metafunction to Support Personalizable Groupware

V. Wulf [1]

University of Bonn, Institute for Computer Science III, Römerstraße 164, 5300 Bonn 1, Germany

Abstract
Negotiability is a supplementary design requirement for groupware, which allows participative activation of functions. It should be applied to global functions, whose usage and modification affect several users. The concept of negotiability will be elaborated and applied to the design of computer integrated telephony.

1. Introduction

The discussion on software-ergonomics, up to now, was mainly concerned with human-centred design of single user applications. Resulting design requirements have become subject of international standardization [1]. Contrary to single user applications, groupware supports computer mediated communication and coope-ration of different users connected by the system. As the field of computers´ appli-cation has widened, the software-ergonomical design requirements have to be supplemented, too. Negotiability is an additional design requirement to handle par-ticipative adaptation of groupware. As a metafunction this feature can be added to a variety of different functions.

Adaptation to changing requirements of different users will be a permanent pro-cess which is caused by the facts that:
- users can be in changing roles (e. g. sender vs. recipient)
- different tasks can be supported by the same system
- tasks are changing during the time of use
- users can be in different contexts of use (e. g. disturbed by other events vs. concentrated on the computer mediated task)
- different users with different personal preferences and styles are connected by the system
- users have different skills in handling the system

---

[1] I would like to thank Anja Hartmann, Thomas Herrmann, and Markus Rohde for intensive discussions on the issues addressed in this paper. This research work has been supported by the German Ministry of Research and Technology within its research program "Labour and Technology" under the grant No. 01 HK 6880.

These changing requirements make it necessary that groupware can be used and modified flexibly. Assuming that individual users have different interests, usage and modification of groupware can become a matter of difficult negotiations between them [2].

To clarify the role negotiability can play in supporting these processes, we will discuss the case of computer integrated telephony. The linkage between telephone and computer systems offers new functions to end users. Functions of the telephone can be controlled via the computer. Data transmitted from the telephone can be stored and evaluated by computer applications. Moreover computer integrated telephony supports synchronous presentation and manipulation of data concerning the interlocutor of a call. Computer integrated telephony belongs to groupware because it is a mean of technically supported communication between caller and recipient. Furthermore, it can support cooperation within a group of users if synchronously presented data are shared by the group.

2. Usage and Modification of Global Functions

Greenberg defines *personalizable groupware* as a groupware whose behaviour can be modified to match the particular needs of group participants (i.e. each member of the group may observe a different behaviour) and the particular needs of the group as a whole (i. e. each group may observe a different collective behaviour) [3].

This definition assumes that groupware has certain functions which should be modified according to the needs of single users. We call these functions *local functions*. Other functions affect a group of users considerably and should be used and accustomized according to their collective needs. These functions will be called *global functions*.

Different ways of personalization of groupware can be classified according to the software-technical complexity of the intended modification and to the degree end users participate in this activity. Concerning the software-technical complexity Henderson/Kyng distinguish three levels of activity [4]:
- choosing between alternative anticipated behaviours,
- constructing new behaviours from existing pieces,
- altering the artifact.

The software-technical complexity influences the division of labor among end users, privileged users (e. g. system administration or group facilitator), and programmers in the process of modification.

In several applications of groupware these modifications are only carried out by priviledged users or programmers [5, 6]. This strategy seems to be adequate either for modification of higher software-technical complexity or in case where end users´ participation is not required.

On the other hand there are systems which allow end users to modify groupware by themselves. These modifications are of lower software-technical complexity. In the Information Lens system, an information manager for mail and news, end users can construct their semistructured templates representing particular types of mail and they can create their own rules to filter incoming mail [7]. Whithin the RAVE system, a computer controlled audio-video network, users can explicitly allow or forbid other users to connect one-way video channels to their offices [8].

Both of these implementations allow single end users to personalize the system according to their needs. As other end-users who might be concerned by this (e.g.

senders of a filtered message) do not have the chance to intervene and to articulate their interests, these functions are implemented as local groupware functions.

Contrary to local functions, personalization of global functions needs the participation of all end users affected. Therefore, in the case of distributed or asynchronous use of groupware, negotiability as a supplementary metafunction should be provided. Concerning different types of modification the application of negotiability should be restricted to those of low software-technical complexity. In this case the difference between modification and usage is rather blurred [4]. Controllability, a design requirement for the usage of single user applications, calls for the existence of functional alternatives, as well [1]. Thus, irrespective of this distinction negotiability should be applied if there are alternative options of anticipated behaviour of global functions.

For instance the SHARE system, a shared window system, offers five different strategies of floor control [3]. In this case negotiability would supply the users with a mechanism to choose the appropriated functional alternative participatively.

Evaluating the CCITT's X.400 standard for message handling systems, Hoeller has proposed to add a mechanism, similar to negotiability, to certain functions [9]. Concerning ISDN telephone systems Hammer/Pordesch/Roßnagel have suggested a similar mechanism which they call "handshaking" [10].

Furthermore, negotiability can be applied to manipulate data whose consistency is controlled participatively. Narayanswamy/Goldman have proposed the concept of lazy consistency. Comparable to negotiability, it contains a mechanism for consistency controll of source code in a collaborative software development environment [11].

3. The Concept of Negotiability

Apart from the activator, global functions affect other end users, as well. Concerning the activation of global functions different users might have diverging or even conflicting interests [2, 9]. These conflicts may occure concerning the choice of alternative options of a function. To find a consentaneous solution of these conflicts we propose negotiability as a metafunction.

Negotiability provides an additional channel of communication within the groupware application. This channel is just built up in the moment when potential conflicts might occur, and abandoned after they are solved. As potential conflicts deal with the choice between a limited number of well defined options, we assume that the process of negotiating a consentaneous solution can be technically supported to a much wider degree than conversations on subjects where the possible options are less structured [12].

Figure 1 gives a survey on the concept of negotiability. The activator A proposes an option X out of the set of alternative options implemented in the system. The affected user B can either agree, disagree or counter-propose another alternative. If he agrees on the proposed option the function is activated in the way the activator intended it. If B disagrees, the process of negotiation is terminated and the system will take a default status. This default option should be carefully chosen that in case of disagreement none of the users´ fundamental rights is violated.

Furthermore B can counter-propose an alternative option of the function. This will be indicated to A who has the same possibilities to act as B had before. After a certain amount of loops or time, this process of negotiation will stop with either a final agreement or disagreement.

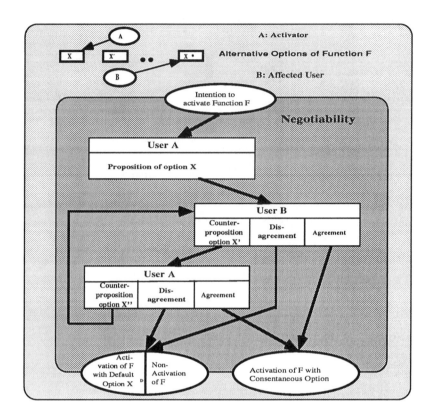

Figure 1: Process of technically supported negotiation

Figure 1 presents the process of negotiation in a very structured manner. It can therefore be easily transformed into a state transition network which is the base for the implementation of the Coordinator [13]. Therefore, the process of negotiations can be divided into single acts.

Structured negotiability means that each act consists of a message just indicating its type and the selected option. It can be easily input by pushing a button either on the screen or on the keyboard. After receiving this message the system will offer to affected users the possibility to answer by clicking another button. Structured negotiability is very time efficient as the single acts are quickly performed. On the other hand there are not any possibilities to explain requests or decisions to each other.

In cases where these informations are considered to be important for such a process *semi-structured negotiability* should be applied. Like before each negotiation act contains its typ and the selected option. But additionally the users have the chance to explain their action via an unstructured field. In a telephone application such a field could consist of a one way voice channel. In e-mail it could be unstructured text which would be added to the message.

4. Applying Negotiability to Computer Integrated Telephony

Applying to negotiability to computer integrated telephony, we will discuss the following functions more in detail:
- initialization of a phone call by automatical dialing from computer's electronic address book,
- storage of inbound phone calls and attempted calls if the interlocator can be identified automatically by features of the ISDN,
- modification of shared data within a group of telephonists, on which are worked during external phone calls.

In the applications which can be found on the German market, all of these functions are treated as local functions. Considering the first function, this approach seems to be adequate because other users are only affected by faster dialing of their number. In the second case such an implementation threatens privacy because data with personal reference can be stored by the activator. The affected user neither knows about this activation nor can he prohibit the activator from storing his data. In the third case an implementation of these functions depends on the pattern of cooperation within the group. If they cooperate in a way that certain data are used and manipulated by a single member of the group an implementation as local function is appropriate. Otherwise usage and modification of these data should be treated as global functions. Thus, the application of negotiability depends on legal and organizational considerations.

Concerning the storage of inbound calls and call attempts negotiability could be realized in a way that the caller gets an information that his activity will be documented. The default value should secure that only in the case of his agreement the storage can be performed. As this function will be frequently used and there are only two alternative options existing, structured negotiability should be applied.

In the case that a telephonist wants to manipulate shared data during an external phone call, negotiability could store his modifications locally and send a message to the affected user of his group. This telephonist either agrees, disagrees or counterproposes a different modification. The final result would be documented in the shared data base. Storing the modifications first locally allows the application of negotiability even if the telephonists do not work synchronously. The default value in case of disagreement should be selected according to the requirements of the field of application. If the intended modifications require explanation, semi structured negotiability seems to be appropriated.

5. Conclusion

Beyond computer integrated telephony, negotiability should be added to a wide range of groupware systems. The selection of global functions should be configurable according to the requirements in the field of applications.

Applying this metafunction to various global functions of one system, it should be designed as uniformly as possible to ease its use. Compared to a change into a different medium, negotiability can be used more time-efficiently. Moreover, the outcome of the negotiations can be realized automatically within the system.

Nevertheless, the usage of negotiability might replace less formalized communication. This might change the flow of communication in an organization. Furthermore, in the case that the available options are no more sufficient to find consentaneous solutions among the users, the embedment of groupware must offer occasions for less formalized, or face to face negotiations to adapt functions by modifications of higher software-technical complexity.

6. References

[1]   ISO 9241: Ergonomic requirements for office work with visual display terminals (VDTs) Part 10: Dialogue Principles, 1st DIS, February 2, 1993.

[2]   K. Schmidt: Riding a Tiger or Computer Supported Cooperative Work, in: L. Bannon, M. Robinson; K. Schmidt, (eds.): Proceedings of the Second European Conference on Computer Supported Cooperative Work, Amsterdam, 1991, 1 - 16.

[3]   S. Greenberg: Personizable Groupware: Accomodating individual roles and group differences, in: L. Bannon; M. Robinson; K. Schmidt (eds.): Proceedings of the Second European Conference on Computer Supported Cooperative Work, Amsterdam, 1991, 17 - 31.

[4]   A. Henderson; M. Kyng: There´s No Place Like Home: Continueing Design in Use; in: J. Greenbaum; M. Kyng: Design at Work - Cooperative Design of Computer Artifacts, Hillsdale, 1991, 219 - 240.

[5]   P. Johnson-Lenz; T. Johnson-Lenz: Post-mechanistic groupware primitives: rhythms, boundaries and containers, in: Greenberg, Saul (ed.): Computersupported Cooperative Work and Groupware. Part 2. International Journal of Man-Machine-Studies, Vol. 34, Number 3, 1991, 395-478.

[6]   M. Turoff; J. Foster; S. R. Hiltz; N. Kenneth: The TEIES Design and Objectives: Computer Mediated Communications and Tailorability, in: Proceedings of the 22 nd Annual Hawai International Conference on System Sciences IEEE Computer Society, 1989, 403 - 411.

[7]   T. W. Malone; K. R. Grant; K.-Y. Lai; R. Rao; D. Rosenblitt: Semistructured Messages are Surprisingly Useful for Computer-Supported Coordination, in: I. Greif (ed.): CSCW: A Book of Readings, Morgan-Kaufmann Publisher, San Mateo, California, 1988, 311-334.

[8]   W. Gaver; T. Moran; A. MacLean; L. Lövstrand; P. Dourish; K. Carter; W. Buxton: Realizing a Video Environment: Europarc´s Rave System, in: Proceedings of CHI (1992) 27 - 35.

[9]   H. P. Höller: Die Determination der Kommunikationstechnik durch OSI-Normen und ihre Bewertung - dargestellt am Beispiel von Message Handling Systemen, PhD Thesis, Bremen, 1992.

[10] V. Hammer, U. Pordesch, A. Roßnagel: Rechtliche Gestaltungsanforderungen an betriebliche ISDN-Telefonsysteme, Berlin Heidelberg, Springer, 1993

[11] K. Narayanaswamy; N. Goldman: "Lazy" Consistency: A Basis for Cooperative Software Development. In: CSCW ´92. Sharing Perspectives. Proceedings of the Conference on Computer-Supported Cooperative Work, ACM Press, New York, 1992, 257 - 264.

[12] T. Herrmann: Dispositionsspielräume bei der Kooperation mit Hilfe vernetzter Systeme, in: M. Frese; Chr. Kasten; C. Skarpelis; B. Zang-Scheucher.(Hrsg.): Software für die Arbeit von morgen. Bilanz und Perspektiven anwendungsorientierter Forschung. Berlin et. al., 1991, 57 - 68.

[13] T. Winograd: A Language/Action Perspective on the Design of Cooperative Work, in: I. Greif (ed.): CSCW: A Book of Readings, Morgan-Kaufmann Publisher, San Mateo, California, 1988, 311 - 334.

An Analysis Technique for User Centred Design

John Kirby and Heather A Heathfield

Medical Informatics Group, Department of Computer Science, University of Manchester, Manchester, M13 9PL, United Kingdom.
Tel: +44-61-275-6133. Fax: +44-61-275-6236. INTERNET: jkirby@cs.man.ac.uk

Abstract
It is argued that the general philosophy of user centred design should be focused on the design of *systems* and that such a focus requires the development of a User Centred Systems Design Methodology. One aspect of such a methodology is the analysis of current user practices and some traditional approaches to this activity are considered and found wanting. An alternative approach - Task Oriented Flow Diagrams - is described and an example is given of its use in the PEN&PAD (Elderly Care) clinical workstation project. Some results of using this approach are briefly present.

1. INTRODUCTION

This paper will describe some initial work on the development of an analysis technique for use within a User Centred System Design Methodology (UCSDM). The technique has been used in the PEN&PAD(Elderly Care) project which is developing a prototype integrated clinical workstation for hospital patient record keeping by a number of healthcare professionals (Heathfield et. al., 1992). Work on this hospital system follows on from four years user centred design work with British General Practitioners in the PEN&PAD(GP) workstation project (Rector et. al., 1992).

As a general philosophy user centred design places the needs of users at the centre of the design process with the aim of producing useful and usable systems (Norman and Draper, 1986). One area of user centred design research has concentrated on creating better human computer interfaces. Despite advances in this area it is becoming clear that better interface design cannot improve human computer interaction when the problems arise from more fundamental aspects of the system (Diaper, 1989).

In recognition of the need to address problems of the underlying system, another area of research activity has sought to incorporate human factors expertise within existing structured design methodologies (Catterall, 1991). But the provision by human factors specialists of high quality information about the needs of users often fails to influence systems design to any significant extent. This is because the designers still operate within the framework of traditional structured design which is a highly prescriptive and essentially system centred framework (Eason, 1991).

Alternative user centred frameworks for systems design usually involve user participation in iterative prototyping cycles with user evaluation. Within such frameworks, approaches to the design, development and construction of the prototypes themselves are often *ad hoc* and informal. One example of such an approach is Supportive Evaluation Methodology (SEM) which was developed in the PEN&PAD (GP) project. In SEM Requirements Workshops provided the starting point for the design of prototypes which were evaluated by users in Formative Evaluation Workshops. The results of these user evaluations was fed back into the next design cycle.

Our overall User Centred System Design Methodology (UCSDM) framework is based on this participatory iterative prototyping approach. However, our experience of attempting to extend and systematize this approach in the PEN&PAD (Elderly Care) project has shown the need for more formal techniques to be employed in the design process.

In this paper, we describe some work in progress on the development of an analysis technique which has been used in an investigation of aspects of the current usage of patient records by a group of nurses. We begin by briefly outlining and discussing the problems encountered with a number of approaches to the analysis of users' activities. This is followed by a description of the basic philosophy and features of a new approach to representing user task analysis and their associated information flows - Task Oriented Flow Diagrams (TOFDs). Next, an example of the use of TOFDs with a group of nurses is presented. Finally, the results of using TOFDs are discussed.

2. ANALYSING WORK PRACTICES

The design process of PEN&PAD(Elderly Care) has begun by analysing the current practices and systems of healthcare workers - doctors and nurses - on two wards in a hospital for elderly patients. This has involved interviews, observations and reading the patient records used by a number of groups of healthcare professional.

Our initial informal approach to the development of an understanding of user tasks raised a number of difficulties:
- no means of unambiguously representing the understanding gained;
- no mechanism for communicating and checking this understanding with users; and
- no obvious way of arriving at an agreed starting point for the design process.

There was, therefore, a clear need for some more formal means of representing our understanding in a way which could help clarify our thinking, was accessible to users and could provide a starting point for design.

Two traditional techniques were considered for representing and communicating our understanding of user activities. The systems analysis technique of traditional data flow diagrams (DFDs) provide a good graphical representation of information flows and provide a good starting point for design (Gane and Sarson, 1979; and Downs et. al., 1992). However, DFDs are highly systems centred in that their ultimate purpose is to provide the basis for writing code and they provide no easy way of representing human tasks.

On the other hand, the Hierarchical Task Analysis technique is focused on user tasks and is clearly user centred (Shepherd, 1989). Unfortunately HTA diagrams provide a poor graphical representation of information flows and do not provide an obvious starting point for the design process.

Because of the failings of these traditional approaches there was a need for a user task focused diagramming technique which could provide a good graphical representation of the information flows associated with user activities and has the potential of being a starting point for the design process. A hybrid of DFDs and HTA has been developed known as Task Oriented Flow Diagrams.

3. TASK ORIENTED FLOW DIAGRAMS

In Task Oriented Flow Diagrams (TOFDs) a clear distinction is made between human task components and system objects. User tasks are represented explicitly in the diagrams in a manner visibly different from the way system objects are shown. Task components are designated in terms of the professional role such as nurse or doctor and have operational and implicit knowledge components. System objects have data storage and process components. Because the current recording system under investigation is entirely paper based, we have only considered system objects to have data storage components.

In addition, the diagrams represent entities which are "external" to the user/information storage system such as, in this medical context, patients and their relatives. Lines in TOFDs represent information flows between aspects of user tasks, system objects and external entities. The symbols used in TOFDs are shown in Figure 1.

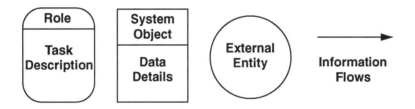

Figure 1. Symbols Used in Task Oriented Flow Diagrams

Following the approach of Annett et. al. (1971) in TOFDs a *task* is defined in terms of its *goals*. These goals are achieved by carrying out a series of *operations* according to a *plan*. Analysis begins by drawing a top level TOFD. This diagram shows the high level goal of the professional role being analysed in terms of flows of information to and from other professional roles and the information system objects. This overall goal is decomposed into a number of suboperations and a lower level TOFD is drawn which shows information flows associated with these suboperations.

An integral part of each TOFD is the plan which indicates some sort of ordering of the suboperations. These plans can be highly conditional and informal including such statements as "if required" or "as appropriate". An understanding of the flexibility of these plans is crucial for building the necessary flexibility into the design system and its user interface.

The suboperations contained within each TOFD can in turn be decomposed into a number of further suboperations and associated plans until a sufficiently detailed analysis has been created. In parallel with the progressive decomposition of tasks there is also a decomposition of

994

the system objects in order to specify which information is required or created by the tasks being analysed.

4. USING TOFDs TO ANALYSE CURRENT RECORD USAGE BY NURSES

TOFDs have been used in the first design and development cycle in the PEN&PAD (Elderly Care) project. This first cycle was mainly concerned with access to patient records for routine daily care - the entry of patient data will be considered in later cycles. TOFDs drawn based on interviews and observations provided the basis for discussions with ad hoc groups of two or three nurses. In all 11 nurses participated in at least one of the group discussions most of which took place over a five week period.

We adopted a talk through technique in which the symbols and meaning of the diagrams were explained to the nurses. The diagrams were readily understood and provided the basis for very constructive dialogues in which many changes were made to the original diagrams.

Figure 2 shows a TOFD for the task "Provide routine daily care". This is a simplified version of the diagram agreed with the groups of nurses which does not show the data entry operations normally associated with the provision of daily routine care to patients.

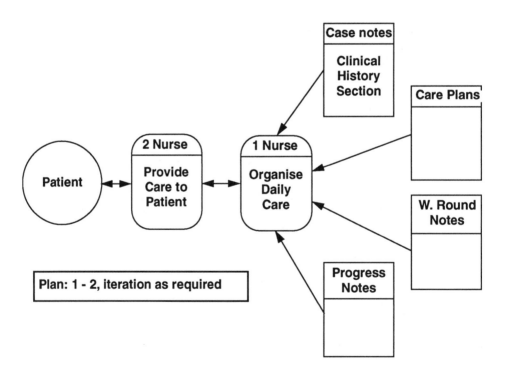

Figure 2. Simplified Task Oriented Flow Diagram for Provide Routine Daily Care

The diagram shows that the information required by the nurse to carry out the operation "Organise Daily Care" is derived from the nursing Progress notes, Ward Round Notes, Nursing Care Plans and the medical Case Notes specifically the Clinical History Section. The simplified plan is shown for completeness.

The operation Organise Daily Care has been further decomposed into suboperations and part of this further decomposition is shown in Figure 3. Here different aspects of the data access tasks shown include "Find out Intended Actions" and "Review Patient Progress". Also the particular information required from the system objects is further specified. The plan for this task is not shown and is somewhat complicated: Which operations and the order in which they are carried out by a particular nurse depends on such issues as the nurse's familiarity with the patient and when the nurse was last on duty.

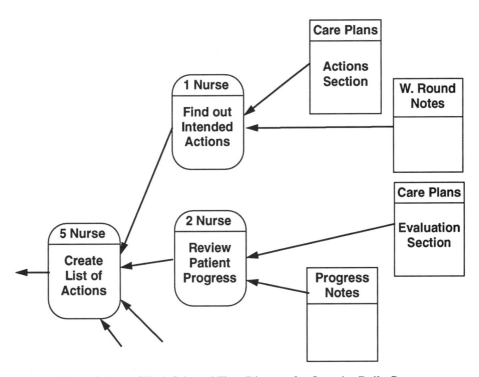

Figure 3. Part of Task Oriented Flow Diagram for Organise Daily Care

5. RESULTS AND CONCLUSIONS

Early results of using the TOFDs approach are very encouraging. TOFDs have proved to be a very successful way of entering into a real dialogue with users about their current practices. This has led to the beginnings of a shared understanding between users and designers of user tasks and their information needs. This understanding has provided the basis for the design of the first PEN&PAD (Elderly Care) prototype clinical workstation.

This first prototype has now been subject to evaluation exercises involving a group of 18 nurses. The overall response of users to the system designed using the analysis described above has been extremely positive. Inevitably problems have been raised by users about certain aspects of the system - this is, after all, one of the purposes of building prototypes. These problems will be addressed in subsequent design cycles. However, we believe that the number and scale of the problems reported are much smaller than would have been the case if we had used a more informal approach.

Our experience of using TOFDs has led us to the view that it is both possible and necessary to translate the general philosophy of user centred design into a practical User Centred Systems Design Methodology complete with appropriate tools and techniques.

Acknowledgements

This work is funded by the UK Computer Board for Universities and Research Councils' K.B.S. initiative. We gratefully acknowledge the help and co-operation of those members of staff at Ladywell Hospital, Salford, UK who have been involved in this work.

6. REFERENCES

Annett J, Duncan K D, Stammers R B & Gray M J (1971). Task Analysis, H.M.S.O., London.

Catterall, B J (1991). Three approaches to the input of human factors in IT systems design: DIADEM, The HUFIT Toolset and the MOD/DTI Human Factors Guidelines. Behaviour and Information Technology, Vol. 10, No. 5, 359-371.

Diaper D (1989). Task Analysis for Knowledge Descriptions (TAKD); the method and an example. In Diaper D (Editor), Task Analysis for Human-Computer Interaction, Ellis Horwood Limited.

Downs E, Clare P & Coe I (1992). Structured Systems Analysis and Design Methodology: Application and Context, Second Edition. Prentice Hall.

Eason, K D (1991). Eronomic perspectives on advances in human-computer interaction. Ergonomics, Vol. 34, No. 6, 721-741.

Gane C P & Sarson T (1979). Structured Systems Analysis: tools and techniques. Prentice-Hall.

Heathfield H A, Kirby J, Nowlan W A & Rector A L (1992). PEN&PAD (Geriatrics): A Collaborative Patient Record System for the Shared Care of the Elderly. In Proceeding of the 16th Annual Symposium on Computer Applications in Medical Care, I.E.E.E. Computer Society Press.

Norman D A & Draper S W (1986). User Centered System Design. Lawrence Erlbaum Associates.

Rector A L, Horan B, Fitter M, Kay S, Newton P D, Nowlan W A, Robinson D & Wilson A (1992). User Centred Design and Development of a General Practice Medical Workstation: The PEN&PAD Experience. In Proceeding of HCI'92, Addison-Wesley.

Shepherd A (1989). Analysis and training in information technology tasks. In Diaper D (Editor), Task Analysis for Human-Computer Interaction, Ellis Horwood Limited.

Cooperating partners : investigating natural assistance

Françoise Darses*, Pierre Falzon* & J.M. Robert°

* Laboratoire d'Ergonomie, Conservatoire National des Arts et Métiers,
41 rue Gay-Lussac, 75005 Paris, France

° Département de Génie Industriel, Ecole Polytechnique de Montréal,
P.O. 6079, Succ. A, Montréal, Québec, Canada H3C 3A7

Abstract
The design of better adapted intelligent systems can benefit from a better knowledge of the natural cooperative behavior between humans. Two studies of natural situations of cooperation are presented, focusing on the type of intervention of each partner in the dialogue. Specific attention is paid to the methodology of analysis. Implications for system design are stressed.

The evolution of technology tends to deeply affect the relationships between humans and their tools. We are shifting from a situation where the human is the user of a machine to a situation where both cooperate in order to reach a common goal. Human-machine interaction can then be seen as the collaboration of two cognitive systems - human and machine - in order to fulfil a task. This *cognitive partnership*, still in its infancy, is one of the key issues of the next few years, from a scientific, industrial and technological standpoint (see Woods, 1986 ; Fisher, 1990). It raises many new questions concerning the modalities of intelligent cooperation.

While interest for cooperative systems grows, it is striking to notice that we do not know much about natural human-human cooperative behavior. Although a number of studies have been conducted, most of them have adopted a psychosociological standpoint more than a cognitive one. The present paper investigates this issue, studying two situations of cooperation.

1. Design dialogues

The first study (conducted by the first two authors) investigates dialogues between an experienced operator and a series of less experienced operators during a task of network design. The experienced operator was instructed to behave cooperatively, but also to avoid to take complete control of problem resolution. Subjects interacted through an electronic link, both by typing and drawing. These dialogues have been gathered by B. Cahour in the course of ESPRIT project MMI2 (Cahour, 1991).

Each dialogue is composed of a succession of interventions (turns) ; each turn is composed of at least one utterance, and represents a basic cooperating behavior. These utterances are coded using a predicate-argument scheme, which has been devised by the experimenters. Predicates are actions (*inform, generate, criticize*), and arguments are the objects of the action (*domain object, procedure or rule ; problem data ; (element of) solution ; goal ; focus*) and the form of the utterance (*assertion, request*). Additionally, criticisms may be positive, negative or neutral (evaluation requests, in particular, are neutral). Table 1 provides examples of the use of this coding scheme on extracts of the corpus (examples are translated from the original French).

- Information on a domain object
        a MPR is a connexion box
- Information request on a domain procedure
        when is the minimum spanning tree to be applied?
- Information on problem data
        the building has two floors
- Solution generation
        I propose 2 thin segments
- Goal generation
        you need some filtering
- Request for focus generation
        which aspect of the problem should be tackled now ?
- Negative criticism of a procedure
        you forgot to take the loops into account when you computed total length
- Request for criticism of a fact on a domain object
        the MPR has 6 I/O, am I right ?

Table 1 : Examples of Basic Cooperating Behaviors (BCBs)

The basic cooperating behaviors (BCBs) performed by each partner were analyzed. It is to be noted that this scheme allowed to take into account all the utterances of the dialogues (with the exception of the very first and last utterances, dialogue initiations and closures). BCBs appear in context, either within a single intervention (a BCB can follow or precede another one in the same intervention), or across interventions (a BCB uttered by A is followed by a BCB uttered by B). When successive BCBs appeared repeatedly in association, seemed to form a pattern, they were grouped into basic cooperative interactions (BCIs), presented in Table 2.

A first observation is that very few direct requests for problem solving are uttered by the less competent operator. This contradicts very strongly the philosophy underlying many help systems, i.e. that the user is to make explicit requests of solution to the system, which should then provide an answer. This mode of assistance (*assistance by response*) is not what these human-human dialogues exhibit.

What is then the cooperation mode of the experienced operator ? A key feature of the interaction is the evaluative, critical activity, which represent a large part of the expert's BCBs : the less experienced operator proposes an element of solution and the more experienced one reacts by evaluating the proposal. Positive evaluations may be followed by solution extensions (addings to the solution state) or by preventive statements (indications of not-to-be-forgotten facts or actions, implied by the solution proposal). Negative evaluations are always accompanied by justifications and often by alternative proposals. Moreover, the experienced operator also acts as a meta-planner, by proposing problems to be tackled or by suggesting to switch to a new design phase.

Thus, it can be seen that the interventions of the experienced operator are not limited to solution proposals (as most classical expert systems behave) : evaluation, planning are essential features of the experienced operator's behavior. When he makes solution proposals, these are often part of a wider assistance move (e.g. negative evaluations).

- Enriching a solution
    Spontaneous solution generation by the expert (spontaneous means : not preceded by an explicit request from the partner), following information on problem data, or a solution generation, or information on a domain object
- Executing a task
    Solution generation following an explicit request from the operator
- Assisting problem representation
    Information generation about the problem following information on problem data
- Orienting problem processing
    Generation of a focus of resolution, following a solution generation by the less experienced operator
- Guiding problem description
    Request by the expert for specific problem data, followed by the provision of this data by the partner (this BCI occurs mostly at the beginning of the dialogue)
- Assisting goal planning
    Generation by the expert of problem processing goals, followed in some cases by preventive information (rules to be applied, facts abouts domain objects)
- Assisting meta-planning
    Request by the expert for a solution generation (following the description of the problem, or the criticism of a solution)
- Positive evaluations
    Positive criticism of solution, following a solution generation (and sometimes an explicit request for criticism), sometimes followed by preventive information or a generation of solution (solution expansion)
- Negative evaluations
    Negative criticism of a solution, following a solution generation (and sometimes an explicit request for criticism), sometimes followed by preventive information or a generation of solution or of goal
- Mitigated evaluations
    Globally positive criticism of a solution, following a solution generation (and sometimes an explicit request for criticism), followed by a modification of the solution ("yes, but" situations)
- Providing additional knowledge or correcting knowledge
    Information on domain rules or object, following an explicit request or an inexact assertion on a rule or an object

Table 2 : Basic Cooperating Interactions (BCIs)

2. Advisory dialogues

The second study (conducted by the last two authors) concerns dialogues between the user of a micro-computer, who has to fulfil various word processing tasks, and an advisor, available on request to provide assistance (these dialogues have been gathered by S. Bouchard, 1991). This situation, as compared to the preceding one, is a learning one : subjects had very little experience of text-editing, and were more focused on the functioning of the system than on task completion. Thus, interactions of a different kind are expected. The analysis presented here focuses on patterns of cooperation. Complementary analyses can be found in Robert & Bouchard (1991) and Robert & Falzon (1992).

We have used a coding scheme similar, but not identical, to the one presented above. In particular, it has proven necessary to add an "action tracking" category, which reflects the utterances by which the advisor corrects the subject while (s)he is performing a procedure. These utterances do not react to a verbal utterance of the subject, but to an action on the interface by the subject. Also, it has appeared that the computer user emitted many requests for confirmation : this category has thus been added.

As a matter of fact, many of the advisor's interventions are solutions (mostly procedures), provided following either a direct request from the user, or a statement of a problem met by the user. However, several other observations are in agreement with the characteristics observed in design dialogues.

First, many interventions of the advisor are spontaneous reactions to a statement of the user, such as : announcement of the procedure the user intends to follow, of the goal to be reached, of the interpretation (s)he makes of some interface object, etc. These statements are interpreted by the advisor as implicit evaluation requests, to which he reacts in different ways : in particular, negative reactions may be followed by corrections, explanations or alternative proposals. Thus, intelligent answering does not consist only in providing an answer to the subjects' requests. This is similar to what was observed in the experiment reported above. Another aspect of this cooperative answering behavior can be seen in the spontaneous provision by the expert of concepts or of explanations about the effect of procedures.

Second, explicit requests for confirmation are uttered by the user. These requests may concern possible goals, the steps of a procedure, the existence of some functionalities, the role of some interface objects, etc. The advisor's reactions to these explicit requests are similar to the reactions to the statements described above.

An additional result concerns explanation strategies. The means used by the advisor in order to assist the user vary extensively : statement of a procedure (in one shot, or step by step ; in the latter case, the advisor controls the execution of the procedure by the user, and provides corrections if necessary), examples, statements of general, declarative pieces of knowledge, analogies, etc.). The execution of the procedure by the advisor also appears among these means, but it is far from being the most frequent mode of assistance.

Lastly, intersting results can be obtained from the analysis of convergence and divergence patterns. A convergence pattern is the list of subject's utterances that may precede a given utterance of the tutor. Conversely, a divergence pattern is the list of tutor's utterances that may follow a given utterance of the subject. Examples of convergence and divergence patterns are shown in figures 1 and 2.

Of course, the arrows of these figures do not correspond to the same frequency. For instance, the top arrow in figure 2 (from "request for confirmation of a procedure" to "confirmation of a procedure") is a "natural" sequence and is more frequent than others. However, the second arrow (from "request for confirmation of a procedure" to "statement of a procedure"), although indicating an hybrid sequence, is also quite frequent (10 occurrences).

The study of the most frequent convergence and divergence links can provide some insight concerning the <u>conversational rules</u> underlying these dialogues. For instance, the arrow "request for confirmation of a procedure" to "statement of a procedure" appearing in figure 2 implies that the advisor does not quite agree with the procedure mentioned by the subject, or that (s)he has doubts on the accuracy of the subject's knowledge of the procedure. However, nothing is said explicitly about this ; but it can be deduced from the succession of the two utterances.

These rules are situation-dependant, i.e. they apply to this specific type of dialogue in which partners have not the same status regarding their domain knowledge. Thus, the rules are not reversible. For this reason, they may not be applicable to peer dialogues.

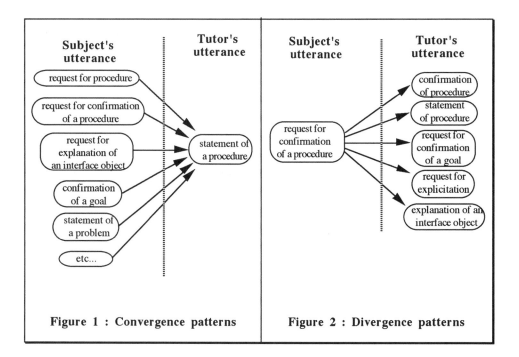

Figure 1 : Convergence patterns   **Figure 2 : Divergence patterns**

3. Conclusion

What general conclusions may be drawn from these two studies for the design of more cooperative systems ?

First, analogous results may be observed : cooperation does not consist in taking charge of the partner's problem, but in exploiting the pieces of solution proposed by the dialogue partner. These observations concur with the results reported by other authors. It is quite striking that, even in the situation of advisory interaction, the less experienced partner is quite active, hypothesizing procedures to be applied or foreseen effects of procedures for instance, as can be seen from the large number of requests for confirmation. This active attitude is likely to have several effects. First, it allows the dialogue partner to elaborate a mental model of the interlocutor's level of skill in the domain. Second, it speeds up the dialogue : if the proposal of the less experienced operator is correct, then it only needs to be acknowledged ; if it is not satisfying (suboptimal, or incorrect proposals), then focused remarks can be provided.

However, differences appear according to the situation of interaction. It is thus necessary to better characterize these situations of interaction and the assistance modalities which are associated to them. In that respect, the extraction of conversational rules from convergence and divergence patterns may allow the cooperation behavior to be better defined.

References

Bouchard, S. (1991) *Analyse du comportement des tuteurs humains dans un contexte d'apprentissage par exploration.* Unpublished Master Dissertation in Applied Sciences, Université de Montréal, Québec, Canada.

Cahour, B. & Falzon, P. (1991) Assistance à l'opérateur et modélisation de sa compétence. *Intellectica*, 12, 2, 1991.

Cahour, B. (1991) *Modélisation de l'interlocuteur et effets sur le dialogue.* Thèse de Doctorat de Psychologie, Université Paris 8, Saint-Denis.

Falzon, P. & Darses, F. (1992) Les processus de coopération dans des dialogues d'assistance. Proceedings of the 27th Congress of the SELF, 23-25 September, Lille, France.

Fisher, G. (1990) Communication requirements for cooperative problem solving systems. *Informations systems*, 15 (1), 21-36.

Robert, J.-M. & Bouchard, S. (1991) Investigating how computer users and human tutors interact with one another. In Y. Quéinnec & F. Daniellou (Eds), *Designing for everyone.* London : Taylor & Francis.

Robert, J.-M. & Falzon, P. (1992) How do tutors help learners ? Communication at the 3rd International Conference on Work with Display Units (WWDU'92), September 1-4, Berlin, Germany.

Woods, D. D. (1986) Cognitive technologies: the design of joint human-machine cognitive systems. *AI Magazine*, Winter (6), 86-92.

V. Hardware Interfaces

The Context-Based Graphic Input System : T-Board

Yasuo Endo[1], Shinji Akimichi[2], Murray Milne[2]

[1] CAD-T Project Team, Takenaka Corporation
1-9-15 Higasiazabu Minatoku Tokyo 106, Japan

[2] Graduate School of Architecture and Urban Planning, UCLA
Los Angeles, California 90024

Abstract

This paper introduces a CAD interface which uses purely graphic input gestures, without the necessity of translating graphic ideas into verbal commands or of using a menu-driven interface. The system infers the user's drawing intentions from pen movements, using basic graphic patterns stored in the knowledge base. The pen tablet mounted on a liquid crystal display, is both the input device and display for this system. It provides designers the similar feeling of drawing with pencil on paper. Another advantage is that designers who speak different languages can effectively collaborate on the same drawing.

1. Introduction

This study seeks to solve fundamental questions about the use of computerized design systems. Menu-driven graphic input systems have several disadvantages in terms of human factors. Information overload, a serious problem, results when there are too many items on a menu at one time, making it cumbersome for the user to select the proper item. Menu-driven systems require switching from one cognitive mode to another which can make the user frustrated. This mode switching disturbs the user's graphic thinking until he/she gets accustomed to it. Despite these shortcomings, menu-driven systems are still popular, mainly because they are the most efficient way of conveying the beginning user's intentions to the system, and in addition, they are easy to implement. But, the system that is the easiest for beginning users to learn may not be the most efficient over the long run. We know that we have to be trained in most systems before we can use them effectively. But why must humans obey the computer's needs? Why do we have to be trained in new esoteric languages for each new system? We do not have to select a menu or type a command in order simply to draw a sketch on a piece of paper with a pencil.

Pencil and paper   Menu-driven interface   A stylus pen and a screen tablet
that "reads" gestures

Fig.1 Comparison of Interfaces

2. Context-Based Graphic Input Method

A freehand sketch recognition system would be an efficient graphic input system for a CAD user, if it could understand his/her sketch properly. However, because of a sketch's ambiguities and complications, even very sophisticated recognition techniques would have trouble recognizing a freehand sketch, especially because of 'rote-latching' (i.e., the system tries to attach one line to another without thought for the meaning of the sketch). Moreover most recognition techniques have no chance to "grab" subtle information from the user's manual drawing actions, because recognition is possible only after the whole sketch is completely done.

An essential difference between the context-based graphic input system and prior systems is that the context-based graphic input system does not wait for a finished sketch to interpret, but instead it is constantly working "on-the-fly" to infer and respond quickly to the user's drawing actions, which include not only creating graphic elements but also deleting, copying or rotating sets of lines, for example. In order to get immediate feedback to the user of the system's interpretation of all the user's pen movements, the user's sketch drawing intentions are intuited based on the recognition of certain patterns of drawing actions. Those heuristics can be stored as a knowledge base which consists of predefined sets of graphic patterns, namely the user's graphic input gestures.

To realize this type of system, the screen tablet was adapted. This tablet has a liquid crystal display mounted on the tablet, which allows the user to pull the stylus pen directly across the screen and to get immediate graphic confirmation from the system. This gives the user a feeling just like using a pencil and paper.

3. Knowledge Base of Graphic Gestures

3.1 Creating Graphic Elements
The knowledge base containing the patterns of graphic input gestures is divided into two categories, creation and modification. Creation gestures are used to draw the primitive graphic elements. For a line drawing, the user just pulls the pen across the screen. The system gives

the user a straight line on the screen immediately after the pen is off the screen. Five other primitive elements can be drawn with the similar gestures, all without selecting any menus nor typing any commands before each gesture (Fig.2).

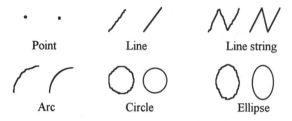

Fig.2 Primitive elements for creation as drawn and as interpreted by the system

Certain relationships between elements are assumed. For example, if the current element is near an existing element, the start or end point of the current element is connected to the existing one (Fig.3). An existing line is extended, if drawn continually from its end in the same direction (Fig.4). A line is to be parallel if drawn approximately parallel to the existing line (Fig.5). A line is to be perpendicular, if drawn perpendicular roughly from the end of the existing line (Fig.6).

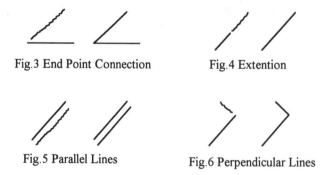

Fig.3 End Point Connection   Fig.4 Extention

Fig.5 Parallel Lines   Fig.6 Perpendicular Lines

3.2 Modifying Graphic Elements

Modification consists of six graphic gestures as follows:

(1) Deletion : A cross drawn on an element will delete the element. The two lines of this cross must be drawn one after another (Fig. 7).

Fig.7 Deletion of one element

(2) Wrapping : A circle or oval or closed polygon drawn around at least one element, followed by a modifying gesture, causes that gesture to be applied to all the enclosed elements. For example, in order to delete several elements simultaneously, wrap them up, then draw the cross outside the wrapper(Fig. 8).

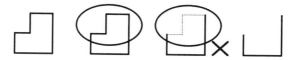

Fig.8 Wrapping multiple elements, then deleting them

When a circle is drawn, it might first be considered as the indication of modification if at least one element is in it. The system will wait for the user's further actions to see if modification gestures follow, otherwise it assumes the user intended to draw just the circle.

(3) Cutting : A short line drawn across an element will cut it into two parts. This cutter disappears if the cutting point becomes the end point of a line or corner of the shape (Fig.9).

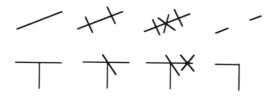

Fig.9 Cutting an element, then deleting it

(4) Translating : In this system the elements in the wrapper will be duplicated by an arrow whose tail originates on the element. They are copied from the arrow tail to the head (Fig. 10).

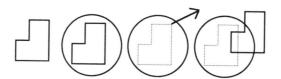

Fig. 10 Translating a set of elements

(5) Copying or Moving : After the elements enclosed by a wrapper are translated, if a cross is drawn on the wrapper then the wrapper is deleted and the original elements remain, in which case they are copied (Fig. 11). If a cross is drawn on the white space outside the wrapper then the original elements disappear, in which case they are moved (Fig. 12).

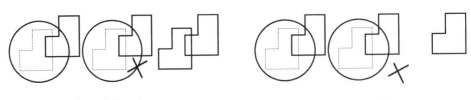

Fig.11 Copying   Fig.12 Moving

(6) Reflecting : The elements in the wrapper followed by a "hinge" line and an arrow will be duplicated symmetrically about the "hinge" line (Fig.13).

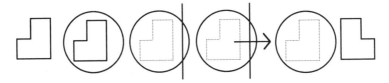

Fig.13 Reflecting about a "hinge" line in the direction of the arrow

(7) Rotating : The elements in the wrapper will be rotated by drawing a pair of intersecting lines, and an arrow. The center of rotation is the intersection of the two lines, the angle of rotation is the angle between them, and the arrow gives the rotation direction (Fig.14).

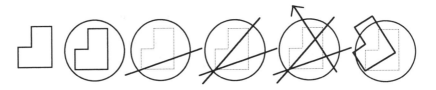

Fig.14 Rotation

(8) Scaling : The elements in the wrapper will be scaled up or down by an arrow whose tail is on the wrapper. The direction of the arrow decides shrinking or magnifying (Fig.15).

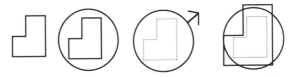

Fig.15 Scaling

4. Results

Each set of creation and modification gestures are sufficiently unique that the system seldom misinterprets them, and in fact, no practical problems have yet been reported. These context-based graphic input gestures are successfully implemented in the T-Board system. Over 500 user's responses to these gestures are favorable, especially regarding the non-menu-driven graphic literacy of the system.

5. Future Work

The purpose of this paper is to convey the concept of a non-menu-driven graphic input system. Therefore it emphasizes the essential part of the system's capabilities, which is how to tell the user's intentions through graphic gestures. There is some future work which needs more study or improvement:

(1) Customizable knowledge base : The sequence of creation and modification can not easily be changed in the present version because it is implemented in the inference system together with the inference engine itself. If the knowledge base could easily be modified corresponding to personal esoteric gestures, the system would become easier to use for each user respectively. For example, when modifying elements, they must first be enclosed by a wrapper. This procedure is often tedious especially when the only one element is to be modified. So the "picking" gesture is being added to the next version to select elements followed by modification gestures.

(2) Menus for efficiency : In order to make the system practical, menus may be required for some basic graphic commands. For instance, there is an icon menu for selecting a line style or weight instead of requiring the user to draw a styled or weighted line with the stylus pen. It may also be reasonable to arrange other optional operations on menus, such as setting a scale of the drawing or managing drawing files.

(3) The size of screen tablet : The size of the screen tablet is approximately B5, which may be too small especially for the architects. They now often have to scroll or zoom the drawing on the screen. These operations might frustrate users, so a large size screen tablet seems warranted.

6. Reference

(1) Murray A. Milne, "Design Tools: Future Design Environments for Visualizing Building Performance," CAAD Futures 91, Gerhard Schmitt, ed., ETH, Zurich, Switzerland, July, 1991.
(2) Yasuo Endo, "The Context-Based Graphic Input System," Thesis at The Graduate School of Architecture and Urban Planning, UCLA, 1984.
(3) Yasuo Endo, Shinji Akimichi, Murray A, Milne, "The Context-Based Graphic Input System," Proceedings of IV-ICCCBE International Conference, Tokyo, Japan, 1991

Segmentation of handwritten text and editing-symbols from ink-data

S.Navaneetha Krishnan and Shinji Moriya

Department of Information and Communication Engineering, Tokyo Denki University,
Tokyo, JAPAN.   e-mail : krishnan@cck.dendai.ac.jp

Abstract

This paper proposes a real-time algorithm for segmenting handwritten text and editing-symbols from ink-data. This algorithm simplifies the development of "mode-less" editors for pen-based computers. Such editors enable users to create documents by writing characters and editing-symbols side-by-side (i.e. in "mode-less" fashion), and then executing the editing-operations corresponding to these editing-symbols. The proposed algorithm uses a segmentation decision-tree, and does not require a character-recognition dictionary. Using this algorithm, we segmented handwritten text and editing-symbols from ink-data (written by twelve writers) with an average segmentation accuracy of 97%.

1. INTRODUCTION

In order to develop a pen-based real-time mode-less editor, it is vital to distinguish (i.e. segment) and identify (i.e. recognise) the handwritten text and editing-symbols in ink-data. Such segmentation and recognition can be done in a single step as in present pen-based computers, or in two steps, i.e. segmentation first and then recognition. Our algorithm follows the latter approach and performs the segmentation step. This makes it easier to develop the algorithms for these two steps independently and also modify them separately.

Present segmenting methods for ink-data suffer from two drawbacks. First, from user's viewpoint, as in PenPoint[1], users are required to write characters in "ink-mode" and edit these written characters in "edit-mode". Second, from research viewpoint, in Okamoto's[2] method, each stroke is recognised, thus requiring a character-recognition dictionary.

As compared to present segmentation methods, the proposed algorithm uses a decision-tree to segment from mode-less ink-data. Developing our algorithm as a decision-tree makes implementation easier and also speeds it up enabling real-time segmentation. The proposed algorithm is also easy to modify since it is structured into sub-trees based on whether the strokes of ink-data are written above/below or near/far-from each other, etc.

2. INK-DATA USED IN THE PROPOSED ALGORITHM

(1) *Contents of ink-data*   In this paper, "ink-data" denotes handwritten text and editing-

symbols written by the writer, and is obtained by sampling in sequence each coordinate point in the locus traced by the tip of stylus pen. While writing this ink–data, no restrictions are placed on the writers regarding writing–speed, number or order of strokes, etc.

The handwritten text portion of the ink–data that we use is composed mainly of Japanese language text, but also includes English alphabets and numerals.

The editing–symbols used are of eight types, which were selected based on (i) frequency of use, (ii) whether users can visually distinguish the editing–symbol, and (iii) whether they conform to JIS (Japan Industrial Standard). To obtain these editing–symbols, we asked fifty-one writers to write and edit using various editing–symbols. From this sample ink–data, we selected those editing–symbols that satisfied the above requirements (i) to (iii).

(2) *"Real–strokes of ink–data"* A "real–stroke" is the locus of points traced by the tip of stylus pen when it is in contact with tablet surface, i.e. when the writer is actually writing. The proposed algorithm examines parameters between two consecutive real strokes.

3. SEGMENTATION ALGORITHM

3.1 Segmentation into sub–lines, and the segmentation decision–tree

The proposed algorithm segments ink–data into "sub–lines" of handwritten text and editing–symbols, as explained below.

(1) *Formation of sub–line* Let us consider that a writer is writing text and editing this text side–by–side. After writing a few characters in some line, let he/she use a delete–symbol to delete written text in this line, and resume writing on this line. Then, this line will be split into three sub–lines. The first sub–line comprises handwritten characters starting from the first character in the line and up to the character written just before delete–symbol. The second sub–line is the delete–symbol itself, and the third sub–line contains characters starting with the character written just after delete–symbol and up to the last character in the line.

It follows from above that our algorithm segments two types of sub–lines, i.e. handwritten text and editing–symbols, and that each editing–symbol is segmented as one sub–line.

(2) *Segmentation decision–tree* To segment handwritten text and editing–symbols, our algorithm examines parameters such as distance, angle, etc. between two consecutive real strokes ("current real stroke" and "next real stroke" of Figure 1), and judges whether current real stroke is the ending stroke of "current sub–line" (sub–line being examined) and next real stroke is the starting stroke of next sub–line. This judgement is made by comparing the above–mentioned parameter values with the conditions of decision–tree of Figure 2.

This decision–tree is divided into four sub–trees (shown shaded) --- Sub–tree$_{far\ below}$, Sub–tree$_{far\ above}$, Sub–tree$_{just\ below}$ and Sub–tree$_{just\ above}$. Here, for example, subscript "far below" denotes the sub–tree examined when next real stroke is "far below" current real stroke.

In Figure 2, the symbols c1~c9 denote the segmenting conditions (listed in Table 1), and "T" and "F" denote their true and false branches. The labels such as Symbol1$_D$, etc. in the true branches of these conditions indicate the type of sub–line that would be segmented when the algorithm reaches these branches. These segmenting conditions are of two types :-

(i) "Direction dependent" conditions such as c3$_D$, c3$_U$, etc. where the subscript "D" stands for "down" and "U" for "up". For example, c3$_D$ is used when next real stroke is written "below" current real stroke, and c3$_U$ is used when next real stroke is "above".

(ii) "Direction independent" conditions such as c1, c2, c5, c6 and c9.

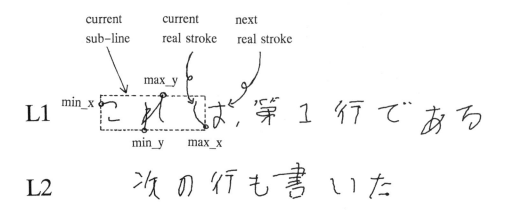

Figure 1. Plot-out of actually written ink-data. The symbols L1 and L2 denote two lines of text that are to be segmented.

Table 1
List of segmenting conditions used in the segmentation algorithm

Condition	Description of segmenting condition
c1	Examines whether current and next real strokes are situated far apart from each other in an arbitrary direction
c2	Examines whether next real stroke is situated below current real stroke
$c3_D$	Examines whether next real stroke is written far below current real stroke
$c3_U$	Examines whether next real stroke is written far above current real stroke
$c4_D$	Examines whether next real stroke is written below current sub-line
$c4_U$	Examines whether next real stroke is written above current sub-line
c5	Examines whether current real stroke is wide and tall
c6	Examines whether next real stroke is wide and tall
$c7_D$	Examines whether current sub-line is sufficiently wide, i.e. whether the width of current sub-line is greater than a threshold value
$c7_U$	Examines whether current sub-line is sufficiently wide
$c8_D$	Examines if the angle between current and next real strokes is sufficiently big, i.e. whether the angle is greater than a threshold angle
$c8_U$	Examines if the angle between current and next real strokes is sufficiently big
c9	Examines whether next real stroke is a delete-symbol

3.2 Steps in the segmentation process

Step 1 Sub-lines of handwritten text and editing-symbols written significantly far apart from each other in an arbitrary direction are segmented. To segment, condition c1 of Figure 2 is

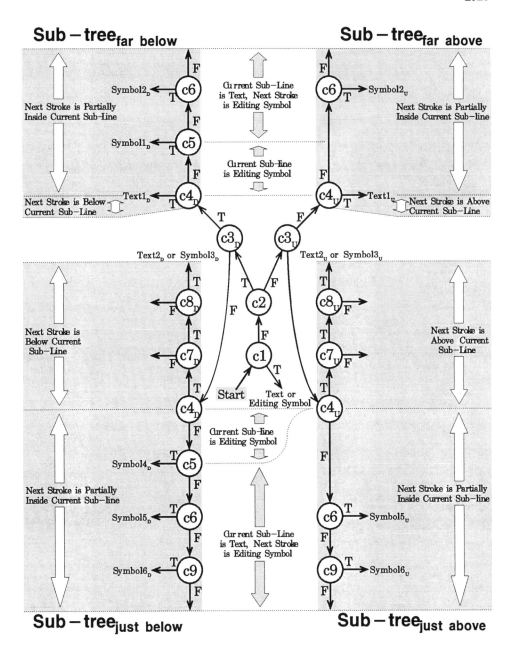

Figure 2. Decision–tree of segmentation algorithm. Shaded portions denote the four sub–trees into which this decision–tree is divided. The symbols c_1~c_9 denote the segmenting conditions, and notations such as "$Symbol1_D$" indicate the type of sub–line that would be segmented when the algorithm reaches such branches.

used, which examines whether or not the straight line distance from the end–point of current real stroke to the starting point of next real–stroke is greater than a threshold value. In our ink–data, condition c1 was capable of segmenting (i) sub–lines of handwritten text, and, (ii) editing–symbols that are used to make the final document more readable and are usually written far away from each other (these editing–symbols are " $\wedge$ " and " $\vee$ ", " $<$ " and " $>$ ", " $\subset\!\!\!\supset$ ", " $\int$ " and " $\bigcirc\!\!\!\nearrow$ "). If the two strokes being examined are far apart,a sub–line is segmented and algorithm goes to step 4,else algorithm goes to step 2.

Step 2 This step is for segmenting sub–lines of handwritten text and editing–symbols that are written relatively near each other, for example, when next real stroke is written far below or far above current real stroke. In such situations, the algorithm uses the set of conditions c2, $c3_D$ or $c3_U$ along with the segmenting conditions contained in Sub–tree$_{far\ below}$ or Sub–tree$_{far\ above}$. If next real stroke is far above or far below current real stroke, a sub–line is segmented and the algorithm goes to step 4, else the algorithm goes to step 3.

Step 3 In this step, (i) handwritten text lying very close to another text sub–line, and, (ii) those editing–symbols which lie partly inside text sub–line, are segmented. Here, the current and next real strokes are relatively near each other, for example, when handwritten text is written near the editing–symbols " $\subset\!\!\supset$ " and " $\supset\!\!\subset$ ", " $\sim\!\!\sim$ " and " $\cup\!\!\cap$ ", and " —— ". In such cases, as next real stroke is just below or just above current real stroke, the segmenting conditions c1 and those of Sub–tree$_{far\ above}$ and Sub–tree$_{far\ below}$ are unable to segment. Therefore, in such cases, the algorithm examines the conditions of Sub–tree$_{just\ below}$ or Sub–tree$_{just\ above}$. After this step, the algorithm goes to step 4.

Step 4 The algorithm advances by one real stroke, i.e. the next real stroke becomes current real stroke, and the new stroke (i.e. the stroke after next real stroke) becomes next real stroke.

In this way, steps 1 to 4 are repeated till the last stroke is reached.

4. EXPERIMENTAL RESULTS

Using the algorithm explained in chapter 3, we performed segmentation experiments on ink–data. The results are shown in Table 2. This ink–data used in our experiments was written by twelve writers on 300 pages of "squared–sheet". The "squared–sheet" consists of uniformly placed squares, where each square holds one written character.

A plot–out of correctly segmented ink–data is shown in Figure 3, in which each rectangle denotes one segmented sub–line. As shown, each editing–symbol is segmented as a sub–line. The curved lines (drawn by hand) at the left and right edges denote that the incomplete rectangles surrounding handwritten text are actually portions of correctly segmented sub–lines.

Table 2
Average segmentation percentage for each type of sub–line (in ink–data of 12 writers)

Average segmentation percentage for each type of sub–line (%)									Overall segmentation percentage (%)
Hand-written text	—	$\cup$ $\cap$	$\subset\!\!\supset$	$\int$	$\vee$ $\wedge$	$<$ $>$	$\bigcirc\!\!\nearrow$		
97.1	96.6	94.2	100	100	100	94.7	96.2	97.6	97.0

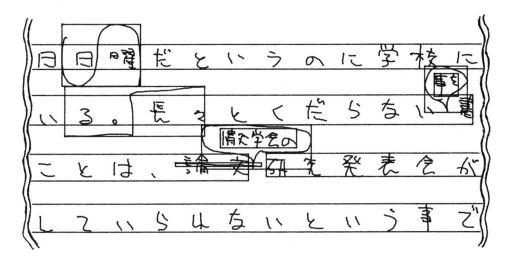

Figure 3. Plot-out of correctly segmented ink-data. Each rectangle denotes a segmented sub-line. The curved lines (drawn by hand) at the left and right edges denote that the incomplete rectangles surrounding handwritten text are portions of correctly segmented sub-lines.

5. CONCLUSION

In this paper, we proposed a real-time algorithm for segmenting handwritten text and editing-symbols from "mode-less" ink-data. This algorithm uses a segmentation decision-tree and does not require a character-recognition dictionary. Using a decision-tree makes our algorithm easier to implement, and also speeds it up enabling real-time segmentation.

Using the proposed algorithm, we segmented handwritten text and editing-symbols with an average accuracy of 97% from ink-data written by twelve writers.

Presently, we are expanding the proposed algorithm to make it capable of segmenting characters also, in addition to editing-symbols. We are developing a pen-based mode-less editor based on this expanded algorithm.

6. REFERENCES

1   Go Corporation, PenPoint User Interface Design Reference, Addison-Wesley Publishing Company Inc. (1992).
2   Okamoto Masayoshi, On-line Handwritten Information Recognition (in Japanese), Human Interface News and Report, Vol.7, No.4, pp.461-468 (1992).
3   Shinji Moriya, Satoshi Shimizu and S.Navaneetha Krishnan, Classification of Handwritten Stroke Data into Lines (in Japanese), Trans. Institute of Electronics, Information and Communication Engineers, Japan, J73-D-II, pp.973-981 (1990).

User Interface Development Tools for Pen Computer Applications

Isamu IWAI and Yoshiyuki MIURA

Information Systems Engineering Laboratory Toshiba Cooperation,
70, Yanagi-cho, Saiwai-ku, Kawasaki, 210 Japan
E-mail : iwai@oayo.ilab.toshiba.co.jp

Abstract

A pen application interface (PAI) has been developed for efficient implementation of application systems for pen based computer. By providing many tools and commands, tool users can substantially shorten the development period.

The PAI includes developing and executing environments. The developing environment consists of a Screen Designing Tool (SDT) for user interface and a Screen Controlling Editor (SCE) for data control. The executing environment provides a process control engine which consists of libraries and program modules in order to execute application systems. The engine has ten kinds of standard input-objects for such business use as button switches, handwriting character input, and list display functions. It also has a hundred kinds of commands for detailed controls. The tool users (developers of systems) determine the location and size of the object on the screen using the SDT, define types and control flow of input date using the SCE.

Without our PAI, the tool users had to use programming language and need skills for developing pen based applications. This means that it requires long developing period for programming, training and system test.

The outstanding advantages of our PAI was proved when we applied it for creating a system of processing application forms, as the developing period was shortened to almost one third, compared with that of traditional programming.

1. INTRODUCTION

A pen computer has lately attracted considerable attention compared with a keyboard computer. A pen computer is small and light, which is very convenient for mobile workers and those who work at plant site. In addition, it is able to input handwritten characters and image data which is difficult to input with keyboard. On top of it, operation of pen computer is so simple and easy that even an inexperienced user can handle. In stead of using cursor keys and mouse for commands, they point out objects directly on the screen using a pen. In other words, they can input characters and figures just as they write with a pencil on the paper [1].

In contrast to key board computers, tablet and display of pen computers are set in one unit. Therefore, pen computer programming has to handle data for data processing and for display synchronously. For every practical use, different types of application systems should be developed and it takes much time and energy using traditional programming. PAI, on the other hand, provides users with packages of complicated processing and tools to combine them. This substantially shortens the developing period.

In this paper, a hardware specification of which PAI is implemented is first described. Next, the construction of PAI and the functions of the application developing tools are given. Then, a handwriting character recognition, an important feature of the pen input, is explained. Finally, an evaluation of the PAI with actual implementing system is presented.

2. Hardware Specification

Currently, a lot of pen based computers are released, and their size and weight are different, respectively. Our PAI is able to execute on the new pen computer "Dynanote" (Japanese version) of Toshiba Corp. [2] This is B5 file size and the weight is 3.3 pounds, which is lighter than other versions. Specification of "Dynanote" is shown in Table 1. The operating system is the popular MS-DOS, and the CPU uses 32 bits microprocessor. At main memory it has four megabyte and has forty megabytes hard disk as offers. The display device is made use of FL-LCD (640x480 pixels, VGA), and input device uses the tablet with code-less pen.

Table 1 General specification of hardware

operating system	MS-DOS V3.1
micro processor	32 bits micro processor (25MHz)
main memory	offers 4MB RAM, max 20MB
display	FL-LCD 9.5-inch 640x480 pixels
hard disk	40MB
weight	3.3 pounds
size	10.6"x8.3"x1.5"

3. Construction of the PAI

One of the main features of the PAI for pen computer applications is to develop application systems without programming. In stead, the PAI provides two developing tools so that tool users without programming knowledge can easily prepare applications. One of the developing tools is a screen designing tool (SDT), which supports to develop the pen user interface. The other tool is a screen controlling editor (SCE) which edits a flow of screen and sets detailed parameters as shown in the Figure 1.

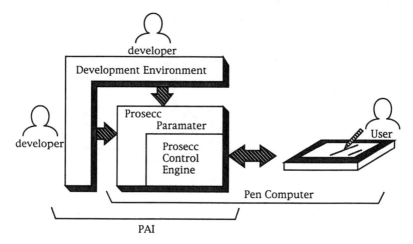

Figure 1   Construction of PAI

(1) Screen designing tool (SDT)

Ten kinds of standard inputting objects for data entry system are previously prepared in the SDT. Their objects are shown as follows.

a. Handwriting inputting object
b. Handwritten character recognition object
c. Table menu selecting object
d. Toggle switch
e. Scroll menu switch
f. Control switch
g. Text data displaying object
h. Kana to Kanji converting object
i. Ten-key object
j. The handwriting data scrolling menu object

First, a tool user designs a visual screen image using figure drawing tools. Next, he selects one from ten kinds of inputting objects in the pop-up menu in order to give a logical meaning and define a detecting area for a pen-point as shown in the Figure 2. At the tool user's operation, a source program of C language is created by being combined program modules or libraries internally. Therefore, he is able to make application program without programming operation.

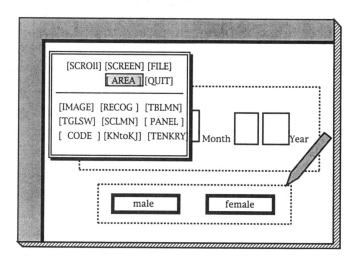

Figure 2 Example of a operation using Screen Designing Tools

(2) Screen controlling editor (SCE)

SCE has somewhat advanced editing function, providing a hundred kinds of commands. While SDT are used screen by screen, SCE controls inter-screen data processing. The tool user establishes more detailed parameters of the inputting objects and controls flows of screen. Therefore, a tool user is able to develop complicated applications by combining these commands. Furthermore, because the SCE has an exceptional processing interface which is able to call source program by C language, he can develop customized objects besides standard ones.

4. Functions of the Handwriting Input Technology

To recognize handwritten characters on the screen, quite an advanced technical skills should be implemented, because Japanese language has about eight thousands kanji characters, eighty three hiraganas, eighty six katakanas, alphanumeric characters and many symbols. In order to help recognition of a number of different types of characters, users have to follow several restrictions, which includes correct number of strokes in a character and the formal stroke orders within a set frame. We developed an advanced character recognition technique in which characters written in improper stroke order can be understood [3].

Since the present character recognition technique is not sufficient to recognize eight thousand chinese characters, we implemented Kana to Kanji converting object into pen computer.

5. Evaluation of the PAI

PAI substantially shortens time for developing applications, which in turn, reduces developers' efforts. Before we developed the PAI, we made pen computer applications by using general programming language. But this did not work efficiently because only a few users have knowledge about pen computers and because it takes much time to program application. Figure 3-A shows number of days spent for developing a pen application (that is a pen based application sheet inputting system include sixty screens) using programming. It took a total of one hundred seventy five days, of which one hundred days were spent for learning programming, forty five days for the screen designing and thirty days for programming input process.

In contrast, by using the PAI, total number of days were shortened to almost one third, or to fifty eight days as shown in the Figure 3-B. Remarkable improvement is observed in short learning period, almost one fifth of normal programming.

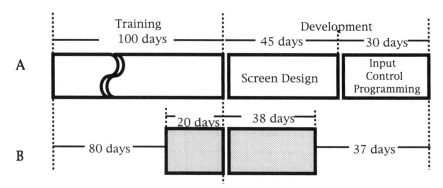

A: development by programing

B: development using the PAI

Figure 3   Comparison of the programming method and PAI

6. Conclusion

PAI excels in developing a pen applications, because it considerably reduced the developing period compared with those using programming, which was proved by a comparison of practical application systems by both ways. The PAI provides not only ten kinds of standard inputting operation objects but also exceptional processing interface that is able to combine C source program. As a result, a user with little knowledge of programming can operate complicated pen applications. Currently, we have developed a variety of demonstration systems for practical use.

For further improvement, we are studying pen gesture objects and graphical user interface.

7. REFERENCES

1 BYTE, Vol. 16, No. 2, 1991
2 Miura, Y., et al. : Development of Application Interface for Pen-Based Machine, Information Processing Society of Japan, 1991 National Convention.
3 Suzuki, K., et al. : Personal Computer with Pen Interface, Toshiba Review, Vol. 48 No. 2 PP.94 (1993)

Cordless Pen and Electronic Stationery

Azuma Murakami

Senior Managing Director,Research Center,WACOM Co.,Ltd.
2-510-1 Toyonodai Ootone-cho,Kita-saitama-gun,
Saitama-ken,349-11 Japan

Abstract
Recently, the pen as an input device has become the focus of attention. As a pioneer of the exploration for using the electronic pen, WACOM began its development by eliminating the need for a cord between a computer and a pen, which had limited free operation.In this development WACOM has been consistent in the pursuit of pen that is friendly to men, i.e. "easy-using" & "easy-writing" pen.
On the basis of my experience, I will discuss in this paper the theme: what is an"easy-using" & "easy-writing" pen ?

1. PEN AS A STATIONERY

First I will discuss on just what is an "easy-using" & "easy-writing pen", and what kind of technical problems we have on the way to its development. The cordless pen, although electronic,must have the same writing touch as that of an ordinary stationery pen.

1-1. Easy-using
For the sake of ease of use it is indispensable that we get rid of the cord between a traditional input device and the computer to realize full freedom of operation. And it is also important to have no batteries to be free from maintenance.

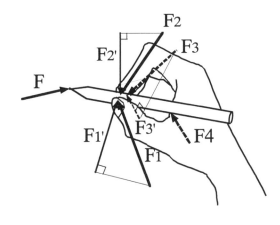

Fig.1 Forces applied by fingers to a pen
(From Ref.No.1)

1-2. Easy-writing

What kind of factors characterize the writing touch of pen? Some consider "easy-writing" should naturally be less fatiguing when used over a long time period.

1-3. Thickness of pen: diameter of pen grip

Cross's ball-point pen has a sectional diameter of 7.5mm, while almost all kinds of pen sold at a store (including ball-point pen, mechanical pen, pencil) have that of 8~9mm, except for a fountain pen with a more larger diameter around 11mm. A recent tendency of stationery is that the diameter of various pens gets larger. (cf.Ref.No.2)

As a reason for their choice of pen thicker, may be more hard to get tired of using, is because the area of touching interface between it and fingers is greater than on a slimmer one. According to the reference, the sectional shape of a triangle or hexagon, namely a poligon of 3's multiple, is prefered for pen grip. This may come from the fact that a pen is supported at 3 points by the thumb, forefinger and middle finger. (cf.Ref.No.2)

1-4. Gripping force

Gripping force of fingers on a pen and its temporal progress was determined by an experiment as a parameter of fatigability. (cf.Ref.No.1)Here the gripping force consists of $F1'$, $F2'$, $F3'$, as components of each finger's force F1, F2, F3 vertical to the pen's axis respectively.(Fig.1) According to the results, gripping force of the thumb is the strongest, and the middle finger is stronger than that of forefinger, which is about one third to a half of the strength. Also, gripping force is revealed to be constant in its strength regardless of the kinds of character being written. The gripping forces of thumb

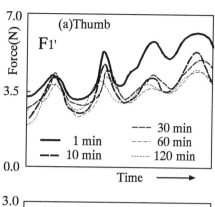

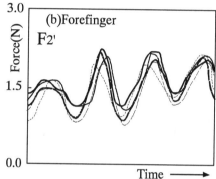

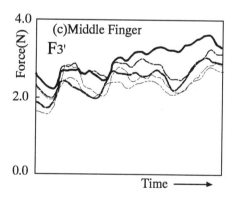

Fig.2 Force applied by each of three active fingers and its temporal progress in writing a Japanese letter "あ"(A) continuously. (From Ref.No.1)

and middle finger decrease as time passes, whereas that of forefinger decreases only slightly. It shows that forefinger only supports the pen, while thumb and middle finger mainly contribute to the writing action.(Fig.2) Hence, a pen that brings on less decrease of gripping forces of the middle finger and thumb can be a "less fatiguing", i.e. an "easy-writing" pen.

1-5. Weight of pen

In general, the weight of a pen is around 10g, and a pen with a weight of 20g or more seems to feel heavy, although this tendency surely depends on the user or usage. Some fountain pens are made heavy intentionally for the purpose of adding a quality.(cf.Ref.No.2)

1-6. Writing pressure

It is an important factor of "easy-writing". For example, when we write something with a pencil, consciously or unconsciously we naturally control the writing pressure, such as when pressing a pencil more firmly if the written trace is too light, or drawing with light pressure in the case of dessin or when sketching. In order to realize the desired shade, a choice among nH, HB,nB, F etc. is available. In writing with a pen, one promptly processes the information of the written results, such as desired shade, from the writing pressure, and feeds it back to the gripping force of fingers.

2. PEN USED FOR ELECTRONIC STATIONERY

Here I will discuss the sketch of the cordless pen,as well as think about the indispensable features required of it.

2-1. Switching and writing pressure

Pens with a mechanical switch for recognition of pen down are often accompanied by a problem of chatter. It is derived from unstable switching in a delicate load range, where the mechanical switch may work due to the continuous variation of the user's writing pressure during operation. Frequent occurence of chatter may make the electric signal irregular and damage the whole system including the pen itself. Therefore, the pen we are going to develop must be one that gets rid of such a problem of chatter.

Another problem is the quick responce of switching. The maximum speed for a man to switch on and off a pen is about 10Hz, i.e. 10 times a second. So a switch which can follow such a maximal motion of human muscles must be substantialized.

According to a report (cf.Ref.No.3) ,the writing pressure varies within a range from 20g to 320g,which the cordless pen must cover.

2-2. Durability

Several ten- to hundred-fold the durability of key board will be required of a cordless pen. Inputting from a key board is carried out by the continuous pressing of a hundred or more keys,but a cordless pen needs to be more durable because of the constant use of the pen top. Hence, the durability required for a cordless pen far surpassing that of key board .

3. THE DEVELOPMENT OF A CORDLESS PEN

On the basis of above pen analysis, we WACOM has set these development targets for the performance of cordless pen as follows. As main features required of the cordless pen, it must:
-1. be cordless
-2. be batteryless
-3. be non-stroke (i.e. little tip travel, or no feeling of it);
-4. have the minimum switching pressure of about 20g.;
-5. have the maximum switching pressure of 320g or more;
-6. be sensitive to the pressure of the pen, so as to assure a natural touch when writing with a pen on paper;
-7. have good response to written trace;
-8. have good reproducibility to writing pressure.
-9. have good durability

4. CHARACTERISTICS OF SENSOR AND EVALUATION OF CORDLESS PEN

4-1.Switching mechanism

The developed cordless pen has a special switching system to avoid as mentioned earlier the trouble of chatter. Instead of the switching mechanism used by traditional electronic pens, it has a mechanism for variable electrostatic capacity varying with a minute stroke variation at the head of pen, which allows the resonance frequency to vary and utilizes it to catch the pen writing pressure. Namely, here the traditional mechanical switch was replaced with a unique method for catching the on-off information using the electrostatic capacitive threshold. (Fig.3,4,5)

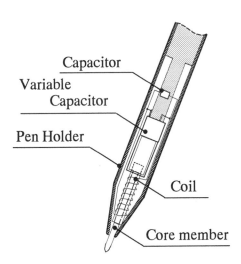

Fig.3   Sectional view of a cordless pen

Capacitor

Variable Capacitor

Pen Holder

Coil

Core member

4-2.Evaluation

Next I will make an evaluation of a cordless pen, which we have developed in accordance with the above conditions.

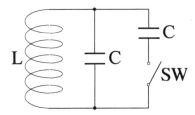

Fig.4 Tuning circuit
(Traditional pen with
a mechanical switch)

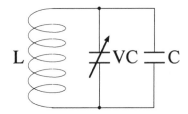

Fig.5 Tuning circuit
(Cordless pen developed
by WACOM)

1. Weight

It weighs approx. 10g, almost the same as a standard ball-point pen sold at any stationery store, and satisfies the condition needed for easy writing.

2. Thickness

It is approx. 10mm thick in sectional diameter, almost equal to a pen sold at any stationery store, and satisfies the conditions necessary for a natural writing touch .

3. Writing pressure

Using a wide range of pressure sensitivity which can be put to use by any user.

4. Reproducibility of writing pressure

As the Fig.6 shows, this cordless pen has such good reproducibility of writing pressure that it can readily be applied to and used for handwriting analysis.

5. Quick switching

Also as shown in Fig.7, substatializes a switch capable of precise on-off operation even when switching is at a frequency of 20Hz.

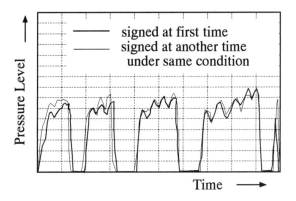

Fig.6 This chart shows the progress of pressure levels of a signature repeated under the same physical and mental conditions, using WACOM's cordless pen.

6. Stroke of pen

As its stroke is limited to only 40 micrometer, it gives little feeling of stroke during normal use.

7. Durability

The developed pen has the same characteristics of writing pressure even after running the test over 10 million times switching test. (Fig.8)

5. CONCLUSION

Thus we have succeeded in realizing an electronic pen as a promising inputting device for use with a computer, and also as extension of a pen as ordinary stationery, which man can use at ease without any sense of incongruity. It means also that we have extented the possibility to make computer more familiar to man. This concept of design may also be extented to a series of easy-using "electronic stationery" such as an electronic eraser, electronic ink, electronic filebox, etc.

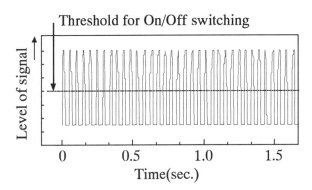

Fig.7   On-Off switching test under 20Hz frequency

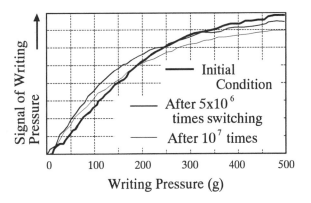

Fig.8   Characteristic curve of writing pressure

6.REFERENCES

1   Kazuaki IWATA,Toshimichi MO RIWAKI & Shoji MIYAKE,"Dynamic analysis of hand writing motion",Human tecnology vol.22.No.5('86),Japan

2   pp48~pp50,"MONO MAGAZINE"No.132,World Photo Press Co.,Ltd.,Japan

3   Katsuhiro NAGANO,Masakazu YOSHIDA,Kiichi IIDA & Yoshihide NAKAMURA,
"Fundamental Research on the Analysis of the Handwriting(2)",Institute of Police Science,Vol.23 No.3 Sept.1970,Japan

The minimal sizes and the quasi-optimal sizes for the input square during pen-input of characters

Xiangshi Ren and Shinji Moriya

Department of Information and Communication Engineering, Tokyo Denki University, Chiyoda-ku, Tokyo 101, Japan. E-mail: ren@cck.dendai.ac.jp

Abstract

In this paper, the authors focus on the precise and minute operation of the tip of the pen of pen-based computers. As the first step, we focus our attention on minute operations that users make when writing characters. In doing so, we attempt to experimentally determine the followings: (i) what is the smallest possible size of the characters or symbols when they are written on the input screen of writing-tablet? (ii) the quasi-optimal sizes of the input square for characters. In this paper, we determine the above two by targeting three kinds of characters: (a) numbers, (b) small English letters, (c) capital English letters. From our experiments, we were able to determine the minimal sizes (i.e., the width and height) of the small English letters, capital English letters and numbers. We also obtained the preliminary approximation of the quasi-optimal sizes (i.e., the width and height) of the square enclosing the above three kinds of characters.

1. INTRODUCTION

Pen-based computers are attracting increasing attention, and there is a need for a pen-based user interface. When using pen-based computers, it is especially preferable that the movements of the user's hand be as small as possible. In this paper, we propose a method of operation in which the tip of the pen is moved by infinitesimal amounts when writing and pointing on the pen-based computer. We call this method of operation as "minute operation".

As the first step in investigating minute operations, in this paper, we focus our attention on "minute writing". We will determine the following experimentally: (i) What is the smallest possible size of the characters that the user can write on the tablet of a pen-based computer? In other words, what is the minimal size of the input square that holds one character? (ii) What is the quasi-optimal size of the input square that holds one written character? Here, we assume that a quasi-optimal exists, and we define it as an approximate value that is obtained on the way towards obtaining the optimal size.

2. METHOD IN WHICH THE EXPERIMENT WERE CONDUCTED

In this chapter, we describe the experimental method for obtaining the minimal size and the quasi-optimal size. Although there are various objects (such as characters, figures, tables

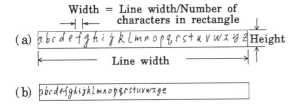

Width = Line width/Number of
characters in rectangle

(a) [abcdefghijklmnopqrstuvwxyz] Height

Line width

(b) [abcdefghijklmnopqrstuvwxyz]

Figure 1. Calculation of the width and height of rectangles.

and mathematical equations) that we could use for investigating minute writing, however we focus on the minute writing of characters. The characters we take up in this paper are as follows: (i) small English letters: a b c d...z, (ii) capital English letters: A B C D...Z, (iii) numbers: 1 2 3...9 0. In our experiments, when the subjects write numbers, they write them as twice as 12345678901234567890 in one line. The reason for doing this is to improve the accuracy when calculating the width of one numerical character.

The hardware which we use in this experiment are: a tablet–cum–display (HD–640A, WACOM Co.), a stylus pen (SP–200A, WACOM Co.), and a personal computer (PC9801–DA, NEC Co.).

We developed a pen–based system (we call this system "experimental tool" or simply "tool") for conducting our experiments regarding minute writing. When using this tool, the subjects adhere to the sequence (1) to (5) when writing one set of the above–mentioned characters.

(1) *The subject selects the first line.* The subject writes three lines, while considering each line as a new line, where each line includes all the characters in a set of the above–mentioned characters. Next, out of these three written lines, the subject selects that one line that he/she feels was written most naturally.

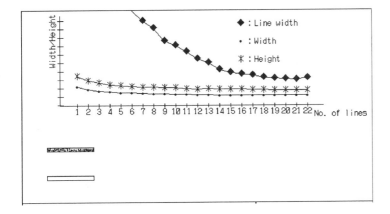

Figure 2. Hard copy of display screen showing a stage in the experiments regarding minute writing. The characters inside the rectangular enclosure are small English letters.

(2) *The tool displays the rectangle that encloses this written line.* Below, we mention the method that the tool follows for determining the rectangle surrounding this single line. Figure 1(a) displays the rectangle which encloses this selected line. Figure 2 shows the hard copy of a snapshot of the tool. The upper rectangle at the bottom left in Figure 2 is an example snapshot of this rectangle. Let us define that the line–width is the width of one written line, i.e., line–width is the difference between the maximum value and the minimum value of x coordinates of all the strokes in the written line. And the width of one character is equal to the line–width divided by the number of characters in the line. The height is defined as the difference between the maximum value and the minimum value of y coordinates of all the strokes in the written line. We call the square with the width and height as the character square.

(3) *The subject writes inside the empty rectangle.* Here, the tool displays an empty rectangle. In Figure 2, the lower rectangle shown at the bottom left is an example of this empty rectangle. The size of this rectangle is exactly the same as that of the upper one. Now, inside the rectangle, the subject writes the same character set which may be smaller in size than the characters written above, starting from the left side of this rectangle. Here, the subject is allowed to write strokes that protrude out from the rectangle, if he/she is unable to fit (i.e. write) the characters inside the rectangle.

(4) *The subject repeats (2) and (3) above.* This tool displays a graph that plots the sizes of character squares in real time (Figure 2). As shown in the graph of Figure 2, there is some up and down wavering when a stroke that the subject writes protrudes from the rectangle. The reason for this wavering is that the tool encloses the written line, including the protruded stroke.

(5) *The experiment ends.* When both the width and height reach a full saturated value, the subject ends the experiment concerning this set of characters. The subject repeats the steps (1) through (5) for the other sets of characters also, until he/she completes the steps for all the sets of characters.

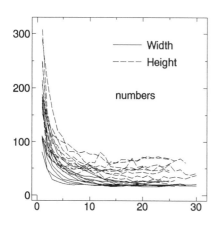

Figure 3. Variation in the size of the character square. The x–axis shows the number of times a line was written, and y–axis represents the width/height [point] of characters inside a particular line. 0.05[mm/point].

3. EXPERIMENT RESULTS

The authors asked ten subjects to perform the above–mentioned experiment concerning each of the small English letters, capital English letters and numbers. Total numbers of the lines written by the ten subjects are 237 (6162 characters), 243 (6318) and 260 (5200) respectively for the small English letters, capital English letters and numbers.

3.1. Variation and the Minimal sizes of Character Squares

Figure 3 shows the sizes of the character squares in the vertical axis, and on the horizontal axis show the number of times each

Table 1
The minimal sizes and the quasi–optimal sizes for the input square during pen–input of characters

three kinds of characters	minimal sizes		quasi–optimal	
	width	height	width	height
numbers	16(0.8)	26(1.3)	63(3.2)	124(6.2)
small English letters	15(0.8)	22(1.1)	67(3.4)	191(9.6)
capital English letters	16(0.8)	30(1.5)	103(5.2)	164(8.2)

In the width and height columns, the number on left represents numbers of points and the right number represents this number in terms of mm.

line was repeatedly written. This figure shows these sizes only for numbers. In order to emphasize the variation in the width and height in the graph, we have used two types of lines (that is, we have not distinguished the individual subjects in this graph). From the graph of Figure 3, we can understand the following. There is considerable individual variation in the height and the width in the first line. And after around the 15th line, although there is a small amount of individual variation, the sizes of the character squares nearly saturate. Almost no variation exists in the saturated values of the widths. The saturated values of the widths are almost identical. The variations in the saturated values of the height are larger than those of the saturated values of the widths, while they are smaller than those of the first lines. The heights of a subject are always larger than the widths of the subject, although this paper does not show this fact in the figures. What we have mentioned above is true for each of the three character sets.

Table 1 shows the minimal sizes of the character squares. Here, by minimal size, we mean that both the line–width and height of a written line are minimum among all the written lines by all subjects concerning a character set (Note: In the data obtained in our experiment, there exists a minimal rectangle for each set of characters. In the case that both the line–width and height do not have minimum values, we could obtain another minimal size which might be slightly different from the above non–existent minimum value. But even then, we will still be able to attain the aim of this paper). Figure 4 shows the characters actually written in the minimum rectangles, each of which corresponds to each of the minimal sizes shown in Table 1. The three lines of characters in Figure 4 were written by different subjects.

3.2. The quasi–optimal size of the character square

In this section, we describe the quasi–optimal size for the character square.

(1) Method of judging optimality and meaning of "quasi–optimal"

There are various aspects in the methods for discussing optimality of character squares. For example, the following are examples of methods that define the "size" of a character square. (f1) the method that investigates the height and the width separately, (f2) the method that investigates the height and the width as a pair which that up the square. In addition, there are two methods for handling a character set as follows: (c1) the method which handles individually each character in a set of characters, (c2) the method which handles the character

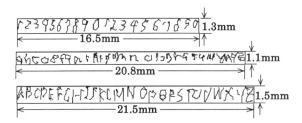

Figure 4. The minimal sizes of rectangles surrounding each line (which contain pen–input characters) for all the ten subjects.

set as a whole. Besides this, there are other aspects, such as, What type of subjects are the target, or, Whether the pen–computer is a desktop or of the compact (i.e., handy) type? In context of the above classification of methods, we have adopted the methods (f2) and (c2).

Also, there are various assessment criterions for optimality of the character squares as follows: Legibility of the character written inside the character square; Is the character cleanly written (i.e., beauty of the written character); How many sets of characters can be written in the square; The amount of time taken for writing; Number of mistakenly written characters or strokes; State of fatigue of hand or eyes in writing; Recognition accuracy for the written characters, etc. In this paper, we focus on whether or not there exists a protruding stroke from the rectangle.

As is clear from the above discussion, there are various methods and assessment criterions for determining the optimality of the character squares. In this paper, we discuss one of the above using only one method and one criterion. Therefore, we cannot use the word "optimal".

(2) The quasi–optimal character square

In this paper, we use a very simple criterion as described below. The following discussions concern one of the three, i.e., one of small English letters, capital English letters or numbers. Thus, we discuss the optimality for each set of characters.

First of all, let us pay attention to the rectangles which contains no protruding stroke. These rectangles are among those which all the subjects wrote in the experiment concerning one set of characters. Next, from among these rectangles, we choose the rectangle for which both the line–width and height are minimum. We call this minimum rectangle as "quasi–optimal rectangle" and the corresponding character square as "quasi–optimal (character) square".

In Table 1, we show the quasi–optimal squares for each set of characters. Figure 5 shows three lines of characters actually written by the subjects. The rectangle surrounding one line in Figure 5 is the quasi–optimal one for the set of characters. These quasi–optimal lines were written by different subjects. The authors observe that the actually written characters inside the quasi–optimal rectangles seem to be naturally written, although there are some variations in how easily we can read them. However, an overall quality evaluation about the written characters still remains to be done as one of our future works.

Regarding the numbers in Table 1, the width (the minimal line–width of the rectangle which does not contain protruding strokes is divided by the number of characters inside the line) is 63 point (3.2 mm) and the height is 124 point (6.2 mm). For the rectangle (90.4% of 260 lines containing numbers, 91.6% of 237 lines containing small English letters, and

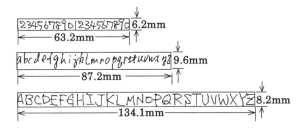

Figure 5. The quasi-optimal sizes of rectangles surrounding each line (which contain pen-input characters) for all the ten subjects.

95.5% of 234 lines containing capital English letters) for which both the line-width and the height are smaller than the quasi-optimal rectangle, the strokes protruding out of rectangle rapidly increase (however, there are cases in which strokes do not protrude).

4. CONCLUSIONS

Let's take a look at Figure 4 which corresponds to the minimal sizes shown in Table 1. We have, up to now, no evidence that a user cannot input gestures in such a minute rectangle. Therefore, a feasibility study still remains to be done for determining whether a writer can write minute gestures. We believe that the minimal sizes shown in this paper are significant because of this feasibility, and that such minimal sizes can become a target or motivation when developing a more miniature pen and tablet (as compared to the present size) in the future.

When a user has to input on a compact(i.e., handy) type pen-based computer with a smaller size screen, he/she will be faced with the situation of writing characters inside smaller size squares. In such a situation, we believe that the quasi-optimal sizes shown in Table 1 will be useful as the first approximation when designing the size of character square. To bring this first approximation close to the optimal size is a future work. It is a new finding that the width is quite smaller than the height.

Among the results of this paper, we believe that the following are universally meaningful: the concept of minute writing, the concept of minimal size and (quasi-)optimal size of input square, the discussion concerning an evaluation of character square, and the experimental method that we followed. However, a portion of the results obtained in our experiments might depend on the hardware and software (the experiment tool) used, and the subjects. Our future work includes a further examination about whether or not some results are dependent, and if they are, then to what extent. It will also be necessary to study minute writing about not only characters but also figures, tables, and mathematical equations, etc.

5. REFERENCES

1 Hiroshi Taninaka, Xiangshi Ren, Shinji Moriya: Micro-Scroll of Pen-based Computer, Proceedings of the 44th Annual Convention IPS Japan, 5th, pp.375-376(1992).

Concept of minute operation and its application to pen-based computers

Shinji Moriya and Hirosi Taninaka

Department of Information and Communication Engineering, Tokyo Denki University, Chiyoda-ku, Tokyo 101, Japan   E-Mail moriya@cck.dendai.ac.jp

Abstract

As compared to conventional computers, pen computers are being steadily miniaturized and are also becoming more portable. As a result of this, the display area as well as the writing area in such computers is getting smaller. In this context, the tip of pen is capable of very fine (i.e. minute) movements. The authors believe that, the above two factors motivate the creation of a pen–input interface in which such minute pen–movements are used to accomplish tasks such as writing, pen–gestures or scrolling.

Pen input can accomplish various operations such as pointing, writing, recognition, gestures, scroll, etc. In this paper, we put forward a method of achieving these operations using the minute movements of pen tip. We call this proposed method as "minute operations " In this paper, we describe the characteristics, associated problems and applications of these minute movements.

1. INTRODUCTION

Research regarding user interfaces unique to the pen is in need in the field of pen–based computers. In this paper, the authors show a new concept of user interface and two examples of its application. The new concept proposed in this paper is "minute operation". Here, by minute operation, the authors mean that when pointing and/or manipulating a computer, the user moves his/her hand by infinitesimal amounts. The first aim of minute operations is to implement the following two aspects in computer operations, namely (i) a user by nature is capable of move his/her hand by minute amounts, (ii) a user can further improve his/her the preciseness of his/her movements through training. The second aim is to realize a new method of operation in which increased effectiveness results from infinitesimal movements. In this paper, the authors employ a stylus pen and a tablet–cum–display as the input devices for minute operations.

We can say safely that, in spite of the fact that a user is capable of moving his/her hand by big amounts as well as minute amounts, no input device has existed that makes the best use of these minute movements. Keyboards and mouse are hardly the input devices for such minute operations. We believe that the pen is capable of such operations. We firmly believe that, when designing machines and/or systems, a designer should aim to bring out the most of the capabilities of the person who will operate such machines/systems.

The concept of minute operations has been conceived by one of the authors, and parts of this concept have been implemented on the pen-based systems[1][2]. This paper discusses the followings points : Minute operations are intrinsic to pen-based user interfaces; What are the parameters that can be used to control minute operations; Two examples of implementation, namely, "micro scroll" and "micro menu".

2. MINUTE OPERATIONS ARE INTRINSIC TO PEN-BASED USER INTERFACES

In this chapter, we describe four essential characteristics of pen-based computers, and show that minute operations embody these four essential characteristics. Pen-based computer has the makings to blend in our daily life in the following four aspects:

[Space conformity]
Pen-based computer conforms well with such "spaces" as paper-sheets, pictures, signboards and message boards that we see in our daily life. There is a clear tendency for the screen sizes of portable electronic devices, like pen-based computers, of moving in the direction of miniaturization. Consequently, the necessity of minute operations will grow.

[Time conformity]
Pen is an input device which makes it possible to input data only and exactly when there is need to input. It is absolutely vital that the user be able to input data and commands in real time, i.e. in conformity with the time in our daily life. It is important that minute operations do not slow down the actual work, but rather improve the speed of working. This means that, when using pen-based computers, the movements of the user's hand should be as small as possible. This shows the necessity of minute operations.

[Psychological conformity]
By developing algorithms such as segmentation and recognition algorithms for ink data, and by designing the pen-based user interfaces suitably, the authors expect that the metaphor "pen, paper, and ink" could lead us to an ultimate user interface which is in conformity with the psychology of the user. For example, minute operations (including minute writing or "blind" minute operation) enable users to write on the screen such that another person (who is viewing) cannot comprehend what is being written. Moreover, by conducting research about the optimal values of minute writing (for example, the optimal square[*] for the input of characters by pen) could also lead us to ultimate elements of pen-based user interfaces.

[Physiological conformity]
The spacial resolution of the tablet and the liquid crystal display of pen-based computers are different, although the display is placed upon the tablet thus uniting two devices into one. It is important to think of this difference in resolution not as a drawback but as an obvious fact of pen-based computers. The reason for this is, the minuteness of the hand's movements is different from the "resolution" of the eyes which receive the output from the display. There is a need for the resolution of the display to approach that of the eye, and for the resolution of the tablet to approach that of the hand. Following this method of reasoning, it is clear that minute operations is important in pen-based computers during input.
Thus, from the above discussion, to realize a user interface which fulfills the essential feature of pen input, obviously minute operations is one of the most influential methods.

3. WHAT CAN BE MANIPULATED MINUTELY WITH THE PEN?

In this chapter, we describe possible parameters which can be manipulated minutely by the pen when conducting minute operations.

(1) Parameters which depend on the hardware structure
Here, we describe parameters concerning the tablet, pen, and display respectively.

[Parameters concerning the pen and the tablet]
Ink-data written with the stylus pen (having a switch at the pen-tip) consists of real strokes and imaginary strokes. A real stroke is the ink data written when switch is "on", and an imaginary stroke is the ink-data when switch is "off". When using this kind of pen, we could have minute operations corresponding to each of these two kinds of strokes. In other words, there are two kinds of minute operation : one, while the pen tip is sliding on the tablet surface, and the other when the pen-tip is moving in the space above the tablet (within the sampling height of the tablet) and outside the sampling height.

The following parameters are also candidates that can be associated with minute operations, namely, the z coordinate value of the pen tip, direction of the pen axis, rotating angle of the pen axis, sampling time of the pen tip position, etc. We could even make use of the value of vertical separation between the pen-tip and tablet surface to realize minute operation, for example, utilizing the locus of the pen-tip when it moves from inside the sampling height towards the outside. As mentioned above, we could utilize each of the hardware parameters about the pen and tablet for minute operation.

[Parameters about the display]
The resolution of the display can be utilized in minute operation. If the resolution of the display is low, the display area can be smaller, corresponding to this resolution. This is because the pen operation on a higher resolution display can be more minute than one on a lower resolution display.

In a pen-based computer, the resolution of the tablet is much higher than that of the display. Therefore, whenever the input area is the same as the output area, it is possible to display only a part of the whole locus of the pen tip. In order to display the whole locus, first, it is necessary to separate the input and output areas, and also we have to greatly increase the output area as compared to the input area.

Thus, to enable minute operation, the output design is important.

(2) Parameters which depends on the structure of document file
We need to pay attention to the data type of a document file operated with the pen. The typical data types are text, image, figure, voice, and ink. A minute operation depends on the data types of such document file.

For instance, when text is being operated with the pen using minute operations, the minimum movement of minute operation will reach a value which depends on the size of one character in width or in height. For image data, the minimum movement may reach a value which depends on the size of one dot.
(3) Parameters about the user
There are various parameters about the users. Some examples are, concerning structure and characteristics of the user's body and the number of users.

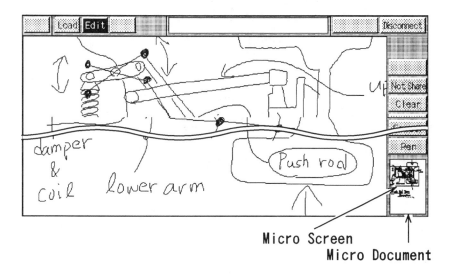

Micro Screen

Micro Document

Figure 1. Hard copy of the display screen of the system which we implemented. The bottom right of the figure shows the micro-scroll. The "micro-scroll" which we implemented has a height of 34mm and width of 22mm.

For example, we could design minute operations in which the user holds one pen; user has five pens attached to each finger of hand (like playing a guitar); user has two pens, one in each hand; task in which one or more persons are using pens; in which the user does not watch his/her hand during the operation (i.e. a blind operation).

4. TWO EXAMPLES OF IMPLEMENTATIONS OF MINUTE OPERATIONS

4.1. A minute operation for scrolling (micro-scroll)

Below, we describe a scrolling method that works on the basis of minute movements of the pen tip. In this method, a small rectangular area on the screen is displayed inside which the user moves the pen tip for scrolling. We call this method "micro-scroll". This method cannot be effective when mouse or arrow keys are used. Rather, an input device like pen is suitable for such minute operations.

This "micro-scroll" is being used daily in the pen-based systems "InkComm"[1] and "InkAssign"[*] developed at the author's laboratory. Here, we discuss the micro-scroll implemented on the telewriting system "InkComm". Telewriting is a real time and bi-directional communication system, using which two persons transmit their handwritten data to each other while simultaneously talking to each other through a telephone. Figure 1 shows one of the screens of "InkComm". The larger area in Figure 1 is the writing and editing screen of "InkComm". A portion of a document file is seen on this writing and editing screen. The rectangular area in the right-hand corner is for micro-scrolling. The "micro-screen" is a scale-down image of the writing and editing screen. The

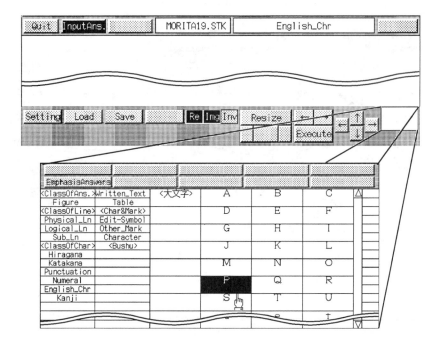

Figure 2 Hard copy of the display screen of the system which we implemented. The bottom right of the figure shows the micro-menu. The "micro-menu" which we implemented has a height of 22mm and width of 22mm.

"micro-document" is a scaled-down image of the whole document. The black pattern is a scaled-down image of ink data. Micro-screen shows one of the positions of the writing and editing screen on micro-document. From above, we can see that, by using the micro-scroll method, user can scroll while seeing an image of the whole document.

There are two methods of scrolling -- continuous scroll and discrete scroll. The purpose of the continuous scroll method is to do a rough scroll by dragging the micro-screen with the pen to a new location. Whereas, in discrete scroll method, the pen-tip is touched on allocation inside the micro-area but outside the micro-screen, and scroll by minute amounts. In this type of micro-scroll, scrolling in any direction, i.e. horizontal, vertical or diagonal, can be done by just one stroke of the pen-tip.

4.2. A minute operation for selecting a menu item (micro-menu)

The authors implemented a pen-based system called "InkAssign[3]" on which the user can select a menu item by minute operation. This system displays a small rectangular area on the screen where the user selects a menu item by tapping the pen tip. We call this small area the "micro-menu". There are two methods by which the user performs a selection, depending on whether he/she is looking at the micro menu or not.

(a) Direct pointing micro-menu : The user taps the pen tip to select while looking at the micro screen where a scaled-down image of a menu is displayed.

(b) Indirect pointing micro-menu: The user taps the pen tip to select while not looking at the micro-menu (whether or not a scaled-down image is displayed), but while looking at a menu which is displayed in the usual size at a different place from the micro-menu. Figure 2 adopts the latter method, and a scaled-down image is not displayed in the micro-menu. The cursor, shown as the icon of a hand on the lower screen in Figure 2, moves together with the pen-tip over the micro-menu of the upper screen. A menu item of the lower screen is selected by pressing the pen tip on the micro-menu.

The system "InkAssign" holds about 8300 items in menu. Figure 2 displays only a part of this menu. When the number of menu items is huge, and when the user's hand has to move to the other screen from the menu screen, the authors believe that micro-menu is a promising method of menu selection.

6. CONCLUSION

Regarding minute operation. All of what we described, excepting the micro-scroll are new.

Distinctive features of minute operation are three folds : it aims to bring out the potential capability of the user's hand; it aims at gaining a larger output from smaller input, and it is essential and unique to pen-input. Minute operations are suitable to pen-based computer with a smaller size screen, but the concept of minute operation is applicable to all user interfaces.

In the near future, the authors would like to design and implement a pen-based user interface which consists of minute operations. This paper showed the first step to a new research field which makes the most of one's potential capability of minute movements, and which helps in getting an interaction style that does not slow down the user when the user's job is going on in the real world.

7. REFERENCES

1 Seiichi Higaki, Hirosi Taninaka, Shinji Moriya :A Telewriting System on a LAN Using a Pen-based Computer as the Terminal, INTERCHI '93.
2 Hirosi Taninaka, Xiangshi Ren, Shinji Moriya : Micro-Scroll of Pen-based Computer, Proceedings of the 44th Annual Convention, Information Processing Society, Japan.
3 Yasuhiro Choh, Toshihiro Morita, Seiichi Higaki, Shinji Moriya : A Pen-based System to Input Correct Answers to Assist in the Development of Recognition and Understanding Algorithms of Ink Data, Proceeding of HCI International'93 5th International Conference on Human-Computer Interaction.

Real-Time Multi-Hand Detection for Human-Computer Interaction

Koichi Ishibuchi, Haruo Takemura, Fumio Kishino

ATR Communication Systems Research Laboratories, 2-2 Hikaridai, Seika-cho, Soraku-gun, Kyoto, Japan

Abstract

This paper proposes a new multi-hand human-computer interface environment based on real-time hand gesture detection. Our real-time hand gesture detection method uses image processing to allow unspecified individuals to convey their intentions to the computer by using their two hands without experiencing the sensation of wearing gloves. The multi-hand detection method, its implementation, and an evaluation of this multi-hand user interface in a virtual reality application are discussed.

1.INTRODUCTION

Gesture-based devices are more intuitive and direct than existing input devices such as keyboards, mice and touch panels. Implementing gestures in a computer-based system would provide an effective interface[1]. Fisher bulit a virtual reality prototype system for telerobotics application[2]. Struman studied the possiblities of using hand gestures in an interactive environment[3]. Most of these studies employed the well-known DataGlove™ as a hand gesture input device. Combined with a magnetic space sensor, it can detect hand gestures to some extent. However, if it is combined with a system's keyboard and mouse, both working efficiency and delicate operation would diminish due to the absence of finger tip sensitivity. When the system is freely utilized by unspecified individuals in a "Virtual Space Teleconferencing System"[4], they must put on the glove and calibrate it every time they use the system. Many gloves would be needed for the system. In environments where complex gesture detection is not required, multi-hand gesture detection method using image processing is a good way to avoid these problems. However, such a method has not yet been reported.

In this paper, we propose a new multi-hand human-computer interface based on real-time hand gesture detection using image processing. Our method allows unspecified individuals to convey their intentions to the computer by using two hands without experiencing the sensation of wearing gloves. The multi-hand detection method, its implementation, and an evaluation of this interface in a virtual reality application are discussed.

2. WHY TWO HANDS?

The importance of two-hand operation has already been reported[5-7]. Hauptmann had subjects indicate via gestures certain manipulations on a graphic image of a 3 inch wire cube on a display screen. This was done by rotating the cube around each main axis in 3-D, transposing the cube by moving it to the left or right from its original position on the screen, and then scaling the cube from its original size to a target size. They used two hands 31 % of the time. Significantly, he found that this tendency to use both hands varied greatly by task, that is, whether the task was to translate, to rotate, or to scale the wire cube. In the translation task, he reports that 1.1 hands on average were seen. In the rotation task, 1.2 on average were seen. In the scaling task, 1.5 hands on average were seen, the most frequent use of two hand. Based on this findings, we focused on the rotation and scaling tasks by two hands.

3. MULTI-HAND DETECTION METHOD

We have already reported a real-time hand shape detection method using image processing for one hand[8-9]. The 3D hand's center of gravity and the finger-tip positions were extracted by two cameras, and the graphic commands GRAB and RELEASE were generated by the numer of extended fingers. In order to attain two-hand operation, the method is extended as shown in Figure 1 and Table 1.

The processes shown in Figure 1 are applied to both stereo images. In the pipe-line image processor, RGB(Red, Green and Blue) analog signals are translated into HSV(Hue, Saturation and Value) digital signals. After the HS images generate the hand probability image IMG1 by using a probability function P(H,S), the run length encoded images IMG4 are calculated. The probability function P(H,S) is

$$P(H,S) = \frac{1}{2\pi\sigma_{H}\sigma_{S}} \exp\left\{ -\frac{(H-m_{H})^{2}}{2\sigma_{H}^{2}} - \frac{(S-m_{S})^{2}}{2\sigma_{S}^{2}} \right\} \quad (1)$$

where m_{H}, m_{S} and σ_{H}, σ_{S} are mean and variance of hue and satulation.

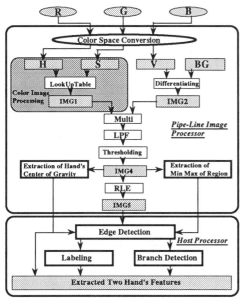

Figure 1. 2D Feature Point Extraction System

Table 1 Created Images

BG	Background image
IMG1	Hand region probability image derived from H,S images
IMG2	Differentiating image between V and BG images
IMG3	Multiplying image between IMG1 and IMG2 images
IMG4	Run length encoded image

In the host processor, by scanning edges from top-right to bottom-left in the run length encoded image IMG4, central points between step-up and step-down edges are detected. At the same time, hand regions are labeled, and finger branches are extracted by the central points as shown in Figure 2. Then, an avarage value of finger directions is extracted by the finger branches. By using the average finger direction, each branch is determined to belong to either hand, left or right, if occlusion does not occur. If occlusion occurs, the branches are predicted by the prediction filter under the assumption that hand shape does not change[10].

Finally, when one finger is recognized as extended, the GRAB command is generated, and when more than two fingers are extended, the RELEASE command is generated, as shown in Figure 2. 3D finger tip positions of both left and right hands are also calculated by triangulation of stereo cameras.

4. IMPLIMENTATION

In order to realize a non-contact two-hand gesture input device that uses neither a glove type device nor a magnetic sensor, these algorithms were implemented and tested. Four sets of MAX-VIDEO20™ (DataCube Inc.) was used as the pipe-line image processor, and SUN4 was used as the host processor. The processing speed was 10 frames/ sec and positional accuracy of the finger tip position was 1.2 cm in a cube-shaped space measuring 45 cm on each side[9]. Detection error of determining the number of fingers was below 10 percent when occlusion did not occur.

The device is implemented in a virtual reality system as shown in Figure 3. Our graphics display is a 70-inch projector connected to the IRIS4DVGX (Silicon Graphics Inc.). In order to compare the non-contact device with glove-type devices, a pair of DataGloves™ (VPL Research Inc.) is also set in the system. The gloves use fiber-optic loops attached to the fabric covering each finger to measure digit flexion. The fiber loops are specially treated to "leak" light when bent. Light sent into one end of the fiber is measured at the other end, the light loss being proportional to how much the

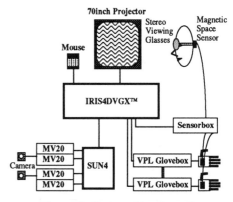

Figure 2. Extracted Hand Shape   Figure 3. System Configuration

digit is bent. In the standard configuration, each DataGlove™ has ten optic fibers, two for each finger. A magnetic space-sensor (Polhemus Navigation Sciences) mounted on the back of the glove gives the position and attitude of the hand. The data rate for hand position and finger-flexion of a single glove is 60Hz. When two gloves are used simultaneously, the effective sampling rate is reduced to 30Hz.

5. EXPELIMENT
5.1 METHOD

Figure 4 illustrates the experimental environment. Two cameras, each with a viewing angles of 34.2° and a resolution of 512x480, are used for detecting two-hand gestures. H=138.0 cm and d=120.0 cm and the angle between cameras is set to 34.2°. The source of the magnetic sensor is also located at the point (0,0,-5) for tracking the user's head position. The unit in each figure is cm. The objects shown in Figure 5 are displayed three dimensionally through the stereo viewing glasses and change their position according to the user's head position.

Three subjects were instructed to grab the shaded object and translate, rotate and scale it in order to put two objects together by using two types of models. Three conditions were tested: using one hand with one DataGlove, using two hands with two sets of DataGlove, and using two hands with the non-contact input device. In one model, the wire and shaded objects were same size, that is, scaling did not occur. In the other, the wire object was one and half size of the shaded object. In this case, translation, rotation and scaling occurred simultaniously. When subjects used one hand, the shaded object was rotated according to the angle of the magnetic sensor attached to the hand. With two hands, the 3D vector, from left to right hand positions, was used for the rotation. This implies that the rotation around the vector was ignored. The shaded object was changed its scale according to the length between two hands. When one hand was used, keeping a left or right mouse button on by another hand made the object to grow or shrink, respectively.

Each subject executed the instruction 10 times, until the two objects were put together in six different conditions. These conditions were called One-sensor without scaling, One-sensor with scaling, Two-sensor without scaling, Two-sensor with scaling, Two-

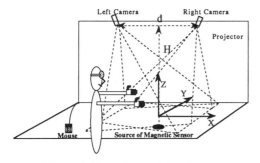

Figure 4. Experimental Environment   Figure 5. Displayed Objects

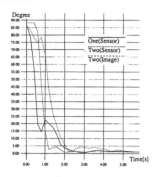

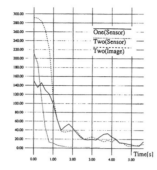

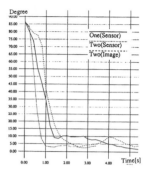

Figure 6.   Rotational Error without scaling

Figure 7.1 Whole Error with scaling

Figure 7.2 Rotational Error with scaling

image without scaling, and Two-image with scaling. At the same time, rotational, scaling and whole errors were measured. The whole error was the square length calculated by using the end points of the central lines of both shaded and wire objects. In the conditions without scaling, when rotational error was below 5°, a color of the ware model was changed as visual feedback. In the conditions with scaling, when whole error was below 20 cm², the sacme feedback was given.

5.2 RESULT

The result of rotational error without scaling is shown in Figure 6. When one-sensor is used, the fastest response in the first second is observed. This means

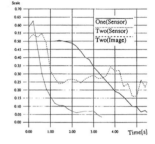

Figure 7.3 Scaling Error

that one hand has quicker response than two hands. However, after 1 second passed, the error of two-sensor is lower than that of one-sensor. The error curve for two-image has the same tendency as for two-sensor without time scale when occlusion does not occur. The sampling rates of two-sensor and of two-image are 30Hz and 10Hz, respectively.

Figures 7.1-7.3 show whole, rotational and scaling error with the scaling task. In Figure 7.1, the response in the first second for one-sensor dropped sharply. As regards rotational error, Figure 7.2 shows the same tendency as seen in Finger 6. However, the response of scaling in the first second for one-sensor can not be observed. This means that in the first second the subjects translated and rotated the wire object, then, scaled it by using the mouse. On the other hand, when two hands are used, both scaling and rotation are observed in the first second. The error curve for two-image has also the same tendency as for two-sensor without time scale. It is clear that if hardware become more faster, our two hand gesture detection method is usefull for virtual object manipulation such as translating, rotating and scaling.

6. SUMMARY

In this paper, we have proposed a new multi-hand human-computer interface environment based on real-time hand gesture detection. The method uses image processing to allow unspecified individuals to convey their intentions to a computer by using their two hands without experiencing the sensation of wearing gloves. This method has been implemented and incorporated into a virtual reality environment. Furthermore, experiments on translating, rotating and scaling virtual object demonstrated the usefulness of this mothod.

7. ACKNOWLEDGMENTS

The authors wish to thank Dr. N. Terashima, President of ATR Communication Systems Research Laboratories, and Dr. K. Habara, Executive Vice President of ATR International, for their thoughtful advice and encouragement of this research. The authors also wish to thank their colleagues, who willingly took part in discussing this study.

8. REFERENCES

1 Brooks and F. P. Jr.: "Grasping Reality Through Illusion", USIT'88: ACM SIGGRAPH/SIGCHI symposium on User interface Software and Technology, 1988.

2 S. S. Fisher, M. McGreevy, J. Humphries and W. Robinett, "Virtual Environment Display System", In Proceesings of ACM Workshop on Interactive Graphics, 77-87, 1986.

3 D. J. Sturman, D. Zeltzer, and S. Pieper, "Hands-on interaction with virtual environments", In Proceedings of the ACM Symposium on User Interface Software and Technology, 1989.

4 F. Kishino: "Communication with realistic sansation(in Japanese)", 3-D image, Vol.4, No.2, 1990.

5 Buxton, William and Brad A. Myers: "A study in two-handed input", In Proceedings of CHI '86 Human Factors in Computing Systems, 321-326, 1986.

6 Hauptmann and Alexander G.: "Speech and gestures for graphic image manipulation", In Proceedings of CHI '89 Human Factors in Computing Systems, 241-245, 1989.

7 Richard A. Bolt and Edward Herranz: "Two-handed gesture in multi-modal natural dialog",In Proceedings of the ACM Symposium on User Interface Software and Technology, 15-18, 1992.

8 K. Ishibuchi, H. Takemura and F. Kishino: "Real Time Hand Shape Recognition Using Pipe-line Image Processor", In Proceedings of the IEEE Internatioanl Workshop on Robot and Human Communication, 111-116, 1992.

9 K. Ishibuchi, H. Takemura and F. Kishino: "Real Time Hand Shape Recognition for Man-Machine Interfaces", In proceedings of the IEEE International Conference on Systems, Man, and Cybernetics, 1407-1412, 1992.

10 K. Ishibuchi, H. Takemura and F. Kishino: "Real Time Hand Shape Recognition for Two-hand Operation(in Japanese)", In Proceesings of IEICE Spring Confernce, A-149, 1992.

Pen-based interfaces for drawing figures with 'Stationery Metaphors'

Masaki Nakagawa, Shinya Kazama, Takashi Satou and Natsuko Fukuda

Dept. of Computer Science, Tokyo Univ. of Agri. and Tech.
2-24-16 Naka-cho, Koganei, Tokyo, 184, JAPAN, e-mail:nakagawa@tuatg.tuat.ac.jp

Abstract
This paper describes figure drawing interfaces on a display integrated tablet where one makes a rough sketch with a pen and then draws a neat copy with virtual drawing tools that are displayed on paper-like images and manipulated with a realistic feel. We call these the 'Stationery Metaphors'. In this paper, we present a hierarchical representation of document structure, how stationery metaphors work within this representation and their advantages.

1. INTRODUCTION

The selection of figure primitives from a menu is a common method used in computer drawing. In these environments, the figure intended to be drawn must be conceptually decomposed into primitives, then those primitives are selected, modified and recomposed into the figure on the screen. On the other hand, with real paper we make a rough sketch with a pen and then make a neat copy with drawing tools. The process of drawing on current computer systems is very different from our familiar actions of drawing with pen on paper.

Handwriting is what is called in cognitive psychology 'automatic' [1], so that creative thinking is not interrupted. Highly dexterous work is automatic and requires no attention what so ever. For work to be made automatic, however, an excessively large amount of time must be spent on training. Typing text can be automated by intensive training, but drawing figures with keyboard and mouse operations is difficult to automate. Consequently, the present conditions require us to prepare a handwritten draft with pen on paper before we perform those unnatural and troublesome operations in order to obtain the benefits of computer processing.

To avoid the problems of mouse and keyboard such as those mentioned above, and to enhance the merits of pen and paper a new device is going to be introduced into human computer interaction. Remarkable progress has been made both in liquid crystal displays and tablet digitizers so that the combination of these technologies, i.e., low cost yet high performance display integrated tablets (DIT) have become available. They are expected to provide paper-like interfaces [2-4].

If so, however, the interfaces should be designed to exploit the automated nature of handwriting. That is, drawing as well as writing should be done without any conscious effort, and without being bothered by troublesome details, so that we can draw figures as easily as possible and still make full use of computing utilities as a way of clarifying our ideas. This helps promote creativity. It is clear that the transportation of mouse-based software to a DIT environment may not extract the true benefits of the device.

We have been working on pen-based interfaces which exploit the automatic nature of handwriting. The concept and scope of the project is described in [5-7]. This paper focuses on drawing.

For drawing as well as writing, we try to introduce and extend the merits of actual drawing with pen on paper. Drawing a sketch with a pen is vital in the process of making and clarifying one's concepts. Therefore, the system allows unrestricted free drawing as well as drawing it up with the virtual drawing tools that are displayed on paper-like images and manipulated with a realistic feel. We call these the 'Stationery Metaphors'. In this paper, we present a hierarchical representation of document structure, how stationery metaphors work within this representation and their advantages.

2. MULTIPLE LEVELS OF REPRESENTATION FOR HANDWRITTEN OBJECTS

A handwritten pattern may represent a code (function), figure or just a pattern as it is. One of the merits of handwriting is that various kinds of objects can be written with a single pen. Given the context they are in, humans can distinguish between these, so that they can be mixed. Taken from a different point of view, handwritten patterns can be interpreted in many ways. For instance, character patterns are usually intended to denote character codes. Similarly, flowchart or circuit diagram symbols as well as their interconnections express functions to be performed rather than just figures. On the other hand, diagrams that represent a systems organization or concept, rough diagrams of processes, or abstracts of real things have no necessity to be interpreted as functions, they may simply be formatted as figures. Moreover, a signature written in that diagram should be kept as its pen-trace pattern, translating it to character codes takes away its meaning.

As shown in Figure 1, when we handle handwritten objects as patterns, countering the fact that we have the same flexibility as with pen and paper, there is little merit of applying editing operations to handwritten objects. On the other hand, when we handle them as figure descriptions, editing and formatting is effective, but there is a decrease in the flexibility of expression. Taking it a step further, if we handle them as functions, the logical merit becomes the greatest, for example, simulation or conversion to programs becomes possible, but the flexibility in regards to expressing handwritten objects becomes even smaller.

Computers cannot judge whether a piece of writing denotes a function, a diagram to be formatted, or just a pattern which needs no processing, so we take as the internal representation a hierarchical representation of: functional representation; figure representation; and handwritten patterns.

Pattern recognition is the process of moving from the lower representation towards higher ones in this hierarchy, while drawing provides lower representations up to the specified representation (for example, if a NAND gate is specified, figure representations and the NAND gate pattern are provided). As the representation goes higher, the logical merit becomes greater, but, the flexibility of expression smaller.

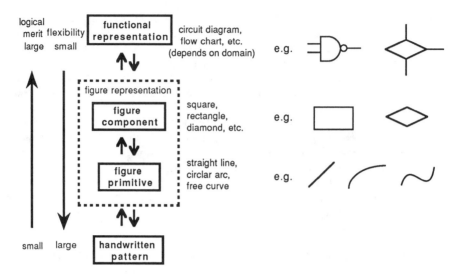

Figure 1. Hierarchy for representing handwritten patterns.

3. DRAWING WITH STATIONERY METAPHORS

The basic concept is that users draw freehand figures and then use stationery metaphors to rule freehand lines as on real paper. When they want to redraw, they can modify figures with gestures as well as erase them partially or totally.

At present, the metaphors of erasers, rulers, compasses and some template metaphors for common figure components have been implemented. Those of templates for functional representations such as flowchart symbols for software diagrams are in the process of being implemented.

3.1 Operations on stationery metaphors

Stationery metaphors can be moved and rotated by pointing and dragging specified areas of the metaphors. When the place is determined, a line is drawn according to the metaphors as the pen is moved along.

As for template metaphors, the shape and size can be also modified by enlarging or reducing height, width or both. Enlargement and reduction can be directed by pen gesture or ratio selection. Moreover, resetting to the original shape and size is done by pointing to the reset area. Thus, various shapes and sizes of oval templates need not be prepared since they can be produced from a circle template. Template metaphors can be created from drawn figures by enclosing the appropriate part with the pen. Of course, user defined templates can be discarded as well.

Figures 2 and 3 show the appearances of the ruler and compass metaphors, respectively. Figure 4 shows an example of drawing up with a compass metaphor.

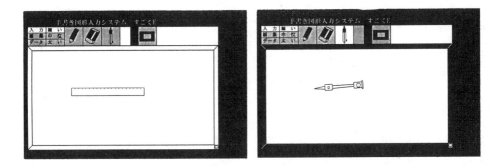

Figure 2. Appearance of a ruler metaphor.   Figure 3. Appearance of a compass metaphor.

Figure 4. Drawing a neat copy with a compass metaphor.

3.2 Automatic adjustment

When we place a drawing tool on paper, we must adjust it so that it fits precisely to already drawn figures. The same problem occurs with the metaphors but it can be partially solved by heuristic processing. Precisely speaking, there are two similar problems. One is to adjust the placement of metaphors as mentioned above and as shown in Figure 5 while the other is to adjust the line drawn to fit already drawn figures as shown in Figure 6. The target of adjustment is different but both require the system to understand the user's intention and apply it when carrying out automatic adjustment. Simple cases such as shown in Figures 5 and 6 have been incorporated but study must be continued into what common sense for figure drawing is, how to capture and how to represent such knowledge and when and how to invoke this knowledge.

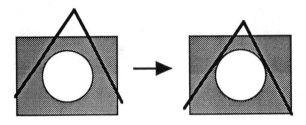

Figure 5. Adjustment of the placement of a metaphor.

Figure 6. Adjustment of the line drawn to fit already drawn figures.

4. HOW STATIONERY METAPHORS WORK WITHIN THE REPRESENTATION

In the above hierarchy of representations, the conventional method of computer drawing by primitive selection deals with functional representations, figure components and partially primitives. Some specialized systems allow the input of only functional representations so that memos or explanatory diagrams cannot be drawn.

On the other hand, in our system freehand drawing provides handwritten patterns, stationery metaphors of rulers and compasses are used to input figure primitives, and templates metaphors deal with figure components and functional representations. Therefore, the environment with stationery metaphors provides all the levels of figure abstraction for us to work with. This type of drawing is a natural extension of drawing with a pen and drawing tools.

5. ADVANTAGES OF STATIONERY METAPHORS

The advantages of stationery metaphors are as follows:
(1) What can be drawn with a real pen and drawing tools can be drawn with stationery met-

aphors.

(2) The manner of drawing figures is almost the same as that with real drawing tools. The system is easy to learn and easy to use, even without referring to a manual.

(3) The problem of parallax caused by the gap between the tablet surface and display surface of a DIT is avoided since a line is drawn on metaphors displayed rather than at the position of the pen.

(4) The ambiguity of a handwritten pattern is disambiguated by the selection of a metaphor. If the straight ruler metaphor is chosen, a straight line primitive is to be inputted, if the compass metaphor is chosen, a circular arc primitive is to be inputted, and so on.

(5) It would be needless to say that the advantages of computer processing are also provided for drawing.

6. TOWARDS EVALUATION

The evaluation of this system should not be made in terms of efficiency alone. We are planning to evaluate it in terms of learnability, flexibility and enjoyability. Prior to this, we demonstrated the prototype system at our university's exhibition. Demonstrations to novices have proved that the concept is especially appealing to children and the younger generation. About 40 people including children and students spent some time on the system, drew figures as they liked and then answered our questionnaires. Among them, 58% reported to have experience using a mouse. We call them the category A subjects while others are called category B. As to the ease of use of pen, 11% in A and 21% in B answered "very easy to use" and 61% in A and 58% in B answered "easy to use". As to the effectiveness of writing a rough sketch before drawing it up, 37% in A and 40% in B reported "very effective" and 58% in A and 50% in B reported "effective". As to the overall drawing prototype system, 44% in A and 46% in B reported "very enjoyable" and 56% in A and 54% in B reported "enjoyable". Their opinions are highly encouraging.

7. REFERENCES

1 J.R. Anderson, Cognitive Psychology and its Implications. 2nd Ed. W.H. Freeman, New York (1985).

2 C. Wolf, J. Rhyne and H. Ellozy, The paper-like interface. Designing and Using Human-Computer Interfaces and Knowledge Based Systems, G. Salvendy and M.L. Smith Ed. Elsevier Science Publishers B.V., Amsterdam (1989).

3 M. Weiser, The computer for the 21st century. Scientific American, (Sep. 1991).

4 Y. Fukunaga, Pen-based interaction technology -seeking the flexibility of paper - (in Japanese). J. of IPS Japan, 33, 7 (July 1992) 820-827.

5 T. Souya, H. Fukushima, N. Takahashi and M. Nakagawa, Handwriting interface for a large character set. Proc. 5th Handwriting Conf. of IGS, Arizona (Oct.1991) 166-168.

6 M. Nakagawa, Robust and fragile technologies of handwriting user interfaces for creative work (in Japanese). Proc. 34th Programming Symposium, IPS Japan (Jan. 1993) 21-32.

7 M. Nakagawa, K. Machii, N. Kato and T. Souya, Lazy recognition as a principle of pen interfaces. Proc. INTERCHI '93 short papers, to appear.

Gesture Specification and Structure Recognition in Handsketch-Based Diagram Editors

Rui Zhao

Cadlab, Cooperation University of Paderborn and Siemens Nixdorf Informationssysteme AG, Bahnhofstr. 32, W-4790 Paderborn, Germany

Abstract

Diagram editing is an attractive application of gestural interfaces and pen-based computers. Within a handsketch-based diagram editor, gesture commands must be specified and recognized. This paper presents a gesture specification mechanism which specifies a gesture command in gesture shape, gesture constraints, and gesture semantics. The structure recognition is based on the two-dimensional relationships between the handsketches and the graphical diagram representations. A Petri net editor is used as an example to illustrate details.

Keywords:

Gestural interface, pen-based computer, visual language, gesture specification, structure recognition, diagram editor, Petri nets.

1   Introduction

In computer-aided design, software engineering, and many other areas, there is growing interest in visual programming. Visual languages used in these domains are mainly graphical diagrams such as Petri nets and entity-relationship charts. For supporting these diagram languages, various diagram editors have been developed. The user interfaces of these diagram editors are mainly menu and command selection based graphical user interfaces improved by direct manipulation techniques such as rubberbanding or dragging. Though the diagram output is greatly supported by many advanced computer graphics techniques, the input of diagrams is a cumbersome process with many complex modes.

The recent advances in pen-based computer technology promise that the pen-based user interface will emerge as a real alternative to the keyboard and mouse based one. Diagram editing is an attractive application of gestural interfaces and pen-based computers which allow the user to communicate with computers in diagram languages by using handsketches so that the user can draw diagrams in the same way as with paper and pen.

While handsketch-based diagram editors offer significant benefits, building such editors is difficult. Recently, there are a number of researches in on-line pattern recognition.

A Survey can be found in [1]. Apart from the problems in recognizing handdrawn graphics and handwritten characters, there has been a lack on concepts of gesture specification and structure recognition for using handsketches to edit diagrams of a visual language. There are well-established methods for specifying textual languages, but this is not the case for visual languages. Most of the existing approaches of parsing visual languages are grammar-based and batch-oriented. Examples are the constrained set grammars [2] and the picture layout grammars [3]. These approaches are not appropriate for specifying gestures in handsketch-based diagram editors. This paper presents concepts and techniques for specifying gestures and recognizing structures in building handsketch-based diagram editors.

2 Gesture Specification

A handsketch-based diagram editor is a graphical structure editor, that is, the editing objects are not just graphical symbols such as in the case of a general drawing editor. They are well-defined diagram elements which can be created and manipulated by handsketches.

A significant feature of handsketch-based diagram editors is that gestures embody several *compound* information such as the user interface in form of handsketches, the underlying diagram syntax, and editing operations together with all of the required parameters.

Our basic idea to specify gesture commands for a handsketch-based diagram editor is to define a set of gesture operators, each of them consists of a gesture shape, a set of gesture constraints, and gesture semantics. In the following, we use a Petri net editor as an example to illustrate our concept and design issues.

Gesture Shapes

A gesture shape is a symbol class whose picture element can be handsketched and recognized by a low-level recognizer which is described in [4]. The main issues for designing gesture shapes are as follows:

- The shape should be intuitive and easy to learn. For "create" commands, the graphical symbol of the object to be created should be used as the gesture shape in the light of our input principle of "what you draw is what you get" (WYDIWYG) [4]. The cross symbol is the standard gesture shape of the delete command, which is abstracted from the paper and pen metaphors of everyday life. Cross is used for delete object in several other gesture-based systems, for example [5].

- The shape should be chosen as general as possible to improve the recognition rate by tolerating the user's drawing mistakes. For example, using an ellipse as the gesture shape for "create place" improves the recognition rate, because the user usually means a circle but draws an ellipse. For the same reason, the shape for "create transition" gesture uses quadrilaterals instead of rectangles. However, the recognizability of each shape must be considered. In case that both parallelograms and rectangles are used in a diagram language with the same constraints for different object types, quadrilaterals are ambiguous, and can therefore not be used.

- The shape should contain enough geometrical information which the corresponding gesture command needs. For example, the "add token" gesture needs only a point to indicate where the token should be inserted, so that a dot is enough. In contrast, the "create transition" gesture requires not only the position but also the size of the transition, so a rectangle can be used as the gesture shape.

Our handsketch-based Petri net editor has ten gestures for creating and manipulating Petri nets. Table 1 shows the set of gesture shapes we chosen.

Table 1: Gesture shapes defined for editing Petri nets

Gesture name	Gesture shape
CreatePlaceGesture	*Ellipse*
CreateTransGesture	*Quadrilateral*
CreateArcGesture	*Opened*
SelectGesture	*Ellipse*
DeleteGesture	*Cross*
ActivateTransGesture	*SharpArrow*
MoveGesture	*SharpArrow*
AddTokenGesture	*Dot*
NameGesture	*HorizontalLine*
ClearGesture	*ZForm*

Gesture Constraints

Matching handsketches with each gesture shape builds the front-end of the gesture recognition. However, the meaning of a gesture shape is similar to the type information in a textual programming language, which is not enough to guarantee the syntactical correctness of a gesture command. Further, there are usually several gesture shapes which belong to the same symbol class which cannot be discriminated one from another without additional information. In our Petri net example, "SharpArrow" is used both as the gesture shapes for "activate transition" gesture and for "move objects" gesture as shown in figure 1. The gesture recognizer can only recognize a "SharpArrow" by considering additional *conditions*. It is a "activate transition" gesture in case that the arrow is drawn over an enabled transition object; and it is a "move objects" gesture, if the gesture is not drawn over an enabled transition, and there are selected objects. Such conditions which make a gesture *valid* are called *gesture constraints*.

Gesture Semantics

One goal in designing our gesture recognizer is to permit easy integration within an object-oriented editor architecture. Different from existing gesture-based systems such as GRANDMA [6], our gesture semantics are not specified in form of interpreters which directly manipulate the editing objects. Instead, our concept for gesture semantics is to generate *normal* editing commands which will be interpreted by the editor framework in the same way as in conventional graphical editors. This has the advantage that the

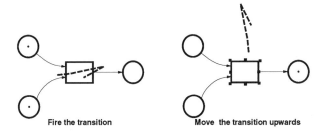

Figure 1: Gesture constraints make possible to use the same gesture shape for different gesture commands.

gesture recognizer is *compatible* with conventional graphical structure editors. Further, the same editing commands can be invoked both by using gestures and by using menu commands.

An editing command usually needs parameters, such as a move command requires the destination position to which the selected object should be moved. In conventional graphical user interfaces, command parameters are collected by using direct manipulation techniques such as dragging or by using dialog forms to prompt the user's input. In contrast to this kind of *explicit* parameter collection, gesture commands have the property that the required command parameters such as "position" or "which object" are contained implicitly in the handsketch or in the spatial relationships between the handsketch and the external representation of the underlying diagram. For example, if one uses an arrow symbol as the move gesture, the destination position can be calculated from the size and position of the handsketched arrow. Therefore, the main task of the command generation is to recognize the command parameters and to create appropriate editing commands.

3   Structure Recognition

A box-and-arc diagram consists of mainly two kinds of structures, namely the *connectivity* and the *hierarchy*. The symbol class of a handsketch identifies the type of the corresponding diagram element. Within the gesture constraints, the diagram syntax can be examined in full detail. Therefore, the key issue of the structure recognition is done by considering the appropriate gesture constraints.

The main task for checking gesture constraints is to examine the spatial relationships between the handsketch which matches the considered gesture shape and the external representation of the underlying diagram. In the following, we consider the recognition of these structures within handsketch-based editing.

Hierarchy

The recognition of the hierarchical structure is to examine the containment relationship between the actual handsketch and the graphical representation of the already recognized diagram fragments. Simply stated, it is to find the smallest node object which contains the sketched object. The external representation of a diagram is organized hierarchically in structured graphics. This provides an efficient structure for searching desired graphical objects because our pictorial hierarchy corresponds to the containment hierarchy of the graphical objects.

Figure 2 shows a screen image of the handsketch-based Petri net editor, in which the user has just sketched a rectangle which is a "create hierarchical transition" gesture. This figure illustrates the recognition of hierarchical structures within hierarchical Petri nets. In this example, the smallest rectangle which contains the handsketched rectangle is that of the transition T1. Therefore, the transition T1 is the hierarchy-parent. Further, the handsketched rectangle contains existing Petri net components, the existing hierarchical structure must be changed. It is obviously that the transition T2 will be a child transition of the new handsketched transition.

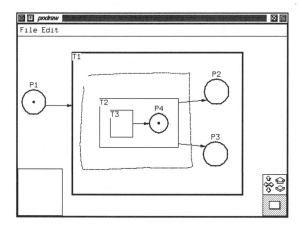

Figure 2: In the handsketch-based Petri net editor, a hierarchical transition can be created by a rectangle gesture.

Connectivity

A connective structure depends at least on one diagram element which belongs to the node type. Therefore, a connection is recognized always in two steps: recognizing the nodes to be connected and recognizing the connection lines. The recognition of nodes is done by matching the gesture shapes and subsequently by checking additional constraints.

In contrast to the hierarchical structures based on the containment relationships, a connective structure is based on the coincident relationships. The gesture constraints defined for a connection gesture deal always with the two endpoints of a handsketched line. The concrete constraints express diagram syntax in form of where the endpoint of a connection line can be positioned. Further, the type of the related diagram elements can be used to constrain the type of the connection. This is particularly useful in case that the same gesture shape is used for different connection types.

The most important task to recognize a connection is to find node objects at the endpoints of the handsketched line, and to check the additional semantic constraints such as places can only be connected with transitions in Petri nets.

4 Conclusion

A mechanism for gesture specification and structure recognition has been described. This mechanism gives the editor programmer a well-defined possibility to specify gesture commands in handsketch-based diagram editors. In order to examine how well our concept for gesture specification and structure recognition works, we built several experimental diagram editors. One of them is the handsketch-based hierarchical Petri net editor which is described in the previous sections. The current implementation is done in C++ by using InterViews and Unidraw [7] for its general graphical editing functionality. An editor framework called Handi [8] is designed and implemented to directly support our concept of gesture specification and structure recognition.

References

[1] C.C Tappert, C.Y Suen, and T. Wakahara. The state of the art in on-line handwriting recognition. *IEEE Transactions on Pattern Analysis and Machine Intelligence*, 12(8):787–808, August 1990.

[2] Richard Helm, Kim Marriott, and Martin Odersky. Building visual language parsers. In *Proceedings of the Conference on Human Factors in Computing Systems (CHI)*, pages 105–112, 1991.

[3] Eric J. Golin. *A Method for the Specification and Parsing of Visual Languages*. PhD thesis, Brown University, 1991.

[4] Rui Zhao. Incremental recognition in gesture-based and syntax-directed diagram editors. In *Proceedings of the ACM Conference on Human Factors in Computing Systems (InterCHI'93)*, Amsterdam, 1993.

[5] C.G. Wolf, J.R. Rhyne, and H.A. Ellozy. The paper-like interface. In *Proceedings of the Third International Conference on Human-Computer Interaction*, volume II, pages 495–501, September 1989.

[6] Dean Rubine. Specifying gestures by example. *ACM SIGGRAPH'91, Computer Graphics*, 25(4), 1991.

[7] John M. Vlissides and Mark A. Linton. Unidraw: A framework for building domain-specific graphical editors. *ACM Transactions on Information Systems*, 8(3):237–268, July 1990.

[8] Rui Zhao. Handi: A framework for building handsketch-based diagram editors. In *Proceedings of the 5th International Conference on Human-Computer Interaction*, Orlando, August 1993.

Musculoskeletal discomfort and job performance of keyboard operators

I.T.S. Yu[a] and H.S.C. Ting[b]

[a]Department of Community & Family Medicine, The Chinese University of Hong Kong; 4/F Lek Yuen Health Centre, Shatin, Hong Kong.

[b]Department of Rehabilitation Sciences, Hong Kong Polytechnic; Hunghom, Hong Kong.

Abstract

A study was performed using a self-administered questionnaire to determine the relationships that might exist between musculoskeletal discomfort and sickness absenteeism and between musculoskeletal discomfort and job performance among keyboard operators in an academic institution.

A high prevalence of musculoskeletal discomfort among keyboard operators was documented. The severity of the discomfort was found to be positively associated with longer sickness absence and possibly also affecting job performance. Although most of the complaints were of a mild degree only, some were found to have adverse effects on the attendance and the job performance. Neck discomfort and shoulder discomfort were of particular concern in that they were both common and were also associated with longer sickness absence as well as worse job performance.

INTRODUCTION

Keyboard operations as part of the office work have attracted much research attention recently both for their productivity and for their association with health problems. Keyboard operators have been reported to be suffering from a variety of physical and psychological problems [1-4]. Among these, musculoskeletal complaints have been given much attention because they are very common among the operators, especially with the introduction of computers / Visual Display Units (VDU) into the workplace [5]. Various risk factors have been investigated, including personal factors such as age and sex which are basically irreversible, as well as modifiable factors such as work station design, VDU design and work stress.

The high prevalence of musculoskeletal complaints might not be of interest to the management if they were not associated with higher absence rate nor adversely affecting job performance. This is why little initiative has been taken by the management (as least in Hong Kong) in an attempt to document the prevalence of musculoskeletal disorders other than for compensation purposes, and to identify the potentially amendable risk factors at work.

OBJECTIVES

The objective of this study was to document the relationship between musculoskeletal discomfort and job performance. More specifically, the study tried to find out the prevalence of musculoskeletal discomfort in various body parts among keyboard operators and to demonstrate that musculoskeletal discomfort could adversely affect job performance and sickness absenteeism. Furthermore, the particular aspects of musculoskeletal discomfort that were important in reducing job performance or causing absence would be identified.

METHODS

The study was carried out in a tertiary educational institution in Hong Kong. Subjects included all typists, clerical officers, personal secretaries, administrative assistants and computer operators who had to operate any kind of keyboard for more than one hour per day. Operators with previous diseases that could cause musculoskeletal problems and those who were pregnant at the time of the study were excluded. A self administered questionnaire was used to collect information on demographic data, job nature and characteristics, experience of musculoskeletal problems and general health conditions, risk factors related and unrelated to work and sickness absence.

Those who reported pain within the three months preceding the interview were asked to evaluate the effect of musculoskeletal discomfort on their job performance. Decrease in work speed, increase in errors and increase in the number of unscheduled rest breaks during keyboard operation and other general office work were measured separately on a scale from 0 (no effect) to 10 (profound influence). Two job performance indices were composed, one related to typing or keyboard operation and the other related to general office work performance. Decrease in work speed, increase in errors and increase in the number of unscheduled rest breaks during work were given equal weight when composing the indices. Six performance scores (type-speed, type-error, type-rest, general-speed, general-error and general-rest), two job performance indices: type performance (type-speed + type-error + type-rest) and general performance (general-speed + general-error + general-rest), and also sickness absenteeism were evaluated for their associations with various musculoskeletal disorders which were then tested using conventional statistical methods.

RESULTS

Sample characteristics
450 questionnaires were sent out and 234 completed questionnaires were returned, giving a response rate of 52%. After excluding those who did not fulfil the inclusion criteria, 221 subjects were included in the subsequent analysis. 189 (86%) of the subjects were female and 116 (53%) were single. Age ranged from 17 to 47 with a mean of 28.7 years. The most common job title was clerk (48%), this was followed by typist (15%), personal secretary (14%), administrative assistant (12%) and computer officer (11%). Most of them were secondary school graduates (78%) while 20% had completed university education.

The majority of them were doing English typing (91%) and using computers (84.2%). The average daily keyboard operation time was 3.39 hours (range 1 - 8 hours), and the majority (73%) worked with the keyboard for less than 4 hours each day. The mean duration in the present job was 5 years and 9 months (range 1 month to 24 years); 60% had worked for 5 years or less, 20% between 5 to 10 years and the remaining 20% over 10 years.

Prevalence of musculoskeletal discomfort
Musculoskeletal discomfort during work was quite prevalent among the keyboard operators, and most of the discomfort consisted of fatigue or soreness and mild pain (see Table 1).

Table 1.
Location and degree of musculoskeletal discomfort

Location	Fatigue/soreness		mild pain		moderate pain		Total	
Neck	71	(32.1%)	32	(14.5%)	21	(9.5%)	124	(56.1%)
Shoulder	65	(29.4%)	31	(14.0%)	22	(10.0%)	118	(53.4%)
Back	59	(26.7%)	29	(13.1%)	16	(7.2%)	104	(47.1%)
Upper limb	11	(5.0%)	8	(3.6%)	5	(2.3%)	24	(10.9%)
Hand/wrist	36	(16.3%)	23	(10.4%)	14	(6.3%)	73	(33.0%)
Any part	88	(39.8%)	38	(17.2%)	22	(10.0%)	148	(67%)

Sickness absence and musculoskeletal discomfort at work
Sickness absence within the three months preceding the questionnaire interview was recorded for all respondents. They were absent for an average of 1.16 days (range 0 - 10). Those who reported having any discomfort within the preceding three months (n=148) had an average of 1.36 days absence due to sickness, while those who did not report musculoskeletal discomfort at work (n=73) had less sickness absence (average of 0.75 day); the difference being statistically significant (p=.001). Further analysis showed that discomfort at different body parts were associated with more days off work but the differences only achieved statistical significance for the neck and shoulder regions (Table 2).

Table 2.
Average sickness absence (days) among keyboard operators with reference to musculoskeletal discomfort

Body Part	With Pain	Without Pain	p value
Neck	1.41	0.85	0.002
Shoulder	1.47	0.82	<0.001
Back	1.35	1.00	0.074
Upper limb	1.46	1.13	0.281
Hand/wrist	1.40	1.05	0.116
Any part	1.36	0.75	0.001

The severity of musculoskeletal discomfort was also found to have an effect on sickness absenteeism (Table 3) which was statistically significant (ANOVA; p=.043). Those having mild and moderate pain had significantly more days off work due to sickness than those who experienced only fatigue or soreness.

Table 3.
Sickness absenteeism according to severity of musculoskeletal discomfort

Discomfort Status	Mean sickness absence (N)	
Fatigue or soreness	1.11 days	(88)
Mild pain	1.82 days	(38)
Moderate or severe pain	1.59 days	(22)

Job performance and musculoskeletal discomfort at work
A higher degree of discomfort was associated with worse performance as indicated by the higher means scores on all performance indices for the group having moderate pain when compared to the other groups, though none of the associations achieved statistical significance (Table 4).

Table 4.
Association of job performance with the degree of discomfort

Performance	Degree of discomfort			ANOVA
Scores (means)	Fatigue	Mild	Moderate	F Probability
Type-speed	3.22	3.34	5.14	.052
Type-error	2.81	2.89	3.95	.260
Type-rest	3.23	3.53	5.23	.053
General-speed	3.20	3.39	4.95	.070
General-error	2.70	2.53	3.64	.289
General-rest	3.11	3.26	4.36	.213
Type performance	9.25	9.76	14.32	.072
General performance	9.02	9.18	12.95	.144

Among the body parts, neck pain was found to have statistically significant associations with type-error, general-speed, general-error, general-rest and general performance; those having neck discomfort had higher mean scores than those without. Similarly, shoulder discomfort had statistically significant associations with type-speed, type-error and type performance. Discomfort at the back and in the upper limbs and hands seemed not to have significant influence on job performance among this group of keyboard operators; in fact, some of the mean scores for those with upper limb discomfort were lower than those without (Table 5).

Table 5.
Discomfort in body parts and job performance

Performance Parameter	Body parts (mean scores for pain/no pain)				
	Neck	Shoulder	Back	Upper limb	Hand/wrist
Type-speed	3.66/2.88	3.93/1.97**	3.68/3.18	4.54/3.34	3.78/3.29
Type-error	3.21/1.92*	3.25/2.00*	3.14/2.66	3.13/2.98	3.18/2.83
Type-rest	3.73/2.96	3.86/2.57	3.61/3.59	4.21/3.48	3.67/3.53
General-speed	3.80/2.04*	3.77/2.50	3.67/3.14	3.54/3.51	3.66/3.37
General-error	3.06/1.42**	2.97/2.13	2.93/2.48	2.71/2.81^	2.95/2.65
General-rest	3.59/2.04*	3.53/2.57	3.51/2.93	3.21/3.36^	3.38/3.29
Type perf.	10.6/7.75	11.1/6.53*	10.4/9.43	11.88/9.8	10.6/9.65
General perf.	10.45/5.5**	10.27/7.2	10.1/8.55	9.46/9.69^	9.98/9.32

* p ≤ .05   ** p ≤ .01   ^ Reversed relationship

DISCUSSIONS

About half of the keyboard operators reported discomfort in each of the following regions: neck, shoulder, back, and one third reported discomfort in the hands and wrists. These prevalence figures for musculoskeletal discomfort were comparable to a previous study conducted on typists only [6]. The response rate in the present study was only 52% and bias might be present in such a way that respondents had a higher tendency to report discomfort and the size of the problem might be over represented.

On the whole, most of the musculoskeletal discomfort experienced by the keyboard operators were considered as minimal or mild, only about one sixth to one fifth of those who experienced discomfort (depending on body parts) were having moderate pain. This may indicate that the subjects under study belonged to a survivor population, those who were really having serious problem might have already quitted their job. On the other hand, the musculoskeletal discomfort, though mild, did have deleterious effects on sickness absenteeism and job performance.

Those keyboard operators who had discomfort in any body part had significantly more sickness absence than those who did not experience any discomfort. The degree of discomfort was also influencing absenteeism, those having mild pain and moderate pain had more days off work than those who only had fatigue or soreness (see table 3). The latter group in turn had more days off work than those who had no musculoskeletal discomfort at all. These findings provided evidence for the hypothesis that musculoskeletal discomfort at work would affect work output by leading to more sickness absence.

The severity of the discomfort also had some influence on the job performance (table 4). Those having moderate pain had poorer job performance scores than those who only experienced fatigue or soreness or mild pain, though a statistically significant result could not be found, probably because of inadequate sample size.

Regarding the location of the musculoskeletal discomfort, neck, shoulders and back were the body parts most commonly affected, but only neck and shoulder discomfort had significant influence on sickness absence from work (table 2), and job performance. Back pain, though common (and also common among different occupational groups studied before), was not very characteristic of keyboard operation and did not affect job performance. Shoulder discomfort seemed to have more influence on typing or keyboard operation while neck discomfort affected the general work performance to a larger extent. A possible explanation might be that during typing or keyboard operation, the shoulders had to sustain a certain amount of static load (unless with an ideal work station design), and if the shoulders were experiencing discomfort, that might lead to lowered tolerance for the static load, thereby giving rise to poorer performance in keyboard operation. On the other hand, general office work required a lot of neck bending while working on the desk top; thus, any neck discomfort would hinder the optimal performance in general office work. Potential confounders, such as age, sex, marital status and job category were evaluated and found not to have any significance influence on the final outcome.

CONCLUSION

This study confirmed the high prevalence of musculoskeletal discomfort among keyboard operators. It also demonstrated that musculoskeletal discomfort did affect job performance and caused sickness absence. This should be of concern to the management. Neck pain and shoulder pain, which are usually more common among clerical workers in general, had a major influence on job performance and sickness absenteeism. Future efforts should be concentrated on identifying the reversible risk factors associated with the development and perpetuation of neck and shoulder pain among keyboard operators so as to reduce their deleterious effects on job performance and attendance.

REFERENCES

1. Knave B.G. Work at video display terminals. An epidemiological health investigation of office employees. 1. Subjective symptoms and discomforts. Scand J Work Environ Health. 1985:457-466.
2. Allen V.R. Health promotion in the office. Am J Occup Ther. 1986; 40(11):764-770.
3. Bammer G. VDUs and musculoskeletal problems at the Australian National University - a case study. In Knave B & Wideback P.G. (eds.), Work with Display Units 86, North-Holland:Elservier Sciences Publishers, 1987.
4. Edwards R.H.T. Hypotheses of peripheral and central mechanisms underlying occupational muscle pain and injury. Eur J Appl Physiol. 1988; 57:275-281.
5. Evans J. Women, men, VDU work and health: a questionnaire survey of British VDU operators. Work and Stress. 1987; 1(3):271-283.
6. Yu I.T.S., Tsang Y.Y. and Liu T.Y. Occupational health problems amongst typist: a questionnaire survey. In: Research Perspectives in Occupational Health and Ergonomics in Asia and Other Countries (ACOH/SEAES Conference Proceedings, November 1991, Bangkok), pp. 251-256.

Evaluating Performance, Discomfort, and Subjective Preference Between Computer Keyboard Designs

S. D. Douglas[a] and A. J. Happ[b]

[a]Office Ergonomic Center, IBM Corp., 1000 N.W. 51 St., MS 2212, Boca Raton, Fl, USA, 33429

[b]Human Factors Department, IBM Corp., 1000 N.W. 51 St., MS 2212, Boca Raton, Fl, USA, 33429

Abstract

Participants performed a data-entry task on three commercially-available QWERTY-layout keyboards. Productivity, error-rate, reported discomfort, and subjective preference were compared.

1. INTRODUCTION

Computer users are best served by a workstation that is either designed or adjustable to accommodate the task requirements and the physique of the person. Proper height and angular settings of the keyboard, screen and chair, with sufficient support for the hands, back, thighs, and feet allow for a healthy and comfortable posture. No matter how adjustable the workstation, however, most keyboards are still configured in the QWERTY layout inherited from manual typewriters. In order to type, the wrists must be turned outward until the fingers lie perpendicular to the key rows. This unnatural positioning of the forearms and wrists can make it uncomfortable to type for long periods of time.

Refer to Table 1. In the current study, we compared the traditional keyboard with an alternative design to determine differences in productivity and discomfort. Both the traditional, an IBM PS/2 Enhanced Keyboard[1], and alternative ("AR," "AD") keyboards are commercially available. The latter employs the QWERTY layout, but splits the alphabetic characters into two keypads, split at the T-Y, G-H, and B-N key junctions. Each keypad rotates outward to enable typing without ulnar deviation, and forms a concave dish in the keyboard. The front of the frame extends as a wrist-rest. Note that less force is required to select ("make") a character. The intent is that a typist can rest the hands and press, rather than strike, the keys. Space keys and back-space- and arrow-keys form thumb-pads.

---

[1]IBM Enhanced Keyboard is a registered trademark of IBM Corporation.

One (AR) retains the function key row; the other (AD) distributes the function keys among the keypads. The brand name of this keyboard is withheld, as the intent was to compare designs, not to stage a competition between manufacturers.

Table 1
Design characteristics of tested keyboards

	IBM PS/2	AR	AD
Key surface dimensions (mm)	13 x 15	13 x 13	13 x 13
Key separation (center to center-mm)	20	20	20
Key force at "make" (N) *	.740	.608	.600
Key displacement at "make" (mm) *	3.32	2.20	2.17

* Key force and travel test performed using Instron Tester 1125, with 2000-gm compression load cell, working in full-scale range of 100 and 200 gms., with a crosshead travel speed of 10 mm/min.

2. METHOD

All nine participants were provided by a temporary-employment firm, and attended a training session the day prior to testing. All three keyboards were demonstrated, and participants performed typing exercises on each. They were also required to demonstrate a sufficient degree of familiarity with WordPerfect 5.1™

A ratio-scale discomfort rating method (Balliett,1991; Borg,1982) was demonstrated. The scale of 0= nothing perceived to 10= very, very strong discomfort enabled ratings on the basis of relative intensity. Breaks could be taken at any time, but subjects were told they would be advised to stop for the duration of the hour if "4- somewhat strong" was reported.

Testing took place over three consecutive days. During each day, participants typed at each keyboard for one hour from one of three provided texts, all of which had been marked with one special command (underline, boldface, italics) per fifty characters of text. Keyboard order was counterbalanced, and all three texts were used by each participant each day.

Participants were seated at adjustable-height ergonomic chairs. A ten-minute warm-up period of typing exercises, to offset carryover effects from the previously-used keyboard, preceded each testing hour. Participants were then given one of the three texts, and were instructed to type at a comfortable rate, and to not spend time proof-reading or scrolling through the text to correct errors. They were also reminded that words (see below) and errors would be counted.

At the 20-, 40-, and 60-minute points of each session, the test administrator instructed participants to stop typing. Without moving, they observed a numbered, sectioned body map (Corlett and Bishop, 1976) that delineated 15 regions: the neck, upper shoulders, shoulders, upper back, middle back, lower back, upper arms, forearms, buttocks, wrists, thighs, lower legs, feet, hands, and fingers. They verbally indicated, by number, the locations of discomfort, and, using the Borg ratio scale, assigned a discomfort intensity rating for each region. When all of the affected regions were reported, participants were instructed to resume typing.

A mandatory 30-minute rest break followed the first and second sessions each day. It was stressed that the break was to last until recovery from all residual discomfort, but additional time was never requested. Following the third session, subjects were dismissed for the day.

3. RESULTS

3.1. Productivity

The 81 typing samples (9 subjects x 3 keyboards x 3 sessions at each) were hand-scored. Characters were counted, rather than words, because of the uniform length of the former.

Errors were grouped by four types: transpositions, substitutions, omissions, and insertions. Multiple errors could be charged per word: a substitution ("cot" instead of "cat") and transposition ("cto") counted for two errors. If a special designator (e.g. underline) was extended beyond the character range indicated on the text, it was scored one insertion error, no matter how far the overrun. An omission error was charged when it did not fully cover the specified range.

Because the alternative keyboards employ space keys, spaces were included in the character count. Extra spaces between words and extra carriage returns, however, were ignored.

Refer to Figure 1. Recall that "AR" applies to the alternative keyboard with the function key row; "AD" to the keyboard with the function keys distributed. A repeated-measures analysis of variance (ANOVA) revealed a significant effect of the keyboard type on character output, $F = 123.07$, $p < .0001$. Duncan Multiple Range tests were performed for mean characters typed, errors, and performance ratio (errors/characters). The mean number of characters typed on the IBM keyboard was 10,195.8 (sd: 4164.6) per hour (approximately 30 words per minute), significantly greater than the 5458.4 (15 wpm, sd: 3015.5 chr/hr) on AR and 5298.1 (14 wpm, sd: 2937.4 chr/hr) on AD.

A two-way repeated-measures ANOVA generated a non-significant F-value for the effect of experience with each keyboard (session) on character output, $F = 0.03$, $p < .9714$. Overall, productivity increased a non-significant 210.5 characters from the first session to the third.

Participants were reminded to type at a natural, comfortable rate, since speed and accuracy were equally important. A Pearson analysis generated a correlation coefficient between characters and total errors per session of -0.16356, $p < .1446$. The negative, non-significant r discounts the possibility of a speed-accuracy trade-off. Performance differences among participants were more likely due to differences in individual typing ability, and to the keyboards themselves.

The distribution of errors over keyboard type and session is shown in Fig. 2. The effect of the keyboard type on errors significantly favors the IBM keyboard. A repeated-measures ANOVA yielded a significant F-value (3.85, $p < .0255$), and a Duncan Means test showed that the 12.04 average errors per hour (1 per 847 characters) was significantly lower than for either AD (33.48/hr, or 1 per 82 characters) or AR (40.41/hr, or 1 per 135 characters). Although the highest average of errors occurs in the second session, no effect of experience on errors was found, $F = 0.19$, $p < .8259$, and the same was true of the effect of experience on performance ratio (errors/characters), F = 0.10, p < .9037.

A General Linear Model procedure was conducted to determine the effect of keyboard order in a given day on productivity and errors. Neither characters typed (F = 0.14, p < .8690), nor errors (F = 0.33, p < .7176) were affected, nor were there significant interactive effects of keyboard and order on productivity (F = 0.06, p < .9927) or errors (F = 1.84, p < .1303). In short, performance was not degraded by the length of time of the test day.

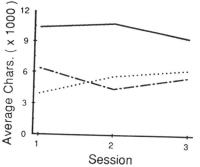 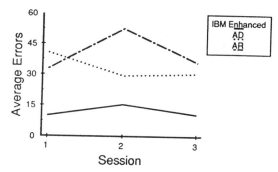

Figure 1. Average characters typed per hour, by keyboard.

Figure 2. Average errors per hour, by keyboard. (Legend applies to both Figs.)

3.2. Discomfort

Participants identified the upper-shoulder region the most frequently on the body map. Receiving the highest average discomfort rating per instance reported (2.18-Moderate) were the shoulders, followed by the upper shoulders (1.95). The thighs and lower legs went unreported throughout the study; the upper legs were mentioned once, and rated 0.5 (very, very weak).

Discomfort reports were made on 120 body regions at the 20- and 40-minute marks. By the end of the hour, either a lower Borg rating or none at all was made for the same region 64 times, or 53.3%, suggesting that some discomfort may originate in adjusting to the workstation and task.

A "4" rating was given prior to the end of the hour on three occasions. Participants were advised to stop, but chose to continue working on all three occasions. Two participants later "recovered" to a lower rating in the respective region. The third rated the affected region a 4 at the end of the hour, but reported full recovery following the 30-minute rest break. In all three instances, the keyboard being used was the traditional model.

Discomfort ratings were summed across regions and 20-minute reporting intervals, and a Friedman ranks analysis showed no significant difference in keyboard type for aggregate discomfort experienced: $Chi^2(2) = 0.76$, p < .6823. A one-way analysis of variance (ANOVA) supports this finding (F= 0.22, p < .8051). The number of body regions in which discomfort was experienced was also aggregated, and a Friedman analysis indicated non-significant differences among the three keyboards: $Chi^2(2) = 1.15$, p < .5623.

A General Linear Models procedure revealed no effect of keyboard order on aggregate discomfort, F = 0.94, p < .3915, nor was there an interactive effect of keyboard type and order on discomfort, F = 1.61, p < .1735.

Finally, in order to perform a Pearson correlation analysis between aggregate discomfort and the performance data, the final discomfort ratings from sessions were summed. This evened the number of data points in each variable. Taken as a whole, the correlation coefficient (r) between the aggregate of final discomfort ratings and the characters typed per hour was -0.11, p < .3345, non-significant. Further, no significant correlation was found between discomfort and performance at a particular keyboard. However, a significant correlation (r = 0.44, p < .0001) was found between total errors and aggregate discomfort.

3.3. Subjective Preference

Following the final testing hour, participants completed a questionnaire, rating their level of agreement (1= strongly agree, 9= strongly disagree) to several statements regarding each keyboard.

The first five statements were made about the alternative-design keyboards. In general, participants were neutral about the idea of keeping either model as part of a job (AR: mean=5.22, sd=1.85; AD: mean=5.33, sd=2.60), even though they expressed moderate agreement that they could eventually be as productive with it as with a traditional keyboard [AR: 3.88(2.20); AD: 4.11 (3.06)]. Note the large standard deviations. A vote for where the function keys were preferred turned out a tie: 3 for a separate row, 3 to distribute, 3 with no preference.

Participants frequently had to pause to find the desired key [AR: 3.11(1.83); AD: 3.33(2.06)], and directly blamed the keyboard design for many of their errors [AR: 3.56(1.59); AD: 3.33 (1.80)]. The statement, "I would perform better with the alternative keyboards if I were a better typist" generated mild disagreement on average [AR: 6.00(3.08); AD: 5.89(3.22)], with responses running the full gamut (1-strongly agree to 9-strongly disagree) of the scale.

The next four statements were made in regard to all three keyboards. All three were generally believed to allow for comfortable positioning of the hands [AR: 3.56(2.24); AD: 4.00(2.73); IBM: 3.44(2.24)], and to not be the cause of cramping or pain in the hands [AR: 5.67(2.69); AD: 6.00(2.40); IBM: 5.89(2.52)].

Strongest agreement [1.77(0.97)] that a keyboard allowed for quick typing was given the IBM model; significantly better than the "No preference" for the alternative models [AR: 5.00 (2.40); AD: 5.00(2.69); F = 5.23, p < .0130]. The IBM keyboard also rated significantly better [2.67(1.80)] for enabling accuracy [AR: 5.67(1.94); AD: 5.78(2.54); F = 6.26, p < .0065]. These were the only statements in which a significant effect on an ANOVA for keyboard type was achieved.

Participants predicted how their productivity would change as they continued to use the alternative models. On a scale of 1=increase greatly to 9=decrease greatly, the mean expectation was very near 3: "increase somewhat" [AR: 2.94(1.18); AD: 2.94(1.63)]. The expectation was slightly higher that comfort with each keyboard would increase [AR: 3.67(0.88); AD: 3.96(2.22)].

Finally, each keyboard received an overall satisfaction rating. On a ten-point scale, the PS/2 Keyboard rated significantly highest [IBM: 8.33(1.43); AR: 5.39(1.58); AD: 5.33(2.63); F = 6.92, p < .0042]. While both alternative designs were rated from 2 to 7, the traditional IBM model was rated between 6 and 10.

4. DISCUSSION

Two versions of an alternative keyboard were compared with a traditional-design model for speed, accuracy, experienced discomfort, and subjective preference.

Productivity (characters/ hour) was highest on the traditional keyboard, and the number of identified errors lowest. On none of the keyboards tested did either productivity significantly increase or errors decrease throughout the study.

Even though the designated limit for discomfort (4- "somewhat strong") was reported only when participants were using the traditional design, there was no overall effect of keyboard type on experienced discomfort, either in terms of aggregate of ratings or of the number of body regions affected. While it may be true that some of the "recovery" in discomfort can be attributed to a period of settling in to the task, it also bears noting that participants were positioned and performing warm-up exercises thirty minutes prior to each session's initial discomfort rating.

Neither the order in which keyboards were used, nor the length of the test day, significantly affected productivity, errors, or discomfort.

Participants felt that the traditional design the one that facilitated both the fastest and the most accurate performance, even though all three were QWERTY keyboards. Even when the QWERTY layout is preserved, there remains a "down-time" to proficiency. Future research would seem to require a test design of longer than three days. Whether that should also entail longer sessions of intense data entry is not as clear. Longer sessions at this task without sufficient break time may compromise the participant's health. Other, less keying-intensive tasks may yield less reliable performance data by incorporating more task-required movements and breaks.

The advertised benefit of the alternative models was to promote more comfortable typing. While it was not proven to do so here, there is, unquestionably, a decrement in performance. Also deserving of further study is not only how long it takes to reach a proficiency level equivalent to that achieved on a traditional keyboard, but also whether the conversion from striking to pressing the keys is itself a damper on productivity. If so, it may be the case that, in selecting a QWERTY-layout keyboard for a given task, the user will have to accept a compromise among speed, accuracy, and discomfort.

5. REFERENCES

1. Balliett, J. A. (1991). The Effect of Degree of Shoulder Flexion on Perceived Exertion and Discomfort at the VDT. Thesis, Miami University, Oxford, OH.
2. Borg, G. A. V. (1982). Psychophysical bases of perceived exertion. Medicine and Science in Sports and Exercise, 14, 377-381.
3. Corlett, E. N. and Bishop, R. B. (1976). A technique for assessing postural discomfort. Ergonomics, 19, 175-182.

The authors are grateful to the following for their valuable contributions: Herb Thomas and Rose Diaz of IBM Boca Raton, and Dr. Marvin Dainoff, Dr. Leonard Mark, and Jim Balliett of the Miami University Center for Ergonomic Research.

Intelligent Keyboard Layout Process

Chin-Chuang Lin[a] , Tzai-Zang Lee[b] and Fu-Shing Chou[a]

[a]National Cheng-kung University, Department of Industrial Management Science, Tainan, Taiwan, R. O. C.

[b]Currently at Purdue University, Correspondence should be sent to Tzai-Zang Lee, School of Industrial Engineering, 1287 Grissom Hall, Purdue University, West Lafayette, In 47907-1287, U. S. A.

Abstract

The main objects of this study were to set up an intelligent keyboard layout process, and use Da-Yi method as an example to evaluate the different layouts. The keyboard layout from this intelligent keyboard layout process come out to be better than the current layout, the process can be applicable to the similar keyboard layout design occasions.

An evaluative experiment was conducted by using 24 subjects to compare their performance (speed, error rate) on the three keyboard layouts. Significant faster key-in speed but no significant difference in error rate was found between redesigned and current layouts. The usefulness of the intelligent keyboard layout process was supported.

Keyword: Intelligent keyboard layout process Da-Yi method Word roots

1. INTRODUCTION

The arrangements of many current Chinese keyboard layouts do not fully consider the proper ergonomic principles of keyboard design. The attempt is made in this study to establish the intelligent keyboard layout process, making the arrangement of the keyboard more favorable so as to improve the efficiency of entering Chinese text into computer. The Da-Yi input method here is taken as an example to test the efficiency of the intelligent keyboard layout process.

First of all, about 170,000 commonly used Chinese words were collected. There words were then decomposed into word roots of Da-Yi code. Word roots frequencies and the coupling relationships of word roots were calculated and fed into computer.

To enter text into computer is a job that need the alternate use of both hands instead of using only one finger. Thus, to design an effective keyboard layout, the coordination of the fingers should be taken into consideration. In considering the alternate use of hand and overlapping use of fingers, this study here develops fingers coordination tapping rate

Fingers coordination tapping rate represents the fingers' sideway motion in one row; however, both hands' moving region on the keyboard is the intersection of rows and columns. Thus, we also establish fingers up-and-down movement tapping rate.

This study combine fingers coordination tapping rate (sideway motion), fingers up-and-down movement tapping rate, and the movement capability of fingers and palms to create a data of keystroke tapping rate.

From literature review, the principles of ergonomic keyboard layout, effect of color, principles of group technology, and arrangement principles were gathered. Then these principles were transmuted into an inductive logic rule base which was programmed into the computer. The computer then generate a new Da-Yi keyboard layout designed by applying the rule base.

The designed principles were summarized as follow:

1. The placement of the keys are arranged according to frequency of word roots, with the most frequently used on the home row [1], and then, on the bottom row, the top row, and finally, on the numerical row.

2. The former word roots with higher coupling relationships are arranged to position on the home row.

3. Those word roots with higher coupling relationships should be arranged on both sides of the keyboard, to the advantage of the alternate use of both hands [2].

4. The movement of hands and fingers are minimized [3].

5. The frequency of same finger tapping is minimized.

6. The word roots with high frequency should be arranged on the pressing positions where more dexterous fingers can handle.

7. The ideal ratio of right / left hand is $100 / 88.87 = 1.125$ [4].

8. The load ratios of the 8 fingers in both hands are, respectively, 7.7%, 9.1%, 10.0%, 21.0%, 22.6%, 11.0%, 9.8%, 8.8% [5].

9. Assignment word roots into keyboard layout begin with the pressing position of the index finger of right hand.

10. Consider first the frequency of word roots, and then coupling relationships. Keystroke tapping rate is also concerned.

11. According to the coupling relationships of word roots, we make a relative analysis and then divide word roots into groups as a reference for keyboard arrangement.

12. The combination of the memory plus visual search may be less efficient than a purely visual search. Considering key grouping principles and for the convenience of visual search [2], this study employs the diagonally organized alphabetic keyboard, which can correspond to finger operation principles.

Among human senses, the visual organ is a more direct one. Color is easy for visual search than texture [6, 7] and also useful for the categorization of information. And color not only exerts great influence on visual feedback during training [8] but also helps beginners in many ways [5]. Color causes lower discriminating error rate than monochrome [9]. For the observer to search the color display, the order of the difficulty of the targets, from the easiest to hardest, was red, blue, green, tan and white [6].

According to previous researches, this study takes such saturated colors as blue, green, red, and yellow into account and creates a coloring keypad based on intelligent process redesign layout, shown in Figure 1.

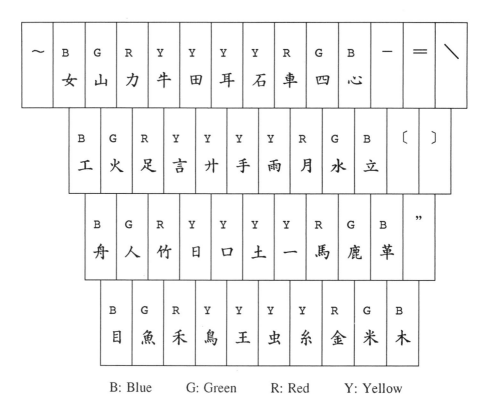

Figure 1. Coloring keypad location on intelligent process redesign layout

2. EXPERIMENT AND RESULTS

24 subjects were randomly assigned to 3 groups, corresponding to 3 kinds of keyboard and working for 20 days, 10 min in each day. Table 1 provides an analysis on input speed. As the table indicated, the influence of the keyboard on mean input speed is significant.

Table 1
An analysis of variance table on input speed

Source	df	SS	MS	F-value	pr>F
Keyboard	2	506.50	253.25	3.58	0.0460
Error	21	1486.53	70.79		
Total	23	1993.03			

As Duncan's multiple comparison and inspection have shown, redesigned and coloring keyboard are considered better than current keyboard 1.

Table 2
Duncan multiple comparison

Duncan Group	Key-in Speed	Frequency	Keyboard
A	96.51	8	Redesigned
A	95.39	8	Coloring
B	86.25	8	Current

Table 3 provides an analysis on error rate. As the table indicates, no significant difference among the keyboards was found.

Table 3
An analysis of variation table on mean error rate

Source	df	SS	MS	F-value	pr>F
Keyboard	2	0.0004	0.0002	0.25	0.7779
Error	21	0.0165	0.0008		
Total	23	0.0169			

3. CONCLUSION

According to the results, using intelligent keyboard layout process to design the keyboard layout will positively improve the efficiency of input operation. Besides, using computer to engage in layout design will avoid those man-made mistakes, making the layout more favorable.

The coloring keypad did not show its superiority possibly due to low input frequencies and short input time in this experiment. So that, the function of color as an aid for memory and identification did not be fully developed. That is also beyond our expectations.

4. Acknowledgements

This research was supported by National Science Council at Taiwan, R. O. C. (NSC80-0415-E006-04).

5. REFERENCE

1 D. A. Norman and D.Fisher, Why Alphabetic Keyboards Are Not Easy to Use: Keyboard Layout Doesn't Much Matter, Human Factors, 24 (1982) 509-519.

2 R. Kinkead, Typing Speed Keying Rater and Optimal Keyboard layouts, Proceedings of the 19th Annual Meeting of the Human Factors Society, Santa Monica, Ca., 159-161 (1975).

3 A. Dvorak, There is a Better Typewriter Keyboard, National Business Education Quarterly, 58-66 (1943).

4 R. E. Hoke, Improvement of Speed and Accuracy in Typewriting, Johns Hopkins studies in Education, 7 (1979) 1-42.

5 F.-S. Chou, T.-Z. Lee and C.-C. Lin, Evaluation and Redesign of Da-Yi Keyboard Layout, J. of National Cheng Kung University: Sci. Eng, & Med. Section, 27 (1992) 69-82. (in Chinese)

6 J. R. Bloomfield, Visual Search with Embedded Targets: Color and Texture Differences, Human Factors, 21 (1979) 317-330.

7 N. Z. Saenz and C. V. Riche, Shape and Color as Dimensions of a Visual Redundant Code, Human Factors, 16 (1974) 308-313.

8 D. G. Alden, R. W. Daniels and A. F. Kanarick, Keyboard Design and Operation: A Review of the Major Issues, Human Factors, 14 (1972) 275-293.

9 C. D. Wickens and A. D. Andre, Proximity Compatibility and Information Display: Effects of Color, Space, and Objectness on Information Integration, Human Factors, 32 (1990) 61-77.

A comparison of keyboard-integrated pointing devices

David F. Loricchio

Design Center/Human Factors
IBM Corporation   Boca Raton, Florida

The IBM Design Center in Boca Raton studied two integrated pointing devices for a portable computer keyboard. The first device was a trackball located on the right side of the typing keys. The second device was a roll bar located below the spacebar on the keyboard. The roll bar rolled up and down and could slide to the left or right. Twenty-one participants used the roll bar, the keyboard-integrated trackball, and an off-keyboard trackball to edit text. Then they wrote their comments about the devices and ranked the devices in order of preference. Participants edited significantly more characters with the trackballs than with the roll bar. Participants significantly preferred the trackballs over the roll bar. While the integrated trackball was clearly better than the roll bar, participants identified a number of problems with both devices.

INTRODUCTION

Recently some computer manufacturers have developed keyboards with integrated pointing devices. Keyboard-integrated pointing devices offer three advantages over pointing devices that are separate from the keyboard: 1) Less hand movement is required because of the shorter distance between the typing keys and the pointing device; 2) The computer requires less desk space because the pointing device is integrated with the keyboard; and 3) If the computer is portable, the user does not have to carry a separate pointing device.

I compared two integrated devices with a trackball that was separate from the keyboard. The first integrated device was a 32-mm diameter trackball located on the right side of the typing keys on the IBM PS/2 keyboard. The second integrated device was a roll bar located below the spacebar on the same type of keyboard. The roll bar was 70 mm long and 3 mm in diameter. Rolling the bar up or down moved the display cursor in a vertical direction. Sliding the bar to the left or right moved the display cursor in a horizontal direction. Rolling and sliding at the same time moved the cursor in a diagonal direction. Two buttons on the side of the roll bar duplicated the functions of the two mouse buttons. The roll bar could be operated with the thumb while the fingers remained on the home row of the keyboard.

I wanted to know if either of the integrated devices was as usable as a conventional off-keyboard trackball. Two of the devices were trackballs. I expected that users would perform a pointing-and-typing task more efficiently with the integrated trackball because it was closer to the typing keys. The roll bar was closer to the typing keys than the integrated trackball but it had the disadvantage of requiring two movements (rolling and sliding). To use either trackball, participants simply rolled the ball in the direction of cursor movement.

METHOD

Participants

Twenty-one employees from a temporary-help employment agency participated in this study. All participants had used a personal computer for two years or more. None of the participants had previous experience with a roll bar or a trackball.

Devices

The three pointing devices were connected to an IBM PS/2 8573 computer with an 8514 display. The integrated trackball was located on the right side of the right shift key. It was 32 mm in diameter and had a control/display ratio of 1:4. The off-keyboard trackball was 54 mm in diameter and had a control/display ratio of 1:1. The roll bar was 70 mm long, 3 mm in diameter, and was below the spacebar on the keyboard. Rolling the bar up or down moved the display cursor in a vertical direction. Sliding the bar to the left or right moved the display cursor in a horizontal direction. Rolling and sliding at the same time moved the cursor in a diagonal direction. Two buttons on the side of the roll bar duplicated the functions of the two mouse buttons. The roll bar could be operated with the thumb while the fingers remained on the home row of the keyboard.

Procedure

Participants used the three devices to edit text that contained misspelled words. Participants moved the cursor to an incorrect character, pressed the selection button to mark the character, and typed the correct character. Participants practiced this task for ten minutes. After practice, participants edited text for three minutes. A participant's score on this task was the number of characters edited in three minutes. After they used a device to edit text, participants wrote comments about the device. Then they used the next device and repeated the procedure. After they used the last device, participants ranked the devices in order of preference. Pairs of latin squares (Lewis, 1989) counterbalanced the order in which the participants used the devices and test materials.

RESULTS

Analysis of variance showed that the type of device used had a significant effect on the number of characters edited (F 2,20=22.79, p=.0001). Participants edited significantly more characters with either trackball than with the roll bar (Multiple comparisons, $p<.05$). Table 1 shows the mean number of characters edited per minute for the three devices.

A Friedman test (Hollander and Wolfe, 1973) showed significant differences in preference for the three devices (Chi square, 2, = 21.24, $p<.01$). Distribution-free multiple comparisons based on the rank sums (Hollander and Wolfe, 1973) showed that the trackballs were significantly preferred over the roll bar ($p<.01$). Table 2 shows the mean preference ranks for the three devices.

TABLE 1. Mean number of characters edited/minute for three devices

On-keyboard trackball	Off-keyboard trackball	Roll bar
13.21	12.08	8.57

TABLE 2. Mean preference ranks for three devices

Off-keyboard trackball	On-keyboard trackball	Roll bar
1.48	1.71	2.81

Participants' Comments

Tables 3-5 describe 95% confidence intervals for participants' comments on the three pointing devices.

Table 3. Comments about the roll bar.

Comment	% Participants	95% Confidence Interval Lower Limit	Upper Limit
Roll bar too sensitive.	90	70	99
Roll bar too narrow.	43	22	66
Roll bar too far left.	19	5	42
Roll bar is a good concept.	19	5	42
Roll bar is too slippery.	9	1	30

Table 4. Comments about the on-keyboard trackball

Comment	% Participants	95% Confidence Interval Lower Limit	Upper Limit
Trackball too sensitive.	71	48	89
Buttons too close to trackball.	19	5	42

Table 5. Comments about the off-keyboard trackball

| | | 95% Confidence Interval | |
Comment	% Participants	Lower Limit	Upper Limit
Trackball too sensitive.	52	30	74
Had to take hand off keyboard.	19	5	42

DISCUSSION

While the integrated trackball was clearly better than the roll bar, the
number of participants reporting problems with the cursor speed or accuracy
was significant for both devices. Small movements in these devices
produced large movements of the cursor on the display. Both devices could
be improved if the control-display rate were increased (cursor
movements were reduced in proportion to the device movements). The roll
bar could be improved if it had a larger diameter, a textured surface, and
a central location. The integrated trackball could be improved if the
selection buttons were moved further away from the trackball.

One difference between the devices was the type of finger movement required
to operate the devices. The trackball requires only one type of finger
movement. The finger rolls the ball in the direction of cursor movement.
The roll bar requires a combination of two different movements, rolling and
sliding. The advantage of the roll bar is that it requires little space
and fits in the area below the spacebar. This location makes it possible
to operate the roll bar with the thumb while the fingers remain on the
keyboard.

REFERENCES

Hollander, M. and Wolfe, D.A. (1973). *Nonparametric
    statistical methods*. New York, N.Y.: John Wiley.

Lewis, J.R. (1989). Pairs of Latin squares to counterbalance
    sequential effects and pairing of conditions and stimuli.
    In *Proceedings of the Human Factors Society 33rd Annual
    Meeting* (pp.1223-1227). Santa Monica, CA: Human Factors Society.

Performance measures in an 'ergonomically' designed keyboard

P. J. McAlindon

Industrial Engineering Department, University of Central Florida,
P. O. Box 25000, Orlando, Florida, USA

Abstract
    The purpose of this paper is to identify and present numerous, and often overlooked, performance measures for the development of an ergonomically designed keyboard. The term ergonomically designed keyboard is commonly used to refer to a number of newly designed keyboards that incorporate human engineering and/or ergonomic principles into their designs. These keyboards attempt to optimize key layout in an effort to reduce finger travel and fatigue, promote a more natural hand, wrist, and arm typing posture through design and support structures, or employ various key activation schema in order to enhance typing performance. All of these keyboards were developed to attempt to remedy a variety of problems associated with the de-facto standard QWERTY keyboard. A more in-depth analysis and evaluation of factors that influence typing performance is presented to better understand the capabilities of the human, the keyboard, the typing task and the way in which they interact.

1. INTRODUCTION

    An abundance of human-computer interaction literature has suggested that newly developed alphanumeric input devices may be more efficient, easier to learn, and may cause less physical trauma than the standard QWERTY keyboard (Hobday, 1988; Kinkead, 1975; Kroemer, 1972; Nakaseko, Grandjean, Hunting, and Gierer, 1985). Numerous studies have found that the QWERTY key layout is difficult to learn and has one of the worst possible character arrangements for touch typing (Dvorak, 1943; Norman and Fisher, 1982). Not only is the QWERTY layout being scrutinized for it's apparent inefficiencies, but concerns over the ergonomic problems accompanying the QWERTY keyboard, including repetitive strain injuries (RSIs), are increasing and warrant investigation. There has been a increase in the concern of muscle and nerve injuries among clerical workers, journalists, and other office workers who use computers or typewriters extensively. The controversy and concern is by no means new. Biegel, 1934, recognized and defined a variety of physical problems caused by the QWERTY keyboard. He pointed out that strength of a keystroke by the little and ring fingers is hampered by having to stretch them to the different rows of keys and that tracks from the home row keys are difficult to follow and often cause errors in typing (Biegel, 1934).

In an effort to quell some of the controversies and concerns associated with typing on a QWERTY keyboard, numerous engineers and ergonomists have radically re-designed the way in which we type. Ergonomic and engineering principles have been applied to the development of several new ergonomically designed keyboards. Keyboard designs range from simple split designs, in which wrist deviations are eliminated, to chordal concepts which utilize a fewer number of keys that are used in conjunction with one another to output characters. Of the dozen or so newly designed keyboards, most incorporate one or more design features that enhance or improve typing performance and reduce or eliminate fatigue or injury associated with typing. These design features include:

- splitting the keyboard to minimize wrist deviations,
- key contouring and flexible key mapping to minimize finger travel,
- built in hand and arm support,
- a ternary capability in which keys rock back and forth to type,
- a capability to rotate and tilt the device into numerous positions, and
- chordal capability in which several keys must be depressed for a single character to be output.

In addition to incorporating these important ergonomic principles into keyboard design, numerous other considerations should be identified and incorporated. Human capability issues related to the typing task and a definition of performance criteria and measurement techniques are required to complete a thorough investigation into developing an ergonomically designed keyboard.

2. HUMAN CAPABILITIES

The Guinness Book of World Records has recorded the world typing record at 159 words per minute (wpm) with only one mistake (Guinness, 1992). Assuming that this was achieved using the QWERTY key layout, numerous performance issues need to be addressed. Is 159 wpm the fastest a human is really capable of typing? Why can't humans type more quickly? Why can't everyone type this quickly? If it isn't a human limitation, can we improve typing speed through better keyboard design? Can we improve performance through better key placement? How long could a person type at such a speed? What types of physical or physiological problems would a high speed typists encounter in the short-term? In the long-term? Researchers have for years been trying to answer such questions. All of these questions can be reduced to a single concept: the concept of performance vs. capability. It behooves designers and developers of keyboards to develop a device that enhances performance by adapting to an individual's capability. It is becoming increasingly important to balance a person's capabilities with the intended performance. Developments for enhancing performance, albeit varied, have focused primarily on increasing wpm measures and have neglected to balance this performance with the capability of the typist. This is especially true for longer-term performance measures and may be a primary contributor to the growing number of RSIs reported each year.

Performance and capability must be defined per unit time (minutes, hours, days). This time element is critical in evaluating and controlling the problems associated with keyboard usage. Problems such as repetitive strain injuries, muscle fatigue, and personnel selection are just a few that need to be evaluated. Numerous researchers have analyzed the time critical aspects of typing performance. Performance studies by Carlson, 1963, and Conrad, 1966, indicate that within subjects low speed correlates to high error rates. Another study, Howell and Kreidler, 1963, found that performance varied as a function of instruction (speed, accuracy, or speed plus accuracy). In understanding and identifying these and other capabilities of a typist, ergonomic issues such as key force, finger repetition, hand and arm posture, along with psychological and physiological considerations, need to be adequately addressed.

2.1. Understanding and identifying human capabilities

Force, repetition, posture, rest, and stress are major factors in controlling and eliminating repetitive strain injuries (RSIs). Analysis of each factor, both independently and in relation to one another, is necessary for designing a keyboard that eliminates or reduces RSIs. Although all factors are equally important in eliminating RSIs, force and repetition are perhaps most important in the development of an ergonomically designed keyboard. A primary objective of a newly designed keyboard should be to reduce or eliminate fatigue factors associated with force and repetition. Force factors relate to the musculature of the fingers and hands that place limitations on their ability to respond in a keyboard task. Haaland, 1962, verified that the thumb is the most resistant to fatigue and that susceptibility to fatigue increases as one moves progressively from the index finger to the little finger. Dreyfuss, 1959, went a step further to say that operating forces should range between 4.1 and 11 ounces. In lieu of this finding, would it be advantageous to correlate key activation force to finger force capability? Or stated another way, should the keys operated with the ring and little fingers be designed to require less force for activation than keys operated by the middle and index fingers? Research suggests that this type of 'balanced' fatigue may have the potential to increase typing performance (Pollock and Gildner, 1963; Harkins, 1965). Additionally, the angle at which the force is applied to activate a key has an affect on fatigue; lateral force results in a more rapid fatigue than downward force (Haaland, 1962). The ring and little fingers have to be stretched when typing characters that are off the home keys. This reduces the strength of the stroke, and leads to the edge of the finger-tip striking the key instead of the center of the tip (Biegel, 1934). As a result of this, lateral forces are required to type with these two fingers. Lateral forces coupled with higher initial susceptibility to fatigue can adversely affect typing performance. Comprehensive research concerning lateral force on typing performance has recently begun primarily due to the development of the ternary method of typing. In spite of this current lack of comprehensive research, a few of the newly designed keyboards did account for lateral force fatigue factors. Most, however, did not. There is still much to discover in developing variable force keys and the associated performance benefits or detriments caused by them.

3. PERFORMANCE MEASUREMENT TECHNIQUES

A paper on performance measures would not be complete without a discussion on performance measurement techniques. A valid, consistent, measure to quantify typing performance is needed to promote future keyboard development and analysis. Inconsistent and invalid measures inhibit promulgation of new ideas and innovation or can discredit a well designed keyboard. There are several measurement techniques used to quantify performance in an ergonomically designed keyboard. Two of most commonly used approaches combine the measurement of speed and accuracy. The first approach utilizes a throughput measure in which an arbitrary correction is made for each error in typing (Alden, Daniels, and Kanarick, 1972). Performance is typically expressed in words per minute (wpm) or net words per minute (nwpm) after an adjustment of strokes subtracted from errors has been made. The second approach measures speed and accuracy in terms of a bits per second (bps) information metric. This approach is based on a more rational grounds for the correction of errors and is typically more difficult to apply (Alden, et. al. 1972). Used appropriately, these measures provide the foundation for future keyboard development.

4. CONCLUSIONS

The emergence of several ergonomically designed keyboards has resulted from an increased awareness and identification of the physical problems associated with the de-facto standard QWERTY keyboard. This realization has led to numerous developments in the way in which one types. Several new ergonomically designed keyboards have had some success in alleviating much of the concern and pain associated with the QWERTY keyboard. Much analysis, however, is still needed to completely understand the typing task and the capabilities of the typist. To increase efficiency, facilitate learning, and to address some of the ergonomic related concerns, a concerted effort must be made to better understand the capabilities of the human, the keyboard, the typing task, and the way in which they interact.

5. REFERENCES

Alden, D. G., Daniels, R. W., and Kanarick, A.F. (1972). Keyboard design and operation: A review of the major issues. Human Factors, 14(4), 275-293.

Biegel, R. A. (1934). An improved typewriter keyboard. The Human Factor, 8, 280-285.

Carlson, R. (1963). Predicting clerical error in an EDP environment. Datamation, 9, 34-36.

Conrad, R. (1966). Short-term memory factor in the design of data-entry keyboards. Journal of Applied Psychology, 50, 353-356.

Dreyfuss, H. (1959). Anthropometric data. Whitney Publications: New York, NY.

Dvorak, A. (1943). There is a better typewriter keyboard. National Business Education Quarterly, 11, 58-66.

Guinness Book of World Records. (1992). New York, N.Y.: Bantam Books.

Haaland, J. (1962). Anatomic and physiological consideration of the use of the thumb for manual control in space flight. Honeywell Memorandum.

Harkins, W. H. (1965). Switch system for consoles. Industrial Design, 1-7.

Hobday, S. W. (1988). A keyboard to increase productivity and reduce postural stress. In F. Aghazadeh (Ed.), Trends in Ergonomics/Human Factors V. New York: North-Holland. 321-330.

Howell, C. and Kreidler, L. (1963). Information processing under contradictory instructional sets. Journal of Experimental Psychology, 65, 30-46.

Kinkead, R. (1975). Typing speed, keying rates, and optimal keyboard layouts. Proceedings of the 19th Annual Meeting of the Human Factors Society. Santa Monica, CA: Human Factors Society, 159-161.

Kroemer, K.H.E. (1972). Human engineering the keyboard. Human Factors, 14, 51-63.

Nakaseko, M., Grandjean, E., Hunting, W., and Gierer, R. (1985). Studies on ergonomically designed alphanumeric keyboards. Human Factors, 27(2), 175-187.

Norman, D. A. & Fisher, D. (1982). Why alphabetic keyboards are not easy to use: Keyboard layout doesn't much matter. <u>Human Factors</u>, <u>24</u>(5), 509-519.

Pollock, W. T., and Gildner, G. G. (1963). Study of computer manual input devices. USAF: Decision Sciences Laboratory, Bedford, Massachusetts, AD 419254.

Facial Animation Synthesis for Human-Machine Communication System

Shigeo MORISHIMA[a] and Hiroshi HARASHIMA[b]

[a]Faculty of Engineering, Seikei University,
3-3-1 Kichijoji-Kitamachi Musashino, Tokyo, 180 Japan

[b]Faculty of Engineering, the University of Tokyo,
7-3-1 Hongo Bunkyo-ku, Tokyo, 113 Japan

Abstract

We've been building a user-friendly human-machine interface with multi-media and it can realize virtual face-to-face communication environment between an user and a machine. In this system, human natural face appears on the display of machine and can talk to user with natural voice and natural expression. Especially in this paper, face expression and animation synthesis schemes utilized in this interface system is presented. We express a human head with 3D model. The surface model is generated by texture mapping with 2D real image. All the motions and expressions are synthesized and controlled automatically by the movement of some feature points on the model.

1. INTRODUCTION

A user friendly human-machine interface using multi-media are focused recently. Our goal is to realize very natural human-machine communication environment by giving a face to computer terminal or communication system. It is a face-to-face type communication system between user and machine. For this purpose, we have already proposed basic schemes including a 3D modeling of face[1], face expression synthesis and coding technique[2], media conversion schemes[3,4], and modeling and rendering method of hair. A real-time animation synthesizer based on Pixel Machine is constructed for the interface prototype system. *Facial Action Coding System (FACS)* [2] is efficient criteria to describe delicate face expression and motion.

Voice is essential to multi-media interface. It's including linguistic information, speaker information, emotional information and so on. If these information can be extracted automatically, natural voice can be an information source of human-machine communication.

This paper reviews and summerizes our facial expression synthesis schemes. After that we propose a new *emotion model* which gives a criteria to decide user's emotion condition and to express emotion transition quantitatively.

We report in this paper some prototypes of computer interface, synchronization method between synthesized motion image and natural voice, scenario making tool to express delicate face expressions and animation scenes appeared in interface display. The basic research of emotion model which is expressed in 2D space is reported at last.

2. FACE EXPRESSION SYNTHESIS

2.1. 3-D Modeling of Human Face

A 3-D wire frame model which approximately represents a human face, is composed of about 600 polygonal elements and was constructed by measuring a mannequin's head. This model is including the teeth's model inside the head. The general surface model is 3-D affine-transformed to harmonize its several feature point positions with those of an input 2-D full-face image. This point adjustment is done by semi-automatical procedures. Some feature points' positions around face, lip, eyes and eyebrows that are necessary for wire frame adjustment are recognized roughly using the results of color information analysis of original image. Some corrections of each feature point can be done by manual operation if necessary.

RGB intensity for a 2-D full-face surface image is then projected and mapped onto an adjusted general face model, following which a 3-D personal facial model is created. This model has a set of points which have 3-D oblique coordinate values and intensity in every polygon.

Once the 3-D facial model is gotten from the 2-D original image, it's easy to rotate the 3-D model in any arbitrary direction or to give many delicate facial actions for lips, jaws, eyes, and eyebrows by controlling lattice points in the wire frame.

Now, we have a high definition wire frame model which has 24000 polygonal elements. This model is constructed by 3D digitizer of Cyberware. This model is expected to make the face expression and its motion more naturally. However, this model doesn't have every feature point positon. So, We control this model hierarchically using normal 3D model with 600 polygons. Figure 1 shows the linkage between high definition model and normal model.

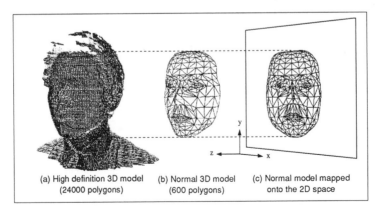

(a) High definition 3D model   (b) Normal 3D model   (c) Normal model mapped
(24000 polygons)   (600 polygons)   onto the 2D space

Figure 1. Two types of wire frame models and their linkages

2.2. Facial Expression Synthesis

Synthesizing the facial images have two main procedures. These are deforming the wire frame model through facial expression parameters and mapping the texture in every polygon onto the surface of the deformed wire frame model. The deforming rules are formulated to simulate the facial muscular actions. Ekman and Friesen decomposed the facial muscular actions into 44 basic actions called *"Action Units" (AUs)* and described the facial expressions as combinations of *AUs* [2].

Upper face has the *AUs* relevant to eyebrows and eyes. The eyebrows have the three types of *AUs*; *"Inner brow raiser (AU1)"*, *"Outer brow raiser (AU2)"*, *"Brow lower (AU4)"*. Lower face has many *AUs*. They include lip actions and jaw rotation. The lips have the five type actions such as up and down, horizontal, oblique and miscellaneous actions. The jaw is rotated round the point beneath the ear. Nodes of the wire frame model in the cheek parts are 3-D affine-transformed to harmonize with the control points of the eyes, lips and jaw. We express each *AU* with the combination of the movements of some specific feature points in the wire frame model. We quantize the movement in each AU into 100 levels between maximum change and no change. So any intermediate expression can be synthesized by combination of *AUs* and their levels.

3. INTERFACE PROTOTYPE

Some prototypes of computer interface are introduced here. Three types of interface system have been designed.

3.1. Interface Driven by Text

The face on display gives messages to user with voice and expression. Speaking scenes are synthesized based on *text to image* media conversion scheme. Mouth shape and duration time of each phoneme are decided after analysis of sentences. Pre-defined mouth shape parameters of each phoneme are located on the keyframe and other frame parameters are decided by 3-D Spline interpolation of keyframe parameters. When phonetic symbol and duration time of each phoneme of sentence are entered into speech synthesis system, synthesized speech signal can be generated synchronizing with the synthesized motion image. Other face expression can be added in the motion image sequence manually using scenario making tool we propose later.

3.2. Interface Driven by Speech

There's natural voice sample in the system, then lip motion can be synthesized by *voice to image* conversion scheme [3,4]. After spectrum analysis of voice, mouth shapes are decided frame by frame, so synchronization between voice and image is automatically completed. This system is useful for voice mail system or voice response system.We proposed parameter conversion methods using vector quantization and neural network. However, clustering or training process takes long time. Sometimes convergence isn't finished. Moreover it's difficult to recognize consonant segment strictly. Face expression based on emotional information may be controlled by voice analysis.

3.3. Interface with Text and Speech

There are both natural voice and text, then lip motion can be synthesized more easily and naturally than previous method. For example, E-mail system can get text sentences and voice mail system can get voice signal. So a multi-media mail system including text, voice and expressions can request both typed-in text and spoken voice from the user.

Automatic speech segmentation and isolated word recognition systems have been proposed . Bottom-up process of this scheme that include segmentation and vowel decision can be expanded to continuous speech, and text can be used as the top-down information for consonant recognition.

The keyframes location and phoneme duration time is decided by recognition and segmentation results. The mouth shapes in keyframe can be decided by phoneme category in text. Smooth and natural lip motion can be realized by 3-D Spline interpolation of parameters between keyframes. Of course, synchronization of speech and image can be done automatically. Face expression control is possible by both voice analysis and manual operation by scenario making tool.

4. SYNCHRONIZATION OF VOICE AND IMAGE

In this section, synchronization method of animation and natural voice using both stored voice and text is introduced especially. Voice recognition for long sentence is difficult problem now. So vowel recognition using template matching and voice sequence segmentation are performed as bottom-up process[6]. After that process, text of sentence is entered and time scale matching between recognized vowels and entered vowels is performed. At last, consonant position is decided by entered text and standard duration table of phoneme. This method can realize an interface using text and speech.

4.1. Vowel Recognition and Segmentation

Vowels in the long Japanese sentence is detected here. Recognition categories are five Japanese vowels that are /a/, /i/, /u/, /e/, /o/, nasals /N/ and voiceless. At first, voice sequience is stored and devided into many segments according to power change and spectrum distance between successive two frames. Each segment is classified into a vowel category by template matching. This result includes more numbers of segments than real phoneme numbers in voice and it has some vowel recognition errors too.

4.2. Time Scale Matching

When text sentence is entered, the order and number of phoneme become clear. Time scale matching is performed by comparing a recognized vowel sequence and a correct vowel sequence of input text. The distance between each phoneme category is pre-determined as normalized Cepstrum distance using training data of specific speaker. The optimum path is decided to minimize the total distance between correct vowel sequence and recognized phoneme sequence using DP Matching method. Many of recognition errors can be restored and segment position of each phoneme of text can be decided by this matching. Each consonant position is located in front of this vowel position and its length is selected by standard duration table. The keyframes for standard mouth shape are located at the start point of each phoneme segment. The shapes of mouth between keyframes are interpolated by 3-d Spline function. Mouth closing moments can be re-generated as well as original motion.

5. SCENARIO MAKING TOOL

We introduce here user-friendly face animation synthesis tool. Delicate face expression and facial animation synthesis scenario for E-mail or system message can be generated by this editing tool. This tool gives an animation making environment to user.

When Japanese or English texts are given to the system, the locations of keyframes in the time axis are decided based on the standard phoneme duration or recognized phoneme segment (Japanese only) from prerecorded voice mentioned at previous section. Next, the face expression can be chosen from the iconic symbol and put it into time axis window by mouth operation. Standard expressions are pre-recorded as the combination of AU's numbers and its intensities. If necessary, user can preview and check the motion image on wire frame model in the window. After choice of original 2-D face image and execution of texture mapping processes, all frame motion pictures can appear on the window. Any kinds of face expressions can be realized by combination of *Action Units* of *FACS* and these intensities quantized by 100 levels. This scenario making tool includes *AU* editor. In this *AU* editor, several kinds of expression can be generated by assigning the *Action Units'* numbers and their intensities in the window. Several expressions edited by this tool are shown in Figure 2.

Figure 2. Several expressions edited by this tool
(neutral, happiness, anger, surprise / disgust, sad, fear)

6. EMOTION MODEL

Emotion model is necessary to express emotional meanings of a parameterized face expresson and it's motion of user and machine quantitatively. We proposed an emotion model based on 5-layered neural network which has generalization and non-linear mapping performance. Figure 3 shows the network structure. Both input and output layer has same number of units. Learning is performed by back-propagation by giving the AU parameters to input and output layers. So identity mapping can be realized and *emotion space* can be constructed in the middle-layer(3rd layer). The mapping from input layer to middle layer means emotion recognition and that from middle layer to output layer corresponds to expression synthesis from the emotion value.

Figure 4 shows the basic emotions' location in the constructed emotion space. Each line means the locus line when AU parameters change from neutral to maximum of each emotion. Training is performed by typical 13 emotion patterns which are expressed by AU parameters. Subjective test of this emotion space by 300 students proves the propriety of this model.

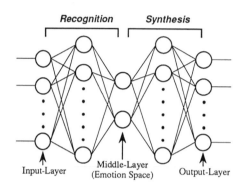

Figure 3. 5-layerd neural network for expression analysis and synthesis

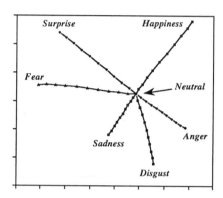

Figure 4. Basic emotions' locations in the emotion space

7. CONCLUSION

This paper presents a prototype of multi-media interface with face. Mouth shape and its motion can be synthesized by analysis of voice and sentence most naturally. Scenario making tool gives the user friendly expression synthesis environment. Emotion space is good to express quantitive meaning of face expression. In near future, computer can understand the user's emotion condition from his face and voice, so it becomes more obedient to user.

8. REFERENCES

1   K.Aizawa, et.al., Model-based analysis synthesis image coding system for a person's face, Signal Processing: Image Comm., Vol.1, No.2, pp.139-152, Elsevier, 1989.
2   P.Ekman et.al., Facial action coding system, Consulting Psychologists Press, 1977.
3   S.Morishima and H.Harashima, "A Media Conversion from Speech to Facial Image for Intelligent Man-Machine Interface", IEEE J-SAC, Vol.9, No.4, 1991.
4   S.Morishima and H.Harashima, Speech-to-Image Media Conversion Based on VQ and Neural Network, Proceedings of ICASSP91, M10.11, pp.2865-2868, 1991.
5   Y.Fukuda and S.Hiki, Characteristic of the mouth shape in the production of Japanese - Stroboscopic Observation, Journal of Acoust. Soc. of Japan, 3.2, pp.75-91, 1982.
6   S.Morishima and H.Harashima, A Proposal of a Knowledge Based Isolated Word Recognition, Proc. ICASSP, 14.5, 1986.

Voice-Responsive Eye-Blinking Feedback for Improved Human-to-Machine Speech Input

Tomio Watanabe

Department of Electrical and Information Engineering, Faculty of Engineering, Yamagata University, Yonezawa, Yamagata 992 JAPAN

Abstract

The synchrony between a speaker's voice and eye-blink, and a listener's eye-blink and nodding plays an important role in regulating human dialogue. This paper reveals significant synchronous as well as lagged relationships between: (a) a speaker's voice and his own eye-blinking response; (b) a speaker's voice and a listener's eye-blinking and nodding responses. On the basis of these findings, an eye-blinking feedback model of a voice reaction system is proposed. The model estimates blinking and nodding responses on the basis of on-off speech characteristics of speech input, and the effectiveness of the model is demonstrated.

1. INTRODUCTION

When people talk to each other, a listener's movements such as nodding and facial expressions are synchronized with a speaker's voice. This synchrony plays an important role in the effective exchange of information. It has been reported that this phenomenon is observed in a neonate in response to the mother's voice [1],[2]. The movement-voice synchrony therefore appears to be an essential part of communication. This reaction mechanism can be adapted to facilitate human-computer information exchange. We have developed a voice-reactive system that, with timing simulates a human nodding. This simulation turns a level meter lamp on and off in response to speech input. This system demonstrates that visual feedback can be effective in assisting effective speech input [3]. Also, we have demonstrated that facial expression graphics can be used to make the human-to-machine speech input environment seem warmer, more interpersonal, and more natural for the speaker [4].

The present paper describes a series of experiments and modeling of eye-blinking and nodding responses. These responses play an important role in regulating the flow of conversation, provide more specific feedback to the speaker, and make the human-to-machine speech input environment more natural. The synchrony between a speaker's voice and eye-blink, and a listener's eye-blink and nodding in actual face-to-face human interactions was evaluated using cross-correlation analysis. From the analysis of synchrony, an eye-blinking feedback model for speech input was proposed. This model incorporated the previously developed voice-responsive nodding model that estimated nod. The model also estimated eye-blinking and nodding responses on the basis of on-off speech characteristics of speech input. We demonstrated the effectiveness of the model in ensuring correct decisions, and accurately simulating the eye-blinking and nodding responses.

2. ANALYSIS OF THE EYE-BLINKING RESPONSE

A Japanese listener nodded in response to a Japanese speaker's message lasting approximately 3 minutes in actual face-to-face interaction. The speaker's voice and eye-blink, and the listener's eye-blink and nodding were recorded on videotape with digital time superimposed on each video frame. There were four speakers and five listeners in the sample.

The eye-blinking parameter B(t) was defined as binary according to whether eye-blink took place or not during each video frame length of 1/30th second. The voice parameter V(t) was also defined in binary terms because the experimenters needed to take note only of the on-off pattern, i.e. talkspurt or silence. Talkspurt or silence was determined in each video frame length of 1/30th second.

Figures 1 (a) and (b) show an example of the time sequence of the speaker's eye-blinking parameter B(t) and his own voice parameter V(t). Figure 1(c) shows a cross-correlogram of the cross-correlation function C(τ) between B(t) and V(t).

$$C(\tau) = \frac{\sum\limits_{i=1}^{n-30\tau} \{V(i/30+\tau)-\mu_V\}\{B(i/30)-\mu_B\}}{\sqrt{\sum\limits_{i=1}^{n}\{V(i/30)-\mu_V\}^2}\sqrt{\sum\limits_{i=1}^{n}\{B(i/30)-\mu_B\}^2}} \quad , \quad \tau = 0, \pm 1/30, \pm 2/30, \cdots$$

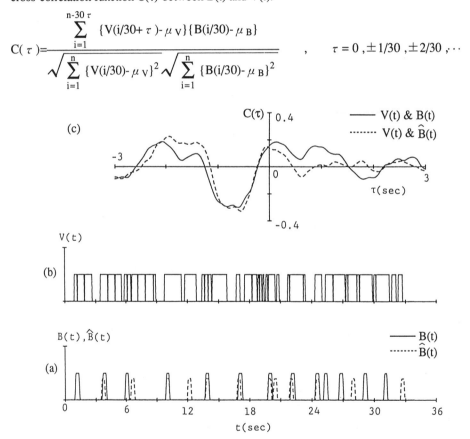

Fig.1 Evaluation of the synchrony between a speaker's voice and his own blinking response. (a) Changing of the speaker's blinking parameter B(t) and the estimated $\hat{B}$(t). (b) Changing of the speaker's voice parameter V(t). (c) Cross-correlation functions between V(t) and B(t), and between V(t) and $\hat{B}$(t) (cross-correlograms).

where μ v is the mean value of V(t) and μ B is the mean value of B(t). We selected a long analyzing period of 34 seconds (1024 frames) and a short one of 12 seconds (360 frames) within the long period. In the region where the time lag $\tau<0$, a significant trough is noted at time lag -0.6 (-18/30) seconds. This indicates that the speaker's eye-blink follows the pause in speech after 0.6 seconds.

Table 1 shows the result of the significant lagged relationship between the speaker's voice V(t) and his own eye-blinking response B(t). In 21 out of 28 in Table 1, the range of time lag where the cross-correlogram shows the significant trough is -0.52 ±0.17 seconds. This indicates the speaker's eye-blink follows his own pause in speech after approximately 0.5 seconds. Figure 2 shows cross-correlograms in 12-second (360 frames) analyzing period (A-F), whose starting times are each shifted by 4 seconds. Computation is based on figures 1 (a) and (b). In the cross-correlograms except F, the significant trough can be observed in the region of time lag -0.4 ±0.1 seconds where the eye-blink follows the pause in speech. The same effects were founded in 21 out of 28 data segments of 34 seconds.

For the relationship between the speaker's voice and the listener's eye-blink response, the significant lagged relationship was noted in 13 out of the same 28 data segments of 34 seconds

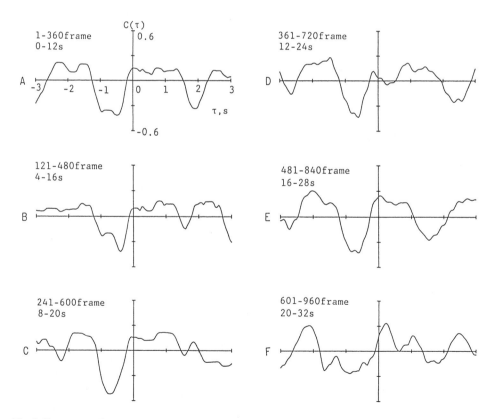

Fig.2 Cross-correlograms in 12-s analyzing periods, whose starting times of analysis are each shifted by 4 s. Computation is based on figures 1(a) and (b).

as shown in Table 1 . The range of time lag is -0.42 ±0.20 seconds. This indicates that the listener's eye-blink also follows the speaker's pause in speech after approximately 0.4 seconds. It was also founded that the listener's eye-blink took place during nodding [5].

Table 1 Significant lagged relationships between: a speaker's voice and his own eye-blinking response; a speaker's voice and a listener's eye-blinking and nodding responses.

Speaker	S 1	S 2					S 3		S 4
Listener	L 1	L 2	L 3	L 4	L 5		L 3	L 4	L 4
Speaker-himself B vs. V	××××	○×○×	○○○○	×	○○○○	○○○○	○○○○	○○○	○○
Listener's B vs. V	××××	○○○○	×○××	○○○×	○××	○××	○××××	○○○	○×
Listener's B vs. M	○○○○	○○○○	×○××	○○○○	○○○○	○○×	○×○×	○×○	○○
M vs. V	○×○×	×○○○	○○×○	○○○○	○○○○	××	○○○○	○○	○○

B: Eye-Bliking, V: Speaker's Voice, M: Listener's Nodding.

3. MODELING

On the basis of these findings, an eye-blinking feedback model was developed. The model consists of a speaker's eye-blinking model and a listener's eye-blinking model.

3.1 Speaker's eye-blinking model
It has been revealed that the speaker's eye-blinking response is related to his own voice signal. I propose a model estimating the eye-blink on the basis of the voice signal. The estimator $\hat{B}(t)$ of B(t) is a moving-average model (MA model), which is expressed as the weighted sum of binary voice signal in each video frame length of 1/30th second:

$$\hat{B}(t)=\sum_{j=1}^{60} a(j)V(t-j) + u(t)$$

where a(j) is the linear prediction coefficient, V(t) is the voice signal, and u(t) is the noise.
The number of coefficient was chosen at 60 on the basis of AIC (Akaike's Information Criterion). This means that the estimator operates over the past 2 (1/30 x 60) seconds. If $\hat{B}(t)$ exceeds the threshold value, the model judges that the time t is the eye-blinking onset, and outputs an eye-blinking response for the mean value 0.33seconds (10 frames).

Using the proposed model, B(t) was estimated on the basis of V(t) in Fig.1. The broken line in Fig.1(a) shows the result of simulation. The threshold value was set at 0.36. The cross-correlogram between $\hat{B}(t)$ and V(t) was also shown by the broken line in Fig.1(c). As is obvious from this figure, the simulated cross-correlogram almost coincides with the original one. This demonstrates the effectiveness of the model.

3.2 Listener's eye-blinking model

It has been reported that the listener's eye-blink frequently takes place during nodding simultaneously, and the eye-blinking interval is regarded as an exponential distribution [5]. By taking note of these two characteristics, I propose a model generating the listener's eye-blink with timing of exponential intervals from each nodding onset in response to speech input, as shown in Fig.3. This model incorporated the previously developed voice-responsive nodding model that estimated nod on the basis of speech characteristics of speech input [3]. The nodding model consists of two stages - macro and micro. The macro stage at the top of the figure estimates the existence of nodding during any given duration unit. A duration unit consists of a talkspurt episode and the following silence episode with a hangover value of 2/30th second. If nodding exists within that duration unit, then the micro stage estimates the nodding onset by examining each frame length of 1/30th second. The present model first estimates a nodding onset by the nodding model, and then generates eye-blinks from the nodding onset to the next nodding onset at the following exponential interval T:

$$T = -\mu \log(1 - \lambda)$$

where μ is the mean interval of B(t) and λ is the uniform random number.

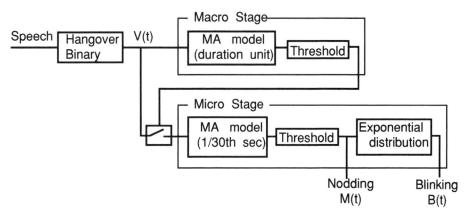

Fig.3 Voice-responsive nodding and eye-blinking model.

Figure 4 shows the result of simulation by using the proposed model. The trough of the simulated correlogram agrees well with that of the original correlogram. However, because the simulation was affected by the nodding model, the simulated cross-correlogram shows the significant peak at time lag 0.8 seconds, which is a representative time lag between a speaker's voice and the listener's nodding [6].

4. CONCLUSION

This paper evaluated the synchrony between a speaker's voice and eye-blink, and a listener's eye-blink and nodding in actual face-to-face interaction by the cross-correlation analysis. We found significant synchronous, and lagged relationships between: (a) a speaker's voice and his own eye-blinking response; (b) a speaker's voice and a listener's eye-blinking and

1096

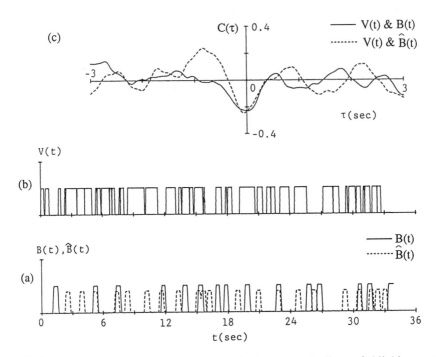

Fig.4 Evaluation of the synchrony between a speaker's voice and a listener's blinking response. (a) Changing of the listener's blinking parameter B(t) and the estimated $\hat{B}$(t). (b) Changing of the speaker's voice parameter V(t). (c) Cross-correlograms.

nodding responses. We also found that the listener's eye-blinking response tends to occur during nodding. On the basis of these findings, an eye-blinking feedback model for speech input was proposed, and the effectiveness was demonstrated. This model would be applicable to a variety of human-computer interactions where visual feedback is possible and may well lead to a more user-friendly system.

This research was supported in part by Tateisi Science and Technology Foundation.

REFERENCES

[1] W.S Condon and L.W. Sander, Science, Vol.183 (1974) 99.
[2] N. Kobayashi, T.Ishii, and T. Watanabe, Early Development and Parenting, Vol.1 (1992) 23.
[3] T. Watanabe and N. Yuuki, Advances in Human Factors/Ergonomics, 12A, M.J. Smith and G.Salvendy (eds.) Elsevier (1989) 396.
[4] T. Watanabe and A. Higuchi, Advances in Human Factors/Ergonomics, 18A, H.J. Bullinger (eds.) Elsevier (1991) 491.
[5] T.Watanabe, Progress in Human Interface, Vol.1 (1992) 35.
[6] T. Watanabe, Jpn.Soc.Mech.Eng. Int. J., Vol.30 (1987) 2040.

Enhancing speech intelligibility using visual images

Christopher Greaves*, Martin Warren*, and Olov Östberg**

*Language Centre, University of Luleå, 951 87 Luleå, Sweden

**The Swedish Agency for Administrative Development, Stockholm, Sweden

Abstract
   This paper describes some further experimental work aimed at assessing the contribution of images to speech intelligibility. The experiments were designed to test the theory that speech is made more intelligible by presenting visual images of speakers along with the speech. These visual images were presented on a video monitor, and the experiments tested subjects at three levels of perception:-
   1. with no image, sound only (Audio);
   2. sound plus head and shoulders of the speaker shown (Audio/Vis);
   3. sound plus full situational context (Audio/Vis+).
   The preliminary conclusions drawn are that the accompaniment of a visual image (Audio/Vis) showing only head and lip movements of the speaker show no significant improved listening comprehension, and that images showing full situational contexts (Audio/Vis+) in this study do not appear to have any additional effect in enhancing intelligibility.

1.   INTRODUCTION

   The experiments described in this paper were inspired by the growing interest and increasing involvement of people in videocommunication. As prices of the technology become less and equipment improves the question of whether and to what extent the use of video images together with sound heightens comprehension has become not one of academic interest but a matter of real practical value. Particularly in education, where video conferencing is now established as a pedagogical tool, a better understanding of these relationships can help us in developing strategies for using this technology to best effect. Previous research has tended to encourage the view that video images do enhance aural comprehension. General support for this is found for example in the findings of McDonald & McGurk (1978) and also the Sign Language and Lip Reading Tests for 'Bit-Saving Video Communication' carried out by the Swedish Handicap Institute (Dopping, 1990). In earlier work carried out at Luleå University aimed at evaluating the contribution of visual images to speech intelligibility, it was found that at least in two out of three experiments visual speech information did indeed contribute to speech perception (Östberg et al, 1992). The set of experiments described here were thus designed to explore more conclusively, and in a way which had a more direct bearing on an educational perspective, the implications of this earlier work.

2. INVESTIGATING SPEECH COMPREHENSION WITH VIDEO SUPPORT

The findings of previous experiments carried out on the effect of visual images on speech intelligibility (Östberg et al 1991) using video images of speakers suggested that there was a definite likelihood that auditory comprehension was thus enhanced by the presence of a visual stimulus, and that language learners in particular might benefit from this. The earlier studies, which were carried out in the Department of Communication and Languages at the University of Luleå, had tested the experimental hypothesis that speech perception would be enhanced by the addition of a video display monitor showing the head and shoulders of the speaker. The setting in the first experiments was a simulated distance teaching activity and small group language laboratory, with the tutor shown reading the stimulus material in video recording, and relayed to groups of students via TV monitors. Although the results from the first set of experiments were encouraging, it was felt that the limited nature of the tests themselves did not give an adequate guide as to how a real learning activity might be performed based on the same principles, and whether the results would be the same.

With this in mind a further set of experiments were devised, with the aim of testing the theory from a more realistic pedagogical perspective than had been applied in the earlier studies. They were again conducted at Luleå University, using students of English as subjects. It was decided to use tests taken from the TOEFL book (ETS, 1989), rather than simulated activities devised for the purposes of the experiment (Östberg et al, 1991). In addition to testing more rigorously the original hypothesis, two further experimental hypotheses were that the less able students would benefit more from having the visual image than the more able students, and that students sitting further way from the TV screen would do less well than those sitting nearer the screen.

3. TEST MATERIALS USED

A videotape of three native English speakers reading the test material was produced by the university media laboratory. The recording was done using a Datapoint Model 2001 MINX Workstation with an attached video recorder. On a 24" TV monitor with good sound and picture quality, the recording was watched by ten groups of five subjects. From the viewing distance of approximately 2 m the sound pressure level of the speech output was approximately 64 dB(A), which is well above the perception threshold. The test material consisted of three types of listening test which are a standard part of the TOEFL test, with tests written entirely by the official TOEFL organisation, which thus ensured that the fullest degree of realism and objectivity in terms of the context of the experiments was achieved.

In the first listening test, twenty short sentences were read. Each sentence was read by only one speaker. After each sentence, there was a pause of 12 seconds before the next sentence was read. On a score sheet the subject marked one of four sentences that was closest in meaning to that which had just been heard. An example is shown as follows:-

Subjects hear: *Mary swam out to the island with her friends*
Subjects read:

    (A) Mary outswam the others
    (B) Mary ought to swim with them
    (C) Mary and her friends swam to the island
    (D) Mary's friends owned the island

Sentence C is closest in meaning to the sentence heard so answer (C) should be chosen. The normal procedure for conducting this test is for students to hear the sentence once from a tape recording. No visual stimulus is provided. For the experiment, the 20 test sentences were presented on video with seven question showing no image (Audio), and seven questions showing the speaker reading the text in head and shoulder views (Audio/Vis). For six of the twenty sentences additional visual information was provided as the main image (Audio/Vis+), giving situational or other visual clues to the meaning, and with the speaker shown only in a small box superimposed on the main picture and displayed in one corner of the screen. For example, one of these test sentences was:-

Kate was really feeling down in the dumps about her latest chemistry assignment.
The main picture accompanying this sentence showed a girl looking extremely miserable, while the head and shoulder image of the speaker appeared in a small box in a corner of the screen.

For the seven Audio/Vis sentences, no such additional contextual or other visual support was given, only the full screen head and shoulders image of the speaker was used. In this, mouth and lip movements were clearly visible. The aim of providing the additional visual information for other six sentences was to reveal the extent to which such additional visual stimuli contributed to enhanced comprehension, and to provide a comparison with the use of only head shoulder images.

In the second type of TOEFL listening test, 15 short conversations between two different speakers are presented on a tape recording. A third speaker then asks a question for the student to select the answer in the same way as the previous test. Here is an example:-

Subjects hear:

Man: *Professor Smith is going to retire soon. What kind of gift shall we give her?*
Woman: *I think she'd like to have a photograph of our class.*
Questioner: *What does the woman think the class should do?*
Subjects read:

    (A) Present Professor Smith with a picture.
    (B) Photograph Professor Smith.
    (C) Put glass over the photograph.
    (D) Replace the broken headlight.

Sentence (A) is the best answer to the question, so this should be selected.

In presenting this second test in the experiment, a third of the test examples were also done showing additional visual information such as situational context (Audio/Vis+). Consider the following example:-

Man: *I can't decide what color to paint my room.*
Woman: *What about white? It'll make the room brighter.*
Questioner: *What does the woman suggest?*

In the video picture the man and woman are seen together looking at some cans of paint, with the woman selecting the white paint. The questioner, however, is seen after this in full screen head and shoulder image. For the other test dialogs, where no situational context was shown, the dialog was presented with each speaker shown separately in full screen head and shoulder image, one after the other. The speakers were not shown together. As with the first type of test, a third of the test questions were presented with extra visual information in order to reveal any marked difference in speech comprehension which might result from this, and to contrast this with the use of only head and shoulder images.

In the third type of TOEFL listening test an extended talk is presented, and students are required after listening to the talk to select answers to questions about it which are put to them by the speaker on the tape. The same procedure for selecting the best answer from a multiple choice set of written options is followed as in the previous tests. The talk was presented on the video using a full screen head and shoulders image of the speaker, but also included a section which graphically illustrated parts of the talk while the speaker continued in the background. The talk concerned the subject of how oil spilled at sea could be recovered using sponges, and the video illustrated this technique showing small pieces of sponge being used to absorb oil, and then collected. The talk was followed by an extended dialog between two speakers, which was presented entirely using head and shoulder images of the individual speakers shown separately. The participants were not shown together. The subjects again selected answers from multiple choice sets to the questions which were posed orally at the end of the dialog.

4. TEST PROCEDURE

The 50 subjects were tested in groups of 5 at a time, arranged so that the subjects were seated at separate desks in 5 rows in front of the TV monitor, with the centre row (C) directly in front of the monitor, and two outer rows on each side arranged as follows:-

Row A   Row B   Row C   Row D   Row E

The test consisted of 50 questions in the three formats described in Section 3 above. One third of the questions were presented under each of the three test conditions.

5. RESULTS OF THE TEST

The results of the tests are summarised in Table 1.

Table 1

Position	Audio	Audio/vis	Audio/Vis+	Average
A	86.47%	88.24%	87.50%	87.40%
B	91.76%	91.76%	92.50%	92.01%
C	78.82%	85.29%	88.13%	84.08%
D	86.47%	92.92%	86.25%	88.55%
E	86.47%	88.24%	88.75%	87.82%
Average	86.00%	89.29%	88.63%	87.97%

Table 1 shows the average scores obtained for the three types of test by the subjects arranged in the respective rows, and also average scores achieved by the whole group. Figure 1 shows a graphic illustration of the results in Table 1.

Figure 1

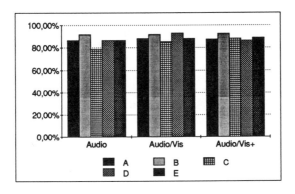

6. STATISTICAL ANALYSIS

Table 2

Factors	Mean	Standard deviation
Audio	86	10.62
Audio/Vis	89.29	9.03
Audio/Vis+	88.63	9.51

The overall mean and the standard deviations were 87.97 and 9.78 respectively.

Table 3: Analysis of variance for scores

Source of variation	Sum of Squares	d.f.	Mean Square	F-ratio	Sig level
MAIN EFFECTS					
A: conditions	303.15927	2	151.57964	1.637	0.1983
B: positions	963.94223	4	240.98806	2.603	0.0387
INTERACTIONS					
AB	488.37188	8	61.046485	0.659	0.7263
RESIDUAL	12497.688	135	92.575470		
TOTAL	14253.172	149			

Table 3 shows that for the population as a whole there are no significant differences between the results obtained under the different conditions Audio, Audio/Vis, and Audio/Vis+. Similarly no significant differences were found arising from the different seating positions of the subjects. However, there are significant differences between the different seating positions at 95% significant level. The results were further analysed using Tukey's comparison test, which showed that there is a significant difference between the seating position of B and C at 95% significant level.

The following conclusions are drawn from these statistical findings:

i) Subjects seated at position B showed higher scores under all conditions whereas subjects seated at position C showed weakest performance under all consitions.

ii) The Audio/Vis condition showed higher performance compared to the Audio and Audio/Vis+ conditions.

iii) When plotted on a graph, the overall scores for all three conditions were found to have a skewed distribution. One reason for this might be that the Audio/Vis+ condition showed a markedly skewed distribution.

iv) Even though seating position B had a significant effect on scores, the scores were found to be asymmetric. However, the scores for the subjects seated at positions A and E were found to be symmetric.

7. DIRECTIONS FOR FURTHER RESEARCH

The results of the experiments described in this paper appear to contradict the intuitive notion that people prefer to be able to make visual contact with each other in communication, and that such visual support serves as an aid to speech intelligibility. It is anticipated that further experiments along these lines should be pursued to throw more light on this, possibly with supporting information gained from subjects via questionnaires so as to identify better the extent of any "feel good" factors. Future experiments also need to be done with more uniform subject populations, perhaps with some pre-testing so as to group subjects as closely as possible into bands of similar abillity.

8. ACKNOWLEDGEMENTS

The authors would especially like to thank Md.Shafiquzzaman Khan of the Department of Ergonomics, Luleå University, for his expert help in providing the statistical validation of the results. We also wish to acknowledge the help given by Jo Fowler in setting up and administering the experiments described in this paper.

9. BIBLIOGRAPHY

1 J. MacDonald & H. McGurk,Visual Influences on speech perception processes, Perception & Psychophysics, vol. 24, 1978. (Pp. 253-257).
2 O. Dopping, Tests with Bit Saving Video Communciation for Sign Language and Lip Reading. Stockholm: Handicap Institute, 1990.
3 O. Östberg, Y. Horie & M. Warren, Contribution of Visual Images to Speech Intelligibility. Human Vision, Visual Processing, and Digital Display III; SPIE Proceedings, 1666, 1992. (Pp 526-533).
4 Listening to TOEFL, Educational Testing Service, Princeton, NJ, 1989.

Evaluation of a gaze using real-time CG eye-animation combined with eye movement detector

Kiyohiro Morii, Fumio Kishino, Nobuji Tetsutani

ATR Communication Systems Research Laboratories, 2-2 Hikaridai, Seika-cho, Soraku-gun, Kyoto 619-02, Japan

Abstract

In a teleconferencing system with realistic sensations, human images are generated by Computer Graphics (CG). This requires animating natural eye movement with CG. In this paper, we describe the results of an experiment on the perception of gaze direction by using CG eye-animation. We then describe a real-time CG eye-animation system combined with an eye movement detector. We also subjectively evaluate the allowable transmission delay time when using this system.

1. INTRODUCTION

In the environment of a conversation or a conference, eye movement and gaze provide important information. We can guess interests or intentions of a participant by his gaze. Researchers at ATR have studied a teleconferencing system with realistic sensations, which can provide remote participants with a cooperative working environment in a room (image space) generated by Computer Graphics (CG)[1]. In this environment, everyone can perceive the visual effect of meeting together. In this system, the human image is a 3-D model generated by CG, which is reconstructed by processing 2-D images acquired through the TV camera. Eye movement information for all participants is obtained by a non-contact eye movement detector[2]. The eyes of each human image are moved according to this information, allowing us to achieve the same eye contact that would occur in an actual conference. This is possible because the human images are synthesized in the image space and stereoscopic images are generated based on the viewer's position. In the field of CG, many facial expression methods have already been investigated[3], but the subjective evaluation of the gaze by a human image generated by CG requires further study.

In this paper, we describe the results of an experiment on the perception of gaze direction using CG eye-animation. In our experiments, we subjectively evaluated the gaze generated by CG using 2-D or 3-D displays, and compared this with the gaze of an actual person. Furthermore, we constructed a system that can animate gaze shift according to an actual person's eye movement in real-time by using an eye movement detector. We also evaluated the allowable transmission delay time using this system.

2. EYE-ANIMATION

We used the 3-D coordinate and texture data of a human face, with eyes opened and closed, obtained by a 3-D digitizer (manufactured by Cyberware Laboratories, USA). We first constructed the eyes by modeling the eye as a sphere, calculating its diameter from the open-eye facial model, and mapping its texture data. Then, the wire-frame of the closed-eye facial model was cut along the eyelids and the vertices of the eyelids were made movable. Using this facial model, we made an eyeless facial model by moving the vertices of the eyelids to the open position. The final 3-D facial model was constructed by synthesizing the eyes in the eyeless facial model[4]. Fig. 1 shows the constructed facial model.

As shown in Fig. 2, gaze is defined as a line connecting the center of the eye, the center of the pupil, and the gaze point. Gaze shift is animated by rotating the eye according to the gaze point shift. This eye animation can be displayed in both 2-D and 3-D using LCD-shuttered stereo glasses.

Fig. 1   Constructed facial model

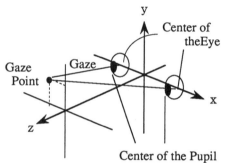

Fig. 2   Gaze

3. PERCEPTION OF GAZE DIRECTION

Using the above eye-animation, we evaluated CG-generated gaze. We investigated how accurately humans can perceive gaze direction of CG human images using 2-D or 3-D displays. This was then compared with the gaze of an actual person.

3.1. Method

We used (a) an actual person, (b) a 2-D CG image, and (c) a 3-D CG image as objects in our experiment. The experimental condition is shown in Fig. 3. The distance between a subject and an object was 150 cm. We placed targets of gaze around the object circularly at a radius of 50 cm in five degree intervals, from the front of the object (0°) to 25° horizontally toward either the left or right side. The object gazed at a target, and the subject judged which target the object gazed at. The subject shifted his gaze below the object before starting the experiment, then judged the gaze of the object when signaled.

There were five subjects, and we conducted the experiment two times and calculated the average. The CG facial image was displayed life-size on a 70-inch screen, then the number of pixels in the eye region were about 30 pixels horizontally. Stereoscopic images were generated according to the experimental condition shown in Fig. 3. Subjects put on LCD-shuttered stereo glasses for the 3-D display. 2-D CG images were projected perspectively. When subjects evaluated 2-D CG images, they also put on LCD glasses in order to match the conditions (e.g. brightness) with 3-D images.

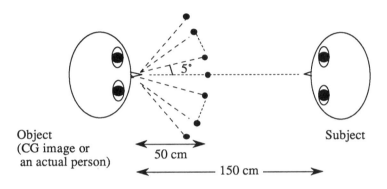

Object
(CG image or
an actual person)

50 cm

150 cm

Subject

Fig. 3   Experimental condition

3.2.   Results and discussion

Experimental results for the actual person are shown in Fig. 4. The horizontal axis in Fig. 4 is actual gaze direction and the vertical axis is judged gaze direction. The plus direction is the right side of the subject. In the field of psychology, it is reported that humans tend to judge the angle of the gaze direction of another person to be wider than the actual direction. In our experiment, when the gaze direction is 0° or 5°, subjects can judge the gaze direction accurately, but when the gaze direction is more than 10°, subjects judge the angle of the gaze direction to be wider than the actual direction.

Experimental results for CG images (2-D and 3-D) and the actual person are shown in Fig. 5. The vertical axis is the difference between judged direction and actual gaze direction. As with the actual person, subjects judge the angle of the gaze direction of the 3-D CG image to be wider than the actual direction. There is a little difference between the results for 3-D CG image and those for the actual person. This is thought to be caused by a subtle difference in eye position and in the figure of eyes, but generally the results are similar.

For the 2-D CG image, subjects judge the angle of the gaze direction to be narrow than the actual direction. This is different than the results of the actual person and the 3-D CG image. This is thought to be caused by the fact that it is hard to judge the gaze direction for a 2-D image. If the subject cannot perceive the distance between the object and targets, then the subject cannot judge the relationship between the gaze and targets.

In a teleconferencing system with realistic sensations, 3-D CG images are synthesized in an image space, so it is assumed that a viewer overestimates the gaze direction of a CG human image. Therefore, we can project a gaze direction or a gaze point of a human image accurately by precisely animating gaze direction in front of the human image and animating the gaze direction at a narrower angle than the actual direction when the gaze direction is wider than 10°. If gaze detection error occurs in sender's side, the viewer senses that the error is significant, so accurately detecting the gaze is very important.

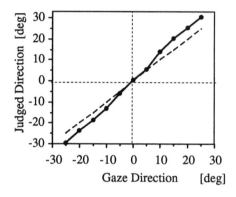

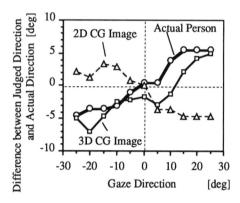

Fig. 4 Experimental results
for the actual person

Fig. 5 Experimental result s for CG images
and the actual person

4. REAL-TIME CG EYE-ANIMATION SYSTEM

In a teleconferencing system with realistic sensations, eye movement detection and animating eye movement with CG is a very important technique for realizing the same eye contact that would occur in an actual conference. We constructed a real-time CG eye-animation system using eye-animation (section 2) and an eye movement detector. Then we subjectively evaluated the allowable delay time when using this system.

4.1. System composition

Fig. 6 shows the composition of the real-time CG eye-animation system. We used a non-contact eye movement detector using active stereo camera[2] or eye tracking system 4100H (manufactured by ASL corporation, USA) as an eye movement detector. Gaze point data V(x, y) is obtained by the eye movement detector. This data is then sent to the Graphic Workstation (IRIS 4D/240 VGX). We use the CG eye-animation described in section 2. Gaze shift is animated by rotating the eye according to the data sent. Using this system, we can animate real-time gaze shift according to the eye movement of an actual person. An example of gaze shift of the CG image and the actual person is shown in Fig. 7.

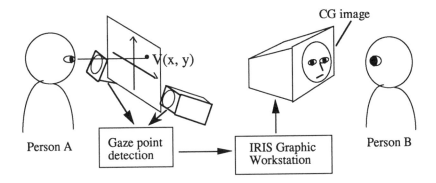

Fig. 6   Composition of the system

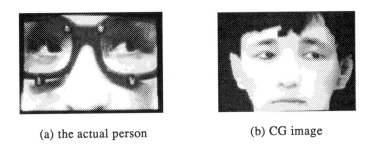

(a) the actual person   (b) CG image

Fig. 7   Gaze shift of the CG image and the actual person

4.2.   Evaluation of the allowable delay time

We subjectively evaluated the allowable delay time using this system.

The subject (person B in Fig. 6) orders the viewer (person A in Fig. 6) to shift his gaze to right, left, up, down. When A shifts his gaze according the instructions of B, the gaze of the CG image shifts too. We evaluate how the subject perceives delay, if there is delay time in data transmission. In our experiment, the delay time changed from 0.1 seconds to 1.0 seconds in 0.1 seconds increments. The CG image was displayed life-size on a 19-inch CRT display. Subjects (seven people) observed the CG image at a distance of 70 cm. Subjects evaluated the delay by classifying them into categories (3: Imperceptible, 2: Slightly Annoying, 1: Annoying).

The experimental result is shown in Fig. 8. The horizontal axis represents the delay time and the vertical axis represents the mean opinion score. It is observed that the allowable delay time (a score of over 2) is about 0.4 seconds. In our system, about 0.05 seconds is needed to generate CG image, but this delay does not influence the evaluation.

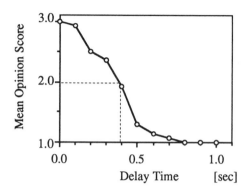

Fig. 8 Experimental result

5. CONCLUSION

In this paper, we have reported the results of an experiment on perception of gaze direction using CG eye-animation. The results show that subjects judged the angle of the gaze direction to be wider than the actual direction for an actual person and the 3-D CG image. However, subjects judged the gaze direction to be narrower for the 2-D CG image. We also constructed a real-time CG eye-animation system in combination with an eye movement detector, and evaluated the allowable delay time when using this system. In our experiment, the allowable delay time is about 0.4 seconds. In future work, We will investigate the perception of gaze direction for an oblique face. Another future work is constructing real-time CG animation that allows for head movement.

6. ACKNOWLEDGMENT

The authors thank Dr.Terashima, president of ATR Communication Systems Research Laboratories, and Dr. Habara, Executive Vice President of ATR Institute International, for their thoughtful advice and encouragement regarding this research. The authors also would like to thank all of the subjects for their cooperation.

7. REFERENCES

1. F. Kishino and K. Yamashita, "Communication with realistic sensations applied to teleconferencing system" (in Japanese), IEICE Technical Report, Vol. IE-89-35, pp.1-6,1989
2. A.Tomono, F.Kishino and Y.Kobayashi,"Pupil extraction processing and gaze point detectionsystem allowing head movement"(in Japanese), IEICE D-II, Vol.76-D-II, 3, pp.636-646
3. D.Terzoupoulos and K.Waters,"Phisically-based facial modelling, analysis, and animation", J. Visualization and Computer Animation, Vol.1, pp.73-80,1990
4. K.Morii, T.Satoh, N.Tetsutani and F.Kishino,"A Technique of eye-animation generated by CG, ...", Proc.SPIE Conf. on Visual Comm. and Image Processing'92, pp.1350-1357,1992

Bidirectional Translation between Sign Language and Japanese for Communication with Deaf-Mute People

Takao KUROKAWA, Tooru MORICHI and Shigeaki WATANABE

Department of Electronics and Information Science, Faculty of Engineering and Design, Kyoto Institute of Technology, Matsugasaki, Sakyo-ku, Kyoto 606, Japan

Abstract

Bidirectional machine translation between sign language and Japanese is proposed as an application of nonverbal interfaces. The translating system employs a sign dictionary for translating sign gesture to Japanese words and vice versa. While sign gesture is tracked by gesture sensors and Japanese sentences are displayed, the system receives Japanese sentences and displays sign gesture animation. It has been confirmed that sign processing works properly.

1. INTRODUCTION

Most of deaf and mute/dumb people in Japan communicate in Japanese sign language (JSL). JSL is mainly expressed in hand gesture although facial expression and trunk gesture sometimes play an important role. Communication between them and hearing persons, however, relies on sign language interpreters. Since the number of the interpreters is extremely limited in Japan, they bear a heavy workload and tend to suffer from cervicobrachial disorder. This situation can be solved if machines capable of translating between sign language and Japanese language come out. Moreover, technology developed for completing such machines will facilitate telecommunication in sign language and crosscultural communication interspersed with gestures proper to each culture.

Some researchers are trying to recognize or translate JSL, but they have not obtained satisfactory results [6-10]. On the other hand our study started with proposing methods of coding gesture [1-3] and we are now attempting to develop a system for translation between JSL and Japanese [4,5]. Major emphasis is placed on that the system is *bidirectional*, or displays not only voices to hearing persons but sign images to signers. Though some believe that written word display will do, sign gesture is a natural language for signers and can contain feelings and stress.

This paper reports the current attainment in our attempt. Since for the time being our efforts are directed to build up sign-related functions of the system, our attention here is chiefly focused on sign gesture processing.

2. BIDIRECTIONAL TRANSLATION

Figure 1 depicts the outline of our system bidirectionally translating between the two languages. The upper blocks show the process for sign language-to-

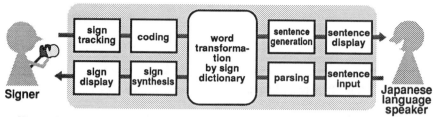

Fig. 1 System bidirectionally translating between sign language and Japanese.

Japanese translation and the lower ones conduct the reverse translation. These two processes share a sign dictionary containing relations between words of the both languages. A signer's gesture is tracked by a pair of hand gesture sensors, the VPL DataGloves and is transcribed into a series of hand shape and hand position codes. The dictionary then transforms them to a Japanese word sequence. Analyzing the given word sequence, a language processing program generates the most possible Japanese sentence. The system's final output can be a voice and/or a character expression of the sentence.

Roughly speaking, Japanese-to-sign language translation goes in the reverse order of the above process. A Japanese sentence received by the system is parsed and transformed to a sequence of root (or dictionary)-formed words that are used as entries of the dictionary. The dictionary works contrariwise in this mode, and its output is a temporal sequence of sign codes corresponding to Japanese words. From this sequence, sign animation is synthesized by rules and is displayed on a CRT screen.

3. JAPANESE SIGN LANGUAGE AND SIGN DICTIONARY

There are three kinds of JSL. We have picked out one that has the same word order as in Japanese sentences but whose vocabulary has its own organization. JSL that we have chosen lacks its counterparts of some particles in Japanese: words indicating the case of their preceding phrases ("wa" and "ga" indicating a subject, "o" an object, and "no" a possessive), the place ("de"), the direction ("e") and such.

In this study, sign language is supposed to be
- expressed with prolonged rest between successive sign words, and
- expressed only with the hands and arms.

A sign word in JSL consists of one or more unit gestures made of a continuous movement and a following rest of the hand and arm [5]. Hand shapes at the resting periods are more significant.

Kurokawa et al. [1-3] introduced a gesture code system by which any gesture can be transcribed into a small number of symbols when enough information about body movements is given. It is composed of three subsystems: the hand-shape, the body-shape and the motion-speed code systems.

As for sign gestures, only hand and body shapes need to be coded. Since we can get limited information on sign gestures from the sensors, the hand-shape code system has been modified as seen in Table 1 [4]. The code H denotes the basic fin-

Table 1 Modified hand-shape codes for sign language

Hi (1 $\leqq i \leqq$ 5) [basic form of hand shape]
Natural extension of a finger i.

Bi (1 $\leqq i \leqq$ 5) [bending]
Bending of a finger i at its first joint. B5: a thumb standing opposite others. Bi: tense extension at its first joint.

Ri (1 $\leqq i \leqq$ 5) [crooking]
Bending of a finger i at its second and third joints.

Fi (1 $\leqq i \leqq$ 5) [fist]
Flexion of a finger i like making a fist.

Ni (1 $\leqq i \leqq$ 5) [counting]
Flexion of a finger i over a bent thumb as Japanese people do so when counting.

Cij ($i, j \in \{1, 2, 5\}$, $i < j$) [contacting]
Contact of a side of a finger i with that of an-other finger j.

X12 [crossing]
Crossing of an index finger over a middle finger.

Underlined letters indicate auxiliary codes. i and j indicate finger numbers: index finger, 1; middle, 2; ring, 3; little, 4 and thumb, 5.

ger configuration of a naturally opened hand. The other six codes are derived as transformations from the basic form. Hand shapes can easily be coded by a computer if quantified data on hand configurations are given. Though this system does not give complete description of sign gestures owing to deficiency of information, it works well for recognition of sign words [4].

On one of the above assumptions, hand position and hand orientation are coded using the body-shape code system. Three positional dimensions (a1, a2 and a3) are adopted to transcribe the right hand position relative to the axial body segments as in Fig. 2(a). The right hand orientation also has three dimensions (h3, h4 and h5) covering the degree of freedom of the wrist joint, and each dimension has nine positional states reflecting the orientation of the palm. The codes of the left hand are determined as in the mirror image of the corresponding right ones.

The sign dictionary is a central unit of the system. Originally it was created as a gesture dictionary to transform a given gesture among its code notation, displayed image and meaning for human-computer interfaces [1]. Here it has been revised so that it can apply to translation between JSL and Japanese. Its entries include two kinds of data: sign gesture codes and Japanese words that are mutually linked by pointers, and data about the right hand gesture and the left hand one are stored in two sections, respective-

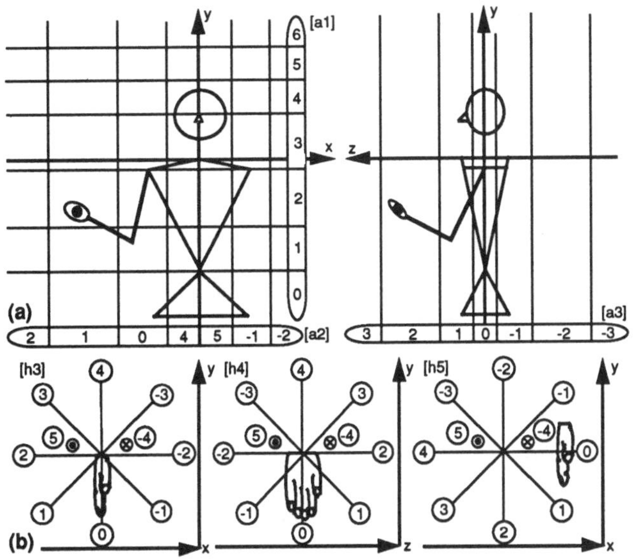

Fig. 2 Codes of hand position (a) and orientation (b). Numbers indicate code numbers.

ly. The dictionary works bidirectionally; it returns a Japanese word when gesture codes enter as a key and vice versa. Search in the dictionary is done by means of a hash method.

4. SIGN LANGUAGE-TO-JAPANESE TRANSLATION

4.1 Sign Gesture Tracking and Segmentation

The DataGloves tracking sign gesture send digitized data of a hand configuration, position and orientation of the both hands to the coding program.

The problem in the coding process is segmentation that determines at what instant a sign word starts or terminates. In the present study this problem is solved by the assumption of a prolonged resting period made in Sec. 3. The squared velocity V^2 of one hand calculated from its position progresses as in Fig. 3. Two sign words must be segmented by a resting period equal to or longer than an appropriate threshold T. Letting a resting period belong to its preceding gesture, one can extract a sign word as indicated in Fig. 3. It may contain one or more short rests, the number of which equals that of units in the sign word. We have decided that static gesture at rest should be coded as the most important information characterizing the sign. This leads to the determination of coding instants along the V^2 curve (O in Fig. 3). Thus each sign word is converted into two sequences of codes, one for a single hand, each sequence consisting of hand shape, hand position and hand orientation codes.

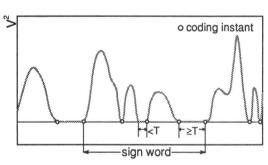

Fig. 3 Time course of squared velocity of one hand and word segmentation.

4.2 Transformation to Japanese Words

The next step is transformation of sign codes to Japanese words using the dictionary. Since varying length of a code sequence is clearly inefficient for search in the dictionary, a combination of the first and the last codes from a code sequence is decided as a key. While the last code is uniquely determined, the first one cannot easily be fixed because a sign word may begin with a preparatory action of varying length depending on the preceding sign gesture. This situation requires to construct several keys having different first code. In the search process, Japanese words the intermediate codes of which do not coincide with those of the original sign codes are rejected.

Thus the results of the search are two groups of possible Japanese words fit to right or left hand gesture. After matching is made between word candidates from the right and the left groups, only the matched words are sent to the Japanese sentence generator in the same order as signs in the tracked sign gesture.

This transformation is exemplified in Fig. 4. In the example just one matched word "kazoku (family)" is obtained.

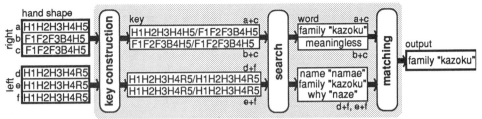

Fig. 4 An example of transformation of gesture codes to a Japanese word. Codes for hand position and orientation are omitted for simplicity.

4.3 Sentence Generation

Analyzing the case and the meaning of words from the given word sequences, the Japanese processing program selects the most possible sequence and generates a complete sentence by supplementing particles and changing root form of words to their appropriate one. The sentence generator's final output is displayed through a speech synthesizer (not implemented now) or a character screen.

5. JAPANESE-TO-SIGN LANGUAGE TRANSLATION

5.1 Parsing and Dictionary Search

The process of Japanese-to-JSL translation is roughly reverse to the above stated process. First a spoken or written sentence is parsed to find particles to be removed and inflecting words. Then the particles are removed and the form of the inflecting words is changed to their root form. Thus the parser produces a sequence of root-formed words that can be keys for search in the dictionary.

If parsing is complete, then dictionary search is rather easy. The output of the dictionary is two sequences of sign gesture codes linked with searched words. The codes are temporally drawn up in each sequence to make sign animation.

5.2 Synthesis of Sign Gesture Animation

The last stage of Japanese-to-JSL translation is synthesis of the animation that features an actor/actress talking by gesture. He/she can express his/her feelings and stress on the whole body gesture including facial expression if necessary, although this function has not been implemented yet.

Images of the animation are synthesized by rules. Sequences of sign gesture codes provide information about the actor's body configuration in every key frame. Successive body configurations are interpolated with smooth gesture movement. The length of moving and resting periods in each sign gesture is estimated based on analysis of actual signs [5]. This yields natural and real sign animation. Unfound words in the dictionary are expressed by finger alphabets.

Examples of images taken from animation are shown in Fig. 5. Most of the sign words used in animation can be understood by signers.

6. CONCLUSIONS

The mechanism and functions of the bidirectional translation system have

1114

Fig. 5 Images from sign animation. "naze (why)"[left] and "kau (to buy)"[right].

been outlined. Though there are many problems to be solved, it has been confirmed that sign gesture processing works properly. One of the remained problems is coding of finger movements seen within a gesture unit. They are important factors of sign gesture characterization.

The next stage in our study is processing of Japanese language. It requires a massive database about word meanings and word relations. Voice recognition and synthesis are also necessary functions in the system.

Our study is being carried out on separate three computers because of their deficient capacity, but we believe that the separate functions can be unified into one system as shown in Fig. 1 when we get a high-performance machine.

Acknowledgments: The authors would like to thank their graduate students Mr. T. Izuchi and Mr. E. Fujishige for their cooperation. This research was partly supported by the MESCJ under Grants-in-Aid No. 02215109 and No. 04452193.

REFERENCES

(1) Kurokawa T. (1992) Gesture coding and a gesture dictionary for a nonverbal interface, IEICE Trans. Fundamentals, **E75-A**, 112-121.

(2) Kurokawa T. & Kambe H. (1989) Description and computerized dictionary of gesture language, Proc. 5th Symp. on Human Interface, 347-352.

(3) Kurokawa T. & Kamiya H. (1989) Trial implementation of a computerized dictionary of manual gesture language, Human Interface News & Rep., **4**, 87-92.

(4) Morichi T. & Kurokawa T. (1992) Gesture coding for machine translation of sign language, Proc. 8th Symp. on Human Interface, 117-122.

(5) Morimoto K., Izuchi T., Fujishige E., Watanabe S., Morichi T. & Kurokawa T. (1992) Analysis of spatio-temporal structure of sign language for its machine translation, Proc. 8th Symp. on Human Interface, 621-626.

(6) Murakami K. & Taguchi H. (1991) Gesture recognition using recurrent neural networks, SIGCHI '91 Conf. Proc., 237-242.

(7) Nagashima Y., Terauchi M., Ohwa G. & Nagashima H. (1992) Investigation about basis design by Japanese sign language conversion concept term dictionaries, 1PSJ Technical Rept. on Human Interface, 44-14, 103-108.

(8) Sagawa H., Sakou H. & Abe M. (1992) Sign language translation system using continuous DP matching, IPSJ Technical Rept. on Human Interface, 44-12, 87-94.

(9) Takahashi T. & Kishino F. (1991) Hand gesture coding based on experiments using hand gesture interface device, SIGCHI Bul., **23**[2], 67-74.

(10) Tamura S. & Kawasaki S. (1986) Recognition system for sign language motion image, IPSJ Technical Rept. on Comput. Vision, 44-1, 1-8.

AUTHOR INDEX

KEYWORD INDEX